P · O · C · K · E · T · S

GERMAN DICTIONARY

GERMAN · ENGLISH
ENGLISH · GERMAN

DORLING KINDERSLEY
London • New York • Moscow • Sydney

A DORLING KINDERSLEY BOOK

Produced for Dorling Kindersley by
PAGE*One*, Cairn House, Elgiva Lane, Chesham,
Buckinghamshire HP5 2JD

PAGEOne **team**   Chris Clark, Matthew Cook,
Bob Gordon, Helen Parker

DK Managing editor   Jane Yorke

German editors   Anke Kornmüller
Christa Wiseman

This edition published in 2002

Published in Great Britain by
Dorling Kindersley Limited, 80 Strand, London WC2R 0RL

6 8 10 9 7 5
Copyright © 1998 Dorling Kindersley Limited, London

See our complete catalogue at **www.dk.com**

A CIP catalogue record for this book is available from
the British Library

ISBN 0-7513-5687-5

Printed and bound by LegoPrint, Italy

GUIDE TO THE IMITATED PRONUNCIATION

The imitated pronunciation in the German–English section is designed to help English speakers pronounce the German words accurately. Read each syllable as though it were an English word, bearing in mind the following conventions:

1 The stressed syllable is printed in **bold type**.

2 **ah** is generally pronounced like the a in Southern English ask:

Abend, ah-bent (evening)

It is, however, shorter when followed by two consonants:

alle, ahll-*e* (all)

3 **ay** represents a sound similar to the ay in day, as pronounced in Scotland:

gehen, gay-*en* (to go)

4 The italic *e* is a neutral vowel like the e in open or the a in local

kommen, kom-*en* (to come)

5 **ow** represents the vowel sound in cow:

aus, owss (from)

6 EE in small capitals is pronounced like the French u in lune (or like an English ee said with pursed lips):

drücken, drEEck-*en* (to press)

7 The italic *r* in the combination **er** must not be pronounced at all; it indicates that the preceding vowel is pronounced like the ur in fur:

hören, her-*r*en (to hear)

8 The italic *k* represents a guttural sound. After a, au, o or u it is pronounced like the ch in Scottish loch:

Bach, bah*k* (brook)

Elsewhere it is like a forcefully pronounced h:

mich, mi*k* (me)

9 g must be pronounced like the g in go:

Gesicht, ge-**zikt** (face)

The soft g in barrage is represented by **zh**:

Genie, zhain-ee (genius)

10 s always represents sound of the s in stand, not in does:

Soße, zoh-*se* (sauce).

4

ABBREVIATIONS

adj	adjective	*mil*	military
abbr	abbreviation	*mus*	music
adv	adverb	*n*	noun
art	article	*naut*	nautical
Brit	Britain	*nt*	neuter
chem	chemistry	*num*	numeral
comm	commerce	o.s.	oneself
comp	computing	*parl*	parliament
conj	conjunction	*pej*	pejorative
elec	electrics	*photog*	photography
etw	something	*pl*	plural
f	feminine	*pref*	prefix
fam	familiar	*prep*	preposition
fig	figuratively	*pron*	pronoun
fin	finance	rail	railways
geog	geography	*refl*	reflexive
gram	grammar	*relig*	religion
interj	interjection	sb	somebody
jd/jdn/jdm	somebody	*sport*	sport
jds	somebody's	sth	something
law	law	*theatre*	theatre
m	masculine	US	United S
mech	mechanics	*v*	ve
med	medicine	*vulg*	vulg

5

ERKLÄRUNG DER NACHGEAHMTEN AUSSPRACHE

Die nachgeahmte Aussprache im Englisch–Deutsch Teil soll dem deutschsprachigen Benutzer des Wörterbuches helfen, die englischen Wörter korrekt auszusprechen. Jede Silbe ist so auszusprechen, als sei sie Teil eines deutschen Wortes. Dabei sind folgende Hinweise zu beachten:

1 Die Betonung liegt auf der **fettgedruckten** Silbe.

2 Das schräg gedruckte *a* wird so wie das a in der deutschen Silbe ank- ausgesprochen:

   uncle, *a*ng-k'l (Onkel)
   come, kamm (kommen)

3 o'a wird in einem Laut ausgesprochen; die Hauptbetonung liegt auf dem o und das k klingt nur leicht nach:

   ought, o'at (sollte)

4 In vielen englischen Wörtern ist der Vokal der unbetonten Silbe kaum hörbar, ähnlich wie das e in Morgen oder Löffel. Dieser tonlose Vokal ist meistens durch ein *schräg* gedrucktes *e* bezeichnet:

   obey, *e*-beh (gehorchen)

Vor l oder n fällt dieser Vokal manchmal ganz weg und wird durch ein ' gekennzeichnet:

   table, teh-b'l (Tisch)
   reckon, reck-'n (rechnen)

5 s am Ende eines Wortes wird gewöhnlich stimmhaft ausgesprochen, ähnlich dem deutschen s zwischen zwei Vokalen, z.B. in Vase. In unserer nachgeahmten Aussprache wird dieses s durch s bezeichnet, das stimmlose s durch ss:

   scissors, ssis-ers (Schere)

Vor oder nach p, t oder k wird das s immer stimmlos ausgesprochen:

   ask, ahsk (fragen)
   must, mast (müssen)
   clasp, klahsp (umarmen)

6 Es gibt im Deutschen keinen Laut, der dem englischen "th" entspricht. Das stimmlose "th" ist mit der Zungenspitze zwischen den Zähnen auszusprechen, wie wenn jemand lispelt.
Es gibt auch ein stimmhaftes "th", das fast wie ein d klingt.
In der nachgeahmten Aussprache wird das stimmlose th mit **th** bezeichnet, das stimmhafte mit **dh**:

   thirty, thör-ti (dreißig)
   this, dhiss (dieser)

ABKÜRZUNGEN

adj	Adjektiv	*mil*	militärisch
abbr	Abkürzung	*mus*	Musik
adv	Adverb	*n*	Substantiv
art	Artikel	*naut*	Seefahrt
Brit	Großbritannien	*nt*	Neutrum
chem	Chemie	*num*	Zahlwort
comm	Handel	o.s.	sich
comp	Computer	*parl*	Parlament
conj	Konjunktion	*pej*	abschätzig
elec	Elektrizität	*photog*	Fotografie
etw	etwas	*pl*	Plural
f	Femininum	*pref*	Präfix
fam	umgangssprachlich	*prep*	Präposition
fig	übertragen	*pron*	Pronomen
fin	Finanzwesen	*rail*	Eisenbahn
geog	Geographie	*refl*	reflexiv
gram	Grammatik	*relig*	Religion
interj	Interjektion	sb	jemand(-en/-em)
jd/jdn/jdm	jemand(-en/-em)	*sport*	Sport
jds	jemands	sth	etwas
law	Rechtswesen	*theatre*	Theater
m	Maskulinum	US	Vereinigte Staaten
mech	Technik	*v*	Verb
med	Medizin	*vulg*	vulgär

7

GERMAN · ENGLISH
DEUTSCH · ENGLISCH

Aal, ahl, *m* eel

Aas, ahss, *nt* carrion

ab, ahp, *adv* off, from, away, down

abändern, ahp-enn-dern, *v* to alter

Abänderung, ahp-enn-der-oong, *f* alteration

abarbeiten (sich), ahp-ahr-by-ten (zik), *v* to overwork oneself

abbeißen, ahp-by-sen, *v* to bite off

abberufen, ahp-be-roof-en, *v* to recall, to summon away

abbestellen, ahp-be-shtell-en, *v* to cancel (orders), to countermand

abbilden, ahp-bild-en, *v* to portray, to delineate

abbitten, ahp-bit-en, *v* to apologize

abbrechen, ahp-brek-en, *v* to break off

abbrennen, ahp-brenn-en, *v* to burn down

abbürsten, ahp-bEErs-ten, *v* to brush off

abdanken, ahp-dahn-ken, *v* to resign, to abdicate

abdecken, ahp-deck-en, *v* to clear (table)

abdrucken, ahp-drook-en, *v* to print

Abend, ah-bent, *m* evening

Abendblatt, ah-bent-blahtt, *nt* evening paper

Abendessen, ah-bent-ess-en, *nt* supper

Abenteuer, ah-ben-toy-er, *nt* adventure

aber, ah-ber, *conj* but

Aberglaube, ah-ber-glow-be, *m* superstition

abergläubisch, ah-ber-gloy-bish, *adj* superstitious

abermal(s), ah-ber-mahl(s), *adv* again, once more

abfahren, ahp-fahr-en, *v* to depart, to start a journey

Abfahrt, ahp-fahrt, *f* departure

Abfall, ahp-fahll, *m* refuse, waste, offal

abfangen, ahp-fahng-en, *v* to catch; to intercept

abfärben, ahp-fair-ben, *v* to run (colours)

abfassen, ahp-fahss-en, *v* to draft; to seize

abfertigen, ahp-fair-tee-gen, *v* to dispatch, to expedite; to snub

abfinden, ahp-finn-den, *v* to satisfy; **sich – mit,** to come to terms with

abfliessen, ahp-fleess-en, *v* to flow off

Abfluß, ahp-flooss, *m* waste pipe; gutter

abführen, ahp-fEEr-en, *v* to march off; to purge

Abführmittel, ahp-fEEr-mitt-el, *nt* purgative

Abgabe, ahp-gah-be, *f* tax; duty

Abgang, ahp-gahng, *m* dispatch; departure; exit; discharge; abortion; waste

abgeben, ahp-gay-ben, *v* to deliver

abgebrannt, ahp-ge-brahnt, *adj* burnt down

abgehen, ahp-gay-en, *v* to go off, to depart

abgelebt, ahp-ge-laypt, *adj* decrepit; antiquated

abgelegen, ahp-ge-lay-gen, *adj* distant, remote

abgemessen, ahp-ge-mess-en, *adj* measured

abgeneigt, ahp-ge-ny'gt, *adj* disinclined

Abgeordnete(r), ahp-ge-ord-ne-te(r), *m & f* delegate, deputy, member of parliament

abgerundet, ahp-ge-roonn-det, *adj* rounded off

Abgesandte(r), ahp-ge-zahnn-te(r), *m & f* envoy, emissary

abgeschmackt, ahp-ge-shmahckt, *adj* insipid; in bad taste

abgesehen (von), ahp-ge-zay-en (fon), *adv* irrespective of, apart from

abgespannt, ahp-ge-shpahnt, *adj* tired out

abgestanden, ahp-ge-shtahnn-den, *adj* stale

abgewiesen, ahp-ge-vee-zen, *adj* rejected

abgewinnen, ahp-ge-vinn-en, *v* to win from

abgewöhnen, ahp-ge-ver-nen, *v* to break a habit, to wean from

abgiessen, ahp-geess-en, *v* to pour off

Abgott, ahp-got, *m* idol

abgöttisch, ahp-gert-ish, *adj* idolatrous

abgrenzen, ahp-grenn-tsen, *v* to delimit

Abgrund, ahp-groont, *m* abyss, precipice

abhacken, ahp-hahck-en, *v* to chop off

abhaken, ahp-hah-ken, *v* to unhook; to tick off

abhalten, ahp-hahll-ten, *v* to detain, to restrain

abhandeln, ahp-hahn-deln, *v* to bargain; to discuss

abhanden kommen, ahp-hahn-den komm-en, *v* to get lost

Abhang, ahp-hahng, *m* slope

abhängen (von), ahp-heng-en (fon), *v* to depend on

abhängig, ahp-heng-ik, *adj* dependent

abhärten, ahp-hair-ten, *v* to harden

abhauen, ahp-how-en, *v* to chop off, to fell

abheben, ahp-hay-ben, *v* to lift off; to cut (cards); to withdraw (money)

abhelfen, ahp-hel-fen, *v* to remedy; to redress

abholen, ahp-hoh-len, *v* to call for; to fetch from

abhören, ahp-her-ren, *v* to examine (students)

abkaufen, ahp-kow-fen, *v* to buy from

abkochen, ahp-kok-en, *v* to boil

Abkomme, ahp-kom-e, *m* descendant

abkommen, ahp-kom-en, *v* to get off/away

abkühlen, ahp-kEEl-en, *v* to cool

Abkunft, ahp-koonft, *f* origin, descent

abkürzen, ahp-kEErt-sen, *v*

to shorten, to abridge

abladen, ahp-lahd-en, *v* to unload

ablassen, ahp-lahss-en, *v* to reduce (price); to desist

Ablaß, ahp-lahss, *m* discharge; outlet

Ablauf, ahp-lowf, *m* drain; course; expiry; start

ablaufen, ahp-lowf-en, *v* to expire; to run down (clock); to flow off

ablecken, ahp-leck-en, *v* to lick off; to file

ablegen, ahp-lay-gen, *v* to lay aside, to take off

ablehnen, ahp-lay-nen, *v* to decline, to refuse

Ablehnung, ahp-lay-noong, *f* refusal

ableiten, ahp-ly-ten, *v* to divert, to derive (grammar)

ablenken, ahp-lenk-en, *v* to divert

ablernen, ahp-lairn-en, *v* to learn by watching

ableugnen, ahp-loyg-nen, *v* to deny

Ableugnung, ahp-loyg-noong, *f* denial

abliefern, ahp-leef-ern, *v* to deliver

Ablieferung, ahp-leef-er-oong, *f* delivery

ablösen, ahp-ler-zen, *v* to detach; to relieve

Ablösung, ahp-ler-zoong, *f* detachment, separation; relief

abmachen, ahp-mahk-en, *v*

to settle; to undo

Abmachung, ahp-mahk-oong, *f* arrangement

abmagern, ahp-mahg-ern, *v* to become thin

abmalen, ahp-mahl-en, *v* to portray

Abmarsch, ahp-marsh, *m* departure (troops)

abmessen, ahp-mess-en, *v* to measure, to survey

abmühen (sich), ahp-mEE-en (zik), *v* to exert oneself

Abnahme, ahp-nahm-e, *f* decrease, diminution; sale

abnehmen, ahp-nay-men, *v* to take off, to decrease; to buy

Abnehmer, ahp-nay-mer, *m* buyer, customer

abneigen, ahp-ny-gen, *v* to turn away

Abneigung, ahp-ny-goong, *f* aversion, disinclination

abnutzen, ahp-noots-en, *v* to wear out

Abnutzung, ahp-noots-oong, *f* wear and tear

Abonnement, ah-bon-ne-mahng, *nt* subscription; season ticket

Abonnent, ah-bon-nent, *m* subscriber

abonnieren, ah-bon-neer-en, *v* to subscribe

Abort, ahp-ort, *m* lavatory; toilet

abputzen, ahp-poots-en, *v* to clean, to cleanse

abquälen, ahp-kvail-en, *v* to torment, to torture

abrahmen, ahp-rahm-en, *v* to skim (milk)

abraten, ahp-raht-en, *v* to dissuade

abräumen, ahp-roy-men, *v* to clear

abrechnen, ahp-rek-nen, *v* to settle; to deduct

Abrechnung, ahp-rek-noong, *f* settlement

Abrechnungshaus, ahp-rek-noongs-hows, *nt* clearing-house

Abrede, ahp-ray-de, *f* denial; agreement

abreden, ahp-ray-den, *v* to dissuade

abreiben, ahp-ry-ben, *v* to rub off; to wear out by friction

Abreise, ahp-ry-ze, *f* departure

abreisen, ahp-ry-zen, *v* to depart

abreißen, ahp-ry-sen, *v* to tear off; to demolish

abrichten, ahp-rik-ten, *v* to train (animals); to adjust

abrufen, ahp-roof-en, *v* to recall

abrunden, ahp-roonn-den, *v* to round off

abrupfen, ahp-roopp-fen, *v* to pluck off

abrutschen, ahp-roott-shen, *v* to slip from

absagen, ahp-zahg-en, *v* to refuse, to put off

Absatz, ahp-zahts, *m* heel (of shoe); sales; paragraph

Absatzgebiet, ahp-zahts-ge-beet, *nt* market, outlet (goods)

abschaffen, ahp-shahff-en, *v* to abolish

Abschaffung, ahp-shahff-oong, *f* abolition

abschälen, ahp-shay-len, *v* to peel, to shell

abschätzen, ahp-shet-sen, *v* to estimate

Abschätzung, ahp-shet-soong, *f* estimate

abscheiden, ahp-shy-den, *v* to separate

Abscheu, ahp-shoy, *m* loathing, abomination

abscheulich, ahp-shoy-lik, *adj* abominable

abschicken, ahp-shik-en, *v* to send off

Abschied, ahp-sheet, *m* farewell; dismissal

abschiessen, ahp-shee-sen, *v* to shoot off

Abschlag, ahp-shlahk, *m* refusal; decline (price)

abschlagen, ahp-shlah-gen, *v* to refuse, to knock off

Abschlagszahlung, ahp-shlahks-tsahl-oong, *f* instalment, part-payment

abschleifen, ahp-shly-fen, *v* to grind off

abschließen, ahp-shlees-en, *v* to lock; to settle (agreement)

Abschluss, ahp-shlooss, *m* conclusion, settlement

abschmelzen, ahp-shmelt-sen, *v* to melt off

abschneiden, ahp-shny-den,

v to cut off

Abschnitt, ahp-shnitt, *m* section

abschrauben, ahp-shrow-ben, *v* to unscrew

abschrecken, ahp-shreck-en, *v* to scare away

abschreiben, ahp-shry-ben, *v* to copy (writing)

Abschrift, ahp-shrift, *f* (written) copy

abschütteln, ahp-shEEtt-eln, *v* to shake off

abschweifen, ahp-shvy-fen, *v* to digress

Abschweifung, ahp-shvy-foong, *f* digression

abschwören, ahp-shver-ren, *v* to retract

absegeln, ahp-zay-geln, *v* to set sail

absehen (von), ahp-zay-en (fon), *v* to refrain from

abseifen, ahp-zy-fen, *v* to clean with soap

abseits, ahp-zites, *adv* aside; apart

absenden, ahp-zen-den, *v* to send off, to dispatch

Absender, ahp-zen-der, *m* sender

absetzen, ahp-zet-sen, *v* to remove (hat); to drop (off); to cancel; to dismiss; to wean

Absetzung, ahp-zet-soong, *f* dismissal; deduction; cancellation; weaning

Absicht, ahp-sikt, *f* intention, design

absichtlich, ahp-sikt-lik, *adj*

intentional

absolvieren, ahp-zol-veer-en, *v* to absolve; to complete studies

absonderlich, ahp-zon-der-lik, *adj* particular, peculiar

absondern, ahp-zon-dern, *v* to separate; **sich –,** to seclude oneself

abspannen, ahp-shpahnn-en, *v* to unharness; to relax

absparen (sich), ahp-shpahr-en (zik), *v* to save up for

abspenstig machen, ahp-shpen-shtik **mahk**-en, *v* to lure away

absperren, ahp-shperr-en, *v* to shut off, to stop

absplittern, ahp-shplitt-ern, *v* to splinter off

abspringen, ahp-shpring-en, *v* to jump off; to break off

abspülen, ahp-shpEEl-en, *v* to rinse

abstammen (von), ahp-shtahmm-en (fon), *v* to be descended/derived (from)

Abstand, ahp-shtahnt, *m* distance; (fig) difference

abstauben, ahp-shtow-ben, *v* to dust

Abstecher, ahp-shtek-er, *m* excursion, short trip

absteigen, ahp-shty-gen, *v* to descend; to put up (hotel)

abstellen, ahp-shtel-en, *v* to turn off

abstempeln, ahp-shtem-

peln, *v* to stamp

absterben, ahp-shtair-ben, *v* to die off

abstimmen, ahp-shtim-en, *v* to put to the vote

Abstimmung, ahp-shtim-oong, *f* vote; division

abstoßend, ahp-shtohs-ent, *adj* repulsive

abstreiten, ahp-shtry-ten, *v* to contest; to dispute

Absturz, ahp-shtoorts, *m* headlong fall; steep slope

abstürzen, ahp-shtEErt-sen, *v* to fall; to descend steeply

Abt, ahpt, *m* abbot

Abtei, ahp-ty, *f* abbey

Abteil, ahp-tile, *nt* compartment

abteilen, ahp-ty-len, *v* to divide, to partition; to classify

Abteilung, ahp-ty-loong, *f* department, division

abtragen, ahp-trahg-en, *v* to pull down (buildings); to wear out (clothes)

abtreiben, ahp-try-ben, *v* to abort

abtrennen, ahp-trenn-en, *v* to unstitch; to separate

abtreten, ahp-tray-ten, *v* to cede

Abtritt, ahp-tritt, *m* exit *theatre*; resignation; abdication

abtrocknen, ahp-trock-nen, *v* to dry; to wipe

abtrünnig, ahp-trEEnn-ik, *adj* disloyal

Abtrünnigkeit, ahp-trEEnn-ik-kite, *f* disloyalty

abwarten, ahp-vahrt-en, *v* to wait for

abwärts, ahp-vairts, *adv* downwards

abwaschen, ahp-vahsh-en, *v* to wash off

abwechseln, ahp-vek-seln, *v* to alternate; to change over

abwechselnd, ahp-vek-selnt, *adj & adv* alternate(ly)

Abwechslung, ahp-vek-sel-oong, *f* change

Abweg, ahp-vaig, *m* mistake, error

Abwehr, ahp-vair, *f* defence; safeguard

abwehren, ahp-vair-en, *v* to protect; to fend/ward off

abweichen, ahp-vy-ken, *v* to deviate, to differ

Abweichung, ahp-vy-koong, *f* deviation

abweisen, ahp-vy-zen, *v* to refuse; to repulse

Abweisung, ahp-vy-zoong, *f* refusal; rebuff

abwendbar, ahp-vent-bar, *adj* preventable

abwenden, ahp-ven-den, *v* to avert, to turn away

abwerfen, ahp-vair-fen, *v* to throw off; to yield

abwesend, ahp-vay-zent, *adj* absent; missing

Abwesenheit, ahp-vay-zen-hite, *f* absence

abwickeln, ahp-vik-eln, *v* to unroll; to settle (business)

Abwicklung, ahp-vik-loong, *f* settlement; completion

abwiegen, ahp-veeg-en, *v* to weigh

abwischen, ahp-vish-en, *v* to wipe off

abzahlen, ahp-tsahl-en, *v* to pay off; to pay in instalments

abzählen, ahp-tsay-len, *v* to count (out), to enumerate

Abzahlung, ahp-tsahl-oong, *f* part payment

Abzählung, ahp-tsay-loong, *f* counting; telling

abzapfen, ahp-tsahpp-fen, *v* to draw off

abzehren, ahp-tsay-ren, *v* to waste; to pine away

Abzehrung, ahp-tsay-roong, *f* emaciation

Abzeichen, ahp-tsyk-en, *nt* badge

abzeichnen, ahp-tsyk-nen, *v* to sketch

abziehen, ahp-tsee-en, *v* to pull down/off; to deduct

Abzug, ahp-tsook, *m* removal; retreat; proof, copy; deduction

abzweigen, ahp-tsvy-gen, *v* to branch off

abzwingen, ahp-tsving-en, *v* to extort; to obtain by force

ach, ahk, *interj* ah, oh, alas

Achse, ahck-se, *f* axis, axle

Achsel, ahck-sel, *f* shoulder

acht, ahkt, *num* eight

Acht, ahkt, *f* care,

attention; **sich in Acht nehmen, zik in ahkt nay-men,** to take care

achtbar, ahkt-bar, *adj* estimable

Achtbarkeit, ahkt-bar-kite, *f* respectability

Achtel, ahk-tel, *nt* eighth (part)

achten, ahk-ten, *v* to esteem, to heed

achtenswert, ahk-tens-vairt, *adj* worthy of esteem

achtfach, ahkt-fahk, *adj* eightfold

achtlos, ahkt-lohs, *adj* careless

Achtlosigkeit, ahkt-loh-zik-kite, *f* carelessness

achtmal, ahkt-mahl, *adv* eight times

achtsam, ahkt-zahm, *adj* careful; attentive (to)

achtseitig, ahkt-zy-tik, *adj* octagonal

Achtung, ahk-toong, *f* attention!, beware!; respect, esteem

achtungsvoll, ahk-toongs-fol, *adj* respectful

achtungswert, ahk-toongs-vairt, *adj* estimable

achtzehn, ahkt-tsain, *num* eighteen

achtzig, ahkt-tsik, *num* eighty

ächzen, ehk-tsen, *v* to groan loudly

Acker, ahck-er, *m* acre; field

Ackerbau, ahck-er-bow, *m* agriculture

ackern, ahck-ern, v to plough

Adel, ah-del, m nobility, nobleness

adelig, ah-del-ik, adj noble, titled

adeln, ah-deln, v to ennoble; to raise to the peerage

Adelstand, ah-del-shtahnt, m nobility

Ader, ah-der, f blood-vessel, vein

Adler, ahd-ler, m eagle

adoptieren, ah-dop-**teer**-en, v to adopt

Adoption, ah-dopts-**yohn**, f adoption

Adreßbuch, ah-**dress**-book, nt directory; address book

Adresse, ah-**dress**-e, f address

Affäre, ah-**fair**-e, f affair

Affe, ahff-e, m monkey, ape

affig, ahff-ik, adj foolish, silly

Afrika, ahff-ree-kah, nt Afrika

AG, abbr **Aktiengesellschaft**

Agent, ah-gent, m agent

Agentur, ah-gen-**toor**, f agency, representation

agieren, ah-**geer**-en, v to act (business)

Ägypten, ay-**gEEp**-ten, nt Egypt

Ahn, ahn, m ancestor

ähneln, ayn-eln, v to resemble

ahnen, ahnn-en, v to foresee, to suspect

ähnlich, ayn-lik, adj similar, like, resembling

Ähnlichkeit, ayn-lik-kite, f likeness, similarity

Ahnung, ahn-oong, f presentiment

ahnungslos, ahn-oongs-lohs, adj unsuspecting

Ähre, air-e, f ear of corn

Aids, aydz, nt Aids

Akademiker, ah-kah-**daym**-ik-er, m university graduate

akademisch, ah-kah-**daym**-ish, adj academic

Akkord, ah-kord, m chord

Akkordarbeit, ah-**kord**-ahr-byt, f piece-work

Akku, ah-koo, m rechargeable battery

akkurat, ah-koo-**raht**, adj tidy; exact; accurate

Akrobat, ah-kroh-**baht**, m acrobat

Akt, ahkt, m act; nude

Akte, ahkk-te, f file; **—nkoffer**, m attaché case; **—ntasche**, f briefcase

Aktenzeichen, ahkk-ten-tsy-ken, nt reference

Aktie, ahkk-tsee-e, f share (in a company)

Aktiengesellschaft, ahkk-tse-en-ge-**zel**-shahft, f public limited company

Aktienkurs, ahkk-tse-en-koors, m share price

Aktion, ahkts-**yohn**, f action; campaign

Aktionär, ahkts-yohn-**air**, m shareholder

aktiv, ahkk-**teev**, adj active

aktuell, ahkk-too-**ell**, adj up-to-date; topical

Akzent, ahkk-tsent, m accent; stress

Alarm, ah-larm, m alarm

albern, ahll-bern, adj silly

Albernheit, ahll-bern-hite, f foolishness, silliness

Alge, ahll-ge, f seaweed

Alkohol, ahll-koh-hohl, m alcohol

alkoholfrei, ahll-koh-hohl-fry, adj non-alcoholic

All, ahll, nt universe

allabendlich, ahll-**ah**-bent-lik, adj every evening

allbekannt, ahll-be-kahnt, adj universally known; notorious

alle(r/s), ahll-e(r/s), pron all; every; everything; adv finished; **—s Gute**, all the best

Allee, ah-lay, f avenue

allein, ah-line, adj & adv alone; only; conj but

allemal, ahll-e-mahl, adv always; every time; **ein für —**, once and for all

allenfalls, ahll-en-fahls, adv if need be; perhaps

allerbeste(r/s), ahll-er-bes-te(r/s), adj very best

allerdings, ahll-er-dings, adv to be sure, surely

Allergie, ahll-er-gee, f allergy

allergisch, ahll-erg-ish, adj allergic

allerhand, ahll-er-**hahnt**, *adj* all kinds of

Allerheiligen, ahll-er-**hyl**-eeg-en, *nt* All Saints' Day

allerlei, ahll-er-**ly**, *adj* all kinds of

allerletzte(r/s), ahll-er-**lets**-te(r/s), *adj* very last

Allerseelen, ahll-er-**zayl**-en, *nt* All Souls' (Day)

allerseits, ahll-er-**zites**, *adv* on every side

alles, ahll-*es*, *pron* everything

allesamt, ahll-*e*-**zahmt**, *adv* all (of them etc.)

allgemein, ahll-ge-**mine**, *adj* general; **im –en,** in general

Allgewalt, ahll-**ge**-vahlt, *f* omnipotence

allgewaltig, ahll-**ge**-vahl-tik, *adj* all-powerful

alljährlich, ahll-**yair**-lik, *adj* annual

Allmacht, ahll-**mahk**t, *f* omnipotence

allmächtig, ahll-**mek**-tik, *adj* omnipotent, almighty

allmählich, ahll-**may**-lik, *adj & adv* gradual(ly)

Alltag, ahll-**tahk**, *m* everyday life

alltäglich, ahll-**tayg**-lik, *adj* daily

allwissend, ahll-**vis**-ent, *adj* omniscient

allzu, ahll-**tsoo**, *adv* much too

Almosen, ahll-**moh**-zen, *nt* alms

Alpen, ahll-**pen**, *pl* alps; **die –,** the Alps

Alphabet, ahll-fah-**bayt**, *nt* alphabet

Alptraum, ahlp-**trowm**, *m* nightmare

als, ahls, *conj* when; than; as; such as

also, ahll-*zo*, *conj* thus; therefore; well!

alt, ahlt, *adj* old, antique

Alter, ahlt-*er*, *nt* age, old age; antiquity

altern, ahlt-**ern**, *v* to age, to grow old

Altersheim, ahlt-*ers*-**hime**, *nt* old people's home

Altersrente, ahlt-*ers*-ren-*te*, *f* old age pension

altersschwach, ahlt-*ers*-shvahk, *adj* decrepit

Altertum, ahlt-*er*-toom, *nt* antiquity

altertümlich, ahlt-*er*-**tEEm**-lik, *adj* ancient, antique

altmodisch, ahlt-**moh**-dish, *adj* old-fashioned

Altpapier, ahlt-**pah**-peer, *nt* waste paper

Altstadt, ahlt-**shtaht**, *f* old town

Alufolie, ah-loo-foh-lee-*e*, *f* aluminium foil

Aluminium, ah-loo-**min**-ee-oom, *nt* aluminium

am (**= an dem**), ahmm, *prep* at the; by the; in the; near the; to the

Amboß, ahmm-bos, *m* anvil

Ambulanz, ahmm-boo-**lahnts**, *f* ambulance; outpatients

Ameise, ah-**my**-*ze*, *f* ant

Amerika, ah-**meh**-ree-kah, *nt* America

Amerikaner, ah-meh-ree-**kah**-ner, *m* American (person)

amerikanisch, ah-meh-ree-**kah**-nish, *adj* American

Amme, ah-*me*, *f* (wet-) nurse

amortisieren, ahmm-ort-ee-**zeer**-en, *v* to pay for itself

Ampel, ahmp-el, *f* traffic lights

Amsel, ahmm-*zel*, *f* blackbird

Amt, ahmt, *nt* office; official position; job

amtlich, ahmt-lik, *adj* official

Amtssiegel, ahmts-**zeeg**-el, *nt* seal of office

Amtszeichen, ahmts-**tsyk**-en, *nt* dialling tone

amüsieren, ahmm-EE-**zeer**-en *v* to amuse; **sich –,** to enjoy oneself

an, ahnn, *prep* at; on; near; by; about; in

Ananas, ahnn-ah-nahs, *f* pineapple

anbahnen, ahnn-bahn-*en*, *v* to initiate; to loom

Anbau, ahnn-bow, *m* cultivation (soil); annex

anbauen, ahnn-**bow**-en, *v* to cultivate (soil); to extend (building)

anbehalten, ahnn-be-hahlt-en, *v* to keep on (clothes)

anbei, ahnn-**by,** *adv*
enclosed; herewith;
annexed

anbeißen, ahnn-by-sen, *v* to
swallow (bait); to bite
(off)

anbeten, ahnn-bay-ten, *v* to
pray to; to worship

Anbeter, ahnn-bay-ter, *m*
worshipper; admirer

anbetteln, ahnn-bet-eln, *v*
to beg from

anbieten, ahnn-beet-en, *v* to
offer

anbinden, ahnn-bin-den, *v*
to tie up; to attach

Anblick, ahnn-blik, *m* sight;
view

anblicken, ahnn-blik-en, *v*
to glance at

anbrechen, ahnn-brek-en, *v*
to break; to begin

anbrennen, ahnn-bren-en, *v*
to burn (food etc.)

anbringen, ahnn-bring-en, *v*
to bring in/on/to; to fix

Anbruch, ahnn-brook, *m*
beginning; break

Andacht, ahnn-dahkt, *f*
devotion; (religious)
service

andächtig, ahnn-dek-tik, *adj*
devout; attentive

andauern, ahnn-dow-ern, *v*
to continue; to last

Anden, ahnn-den, *pl* Andes

Andenken, ahnn-denn-ken,
nt souvenir; memory

andere(r/s), ahnn-der-e(r/s),
adj other; different

andererseits, ahnn-der-er-

zites, *adv* on the other
hand

ändern, en-dern, *v* to
change; to alter

andernfalls, ahnn-dern-
fahls, *adv* otherwise

anders, ahnn-ders, *adv*
otherwise; differently

anderswo, ahnn-ders-voh,
adv elsewhere

anderthalb, ahnn-dert-
hahlp, *num* one and a half

Änderung, en-der-oong, *f*
alteration; change

anderweitig, ahnn-der-vy-
tik, *adv* otherwise;
elsewhere

andeuten, ahnn-doyt-en, *v*
to hint; to notify

Andeutung, ahnn-doyt-
oong, *f* hint; intimation

Andrang, ahnn-drahng, *m*
crowd; congestion

andrehen, ahnn-dray-en, *v*
to turn on

androhen, ahnn-droh-en, *v*
to threaten; to menace

aneignen, ahnn-y-gnen, *v*
sich etw –, to appropriate
sth; to acquire sth

aneinander, ahnn-ine-**ahnn**-
der, *adv* one against
another; together

anekeln, ahnn-ayk-eln, *v* to
disgust; to sicken

anerkennen, ahnn-air-ken-
en, *v* to acknowledge

Anerkennung, ahnn-
air-ken-oong, *f*
acknowledgement;
recognition

anfachen, ahnn-fahk-en, *v*
to fan (flame)

anfahren, ahnn-fahr-en, *v* to
arrrive; to deliver; to stop
at; to run into, to hit

Anfall, ahnn-fahl, *m* attack;
spasm

anfallen, ahnn-fahl-en, *v* to
attack

Anfang, ahnn-fahng, *m*
beginning

anfangen, ahnn-fahng-en, *v*
to begin, to commence

Anfänger, ahnn-feng-er, *m*
beginner, novice

anfänglich, ahnn-feng-lik,
adj & adv original(ly); at
first

anfangs, ahnn-fahngs, *adv*
in the beginning

anfassen, ahnn-fahss-en, *v* to
take hold of

anfertigen, ahnn-fairt-ig-en,
v to manufacture; to make

Anfertigung, ahnn-fairt-ig-
oong, *f* manufacturing;
making

anfeuchten, ahnn-foyk-ten,
v to moisten

anflehen, ahnn-flay-en, *v* to
implore

anfordern, ahnn-for-dern, *v*
to demand; to claim

Anforderung, ahnn-for-der-
oong, *f* demand; claim

Anfrage, ahnn-frah-ge, *f*
enquiry; question

anfragen, ahnn-frah-gen, *v*
to enquire

anfreunden (sich), ahnn-
froyn-den (zik), *v* to

make friends

anfügen, ahnn-fEE-gen, *v* to join on; to add

anführen, ahnn-fEEr-en, *v* to lead; to quote; to dupe

Anführer, ahnn-fEEr-er, *m* leader; guide

Angabe, ahnn-gah-be, *f* declaration; statement; boasting

angeben, ahnn-gay-ben, *v* to declare; to denounce; to boast

Angeberei, ahnn-gey-ber-y, *f* showing off

angeblich, ahnn-gayp-lik, *adj* alleged; pretended

angeboren, ahnn-ge-bohr-en, *adj* inborn, innate

Angebot, ahnn-ge-boht, *nt* offer; bid

angebracht, ahnn-ge-brahkt, *adj* appropriate, fitting

angeheitert, ahnn-ge-hy-tert, *adj* tipsy

angehen, ahnn-gay-en, *v* to concern; to be tolerable

angehend, ahnn-gay-ent, *adj* incipient; (fig) budding

angehören, ahnn-ge-her-ren, *v* to belong to

angehörig, ahnn-ge-her-ik, *adj* belonging to

Angehörige(r), ahnn-ge-her-ig-e(r), *m & f* relative

Angeklagte(r), ahnn-ge-klahk-te(r), *m & f* accused

Angel, ahng-el, *f* fish-hook; door-hinge

Angelegenheit, ahnn-ge-lay-gen-hite, *f*

business; affair

angeln, ahng-eln, *v* to fish

angemessen, ahnn-ge-mess-en, *adj* appropriate

angenehm, ahnn-ge-naym, *adj* agreeable, pleasant

angesehen, ahnn-ge-say-en, *adj* respected

Angesicht, ahnn-ge-zikt, *nt* countenance; face

angesichts, ahnn-ge-zikts, *prep* in view of

Angestellte(r), ahnn-ge-shell-te(r), *m & f* employee

angetrunken, ahnn-ge-troonk-en, *adj* drunk

angewöhnen, ahnn-ge-ver-nen, *v* to accustom

Angewohnheit, ahnn-ge-vohn-hite, *f* habit

angezogen, ahnn-ge-tsoh-gen, *adj* dressed; stretched

angreifen, ahnn-gry-fen, *v* to attack; to touch

Angreifer, ahnn-gry-fer, *m* aggressor; assailant

angrenzend, ahnn-grent-sent, *adj* adjacent, bordering

Angriff, ahnn-griff, *m* attack, assault

Angst, ahnkst, *f* anxiety, fear; – **haben (vor),** to be afraid (of)

ängstigen (sich), eng-stee-gen (zik), *v* to worry, to be worried

ängstlich, engst-lik, *adj* anxious; timid

Ängstlichkeit, engst-lik-

kite, *f* anxiousness, uneasiness

anhaben, ahnn-hahb-en, *v* to have on; to wear

anhalten, ahnn-hahlt-en, *v* to stop

Anhalter, ahnn-hahlt-er, *m* hitch-hiker

Anhaltspunkt, ahnn-hahlts-poonkt, *m* clue

Anhang, ahnn-hahng, *m* appendix; following, supporters

anhängen, ahnn-heng-en, *v,* to append, to add to

Anhänger, ahnn-heng-er, *m* follower, adherent; trailer; pendant

anhänglich, ahnn-heng-lik, *adj* attached, faithful

Anhängsel, ahnn-heng-sel, *nt* appendage; hanger-on; tag

anhäufen, ahnn-hoyf-en, *v* to accumulate

Anhäufung, ahnn-hoyf-oong, *f* accumulation; congestion

anheften, ahnn-heft-en, *v* to fasten, to tack on

Anhöhe, ahnn-her-e, *f* hill, rising ground; height

anhören, ahnn-her-ren, *v* to listen to; to hear

Ankauf, ahnn-kowf, *m* purchase

ankaufen, ahnn-kowf-en, *v* to purchase

Ankäufer, ahnn-koyf-er, *m* purchaser

Anker, ahng-ker, *m* anchor

Ankerplatz, ahng-ker-plahts, *m* anchorage

anketten, ahnn-ket-en, *v* to chain up

Anklage, ahnn-klahg-*e*, *f* accusation, charge

anklagen, ahnn-klahg-en, *v* to accuse

Ankläger, ahnn-klay-ger, *m* accuser; complainant

anklammern (sich), ahnn-klahmm-ern (zik), *v* to cling to

Anklang, ahnn-klahng, *m* accord; approval

ankleben, ahnn-klay-ben, *v* to stick on; to affix

ankleiden, ahnn-kly-den, *v* to dress; to attire

anklopfen, ahnn-klopp-fen, *v* to knock at the door

anknüpfen, ahnn-k'nEEp-fen, *v* to fasten/tie on; to enter into (conversation etc.)

ankommen, ahnn-komm-en, *v* to arrive; – **auf,** owf, to depend (on)

ankreuzen, ahnn-kroyts-en, *v* to mark with a cross

ankündigen, ahnn-kEEn-de-gen, *v* to announce

Ankunft, ahnn-koonft, *f* arrival

anlächeln, ahnn-lek-eln, *v* to smile at

Anlage, ahnn-lah-ge, *f* (industrial) plant; investment; aptitude; enclosure; park

Anlaß, ahnn-lahss, *m* reason, cause, motive

anlassen, ahnn-lahss-en, *v* to leave on; to start up

Anlasser, ahnn-lahss-er, *m* starter (car)

anläßlich, ahnn-les-lik, *prep* on the occasion of

Anlauf, ahnn-lowf, *m* run-up; attempt; onset

anlaufen, ahnn-low-fen, *v* to begin; to start; (windows) to steam up

anlegen, ahnn-lay-gen, *v* to lay on/against; to invest; to aim at

anlehnen, ahnn-lay-nen, *v* to lean against; to leave ajar

Anleihe, ahnn-ly-*e*, *f* loan

anleiten, ahnn-ly-ten, *v* to guide; to instruct

Anleitung, ahnn-ly-toong, *f* instructions

Anliegen, ahnn-leeg-en, *nt* request; desire

Anlieger, ahnn-leeg-er, *m* resident

anlocken, ahnn-lock-en, *v* to attract; to lure

anlöten, ahnn-lert-en, *v* to solder on

anlügen, ahnn-lEEg-en, *v* to lie to

anmachen, ahnn-mahk-en, *v* to turn on; to fasten

anmaßend, ahnn-mahs-ent, *adj* arrogant

Anmaßung, ahnn-mahs-oong, *f* arrogance

anmelden, ahnn-mel-den, *v* to announce; to register;

sich –, to make an appointment; to register

Anmeldung, ahnn-mel-doong, *f* announcement; appointment; registration

anmerken, ahnn-mairk-en, *v* to note; to annotate

Anmerkung, ahnn-mairk-oong, *f* annotation

Anmut, ahnn-mooht, *f* grace, gracefulness

anmutig, ahnn-mooht-ik, *adj* graceful

annageln, ahnn-nahg-eln, *v* to nail on

annähen, ahnn-nay-en, *v* to sew on

annähern, ahnn-nay-ern, *v* to approach

annähernd, ahnn-nay-ernt, *adj* approximate

Annahme, ahnn-nahm-*e*, *f* acceptance; assumption

annehmbar, ahnn-naym-bahr, *adj* acceptable

annehmen, ahnn-naym-en, *v* to accept; to assume

Annehmlichkeit, ahnn-naym-lik-kite, *f* agreeableness

Annonce, ahnn-nohnn-se, *f* advertisement

annoncieren, ahnn-nonn-see-ren, *v* to advertise

Anorak, ahnn-or-ahkk, *m* anorak

anordnen, ahnn-ord-nen, *v* to order; to arrange

Anordnung, ahnn-ord-noong, *f* arrangement; direction

anormal, ah-nohr-mahl, *adj*
abnormal

anpacken, ahnn-pahck-en, *v*
to seize

anpassen, ahnn-pahss-en, *v*
to adapt; to fit

anpflanzen, ahnn-pflahnt-
sen, *v* to plant; to
cultivate

Anpflanzung, ahnn-
pflahnt-soong, *f*
cultivation; plantation

anpreisen, ahnn-pry-sen, *v*
to commend; to extol

Anprobe, ahnn-proh-be, *f*
trying on

anprobieren, ahnn-proh-
beer-en, *v* to try on

anraten, ahnn-raht-en, *v* to
advise; to recommend

anrechnen, ahnn-rek-nen, *v*
to charge; take into
account

Anrecht, ahnn-rekt, *nt*
right, entitlement;
subscription

Anrede, ahnn-ray-de, *f*
address; speech

anreden, ahnn-ray-den, *v* to
address

anregen, ahnn-ray-gen, *v* to
stimulate; to prompt; to
activate

anregend, ahnn-ray-gent,
adj stimulating

Anregung, ahnn-ray-goong,
f stimulation; stimulus

Anreiz, ahnn-rites, *m*
incentive

anrempeln, ahnn-rem-peln,
v to jostle; to bump into

anrichten, ahnn-rik-ten, *v*
to prepare (food); to cause

anrücken, ahnn-rEEck-en, *v*
to move near; to approach

Anruf, ahnn-roof, *m* phone
call; **–beantworter,** *m*
answerphone

anrufen, ahnn-roof-en, *v* to
call; to ring up

anrühren, ahnn-rEEr-en, *v*
to touch; to blend

ansagen, ahnn-zahg-en, *v* to
announce

Ansager, ahnn-zahg-er, *m*
(radio/tv) announcer

ansammeln, ahnn-zahmm-
eln, *v* to collect; to amass

ansässig, ahnn-zess-ik, *adj*
domiciled; settled

Ansatz, ahnn-zahts, *m* base;
starting point; approach

anschaffen, ahnn-shahff-en,
v to procure; to furnish; to
remit

Anschaffung, ahnn-shahff-
oong, *f* acquisition

anschauen, ahnn-show-en,
v to look at

Anschauung, ahnn-show-
oong, *f* point of view

Anschein, ahnn-shine, *m*
appearance; semblance

anscheinend, ahnn-shine-
ent, *adj* seeming

anschicken (sich), ahnn-
shik-en (*zik*), *v* to get
ready for

Anschlag, ahnn-shlahg, *m*
placard; plot; touch;
estimate

anschlagen, ahnn-shlahg-

en, *v* to strike (key); to
tap; to fix to; to put up; to
estimate

anschließen, ahnn-shlees-
en, *v* to lock; to attach;
sich etw –, to follow sth

Anschluß, ahnn-shlooss, *m*
connection

anschmiegen (sich), ahnn-
shmeeg-en (*zik*), *v* to
nestle against; to cling to

anschmieren, ahnn-shmeer-
en, *v* to smear on; to cheat
(sb)

anschnallen (sich), ahnn-
shnahll-en (*zik*), *v* to
fasten one's seat belt

anschnauzen, ahnn-shnowt-
sen, *v* to reprimand

anschneiden, ahnn-shny-
den, *v* to cut into; to
broach

anschrauben, ahnn-shrow-
ben, *v* to screw on

anschreiben, ahnn-shry-
ben, *v* to write up; to write
to

anschreien, ahnn-shry-en, *v*
to shout at

Anschrift, ahnn-shrift, *f*
address

Anschuldigung, ahnn-
shooll-dig-oong, *f*
accusation, indictment

anschwärzen, ahnn-shvairt-
sen, *v* to blacken

ansehen, ahnn-zay-en, *v* to
look at; to consider

Ansehen, ahnn-zay-en, *nt*
appearance; reputation

ansehnlich, ahnn-zayn-lik,

adj considerable; good-looking

Ansicht, ahnn-zikt, *f* view; prospect; opinion; **–skarte,** *f* (picture) postcard; **–ssache,** *f* matter of opinion

Ansiedlung, ahnn-zeed-loong, *f* colony; settlement

anspannen, ahnn-shpahnn-en, *v* to stretch; to strain; to harness

anspielen (auf), ahnn-shpeel-en (owf), *v* to hint

Anspielung, ahnn-shpeel-oong, *f* allusion

anspornen, ahnn-shporn-en, *v* to spur on

Ansprache, ahnn-shprahk-e, *f* address; speech

ansprechen, ahnn-shprek-en, *v* to speak to; to address

Anspruch, ahnn-shprook, *m* claim, pretension

anspruchslos, ahnn-shprooks-lohs, *adj* modest

anspruchsvoll, ahnn-shprooks-fol, *adj* demanding

anspucken, ahnn-shpoock-en, *v* to spit at

Anstalt, ahnn-shtahlt, *f* institution

Anstand, ahnn-shtant, *m* decorum; decency

anständig, ahnn-shten-dik, *adj* decent; becoming

Anständigkeit, ahnn-shten-dik-kite, *f* decency

anstatt, ahnn-shtahtt, *prep* instead of

anstaunen, ahnn-shtow-nen, *v* to look at in amazement

anstecken, ahnn-shteck-en, *v* to pin to; to set alight; to infect

ansteckend, ahnn-shteck-ent, *adj* infectious, contagious

Ansteckung, ahnn-shteck-oong, *f* infection

ansteigen, ahnn-shty-gen, *v* to ascend, to climb

anstellen, ahnn-shtell-en, *v* to appoint; to employ

Anstellung, ahnn-shtell-oong, *f* appointment, employment, position

anstiften, ahnn-shtift-en, *v* to instigate

Anstiftung, ahnn-shtift-oong, *f* instigation; provocation

anstimmen, ahnn-shtimm-en, *v* to intonate; to tune

Anstoß, ahnn-shtohs, *m* impetus; offence

anstoßen, ahnn-shtohs-en, *v* to knock against; to clink (glasses)

anstößig, ahnn-shters-ik, *adj* offensive; obnoxious

anstreichen, ahnn-shtry-ken, *v* to paint

anstrengen, ahnn-shtreng-en, *v* to exert; to strain; **sich –,** to make an effort

anstrengend, ahnn-shtreng-ent, *adj* tiring

Anstrengung, ahnn-shtreng-oong, *f* exertion; effort

Anstrich, ahnn-shtrik, *m* coat of paint

Ansturm, ahnn-shtoorm, *m* rush; attack

anstürmen, ahnn-shtEErm-en, *v* to charge against

Antarktis, ahnt-ahrk-tis, *f* Antarctica

antarktisch, ahnt-ahrk-tish, *adj* Antarctic

Anteil, ahnn-tile, *m* share, portion; sympathy

Antenne, ahnn-ten-e, *f* antenna; aerial

Antibiotikum, ahnn-te-be-**oh-**te-koom, *nt* anti-biotic

antik, ahnn-teek, *adj* antique

Antiquar, ahnn-tee-**kvahr,** *m* antiquarian

Antiquariat, ahnn-tee-kvahr-e-**aht,** *nt* secondhand bookshop

Antiquitäten, ahnn-tee-kvee-**tay-**ten, *pl* antiques

Antlitz, ahnt-lits, *nt* countenance

Antrag, ahnn-trahg, *m* proposal

antreffen, ahnn-treff-en, *v* to meet; to come across

antreiben, ahnn-try-ben, *v* to drive (on/against); to urge (on)

antreten, ahnn-tray-ten, *v* to begin; to line up; to assemble; to compete

Antrieb, ahnn-treep, *m*

impulse; incentive; drive

Antritt, ahnn-tritt, *m*
beginning

antun, ahnn-toon, *v* to
inflict

Antwort, ahnt-vort, *f*
answer, reply

antworten, ahnt-vort-en, *v*
to answer, to reply

anvertrauen, ahnn-fair-
trow-en, *v* to entrust

anwachsen, ahnn-vahks-en,
v to grow (on); to increase

Anwalt, ahnn-vahlt, *m*
lawyer; solicitor; barrister

anwärmen, ahnn-vairm-en,
v to warm up

anweisen, ahnn-vy-zen, *v* to
instruct; to transfer
(money)

Anweisung, ahnn-vy-zoong,
f direction; instruction;
payment; postal order

anwendbar, ahnn-vent-bar,
adj applicable (to)

anwenden, ahnn-ven-den, *v*
to use; to apply to

Anwendung, ahnn-ven-
doong, *f* use; application

anwesend, ahnn-vay-zent,
adj present

Anwesenheit, ahnn-vay-
zen-hite, *f* presence

anwidern, ahnn-veed-ern, *v*
to disgust

Anzahl, ahnn-tsahl, *f*
number; quantity

anzahlen, ahnn-tsahl-en, *v*
to pay a deposit

Anzahlung, ahnn-tsahl-
oong, *f* deposit;

part-payment

anzapfen, ahnn-tsahpp-fen,
v to breach; to tap
(trees/telephones)

Anzeichen, ahnn-tsy-ken, *nt*
mark, sign, indication

Anzeige, ahnn-tsy-ge, *f*
advertisement; notice;
advice; denunciation; –
gegen jdn erstatten, to
report sb to the police

anzeigen, ahnn-tsy-gen, *v* to
report sb to the police; to
denounce

Anzeiger, ahnn-tsy-ger, *m*
indicator; advertiser

anziehen, ahnn-tsee-en, *v* to
draw towards; to attract;
to put on (clothes)

Anziehung, ahnn-tsee-
oong, *f* attraction

Anzug, ahnn-tsook, *m* suit
(of clothes); approach

anzüglich, ahnn-tsEEk-lik,
adj suggestive; pointed

Anzüglichkeit, ahnn-tsEEk-
lik-kite, *f* suggestiveness

anzünden, ahnn-tsEEn-den,
v to light

apart, ah-part, *adj*
distinctive

Apfel, ahpp-fel, *m* apple

Apfelbaum, ahpp-fel-bowm,
m apple-tree

Apfelkuchen, ahpp-fel-
kook-en, *m* apple tart

Apfelsine, ahpp-fel-seen-e, *f*
orange

Apfelwein, ahpp-fel-vine, *m*
cider

Apotheke, ah-poh-tay-ke, *f*

chemist's (shop)

Apotheker, ah-poh-tay-ker,
m chemist

Apparat, ah-pah-raht, *m*
appliance; camera;
telephone

Appartement, ah-pahrt-e-
mong, *nt* flat

Appell, ah-pell, *m* appeal;
roll call

appellieren, ah-pell-eer-en,
v to appeal (court)

Appetit, ahp-pay-teet, *m*
appetite; **guten –,** bon
appétit

applaudieren, ahp-plow-
deer-en, *v* to applaud

Applaus, ahp-lows, *m*
applause

Aprikose, ah-pre-koh-ze, *f*
apricot

April, ah-pril, *m* April

Aquarell, ahkk-vah-rel, *nt*
water-colour; **–farbe,** *f*
water-colour paint

Araber, ah-rahb-er, *m* Arab

arabisch, ah-rahb-ish, *adj*
Arabian, Arabic

Arbeit, ahr-bite, *f* work,
labour

arbeiten, ahr-bite-en, *v* to
work

Arbeiter, ahr-bite-er, *m*
workman, worker,
labourer

Arbeitgeber, ahr-bite-gay-
ber, *m* employer

Arbeitnehmer, ahr-bite-
nay-mer, *m* employee

Arbeitsamt, ahr-bites-ahmt,
nt employment exchange

Arbeitserlaubnis, ahr-bites-er-lowb-nis, *f* work permit

arbeitsfähig, ahr-bites-fay-ik, *adj* able-bodied

Arbeitslohn, ahr-bites-lohn, *m* wages; pay

arbeitslos, ahr-bites-lohs, *adj* unemployed

Arbeitslosigkeit, ahr-bites-loh-zik-kite, *f* unemployment

Arbeitsplatz, ahr-bites-plahts, *m* place of work

Arbeitstag, ahr-bites-tahk, *m* working day

Arbeitszeit, ahr-bites-tsite, *f* working hours

Arbeitszimmer, ahr-bites-tsim-*er*, *nt* study

Architektur, ahr-kee-teck-toor, *f* architecture

arg, ahrk, *adj* bad; severe; tremendous; wicked

Argentinien, ahrg-enn-tee-nee-en, *nt* Argentina

Argentinier, ahrg-enn-tee-nee-*er*, *m* Argentinian (person)

argentinisch, ahrg-enn-tee-nish, *adj* Argentinian

Ärger, airg-*er*, *m* annoyance; anger

ärgerlich, airg-er-lik, *adj* annoyed; annoying

ärgern, airg-ern, *v* to annoy; to provoke

Ärgernis, airg-er-nis, *nt* annoyance; scandal

arglos, ahrk-lohs, *adj* innocent; ingenuous

Argwohn, ahrk-vohn, *m* suspicion, mistrust

argwöhnisch, ahrk-vern-ish, *adj* suspicious

Aristokratie, ah-ree-stoh-krah-tee, *f* aristocracy

Arktis, ahrk-tis, *f* the Arctic

arktisch, ahrk-tish, *adj* Arctic

Arm, ahrm, *m* arm

arm, ahrm, *adj* poor

Armband, ahrm-bahnt, *nt* bracelet

Armbanduhr, ahrm-bahnt-oor, *f* wristwatch

Arme(r), ahrm-e(r), *m & f* poor man/woman

Armee, ahrm-ay, *f* army

Ärmel, air-mel, *m* sleeve; –kanal, *m* English Channel

Armenhaus, ahrm-en-hows, *nt* almshouse

ärmlich, airm-lik, *adj* miserable, poor

armselig, ahrm-zay-lik, *adj* wretched; poor

Armseligkeit, ahrm-zay-lik-kite, *f* wretchedness

Armsessel, ahrm-zess-el, *m* armchair

Armut, ahr-moot, *f* poverty

arrangieren, ahr-rahng-zheer-en, *v* to arrange

Arsen, ahr-zayn, *nt* arsenic

Art, ahrt, *f* sort, kind; species; manner

Arterie, ahr-tair-ee-e, *f* artery

artig, ahr-tik, *adj* well-behaved; polite

Artikel, ahr-tik-el, *m* article

Artist, ahr-tist, *m* artiste

Arzneimittel, ahrts-ny-mit-tel, *nt* medicine; drug

Arzt, ahrtst, *m* (male) doctor

Ärztin, airtst-in, *f* (female) doctor

ärztlich, airtst-lik, *adj* medical, medicinal

As, ahss, *nt* ace

Asche, ahsh-e, *f* ash(es)

Aschenbecher, ahsh-en-bek-*er*, *m* ashtray

Aschenbrödel, ahsh-en-brer-del, *nt* Cinderella

Aschermittwoch, ahsh-er-mit-vok, *m* Ash Wednesday

Asiat, ah-zee-**aht**, *m* Asian (person)

asiatisch, ah-zee-ah-**tish**, *adj* Asian

Asien, ah-zee-en, *nt* Asia

Ast, ahst, *m* branch (tree)

Asthma, ahst-mah, *nt* asthma

Astrologie, ahst-roh-loh-gee, *f* astrology

Asyl, ah-z**EEl**, *nt* sanctuary; (political) asylum

Atelier, ah-tel-e-eh, *nt* studio

Atem, ah-tem, *m* breath; respiration

Atembeklemmung, ah-tem-be-klemm-oong, *f* difficulty in breathing; asthma

Atemholen, ah-tem-hoh-len, *nt* breathing

atemlos, ah-tem-lohs, *adj* breathless

Atemlosigkeit, ah-tem-loh-zik-kite, *f* breathlessness

Atemnot, ah-tem-noht, *f* difficult breathing

Atemzug, ah-tem-tsook, *m* breath

Athen, ah-tain, *nt* Athens

Äther, ay-ter, *m* ether

Athlet, ahtt-lait, *m* athlete

Atlantik, ahtt-lahnn-tik, *m* Atlantic (ocean)

atlantisch, ahtt-lahnn-tish, *adj* Atlantic

Atlas, aht-lass, *m* atlas; satin

atmen, aht-men, *v* to breathe

Atmosphäre, ahtt-mohs-fair-e, *f* atmosphere

Atmung, aht-moong, *f* breath; respiration

Atombombe, ah-tohm-bom-be, *f* atom bomb

Atomwaffen, ah-tohm-vahff-en, *pl* atomic weapons

Attentat, ahtt-en-taht, *nt* assassination attempt

Attest, ahtt-est, *nt* certificate, attestation

attestieren, ahtt-est-eer-en, *v* to attest, to certify

Attraktion, ahtt-rahkts-yohn, *f* attraction

attraktiv, ahtt-rahk-teef, *adj* attractive

ätzen, et-sen, *v* to corrode; to cauterize; to etch

au, ow, *interj* ouch!

auch, owk, *conj* also, likewise, as well

auf, owf, *prep* (up)on; *adv* up(wards); open

aufatmen, owf-aht-men, *v* to give a sigh of relief

aufbauen, owf-bow-en, *v* to build up, to erect

aufbäumen (sich), owf-boy-men (zik), *v* to rear; to prance (horse)

aufbauschen, owf-bow-shen, *v* to puff (up)

aufbehalten, owf-be-hahl-ten, *v* to keep on (hat)

aufbessern, owf-bess-ern, *v* to raise (wages); to improve

aufbewahren, owf-be-vahr-en, *v* to keep; to take of

Aufbewahrung, owf-be-vahr-oong, *f* (safe-) keeping

aufbieten, owf-beet-en, *v* to summon; to muster

aufblasen, owf-blah-zen, *v* to inflate

aufbleiben, owf-bly-ben, *v* to stay open; to stay up late

aufblühen, owf-blEE-en, *v* to flourish

aufbrauchen, owf-browk-en, *v* to use up, to consume

aufbrausen, owf-brow-zen, *v* to fizz; to fly into a rage

aufbrechen, owf-brek-en, *v* to break open; to start (journey)

aufbringen, owf-bring-en, *v* to rear; to introduce; to raise (money)

aufdecken, owf-deck-en, *v* to uncover; to expose

Aufdeckung, owf-deck-oong, *f* exposure

aufdrehen, owf-dray-en, *v* to turn on

aufdringlich, owf-dring-lik, *adj* obtrusive, insistent

aufdrucken, owf-drook-en, *v* to print (on); to imprint; to stamp

aufeinander, owf-ine-ahnn-der, *adv* one upon another, one after another

Aufenthalt, owf-ent-hahlt, *m* stay; delay; **—serlaubnis**, *f* residence permit

auferlegen, owf-air-lay-gen, *v* to impose

auferstehen, owf-air-shtay-en, *v* to rise from the dead

Auferstehung, owf-air-shtay-oong, *f* resurrection

aufessen, owf-ess-en, *v* to eat up, to consume

auffahren, owf-fahr-en, *v* to fly into a rage

Auffahrt, owf-fahrt, *f* drive

auffallend, owf-fahll-ent, *adj* striking; conspicuous

auffällig, owf-fel-lik, *adj* striking; conspicuous

auffangen, owf-fahng-en, *v* to catch; to intercept

auffassen, owf-fahss-en, *v* to comprehend, to conceive (ideas); to perceive

Auffassung, owf-fahss-oong, *f* conception,

comprehension

auffordern, owf-for-dern, *v* to ask; to invite

Aufforderung, owf-for-der-oong, *f* invitation

auffressen, owf-fress-en, *v* to eat up; to devour

aufführen, owf-fEEr-en, *v* to stage, to perform; to list

Aufführung, owf-fEEr-oong, *f* performance

Aufgabe, owf-gah-be, *f* task; exercise; registration; retirement; surrender; giving up

Aufgang, owf-gahng, *m* ascent; staircase; appearance; emergence

aufgeben, owf-gay-ben, *v* to give (up); to register; to check in

aufgeblasen, owf-ge-blah-zen, *adj* puffed up

Aufgebot, owf-ge-boht, *nt* public notice; banns

aufgebracht, owf-ge-brahkt, *adj* outraged

aufgehen, owf-gay-en, *v* to open; to rise (sun, curtain)

aufgeklärt, owf-ge-klairt, *adj* enlightened

aufgeregt, owf-ge-raykt, *adj* excited, agitated

aufgeweckt, owf-ge-veckt, *adj* lively; bright

aufgreifen, owf-gry-fen, *v* to seize, to take up

aufhalten, owf-hahlt-en, *v* to hold open; to detain

aufhängen, owf-heng-en, *v* to hang

aufhäufen, owf-hoyf-en, *v* to pile up

aufheben, owf-hay-ben, *v* to lift up; to keep up

aufheitern, owf-hy-tern, *v* to brighten up

Aufheiterung, owf-hy-ter-oong, *f* brightening

aufhetzen, owf-het-sen, *v* to rouse, to incite

aufhorchen, owf-hor-ken, *v* to prick up one's ears

aufhören, owf-her-ren, *v* to stop, to finish

aufkaufen, owf-kowf-en, *v* to buy up

aufklappen, owf-klahpp-en, *v* to open up/out

aufklären, owf-klair-en, *v* to clear up; to enlighten

Aufklärung, owf-klair-oong, *f* enlightenment

aufknacken, owf-k'nahck-en, *v* to crack open

aufknöpfen, owf-k'nerp-fen, *v* to unbutton

aufkommen, owf-komm-en, *v* to (a)rise; to come up/out; to pay (for)

aufladen, owf-lahd-en, *v* to load; to charge with

Auflage, owf-lahg-e, *f* edition (books); imposition

auflassen, owf-lahss-en, *v* to leave open; to shut down

Auflauf, owf-lowf, *m* crowd; mob; baked pudding

auflegen, owf-lay-gen, *v* to apply; to lay on

auflesen, owf-lay-zen, *v* to pick up; to glean

auflösen, owf-ler-zen, *v* to (dis)solve; to loosen

Auflösung, owf-ler-zoong, *f* dissolution; solution

aufmachen, owf-mahk-en, *v* to open, to undo

Aufmachung, owf-mahk-oong, *f* outfit; format

aufmerken, owf-mairk-en, *v* to mark, to take note

aufmerksam, owf-mairk-zahm, *adj* attentive

Aufmerksamkeit, owf-merk-sahm-kite, *f* attention, attentiveness

aufmuntern, owf-moon-tern, *v* to cheer up, to rouse

Aufnahme, owf-nahm-e, *f* taking up; reception

aufnehmen, owf-nay-men, *v* to take up/in

aufopfern (sich), owf-op-fern (zik), *v* to sacrifice (oneself)

aufpassen, owf-pahss-en, *v* to be careful; to pay attention

aufpolstern, owf-pol-stern, *v* to upholster

aufpumpen, owf-poom-pen, *v* to pump up

aufräumen, owf-roy-men, *v* to clear (up); to tidy (up)

aufrecht, owf-rekt, *adj* upright, erect

aufregen, owf-ray-gen, *v* to excite, to stir up

Aufregung, owf-ray-goong,

f excitement

aufreißen, owf-ry-sen, v to tear open (or up)

aufreizen, owf-ry-tsen, v to incite, to provoke

aufrichten, owf-rik-ten, v to erect

aufrichtig, owf-rik-tik, adj sincere, honest

Aufrichtigkeit, owf-rik-tik-kite, f sincerity, honesty

Aufruf, owf-roof, m calling up; appeal

Aufruhr, owf-roor, m uproar, riot, rebellion

aufrührerisch, owf-rEER-er-ish, adj mutinous

aufsagen, owf-zahg-en, v to recite

aufsammeln, owf-zahmm-eln, v to collect

Aufsatz, owf-sahts, m essay; upper part

aufschauen, owf-show-en, v to look up

aufschieben, owf-shee-ben, v to postpone, to put off

Aufschlag, owf-shlahk, m impact; service (tennis)

aufschlagen, owf-shlahg-en, v to crash; to serve (tennis)

aufschließen, owf-shlees-en, v to unlock

Aufschluß, owf-shlooss, m disclosure, explanation

aufschneiden, owf-shny-den, v to cut open; to boast

Aufschneider, owf-shny-der, m boaster

Aufschnitt, owf-shnitt, m cut; cold meat

aufschrauben, owf-shrow-ben, v to screw on

aufschrecken, owf-shreck-en, v to startle

Aufschrei, owf-shry, m outcry; shriek

aufschreiben, owf-shry-ben, v to write down

Aufschrift, owf-shrift, f inscription; address

Aufschub, owf-shoop, m delay; adjournment

aufschütten, owf-shEEtt-en, v to pour on

Aufschwung, owf-shvoong, m swinging up; comm revival, upturn

Aufsehen, owf-zay-en, nt sensation, scandal

Aufseher, owf-zay-er, m overseer, inspector

aufsetzen, owf-zet-sen, v to put on; to set up

Aufsicht, owf-zikt, f supervision; care; inspection; **–srat,** m board of inspection

aufsitzen, owf-zit-sen, v to sit up; to mount (horse)

aufsparen, owf-shpahr-en, v to save up

aufsperren, owf-shpair-ren, v to open wide

aufsprengen, owf-shpreng-en, v to burst open; to blast open

aufspringen, owf-shpring-en, v to jump up; to bounce; to burst open

aufstacheln, owf-shtahk-eln, v to goad; to spur on

Aufstand, owf-shtahnt, m rising, rebellion

aufständisch, owf-shten-dish, adj rebellious

aufstapeln, owf-shtah-peln, v to pile/stack up

aufstehen, owf-shtay-en, v to rise, to get up

aufsteigen, owf-shty-gen, v to climb; to rise; to mount

aufstellen, owf-shtell-en, v to set up, to erect

Aufstellung, owf-shtell-oong, f erection; drawing up; list, inventory

Aufstieg, owf-shteek, m ascent

aufsuchen, owf-sook-en, v to look up; to visit

auftauchen, owf-towk-en, v to rise; to emerge

auftauen, owf-tow-en, v to thaw

aufteilen, owf-ty-len, v to divide

Aufteilung, owf-ty-loong, f division

auftischen, owf-tish-en, v to serve up, to dish up

Auftrag, owf-trahk, m order; commission; task; **–geber,** m client; customer; **–nehmer,** m person/firm accepting an order; contractor

auftreiben, owf-try-ben, v to raise; to find

auftreten, owf-tray-ten, v to appear; to step on

Auftritt, owf-tritt, *m*
appearance; entrance

aufwachen, owf-vahk-en, *v*
to wake up, to awake

aufwachsen, owf-vahk-sen,
v to grow up

aufwärmen, owf-vair-men, *v*
to warm up

aufwarten, owf-vahrt-en, *v*
to wait on

aufwärts, owf-vairts, *adv*
upwards

aufwaschen, owf-vahsh-en,
v to wash (up/down)

aufwecken, owf-veck-en, *v*
to awaken; to rouse

aufweisen, owf-vy-zen, *v* to
show (results)

aufwenden, owf-ven-den, *v*
to spend; to devote

aufwendig, owf-vend-ik, *adj*
costly; lavish

aufwerfen, owf-vairf-en, *v*
to throw up/open; to raise
(question, problem)

aufwerten, owf-vair-ten, *v*
to revalue; to increase in
value

aufwickeln, owf-vik-eln, *v*
to coil; to wind up

aufwiegeln, owf-veeg-eln, *v*
to stir up, to provoke

aufwirbeln, owf-veer-beln, *v*
to swirl up

aufwischen, owf-vish-en, *v*
to wipe up, to mop up

aufwühlen, owf-vEEl-en, *v*
to toss/rip up

aufzählen, owf-tsay-len, *v* to
list

aufzehren, owf-tsay-ren, *v*

to consume

aufzeichnen, owf-tsy'k-nen,
v to sketch; to record; to
note

Aufzeichnung, owf-tsy'k-
noong, *f* sketch; record;
recording; note

aufziehen, owf-tsee-en, *v* to
wind up; to pull up; to
rear

Aufzug, owf-tsook, *m* lift;
act; procession

Augapfel, owk-ahpp-fel, *m*
eyeball

Auge, ow-ge, *nt* eye; bud;
spot

Augenarzt, ow-gen-ahrts-t,
m ophthalmologist

Augenblick, ow-gen-blik, *m*
moment, instant

augenblicklich, ow-gen-
blik-lik, *adv* at present

Augenbraue, ow-gen-brow-
e, *f* eyebrow

Augenlicht, ow-gen-likt, *nt*
(eye)sight

Augenlid, ow-gen-leet, *nt*
eyelid

Augenschein, ow-gen-
shine, *m* appearance

augenscheinlich, ow-gen-
shine-lik, *adj* apparent

Augenwimper, ow-gen-vim-
per, *f* eyelash

Augenzeuge, ow-gen-tsoy-
ge, *m* eye-witness

August, ow-goost, *m*
August

Auktion, owkts-yohn, *f*
auction

Auktionator, owkts-yohn-

ah-tohr, *m* auctioneer

aus, owss, *prep* out of; of;
from; made of; *adv*
finished; over; off

ausarbeiten, ows-ahr-by-
ten, *v* to work out

ausarten, ows-ahrt-en, *v* to
degenerate

ausatmen, ows-aht-men, *v*
to breathe out, to exhale

ausbedingen, ows-be-ding-
en, *v* to stipulate

ausbessern, ows-bes-ern, *v*
to repair, to restore

ausbeuten, ows-boy-ten, *v*
to exploit

ausbezahlen, ows-be-tsahl-
en, *v* to pay out

ausbilden, ows-bil-den, *v* to
train

Ausbildung, ows-bil-doong,
f training; development

ausblasen, ows-blah-zen, *v*
to blow out

ausbleiben, ows-bly-ben, *v*
to stay out; to fail to
appear

Ausblick, ows-blik, *m*
prospect; view

ausbrechen, ows-brek-en, *v*
to break out

ausbreiten, ows-bry-ten, *v*
to spread out

ausbrennen, ows-bren-en, *v*
to burn out

Ausbruch, ows-brook, *m*
outbreak; eruption

ausbrüten, ows-brEEt-en, *v*
to hatch; to incubate

ausbürsten, ows-bEErst-en, *v*
to brush thoroughly

Ausdauer, ows-dow-er, *f* endurance; perseverance

ausdehnen, ows-day-nen, *v* to stretch; to expand

Ausdehnung, ows-day-noong, *f* extension; enlargement; dimension

ausdenken, ows-deng-ken, *v* to think out; to imagine

ausdienen, ows-deen-en, *v* to serve one's time

ausdrehen, ows-dray-en, *v* to turn out

Ausdruck, ows-droock, *m* expression

ausdrücken, ows-drEEck-en, *v* to express; to squeeze out

ausdrücklich, ows-drEEck-lik, *adj* positive; explicit

ausdruckslos, ows-droocks-lohss, *adj* without expression

ausdrucksvoll, ows-droocks-foll, *adj* expressive; significant

Ausdünstung, ows-dEEnn-stoong, *f* evaporation; perspiration

auseinander, ows-ine-ahnn-der, *adj* asunder; apart; separate

Auseinandersetzung, ows-ine-ahnn-der-zets-oong, *f* discussion; argument; examination; analysis

auserlesen, ows-air-lay-zen, *adj* choice; select

auserwählen, ows-air-vay-len, *v* to choose

auserwählt, ows-air-vailt, *adj* elect; predestined

ausfahren, ows-fahr-en, *v* to drive out

Ausfahrt, ows-fahrt, *f* drive; excursion; exit, way out

Ausfall, ows-fahll, *m* loss; cancellation; retirement; result, outcome

ausfallen, ows-fahll-en, *v* to turn out; to fall out; to fail, to break down; to be cancelled

ausfechten, ows-fek-ten, *v* to fight out

ausfegen, ows-fay-gen, *v* to sweep out

ausfertigen, ows-fairt-ig-en, *v* to expedite; to draw up (documents)

ausfindig machen, ows-fin-dig **mahk**-en, *v* to find (out)

Ausflucht, ows-flookt, *f* excuse

Ausflug, ows-floock, *m* excursion; trip

Ausflügler, ows-flEEg-ler, *m* tripper

Ausfluß, ows-flooss, *m* outflow; discharge

ausfragen, ows-frahg-en, *v* to question

Ausfuhr, ows-foor, *f* export

ausführen, ows-fEEr-en, *v* to carry out; to export

ausführlich, ows-fEEr-lik, *adj* detailed; ample

Ausführung, ows-fEEr-oong, *f* execution; completion; model

ausfüllen, ows-fEEll-en, *v* to fill out (form)

Ausgabe, ows-gah-be, *f* edition; issue; expense

Ausgang, ows-gahng, *m* exit, way out; upshot

ausgeben, ows-gay-ben, *v* to spend; to yield

ausgebreitet, ows-ge-bry-tet, *adj* spread out

ausgebucht, ows-ge-bookt, *adj* fully booked

ausgefallen, ows-ge-fahll-en, *adj* exceptional

ausgehen, ows-gay-en, *v* to go out; to proceed from

ausgelassen, ows-ge-lahss-en, *adj* boisterous; unrestrained; left out

ausgemacht, ows-ge-mahkt, *adj* made out; agreed (upon)

ausgenommen, ows-ge-nomm-en, *conj* except

ausgesucht, ows-ge-sookt, *adj* choice; exceptional

ausgezeichnet, ows-ge-tsy'k-net, *adj* distinguished; excellent

ausgießen, ows-geess-en, *v* to pour out

Ausgleich, ows-gly'k, *m* balance; settling

ausgleiten, ows-gly-ten, *v* to slip, to slide

ausgraben, ows-grahb-en, *v* to dig out

Ausguck, ows-goock, *m* look-out

Ausguß, ows-gooss, *m* sink; drain

aushalten, ows-hahll-ten, *v*

29

to hold out; to sustain;
to bear

aushandeln, ows-hahnn-
deln, *v* to negotiate

aushändigen, ows-hen-dig-
en, *v* to hand over

aushängen, ows-heng-en, *v*
to hang out

ausharren, ows-hahrr-en, *v*
to persevere

ausheben, ows-hay-ben, *v*
to levy; to lift out; to raid

aushelfen, ows-hel-fen, *v* to
help out

Aushilfe, ows-hil-fe, *f* aid;
temporary help

ausholen, ows-hohl-en, *v* to
raise one's arm to strike

aushorchen, ows-hor-ken, *v*
to sound

aushungern, ows-hoong-
ern, *v* to famish; to starve
out

auskämmen, ows-kem-en,
to comb out

auskennen (sich), ows-ken-
en (zik), *v* to know one's
way; to be knowledgeable

auskleiden (sich), ows-kly-
den (zik), *v* to undress; to
take off (clothes)

ausklopfen, ows-klop-fen, *v*
to beat out

auskneifen, ows-k'ny-fen, *v*
to run away

auskochen, ows-kok-en, *v*
to boil thoroughly

auskommen, ows-kom-en, *v*
to manage (to live); to get
on with (sb)

auskundschaften, ows-

koont-shahft-en, *v* to
reconnoitre

Auskunft, ows-koonft, *f*
information

auslachen, ows-lahk-en, *v*
to laugh at; to deride

ausladen, ows-lahd-en, *v* to
unload

Auslage, ows-lahg-e, *f*
outlay; (shop) display

Ausland, ows-lahnt, *nt*
foreign countries; **im –,**
abroad; **ins – gehen,** to go
abroad

Ausländer, ows-len-der, *m*
foreigner

ausländisch, ows-len-dish,
adj foreign; alien

Auslandsgespräch, ows-
lahnts-ge-shpraik, *nt*
international call

Auslandsreise, ows-lahnts-
ry-ze, *f* trip abroad

auslassen, ows-lahss-en, *v*
to omit; to let out

auslaufen, ows-lowf-en, *v* to
run out; to stop running

ausleeren, ows-lay-ren, *v* to
empty

auslegen, ows-lay-gen, *v* to
spread out; to display; to
lay out; to interpret

Auslegung, ows-lay-goong,
f interpretation;
explanation

ausleihen, ows-ly-en, *v* to
lend; **sich etw –,** to
borrow sth

ausliefern, ows-leef-ern, *v*
to deliver; to hand over;
to extradite

Auslieferung, ows-leef-er-
oong, *f* delivery;
extradition

auslöschen, ows-lersh-en, *v*
to extinguish; to
obliterate

auslösen, ows-ler-zen, *v* to
cause; to start

ausmachen, ows-mahk-en, *v*
to put out; to switch off;
Macht es Ihnen etw aus?
Do you mind?

Ausmarsch, ows-marsh, *m*
marching out; departure
(troops)

Ausmaß, ows-mahss, *nt*
scale; extent

ausmessen, ows-mess-en, *v*
to measure; to take the
dimensions

Ausnahme, ows-nahm-e, *f*
exception; **–zustand,** *m*
state of emergency

ausnahmslos, ows-nahms-
lohs, *adv* without
exception

ausnahmsweise, ows-
nahms-vy-ze, *adv* as an
exception

ausnehmen, ows-nay-men,
v to except; to make out

ausnutzen, ows-noots-en,
ausnützen, ows-nEEts-en,
v to exploit; to utilize

auspacken, ows-pahck-en, *v*
to unpack

auspfeifen, ows-pfy-fen, *v* to
hiss at

ausplaudern, ows-plow-
dern, *v* to have a good
chat

ausplündern, ows-plEEnn-dern, *v* to loot

auspressen, ows-press-en, *v* to squeeze out

ausprobieren, ows-proh-beer-en, *v* to try out

Auspuff, ows-pooff, *m* exhaust (pipe, valve)

ausrauben, ows-row-ben, *v* to rob; to pillage

ausräumen, ows-roy-men, *v* to clear away

ausrechnen, ows-rek-nen, *v* to work out; to calculate

Ausrede, ows-ray-de, *f* excuse; plea

ausreden, ows-ray-den, *v* to finish speaking; **jdm etw –**, to talk sb out of sth

ausreichen, ows-ry-ken, *v* to suffice

ausreichend, ows-ry-kent, *adj* adequate

Ausreise, ows-ry-ze, *f* departure; **–erlaubnis**, *f* exit permit

ausreisen, ows-ry-zen, *v* to leave the country

ausreißen, ows-ry-sen, *v* to tear out; to run away

ausreiten, ows-ry-ten, *v* to go (out) riding

ausrenken, ows-renk-en, *v* to put out of joint

ausrichten, ows-rik-ten, *v* to align; to tell; to pass on

ausrotten, ows-rot-en, *v* to root out; to eradicate

Ausruf, ows-roof, *m* exclamation

ausrufen, ows-roof-en, *v* to

exclaim; to call out

Ausrufezeichen, ows-roof-e-tsy-ken, *nt* exclamation mark

ausruhen, ows-roo-en, *v* to rest

ausrupfen, ows-roop-fen, *v* to pluck out

ausrüsten, ows-rEEst-en, *v* to furnish; to provide with; to equip

Ausrüstung, ows-rEEst-oong, *f* equipment; outfit

ausrutschen, ows-root-shen, *v* to slip

Aussage, ows-zahg-e, *f* assertion; statement

aussagen, ows-zahg-en, *v* to say; to testify

aussätzig, ows-zets-ik, *adj* leprous

aussaugen, ows-zow-gen, *v* to suck dry; to exhaust

ausschalten, ows-shahlt-en, *v* to eliminate; to switch off

Ausschank, ows-shahnk, *m* bar, pub

ausschauen, ows-show-en, *v* to have the appearance; **nach etw –**, to look out for sth

ausscheiden, ows-shy-den, *v* to separate from; to secrete

Ausscheidung, ows-shy-doong, *f* separation; secretion

ausschenken, ows-shenk-en, *v* to pour out

ausscheuern, ows-shoy-ern,

v to scour

ausschiffen, ows-shif-en, *v* to disembark; to put to sea

ausschimpfen, ows-shimp-fen, *v* to tell off

ausschildern, ows-shild-ern, *v* to signpost

ausschlafen, ows-shlahf-en, *v* to sleep enough

Ausschlag, ows-shlahk, *m* rash; swing; **den – geben**, to tip the balance

ausschlagen, ows-shlahg-en, *v* to refuse (offers)

ausschließen, ows-shleess-en, *v* to shut out

ausschließlich, ows-shleess-lik, *adj* exclusive; *adv* exclusively

Ausschluß, ows-shlooss, *m* exclusion

ausschmücken, ows-shmEEck-en, *v* to adorn

ausschneiden, ows-shny-den, *v* to cut out

Ausschnitt, ows-shnitt, *m* cutting; cut out

ausschöpfen, ows-sherp-fen, *v* to scoop out

ausschreiben, ows-shry-ben, *v* to write in full; to announce

Ausschreibung, ows-shry-boong, *f* invitation for tenders

Ausschreitungen, ows-shry-toong-en, *fpl* riot

Ausschuß, ows-shooss, *m* rubbish; committee

ausschütten, ows-shEEtt-en, *v* to pour out

ausschwatzen, ows-shvaht-sen, v to blab

ausschweifend, ows-shvy-fend, adj debauched; extravagant

Ausschweifung, ows-shvy-foong, f excess; dissipation

aussehen, ows-zay-en, v to look (have the appearance)

Aussehen, ows-zay-en, nt appearance

aussein, ows-sine, v to be out; to be over; to be switched off

außen, ows-en, adv outside; without

Außenhandel, ows-sen-hahn-del, m foreign trade

Außenminister, ows-sen-mee-nis-ter, m foreign minister

Außenpolitik, ows-sen-pohlee-teek, f foreign policy

außenpolitisch, ows-sen-poh-lee-tish, adj as regards foreign affairs

Außenseite, ows-sen-zy-te, f outside; surface; **–r**, m outsider

außer, ows-ser, prep out of, beside(s), except; conj except; **– Betrieb**, out of order

außerdem, ows-ser-daim, adv besides; moreover

äußere(r/s), oys-ser-e(r/s), adj outer; external

Äußere, oys-ser-e, nt appearance; outer part

außerehelich, ows-ser-ay-e-lik, adj illegitimate

außergewöhnlich, ows-ser-ge-vern-lik, adj extraordinary

außerhalb, ows-ser-hahlp, prep & adv outside; externally

äußerlich, oys-ser-lik, adj outward; apparent; external

äußern, oys-sern, v to manifest; to show

außerordentlich, ows-ser-ord-ent-lik, adj extraordinary

äußerst, oys-serst, adv extremely, exceedingly, most

Äußerung, oys-ser-oong, f utterance

aussetzen, ows-zet-sen, v to object; to disembark

Aussicht, ows-sikt, f view; prospect; outlook

aussichtslos, ows-sikts-lohs, adj hopeless

aussöhnen, ows-zern-en, v to make up (quarrel)

Aussöhnung, ows-zern-oong, f reconciliation

aussondern, ows-zon-dern, v to single out; to reject

aussortieren, ows-zort-eer-en, v to sort

ausspannen, ows-shpahnn-en, v to stretch out; to relax; to unharness

aussperren, ows-shpairr-en, v to lock out

Aussprache, ows-shprahk-e, f pronunciation; discussion

aussprechen, ows-shprek-en, v to pronounce; to say; to finish speaking

Ausspruch, ows-shproock, m saying

ausspucken, ows-shpoock-en, v to spit out

ausspülen, ows-shpEEl-en, v to rinse; to wash out

ausstaffieren, ows-shtahff-eer-en, v to equip

Ausstand, ows-shtahnt, m strike

Ausstattung, ows-shtahtt-oong, f equipment

aussteigen, ows-shty-gen, v to get out; to alight

ausstellen, ows-shtell-en, v to exhibit

Ausstellung, ows-shtell-oong, f exhibition; show

aussterben, ows-shtairb-en, v to die out

Aussteuer, ows-shtoy-er, f dowry

Ausstieg, ows-shteeg, m exit

ausstopfen, ows-shtopp-fen, v to stuff; to pad

ausstoßen, ows-shtols-en, v to eject

ausstrahlen, ows-shtrahl-en, v to radiate

Ausstrahlung, ows-shtrahl-oong, f emission (rays)

ausstrecken, ows-shtreck-en, v to stretch out; to put out (hand)

ausstreichen, ows-shtry-ken, v to cross out

ausstreuen, ows-**shtroy**-en, *v* to strew (out)

ausströmen, ows-**shtrer**-men, *v* to stream out

aussuchen, ows-**zook**-en, *v* to choose, to pick

Austausch, ows-**towsh**, *m* exchange; barter

austauschen, ows-**towsh**-en, *v* to exchange

austeilen, ows-**ty**-len, *v* to distribute; to hand out; to dispense; to deal (cards)

Auster, ows-**ter**, *f* oyster

austragen, ows-**trahg**-en, *v* to carry out; to deliver (mail)

Australien, ows-**trah**-lee-en, *nt* Australia

australisch, ows-**trah**-lish, *adj* Australian

austreiben, ows-**try**-ben, *v* to drive out; to expel

austreten, ows-**tray**-ten, *v* to step out; **aus etw –**, to leave

austrinken, ows-**trink**-en, *v* to drink up

Austritt, ows-**tritt**, *m* outflow; discharge; leaving; resignation

austrocknen, ows-**trock**-nen, *v* to dry up/out; to drain; to parch

ausüben, ows-**EEb**-en, *v* to exercise; to practise; to execute

Ausübung, ows-**EEb**-oong, *f* practice; exercise; execution

Ausverkauf, ows-**fair**-kowf, *m* (clearance) sale

ausverkauft, ows-**fair**-kowft, *adj* sold out

Auswahl, ows-**vahl**, *f* selection, choice

auswählen, ows-**vail**-en, *v* to select, to choose

Auswanderer, ows-**vahnn**-der-er, *m* emigrant

auswandern, ows-**vahnn**-dern, *v* to emigrate

Auswanderung, ows-**vahnn**-der-oong, *f* emigration; exodus

auswärtig, ows-**vairt**-ik, *adj* foreign

auswärts, ows-**vairts**, *adv* abroad; outward

auswaschen, ows-**vahsh**-en, *v* to wash out

Ausweg, ows-**vaig**, *m* way out; loophole; expedient

ausweichen, ows-**vy**-ken, *v* to make way

Ausweis, ows-**vice**, *m* identity card

ausweisen, ows-**vy**-zen, *v* to expel; to deport; **sich –**, to give proof of one's identity

Ausweisung, ows-**vy**-zoong, *f* eviction; expulsion

auswendig, ows-**ven**-dig, *adv* from memory, by heart

auswickeln, ows-**vik**-eln, *v* to unwrap

auswischen, ows-**vish**-en, *v* to wipe out

Auswuchs, ows-**vooks**, *m* (out)growth

auszahlen, ows-**tsahl**-en, *v* to pay out

Auszahlung, ows-**tsahl**-oong, *f* paying out

auszeichnen, ows-**tsy'k**-nen, *v* to distinguish

Auszeichnung, ows-**tsy'k**-noong, *f* distinction; honours (exam)

ausziehen, ows-**tsee**-en, *v* to move out; to take off; to undress

Auszubildende(r), ows-**tsoo**-bil-den-de(r), *m & f* trainee

Auszug, ows-**tsook**, *m* exodus; removal; statement (accounts)

Auto, ow-**toh**, *nt* car; **–bahn**, *f* motorway; **–bahngebühr**, *f* motorway toll; **–bus**, *m* bus; **–fähre**, *f* car ferry; **–fahrer**, *m* driver

Automat, ow-toh-**maht**, *m* (vending/slot) machine

automatisch, ow-toh-**mah**-tish, *adj* automatic

Autor, ow-**tohr**, *m* author

Autorität, ow-tohr-ee-**tait**, *f* authority

Autounfall, ow-toh-**oonn**-fahll, *m* car accident

Autovermietung, ow-toh-**fair**-meet-oong, *f* car hire

Axt, ahkst, *f* axe

B

Baby, bay-bee, *nt* baby;
  –nahrung, *f* baby food;
  –sitter, *m* baby-sitter
Bach, bah*k*, *m* brook; stream
Backe, bah*ck-e*, *f* cheek
backen, bah*ck-en*, *v* to bake
Backenbart, bah*ck-en*-bart,
  m sideboards
Backenzahn, bah*ck-en*-
  tsahn *m* molar
Bäcker, beck-*er*, *m* baker
Bäckerei, beck-*e*-**ry**, *f*
  bakery; baker's shop
Backform, bah*ck-*form, *f*
  baking tin
Backofen, bah*ck-*oh-fen, *m*
  oven
Backpulver, bah*ck-*pool-fer,
  nt baking-powder
Backstein, bah*ck-*shtine, *m*
  brick
Bad, baht, *nt* bath; spa;
  –eanstalt, *f* swimming
  baths; **–eanzug**, *m*

swimming costume;
  –ehose, *f* swimming
  trunks; **–ekappe**, *f*
  swimming cap; **–emantel**,
  m bath robe; **–emeister**, *m*
  pool attendant
baden, bahd-*en*, *v* to bath(e)
Badeort, bahd-*e*-ort, *m* spa;
  resort
Badewanne, bahd-*e*-
  vahnn*e*, *f* bath tub
Badezimmer, bahd-*e*-
  tsimmer, *nt* bathroom
Bagger, bahg-*ger*, *m*
  excavator
baggern, bahg-*gern*, *v* to
  excavate, to dredge
Bahn, bahn, *f* railway; track;
  lane; orbit; **–Card**, *f*
  railcard
bahnen, bahn-*en*, *v* to make
  the way
Bahnhof, bahn-hohf, *m*
  railway station

Bahnsteig, bahn-shtyk, *m*
  (station) platform
Bahnübergang, bahn-EE-ber-
  gahng, *m* level crossing
Bahre, bahr-*e*, *f* stretcher;
  bier
Baisse, bay-s*e*, *f* fall (prices);
  slump
Bakterien, bahck-**tair**-i-en,
  pl bacteria
bald, bahlt, *adv* soon; almost
baldig, bahl-dik, *adj* early;
  speedy
balgen, bahlg-en, *v* to
  scuffle; to romp
Balken, bahlk-en, *m* beam;
  joist
Balkon, bahl-kohn, *m*
  balcony; circle
Ball, bahll, *m* ball; dance
ballen, bahll-en, *v* to form
  into a ball
Ballen, bahll-en, *m* bale;
  pack
Ballett, bahl-let, *nt* ballet
Ballsaal, bahll-zahl, *m*
  ballroom
Banane, ba-nah-n*e*, *f*
  banana
Band, bahnt, *m* volume,
  tome; *nt* ribbon; band;
  tape
Bande, bahnd-*e*, *f* band,
  horde, gang
bändigen, bend-ig-en, *v* to
  tame
Bandmaß, bahnt-mahs, *nt*
  tape-measure
bange, bahng-*e*, *adj & adv*
  afraid, anxious(ly)
Bank, bahnk, *f* bench;

comm bank; **–anweisung,** *f* banker's order

Bankier, bahnk-e-eh, *m* banker

Bankkonto, bahnk-kon-to, *nt* bank account

Bankleitzahl, bahnk-lyt-tsahl, *f* bank sort-code number

bankrott, bahnk-**rott,** *adj* bankrupt

Bankrott, bahnk-**rott,** *m* bankruptcy; failure; crash

Bankverbindung, bahnk-fair-bin-doong, *f* banking arrangements

Bankwesen, bahnk-vay-zen, *nt* banking

bannen, bahnn-en, *v* to captivate; to enchant

bar, bahr, *adj* bare; in cash

Bär, bair, *m* bear

barfuß, bahr-foos, *adj* barefoot(ed)

Bargeld, bahr-gelt, *nt* cash

bargeldlos, bahr-gelt-lohs, *adj* cashless; *adv* without using cash

barmherzig, bahrm-**hairt**-sik, *adj* merciful; charitable

Barmherzigkeit, bahrm-**hairt**-sik-kite, *f* mercy; compassion

Barren, bahr-ren, *m* (metal) bar; ingot

Barrikade, bahr-re-kah-de, *f* barricade

barsch, bahr-sh, *adj* rude; rough; harsh

Bart, bahrt, *m* beard

bärtig, bairt-ik, *adj* bearded

Barzahlung, bahr-tsahl-oong, *f* cash payment

Base, bah-ze, *f chem* base

Basilikum, bahs-se-le-koom, *nt* basil

Baß, bahss, *m* bass (voice); **–geige,** *f* double bass

basteln, bahss-teln, *v* to do handicrafts, to make

Batterie, bah-te-**ree,** *f* battery

Bau, bow, *m* building; construction; erection

Bauch, bowk, *m* belly; abdomen; **–redner,** *m* ventriloquist; **–schmerzen,** *pl* stomach ache

bauen, bow-en, *v* to build

Bauer, bow-er, *m* peasant; farmer; pawn (chess)

Bäuerin, boy-er-in, *f* farmer, farmer's wife

Bauernfänger, bow-ern-**feng**-er, *m* confidence trickster

Bauernhaus, bow-ern-hous, *nt* farmhouse

Bauernhof, bow-ern-hof, *m* farmyard

baufällig, bow-fell-ik, *adj* dilapidated

Baugelände, bow-ge-len-de, *nt* building site; building land

Baum, bowm, *m* tree; **–schule,** *f* (tree) nursery; **–stamm,** *m* trunk (of tree); **–wolle,** *f* cotton

baumeln, bowm-eln, *v*

to dangle

Bauplan, bow-plahn, *m* architect's plan

bauschen, bow-shen, *v* to puff out

Bausparkasse, bow-shpahr-kahs-se, *f* building society

Baustein, bow-shtine, *m* building stone

Baustelle, bow-shtel-le, *f* building site

Bayer, by-er, *m* Bavarian (person)

bay(e)risch, by(-e)-rish, *adj* Bavarian

Bayern, by-ern, *nt* Bavaria

Bazillus, bah-tsil-loos, *m* bacillus

beabsichtigen, be-**ahp**-sik-tig-en, *v* to intend

beachten, be-**ahk**-ten, *v* to heed; to take notice

beachtenswert, be-**ahk**-tens-vairt, *adj* noteworthy

Beachtung, be-**ahk**-toong, *f* attention, notice

Beamte(r), be-**ahm**-te(r), *m* official; civil servant

Beamtin, be-**ahm**-tin, *f* official; civil servant

beängstigend, be-**engst**-ig-end, *adj* alarming

beanspruchen, be-**ahnn**-shprook-en, *v* to claim; to take up; to demand

beantragen, be-**ahnn**-trahg-en, *v* to apply for; to propose

beantworten, be-**ahnt**-vort-en, *v* to answer (to)

Beantwortung, be-**ahnt**-

vort-oong, *f* answer

bearbeiten, be-**ar**-by-ten, *v* to work (on sth), to deal with

beaufsichtigen, be-**owf**-zik-tig-en, *v* to supervize

beauftragen, be-**owf**-trahg-en, *v* to hire; to commission; to instruct

bebauen, be-**bow**-en, *v* to build upon; to cultivate (land)

beben, bay-ben, *v* to quiver

Becher, bek-er, *m* beaker; cup

Becken, beck-en, *nt* basin; pelvis; cymbals *(pl)*

bedächtig, be-**dek**-tik, *adj* deliberate; measured

Bedächtigkeit, be-**dek**-tik-kite, *f* deliberateness

bedanken (sich), be-**dahnk**-en (zik), *v* to thank

Bedarf, be-**dahrf**, *m* need; requirement; demand

bedauerlich, be-**dow**-er-lik, *adj* regrettable

bedauern, be-**dow**-ern, *v* to regret; to sympathize; to pity

bedecken, be-**deck**-en, *v* to cover (with)

bedenken, be-**denk**-en, *v* to reflect; to think over

bedenklich, be-**denk**-lik, *adj* serious; critical

Bedenkzeit, be-**denk**-tsyt, *f* time for reflection

bedeuten, be-**doyt**-en, *v* to mean, to signify

bedeutend, be-**doyt**-ent, *adj* important, significant

Bedeutung, be-**doyt**-oong, *f* meaning; significance; importance

bedeutungsvoll, be-**doyt**-oongs-foll, *adj* significant

bedienen, be-**deen**-en, *v* to serve; to operate

Bedienung, be-**deen**-oong, *f* service; waiter/waitress; service charge; **–sanleitung**, *f* operating instructions

bedingt, be-**dingt**, *adj* qualified; conditional

Bedingung, be-**ding**-oong, *f* condition; terms

bedrängen, be-**dreng**-en, *v* to pester; to put under pressure

bedrohen, be-**droh**-en, *v* to threaten

Bedrohung, be-**droh**-oong, *f* threat

bedürfen, be-**dEErf**-en, *v* to need, to require

Bedürfnis, be-**dEErf**-niss, *nt* want, need

bedürftig, be-**dEErf**-tik, *adj* needy, poor

beehren, be-**air**-en, *v* to honour with; to favour

beeilen (sich), be-**ile**-en, (zik), *v* to hurry

beeinflussen, be-ine-**flooss**-en, *v* to influence

beeinträchtigen, be-ine-**trek**-tig-en, *v* to restrict; to impair; to spoil

beenden, be-**end**-en, *v* to end, to finish

Beendung, be-**end**-oong, *f* termination; completion

beerben (jdn), be-**airb**-en, *v* to inherit (from sb)

beerdigen, be-**aird**-ig-en, *v* to bury

Beerdigung, be-**aird**-ig-oong, *f* funeral

Beere, bair-e, *f* berry

Beet, bait, *nt* (flower/vegetable) bed

befähigen, be-**fay**-ig-en, *v* to qualify; to enable

Befähigung, be-**fay**-ig-oong, *f* capacity; qualification; talent

befallen, be-**fahll**-en, *v* to overcome; to attack

Befangenheit, be-**fahng**-en-hite, *f* self-consciousness; *law* bias

befassen (sich mit), be-**fahss**-en (zik mitt), *v* to occupy o.s. with

Befehl, be-**fail**, *m* command, order

befehlen, be-**fail**-en, *v* to command, to order

befestigen, be-**fest**-ig-en, *v* to fasten; to fortify

Befestigung, be-**fest**-ig-oong, *f* fastening; fortification

Befinden, be-**finn**-den, *nt* state of health

befinden (sich), be-**finn**-den (zik), *v* to be; to feel

beflissen, be-**fliss**-en, *adj* zealous, studious

befolgen, be-**foll**-gen, *v* to follow; to observe (order)

befördern, be-**ferd**-ern, v to transport; to send; to promote

Beförderung, be-**ferd**-er-oong, f promotion; transport

befragen, be-**frahg**-en, v to question; to consult

befreien, be-**fry**-en, v to free, to liberate; to exempt

Befreiung, be-**fry**-oong, f release; liberation; exemption

befremden, be-**fremm**-den, v to seem odd

befreunden (sich mit jdm), be-**froynd**-en, v to make friends with

befreundet, be-**froynd**-et, adj friends with

Befruchtung, be-**frookt**-oong, f pollination; **künstliche –**, artificial insemination

begabt, be-**gahpt**, adj talented, gifted

Begabung, be-**gahb**-oong, f talent

begeben (sich), be-**gay**-ben (zik), v to proceed; to occur

Begebenheit, be-**gay**-ben-hite, f event

begegnen, be-**gaig**-nen, v to meet (by chance)

Begegnung, be-**gaig**-noong, f (chance) meeting

begehen, be-**gay**-en, v to commit; to celebrate

begehren, be-**gair**-en, v to desire; to wish for

begehrt, be-**gairt**, adj in demand

begeistern, be-**gy**-stern, v to inspire; **sich für etw–**, to be keen on sth

Begeisterung, be-**gy**-ster-oong, f enthusiasm

Begier, be-**geer**, f eagerness; desire; passion

begierig, be-**geer**-ik, adj eager for; keen; desirous

begießen, be-**geess**-en, v to water; fam to drink to

Beginn, be-**ginn**, m beginning

beginnen, be-**ginn**-en, v to begin, to start

beglaubigen, be-**glow**-big-en, v to certify

Beglaubigung, be-**glow**-bi-goong, f certification

begleichen, be-**gly**-ken, v to settle (accounts); to pay

begleiten, be-**gly**-ten, v to accompany; to escort

Begleiter, be-**gly**-ter, m companion; escort; mus accompanist

beglücken, be-**glEEck**-en, v to make a person happy

beglückwünschen, be-**glEEck**-vEEnn-shen, v to congratulate

begnadigen, beg-**nahd**-ig-en, v to pardon; to amnesty

Begnadigung, beg-**nahd**-ig-oong, f pardon; amnesty

begnügen (sich mit), beg-**nEEg**-en (zik mitt), v to be satisfied with

begraben, be-**grahb**-en, v to bury

Begräbnis, be-**grape**-niss, nt burial; funeral

begreifen, be-**gry**-fen, v to understand; to comprehend

begreiflich, be-**grife**-lik, adj comprehensible

begrenzen, be-**grent**-sen, v to limit

Begriff, be-**griff**, m idea; concept; notion

begründen, be-**grEEnn**-den, v to justify

Begründung, be-**grEEnn**-doong, f justification; reason; argument

begrüßen, be-**grEEs**-en, v to greet, to welcome

Begrüßung, be-**grEEs**-oong, f greeting; welcome

begünstigen, be-**gEEnn**-stig-en, v to favour

begutachten, be-**goot**-ahk-ten, v to assess

behaart, be-**hahrt**, adj hairy

behäbig, be-**hay**-bik, adj portly; solid

behaglich, be-**hahk**-lik, adj comfortable; cosy

behalten, be-**hahllt**-en, v to keep; to retain

Behälter, be-**hell**-ter, m container; reservoir

behandeln, be-**hahnn**-deln, v to treat

Behandlung, be-**hahnnd**-loong, f treatment

beharren (auf etw), be-**hahrr**-en, v to persevere; to insist

behaupten, be-howp-ten, *v* to claim; to assert; to maintain

Behauptung, be-howp-toong, *f* claim; assertion

behend, be-hent, *adj* agile, nimble

beherrschen, be-hairsh-en, *v* to rule; to govern; to dominate; to control; to master

behilflich, be-hilf-lik, *adj* helpful

behindert, be-hin-dert, *adj* disabled

Behinderte(r), be-hin-derte(r), *m & f* disabled person

Behörde, be-herd-en, *f* authority

behördlich, be-herd-lik, *adj* official; authoritative

behüten, be-hEEt-en, *v* to look after; to guard

behutsam, be-hoot-zahm, *adj* cautious; careful

bei, by, *prep* near (to); at (the house of); on; in

beibehalten, by-be-hahllt-en, *v* to keep; to retain

beibringen, by-bring-en *v* to teach; to bring forward

Beichte, byk-te, *f* confession

beichten, byk-ten, *v* to confess

beide, by-de, *adj* both

beiderlei, by-der-ly, *adj* both kinds; of both sorts

beiderseits, by-der-zites, *adv* on both sides

beieinander, by-ine-ahnn-der, *adv* together

Beifall, by-fahll, *m* applause; assent; approval

beifügen, by-fEEg-en, *v* to enclose; to append

Beifügung, be-fEEg-oong, *f* enclosure; addition; appendage

Beigeschmack, by-ge-shmahck, *m* aftertaste

Beil, bile, *nt* hatchet; chopper; axe

Beilage, by-lahg-e, *f* supplement (of a journal); side dish; vegetables

beilegen, by-lay-gen, *v* to add; to enclose; to impute; to settle (disputes)

Beileid, by-lite, *nt* condolence; sympathy

beiliegend, by-leeg-end, *adj* enclosed

beim, bime (= bei dem, by daim), *prep* with the; at the; near the

beimessen, by-mess-en, *v* to attribute; to ascribe

Bein, bine, *nt* leg; bone

beinahe, by-nah-e, *adv* almost; nearly

Beiname, by-nahm-e, *m* nickname; epithet

Beinbruch, bine-brook, *m* fracture of the leg

beipacken, by-pahck-en, *v* to pack up with

Beipackzettel, by-pahck-tse-tel, *m* instruction leaflet

beisammen, by-zahmm-en, *adv* together

Beisammensein, by-zahmm-en-zine, *nt* get-together

Beischlaf, by-shlahf, *m* sexual intercourse

beiseite, by-zyte, *adv* aside, on one side

beisetzen, by-zet-sen, *v* to bury

Beisetzung, by-zet-soong, *f* funeral

Beispiel, by-shpeel, *nt* example

beispiellos, by-shpeel-lohs, *adj* unprecedented

beispielsweise, by-shpeels-vy-ze, *adv* for instance; for example

beispringen, by-shpring-en, *v* to rush to help

beißen, by-sen, *v* to bite

Beißzange, bice-tsahng-e, *f* pliers, pincers

Beistand, by-stahnt, *m* assistance, support

beistehen, by-shtay-en, *v* to help; to stand by (sb)

Beitrag, by-trahk, *m* contribution

beitragen, by-trahg-en, *v* to contribute

beitreten, by-trait-en, *v* to join (club etc.)

Beitritt, by-tritt, *m* enrolment; joining

Beiwagen, by-vahg-en, *m* side-car (of motorbike)

beiwohnen, by-wohn-en, *v* to be present

beizeiten, by-tsy-ten, *adv* in time

beizen, by-tsen, *v* to

stain (wood)

bejahen, be-**yah**-en, *v* to answer in the affirmative; to agree with

bejahrt, be-**yahrt**, *adj* aged, advanced in years

bekämpfen, be-**kemp**-fen, *v* to fight against

bekannt, be-**kahnnt**, *adj* well-known; renowned; familiar

Bekannte(r), be-**kahnnt**-e(r), *m & f* acquaintance

bekanntlich, be-**kahnnt**-lik, *adv* as is well known

bekanntmachen, be-**kahnnt**-mahk-en, *v* to introduce; to advertise; to announce

Bekanntmachung, be-**kahnnt**-mahk-oong, *f* (public) notice; proclamation; announcement

Bekanntschaft, be-**kahnnt**-shahft, *f* acquaintance

bekehren, be-**kair**-en, *v* to convert

Bekehrung, be-**kair**-oong, *f* conversion

bekennen, be-**ken**-en, *v* to admit; to profess

Bekenntnis, be-**kent**-nis, *nt* confession; denomination

beklagen (sich), be-**klahg**-en (zik), *v* to complain

beklagenswert, be-**klahg**-ens-vairt, *adj* pitiable; pathetic

Beklagte(r), be-**klahk**-te(r), *m & f* defendant; accused

bekleiden, be-**kly**-den, *v* to clothe; to fill a post; to occupy

Bekleidung, be-**kly**-doong, *f* clothing

beklommen, be-**klomm**-en, *adj* uneasy; oppressed

bekommen, be-**komm**-en, *v* to receive, to get

bekömmlich, be-**kermm**-lik, *adj* (easily) digestible

bekräftigen, be-**kreff**-tig-en, *v* to confirm

Bekräftigung, be-**kreff**-tig-oong, *f* confirmation

bekränzen, be-**krent**-sen, *v* to deck with wreaths

bekreuzigen (sich), be-**kroyt**-sig-en (zik), *v* to cross o.s.

bekümmern (sich), be-**kEEmm**-ern (zik), *v* to be concerned about; to trouble o.s. about

beladen, be-**lahd**-en, *v* to load with

Belag, be-lahg, *m* coating; layer

belagern, be-**lahg**-ern, *v* to besiege; to beleaguer

Belagerung, be-**lahg**-er-oong, *f* siege

Belang, be-**lahng**, *m* importance; consequence

belangen, be-**lahng**-en, *v* to sue, to prosecute; to concern

belanglos, be-**lahng**-lohs, *adj* insignificant

belasten, be-**lahst**-en, *v* to burden; to worry; to

incriminate; to debit

belästigen, be-**lesst**-ig-en, *v* to pester; to molest

Belastung, be-**lahsst**-oong, *f* load; debit

belaufen (sich auf), be-**lowf**-en (zik owf), *v* to amount to

beleben, be-**lay**-ben, *v* to animate, to liven up; to come alive

belebt, be-**laipt**, *adj* animated, lively; busy (street)

Belebung, be-**laib**-oong, *f* revival; animation

Beleg, be-**laik**, *m* receipt; proof; voucher

belegen, be-**laig**-en, *v* to cover; to spread; to prove; to reserve

belehren, be-**lair**-en, *v* to instruct; to inform

Belehrung, be-**lair**-oong, *f* instruction; information

beleidigen, be-**ly**-dig-en, *v* to insult; to offend

Beleidigung, be-**ly**-dig-oong, *f* insult; offence

belesen, be-**lay**-zen, *adj* well-read; scholarly

beleuchten, be-**loyk**-ten, *v* to illuminate; to light (up); to elucidate

Beleuchtung, be-**loyk**-toong, *f* illumination; lighting; elucidation

Belgien, **bel**-gi-en, *nt* Belgium

Belgier, **bel**-gi-er, *m* Belgian (person)

belgisch, bel-gish, *adj*
Belgian

belichten, be-*lik*-ten, *v*
photog to expose

beliebig, be-*leeb*-ik, *adj* any;
according to one's liking

beliebt, be-*leept*, *adj* (well)
liked; popular

bellen, bel-en, *v* to bark; to
bay

belohnen, be-*loh*-nen, *v* to
reward

Belohnung, be-*loh*-noong, *f*
reward

Belüftung, be-*lEEft*-oong, *f*
ventilation

belügen, be-*lEEg*-en, *v* to lie
(to sb); to deceive (sb)

belustigen (sich), be-*loost*-
tig-en (*zik*), *v* to amuse
(o.s.)

Belustigung, be-*loost*-tig-
oong, *f* amusement;
diversion

bemächtigen (sich), be-
mek-tig-en (*zik*), *v* to
seize, to take possession of

bemalen, be-*mahl*-en, *v* to
paint

bemannen, be-*mahnn*-en, *v*
to man; to equip

Bemannung, be-*mahnn*-
oong, *f* crew

bemerken, be-*mairk*-en, *v* to
notice; to remark; **–swert**,
adj remarkable; noticeable

Bemerkung, be-*mairk*-oong,
f remark; observation;
note

bemitleiden, be-*mit*-ly-den,
v to pity

bemittelt, be-*mit*-elt, *adj*
well-off, well-to-do

bemühen (sich), be-*mEE*-en
(*zik*), *v* to endeavour

Bemühung, be-*mEE*-oong, *f*
trouble; endeavour

benachbart, be-*nahk*-bart,
adj neighbouring,
adjoining

benachrichtigen, be-*nahk*-
rik-tig-en, *v* to inform

Benachrichtigung, be-*nahk*-
rik-tig-oong, *f* notification

benachteiligen, be-*nahk*-ty-
lig-en, *v* to prejudice, to
wrong

benannt, be-*nahnt*, *adj*
called, named

benehmen (sich), be-*nay*-
men (*zik*), *v* to behave

Benehmen, be-*nay*-men, *nt*
behaviour

beneiden, be-*ny*-den, *v* to
envy; to begrudge

beneidenswert, be-*ny*-dens-
vairt, *adj* enviable

benennen, be-*nen*-en, *v* to
name, to call

Benennung, be-*nen*-oong, *f*
name, naming

Bengel, beng-el, *m* rascal,
urchin; lout

benötigen, be-*nert*-ig-en, *v*
to require; to need

benutzen (or **benützen**), be-
noott-sen (or ben*EEtt*-
sen), *v* to use

Benutzer, be-*nootts*-er, *m*
user

Benutzung, be-*noots*-oong,
f use

Benzin, ben-*tseen*, *nt* petrol

beobachten, be-oh-*bahk*-
ten, *v* to observe, to
watch; to examine

Beobachter, be-oh-*bahk*-ter,
m observer

Beobachtung, be-oh-*bahk*-
toong, *f* observation

bepacken, be-*pahck*-en, *v* to
load, to pack

bepflanzen, be-*pflahnt*-sen,
v to plant with

bequem, bek-*vaim*, *adj*
comfortable, cosy, snug

bequemen (sich), bek-*vaim*-
en (*zik*), *v* to bring o.s. to

bequemlich, bek-*vaim*-lik,
adj convenient

Bequemlichkeit, bek-*vaim*-
lik-kite, *f* comfort;
laziness; snugness

beraten, be-*raht*-en, *v* to
advise, to counsel

Berater, be-*raht*-er, *m*
adviser

beratschlagen (sich), be-
raht-shlahg-en (*zik*), *v* to
discuss

Beratung, be-*raht*-oong, *f*
advice; consultation;
–sstelle, *f* advice centre

berauben, be-*row*-ben, *v* to
rob, to deprive

berauschen, be-*row*-shen, *v*
to intoxicate

berechnen, be-*rek*-nen, *v* to
calculate

berechnend, be-*rek*-nent,
adj calculating

Berechnung, be-*rek*-noong,
f calculation

berechtigen, be-**rek**-tig-en, *v* to entitle; to justify

berechtigt, be-**rek**-tigt, *adj* entitled; qualified; justified

Berechtigung, be-**rek**-tig-oong, *f* authorisation; justification

beredsam, be-**rait**-zahm, *adj* eloquent

Beredsamkeit, be-**rait**-zahm-kite, *f* eloquence

Bereich, be-**ryk**, *m* area, scope; sphere

bereichern (sich), be-**ry**-kern (zik), *v* to enrich (o.s.)

bereifen, be-**ry**-fen, *v* to fit tyres to

Bereifung, be-**ry**-foong, *f* set of tyres

bereit, be-**rite**, *adj* ready, prepared

bereiten, be-**ry**-ten, *v* to prepare, to get ready

bereits, be-**rites**, *adv* already

Bereitschaft, be-**rite**-shahft, *f* readiness; alertness; **–sdienst**, *m* emergency service

bereitwillig, be-**rite**-vil-ik, *adj* willing, obliging

Bereitwilligkeit, be-**rite**-vil-ig-kite, *f* willingness, obligingness

bereuen, be-**roy**-en, *v* to regret, to repent

Berg, bairk, *m* mountain; hill

bergab, bairk-**ahpp**, *adv* downhill

Bergarbeiter, bairk-**ar**-by-ter, *m* miner

bergauf, bairk-**owf**, *adv* uphill

Bergbau, bairk-bow, *m* mining

bergen, bairg-en, *v* to save, to shelter; to protect

Berggipfel, bairk-gip-fel, *m* mountain peak

bergig, bairg-ik, *adj* mountainous, hilly

Bergmann, bairk-mahnn, *m* miner

Bergsteigen, bairk-shty-gen, *nt* mountaineering

Bergsteiger, bairk-shty-ger, *m* mountaineer

Bergwerk, bairk-vairk, *nt* mine; (coal-)pit

Bericht, be-**rikt**, *m* report; account, particulars

berichten, be-**rikt**-en, *v* to report

Berichterstatter, be-**rikt**-er-shtahtt-er, *m* reporter; correspondent

berichtigen, be-**rikt**-ig-en, *v* to correct; to rectify

Berichtigung, be-**rikt**-ig-oong, *f* correction

berieseln, be-**reez**-eln, *v* to irrigate

Bernstein, bairn-shtine, *m* amber

bersten, bairst-en, *v* to burst, to explode

berüchtigt, be-**rEEk**-tigt, *adj* notorious, ill-famed

berücksichtigen, be-**rEEck**-sikt-ig-en, *v* to take into consideration

Berücksichtigung, be-**rEEck**-sikt-ig-oong, *f* consideration

Beruf, be-**roof**, *m* profession; occupation

berufen, be-**roof**-en, *v* to appoint

berufen (sich auf), be-**roof**-en (zik owf), *v* to refer to

beruflich, be-**roof**-lik, *adj* professional

Berufsausbildung, be-**roofs**-ows-bild-oong, *f* professional training

Berufsberater, be-**roofs**-be-raht-er, *m* careers adviser

Berufsberatung, be-**roofs**-be-raht-oong, *f* vocational guidance

Berufsgeheimnis, be-**roofs**-ge-hym-nis, *nt* professional secret

Berufskrankheit, be-**roofs**-krahnnk-hite, *f* occupational disease

Berufsschule, be-**roofs**-shoo-le, *f* vocational school; technical college

Berufssportler, be-**roofs**-shport-ler, *m* professional sportsman

berufstätig, be-**roofs**-tait-ik, *adj* employed

Berufsverkehr, be-**roofs**-fer-kair, *m* rush hour traffic

Berufung, be-**roof**-oong, *f* *law* appeal

beruhen (auf), be-**roo**-en (owf), *v* to be attributable (to)

beruhigen, be-**roo**-ig-en, *v* to calm, to soothe, to quieten; to reassure

Beruhigung, be-**roo**-ig-oong, *f* calming, soothing

berühmt, be-**rEEmt**, *adj* celebrated, famous

Berühmtheit, be-**rEEmt**-hite, *f* fame, celebrity

berühren, be-**rEEr**-en, *v* to touch

Berührung, be-**rEEr**-oong, *f* touch; contact

besagt, be-**zahkt**, *adj* aforesaid, mentioned, said

besänftigen, be-**zenft**-ig-en, *v* to calm; to appease

Besatz, be-**zahtts**, *m* trimming

Besatzung, be-**sahtts**-oong, *f* garrison; crew

besaufen (sich), be-**zowf**-en (zik), *v fam* to get drunk

beschädigen, be-**shay**-dig-en, *v* to damage, to injure

Beschädigung, be-**shay**-dig-oong, *f* damage

beschaffen, be-**shahff**-en, *v* to procure, to get

beschaffen, be-**shahff**-en, *adj* constituted

Beschaffenheit, be-**shahff**-en-hite, *f* composition; constitution

Beschaffung, be-**shahff**-oong, *f* acquisition

beschäftigen, be-**sheff**-tig-en, *v* to occupy; to employ

beschäftigt, be-**sheff**-tigt, *adj* busy

Beschäftigung, be-**sheff**-tig-

oong, *f* occupation, employment

beschämen, be-**shay**-men, *v* to (put to) shame

Bescheid, be-**shy't**, *m* information; reply; instruction(s)

bescheiden, be-**shy**-den, *adj* moderate; modest

Bescheidenheit, be-**shy**-den-hite, *f* modesty

bescheinen, be-**shy**-nen, *v* to shine on

bescheinigen, be-**shy**-nig-en, *v* to certify, to attest

Bescheinigung, be-**shy**-nig-oong, *f* attestation, certificate

beschenken, be-**shenk**-en, *v* to give (sb) a present

bescheren, be-**shair**-en, *v* to give (sb) Christmas presents

Bescherung, be-**shair**-oong, *f* the giving of Christmas presents

beschießen, be-**shees**-en, *v* to bombard, to fire on

Beschießung, be-**shees**-oong, *f* bombardment

beschimpfen, be-**shim**-fen, *v* to abuse; to affront

beschirmen, be-**sheerm**-en, *v* to protect; to shield

Beschlag, be-**shlahk**, *m* (metal) fitting; condensation; tarnish

beschlagen, be-**shlahg**-en, *v* to put metal fittings on; to mist over; to shoe (horse)

Beschlagnahmung, be-

shlahk-nahm-oong, *f* confiscation, seizure

beschleunigen, be-**shloin**-ig-en, *v* to accelerate, to speed up

Beschleunigung, be-**shloin**-ig-oong, *f* acceleration, increase of speed

beschließen, be-**shlees**-en, *v* to decide, to resolve

Beschluß, be-**shlooss**, *m* decision; resolution

beschlußfähig, be-**shlooss**-fay-ik, *adj* forming a quorum

beschmieren, be-**shmeer**-en, *v* to spread, to smear (with)

beschmutzen, be-**shmoott**-sen, *v* to soil

beschneiden, be-**shny**-den, *v* to clip; to circumcise

Beschneidung, be-**shny**-doong, *f* clipping; circumcision

beschönigen, be-**shern**-ig-en, *v* to gloss over; to palliate

Beschönigung, be-**shern**-ig-oong, *f* glossing over; extenuation

beschränken, be-**shrenk**-en, *v* to limit

beschränkt, be-**shrenkt**, *adj* limited; dull

Beschränkung, be-**shrenk**-oong, *f* limitation

beschreiben, be-**shry**-ben, *v* to write on; to describe

Beschreibung, be-**shry**-boong, *f* description

beschuldigen, be-shooll-dig-en, v to accuse; to charge with a crime

Beschuldigung, be-shooll-dig-oong, f accusation; charge

beschützen, be-shEEtt-sen, v to protect

Beschützer, be-shEEtt-ser, m defender, protector

Beschützung, be-shEEtt-soong, f protection

Beschwerde, be-shvaird-e, f complaint

beschweren (sich), be-shvair-en (zik), v to complain

beschwerlich, be-shvair-lik, adj exhausting; troublesome

beschwichtigen, be-shvik-ti-gen, v to pacify; to appease; to calm

Beschwichtigung, be-shvik-tig-oong, f conciliation; appeasement

beschwindeln, be-shvin-deln, v to cheat; to swindle; to tell lies

beschwören, be-shver-en, v to confirm by oath; to swear to; to implore; to conjure (spirits)

Beschwörung, be-shver-oong, f confirmation by oaths; entreaty; raising of spirits

besehen, be-zay-en, v to inspect; to view

beseitigen, be-zyt-ig-en, v to do away with, to eliminate

Besen, bay-zen, m broom

besessen, be-zes-en, adj possessed, frantic

Besessene(r), be-zes-en-e(r), m & f possessed/frantic person

besetzen, be-zett-sen, v to fill (a space/seat; a vacancy); to occupy

Besetzung, be-zetts-oong, f cast theatre; occupation

besichtigen, be-zik-tig-en, v to visit; to view; to inspect

Besichtigung, be-zik-tig-oong, f visit; inspection

besiegen, be-zeeg-en, v to conquer; to vanquish

besinnen (sich), be-zin-en (zik), v to think; to reflect

Besinnung, be-zin-oong, f consciousness

Besitz, be-zits, m possession; property; estate

besitzen, be-zit-sen, v to possess, to have

Besitzer, be-zit-ser, m owner, proprietor

Besitzung, be-zits-oong, f possession; estate

besohlen, be-zohl-en, v to sole (shoes)

besonders, be-zon-ders, adv especially; particularly

besonnen, be-zon-en, adj cautious; thoughtful

besorgen, be-zorg-en, v to acquire; to deal with; to take care of

Besorgnis, be-zork-niss, f concern; fear

besorgt, be-zorkt, adj

apprehensive; anxious

Besorgung, be-zorg-oong, f errand; acquisition; purchase

besprechen, be-shprek-en, v to discuss; to review; to record

Besprechung, be-shprek-oong, f discussion; meeting; review

bespritzen, be-shprit-sen, v to squirt with water

besser, bess-er, adj better

bessern, bess-ern, v to better, to improve

Besserung, bess-er-oong, f improvement; reform(ation); recovery

Bestand, be-shtahnt, m existence; duration; stock

beständig, be-shten-dik, adj constant; permanent

Beständigkeit, be-shten-dig-kite, f stability

Bestandteil, be-shtahnt-tile, m ingredient

bestärken (in etw), be-shtairk-en, v to confirm in sth

bestätigen, be-shtayt-ig-en, v to confirm; to corroborate; to acknowledge

Bestätigung, be-shtayt-ig-oong, f confirmation

bestatten, be-shtaht-en, v to bury

Bestattung, be-shtaht-oong, f burial; funeral

beste(r/s), **best**-e(r/s), adj best

bestechen, be-**shtek**-en, v to bribe; to corrupt

bestechlich, be-**shtek**-lik, adj open to bribery; corruptible

Bestechung, be-**shtek**-oong, f corruption; bribery

Besteck, be-**shteck**, nt cutlery

bestehen, be-**shtay**-en, v to consist (**aus** of); to exist; to insist (**auf** on); to pass (exam)

bestehlen, be-**shtay**-len, v to rob, to steal from

besteigen, be-**shty**-gen, v to climb; to mount; to board (ship, bus, aeroplane); to ascend (throne)

Besteigung, be-**shty**-goong, f climb; ascent; accession

bestellen, be-**shtel**-en, v to order (goods); to give messages; to cultivate (soil)

Bestellung, be-**shtel**-oong, f order; commission; cultivation (soil)

bestens, best-ens, adv very well

besteuern, be-**shtoy**-ern, v to tax

Besteuerung, be-**shtoy**-er-oong, f taxation

Bestie, best-e-e, f beast, brute

bestimmen, be-**shtim**-en, v to decide; to appoint

bestimmt, be-**shtimt**, adj firm; certain; definite

Bestimmung, be-**shtim**-

oong, f regulation; purpose

Bestimmungsort, be-**shtim**-oongs-ort, m destination

bestrafen, be-**shtrahf**-en, v to punish; to chastise; to fine

Bestrafung, be-**shtrahf**-oong, f punishment; reprimand; fine

Bestrahlung, be-**shtrahl**-oong, f radiation; radiotherapy

bestreben, be-**shtray**-ben, v to endeavour

Bestrebung, be-**shtray**-boong, f endeavour

bestreichen, be-**shtry**-ken, v to spread; to coat

bestreiten, be-**shtry**-ten, v to contest; to dispute; challenge; to deny

bestreuen, be-**shtroy**-en, v to sprinkle (with)

bestürmen, be-**shtEErm**-en, v to overwhelm; to molest

bestürzt, be-**shtEErtst**, adj disconcerted; alarmed

Bestürzung, be-**shtEErts**-oong, f consternation

Besuch, be-**sook**, m visit, call; attendance

besuchen, be-**sook**-en, v to (pay a) visit (to); to attend

Besucher, be-**sook**-er, m visitor

betätigen (sich), be-**tay**-tig-en (zik), v to be engaged (in)

betäuben, be-**toyb**-en, v to stun; to anaesthetize

Betäubung, be-**toyb**-oong f anaesthetic

beteiligen, be-**ty**-lig-en, v to participate, to take part (in)

Beteiligung, be-**ty**-lig-oong, f participation

beten, bay-ten, v to pray; to say one's prayers

betiteln, be-**teet**-eln, v to give a title to

Beton, bay-tong, m concrete

betonen, be-**tohn**-en, v to emphasize, to stress

Betonung, be-**tohn**-oong, f emphasis; stress

betören, be-**ter**-en, v to beguile

Betracht, be-**trahkt**, m consideration; respect

betrachten, be-**trahkt**-en, v to look at; to regard

beträchtlich, be-**trekt**-lik, adj considerable

Betrachtung, be-**trahkt**-oong, f consideration

Betrag, be-**trahk**, m amount; sum

Betragen, be-**trahg**-en, nt behaviour

betragen, be-**trahg**-en, v to amount to

betragen (sich), be-**trahg**-en (zik), v to behave o.s.

Betreff, be-**tref**, m regard ; respect

betreffen, be-**tref**-en, v to concern, to relate to

betreffs, be-**trefs**, prep concerning, with regard to

betreiben, be-**try**-ben, v to

pursue; to carry on (trade)

betreten, be-**trayt**-en, v to enter

Betrieb, be-**treep**, m firm; plant; operation; bustle; **–sferien,** f company holidays; **–sklima,** nt working atmosphere; **–skosten,** pl running costs; **–sleiter,** m (works) manager; **–sleitung,** f management; **–srat,** m works committee; **–sstörung,** f malfunction; **–ssystem,** nt comp operating system; **–swirtschaft,** business management

betrinken (sich), be-**tring**-ken (zik), v to get drunk

betroffen, be-**trof**-en, adj perplexed; surprised

betrüben, be-**trEEb**-en, v to grieve; to afflict

Betrug, be-**trook**, m deception; fraud

betrügen, be-**trEEg**-en, v to deceive; to defraud; to cheat; to be unfaithful to

Betrüger, be-**trEEg**-er, m deceiver; cheat

Betrügerei, be-**trEEg**-e-ry, f deception, cheating

betrunken, be-**troonk**-en, adj drunk

Betrunkenheit, be-**troonk**-en-hite, f drunkenness

Bett, bet, nt bed

Bettdecke, bet-**deck**-e, f blanket; quilt

Bettelei, bet-e-**ly**, f begging

betteln, bet-**eln**, v to beg

Bettlaken, bet-**lahk**-en, nt sheet

Bettler, bet-ler, m beggar

Bettuch, bet-**took**, nt sheet

Bettwäsche, bet-**vesh**-e, f bed-linen

beugen, boyg-en, v to bend; gram to inflect, to decline, to conjugate

Beugung, boyg-oong, f bend(ing); inflexion

Beule, boyl-e, f hump; bump; swelling; bruise

beunruhigen, be-**oonn**-roo-ig-en, v to disturb; to alarm; to worry

Beunruhigung, be-**oonn**-roo-ig-oong, f alarm; uneasiness; worry

beurkunden, be-**oor**-koonn-den, v to certify; to document; to verify

beurlauben, be-**oor**-low-ben, v to give time off

beurteilen, be-**oor**-tyl-en, v to judge; to estimate

Beurteilung, be-**oor**-tyl-oong, f judgment; criticism

Beute, boyt-e, f booty; prey; victim

Beutel, boyt-el, m purse; small bag; pouch

bevölkern, be-**ferl**-kern, v to people; to populate

Bevölkerung, be-**ferl**-ker-oong, f population; inhabitants

bevollmächtigen, be-**foll**-mek-tig-en, v to authorize;

to give power of attorney

bevollmächtigt, be-**foll**-mek-tigt, adj authorized

bevor, be-**fohr**, conj before; **–munden,** v to impose one's will on sb; **–stehend,** adj imminent

bevorzugen, v to prefer

bewachen, be-**vahk**-en, v to guard, to watch

bewachsen, be-**vahk**-sen, v to grow over

Bewachung, be-**vahk**-oong, f watching; guarding; guard

bewaffnen, be-**vahff**-nen, v to arm

Bewaffnung, be-**vahff**-noong, f armament

bewahren, be-**vahr**-en, v to keep

bewähren (sich), be-**vair**-en (zik), v to stand the test; to prove o.s.

Bewährung, be-**vair**-oong, f probation

bewaldet, be-**vahl**-det, adj wooded

bewältigen, be-**velt**-ig-en, v to accomplish; to overcome

bewandert, be-**vahnn**-dert, adj knowledgeable; skilled

bewässern, be-**ves**-ern, v to irrigate, to water

Bewässerung, be-**ves**-er-oong, f irrigation

bewegen, be-**vayg**-en, v to move; to stir; to budge

Beweggrund, be-**vayk**-groont, m motive

beweglich, be-**vayk**-lik, *adj*
movable, mobile; agile

Beweglichkeit, be-**vayk**-lik-kite, *f* mobility

Bewegung, be-**vayg**-oong, *f*
movement; exercise

beweinen, be-**vy**-nen, *v* to
mourn, to weep for

Beweis, be-**vice,** *m* proof,
evidence

beweisen, be-**vy**-zen, *v* to
prove; to substantiate

bewerben (sich), be-**vairb**-en (zik), *v* to apply for

Bewerber, be-**vairb**-er, *m*
applicant; candidate

Bewerbung, be-**vairb**-oong,
f application; candidature

bewerkstelligen, be-**vairk**-shtel-ig-en, *v* to achieve,
to accomplish

bewilligen, be-**vil**-ig-en, *v* to
grant, to allow

Bewilligung, be-**vil**-ig-oong,
f granting; allowance

bewirken, be-**veerk**-en, *v* to
effect; to cause

bewirten, be-**veert**-en, *v* to
entertain (guests)

bewirtschaften, be-**veert**-shahft-en, *v* to cultivate
(soil); to manage

Bewirtung, be-**veert**-oong, *f*
hospitality

bewohnen, be-**vohn**-en, *v* to
inhabit

Bewohner, be-**vohn**-er, *m*
inhabitant; resident

bewundern, be-**voonn**-dern,
v to admire

Bewunderung, be-**voonn**-der-oong, *f* admiration

bewußt, be-**voosst,** *adj*
conscious, aware

bewußtlos, be-**voosst**-lohs,
adj unconscious, senseless

Bewußtlosigkeit, be-**voosst**-loh-zig-kite, *f*
unconsciousness

Bewußtsein, be-**voosst**-zine,
nt consciousness

bezahlen, bet-**sahl**-en, *v* to
pay

Bezahlung, bet-**sahl**-oong, *f*
payment; pay; salary

bezaubern, bet-**sow**-bern, *v*
to enchant; to charm

bezeichnen, bet-**sy'k**-nen, *v*
to mark; to call; to
designate

Bezeichnung, bet-**sy'k**-noong, *f* mark; name;
designation

bezeigen, bet-**sy**-gen, *v* to
show; to give signs of

Bezeigung, bet-**sy**-goong, *f*
manifestation; show

bezeugen, bet-**soyg**-en, *v* to
(bear) witness, to testify

Bezeugung, bet-**soyg**-oong, *f*
testimony

beziehen, bet-**see**-en, *v*
to move into; to cover;
to obtain; **sich auf
etw/jdn –,** *v* to refer
to sb

Beziehung, bet-**see**-oong, *f*
reference; connection;
relationship

beziehungsweise, bet-**see**-oongs-vy-ze, *adv*
respectively; that is

Bezirk, bet-**seerk,** *m* district;
borough

Bezug, bet-**sook,** *m*
cover(ing); regard;
reference

bezüglich, bet-**sEEk**-lik, *adj*
& *prep* concerning, with
regard to

bezwecken, bet-**sveck**-en, *v*
to aim at

bezweifeln, bet-**svy**-feln, *v*
to doubt; to question

bezwingen, bet-**sving**-en, *v*
to master; to overcome

BH, baih-hah, *m* bra

Bibel, beeb-el, *f* Bible

Biber, beeb-er, *m* beaver

Bibliothek, beeb-le-oh-**take,**
f library; study

Bibliothekar, beeb-le-oh-take-**ar,** *m* librarian

bieder, beed-er, *adj* honest;
straightforward; plain

Biederkeit, beed-er-kite, *f*
straightforwardness

biegen, beeg-en, *v* to bend;
to inflect; to curve

biegsam, beek-zahm, *adj*
pliable; bendy

Biegung, beeg-oong, *f* bend;
curve; inflexion

Biene, bee-ne, *f* bee

Bienenkorb, been-en-korp,
m bee-hive

Bienenzucht, been-en-tsookt, *f* bee keeping

Bier, beer, *nt* beer

Biergarten, beer-gart-en, *m*
beer garden

bieten, beet-en, *v* to offer; to
show; to bid

Bikini, be-kee-nee, m bikini

Bilanz, be-lahnts, f balance(-sheet)

Bild, bilt, nt picture, image, illustration

bilden, bild-en, v to form; to educate

Bilderrahmen, bild-er-rahm-en, m picture frame

Bildfläche, bilt-flaik-e, screen; fig scene

Bildhauer, bilt-how-er, m sculptor

Bildhauerei, bilt-how-e-ry, f sculpture

bildlich, bilt-lik, adj figurative, metaphorical

Bildnis, bilt-niss, nt image, likeness

Bildschirm, bilt-shirm, m (television) screen; monitor; –text, m teletext

bildschön, bilt-shern, adj lovely; dazzlingly beautiful

Bildung, bild-oong, f education; formation

Billard, bil-yart, nt billiards; billiard-table

billig, bil-ik, adj cheap; equitable; just

billigen, bil-ig-en, v to approve of, to consent to

Billigkeit, bil-ik-kite, f cheapness; fairness

Billigung, bil-ig-oong, f assent, approval

Billion, bil-yohn, f Brit billion, (US) trillion

bimmeln, bim-eln, v to ring; to tinkle

Bimsstein, bims-shtine, m pumice-stone

Binde, bin-de, f band; bandage; sanitary towel

binden, bin-den, v to bind; to tie; to fasten

Bindestrich, bin-de-shtrik, m hyphen

Bindfaden, bint-fahd-en, m string; twine

binnen, bin-en, prep within (time)

Bio-, bee-oh, pref bio-; **–graphie,** f biography; **–laden,** m health food shop; **–loge** (-login), m & f biologist; **–logie,** f biology

Birnbaum, beern-bowm, m pear-tree

Birne, beern-e, f pear

bis, bis, prep till, until; as far as

bisher, bis-hair, adv until now; so far

bisherig, bis-hair-ik, adj present

Biskuit, bis-kvit, m sponge cake

Biß, bis, m bite; biting; sting

bißchen (ein), bis-ken (ine), adv (a) little (bit); somewhat

Bissen, bis-en, m morsel; mouthful

bissig, bis-ik, adj snappish; vicious; biting; caustic

bisweilen, bis-vy-len, adv sometimes, at times

Bit, bit, nt comp bit

Bitte, bit-e, f request; petition

bitte, bit-e, interj please; **wie b–?,** pardon?

bitten, bit-en, v to ask, to implore; to demand

bitter, bit-er, adj bitter

Bitterkeit, bit-er-kite, f bitterness; sharpness

bitterlich, bit-er-lik, adj & adv bitter(ly)

Bittschrift, bit-shrift, f petition

blähen, blay-en, v to blow out; (sich) to swell

Blähungen, blay-oong-en, pl med wind, flatulence

blamieren, blahm-eer-en, v to show up; to expose to ridicule

blank, blahnnk, adj shining; bright; glittering

Blase, blahz-e, f bubble; blister; med bladder

Blasebalg, blah-ze-bahlk, m bellows

blasen, blahz-en, v to blow

Blasenentzündung, blahz-en-en-tsEEnd-oong, f cystitis

blasiert, blahz-eert, adj jaded; blasé

Blasinstrument, blahs-in-stroo-ment, nt wind instrument

blaß, blahss, adj pale

Blässe, bless-e, f paleness; pallor

Blatt, blahtt, nt leaf; blade; petal; sheet

blättern, blet-ern, v to turn over the pages of a book

Blätterteig, blet-er-tyg, m

puff pastry

blau, blow, *adj* blue

Blech, blek, *nt* sheet-metal; tin; *fam* nonsense

Blechinstrument, blek-in-stroo-**ment,** *nt* brass instrument

Blei, bly, *nt* lead (metal)

bleiben, bly-ben, *v* to stay, to remain

bleich, bly'k, *adj* pale, faded

bleichen, bly-ken, *v* to bleach; to turn pale

bleiern, bly-ern, *adj* leaden

Bleistift, bly-shtift, *m* pencil

Blende, blend-e, *f* aperture

blenden, blend-en, *v* to blind; to dazzle

Blick, blik, *m* glance; look; glimpse; peep

blicken, blik-en, *v* to look; to glance

blind, blinnt, *adj* blind

Blinddarm, blint-dahrm, *m med* appendix;
–entzündung, *f* appendicitis

Blindenschrift, blin-den-shrift, *f* braille

Blindgänger, blint-geng-er, *m* unexploded shell; dud; dead loss

Blindheit, blint-hite, *f* blindness

blindlings, blint-links, *adv* at random

blinken, blink-en, *v* to shine; to gleam

blinzeln, blint-seln, *v* to blink; to wink

Blitz, blits, *m* lightning; flash; **–ableiter,** *m* lightning-conductor; **–licht,** *nt* flash

blitzblank, blits-blahnk, *adj* spick and span

blitzen, blits-en, *v* to be like lightning; to sparkle; *photog* to use flash

blitzschnell, blits-shnel, *adj* quick as a flash

Block, block, *m* block; (writing) pad

Blockade, block-ah-de, *f* blockade

blockieren, block-eer-en, *v* to blockade

blöd, blerd, *adj fam* stupid

Blödsinn, blerd-zin, *m* nonsense; imbecility; idiocy

blödsinnig, blerd-zin-ik, *adj* idiotic; imbecile

blond, blont, *adj* fair-haired

Blondine, blond-een-e, *f* blonde

bloß, blohs, *adj* plain; naked, bare; mere; *adv* simply, only, merely

Blöße, blers-e, *f* nudity; clearing; opening

blühen, blEE-en, *v* to bloom; to blossom; to flower

Blume, bloom-e, *f* flower; bloom; bouquet (of wine)

Blumenkohl, bloom-en-kohl, *m* cauliflower

Blumenstrauß, bloom-en-shtrows, *m* bouquet (of flowers)

Blumentopf, bloom-en-top'f, *m* flower-pot

Bluse, blooz-e, *f* blouse; smock

Blut, bloot, *nt* blood

Blutader, bloot-ahd-er, *f* vein

Blutarmut, bloot-arm-oot, *f* anæmia

Blutdruck, bloot-droock, *m* blood pressure

Blüte, blEEt-e, *f* blossom; flower

bluten, bloot-en, *v* to bleed

Blütenblatt, blEEt-en-blahtt, *nt* petal

Blütenstaub, blEEt-en-shtowp, *m* pollen

Blütezeit, blEEt-e-tsite, *f* prosperous time; heyday

Blutgefäß, bloot-ge-faiss, *nt* blood-vessel

blutgierig, bloot-geer-ik, *adj* bloodthirsty

Blutgruppe, bloot-groop-e, *f* blood group

blutig, bloot-ik, *adj* bloody; gory

Blutkörperchen, bloot-kerp-er-ken, *nt* blood-corpuscle

Blutprobe, bloot-prohb-e, *f* blood test

blutsverwandt, bloots-fair-vahnnt, *adj* closely related

Blutverlust, bloot-fair-loost, *m* loss of blood

Blutvergießen, bloot-fair-gees-en, *nt* bloodshed

Bock, bock, *m* buck; ram; billy-goat

Boden, bohd-en, *m* floor; ground; bottom; loft, attic

bodenlos, bohd-en-lohs, *adj*
bottomless; abysmal

Bodensatz, bohd-en-zahtts,
m sediment; grounds;
dregs

Bodenschätze, bohd-en-
shets-*e*, *pl* mineral
resources

Bogen, bohg-en, *m* arch;
bow; bend; sheet
(of paper)

Bogenlicht, bohg-en-likt, *nt*
arc-light

Bohle, bohl-*e*, *f* (thick)
plank, board; sleeper

Bohne, bohn-*e*, *f* bean

bohren, bohr-en, *v* to bore;
to drill

Bohrer, bohr-*er*, *m* gimlet;
drill

Bohrinsel, bohr-in-zel, *f* oil
rig

Bolzen, bolt-sen, *m* bolt;
rivet; pin

Bombe, bom-be, *f* bomb

Bonbon, bom-bong, *m & nt*
sweet

Boot, boht, *nt* boat

Bord, bort, *m* border; edge;
an –, naut aboard, on
board

Bordell, bord-ell, *nt* brothel

borgen, borg-en, *v* to
borrow; to lend

borniert, born-eert, *adj*
narrow-minded

Börse, ber-ze, *f* stock
exchange; purse

Borste, borst-*e*, *f* bristle

bösartig, bers-art-ik, *adj* ill-
natured; malicious

Böschung, bersh-oong, *f*
slope; embankment

böse, berz-*e*, *adj* bad; evil;
wicked

Bösewicht, berz-e-vikt, *m*
scoundrel

boshaft, bohs-hahft, *adj*
malicious; wicked

Boshaftigkeit, bohs-hahft-
ig-kite, *f* malice

böswillig, bers-vil-ik, *adj*
malevolent

Botanik, boht-**ahn**-ik, *f*
botany

Bote, boht-*e*, *m* messenger;
courier

Botschaft, boht-shahft, *f*
message; errand; news;
embassy; **–er,** *m*
ambassador

boxen, box-en, *v* to box

boykottieren, boy-kott-eer-
en, *v* to boycott

Branche, brahng-she, *f* line
of business; branch;
–nverzeichnis, *nt* yellow
pages

Brand, brahnnt, *m* fire

branden, brahn-den, *v* to
surge; to roll

Brandstiftung, brahnnt-
shtif-toong, *f* arson

Brandung, brahn-doong, *f*
surf

Branntwein, brahnnt-vine,
m brandy

Brasilianer, brah-zee-lee-ah-
ner, *m* Brazilian (person)

brasilianisch, brah-zee-lee-
ah-nish, *adj* Brazilian

Brasilien, brah-zee-lee-en,
nt Brazil

braten, braht-en, *v* to fry; to
roast; to bake

Braten, braht-en, *m* roast,
joint (of meat)

Brathuhn, braht-hoon, *nt*
roast chicken

Bratkartoffeln, braht-kart-
off-eln, *pl* fried potatoes

Bratpfanne, braht-fahnn-*e*,
f frying-pan

Bratsche, braht-she, *f* viola;
(bass-)viol

Bratwurst, braht-voorst, *f*
fried sausage

Brauch, browk, *m* usage;
custom

brauchbar, browk-bar, *adj*
useful; useable

brauchen, browk-en, *v* to
use; to employ; to need

brauen, brow-en, *v* to brew;
to mix

Brauerei, brow-*e*-ry, *f*
brewery

braun, brown, *adj* brown

Braunkohle, brown-kohl-*e*,
f brown-coal; lignite

Brause, brow-ze, *f* shower;
lemonade

brausen, brow-zen, *v* to
rush; to roar; to sprinkle

Braut, browt, *f* fiancée;
bride

Bräutigam, broy-tee-gahm,
m fiancé; bridegroom

Brautjungfer, browt-yoong-
fer, *f* bridesmaid

Brautpaar, browt-pahr, *nt*
bride and bridegroom

brav, brahf, *adj* honest;

upright; good

brechen, brek-en, v to break; to crack; to vomit

Brei, bry, m mush, pulp, paste

breit, brite, adj broad; wide

Breite, bry-te, f breadth; width

Breitengrad, bry-ten-graht, m degree of latitude

Bremse, brem-ze, f brake

bremsen, brem-zen, v to brake

brennen, brenn-en, v to burn; to cauterize; to brand

Brennglas, brenn-glahs, nt burning-glass

Brennessel, bren-nes-el, f stinging nettle

Brennpunkt, brenn-poonkt, m focus

Brennspiritus, brenn-shpeer-it-ooss, m (methylated) spirits

Brennstoff, brenn-shtof, m fuel

Brett, bret, nt board; plank

Brettspiel, bret-shpeel, nt board game

Brief, breef, m letter; epistle

Briefbogen, breef-bohg-en, m sheet of writing paper

Briefkasten, breef-kahsst-en, m letter-box

Briefmarke, breef-mark-e, f (postage-)stamp

Briefpapier, breef-pah-peer, nt writing paper

Briefpost, breef-posst, f letter-post

Brieftasche, breef-tahsh-e, f wallet

Briefträger, breef-trayg-er, m postman

Briefumschlag, breef-oomm-shlahk, m envelope

Briefwechsel, breef-veck-sel, m correspondence

Brillant, brill-**yahnt**, m (cut) diamond

Brille, bril-e, f (pair of) spectacles

bringen, bring-en, v to bring; to convey; to take

Brise, breez-e, f breeze

Brite, breet-e, m Briton

britisch, brit-ish, adj British

bröckeln, brer-keln, v to crumble; to break in small pieces

Brocken, brock-en, m fragment; scrap; crumb

brodeln, brohd-eln, v to bubble (up); to simmer

Brokkoli, brock-oh-lee, pl broccoli

Brombeere, brom-bair-e, f bramble; blackberry

Brosche, brosh-e, f brooch

Broschüre, brosh-**EER**-e, f pamphlet; leaflet

Brot, broht, nt bread

Brötchen, brert-ken, nt (bread) roll

brotlos, broht-lohs, adj without means of support

Bruch, brook, m break(ing); fracture; rupture

Bruchstück, brook-st**EE**k, nt fragment; piece

Bruchzahl, brook-tsahl,

f fraction

Brücke, br**EE**ck-e, f bridge; viaduct

Bruder, brood-er, m brother

brüderlich, br**EE**d-er-lik, adj brotherly; fraternal

Brühe, br**EE**-e, f broth

brüllen, br**EE**ll-en, v to bellow; to bawl; to roar

brummen, broomm-en, v to growl; to hum

brünett, br**EE**n-ett, adj brunette

Brunnen, broonn-en, m well; spring; fountain

Brunnenkresse, broonn-en-kress-e, f water-cress

Brüssel, br**EE**s-el, nt Brussels

Brust, broosst, f breast; chest; bosom

brüsten (sich), br**EE**sst-en (zik), v to pride o.s.; to boast about sth

Brustkasten, broosst-kahsst-en, m chest; thorax

Brustkrebs, broosst-kreps, m breast cancer

Brüstung, br**EE**sst-oong, f parapet

Brut, broot, f brood; brooding; offspring

brutal, broot-**ahl**, adj brutal

Brutalität, broot-ahl-ee-**tait**, f brutality

brüten, br**EE**t-en, v to hatch; to sit on (eggs)

Brutkasten, broot-kahst-en, m incubator

brutto, broott-oh, adv gross

Bruttolohn, broott-oh-lohn, m gross wages

Bruttosozialprodukt, broott-oh-soh-tsee-**ahl**-proh-doockt, *nt* gross national product

Buch, book, *nt* book; volume; **–binder,** *m* bookbinder

Buche, book-e, *f* beech

buchen, book-en, *v* to book; to enter in the books

Bücherei, bEEk-e-ry, *f* library

Bücherregal, bEEk-er-reg-ahl, *nt* bookshelves

Buchführung, book-fEEr-oong *f* bookkeeping

Buchhalter, book-hahlt-er, *m* bookkeeper

Buchhaltung, book-hahlt-oong, *f* bookkeeping

Buchhandel, book-hahnd-el, *m* bookselling, book trade

Buchhandlung, book-hahnd-loong, *f* bookshop

Buchmacher, book-mak-er, *m* bookmaker

Buchsbaum, boocks-bowm, *m* box (tree)

Büchse, bEEck-se, *f* box; tin; rifle

Büchsenfleisch, bEEck-sen-fly'sh, *nt* tinned meat

Büchsenöffner, bEEck-sen-erff-ner, *m* tin opener

Buchstabe, book-shtahb-e, *m* (alphabet) letter; type

buchstabieren, book-shtahb-**eer**-en, *v* to spell

buchstäblich, book-shtayp-lik, *adj* literal

Bucht, bookt, *f* bay, cove;

Buchung, book-oong, *f* booking; entry

Buckel, boock-el, *m* hump, hunch; hunchback

bucklig, boock-lik, *adj* hunchbacked

bücken (sich), bEEck-en (zik), *v* to stoop; to bow

Bückling, bEEck-ling, *m* a kind of smoked herring

Bude, bood-e, *f* booth; stall; *fam* digs

Büfett, bEE-fett, *nt* sideboard

Büffel, bEEff-el, *m* buffalo, bison

Bug, boohk, *m naut* bow; hock, shoulder blade

Bügel, bEEg-el, *m* coathanger; stirrup; bow

Bügeleisen, bEEg-el-i-zen, *nt* iron

bügelfrei, bEEg-el-fry, *adj* non-iron

bügeln, bEEg-eln, *v* to iron, to press

Bühne, bEEn-e, *f theatre* stage; platform; **–nbild,** *nt* (stage) set

Bühnenstück, bEEn-en-shtEEck, *nt* (stage-)play

Bulle, booll-e, *m* bull; *fam* copper

Bummel, boomm-el, *m* stroll; jaunt

bummeln, boomm-eln, *v* to stroll; to dawdle

Bummelzug, boomm-el-tsook, *m* slow train

Bund, boont, *m* union,

alliance; league

Bund, boont, *nt* bundle, bunch; packet

Bündel, bEEnd-el, *nt* bundle; packet, parcel

Bundes-, boond-es, *pref* federal; **–bürger,** *m* German citizen; **–kanzler,** *m* Federal Chancellor; **–land,** *nt* state; Federal Republic; **–präsident,** *m* Federal President; **–rat,** *m* upper house of German parliament; **–tag,** *m* German parliament; **–wehr,** *f* German armed forces

Bündnis, bEEnt-niss, *nt* alliance, union

bunt, boont, *adj* multicoloured

Buntstift, boont-shtift, *m* crayon

Bürde, bEErd-e, *f* burden, load

Burg, boork, *f* castle; stronghold

Bürge, bEErg-e, *m* security; bail; guarantor

bürgen, bEErg-en, *v* to guarantee; to stand bail; to vouch for

Bürger, bEErg-er, *m* citizen; **–krieg,** *m* civil war

bürgerlich, bEErg-er-lik, *adj* middle class; civilian

Bürgermeister, bEErg-er-myst-er, *m* mayor

Bürgersteig, bEErg-er-shtyg, *m* footpath; pavement

Bürgschaft, bEErk-shahft, *f*
pledge, guarantee

Büro, bEEr-oh, *nt* office

Bürokratie, bEEr-oh-kraht-ee, *f* bureaucracy

bürokratisch, bEEr-oh-kraht-ish, *adj* bureaucratic

Bursche, boorsh-*e*, *m* youth,
young man

Bürste, bEErs-*te*, *f* brush

bürsten, bEErs-*ten*, *v* to
brush

Bus, boos, *m* bus; coach

Busch, boosh, *m* bush,
shrub; plume; tuft

Büschel, bEEsh-*el*, *nt* whisp;
cluster; tuft

buschig, boosh-*ik*, *adj*
bunchy; tufted; bushy

Busen, booz-*en*, *m* bosom,
breast, bust

Bushaltestelle, boos-hahlt-*e*-stel-*le*, *f* bus stop

Buße, boos-*e*, *f* penitence;
repentance, atonement;
fine

büßen, bEEs-*en*, *v* to atone;
to expiate (crime); to do
penance

Büste, bEEst-*e*, *f* bust

Büstenhalter, bEEst-*en*-hahlt-*er*, *m* bra

Butter, boott-*er*, *f* butter

Butterblume, boott-*er*-bloom-*e*, *f* buttercup

Butterbrot, boott-*er*-broht,
nt bread and butter

bzgl., *abbr* bezüglich

bzw., *abbr* beziehungsweise

C

ca. (= circa), tseer-kah, *adv* about, approximately

Camcorder, kem-korder, *m* camcorder

campen, kemp-en, *v* to camp

Campingbus, kemp-ing-boos, *m* dormobile

Campingplatz, kemp-ing-plahts, *m* camp site

CD-Spieler, see-dee-shpeel-er, *m* CD-player

Cello, tchel-loh, *nt* cello

Celsius, tsel-ze-ooss, *nt* centigrade

Champagner, shahmm-pahnn-yer, *m* champagne

Champignon, shahmm-pin-yong, *m* mushroom

Chance, shahn-se, *f* chance, opportunity

Charakter, kah-rahck-ter, *m* character, nature

charakterfest, kah-rahck-ter-fest, *adj* firm of character

charakterisieren, kah-rahck-ter-eez-eer-en, *v* to depict; to characterize

Charakterzug, kah-rahck-ter-tsook, *m* trait of character

Charme, shahrm, *m* charm

Charterflug, tchahrt-er-floog, *m* charter flight

Chef, shef, *m* principal, manager, chief, boss

Chemie, keh-mee, *f* chemistry

Chemikalien, keh-me-kahl-yen, *pl* chemicals, drugs

Chemiker, keh-mik-er, *m* (scientific) chemist

chemisch, keh-mish, *adj* chemical; **–e Reinigung,** *f* dry-cleaning

Chiffre, shif-re, *f* cipher; box number

China, kee-nah, *nt* China

Chinese, kee-nay-ze, *m*, **Chinesin,** kee-nay-zin, *f* Chinese (person)

chinesisch, kee-nay-zish, *adj* Chinese

Chinin, kee-neen, *nt* quinine

Chip, tchip, *m* crisp; *comp* chip; **–karte,** smart card

Chirurg, kee-roork, *m* surgeon

Chor, kohr, *m* chorus, choir

Choral, kohr-ahl, *m* hymn, anthem

Christ, krist, *m* Christian; **–baum,** *m* Christmas-tree; **–entum,** *nt* Christianity; **–fest,** *nt* Christmas; **–kind,** *nt* Infant Jesus, Christ Child

christlich, krist-lik, *adj* Christian

Cola, koh-lah, *fam* Coke ®

Computer, kohm-pyoot-er, *m* computer; **–spiel,** *nt* computer game

Cousin, koo-zeng, *m* (male) cousin

Cousine, koo-zeen-e, *f* (female) cousin

Creme, kraim, *f* cream; (shoe) polish

D

da, dah, *adv* there; here; then; *conj* as, since, because

dabei, dah-by, *adv* thereby, by it; **–sein,** *v* to be present; to be involved; **–stehen,** *v* to stand around

Dach, dah*k*, *nt* roof; **–boden,** *m* loft; **–decker,** *m* tiler; roofer; slater; **–gepäckträger,** *m* roof rack; **–rinne,** *f* gutter

Dachs, dah*ks*, *m* badger

Dachstube, dah*k*-shtoob-e, *f* garret, attic

Dackel, dah*kk*-el, *m* dachshund

dadurch, dah-doohr*k*, *adv* by that means; thereby

dafür, dah-fEER, *adv* in return for, for that; in place of

dagegen, dah-gay-gen, *adv*
& *conj* against it, in return; on the contrary

daheim, dah-hime, *adv* at home; indoors

daher, dah-hair, *adv* from that; hence

dahin, dah-hin, *adv* there (thither)

dahingegen, dah-hin-gay-gen, *adv* on the other hand; on the contrary

dahinter, dah-hint-er, *adv* behind it

damals, dah-mahls, *adv* at that time

Damast, dahmm-ast, *m* damask

Dame, dahm-e, *f* lady; (chess) queen

damit, dah-mit, *adv* & *conj* with it; so that

Damm, dahmm, *m* dam, dike; embankment, sea-wall

dämmen, dem-en, *v* to dam; to (hold in) check

dämmerig, dem-er-ik, *adj* dim, dusky

dämmern, dem-ern, *v* to dawn

Dämmerung, dem-er-oong, *f* twilight; dawn

Dampf, dahmf, *m* steam; vapour

dampfen, dahm-fen, *v* to steam; to emit steam

dämpfen, dem-fen, *v* to suppress, to check; to muffle, to deaden

Dampfer, dahm-fer, *m* steamer

Dampfkessel, dahmf-kess-el, *m* steam-boiler

Dampfmaschine, dahmf-mah-sheen-e, *f* steam-engine

Dampfschiff, dahmf-shif, *nt* steamship

Dampfwalze, dahmf-vahlt-se, *f* steam-roller

danach, dah-nah*k*, *adv* after that; later on

Däne, day-ne, *m* Dane, Danishman

Dänemark, day-ne-mahrk, *nt* Denmark

daneben, dah-nay-ben, *adv* beside it; next to it

Dänin, day-nin, *f* Dane, Danishwoman

dänisch, day-nish, *adj* Danish

Dank, dahngk, *m* gratitude, thanks; reward; **vielen –,** many thanks

dankbar, dahngk-bar, *adj*
grateful, thankful

Dankbarkeit, dahngk-bar-
kite, *f* gratitude

danke, dahngk-*e*, *interj*
thank you

danken, dahngk-en, *v* to
thank

dann, dahnn, *adv* then; after
that, afterwards

daran, dah-rahnn, *adv* on it;
against it; near it

darauf, dah-rowf, *adv* on it

daraus, dah-rows, *adv* from
there; from it

Darbietung, dahr-beet-
oong, *f* performance,
presentation

darin, dah-rin, *adv* in it

darlegen, dahr-lay-gen, *v* to
show; to exhibit; to
explain

Darleh(e)n, dahr-lay(-*e*-)n,
nt loan

Darm, darm, *m* intestine,
gut

darstellen, dahr-shtel-en, *v*
to present, to show; to
produce

Darsteller, dahr-shtel-er, *m*
actor

Darstellung, dahr-shtel-
oong, *f* presentation

darüber, dah-rEEb-er, *adv*
over it; about it

darum, dah-roomm, *adv*
about it; therefore

darunter, dah-roont-er, *adv*
underneath; among

das, see **der**

Dasein, dah-zine, *nt*

existence, being

daß, dahss, *conj* that

Datei, daht-y, (data) file

Daten, daht-en, *pl* data

Datenbank, daht-en-bahnk,
f database

Datenschutz, daht-en-
shoots, *m* data protection

Datenverarbeitung, daht-
en-fer-ahr-bite-oong, *f*
data processing

datieren, daht-eer-en, *v* to
date

Dattel, daht-el, *f* date (fruit)

Datum, daht-oomm, *nt* date
(calendar)

Dauer, dow-er, *f* duration;
length of time

dauerhaft, dow-er-hahfft,
adj durable, lasting

Dauerkarte, dow-er-kahr-te,
f season ticket

dauern, dow-ern, *v* to last,
to continue

Dauerwelle, dow-er-vel-le, *f*
perm

Daumen, dowm-en, *m*
thumb

Daunendecke, down-en-
deck-e, *f* duvet

davon, dah-fon, *adv* from it;
of it

davor, dah-fohr, *adv* in front
of it

dazu, dah-tsoo, *adv* with it

dazwischen, dah-tsvish-en,
adv between them; among
them

Deck, deck, *nt* deck

Decke, deck-e, *f* cover(ing);
ceiling; layer

Deckel, deck-el, *m* lid;
cover (of book)

decken, deck-en, *v* to cover;
to reimburse

Deckung, deck-oong, *f*
cover, shelter, protection

Defekt, de-feckt, *m* fault,
defect

Degen, day-gen, *m* sword

dehnen, dayn-en, *v* to
stretch; to extend

Deich, dy'k, *m* dike; dam;
embankment

dein, deine(r/s), dine, dine-
e(r/s), *adj* your; *pron* yours

Dekoration, day-koh-rah-
tse-ohn, *f* decoration;
window display

delikat, day-le-kaht, *adj*
delicious

Delikatessen, day-le-kaht-
ess-en, *pl* delicatessen
(food), delicacies;
–geschäft *nt*, **–laden** *m*,
–handlung *f* delicatessen
(shop)

Delikt, de-likt, *nt* offence

dem, daym, *art* (*dative m &*
nt) (to) the; *pron* (to)
whom

dementsprechend, daym-
ent-shprek-ent, *adv*
accordingly

demgemäß, daym-ge-mace,
adv correspondingly;
accordingly

demnach, daym-nahk, *adv*
therefore; accordingly

demnächst, daym-naikst,
adv shortly, soon

Demokratie, day-moh-krah-

tee, f democracy

demokratisch, day-moh-**kraht**-ish, *adj* democratic

Demonstration, day-mohn-strahts-**yohn,** f demonstration

demonstrieren, day-mohn-**streer**-en, *v* to demonstrate

Demut, day-moot, f humility

demütig, day-mEEt-ik, *adj* humble; **–en,** *v* to humble; to humiliate

Demütigung, day-mEEt-ig-oong, f humiliation; abasement

den, dayn, *definite art (accusative m & dative pl)* (to) the

denen, dayn-en, *pron (dative pl)* to them, to those

denkbar, denk-bar, *adj* imaginable

denken, deng-ken, *v* to think

Denkmal, dengk-mahl, *nt* monument, memorial; **–schutz,** m protection of historical monuments

denkwürdig, dengk-vEErd-ik, *adj* notable; memorable

denn, den, *conj* for, because, since

dennoch, den-ok, *adv & conj* nevertheless; however; still

Deodorant, day-oh-dor-ahnt, *nt* deodorant

deponieren, day-pon-**eer**-en, *v* to deposit

Deponie, day-pohn-ee, f dump

deprimieren, day-preem-**eer**-en, *v* to depress

der, die, das, der, dee, dahs, *definite art* the; *pron* who, which

derb, dairp, *adj* firm, robust; rude, rough, coarse

deren, dair-en, *pron (genitive f & pl)* whose, of whom, of which

dergleichen, dair-gly-ken, *pron* such

derjenige, dair-yayn-ig-e, *pron* the one who

derselbe, dair-zel-be, *pron* the same

des, dess, *definite art (genitive m & nt)* of the

desgleichen, dess-gly-ken, *adv* likewise

deshalb, dess-hahlp, *adv & conj* because of that, therefore

dessen, dess-en, *pron (genitive m & n)* whose

Dessert, dess-er, *nt* dessert

desto, dess-toh, *adv* so much; **– besser, bess**-er, so much the better

deswegen, dess-vaig-en, *adv & conj* because of that; therefore

Dezember, day-**tsemm**-ber, m December

Detail, day-tie, *nt* detail

Detektiv, day-tek-**teef,** m detective

deuten, doyt-en, *v* to point out; to explain

deutlich, doyt-lik, *adj* distinct, clear, intelligible

deutsch, doytsh, *adj* German

Deutsche(r), doyt-she(r), m & f German (person)

Deutschland, doytsh-lahnt, *nt* Germany

Deutung, doyt-oong, f interpretation, explanation

Devise, day-**veez**-e, f device, motto; **–n,** *pl* foreign currency; foreign exchange

Dia, dee-ah, *nt photog* slide; transparency

Dialekt, dee-ah-**lekt,** m dialect

Dialog, dee-ah-**lohk,** m dialogue

Diät, dee-**ait,** f diet

Diamant, dee-ah-**mahnt,** m diamond

dich, dik, *pron (accusative)* you

dicht, dikt, *adj* dense; tight; solid

dichten, dik-ten, *v* to seal; to write poetry

Dichter, dik-ter, m poet, writer

Dichtkunst, dikt-koonst, f (art of) poetry

Dichtung, dikt-oong, f poetry

dick, dik, *adj* thick; fat, stout

Dicke, dik-e, f thickness; stoutness

Dickkopf, dik-kop'f, m stubborn person

die, see **der**

Dieb, deep, *m* thief, robber

Diebstahl, deep-shtahl, *m* theft, robbery

Diele, deel-*e*, *f* floorboard; plank; hall(way)

dienen, deen-en, *v* to serve

Diener, deen-*er*, *m* servant, footman, valet

dienlich, deen-lik, *adj* useful; expedient

Dienst, deenst, *m* service; duty; favour; **–bote,** *m* domestic servant

Dienstag, deens-tahk, *m* Tuesday

diensthabend, deenst-hahb-ent, *adj* on duty

Dienstleistung, deenst-lyst-oong, *f* service

Dienstreise, deenst-ryz-*e*, *f* business trip

diesbezüglich, dees-bet-sEEk-lik, *adj* referring to this

dies, diese(r/s), dees, deez-*e*(r/s), *pron* this, that

diesmal, dees-mahl, *adv* this time; for (this) once

diesseits, dees-zites, *adv & prep* on this side

digital, dee-gee-tahl, *adj* digital

Diktat, dik-taht, *nt* dictation

Diktatur, dik-tah-toor, *f* dictatorship

diktieren, dik-teer-en, *v* to dictate

Ding, ding, *nt* thing; subject; matter

Diplom, deep-lohm, *nt* diploma; (university) degree

Diplomat, deep-lohm-aht, *m* diplomat

Diplomatie, deep-lohm-aht-ee, *f* diplomacy

direkt, dee-reckt, *adj* direct

Direktor, dee-reckt-ohr, *m* director; (school) headmaster

Direktübertragung, dee-reckt-EEber-trahg-oong, *f* live broadcast

Dirigent, dee-ree-gent, *m mus* conductor

dirigieren, dee-ree-geer-en, *v mus* to conduct

Diskont, dis-kont, *m* discount, rebate

Diskussion, dis-kooss-yohn, *f* discussion; debate

diskutieren, dis-koot-eer-en, *v* to discuss; to debate

disponieren (über jdn), dees-pohn-eer-en, *v* to tell (sb) what to do; to make arrangements

Distel, dist-el, *f* thistle

distinguiert, dist-ing-geert, *adj* distinguished

doch, dok, *conj & adv* still, yet, however; yes, indeed

Docht, dokt, *m* wick

Dogge, dog-*e*, *f* mastiff

Dohle, dohl-*e*, *f* jackdaw

Dokument, doh-koo-ment, *nt* document; **–arbericht,** *m* documentary

Dolch, dolk, *m* dagger

dolmetschen, dol-metsh-en, *v* to interpret

Dolmetscher, dol-metsh-er, *m* interpreter

Dom, dohm, *m* cathedral

Donau, doh-now, *f* Danube

Donner, don-er, *m* thunder

donnern, don-ern, *v* to thunder

Donnerstag, don-ers-tahk, *m* Thursday

doof, dohf, *adj* stupid

Doppel, dop-el, *nt* double, duplicate; **–bett,** *nt* double bed; **–stecker,** *m* two-way adaptor

doppelt, dop-elt, *adj* double, twin

Doppelzimmer, dop-el-tsim-er, *nt* double room

Dorf, dorf, *nt* village

Dorn, dorn, *m* thorn, prickle

dornig, dorn-ik, *adj* thorny

Dörrobst, der-ohpst; *nt* dried fruit

dort, dort, *adv* there

dorther, dort-hair, *adv* from there

dorthin, dort-hin, *adv* there (thither)

dortig, dort-ik, *adj* there (of that place)

Dose, doh-ze, *f* tin; can; box; **–nöffner,** *m* tin-opener

Dotter, dot-er, *m* yolk of an egg

Dozent, doht-sent *m* university lecturer

Drache, drahk-*e*, *m* dragon

Drachen, drahk-en, *m* kite; **–fliegen,** *nt* hang-gliding

Draht, draht, *m* wire

Drama, drah-mah, *nt* drama

dramatisch, drah-**mah**-tish, *adj* dramatic

Drang, drahng, *m* throng; pressure; urge

drängen, dreng-en, *v* to press, to push

draußen, drows-en, *adv* outside; outdoors

Dreck, dreck, *m* dirt, filth

dreckig, dreck-ik, *adj* dirty, filthy

drehen, dray-en, *v* to turn, to twist; to wind

drei, dry, *num* three

Dreieck, dry-eck, *nt* triangle

dreieckig, dry-eck-ik, *adj* triangular; three-cornered

dreierlei, dry-er-ly, *adj* of three kinds

dreifach, dry-fahk, *adj* threefold; treble; triple

dreimal, dry-mahl, *adv* three times; thrice

dreiseitig, dry-zy-tik, *adj* trilateral

dreißig, dry-sik, *num* thirty

dreist, dry'st, *adj* bold, audacious; impudent

dreizehn, dry-tsain, *num* thirteen

dreschen, dresh-en, *v* to thresh; *fam* to thrash

dressieren, dres-eer-en, *v* to train (animals)

dringen, dring-en, *v* to force; to urge; to penetrate; **auf etwas –,** to insist on sth

dringend, dring-ent, *adj* urgent, pressing

drinnen, drinn-en, *adv* inside

dritte(r/s), dritt-e(r/s), *adj* third

Drittel, dritt-el, *nt* third (part)

drittens, dritt-ens, *adv* thirdly

droben, drohb-en, *adv* above, up there; on high

Droge, drohg-e, *f* drug

drogenabhängig, drohg-en-ahp-heng-ik, *adj* addicted to drugs

Drogenmißbrauch, drohg-en-miss-browk, *m* drug abuse

Drogerie, drohg-er-ee, *f* chemist's shop; drugstore

drohen, droh-en, *v* to threaten, to menace

dröhnen, drern-en, *v* to rumble, to roar, to boom

Drohung, droh-oong, *f* threat, menace

drollig, drol-lik, *adj* droll, funny, quaint

Droschke, drosh-ke, *f* (horse-drawn) carriage

Drossel, dross-el, *f* thrush

drüben, drEEb-en, *adv* over there

Druck, droock, *m* pressure; depression; print(ing)

drucken, droock-en, *v* to print; to typeset

drücken, drEEck-en, *v* to press, to squeeze; to oppress

Drucker, droock-er, *m* printer

Druckerei, droock-e-ry, *f* printing-works

Drucksache, droock-sahk-e, *f* printed matter

Druckschrift, droock-shrift, *f* block letters

drunten, droonnt-en, *adv* below, down there

Drüse, drEEz-e, *f* gland

Dschungel, tshoong-el, *m* jungle

du, doo, *pron* you

Dudelsack, dood-el-zahck, *m* bagpipes

Duft, dooft, *m* odour, fragrance

duften, dooft-en, *v* to smell (be fragrant)

dulden, doold-en, *v* to tolerate, to suffer

duldsam, doolt-zahm, *adj* (long-)suffering; tolerant

dumm, doomm, *adj* stupid, thick

Dummheit, doomm-hite, *f* stupidity

Dummkopf, doomm-kop'f, *m* blockhead; idiot

dumpf, doomf, *adj* dull, muffled; stuffy, close

düngen, dEEng-en, *v* to manure, to fertilize

Dünger, dEEng-er, *m*, manure, dung, fertilizer

dunkel, doong-kel, *adj* dark; gloomy, murky

Dunkelheit, doong-kel-hite, *f* darkness

dunkeln, doong-keln, *v* to

grow dark

dünn, dEEnn, *adj* thin; lean

Dunst, doonst, *m* vapour, steam; mist

dünsten, dEEns-ten, *v* to steam; to stew

dunstig, doons-tik, *adj* vaporous; hazy, misty

Dur, door, *nt mus* major

durch, doohrk, *prep* through; by (means of)

durchaus, doohrk-ows, *adv* throughout; quite; thoroughly

durchblicken, doohrk-blik-en, *v* to peep/glance through

durchbohren, doohrk-bohr-en, *v* to pierce through

durchbrechen, doohrk-brek-en, *v* to break through

durchbringen, doohrk-bring-en, *v* to get through; to support

durchdringen, doohrk-dring-en, *v* to permeate

durcheinander, doohrk-yn-ahnd-er, *adj* confused; in a mess; muddled

Durchfahrt, doohrk-fahrt, *f* thoroughfare, passage

Durchfall, doohrk-fahll, *m* diarrhoea

durchfallen, doohrk-fahll-en, *v* to fall through; to fail

durchfinden (sich), doohrk-finn-den (zik), *v* to find one's way through

durchführen, doohrk-fEEr-

en, *v* to carry through; to achieve

Durchführung, doohrk-fEEr-oong, *f* implementation; carrying out

Durchgang, doohrk-gahng, *m* passing through; passage; way through

durchgehend, doohrk-gai-ent, *adj* continuous; through (train)

durchkommen, doohrk-kom-en, *v* to get through; to pass (exam)

durchkreuzen, doohrk-kroyts-en, *v* to traverse

durchlassen, doohrk-lahss-en, *v* to let through

durchlaufen, doohrk-lowf-en, *v* to run through

durchlesen, doohrk-lai-zen, *v* to read through

durchmachen, doohrk-mahk-en, *v* to experience (hardship etc.)

Durchmesser, doohrk-mess-er, *m* diameter

durchnässen, doohrk-ness-en, *v* to seep through; to make wet; to soak

durchnehmen, doohrk-naym-en, *v* to go through

Durchreise, doohrk-ry-ze, *f* journey through

durchreisen, doohrk-ry-zen, *v* to travel through

Durchsage, doohrk-sag-e, *f* announcement

durchschauen, doohrk-show-en, *v* to see through

Durchschlag, doohrk-shlahk, *m* carbon copy

durchschlagen, doohrk-shlahg-en, *v* to break through; to knock through; **sich–,** to rough it

durchschneiden, doohrk-shny-den, *v* to cut through

Durchschnitt, doohrk-shnit, *m* average

durchschnittlich, doohrk-shnit-lik, *adj* average

durchsehen, doohrk-zay-en, *v* to look through

durchsetzen, doohrk-sets-en, *v* to enforce; **sich –,** to get one's way; to succeed

durchsichtig, doohrk-zik-tik, *adj* transparent

durchstellen, doohrk-shtel-en, *v* (telephone) to put through

durchstöbern, doohrk-shterb-ern, *v* to ransack

durchstreichen, doohrk-shtryk-en, *v* to cross out

durchsuchen, doohrk-sook-en, *v* to search

Durchsuchung, doohrk-sook-oong, *f* search

durchtrieben, doohrk-treeb-en, *adj* cunning

durchweg, doohrk-vek, *adv* through out

durchziehen, doohrk-tsee-en, *v* to pull through

Durchzug, doohrk-tsoog, *m* passage; draught

dürfen, dEErf-en, *v* to be allowed; may

dürftig, dEErft-*ik, adj* needy;
inadequate

dürr, dEErr, *adj* dry; barren;
arid; scrawny

Dürre, dEErr-*e, f* aridity;
drought

Durst, doohrst, *m* thirst; –
haben, *v* to be thirsty

durstig, doorst-*ik, adj* thirsty

Dusche, doosh-*e, f* shower

duschen, doosh-*en, v* to
(have a) shower

düster, dEEst-*er, adj* dark;
gloomy; dim

Düsenflugzeug, dEE-zen-
floog-tsoyg, *nt* jet (plane)

Düsternis, dEEst-er-niss, *f*
darkness, gloom

Dutzend, doot-sent, *nt*
dozen

duzen, doot-sen, *v* to address
a person as **du**

D-Zug, day-tsook, *m* fast
train

Ebbe, eb-e, f ebb-tide

eben, ay-ben, adj & adv even, level, flat; exact; just so

Ebene, ay-ben-e, f plain, level ground

ebenfalls, ay-ben-fahls, adv likewise; also

Ebenholz, ay-ben-holts, nt ebony

ebenso, ay-ben-zo, adv just so, just as

ebnen, ayb-nen, v to level, to flatten

echt, ekt, adj genuine; true; real

Echtheit, ekt-hite, f genuineness

Ecke, eck-e, f corner, angle, nook, edge

eckig, eck-ik, adj cornered; angular

edel, ay-del, adj noble; high-born; precious

Edelmetall, ayd-el-mett-ahll, nt rare metal

Edelstein, ay-el-shtine, m precious stone; jewel

Efeu, ay-foy, m ivy

Effekten, ef-fek-ten, pl effects; stock(s), securities

egal, ay-gahl, adj all the same; indifferent

ehe, ay-e, adv before; formerly

Ehe, ay-e, f matrimony; marriage; –beratung, f marriage counselling; –bruch, m adultery; –frau, f wife

ehelich, ay-e-lik, adj conjugal, matrimonial

ehemalig, ay-e-mahl-ik, adj former, previous

ehemals, ay-e-mahls, adv formerly

Ehemann, ay-e-mahnn, m husband

Ehepaar, ay-e-par, nt married couple

eher, ay-er, adv earlier; sooner

ehrbar, air-bar, adj honourable, respectable, decent

Ehre, air-e, f honour; repute, credit

ehren, air-en, v to honour

Ehrenamt, air-en-ahmt, nt honorary post

ehrenamtlich, air-en-ahmt-lik, adj honorary

Ehrengast, air-en-gahst, m guest of honour

ehrenhaft, air-en-hahft, adj honourable

Ehrenwort, air-en-vort, nt word of honour

Ehrfurcht, air-foorkt, f veneration; awe

Ehrgeiz, air-gites, m ambition

ehrgeizig, air-gite-sik, adj ambitious

ehrlich, air-lik, adj honest, fair; true

Ehrlichkeit, air-lik-kite, f honesty; reliability

ehrwürdig, air-vEErd-ik, adj venerable, reverend

Ei, i, nt egg

Eiche, i-ke, f oak(-tree)

Eichel, i-kel, f acorn

Eichhörnchen, i'k-hern-ken, nt squirrel

Eid, ite, m oath

Eidechse, i-deck-se, f lizard

Eierbecher, i-er-bek-er, m egg cup

Eierkuchen, i-er-kook-en, *m* omelet

Eierlikör, i-er-leek-er, *m* advocaat

Eierstock, i-er-shtock, *m med* ovary

Eierschale, i-er-shahl-e, *f* egg-shell

Eifer, i-fer, *m* zeal, eagerness; ardour

Eifersucht, i-fer-sookt, *f* jealousy

eifersüchtig, i-fer-sEEkt-ik, *adj* jealous

eifrig, i-frik, *adj* zealous, eager, keen

Eigelb, i-gelp, *nt* egg yolk

eigen, i-gen, *adj* own; particular; singular

Eigenart, i-gen-ahrt, *f* peculiarity; singularity

Eigenheim, i-gen-hym, *nt* owner-occupied house

eigenmächtig, i-gen-mekt-ik, *adj* arbitrary

Eigenname, i-gen-nahm-e, *m* proper name

eigennützig, i-gen-nEEtt-sik, *adj* selfish, self-seeking

eigens, i-gens, *adv* purposely; expressly

Eigenschaft, i-gen-shahft, *f* attribute; property

Eigensinn, i-gen-zinn, *m* obstinacy, caprice

eigensinnig, i-gen-zinn-ik, *adj* wilful; capricious; obstinate

eigentlich, i-gent-lik, *adj* real, true; essential; *adv* actually

Eigentum, i-gen-toom, *nt* property, estate

Eigentümer, i-gen-tEEm-er, *m* proprietor, owner

eigentümlich, i-gen-tEEm-lik, *adj* odd; peculiar; typical

Eigentumswohnung, i-gen-tooms-vohn-oong, *f* owner-occupied flat

eigenwillig, i-gen-vil-ik, *adj* wilful, self-willed

eignen (sich), i-gnen (zik), *v* to be suitable

Eilbote, ile-boht-e, *m* courier

Eilbrief, ile-breef, *m* express letter

Eile, i-le, *f* hurry, haste; promptness, speed

eilen, i-len, *v* to hurry

Eilgut, ile-goot, *nt* express freight

eilig, i-lik, *adj* pressing, urgent; speedy, quick

Eilzug, ile-tsoog, *m* semi-fast train

Eimer, i-mer, *m* bucket

ein(e/s), ine(-e/s), *indefinite art* a, an; one

einander, ine-**ahnn**-der, *adv* one another; each other

einatmen, ine-aht-men, *v* to inhale

Einbahnstraße, ine-bahn-shtrahss-e, *f* one-way street

Einband, ine-bahnt, *m* binding, cover (of book)

einbilden (sich), ine-bil-den (zik), *v* to imagine

Einbildung, ine-bil-doong, *f* imagination, fancy

Einbildungskraft, ine-bil-doongs-krahft, *f* (power of) imagination

Einblick, ine-blik, *m* insight

einbrechen, ine-brek-en, *v* to break in/through

Einbrecher, ine-brek-er, *m* burglar

einbringen, ine-bring-en, *v* to bring in

Einbruch, ine-brook, *m* burglary

einchecken, ine-tsheck-en, *v* to check in

eincremen, ine-kraim-en, *v* to put cream on

eindämmen, ine-dem-en, *v* to dam

eindeutig, ine-doyt-ik, *adj* unequivocal

eindringen, ine-dring-en, *v* to penetrate

eindringlich, ine-dring-lik, *adj* intrusive; forcible

Eindruck, ine-droock, *m* impression; imprint

einerlei, ine-er-ly, *adj* of the same kind, all the same

einerseits, ine-er-zites, *adv* on the one hand

einfach, ine-fahk, *adj* simple, single, plain

Einfahrt, ine-fahrt, *f* gateway, doorway, drive

Einfall, ine-fahll, *m* idea

einfallen, ine-fahll-en, *v* to fall in; to occur

einfältig, ine-felt-ik, *adj* simple-minded, foolish

einfangen, ine-fahng-en, *v* to capture; to arrest

einfarbig, ine-fahrb-ik, *adj* one colour

Einfassung, ine-fahss-oong, *f* border, edge

Einfluß, ine-flooss, *m* influence; influx

einflußreich, ine-flooss-ry'k, *adj* influential

einförmig, ine-ferm-ik, *adj* uniform; monotonous

einfrieren, ine-freer-en, *v* to freeze

Einfuhr, ine-foor, *f* import(ation)

einführen, ine-fEEr-en, *v* to import; to introduce

Einführung, ine-fEEr-oong, *f* introduction; import

Eingabe, ine-gahb-e, *f* petition; address

Eingang, ine-gahng, *m* entry; arrival; opening

eingeben, ine-gay-ben, *v* to give; *comp* to enter

eingebildet, ine-ge-bil-det, *adj* conceited

Eingeborene(r), ine-ge-bohr-e-ne(r), *m & f* native

Eingebung, ine-gay-boong, *f* inspiration

eingehen, ine-gay-en, *v* to arrive; to shrink; to perish; **auf etwas –,** to go into sth

eingehend, ine-gay-ent, *adj* in detail; thorough

Eingemachte(s), ine-ge-mahk-te(s), *nt* bottled fruit/vegetables

eingenommen, ine-ge-nom-en, *adj* prejudiced

eingeschlossen, ine-ge-shlos-en, *adj* enclosed; locked up

eingeschrieben, ine-ge-shreeb-en, *adj* registered (letter)

Eingeständnis, ine-ge-shtent-niss, *nt* confession

eingestehen, ine-ge-shtay-en, *v* to confess

Eingeweide, ine-ge-vy-de, *nt* intestines, bowels

eingießen, ine-gees-en, *v* to pour into

eingreifen, ine-gry-fen, *v* to intervene; to meddle

Eingriff, ine-griff, *m* intervention

einhalten, ine-hahlt-en, *v* to stop; to fulfil

einhängen, ine-henng-en; to hang; to hang up (telephone)

einheimisch, ine-hy-mish, *adj* native, indigenous

Einheimische(r), ine-hy-mish-e(r), *m & f* local (person)

Einheit, ine-hite, *f* unit(y); union; uniformity

einheitlich, ine-hite-lik, *adj* uniform; homogeneous

einher, ine-her, *adv* along

einholen, ine-hohl-en, *v* to overtake; to bring in

einhüllen, ine-hEEll-en, *v* to envelop, to wrap

einig, ine-ik, *adj* in agreement, unanimous

einige, ine-ig-e, *pron* a few, several

einigen, ine-ig-en, *v* to unite; **sich auf etw –,** to agree on sth

einigermaßen, ine-ig-er-mahss-en, *adv* somewhat

Einigkeit, ine-ig-kite, *f* unity, agreement

Einigung, ine-ig-oong, *f* agreement; unification

einimpfen, ine-im-fen, *v* to inoculate; to vaccinate

Einkauf, ine-kowf, *m* purchase, buying

einkaufen, ine-kowf-en, *v* to purchase, to buy; **– gehen,** to go shopping

Einkäufer, ine-koyf-er, *m* buyer

Einkaufswagen, ine-kowfs-vah-gen, *m* shopping trolley

einkehren, ine-kayr-en, *v* to stop off

Einklang, ine-klahng, *m* unison, accord, harmony

Einkommen, ine-kom-en, *nt* income; revenue

Einkünfte, ine-kEEnnft-e, *pl* revenue

einladen, ine-lahd-en, *v* to invite; to load into

Einladung, ine-lahd-oong, *f* invitation

Einlage, ine-lahg-e, *f* enclosure; investment

Einlaß, ine-lahss, *m* admission; letting-in

einlassen, ine-lahss-en, *v* to admit; to enter

einlaufen, ine-lowf-en, v to shrink

einleben (sich), ine-lay-ben (zik), v to settle down

einleiten, ine-ly-ten, v to introduce; to initiate

Einleitung, ine-ly-toong, f introduction, preface

einlösen, ine-lerz-en, v to redeem, to honour (bills)

einmachen, ine-mahk-en, v to preserve; to bottle

einmal, ine-mahl, adv once, once upon a time; just; noch –, once more

Einmaleins, ine-mahl-ines, nt multiplication-table

einmalig, ine-mahl-ik, adj unique, single

Einmarsch, ine-marsh, m marching-in, entry

einmischen(sich), ine-mish-en (zik), v to interfere; to meddle

Einnahme, ine-nahm-e, f occupation; takings

einnehmen, ine-naym-en, v to take medicine; to take in; to collect (taxes); to conquer

Einöde, ine-erd-e, f wilderness, desert

einpacken, ine-pahck-en, v to pack (up)

einpflanzen, ine-flahnt-sen, v to plant; med to implant

einprägen, ine-prayg-en, v to impress; to imprint; sich etw –, to memorize sth

einquartieren, ine-kvahrt-eer-en, v to quarter, to billet

einrahmen, ine-rahm-en, v to frame

einräumen, ine-roym-en, v to put in order; to accord, to grant (credit etc.)

einreden, ine-rayd-en, v to talk (sb) into

einreichen, ine-ry-ken, v to hand over; to deliver

Einreise, ine-ry-ze, f entry; –bestimmungen, fpl entry regulations

einrichten, ine-rik-ten, v to arrange; to put in order; to furnish

Einrichtung, ine-rik-toong, f arrangement; furniture, furnishing

einrücken, ine-rEEck-en, v to insert (advertisement); to indent

eins, ines, num one

einsam, ine-zahm, adj solitary, lonely, secluded

Einsamkeit, ine-zahm-kite, f solitude, isolation

einsammeln, ine-zahmm-eln, v to gather

Einsatz, ine-zahts, m insertion; stake (at games)

einschalten, ine-shahlt-en, v to put in; to interpolate; to switch on

einschätzen, ine-shett-sen, v to assess, to value

einschenken, ine-shenk-en, v to pour in/out

einschiffen (sich), ine-shif-en (zik), v to embark

einschl. abbr **einschließlich**

einschlafen, ine-shlahf-en, v to go to sleep

einschlagen, ine-shlahg-en, v to knock in; to wrap up; to smash; to strike (lightning)

einschließen, ine-shlees-en, v to lock (up); to enclose; to include

einschließlich, ine-shlees-lik, adj inclusive of

Einschnitt, ine-shnit, m incision, cut, slit

einschränken, ine-shrenk-en, v to restrict; sich –, to cut down

Einschränkung, ine-shrenk-oong, f restriction

Einschreiben, ine-shry-ben, nt registered letter

einschreiben, ine-shry-ben, v to write in (a book); sich –, to register; to enrol

einschreiten, ine-shry-ten, v to interpose

einschüchtern, ine-shEEk-tern, v to intimidate

einsehen, ine-zay-en, v to look into; to understand

einseitig, ine-zy-tik, adj one-sided

einsenden, ine-zen-den, v to send in; to forward

einsetzen, ine-zet-sen, v to insert; to stake; sich für etw –, to support sth

Einsicht, ine-zikt, f insight; inspection

einsichtsvoll, ine-zikts-fol, adj intelligent; judicious

Einsiedler, ine-zeed-ler, *m* hermit, recluse

einsilbig, ine-zil-bik, *adj* of one syllable

einspannen, ine-shpahnn-en, *v* to put (in); to harness; to stretch over a frame

einsperren, ine-shpair-en, *v* to lock up

Einspruch, ine-shprook, *m* objection, protest

einspurig, ine-shpoor-ik, *adj* single-lane

einst, ine'st, *adv* once upon a time

einstecken, ine-shteck-en, *v* to pocket

einstehen (für), ine-shtay-en, *v* to stand up (for)

einsteigen, ine-shty-gen, *v* to get into

einstellen, ine-shtel-en, *v* to stop; to adjust; to focus; to employ

einstig, ine'st-ik, *adj* former

einstimmig, ine-shtim-ik, *adj* unanimous

einstmals, ine'st-mahls, *adv* at one time

einstöckig, ine-shterck-ik, *adj* two-storeyed

einstudieren, ine-shtood-eer-en, *v* to rehearse

Einsturz, ine-shtoorts, *m* collapse, downfall, crash

einstürzen, ine-shtEErt-sen, *v* to collapse

einstweile, ine'st-vile-en, *adv* meanwhile, for the present

einstweilig, ine'st-vile-ik, *adj* temporary

eintauchen, ine-towk-en, *v* to immerse; to dip in

einteilen, ine-ty-len, *v* to divide; to classify

einteilig, ine-ty-lik, *adj* one-piece

eintönig, ine-tern-ik, *adj* monotonous; tedious

Eintopf, ine-topf, *m* stew

Eintracht, ine-trahkt, *f* harmony; union

eintragen, ine-trahg-en, *v* to enter; **sich –**, to put one's name down

einträglich, ine-traik-lik, *adj* profitable, productive

Eintragung, ine-trahg-oong, *f* entry (in books)

eintreffen, ine-tref-en, *v* to arrive; to come

eintreiben, ine-try-ben, *v* to drive in; to collect

eintreten, ine-tray-ten, *v* to step in; to occur

Eintritt, ine-tritt, *m* entry, entrance, admission

Eintrittskarte, ine-trits-kart-e, *f* admission ticket

Einvernehmen, ine-fair-naym-en, *nt* agreement

einverstanden, ine-fair-shtann-den, *adj* agreed

Einwand, ine-vahnt, *m* objection

Einwanderer, ine-vahnn-der-er, *m* immigrant

einwandern, ine-vahnn-dern, *v* to immigrate

Einwanderung, ine-vahn-

der-oong, *f* immigration

einwandfrei, ine-vahnt-fry, *adj* perfect, faultless

einweihen, ine-vy-en, *v* to dedicate; to consecrate; to inaugurate

Einweihung, ine-vy-oong, *f* inauguration

einwenden, ine-ven-den, *v* to object, to protest

Einwendung, ine-ven-doong, *f* objection, protest

einwerfen, ine-verf-en, *v* to post; to smash; to throw in

einwickeln, ine-vik-eln, *v* to wrap; to envelop

einwilligen, ine-vil-ig-en, *v* to consent, to agree

Einwilligung, ine-vil-ig-oong, *f* consent, assent

einwirken, ine-veerk-en, *v* to have an effect; to influence

Einwohner, ine-vohn-er, *m* inhabitant, resident

Einwurf, ine-voorf, *m* objection, rejoinder; slot

Einzahl, ine-tsahl, *f* singular

einzahlen, ine-tsahl-en, *v* to pay in

Einzel-, ine-tsel, *pref* single; **–fahrschein**, *m* one-way ticket; **–fall**, *m* individual case; **–handel**, *m* retail trade; **–heit**, *f* detail; **–kind**, *nt* single child

einzeln, ine-tseln, *adj* single, individual, particular

Einzelzimmer, ine-tsel-tsim-er, *nt* single room

einziehen, ine-tsee-en, v to draw/pull in(to); to collect (money); to withdraw from circulation; to move in

einzig, ine-tsik, adj only, sole, single, unique

Einzug, ine-tsook, m entry, entrance; moving in

Eis, ice, nt ice

Eisbahn, ice-bahn, f ice-rink

Eisbär, ice-bear, m polar bear

Eisbein, ice-bine, nt boiled knuckle of pork

Eisberg, ice-bairk, m iceberg

Eisen, ize-en, nt iron

Eisenbahn, ize-en-bahn, f railway

eisern, ize-ern, adj made of iron

eisig, ize-ik, adj icy, chilly

Eisschrank, ice-shrahngk, m refrigerator

Eiszapfen, ice-tsahpp-fen, m icicle

eitel, ite-el, adj vain; futile; coquetish

Eitelkeit, ite-el-kite, f vanity; futility

Eiter, ite-er, m pus

eitern, ite-ern, v to fester, to ulcerate; to suppurate

Eiweiß, i-vice, nt white of egg; protein

Ekel, ayk-el, m disgust; loathsome person

ekelhaft, ayk-el-hahfft, adj disgusting, loathsome

ekeln, ayk-eln, v to feel

disgust; **sich vor etw –,** to be disgusted at sth

elektrisch, ay-leck-trish, adj electric, electrical

Elektrizität, ay-leck-tree-tsee-**teht,** f electricity

Elend, ayl-ent, nt misery, wretchedness; calamity

elend, ayl-ent, adj miserable, wretched; needy

elf, elf, num eleven

Elfe, el-fe, f elf, fairy

Elfenbein, elf-en-bine, nt ivory

Elftel, elf-tel, nt eleventh (part)

Ellbogen, el-bohg-en, m elbow

Elster, el-ster, f magpie

Eltern, el-tern, pl parents

Emaille, ay-mahll-ye, nt enamel

Empfang, emp-fahng, m receipt, reception

empfangen, emp-fahng-en, v to receive

Empfänger, emp-feng-er, m recipient; addressee

Empfängnis, emp-feng-niss, f conception; **–verhütung,** f contraception

Empfangsschein, emp-fahngs-shine, m receipt

empfehlen, emp-fayl-en, v to recommend

empfinden, emp-fin-den, v to feel; to perceive

empfindlich, emp-fint-lik, adj sensitive; delicate

Empfindlichkeit, emp-fint-lik-kite, f sensitivity

Empfindung, emp-fin-doong, f perception, sensation, feeling

empor, em-pohr, adv up(wards)

empören, em-per-en, v to (drive to) revolt

Empörung, em-per-oong, f rising, revolt, rebellion

emsig, em-zik, adj industrious; busy; assiduous

Ende, en-de, nt end; result; conclusion; **zu – sein,** to be finished

enden, en-den, v to end, to finish

endgültig, ent-gEEl-tik, adj final; conclusive

endlich, ent-lik, adj final; finite; adv at last

endlos, ent-lohs, adj endless

Endstation, ent-shtats-yohn, f terminus

Endung, end-oong, f ending; termination

Energie, en-er-gee, f energy; **–verbrauch,** m energy consumption

energisch, en-ehrg-ish, adj energetic

eng, eng, adj narrow; tight; cramped

Enge, eng-e, f narrowness; tightness; geog straits

Engel, eng-el, m angel

engherzig, eng-hairt-sik, adj narrow-minded

England, eng-lahnt, nt England

Engländer, eng-len-der, m

Englishman; **–in,** f
Englishwoman

englisch, eng-lish, *adj*
English

en gros, ahng groh, *adv*
wholesale

Enkel, eng-kel, *m*
grandchild; grandson

Enkelin, eng-kel-in, f
granddaughter

entarten, ent-**art**-en, *v* to
degenerate

entbehren, ent-**bair**-en, *v* to
spare; to miss

Entbehrung, ent-**bair**-oong,
f privation, want

entbinden, ent-**bin**-den, *v* to
release; to absolve; to
deliver of a child

Entbindung, ent-**bin**-doong,
f delivery; release

entblößen, ent-**blers**-en, *v*
to bare; to deprive of

entdecken, ent-**deck**-en, *v*
to discover

Entdecker, ent-**deck**-er, *m*
discoverer

Entdeckung, ent-**deck**-
oong, f discovery

Ente, ent-e, f duck

entehren, ent-**air**-en, *v* to
dishonour; to disgrace

Entenbraten, ent-en-braht-
en, *m* roast duck

entfallen, ent-**fahll**-en, *v* to
fall from a person's hands

entfalten, ent-**fahllt**-en, *v* to
unfold; to develop

entfernen, ent-**fairn**-en, *v* to
remove; to retire

entfernt, ent-**fairnt**, *adj*

distant, remote, far

Entfernung, ent-**fairn**-oong,
f distance; removal;
withdrawal

entflammen, ent-**flahmm**-
en, *v* to inflame; to set
ablaze

entfliehen, ent-**flee**-en, *v* to
flee from, to escape

entführen, ent-**fEEr**-en, *v* to
carry off; to abduct; to
kidnap

Entführer, ent-**fEEr**-er, *m*
kidnapper

Entführung, ent-**fEEr**-oong,
f kidnapping; abduction

entgegen, ent-**gayg**-en, *adv*
against; towards

entgegensehen, ent-**gayg**-
en-zay-en, *v* to look
forward to

entgegnen, ent-**gayg**-nen, *v*
to retort; to reply

Entgegnung, ent-**gayg**-
noong, f reply; retort

entgehen, ent-**gay**-en, *v* to
escape; to elude

Entgelt, ent-gelt, *nt*
remuneration;
recompense

entgleisen, ent-**gly**-zen, *v* to
derail

enthalten, ent-**hahlt**-en, *v* to
contain; **sich –,** to refrain

enthaltsam, ent-**hahlt**-
sahm, *adj* abstinent

enthüllen, ent-**hEEll**-en, *v* to
unveil; to uncover

entkommen (aus), ent-
kom-en, *v* to escape
(from)

entladen, ent-**lahd**-en, *v* to
unload; to discharge; **sich
–,** to discharge

Entladung, ent-**lahd**-oong, f
discharge; explosion

entlang, ent-**lahng,** *adv &*
prep along, by the side of

entlassen, ent-**lahss**-en, *v* to
dismiss; to discharge

Entlassung, ent-**lahss**-oong,
f dismissal

entlaufen, ent-**lowf**-en, *v* to
run away

entmutigen, ent-**moot**-ig-en,
v to discourage

entnehmen, ent-**naym**-en, *v*
to take from

enträtseln, ent-**rayt**-seln, *v*
to decipher

entreißen, ent-**rice**-en, *v* to
snatch from

entrinnen, ent-**rin**-en, *v* to
run from

entrüsten, ent-**rEEst**-en, *v* to
incense, outrage; **sich –,**
to become indignant

Entrüstung, ent-**rEEst**-oong,
f indignation

entsagen, ent-**zahg**-en, *v* to
renounce, to resign

entschädigen, ent-**shayd**-ig-
en, *v* to indemnify

Entschädigung, ent-**shayd**-
ig-oong, f
indemnification;
compensation

entscheiden, ent-**shy**-den, *v*
to decide

Entscheidung, ent-**shy**-
doong, f decision

entschieden, ent-**sheed**-en,

adj decided

Entschiedenheit, ent-sheed-en-hite, *f* determination; firmness

entschließen (sich), ent-shlees-en (*zik*), *v* to decide, to determine

entschlossen, ent-shloss-en, *adj* determined

Entschluß, ent-shlooss, *m* decision; resolve

entschuldigen, ent-shoold-ig-en, *v* to excuse; **sich –,** to apologize

Entschuldigung, ent-shoolld-ig-oong, *f* excuse; apology

entschwinden, ent-shvind-en, *v* to vanish; to die away

entsetzen, ent-zet-sen, *v* to horrify

Entsetzen, ent-set-sen, *nt* horror; dismissal

entsetzlich, ent-zets-lik, *adj* awful, horrible

entsinnen (sich), ent-zin-en (*zik*), *v* to remember

Entsorgung, ent-sorg-oong, *f* waste disposal

entsprechen, ent-shprek-en, *v* to correspond to

entspannen (sich), ent-shpahnn-en (*zik*), *v* to relax

Entspannung, ent-spahnn-oong, *f* relaxation

entspringen, ent-shpring-en, *v* to escape; to originate, to spring from

entstehen, ent-shtay-en, *v*

to arise; to come into existence

Entstehung, ent-shtay-oong, *f* origin, formation

entstellen, ent-shtel-en, *v* to disfigure, to deface

enttäuschen, ent-toysh-en, *v* to disappoint

Enttäuschung, ent-toysh-oong, *f* disappointment

entwaffnen, ent-vahff-nen, *v* to disarm

entwässern, ent-vess-ern, *v* to drain (land)

entweder, ent-vaid-er, *conj* either

entweichen, ent-vy-ken, *v* to escape; to disappear

entwenden, ent-vend-en, *v* to misappropriate

entwerfen, ent-vairf-en, *v* to design, to draft

entwerten, ent-vairt-en, *v* to devalue

Entwerter, ent-vairt-er, *m* ticket validating machine

entwickeln, ent-vik-eln, *v* to develop; to unroll

Entwicklung, ent-vik-loong, *f* development; **–sland,** *nt* developing country

Entwurf, ent-voorf, *m* design, sketch, outline

entziehen, ent-tsee-en, *v* to withdraw from

Entziehung, ent-tseeh-oong, *f* withdrawal; **–skur,** *f* treatment for addiction

entziffern, ent-tsiff-ern, *v* to decipher; to solve

entzücken, ent-tsEEck-en, *v* to charm, to enchant

Entzücken, ent-tsEEck-en, *nt* delight, rapture

Entzug, ent-tsoog, *m* withdrawal; **–serscheinungen,** *pl* withdrawal symptoms

entzünden, ent-tsEEnd-en, *v* to inflame

Entzündung, ent-tsEEnd-oong, *f* inflammation

entzwei, ent-tsvy, *adv* in two; asunder

Epidemie, epee-de-mee, *f* epidemic

Epoche, e-pok-e, *f* epoch

er, air, *pron* he; it

erbarmen (sich), air-barm-en (*zik*), *v* to have mercy on

erbärmlich, air-bairm-lik, *adj* pitiable, miserable, wretched

Erbe, airb-e, *m* heir, successor

Erbe, airb-e, *nt* inheritance, bequest

erben, air-ben, *v* to inherit

erbeuten, air-boyt-en, *v* to capture; to take as booty

erbieten (sich), air-beet-en (*zik*), *v* to volunteer

erbitten, air-bit-en, *v* to ask; to petition for

erblassen, air-blahss-en, *v* to turn pale

erblich, airp-lik, *adj* hereditary

erblicken, air-blik-en, *v* to behold, to view

erblinden, air-**blin**-den, *v* to go blind

erbrechen, air-**brek**-en, *v* to vomit

Erbschaft, airp-shahft, *f* inheritance; legacy

Erbse, airp-se, *f* pea

Erbsensuppe, airp-sen-zoop-e, *f* pea-soup

Erdbeben, airt-bayb-en, *nt* earthquake

Erdbeere, airt-bair-e, *f* strawberry

Erdboden, airt-bohd-en, *m* soil; surface of the earth

Erde, aird-e, *f* earth; world, globe

erdenklich, air-denk-lik, *adj* imaginable

Erdgas, airt-gahs, *nt* natural gas

Erdgeschoß, airt-ge-shohss, *nt* ground floor

erdichten, air-dik-ten, *v* to invent; to feign

Erdnuß, airt-nooss, *f* peanut

erdrosseln, air-dross-eln, *v* to throttle, to strangle

erdrücken, air-**drEEck**-en, *v* to smother

Erdteil, airt-tyl, *m* continent

ereignen (sich), air-i-gnen (zik), *v* to happen

Ereignis, air-i-gniss, *nt* occurrence; event; accident

erfahren, air-**fahr**-en, *v* to hear, to learn

Erfahrung, air-**fahr**-oong, *f* experience

erfassen, air-fahss-en, *v* to seize, to grasp

erfinden, air-fin-den, *v* to invent, to devise

Erfinder, air-fin-der, *m* inventor

Erfindung, air-fin-doong, *f* invention; contrivance, device

Erfolg, air-folk, *m* success; result, issue; outcome

erfolgen, air-folg-en, *v* to result; to take place

erfolglos, air-folg-lohs, *adj* unsuccessful

erfolgreich, air-folg-ryk, *adj* successful

erforderlich, air-ford-er-lik, *adj* necessary

erfordern, air-ford-ern, *v* to require, to necessitate

erforschen, air-forsh-en, *v* to explore

erfreuen, air-froy-en, *v* to gladden, to delight

erfreulich, air-froy-lik, *adj* pleasing; gratifying

erfrieren, air-free-ren, *v* to die of cold

erfrischen, air-frish-en, *v* to refresh

Erfrischung, air-frish-oong, *f* refreshment

erfüllen, air-f**EEll**-en, *v* to fulfil; to fill with

Erfüllung, air-f**EEll**-oong, *f* fulfilment; compliance

ergänzen, air-gent-sen, *v* to complete

ergeben (sich), air-gayb-en (zik), *v* to surrender; to result

Ergebenheit, air-gayb-en-hite, *f* devotion; attachment

Ergebnis, air-gayp-niss, *nt* result; issue, conclusion

ergiebig, air-geeb-ik, *adj* productive; prolific

ergießen, air-gees-en, *v* to pour/flow from

ergreifen, air-gry-fen, *v* to seize, to catch hold of; to move

ergreifend, air-gryf-ent, *adj* moving

erhaben, air-hahb-en, *adj* sublime; illustrious

erhalten, air-hahlt-en, *v* to receive; to preserve

Erhaltung, air-hahlt-oong, *f* preservation

erheben, air-hayb-en, *v* to raise, to lift

erheblich, air-hayp-lik, *adj* considerable

erhellen, air-hell-en, *v* to light up; to clear up

erhöhen, air-her-en, *v* to raise; to enhance; to increase

Erhöhung, air-her-oong, *f* elevation; increase

erholen (sich), air-hohl-en (zik), *v* to recover

Erholung, air-hohl-oong, *f* rest; recovery

erinnern (an), air-in-ern (ahnn), *v* to remind; **sich–,** to remember

Erinnerung, air-in-er-oong, *f* remembrance

erkälten (sich), air-kelt-en (zik), v to catch cold

erkältet sein, air-kelt-et sine, v to have a cold

Erkältung, air-kelt-oong, f cold, chill, catarrh

erkennen, air-ken-en, v to recognize

erkenntlich, air-kent-lik, adj cognizant; grateful

Erkenntnis, air-kent-niss, f perception; knowledge; understanding

Erkennung, air-ken-oong, f recognition

Erker, airk-er, m alcove, balcony

erklären, air-klair-en, v to explain; to elucidate; to declare

erklärlich, air-klair-lik, adj comprehensible

Erklärung, air-klair-oong, f explanation; declaration

erkranken, air-krank-en, v to fall ill

erkundigen (sich), air-koond-ig-en (zik), v to inquire; to make inquiries

Erkundigung, air-koond-ig-oong, f inquiry

erlangen, air-lahng-en, v to reach, to attain

Erlaß, air-lahss, m remission; relief; enactment

erlassen, air-lahss-en, v to publish (laws); to waive (debts etc.)

erlauben, air-lowb-en, v to permit, to allow

Erlaubnis, air-lowp-niss, f permission

erläutern, air-loyt-ern, v to make clear; to elucidate

Erle, airl-e, f alder(-tree)

erleben, air-layb-en, v to experience

Erlebnis, air-layp-niss, nt experience

erledigen, air-layd-ig-en, v to settle; to adjust

Erledigung, air-layd-ig-oong, f settlement

erleichtern, air-ly'k-tern, v to make easy

Erleichterung, air-ly'k-ter-oong, f relief; facility

erleiden, air-ly-den, v to suffer, to sustain; to bear

erlernen, air-lairn-en, v to learn, to acquire

erliegen, air-leeg-en, v to succumb

Erlös, air-lers, m proceeds

erlöschen, air-lersh-en, v to be extinguished

erlösen, air-lerz-en, v to save, to redeem

Erlösung, air-lerz-oong, f release; salvation

ermächtigen, air-mek-tig-en, v to empower

Ermächtigung, air-mek-tig-oong, f authority

ermahnen, air-mahn-en, v to admonish, to warn

ermäßigen, air-maiss-ig-en, v to moderate; to reduce

Ermäßigung, air-maiss-ig-oong, f reduction

ermitteln, air-mit-eln, v to

ascertain, to find out; **gegen jdn –**, to investigate sb

Ermittlung, air-mit-loong, f ascertainment; investigation

ermöglichen, air-merg-lik-en, v to make possible

ermorden, air-mord-en, v to murder; to assassinate

Ermordung, air-mord-oong, f murder

ermüden, air-mEEd-en, v to tire

ermuntern, air-moont-ern, v to rouse; to liven up

ermutigen, air-moot-ig-en, v to encourage

ernähren, air-nair-en, v to nourish; **sich – von**, to live on

Ernährung, air-nair-oong, f nourishment

ernennen, air-nen-en, v to appoint; to nominate

erneuern, air-noy-ern, v to renew; to renovate

erniedrigen, air-need-rig-en, v to lower

Ernst, airnst, m seriousness; severity

ernst, airnst, adj serious, earnest; solemn, grave

ernsthaft, airnst-hahft, adj serious, earnest

ernstlich, airnst-lik, adj earnest, fervent

Ernte, airnt-e, f harvest (-time); crop

ernten, airnt-en, v to harvest, to reap

erobern, air-ohb-ern, *v* to conquer, to capture

Eroberung, air-ohb-er-oong, *f* capture, conquest

eröffnen, air-erff-nen, *v* to open; to inaugurate

Eröffnung, air-erff-noong, *f* opening; inauguration

erörtern, air-ert-ern, *v* to discuss, to argue

Erörterung, air-ert-er-oong, *f* discussion, debate

Erotik, air-oht-ik, *f* eroticism

erotisch, air-oht-ish, *adj* erotic

erpressen, air-press-en, *v* to extort; to blackmail

Erpresser, air-press-er, *m* blackmailer

Erpressung, air-press-oong, *f* extortion, blackmail

erproben, air-prohb-en, *v* to try; to experience

erraten, air-raht-en, *v* to guess

erregen, air-rayg-en, *v* to excite; to agitate

Erregung, air-rayg-oong, *f* irritation; agitation; excitement

erreichen, air-ry-ken, *v* to reach; to attain

errichten, air-rik-ten, *v* to erect; to set up

erröten, air-rert-en, *v* to blush, to redden

Errungenschaft, air-roong-en-shahft, *f* achievement

Ersatz, air-zahts, *m* substitute; compensation;

–dienst, *m* community service (as alternative to military service); **–reifen,** *m* spare tyre; **–teil,** spare part

erscheinen, air-shy-nen, *v* to appear

Erscheinung, air-shy-noong, *f* appearing; phenomenon

erschießen, air-sheess-en, *v* to shoot dead

erschlagen, air-shlahg-en, *v* to kill

erschöpfen, air-sherp-fen, *v* to exhaust

Erschöpfung, air-sherp-foong, *f* exhaustion

erschrecken, air-shreck-en, *v* to frighten

erschüttern, air-shEEtt-ern, *v* to shake up

ersetzen, air-zet-sen, *v* to replace; to substitute

ersichtlich, air-zikt-lik, *adj* visible, manifest

ersparen, air-shpahr-en, *v* to save, to economize

Ersparnis, air-shpahr-niss, *f* economy

erst, airst, *adv* at first; previously; only (just)

erstarren, air-shtahrr-en, *v* to stiffen; to grow numb/rigid

erstatten, air-shtahtt-en, *v* to restore; to render; to reimburse

Erstattung, air-shtatt-oong, *f* refund

erstaunen, air-shtown-en, *v*

to be astonished

erstaunlich, air-shtown-lik, *adj* astonishing, amazing

erste(r/s), airst-*e*(r/s) *adj* first

erstechen, air-shtek-en, *v* to stab to death

erstehen, air-shtay-en, *v* to buy, to purchase

ersteigen, air-shty-gen, *v* to mount, to climb

erstens, airst-ens, *adv* first; in the first place

ersticken, air-shtik-en, *v* to stifle; to suffocate

erstklassig, airst-klahss-ik, *adj* first class

erstmals, airst-mahls, *adv* for the first time

erstrecken, air-shtreck-en, *v* to reach up to

ersuchen, air-sook-en, *v* to request

ertappen, air-tahpp-en, *v* to catch (in the act)

erteilen, air-ty-len, *v* to bestow upon, to confer upon

ertönen, air-tern-en, *v* to sound

Ertrag, air-trahk, *m* yield, produce, return

ertragen, air-trahg-en, *v* to bear; to tolerate

erträglich, air-traik-lik, *adj* bearable, tolerable

ertrinken, air-trink-en, *v* to drown

erwachen, air-vahk-en, *v* to awake

erwachsen, air-vahck-sen,

adj grown-up, adult

Erwachsene(r), air-vahck-sen-*e*(r), *m & f* adult

erwähnen, air-**vain**-en, *v* to mention, to refer to

erwärmen, air-**vairm**-en, *v* to warm

erwarten, air-**vart**-en, *v* to expect, to await

Erwartung, air-**vart**-oong, *f* expectation

erwecken, air-**veck**-en, *v* to awake; to rouse

erweitern, air-**vy**-tern, *v* to enlarge, to widen

Erwerb air-**vairp**, *m* gain, profit; acquisition

erwerben, air-**vairb**-en, *v* to acquire; to earn

erwerbslos, air-**vairbs**-lohs, *adj* unemployed

erwidern, air-**veed**-ern, *v* to reply, to reciprocate

erwünscht, air-**vEEnsht**, *adj* desired, desirable

erwürgen, air-**vEErg**-en, *v* to strangle

Erz, airts, *nt* ore, metal

erzählen, air-**tsail**-en, *v* to relate, to narrate, to tell

Erzählung, air-**tsail**-oong, *f* tale, story, narrative

Erzbischof, airts-bish-ohf, *m* archbishop

erzeugen, air-**tsoyg**-en, *v* to produce; to engender

Erzeugnis, air-**tsoyk**-niss, *nt* product, produce

Erzeugung, air-**tsoyg**-oong, *f* production

erziehen, air-**tsee**-en, *v* to

rear; to educate

Erziehung, air-**tsee**-oong, *f* rearing; education

erzielen, air-**tseel**-en, *v* to achieve

erzwingen, air-**tsving**-en, *v* to enforce; to obtain by force

es, ess, *pron* it

Esche, esh-*e*, *f* ash (tree)

Esel, ay-zel, *m* donkey, ass

Espe, esp-*e*, *f* aspen

eßbar, ess-bar, *adj* eatable, edible

essen, ess-en, *v* to eat

Essig, ess-ik, *m* vinegar

Eßlöffel, ess-lerff-el, *m* tablespoon

Eßzimmer, ess-tsimm-er, *nt* dining room

etablieren, ay-tahb-leer-en, *v* to establish, to set up; **sich –**, to become established

Etage, ay-tah-zhe, *f* storey; floor (of building)

Etat, ay-tah, *m* balance-sheet; budget

Etikett, ay-tee-ket, *nt* label, ticket

etliche, et-lik-*e*, *pron* some; a few

Etui, ay-twee, *nt* case

etwa, et-vah, *adv* about, approximately; perhaps

etwaig, et-vah-ik, *adj* possible; incidental

etwas, et-vahss, *pron* something, some; somewhat

euch, oyk, *pron* (accusative

& dative) you, to you

euer, eure(r/s), oy-er, oyr-*e*(r/s), *adj* your; *pron* yours

Eule, oyl-*e*, *f* owl

Euro, oy-roh, *m* Euro

Europa, oy-roh-pah, *nt* Europe

Europäer, oy-roh-pay-er, *m* European (person)

europäisch, oy-roh-pay-ish, *adj* European; **E–e Union**, *f* European Union

evangelisch, ay-fahng-ayl-ish, *adj* evangelical; Protestant

Evangelium, ay-fahng-ayl-e-oomm, *nt* gospel

eventuell, ay-vent-oo-el, *adj & adv* possible; possibly

ewig, ayv-ik, *adj* eternal, everlasting, endless

Ewigkeit, ayv-ik-kite, *f* eternity

Examen, ecks-ahm-en, *nt* examination

Exemplar, ecks-emp-lahr, *nt* sample; copy

Exil, ecks-eel, *nt* exile

exotisch, ecks-oht-ish, *adj* exotic

Expedition, eck-pay-dits-yohn, *f* expedition

Experte, ecks-per-te, *m* expert

Export, ecks-port, *m* export

exportieren, ecks-port-eer-en, *v* to export

extra, eck-strah, *adj* separate; extra

Extrablatt, ecks-trah-blahtt, *nt* special edition

F

fabelhaft, fahb-el-hahft, adj fabulous; fam fantastic

Fabrik, fah-breeck, f factory, works

Fabrikant, fah-brik-ahnt, m manufacturer

Fabrikat, fah-brik-aht, nt manufactured article; make

Fach, fahk, nt division; branch, line of business; –arbeiter, m skilled worker; –arzt, m med specialist; –ausdruck, m technical term

Fächer, fek-er, m fan

Fachmann, fahk-mahnn, m expert, specialist

fachmännisch, fahk-men-ish, adj expert

Fackel, fahck-el, f (lighted) torch

fad, faht, adj tasteless, insipid, dull

Faden, fahd-en, m thread; fathom

fadenscheinig, fahd-en-shine-ik, adj threadbare; shabby

fähig, fay-ik, adj capable, able, competent

Fähigkeit, fay-ik-kite, f capability, fitness, aptitude

fahnden, fahn-den, v to search for (police)

Fahndung, fahnd-oong, f police search

Fahne, fahn-e, f flag, colours, banner

Fahrausweis, fahr-ows-vise, m ticket

Fahrbahn, fahr-bahn, f carriageway

Fähre, fay-re, f ferry

fahren, fahr-en, v to ride, to drive; to travel; to convey

Fahrer, fahr-er, m driver

Fahrgeld, fahr-gelt, nt fare

Fahrkarte, fahr-kart-e, f (travel) ticket; –nautomat, m ticket machine; –nschalter, m ticket-office

fahrlässig, fahr-less-ik, adj careless, negligent

Fahrplan, fahr-plahn, m timetable

Fahrprüfung, fahr-prEEf-oong, f driving test

Fahrrad, fahr-raht, nt cycle, bicycle; –weg, m cycle lane

Fahrschein, fahr-shine, m (bus/tram) ticket; –entwerter, m ticket machine

Fahrschule, fahr-shool-e, f driving school

Fahrstuhl, fahr-shtool, m lift

Fahrt, fahrt, f journey, drive, ride, voyage, trip; –kosten, pl travelling expenses; –richtung, f direction (of travel)

Fährte, fairt-e, f track, trail

Fahrzeit, fahr-tsite, f journey time

Fahrzeug, fahr-tsoyk, nt vessel, craft; vehicle, conveyance

Falke, fahlk-e, m falcon; hawk

Fall, fahll, m case; fall

Falle, fahll-e, f trap, snare

fallen, fahll-en, v to fall; to decrease

fällen, fel-en, v to fell, to

7 3

cut down (trees)

fällig, fel-ik, *adj* due, payable

falls, fahls, *conj* in case; provided that

Fallschirm, fahll-sheerm, *m* parachute

falsch, fahlsh, *adj* wrong, false, forged; mistaken

fälschen, fel-shen, *v* to forge, to adulterate

Fälschung, felsh-oong, *f* falsification; forgery

Falte, fahlt-*e*, *f* fold; wrinkle; pleat, crease

falten, fahlt-en, *v* to fold; to crease, to crumple

faltig, fahlt-ik, *adj* wrinkled, creased, crumpled

Familie, fahm-eel-ye, *f* family; tribe, stock; **–nname,** *m* surname; **–nstand,** *m* marital status

Fang, fahng, *m* catch, capture; prey, booty

fangen, fahng-en, *v* to catch, to capture, to trap

Farbe, fahrb-*e*, *f* colour, colouring, tint; paint

farbecht, fahrb-ekt, *adj* colour-fast

farbenblind, fahrb-en-blint, *adj* colour-blind

Farbfernsehen, fahrb-fairn-zay-en, *nt* colour television

Farbfilm, farb-film, *m* colour film

färben, fairb-en, *v* to dye; to colour; to tint

farbig, farb-ik, *adj* coloured

Farbige(r), farb-ig-*e*(r), *m*

& f coloured person

Farbstoff, farp-shtof, *m* dye, pigment

Farn, farn, *m* bracken, fern

Fasan, fah-zahn, *m* pheasant

Fasching, fahsh-ing, *m* carnival

Faschismus, fash-is-moos, *m* fascism

Faschist, fash-ist, *m* fascist

Faser, fah-zer, *f* fibre; filament; string

faserig, fah-zer-ik, *adj* fibrous; stringy

Faß, fahss, *nt* vat, cask, barrel, keg

fassen, fahss-en, *v* to seize, to take hold of; **sich –,** to compose oneself

fast, fahsst, *adv* almost, nearly

fasten, fahsst-en, *v* to fast

Fastnacht, fahsst-nahkt, *f* carnival-time

fatal, fahtt-ahl, *adj* disagreeable, vexatious; awkward

fauchen, fowk-en, *v* to hiss

faul, fowl, *adj* rotten, putrid; lazy, indolent

faulen, fowl-en, *v* to rot, to putrify

faulenzen, fowl-ent-sen, *v* to laze around, to lead an idle life

Faulheit, fowl-hite, *f* laziness, idleness

Fäulnis, foyl-niss, *f* rottenness; putrefaction

Faulpelz, fowl-pelts, *m* lazybones, idle person

Faust, fowst, *f* fist

Fax, fax, *nt* fax

faxen, fax-en, *v* to fax

Februar, fay-broo-ahr, *m* February

fechten, fekt-en, *v* to fence, to fight with swords

Feder, fayd-er, *f* feather; pen(-nib), quill; *mech* spring

Federhalter, fayd-er-hahlt-er, *m* pen-holder

federn, fayd-ern, *v* to be springy/elastic

Fee, fay, *f* fairy, elf

Fegefeuer, fay-ge-foy-er, *nt* purgatory

fegen, fayg-en, *v* to sweep; to wipe; to scour

Fehde, fayd-*e*, *f* feud, dispute, quarrel

fehlen, fayl-en, *v* to miss; to mistake; to be wrong

Fehler, fayl-er, *m* mistake; defect, blemish, flaw

fehlerhaft, fayl-er-hahfft, *adj* faulty, defective

fehlerlos, fayl-er-lohs, *adj* flawless

Fehlgeburt, fayl-ge-boort, *f* miscarriage

Fehlgriff, fayl-grif, *m* bad choice; mistake

Fehlschlag, fayl-shlahk, *m* failure

fehlschlagen, fayl-shlahg-en, *v* to miss; to fail

Feier, fy-er, *f* celebration

Feierabend, fy-er-ahb-ent, *m* closing time

feierlich, fy-er-lik, *adj*

ceremonious; dignified, grave

feiern, fy-ern, v to celebrate; to honour

Feiertag, fy-er-tahk, m feast-day, festival, holiday

feig(e), fy'k (fy'g-e), adj cowardly, timid; faint-hearted

Feige, fy-ge, f fig

Feigheit, fike-hite, f cowardice; timidity

Feigling, fike-ling, m coward

Feile, file-e, f file, rasp

feilen, file-en, v to file; to polish

fein, fine, adj fine, slender; elegant, graceful; refined

Feind, fine't, m enemy, foe, adversary

feindlich, fine't-lik, adj hostile, opposed, unfriendly

Feindschaft, fine't-shahft, f enmity, hostility

feindselig, fine't-zail-ik, adj hostile, inimical

feinfühlig, fine-fEEl-ik, adj sensitive, delicate

Feinheit, fine-hite, f fineness, subtlety; refinement

Feinschmecker, fine-shmeck-er, m gourmet

Feld, felt, nt field

Feldherr, felt-hairr, m commander-in-chief

Feldstecher, felt-shtek-er, m binoculars; field glasses

Feldzug, felt-tsook, m

campaign

Fell, fel, nt skin, hide

Fels, fels, m rock; cliff; crag

Felsen, fel-zen, m rock; cliff; crag

Fenster, fenst-er, nt window; –**bank**, f window-sill; –**laden**, m shutter; –**scheibe**, f window-pane

Ferien, fair-yen, pl holidays; – **haben**, v to be on holiday; –**haus**, nt holiday home; –**wohnung**, f holiday apartment

fern, fairn, adj & adv far, distant, remote

Fernbedienung, fairn-be-deen-oong, f remote control

Ferne, fair-ne, f distance

ferner, fair-ner, adv further(more); farther; moreover

Ferne(r) Osten, fair-ne(r) ost-en, m Far East

Ferngespräch, fairn-ge-shpraik, nt long-distance call

Fernglas, fairn-glahss, nt binoculars

Fernrohr, fairn-rohr, nt telescope

Fernsehapparat, fairn-zay-ahp-ah-raht, m television set

fernsehen, fairn-zay-en, v to watch television

Fernsehen, fairn-zay-en, nt television

Fernsprecher, fairn-shprek-er, m telephone

Fernsteuerung, fairn-shtoy-er-oong, f remote control

Fernverkehr, fairn-fer-kair, m through traffic

Ferse, fair-ze, f heel

fertig, fairt-ik, adj ready, prepared; skilled; finished

Fertiggericht, fairt-ik-ge-rikt, nt pre-cooked meal

Fertigkeit, fairt-ik-kite, f skill, dexterity

fertigmachen, fairt-ik-mak-en, v to finish, to get done

fertigstellen, fairt-ik-shtel-en, v to complete; to finish

fesch, fesh, adj smart, fashionable

Fessel, fes-el, f fetters, shackle; ankle

fesseln, fes-eln, v to fetter, to chain; to shackle

fest, fest, adj firm, fast; constant

Fest, fest, nt festival; party; fête

Festessen, fest-ess-en, nt banquet

festhalten, fest-hahlt-en, v to hold fast; to detain

Festigkeit, fest-ik-kite, f firmness

festklammern (sich), fest-klahmm-ern (zik), v to cling

Festland, fest-lahnt, nt mainland, continent

festlich, fest-lik, adj festive; solemn; splendid

Festlichkeit, fest-lik-kite, f festivity

festmachen, fest-mah*k*-en, *v*
to fix, to attach

festnageln, fest-nahg-eln, *v*
to nail fast; to clinch

Festnahme, fest-nahm-*e*, *f*
arrest

festnehmen, fest-naym-en,
v to arrest

Festplatte, fest-plahtt-*e*, *f*
(hard) disk

festsetzen, fest-zet-sen, *v* to
arrange; to stipulate

Festspiele, fest-shpeel-*e*, *pl*
festival

feststellen, fest-shtel-en, *v*
to ascertain; to fix

Feststellung, fest-shtel-
oong, *f* evidence

Festtag, fest-tahk, *m*
holiday, feast-day

Festung, fest-oong, *f*
fortress, stronghold

fett, fet, adj fat, greasy

Fett, fet, nt fat, grease

fettarm, fet-ahrm, *adj* low
fat

fettig, fet-ik, *adj* fatty, greasy,
oily

Fetzen, fet-sen, *m* shred,
scrap, rag

feucht, foykt, adj damp,
moist, humid

Feuchtigkeit, foykt-ik-kite,
f moisture, humidity

Feuer, foy-er, *nt* fire;
–löscher, *m* fire
extinguisher

feuern, foy-ern, *v* to fire; to
light

Feuerstein, foy-er-shtine, *m*
flint

Feuerwehr, foy-er-vair, *f*
fire-brigade

Feuerwerk, foy-er-vairk, *nt*
firework(s)

Feuerzeug, foy-er-tsoyk, *nt*
(cigarette) lighter

feurig, foyr-ik, *adj* fiery;
ardent, passionate

Fichte, fik-te, *f* pine(-tree);
spruce

Fieber, feeb-er, *nt* fever,
(high) temperature

fieberhaft, feeb-er-hahft, *adj*
feverish, febrile

Figur, fee-goor, *f* figure

Filet, fee-lay, *nt* fillet

Filiale, fil-yahl-*e*, *f* comm
branch

Film, film, m film

filmen, film-en, *v* to film

Filmkamera, film-kahm-er-
ah, *f* cine camera

Filter, filt-er, *m* filter;
–zigarette, *f* filter cigarette

Filz, filts, m felt; **–stift,** *m*
felt tip pen

Finanz, fin-ahnts, *f* finance;
–amt, *nt* Inland Revenue

finanziell, fin-ahnts-*e*-**ell,**
adj financial

finden, fin-den, *v* to find

Findigkeit, fin-dik-kite, *f*
cleverness, shrewdness

Findling, fint-ling, *m*
foundling

Finger, fing-er, *m* finger

Fingerhut, fing-er-hoot, *m*
thimble; foxglove

Fingerzeig, fing-er-tsike, *m*
indication, hint

Fink, fink, m finch

Finne, fin-*e*, *m*, **Finnin, fin**-
in, *f* Finn

finnisch, fin-ish, *adj* Finnish

Finnland, fin-lahnt, *nt*
Finland

finster, fin-ster, *adj* dark,
gloomy

Finsternis, fin-ster-nis, *f*
darkness, gloom

Firma, feer-mah, *f* firm,
company

Firmenwagen, feer-men-
vahg-en, *m* company car

Fisch, fish, m fish

fischen, fish-en, *v* to fish

Fischer, fish-er, *m* fisherman

Fischfang, fish-fahng, *m*
fishing

Fischotter, fish-ot-er, *m*
otter

Fitneß, fit-ness, *f* fitness

fix, fix, adj fast, fixed;
prompt, quick, nimble

flach, flahk, *adj* flat, plain,
even

Fläche, flek-*e*, *f* surface,
plain, plane, level

Flachs, flahx, m flax

flackern, flahck-ern, *v* to
flicker; to flare, to blaze

Flagge, flahgg-*e*, *f* flag

Flamme, flahmm-*e*, *f* flame

Flannell, flahnn-el, *m*
flannel

Flasche, flahsh-*e*, *f* bottle;
flask; **–nöffner,** *m* bottle
opener

flattern, flahtt-ern, *v* to
flutter; to be fickle

flau, flow, adj feeble; faint

Flaum, flowm, m down, fluff

flechten, flek-ten, v to braid; to intertwine

Fleck, fleck, m spot; place; piece of land; **blauer –,** m bruise

fleckig, fleck-ik, adj stained, spotted, marked

Fledermaus, flaid-er-mows, f bat

Flegel, flaig-el, m flail; boor; churl

flehen, flay-en, v to implore, to beseech

flehentlich, flay-ent-lik, adj urgent, fervent

Fleisch, fly'sh, nt flesh; meat

Fleischbrühe, fly'sh-brEE-e, f meat broth

Fleischer, fly-sher, m butcher

Fleiß, flice, m application, industry, diligence

fleißig, flice-ik, adj assiduous, industrious, diligent

Flicken, flick-en, m patch

flicken, flik-en, v to patch, to mend, to repair

Flieder, fleed-er, m lilac

Fliege, fleeg-e, f fly; bow-tie

fliegen, fleeg-en, v to fly; to race (along)

Flieger, fleeg-er, m flier; airman

fliehen, flee-en, v to flee; to fly

Fließband, flees-bahnt, nt assembly line

fließen, flees-en, v to flow, to run, to gush

fließend, flees-ent, adj &

adv flowing(ly); fluent(ly)

flimmern, flim-ern, v to glitter, to glisten, to shimmer

flink, flink, adj agile, quick, nimble

Flinte, flint-e, f gun, musket, rifle

Flitterwochen, flit-er-vok-en, pl honeymoon

Flocke, flock-e, f flake; piece of wool

flockig, flock-ik, adj flaky, fluffy

Floh, floh, m flea; **–markt,** m flea market

Floß, flohs, nt raft, float

Flosse, flos-e, f fin

Flöte, flert-e, f flute

flott, flot, adj quick; lively; fun-loving

Flotte, flot-e, f fleet, navy

Fluch, flook, m curse; malediction, imprecation

fluchen, flook-en, v to curse, to swear

Flucht, flookt, f flight, escape; suite (of rooms)

flüchten, flEEkt-en, v to take flight, to flee

flüchtig, flEEkt-ik, adj fugitive, flying; hasty

Flüchtigkeit, flEEkt-ik-kite f carelessness

Flüchtling, flEEkt-ling, m fugitive; exile; refugee

Flug, flook, m flight, flying; **–blatt,** nt pamphlet; **–gesellschaft,** f airline; **–hafen,** m airport; **–schein,** m flight ticket;

pilot's licence; **–steig,** m boarding gate; **–verbindung,** f connecting flight; **–zeug,** nt aeroplane

Flügel, flEEg-el, m wing; grand piano

Flunder, floonn-der, f flounder

Flur, floohr, f field; m entrance(-hall)

Fluß, floohs, m river; running water; stream

flüssig, flEEss-ik, adj liquid, fluid

Flüssigkeit, flEEss-ig-kite, f liquid, fluid; liquidity

flüstern, ffEEsst-ern, v to whisper

Flut, floot, f flood, waves; high tide

fluten, floot-en, v to swell, to flow, to rise

Flutlicht, floot-likt, nt floodlight

Fohlen, fohl-en, nt foal; colt

Folge, fol-ge, f succession; sequence; conclusion; obedience

folgen, fol-gen, v to follow

folgendermaßen, fol-gend-er-mahss-en, adv as follows

folgern, fol-gern v to draw a conclusion

folglich, folk-lik, adv & conj consequently; hence

folgsam, folk-zahm, adj obedient, submissive

Folgsamkeit, folk-zahm-kite, f obedience

Folie, fohl-ee-*e*, *f* foil

Folter, folt-*er*, *f* torture

foltern, folt-*ern*, *v* to torture

Fön, fern, *m* hair dryer

fönen, fern-*en*, *v* to blow dry

förderlich, ferd-*er*-lik, *adj* conducive, useful

fordern, ford-*ern*, *v* to demand, to challenge

fördern, ferd-*ern*, *v* to further, to promote

Forderung, ford-*er*-oong, *f* demand; claim, debt, challenge

Forelle, foh-**rel**-*e*, *f* trout

Form, form, *f* shape, form; ceremony, usage

Format, form-**aht**, *nt* size

formatieren, form-aht-eer-en, *v* to format

Formel, form-*el*, *f* formula; schedule; form

formen, form-*en*, *v* to form, to fashion, to mould

förmlich, ferm-lik, *adj* formal, in due form; downright

Formular, form-oo-**lahr**, *nt* (blank) form

forschen, forsh-*en*, *v* to inquire, to investigate

Forscher, forsh-*er*, *m* investigator, inquirer, scholar

Forschung, forsh-oong, *f* research

Forst, forst, *m* forest

Förster, ferst-*er*, *m* forester

fort, fort, *adv* away

fortan, fort-**ahn**, *adv*

henceforth; in future

Fortbildung, fort-bild-oong, *f* further education

fortfahren, fort-fahr-en, *v* to continue, to go on

fortlaufend, fort-lowf-ent, *adj* uninterrupted

fortpflanzen, fort-pflahnt-sen, *v* to reproduce

Fortpflanzung, fort-pflahnt-soong, *f* reproduction

Fortschritt, fort-shrit, *m* progress; improvement

fortschrittlich, fort-shrit-lik, *adj* progressive

fortsetzen, fort-zet-sen, *v* to continue

Fortsetzung, fort-zet-soong, *f* continuation

fortwährend, fort-vair-ent, *adj* continual; lasting

fortziehen, fort-tsee-en, *v* to move away

Foto, foh-toh, *nt* photograph; **–apparat,** *m* camera; **–graf,** *m* photographer; **–grafie,** *f* photography

fotografieren, foh-toh-grahf-eer-en, *v* to take photographs

Fotokopie, foh-toh-koh-pee, *f* photocopy

fotokopieren, foh-toh-koh-peer-en, *v* to photocopy

Foyer, fwah-yeh, *nt* foyer, entrance-hall

Fracht, frahkt, *f* freight; charge for carriage

Frachtbrief, frahkt-breef, *m* bill of lading

Frack, frahck, *m* tails

Frage, frahg-*e*, *f* question, inquiry; **–bogen,** *m* questionnaire

fragen, frahg-en, *v* to ask, to question, to inquire

Fragezeichen, frahg-e-tsy-ken, *nt* question mark

fraglich, frahk-lik, *adj* questionable

frankieren, frahnk-eer-en, *v* to pay postage

franko, frahnk-oh, *adv* post-paid; (carriage) free

Frankreich, frahnk-ry'k, *nt* France

Franzose, frahnn-tsoh-ze, *m* Frenchman

Französin, frahnn-tser-zin, *f* Frenchwoman

französisch, frahnn-tser-zish, *adj* French

frappant, frahpp-ahnt, *adj* striking

Fraß, frahss, *m* food, *fam* grub

Fratze, frahtt-se, *f* grimace, ugly face; tomfoolery

Frau, frow, *f* woman; wife; Mrs; **–enarzt,** *m* gynaecologist; **–enbewegung,** *f* feminist movement

Fräulein, froy-line, *nt* young lady; Miss

frech, frek, *adj* impudent; bold, daring

Frechheit, frek-hite, *f* impudence; offensiveness

frei, fry, *adj* free, at liberty; independent

Freibad, fry-baht, *nt* open-air swimming pool

freiberuflich, fry-be-roof-lik, *adj* self-employed, freelance

freigebig, fry-gay-bik, *adj* generous; liberal

freihalten, fry-hahlt-en, *v* to pay for (sb)

Freiheit, fry-hite, *f* freedom, liberty

Freiherr, fry-herr, *m* baron

freilich, fry-lik, *adv* certainly, to be sure, admittedly

Freimaurer, fry-mowr-er, *m* freemason

Freimut, fry-moot, *m* frankness, candour

freisprechen, fry-shprek-en, *v* to acquit; to absolve

Freispruch, fry-shprook, *m* acquittal

Freitag, fry-tahk, *m* Friday

freiwillig, fry-vil-ik, *adj* voluntary; spontaneous

Freizeit, fry-tsite, *f* leisure, free time; **–kleidung,** *f* casual wear; **–park,** *m* theme park

fremd, fremt, *adj* strange; foreign; curious, odd

fremdartig, fremt-art-ik, *adj* strange, singular, odd

Fremde, frem-de, *f* foreign/strange country

Fremde(r), frem-de(r), *m & f* stranger, foreigner; **–nführer,** *m* (tourist) guide; **-nverkehrsamt,** *nt* tourist

office

Fremdsprache, fremt-shprahk-e, *f* foreign language

fressen, fress-en, *v* to eat (of animals)

Frettchen, fret-ken, *nt* ferret

Freude, froyd-e, *f* joy(fulness), gladness, delight

freudestrahlend, froyd-e-shtrahl-ent, *adj* radiant with joy

freuen, froy-en, *v* to please; to rejoice; **sich –,** to be happy; **sich auf etw –,** to look forward to sth

Freund, froynt, *m* friend

freundlich, froynt-lik, *adj* friendly, amiable, kind

Freundlichkeit, froynt-lik-kite, *f* kindness

Freundschaft, froynt-shahft, *f* friendship

freundschaftlich, froynt-shahft-lik, *adj* friendly

Friede, freed-e, *m* peace, concord

Friedensschluß, freed-enss-shlooss, *m* peace agreement

friedfertig, freet-fairt-ik, *adj* peaceable

Friedhof, freet-hohf, *m* churchyard, cemetery

friedlich, freed-lik, *adj* peaceable

frieren, freer-en, *v* to freeze; to feel cold

frisch, frish, *adj* fresh; cool

Frische, frish-e, *f* freshness;

coolness

Friseur, free-zer, *m* hairdresser

frisieren, free-zeer-en, *v* to do sb's hair

Frist, frist, *f* space of time; interval; date; delay

fristen, frist-en, *v* to delay, to put off; to reprieve

Frisur, free-zoor, *f* hairstyle

froh, froh, *adj* glad, joyful, delighted

fröhlich, frer-lik, *adj* cheerful, glad

Fröhlichkeit, frer-lik-kite, *f* cheerfulness; joyfulness

frohlocken, froh-lock-en, *v* to exult; to rejoice

Frohsinn, froh-zin, *m* cheerfulness

fromm, from, *adj* pious, religious, devout

Frömmigkeit, frermm-ik-kite, *f* piety, godliness

Frosch, frosh, *m* frog

Frost, frost, *m* frost; frosty weather; severe cold

Frostbeule, frost-boy-le, *f* chilblain

frösteln, frerst-eln, *v* to shiver; to feel chilly

frostig, frost-ik, *adj* frosty; frozen

Frostschutzmittel, frost-shoots-mitt-el, *nt* antifreeze

Frucht, frookt, *f* fruit

fruchtbar, frookt-bahr, *adj* fruitful, fertile, fruit-bearing

Fruchtbarkeit, frookt-bahr-kite, f fruitfulness

Fruchtsaft, frookt-sahft, m
fruit juice

früh, frEE, adj early; **heute –,**
this morning

Frühe, frEE-e, f (early)
morning

früher, frEE-er, adj earlier,
sooner; adv formerly

Frühjahr, frEE-yahr, nt
spring

Frühling, frEE-ling, m spring

Frühstück, frEE-shtEEck, nt
breakfast

frühzeitig, frEE-tsite-ik, adj
& adv early; premature(ly)

Fuchs, fooks, m fox;
chestnut horse; freshman

fuchteln, fookt-eln, v to
gesticulate; to brandish

Fuge, foog-e, f joint; seam;
fugue

fügen, fEEg-en, v to join, to
put together; **sich –,** to
submit, to accommodate
oneself

fügsam, fEEg-zahm, adj
tractable, accommodating

fühlbar, fEEl-bar, adj
sensible, palpable;
perceptible

fühlen, fEEl-en, v to feel, to
touch; to sense

Fuhre, foor-e, f cart-load

führen, fEEr-en, v to lead, to
conduct, to guide; to
manage; to stock

Führer, fEEr-er, m leader;
driver; manager; guide:
guide-book

Führerschein, fEEr-er-shine,

m driving licence

Führung, fEEr-oong, f
conduct; guidance,
management

Fülle, fEEll-e, f plenty,
abundance, profusion

Füllen, fEEll-en, nt foal,
colt, filly

füllen, fEEll-en, v to fill

Füller, fEEll-er, m fountain-
pen

Füllung, fEEll-oong, f filling

Fund, foont, m find

Fundbüro, foont-bEEr-oh, nt
lost-property office

fünf, fEEnf, num five

fünfzehn, fEEnf-tsayn, num
fifteen

fünfzig, fEEnf-tsik, num fifty

Funk, foonk, m radio

Funke, foonk-e, m spark,
flash, flashing light

funkeln, foonk-eln, v to
sparkle, to flash

Funkspruch, foonk-
shprook, m radio signal

Funktelefon, foonk-te-le-
fohn, nt cell-phone

Funktion, foonk-tse-ohn, f
function

funktionieren, foonk-
tsyohn-eer-en, v to
function

für, fEEr, prep for

Furcht, foorkt, f fear,
apprehension, anxiety

furchtbar, foorkt-bar, adj
fearful, frightful, horrible

fürchten, fEErk-ten, v to
fear, to be afraid of

fürchterlich, fEErk-ter-lik,

adj dreadful, terrible

furchtsam, foorkt-zahm, adj
timid, apprehensive

Fürsorge, fEEr-zorg-e,
f care, solicitude;
–unterstützung, f
social security

Fürsprache, fEEr-shprah-ke,
f intercession, plea

Fürst, fEErst, m prince

Fürstentum, fEErst-en-
toom, nt principality

fürstlich, fEErst-lik, adj
princely

Fuß, foos, m foot, paw;
–ball, m football; **–boden,**
m floor(ing)

Fußgänger, foos-geng-er, m
pedestrian; **–zone,** f
pedestrian precinct

Fußtritt, foos-tritt, m kick

Futter, foott-er, nt food;
fodder; lining (cloth)

Futteral, foott-er-ahl, nt
case, covering, sheath

füttern, fEEtt-ern, v to feed;
to line

G

g, *abbr* **Gramm**

Gabe, gahb-*e,* *f* gift, present; talent

Gabel, gahb-*el,* *f* fork

gaffen, gahff-*en,* *v* to gape; to yawn

gähnen, gain-*en,* *v* to yawn

Galeere, gah-lair-*e,* *f* galley

Galerie, gah-lair-*ee,* *f* gallery

Galgen, gahll-gen, *m* gallows, gibbet

Galle, gahll-*e,* *f* gallbladder; gall, bile; venom

Gang, gahng, *m* walk; path; corridor; course; **–schaltung,** *f* gears

Gans, gahns, *f* goose

Gänseblume, gen-*ze*-bloom-*e,* *f* daisy

Gänsebraten, gen-*ze*-braht-en, *m* roast goose

Gänsehaut, gen-*ze*-howt, *f* goose-flesh; goose-pimples

Gänserich, gen-*ze*-rik, *m* gander

ganz, gahnts, *adj* whole, complete, all; *adv* quite

gänzlich, gents-lik, *adj* entire, total, quite

gar, gahr, *adj* done, (well) cooked, *adv* fully, quite; **– nicht,** not at all

Garage, gahr-ahzh-*e,* *f* garage

Garantie, gahr-ahnn-tee, *f* guarantee

Garbe, gahrb-*e,* *f* sheaf; beam (of light)

Garderobe, gahr-de-rohb-*e,* *f* wardrobe; cloakroom; dressing-room

Gardine, gahrd-een-*e,* *f* curtain

gären, gay-ren, *v* to ferment; to effervesce

Garn, gahrn, *nt* thread, yarn, twine

garnieren, gahrn-eer-*en,* *v* to trim; to garnish

Garnison, gahrn-ee-zohn, *f* garrison

Garnitur, gahrn-ee-toor, *f* trimming, uniform; (matching) set

garstig, gahrst-ik, *adj* nasty, objectionable; loathsome

Garten, gahrt-en, *m* garden

Gärtner, gairt-ner, *m* gardener

Gärtnerei, gairt-ne-ry, *f* gardening, horticulture; garden centre; nursery

Gas, gahs, *nt* gas; **–herd,** *m* gas cooker; **–pedal,** *nt* accelerator pedal

Gasse, gahss-*e,* *f* (narrow) street, alley, lane

Gast, gahst, *m* guest, visitor; **–arbeiter,** *m* immigrant worker; **–freundschaft,** *f* hospitality; **–geber,** *m* host; **–haus,** *nt* inn; restaurant; **–hof,** *m* inn, hotel; **–spiel,** *nt* guest performance; **–stätte,** *f* restaurant; **–wirt,** *m* landlord, innkeeper

Gatte, gahtt-*e,* *m* husband

Gattin, gahtt-in, *f* wife

Gattung, gahtt-oong, *f* kind, sort; species, genus; breed

Gaukler, gowk-ler, *m* juggler, conjurer, magician

Gaul, gowl, *m* (inferior) horse, nag, old crock

Gaumen, gowm-en, *m* gum(s); palate

Gauner, gown-er, *m* swindler, sharper, rogue

geb., *abbr* **geboren**

Gebäck, ge-**beck,** *nt* biscuits, pastries

Gebärde, ge-**baird**-e, *f* gesture; gesticulation

gebärden (sich), ge-**baird**-en (zik); *v* to behave

gebären, ge-**bair**-en, *v* to give birth

Gebäude, ge-**boyd**-e, *nt* structure, building

geben, gay-ben, *v* to give, to bestow, to present

Gebet, ge-**bait,** *nt* prayer, praying

Gebiet, ge-**beet,** *nt* territory; area; sphere

gebieten, ge-**beet**-en, *v* to command, to order

gebieterisch, ge-**beet**-er-ish, *adj* imperious

gebildet, ge-**bild**-et, *adj* educated

Gebirge, ge-**beer**-ge, *nt* mountain-range

Gebiß, ge-**biss,** *nt* set of teeth, denture; (bridle) bit

geboren, ge-**bohr**-en, *adj* born; née

Gebot, ge-**boht,** *nt* command(ment), order

gebraten, ge-**braht**-en, *adj* fried

Gebrauch, ge-**browk,** *m* use; application; usage

gebrauchen, ge-**browk**-en, *v* to use; to apply

gebräuchlich, ge-**broyk**-lik, *adj* in use, current

gebraucht, ge-**browkt,** *adj* second-hand

gebrechlich, ge-**brek**-lik, *adj* weak, feeble, fragile, frail

Gebrüder, ge-**brEEd**-er, *pl comm* Brothers

Gebühr, ge-**bEEr,** *f* due, duty, obligation, fee; **–eneinheit,** *f* (telephone) unit

Geburt, ge-**boort,** *f* birth; confinement; **–enkontrolle,** *f* birth control

gebürtig, ge-**bEErt**-ik, *adj* native

Geburtsdatum, ge-**boorts**-daht-oomm, *nt* date of birth

Geburtsort, ge-**boorts**-ohrt, *m* place of birth

Geburtstag, ge-**boorts**-tahk, *m* birthday

Gebüsch, ge-**bEEsh,** *nt* bushes, thicket, copse

Gedächtnis, ge-**dekt**-nis, *nt* memory

Gedanke, ge-**dahng**-ke, *m* thought, idea

Gedankenstrich, ge-**dahng**-ken-shtrik, *m* dash

Gedärme, ge-**dairm**-e, *pl* entrails, bowels, intestines

gedeihen, ge-**dy**-en, *v* to prosper, to thrive

gedenken, ge-**deng**-ken, *v* to remember

Gedicht, ge-**dikt,** *nt* poem, verse(s)

gediegen, ge-**deeg**-en, *adj* solid; genuine; pure

Gedränge, ge-**dreng**-e, *nt* crowd; trouble, straits

Geduld, ge-**doolt,** *f* patience

gedulden (sich), ge-**doold**-en (zik), *v* to have patience

geduldig, ge-**doold**-ik, *adj* patient; indulgent

geeignet, ge-**yg**-net, *adj* suitable, right

Gefahr, ge-**far,** *f* danger, risk

gefährden, ge-**faird**-en, *v* to endanger

gefährlich, ge-**fair**-lik, *adj* dangerous, risky

Gefährte, ge-**fairt**-e, *m* companion, associate

Gefallen, ge-**fahll**-en, *m* favour, service

gefallen, ge-**fahll**-en, *v* to please

gefällig, ge-**fel**-ik, *adj* kind; obliging

gefälligst, ge-**fel**-igst, *adv* kindly, if you please

gefangen, ge-**fahng**-en, *adj* captured

Gefangene(r), ge-**fahng**-en-e(r), *m & f* prisoner

Gefangenschaft, ge-**fahng**-en-shahft, *f* captivity

Gefängnis, ge-**feng**-niss, *nt* prison, jail

Gefäß, ge-**fes,** *nt* vessel, receptacle

Gefecht, ge-**fekt,** *nt* combat, action, engagement

Gefieder, ge-**feed**-er, *nt* plumage, feathers

Geflügel, ge-**flEEg**-el, *nt* poultry

Gefolge, ge-**folg**-e, *nt* retinue, entourage;

cortege

gefräßig, ge-fres-ik, *adj*
gluttonous; ravenous

Gefreite(r), ge-fry-te(r), *m*
& *f* lance-corporal

gefrieren, ge-freer-en, *v* to
freeze, to congeal

Gefrierfach, ge-freer-fahk,
nt freezer compartment

Gefriertruhe, ge-freer-troo-
e, *f* freezer

Gefühl, ge-fEEl, *nt* feeling,
emotion, sense; touch

gegen, gayg-en, *prep*
towards; against; about

Gegend, gayg-ent, *f* country,
region; scenery

Gegensatz, gayg-en-zahts, *m*
contrast

gegenseitig, gayg-en-zite-ik,
adj opposite; mutual

Gegenstand, gayg-en-
shtahnt, *m* object; theme,
topic

Gegenteil, gayg-en-tile, *nt*
opposite, contrary, reverse

gegenüber, gayg-en-EEb-er,
adv opposite, facing

Gegenverkehr, gayg-en-fer-
ker, *m* oncoming traffic

Gegenwart, gayg-en-vahrt, *f*
presence; present

gegenwärtig, gayg-en-vairt-
ik, *adj* nowadays

Gegner, gayg-ner, *m*
opponent, adversary

Gehalt, ge-hahlt, *nt* salary

gehässig, ge-hess-ik, *adj*
spiteful; hateful

Gehäuse, ge-hoy-ze, *nt* box,
case, casing, shell

Gehege, ge-hay-ge, *nt*
enclosure; park, preserve

geheim, ge-hime, *adj* secret;
hidden; mysterious

Geheimdienst, ge-hime-
deenst, *m* secret service

Geheimnis, ge-hime-niss, *nt*
secret, mystery

gehen, gay-en, *v* to go; to
walk; to work; **wie
geht's?,** how are things?;
es geht, it's all right

Gehilfe, ge-hilf-e, *m*
assistant, colleague; clerk

Gehirn, ge-heern, *nt*
brain(s); intellect;
–erschütterung, *f*
concussion

Gehölz, ge-herlts, *nt* copse,
thicket, wood

Gehör, ge-her, *nt* hearing

gehorchen, ge-hork-en, *v* to
obey

gehören, ge-her-en, *v* to
belong; to be due

gehorsam, ge-hohr-zahm,
adj obedient, docile

Gehweg, gay-wayk, *m*
pavement

Geier, gy-er, *m* vulture

Geige, gy-ge, *f* violin, fiddle

geigen, gy-gen, *v* to play the
violin

geil, gy'l, *adj* lewd

Geisel, gy-zel, *f* hostage

Geißel, gy-sel, *f* whip

geißeln, gy-seln, *v* to whip

Geist, gy'st, *m* ghost, spirit,
spectre; intellect, mind

geisterhaft, gy-ster-hahft,
adj ghostly

geisteskrank, gy-stes-
krahnk, *adj* mentally ill

geistig, gy-stik, *adj* spiritual;
intellectual, mental;
chem alcoholic

geistlich, gy-stlik, *adj*
spiritual, sacred; clerical

Geistliche(r), gy-stlik-e(r),
m clergyman

geistreich, gy-stry'k, *adj*
witty, clever, smart

Geiz, gy'ts, *m* avarice, greed,
meanness

geizen, gy-tsen, *v* to be
avaricious/mean

Geizhals, gy'ts-hahls, *m*
miser, skinflint

geizig, gy-tsik, *adj*
avaricious, greedy, mean

Gelächter, ge-lek-ter, *nt*
laughter, laughing

Gelage, ge-lahg-e, *nt* feast,
carousal

gelähmt, ge-laymt, *adj*
paralysed

Gelände, ge-lend-e, *nt*
ground; grounds; terrain

Geländer, ge-lend-er, *nt*
rail(ing), balustrade

gelangen, ge-lahng-en, *v* to
arrive at, to reach

gelangweilt, ge-lahng-wylt,
adj bored

gelassen, ge-lahss-en, *adj*
calm, unruffled

geläufig, ge-loyf-ik, *adj*
fluent; ready; with ease

gelaunt, ge-lownt, *adj*
gut/schlecht –, in a
good/bad mood

gelb, gelp, *adj* yellow

Gelbsucht, gelp-sookt, f jaundice

Geld, gelt, nt money; **–automat**, m cash dispenser; **–beutel**, m wallet; **–schein**, m bank note; **–strafe**, f fine; **–wechsel**, m exchange

gelegen, ge-lay-gen, adj situated, lying; appropriate

Gelegenheit, ge-laig-en-hite, f opportunity

Gelegenheitskauf, ge-laig-en-hites-kowf, m chance purchase, bargain, job-lot

gelegentlich, ge-laig-ent-lik, adj occasional, incidental

gelehrig, ge-lair-ik, adj teachable; tractable; docile

gelehrt, ge-lairt, adj learned, well-read, scholarly

Gelehrte(r), ge-lairt-e(r), m & f scholar, scientist

Geleise, ge-ly-ze, nt track, rails

Geleit, ge-lite, nt escort, accompaniment

geleiten, ge-ly-ten, v to escort, to accompany

Gelenk, ge-lenk, nt joint, articulation; link

gelenkig, ge-lenk-ik, adj jointed; flexible

Geliebte(r), ge-leep-te(r), m & f loved one, lover

gelingen, ge-ling-en, v to succeed, to be successful

geloben, ge-lohb-en, v to vow

gelten, gelt-en, v to have value, to be valid; to apply

Geltung, gelt-oong, f worth; validity; prominence

Gelüste, ge-lEEst-e, pl desire, longing

gemächlich, ge-maik-lik, adj leisurely, unhurried

Gemälde, ge-meld-e, nt painting

gemäß, ge-mes, adj & adv in accordance with; appropriate

gemein, ge-mine, adj common; ordinary; general; low, mean

Gemeinde, ge-mine-de, f community; parish

Gemeinheit, ge-mine-hite, f meanness; vulgarity

gemeinsam, ge-mine-zahm, adj common, mutual

Gemeinschaft, ge-mine-shahft, f community; fellowship

Gemenge, ge-meng-e, nt mixing, mingling; crowd

gemessen, ge-mes-en, adj measured; strict; slow

Gemetzel, ge-mets-el, nt slaughter, massacre

Gemisch, ge-mish, nt mixture

Gemse, gem-ze, f chamois

Gemurmel, ge-moorm-el, nt murmur(ing), muttering

Gemüse, ge-mEEz-e, nt vegetable(s); **–händler**, **–laden**, m greengrocer('s)

gemustert, ge-moost-ert, adj patterned

Gemüt, ge-mEET, nt feeling; soul; mind; nature

gemütlich, ge-mEEt-lik, adj comfortable, cosy, snug; agreeable

Gemütlichkeit, ge-mEEt-lik-kite, f comfort, cosiness, snugness

Gen, gayn, nt gene

genau, ge-now, adj exact, precise; strict

genehmigen, ge-naym-ig-en, v to permit; to approve

Genehmigung, ge-naym-ig-oong, f permission; approval

geneigt, ge-ny'kt, adj sloping; inclined; disposed

General, gen-e-rahl, m general; **–probe**, f dress rehearsal; **–streik**, m general strike

genesen, ge-nayz-en, v to recover, to get well

Genf, genf, nt Geneva

Genick, ge-nik, nt neck; nape

Genie, zhain-ee, nt genius

genieren (sich), shain-eer-en (zik), v to be embarrassed

genießen, ge-nees-en, v to enjoy

Genosse, ge-nos-e, m companion, comrade, associate

Genre, zhahn-re, nt kind; sort; species

genug, ge-nook, adv enough

Genüge, ge-nEEg-e, f sufficiency; **zur –**, enough

genügen, ge-**nEEg**-en, v to suffice

genügsam, ge-**nEEk**-zahm, adj undemanding; modest

Genugtuung, ge-**nook**-too-oong, f satisfaction

Genuß, ge-**nooss**, m enjoyment; consumption (of food)

geöffnet, ge-**erf**-net, adj open

Geographie, gay-oh-grahf-ee, f geography

Gepäck, ge-**peck**, nt luggage, baggage; **–aufbewahrung**, f left-luggage; **–schein**, m luggage ticket; **–träger**, m porter

gerade, ge-**rahd**-e, adj & adv straight; direct; just

geradeaus, ge-**rahd**-e-ows, adv straight ahead

Gerät, ge-**rayt**, nt tools, utensils, implements

geraten, ge-**raht**-en, v to hit upon, to get (in)to; to turn out

geräuchert, ge-**royk**-ert, adj smoked

geräumig, ge-**roym**-ik, adj spacious, roomy, extensive

Geräusch, ge-**roysh**, nt noise, sound

gerben, **gairb**-en, v to tan (hides)

gerecht, ge-**rekt**, adj just, fair, righteous

Gerechtigkeit, ge-**rekt**-tik-kite, f justice, fairness

Gerede, ge-**raid**-e, nt talk; gossip

Gericht, ge-**rikt**, nt court (of law), tribunal; dish, course

gerichtlich, ge-**rikt**-lik, adj judicial, legal, lawful

gering, ge-**ring**, adj slight, unimportant; humble; low; **–fügig**, adj trifling, petty

geringschätzig, ge-**ring**-shet-sik, adj disdainful

gerinnen, ge-**rin**-en, v to curdle; to clot

Gerippe, ge-**rip**-e, nt skeleton; framework

gern(e), **gairn**(-e), adv gladly, with pleasure, willingly; **– haben**, v to like; **etw – tun**, to like doing sth

Gerste, **gairst**-e, f barley

Geruch, ge-**rook**, m (sense of) smell; odour

Gerücht, ge-**rEEkt**, nt rumour, hearsay

Gerümpel, ge-**rEEmp**-el, nt junk

Gerüst, ge-**rEEst**, nt scaffold(ing); stage; platform

gesamt, ge-**zahmt**, adj whole, entire, total

Gesamtschule, ge-**zahmt**-shool-e, f comprehensive school

Gesandte(r), ge-**zahnt**-e(r), m & f ambassador

Gesandtschaft, ge-**zahnt**-shahft, f embassy

Gesang, ge-**zahng**, m singing; song

Gesäß, ge-**zes**, nt seat; bottom, backside

Geschäft, ge-**sheft**, nt business; affair; trade

geschäftig, ge-**sheft**-ik, adj busy, active

geschäftlich, ge-**sheft**-lik, adj relating to business

Geschäfts-, ge-**shefts**, pref business; **–frau**, businesswoman; **–führer**, m manager; **–mann**, m businessman; **–reise**, f business trip; **–schluß**, closing time; **–zeit**, f business hours

geschehen, ge-**shay**-en, v to happen, to occur

Geschehnis, ge-**shay**-niss, nt occurrence

gescheit, ge-**shite**, adj intelligent, shrewd, sensible

Geschenk, ge-**shenk**, nt present; gift

Geschichte, ge-**shikt**-e, f story, tale; history

Geschick, ge-**shik**, nt fate, destiny; aptitude

geschickt, ge-**shikt**, adj skilled, skilful; agile

geschieden, ge-**sheed**-en, adj divorced

Geschirr, ge-**sheer**, nt crockery, pots and pans; **–spülmaschine**, f dishwasher; **–spülmittel**, nt washing-up liquid; **–tuch**, nt dish cloth

Geschlecht, ge-**shlekt**, nt sex; gender; species; kind; generation

geschlechtlich, ge-shlekt-lik, *adj* sexual; generic

Geschlechtskrankheit, ge-shlekts-krahnk-hite, *f* venereal disease

Geschlechtsteil, ge-shlekts-tile, *nt* genitals

Geschlechtsverkehr, ge-shlekts-fer-kair, *m* sexual intercourse

geschlossen, ge-shlos-en, *adj* closed

Geschmack, ge-shmahck, *m* taste, flavour

geschmeidig, ge-shmy-dik, *adj* supple, flexible

Geschöpf, ge-sherpf, *nt* creature

Geschoß, ge-shoss, *nt* projectile, missile

Geschrei, ge-shry, *nt* shouts, shouting, shrieking, screaming

Geschütz, ge-shEEts, *nt* cannon, (big) gun

Geschwätz, ge-shvets, *nt* talk, gossip

geschwätzig, ge-shvets-ik, *adj* talkative, garrulous

geschwind, ge-shvint, *adj* quick, swift, prompt

Geschwindigkeit, ge-shvind-ig-kite, *f* speed, velocity; **–beschränkung**, *f* speed limit

Geschwister, ge-shvist-er, *pl* brother(s) and sister(s)

Geschworene(r), ge-shvohr-en-e(r), *m & f* juror

Geschwulst, ge-shvoolst, *f* swelling, inflation

Geschwür, ge-shvEEr, *nt* boil, ulcer, abscess

gesellig, ge-zel-ik, *adj* companionable, sociable

Geselligkeit, ge-zel-ig-kite, *f* sociability

Gesellschaft, ge-zel-shahft, *f* society; company; party

gesellschaftlich, ge-zel-shahft-lik, *adj* social, sociable

Gesetz, ge-zets, *nt* law, statute

gesetzlich, ge-zets-lik, *adj* lawful, legal

Gesicht, ge-zikt, *nt* face, countenance; **–ausdruck**, *m* facial expression; **–spunkt**, *m* point of view

Gesindel, ge-zin-del, *nt* mob, rabble

Gesinnung, ge-zinn-oong, *f* disposition, mind, feeling

gespannt, ge-shpahnt, *adj* tense; taut; curious

Gespenst, ge-shpenst, *nt* ghost

Gespräch, ge-shprayk, *nt* conversation; dialogue

gesprächig, ge-shprayk-ik, *adj* talkative

Gestalt, ge-shtahlt, *f* form(ation), figure, shape

gestalten, ge-shtahlt-en, *v* to shape, to form

Geständnis, ge-shtent-nis, *nt* confession

Gestank, ge-shtahnk, *m* stench, stink

gestatten, ge-shtahtt-en, *v* to permit, to allow

gestehen, ge-shtay-en, *v* to confess, to admit

Gestell, ge-shtell, *nt* stand; trestle; jack

gestern, gest-ern, *adv* yesterday

gestört, ge-shtert, *adj* disturbed

Gesträuch, ge-shtroyk, *nt* bushes, shrubs, shrubbery

gestreift, ge-shtry'ft, *adj* striped, streaky

gestrig, ges-trik, *adj* yesterday's

Gestüt, ge-shtEEt, *nt* stud (farm)

Gesuch, ge-sook, *nt* petition; request, demand

gesund, ge-soont, *adj* healthy, well; wholesome; **– werden**, *v* to get better

Gesundheit, ge-zoont-hite, *f* health

Getöse, ge-terz-e, *nt* din, racket, row

Getränk, ge-trenk, *nt* drink, beverage; **–ekarte**, *f* wine list

getrauen (sich), ge-trow-en (zik), *v* to venture, to dare

Getreide, ge-try-de, *nt* cereals, corn, grain

getrennt, ge-trennt, *adj* separate(d)

getreu, ge-troy, *adj* faithful, true

Getriebe, ge-treeb-e, *nt* gear box

getrost, ge-trohst, *adj* confident, hopeful

Getümmel, ge-tEEmm-el, *nt* turmoil, tumult; crowd

Gewächs, ge-veks, *nt* growth, plant; **–haus**, *nt* greenhouse

Gewähr, ge-vair, *f* guarantee, security

gewähren, ge-vair-en, *v* to grant, to give

gewährleisten, ge-vair-ly-sten, *v* to guarantee

Gewalt, ge-vahlt, *f* force, power, might

gewaltig, ge-vahlt-ik, *adj* mighty, strong; immense

gewaltsam, ge-vahlt-zahm, *adj* forcible; violent

gewalttätig, ge-vahlt-tait-ik, *adj* violent

Gewand, ge-vahnnt, *nt* garment, gown, attire

gewandt, ge-vahnt, *adj* agile, active, supple

Gewebe, ge-vayb-e, *nt* web, fabric; tissue

Gewehr, ge-vair, *nt* rifle, gun; weapon

Geweih, ge-vy, *nt* horns, antlers

Gewerbe, ge-vairb-e, *nt* trade, profession, line of business

Gewerkschaft, ge-vairk-shahft, *f* trade-union

Gewicht, ge-vikt, *nt* weight; stress

gewillt, ge-vilt, *adj* willing, disposed, inclined

Gewinn, ge-vin, *m* profit(s); winning(s); gain

gewinnen, ge-vin-en, *v* to win; to gain; to extract

gewiß, ge-vis, *adj* certain, sure

Gewissen, ge-vis-en, *nt* conscience

gewissenhaft, ge-vis-en-hahft, *adj* conscientious

Gewissensbisse, ge-vis-ens-bis-e, *pl* pang (of conscience)

gewissermaßen, ge-vis-er-mahss-en, *adv* to a certain extent, in a way

Gewißheit, ge-vis-hite, *f* certainty

Gewitter, ge-vit-er, *nt* thunder(storm)

gewogen, ge-vohg-en, *adj* kindly disposed

gewöhnen, ge-vern-en, *v* to accustom; **sich an etw –**, *v* to get used to sth

Gewohnheit, ge-vohn-hite, *f* custom, usage, habit

gewöhnlich, ge-vern-lik, *adj* usual; ordinary; vulgar

gewohnt, ge-vohnt, *adj* accustomed

Gewölbe, ge-verl-be, *nt* vault; arch

Gewühl, ge-vEEl, *nt* rummaging, wriggling; crowd, throng

Gewürz, ge-vEErts, *nt* spice, seasoning, condiment

Gezeiten, ge-tsy-ten, *pl* tide(s)

geziert, ge-tseert, *adj* affected

Gezwitscher, ge-tsvit-sher, *nt* twittering, chirping

Gicht, gikt, *f* gout

Giebel, geeb-el, *m* gable end

Gier, geer, *f* greed(iness); lust

gierig, geer-ik, *adj* greedy; lustful

gießen, gees-en, *v* to pour; to spill; to cast metal

Gießkanne, gees-kahnn-e, *f* watering-can

Gift, gift, *nt* poison; venom

giftig, gift-ik, *adj* poisonous; venomous

Ginster, gins-ter, *m* gorse, broom

Gipfel, gip-fel, *m* summit, top, peak

Gips, gips, *m* plaster

Giraffe, gee-rahff-e, *f* giraffe

Girlande, geer-lahnd-e, *f* garland, festoon

Girokonto, dsheer-oh-kohnn-toh, *nt* current account

Gitarre, gee-tahrr-e, *f* guitar

Gitter, git-er, *nt* railing, fence, grille

Glanz, glahnts, *m* brilliance, radiance, brightness

glänzen, glent-sen, *v* to shine, to sparkle

Glas, glahs, *nt* glass

gläsern, glay-zern, *adj* of glass, vitreous

glatt, glahtt, *adj* smooth, even, polished

Glatteis, glahtt-ice, *nt* (black) ice

glätten, glet-en, *v* to smooth, to press; **sich –**, to become smooth

Glatze, glahtt-se, f bald head, bald patch

Glaube, glow-be, m belief; faith; trust

glauben (an), glowb-en, v to believe (in)

gläubig, gloy-bik, adj believing; faithful; orthodox

Gläubiger, gloy-big-er, m creditor

gleich, gly'k, adj like; equal; at once; presently

Gleichberechtigung, gly'k-be-rekt-ig-oong, f equal rights

gleichen, gly'k-en, v to be similar to, to resemble

gleichfalls, gly'k-fahlls, adv also; the same to you

Gleichgewicht, gly'k-ge-vikt, nt equilibrium

gleichgültig, gly'k-gEElt-ik, adj indifferent

gleichmäßig, gly'k-mes-ik, adj even, uniform

Gleichmut, gly'k-moot, m equanimity

Gleichnis gly'k-nis, nt simile; parable; image, likeness

gleichsam, gly'k-zahm, adv so to speak, as it were

Gleichstrom gly'k-shtrohm, m direct current

gleichzeitig, gly'k-tsy-tik, adj at the same time

Gleis, gly's, nt rails, track; platform

gleiten, gly-ten, v to glide, to slide

Gleitzeit, gly't-tsite, f flexitime

Gletscher, glet-sher, m glacier

Glied, gleet, nt limb; joint; link

gliedern, gleed-ern, v to order, to structure

glimmen, glim-en, v to glimmer, to glow

glimpflich, glimp-flik, adj moderate, indulgent

glitzern, glit-sern, v to glitter, to sparkle

global, gloh-bahl, adj global

Glocke, glock-e, f bell

Glockenblume, glock-en-bloom-e, f bluebell

Glockenspiel, glock-en-shpeel, nt chimes; mus glockenspiel

glotzen, glot-sen, to stare

Glück, glEEck, nt (good) fortune, (good) luck; chance; happiness; – **haben,** v to be lucky

glücken, glEEck-en v to succeed

glücklich, glEEck-lik, adj fortunate; happy; –**erweise,** adv fortunately

Glücksspiel, glEEcks-shpeel, nt game of chance

Glückwunsch, glEEck-voonsh, m congratulation

glühen, glEE-en, v to glow; to make red-hot

Glühbirne, glEE-beern-e, f light bulb

Glut, gloot, f glow; heat; ardour

GmbH, gay em bay hah, abbr limited company

Gnade, g'nah-de, f grace; mercy, leniency, favour

gnädig, g'nayd-ik, adj gracious, merciful, lenient

Gold, golt, nt gold

golden, gol-den, adj golden, made of gold

Goldfisch, golt-fish, m goldfish

Golf, golf, m gulf; nt golf; –**platz,** m golf course

gönnen, gern-en, v not to grudge

Gönner, gern-er, m wellwisher, patron, protector

Gosse, goss-e, f gutter

Gott, got, m God, god, idol

Gottesdienst, got-es-deenst, m service, mass

Gottheit, got-hite, f deity

Göttin, gert-in, f goddess

göttlich, gert-lik, adj divine, godlike; funny, amusing

gottlob, got-lohp, interj thank God, thank goodness

Götze, gert-se, m idol

Grab, grahp, nt grave, tomb

Graben, grah-ben, m ditch, trench

graben, grah-ben, v to dig

Grabstein, grahp-shtine, m gravestone, tombstone

Grad, graht, m degree; grade

Graf, grahf, m count, earl

Grafschaft, grahf-shahft, f county, shire; earldom

Gram, grahm, m grief, sorrow, sadness

grämen (sich), gray-men (zik), v to grieve

Gramm, grahmm, nt gram(me)

Grammatik, grahmm-ahtt-ik, f grammar

Granate, grahnn-aht-e, f shell, grenade

Gras, grahs, nt grass

grasen, grah-zen, v to graze

Grashalm, grahs-hahlm, m blade of grass

grassieren, grahss-eer-en, v to be rife/rampant

gräßlich, gress-lik, adj horrible, awful, terrible

Grat, graht, m sharp edge

Gräte, grayt-e, f fish-bone

gratis, grah-tis, adj free (of charge)

gratulieren (zu), graht-oo-leer-en (tsoo), v to congratulate (on)

grau, grow, adj grey

Grauen, grow-en, nt fear, dread, horror

grauenhaft, grow-en-hahft, adj sinister, horrible

grauhaarig, grow-hahr-ik, adj grey-haired

grausam, grow-zahm, adj cruel, barbarous, inhuman

gravieren, grahv-eer-en, v to engrave

graziös, grah-tsee-erss, adj graceful

greifen, gry-fen, v to seize

Greis, grice, m very old man

grell, grel, adj shrill, harsh, piercing; glaring, gaudy

Grenze, grent-se, f border,

frontier; limit, edge

grenzen, grent-sen, v to border, to verge

Grenzkontrolle, grents-kon-troll-e, f border control

Greuel, groy-el, m horror, abomination; atrocity

Grieche, gree-ke, m Greek (man)

Griechenland, gree-ken-lahnt, nt Greece

Griechin, gree-kin, f Greek (woman)

griechisch, gree-kish, adj Greek

Grieß, greess, m grit, gravel; semolina

Griff, grif, m grip, seizure, capture; handle

Grill, grill, m barbecue

Grille, grill-e, f cricket

grillen, grill-en, v to grill

Grimm, grim, m anger, fury

grimmig, grim-ik, adj furious; fierce

grinsen, grin-zen, v to grin

Grippe, grip-e, f flu

grob, grohp, adj rude, coarse, uncouth

Grobheit, grope-hite, f rudeness, coarseness

Groll, groll, m resentment, grudge, malice

grollen, groll-en, v to rumble; to have a grudge

groß, grohs, adj great, big, large, spacious; tall

großartig, grohs-art-ik, adj grand, sublime

Großbritannien, grohs-brit-

ahn-ee-en, nt Great Britain

Größe, grers-e, f greatness; size

Großeltern, grohs-elt-ern, pl grandparents

großenteils, grohs-en-tiles, adv to a large extent

Großhandel, grohs-hahnd-el, m wholesale (trade)

großjährig, grohs-yair-ik, adj of age; major

Großmacht, grohs-mahkt, f power(ful nation)

Großmut, grohs-moot, f generosity

Großmutter, grohs-moott-er, f grandmother

Großstadt, grohs-shtahtt, f large town/city

größtenteils, grerst-en-tiles, adv chiefly, mostly

Großvater, grohs-faht-er, m grandfather

großziehen, grohs-tsee-en, v to rear, to bring up

großzügig, grohs-tsEEg-ik, adj on a grand scale

Grübchen, grEEp-ken, nt dimple

Grube, groob-e, f pit, mine; hollow, cavity

grübeln, grEEb-eln, v to brood, to ponder

Gruft, grooft, f tomb, vault

grün, grEEn, adj green

Grund, groont, m ground; soil; bottom (of sea); cause, reason; **–besitz,** m property

gründen, grEEnn-den, v to

found, to establish

Gründer, grEEn-der, *m* founder

Grundgesetz, groont-ge-zets, *nt* (German) Constitution

Grundlage, groont-lahg-e, *f* elements, rudiments

gründlich, grEEnt-lik, *adj* solid, profound; thorough

Grundriß, groont-riss, *m* ground plan; sketch

Grundsatz, groont-zahts, *m* principle; axiom

Grundschule, groont-shool-e, *f* primary school

Grundstein, groont-shtine, *m* foundation stone

Grundstück, groont-shtEEk, *nt* plot (of land)

Gründung, grEEnn-doong, *f* foundation

grunzen, groont-sen, *v* to grunt

Gruppe, groopp-e, *f* group, clump, cluster; **–nermäßigung,** *f* group discount

gruselig, grooz-el-ik, *adj* ghastly, shuddering

Gruß, groos, *m* greeting, regard(s); **viele Grüße,** best wishes; **Grüße an,** regards to

grüßen, grEEs-en, *v* to greet, to salute

gucken, goock-en, *v* to look, to peep

Gulasch, gool-ahsh, *nt* goulash

Gulden, goold-en, *m* florin; Dutch guilder

gültig, gEElt-ik, *adj* valid, current; legal, legitimate

Gültigkeit, gEElt-ik-kite, *f* validity

Gummi, goomm-ee, *m & nt* rubber; gum; **–band,** *nt* elastic band; **–reifen,** *m* tyre; **–stiefel,** *m* rubber boot; wellington

Gunst, goonst, *f* favour, kindness, goodwill

günstig, gEEnst-ik, *adj* favourable, advantageous

Gurgel, goorg-el, *f* throat, gullet

gurgeln, goorg-eln, *v* to gargle, to gurgle

Gurke, goork-e, *f* cucumber; **saure –,** gherkin

Gurt, goort, *m* girth, girdle; belt, strap

Gürtel, gEErt-el, *m* girdle, belt

Guß, gooss, *m* pouring; shower, downpour; icing; founding; casting

Gußeisen, gooss-ize-en, *nt* cast-iron

gußeisern, gooss-ize-ern, *adj* made of cast-iron

gut, goot, *adj* good; *adv* well

Gut, goot, *nt* commodity, goods; farm; possession

Gutachten, goot-ahk-ten, *nt* expert opinion

Gutdünken, goot-dEEng-ken, *nt* judgment, opinion

Güte, gEEt-e, *f* goodness, kindness, virtue; quality

Güterbahnhof, gEEt-er-bahn-hof, *m* goods-station

Güterzug, gEEt-er-tsoog, *m* goods train

Guthaben, goot-hahb-en, *nt* credit

gutheißen, goot-hice-en, *v* to approve, to sanction

gütig, gEEt-ik, *adj* gracious, good-hearted

gutmütig, goot-mEEt-ik, *adj* good-natured

Gutschein, goot-shine, *m* voucher; credit note

gutschreiben, goot-shry-ben, *v* to credit (to)

gutwillig, goot-vill-ik, *adj* obliging, willing

Gymnasium, gim-nahz-yoom, *nt* grammar school

H

Haag, hahg, **Den –,** *nt* The Hague

Haar, hahr, *nt* hair; **–festiger,** *m* setting lotion; **–nadel,** *f* hairpin; **–schnitt,** *m* haircut, hairstyle; **–spange,** *f* hairslide

haarsträubend, hahr-shtroyb-ent, *adj* shocking, hair-raising

Habe, hah-be, *f* property, possession(s), fortune, belongings

haben, hah-ben, *v* to have

Habgier, hahp-geer, *f* avarice, greed

Habicht, hahb-ikt, *m* hawk

Habseligkeiten, hahp-zail-ik-kite-en, *pl* possessions, belongings; effects

Habsucht, hahp-sookt, *f* avarice, greed

Hacke, hahck-e, *f* hoe, pick-axe; heel

hacken, hahck-en, *v* to pick, to peck; to hack

Hafen, hahf-en, *m* port, harbour; **–stadt,** *f* port

Hafer, hahf-er, *m* oats

Haferbrei, hahf-er-bry, *m* porridge

Haft, hahft, *f* detention, confinement, imprisonment

Haftbefehl, hahft-be-fail, *m* warrant for arrest

haften, hahft-en, *v* to adhere, to be fixed to

Haftpflicht, hahft-pflikt, *f* liability, responsibility

Haftung, haft-oong, *f* liability; adhesion

Hagel, hahg-el, *m* hail; shower (e.g. of stones)

hageln, hahg-eln, *v* to hail

hager, hahg-er, *adj* haggard; lean, thin; slender

Hahn, hahn, *m* cock(-erel), rooster; tap

Hähnchen, hain-ken, *nt* chicken

Hai, hy, *m* shark

häkeln, hay-keln, *v* to crochet

Haken, hahk-en, *m* hook; peg; crook; **–kreuz,** *nt* swastika

halb, hahlp, *adj* half

halber, hahlb-er, *prep* owing to, on account of

halbieren, hahll-beer-en, *v* to halve, to divide into halves

Halbinsel, hahlb-in-zel, *f* peninsula

halbjährlich, hahlp-yair-lik, *adj* half-yearly; bi-annual

Halbkreis, hahlp-krice, *m* semi-circle

Halbkugel, hahlp-koog-el, *f* hemisphere

Halbpension, hahlp-pents-yohn, *f* half-board

halbstündlich, hahlp-shtEEnt-lik, *adj* half-hourly

halbwegs, hahlp-vaiks, *adv* tolerably, half-way

Halbzeit, hahlp-tsite, *f* half time

Hälfte, helf-te, *f* half

Halle, hahll-e, *f* hall; covered area; gallery

hallen, hahll-en, *v* to (re)sound

Hallenbad, hahll-en-baht, *nt* indoor swimming pool

Halm, hahlm, *m* blade, stalk

Hals, hahls, *m* neck, throat

Halsband, hahlls-bahnt, *nt* necklace, collar

Halsschmerzen, hahls-shmairt-sen, *pl* sore throat

halsstarrig, hahls-shtar-rik, *adj* stubborn

Halstuch, hahls-took, *nt* scarf

Halsweh, hahls-vay, *nt* sore throat

Halt, hahlt, *m* halt, stop; stability; firmness

haltbar, hahlt-bar, *adj* durable, solid, firm

Haltbarkeit, hahlt-bahr-kite, *f* durability

halten, hahlt-en, *v* to hold; to stop; to keep

Haltestelle, hahlt-e-shtell-e, *f* (bus/tram) stop

Halteverbot, hahlt-te-fer-boht, *nt* no stopping

Haltung, hahlt-oong, *f* bearing, carriage; conduct

Halunke, hahll-oonk-e, *m* scoundrel, rogue, ruffian

hämisch, hay-mish, *adj* spiteful, malicious

Hammel, hahmm-el, *m* mutton

Hammelbraten, hahmm-el-braht-en, *m* roast mutton

Hammelfleisch, hahmm-el-fly'sh, *nt* mutton

Hammer, hahmm-er, *m* hammer

hämmern, hemm-ern, *v* to hammer, to forge

Hamster, hahmm-ster, *m* hamster; hoarder

Hand, hahnt, *f* hand

Handarbeit, hahnt-ahr-bite, *f* needlework; manual work

Handbremse, hahnt-bremm-ze, *f* hand brake

Handel, hahnn-del, *m* trade; transaction

handeln, hahnn-deln, *v* to trade; to act, to proceed; to bargain, to deal; **sich um etw —,** to be about sth

Handelsbilanz, hahnd-els-bee-lants, *f* balance of trade

Handelskammer, hahnd-els-kahmm-er, *f* chamber of commerce

Handelsschule, hahnd-els-shool-e, *f* business school

handfest, hahnnt-fest, *adj* sturdy, stalwart, strong

Handfläche, hahnnt-flek-e, *f* palm (of hand)

Handgelenk, hahnnt-ge-lenk, *nt* wrist

Handgepäck, hahnnt-ge-peck, *nt* hand luggage

handgeschrieben, hahnnt-ge-shreeb-en, *adj* handwritten

handgreiflich, hahnnt-grife-lik, *adj* violent

Handgriff, hahnnt-grif, *m* grip; manipulation

handhaben, hahnnt-hahb-en, *v* to handle

Handkoffer, hahnnt-kof-er, *m* suitcase

Händler, hend-ler-, *m* trader, dealer

Handlung, hahnd-loong, *f* action; deed; shop

Handschelle, hahnt-shell-e, *f* handcuff

Handschrift, hahnt-shrift, *f* handwriting

Handschuh, hahnt-shoo, *m* glove

Handtasche, hahnt-tahsh-e, *f* handbag

Handtuch, hahnt-took, *nt* towel

Handwerk, hahnt-vairk, *nt* (handi)craft; trade

Handwerker, hahnt-vairk-er, *m* craftsman

Handy, hand-i, *nt* mobile phone

Hanf, hahnf, *m* hemp

Hang, hahng, *m* incline; slope; inclination

Hängebrücke, heng-e-brEEck-e, *f* suspension-bridge

Hängematte, heng-e-mahtt-e, *f* hammock

hängen, heng-en, *v* to hang, to suspend

Hanswurst, hahns-voorst, *m* buffoon, clown

Hantel, hahnt-el, *f* dumbbell

hantieren, hahnt-eer-en, *v* to handle, to manipulate

Happen, hahpp-en, *m* mouthful, morsel, bit

Harfe, harf-e, *f* harp

Harke, hark-e, *f* rake

harken, hark-en, *v* to rake

harmlos, harm-lohs, *adj*

harmless; innocuous

harmonisch, hahr-**mo**-nish, *adj* harmonious

Harn, harn, m urine

harren (auf), har-ren (owf), *v* to wait (for)

hart, hart, *adj* hard, firm, solid, severe

Härte, hairt-e, f hardness; hardiness; roughness

härten, hairt-en, v to harden; to temper (iron)

hartgekocht, hart-*ge*-kokt, *adj* hard-boiled

hartherzig, hart-hairt-sik, *adj* hard-hearted

hartnäckig, hart-neck-ik, *adj* stubborn, stiff-necked; chronic

Harz, harts, nt resin, rosin, gum

Haschisch, hahsh-ish, nt hashish

Hase, hah-ze, m hare

Haselnuß, hah-zel-nooss, f hazel-nut

Haß, hahss, m hate, hatred

hassen, hahss-en, v to hate

häßlich, hess-lik, *adj* ugly; hideous

Häßlichkeit, hess-lik-kite, f ugliness

Hast, hahst, f haste, hurry

hasten, hahst-en, v to hasten, to hurry

hastig, hahst-ik, *adj* hasty, hurried

Haube, howb-e, f woman's bonnet; crest

Hauch, howk, m breath, exhalation

hauchen, howk-en, v to breathe, to exhale

Haue, how-e, f *fam* beating, spanking

hauen, how-en, v to beat; to hew, to cut

Haufen, howf-en, m heap, group, mass; crowd

häufen, hoyf-en, v to heap (up), to accumulate; **sich —,** to mount up

haufenweise, howf-en-vy-ze, *adv fam* in heaps

häufig, hoyf-ik, *adj* frequent; numerous; usual

Haupt, howpt, nt head; chief(tain); **Haupt–** *pref* principal, main

Hauptbahnhof, howpt-bahn-hohf, m main station

Hauptdarsteller, howpt-dahr-shtell-er, m leading actor

Hauptgericht, howpt-*ge*-rikt, nt main course

Häuptling, hoypt-ling, m chieftain, captain

Hauptmann, howpt-mahnn, m captain

Hauptquartier, howpt-kvart-eer, nt headquarters

Hauptrolle, howpt-roll-e, f leading part

Hauptsache, howpt-sahk-e, f main thing

hauptsächlich, howpt-sek-lik, *adj* principal

Hauptsaison, howpt-say-zong, f high season

Hauptspeise, howpt-shpy-ze, f main course

Hauptstadt, howpt-shtahtt, f capital, metropolis

Hauptstraße, howpt-shtrahss-e, f main street

Hauptverkehrszeit, howpt-fer-kairs-tsite, f rush hour

Hauptwort, howpt-vort, nt noun, substantive

Haus, howss, nt house

Hausarbeit, hows-ahr-byt, f housework; homework

Hausarzt, hows-artst, m family doctor

Häuserblock, hoy-zer-block, m block (of houses)

Hausflur, hows-floohr, m (entrance-)hall

Hausfrau, hows-frow, f housewife

Haushalt, hows-hahlt, m household

haushalten, hows-hahlt-en, v to keep house

Haushälterin, hows-helt-er-in, f housekeeper

Hausherr, hows-hairr, m master of the house

hausieren, howz-eer-en, v to hawk, to peddle

Hausierer, howz-eer-er, m pedlar, hawker

häuslich, hoys-lik, *adj* domestic(ated)

Hausmeister, hows-myst-er, m caretaker

Hausnummer, hows-noomm-er, f house number

Hausschuh, hows-shoo, m slipper

Hausschlüssel, hows-shlEEss-el, *m* front-door key

Haustier, hows-teer, *nt* pet

Haustür, hows-tEEr, *f* front door

Hauswirt, hows-veert, *m* landlord

**Haut, howt, *f* skin, hide, coat; peel

häuten, hoyt-en, *v* to skin, to flay

Hautfarbe, howt-fahr-be, *f* skin colour; complexion

Hebamme, haip-ahmm-e, *f* midwife

Hebel, hay-bel, *m* lever

heben, hay-ben, *v* to lift, to raise

hebräisch, heb-ray-ish, *adj* Hebrew

Hebriden, heb-ree-den, *pl* Hebrides

**Hecht, hekt, *m* pike, jack

Hecke, heck-e, *f* hedge(-row); thorny bushes

**Heer, hair, *nt* army; legion; **–führer, *m* commander (-in-chief)

Hefe, hayf-e, *f* yeast

**Heft, heft, *nt* exercise-book; knife-handle

heften, heft-en, *v* to fasten, to stick; to stitch

heftig, heft-ik, *adj* violent, vehement

Heftpflaster, heft-pflahst-er, *nt* (sticking) plaster

hegen, hayg-en, *v* to preserve; to cherish

Heide, hy-de, *f* heath,

common; *m* heathen

Heidekraut, hy-de-krowt, *nt* heather

Heidelbeere, hy-del-bair-e, *f* bilberry

Heidentum, hy-den-toom, *nt* paganism

heidnisch, hide-nish, *adj* pagan

heikel, hy-kel, *adj* delicate, tricky; awkward

**heil, hile, *adj* sound, whole, intact; cured

Heiland, hy-lahnt, *m* Saviour, Redeemer

heilbar, hile-bahr, *adj* curable

Heilbutt, hile-boott, *m* halibut

heilen, hile-en, *v* to heal, to cure

heilig, hile-ik, *adj* holy, sacred, hallowed, saintly

Heiligabend, hile-ig-ahb-ent, *m* Christmas Eve

Heilige(r), hile-ig-e(r), *m &* *f* saint

Heiligenbild, hile-ig-en-bilt, *nt* image of a saint

Heiligenschein, hile-ig-en-shine, *m* halo

Heiligtum, hile-ik-toom, *nt* sanctuary, sanctum

heilkräftig, hile-kreft-ik, *adj* curative, healing

heillos, hile-lohs, *adj* hopeless; frightful

Heilmittel, hile-mitt-el, *nt* remedy; cure

Heilpraktiker, hile-prahck-tik-er, *m* non-medical

practitioner

heilsam, hile-zahm, *adj* wholesome, beneficial

Heilsarmee, hiles-arm-ay, *f* Salvation Army

Heilung, hile-oong, *f* cure

**Heim, hime, *nt* home

Heimat, hime-aht, *f* home; native place

heimatlos, hime-aht-lohs, *adj* homeless

Heimcomputer, hime-kom-pyu-ter, *m* home computer

Heimfahrt, hime-fahrt, *f* homeward journey

Heimkehr, hime-kair, *f* return home

heimlich, hime-lik, *adj* secret, clandestine

Heimreise, hime-ry-ze, *f* journey home

heimsuchen, hime-sook-en, *v* to afflict

heimtückisch, hime-tEEck-ish, *adj* treacherous, spiteful

Heimweg, hime-vaik, *m* way home

Heimweh, hime-vay, *nt* home-sickness, nostalgia

Heirat, hy-raht, *f* marriage

heiraten, hy-raht-en, *v* to marry, to get married

Heiratsantrag, hy-rahts-ahn-trahk, *m* (marriage) proposal

heiser, hy-zer, *adj* hoarse, husky, raucous

**heiß, hice, *adj* hot

heißen, hy-sen, *v* to call; to be called; to name; to bid;

to signify

Heißhunger, hice-hoong-er, *m* ravenous appetite

heiter, hite-er, *adj* bright, serene, clear; cheerful, gay

Heiterkeit, hite-er-kite, *f* cheerfulness

heizen, hite-sen, *v* to heat, to light a fire

Heizkörper, hites-ker-per, *m* radiator

Heizung, hites-oong, *f* heating

hektisch, heck-tish, *adj* hectic

Held, helt, *m* hero; champion

helfen, help-en, *v* to help, to aid; to promote; to support

Helfer, help-er, *m* helper

Helfershelfer, hel-fers-helfer, *m* accomplice

hell, hel, *adj* clear; shrill; bright; brilliant; light

Helle, hel-e, *f* clearness, brightness, brilliance

Hellseher, hel-zay-er, *m* clairvoyant

Helm, helm, *m* helmet; *m & nt* helm, rudder

Hemd, hemt, *nt* shirt

hemmen, hem-en, *v* to stop, to check, to impede

Hemmung, hem-oong, *f* inhibition

Hengst, hengst, *m* stallion

Henkel, heng-kel, *m* handle

Henker, heng-ker, *m* hangman, executioner

Henne, hen-e, *f* hen, fowl

her, hair, *adv* here

herab, hair-ahp, *adv* down(wards)

herablassen (sich), hair-ahp-lahss-en (zik), *v* to condescend

heran, hair-ahnn, *adv* this way, near this place

heranwachsen, hair-ahnn-vahks-en, *v* to grow up

herauf, hair-owf, *adv* up(ward), up here; uphill

heraus, hair-owss, *adv* out of

herausfordern, hair-ows-ford-ern, *v* to challenge

herausgeben, hair-ows-gaib-en, *v* to hand over; to give in change; to publish

herausstellen (sich), hair-ows-shtel-en (zik), *v* to prove to be, to turn out to be

herb, hairp, *adj* harsh, acrid; sharp, bitter

herbei, hair-by, *adv* hither, here, this way

herbeiführen, hair-by-fEEr-en, *v* to bring about

Herberge, hair-bairg-e, *f* shelter; lodging; hostel

Herbst, hairpst, *m* autumn

herbstlich, hairpst-lik, *adj* autumnal

Herd, hairt, *m* hearth; oven

Herde, haird-e, *f* herd, flock

herein, hair-ine, *adv* in(to) this place; come in!

hereinfallen, hair-ine-fahll-en, *v* to be cheated

hereinkommen, hair-ine-kohmm-en, *v* to come in

hereinlegen, hair-ine-laig-en, *v* to put in(to); to swindle

Herfahrt, hair-fahrt, *f* journey here

hergeben, hair-gaib-en, *v* to give up, to hand over

Hering, hair-ing, *m* herring

herkommen, hair-kom-en, *v* to come here

Herkunft, hair-koonft, *f* arrival; descent, origin

Herr, hairr, *m* master, lord; Mr, sir; Lord; **–entoilette,** *f* men's toilet

herrichten, hair-rik-ten, *v* to prepare, to set in order

herrisch, hair-rish, *adj* domineering

herrlich, hair-lik, *adj* magnificent, delightful

Herrschaft, hair-shahft, *f* dominion, rule

herrschen, hair-shen, *v* to rule

Herrscher, hair-sher, *m* ruler, sovereign

herrühren, hair-rEEr-en, *v* to originate from

herstellen, hair-shtel-en, *v* to produce

Hersteller, hair-shtel-er, *m* producer; manufacturer

Herstellung, hair-shtel-oong, *f* production; manufacture

herüber, hair-EEb-er, *adv* over here; across

herum, hair-oomm, *adv* (a)round, round about

herumkommen, hair-**oomm**-kom-en, *v* to get round (places)

herunter, hair-**oonnt**-er, *adv* down(wards)

hervor, hair-**for**, *adv* forward, forth

hervorbringen, hair-**for**-bring-en, *v* to bring out/forth

hervorgehen, hair-**for**-gay-en, *v* to result from

hervorheben, hair-**for**-haib-en, *v* to accentuate, to emphasize

hervorragend, hair-**for**-rahg-ent, *adj* prominent; eminent; distinguished

hervorrufen, hair-**for**-roof-en, *v* to cause

hervortreten, hair-**for**-trait-en, *v* to step forward; to stand out (in relief)

Herz, hairts, *nt* heart

herzhaft, hairts-hahft, *adj* bold; hearty

Herzinfarkt, hairts-in-fahrkt, *m* heart attack

Herzklopfen, hairts-klohpf-en, *nt* palpitations

herzlich, hairts-lik, *adj* cordial, heartfelt, sincere; **–en Dank,** many thanks; **–en Glückwunsch,** congratulations; **–e Grüße,** best wishes

Herzog, hairt-sohk, *m* duke

Herzschlag, hairts-shlahk, *m* heart-beat; apoplexy

Hetze, het-se, *f* hunt; rush; hurry

hetzen, het-sen, *v* to hound; to rush; to hurry

Hetzerei, het-se-ry, *f* rushing

Heu, hoy, *nt* hay

Heuchelei, hoy-kel-ly, *f* hypocrisy; sham; cant

heucheln, hoy-keln, *v* to feign; to simulate

heuchlerisch, hoyk-ler-ish, *adj* hypocritical

heuer, hoy-er, *adv* this year

heulen, hoyl-en, *v* to howl, to roar, to shriek

heurig, hoy-rik, *adj* this year's

Heuschnupfen, hoy-shnoopf-en, *m* hay fever

Heuschrecke, hoy-shreck-e, *f* grasshopper

heute, hoyt-e, *adv* today; **– früh/abend,** this morning/evening

heutig, hoyt-ik, *adj* today's; of this day; present

heutzutage, hoyt-tsoo-tahg-e, *adv* nowadays

Hexe, hex-e, *f* witch, sorceress, enchantress

hexen, hex-en, *v* to practise magic/witchcraft

Hieb, heep, *m* stroke, blow, cuff, smack

hier, heer, *adv* here

hierauf, heer-owf, *adv* hereon, hereupon

hierbei, heer-by, *adv* herewith, hereby; enclosed

hierbleiben, heer-bly-ben, *v* to stay here

hierher, heer-**hair**, *adv* here (hither)

hierhin, heer-**hin**, *adv* here (hither)

hierlassen, heer-lahss-en, *v* to leave here

hierzulande, heer-tsoo-lahnn-de, *adv* in this country

hiesig, hee-zik, *adj* in this place/town

Hilfe, hilf-e, *f* help, aid, assistance, relief, support

hilflos, hilf-lohs, *adj* helpless

hilfreich, hilf-ry'k, *adj* helpful; charitable

Hilfskraft, hilfs-krahft, *f* assistant

Hilfsmittel, hilfs-mit-el, *nt* remedy, help; expedient

Himbeere, him-bair-e, *f* raspberry

Himmel, him-el, *m* heaven; sky; **–bett,** *nt* bed with canopy; **–fahrt,** *f* Ascension; **–reich,** *nt* kingdom of heaven; **–srichtung,** *f* direction; point of compass

himmlisch, him-lish, *adj* heavenly, divine

hin, hin, *adv* there; along; down; **– und zurück,** there and back

hinab, hin-ahpp, *adv* down (there), downwards)

hinauf, hin-owf, *adv* up (there)

hinaus, hin-owss, *adv* out (there); **–gehen,** *v* to go (there) out; to leave; **–werfen,** *v* to throw out

hinderlich, hin-der-lik, *adj* obstructive

hindern, hin-dern, *v* to hinder, to prevent

Hindernis, hin-der-niss, *nt* hindrance

hindeuten, hin-doyt-en, *v* to point to

hindurch, hin-**doohrk,** *adv* through(out)

hinein, hin-**ein,** *adv* into, in(side); **–gehen,** *v* to go in(to); **–passen,** *v* to fit in

hinfahren, hin-fahr-en, *v* to drive to a place

Hinfahrt, hin-fahrt, *f* outward journey

hinfallen, hin-fahll-en, *v* to fall down

hinfällig, hin-fel-ik, *adj* invalid; untenable

Hingabe, hin-gahb-e, *f* devotion

hingeben (sich), hin-gayb-en (zik), *v* to devote (o.s.)

hingegen, hin-**gayg**-en, *adv* on the other hand; on the contrary

hingerissen, hin-ge-ris-en, *adj* carried away

hinhalten, hin-hallt-en, *v* to hold out; to put off

hinken, hin-ken, *v* to limp

hinkommen, hin-kom-en, *v* to reach/get to a place

hinlegen, hin-layg-en, *v* to lay down; to put down; **sich —,** *v* to lie down

hinreichend, hin-ry'k-ent,

adj adequate, sufficient

Hinreise, hin-ry-ze, *f* outward journey

hinreißen, hin-ry-sen, *v* to tear along; to carry away

hinrichten, hin-rik-ten, *v* to execute

Hinrichtung, hin-rik-toong, *f* execution

hinschaffen, hin-shahff-en, *v* to convey there

hinsetzen, hin-zets-en, *v* to put down; **sich —,** *v* to sit down

hinsichtlich, hin-zikt-lik, *prep* with regard to

hinten, hint-en, *adv* behind; at the back

hinter, hint-er, *prep* behind

Hinterbliebene(r), hint-er-**bleeb**-en-e(r), *m & f* bereaved person

hintereinander, hint-er-ine-ahnd-er, *adv* one after the other

hintergehen, hint-er-gay-en, *v* to deceive, to dupe

Hintergrund, hint-er-groont, *m* background

Hinterhalt, hint-er-halt, *m* ambush

hinterher, hint-er-**hair,** *adv* behind; afterwards

hinterlassen, hint-er-**lahss**-en, *v* to bequeath; to leave behind

hinterlegen, hint-er-**laig**-en, *v* to deposit

Hinterlist, hint-er-list, *f* cunning, deception, fraud

Hinterrad, hint-er-raht, *nt*

rear wheel

hinterrücks, hint-er-**rEEcks,** *adv* from behind

hinüber, hin-**EEb**-er, *adv* over (there), across

hin und her, hin oont hair, *adv* to and fro

hinunter, hin-**oonnt**-er, *adv* down(wards); downstairs

Hinweg, hin-veeck, *m* the way there

hinweg, hin-**veck,** *adv* away

Hinweis, hin-vice, *m* reference; indication

hinweisen (auf), hin-vy-zen (owf), *v* to point (to); to indicate

hinziehen (sich), hin-tsee-en (zik), *v* to drag on

hinzu, hin-**tsoo,** *adv* to (a place); in addition

hinzufügen, hin-**tsoo-fEEg**-en, *v* to add to

hinzuziehen, hin-**tsoo-tsee**-en, *v* to consult

Hirn, heern, *nt* brain

hirnverbrannt, heern-**fair**-brahnt, *adj* crazy

Hirsch, heersh, *m* stag

Hirt, heert, *m* shepherd, herdsman

hissen, his-en, *v* to hoist

Historiker, his-**tohr**-ik-er, *m* historian

historisch, his-**tohr**-ish, *adj* historical

Hitze, hit-se, *f* heat, warmth

hitzig, hit-sik, *adj* hot (-headed), hasty, impetuous

Hitzkopf, hits-kopp'f, *m*

hot-headed person

Hitzschlag, hits-shlahk, *m* heat-stroke, sunstroke

H-Milch, hah-milk, *f* long-life milk

Hobby, hobb-ee, *nt* hobby

Hobel, hobb-el, *m* (wood) plane

hobeln, hobb-eln, *v* to plane

Hobelspäne, hobb-el-shpay-ne, *pl* (wood) shavings

hoch, hohk, *adj* high, elevated, lofty

Hochachtung, hohk-ahk-toong, *f* respect, (high) esteem

hochachtungsvoll, hohk-ahk-toongs-foll, *adv* faithfully

Hochamt, hohk-ahmt, *nt* High Mass

Hochbetrieb, hohk-be-treep, *m* peak period

hochdeutsch, hohk-doytsh, *adj* high German

hochgradig, hohk-grahd-ik, *adj* absolute; utter

hochhalten, hohk-hahlt-en, *v* to hold up

Hochhaus, hohk-hows, *nt* high-rise block

Hochkonjunktur, hohk-kon-yoonkt-oor, *f* economic boom

Hochmut, hohk-moot, *m* haughtiness, pride

hochmütig, hohk-mEEt-ik, *adj* haughty, proud

hochnäsig, hohk-nay-zik, *adj* arrogant

Hochsaison, hohk-zay-zohn, *f* high season

Hochschule, hohk-shool-e, *f* university; college

Hochsommer, hohk-zom-er, *m* midsummer

Hochsprung, hohk-hproong, *m* high jump

höchst, herkst, *adv* highest; extremely

Hochstapler, hohk-shtahp-ler, *m* con man

höchstens, herk-stens, *adv* at the most

Höchstgeschwindigkeit, herkst-ge-shvind-ik-kite, *f* maximum speed

Hochverrat, hohk-fair-raht, *m* high treason

Hochwasser, hohk-vahss-er, *nt* high tide; flood

Hochzeit, hohk-tsite, *f* wedding, marriage

Hochzeitsreise, hohk-tsites-ry-ze, *f* honeymoon

hocken, hock-en, *v* to squat

Hocker, hock-er, *m* stool

Höcker, herck-er, *m* knob; bump; hump; hunch

Hoden, hohd-en, *m* testicle

Hof, hohf, *m* court(yard); farm

hoffen, hof-en, *v* to hope, to expect, to await

hoffentlich, hof-ent-lik, *adv* hopefully

Hoffnung, hof-noong, *f* hope, expectation

höflich, herf-lik, *adj* polite, courteous; courtly

Höflichkeit, herf-lik-kite, *f* politeness, courtesy

Höhe, her-e, *f* height, altitude; level; *mus* pitch

Höhepunkt, her-e-poonkt, *m* high point; peak

höher, her-er, *adj & adv* higher

hohl, hohl, *adj* hollow(ed out); concave

Höhle, herl-e, *f* cave(rn), hole, burrow; hovel

Hohlmaß, hohl-mahs, *nt* measure of capacity; dry measure

Hohn, hohn, *m* scorn, derision; sneer

höhnisch, hern-ish, *adj* scornful; sneering, mocking

holen, hohl-en, *v* to fetch, to come for

Holland, hol-ahnt, *nt* Holland

Holländer, hol-end-er, *m* Dutchman; **–in,** *f* Dutchwoman

holländisch, hol-end-ish, *adj* Dutch

Hölle, herll-e, *f* hell, inferno; limbo

höllisch, herll-ish, *adj* hellish, diabolical, infernal

holperig, holp-er-ik, *adj* uneven, rough, rugged

Holunder, hohl-oond-er, *m* elder

Holz, holts, *nt* wood; timber; grove

hölzern, herlt-sern, *adj* wooden; clumsy, stiff

Holzkohle, holts-kohl-e, *f*

charcoal

Holzschnitt, holts-shnit, *m*
wood-carving

Homöopathie, hohm-er-oh-paht-**ee**, *f* homeopathy

homosexuell, hoh-moh-sex-oo-**el**, *adj* homosexual

Honig, hohn-ik, *m* honey

Honorar, on-ohr-**ar**, *nt*
(professional) fee

honorieren, hon-oh-**reer**-en, *v* to remunerate

Hopfen, hop-fen, *m* hop
(-plant), hops

hopsen, hop-sen, *v* to hop,
to skip

horchen, hork-en, *v* to
listen

Horde, hord-e, *f* horde,
wandering tribe; band

hören, her-ren, *v* to hear; to
listen to

Hörer, her-er, *m* listener;
(telephone) receiver

Horizont, hoh-ree-**tsont**, *m*
horizon

Hormon, hor-**mohn**, *nt*
hormone

Horn, horn, *nt* horn; *mus*
(French) horn

Hornhaut, horn-howt, *f*
horny skin; cornea

Hornisse, horn-**iss**-e, *f*
hornet

Horoskop, hor-oss-**kohp**, *nt*
horoscope

Hörsaal, her-zahl, *m*
lecture-hall

Hose, hoh-ze, *f* trousers,
breeches

Hosenträger, hohz-en-trayg-

er, *m* (pair of) braces

Hospiz, hos-**peets**, *nt*
hospice

Hostie, host-ye, *f* host;
consecrated wafer

Hotel, hoh-**tell**, *nt* hotel;
–verzeichnis, *nt* hotel
register

hübsch, hEEpsh, *adj* pretty;
polite; nice

Hubschrauber, hoop-
shrowb-er, *m* helicopter

Huf, hoof, *m* hoof

Hufeisen, hoof-ay-zen, *nt*
horseshoe

Hüfte, hEEft-e, *f* hip,
haunch

Hügel, hEEg-el, *m* hill,
hillock

hügelig, hEEg-el-ik, *adj* hilly

Huhn, hoon, *nt* hen,
chicken; fowl

Hühnerauge, hEEn-er-owg-
e, *nt med* corn

Hühnerbraten, hEEn-er-
braht-en, *m* roast chicken

Hühnerhof, hEEn-er-hohf,
m poultry farm

huldigen, hoold-ig-en, *v* to
render homage

Hülle, hEEl-e, *f* wrapping;
wrapper, covering;
garment

Hülle und Fülle, hEEl-e
oont **fEEl**-e, *f* abundance

hüllen, hEEl-en, *v* to wrap,
to envelop

Hülse, hEEl-ze, *f* husk, shell,
pod; **–nfrucht,** *f* pulse
(vegetable)

human, hoo-**mahn**, *adj*

humane

Hummel, hoomm-el, *f*
(bumble-)bee

Hummer, hoomm-er, *m*
lobster

Humor, hoo-**mohr**, *m*
humour; **–** **haben,** *v* to
have a sense of humour

humpeln, hoomp-eln, *v* to
limp, to hobble

Hund, hoont, *m* dog, hound

Hundehütte, hoond-e-
hEEtt-e, *f* dog-kennel

hundert, hoond-ert, *num*
hundred

hundertprozentig, hoond-
ert-pro-**tsent**-ik, *adj* one
hundred percent

Hündin, hEEnd-in, *f* bitch

Hüne, hEEn-e, *m* giant

Hunger, hoong-er, *m*
hunger; starvation;
famine; **–** **haben,** *v* to be
hungry

hungern, hoong-ern, *v* to
feel hungry; to be starving

Hungersnot, hoong-ers-
noht, *f* famine

hungrig, hoong-rik, *adj*
hungry; starving

Hupe, hoop-e, *f* car horn

hüpfen, hEEp-fen, *v* to hop,
to skip, to jump

Hürde, hEErd-e, *f* hurdle;
fold, pen

Hure, hoor-e, *f* whore

huschen, hoosh-en, *v* to
scurry, to whisk

husten, hoost-en, *v* to
cough

Husten, hoost-en, *m* cough;

–**saft**, *m* cough mixture

Hut, hoot, *m* hat

hüten, hEEt-*en*, *v* to guard, to watch over; **sich –,** *v* to be on one's guard

Hütte, hEEtt-*e*, *f* hut, cabin, cottage; foundry

Hyäne, he-**ayn**-*e*, *f* hyena

Hygiene, hee-gee-**ayn**-*e*, *f* hygiene

Hypothek, hip-oh-**take**, *f* mortgage

hysterisch, hist-**air**-ish, *adj* hysterical

I

IC, ee-tsay, *abbr* Intercity-Zug

ICE, ee-tsay-ay, *abbr* Intercity-Expreßzug

ich, ik, *pron* I, (*emphatic*) me

Ideal, ee-day-ahl, *nt* ideal

ideal, ee-day-ahl, *adj* ideal

idealistisch, ee-day-ahl-is-tish, *adj* idealistic

Idee, ee-day, *f* idea

identisch, ee-dent-ish, *adj* identical

Identität, ee-dent-ee-tayt, *f* identity

Idiot, ee-dee-oht, *m* idiot

idyllisch, ee-dEEll-ish, *adj* idyllic

Igel, eeg-el, *m* hedgehog

ihm, eem, *pron* (*dative m & nt*) (to) him; (to) it

ihn, een, *pron* (*accusative m*) him; it

ihnen, een-en, *pron* (*dative pl*) (to) them

Ihnen, een-en, *pron* (*dative*) (to) you

ihr, eer, *pron* (*pl & dative f*) (to) her; you

ihr, ihre(r/s), eer, eer-e(r/s), *adj* her; their; *pron* hers; theirs

Ihr, Ihre(r/s), eer, eer-e(r/s), *adj* your; *pron* yours

illegal, ill-e-gahl, *adj* illegal

illustrieren, ill-oos-treer-en, *v* to illustrate

Illustrierte, ill-oos-treert-e, *f* magazine

im (= in dem), im, in the

Imbiß, im-bis, *m* snack; –stube, *f* snack bar

immer, im-mer, *adv* always; continually; – mehr, more and more; – wieder, again and again; für –, for ever; –noch, still; – schlimmer, worse and worse

Immobilien, im-moh-bee-lee-en, *pl* property; –makler, *m* estate agent

impfen, imp-fen, *v* to vaccinate, to inoculate

Impfung, imp-foong, *f* vaccination

imponieren, im-pohn-eer-en, *v* to impress

Import, im-port, *m* import

importieren, im-port-eer-en, *v* to import

imposant, im-poh-zahnt, *adj* imposing

impotent, im-poh-tent, *adj* impotent

imstande, im-shtahnd-e, *adj* – sein, to be able (to)

in, in, *prep* in; at; to

Inbegriff, in-be-grif, *m* essence; inclusion

indem, in-daym, *conj* while, whilst; by, in

Inder, in-der, *m* Indian (person)

Indianer, in-dee-ahn-er, *m* American Indian

Indien, in-dee-en, *nt* India

indisch, in-dish, *adj* Indian

industrialisieren, in-doos-tree-ahl-ee-seer-en, *v* to industrialize

Industrie, in-doos-tree, *f* industry

ineinander, in-ine-ahnn-der, *adv* into one another

Infektion, in-fekts-yohn, *f* infection; –skrankheit, *f* infectious disease

infizieren, in-fee-tseer-en, *v* to infect

Inflation, in-flahts-yohn, *f*

inflation

infolge, in-**folg**-e, *prep* in consequence of

Informatik, in-for-**mah**-tik, *f* computer science

Information, in-for-mahts-**yohn**, *f* information

informieren, in-form-**eer**-en, *v* to inform

Ingenieur, in-zhayn-**yer**, *m* engineer

Ingwer, ing-ver, *m* ginger

Inhaber, in-**hahb**-er, *m* possessor; bearer; holder

Inhalt, in-hahlt, *m* content; –**sverzeichnis,** *nt* table of contents

Initiative, in-ee-tsee-ah-**teev**-e, *f* initiative

inklusive, in-kloo-**seev**-e, *adj* inclusive

Inland, in-lahnt, *nt* interior (of country); –**flug,** *m* domestic flight

inländisch, in-**lend**-dish, *adj* native, home, inland

inmitten, in-**mit**-en, *prep* in the middle/centre of

innehalten, in-e-**hahlt**-en, *v* to stop

innen, in-en, *adv* inside

Innenminister, in-en-min-ist-er, *m* Home Secretary

Innenpolitik, in-en-poh-lee-teek, *f* domestic policy

Innenstadt, in-en-**shtahtt**, *f* town centre

innerhalb, in-er-hahlp, *adv* inside; *prep* within

innerlich, in-er-lik, *adj* inner, within, internal

innig, in-ik, *adj* intimate, heartfelt, fond

Innung, in-oong, *f* corporation, guild; craft

ins (= **in das**), ins, into the

Insasse, in-zahss-e, *m* inmate; occupant

insbesondere, ins-be-zon-der-e, *adv* in particular

Inschrift, in-shrift, *f* inscription

Insekt, in-zekt, *nt* insect

Insel, in-zel, *f* island, isle

Inserat, in-zair-aht, *nt* advertisement

inserieren, in-zer-eer-en, *v* to advertise

insgesamt, ins-ge-**zahmt**, *adv* altogether

Installateur, in-shtahll-ah-ter, *m* plumber

inständig, in-shtend-ik, *adj* earnest, pressing, urgent

Instinkt, in-**stinkt**, *m* instinct

instinktiv, in-stink-**teef**, *adj* instinctive

Institut, in-stee-**toot**, *nt* institute

Instrument, in-stroo-**ment**, *nt* instrument

intelligent, in-tel-ee-**gent**, *adj* intelligent

Intendant, in-ten-**dahnt**, *m* director; theatre manager

intensiv, in-ten-**seef**, *adj* intensiv

Intensivstation, in-ten-seef-shtahts-yohn, *f* intensive care unit

Intercity Expreßzug, in-ter-

sit-ee ex-press-tsook, *m* high speed train

Intercity-Zug, in-ter-**sit**-ee-tsook, *m* intercity train

interessant, in-ter-ess-**ahnt**, *adj* interesting

Interesse, in-ter-**ess**-e, *nt* interest

interessieren, in-te-ress-**eer**-en, *v* to interest; **sich für etw –,** to be interested in sth

Internat, in-tair-**naht**, *nt* boarding school

international, in-ter-nahts-yohn-**ahl**, *adj* international

intim, in-**teem**, *adj* intimate

intolerant, in-tohl-er-**ahnt**, *adj* intolerant

Invasion, in-vahz-**yohn**, *f* invasion

Inventur, in-ven-**toor**, *f* stocktaking

investieren, in-ves-**teer**-en, *v* to invest

inzwischen, int-**svish**-en, *adv* meanwhile

irdisch, eerd-ish, *adj* earthly, worldly

Ire, eer-e, *m* Irishman

irgend, eerg-ent, *adv* any; –**jemand,** *pron* anybody; –**wie,** *adv* somehow; –**wann,** *adv* some time; –**wo,** *adv* somewhere

Irin, eer-in, *f* Irishwoman

irisch, eer-ish, *adj* Irish

Irland, eer-lahnt, *nt* Ireland, Eire

Irländer, eer-len-der, *m*

Irishman; **–in,** *f*
Irishwoman

Ironie, eer-oh-**nee,** *f* irony

ironisch, eer-oh-nish, *adj*
ironic

irre, eer-*e*, *adj & adv* mad,
insane; muddled, confused

Irre(r), eer-*e*(r), *m & f*
madwoman (madman)

irreführen, eer-*e*-fEEr-en, *v*
to lead astray

irremachen, eer-*e*-mah*k*-en,
v to bewilder

irren, eer-en, *v* to err, to go
astray; to stray; **sich –,** *v*
to be mistaken

Irrenanstalt, eer-en-ahnn-
shtahlt, *f* lunatic asylum

Irrgarten, eer-gart-en, *m*
maze

irrig, eer-ik, *adj* erroneous,
wrong, false

Irrsinn, eer-zin, *m* insanity,
lunacy

irrsinnig, eer-zin-ik, *adj*
insane, mentally deranged

Irrtum, eer-toom, *m* error,
mistake; oversight

irrtümlich, eer-tEEm-lik, *adj*
erroneous

Islam, ees-lahm, *m* Islam

isolieren, ees-oh-**leer**-en, *v*
to isolate; to insulate

Isolierung, ee-zoh-**leer**-
oong, *f* isolation;
insulation

Israel, ees-rah-ayl, *nt* Israel

Israeli, ees-rah-**ay**-lee, *m &
f* Israeli (person)

israelisch, ees-rah-**ay**-lish,
adj Israeli

Italien, ee-tah-lee-en, *nt*
Italy

Italiener, ee-tah-lee-**ay**-n*e*r,
m Italian (person)

italienisch, ee-tah-lee-**ay**-
nish, *adj* Italian

J

ja, yah, *adv* yes

Jacht, yah*k*t, *f* yacht

Jacke, yahk-*e*, *f* jacket, coat

Jagd, yahkt, *f* hunt(ing); chase; shooting; **–hund,** *m* hunting dog

jagen, yahg-en, *v* to hunt, to chase

Jäger, yayg-er, *m* hunter; rifleman

jäh, yay, *adj* sudden, impetuous; steep

Jahr, yahr, *nt* year

jahrelang, yahr-*e*-lahng, *adv* lasting for years

Jahresbeitrag, yahr-es-by-trahk, *m* annual subscription

Jahreskarte, yahr-es-kahr-te, *f* annual season ticket

Jahrestag, yahr-es-tahk, *m* anniversary

Jahreswechsel, yahr-es-veck-sel, *m* new year

Jahreszahl, yahr-es-tsahl, *f* date, year

Jahreszeit, yahr-es-tsite, *f* season, time of year

Jahrgang, yahr-gahng, *m* year; vintage; volume (of publication)

Jahrhundert, yahr-hoonn-dert, *nt* century

jährlich, yair-lik, *adj* annual, yearly

Jahrmarkt, yahr-markt, *m* fair

Jahrtausend, yahr-tow-zent, *nt* millennium

Jahrzehnt, yahr-tsaynt, *nt* decade

Jähzorn, yay-tsorn, *m* sudden anger; irritability

Jalousie, zhahll-oo-zee, *f* Venetian blind

Jammer, yahmm-er, *m* great misery, calamity

jämmerlich, yem-er-lik, *adj* wretched, pitiable

jammern, yahmm-ern, *v* to lament; to wail

Januar, yahnn-oo-ahr, *m* January

Japan, yah-pahnn, *nt* Japan

Japaner, yah-pahn-er, *m* Japanese (person)

japanisch, yah-pahn-ish, *adj* Japanese

jäten, yay-ten, *v* to weed

jauchzen, yowk-tsen, *v* to rejoice; to exult

je, yay, *adv* ever; each, every; *conj* **– nach,** according to

jede(r/s), yayd-e(r/s) *pron* each, every

jedenfalls, yayd-en-fahls, *adv* in any case

jedermann, yayd-er-mahnn, *pron* everybody; anybody

jederzeit, yayd-er-tsy't, *adv* at any time, always

jedesmal, yayd-es-mahl, *adv* each/every time

jedoch, yay-doch, *adv* however, still, nevertheless

jeher, yay-hair, *adv* von/seit –, always

jemals, yay-mahls, *adv* ever

jemand, yay-mahnt, *pron* someone, anyone,

anybody

jene(r/s) yayn-*e*(r/s) *pron*
that one

jenseits, yayn-zites, *prep* on
the other side

jetzig, yet-sik, *adj* actual, of
the present time

jetzt, yetst, *adv* now

jeweils, yay-viles, *adv* at a
time

Jh., *abbr* **Jahrhundert**

joggen, dshogg-*en*, *v* to jog

Joghurt, yoh-koort, *nt*
yogurt

Johannisbeere, yoh-**hahnn**-
is-bair-*e*, *f* redcurrant,
blackcurrant

Journalismus, zhoor-nahl-
ees-moos, *m* journalism

Jubel, yoob-el, *m* jubilation,
exultation

jubeln, yoob-eln, *v* to
jubilate, to rejoice

jucken, yoock-en, *v* to itch

jüdisch, yEEd-ish, *adj* Jewish

Jugend, yoog-ent, *f* youth;
–herberge, *f* youth hostel

jugendlich, yoog-ent-lik, *adj*
youthful

Jugendliche(r), yoog-ent-
lik-*e*(r), *m & f* adolescent

Juli, yoo-li, *m* July

jung, yoong, *adj* young,
youthful

Junge, yoong-*e*, *m* boy, lad;
nt young (animals)

Jünger, yEEng-er, *m* disciple,
follower

Jungfrau, yoong-frow, *f*
virgin

Junggeselle, yoong-ge-zel-*e*,

m bachelor

Jüngling, yEEng-ling; *m*
youth, young man

jüngst, yEEngst, *adv* recently,
a short time ago

Juni, yoo-ni, *m* June

Jurist, yoor-**ist**, *m* lawyer,
jurist

Justiz, yoos-**teets**, *f* judiciary

Juwel, yoo-**vail**, *nt* jewel,
gem

Juwelier, yoo-vail-**eer**, *m*
jeweller

K

Kabel, kahb-el, *nt* cable;
  –fernsehen, *nt* cable
  television
Kabeljau, kahb-el-yow, *m*
  cod
Kabine, kahb-een-e, *f* cabin
Kachel, kahk-el, *f* (glazed)
  tile
Käfer, kay-fer, *m* beetle
Kaffee, kahff-ay, *m* coffee
Käfig, kay-fik, *m* cage
kahl, kahl, *adj* bare, bleak;
  bald
Kahn, kahn, *m* skiff, small
  boat; barge
Kai, kay, *m* quay, jetty
Kaiser, ky-zer, *m* emperor
kaiserlich, ky-zer-lik, *adj*
  imperial
Kaiserreich, ky-zer-ry'k, *nt*
  empire
Kaiserschnitt, ky-zer-shnit,
  m Caesarean (section)
Kakadu, kah-kah-doo, *m*
cockatoo
Kakao, kah-kow, *m* cocoa
Kaktus, kahk-toos, *m*
  cactus
Kalb, kahlp, *nt* calf
Kalbfleisch, kahlp-fly'sh, *nt*
  veal
Kalender, kahl-end-er, *m*
  calendar, almanac
Kalk, kahlk, *m* lime, chalk
Kalorie, kahl-oh-ree, *f*
  calorie
kalt, kahlt, *adj* cold; frigid;
  –blütig, *adj* cold-blooded;
  cool-headed
Kälte, kelt-e, *f* cold; frigidity
Kamel, kahmm-ail, *nt* camel
Kamera, kahmm-er-ah, *f*
  camera
Kamerad, kahmm-er-aht, *m*
  comrade, companion;
  –schaft, *f* comradeship
Kamille, kahmm-il-e, *f*
  camomile

Kamin, kahmm-een, *m*
  chimney (pot); fireplace
Kamm, kahmm, *m* comb;
  crest, ridge (of mountain)
kämmen, kem-en, *v* to
  comb
Kammer, kahmm-er, *f*
  chamber, small room
Kampf, kahmpf, *m* combat,
  fight
kämpfen, kemp-fen, *v* to
  fight, to struggle
Kämpfer, kemp-fer, *m*
  fighter, combatant,
  warrior
kampflustig, kahmpf-loost-
  ik, *adj* belligerent
Kanada, kah-nah-dah, *nt*
  Canada
Kanadier, kah-nah-dee-er, *m*
  Canadian (person)
kanadisch, kah-nah-dish,
  adj Canadian
Kanal, kahnn-ahl, *m*
  channel; canal; **–inseln,** *pl*
  Channel Islands
Kanalisation, kahnn-ahl-e-
  zahts-yohn, *f* drainage
Kanaltunnel, kahnn-ahl-
  toon-el, *m* Channel
  Tunnel
Kanarienvogel, kahnn-ahr-
  ee-en-fohg-el, *m* canary
Kandidat, kahnn-dee-daht,
  m candidate
Kaninchen, kahnn-een-ken,
  nt rabbit
Kännchen, ken-ken, *nt* pot
Kanne, kahnn-e, *f* can, pot,
  jug; tankard
Kanone, kahnn-ohn-e, *f*

cannon

Kante, kahnt-e, f edge, border, corner

kantig, kahnt-ik, adj edged, angular

Kantine, kahnn-teen-e, f canteen

Kanzel, kahnt-sel, f pulpit

Kanzlei, kahnt-se-ly, f government office; office, chambers

Kanzler, kahnt-sler, m chancellor

**Kap, kahpp, nt cape, promontory, headland

Kapelle, kahpp-el-e, f chapel; *mus* band

kapern, kahpp-ern, v to capture; to commandeer

kapieren, kahpp-eer-en, v to grasp, to understand

Kapital, kahpp-ee-tahl, nt capital; **–anlage,** f investment

Kapitalismus, kahpp-ee-tahl-is-moos, m capitalism

Kapitän, kahpp-e-tain, m captain

Kapitel, kahpp-it-el, nt chapter

Kappe, kahpp-e, f cap; hood

Kapsel, kahpp-sel, f capsule, casing

kaputt, kahpp-oott, adj ruined; smashed, broken

Kapuze, kahpp-oots-e, f hood

Karaffe, kar-ahff-e, f carafe; decanter

Karfreitag, kar-fry-tahk, m Good Friday

**karg, kark, adj mean; economical; parsimonious; scanty

Karibik, kah-ree-beek, f Caribbean (Sea)

karibisch, kah-ree-bish, adj Caribbean

kariert, kar-eert, adj chequered

Karneval, kar-ne-vahl, m carnival

**Karo, kar-oh, nt check; diamond (shape/card)

Karosserie, kar-oss-er-ee, f bodywork

Karotte, kar-ott-e, f carrot

Karpfen, karp-fen, m carp

Karren, kar-en, m cart, dray, barrow

Karriere, kar-ee-ayr-e, f career; **– machen,** to make a career for o.s.

Karte, kart-e, f card; map, chart; ticket; **–nspiel,** nt card game; **–ntelefon,** nt card phone

Kartoffel, kart-off-el, f potato

Kartoffelbrei, kart-off-el-bry, m mashed potatoes

Karton, kart-ong, m cardboard(-box)

Karussell, kar-ooss-el, nt roundabout, merry-go-round

Käse, kay-ze, m cheese

Käseglocke, kay-ze-glock-e, f cheese-cover

Kaserne, kah-zern-e, f barracks

Kasse, kahss-e, f cash(-

box); till; box-office

Kassette, kahss-et-e, f cassette; box

kassieren, kahss-eer-en, v to cash, to collect; to confiscate

Kassierer, kahss-eer-er, m cashier

Kastanie, kahss-tahn-ye, f chestnut

Kasten, kahsst-en, m box, trunk, case

kastrieren, kahss-treer-en, v to castrate

Katalog, kah-tah-lohk, m catalogue

Katastrophe, kah-tah-strohf-e, f disaster

Kater, kaht-er, m tom cat; hangover

Katholik, kaht-ohl-eeck, m Catholic

katholisch, kaht-ohl-ish, adj Catholic

Katze, kahtt-se, f cat

Katzensprung, kahtt-sen-shproong, m stone's throw

Kauderwelsch, kowd-er-velsh, nt gibberish

kauen, kow-en, v to chew, to masticate

kauern, kow-ern, v to cower, to crouch (down)

**Kauf, kowf, m buying, purchase

kaufen, kowf-en, v to buy, to purchase

Käufer, koyf-er, m purchaser, buyer; customer

Kaufhaus, kowf-hows, nt department store

kaufkräftig, kowf-kreft-ik, *adj* having purchasing power/disposable income

käuflich, koyf-lik, *adj* for sale, purchasable

kauflustig, kouf-loost-ik, *adj* inclined to buy

Kaufmann, kowf-mahnn, *m* dealer, merchant

Kaugummi, kow-goom-ee, *m* chewing gum

kaum, kowm, *adv* hardly, scarcely, barely

Kaution, kowts-yohn, *f* security, bail

keck, keck, *adj* bold, daring; impudent, cheeky

Kegel, kay-gel, *m* skittle; cone

Kegelbahn, kay-gel-bahn, *f* skittle-alley

kegeln, kay-geln, *v* to play skittles; to bowl

Kehle, kayl-e, *f* throat, gullet

Kehlkopf, kayl-kop'f, *m* larynx

kehren, kayr-en, *v* to sweep; to turn (over)

Kehrseite, kayr-zy-te, *f* reverse; wrong side

keifen, ky-fen, *v* to chide, to scold, to squabble

Keil, kile, *m* wedge; key; **–riemen,** *m* fan belt

Keim, kime, *m* germ; seed-bud; ovum

keimen, ky-men, *v* to germinate, to sprout

keine(r/s), kyn-e(r/s), *pron* no, not a, not any

keinerlei, ky-ner-ly, *adj* not of any kind

keinesfalls, ky-nes-fahls, *adv* on no account

keineswegs, ky-nes-vaygs, *adv* by no means

Keks, kayks, *m* biscuit

Kelch, kelk, *m* goblet, cup; chalice

Kelle, kel-e, *f* scoop, ladle

Keller, kel-er, *m* cellar, basement; vault

Kellner, kel-ner, *m* waiter

keltern, kelt-ern, *v* to press (grapes)

kennen, ken-en, *v* to know, to be acquainted with; **–lernen,** *v* to get to know; **sich –lernen,** *v* to get to know each other; to meet

Kenner, ken-er, *m* expert, connoisseur

Kenntnis, kent-niss, *f* knowledge, information

Kennzeichen, ken-tsy-ken, *nt* sign, mark

kennzeichnen, ken-tsy-k'nen, *v* to characterize

kentern, kent-ern, *v* to capsize

Keramik, kay-rahm-ik, *f* ceramics; pottery

Kerbe, kair-be, *f* notch

Kerker, kairk-er, *m* jail, prison, dungeon

Kerl, kairl, *m* fellow, chap; individual

Kern, kairn, *m* kernel, pip, nucleus, pith; **–energie,** *f* nuclear energy

kerngesund, kairn-ge-zoont, *adj* thoroughly healthy

kernig, kairn-ik, *adj* full of pips; pithy; solid, robust

kernlos, kairn-lohs, *adj* seedless

Kerze, kairt-se, *f* candle, taper

kerzengerade, kairt-sen-ge-rad-e, *adj* straight as an arrow

Kerzenständer, kairt-sen-shtend-er, *m* candleholder

Kessel, kes-el, *m* kettle; cauldron; boiler

Kette, ket-e, *f* chain; range (of mountains)

ketten, ket-en, *v* to chain

Ketzer, ket-ser, *m* heretic

Ketzerei, ket-se-ry, *f* heresy

keuchen, koy-ken, *v* to gasp, to pant, to wheeze

Keuchhusten, koyk-hoost-en, *m* whooping-cough

Keule, koyl-e, *f* club, cudgel; leg (of meat)

keusch, koysh, *adj* chaste, pure, immaculate

Kfz., kah eff tset, *abbr* **Kraftfahrzeug**

kg, *abbr* **Kilogramm**

kichern, kik-ern, *v* to giggle, to titter, to chuckle

Kiefer, keef-er, *m* jaw (-bone); *f* pine, fir

Kiel, keel, *m* quill(-pen); float (angling); keel

Kieme, keem-e, *f* gills

Kies, kees, *m* gravel

Kieselstein, keez-el-shtine, *m* pebble

kikeriki, keek-e-reek-ee,

interj cock-a-doodle-doo

Kilo(gramm), keel-oh
(-grahmm), *nt* kilo(gram)

Kilometer, keel-oh-mayt-er,
m kilometre; **–zähler,** *m*
mileometer, odometer

Kind, kint, *nt* child

Kinderei, kin-de-ry, *f*
childishness, nonsense

Kindergarten, kin-der-gahr-
ten, *m* nursery school

Kindergeld, kin-der-gelt, *nt*
child benefit

Kinderheim, kin-der-hime,
nt children's home

Kindermädchen, kin-der-
maid-ken, *nt* nanny

Kinderwagen, kin-der-vahg-
en, *m* pram

kinderleicht, kin-der-ly'kt,
adj very easy

Kinderzimmer, kin-der-
tsim-er, *nt* nursery

Kindheit, kint-hite, *f*
childhood, infancy

kindisch, kin-dish, *adj*
childish; foolish

kindlich, kint-lik, *adj*
childlike; simple

Kinn, kin, *nt* chin, lower
jaw

Kino, keen-oh, *nt* cinema

Kiosk, kee-osk, *m* kiosk

kippen, kip-en, *v* to tilt, to
tip (over), to lose one's
balance

Kirche, keerk-e, *f* church

Kirchenchor, keerk-en-kor,
m church choir

Kirchengemeinde, keerk-
en-ge-mine-de, *f* parish

Kirchhof, keerk-hohf, *m*
churchyard, cemetery

Kirchturm, keerk-toorm, *m*
steeple, spire

Kirmes, keerm-es, *f* country
fair

Kirsche, keersh-e, *f* cherry

Kissen, kis-en, *nt* cushion,
pillow; **–bezug,** *m*
pillowcase

Kiste, kist-e, *f* box, case,
chest

Kitsch, kitsh, *m* kitsch

kitschig, kitsh-ik, *adj*
kitschy, trashy

Kitt, kit, *m* putty; cement

Kittel, kit-el, *m* smock,
overall, frock

kitten, kit-en, *v* to cement;
to putty

kitzelig, kit-sel-ik, *adj*
ticklish; sensitive; delicate

kitzeln, kit-seln, *v* to tickle,
to itch

klaffen, klahff-en, *v* to
gape, to yawn

kläffen, klef-en, *v* to bark,
to yap, to yelp

Klage, klahg-e, *f* complaint,
wailing, lamentation;
legal action

klagen, klahg-en, *v* to
complain, to wail; to take
legal action

Kläger, klayg-er, *m*
complainant, plaintiff

kläglich, klayk-lik, *adj*
plaintive; lamentable

Klammer, klahmm-er, *f*
clasp; peg; bracket

klammern, klahmm-ern, *v*

to clasp; to cramp; **sich –
(an),** *v* to cling (to)

Klang, klahng, *m* sound,
ring, tone

Klappe, klahpp-e, *f* flap,
tray; valve

klappen, klahpp-en *v* to
click; to tally; to work
well

klapperig, klahpp-er-ik, *adj*
rattling, shaky

klappern, klahpp-ern, *v* to
rattle, to clatter

Klapperschlange, klahpp-er-
shlahng-e, *f* rattle-snake

Klapperstorch, klahpp-er-
shtork, *m* stork

Klappstuhl, klahpp-shtool,
m folding chair

Klaps, klahps, *m* tap, slap;
bang

klar, klar, *adj* clear, lucid;
transparent

klären, klair-en, *v* to clarify;
to purify; to become clear

Klarheit, klar-hite, *f* clarity,
brightness

Klarinette, klah-ree-net-e, *f*
clarinet

klarlegen, klar-layg-en, *v* to
clarify, to explain

klarmachen, klar-mah-ken,
v jdm. etw –, to make sth
clear to sb

Klarsichtfolie, klar-zikt-foh-
lee-e, *f* cling film;
transparent film

Klärung, klair-oong, *f*
clarification

Klasse, klahss-e, *f* class;
division

Klassik, klahss-ik, *f* classic period

klassisch, klahss-ish, *adj* classical

Klatsch, klahtsh, *m* gossip

klatschen, klahtsh-en, *v* to clap; to smack; to gossip

klatschnaß, klahtsh-nahss, *adj* soaked to the skin

Klaue, klow-e, *f* claw, talon, fang

klauen, klow-en, *v* to pinch

Klausel, klow-zel, *f* clause, proviso

Klavier, klah-veer, *nt* piano(forte)

kleben, klayb-en, *v* to adhere, to stick, to affix

klebrig, klayb-rik, *adj* adhesive, sticky, gluey

Klebstoff, klayp-shtof, *m* glue, adhesive

kleckern, kleck-ern, *v* to slobber, to make a mess

Klecks, klecks, *m* ink-blot, blotch

klecksen, kleck-sen, *v* to make blots

Klee, klay, *m* clover, shamrock; –blatt, *nt* cloverleaf

Kleid, klite, *nt* dress, garment, gown; –er, *pl* clothes, dresses

kleiden, kly'd-en, *v* to dress, to clothe

Kleiderbügel, kly'd-er-bEEg-el, *m* coat hanger

Kleiderschrank, kly'd-er-shrahnk, *m* wardrobe

kleidsam, kly'd-sahm, *adj* becoming, fitting

Kleidung, kly'd-oong, *f* clothing; –sstück, *nt* garment

klein, kline, *adj* small, little; short, insignificant

Kleingeld, kline-gelt, *nt* (small) change

Kleinigkeit, kline-ik-kite, *f* trifle, trivial matter

kleinlaut, kline-lowt, *adj* dejected, downcast

kleinlich, kline-lik, *adj* petty; narrow-minded

Kleinod, kline-oht, *nt* jewel, gem, treasure

Kleinstadt, kline-shtahtt, *f* small town

Kleister, kly-ster, *m* paste

Klemme, klem-e, *f* clamp, vice; tight corner

klemmen, klem-en, *v* to squeeze, to pinch, to jam

Klempner, klemp-ner, *m* plumber

Klette, klet-e, *f* bur(dock)

klettern, klet-ern, *v* to climb, to clamber

Klima, kleem-ah, *nt* climate

Klimaanlage, kleem-ah-ahnn-lah-ge, *f* air-conditioning

klimpern, klim-pern, *v* to jingle, to tinkle; to strum

Klinge, kling-e, *f* blade

Klingel, kling-el, *f* bell

klingeln, kling-eln, *v* to ring a bell

klingen, kling-en, *v* to sound, to resound

Klinik, klee-nik, *f* clinic, hospital

Klinke, klink-e, *f* door-handle; latch; catch

Klippe, klip-e, *f* cliff, crag; reef, rock

klirren, kleerr-en, *v* to clatter, to clash, to rattle

Klo, kloh, *nt fam* loo

klobig, klohb-ik, *adj* rude, rough, clumsy

klopfen, klop-fen, *v* to knock, to tap, to rap, to beat

Klops, klops, *m* meatball

Kloß, klohs, *m* dumpling; lump, clod

Kloster, klohs-ter, *nt* cloister, monastery, convent

Klotz, klots, *m* log, block; trunk/stump (of tree)

klotzig, klot-sik, *adj* clumsy, heavy; enormous

Klub, kloop, *m* club

Kluft, klooft, *f* gap, cleft, chasm; *fam* clothes

klug, klook, *adj* clever; sensible; prudent; wise

Klugheit, klook-hite, *f* prudence, wisdom

Klumpen, kloomp-en, *m* lump, mass; clot

km., *abbr* Kilometer

knabbern, k'nahbb-ern, *v* to gnaw, to nibble

Knabe, k'nahb-e, *m* boy, lad

knabenhaft, k'nahb-en-hahft, *adj* boyish

knacken, k'nahck-en, *v* to crack, to snap

Knacks, k'nahcks, *m* crack

Knackwurst, k'nahck-voorst, *f* smoked sausage

Knall, k'nahll, *m* crack, crash, bang

Knallbonbon, k'nahll-bon-bong, *nt* (Christmas) cracker

knallen, k'nahll-en, *v* to crack

knallrot, k'nahll-roht, *adj* bright red

knapp, k'nahpp, *adj* tight (-fitting); scanty; narrow

Knappheit, k'nahpp-hite, *f* tightness; scantiness

knarren, k'narr-en, *v* to creak, to grate, to squeak

knattern, k'nahtt-ern, *v* to rattle, to crackle

Knäuel, k'noy-el, *nt* ball (of thread); tangle; throng

knauserig, k'nowz-er-ik, *adj* mean, stingy

knausern, k'nowz-ern, *v* to be mean/stingy

Knebel, k'nayb-el, *m* gag; toggle, catch

knebeln, k'nayb-eln, *v* to gag

Knecht, k'nekt, *m* servant; labourer

kneifen, k'ny-fen, *v* to pinch, to nip

Kneipe, k'ny-pe, *f* pub, inn

kneten, k'nayt-en, *v* to knead, to mix, to mould

Knick, k'nik, *m* break, bend; flaw

knicken, k'nik-en, *v* to crack, to break, to split

Knicks, k'niks, *m* curtsy

knicksen, k'nik-sen, *v* to curtsy

Knie, k'nee, *nt* knee

knien, k'nee-en/k'neen, *v* to kneel

Kniff, k'nif, *m* pinch(ing); fold; knack, trick

knipsen, k'nip-sen, *v* to punch (tickets); to snap

Knirps, k'neerps, *m* little boy, nipper

knirschen, k'neersh-en, *v* to creak; to gnash

knistern, k'nist-ern, *v* to crackle, to rustle

knitterfrei, k'nit-ter-fry, *adj* non-crease

knittern, k'nit-tern, *v* to crease

Knoblauch, k'nohp-lowk, *m* garlic; **–zehe**, *f* clove of garlic

Knöchel, k'nerk-el, *m* knuckle; ankle

Knochen, k'nok-en, *m* bone

knochig, k'nok-ik, *adj* bony

Knödel, k'nerd-el, *m* dumpling

Knolle, k'nohll-e, *f* bulb, tuber

Knopf, k'nopf, *m* button, knob

knöpfen, k'nerpp-fen, *v* to button

Knopfloch, k'noppf-lok, *nt* button-hole

Knorpel, k'norp-el, *m* cartilage, gristle

knorpelig, k'norp-el-ik, *adj* gristly

knorrig, k'norr-ik, *adj* gnarled, knotted

Knospe, k'nosp-e, *f* bud

knospen, k'nosp-en, *v* to bud, to shoot, to sprout

Knoten, k'noht-en, *m* lump; knot; node; plot

knoten, k'noht-en, *v* to knot

knüpfen, k'nEEpp-fen, *v* to tie, to knot

Knüppel, k'nEEpp-el, *m* cudgel, club

knurren, k'noorr-en, *v* to growl, to snarl

knurrig, k'noorr-ik, *adj* snarling, growling; grumbling

knusperig, k'noosp-er-ik, *adj* crisp

k.o., kah oh, *adj* knocked-out; exhausted

Kobold, koh-bolt, *m* goblin, imp

Koch, kok, *m* cook; **–buch**, *nt* cookery book

kochen, kok-en, *v* to cook; to boil

Kochgelegenheit, kok-*ge*-laig-en-hite, *f* cooking facilities

Kochgeschirr, kok-ge-sheerr, *nt* cooking utensils

Kochplatte, kok-plahtt-e, *f* hot-plate

Kochtopf, kok-topf, *m* saucepan

Köder, ker-der, *m* bait, lure

Koffein, koh-fay-een, *nt* caffeine

koffeinfrei, koh-fay-een-fry, *adj* decaffeinated

Koffer, kof-er, m suitcase;
–kuli, m trolley; **–radio,** nt
portable radio; **–raum,** m
boot

Kohl, kohl, m cabbage

Kohle, kohl-e, f coal,
carbon; charcoal

Kohlengrube, kohl-en-
groob-e, f coal-pit

kohlensäurehaltig, kohl-en-
zoyr-e-hahll-tik, adj
carbonated

Kohlkopf, kohl-kopf, m
cabbage

kohlrabenschwarz, kohl-
rabh-en-shvahrts, adj
pitch black

Kohlrübe, kohl-rEEb-e, f
turnip

Koje, koh-ye, f berth, small
cabin

Kokain, koh-kah-een, nt
cocain

Kokosnuß, koh-kos-nooss, f
coconut

Koks, kohks, m coke

Kolben, kolb-en, m butt (of
gun); piston

Kolik, kohl-eek, f colic

Kollege, kol-ayg-e, m
colleague

Kollegium, kol-layg-e-
oomm, nt staff; working
party

Koller, kol-er, m rage, frenzy

Kolonie, kol-on-ee, f colony

Kolonne, ko-lon-e, f convoy

kolossal, kol-os-ahl, adj
colossal, enormous, huge

Kombination, kom-bee-
nahts-yohn, f

combination

kombinieren, kom-bee-
neer-en, v to combine

Komfort, kom-for, m luxury

Komiker, koh-mik-er, m
comedian; comic
actor/author

komisch, kohm-ish, adj
funny, comical

Komitee, koh-mit-tay, nt
committee

Komma, kom-mah, nt
comma

Kommando, kom-**mahnn**-
doh, nt (word of)
command, order;
detachment

kommen, kom-en, v to
come; **zu sich –,** v to
come round; **– lassen,** v to
send for

Kommission, kom-miss-
yohn, f commission;
committee

Kommode, kom-**mohd**-e, f
chest of drawers

Kommunikation, kom-moo-
nee-kahts-yohn, f
communication

Kommunismus, kom-moo-
nis-mooss, m communism

kommunistisch, kom-moo-
nis-tish, adj communist

Komödie, kom-**erd**-ee-e, f
comedy, play

Kompagnon, kom-pahnn-
yong, m partner (in
business)

Kompaß, kom-pahss, m
compass

komplex, kom-plex, adj

complicated

Kompliment, kom-plee-
ment, nt compliment

kompliziert, kom-plee-
tseert, adj complicated

Komplott, kom-**plot,** nt plot,
conspiracy

komponieren, kom-pohn-
eer-en, v to compose

Komponist, kom-pohn-**ist,**
m composer

Kompott, kom-pot, nt
stewed fruit

Kompromiß, kom-pro-**miss,**
m compromise

kompromittieren (sich),
kom-proh-mit-**eer**-en
(zik), v to expose oneself

Kondition, kon-deets-**yohn,**
f condition; stamina; state
of health

Konditor, kon-**deet**-ohr, m
pastry-cook

Konditorei, kon-deet-oh-**ry,**
f patisserie, cake shop;
café

Kondom, kon-**dohm,** nt
condom

Konfektion, kon-fekts-
yohn, f ready-to-wear
clothing

Konferenz, kon-fair-**ents,** f
conference; **–zentrum,** nt
congress centre

Konfession, kon-fes-**yohn,** f
denomination

Konfitüre, kon-fee-t**EEr**-e, f
jam

Konflikt, kon-**flikt,** m
conflict

Kongreß, kong-gres, m

congress

König, kern-ik, *m* king

Königin, kern-ig-in, *f* queen

Königreich, kern-ig-ry'k, *nt* kingdom, realm

Konkurrent, kong-koor-**rent,** *m* competitor

Konkurrenz, kong-koor-**rents,** *f* competition

konkurrieren, kong-koor-**reer**-en, *v* to compete

Konkurs, kong-**koors,** *m* bankruptcy, insolvency

können, kern-en, *v* to be able to, to be capable of; to know how to; to be allowed to

konsequent, kon-ze-**kvent,** *adj* consistent

Konsequenz, kon-ze-**kvents,** *f* consistency; consequence

konservativ, kon-zair-vah-**teef,** *adj* conservative

Konserve, kon-**zairv**-e, *f* tinned/bottled food

konservieren, kon-zairv-**eer**-en, *v* to preserve

Konsortium, kon-**zorts**-ee-oomm, *nt* syndicate; ring

Konsulat, kon-zoo-**laht,** *nt* consulate

Konsum, kon-**zoom,** *m* consumption (of goods)

Konsument, kon-zoom-**ent,** *m* consumer

Kontinent, kon-tee-**nent,** *m* continent

Konto, kon-toh, *nt* account

Kontrolle, kon-**trol**-e, *f* control

Konzept, kon-**tsept,** *nt* rough draft; copy; concept

Konzert, kon-**tsairt,** *nt* concert

Kopf, kop'f, *m* head; skull; sense

köpfen, kerp-fen, *v* to behead; to lop (trees)

Kopfhaut, kop'f-howt, *f* scalp

Kopfkissen, kop'f-kis-en, *nt* pillow

Kopfsalat, kop'f-zahll-aht, *m* (round-headed) lettuce

Kopfschmerzen, kop'f-shmairts-en, *pl* headache

Kopftuch, kop'f-took, *nt* headscarf

kopfüber, kop'f-EEb-er, *adv* head over heels

Kopfweh, kop'f-vay, *nt* headache

Kopie, koh-pee, *f* copy

kopieren, koh-peer-en, *v* to copy

Kopiergerät, koh-peer-ge-rait, *nt* photocopier

Korb, korp, *m* basket, hamper, crate

Kork, kork, *m* cork; **–enzieher,** *m* corkscrew

Korn, korn, *nt* grain; corn

körnig, kern-ik, *adj* granular, grainy

Körper, kerp-er, *m* body; substance

körperbehindert, kerp-er-be-hin-dert, *adj* disabled

Körpergeruch, kerp-er-ge-rook, *m* body odour

körperlich, kerp-er-lik, *adj*

bodily, physical; substantial

Körperteil, kerp-er-tile, *m* part of the body

korrekt, kor-**rekt,** *adj* correct

Korrektur, kor-rek-**toor,** *f* correction

korrigieren, kor-ree-**geer**-en, *v* to correct; to revise

Korruption, kor-roopts-**yohn,** *f* corruption

Kosename, koh-ze-nahm-e, *m* pet name

Kosmetik, kos-may-tik, *f* cosmetics

Kost, kost, *f* food; diet

kostbar, kost-bar, *adj* precious, valuable; splendid

Kosten, kost-en, *pl* cost(s), charges; expenses

kosten, kost-en, *v* to cost; to taste, to try (food)

Kostenanschlag, kost-en-ahnn-shlahk, *m* estimate

kostenlos, kost-en-lohs, *adj* free (of charge)

köstlich, kerst-lik, *adj* delicious, dainty; precious

kostspielig, kost-shpeel-ik, *adj* costly, dear

Kostüm, kost-EEm, *nt* costume; suit

Kot, koht, *m* mud, filth; excrement; dung

Kotelett, kot-let, *nt* cutlet, chop

Kontaktlinsen, kon-tahkt-lin-zen, *pl* contact lenses

Kotflügel, koht-flEEg-el, *m*

mud-guard

kotzen, kot-sen, *v fam* to
vomit

Krabbe, krahbb-e, *f* crab,
shrimp

krabbeln, krahbb-eln, *v* to
wriggle; to crawl

krach, krahk, *interj* bang,
crash, crack

Krach, krahk, *m* crash;
smash; *fam* row, quarrel

krachen, krahk-en, *v* to
crash; to burst

krächzen, krek-tsen, *v* to
croak, to caw

Kraft, krahft, *f* strength,
power; force, validity

kraft, krahft, *prep* by virtue
of

Kraftfahrzeug, krahft-fahr-
tsoyk, *nt* motor vehicle

kräftig, kreft-ik, *adj* strong,
vigorous, powerful

kräftigen, kreft-ig-en, *v* to
strengthen

Kraftwerk, krahft-vairk, *nt*
power-station

Kragen, krahg-en, *m* collar

Krähe, kray-e, *f* crow

krähen, kray-en, *v* to crow

Kralle, krahll-e, *f* claw,
talon

krallen, krahll-en, *v* to
scratch, to claw

Kram, krahm, *m* junk; stuff;
business

kramen, krahm-en, *v* to
rummage

Krampf, krahmp'f, *m* cramp,
spasm, convulsion

krampfhaft, krahmp'f-

hahft, *adj* convulsive,
spasmodic

Kran, krahn, *m* crane; tap

krank, krahnk, *adj* ill, sick,
diseased

Kranke(r), krahnk-*e*(r), *m*
& f sick person, patient

Krankenschein, krahnk-en-
shine, *m* health insurance
card

**Krankenschwester,
krah**nk-en-shvest-er, *f*
nurse

kränkeln, krenk-eln, *v* to be
ill

kränken, krenk-en, *v* to
offend, to hurt

Krankenhaus, krahnk-en-
hows, *nt* hospital

Krankenkasse, krahnk-en-
kahss-e, *f* health insurance

Krankenpfleger, krahnk-
en-p'flayg-er, *m* nurse,
orderly

Krankenwagen, krahnk-en-
wahg-en, *m* ambulance

krankhaft, krahnk-hahft,
adj morbid, diseased;
pathological

Krankheit, krahnk-hite, *f*
illness, disease

kränklich, krenk-lik, *adj*
sickly, delicate

Kranz, krahnts, *m* wreath,
garland

kratzen, krahts-en, *v* to
scratch, to scrape; to
scrawl

kraus, krows, *adj* curly,
frizzled; crisp

kräuseln, krowz-eln, *v* to

curl, to frizzle, to crimp

Kraut, krowt, *nt* plant, herb;
cabbage

Krawall, krah-vahll, *m* riot;
brawl

Krawatte, krah-vahtt-e, *f* tie

Krebs, krapes, *m* crayfish;
med cancer

Kreide, kry-de, *f* chalk

Kreis, krice, *m* circle;
district, parish

kreischen, kry-shen, *v* to
scream, to yell, to shriek

Kreisel, kry-zel, *m* spinning-
top

kreisen, kry-zen, *v* to circle,
to revolve, to orbit

kreisförmig, krice-ferm-ik,
adj circular

Kreislauf, krice-lowf, *m*
circulation

Kreissäge, krice-zayg-e, *f*
circular-saw

Kreisstadt, krice-shtahtt, *f*
county-town

krepieren, kray-peer-en, *v*
to die, to perish

Krepp, krep, *m* crepe

Kresse, kres-e, *f* cress

Kreta, kray-tah, *nt* Crete

Kreuz, kroyts, *nt* cross;
(small of the) back

kreuzen, kroyts-en, *v* to
cross

Kreuzfahrt, kroyts-fahrt, *f*
crusade

Kreuzgang, kroyts-gahng, *m*
cloister; cutting

kreuzigen, kroyts-ig-en, *v*
to crucify

Kreuzverhör, kroyts-fair-her, nt, cross-examination

Kreuzzug, kroyts-tsook, m crusade, Holy War

kribbeln, krib-eln, v to prickle, to tingle; to swarm

kriechen, kreek-en, v to creep, to crawl

Krieg, kreek, m war(fare)

kriegen, kreeg-en, v fam to receive, to get

kriegerisch, kreeg-er-ish, adj warlike, martial

Kriegserklärung, kreeks-er-klair-oong, f declaration of war

Kriegsgefangene(r), kreeks-ge-fahng-en-e(r), m & f prisoner of war

Kriegsgefangenschaft, kreeks-ge-fahng-en-shaft, f captivity

Kriegsgericht, kreeks-ge-rikt, nt courtmartial

Kriegsgesetz, kreeks-ge-sets, nt martial law

Kriegszustand, kreeks-tsoo-shtahnt, m state of war

Kriminalbeamte(r), krim-in-**ahl**-be-ahmt-e(r), m detective

kriminell, krim-in-**ell,** adj criminal

Krimi, kree-mee, m thriller

Krippe, krip-e, f manger, crib; creche

Krise, kree-ze, f crisis

Kritik, krit-**eek,** f criticism, critique, review

Kritiker, krit-ik-er, m critic, reviewer

kritisieren, krit-eez-**eer**-en, v to criticise

kritzeln, krit-seln, v to scratch; to scribble

Krokodil, kroh-koh-**deel,** nt crocodile

Krone, krohn-e, f crown

krönen, krern-en, v to crown

Kronprinz, krohn-prints, m Crown Prince

Kröte, krert-e, f toad

Krücke, krEEck-e, f crutch; crook

Krug, krook, m jug, pitcher

krümelig, krEEm-el-ik, adj crumbly, crumbling

krumm, kroomm, adj crooked, bent, curved

krümmen, krEEmm-en, v to wind, to twist, to bend

Krümmung, krEEmm-oong, f curve, bend

Krüppel, krEEpp-el, m cripple, deformed person

Kruste, kroost-e, f crust; crackling

Kuba, koo-bah, nt Cuba

Kübel, kEEb-el, m vat, bucket

Küche, kEEk-e, f kitchen; cooking

Kuchen, kook-en, m cake

Kuckuck, kook-kook, m cuckoo

Kugel, koog-el, f ball, globe, sphere; bullet

kugelrund, koog-el-roont, adj round, spherical

Kugelschreiber, koog-el-shry-ber, m biro

Kuh, koo, f cow

kühl, kEEl, adj cool, fresh; cold, unfeeling

Kühle, kEEl-e, f coolness, freshness

kühlen, kEEl-en, v to cool

Kühler, kEEl-er, m radiator (of car); ice-bucket; **–haube,** f bonnet (of car)

Kühlschrank, kEEl-shrahnk, m refrigerator

kühn, kEEn, adj bold, brave, intrepid, rash

Küken, kEEk-en, nt chick

kulant, kool-**ahnt,** adj fair; obliging

Kulanz, kool-**ahnts,** f fairness, promptness

Kulisse, kool-**iss**-e, f (theatre) scene, wings

Kult, koolt, m cult

Kultur, koolt-**oor,** f culture; civilization; cultivation (soil); **–beutel,** m toilet bag

kulturell, koolt-oor-**ell,** adj cultural

Kultusminister, koolt-oos-min-ist-er, m minister of education

Kümmel, kEEmm-el, m caraway; kümmel (liqueur)

Kummer, koomm-er, m grief, sorrow

kümmerlich, kEEmm-er-lik, adj wretched, miseable, grievous

kümmern, kEEmm-ern, v to concern; **sich um etw/jdn –,** v to look after sth/sb

kündbar, kEEnt-bar, *adj*
    subject to notice;
    redeemable
Kunde, koond-e, *m*
    customer, client;
    –ndienst, *m* after-sales
    service
kundgeben, koont-gayb-en,
    v to publish, to notify
Kundgebung, koont-gayb-
    oong, *f* manifestation
kündigen, kEEnd-ig-en, *v* to
    give notice; to cancel
Kundschaft, koont-shahft, *f*
    customers; clientele;
    reconnaissance
Kundschafter, koont-
    shahft-er, *m* scout, spy
künftig, kEEnf-tik, *adj* future
Kunst, koonst, *f* art; skill,
    cleverness; **–faser,** *f*
    synthetic fibre;
    –gegenstand, *m* art object
Kunstgeschichte, koonst-
    ge-shik-te, *f* history of art
Kunstgewerbe, koonst-ge-
    vair-be, *nt* arts and crafts
Kunstkenner, koonst-ken-
    er, *m* art expert,
    connoisseur
Künstler, kEEnst-ler, *m*
    artist; artiste
künstlerisch, kEEnst-ler-ish,
    adj artistic
künstlich, kEEnst-lik, *adj*
    artificial; ingenious
Kunstsammler, koonst-
    sahm-ler, *m* art collector
Kunstseide, koonst-zy-de, *f*
    artificial silk
Kunststoff, koonst-shtoff,

m synthetic material
Kunststück, koonst-
    shtEEck, *nt* clever trick,
    feat
Kunstwerk, koonst-vairk,
    nt work of art
kunterbunt, koont-er-
    boont, *adj* gaudy,
    variegated; jumbled
Kupfer, koopp-fer, *nt* copper
Kupferstich, koopp-fer-
    shtik, *m* engraving
Kuppe, koopp-e, *f*
    mountain-peak
Kuppel, koopp-el, *f* cupola,
    dome
kuppeln, koopp-eln, *v* to
    pair; to matchmake; *mech*
    to engage the clutch
Kupplung, koopp-loong, *f*
    clutch
Kurbel, koorb-el, *f* crank-
    handle, winch-handle
kurbeln, koorb-eln, *v* to
    turn a handle, to crank
Kürbis, kEErb-iss, *m*
    pumpkin
Kur, koor, *f* cure; stay at a
    health spa; **–gast,** *m*
    visitor to a spa
kurieren, koor-eer-en, *v* to
    cure
Kurort, koor-ort, *m* health-
    resort; spa
Kurpfuscher, koor-p'foosh-
    er, *m* quack, charlatan
Kurs, koors, *m* rate of
    exchange; course
Kursbuch, koors-book, *nt*
    (train) timetable
kurz, koorts, *adj* short

Kürze, kEErt-se, *f* shortness;
    brevity
kürzen, kEErt-sen, *v* to
    shorten; to cut down
kurzerhand, koort-ser-
    hahnt, *adv* abruptly
kurzfristig, koorts-frist-ik,
    adj short-term
Kurzgeschichte, koorts-ge-
    shik-te, *f* short story
kürzlich, kEErts-lik, *adv*
    lately, recently
Kurzschluß, koorts-shlooss,
    m short-circuit
kurzsichtig, koorts-zikt-ik,
    adj short-sighted
Kürzung, kEErts-oong, *f*
    abridgement
Kurzwelle, koorts-vel-le, *f*
    short wave
Kusine, koo-zeen-e, *f* cousin
Kuß, kooss, *m* kiss
küssen, kEEss-en, *v* to kiss
Küste, kEEst-e, *f* coast,
    beach, shore
Küster, kEEst-er, *m* verger,
    sexton
Kutsche, koott-she, *f* coach,
    carriage
Kutscher, koott-sher, *m*
    coachman
Kutte, koott-e, *f* (monk's)
    habit
Kuvert, koo-**vair**, *nt*
    envelope, wrapper, cover

L

l, *abbr* **Liter**

Lache, lahk-*e*, *f* puddle, pool; laughter

lächeln, lek-*e*ln, *v* to smile

lachen, lahk-*e*n, *v* to laugh

lächerlich, lek-*er*-lik, *adj* laughable, ludicrous, ridiculous

Lachs, lahx, *m* salmon

Lack, lahck, *m* lacquer, varnish

lackieren, lahck-eer-*e*n, *v* to lacquer

Lackleder, lahck-laid-*er*, *nt* patent-leather

Lade, lah-*de*, *f* drawer

Laden, lah-den, *m* shop; shutter

laden, lah-den, *v* to load, to charge; to invite

Ladendiebstahl, lah-den-deep-shtahl, *m* shoplifting

Ladentisch, lah-den-tish, *m* counter (in shop)

Laderaum, lah-de-rowm, *m* hold (of a ship)

Ladung, lah-doong, *f* load, cargo; summons

Lage, lah-ge, *f* position, situation

Lager, lah-ger, *nt* camp; storehouse; stock

Lagerhaus, lah-ger-hows, *nt* warehouse

lagern, lah-gern, *v* to be stored/warehoused; to store

lahm, lahm, *adj* paralysed, limping, lame

lähmen, laym-*e*n, *v* to paralyse, to make lame

Lähmung, laym-oong, *f* paralysis

Laie, ly-*e*, *m* layman, novice; outsider

Laken, lahk-*e*n, *nt* (linen) sheet; shroud

Lakritze, lahck-rit-*se*, *f* liquorice

lallen, lahll-*e*n, *v* to mumble, to babble

Lamm, lahmm, *nt* lamb

Lampe, lahmp-*e*, *f* lamp, light

Lampenfieber, lahmp-en-feeb-*er*, *nt* stage-fright

Lampenschirm, lahmp-en-sheerm, *m* lampshade

Land, lahnt, *nt* land, country, territory; state

Landebahn, lahnn-de-bahn, *f* runway

landeinwärts, lahnt-ine-vairts, *adv* inland

landen, lahnd-*e*n, *v* to land, to disembark

Landessprache, lahnn-des-shprahk-*e*, *f* national language

landesüblich, lahnn-des-EEp-lik, *adj* customary in a country

Landesverrat, lahnn-des-fair-raht, *m* treason

Landeswährung, lahnn-des-vair-oong, *f* national currency

Landgericht, lahnt-ge-rikt, *nt* provincial court

Landhaus, lahnt-hows, *nt* country house

Landkarte, lahnt-kart-*e*, *f* map

landläufig, lahnt-loyf-ik, *adj* customary in a country

ländlich, lent-lik, *adj* rural

Landschaft, lahnt-shaft, *f* landscape, scenery

Landsitz, lahnt-zits, *m*

country-seat, villa

Landsmann, lahnts-mahn, *m* fellow country-man

Landstraße, lahnt-shtrahs-e, *f* country road

Landstreicher, lahnt-shtry-ker, *m* vagrant

Landung, lahnd-oong, *f* landing; **–sbrücke,** *f* landing-stage

Landwirt, lahnt-veert, *m* farmer; **–schaft,** *f* agriculture

lang, lahng, *adj* long; tall

lange, lahng-e, *adv* (for) a long time

Länge, leng-e, *f* length

langen, lahng-en, *v* to suffice; to reach, to touch

Längengrad, leng-en-graht, *m* degree of longitude

Langeweile, lahng-e-vy-le, *f* boredom, tediousness

langfristig, lahng-frist-ik, *adj* long-term

langjährig, lahng-yair-ik, *adj* (of) long standing

länglich, leng-lik, *adj* long, elongated

längs, lengs, *adv & prep* along

langsam, lahng-zahm, *adj* slow

längst, lengst, *adj* longest, *adv* long ago

langweilen, lahng-vy-len, *v* to tire, to bore; **sich –,** *v* to be bored

langweilig, lahng-vy-lik, *adj* boring, tedious

Langwelle, lahng-vel-e, *f*

long-wave

langwierig, lahng-veer-ik, *adj* lengthy, long lasting

längstens, leng-stens, *adv* at the latest

Lappalie, lahpp-ahl-ye, *f* trifle, petty matter

Lappen, lahpp-en, *m* rag, shred; duster

läppisch, lep-ish, *adj* foolish, nonsensical

Lärche, lair-ke, *f* larch (tree)

Lärm, lairm, *m* noise, din

lärmen, lairm-en, *v* to make a noise, to clamour

Larve, lahrf-e, *f* mask; pretty face; larva, grub

lassen, lahss-en, *v* to let, to allow (to); to leave; **etw machen –,** *v* to have sth done

lässig, less-ik, *adj* lazy, idle, indolent; neglectful

Last, lahst, *f* burden; charge; trouble

Laster, lahst-er, *nt* vice

lasterhaft, lahst-er-hahft, *adj* vicious, depraved

Lästermaul, lest-er-mowl, *nt* scandal-monger

lästern, lest-ern, *v* to blaspheme, to slander

Lästerung, lest-er-oong, *f* blasphemy; slander

lästig, lest-ik, *adj* burdensome, troublesome

Lastkraftwagen, last-krahft-vahg-en, *m* heavy-goods vehicle

Lasttier, lahst-teer, *nt* beast

of burden; drudge

Lastwagen, lahst-vah-gen, *m* lorry

Latein, lah-tine, *nt* Latin; **–amerika,** *nt* Latin America

Laterne, lahtt-airn-e, *f* lantern

Laternenpfahl, laht-airn-en-p'fahl, *m* lamp-post

latschen, laht-shen, *v* to shuffle along; to slouch

Latte, lahtt-e *f* slat; bar

Latz, lahts, *m* bib

lau, low, *adj* lukewarm, tepid; half-hearted

Laub, lowp, *nt* foliage, leaves; **–baum,** *m* deciduous tree

Laube, lowb-e, *f* arbour, porch

Laubfrosch, lowp-frosh, *m* green frog

Laubsäge, lowp-zaig-e, *f* fret-saw

Lauch, lowk, *m* leek

lauern, low-ern, *v* to lie in wait

Lauf, lowf, *m* run(ning); path, track; (gun) barrel

Laufbahn, lowf-bahn, *f* career; running track

Laufbursche, lowf-boorsh-e, *m* errand-boy

laufen, lowf-en, *v* to run; to flow

Läufer, loyf-er, *m* runner; narrow carpet; (chess) bishop

Laufmasche, lowf-mahsh-er, *f* ladder (in tights)

Laufwerk, lowf-vairk, *nt*
disk drive

Lauge, lowg-*e f* lye; salt
solution

Laune, lown-*e, f* mood,
humour

launenhaft, lown-en-haft,
adj capricious, moody

launisch, lown-ish, *adj*
moody

Laus, lows, *f* louse

lauschen, lowsh-en, *v*
eavesdrop, to listen

laut, lowt, *adj* loud; noisy;
prep according to

Laut, lowt, *m* sound, tone,
note

Laute, lowt-*e, f* lute

lauten, lowt-en, *v* to sound;
to express, to phrase

läuten, loyt-en, *v* to ring, to
peal, to tinkle

lauter, lowt-er, *adj* pure; *adv*
nothing but

läutern, loyt-ern, *v* to purify,
to chasten, to ennoble

Lautschrift, lowt-shrift, *f*
phonetic alphabet

Lautsprecher, lowt-shprek-
er, *m* loudspeaker

lauwarm, low-varm, *adj*
lukewarm

Lavendel, lah-vend-el, *m*
lavender

Lawine, lah-veen-*e, f*
avalanche

Leben, lay-ben, *nt* life,
existence

leben, lay-ben, *v* to live, to
exist

lebend, lay-bent, *adj* living

lebendig, lay-bend-ik, *adj*
alive, lively; live

**Lebenserwartung, lay-bens-
er-vahrt**-oong, *f* life
expectancy

**Lebensfreude, lay-bens-
froyd**-*e, f* joy of life

**Lebensgefahr, lay-bens-ge-
fahr**, *f* mortal danger

**lebensgefährlich, lay-bens-
ge-fair-lik**, *adj* extremely
dangerous; critical

**Lebensgefährte, lay-bens-
ge-fair-te**, *m* partner

lebensgroß, lay-bens-grohs,
adj life-size

**lebenslänglich, lay-bens-
leng-lik**, *adj* lifelong

Lebenslauf, lay-bens-lowf,
m curriculum vitae

Lebenslust, lay-bens-loost, *f*
joy of living; gaiety

**Lebensmittel, lay-bens-mit-
el**, *pl* provisions, food;
–vergiftung, *f* food
poisoning

**Lebensunterhalt, lay-bens-
oont-er-hahlt**, *m*
livelihood

**Lebensversicherung, lay-
bens-fair-zik-er-oong**, *f* life
insurance

**Lebensweise, lay-bens-vy-
ze**, *f* way of life

**lebenswichtig, lay-bens-vik-
tik**, *adj* vital

**Lebenszweck, lay-bens-
tsveck**, *m* purpose in life

Leber, lay-ber, *f* liver

Leberfleck, lay-ber-fleck, *m*
mole, birth-mark

Lebertran, lay-ber-trahn, *m*
cod-liver oil

Leberwurst, lay-ber-voorst,
f liver-sausage

Lebewesen, lay-be-vaiz-en,
nt living creature

Lebewohl, lay-be-vohl, *nt*
farewell

lebhaft, laip-hahft, *adj*
lively, vivacious

Lebkuchen, laip-kook-en, *m*
gingerbread

lechzen, lek-tsen, *v* to be
parched; to yearn for

leck, leck, *adj* leaky, leaking

Leck, leck, *nt* leak; outlet

lecken, leck-en, *v* to lick; to
leak

lecker, leck-er, *adj* dainty,
delicious

**Leckerbissen, leck-er-bis-
en**, *m* delicacy; titbit

Leckerei, leck-e-ry, *f*
delicacy; titbit

Leckermaul, leck-er-mowl,
nt sweet-toothed person

Leder, lay-der, *nt* leather;
hide

ledern, lay-dern, *adj* (made
of) leather; leathery,
tough

ledig, lay-dik, *adj* single,
unmarried

lediglich, lay-dik-lik, *adv*
purely, simply, solely

leer, lair, *adj* empty,
unoccupied, vacant

Leere, lair-*e, f* void,
vacuum, space

leeren, lair-en, *v* to empty,
to vacate

legen, lay-gen, *v* to lay, to put; **sich –,** *v* to lie down; to abate, to die down

legieren, lay-geer-en, *v* to alloy (metals)

Legierung, lay-geer-oong, *f* alloy(ing)

Legitimation, lay-geet-eem-ahts-yohn, *f* proof of identity

legitimieren (sich), lay-geet-eem-**eer-**en (zik), *v* to prove one's identity

Lehm, laim, *m* loam; clay

lehmig, laim-ik, *adj* loamy, clayey

Lehne, lain-e, *f* (of chair) back ; arm-rest

lehnen, lain-en, *v* to lean, to recline; to prop

Lehnstuhl, lain-shtool, *m* arm-chair, easy-chair

Lehrbuch, lair-book, *nt* text-book

Lehre, lair-e, *f* advice, tuition; apprenticeship; science

lehren, lair-en, *v* to teach, to instruct

Lehrer, lair-er, *m* teacher

Lehrfach, lair-fahk, *nt* subject

Lehrgang, lair-gahng, *m* course (of lessons)

Lehrling, lair-ling, *m* apprentice, beginner

Lehrmeister, lair-my-ster, *m* master

Lehrplan, lair-plahn, *m* curriculum, teaching plan

lehrreich, lair-ry'k, *adj* instructive

Lehrsatz, lair-zahts, *m* proposition; doctrine

Lehrstuhl, lair-shtool, *m* professor's chair

Lehrzeit, lair-tsite, *f* apprenticeship

Leib, lipe, *m* body; belly; abdomen

Leibgericht, lipe-ge-rikt, *nt* favourite dish

leibhaftig, lipe-hahft-ik, *adj* real, personified

leiblich, lipe-lik, *adj* physical; bodily; natural, by birth

Leibrente, lipe-rent-e, *f* life annuity

Leibwache, lipe-vak-e, *f* bodyguard

Leiche, ly-ke, *f* corpse, dead body

leichenblaß, ly-ken-blahss, *adj* deathly pale

Leichenwagen, ly-ken-vahg-en, *m* hearse

Leichnam, ly'k-nahm, *m* corpse

leicht, ly'kt, *adj* light (in weight); easy, light; slight

Leichtathletik, ly'kt-aht-lay-tik, *f* athletics

leichtfertig, ly'kt-fairt-ik, *adj* light-hearted, frivolous

leichtfüßig, ly'kt-fEEss-ik, *adj* light-footed, nimble

leichtgläubig, ly'kt-gloyb-ik, *adj* credulous

leichtherzig, ly'kt-hairt-sik, *adj* light-hearted

leichthin, ly'kt-hin, *adv* lightly

Leichtigkeit, ly'kt-ik-kite, *f* lightness; ease

leichtlebig, ly'kt-laib-ik, *adj* easy-going, happy-go-lucky

Leichtsinn, ly'kt-zin, *m* carelessness, recklessness

leichtsinnig, ly'kt-zin-ik, *adj* careless, reckless

leid, lite, *adj* es tut mir –, I am sorry

Leid, lite, *nt* injury; wrong; harm; grief; pain

leiden, ly-den, *v* to suffer; etw/jdn nicht – können, to dislike sth/sb

Leiden, ly-den, *nt* suffering; illness; **–schaft,** *f* passion

leidenschaftlich, ly-den-shahft-lik, *adj* passionate

leider, ly-der, *interj* unfortunately

leidlich, lite-lik, *adj* bearable; passable

Leier, ly-er, *f* lyre; hurdy-gurdy; (same old) story

Leierkasten, ly-er-kahst-en, *m* barrel-organ

leiern, ly-ern, *v* to grind out a tune; to turn a handle

leihen, ly-en, *v* to lend; sich etw –, *v* to borrow sth

Leihgebühr, ly-ge-bEEr, *f* hire charge

Leihhaus, ly-hows, *nt* pawnshop

leihweise, ly-vy-ze, *adv* on loan

Leim, lime, *m* glue

leimen, lime-en, *v* to glue

Leine, line-*e,* f cord, line, thin rope; leash

Leinen, line-*en,* nt linen (goods)

Leintuch, line-took, nt sheet

Leinwand, line-vahnt, f canvas; screen

leise, ly-ze, *adj* soft, gentle, low

Leiste, ly-ste, f strip; border, skirting; groin

leisten, ly-sten, v to render, to perform; **sich etw –,** to afford

Leistung, ly-stoong, f accomplishment; capacity

leistungsfähig, ly-stoongs-fay-ik, *adj* efficient

leiten, lite-en, v to lead, to conduct; to manage

Leiter, lite-er, m leader, conductor; manager; f ladder, steps

Leitfaden, lite-fahd-en, m clue

Leitsatz, lite-zahts, m guiding rule

Leitung, lite-oong, f lead(ing), conduct(ing); management; **–swasser,** nt tap water

Lektion, lekts-yohn, f lesson, lecture

Lektor, leck-tohr, m editor

Lektüre, leck-tEEr-e, f reading (matter)

Lende, lend-e, f loin; hip

lenken, lenk-en, v to turn; to bend; to drive; to direct

Lenkrad, lenk-raht, nt steering wheel

Lenkstange, lenk-shtahng-e, f handlebars

Lepra, lay-prah, f leprosy

Lerche, lairk-e, f skylark

lernbegierig, lairn-be-geer-ik, *adj* eager to learn

lernen, lairn-en, v to learn, to study; to serve apprenticeship

Lesbierin, les-bee-er-in, f lesbian

lesbisch, les-bish, *adj* lesbian

Lese, lay-ze, f picking; harvest; vintage

Lesebrille, lay-ze-bril-le, f reading glasses

lesen, lay-zen, v to read

Leser, lay-zer, m reader

leserlich, lay-zer-lik, *adj* legible; easy to read

Lesezeichen, lay-ze-tsy-ken, nt bookmark

letzte(r/s), lets-te(r/s), *adj* last; latest, ultimate, final

letztens, lets-tens, *adv* lastly, finally

letzthin, letst-hin, *adv* lately

leuchten, loyk-ten, v to shine, to give light

Leuchter, loyk-ter, m candlestick; chandelier

Leuchtfeuer, loykt-foy-er, nt beacon

Leuchtturm, loykt-toorm, m lighthouse

leugnen, loyg-nen, v to deny; to retract

Leumund, loy-moont, m repute, reputation; fame

Leumundszeugnis, loy-moonts-tsoyk-niss, nt character reference

Leute, loyt-e, pl people

leutselig, loyt-zayl-ik, *adj* affable, condescending

Lexikon, lek-see-kohn, nt encyclopedia

Libelle, lee-bel-e, f dragon-fly

liberal, lee-be-rahl, *adj* liberal

Licht, likt, nt light; brightness; illumination; **–bild,** nt photograph; transparency

lichtempfindlich, likt-emp-find-lik, *adj* light sensitive

Lichtschalter, likt-shahlt-er, m light switch

Lichtschutzfaktor, likt-shoots-fahk-tor, m (sun) protection factor

Lichtstrahl, likt-strahl, m ray of light

Lichtung, likt-oong, f clearing; glade

Lid, leet, nt (eye-)lid

lieb, leep, *adj* dear, beloved

liebäugeln, leep-oyg-eln, v to ogle

Liebe, leeb-e, f love, affection, fondness

Liebelei, leeb-e-ly, f flirtation

lieben, leeb-en, v to love, to be fond of

liebenswürdig, leeb-ens-vEErd-ik, *adj* amiable, lovable

lieber, leeb-er, *adj* dearer;

adv rather

Liebesbrief, leeb-es-breef, *m* love letter

Liebeserklärung, leeb-es-air-klair-oong, *f* declaration of love

Liebeskummer, leeb-es-koom-er, *m* – **haben,** to be lovesick

Liebespaar, leeb-es-pahr, *nt* courting couple

liebevoll, leeb-e-fol, *adj* loving, affectionate; kind-hearted

liebgewinnen, leep-ge-vin-en, *v* to become fond of

liebhaben, leep-hahb-en, *v* to love, to be fond of

Liebhaber, leep-hahb-er, *m* lover; connoisseur, enthusiast

Liebhaberei, leep-hahb-e-ry, *f* hobby

liebkosen, leep-koz-en, *v* to caress, to fondle

lieblich, leep-lik, *adj* lovely; agreeable, pleasing

Liebling, leep-ling, *m* darling, pet; **Lieblings-,** *pref* favourite

Liebschaft, leep-shahft, *f* love-affair

Lied, leet, *nt* song

liederlich, leed-er-lik, *adj* slovenly; dissolute

Lieferant, leef-er-ahnt, *m* supplier, contractor

liefern, leef-ern, *v* to deliver, to supply

Lieferung, leef-er-oong, *f* delivery; consignment;

supply

Lieferwagen, leef-er-vah-gen, *m* (delivery) van

Lieferzeit, leef-er-tsite, *f* delivery time

liegen, leeg-en, *v* to lie, to be (situated)

liegenlassen, leeg-en-lahs-sen, *v* to leave behind

Liegesitz, leeg-e-sits, *m* reclining seat

Liegestuhl, leeg-e-shtool, *m* deck chair

Liegewagen, leeg-e-vah-gen, *m* couchette

Liga, leeg-ah, *f* league

Likör, le-ker, *m* liqueur, cordial

lila, lee-lah, *adj* lilac (-coloured)

Lilie, leel-ee-e, *f* lily

Limonade, lee-moh-**nah**-de, *f* lemonade

Linde, lin-de, *f* lime tree, linden

lindern, lin-dern, *v* to soften; to alleviate, to ease

Lineal, lin-e-ahl, *nt* ruler; rule

Linie, leen-ee-e, *f* line, rule; lineage; **–nflug,** *m* scheduled flight

Linke, link-e, *f* (political) left

linkisch, link-ish, *adj* clumsy, awkward

links, links, *adv* on/to the left; on the reverse/wrong side

Linkshänder, links-hend-er, *m* left-handed person

Linksverkehr, links-fer-kair, *m* driving on the left

Linse, lin-ze, *f* lentil; lens

Lippe, lip-e, *f* lip; **–nstift,** *m* lipstick

lispeln, lisp-eln, *v* to lisp; to murmur; to ripple

List, list, *f* craftiness, cunning, artifice

Liste, list-e, *f* list, register, schedule

listig, list-ik, *adj* cunning, crafty, wily

Listigkeit, list-ik-kite, *f* craftiness

Liter, lee-ter, *m & nt* litre

Literatur, lit-er-ah-**toor,** *f* literature

Litfaßsäule, lit-fahss-zoyl-e, *f* advertising column

Litze, lit-ze, *f* braid; flex

Lizenz, lee-tsents, *f* license

Lkw, el kah vay, *abbr* **Lastkraftwagen,** *m* HGV

Lob, lohp, *nt* praise, applause; good mark

loben, lohb-en, *v* to praise

lobenswert, lohb-ens-vairt, *adj* praiseworthy

löblich, lerp-lik, *adj* laudable, praiseworthy

Loch, lok, *nt* hole; opening; aperture

lochen, lok-en, *v* to perforate

löcherig, lerk-er-ik, *adj* full of holes, perforated

Locke, lock-e, *f* curl, lock, ringlet

locken, lock-en, *v* to curl; to allure

Lockenwickler, lock-*en*-vik-ler, *m* curler

locker, lock-*er*, *adj* loose; spongy

lockern, lock-*ern*, *v* to loosen; to slacken

lockig, lock-*ik*, *adj* curly

Lockmittel, lock-*mit*-el, *nt* bait; temptation

lodern, lohd-*ern*, *v* to blaze

Löffel, lerff-*el*, *m* spoon; ladle

löffeln, lerff-*eln*, *v* to ladle; to eat with a spoon

löffelweise, lerff-el-*vy*-ze, *adv* by spoonfuls

Loge, lohzh-*e*, *f* (theatre) box; lodge

Logik, lohg-*ik*, *f* logic

logisch, lohg-*ish*, *adj* logical

Lohn, lohn, *m* reward, recompense; wage(s)

lohnen (sich), lohn-*en* (*zik*), *v* to be profitable

Lohnerhöhung, lohn-*er*-her-oong, *f* pay rise

Lohnsteuer, lohn-*shtoy*-er, *f* income tax

Lokal, loh-kahl, *nt* premises; restaurant

Lokomotive, loh-koh-moh-tee-ve, *f* locomotive

Lorbeer, lor-bair, *m* laurel, bay(-tree)

Lorbeerkranz, lor-bair-krahnts, *m* laurel-wreath

Los, lohs, *nt* lot, lottery-ticket; fate, destiny

los, lohs, *adj* loose, slack; **etw – sein,** *v* to be rid of sth; **Was ist –?** What is the matter?

losbekommen, lohs-*be*-kom-en, *v* to loosen

losbinden, lohs-bin-den, *v* to untie

löschen, lersh-*en*, *v* to extinguish; to quench; to blot (out); to unload (ship)

lose, loh-ze, *adj* loose; movable; dissipated

Lösegeld, lerz-*e*-gelt, *nt* ransom

losen, loh-zen, *v* to draw lots, to toss

lösen, lerz-*en*, *v* to loosen; to sever; to (dis)solve; to take (tickets); **sich –,** *v* to come loose; to dissolve; to solve itself

losfahren, lohs-fahr-en, *v* to ride/drive off

losgehen, lohs-gay-en, *v* to go off; to start

loskaufen, lohs-kowf-en, *v* to ransom, to redeem

loskommen, lohs-kom-en, *v* to get off; to be set free

loslassen, lohs-lahss-en, *v* to let go; to release

löslich, lers-lik, *adj* soluble

losmachen, lohs-mahk-en, *v* to untie, to undo, to free

losschießen, lohs-shees-en, *v* to fire (away); to start firing

losschrauben, lohs-shrowb-en, *v* to unscrew

losspringen, lohs-shpring-en, *v* to snap off; to jump at

losstürmen, lohs-shtEErm-en, *v* to (take by) storm

lostrennen, lohs-tren-en, *v* to sever; to unstitch

Losung, lohz-oong, *f* casting lots; password

Lösung, lerz-oong, *f* solution

loswerden, lohs-vaird-en, *v* to get rid of

losziehen, lohs-tsee-en, *v* to set out/off

Lot, loht, *nt* plumbline

löten, lert-en, *v* to solder

Lotleine, loht-line-e, *f* plumbline

Lotse, loht-se, *m* pilot (ship)

lotsen, loht-sen, *v* to pilot; *fam* to drag (sb) along

Lotterie, lot-e-ree, *f* lottery

Lotto, lot-oh, *nt* national lottery

Löwe, ler-*ve*, *m* lion; **–nmaul,** *nt* snapdragon; **–nzahn,** *m* dandelion

Luchs, looks, *m* lynx; artful person

Lücke, lEEck-e, *f* gap, hiatus, breach, break

Luder, lood-er, *nt* abomination; beast

Luft, looft, *f* air; gas; breath; **–ballon,** *m* balloon

Luftdruck, looft-droock, *m* air-pressure

lüften, lEEft-en, *v* to ventilate; to raise (hat)

Luftfahrt, looft-fahrt, *f* aviation

Luftfracht, looft-frakt, *f* air freight

luftig, looft-ik, *adj* airy; lofty; light as air

Luftkissenfahrzeug, looft-kis-en-fahr-tsoyk, *nt* hovercraft

luftleer, looft-lair, *adj* void of air

Luftlinie, looft-leen-ye, *f* bee-line, as the crow flies

Luftmatratze, looft-mah-trah-tse, *f* lilo, air mattress

Luftpirat, looft-peer-aht, *m* hijacker

Luftpost, looft-post, *f* air mail

Luftpumpe, looft-poom-pe, *f* (air) pump

Luftschloß, looft-shloss, *nt* castle in the air

Luftstoß, looft-shtos, *m* gust of wind

Luftverschmutzung, looft-fer-shmoots-oong, *f* air pollution

Luftwaffe, looft-vahff-e, *f* air force

Luftzug, looft-tsook, *m* draught (of air), air-current

Lüge, lEEg-e, *f* lie, falsehood

lügen, lEEg-en, *v* to lie, to tell lies

Lügner, lEEg-ner, *m* liar

lügnerisch, lEEg-ner-ish, *adj* lying, untruthful

Luke, look-e, *f* hatchway; dormer-window

Lümmel, lEEmm-el, *m* lout

Lump, loomp, *m* rogue

Lumpen, loomp-en, *pl* rags

lumpig, loomp-ik, *adj* tattered, shabby; measly

Lunge, loong-e, *f* lung

Lungenentzündung, loong-en-ent-tsEEnd-oong, *f* pneumonia

lungern, loong-ern, *v* to loiter, to hang about

Lunte, loont-e, *f* fuse; brush (fox)

Lupe, loop-e, *f* magnifying glass

Lust, loost, *f* desire; inclination; joy; **– auf/zu etw haben,** *v* to feel like doing sth

Lustbarkeit, loost-bar-kite, *f* festivity, revelry

Lüster, lEEst-er, *m* lustre, chandelier

lüstern, lEEst-ern, *adj* longing for; lustful

lustig, loost-ik, *adj* happy, jolly; amusing

lustlos, loost-lohs, *adj* unenthusiastic

Lustspiel, loost-shpeel, *nt* comedy

lutschen, loott-shen, *v* to suck

Luxus, loox-ooss, *m* luxury

Lyrik, lEEr-ik, *f* lyric poetry, verse

machbar, mah*k*-bar, *adj* possible, feasible

machen, mah*k*-en, *v* to make, to do, to matter

Machenschaften, mah*k*-en-shahf*t*-en, *pl* machination, intrigue

Macht, mahkt, *f* might, power; **–befugnis**, *f* authority; **–haber**, *m* person in power

mächtig, mekt-ik, *adj* mighty, powerful, considerable

Machtkampf, mahkt-kahmpf, *m* power struggle

Machtstellung, mahkt-shtell-oong, *f* position of power

Machtwechsel, mahkt-veks-el, *m* change of power

Mädchen, mait-ken, *nt* girl, maid, maiden

Made, mahd-e, *f* maggot, grub, mite

Mädel, maid-el, *nt fam* girl

madig, mahd-ik, *adj* maggoty, worm-eaten; **jdm etw – machen**, *v* to put sb off sth

mag, mahg, (from **mögen**) likes, may

Magen, mahg-en, *m* stomach; **–geschwür**, *nt* stomach ulcer; **–schmerzen**, *pl* stomach pains

mager, mahg-er, *adj* lean, thin

Magermilch, mahg-er-milk, *f* skimmed milk

Magistrat, mahgg-ist-raht, *m* town-council, corporation; **–ur**, *f* municipal council

Mahagoni, mah-hah-gohn-ee, *nt* mahogany

mähen, may-en, *v* to mow, to cut (grass), to reap

Mahl, mahl, *nt* meal, feast

mahlen, mahl-en, *v* to grind, to mill

Mahlzeit, mahl-tsite, *f* meal, repast

Mähne, mayn-e, *f* mane; *fam* head of hair

mahnen, mahn-en, *v* to remind, to admonish

Mahnung, mahn-oong, *f* warning

Mai, my, *m* May; **–glöckchen**, *nt* lily-of-the-valley; **–käfer**, *m* cockchafer, May bug

Mailand, my-lahnt, *nt* Milan

Mais, mice, *m* maize, Indian corn; **–kolben**, *m* corn (on the) cob

makaber, ma-kahb-er, *adj* macabre

Makel, mahk-el, *m* stain, blot; blemish

makellos, mahk-el-lohs, *adj* immaculate

Mäkelei, mayk-e-ly, *f* fault finding

mäkeln, mayk-eln, *v* to find fault, to carp

Makler, mahk-ler, *m* broker, commission-agent

Makrele, mahk-rayl-e, *f* mackerel

Makrone, mahk-rohn-e, *f* macaroon

Makulatur, mahk-oo-laht-oor, *f* waste-paper; *fig* rubbish

Mal, mahl, *nt* mole,

(birth)mark; time(s)

malen, mahl-en, v to paint, to depict

Maler, mahl-er, m painter, artist

Malerei, mahl-e-**ry,** f (art of) painting

malerisch, mahl-er-ish, adj picturesque, artistic

Malheur, mahl-**er,** nt misfortune, accident

Mallorca, mahl-**or**-kah, nt Majorca

Malz, mahlts, nt malt; **–bier,** nt malt beer; **–kaffee,** m malt coffee; coffee substitute

Mama, mah-mah, f mum

man, mahnn, pron one, people, they

Manager, man-edsh-er, m manager

manch(e/er/es), mahnnk(-e/er/es), adj many (a)

mancherlei, mahnnk-er-**ly,** adj different (kinds of), many, various, diverse

manchmal, mahnnk-mahl, adv sometimes

Mandarine, mahnn-dah-**reen**-e, f tangerine

Mandat, mahnn-**daht,** nt mandate, authorization; decree

Mandel, mahnn-del, f almond; tonsil

Mangel, mahng-el, m want, lack, scarcity, absence, shortcoming; **–erscheinung,** f shortage; med deficiency symptom

mangelhaft, mahng-el-hahft, adj defective, imperfect, insufficient

mangeln, mahng-eln, v to be wanting (in)

mangels, mahng-els, prep for lack of

Mango, mahng-goh, f mango

Manie, mahnn-ee, f mania

Manier, mahnn-eer, f manner, mode, fashion; **–en,** pl manners

manierlich, mahnn-eer-lik, adj well-mannered, well-bred; polite

Manifest, mahnn-ee-**fest,** nt manifesto

Manko, mahng-koh, nt deficiency, shortage; shortness

Mann, mahnn, m man; husband; **–esalter,** nt manhood; **–schaft,** f crew, (ship's) company; team; gang of men

Männchen, men-ken, nt little man, manikin; male animal

Mannequin, mahnn-e-kang, nt (fashion) model

mannhaft, mahnn-hahfft, adj manly, virile, brave

mannigfach, mahnn-ik-fahk, adj manifold, varied

mannigfaltig, mahnn-ik-fahlt-ik, adj manifold, multifarious

männlich, men-lik, adj male, masculine

Mansarde, mahnn-**zard**-e, f attic, garret

manschen, mahnn-shen, v fam to mess around

Manschette, mahnn-**shet**-e, f cuff, wristband; **–nknopf,** m cuff-link

Mantel, mahnn-tel, m mantle, coat, cloak; casing

Manufaktur, mahnn-oo-fahck-**toor,** f factory; (textile) mill; **–waren,** pl manufactured goods (especially textiles)

Manuskript, mahnn-oo-**skript,** nt manuscript

Mappe, mahpp-e, f portfolio, album, satchel

Marathon, mah-rah-tohnn, m marathon

Märchen, mair-ken, nt fairytale, fable, romance; **–prinz,** m Prince Charming

märchenhaft, mair-ken-hahft, adj legendary, like a fairy-tale

Margarine, mahr-gah-**ree**-ne, f margarine

Marienkäfer, mah-ree-en-kayf-er, m lady-bird

Marihuana, mah-ree-hwah-nah, nt marijuana

Marine, mah-**reen**-e, f navy, fleet

marinieren, mah-ree-**neer**-en, v to pickle, to marinate

Mark, mark, nt marrow; pith; vigour; f (German) mark

markant, mark-**ahnt,** adj

clear-cut, striking, marked

Marke, mark-*e*, *f* token, sign; stamp; brand; **–nartikel**, *m* proprietary article

markieren, mark-**eer**-en, *v* to emphasize; to pretend

Markstein, mark-**shtine**, *m* milestone; boundary stone; epoch

Markt, markt, *m* market; fair; trade, business; **–bude**, *f* market-stall; **–flecken**, *m* market-town; **–forschung,** *f* market research; **–lücke**, *f* gap in the market; **–platz**, *m* market-place; **–wirtschaft,** *f* market economy

Marmelade, mar-me-**lahd**-*e*, *f* jam

Marmor, mar-mohr, *m* marble; **–bild**, *nt* marble statue

Marokko, mah-**rock**-oh, *nt* Morocco

Marone, mah-**rohn**-*e*, *f* sweet chestnut

Marsch, marsh, *m* march; *f* marshy land

marschbereit, marsh-be-rite, *adj* ready to march

marschieren, marsh-**eer**-en, *v* to march

Marter, mar-ter, *f* torture, torment, agony

martern, mar-tern, *v* to torture, to torment, to put on the rack

Märtyrer, mairt-**EE**-rer, *m* martyr; **–tum**, *nt* martyrdom

März, mairts, *m* March

Marzipan, mar-tsee-pahn, *nt* marzipan

Masche, mahsh-*e*, *f* mesh, stitch

Maschine, mahsh-ee-ne, *f* machine, engine

maschinell, mahsh-ee-**nel**, *adj* machine-made, mechanical

Maschinenbauer, mahsh-ee-nen-bow-er, *m* mechanical engineer

Maschinengewehr, mash-ee-nen-gay-ver, *nt* machine gun

Maschinenschaden, mash-ee-nen-shah-den, *m* mechanical fault

Masern, mah-zern, *pl* measles

Maß, mahss, *nt* measure; rate, proportion; extent; size; *f* litre (of beer)

Masse, mahss-*e*, *f* bulk, mass, volume; quantity; **–nartikel**, *m* mass-produced article; **–medien**, *pl* mass media

massenhaft, mahss-en-hahft, *adj & adv* massed together, numerous; *fam* heaps of

Massenkarambolage, mahss-en-kah-rahmm-boh-**lah**-zhe, *f* multiple car accident

maßgebend, mahss-gayb-ent, *adj* decisive,

authoritative, leading

massieren, mahss-**eer**-en, *v* to massage

massig, mahss-ik, *adj* solid, massive, bulky

mäßig, mace-ik, *adj* moderate; temperate; frugal

mäßigen, mace-ig-en, *v* to moderate; to modify

Maßkrug, mahss-krook, *m* litre (beer) mug

Maßnahme, mahss-nahm-*e*, *f* step; measure

Maßregel, mahss-rayg-el, *f* measure

Maßstab, mahss-shtahp, *m* rule(r); scale

Mast, mahst, *m* mast, pole, pylon; *f* fattening, feed

mästen, mest-en, *v* to fatten; to batten

Material, maht-air-ee-**ahl**, *nt* material

Materie, maht-**air**-ee-*e*, *f* matter; subject

Mathematik, mahtt-*e*-mah-**tick**, *f* mathematics

Matratze, maht-**rahtt**-se, *f* mattress

Matrose, maht-**roh**-ze, *m* seaman, sailor, mariner

Matsch, mahttsh, *m* slush, slop, pulp, mash

matschig, mahtsh-ik, *adj* muddy, messy, sloppy

matt, mahtt, *adj* exhausted, jaded, lifeless; dull; faint; mat; (chess) mate

Matte, mahtt-*e*, *f* mat(ting);

mead, meadow

Mauer, mow-er, *f* wall; partition; **–blümchen,** *nt* wallflower

mauern, mow-ern, *v* to build walls

Maul, mowl, *nt* snout; muzzle; *fam* big mouth; **–beere,** *f* mulberry; **–esel,** *m* mule; **–korb,** *m* muzzle (of animal); **–sperre,** *f* lock-jaw; **–tier,** *nt* mule; **–wurf,** *m* mole

Maurer, mowr-er, *m* bricklayer, mason; builder

Maus, mows, *f* mouse

mäuschenstill, moys-ken-shtill, *adj* quiet as a mouse

Mausefalle, mow-ze-fahll-e, *f* mouse-trap

mausen, mowz-en, *v* to catch mice; to sneak

mausern, mow-zern, *v* to moult

mausetot, mow-ze-toht, *adj* stone-dead

Maut, mowt, *f* toll; **–gebühr,** *f* toll (charge); **–straße,** *f* toll road

maximal, mahks-ee-mahl, *adj & adv* maximal, maximum; maximally, at most

Mayonnaise, mah-yoh-neh-ze, *f* mayonnaise

Mechanik, mek-ahn-ik, *f* mechanics, mechanism; **–er,** *m* mechanic; fitter

Mechanismus, mek-ahn-is-mooss, *m* mechanism

meckern, meck-ern, *v* to

bleat

Medaille, may-dahll-ye, *f* medal

Medien, meh-dee-en, *pl* the media

Medikament, may-dee-kah-ment, *nt* medicine

Medizin, may-dee-tseen, *f* medicine, physic; medication; **–er,** *m* doctor

Meer, mair, *nt* sea, ocean; **–busen,** *m* gulf, bay; **–enge,** *f* straits, channel

Meeresfrüchte, mair-es-frEEk-te, *pl* seafood

Meeresspiegel, mair-es-shpeeg-el, *m* sea-level

Meerrettich, mair-ret-ik, *m* horse-radish

Meerschweinchen, mair-shvine-ken, *nt* guinea-pig

Megaphon, maig-ah-fohn, *nt* megaphone

Mehl, mail, *nt* flour, meal

mehlig, mail-ik, *adj* floury, mealy

Mehlspeise, mail-shpy-ze, *f* floury food; pudding

mehr, mair, *adv* more

mehrdeutig, mair-doyt-ik, *adj* ambiguous

mehren, mair-en, *v* to multiply, to increase

mehrere, mair-e-re, *adj* several, a few, different

mehrfach, mair-fahk, *adj* manifold; *adv* repeatedly, on several occasions

Mehrheit, mair-hite, *f* majority; plurality

mehrmal(s), mair-mahl(s),

adv several times

Mehrwertsteuer, mair-vairt-shtoy-er, *f* value added tax

Mehrzahl, mair-tsahl, *f* greater part, majority

meiden, my-den, *v* to avoid, to shun

Meile, my-le, *f* mile

meilenweit, my-len-vite, *adj* stretching for miles, miles away

mein, meine(r/s), mine, mine-e(r/s), *adj* my; *pron* mine

Meineid, mine-ite, *m* perjury, false oath

meinen, mine-en, *v* to mean, to signify; to think; to assert

meinerseits, mine-er-zites, *adv* for my part

meinesgleichen, my-nes-gly-ken, *pron* people like myself

meinesteils, my-nes-tiles, *adv* for my part

meinethalben, my-net-hahllb-en, *adv* on my account, for my sake

meinetwegen, my-net-vay-gen, *adv* on my account, for my sake

meinetwillen, my-net-vil-en, *adv* on my account, for my sake

Meinung, my-noong, *f* opinion; intention, wish

Meißel, my-sel, *m* chisel

meißeln, my-seln, *v* to carve, to chisel

meist, my'st, *adj* most, greatest

meistbietend, my'st-beet-ent, *adj* bidding most (at auctions)

meistens, my-stens, *adv* mostly, in most cases, generally

Meister, my-ster, *m* master; champion (sport)

meisterhaft, my-ster-hahft, *adj* masterly; *adv* to perfection

meistern, my-stern, *v* to master

Meisterschaft, my-ster-shahft, *f* championship, mastery

Meisterwerk, my-ster-vairk, *nt* masterpiece

Meistgebot, my'st-ge-boht, *nt* highest bid

Melasse, may-lahss-e, *f* molasses, treacle

melden, meld-en, *v* to announce, to inform, to report; **sich –**, to get in touch; to report

Meldung, meld-oong, *f* notification; report

melken, melk-en, *v* to milk

Melone, mel-oh-ne, *f* melon

Memme, mem-e, *f* coward

Menge, meng-e, *f* crowd, quantity, swarm

mengen, meng-en, *v* to mix; **sich –**, *v* to meddle

Meningitis, men-in-gee-tis, *f* meningitis

Mensch, mensh, *m* man, human being; *nt* hussy

Menschenalter, men-shen-ahlt-er, *nt* generation; lifetime

Menschenfeind, men-shen-fy'nt, *m* misanthrope

Menschenfreund, men-shen-froynt, *m* philanthropist

Menschenkenner, men-shen-ken-er, *m* judge of character

menschenmöglich, men-shen-merk-lik, *adj* feasible; humanly possible

menschenscheu, men-shen-shoy, *adj* unsociable, shy

Menschenschlag, men-shen-shlahk, *m* kind of people

Menschenverstand, men-shen-fair-shtahnt, *m* common-sense

Menschheit, mensh-hite, *f* mankind; humankind

menschlich, mensh-lik, *adj* human(e)

Menschlichkeit, mensh-lik-kite, *f* humaneness

Menstruation, mens-troo-ahts-yohn, *f* menstruation

Mensur, men-zoor, *f* fencing bout; duel

Mentalität, men-tahl-ee-tait, *f* mentality

merken, mairk-en, *v* to mark, to note, to observe

merkenswert, mairk-ens-vairt, *adj* noteworthy

merklich, mairk-lik, *adj* perceptible; visible

Merkmal, mairk-mahl, *nt* characteristic

merkwürdig, mairk-vEErd-ik, *adj* strange, curious

merkwürdigerweise, mairk-vEErd-ig-er-vy-ze, *adv* curiously (enough)

meßbar, mess-bahr, *adj* measurable

Meßbecher, mess-bek-er, *m* measuring jug

Messe, mess-e, *f* mass; fair; **–gelände**, *nt* exhibition centre; **–halle**, *f* exhibition hall

messen, mess-en, *v* to measure; to gauge

Messer, mess-er, *nt* knife

Messing, mess-ing, *nt* brass

Metall, met-ahll, *nt* metal

metallisch, met-ahll-ish, *adj* metallic

Meter, mayt-er, *m* metre; **–maß**, *nt* (metric) measuring tape; metre rule

Methode, met-oh-de, *f* method

Metier, met-ee-ay, *nt* calling, vocation

Mettwurst, met-voorst, *f* (soft) German sausage

metzeln, mets-eln, *v* to massacre

Metzger, mets-ger, *m* butcher

Meuchelmord, moyk-el-mort, *m* assassination

Meuchelmörder, moyk-el-merd-er, *m* assassin

meuchlerisch, moyk-ler-ish, *adj* treacherous, like an assassin

Meute, moyt-e, f pack (of hounds)

Meuterei, moyt-e-ry, f mutiny

Meuterer, moyt-er-er, m mutineer

meutern, moyt-ern, v to mutiny

Mexiko, mek-sik-oh, nt Mexico

mich, mik, pron (accusative) me

Mieder, meed-er, nt girdle, bodice

Miene, meen-e, f mien, air, look

Miete, meet-e, f hire; rent; tenancy

mieten, meet-en, v to hire, to rent; to charter

Mieter, meet-er, m tenant

Mietskaserne, meets-kah-zairn-e, f tenement-building

Mietvertrag, meet-fer-trahk, m lease

Mietwagen, meet-vah-gen, m hire car

Migräne, mee-gray-ne, f migraine

Mikrofon, meek-roh-fohn, nt microphone

Mikrowelle, meek-roh-vel-e, f microwave

Milch, milk, f milk; soft roe (of fish)

milchig, milk-ik, adj milky

Milchspeise, milk-shpy-ze, f milk diet; milk-pudding

Milchstraße, milk-shtrahs-e, f milky-way

Milchwirtschaft, milk-veert-shahft, f dairy-farm

mild(e), milt (mild-e), adj mild, gentle, soft; lenient

Milde, mild-e, f mildness, gentleness, softness; leniency

mildern, mild-ern, v to soothe; to mitigate

mildherzig, milt-hairt-sik, adj tender-hearted

mildtätig, milt-tait-ik, adj charitable

Milieu, mil-yer, nt sphere; atmosphere, tone

militant, mee-lee-tahnt, adj militant

Milz, milts, f spleen

minder, min-der, adj & adv less(er); smaller; minor

Minderheit, min-der-hite, f minority

minderjährig, min-der-yair-ik, adj under age

mindern, min-dern, v to lessen, to decrease

minderwertig, min-der-vairt-ik, adj inferior

mindest, min-dest, adv least, lowest, smallest

Mindestalter, min-dest-ahll-ter, nt minimum age

mindestens, min-dest-ens, adv at least, no less than

Mindestmaß, min-dest-mahs, nt minimum

Mine, meen-e, f mine

Mineralwasser, min-e-rahl-vahss-er, nt mineral water

Minibus, min-e-booss, m minibus

Minimum, min-im-oom, nt minimum

Minirock, min-e-rock, m mini-skirt

Ministerium, min-ist-air-ee-oomm, nt ministry

Ministerpräsident, minn-ist-er-pray-zee-dent, m prime minister

Minorität, mcen-o-ree-tayt, f minority

Minute, meen-oot-e, f minute

Minze, min-tse, f mint

mir, meer, pron (dative) (to) me

Mischbrot, mish-broht, nt bread (made from a mixture of flours)

mischen, mish-en, v to mix; to alloy; to mingle; to shuffle (cards)

Mischling, mish-ling, m hybrid, cross-breed

Mischmasch, mish-mahsh, m jumble; mess

mißachten, miss-ahkt-en, v to disregard; to despise, to disdain

Mißbehagen, miss-be-hahg-en, nt uneasiness; discontent

mißbilligen, miss-bil-ig-en, v to disapprove (of)

Mißbrauch, miss-browk, m misuse, abuse

mißbrauchen, miss-browk-en, v to misuse

missen, miss-en, v to miss; to go without

Mißerfolg, miss-air-folk, m

failure, ill-success

Missetat, miss-e-taht, f
misdeed; crime

Missetäter, miss-e-tayt-er, m
evil-doer; criminal

mißfallen, miss-fahll-en, v
to displease

Mißgeburt, miss-ge-boort, f
deformed person

Mißgeschick, miss-ge-shick,
nt misfortune

mißgestaltet, miss-ge-
shtahlt-et, adj misshapen,
deformed

mißgestimmt, miss-ge-
shtimt, adj depressed, low-
spirited

mißgönnen, miss-gern-en, v
to begrudge

Mißgunst, miss-goonst, f
jealousy, envy; grudge

mißhandeln, miss-hahnn-
deln, v to ill-treat, to
maltreat

Missionar, miss-yohn-**ahr**,
m, missionary

Mißkredit, miss-kraid-it, m
discredit

mißlich, miss-lik, adj
awkward, delicate;
doubtful

mißliebig, miss-leeb-ik, adj
unpopular; obnoxious

mißlingen, miss-ling-en, v to
fail, to be abortive

mißmutig, miss-moot-ik, adj
discontented, bad-
tempered

mißraten, miss-raht-en, adj
badly brought up

Mißstand, miss-shtahnt, m

disgrace, outrage; bad
state of affairs

Mißtrauen, miss-trow-en, nt
mistrust, distrust

mißtrauen, miss-trow-en, v
to distrust, to mistrust

mißtrauisch, miss-trow-ish,
adj distrustful, suspicious

Mißverständnis, miss-fer-
shtent-niss, nt
misunderstanding

mißverstehen, miss-fer-
shtay-en, v to
misunderstand

Mißwirtschaft, miss-veert-
shahfft, f mismanagement

Mist, mist, m manure, dung;
rubbish

mit, mit, prep with; adv too;
along (with)

Mitarbeit, mit-ahr-bite, f
co-operation, assistance;
–er, m co-worker,
colleague

mitbringen, mit-bring-en, v
to bring along

Mitbringsel, mit-bring-zel,
nt gift, souvenir

miteinander, mit-ine-**ahnn**-
der, adv with one another

Mitesser, mit-ess-er, m
blackhead

Mitgefühl, mit-ge-fEEl, nt
sympathy

Mitgift, mit-gift, f dowry

Mitglied, mit-gleet, nt
member

Mithilfe, mit-hilf-e, f aid,
help, assistance

mithin, mit-hin, adv
therefore consequently;

thus, so

mitkommen, mit-komm-en,
v to come along

Mitleid, mit-lite, nt
sympathy; compassion

Mitleidenschaft, mit-ly-den-
shahft, f jdn in – ziehen, v
to affect sb
(detrimentally)

mitmachen, mit-mahk-en, v
to join in, to participate

Mitmensch, mit-mensh, m
fellow-man

mitreden, mit-rayd-en, v to
join in (a conversation)

Mitschuld, mit-shoolt, f
complicity

Mittag, mit-tahk, m midday,
noon; lunch break;
–essen, nt lunch;
–(s)schlaf, m afternoon
nap, siesta

mittags, mit-tahks, adv at
noon/midday

Mittäter, mit-tayt-er, m
accomplice

Mitte, mit-e, f middle,
centre; midst

mitteilen, mit-tile-en, v to
inform, to advise

Mitteilung, mit-tile-oong, f
communication,
information

mittel, mit-el, adj central,
middle; medium

Mittel, mit-el, m means;
remedy, medicine;
medium

Mittelalter, mit-el-ahlt-er, nt
Middle Ages

mittelbar, mit-el-bar, adj

intermediate; indirect

Mitteleuropa, mit-el-oy-roh-pah, *nt* Central Europe

Mittelgebirge, mit-el-ge-bir-ge, *nt* low mountain range

mittellos, mit-el-lohs, *adj* impoverished; powerless

mittelmäßig, mit-el-maiss-ik, *adj* mediocre, middling

Mittelmeer, mit-el-mair, *nt* Mediterranean

Mittelpunkt, mit-el-poonkt, *m* centre, focus

mittels, mit-els, *prep* by means of

Mittelstand, mit-el-shtahnt, *m* middle-classes

Mittelstufe, mit-el-shtoof-e, *f* intermediate classes/years (in school)

Mittelweg, mit-el-vaik, *m* middle course

mitten, mit-en, *adv* in the midst of; **–durch,** *adv* right through the centre

Mitternacht, mit-er-nahkt, *f* midnight

mittlere(r/s), mit-ler-e(r/s), *adj* middle, central; intermediate

mittlerweile, mit-ler-vy-le, *adv* meanwhile

mittun, mit-toon, *v* to join/help in

mitunter, mit-oont-er, *adv* occasionally

Mitwelt, mit-velt, *f* contemporary world

mitwirken, mit-virk-en, *v* to co-operate in

Mittwoch, mit-vok, *m* Wednesday

mitzählen, mit-tsayl-en, *v* to take into account

Möbel, merb-el, *nt* (piece of) furniture

Mobiliar, moh-bil-ee-ahr, *nt* household effect(s), furniture

Mobiltelefon, moh-beel-tay-le-fohn, *nt* mobile phone

möblieren, merb-leer-en, *v* to furnish

Mode, mohd-e, *f* fashion; vogue, craze, fad

Modell, moh-**dell**, *nt* model, mould; pattern

modellieren, moh-del-**eer**-en, *v* to model, to mould

Moder, mohd-er, *m* mould(ering), mustiness

moderig, mohd-er-ik, *adj* musty, mouldy, decaying

modern, mohd-**ern**, *v* to rot; to go mouldy

modern, mohd-**airn**, *adj* modern

Modeschöpfer, mohd-e-sherpp-fer, *m* fashion designer

Modewort, mohd-e-vort, *nt* fashionable word, buzz word

modisch, mohd-ish, *adj* stylish, fashionable

mogeln, mohg-eln, *v* to cheat, to trick

mögen, merg-en, *v* to like (to); may

möglich, merk-lik, *adj* possible

möglicherweise, merk-lik-er-vy-ze, *adv* possibly

Möglichkeit, merk-lik-kite, *f* possibility

Mohn, mohn, *m* poppy

Möhre, mer-re, *f* carrot

Mohrrübe, mohr-rEEb-e, *f* carrot

Mokka, mock-ah , *m* Mocha coffee

Molkerei, molk-e-ry, *f* dairy-farm(ing)

Moll, mol, *nt mus* minor

mollig, mol-ik, *adj* comfortable, cosy, snug; plump

Moment, moh-**ment**, *m* moment; *nt* motive; momentum; **–aufnahme,** *f* snap-shot

momentan, moh-men-**tahn**, *adj* momentary; immediate

Monat, moh-naht, *m* month; **–sheft,** *nt* (monthly) magazine

monatlich, moh-**naht**-lik, *adj* monthly

Monatskarte, moh-**nahts**-kahr-te, *f* monthly ticket

Mönch, mernk, *m* monk; friar

Mond, mohnt, *m* moon; **–finsternis,** *f* eclipse of the moon; **–schein,** *m* moonshine, moonlight; **–sichel,** *f* crescent (moon)

mondsüchtig, mohnt-zEEkt-ik, *adj* moonstruck; somnambulistic

Monopol, mo-noh-**pohl**, *nt* monopoly

Montag, mohn-tahk, *m*
Monday

Montage, mon-tah-she, *f*
installation, erection,
assembly

montieren, mont-eer-en, *v*
to instal, to erect, to
assemble

Moor, mohr, *nt* swamp, bog,
fen, marsh

Moos, mohs, *nt* moss

moosig, moh-zik, *adj* mossy

Moral, moh-rahl, *f* morality

Morast, mo-rahst, *m* bog,
swampy soil, mud, morass

Mord, mort, *m* murder

morden, mord-en, *v* to
murder

Mörder, merd-er, *m*
murderer

mörderisch, merd-er-ish, *adj*
murderous; *fig* dreadful

Mordgier, mort-geer, *f*
bloodthirstiness

Mordskerl, morts-kairl, *m*
fig devil

mordsmäßig, morts-maiss-
ik, *adj* enormous, awful

Mordsspaß, morts-shpahs,
m great fun

Mordsspektakel, morts-
shpeck-**tahk**-el, *m* terrible
noise

Morgen, morg-en, *m*
morning

morgen, morg-en, *adv*
tomorrow; **– abend,** *adv*
tomorrow evening **– früh,**
adv tomorrow morning

Morgenblatt, morg-en-
blahtt, *nt* (morning)
newspaper

morgendlich, morg-ent-lik,
adj of/in the morning

Morgengrauen, morg-en-
grow-en, *nt* daybreak

Morgenland, morg-en-
lahnt, *nt* Orient, East

Morgenrock, morg-en-rock,
m housecoat, dressing-
gown

Morgenrot, morg-en-roht,
nt sunrise, dawn

morgens, morg-ens, *adv* in
the morning; every
morning

morsch, morsh, *adj* rotten,
decayed

Mörser, merz-er, *m* mortar

Mörtel, mert-el, *m* mortar;
plaster

Moschee, mosh-ay, *f*
mosque

Moschus, mosh-ooss, *m*
musk

Moselwein, moh-zel-vine, *m*
Moselle (wine)

Moskau, moss-kow, *nt*
Moscow

Moskito, moss-kee-toh, *m*
mosquito

Moslem, moss-laim, *m*
Muslim

moslemisch, moss-laim-ish,
adj muslim

Most, mosst, *m* new wine,
unfermented fruit juice

motivieren, moh-teev-eer-
en, *v* to motivate

Motor, moh-tohr, *m* engine,
motor; **–boot,** *nt* motor
boat; **–fahrzeug,** *nt* motor
vehicle; **–haube,** *f* bonnet;
–schaden, *m* engine
failure

Motorrad, mo-tohr-raht, *nt*
motor-cycle

Motte, mot-e, *f* moth

moussieren, mooss-eer-en, *v*
to fizz

Möwe, merv-e, *f* (sea-)gull,
mew

Mücke, mEEck-e, *f* gnat,
midge

mucken, moock-en, *v* to
growl, to mutter

Mückenstich, mEEck-en-
shtik, *m* gnat-bite

müde, mEEd-e, *adj* tired,
fatigued

Müdigkeit, mEEd-ik-kite, *f*
tiredness, fatigue

muffig, mooff-ik, *adj* sulky,
stuffy, fusty

Mühe, mEE-e, *f* trouble;
labour; effort; pains

mühelos, mEE-e-lohs, *adj*
without effort

mühen (sich), mEE-en (zik),
v to take pains, to make
an effort

Mühle, mEEl-e, *f* mill;
grinder

Mühsal, mEE-zahl, *f*
hardship, trouble; toil

mühsam, mEE-zahmm, *adj*
wearisome; troublesome;
painstaking

mühselig, mEE-zail-ik, *adj*
laborious; wretched

Mulde, moold-e, *f* hollow;
trough; skip (for rubbish)

Müll, mEEll, *m* rubbish,

refuse; **–eimer,** *m* dustbin

Müller, mEEll-er, *m* miller

Mumie, moom-ee-e, *f* mummy

München, mEEn-ken, *nt* Munich

Mund, moont, *m* mouth

Mundart, moont-art, *f* dialect; idiom

munden, moon-den, *v* to taste good

münden, mEEn-den, *v* to run into (river)

mundgerecht, moont-ge-rekt, *adj* palatable; suitable

mündig, mEEn-dik, *adj* of age; mature, responsible

mündlich, mEEnt-lik, *adj* verbal; oral

Mundstück, moont-shtEEck, *nt* mouthpiece; tip (of cigarette)

Mündung, mEEn-doong, *f* mouth (of river); estuary; muzzle (of gun)

munkeln, moonk-eln, *v* to rumour; to whisper

Münster, mEEnst-er, *nt* cathedral; minster

munter, moont-er, *adj* vigorous; lively; merry

Münze, mEEnt-se, *f* coin(age); cash; mint

Münztelefon, mEEnts-tay-le-fohn, *nt* pay-phone

mürb(e), mEErb(-e), *adj* crumbly; rotten; soft, tender; ripe; well-done

Mürbeteig, mEEr-be-tike, *m* shortcrust pastry

murmeln, moorm-eln, *v* to

murmur

murren, moorr-en, *v* to grumble, to murmur

mürrisch, mEErr-ish, *adj* sulky, ill-tempered, sullen

Mus, moos, *nt* mush; puree; jam

Muschel, moosh-el, *f* mussel; shell

Muscheltier, moosh-el-teer, *nt* shell-fish

Museum, moo-**zai**-oom, *nt* museum

Musik, moo-**zeek,** *f* music

musikalisch, moo-zee-**kahl**-ish, *adj* musical

Musikant, moo-zee-**kahnt,** *m* (amateur) musician

Musikautomat, moo-**zeek**-ow-toh-maht, *m* musical box

Musiker, moo-**zeek**-er, *m* (professional) musician

musizieren, moo-zee-**tseer**-en, *v* to play music

Muskat(nuß), moos-**kaht**(-nooss), *m* (*f*), nutmeg

Muskel, mooss-kel, *m* muscle

muskulös, moos-koo-**lers,** *adj* muscular

Muße, moos-e, *f* leisure; spare time

Müsli, mEEs-lee, *nt* muesli

müssen, mEEss-en, *v* to have to, to be obliged to, must

müßig, mEEss-ik, *adj* idle, lazy; useless

Müßiggang, mEEss-ik-gahng, *m* idleness, sloth

Muster, moost-er, *nt* sample; design; pattern; model; **–beispiel,** *nt* typical example

mustergültig, moost-er-gEElt-ik, *adj* exemplary, model

musterhaft, moost-er-hahft, *adj* exemplary, model

mustern, moost-ern, *v* to muster; to review; to figure

Mut, moot, *m* courage, bravery

mutig, moot-ik, *adj* courageous, brave

mutlos, moot-lohs, *adj* disheartened, despondent

mutmaßen, moot-mahs-en, *v* to presume

mutmaßlich, moot-mahs-lik, *adj* presumably

Mutter, moott-er, *f* mother; **–leib,** *m* womb

mütterlich, mEEtt-er-lik, *adj* motherly, maternal

Muttermal, moott-er-mahl, *nt* birthmark, mole

Muttermilch, moott-er-milk, *f* mother's milk

mutterseelenallein, moott-er-zail-en-ahll-ine, *adj* all alone

Mutwille, moot-vil-e, *m* wilfulness, malice

mutwillig, moot-vil-ik, *adj* mischievous; wilful

Mütze, mEEtt-se, *f* cap, bonnet

MwSt, *abbr* **Mehrwertsteuer,** VAT

N

na! nah, *interj* now! now then! well!

na gut, nah goot, *interj* okay then

Nabel, nahb-el, *m* navel

nach, nahk, *prep & adv* after; to(wards); according to; past

nachäffen, nahk-eff-en, *v* to ape, to copy

nachahmen, nahk-ahm-en, *v* to imitate, to copy

Nachbar, nahk-bar, *m* neighbour; **–schaft**, *f* neighbours; proximity; **–staat**, *m* neighbouring state

nachdem, nahk-**daim**, *adv & conj* after(wards)

nachdenken, nahk-deng-ken, *v* to reflect

nachdenklich, nahk-deng-klik, *adj* meditative, pensive

Nachdruck, nahk-droock, *m* emphasis; (print) reproduction

nachdrücklich, nahk-drEEck-lik, *adj* emphatic

nacheinander, nahk-ine-**ahnn**-der, *adv* one after the other

Nachfolger, nahk-folg-er, *m* successor

nachforschen, nahk-forsh-en, *v* to investigate

Nachfrage, nahk-frahg-e, *f* demand; inquiry

nachfüllen, nahk-fEEll-en, *v* to refill

nachgeben, nahk-gayb-en, *v* to give in

nachgehen, nahk-gay-en, *v* to go after; to attend to; to investigate; (clock) to be slow

Nachgeschmack, nahk-ge-shmahck, *m* after-taste

nachgiebig, nahk-geeb-ik, *adj* indulgent; yielding; submissive

nachgrübeln, nahk-grEEb-eln, *v* to muse over

nachhelfen, nahk-helf-en, *v* to give help; to push forward

nachher, nahk-hair, *adv* afterwards; later on

Nachhilfe, nahk-hilf-e, *f* assistance, aid

nachholen, nahk-hohl-en, *v* to make up for; to recover

Nachhut, nahk-hoot, *f* rearguard

Nachkomme, nahk-kom-e, *m* descendant

nachkommen, nahk-kom-en, *v* to come after; to comply with

Nachlaß, nahk-lahss, *m* reduction; estate

nachlassen, nahk-lahss-en, *v* to bequeath; to abate; to deteriorate

Nachlassenschaft, nahk-lahss-en-shahft, *f* inheritance

nachlässig, nahk-less-ik, *adj* careless, negligent

nachlösen, nahk-lers-en, *v* to buy a ticket/supplement on the train

nachmachen, nahk-mahk-en, *v* to imitate; to counterfeit

Nachmittag, nahk-mit-ahg, *m* afternoon

nachmittags, nahk-mit-ahks, *adv* in/during the

afternoon

Nachnahme, nahk-nahm-*e*, *f* reimbursement; c.o.d.

nachrechnen, nahk-rek-nen, *v* to check, to verify

Nachricht, nahk-rikt, *f* information, report, news; **–en**, *pl* the news

Nachruf, nahk-roof, *m* obituary notice

nachrufen, nahk-roof-en, *v* to call after (sb)

Nachsaison, nahk-zay-zong, *f* off-season

nachschicken, nahk-shick-en, *v* to forward (mail)

nachschlagen, nahk-shlahg-en, *v* to look up (in a book)

Nachschub, nahk-shoop, *m* reinforcements; new batch

nachsehen, nahk-zay-en, *v* to look up a thing; to gaze after

nachsenden, nahk-zen-den, *v* to forward (mail)

Nachsicht, nahk-zikt, *f* indulgence, toleration

nachsichtig, nahk-zik-tik, *adj* indulgent, lenient

nachsinnen, nahk-zin-en, *v* to reflect, to ponder

nachsitzen, nahk-zits-en, *v* to be kept in school

Nachspeise, nahk-shpy-ze, *f* dessert, sweet, pudding

nächst(e/r), naykst(-e/er), *adj* nearest; *adv* next, nearest

nachstehen, nahk-shtay-en, *v* to rank after

nachstellen, nahk-shtel-en, *v* to put back (clocks), to adjust; to pursue (sb)

Nächstenliebe, nayk-sten-leeb-*e*, *f* love of one's neighbour

nächstens, nayk-stens, *adv* shortly, very soon

nachstöbern, nahk-shterb-ern, *v* to rummage (after)

nachsuchen, nahk-zook-en, *v* to (have a) look

Nacht, nahkt, *f* night

Nachteil, nahk-tile, *m* drawback; injury, loss

nachteilig, nahk-ty-lik, *adj* detrimental, injurious

Nachthemd, nahkt-hemt, *nt* night-shirt

Nachtigall, nahkt-ee-gahll, *f* nightingale

Nachtisch, nahk-tish, *m* dessert, sweet, pudding

Nachtleben, nahkt-lay-ben, *nt* nightlife

nächtlich, naykt-lik, *adj* at night, nocturnal

Nachtmahl, nahkt-mahl, *nt* supper

Nachtrag, nahk-trahk, *m* postscript, supplement

nachtragen, nahk-trahg-en, *v* to bear a grudge, to append

nachträglich, nahk-traik-lik, *adj* supplementary; belated

nachts, nahkts, *adv* at/during the night

nachtwandeln, nahkt-vahhn-deln, *v* to walk in one's sleep

Nachweis, nahk-vice *m* information, particulars, proof

nachweisbar, nahk-vice-bar, *adj* manifest, demonstrable

nachweisen, nahk-vy-zen, *v* to indicate, to prove

nachweislich, nahk-vice-lik, *adj* evident, demonstrable

Nachwelt, nahk-velt, *f* posterity

Nachwuchs, nahk-vooks, *m* new generation(s); young shoot(s)

nachzahlen, nahk-tsahl-en, *v* to pay in addition

nachzählen, nahk-tsayl-en, *v* to count over

nachziehen, nahk-tsee-en, *v* to draw (drag) after; to follow

Nachzügler, nahk-tsEEg-ler, *m* straggler

Nacken, nahck-en, *m* nape/scruff of the neck

nackt, nahckt, *adj* naked, bare, nude

Nadel, nahd-el, *f* needle

Nadelwald, nahd-el-wahlt, *m* coniferous forest

Nagel, nahg-el, *m* nail

nageln, nahg-eln, *v* to nail

nagelneu, nahg-el-noy, *adj* brand-new

nagen, nahg-en, *v* to gnaw, to nibble

**nahe, nah-*e*, *adj & adv* near(ly), close to

**Nähe, nay-*e*, *f* proximity; neighbourhood

**nahebei, nah-*e*-by, *adv* close

by, nearly

nahelegen, nah-*e*-lay-gen, *v*
to urge sb to do sth

naheliegen, nah-*e*-lee-gen, *v*
to be obvious, near at
hand

nahen, nah-en, *v* to
approach, to draw near

nähen, nay-en, *v* to sew; to
do needlework

näher, nay-er, *adj* nearer,
closer

Nähere(s), nay-er-es, *nt*
particulars, details

näherkommen, nay-er-
komm-en, *v* to approach;
sich –, *v* to get closer

nähern (sich), nay-ern
(zik), *v* to approach

Nähgarn, nay-garn, *nt*
sewing cotton

nähren, nayr-en, *v* to
nourish, to feed

nahrhaft, nahr-hahft, *adj*
nourishing; rich,
substantial

Nahrung, nahr-oong, *f*
food, sustenance

Nahrungsmittel, nahr-
oongs-mit-el, *nt* foodstuff

Naht, naht, *f* seam; joint

Nahverkehr, nah-fer-kair, *m*
local traffic

Name, nahm-*e*, *m* name;
reputation

namens, nahm-ens, *adv* by
the name of, called,
named; *prep* on behalf of

Namensvetter, nahm-ens-
fet-er, *m* namesake

namentlich, nahm-ent-lik,

adj & adv by name;
especially, particularly

namhaft, nahm-hahft, *adj*
named, by name;
renowned

nämlich, naim-lik, *adj & adv*
the same; namely, that is
to say

Napf, nahp'*f*, *m* basin, bowl,
dish, mug

Napfkuchen, nahp'**f**-kook-
en, *m* kind of madeira
cake

Narbe, narb-*e*, *f* scar, mark

Narr, nahrr, *m* fool

Narrenstreich, nahrr-en-
shtry'k, *m* foolish trick

Narrheit, nahrr-hite, *f*
foolishness, folly

närrisch, nairr-ish, *adj*
foolish, crazy; funny

Narzisse, nahrr-tsis-*e*, *f*
narcissus, daffodil

naschen, nahsh-en, *v* to
enjoy dainties on the sly,
to nibble

naschhaft, nahsh-hahft, *adj*
having a sweet tooth

**Naschkätzchen, –katze,
nahsh**-kets-ken, –kahts-*e*,
nt f person with a sweet
tooth

Naschwerk, nahsh-vairk, *nt*
sweetmeats

Nase, nahz-*e*, *f* nose; snout,
proboscis

Nasenloch, nahz-en-lok, *nt*
nostril

naseweis, nahz-*e*-vice, *adj*
forward, pert

Nashorn, nahs-horn, *nt*

rhinoceros

naß, nahss, *adj* wet; moist,
damp, humid

Nässe, ness-*e*, *f* wet(ness);
moisture

nässen, ness-en, *v* to wet, to
moisten

naßkalt, nahss-kahlt, *adj*
wet and cold

Nation, nahts-yohn, *f*
nation

Nationalfeiertag, nahts-
yohn-**ahl**-fy-er-tahk, *m*
national holiday

Nationalflagge, nahts-yohn-
ahl-flahgg-*e*, *f* national
flag

Nationalhymne, nahts-
yohn-**ahl**-hEEm-ne, *f*
national anthem

Nationalmannschaft, nah-
tse-ohn-**ahl**-mahnn-
shahft, *f* national team

Nationalpark, nahts-yohn-
ahl-park, *m* national park

Natter, nahtt-er, *f* viper,
adder, asp

Natur, nah-toor, *f* nature

Naturerscheinung, nah-
toor-air-shy-noong, *f*
natural phenomenon

Naturforscher, nah-toor-
forsh-er, *m* naturalist

Naturgeschichte, nah-toor-
ge-shik-te, *f* natural
history

naturgetreu, nah-toor-ge-
troy, *adj* true to nature,
life-like

Naturkatastrophe, nah-
toor-kah-tah-stroh-fe, *f*

natural disaster

natürlich, nah-**tEEr**-lik, *adj & adv* natural(ly); of course

Naturprodukt, nah-**toor**-pro-dookt, *nt* natural product

naturrein, nah-**toor**-rine, *adj* pure

Naturschutz, nah-**toor**-shoots, *m* nature conservation; **–gebiet,** *nt* nature reserve

Neapel, nay-**ah**-pel, *nt* Naples

Nebel, nayb-el, *m* fog; mist; haze

neb(e)lig, nayb-(e-)lik, *adj* foggy; misty; hazy

neben, nayb-en, *prep* next to, beside(s); side by side

nebenan, nayb-en-**ahnn,** *adv* next door, adjoining

nebenbei, nayb-en-by, *adv* at the same; incidentally

nebeneinander, nayb-en-ine-**ahnn**-der, *adv* side by side

Nebenfluß, nayb-en-flooss, *m* tributary

nebenher, nayb-en-**hair,** *adv* in addition; at the same time; besides

Nebensache, nayb-en-sahk-e, *f* minor matter, trifle

nebensächlich, nayb-en-sayk-lik, *adj* subordinate

Nebensaison, nayb-en-zay-zong, *f* low season

Nebenstraße, nayb-en-shtrahs-e, *f* side-street

Nebenwirkung, nai-ben-virk-oong, *f* side-effect

nebst, naip'st, *prep* (together) with

necken, neck-en, *v* to tease

neckisch, neck-ish, *adj* teasing, amusing

Neffe, nef-e, *m* nephew

negativ, neg-ah-teef, *adj* negative

nehmen, naym-en, *v* to take; to receive, to accept

Neid, nite, *m* envy, jealousy

neidisch, ny-dish, *adj* envious, jealous

Neige, ny-ge, *f* slope; depression; end; dregs

neigen, ny-gen, *v* to bend; to bow, to tilt; to incline

Neigung, ny-goong, *f* slope, incline, gradient; inclination, liking

nein, nine, *adv* no

Nektarine, neck-tah-ree-ne, *f* nectarine

Nelke, nelk-e, *f* carnation, pink; clove

nennen, nen-en, *v* to name, to call; to mention

nennenswert, nen-ens-vairt, *adj* worth mentioning

Neon, nay-on, *nt* neon; **–lampe,** *f* neon lamp; **–röhre,** *f* neon tube

Nerv, nairf, *m* nerve

nervig, nairv-ik, *adj* strong, terse; pithy

nervös, nairv-ers, *adj* excitable, irritable; nervy, having weak nerves

Nerz, nairts, *m* mink

Nessel, nes-el, *f* nettle

Nest, nest, *nt* nest; eyrie; small town/village

Nesthäkchen, nest-haik-ken, *nt* youngest child, baby of family

nett, net, *adj* nice; neat, tidy, pretty

netto, net-oh, *adv* net, clear

Netz, nets *nt* net, network

neu, noy, *adj* new, novel; original; fresh

Neubau, noy-bow, *m* building under construction, new building

neuerdings, noy-er-dings, *adv* lately, latterly, of late; anew

Neuerung, noy-er-oong, *f* innovation, reform; novelty

neu(e)stens, noy-(e-)stens, *adv* of late, recently

Neugier(de), noy-geer(-de), *f* curiosity

neugierig, noy-geer-ik, *adj* curious, inquisitive, nosy

Neuheit, noy-hite, *f* newness

Neuigkeit, noy-ik-kite, *f* (piece of) news; novelty

Neujahr, noy-yar, *nt* New Year('s Day)

neulich, noy-lik, *adj & adv* recent(ly); the other day

Neuling, noy-ling, *m* novice, beginner

Neumond, noy-mohnt, *m* new moon

neun, noyn, *num* nine

neunzehn, noyn-tsain, *num* nineteen

neunzig, noyn-tsik, *num* ninety

neurotisch, noy-roht-ish, *adj* neurotic

Neuseeland, noy-zay-lahnt, *nt* New Zealand

Neuzeit, noy-tsite, *f* modern times

neuzeitlich, noy-tsite-lik, *adj* modern, up-to-date

nicht, nikt, *adv* not

Nichte, nik-te, *f* niece

nichtig, nik-tik, *adj* void; vain, idle

Nichtraucher, nikt-rowk-er, *m* non-smoker

nichts, nikts, *pron* nothing, nought

nichtsdestoweniger, nikts-dest-oh-**vayn**-ig-er, *adv* nevertheless

Nichtsnutz, nikts-noots, *m* good-for-nothing

nichtssagend, nikts-zahg-ent, *adj* meaningless

nichtswürdig, nikts-vEErd-ik, *adj* worthless, vile

nicken, nick-en, *v* to nod

nie, nee, *adv* never

nieder, need-er, *adj & adv* common, low; down

niederdrücken, need-er-drEEck-en, *v* to press down; to oppress

Niedergang, need-er-gahng, *m* decline

niedergeschlagen, need-er-ge-shlahg-en, *adj* depressed, dejected

Niederlage, need-er-lahg-e, *f* defeat

Niederlande, need-er-lahnn-de, *pl* Netherlands

Niederländer, need-er-lender, *m* Dutchman; **–in,** *f* Dutchwoman

niederländisch, need-er-lendish, *adj* Dutch

niederlassen (sich), need-er-lahss-en (zik), *v* to settle; to establish o.s.

Niederlassung, need-er-lahss-oong, *f* settlement; branch

niedermetzeln, need-er-metseln, *v* to massacre

Niederschlag, need-er-shlahg, *m* precipitation; sediment

niederschlagen, need-er-shlah-gen, *v* to knock down; to cast down; to suppress

niederste(r), need-erst-e(r), *adj* lowest

Niedertracht, need-er-trahkt, *f* infamy, vileness

niederträchtig, need-er-trek-tik, *adj* vile, mean, base, infamous

Niederung, need-er-oong, *f* lowland, plain

niedlich, need-lik, *adj* dainty, neat; nice, pretty

niedrig, need-rik, *adj* low; base, vulgar

niemals, nee-mahls, *adv* never, at no time

niemand, nee-mahnt, *pron* nobody

Niere, neer-e, *f* kidney

nieseln, neez-eln, *v* to drizzle

niesen, neez-en, *v* to sneeze

Niete, neet-e, *f* blank (cartridge); dead loss; no-hoper

nieten, neet-en, *v* to rivet

Nikotin, nee-ko-teen, *nt* nicotine

Nil, neel, *m* Nile; **–pferd,** *nt* hippopotamus

nimmer, nim-er, *adv* never

nimmersatt, nim-er-saht, *adj* insatiable

nippen, nip-en, *v* to sip

Nippes, nip-es, *pl* knick-knacks, small ornaments

nirgend(s), neerg-ent(s), *adv* nowhere

Nische, neesh-e, *f* niche, recess

nisten, nist-en, *v* to (make a) nest

Niveau, nee-voh, *nt* level

Nixe, nix-e, *f* nymph, water-sprite

nobel, nohb-el, *adj* generous, liberal; noble

noch, nok, *adv* still, yet, besides; nor

nochmals, nok-mahls, *adv* once more, again

Nonne, non-e, *f* nun

Nord-, nort, *pref* North, northern

Norden, nord-en, *m* north

Nordirland, nort-eer-lahnt, *nt* Northern Ireland

nordisch, nord-ish, *adj* northern;

northerly; Norse

nördlich, nert-lik, *adj*
northerly, northern;
arctic; *adv* north (of)

Nordlicht, nord-likt, *nt*
aurora borealis, northern
lights

Nordpol, nort-pohl, *m*
North Pole

Nordsee, nort-zay, *f* North
Sea

nörgeln, nerg-eln, *v* to
grumble, to find fault
with, to nag

Norm, norm, *f* pattern,
model, standard

Norwegen, nor-vay-gen, *nt*
Norway

Norweger, nor-vay-ger, *m*
Norwegian (person)

norwegisch, nor-vay-gish,
Norwegian

Not, noht, *f* need, necessity;
distress, want; danger;
trouble

Notar, noht-ar, *m* notary,
solicitor

notariell, noht-ar-ee-yel, *adj*
notarial

Notausgang, noht-ows-
gahng, *m* emergency exit

Notbehelf, noht-be-helf, *m*
stop-gap, makeshift,
expedient

Notbremse, noht-brem-se, *f*
emergency brake

notdürftig, noht-dEErft-ik,
adj meagre, poor;
makeshift

Note, noht-e, *f mus*
note; mark, certificate

(school); remark

Noten, noht-en, *pl* (sheet)
music

Notfall, noht-fahll, *m*
emergency

notgedrungen, noht-ge-
droong-en, *adj* from
necessity

notieren, noht-eer-en, *v* to
note, to jot down

nötig, nert-ik, *adj* necessary,
required

nötigen, nert-ig-en, *v* to
force, to oblige; to invite;
to urge

Notiz, noht-eets, *f* notice,
cognizance;
memorandum; **–block,**
–buch, *nt* notebook

Notstand, noht-shtahnt, *m*
(state of) emergency;
urgent need

Notwehr, noht-vair, *f* self-
defence

notwendig, noht-ven-dik,
adj necessary

Novelle, noh-vel-e, *f* short
story

November, noh-vem-ber, *m*
November

Nu, noo, *nt* moment,
instant

Nuance, noo-ahng-se, *f*
shade, tint

nüchtern, nEEk-tern, *adj*
sober; fasting; temperate,
frugal

Nudel, nood-el, *f* noodle,
vermicelli; **–n,** *pl* pasta

Null, nooll, *f* nought

null, nooll, *adj* void;

num zero

Nullpunkt, nooll-poonkt, *m*
zero; freezing-point

numerieren, noomm-er-eer-
en, *v* to number

Nummer, noomm-er, *f*
number; copy, issue; size

nun, noon, *adv* now, at
present; then; well now!

nunmehr, noon-mair, *adv &*
conj now, by (from) this
time

nur, noor, *adv* only, solely

Nürnberg, nEErn-bairg, *nt*
Nuremberg

Nuß, nooss, *f* nut;
–knacker, *m* nut-cracker

Nüster, nEEst-er, *f* nostril
(of animals)

nutz(e), noots(-e), *adj*
profitable, useful

Nutz(en), noots(-en), *m*
utility, use; gain,
advantage

nutzen, noots-en, *v* to be
useful

nützen, nEEts-en, *v* to use

nützlich, nEEts-lik, *adj*
useful

nutzlos, noots-lohs, *adj*
useless

Nylon, ny-lon, *nt* nylon;
–hemd, *nt* nylon shirt;
–strümpfe, *fpl* nylon
stockings

protection, care, guardianship

obig(e/er/es), oh-bik (**oh**-big-e/er/es), *adj* foregoing, above(-mentioned)

Oblate, ob-laht-e, *f* wafer

obligatorisch, ob-lig-ah-**tohr**-ish, *adj* obligatory, compulsory

Obmann, op-mahn, *m* chief, chairman, foreman

Obrigkeit, oh-brik-kite, *f* public authorities

Obst, ohp'st, *nt* fruit

obwohl, ob-vohl, *conj* although, though

Ochs(e), oks(-e), *m* ox, bullock

ode, erd-e, *adj* deserted, dreary

Öde, erd-e, *f* desert, wasteland

oder, oh-der, *conj* or

Ofen, oh-ffen, *m* stove, fire-place; oven; furnace

offen, off-en, *adj* open; candid, frank

offenbar, off-en-**bahr**, *adj* obvious, manifest, evident; **–en**, *v* to reveal, to manifest

offenherzig, off-en-hairt-sik, *adj* openhearted, frank

offensichtlich, off-en-**zikt**-lik, *adj* obvious

offenstehen, off-en-shtay-en; *v* to be open/permitted

öffentlich, erf-ent-lik, *adj* public

Öffentlichkeit, erf-ent-lik-kite, *f* public

ob, op, *conj* whether, if

Obacht, oh-bahkt, *f* attention, heed

Obdach, op-dahk, *nt* shelter, lodging

obdachlos, op-dahk-lohs, *adj* homeless

oben, oh-ben, *adv* above, upstairs; overhead

obenan, oh-ben-ahnn, *adv* at the top/head of

obendrein, oh-ben-drine, *adv* into the bargain, over and above

Ober, oh-ber, *m* waiter

ober(e/er/es), oh-ber(-e/er/es), *adj* upper, higher, superior

Oberbefehlshaber, oh-ber-be-**fails**-hahb-er, *m* commander-in-chief

Oberfläche, oh-ber-flek-e, *f* surface

oberflächlich, oh-ber-flek-

lik, *adj* superficial, shallow

oberhalb, oh-ber-hahlp, *prep* above

Oberhaupt, oh-ber-howpt, *nt* chief, sovereign, head

Oberhemd, oh-ber-hemt, *nt* shirt

Oberkellner, oh-ber-kel-ner, *m* head-waiter

Oberkiefer, oh-ber-keef-er, *m* upper jaw

Oberkörper, oh-ber-kerp-er, *m* upper part of body, torso

Oberleder, oh-ber-layd-er, *nt* uppers (shoe)

Oberlicht, oh-ber-likt, *nt* sky-(top-)light

Oberschenkel, oh-ber-sheng-kel, *m* thigh

Oberst, oh-berst, *m* colonel

obgleich, op-**gly'k**, *conj* although, though

Obhut, op-hoot, *f*

offerieren, of-er-*eer*-en, *v* to offer

Offerte, of-*airt*-e, *f* offer

öffnen, *erf*-nen, *v* to open

oft, oft, *adv* often, frequently

oh, oh, *interj* oh

ohne, *oh*-ne, *prep* without

ohnegleichen, *oh*-ne-gly-ken, *adj* unparalleled

Ohnmacht, *ohn*-mahkt, *f* fainting fit, fainting

ohnmächtig, *ohn*-mekt-ik, *adj* unconscious; powerless

Ohr, ohr, *nt* ear

Öhr, er, *nt* eye (of needle); eyelet

Ohrfeige, *ohr*-fy-ge, *f* box on the ear

Ohrring, *ohr*-ring, *m* earring

Ökoladen, *er*-koh-lahd-en, *m* health-food shop

Oktober, ok-*toh*-ber, *m* October

Öl, erl, *nt* oil

Ölbild, *erl*-bilt, *nt* oil-painting

Oldtimer, *old*-time-er, *m* vintage car

ölen, *erl*-en, *v* to oil, to lubricate

Ölfarbe, *erl*-farb-e, *f* oil-paint

ölig, *erl*-ik, *adj* oily; unctuous

Olympiade, oh-lEEmp-ee-*ahd*-e, *f* Olympic Games

Oma, *oh*-mah, *f* granny

Onkel, *ong*-kel, *m* uncle

Oper, *oh*-per, *f* opera

Operette, oh-per-*et*-e, *f* light opera, musical comedy

Opfer, *op*-fer, *nt* victim; sacrifice; martyr

Opferlamm, *op*-fer-lahmm, *nt* sacrificial lamb; innocent victim

opfern, *op*-fern, *v* to sacrifice

Orange, oh-*rahng*-zhe, *f* orange; **–nsaft**, *m* orange juice

Orden, *ord*-en, *m* order; distinction, decoration

ordentlich, *ord*-ent-lik, *adj* ordinary; orderly; regular

ordinär, ord-in-*air*, *adj* vulgar, common

ordnen, *ord*-nen, *v* to regulate; to put in order; to settle

Ordnung, *ord*-noong, *f* order, arrangement

Orgel, *org*-el, *f* organ

orgeln, *org*-eln, *v* to play/grind a (barrel-)organ

orientieren (sich), or-ee-ent-*eer*-en (zik), *v* to find one's way; to collect information

Orientierung, or-ee-ent-*eer*-oong, *f* orientation; **–ssinn**, *m* sense of orientation

Orkan, or-*kahn*, *m* hurricane, gale

Ort, ort, *m* place, spot, locality; town

örtlich, *ert*-lik, *adj* local

ortsansässig, orts-*ahnn*-saiss-ik, *adj* local

Ortschaft, *ort*-shahft, *f* locality; township, place

Ortssinn, *orts*-sin, *m* sense of direction

Öse, *erz*-e, *f* loop, eye

Ost-, ost, *pref* East, eastern

Osten, *ost*-en, *m* east; East, Orient

Osterei, ohst-er-*i*, *nt* Easter-egg

Osterglocke, ohst-er-glock-e, *f* daffodil

Ostermontag, ohst-er-*mohn*-tahk, *m* Easter Monday

Ostern, *ohst*-ern, *pl* Easter

Österreich, *erst*-e-rike, *nt* Austria

Österreicher, *erst*-e-rike-er, *m* Austrian (person)

österreichisch, *erst*-e-rike-ish, *adj* Austrian

östlich, *erst*-lik, *adj* eastern, easterly

Ostsee, *ost*-zay, *f* Baltic (Sea)

Otter, *ot*-er, *m* otter; *f* adder

Ozon, oh-*tsohn*, *nt* ozone; **–loch**, *nt* ozone hole; **–schicht**, *f* ozone layer

P

Paar, pahr, *nt* pair; couple

paar, pahr, *adj* ein –, a few

paaren, pahr-en, *v* to pair, to couple; to match

Pacht, pahkt, *f* lease, tenancy; tenure

pachten, pahkt-en, *v* to lease, to rent; to farm

Pächter, pekt-er, *m* tenant (-farmer); leaseholder, lessee

Pack, pahck, *nt*; pack, packet, package; rabble, mob

Päckchen, peck-ken, *nt* small package/parcel

packen, pahck-en, *v* to pack; to seize

Packesel, pahck-ay-zel, *m* pack-mule; drudge

paffen, pahff-en, *v* to puff, to smoke

Paket, pah-**kait**, *nt* parcel, package, packet

Palast, pah-**lahst**, *m* palace

panieren, pah-neer-en, *v* to coat with breadcrumbs

Paniermehl, pah-neer-mail, *nt* breadcrumbs

Panne, pahnn-e, *f* breakdown (of car etc.)

Pantoffel, pahnn-**toff**-el, *m* slipper; **–held**, *m* hen-pecked husband

Pantomime, pahnn-toh-**mee**-me, *m* mime; *f* mime show

Panzer, pahnt-ser, *m* armour, (coat of) mail; tank

panzern, pahnt-sern, *v* to armour-plate

Papa, pahpp-ah, *m* dad

Papagei, pah-pah-**guy**, *m* parrot

Papier, pah-peer, *nt* paper

Papierkorb, pah-peer-korp, *m* waste-paper basket

Papiertaschentuch, pah-peer-tah-shen-took, *nt* paper handkerchief

Pappe, pahpp-e, *f* cardboard; paste

Pappel, pahpp-el, *f* poplar

Pappendeckel, pahpp-en-deck-el, *m* cardboard, pasteboard

Pappschachtel, pahpp-shahk-tel, *f* cardboard box

Paprika, pahpp-ree-kah, *m* paprika; capsicum, pepper

Papst, pahpst, *m* Pope, Pontiff

päpstlich, paipst-lik, *adj* papal, pontifical; papist

Parabolantenne, pah-rah-bohl-ahnn-ten-e, *f* satellite dish

Parfüm, par-**fEEm**, *nt* perfume, scent

parieren, pah-reer-en, *v* to obey; to stop short; to wager; to parry

Paris, pah-rees, *nt* Paris

Parkett, par-kett, *nt* parquet (floor); stalls *theatre*

Parkhaus, park-hows, *nt* multi-storey car park

Parkkralle, park-krahll-e, *f* wheel clamp

Parklücke, park-lEEk-e, *f* parking space

Parkplatz, park-plahts, *m* car park, parking place

Parkuhr, park-oohr, *f* parking meter

Parkverbot, park-fair-boht, *nt* parking ban

Partei, par-ty, *f* party (political, contracting);

faction

parteiisch, par-**ty**-ish, *adj*
one-sided, biassed

Parterre, par-**tair,** *nt*
ground-floor; pit *theatre*

Partie, part-ee, *f* outing;
parcel; game

Partitur, part-ee-**toor,** *f mus*
score

Partner, part-ner, *m* partner;
–stadt, *f* twin town

Party, part-ee, *f* party

Parzelle, par-**tsel**-e, *f* plot
(of land), lot

Paß, pahss, *m* passport;
(mountain) pass; passage

Passagier, pahss-ah-**zheer,** *m*
passenger

Passant, pahss-**ahnnt,** *m*
passer-by

passen, pahss-en, *v* to fit; to
pass; to suit

passieren, pahss-**eer**-en, *v* to
pass, to cross; to happen,
to occur

passiv, pahss-eef, *adj* passive

Passivrauchen, pahss-eef-
rowk-en, *nt* passive
smoking

Paste, pahss-te, *f* paste; paté

Pastete, pahss-**tait**-e, *f* pie,
tart

pasteurisiert, pahss-ter-ree-
zeert, *adj* pasteurized

Pastinake, pahss-tee-**nahck**-
e, *f* parsnip

Pastor, pahss-tohr, *m*
(Protestant) clergyman

Pate, paht-e, *m* godfather;
–nkind, *nt* godchild

Patient, pahts-**yent,** *m*

patient

Patrone, pah-**trohn**-e, *f*
cartridge; model, pattern

Patrouille, pah-**trooll**-ye, *f*
patrol

Patsche, pahtt-she, *f* puddle;
mess; paw

patzig, pahtt-sik, *adj*
insolent, saucy

Pauke, powk-e, *f* drum,
tympanum

pauken, powk-en, *v* to beat
a drum, to thump; to fight
a duel; to cram

Pauschalreise,
Pauschalurlaub, pow-
shahl-ry-ze, pow-**shahl**-
oor-lowp, *f m* package
holiday

Pause, pow-ze, *f* interval;
pause, rest

Pazifik, pah-**tsee**-fick, *m*
Pacific Ocean

PC, peh-tseh, *m abbr*
Personal**c**omputer, PC

Pech, pek, *nt* pitch; hard
luck

Pechvogel, pek-fohg-el, *m*
unlucky person

Pein, pine, *f* pain, torment,
torture

peinigen, pine-ig-en, *v* to
torment

peinlich, pine-lik, *adj* very
careful; painful, awkward

Peitsche, pite-she, *f* whip,
lash

Pelle, pel-e, *f* skin, peel

pellen, pel-en, *v* to peel, to
skin

Pellkartoffeln, pel-kahrt-of-

eln, *pl* jacket potatoes

Pelz, pelts, *m* fur, pelt, skin

Pendel, pen-del, *nt*
pendulum; **–verkehr,** *m*
shuttle service; commuter
traffic

Pendler, pend-ler, *m*
commuter

penibel, pen-**eeb**-el, *adj*
fastidious; painful;
difficult to please

Penicillin, pen-ee-tsil-**een,**
nt penicillin

Pension, pahngs-**yohn,** *f*
pension; guest house; **–är,**
m pensioner; **–at,** *nt* girls'
boarding-school; **–ierung,**
f retirement

Pergament, pair-gah-**ment,**
nt parchment; grease-
proof paper

Perle, pairl-e, *f* pearl; bead

perlen, pairl-en, *v* to
sparkle; to fizz

Perlmutt(er), pairl-**moott**(-
er), *nt (f)*, mother-of-pearl

Personal, pair-zohn-**ahl,** *nt*
personnel, staff; cast

Personalcomputer, pair-
zohn-**ahl**-kom-pyoo-ter, *m*
personal computer

Personalien, pair-zohn-**ahl**-
yen, *pl* (full) personal
particulars

persönlich, pair-**zern**-lik, *adj*
personal

Perücke, pair-**EEck**-e, *f* wig

Pessimist, pes-ee-**mist,** *m*
pessimist

Pest, pest, *f* plague,
pestilence; epidemic

Petersilie, pait-er-**zeel**-ye, *f* parsley

petzen, pet-sen, *v* to tell tales, to inform

Pfad, p'faht, *m* path

Pfadfinder, p'**faht**-fin-der, *m* path-finder; (Boy-)Scout

Pfaffe, p'**fahff**-e, *m* *fam* parson; priest

Pfahl, p'fahl, *m* post, pole, stake, prop

Pfand, p'fahnt, *nt* pledge, security; forfeit

pfänden, p'**fend**-en, *v* to seize as a pledge

Pfänderspiel, p'**fen**-der-shpeel, *nt* game of forfeits

Pfandflasche, p'**fahnt**-flahsh-e, *f* returnable bottle

Pfandleiher, p'**fahnt**-ly-er, *m* pawnbroker

Pfanne, p'**fahnn**-e, *f* (frying) pan

Pfannkuchen, p'**fahnn**-kookh-en, *m* pancake, fritter; doughnut

Pfarrer, p'**fahrr**-er, *m* vicar, minister

Pfau, p'fow, *m* peacock

Pfeffer, p'**fef**-er, *m* pepper; **–kuchen,** *m* gingerbread; **–minz,** *nt* peppermint

pfeffern, p'**fef**-ern, *v* to (season with) pepper; to chuck (out)

Pfeife, p'**fy**-fe, *f* (organ) pipe; whistle

pfeifen, p'**fy**-fen, *v* to whistle; to pipe; to squeak

Pfeil, p'file, *m* arrow; dart;

bolt

Pfeiler, p'**fy**-ler, *m* pillar, column, post

Pfennig, p'**fenn**-ik, *m* pfennig

pferchen, p'**fairk**-en, *v* to pen/cram together

Pferd, p'fairt, *nt* horse; **–estärke,** *f* horse-power

Pfiff, p'fif, *m* whistle; trick, ruse

pfiffig, p'**fif**-ik, *adj* cunning, sly

Pfingsten, p'**fing**-sten, *nt* Whitsun

Pfirsich, p'**feer**-zik, *m* peach

Pflanze, p'**flahnt**-se, *f* plant; *fam* person

pflanzen, p'**flahnt**-sen, *v* to plant

Pflaster, p'**flahst**-er, *nt* plaster; flagging; pavement

pflastern, p'**flahst**-ern, *v* to plaster; to pave

Pflasterstein, p'**flahst**-er-shtine, *m* paving-stone

Pflaume, p'**flowm**-e, *f* plum; **–nkucken,** *m* plum-tart; **–nmus,** *nt* (thick) plum-jam

Pflege, p'**flaig**-e, *f* care, nursing; maintenance; **–kind,** *nt* foster-child

pflegen, p'**flaig**-en, *v* to nurse; to tend; to care for; to apply oneself to

Pflicht, p'flikt, *f* duty; obligation; **–eifer,** *m* zeal; **–gefühl,** *nt* sense of duty

Pflock, p'flock, *m* peg,

wooden pin

pflücken, p'**flEEck**-en, *v* to pick; to pluck

Pflug, p'flook, *m* plough

pflügen, p'**flEEg**-en, *v* to plough

Pforte, p'**fort**-e, *f* gate, doorway, portal

Pförtner, p'**fert**-ner, *m* porter; doorkeeper; turn-key

Pfote, p'**foht**-e, *f* paw, foot; scrawl

Pfropf(en), pfrop'f(-en), *m* bung; stopper, cork; clot; blockage

Pfuhl, p'fool, *m* pool, puddle, pit

pfui, p'**foo**-ee, *interj* ugh, yuk; tut tut

Pfund, p'foont, *nt* pound (money and weight)

pfuschen, p'**foosh**-en, *v* to botch, to bungle

Pfütze, p'**fEEt**-se, *f* puddle, mud-hole

Phantasie, fahnt-ah-**zee,** *f* imagination, fancy

phantasieren, fahnt-ah-**zeer**-en, to fantasize; to improvise

Philister, fi-**list**-er, *m* Philistine; uncultured person

phlegmatisch, fleg-**mah**-tish, *adj* lethargic, apathetic

Phobie, foh-**bee,** *f* phobia

Photograph, see **Fotograf**

Photographie, see **Fotografie**

photographieren, see

fotografieren

Physik, fEE-zick, *f* physics

Pickel, pick-el, *m* pimple; pickaxe

Picknick, pick-nick, *nt* picnic

piep(s)en, peep(s)-en, *v* to chirp, to squeak

Piepmatz, peep-mahts, *m* dicky-bird

piesacken, pee-sahck-en, *v* to torment, to torture

Pik, peek, *nt* (cards) spades

pikfein, peek-fine, *adj* very smart, elegant

Pilger, pil-ger, *m* pilgrim

pilgern, pil-gern, *v* to go on a pilgrimage

Pille, pil-e, *f* pill

Pilz, pilts, *m* mushroom, toadstool; fungus

Pinsel, pin-zel, *m* paintbrush

pinseln, pin-zeln, *v* to paint, to handle a brush

Pionier, pee-yohn-**eer,** *m* pioneer

pirschen, peersh-en, *v* to stalk (prey)

Piste, pis-te, *f* course; piste; runway

Pizza, pits-ah, *f* pizza

Pkw, peh-kah-weh, *m abbr* **Personenkraftwagen,** car, light goods vehicle

plädieren, play-**deer**-en, *v* to plead, to act as advocate

Plage, plahg-e, *f* worry, care; torment; nuisance

plagen, plahg-en, *v* to annoy, to torment; to

tease

Plakat, plah-**kaht,** *nt* placard, poster

Plan, plahn, *m* plan, scheme, project; plain, level country

planen, plahn-en, *v* to plan, to scheme, to plot

Planke, plahng-ke, *f* plank, thick board

Plänkelei, pleng-ke-**ly,** *f* squabble

planmäßig, plahn-mace-ik, *adj* according to plan, systematic

planschen, plahn-shen, *v* to splash, to paddle

Plappermaul, plahpp-er-mowl, *nt* chatterbox, prattler

plappern, plahpp-ern, *v* to chatter, to babble

Plastik, plahss-tick, *f* sculpture; *nt* plastic, polythene; **–beutel,** *m* plastic bag; **–folie,** *f* plastic film; **–tüte,** *f* plastic bag

Platane, plaht-**ahn**-e, *f* plane tree

plätschern, plet-shern, *v* to splash; to ripple

platschnaß, plahtsh-**nahss,** *adj* soaking wet

platt, plahtt, *adj* flat, even, level

Plattdeutsch, plahtt-doytsh, *nt* Low German

Platte, plahtt-e, *f* plate; dish; bare spot; board

plätten, plet-en, *v* to flatten; to iron; to press

Plattenspieler, plahtt-en-shpeel-er, *m* record player

Platz, plahts, *m* place, spot; square

Plätzchen, plets-ken, *nt* biscuit; small place

platzen, plahts-en, *v* to burst; to crack

Platzkarte, plahts-kart-e, *f* seat reservation

Platzmangel, plahts-mahng-el, *m* lack of space

Plauderei, plowd-e-**ry,** *f* chat, gossip(ing)

plaudern, plowd-ern, *v* to chat, to gossip

Pleite, ply-te, *f* bankruptcy, failure

Plombe, plom-be, *f* lead seal; filling (in tooth)

plombieren, plom-**beer**-en, *v* to seal; to fill (teeth)

plötzlich, plerts-lik, *adj* sudden, unexpected; *adv* suddenly

plump, ploomp, *adj* blunt, clumsy, coarse

plumps, ploomps, *interj* thump! thud! splash!

Plunder, ploonn-der, *m* rubbish, lumber, junk

plündern, plEEn-dern, *v* to plunder, to loot

Plüsch, plEEsh, *m* plush

PLZ, *abbr* **Postleitzahl**

Po, poh, *m* bottom, bum

pochen, pok-en, *v* to rap, to beat, to knock

Pointe, pwang-te, *f* point (of

a joke etc.)

Pokal, poh-**kahl,** m cup, goblet

pökeln, perk-eln, v to pickle, to salt

Polen, poh-len, nt Poland

polieren, poh-**leer**-en, v to polish

Politur, poh-lee-**toor,** f polish, gloss

Polizei, poh-lee-**tsy,** f police; **–beamte(r),** m policeman; **–revier,** nt police-station; **–stunde,** f (pub) closing time; **–wache,** f police-station

Polizist, poh-lee-**tsist,** m policeman

polnisch, pol-nish, adj Polish

Polster, polst-er, nt cushion; upholstery; stuffing; **–möbel,** pl upholstered furniture

polstern, pol-stern, v to upholster, to stuff

Polterabend, polt-er-ahb-ent, m party on the eve of a wedding

poltern, polt-ern, v to crash (about)

Polyester, pohl-ee-**aist**-er, m polyester

Pommes frites, pom frit, pl chips, French fries

Popcorn, pop-korn, nt popcorn

Popmusik, pop-moo-zeek, f pop (music)

Pornographie, por-noh-**grahff**-ee, f pornography

Porree, por-ay, m leek

Portemonnaie, port-mon-ay, nt purse

Portier, port-yeh, m doorkeeper, porter

Porto, port-oh, nt postage

Portugal, port-oo-gahll, nt Portugal

portugiesisch, port-oo-geez-ish, adj Portuguese

Porzellan, por-tsel-lahn, nt porcelain, china

Posaune, poh-**zown**-e, f trombone, trumpet

Positur, poh-zee-**toor,** f posture, attitude

possierlich, pos-eer-lik, adj comical; funny

Post, post, f mail, post (-office); **–amt,** nt post-office (building); **–anweisung,** f money-order; **–bote,** m postman; **–fach,** nt post-office/P.O. box; **–karte,** f postcard

Posten, post-en, m item; lot; sentry; post

postlagernd, post-**lahg**-ernt, adj poste restante

Postleitzahl, post-**lite**-tsahl, f post code

Poststempel, post-**shtem**-pel, m postmark

postwendend, post-**ven**-dent, adv by return of post

poussieren, pooss-**eer**-en, v to flirt, to court

Pracht, prahkt, f splendour, pomp

prächtig, prek-tik, adj splendid, gorgeous, fine

Prachtkerl, prahkt-**kairl,** m splendid fellow; beauty

Prachtstück, prahkt-**stEEck,** nt showpiece

prachtvoll, prahkt-fol, adj (very) fine, magnificent

prägen, pray-gen, v to mint; to coin; to emboss, to stamp

prahlen, prahl-en, v to boast, to brag

Prahlerei, prahl-e-ry, f boasting

prahlerisch, prahl-er-ish, adj boastful

Prahlhans, prahl-hahns, m boaster

praktisch, prahck-tish, adj practical; useful

praktizieren, prahck-tee-**tseer**-en, v to practise (medicine etc.)

Praline, prahl-ee-ne, f truffle chocolate

prall, prahll, adj stretched tight; plump

prallen, prahll-en, v to crash into, to collide with

Prämie, praim-ye, f premium; bonus; prize

präm(i)ieren, praim-(ee-)eer-en, v to give an award/bonus

prangen, prahng-en, v to shine; to be resplendent

Präparat, pray-pah-**raht,** nt preparation; medicine

präparieren, pray-pah-**reer**-en, v to preserve; to dissect

Prärie, pray-ree, f prairie

präsentieren, pray-zent-**eer**-en, *v* to present

Präservativ, pray-zer-vah-teef, *nt* condom

Präsidium, pray-zeed-ee-oomm, *nt* presidency; headquarters

prasseln, **prahss**-eln, *v* to patter; to crackle

prassen, **prahss**-en, *v* to lead the high life

prätentiös, pray-ten-se-**erss**, *adj* pretentious

Praxis, **prahck**-siss, *f* practice; experience; connexion; (doctor's) surgery

predigen, **pray**-dee-gen, *v* to preach; to sermonize

Prediger, **pray**-dee-ger, *m* preacher, clergyman

Predigt, **pray**-dikt, *f* sermon

Preis, price, *m* price; prize

Preiselbeere, **pry**-sel-bair-e, *f* cranberry

preisen, **pry**-zen, *v* to praise; to extol

preisgeben, **price**-gay-ben, *v* to abandon; to expose; to betray

preisgekrönt, **price**-ge-krernt, *adj* prize-winning, award-winning

preisgünstig, **price**-gEEnst-ik, *adj* good value, inexpensive

Preisliste, **price**-list-e, *f* price-list

Preisschild, **price**-shilt, *nt* price tag

preiswert, **price**-vairt, *adj* good value

prellen, **prel**-en, *v* to overcharge; to dupe; to rebound

Presse, **press**-e, *f* press; journalism; **–agentur**, *f* press agency; **–bericht**, *m* news item, news story; **–fotograf**, *m* press photographer; **–freiheit**, *f* freedom of the press

pressen, **press**-en, *v* to press, to squeeze

pressieren, press-**eer**-en, *v* to be urgent

prickeln, **prick**-eln, *v* to prickle, to sting; to bubble

Priester, **preest**-er, *m* priest

prima, **preem**-ah, *adj & interj* excellent, great

Primel, **preem**-el, *f* cowslip, primrose

Prinz, prints, *m* prince

Prinzessin, prin-**tsess**-in, *f* princess

Prinzip, prin-**tseep**, *nt* principle

prinzipiell, prin-tseep-ee-**ell**, *adj & adv* on principle

Prise, **preez**-e, *f* pinch (of salt etc.)

Pritsche, **prit**-she, *f* flat-bed (of lorry); plank-bed

Privatdozent, pree-vaht-doh-tsent, *m* private lecturer

Privatfernsehen, pree-**vaht**-fairn-say-en, *nt* commercial television

privatisieren, pree-vaht-e-zeer-en, *v* to privatise

Privatschule, pree-**vaht**-shoo-le, *f* private school

pro, proh, *prep* for, per

Probe, **proh**-be, *f* trial, test; rehearsal; sample

proben, **proh**-ben, *v* to try; to rehearse

probeweise, **proh**-be-vy-ze, *adv* experimentally

probieren, proh-**beer**-en, *v* to try; to rehearse

Produzent, proh-doo-**tsent**, *m* producer, grower, maker

produzieren, proh-doo-tseer-en, *v* to produce, to make

Profi, **proh**-fee, *m* professional (sport etc.)

profitieren, proh-feet-**eer**-en, *v* to profit from

Prokurist, proh-koor-**ist**, *m* head-clerk (authorized to sign)

Propaganda, pro-pah-**gahnn**-dah, *f* propaganda

prophezeien, proh-fe-**tsy**-en, *v* to prophesy

prosit, **proh**-zit, *interj* cheers, to your health

Prospekt, proh-**spekt**, *m* brochure, leaflet; prospectus

prost, prohst, *interj* cheers, to your health

protegieren, proh-te-zheer-en, *v* to favour, to patronize

protestieren, proh-test-**eer**-en, *v* to protest

Protokoll, proh-toh-kol, *nt* minutes, record; protocol

protzen, prot-sen, v to boast, to show off

protzig, prot-sik, adj boastful

Proviant, proh-vee-**ahnt**, m provisions

Provinz, proh-**vints**, f province, county, country

Provision, proh-vee-zee-**ohn**, f commission

provisorisch, proh-ve-**zohr**-ish adj temporary, provisional

Prozedur, proh-tsay-**doohr**, f procedure, process

Prozent, proh-**tsent**, nt per cent

Prozess, proh-**tsess**, m lawsuit; process

prozessieren, proh-tsess-**eer**-en, v to litigate

prüde, prEEd-e, adj prudish

prüfen, prEEf-en, v to test, to examine

Prüfung, prEEf-oong, f examination; affliction

Prügel, prEEg-el, m cudgel; pl thrashing; **–ei**, f fight, scuffle; **–knabe**, m scapegoat, whipping-boy

prügeln, prEEg-eln, v to thrash; **sich –**, to have a fight

Prügelstrafe, prEEg-el-shtrah-fe, f corporal punishment

Prunk, proonk, m pomp, splendour

prunken, proonk-en, v to be resplendent; to flaunt

prusten, proost-en, v to sneeze; to burst out laughing

PS, abbr Pferdestärke, hp

Psyche, psEE-ke, f psyche

Psychiater, psEEk-**yah**-ter, m psychiatrist

Psychoanalytiker, psEEk-oh-ah-nah-**lEEt**-ee-ker, m psychoanalyst

psychologisch, psEEk-oh-**loh**-gish, adj psychological

Psychopath, psEEk-oh-**paht**, m psychopath

Psychotherapeut, psEEk-oh-tair-ah-**poyt**, m psychotherapist

Publikum, poob-lee-koomm, nt audience

Pudel, pood-el, m poodle

Pudding, poodd-ing, m blancmange

Puder, pood-er, m powder

pudern, pood-ern, v to powder

Puderquaste, pood-er-kvahst-e, f powder-puff

Puff, pooff, m bang; thump; pouffe; fam brothel

Puffärmel, pooff-airm-el, m puff(ed) sleeve

Puffer, pooff-er, m buffer; (potato) pancake

Pulle, pooll-e, f fam bottle

Pullover, pooll-**oh**-ver, m pullover

Puls, pools, m pulse

Pulsader, pools-ahd-er, f artery

pulsieren, pooll-**zeer**-en, v to pulsate; to throb

Pulsschlag, pools-shlahk, m pulsation, beating of pulse

Pult, poolt, nt (writing-) desk

Pulver, pool-ver, nt powder

Pumpe, poomp-e, f pump

pumpen, poomp-en, v to pump; fam to borrow/lend

Pumpernickel, poomp-er-nick-el, m black rye-bread

Pumphose, poomp-hoh-ze, f baggy trousers

Punkt, poonkt, m point; full-stop, period

pünktlich, pEEnkt-lik, adj punctual; exact

Pünktlichkeit, pEEnkt-lik-kite, f punctuality

Pupille, pooh-**pil**-e, f pupil (of eye)

Puppe, poopp-e, f doll, puppet; pupa, cocoon

pur, poor, adj pure, sheer

Püree, pEEr-ay, nt mash, puree

pürieren, pEEr-eer-en, v to liquidize

purpurfarbig, poor-poor-fahr-bik, adj crimson

Purzelbaum, poort-sel-bowm, m somersault

purzeln, poort-seln, v to tumble

pusten, poost-en, v to blow, to puff

Pute, poot-e, f turkey(-hen)

Puter, poot-er, m turkey (-cock)

Putsch, pootsh, m coup d'état, revolt, putsch

Putz, poots, m decoration; millinery; finery; plaster

putzen, poots-en, v to

polish; to clean(se); to
adorn

putzig, poots-ik, *adj* droll,
funny

Putzfrau, poots-frow, *f*
cleaning lady

Putzkolonne, poots-ko-lo-
ne, *f* cleaning staff

Putzmittel, poots-mit-*el*, *nt*
cleanser; polishing
material

Putzzeug, poots-tsoyk, *nt*
polishing material(s)

Puzzle(spiel), poozz-*el*
(-shpeel), *nt* jigsaw •

Pyrenäen, pEE-ray-**nay**-*en*,
pl Pyrenees

Q

quantum

Quappe, kvahpp-e, *f* tadpole

Quark, kvahrk, *m* curds, cream-cheese; *fam* trash

Quart, kvahrt, *f mus* fourth

Quartal, kvahrt-ahl, *nt* quarter (of a year)

Quarz, kvahrts, *nt* quartz

quasi, kvah-zee, *adv* so to speak, as it were

quasseln, kvahss-eln, *v* to chatter

Quasselstrippe, kvahss-el-shtrip-e, *f* chatterbox

Quaste, kvahst-e, *f* tassel, pom-pom

Quatsch, kvahtsh, *m* nonsense, rubbish

quatschen, kvahtt-shen, *v* to talk rubbish; **kvahtt**-shen, *v* to squash

Quecksilber, kveck-sil-ber, *nt* mercury, quick-silver

Quelle, kvel-e, *f* spring, source, fountain

quellen, kvel-en, *v* to pour, to stream, to well (up); to swell

Quengelei, kveng-e-ly, *f* bother, nagging, fault-finding

quengelig, kveng-el-ik, *adj* nagging, grumbling

quengeln, kveng-eln, *v* to nag, to grumble, to find fault

quer, kvair, *adj* slanting; *adv* across, diagonally; – **durch**, *adv* right across/through

Quere, kvair-e, *f* diagonal

Quacksalber, kvahck-zahlb-er, *m* quack (doctor); **–ei**, *f* quackery, quack medicine

Quader, kvahd-er, *m* cuboid

Quadrat, kvah-draht, *nt* square

quaken, kvahk-en, *v* to croak; to quack

Qual, kvahl, *f* torment, intense suffering

quälen, kvay-len, *v* to torture, to torment;

Quälerei, kvay-le-ry, *f* torture; worry

quälerisch, kvay-ler-ish, *adj* tormenting, annoying

Quälgeist, kvail-gy'st, *m* tormenter

Qualität, kvahl-ee-tait, *f* quality, kind, variety

Qualifikation, kvahl-ee-fee-kahts-yohn, *f* qualification

qualifiziert, kvahl-ee-fee-tseert, *adj* qualified

Qualle, kvahll-e, *f* jelly-fish

Qualm, kvahlm, *m* (thick) smoke; fumes

qualmen, kvahll-men, *v* to give off fumes/thick smoke; *fam* to smoke (cigarettes)

qualmig, kvahll-mik, *adj* smoky, full of fumes

qualvoll, kvahl-fol, *adj* agonizing

Quantität, kvahnn-tee-tait, *f* quantity

Quantum, kvahnn-toomm, *nt* quantity; quota;

Querflöte, kvair-flert-*e*, *f*
flute

Querkopf, kvair-kop'f, *m*
obstinate person

Querschnitt, kvair-shnitt,
m cross-section

Querstraße, kvair-shtrahs-
e, *f* side-street, turning

quetschen, kvet-shen, *v* to
crush, to pinch

Quetschung, kvet-shoong, *f*
bruise

quieken, kveek-*en*, *v* to
squeak, to squeal

quietschen, kveet-shen, *v* to
squeak, to creak

Quirl, kvirl, *m* whisk

quirlen, kvirl-en, *v* to
whisk; to twirl

Quitte, kvit-*e*, *f* quince

quittieren, kvit-**eer**-en, *v* to
give a receipt; to quit

Quittung, kvit-oong, *f*
receipt; penalty

Quiz, kvis, *nt* Quiz;
–sendung, *f* quiz show

Quote, kvoht-*e*, *f* share,
quota

R

Rabatt, rah-bahtt, *m* rebate, discount

Rabbiner, rah-been-er, *m* rabbi

Rabe, rah-be, *m* raven

rabenschwarz, rah-ben-shvahrts, *adj* jet-black

rabiat, rah-be-aht, *adj* rabid; rough; furious

Rache, rahk-e, *f* revenge, vengeance

Rachen, rahk-en, *m* throat, pharynx

rächen, rek-en, *v* to revenge, to avenge

Rad, raht, *nt* wheel; cycle; bike

Radar, rahd-ahr, *m & nt* radar; **–falle,** *f* speed trap; **–kontrolle,** *f* radar speed check

Radau, rah-dow, *m* loud noise, row

Raddampfer, raht-dahmp-

fer, *m* paddle-steamer

radebrechen, rahd-e-brek-en, *v* to speak a language imperfectly

radeln, raht-eln, *v* to cycle

rädern, ray-dern, *v* to put on wheels

radfahren, raht-fahr-en, *v* to cycle

Radfahrer, raht-fahr-er, *m* cyclist

radieren, rah-deer-en, *v* to erase; to etch

Radiergummi, rah-deer-goomm-ee, *m* (india-) rubber

Radiermesser, rah-deer-mess-er, *nt* pen-knife

Radierung, rah-deer-oong, *f* etching; erasure

Radieschen, rah-dees-ken, *nt* radish

radikal, rah-dee-kahl, *adj* radical

radioaktiv, rah-dee-oh-ahk-teef, *adj* radioactive

Radiosender, rah-dee-oh-zen-der, *m* radio station

Radler, rahd-ler, *m* cyclist

radschlagen, raht-shlahg-en, *v* to turn a somersault

Radweg, raht-vaig, *m* cycleway, cycle path

raffen, rahff-en, *v* to amass; to gather; to take in (seams)

Raffinerie, rahff-een-er-ee, *f* refinery

raffiniert, rahff-een-eert, *adj* cunning; refined

Rahm, rahm, *m* cream

rahmen, rahm-en, *v* to frame; to form cream; to skim

Rahmen, rahm-en, *m* frame

Rakete, rah-kayt-e, *f* rocket

rammen, rahmm-en, *v* to ram; to stamp firm

Rampe, rahmp-e, *f* ramp, platform

Ramsch, rahmsh, *m* job-lot; junk; **–ware,** *f* cheap goods

ran, rahnn, *abbr* **heran**

Rand, rahnt, *m* edge; rim; brink

randalieren, rahnn-dah-lee-ren, *v* to (go on the) rampage

Rang, rahng, *m* rank, station; circle *theatre*

rangieren, rahng-zheer-en, *v* to shunt; to take rank

Ranke, rahng-ke, *f* tendril,

shoot

ranken, rahng-ken v to creep, to climb (of plants)

Ranzen, rahnt-sen, m satchel

ranzig, rahnt-sik, adj rancid, rank

Rappe, rahpp-e, m black horse

rappeln, rahpp-eln, v to rattle

Raps, rahpps, m rape(-seed), colza

rar, rahr, adj rare, scarce; exquisite

Rarität, rahr-ee-**tait**, f rarity; curio(sity)

rasch, rahsh, adj quick, brisk, speedy

rascheln, rahsh-eln, v to rustle; to crackle

Rasen, rahz-en, m lawn, turf; **–mäher,** m lawn-mower

rasen, rahz-en, v to rage; to rush; to be frenzied

Raserei, rahz-e-**ry,** f frenzy, madness

Rasierapparat, rahz-eer-ahpp-ah-raht, m (electric) shaver

rasieren, rahz-eer-en, v to shave

Rasierklinge, rahz-eer-kling-e, f razor-blade

Rasierpinsel, rahz-eer-pin-zel, m shaving-brush

Raspel, rahsp-el, f rasp

raspeln, rahsp-eln, v to rasp; to scrape

Rasse, rahss-e, f race, breed,

stock

rasseln, rahss-eln, v to rattle; to clank

rassig, rahss-ik, adj racy, sleek; spirited, lively

Rassismus, rahss-is-mooss, m racism

Rassist, rahss-ist, m racist

**Rast, rahst, f rest; recreation; halt

rasten, rahst-en, v to rest; to halt

Rat, raht, m advice; council(lor)

Rate, raht-e, f instalment; rate

raten, raht-en, v to advise; to guess (see **erraten**)

ratenweise, raht-en-vy-ze, adv in instalments

Ratgeber, raht-gayb-er, m adviser, counsellor

Rathaus, raht-hows, nt town-hall

rationalisieren, rahts-yohn-ahl-ee-zee-ren, v to rationalise

rationell, rahts-yohn-ell, adj rational; efficient

ratlos, raht-lohs, adj helpless, at a loss

ratsam, raht-zahmm, adj advisable; commendable

Ratschlag, raht-shlahk, m advice, counsel

Rätsel, rayt-sel, nt riddle, puzzle; mystery

rätselhaft, rayt-sel-hahft, adj mysterious; puzzling

Ratsherr, rahts-hair, m councillor

Ratskeller, rahts-kel-er, m cellar under the town-hall

Ratte, rahtt-e, f rat; **–nfänger,** m rat-catcher; Pied Piper

rattern, rahtt-ern, v to rattle

Raub, rowp, m robbery; abduction; prey

rauben, row-ben, v to rob, to steal

Räuber, roy-ber, m robber, thief

Raubgier, rowp-geer, f rapacity

Raubtier, rowp-teer, nt beast of prey

Raubvogel, rowp-fohg-el, m bird of prey

Rauch, rowk, m smoke

rauchen, rowk-en, v to smoke

Raucher, rowk-er, m smoker; **–abteil,** nt smoking compartment

Rauchfang, rowk-fahng, m chimney

rauchig, rowk-ik, adj smoky

räuchern, royk-ern, v to cure with smoke; to fumigate

'rauf, rowf, abbr **herauf**

Raufbold, rowf-bolt, m bully

raufen, rowf-en, v to pull up/out; to brawl

rauh, row, adj rough, rugged; severe, harsh

Raum, rowm, m room, space; locality

räumen, roym-en, v to clear; to remove

Raumfahrt, rowm-fart, *f* space travel

räumlich, roym-lik, *adj* in regard to space, spatial

Räumlichkeit, roym-lik-kite, *f* space; **–en**, *pl* rooms, premises

raunen, rown-en, *v* to whisper

Raupe, rowp-e, *f* caterpillar

'aus, rowss, *abbr* **heraus**

Rausch, rowsh, *m* ecstasy; intoxication

rauschen, rowsh-en, *v* to rush; to rustle; to roar

Rauschgift, rowsh-gift, *nt* drug; **–süchtige(r)**, *m & f*, drug addict

räuspern (sich), roysp-ern (zik), *v* to clear one's throat

Razzia, rahtt-see-ah, *f* raid

Reagenzglas, ray-ah-gents-glahs, *nt* test tube

reagieren, ray-ah-geer-en, *v* to react; to respond

Realschule, ray-ahl-shool-e, *f* type of secondary school

Realität, ray-ahl-ee-tait, *f* reality

realitätsfern, **realitätsfremd**, ray-ahl-ee-taits-fairn, -fremt, *adj* unrealistic

Rebe, ray-be, *f* vine; shoot

Rebhuhn, rayp-hoon, *nt* partridge

Rechen, rek-en, *m* rake; rack

Rechenschaft, rek-en-shahft, *f* account

Recherche, ray-shair-she, *f* investigation, inquiry

rechnen, rek-nen, *v* to reckon, to calculate

Rechnung, rek-noong, *f* bill, invoice; account

Rechnungsauszug, rek-noongs-ows-tsook, *m* statement of account

recht, rekt, *adj* right; right-hand; correct

Recht, rekt, *nt* right, privilege; justice; law

rechtfertigen, rekt-fairt-ig-en, *v* to justify; to defend

rechthaberisch, rekt-hahb-er-ish, *adj* dogmatic, pig-headed

rechtlich, rekt-lik, *adj* lawful, legal; fair

rechtmäßig, rekt-mace-ik, *adj* rightful, lawful

rechts, rekts, *adv* on the right; *adj* right

Rechtsanwalt, rekts-ahnn-vahlt, *m* solicitor; lawyer; barrister

rechtschaffen, rekt-shahff-en, *adj* upright, just

Rechtschreibung, rekt-shry-boong, *f* orthography

Rechtsfall, rekts-fahll, *m* case (court)

rechtsgültig, rekts-gEElt-ik, *adj* valid in law

Rechtshänder, rekts-hen-der, *m* right-handed person

rechtskräftig, rekts-kreft-ik, *adj* valid, legal

rechtsum, rekts-oomm, *adv* to the right; about (turn)

Rechtsverkehr, rekts-fair-kair, *m* right-hand traffic

rechtswegen, rekts-vaig-en, *adv* by rights

rechtzeitig, rekt-tsy-tik, *adv* in good time, punctually

recken, reck-en, *v* to stretch

recyceln, ree-sike-eln, *v* to recycle

Recycling, ree-sike-ling, *nt* recycling

Redakteur, ray-dahck-ter, *m* editor

Redaktion, ray-dahckts-yohn, *f* editor's office; editing

Rede, ray-de, *f* speech; talk; address

Redefreiheit, ray-de-fry-hite, *f* freedom of speech

redegewandt, ray-de-ge-vahnt, *adj* eloquent

reden, ray-den, *v* to talk, to speak

Redensart, ray-dens-art, *f* (hackneyed/empty) phrase; idiom

redigieren, ray-dee-geer-en, *v* to edit

redlich, rayt-lik, *adj* upright; open; straightforward

Redner, rayd-ner, *m* orator; speaker

redselig, rayd-zail-ik, *adj* talkative

Reeder, rayd-er, *m* ship-owner; shipper

Reederei, rayd-e-ry, *f* shipping (-business)

reel, ray-el, *adj* fair, honest;

respectable; real

Referendar, ref-*e*-ren-**dar,** *m* trainee; student (teacher); articled clerk

Referent, ref-*e*-rent, *m* speaker, reporter

reflektieren, ref-lek-**teer**-en, *v* to reflect; to think

Refrain, ray-**freng,** *m* chorus of a song

Regal, ray-**gahl,** *nt* shelves, shelving, pigeon-holes

rege, ray-ge, *adj* lively, brisk, active

Regel, ray-gel, *f* rule; regulation

regelmäßig, ray-gel-mace-ik, *adj* regular; orderly

regeln, ray-geln, *v* to regulate; to arrange

regelrecht, ray-gel-rekt, *adj* real, proper

regen (sich), ray-gen (zik), *v* to stir, to move

Regen, ray-gen, *m* rain; **–bogen,** *m* rainbow; **–mantel,** *m* raincoat; **–schirm,** *m* umbrella; **–wald,** *m* rain forest; **–wurm,** *m* earth-worm

Regie, ray-zhee, *f* production; direction (film)

regieren, ray-**gheer**-en, *v* to rule, to govern

Regierung, ray-**gheer**-oong, *f* government

Regisseur, ray-zhee-ser, *m* producer; (film) director

regnen, rayg-nen, *v* to rain

regnerisch, rayg-ner-ish, *adj*

rainy

Reh, ray, *nt* deer, roe(-buck)

Rehbraten, ray-braht-en, *m* roast venison

reiben, ry-ben, *v* to rub; to grate

Reiberei, ry-be-ry, *f* friction

reich, ry'k, *adj* rich

Reich, ry'k, *nt* empire, realm

reichen, ry'k-en, *v* to reach, to stretch; to pass

reichhaltig, ry'k-hahlt-ik, *adj* plentiful, abundant

reichlich, ry'k-lik, *adj* copious, plentiful

Reichtum, ry'k-toom, *m* riches, wealth

reif, rife, *adj* ripe, mature

Reif, rife, *m* ring; hoop; frost

Reife, ry-fe, *f* maturity, ripeness

reifen, ry-fen, *v* to ripen, to mature

Reifen, ry-fen, *m* hoop; tyre

reiflich, rife-lik, *adj* mature

Reihe, ry-e, *f* row; range; succession; turn

reihen, ry-en, *v* to string, to arrange in rows; to tack (sewing)

Reihenfolge, ry-en-folg-e, *f* succession, sequence

Reiher, ry-er, *m* heron

Reim, rime, *m* rhyme

reimen, ry-men, *v* to rhyme, to make up rhymes

rein, rine, *adj* pure; clean; chaste; net

reinigen, ry-nig-en, *v* to clean(se); to purify

Reinigung, ry-nee-goong, *f*

clean(s)ing; purification; dry cleaning

reinlich, rine-lik, *adj* clean; tidy

Reis, rice, *m* rice

Reise, ry-ze, *f* voyage, journey, trip; **–büro,** *nt* travel agency

reisefertig, ry-ze-fair-tik, *adj* ready for a journey

Reiseführer, *m* (tour) guide; guidebook

reisen, ry-zen, *v* to travel

Reisekrankheit, ry-ze-krahnk-hite, *f* travel sickness

Reisende(r), ry-zen-de(r), *m & f* traveller; passenger

Reisepaß, ry-ze-pahss, *m* passport

Reisescheck, ry-ze-sheck, *m* traveller's cheque

Reisetasche, ry-ze-tah-she, *f* travelling-bag, grip

Reisig, ry-zik, *nt* brushwood, faggots

reißen, ry-sen, *v* to tear; to pull; to break, to snap

Reitbahn, rite-bahn, *f* bridle path

reiten, ry-ten, *v* to ride (a horse)

Reiter, ry-ter, *m* rider

Reithose, rite-hoh-ze, *f* riding breeches; jodhpurs

Reitweg, rite-wayk, *m* bridle path

Reiz, rites, *m* irritation; charm

reizbar, rites-bahr, *adj* irritable, touchy

reizen, rites-en, v to irritate; to stimulate; to incite; to charm

reizend, rites-ent, adj charming, delightful

reizvoll, rites-fol, adj attractive; fascinating

Reklamation, ray-klah-mahts-yohn, f complaint; protest

Reklame, ray-klah-me, f advertising, advertisement; publicity

reklamieren, ray-klah-meer-en, v to complain; to claim

rempeln, rem-peln, v to jostle

Rennbahn, ren-bahn, f race-course

rennen, ren-en, v to run, to rush

Rennpferd, ren-pfairt, nt race-horse

Renommee, ray-nom-ay, nt renown; reputation

renommiert, ray-nom-eert, adj renowned

renovieren, ray-noh-veer-en, v to renovate, to redecorate; to refurbish

rentabel, ren-tahb-el, adj lucrative, profitable

Rente, rent-e, f pension; income; annuity

rentieren (sich), rent-eer-en (zik), v to be worthwhile/profitable, to pay

Rentner, rent-ner, m pensioner

Reparatur, ray-pah-raht-oor, f repair(ing); **–werkstatt**, f garage; repair shop

reparieren, ray-pah-reer-en, v to repair

Reservierung, ray-zer-veer-oong, f booking, reservation

Residenz, ray-zee-dents, f residence; seat (mansion)

respektieren, res-peck-teer-en, v to respect

Rest, rest, m rest, remainder; remnant

restlos, rest-lohs, adj & adv complete(ly), total(ly)

Resultat, ray-zooll-taht, nt result; outcome

retour, ray-toor, adv back

retten, ret-en, v to save, to rescue

Rettich, ret-ik, m radish

Rettung, ret-oong, f rescue; salvation; escape

Reue, roy-e, f penitence, repentance

revanchieren (sich), ray-vahng-sheer-en (zik), v to return a compliment/service; to have one's revenge

revidieren, ray-vee-deer-en, v to examine

Revision, ray-veez-yohn, f auditing; examination; appeal

Revisor, ray-vee-zohr, m auditor

Rezension, ray-tsents-yohn, f review (of book etc.)

Rezept, ray-tsept, nt recipe; prescription

Rezeption, ray-tsepts-yohn, f reception (hotel etc.)

Rhabarber, rah-barb-er, m rhubarb

Rhein, rine, m Rhine

Rheinwein, rine-vine, m Rhine wine, hock

richten, rik-ten, v to set, to straighten; to direct; to judge

Richter, rik-ter, m judge

Richtgeschwindigkeit, rikt-ge-shvind-ik-kite, f recommended speed

richtig, rik-tik, adj right, correct; just; fair

Richtigkeit, rik-tik-kite, f correctness; fairness

Richtlinie, rikt-leen-ye, f guideline; directive

Richtung, rikt-oong, f direction, course

riechen, reek-en, v to smell

Riege, reeg-e, f team, squad

Riegel, reeg-el, m bolt

Riemen, reem-en, m strap, thong

Riese, reez-e, m giant; ogre

rieseln, reez-eln, v to trickle; to fall (snow)

riesenartig, reez-en-art-ik, adj like a giant

Riesenerfolg, reez-en-air-folk, m huge success

riesengroß, reez-en-grohs, adj gigantic

riesig, reez-ik, adj colossal, enormous

Riff, rif, nt reef; sandbank

Rille, ril-*e*, *f* groove; furrow

Rind, rint, *nt*, cow; beef

Rinde, rin-*de*, *f* bark, rind; crust

Rindfleisch, rint-fly'sh, *nt* beef

Rindvieh, rint-fee, *nt* cattle;*fam* blockhead

Ring, ring, *m* ring; circle; round

Ringbahn, ring-bahn, *f* circle line

ringeln, ring-eln, *v* to curl; to coil

ringen, ring-en, *v* to wrestle; to wring (hands)

ringsherum, ringsumher, rings-hair-oomm, -oomm-hair, *adv* round about

Ringstraße, ring-strahs-*e*, *f* ring road

Rinne, rin-*e*, *f* groove; gully, sewer

rinnen, rin-en, to trickle; to flow; to leak

Rinnstein, rin-shtine, *m* gutter

Rippe, rip-*e*, *f* rib; frame(work)

Rippenspeer, rip-en-shpair, *m* roast loin of pork

Risiko, ree-zee-koh, *nt* risk

riskant, risk-ahnt, *adj* risky

riskieren, risk-eer-en, *v* to risk

Riß, ris, *m* tear, fissure; gap, crack

rissig, ris-ik, *adj* cracked

Ritt, rit, *m* ride

Ritter, rit-er, *m* knight; cavalier

Rittergut, rit-er-goot, *nt* gentleman's estate

ritterlich, rit-er-lik, *adj* chivalrous; knightly

rittlings, rit-lings, *adj* astride

Ritze, rits-*e*, *f* slit; fissure; scratch

ritzen, rit-sen, *v* to slit; to scratch; to graze

Rizinusöl, rit-see-nooss-erl, *nt* castor-oil

Robbe, rob-*e*, *f* seal

Roboter, roh-boh-ter, *m* robot

röcheln, rerk-eln, *v* to groan; to give a death rattle

Rock, rock, *m* coat; skirt

Rogen, rohg-en, *m* hard roe

Roggen, rogg-en, *m* rye; –brot, *nt* rye-bread

roh, roh, *adj* raw; rough; brutal

Roheit, roh-hite, *f* rawness; roughness; brutality

Rohr, rohr, *nt* cane; tube; pipe; barrel (of gun)

Röhre, rer-*e*, *f* tube; channel; oven

Rohrstock, rohr-shtock, *m* cane, stick

Rolle, rol-*e*, *f* roller; reel; spool; roll; rôle

rollen, rol-en, *v* to roll; to rumble

Rollmops, rol-mops, *m* pickled herring, roll-mop

Rollo, rol-oh, *nt* roller-blind

Rollschuh, rol-shoo, *m* roller-skate

Rollstuhl, rol-shtool, *m* wheelchair; –fahrer, *m* wheelchair user

Rolltreppe, rol-trep-*e*, *f* escalator

Rom, rohm, *nt* Rome

Roman, roh-mahn, *m* novel

Röntgenstrahlen, rernt-gen-shtrahl-en, *pl* X-rays

rosa, roh-zah, *adj* pink

Rose, roh-ze, *f* rose

Rosenkohl, roh-zen-kohl, *m* brussels sprouts

rosig, roh-zik, *adj* rosy

Rosine, roh-zeen-*e*, *f* raisin; sultana

Roß, ross, *nt* horse, steed

Rost, rost, *m* rust; grate; gridiron

Rostbraten, rosst-braht-en, *m* roast joint (of beef)

rosten, rosst-en, *v* to rust

rösten, rerst-en, *v* to grill, to roast, to fry

rostig, rost-ik, *adj* rusty

rot, roht, *adj* red

rotbäckig, roht-beck-ik, *adj* rosy-cheeked

Röte, rert-*e*, *f* redness

rothaarig, roht-hahr-ik, *adj* red-haired

Rotkehlchen, roth-kayl-ken, *nt* robin (redbreast)

Rotkraut, roht-krowt, *nt* red cabbage

Rotlichtbezirk, roht-likt-be-tsirk, *m* red-light district

Rotwein, roht-vine, *m* red wine

Rotte, rot-*e*, *f* gang, band; swarm

Rotwild, roht-vilt, *nt* red

deer

Roulade, rool-**ahd**-e, f beef olive

routiniert, root-een-**eert**, adj experienced

Rowdy, row-dee, m vandal

Rübe, rEEb-e, f turnip

rüber, rEEb-er, abbr **herüber**

Rubin, roob-een, m ruby

ruchlos, rook-lohs, adj wicked, malicious

Ruck, roock, m jerk, push

Rückblick, rEEck-blick, m retrospect

Rücken, rEEck-en, m back; rear; ridge

rücken, rEEck-en, v to move, to shift

Rückenmark, rEEck-en-mark, nt spinal cord

Rückfahrkarte, rEEck-fahr-kart-e, f return ticket

Rückfahrt, rEEck-fahrt, f return journey

Rückfall, rEEck-fahll, m relapse

Rückflug, rEEck-flook, m return flight

Rückgabe, rEEck-gahb-e, f return, restitution

Rückgang, rEEck-gahng, m fall; decline

Rückgrat, rEEck-graht, nt backbone; spine

Rückhalt, rEEck-hahlt, m reserve; support

Rückkehr, Rückkunft, rEEck-kair, -koonft, f return

rücklings, rEEck-lings, adj backwards

Rückreise, rEEck-ry-ze, f return journey

Rucksack, roock-zahck, m rucksack

Rückseite, rEEck-zy-te, f back, reverse

Rücksicht, rEEck-sikt, f consideration, regard

Rücksichtnahme, rEEck-sikt-nahm-e, f (taking into) consideration

Rücksprache, rEEck-shprahk-e, f consultation

rückständig, rEEck-shtend-ik, adj in arrears

Rücktritt, rEEck-trit, m retirement, resignation

rückwärts, rEEck-vairts, adv back(wards)

Rückweg, rEEck-vayk, m way back/home

ruckweise, roock-vy-ze, adv by jerks

Rückzug, rEEck-tsook, m retreat

Rudel, rood-el, m crowd; pack; herd

Ruder, rood-er, nt oar; rudder; helm

rudern, rood-ern, v to row

Ruf, roof, m call, shout, sound; reputation

rufen, roof-en, v to call, to shout

Rufnummer, roof-noomm-er, f telephone number

Rüffel, rEEff-el, m reprimand

Rüge, rEEg-e, f reproach, blame

rügen, rEEg-en, v to

reproach, to blame

Ruhe, rooh-e, f silence, quiet; recreation; rest

ruhen, rooh-en, v to rest

Ruhestand, rooh-e-shtahnt, m retirement

Ruhetag, rooh-e-tahg, m rest day, holiday

ruhig, rooh-ik, adj quiet; tranquil; calm; interj be quiet!

Ruhm, room, m glory; fame; praise

rühmen, rEEm-en, v to praise; to extol

rühmlich, rEEm-lik, adj praiseworthy; glorious

Ruhr, roor, f diarrhoea, dysentery

Rührei, rEEr-i, nt scrambled egg(s)

rühren, rEEr-en, v to stir; to move; to strike

rührend, rEEr-ent, adj touching, affecting

rührig, rEEr-ik, adj alert; active

Rührung, rEEr-oong, f emotion

Rumänien, roo-main-ee-en, nt Rumania

Rummel, roomm-el, m (loud) noise; trick(s); –platz, m fairground

Rumpelkammer, roomm-pel-kahmm-er, f lumber-room

Rumpf, roomp'f, m trunk; torso; hull

rümpfen, rEEmp-fen, v to wrinkle; to curl

rund, roont, *adj* round, circular; globular

Runde, roonn-de, *f* circle

runden, roonn-den, *v* to (make/become) round

Rundfahrt, roonnt-fahrt, *f* round trip; excursion

Rundfunk, roont-foonk, *m* broadcasting; **–sendung,** *f* (radio) broadcast/programme

rundherum, roont-hair-oomm, *adv* round about

Rundreise, roont-ry-ze, *f* circular tour, round trip

Rundschau, roont-show, *f* review

Rundschreiben, roont-shry-ben, *nt* circular letter

rundum, roont-oomm, *adv* round about

Rundwanderweg, roont-vahnn-der-vaig, *m* circular path

Runkelrübe, roonk-el-rEEb-e, *f* swede

Runzel, roonn-tsel, *f* wrinkle; pucker

runzelig, roonn-tsel-ik, *adj* wrinkled, puckered

runzeln, roonn-tseln, *v* to wrinkle; to pucker

Rüpel, rEEp-el, *m* lout, yob(bo)

rupfen, roopp-fen, *v* to pluck; to pick

ruppig, roopp-ik, *adj* rough; gruff; wild

Ruß, roos, *m* soot

Russe, roos-e, *m* Russian (man)

Rüssel, rEEss-el, *m* trunk, snout

rußig, roos-ik, *adj* sooty; smutty

Russin, roos-in, *f* Russian (woman)

russisch, roos-ish, *adj* Russian

Rußland, ross-lahnt, *nt* Russia

rüsten, rEEst-en, *v* to arm; to equip

rüstig, rEEst-ik, *adj* active; nimble

Rüstung, rEEst-oong, *f* armour; preparation

Rute, root-e, *f* rod, birch, switch; brush

Rutschbahn, rootsh-bahn, *f* (children's) slide

rutschen, roott-shen, *v* to slide, to glide

rütteln, rEEtt-eln, *v* to shake (up); to jog

S

Saal, zahl, *m* hall, large room; ward

Saat, zaht, *f* seed(s); young crop(s); **–krähe**, *f* rook

sabbern, zahbb-ern, *v* to slobber, to slaver

Säbel, zay-bel, *m* sword

sachdienlich, zahk-deen-lik, *adj* suitable; serviceable; relevant

Sache, zahk-*e*, *f* thing; matter; affair

Sachkenner, zahk-ken-er, *m* expert; connoisseur

sachkundig, zahk-koonn-dik, *adj* expert

Sachlage, zahk-lahg-*e*, *f* circumstances

sachlich, zahk-lik, *adj* objective; matter-of-fact

sächlich, zek-lik, *adj* neuter

sacht(e), zahkt(-*e*), *adj* gentle, soft; gradual

Sachverhalt, zahk-fair-hahlt, *m* facts of the case

Sachverständige(r), zahk-fair-shten-dig-*e*(r), *m & f*, expert

Sack, zahck, *m* sack; bag; pocket; **–gasse**, *f* cul-de-sac

säen, zay-en, *v* to sow

Safran, zahff-rahn, *m* saffron

Saft, zahft, *m* sap, juice; fluid

saftig, zahft-ik, *adj* juicy; obscene

Sage, zahg-*e*, *f* saga, legend; rumour

Säge, zayg-*e*, *f* saw; **–mehl**, *nt* sawdust

sagen, zahg-en, *v* to say, to tell

sägen, zayg-en, *v* to saw

sagenhaft, zahg-en-hahft, *adj* legendary; mythical; fabulous

Sägespäne, zayg-*e*-shpayn-*e*, *pl* wood-shavings; sawdust

Sahne, zahn-*e*, *f* cream

Saison, zay-zong, *f* season

Saite, zy-t*e*, *f* string (of an instrument)

Salami, zahl-ah-mee, *f* salami

Salat, zahl-aht, *m* salad; lettuce; **–soße**, *f* salad dressing

Salbe, zahlb-*e*, *f* ointment; balm

Salbei, zahlb-i, *m & f* sage

salben, zahlb-en, *v* to anoint

Salbung, zahlb-oong, *f* anointment; unction

Saldo, zahl-oh, *m* balance, remainder

Saline, zahl-een-*e*, *f* salt-mine, salt works

Salmonelle, zahlm-ohn-ell-*e*, *f* salmonella

Salon, zahl-ong, *m* drawing-room; saloon; lounge

salonfähig, zahl-ong-fay-ik, *adj* presentable

salopp, zahl-op, *adj* casual

Salz, zahlts, *nt* salt; seasoning

salzarm, zahlts-ahrm, *adj* low in salt

salzen, zahlt-sen, *v* to salt; to season

salzig, zahlts-ik, *adj* salt(y)

Salzkartoffeln, zahlts-kahr-tof-eln, *pl* boiled potatoes

Salzstreuer, zahlts-shtroy-er, *m* salt cellar

Same(n), zahm-*e*(n), *m* seed

Sammelbecken, zahmm-el-

161

beck-en, *nt* reservoir

sammeln, zahmm-eln, *v* to
collect, to gather

Sammler, zahmm-ler, *m*
collector, gatherer

Sammlung, zahmm-loong, *f*
collection

Samstag, zahmms-tahk, *m*
Saturday

Samt, zahmmt, *m* velvet

samt, zahmmt, *adv* together;
– und sonders, *adv* each
and every

sämtlich, zemt-lik, *adj* all,
complete

Sand, zahnt, *m* sand; grit

sandig, zahnn-dik, *adj* sandy;
gritty

Sandkuchen, zahnnt-kook-
en, *m* Madeira cake

Sandstrand, zahnt-shtrahnt,
m sandy beach

Sanduhr, zahnt-oor, *f* hour-
glass

sanft, zahnft, *adj* gentle,
sweet; soft, smooth

Sänfte, zenf-te, *f* sedan-
chair

Sanftmut, zahnft-moot, *f*
gentleness

Sänger, zeng-er, *m* singer

Sanitäter, zahnn-ee-**tayt**-er,
m first-aider, stretcher-
bearer

Sanitätswagen, zahnn-ee-
tayts-vahg-en, *m*
ambulance

Sardelle, zard-el-*e*, *f*
anchovy

Sarg, zark, *m* coffin

Satellit, zahtt-e-**leet**, *m*

satellite; **–enfernsehen,** *nt*
satellite TV

satt, zahtt, *adj* satisfied;
sated

Sattel, zahtt-el, *m* saddle

sattelfest, zahtt-el-fest, *adj*
firm in the saddle; well
versed

satteln, zahtt-eln, *v* to
saddle

sättigen, zet-ig-en, *v* to
satisfy; to appease

Satz, zahtts, *m* sentence; set;
leap; fixed sum; *mus*
movement; **–ung,** *f* rule;
statute; dogma

Sau, zow, *f* sow

sauber, zow-ber, *adj* clean;
neat, tidy; fine

säuberlich, zoy-ber-lik, *adj*
clean; decent

säubern, zoyb-ern, *v* to
clean(se)

Saubohne, zow-bohn-*e*, *f*
broad-bean

Sauce, zoh-se, *f* gravy, sauce

sauer, zow-er, *adj* sour, acid,
tart; cross

Sauerampfer, zow-er-ahmp-
fer, *m* sorrel

Sauerbraten, zow-er-braht-
en, *m* joint soaked in
vinegar

Sauerei, zow-e-ry, *f* mess,
dirty business

Sauerkraut, zow-er-krowt,
nt pickled shredded
cabbage

säuerlich, zoy-er-lik, *adj*
acidic

säuern, zoy-ern, *v* to make

sour; to leaven

Sauerstoff, zow-er-shtof, *m*
oxygen

Saufbold, zowf-bolt, *m*
drunkard

saufen, zowf-en, *v* to swill,
to drink (animals); *fam* to
booze

Säufer, zoy-fer, *m* drunkard

Sauferei, zowf-e-ry, *f* hard
drinking

saugen, zowg-en, *v* to suck

säugen, zoyg-en, *v* to suckle,
to nurse

Säugetier, zoyg-e-teer, *nt*
mammal

Säugling, zoyg-ling, *m* baby

Säule, zoyl-*e*, *f* column,
pillar

Saum, zowm, *m* seam, hem;
edge

saumäßig, zow-mace-ik, *adj*
lousy; tremendous

säumen, zoym-en, *v* to
delay; to hem

Sauna, zow-nah, *f* sauna

Säure, zoyr-*e*, *f* acid;
sourness

saurer Regen, zow-rer ray-
gen, *m* acid rain

säuseln, zoy-zeln, *v* to
murmur; to rustle; to purr

sausen, zow-zen, *v* to rush,
to dash, to whiz

SB, *abbr* **Selbstbedienung**

S-Bahn, ess-bahn, *f*
suburban railway

Scampi, skahmm-pee, *pl*
scampi

schaben, shahb-en, *v* to
scrape, to grate; to rasp

schäbig, shay-bik, *adj* shabby; mean

Schablone, shahb-lohn-e, *f* stencil; routine

Schach, shahk, *nt* chess

schachern, shahk-ern, *v* to barter; to haggle

schachmatt, shahk-mahtt, *adj* checkmate

Schacht, shahkt, *m* shaft, pit; hollow

Schachtel, shahk-tel, *f* (cardboard) box

schade, shahd-e, *adj* what a pity!

Schädel, shay-del, *m* skull

schaden, shahd-en, *v* to harm; to injure

Schaden, shahd-en, *m* damage; hurt; loss; **–ersatz,** *m* compensation; **–freude,** *f* malice, gloating

schadenfroh, shahd-en-froh, *adj* malicious, gloating

schadhaft, shaht-hahft, *adj* defective; damaged

schädigen, shayd-ig-en, *v* to harm; to wrong

schädlich, shayt-lik, *adj* harmful, hurtful

schadlos, shaht-lohs, *adj* unhurt; indemnified

Schadstoff, shaht-shtof, *m* pollutant, harmful substance

Schaf, shahf, *nt* sheep; *fam* stupid person

Schäfer, shayf-er, *m* shepherd

Schäferhund, shayf-er-hoont, *m* sheepdog; German shepherd dog

schaffen, shahff-en, *v* to create; to be busy; to do, to manage

Schaffner, shahff-ner, *m* guard, conductor

Schafott, shahff-ot, *nt* scaffold

Schaft, shahft, *m* shaft, stock; leg (of boot); shank

Schakal, shah-kahl, *m* jackal

schal, shahl, *adj* stale, flat, insipid

Schal, shahl, *m* shawl, muffler

Schale, shahl-e, *f* shell; peel; bowl, basin

schälen, shayl-en, *v* to peel, to shell

Schalk, shahlk, *m* rogue, joker

schalkhaft, shahlk-hahft, *adj* roguish; arch

Schall, shahll, *m* sound, noise; peal

schalldicht, shahll-dikt, *adj* soundproof

schallen, shahll-en, *v* to sound; to ring

Schaltbrett, shahlt-bret, *nt* switchboard; dashboard

schalten, shahlt-en, *v* to command; to switch; to change gear

Schalter, shahlt-er, *m* booking-office, counter; switch; **–stunden,** *pl* hours of business

Schaltjahr, shahlt-yahr, *nt* leap-year

Scham, shahm, *f* shame; modesty; bashfulness

schämen (sich), shaym-en (zik), *v* to be ashamed; to be shy

Schamgefühl, shahm-ge-fEEl, *nt* feeling of shame

schamhaft, shahm-hahft, *adj* shy; modest, coy

schamrot, shahm-roht, *adj* blushing

schampunieren, shahm-poo-neer-en, *v* to shampoo

Schande, shahnd-e, *f* shame, disgrace

schänden, shend-en, *v* to dishonour; to outrage; to violate

schändlich, shent-lik, *adj* shameful, disgraceful

Schank, shahnk, *m* sale of alcohol; bar; **–tisch,** *m* bar

Schanze, shahnt-se, *f* earthwork, trench

Schar, shahr, *f* troop; host; flock; plough-share

scharen, shahr-en, *v* to collect

scharf, shahrf, *adj* sharp; harsh; keen, smart

Scharfblick, shahrf-blick, *m* perspicacity; insight

Schärfe, shairf-e, *f* sharpness; keenness; severity

schärfen, shairf-en, *v* to sharpen; to strengthen

Scharfrichter, shahrf-rik-ter, *m* executioner

Scharfsicht, shahrf-zikt, *f* sharp sight

Scharfsinn, shahrf-zin, *m* acumen

Scharlach, shahr-lahk, *m* scarlet; scarlet fever

Scharmützel, shahr-mEEtt-sel, *nt* skirmish

**Scharnier, shahr-neer, *nt* hinge

Schärpe, shairp-e, *f* sash; sling

scharren, shahr-en, *v* to scrape; to scratch

Scharte, shahrt-e, *f* notch; loophole; gap

Schatten, shahtt-en, *m* shadow; shade

Schattierung, shahtt-eer-oong, *f* shading; tint

schattig, shahtt-ik, *adj* shaded

**Schatz, shahts, *m* treasure; riches; loved one

Schatzamt, shahts-ahmt, *nt* exchequer

schätzen, shets-en, *v* to estimate; to esteem

Schätzung, shets-oong, *f* estimate; estimation

Schau, show, *f* show, view; performance; **–bild,** *nt* diagram, graph

Schauder, show-der, *m* shudder(ing); horror

schauderhaft, show-der-hahft, *adj* dreadful

schaudern, show-dern, *v* to shudder

schauen, show-en, *v* to see; to gaze

Schauer, show-er, *m* shower; shudder

schauerlich, show-er-lik, *adj* gruesome

Schaufel, show-fel, *f* shovel; paddle(-boat)

schaufeln, show-feln, *v* to shovel

Schaufenster, show-fenst-er, *nt* shop-window; **–bummel,** *m* window shopping

Schaukel, show-kel, *f* swing, see-saw

schaukeln, show-keln, *v* to rock, to swing

Schaum, showm, *m* foam, froth, surf; lather

schäumen, shoym-en, *v* to foam, to froth

Schauplatz, show-plahts, *m* scene; theatre (of war)

Schauspiel, show-shpeel, *nt* scene; drama; **–er,** *m* actor, player; **–haus,** *nt* theatre

Scheck, sheck, *m* cheque

scheckig, sheck-ik, *adj* piebald; speckled

Scheckkarte, sheck-kahrt-e, *f* bank card, cheque card

Scheibe, shy-be, *f* disc; slice; pane; target; **–nwischer,** *m* windscreen wiper

Scheide, shy-de, *f* sheath; case; division; vagina

scheiden, shy-den, *v* to part, to separate; to divorce

Scheideweg, shy-de-vayk, *m* crossroads

Scheidung, shy-doong, *f* separation; divorce

Schein, shine, *m* shine; semblance; note, bill

scheinbar, shine-bar, *adj* apparent

scheinen, shine-en, *v* to shine; to seem

scheinheilig, shine-hile-ik, *adj* hypocritical

Scheinwerfer, shine-vair-fer, *m* searchlight; spotlight

Scheit, shy't, *nt* log; splinter

Scheitel, shy-tel, *m* crown of head; (hair) parting

scheiteln, shy-teln, *v* to part (hair)

Scheiterhaufen, shy-ter-howf-en, *m* stake, (funeral-)pyre

scheitern, shy-tern, *v* to fail; to be wrecked

Schelle, shel-e, *f* bell

schellen, shel-en, *v* to ring a bell

Schellfisch, shel-fish, *m* haddock

Schelte, shelt-e, *f* scolding

schelten, shelt-en, *v* to scold, to reprimand

Schema, shaym-ah, *nt* model; pattern

Schemel, shaym-el, *m* stool

Schenke, sheng-ke, *f* inn, tavern

Schenkel, sheng-kel, *m* thigh; shank; angle

schenken, sheng-ken, *v* to give (as a present); to pour out; to grant

Schenkung, shenk-oong, *f* donation

Scherbe, shairb-e, *f*
fragment; shard

Schere, shair-e, *f* shears,
scissors; shafts

scheren, shair-en, *v* to
shear, to clip; **sich um
etw –,** *v* to care about sth;
scher dich! *interj* scram!

Schererei, shair-e-ry, *f*
annoyance, trouble

Scherz, shairts, *m* joke

scherzen, shairt-sen, *v* to
joke

scherzhaft, shairts-hahft,
adj jovial

Scheu, shoy, *f* shyness;
timidity; fear

scheu, shoy, *adj* shy; timid

scheuchen, shoyk-en, *v* to
scare away

Scheuer, shoy-er, *f* barn;
shelter

scheuern, shoy-ern, *v* to
scrub, to scour

Scheune, shoyn-e, *f* barn

Scheusal, shoy-zahl, *nt*
monster

scheußlich, shoys-lik, *adj*
horrible, awful

Schicht, shikt, *f* layer,
stratum; shift; class

schichten, shikt-en, *v* to
layer, to stack

Schick, shick, *m* smartness,
chic

schick, shick, *adj* smart,
chic

schicken, shick-en, *v* to
send, to dispatch

schicklich, shick-lik, *adj*
seemly; decent

Schicksal, shick-zahl, *nt*
fate, destiny

Schiebedach, sheeb-e-dahk,
nt sun roof

schieben, sheeb-en, *v* to
push, to slide; to wangle

Schieber, sheeb-er, *m* slider;
pusher; wangler

Schiebung, sheeb-oong, *f*
pushing; wangling

Schiedsgericht, sheets-ge-
rikt, *nt* court of arbitration

Schiedsrichter, sheets-rik-
ter, *m* arbitrator, referee;
umpire

schief, sheef, *adj* crooked;
slanting; sloping

Schiefer, sheef-er, *m* slate

schielen, sheel-en, *v* to
squint, to be cross-eyed

Schienbein, sheen-bine, *nt*
shin(-bone)

Schiene, sheen-e, *f* splint;
rail; bar; hoop

Schienennetz, sheen-en-
nets, *nt* railway-system

schier, sheer, *adj* pure; sheer;
adv nearly

schießen, shees-en, *v* to
shoot, to fire

Schießscheibe, shees-shy-
be, *f* target

Schiff, shif, *nt* ship, vessel,
craft; nave; shuttle

Schiffahrt, shif-fahrt, *f*
shipping, navigation

schiffbar, shif-bahr, *adj*
navigable

Schiffbruch, shif-brook, *m*
shipwreck

schiffen, shif-en, *v* to ship;

to navigate

Schild, shilt, *nt* shield; sign-
board

schildern, shild-ern, *v* to
describe

Schilderung, shild-er-oong,
f description; sketch

Schildkröte, shilt-krert-e, *f*
tortoise, turtle

Schildpatt, shilt-pahtt, *nt*
tortoise-shell

Schildwache, shilt-vahk-e, *f*
sentry

Schilf(rohr), shilf(-rohr), *nt*
reed

schillern, shil-ern, *v* to
shimmer

Schimmel, shim-el, *m*
mildew, mould; white
horse

schimmelig, shim-el-ik, *adj*
mildewed, mouldy

schimmeln, shim-eln, *v* to
go mouldy

Schimmer, shim-er, *m*
glimmer; gleam; pomp

schimmern, shim-ern, *v* to
gleam; to glitter

Schimpf, shimp'f, *m* insult;
indignity; disgrace

schimpfen, shimp'f-en, *v* to
scold; to grumble; to abuse

schimpflich, shimp'f-lik, *adj*
disgraceful

Schimpfwort, shimp'f-vort,
nt swear word

schinden, shin-den, *v* to
maltreat, to overwork; to
flay

Schinder, shin-der, *m*
knacker; slave-driver; **–ei,**

f drudgery, grind

Schinken, shing-ken, *m* ham; **-speck,** *m* bacon

Schippe, ship-*e*, *f* spade; shovel; spades (cards)

schippen, ship-en, *v* to shovel

Schirm, sheerm, *m* umbrella; shelter; protection; peak (of cap); **-herrschaft,** *f* patronage

schlabbern, shlahbb-ern, *v* to slobber

Schlacht, shlahkt, *f* battle, action

schlachten, shlahkt-en, *v* to slaughter; to kill

Schlachter, shlahkt-er, *m* butcher; **-ei,** *f* butcher's shop

Schlächter, shlekt-er, *m* butcher; **-ei,** *f* butcher's shop

Schlachtfeld, shlahkt-felt, *nt* battle-field

Schlachthaus, shlahkt-hows, *nt* slaughter-house, abattoir

Schlachthof, shlahkt-hohf, *m* slaughter-house, abattoir

Schlacke, shlahck-*e*, *f* slag

Schlackwurst, shlahck-voorst, *f* kind of sausage

Schlaf, shlahf, *m* sleep; **-abteil,** *nt* sleeping compartment; **-anzug,** *m* pyjamas

Schläfe, shlay-*fe*, *f* temple (forehead)

schlafen, shlahf-en, *v*

to sleep

Schläfer, shlayf-er, *m* sleeper

schläfrig, shlayf-rik, *adj* sleepy, drowsy

schlaff, shlahff, *adj* slack, limp, flabby

Schlaflosigkeit, shlahf-lohz-ik-kite, *f* sleeplessness

Schlafmittel, shlahf-mit-el, *nt* sleeping-draught

Schlafsack, shlahf-zahck, *m* sleeping-bag

Schlaftablette, shlahf-tah-blet-*e*, *f* sleeping-pill

schlaftrunken, shlahf-troong-ken, *adj* heavy with sleep

Schlafwagen, shlahf-vahg-en, *m* sleeping-car

schlafwandeln, shlahf-vahnn-deln, *v* to sleep-walk

Schlafzimmer, shlahf-tsim-er, *nt* bedroom

Schlag, shlahk, *m* blow, stroke; slap; shock; beat; knock; kind; **-anfall,** *m* stroke; **-baum,** *m* barrier

schlagen, shlahg-en, *v* to beat; to strike, to hit, to knock

Schlager, shlahg-er, *m* hit (-song); bargain; draw (attraction)

Schläger, shlayg-er, *m* brawler; bat, racket, club; rapier

Schlägerei, shlayg-*e*-**ry,** *f* brawl

schlagfertig, shlahk-fairt-ik,

adj quick-witted

Schlagloch, shlahk-lok, *nt* pothole

Schlagsahne, shlahk-zahn-*e*, *f* whipped cream

Schlagwort, shlahk-vort, *nt* catchword, slogan

Schlamm, shlahmm, *m* mud, slime

schlammig, shlahmm-ik, *adj* muddy, slimy

Schlange, shlahng-*e*, *f* snake, serpent; queue

schlank, shlahnk, *adj* slim, slight, slender

Schlankheitskur, shlahnk-hites-koor, *f* (slimming) diet

schlapp, shlahpp, *adj* slack, limp; worn-out; run-down

Schlappe, shlahpp-*e*, *f* defeat; loss

Schlapphut, shlahpp-hoot, *m* floppy hat

schlau, shlow, *adj* sly, clever

Schlauch, shlowk, *m* tube; hose; **-boot,** *nt* rubber dinghy

Schläue, shloy-*e*, *f* cunning

Schlauheit, shlow-hite, *f* cleverness; cunning

schlecht, shlekt, *adj* bad, evil; wicked

schlechterdings, shlekt-er-dings, *adv* absolutely; virtually

schlechthin, shlekt-hin, *adv* plainly

Schlechtigkeit, shlekt-ik-kite, *f* wickedness; evil

Schlegel, shlayg-el, *m*

drumstick; mallet

Schlehdorn, shlay-dorn, m blackthorn, sloe

Schlehe, shlay-e, f sloe

Schleie, shly-e, f tench

schleichen, shly-ken, v to creep, to prowl

Schleichhandel, shly'k-hahnd-el, m illicit trade

Schleier, shly-er, m veil

schleierhaft, shly-er-hahft, *adj* hazy; veiled

Schleife, shly-fe, f loop; knot, bow

schleifen, shly-fen, v to grind, to sharpen, to polish; to drag; to demolish

Schleifstein, shlife-shtine, m grindstone

Schleim, shlime, m slime; phlegm, mucus

schleimig, shly-mik, *adj* slimy

schlemmen, shlem-en, v to feast, to live it up

Schlemmer, shlem-er, m glutton; gourmet

schlendern, shlend-ern, v to saunter

schlenkern, shlenk-ern, v to dangle; to jerk

Schleppdampfer, shlep-dahmp-fer, m tug(-boat)

Schleppe, shlep-e, f train (of dress)

schleppen, shlep-en, v to drag; to trail

Schlepper, shlep-er, m hauler; tug(-boat); smuggler

Schleuder, shloy-der, f sling; centrifuge

schleudern, shloy-dern, v to sling, to fling; to skid

schleunig(st), shloy-nig(st), *adj* prompt

Schleuse, shloy-ze, f lock, sluice

Schlich(e), shlik(-e), m (pl) trick, dodge

schlicht, shlikt, *adj* simple, homely, honest

schlichten, shlikt-en, v to arrange; to settle (a dispute)

schließen, shlees-en, v to lock; to close, to shut; to conclude

Schließfach, shlees-fak, nt locker

schließlich, shlees-lik, *adj* final; conclusive; *adv* finally, ultimately

Schliff, shlif, m cut; polish

schlimm, shlim, *adj* evil, bad; severe; serious; ill

Schlinge, shling-e, f sling; noose; snare

Schlingel, shling-el, m rascal

schlingen, shling-en, v to wind, to wrap; to gulp

schlingern, shling-ern, v *naut* to roll

Schlingpflanze, shling-pflahnt-se, f climbing plant, creeper

Schlips, shlips, m tie

Schlitten, shlit-en, m sledge, sleigh

schlittern, shlit-ern, v

to slide

Schlittschuh, shlit-shoo, m skate; – laufen, v to skate

Schlittschuhbahn, shlit-shoo-bahn, f ice-rink

Schlitz, shlits, m slit; slot; crack

schlitzen, shlit-sen, v to slit; to slash

Schloß, shloss, nt castle, palace; lock; clasp

Schlosser, shloss-er, m locksmith

Schlot, shloht, m chimney; funnel

schlottern, shlot-ern, v to shake; to hang loosely

Schlucht, shlookt, f gorge, gully, ravine

schluchzen, shlook-tsen, v to sob

Schluck, shloock, m mouthful, gulp; draught

schlucken, shloock-en, v to swallow; to gulp

Schlummer, shloomm-er, m slumber, light sleep

schlummern, shloomm-ern, v to slumber

Schlund, shloont, m gullet

schlüpfen, shlEEp-fen, v to slip

schlüpfrig, shlEEp'f-rik, *adj* slippery; precarious

Schlupfloch, shloopp'f-lok, nt hiding-place; loop-hole

Schlupfwinkel, shloopp'f-vink-el, m hiding place, nook

schlürfen, shlEErf-en, v to drink (noisily); to slurp

schlurfen, shloorf-en, v to shuffle

Schluß, shlooss, m closing, end; conclusion

Schlüssel, shlEEss-el, m key; clef; **–bein,** nt collar-bone; **–blume,** f primrose; **–bund,** nt bunch of keys; **–loch,** nt keyhole

schlüssig, shlEEss-ik, adj logical, conclusive

Schlußverkauf, shlooss-fair-kowf, m clearance sale

Schmach, shmahk, f dishonour; disgrace; insult

schmachten, shmahkt-en, v to languish; to be parched

schmächtig, shmekt-ik, adj delicate; slight, slim

schmackhaft, shmahck-hahft, adj tasty, palatable

schmähen, shmay-en, v to vilify; to slander

schmählich, shmay-lik, adj abusive; disgraceful; adv badly, sadly

schmal, shmahl, adj narrow; slender; meagre

schmälern, shmayl-ern, v to narrow; to lessen

Schmälerung, shmayl-er-oong, f reduction, diminution

Schmalz, shmahlts, nt lard, dripping

schmarotzen, shmah-rot-sen, v to sponge

Schmarotzer, shmah-rot-ser, m sponger; cadger; parasite

Schmarren, shmahrr-en, m nonsense; dish made of pancakes

schmatzen, shmahtt-sen, v to smack one's lips; to eat noisily

Schmaus, shmows, m feast

schmecken, shmeck-en, v to taste

Schmeichelei, shmy-ke-ly, f flattery

schmeicheln, shmy-keln, v to coax; to flatter

Schmeichler, shmy'k-ler, m flatterer; wheedler

schmeichlerisch, shmy'k-ler-ish, adj wheedling; flattering

schmeißen, shmy-sen, v to throw, to chuck

Schmelz, shmelts, m glaze, enamel; melodiousness

schmelzen, shmelt-sen, v to melt; to smelt

Schmerz, shmairts, m pain, ache; grief; suffering

schmerzen, shmairt-sen, v to ache, to hurt

Schmerzensgeld, shmairt-sens-gelt, nt damages

schmerzhaft, shmairts-hahft, adj painful

schmerzlich, shmairts-lik, adj painful; grievous

Schmerzmittel, shmairts-mit-el, nt painkiller

Schmetterling, shmet-er-ling, m butterfly

schmettern, shmet-ern, v to shatter; to resound; to warble

Schmied, shmeet, m smith

Schmiede, shmeed-e, f smithy

Schmiedeeisen, shmeed-e-ize-en, nt wrought iron

schmieden, shmeed-en, v to forge; to devise

schmiegen, shmeeg-en, v to adhere, to nestle; to bend

schmiegsam, shmeek-zahm, adj flexible

Schmiere, shmeer-e, f grease, ointment; flea-pit; look-out

schmieren, shmeer-en, v to smear; to grease; to bribe

Schmierfink, shmeer-fink, m fam muck-raker

schmierig, shmeer-ik, adj smeary; greasy; dirty

Schminke, shming-ke, f make-up

schminken, shming-ken, v to make up, to put on make-up

schmollen, shmol-en, v to sulk; to pout

Schmorbraten, shmohr-braht-en, m pot roast

schmoren, shmohr-en, v to stew

Schmuck, shmoock, m finery; jewellery; decoration

schmuck, shmoock, adj trim; spruce; smart

schmücken, shmEEck-en, v to adorn; to decorate

Schmucksachen, shmoock-sak-en, pl jewels

Schmuggel, shmoogg-el, m smuggling

schmuggeln, shmoogg-eln, *v* to smuggle

Schmuggler, shmoogg-ler, *m* smuggler

schmunzeln, shmoont-seln, *v* to smile broadly; to smirk

Schmutz, shmoots, *m* dirt, filth

schmutzen, shmoots-en, *v* to soil (easily)

schmutzig, shmoots-ik, *adj* dirty, filthy; squalid

Schnabel, shnahb-el, *m* beak, bill

schnäbeln, shnayb-eln, *v* to bill and coo

Schnalle, shnahll-*e*, *f* buckle, clasp; *fam* silly woman

schnallen, shnahll-en, *v* to buckle, to fasten

schnalzen, shnahlt-sen, *v* to click; to snap

schnappen, shnahpp-en, *v* to snap; to catch; to tip

Schnappschuß, shnahpp-shooss, *m* snapshot

Schnaps, shnahps, *m* liquor; spirits

schnarchen, shnark-en, *v* to snore; to snort

schnarren, shnahrr-en, *v* to whiz; to rattle

schnattern, shnahtt-ern, *v* to rattle; to cackle

schnauben, shnowb-en, *v* to snort; to pant

schnaufen, shnowf-en, *v* to breathe hard; to snort

Schnauzbart, shnowts-bart, *m* moustache

Schnauze, shnowt-*se*, *f* snout, mouth (animals); jaw

schnauzen, shnowt-sen, *v* to scold roughly

Schnecke, shneck-*e*, *f* snail, slug

Schnee, shnay, *m* snow

Schneeball, shnay-bahll, *m* snowball

schneebedeckt, shnay-be-deckt, *adj* snow-covered

Schneeflocke, shnay-flock-*e*, *f* snowflake

Schneegestöber, shnay-ge-shter-ber, *nt* light snowstorm

Schneeglöckchen, shnay-glerck-ken, *nt* snowdrop

Schneeketten, shnay-ket-en, *pl* snow chains

Schneeregen, shnay-rayg-en, *m* sleet

Schneeschuh, shnay-shoo, *m* snow-shoe

Schneesturm, shnay-shtoorm, *m* snowstorm, blizzard

Schneewehe, shnay-vay-*e*, *f* snow-drift

Schneewittchen, shnay-vit-ken, *nt* Snow White

Schneid, shnite, *m* smartness

Schneide, shny-de, *f* cutter, cutting-edge

schneiden, shny-den, *v* to cut; to clip; to prune

Schneider, shny-der, *m* tailor; cutter

Schneiderei, shny-de-ry, *f* tailoring; dressmaking

schneidern, shny-dern, *v* to do tailoring/dress-making, to sew

schneidig, shny-dik, *adj* sharp, smart

schneien, shny-en, *v* to snow

schnell, shnell, *adj* quick; rapid; brisk

schnellen, shnell-en, *v* to toss; to jerk

Schnelligkeit, shnell-ik-kite, *f* rapidity; velocity

Schnellimbiß, shnell-im-bis, *m* snack; snack bar

Schnellkochtopf, shnell-kok-topf, *m* pressure cooker

Schnellzug, shnell-tsook, *m* express train

Schnepfe, shnep-fe, *f* snipe

schneuzen (sich), shnoyt-sen (zik), *v* to blow one's nose

schniegeln (sich), shneeg-eln (zik), *v* to smarten o.s. up

schnippisch, shnip-ish, *adj* snappish, uppish

Schnitt, shnit, *m* cut(ting); slash, wound; pattern

Schnittbohnen, shnit-bohn-en, *pl* French beans

Schnitte, shnit-*e*, *f* slice, cut; sandwich

Schnittlauch, shnit-lowk, *m* chive

Schnittmuster, shnit-moost-er, *nt* (dress)

pattern

Schnitzel, shnit-sel, *nt* chip, cut, scrap; cutlet

schnitzen, shnit-sen, *v* to carve

Schnitzer, shnit-ser, *m* (wood) carver; howler, blunder

Schnitzerei, shnit-se-**ry**, *f* carving

schnöde, shnerd-*e*, *adj* vile, base, despicable

Schnorchel, shnork-el, *m* snorkel

schnorcheln, shnork-eln, *v* to go snorkelling

Schnörkel, shnerk-el, *m* flourish; scroll; spiral

schnorren, shnorr-en, *v* to cadge; to beg; to scrounge

Schnorrer, shnorr-er, *m* cadger; beggar; scrounger

schnüffeln, shnEEff-eln, *v* to sniff; to spy out

Schnupfen, shnoopp-fen, *m* (head) cold

schnupfen, shnoopp-fen, *v* to take snuff

Schnupftabak, shnoopp'f-tah-bahck, *m* snuff

schnuppe, shnoopp-*e*, *adj* jdm – sein, to be all the same to sb

schnuppern, shnoopp-ern, *v* to sniff; to scent

Schnur, shnoor, *f* string, cord; braid

schnüren, shnEEr-en, *v* to cord; to tie; to lace

schnurgerade, shnoor-ge-rahd-*e*, *adj* straight as a die

schnurlos, shnoor-lohs, *adj* cordless

Schnurrbart, shnoorr-bart, *m* moustache

schnurren, shnoorr-en, *v* to purr; to buzz

Schnürriemen, shnEEr-reem-en, *m* (shoe-)lace

Schnürschuhe, shnEEr-shoo-*e*, *pl* lace-up shoes

Schnürsenkel, shnEEr-zen-kel, *m* shoe-lace

schnurstracks, shnoor-shtrahcks, *adv* straight away

Schober, shoh-ber, *m* shed; stack

Schöffe, sherff-*e*, *m* juror; –namt, *nt* jury service

Schokolade, shoh-koh-lah-de, *f* chocolate

Scholle, shol-*e*, *f* clod; lump; floe; plaice

schon, shohn, *adv* already; as yet, so far; indeed, sure enough; anyway

schön, shern, *adj* beautiful; fine; nice

schonen, shohn-en, *v* to spare; to take care; to preserve

Schoner, shohn-er, *m* schooner; antimacassar

Schönheit, shern-hite, *f* beauty; good looks; –soperation, *f* plastic surgery

Schonkost, shohn-kost, *f* (special) diet

Schopf, shop'f, *m* shock/tuft of hair

schöpfen, sherpp-fen, *v* to draw (water, breath etc.); to bale (water); to create

Schöpfer, sherpp-fer, *m* Creator; maker; producer

schöpferisch, sherpp-fer-ish, *adj* creative

Schöpfung, sherpp-foong, *f* creation; production

Schorf, shorf, *m* scab

Schornstein, shorn-shtine, *m* chimney; funnel; –feger, *m* chimney-sweep

Schoß, shohs, *m* shoot (plant); lap; womb

Schoßhund, shohs-hoont, *m* lap-dog

Schote, shoht-*e*, *f* pod, husk

Schotte, shot-*e*, *m* Scot, Scotsman

Schottin, shot-in, *f* Scot, Scotswoman

schottisch, shot-ish, *adj* Scottish

Schottland, shot-lahnt, *nt* Scotland

schräg, shrayk *adj* slanting, oblique; sloping; – gegenüber, *adv* diagonally across

Schramme, shrahmm-*e*, *f* scratch; scar

Schrank, shrahnk, *m* cupboard; cabinet; wardrobe

Schranke, shrahng-ke, *f* barrier; fencing

Schraube, shrowb-*e*, *f* screw

schrauben, shrowb-en, *v* to screw

Schraubenschlüssel,

shrowb-en-shlEEss-el, *m* spanner

Schraubenzieher, shrowb-en-tsee-er, *m* screwdriver

Schreck(en), shreck(-en), *m* shock; terror

schrecken, shreck-en, *v* to frighten, to scare

schrecklich, shreck-lik, *adj* terrible; fearful

Schrei, shry, *m* cry, shout, shriek, scream

schreiben, shry-ben, *v* to write

Schreibheft, shripe-heft, *nt* exercise book

Schreibkraft, shripe-krahft, *f* typist

Schreibmaschine, shripe-mah-sheen-e, *f* typewriter

Schreibtisch, shripe-tish, *m* writing-desk

Schreibwaren, shripe-wahren, *pl* stationery

schreien, shry-en, *v* to cry, to scream, to yell

Schrein, shry, *m* shrine

Schreiner, shrine-er, *m* joiner, cabinet-maker

schreiten, shry-ten, *v* to step, to stride

Schrift, shrift, *f* writing; character; manuscript

Schriftführer, shrift-fEEr-er, *m* secretary (of an organisation)

Schriftleiter, shrift-ly-ter, *m* editor

Schriftleitung, shrift-ly-toong, *f* editorial office

schriftlich, shrift-lik, *adj*

in writing

Schriftsteller, shrift-shtel-er, *m* writer; author

Schriftstück, shrift-shtEEck, *nt* document

Schriftverkehr, shrift-fair-kair, *m* correspondence

schrill, shrill, *adj* shrill, grating

Schritt, shrit, *m* step; pace; footstep

schrittweise, shrit-vy-ze, *adv* step by step

schroff, shrof, *adj* gruff, rough; rugged

schröpfen, shrerpp-fen, *v* to fleece; to bleed

Schrot, shroht, *nt* shot; wholemeal

Schrott, shrot, *m* srap metal; *fam* rubbish

schrubben, shroobb-en, *v* to scrub

Schrubber, shroobb-er, *m* scrubbing-brush

schrumpfen, shroomp-fen, *v* to shrink

Schub, shoop, *m* batch; push, shove

Schubkarre(n), shoop-karr-e(n), *m & f,* wheelbarrow

Schublade, shoob-lahd-e, *f* drawer

schüchtern, shEEk-tern, *adj* shy, timid, bashful

Schuft, shooft, *m* scoundrel, rogue

schuften, shooft-en, *v* to work very hard

Schuh, shoo, *m* shoe; **–creme,** *f* shoe polish;

–größe, *f* shoe size;

–löffel, *m* shoehorn;

–macher, *m* cobbler; shoemaker; **–putzer,** *m* boot-black; **–riemen,** *m* shoelace; **–werk,** *nt* footwear

Schularbeiten, shool-ar-bite-en, *pl* homework

Schuld, shoolt, *f* guilt; debt; fault

schuldbewußt, shoolt-be-woost, *adj* feeling guilty

schulden, shoold-en, *v* to owe; to be indebted

schuldig, shoold-ik, *adj* guilty; indebted

Schuldigkeit, shoold-ik-kite, *f* obligation, duty; debt

Schuldner, shoold-ner, *m* debtor

Schuldschein, shoolt-shine, *m* I.O.U., promissory note

Schule, shool-e, *f* school; college

schulen, shool-en, *v* to train, to school

Schüler, shEEl-er, *m* scholar, pupil, student

Schulferien, shool-fair-ee-en, *pl* school holidays

Schulklasse, shool-klahss-e, *f* (school) class/form

schulpflichtig, shool-p'flikt-ik, *adj* of school age

Schulunterricht, shool-oon-ter-ikt, *m* (school) lessons

Schulter, shoolt-er, *f* shoulder; **–blatt,** *nt*

shoulder-blade

schultern, shoolt-ern, v to shoulder

Schulzwang, shool-tsvahng, m compulsory education

Schund, shoont, m trash; rubbish

Schuppe, shoopp-e, f scale; –n, pl dandruff

Schuppen, shoopp-en, m shed, shelter

schuppen, shoopp-en, v to scale, to remove scales

schüren, shEEr-en, v to rake/poke (a fire); fig to stir up, to fan flames

Schurke, shoork-e, m rascal, villain

Schürze, shEErt-se, f apron; pinafore

Schuß, shooss, m shot; shoot(ing)

Schüssel, shEEss-el, f dish, bowl; basin

Schußwaffen, shooss-vahff-en, pl firearms

Schuster, shooss-ter, m cobbler, shoemaker

schustern, shooss-tern, v to cobble; to botch

Schutt, shoott, m refuse; rubbish

schütteln, shEEtt-eln, v to shake

schütten, shEEtt-en, v to pour; to shoot; to throw

Schutz, shoots, m protection; screen; shelter

Schütze, shEEts-e, m marksman; hunter

schützen, shEEts-en, v to

protect, to guard

Schutzengel, shoots-eng-el, m guardian angel

Schützengraben, shEEts-en-grahb-en, m trench

Schutzhütte, shoots-hEEtt-e, f (mountain) shelter

Schutzmarke, shoots-mark-e, f trade-mark

Schutztruppe, shoots-troopp-e, f colonial troops

schwach, shvahk, adj weak, feeble; delicate

Schwäche, shvek-e, f weakness

schwächen, shvek-en, v to weaken; to lessen

Schwachheit, shvahk-hite, f weakness

schwächlich, shvek-lik, adj delicate, weakly

Schwächling, shvek-ling, m weakling

schwachsichtig, shvahk-zik-tik, adj weak-sighted

schwachsinnig, shvahk-zin-ik, adj feeble-minded

Schwächung, shvek-oong, f weakening

Schwager, shvahg-er, m brother-in-law

Schwägerin, shvayg-er-in, f sister-in-law

Schwalbe, shvahlb-e, f swallow; –nschwanz, m swallow-tail

Schwall, shvahll, m surge; heaving mass/crowd

Schwamm, shvahmm, m sponge; fungus

schwammig, shvahmm-ik,

adj spongy; fungoid

Schwan, shvahn, m swan

schwanger, shvahng-er, adj pregnant

Schwangerschaft, shvahng-er-shahft, f pregnancy

Schwank, shvahnk, m farce; burlesque; joke

Schwankung, shvahnk-oong, f fluctuation; uncertainty

Schwanz, shvahnts, m tail

schwänzeln, shvent-seln, v to wag (tail); fig to crawl

schwänzen, shvent-sen, v to saunter; to play truant

Schwarm, shvahrm, m swarm; flock; crowd

schwärmen, shvairm-en, v to swarm; to skirmish; to enthuse

Schwarte, shvart-e, f rind; skin

schwarz, shvarts, adj black; swarthy

Schwarzbrot, shvarts-broht, nt (dark) rye-bread

Schwärze, shvairts-e, f blackness; blacking

schwärzen, shvairts-en, v to blacken; to darken

Schwarze Meer, shvarts-e mair, nt Black Sea

Schwarzmarkt, shvarts-mahrkt, m black market

Schwarzseher, shvarts-zay-er, m pessimist

Schwarzwald, shvarts-vahlt, m Black Forest

schwatzen, (schwätzen), shvahts-en, (shvets-en), v

to chatter

Schwätzer, shvets-*er*, *m* chatterbox

schwatzhaft, shvahts-hahft, *adj* talkative, chatty

schweben, shvayb-en, *v* to hover, to float; to be suspended

Schweden, shvay-den, *nt* Sweden

schwedisch, shvay-dish, *adj* Swedish

Schwefel, shvay-fel, *m* sulphur

schwefelig, shvayf-el-ik, *adj* sulphurous

Schweif, shvife, *m* tail

schweifen, shvy-fen, *v* to roam, to ramble; to curve

schweigen, shvy-gen, *v* to be silent

schweigsam, shvike-zahm, *adj* silent; taciturn

Schwein, shvine, *nt* pig, swine; good luck; –ebraten, *m* roast pork; –efleisch, *nt* pork; –ehund, *m* *pej* pig; –erei, *f* dirtiness; mess; –eschmalz, *nt* lard; –skotelett, *nt* pork-chop

Schweiß, shvice, *m* sweat

schweißtriefend, shvice-treef-ent, *adj* dripping with sweat

Schweiz, shvites, *f* Switzerland

schweizerisch, shvy-tser-ish, *adj* Swiss

Schweizer Käse, shvy-tser **kay-**ze, *m*

Emmental cheese

schwelgen, shvelg-en, *v* to indulge oneself

Schwelle, shvel-e, *f* threshold; beam; sleeper (train)

schwellen, shvel-en, *v* to swell; to swirl

Schwemme, shvem-e, *f* watering place; *fam* bar, pub

Schwengel, shveng-el, *m* clapper; handle; lout

schwenken, shveng-ken, *v* to brandish; to swing (round)

schwer, shvair, *adj* heavy; difficult, hard; serious; –behindert, *adj* severely handicapped

Schwere, shvair-e, *f* heaviness, weight; severity

schwerfallen, shvair-fahll-en, *v* to be(come) difficult

schwerfällig, shvair-fel-ik, *adj* ponderous; slow; clumsy

schwerhörig, shvair-her-ik, *adj* hard of hearing

Schwerkraft, shvair-krahft, *f* gravity

schwerlich, shvair-lik, *adv* scarcely; with difficulty

Schwermut, shvair-moot, *f* melancholy

Schwerpunkt, shvair-poonkt, *m* centre of gravity; *fig* emphasis, focal point

Schwert, shvairt, *nt* sword

Schwester, shvest-er, *f*

sister; nurse

schwesterlich, shvest-er-lik, *adj* sisterly

Schwieger–, shveeg-er, *pref* -in-law; –eltern, *pl* parents-in-law; –mutter, *f* mother-in-law; –sohn, *m* son-in-law; –tochter, *f* daughter-in-law; –vater, *m* father-in-law

Schwiele, shveel-e, *f* callus; welt

schwierig, shveer-ik, *adj* difficult; precarious; delicate

Schwierigkeit, shveer-ik-kite, *f* difficulty

Schwimmbad, shvim-baht, *nt* swimming pool

schwimmen, shvim-en, *v* to swim; to float

Schwimmweste, shvim-vest-e, *f* life jacket

Schwindel, shvin-del, *m* giddiness; swindle

Schwindelei, shvin-de-ly, *f* swindling

schwind(e)lig, shvind(-e)-lik, *adj* giddy, dizzy

schwindeln, shvind-eln, *v* to swindle, to cheat; to be dizzy

schwinden, shvind-en, *v* to dwindle, to grow less; to vanish

Schwindler, shvind-ler, *m* swindler, cheat

Schwinge, shving-e, *f* wing, pinion

schwingen, shving-en, *v* to swing, to wield

Schwips, shvips, *m* (slight) intoxication

schwirren, shvir-en, *v* to whir, to whiz, to hum

Schwitzbad, shvits-baht, *nt* Turkish bath

schwitzen, shvits-en, *v* to sweat, to perspire

schwören, shver-en, *v* to swear

schwul, shvool, *adj* gay (homosexual)

schwül, shvEEl, *adj* sultry, close

Schwung, shvoong, *m* swing(ing); rise; ardour

schwunghaft, shvoong-hahft, *adj* lively, brisk

schwungvoll, shvoong-fol, *adj* full of energy

Schwur, shvoor, *m* oath; **–gericht**, *nt* sessional court

sechs, zecks, *num* six

Sechseck, zecks-eck, *nt* hexagon

sechste(r), zecks-te(r), *adj* sixth

Sechstel, zecks-tel, *nt* sixth

sechzehn, zek-tsayn, *num* sixteen

sechzig, zek-tsik, *num* sixty

See, zay, *m* lake; *f* sea, ocean

Seebad, zay-baht, *nt* seaside resort

seefest, zay-fest, *adj* seaworthy; not subject to sea-sickness

Seehund, zay-hoont, *m* seal

seekrank, zay-krahnk, *adj* sea-sick

Seele, zayl-e, *f* soul

Seelenheil, zayl-en-hile, *nt* salvation

Seelenruhe, zayl-en-roo-e, *f* tranquillity of mind

Seelöwe, zay-lerv-e, *m* sea-lion

Seelsorger, zayl-zorg-er, *m* minister (of religion)

Seemacht, zay-mahkt, *f* naval power

Seemöwe, zay-merv-e, *f* sea-gull

Seeräuber, zay-royb-er, *m* pirate

seetüchtig, zay-tEEkt-ik, *adj* seaworthy

Seezunge, zay-tsoong-e, *f* sole (fish)

Segel, zay-gel, *nt* sail; **–boot**, *nt* sailing boat, yacht; **–fliegen**, *nt* gliding

segeln, zay-geln, *v* to sail

Segelschiff, zay-gel-shif, *nt* sailing ship

Segeltuch, zay-gel-took, *nt* canvas, sail-cloth

Segen, zay-gen, *m* blessing

Segler, zayg-ler, *m* sailor, navigator; yachtsman

segnen, zayg-nen, *v* to bless

sehen, zay-en, *v* to see; to look

Sehenswürdigkeit, zay-ens-vEErd-ik-kite, *f* sight, place of interest

Sehkraft, zay-krahft, *f* (eye)sight

Sehne, zay-ne, *f* sinew, tendon; string (bow)

sehnen (sich), zayn-en

(zik), *v* to long (for)

sehnig, zayn-ik, *adj* sinewy; muscular

sehnlich(st), zayn-lik(st), *adj* ardent, eager

Sehnsucht, zayn-zookt, *f* longing, yearning

sehnsüchtig, zayn-zEEk-tik, *adj & adv* longing(ly); yearning

sehr, zair, *adv* very; greatly; highly; badly

seicht, zy'kt, *adj* shallow; superficial

Seide, zy-de, *f* silk

Seidel, zy-del, *nt* tankard, pot

seiden, zy-den, *adj* of silk, silken

Seidenpapier, zy-den-pah-peer, *nt* tissue-paper

Seidenraupe, zy-den-rowp-e, *f* silkworm

Seife, zy-fe, *f* soap; **–nschaum**, *m* lather

Seil, zile, *nt* rope, cable, line; **–bahn**, *f* cable railway

sein, zine, *v* to be; to exist

sein, **seine(r/s)**, zine, zine-e(r/s), *adj & pron* his, its

seiner, zine-er, *pron* (genitive *m & nt*) of him/it

seinerseits, zine-er-zites, *adv* on his/its part

seinesgleichen, zine-es-gly-ken, *pron* people like him

seinethalben, **seinetwegen**, **seinetwillen**, zine-net-hahllb-en, -vaig-en, vil-en, *adv* for his sake

seit, zite, *prep* since; *conj* since, seeing that

seitdem, zite-daym, *adv* since (then)

Seite, zy-*te*, *f* side; page; party

Seitengasse, zy-ten-gahss-e, *f* side-street

seitens, zy-tens, *prep* on the part of

seither, zite-hair, *adv* since then

seitlich, zite-lik, *adj* beside, at the side

seitwärts, zite-vairts, *adv* sideways

Sekretär, zeck-re-tair, *m* writing-desk; secretary

Sekt, zeckt, *m* sparkling wine

Sektion, zeckts-yohn, *f* division; dissection; post-mortem

sekundär, zeck-oonn-dair, *adj* secondary, subordinate

Sekunde, zeck-oonn-de, *f* second

selber, zelb-er, *pron* my/ your/him/her/it/oneself/ our/your/themselves

selbst, zelp'st, *adv* even; *pron* my/your/him/her/it/ oneself/our/your/ themselves; in person

selbständig, zelp-shtend-ik, *adj* independent; self-employed

Selbstbedienung, zelpst-be-deen-oong, *f* self-service

selbstbewußt, zelpst-be-voost, *adj* self-confident

Selbstgefühl, zelpst-ge-fEEl, *nt* self-assurance, ego

selbstgemacht, zelpst-ge-makt, *adj* home-made

Selbstgespräch, zelpst-ge-shprayk, *nt* soliloquy

selbstlos, zelpst-lohs, *adj* unselfish

Selbstmord, zelpst-mort, *m* suicide

Selbstmörder, zelpst-merd-er, *m* (person committing) suicide

selbstredend, zelpst-rayd-ent, *adj* self-evident

selbstsicher, zelpst-zik-er, *adj* self-assured, self-confident

selbstsüchtig, zelpst-zEEkt-ik, *adj* selfish

Selbstversorgung, zelpst-fair-zohrg-oong, *f* self-catering

Selbstvertrauen, zelpst-fair-trow-en, *nt* self-confidence

selbstverständlich, zelpst-fair-shtent-lik, *adv* of course

selig, zayl-ik, *adj* relig blessed; happy

Sellerie, zel-er-ee, *m & f* celery

selten, zelt-en, *adj* rare, seldom, scarce

seltsam, zelt-zahm, *adj* curious, strange

Semester, zay-mest-er, *nt* term (university)

senden, zend-en, *v* to send; to broadcast

Sendung, zend-oong, *f*

consignment; dispatch; programme

Senf, zenf, *m* mustard

sengen, zeng-en, *v* to single, to scorch

Senior, zehn-yohr, *m* (old-age) pensioner; **–enheim,** *nt* old people's home; **–enpaß,** *m* senior citizen's pass/railcard

senken, zeng-ken, *v* to sink, to lower; to dip

senkrecht, zenk-rekt, *adj* vertical

Sense, zen-ze, *f* scythe

sensibel, zen-zee-bel, *adj* sensitive

September, zep-tem-ber, *m* September

servieren, zairv-eer-en, *v* to serve

Serviette, zairv-ee-ett-e, *f* napkin

Sessel, zess-el, *m* easy-chair; **–lift,** *m* chairlift

setzen, zets-en, *v* to set, to place; **sich –,** *v* to sit down

Seuche, zoyk-e, *f* epidemic; plague

seufzen, zoyf-tsen, *v* to sigh

Sexismus, seks-is-mooss, *m* sexism

sexistisch, seks-ist-ish, *adj* sexist

sezieren, zay-tseer-en, *v* to dissect

Shampoo, shahmm-poo, *nt* shampoo

sich, zik, *refl pron* oneself

Sichel, zik-el, *f* sickle

sicher, zik-er, *adj* certain,

sure; safe, secure

Sicherheit, zik-er-hite, *f* security; safety; certainty; **–sgurt,** *m* safety belt; **–snadel,** *f* safety pin

sicherlich, zik-er-lik, *adv* surely, certainly

sichern, zik-ern, *v* to secure; to safeguard; to ensure

sicherstellen, zik-er-shtel-en, *v* to secure; to make sure

Sicht, zikt, *f* sight, vision; view

sichtbar, zikt-bahr, *adj* visible; perceptible

sichten, zikt-en, *v* to sight

sichtlich, zikt-lik, *adj* visible; *adv* evidently

sickern, zick-ern, *v* to ooze; to trickle

Sie, zee, *pron* (formal) you

sie, zee, *pron* she, her; it; they, them

Sieb, zeep, *nt* sieve; strainer

sieben, zee-ben, *v* to sift, to sieve; *num* seven

sieb(en)te, zeeb(-en)-te, *adj* seventh

siebzehn, zeep-tsain, *num* seventeen

siebzig, zeep-tsik, *num* seventy

siechen, zeek-en, *v* to pine away; to be in ill-health

siedeln, zeed-eln, *v* to settle

sieden, zeed-en, *v* to boil; to seethe

Siedler, zeed-ler, *m* settler, colonist

Siedlung, zeed-loong, *f* housing estate

Sieg, zeek, *m* victory

Siegel, zeeg-el, *nt* seal; signet

siegen, zeeg-en, *v* to be victorious

Sieger, zeeg-er, *m* victor

siegreich, zeek-ry'k, *adj* victorious

Silbe, zilb-e, *f* syllable

Silber, zilb-er, *nt* silver

silbern, zilb-ern, *adj* of silver

Silvester(abend), zil-vest-er(-ahb-ent), *nt* (*m*), New Year's Eve

singen, zing-en, *v* to sing

sinken, zing-ken, *v* to sink

Sinn, zin, *m* sense; mind; nature; disposition

sinnen, zin-en, *v* to ponder; to reflect, to meditate

sinnlich, zin-lik, *adj* sensual; sensuous; sensory

Sinnlichkeit, zin-lik-kite, *f* sensuality; sensuousness

sinnlos, zin-lohs, *adj* pointless; meaningless

sinnvoll, zin-fol, *adj* meaningful; wise; sensible

Sintflut, zint-floot, *f* deluge, flood

Sippe, zip-e, *f* relations, family, clan

Sippschaft, zip-shahft, *f* relations, family, clan

Sitte, zit-e, *f* habit, custom, usage; **–n,** *pl* morals

sittlich, zit-lik, *adj* moral; respectable

Sittlichkeit, zit-lik-kite, *f* morality; moral code

sittsam, zit-zahm, *adj* modest; respectable; decent

Sitz, zits, *m* seat; residence

sitzen, zit-sen, *v* to sit, to be seated; to fit

Sitzplatz, zits-plahts, *m* seat

Sitzung, zit-soong, *f* meeting; session

Skala, skah-lah, *f mus* scale

Skandal, skahnn-dahl, *m* noise; scandal

Skandinavien, skahnn-dee-nah-vee-en, *pl* Scandinavia

Skat, skaht, *m* German card game

Skateboard, skayt-bort, *nt* skateboard

Ski, shee, *m* ski; **–lauf,** *m* skiing; **–laufen,** *v* to ski; **–läufer,** *m* skier; **–lift,** *m* ski lift; **–piste,** *f* ski slope, piste

Skizze, skit-se, *f* sketch; draft

skizzieren, skit-seer-en, *v* to sketch

Sklave, sklahv-e, *m* slave

Sklaverei, sklahv-e-ry, *f* slavery

Skonto, skont-oh, *m* discount, rebate

Slowakei, slo-vah-ky, *f* Slovakia

Slowenien, slo-vay-nee-en, *nt* Slovenia

Smaragd, smah-rahkt, *m* emerald

Smog, smog, *m* smog

Smoking, smoh-king, *m*

dinner jacket

sb., *abbr* for **siehe oben, zee-e oh**-ben, see above

so, zoh, *adv* so, like this; such; *conj* therefore

sobald, zoh-**bahlt**, *conj* as soon as

Socke, zohck-e, *f* sock

Sockel, zock-el, *m* base, foot

sodann, zoh-**dahnn**, *adv* after that; then

soeben, zoh-**ayb**-en, *adv* just now

sofern, zoh-**fairn**, *conj* in so far as; if

sofort, zoh-**fort**, *adv* at once, immediately

Software, soft-wair, *f* software

sog., *abbr* **sogenannt,** zoh-ge-nahnt, *adj* so-called

sogar, zoh-**gar**, *adv* even

sogleich, zoh-**gly'k**, *adv* at once, immediately

Sohle, zohl-e, *f* (in)sole; bottom, floor

Sohn, zohn, *m* son

Soja, zoh-jah, *f* soya; –**bohne,** *f* soya bean; –**soße,** *f* soya sauce

solange, zoh-**lahng**-e, *conj* so long as

solch, zolk, *pron* such; – **ein(e),** such a

solche(r/s), zol-**ke**(r/s), *adj* such; **ein(e) –,** such a

Soldat, zol-**daht**, *m* soldier

Söldner, zerlt-ner, *m* hireling, mercenary

solid(e), zol-**eed**(-e), *adj* steady, respectable; solid

sollen, zol-en, *v* to be obliged to; to have to; ought to; shall

Solo, zoh-loh, *nt* solo

somit, zoh-**mit**, *adv* hence, therefore, thus

Sommer, zom-er, *m* summer; –**sprossen,** *pl* freckles

Sonderangebot, zon-der-ahnn-ge-boht, *nt* special offer

sonderbar, zon-der-bar, *adj* strange; unusual

sondergleichen, zon-der-gly-ken, *adj* unequalled

sonderlich, zon-der-lik, *adj* notable; *adv* particularly

Sonderling, zon-der-ling, *m* eccentric (person)

sondern, zon-dern, *conj* but (after negation)

Sonnabend, zon-ah-bent, *m* Saturday

Sonne, zon-e, *f* sun

sonnen (sich), zon-en (zik), *v* to sun oneself; to bask

Sonnenaufgang, zon-en-owf-gahng, *m* sunrise

Sonnenblume, zon-en-bloom-e, *f* sunflower

Sonnenbad, zon-en-baht, *nt* sunbathing

Sonnenbrand, zon-en-brahnt, *m* sunburn

Sonnenbräune, zon-en-broy-ne, *f* sun tan

Sonnenbrille, zon-en-brill-e, *f* sun glasses

Sonnencreme, zon-en-kraim, *f* sun cream

Sonnenenergie, zon-en-en-

air-gee, *f* solar power

sonnenklar, zon-en-klahr, *adj* clear as day

Sonnenkollektor, zon-en-kol-ek-tohr, *m* solar panel

Sonnenschein, zon-en-shine, *m* sunshine

Sonnenschirm, zon-en-sheerm, *m* sunshade, parasol

Sonnenschutz, zon-en-shoots, *m* sun protection

Sonnenstich, zon-en-shtik, *m* sunstroke

Sonnenstrahl, zon-en-shtrahl, *m* sunbeam

Sonnenuntergang, zon-en-oont-er-gahng, *m* sunset

sonnenverbrannt, zon-en-fair-brahnnt, *adj* sunburnt

sonnig, zon-ik, *adj* sunny

Sonntag, zon-tahk, *m* Sunday

sonst, zonst, *adv* otherwise; besides

sonstige(r/s), zons-ti-ge(r/s), *adj* former; other

sonstwie, zonst-vee, *adv* in some other way

sonstwo, zonst-voh, *adv* elsewhere

sonstwoher, zonst-voh-hair, *adv* from elsewhere

Sorge, zorg-e, *f* sorrow; anxiety; worry

sorgen, zorg-en, *v* to attend to; to procure; **sich –,** to worry

Sorgfalt, zorg-fahlt, *f* attention; care

sorgfältig, zorg-felt-ik, *adj*

careful; attentive; exact

sorgsam, zorg-zahm, *adj* particular; careful

Sorte, zort-se, *f* kind, sort; variety

sortieren, zort-eer-en, *v* to (as)sort; to arrange

Soße, zoh-se, *f* sauce, gravy

Souffleur, zooff-ler, *m* prompter

soviel, zoh-feel, *conj* as far as

soweit, zoh-vite, *conj* in so far as

sowie, zoh-vee, *conj* as soon as; as well as

sowieso, zoh-vee-soh, *adv* in any case

sowohl, zoh-vohl, *conj* as well; **– ... als auch ...**, *conj* both ... and ...

Sozialhilfe, zo-tsee-**ahl**-hilf-e, *f* income support

Sozialversicherung, zo-tsee-**ahl**-fair-zik-er-oong, *f* social security

spähen, shpay-en, *v* to look out for; to spy

Spalier, sphah-leer, *nt* trellis; row, line (of people)

Spalt, shpahlt, *m* cleft; slit; crevasse

Spalte, shpahlt-e, *f* column; cleft; slit; crevasse

spalten, shpahlt-en, *v* to split; to crack

Span, shpahn, *m* chip, splinter

Spanferkel, shpahn-fairk-el, *nt* suckling pig

Spange, shpahng-e, *f* buckle, clasp

Spanien, shpah-nee-en, *nt* Spain

spanisch, shpah-nish, *adj* Spanish

Spann, shpahnn, *m* instep

Spanne, shpahnn-e, *f* span; stretch

spannen, shpahnn-en, *v* to stretch; to tighten; to tie

Spannung, shpahnn-oong, *f* tension; tightness; strain; suspense; voltage

Sparbüchse, shpahr-bEEks-e, *f* money box

sparen, shpahr-en, *v* to save; to spare

Spargel, shpahrg-el, *m* asparagus

Sparkasse, shpahr-kahss-e, *f* savings bank

spärlich, shpair-lik, *adj* scanty, sparse; meagre

sparsam, shpahr-zahm, *adj* saving; thrifty; economical

Sparschwein, shpahr-shvine, *nt* piggy bank

Spaß, shpahss, *m* fun; joking; amusement

spaßen, shpahs-en, *v* to joke

spaßhaft, shpahs-hahft, *adj* funny; for fun

spaßig, shpahs-ik, *adj* amusing, funny

spät, shpayt, *adj* late, belated

Spaten, shpaht-en, *m* spade

späterhin, shpayt-er-hin, *adv* later on

spätestens, shpayt-est-ens, *adv* at the latest

Spatz, shpahts, *m* sparrow

spazieren, shpaht-seer-en, *v* to stroll; **–fahren,** *v* to go for a drive; **–gehen,** *v* to go for a walk

Spazierfahrt, shpaht-seer-fahrt, *f* drive, ride

Spaziergang, shpaht-seer-gahng, *m* walk, ramble; stroll

Spazierstock, shpaht-seer-shtock, *m* walking-stick

Specht, sphpekt, *m* woodpecker

Speck, shpeck, *m* bacon

Spediteur, shpay-de-ter, *m* forwarding-agent; furniture remover

Speer, shpair, *m* spear; lance; javelin (sport)

Speiche, shpy-ke, *f* spoke (wheel)

Speichel, shpy-kel, *m* spittle, saliva

Speicher, shpy-ker, *m* granary; warehouse; attic

speichern, shpy-kern, *v* to store; to warehouse

Speise, shpy-ze, *f* food; nourishment; **–kammer,** *f* pantry; **–karte,** *f* menu; **–lokal,** *nt* restaurant

speisen, shpy-zen, *v* to eat, to dine

Speisesaal, shpy-ze-zahl, *m* dining-room

Speisewagen, shpy-ze-vahg-en, *m* restaurant-car

Speisezimmer, shpy-ze-tsim-er, *nt* dining-room

Spektakel, shpeck-tahk-el,

m noise, row

Spelunke, shpay-loong-ke, f *fam* dive

Spende, shpend-e, f donation, gift; distribution

spenden, shpend-en, v to donate; to give

spendieren, shpend-eer-en, v to buy (for), to stand (drink etc.)

Sperber, shpairb-er, m sparrow-hawk

Sperling, shpair-ling, m sparrow

Sperre, shpairr-e, f closure; blockade; stoppage

sperren, shpairr-en, v to bar, to obstruct; to interrupt

Sperrsitz, shpairr-zits, m stall *theatre*

Sperrstunde, shpairr-shtoond-e, f closing time

Spesen, shpay-zen, pl expenses; charges

spicken, shpick-en, v to lard; to bribe; *fam* to crib

Spiegel, shpeeg-el, m mirror

Spiegelei, shpeeg-el-i, nt fried egg

spiegelglatt, shpeeg-el-glahtt, adj smooth as glass

spiegeln, shpeeg-eln, v to reflect; to shine

Spiel, shpeel, nt play; game; pastime

spielen, shpeel-en, v to play; to perform; to gamble

Spieler, shpeel-er, m player; gambler

Spielerei, shpeel-e-ry, f

play(ing); pastime; triviality

Spielhölle, shpeel-herll-e, f gambling den

Spielsachen, shpeel-sahk-en, pl toys

Spielverderber, shpeel-fair-dairb-er, m spoil-sport

Spielwaren, shpeel-vahr-en, pl toys

Spielzeug, shpeel-tsoyk, nt plaything(s), toy(s)

Spieß, shpees, m spear; pike; (roasting-)spit

Spießbürger, shpees-bEErg-er, m bourgeois, Philistine

Spießer, shpees-er, m bourgeois, Philistine

Spinat, shpeen-aht, m spinach

Spind, shpint, m & nt locker, cupboard

Spindel, shpin-del, f spindle

Spinne, shpinn-e, f spider

spinnen, shpinn-en, v to spin; to purr; *fam* to imagine things, to be mad

Spinnwebe, shpinn-vaib-e, f spider's web

Spion, shpee-ohn, m spy; scout

Spionage, shpee-ohn-ahzh-e, f espionage, spying

spionieren, shpee-ohn-eer-en, v to spy; to pry

Spiritismus, shpeer-ee-tis-mooss, m spiritualism

Spirituosen, shpeer-it-oo-ohz-en, pl spirits

Spital, shpee-tahl, nt hospital

spitz, shpits, adj pointed; sharp

Spitz, shpits, m Pomeranian (dog)

Spitzbube, shpits-boob-e, m rogue; rascal, scamp

Spitze, shpit-se, f point; peak; tip; spire; lace

Spitzel, shpit-sel, m detective; police spy

spitzen, shpit-sen, v to point; to sharpen

spitzfindig, shpits-fin-dik, adj nit-picking

Spitzname, shpits-nahm-e, m nickname

Splitter, shplitt-er, m splinter

splittern, shplitt-ern, v to splinter; to shatter

splitternackt, shplitt-er-nahckt, adj stark naked

sponsern, shpon-sern, v to sponsor

Sponsor, shpon-sohr, m sponsor

Sporn, shporn, m spur

spornen, shporn-en, v to spur

sportlich, shport-lik, adj relating to sport

Spott, shpott, m mockery; derision

spottbillig, shpot-bil-ik, adj dirt-cheap

Spöttelei, shpertt-e-ly, f mocking (remark)

spötteln, shpertt-eln, v to mock, to poke fun at

spotten, shpot-en, v to mock; to jeer

Spötter, shpertt-er, m
mocker; blasphemer

spöttisch, shpertt-ish, adj
mocking, sneering,
derisive

Spottpreis, shpot-price, m
ridiculous(ly low) price

Sprache, sphrahk-e, f
language; speech

Sprachfehler, shprahk-fail-
er, m speech defect

sprachkundig, shprahk-
koond-ik, adj good at
(foreign) languages

Sprachkurs, shprahk-koors,
m language course

sprachlos, shprahk-lohs, adj
speechless

Sprachrohr, shprahk-rohr,
nt megaphone; fig
mouthpiece

Spray, shpray, nt spray;
–dose, f aerosol, spray

sprechen, shprek-en, v to
speak, to talk; to converse

Sprecher, shprek-er, m
speaker; spokesman; news
reader

Sprechstunde, shprek-
shtoonn-de, f office-hour;
surgery

Sprechzimmer, shprek-tsim-
er, nt consulting-room

spreizen, shpry-tsen, v to
spread out

sprengen, shpreng-en, v to
force apart; to blow up; to
sprinkle

Sprengstoff, shpreng-shtof,
m explosive

sprenkeln, shpreng-keln, v

to speckle, to spot

Spreu, shproy, f chaff

Sprichwort, shprik-vort, nt
proverb

sprichwörtlich, shprik-vert-
lik, adj proverbial

sprießen, shprees-en, v to
sprout, to germinate

Springbrunnen, shpring-
broonn-en, m fountain

springen, shpring-en, v to
jump; to spring; to burst;
to crack

Springer, shpring-er, m
jumper; knight (chess)

Spritze, shprit-se, f syringe;
hose; injection

spritzen, shprit-sen, v to
squirt; to splash

spröde, shprerd-e, adj
fragile; brittle; rough; coy,
prudish

Sproß, shpross, m shoot,
sprout; offspring

Sprosse, shpross-e, f rung,
step

sprossen, shpross-en, v to
sprout, to shoot

Sprößling, shprerss-ling, m
shoot, sprout; offspring

Spruch, shprook, m
sentence; verdict; maxim,
saying

Sprudel, shprood-el, m
bubbling spring; flow;
sparkling water

sprudeln, shprood-eln, v to
gush forth, to bubble

Sprühdose, shprEE-doh-ze, f
aerosol

sprühen, shprEE-en, v to

sparkle; to send out sparks

Sprung, shproong, m jump,
leap; **–brett,** nt diving-
board, springboard (also
fig); **–feder,** f (spiral)
spring

sprungfertig, shproong-
fairt-ik, adj ready to jump

Spucke, shpoock-e, f
spit(tle)

spucken, shpoock-en v to
spit

Spucknapf, shpoock-nahp'f,
m spittoon

Spuk, shpook, m spook,
spectre, ghost

spuken, shpook-en, v to
haunt, to walk (ghosts)

Spule, shpool-e, f bobbin,
spool; coil

spulen, shpool-en, v to reel;
to spin

spülen, shpEEl-en, v to
rinse; to wash up

Spülmaschine, shpEEl-mah-
shee-ne, f dishwasher

Spülmittel, shpEEl-mit-el, nt
washing-up liquid

Spur, shpoor, f spoor; track;
trail

spüren, shpEEr-en, v to
perceive, to feel

spurlos, shpoor-lohs, adj
without (leaving any)
trace

Spurweite, shpoor-vite-e, f
gauge (of railway); track
(of car)

sputen (sich), shpoot-en
(zik), v to make haste

Staat, shtaht, m state;

show, pomp

staatlich, shtaht-lik, *adj* (of the) state

Staatsangehörige(r), shtahts-ahnn-ge-her-rig-e(r), *m & f* subject (of a state), national

Staatsanwalt, shtahts-ahnn-vahlt, *m* public prosecutor

Staatsbeamte(r), shtahts-be-ahmt-e(r), *m* civil servant

Staatsdienst, shtahts-deenst, *m* civil service

Staatswesen, shtahts-vayz-en, *nt* state

Stab, shtahp, *m* staff, stick; bar

Stachel, shtahk-el, *m* spike; sting; thorn; prickle; barb; **–beere**, *f* gooseberry; **–draht**, *m* barbed wire

stachelig, shtahk-el-ik, *adj* thorny, prickly

Stachelschwein, shtahk-el-shvine, *nt* porcupine

Stadion, shtahd-yohn, *nt* stadium

Stadt, shtahtt, *f* town

Städter, shtayt-er, *m* town-/city-dweller

städtisch, shtayt-ish, *adj* municipal; urban

Stadtmitte, shtahtt-mit-e, *f* town/city centre

Stadtplan, shtahtt-plahn, *m* street plan

Stadtrat, shtahtt-raht, *m* town-council(lor)

Stadtrundfahrt, shtatt-roont-fahrt, *f* city tour

Stadtteil, shtahtt-tile, *m* district, quarter

Stadtverordnete(r), shtahtt-fair-ord-net-e(r), *m & f* town councillor

Staffel, shtahff-el, *f* degree, step; bracket; (sport) relay

Staffelei, shtahff-e-ly, *f* easel

Stahl, shtahl, *m* steel

stählen, shtayl-en, *v* to steel; to harden

stählern, shtayl-ern, *adj* (of/like) steel

Stall, shtahll, *m* stable, stall, sty; **–knecht**, *m* stable-boy, groom; **–ung**, *f* stabling; mews

Stamm, shtahmm, *m* stem, stalk; trunk; tribe; stock; **–baum**, *m* genealogical tree; pedigree

stammeln, shtahmm-eln, *v* to stammer

stammen, shtahmm-en, *v* to descend (from); to spring (from)

Stammgast, shtahmm-gahsst, *m* regular customer (in pub)

stämmig, shtem-ik, *adj* robust, stocky, sturdy

Stammkneipe, Stammlokal, shtahmm-knipe-e, -loh-kahl, *f nt* favourite pub, local

Stammtisch, shtahmm-tish, *m* table reserved for regular customers (in pub)

stampfen, shtahmp-fen, *v* to stamp; to trample; to paw

Stand, shtahnt, *m* stand;

position; state; **–bild**, *nt* statue

Ständchen, shtent-ken, *nt* serenade

Ständer, shtend-er, *m* stand; post; pedestal

Standesamt, shtahnd-es-ahmt, *nt* register office

Standesbeamte(r), shtahnd-es-be-ahmt-e(r), *m* registrar

standesgemäß, shtahnd-es-ge-mace, *adj* according to one's station

standhaft, shtahnt-hahft, *adj* firm, steadfast, resolute

standhalten, shtahnt-hahlt-en, *v* to stand firm

ständig, shtend-ik, *adj* constant; permanent

Standort, shtahnt-ort, *m* location, position; base

Standpunkt, shtahnt-poonkt, *m* point of view; position

Standuhr, shtahnt-oor, *f* clock

Stange, shtahng-e, *f* rod, perch, stake

stänkern, shtenk-ern, *v* to make mischief

Stanniol, shtahnn-yohl, *nt* tin foil, silver paper

stanzen, shtahnt-sen, *v* to stamp, to punch

Stapel, shtahp-el, *m* stack, pile; store, depot; stocks; **–lauf**, *m* launch(ing)

stapeln, shtahp-eln, *v* to heap up; to stack

Star, shtar, *m* starling;

cataract (eye); (pop/film etc.) star

stark, shtark, *adj* strong; sturdy; severe

Stärke, shtairk-*e*, *f* strength, power; starch

stärken, shtairk-en, *v* to strengthen; to starch

Stärkung, shtairk-oong, *f* strengthening; reinforcement

starr, shtarr, *adj* rigid, stiff; fixed, staring

starren, shtarr-en, *v* to stare; to be(come) numb

Starrheit, shtarr-hite, *f* rigidity; numbness

starrköpfig, shtarr-kerpp-fik, *adj* stubborn; headstrong

Starrsinn, shtarr-zin, *m* stubbornness

Startbahn, shtart-bahn, *f* runway

Station, shtahts-yohn, *f* station; bus stop; (hospital) ward; **–vorsteher**, *m* station-master

Statist, shtaht-ist, *m* supernumerary, *theatre* extra

statt, shtahtt, *prep* instead of

Stätte, shtet-*e*, *f* place; abode; site

stattfinden, shtahtt-fin-den, *v* to take place

statthaft, shtahtt-hahft, *adj* permitted; legal

Statthalter, shtahtt-hahlt-er, *m* governor, viceroy

stattlich, shtahtt-lik, *adj* splendid, stately; commanding

Stau, shtow, *m* traffic jam; blockage

Staub, shtowp, *m* dust; (fine) powder

stauben, shtowb-en, *v* to give off/create dust

stäuben, shtoyb-en, *v* to dust; to powder

Staubgefäß, shtowp-ge-face, *nt* stamen

staubig, shtowb-ik, *adj* dusty; powdery

Staubsauger, shtowp-sow-ger, *m* vacuum cleaner

Staude, shtowd-*e*, *f* bush, shrub

stauen, shtow-en, *v* to stow; to dam

staunen, shtown-en, *v* to be surprised/astonished

Stausee, shtow-zay, *m* reservoir

Std., *abbr* **Stunde**, hour; o'clock

stechen, shtek-en, *v* to stab; to pierce; to prick

Stechginster, shtek-ginst-er, *m* gorse, furze

Stechpalme, shtek-pahlm-*e*, *f* holly

Steckbrief, shteck-breef, *m* warrant

Steckdose, shteck-doh-ze, *f* (electrical) socket

Stecken, shteck-en, *m* staff, stick

stecken, shteck-en, *v* to stick; to be stuck; to put, to set; **–bleiben**, *v* to

be/get stuck

Steckenpferd, shteck-en-p'fairt, *nt* hobby-horse; fad

Steckling, shteck-ling, *m* shoot, cutting, slip

Stecknadel, shteck-nahd-el, *f* pin

Steckrübe, shteck-rEEb-*e*, *f* swede

Steg, shtayk, *m* path; foot-bridge; bridge (of violin)

Stegreif, shtayk-rife, *m* **aus dem – spielen**, to improvise

stehen, shtay-en, *v* to stand, to be standing (up); **–bleiben**, *v* to stop; to remain standing

Stehkragen, shtay-krahg-en, *m* stand-up collar

stehlen, shtayl-en, *v* to steal

Stehplatz, shtay-plahts, *m* standing-room

steif, shtife, *adj* stiff, rigid; thick

steifen, shty-fen, *v* to stiffen; to starch

Steig, shtike, *m* steep track; **–bügel**, *m* stirrup

steigen, shty-gen, *v* to climb, to mount; to rise

steigern, shty-gern, *v* to raise; to increase; to intensify

Steigerung, shty-ger-oong, *f* increase; raising; comparing

Steigung, shty-goong, *f* rise; gradient

steil, shtile, *adj* steep, sheer

Stein, shtine, *m* stone

steinalt, shtine-ahlt, *adj* very old

Steinbock, shtine-bock, *m* ibex; capricorn

Steinbruch, shtine-brook, *m* quarry

Steinbutt, shtine-boott, *m* turbot

steinern, shtine-ern, *adj* (of) stone; (of) earthenware

Steingut, shtine-goot, *nt* earthenware

steinhart, shtine-hart, *adj* as hard as stone

steinig, shtine-ik, *adj* stony; rocky

steinigen, shtine-ig-en, *v* to stone (to death)

Steinkohle, shtine-kohl-e, *f* hard coal

Steinmetz, shtine-mets, *m* stone-mason

Steinpflaster, shtine-p'flahst-er, *nt* stone paving

steinreich, shtine-ry'k, *adj* very rich

Steiß, shtice, *m* rump, buttock; posterior

Stelldichein, shtel-dik-ine, *nt* appointment; rendezvous

Stelle, shtel-e, *f* place, spot; job; situation; digit

stellen, shtel-en, *v* to place; to stand; to set

stellenweise, shtel-en-vy-ze, *adv* in places

Stellung, shtel-oong, *f* position; placement, employment

Stellvertreter, shtel-fair-traiyt-er, *m* representative; substitute, deputy

Stelze, shtelt-se, *f* stilt

Stemmeisen, shtem-i-zen, *nt* crowbar

stemmen, shtem-en, *v* to support; to dam; to stem

Stempel, shtemp-el, *m* stamp; mark; pistil

stempeln, shtemp-eln, *v* to stamp; to mark

Stengel, shteng-el, *m* stem, stalk; handle

Steppdecke, shtep-deck-e, *f* quilt

steppen, shtep-en, *v* to quilt

Sterbebett, shtairb-e-bet, *nt* death-bed

sterben, shtairb-en, *v* to die

sterbenskrank, shtairb-ens-krahnk, *adj* fatally/terminally ill

sterblich, shtairp-lik, *adj* mortal

Sterblichkeit, shtairp-lik-kite, *f* mortality

Stereoanlage, shtay-ray-oh-ahnn-lah-ge, *f* stereo (system)

Stern, shtairn, *m* star; asterisk

Sterndeuter, shtairn-doyt-er, *m* astrologer

sternhell, shtairn-hel, *adj* starry

Sternkunde, shtairn-koonn-de, *f* astronomy

Sternschnuppe, shtairn-shnoop-e, *f* shooting star

Sternwarte, shtairn-vart-e, *f* observatory

Sternzeichen, shtairn-tsyk-en, *nt* star sign

stet, shtayt, *adj* fixed, steady; constant

stetig, shtayt-ik, *adj* steady; continual; constant

stets, shtayts, *adv* always, ever

Steuer, shtoy-er, *nt* rudder, tiller; *f* tax, duty; **–berater,** *m* tax consultant; **–bord,** *nt* starboard; **–mann,** *m* helmsman; mate

steuern, shtoy-ern, *v* to steer, to navigate; to control

Steuerung, shtoy-er-oong, *f* steering(-wheel); control

Stewardeß, st'yoo-ahr-dess, *f* stewardess

Stich, shtik, *m* stitch; sting; bite; stab

sticheln, shtik-eln, *v* to sneer; to tease

stichhaltig, shtik-hahlt-ik, *adj* plausible, sound

Stichwaffe, shtik-vahff-e, *f* foil, sword, dagger

Stichwort, shtik-vort, *nt* cue; catch-word; headword

sticken, shtick-en, *v* to embroider

Stickerei, shtick-e-ry, *f* embroidery

stickig, shtick-ik, *adj* stuffy, choking

Stickstoff, shtick-shtof, *m* nitrogen

Stief–, shteef, *pref* step-; **–bruder,** *m* stepbrother;

–**mutter,** f stepmother;
–**schwester,** f stepsister;
–**sohn,** m stepson;
–**tochter,** f stepdaughter;
–**vater,** m stepfather
Stiefel, shteef-el, m boot
stiefeln, shteef-eln, v fam to
hoof it
Stiefmütterchen, shteef-
mEEtt-er-ken, nt pansy
Stiege, shteeg-e, f stair(s)
Stieglitz, shteeg-lits, m
goldfinch
Stiel, shteel, m handle;
stalk; stem
stier, shteer, adj staring;
vacant
Stier, shteer, m bull; steer
stieren, shteer-en, v to
stare; to look vacant
Stierkampf, shteer-kahmp'f,
m bull-fight
Stift, shtift, m peg; tag; bolt;
pencil; nt convent;
charitable foundation
stiften, shtift-en, v to found;
to create; to endow
Stiftung, shtift-oong, f
foundation; endowment;
–**sfest,** nt commemoration
day
Stigma, s(h)tig-mah, nt
stigma
Stil, shteel, m style
still, shtil, adj still, quiet;
silent; peaceful
Stille, shtil-e, f quiet,
stillness; calm
Stilleben, shtil-layb-en, nt
still-life
stillen, shtil-en, v to still; to

stanch; to appease; to
quench; to breast-feed
Stille(r) Ozean, shtil-e(r)
oh-tsay-ahn, m Pacific
Ocean
stillschweigend, shtil-shvy-
gent, adj silent; tacit
Stillstand, shtil-shtahnt, m
stoppage
Stimmband, shtim-bahnt, nt
vocal chord
Stimme, shtim-e, f voice;
vote
stimmen, shtim-en, v to
tally; to tune; to
harmonize
Stimmgabel, shtim-gahb-el,
f tuning-fork
Stimmung, shtim-oong, f
mood, humour;
atmosphere
Stimmwechsel, shtim-
vecks-el, m breaking of
the voice
stinken, shtink-en, v to
stink
Stinktier, shtink-teer, nt
skunk
Stirn, shteern, f forehead;
brow; –**runzeln,** nt
frown(ing)
stöbern, shterb-ern, v to
rummage
stochern, shtok-ern, v to
poke, to stir up
Stock, shtock, m stick; cane;
storey
stocken, shtock-en, v to
stop (short); to slacken
stockfinster, shtock-finst-er,
adj pitch-dark

Stockfisch, shtock-fish, m
dried cod
Stockung, shtock-oong, f
stoppage; block;
congestion
Stockwerk, shtock-vairk, nt
storey
Stoff, shtof, m stuff;
substance; fabric, material;
subject
Stoffel, shtof-el, m
blockhead
stöhnen, shtern-en, v to
groan, to moan
Stollen, shtol-en, m tunnel,
gallery (in mine); fruit
loaf
stolpern, shtolp-ern, v to
stumble
stolz, shtolts, adj proud;
haughty
Stolz, shtolts, m pride;
vanity
stolzieren, shtolts-eer-en, v
to stalk, to strut
stopfen, shtop-fen, v to
stuff, to cram; to darn
Stoppel, shtop-el, f stubble
Stöpsel, shterpp-sel, m
stopper
stöpseln, shterpp-seln, v to
stop (up); to cork
Stör, shter, m sturgeon
Storch, shtork, m stork
stören, shter-en, v to
disturb; to interrupt
Störenfried, shter-en-freet,
m mischief-maker
stornieren, shtorn-eer-en, v
to cancel
störrisch, shter-ish, adj

stubborn; wayward

Störung, shter-oong, *f*
disturbance; interruption

Stoß, shtohs, *m* thrust, push;
stroke; blow; blast; heap

stoßen, shtohs-en, *v* to
push; to thrust; to pound;
to knock

Stoßzahn, shtohs-tsahn, *m*
tusk

stottern, shtot-ern, *v* to
stutter, to stammer

Str., *abbr* **Straße**

stracks, shtrahcks, *adv*
straight away; directly

strafbar, shtrahf-bar, *adj*
punishable; criminal

Strafe, shtrahf-e, *f*
punishment; penalty;
chastisement

strafen, shtrahf-en, *v* to
punish; to correct

straff, shtrahff, *adj* taut,
tight; stretched; severe

straffen, shtrahff-en, *v* to
tighten, to stretch

Strafgesetz, shtrahf-ge-zets,
nt criminal code

sträflich, shtrayf-lik, *adj*
criminal; punishable

Sträfling, shtrayf-ling, *m*
convict

Strafrecht, shtrahf-rekt, *nt*
criminal law

Strafsache, shtrahf-sahk-e, *f*
criminal case

Strafzettel, shtrahf-tset-el,
m (speeding, parking etc.)
ticket

Strahl, shtrahl, *m* beam, ray;
jet

strahlen, shtrahl-en, *v* to
beam; to radiate; to shine

Strahlung, shtrahl-oong, *f*
radiation

Strähne, shtrayn-e, *f* strand;
plait

stramm, shtrahmm, *adj*
sturdy; stiff

strampeln, shtrahmp-eln, *v*
to struggle; to fidget, to
kick

Strand, shtrahnt, *m* beach,
shore, strand

stranden, shtrahnd-en, *v* to
be stranded; to founder

Strang, shtrahng, *m* rope;
track; trace

Strapaze, shtrah-paht-se, *f*
hardship; toil; exertion

Straße, shtrahs-e, *f* street,
road; straits; –**nbahn,** *f*
tramway; –**nfest,** *nt* street
fair; –**nkarte,** *f* road map;
–**nmusikant,** *m* busker;
–**nverkehr,** *m* traffic

Strategie, shtrah-tay-gee, *f*
strategy

sträuben (sich), shtroyb-en
(zik), *v* to stand on end; to
struggle against

Strauch, shtrowk, *m* bush,
shrub

straucheln, shtrowk-eln, *v*
to stumble

Strauß, shtrows, *m* ostrich;
bouquet

streben, shtrayb-en, *v* to
aspire; to strive

Streber, shtrayb-er, *m*
ambitious person

strebsam, shtrayp-zahm, *adj*
zealous; ambitious

Strecke, shtreck-e, *f* stretch;
tract; track

strecken, shtreck-en, *v* to
stretch, to extend

Streich, shtry'k, *m* stroke;
trick; action

streicheln, shtry-keln, *v* to
stroke, to pat

streichen, shtry-ken, *v* to
stroke; to delete; to
spread; to paint

Streichholz, shtry'k-holts,
nt match

Streifband, shtrife-bahnt, *nt*
wrapper

Streifen, shtrife-en, *m* strip,
stripe

streifen, shtrife-en, *v* to
brush against; to touch; to
roam

Streifzug, shtrife-tsook, *m*
expedition, incursion

Streik, shtrike, *m* strike

streiken, shtrike-en, *v* to
strike; to down tools

Streit, shtrite, *m* dispute,
quarrel; fight

streiten, shtrite-en, *v* to
quarrel, to dispute

Streitfrage, shtrite-frah-ge, *f*
dispute

streitig, shtrite-ik, *adj*
contested, in dispute

Streitigkeit, shtrite-ik-kite,
f dispute; quarrel

Streitkräfte, shtrite-kreft-e,
pl mil forces

streitsüchtig, shtrite-sEEkt-
ik, *adj* quarrelsome

streng, shtreng, *adj* strict;

severe; harsh

Strenge, shtreng-*e*, *f*
severity; strictness

Streß, shtres, *m* stress

streuen, shtroy-en, *v* to
strew, to scatter

Streuselkuchen, shtroy-sel-kook-en, *m* cake with
crumble topping

Strich, shtrik, *m* stroke, line

Strick, shtrick, *m* cord,
rope, line

stricken, shtrick-en, *v* to
knit

Strickwaren, shtrick-vahr-en, *pl* knitwear

striegeln, shtreeg-eln, *v* to
brush

Striemen, shtreem-en, *m*
stripe; weal

Strippe, shtrip-*e*, *f* string;
strap; *fam* phone

Stroh, shtroh, *nt* straw;
–dach, *nt* thatched roof;
–feuer, *nt fig* passing
fancy; **–halm,** *m*
(drinking) straw; **–mann,**
m scarecrow; dummy;
–witwer, *m* grass-widower

Strolch, shtrolk, *m* tramp;
rascal

Strom, shtrom, *m* stream;
current; large river;
–ausfall, *m* power cut;
–bett, *nt* river-bed

strömen, shtrerm-en, *v* to
stream; to flow, to run

Stromschnelle, shtrohm-shnel-*e*, *f* rapid(s)

Strömung, shtrerm-oong, *f*
current; streaming,

flowing

Strophe, shtrohf-*e*, *f* verse;
stanza

strotzen, shtrot-sen, *v* to be
full (of); to be crammed
(with)

Strudel, shtrood-el, *m*
whirlpool, eddy; strudel

strudeln, shtrood-eln, *v* to
swirl; to eddy

Strumpf, shtroomp'f, *m*
stocking; sock; **–band,** *nt*
garter; **–hose,** *f* (pair of)
tights; **–waren,** *pl* hosiery

Strunk, shtroonk, *m* stump,
stalk

struppig, shtroopp-ik, *adj*
dishevelled; scrubby

Stube, shtoob-*e*, *f* room

stubenrein, shtoob-en-rine,
adj house-trained

Stück, shtEEck, *nt* piece;
portion; play; **–chen,** *nt*
little piece

stückeln, shtEEck-eln, *v* to
cut into (small) pieces

stückig, shtEEck-ik, *adj* in
pieces

stückweise, shtEEck-vy-ze,
adv piecemeal

Stückwerk, shtEEck-vairk,
nt patchwork; piece-work

Student, shtoo-dent, *m*
(university) student

Studienplan, shtoo-dee-en-plahn, *m* syllabus

studieren, shtoo-deer-en, *v*
to study

Studium, shtood-ee-oomm,
nt study, studies

Stufe, shtoof-*e*, *f* step;

grade; rung; standard

stufenweise, shtoof-en-vy-ze, *adv* by steps/degrees

Stuhl, shtool, *m* chair;
–gang, *m* bowel
movement

Stulle, shtooll-*e*, *f* piece of
bread and butter;
sandwich

stülpen, shtEElp-en, *v* to
turn up/out/in

stumm, shtoomm, *adj* dumb,
mute

Stummel, shtoomm-el, *m*
stump; fag-end

Stümper, shtEEmp-er, *m*
botcher, bungler, clumsy
person

stümpern, shtEEmp-ern, *v* to
botch, to bungle

stumpf, shtoomp'f, *adj* blunt

Stumpf, shtoomp'f, *m*
stump; fag-end

Stumpfsinn, shtoomp'f-zin,
m stupidity; dullness

Stunde, shtoonn-*de*, *f* hour;
lesson

stunden, shtoonn-den, *v* to
give time for payment

Stundenkilometer,
shtoonn-den-kee-loh-may-ter, *m* kilometers per
hour

stundenlang, shtoonn-den-lahng, *adv* for hours

Stundenplan, shtoonn-den-plahn, *m* timetable

stündlich, shtEEnt-lik, *adj*
hourly

stur, shtoor, *adj* obstinate

Sturm, shtoorm, *m*

storm, gale

stürmen, shtEErm-en, *v* to storm; to charge; to dash

Stürmer, shtEErm-er, *m* forward (sport); *fam* go-getter

stürmisch, shtEErm-ish, *adj* stormy; impetuous

Sturz, shtoorts, *m* (down)fall; crash; collapse; **–bach**, *m* mountain stream

stürzen, shtEErt-sen, *v* to fall; to collapse; to crash; to dash

Stute, shtoot-e, *f* mare

Stütze, shtEEtt-se, *f* support; stay; help

stutzen, shtoott-sen, *v* to trim, to cut short; to hesitate

stützen, shtEEtt-sen, *v* to support; to rely

stutzig, shtoott-sik, *adj* startled; perplexed

Styropor®, shtEEr-oh-pohr, *nt* polystyrene

s.u., *abbr* **siehe unten**, zee-e oont-en, see below

subtrahieren, zoopp-trah-heer-en, *v* to subtract

Subvention, zoopp-vents-yohn, *f* subsidy

subventionieren, zoopp-vents-yohn-eer-en, *v* to subsidize

Suche, zook-e, *f* search

suchen, zook-en, *v* to seek, to look for

Sucht, zookt, *f* mania, passion; addiction

süchtig, zEEk-tik, *adj* addicted

Süd-, zEEt, *pref* South, southern; **–früchte**, *pl* citrus/tropical fruits; **–see**, *f* South Pacific

Sudelei, zood-e-ly, *f* scrawl; graffiti

sudeln, zood-eln, *v* to scrawl; to daub

Süden, zEEd-en, *m* South

südlich, zEEt-lik, *adj* southern, southerly

Suff, zooff, *m fam* drunkenness, drink(ing)

süffig, zEEff-ik, *adj* light and sweet (beverage)

Sühne, zEEn-e, *f* atonement; reconciliation

sühnen, zEEn-en, *v* to expiate; to atone

Summe, zoomm-e, *f* sum, amount; total

summen, zoomm-en, *v* to buzz, to hum

Summer, zoomm-er, *m* buzzer

Sumpf, zoomp'f, *m* bog, swamp, marsh

sumpfig, zoomp-fik, *adj* boggy, marshy

Sünde, zEEnn-de, *f* sin, trespass; **–bock**, *m* scapegoat; **–r**, *m* sinner

sündhaft, zEEnt-hahft, *adj* sinful

sündigen, zEEnn-dig-en, *v* to sin

Supermarkt, zoop-er-mahrkt, *m* supermarket

Suppe, zoopp-e, *f* soup,

broth; **–nfleisch**, *nt* boiled beef; **–nlöffel**, *m* soup spoon

Surfbrett, serf-bret, *nt* surfboard

surfen, serf-en, *v* to surf

surren, zoorr-en, *v* to buzz, to whiz

süß, zEES, *adj* sweet

süßen, zEEs-en, *v* to sweeten

Süßholz, zEEs-holts, *nt* liquorice; soft-soap

Süßigkeit, zEEs-ik-kite, *f* sweets, sweetness

süßlich, zEEs-lik, *adj* (slightly) sweet; sickly, sugary

Süßstoff, zEEs-shtoff, *m* artificial sweetener

Süßwasser, zEEs-vahss-er, *nt* fresh water

Sweatshirt, svet-shert, *nt* sweatshirt

synthetisch, zEEn-tayt-ish, *adj* synthetic

Szene, s'tsayn-e, *f* scene

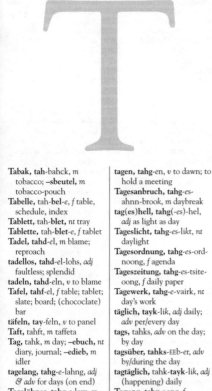

Tabak, tah-bahck, *m* tobacco; **–sbeutel,** *m* tobacco-pouch

Tabelle, tah-bel-e, *f* table, schedule, index

Tablett, tah-blet, *nt* tray

Tablette, tah-blet-e, *f* tablet

Tadel, tahd-el, *m* blame; reproach

tadellos, tahd-el-lohs, *adj* faultless; splendid

tadeln, tahd-eln, *v* to blame

Tafel, tahf-el, *f* table; tablet; slate; board; (chocolate) bar

täfeln, tay-feln, *v* to panel

Taft, tahft, *m* taffeta

Tag, tahk, *m* day; **–ebuch,** *nt* diary, journal; **–edieb,** *m* idler

tagelang, tahg-e-lahng, *adj & adv* for days (on end)

Tagelöhner, tahg-e-lern-er, *m* (day-)labourer

tagen, tahg-en, *v* to dawn; to hold a meeting

Tagesanbruch, tahg-es-ahnn-brook, *m* daybreak

tag(es)hell, tahg(-es)-hel, *adj* as light as day

Tageslicht, tahg-es-likt, *nt* daylight

Tagesordnung, tahg-es-ord-noong, *f* agenda

Tageszeitung, tahg-es-tsite-oong, *f* daily paper

Tagewerk, tahg-e-vairk, *nt* day's work

täglich, tayk-lik, *adj* daily; *adv* per/every day

tags, tahks, *adv* on the day; by day

tagsüber, tahks-EEb-er, *adv* by/during the day

tagtäglich, tahk-tayk-lik, *adj* (happening) daily

Tagung, tahg-oong, *f* session, conference; **–sort,**

m venue

Taille, tahll-ye, *f* waist

Takt, tahckt, *m* rhythm, time; tact

Tal, tahl, *nt* valley, dale

Talg, tahlk, *m* tallow, suet

Talk, tahlk, *m* talc(um)

Talkessel, tahl-kess-el, *m* circular valley

Talsperre, tahl-shpairr-e, *f* dam across valley

talwärts, tahl-vairts, *adv* towards the valley

Tampon, tahmm-pong, *m* tampon

Tändelei, tend-e-ly, *f* dallying, trifling; dawdling

tändeln, tend-eln, *v* to dally, to trifle; to dawdle

Tang, tahng, *m* sea-weed

Tank, tahnck, *m* tank; **–stelle,** *f* petrol station

Tanne, tahnn-e, *f* fir(-tree); **–nbaum,** *m* fir/Christmas tree; **–nnadel,** *f* pine needle; **–nwald,** *m* forest of fir-trees; **–nzapfen,** *m* fir-cone

Tante, tahnt-e, *f* aunt

Tanz, tahnts, *m* dance

tänzeln, tent-seln, *v* to frisk; to amble; to prance

tanzen, tahnt-sen, *v* to dance

Tänzer, tent-ser, *m* dancer

Tanzfläche, tahnts-flaik-e, *f* dance-floor

Tanzlokal, tahnts-loh-kahl, *nt* dance-hall

Tanzstunde, tahnts-shtoonn-de, *f*

dancing-lesson

Tapete, tahpp-**ayt**-e, f
wallpaper

tapezieren, tahpp-e-**tseer**-en, v to wallpaper

Tapezierer, tahpp-e-**tseer**-er, m (interior) decorator

tapfer, tahpp-fer, adj brave, valiant, plucky

Tapferkeit, tahpp-fer-kite, f valour, bravery

tappen, tahpp-en, v to grope; to walk clumsily

Tarnung, tarn-oong, f camouflage

Tasche, tahsh-e, f pocket; bag, pouch; **–buch,** nt paperback (book); **–dieb,** m pickpocket; **–krebs,** m common crab; **–lampe,** f torch; **–messer,** nt penknife; **–tuch,** nt handkerchief

Tasse, tahss-e, f cup

Taste, tahst-e, f (piano etc.) key

tasten, tahst-en, v to grope, to feel one's way

Tat, taht, f deed, action; achievement; **–bestand,** m facts of the matter

Täter, tayt-er, m doer; culprit, perpetrator

tätig, tayt-ik, adj active, busy, engaged (in)

Tätigkeit, tayt-ik-kite, f activity, action; occupation

Tatkraft, taht-krahft, f energy

tätlich, tayt-lik, adj

violent; physical

Tatsache, taht-zahk-e, f fact

tatsächlich, taht-**zaik**-lik, adj & adv actual(ly)

Tatze, tahtt-se, f paw

Tau, tow, nt cable, rope; m dew

taub, towp, adj deaf, hard of hearing; hollow

Taube, towb-e, f pigeon, dove; **–nschlag,** m dovecote

Taubheit, towp-hite, f deafness

taubstumm, towp-shtoom, adj deaf and dumb

tauchen, towk-en, v to dip; to plunge; to dive

Taucher, towk-er, m diver; **–anzug,** m wetsuit

tauen, tow-en, v to thaw; to cover with dew

Taufbecken, towf-beck-en, nt (baptismal) font

Taufe, towf-e, f baptism, christening

taufen, towf-en, v to baptize, to christen

Taufname, towf-nahm-e, m Christian name

Taufpate, towf-paht-e, m godfather

Taufschein, towf-shine, m baptism certificate

taugen, towg-en, v to be of value; to serve a purpose

Taugenichts, towg-e-nikts, m good-for-nothing

tauglich, towk-lik, adj serviceable; fit; useful

Taumel, towm-el, m

giddiness; delirium; frenzy

taumeln, towm-eln, v to totter, to stagger; to tumble

Tausch, towsh, m exchange; barter

tauschen, towsh-en, v to exchange; to barter

täuschen, toysh-en, v to deceive, to trick, to delude

Täuschung, toysh-oong, f delusion; deception

tausend, towz-ent, num thousand

Tauwetter, tow-vet-er, nt thaw

Taxe, tahcks-e, f rate, charge; tax

Taxi, tahcks-ee, nt taxi

taxieren, tahcks-eer-en, v to estimate, to assess

Technik, tek-nick, f technology; technique, skill; **–er,** m engineer; technician

Technologie, tek-noh-loh-gee, f technology

Tee, tay, m tea; (herb) infusion; **–beutel,** m tea bag; **–gebäck,** nt cake, biscuits; **–kanne,** f teapot; **–löffel,** m teaspoon

Teer, tayr, m tar

teeren, tayr-en, v to tar

Teich, ty'k, m pond

Teig, tike, m dough, paste

Teil, tile, m part, share, division

teilen, tile-en, v to share; to divide; to distribute

Teilhaber, tile-hahb-er, m partner

Teilnahme, tile-nahm-e, f sympathy; participation

teilnahmslos, tile-nahms-lohs, adj apathetic

teilnehmen, tile-naym-en, v to take part; to join (in)

teils, tiles, adv partly, in part

Teilung, tile-oong, f division; partition

teilweise, tile-vy-ze, adv partially, partly

Teilzahlung, tile-tsahl-oong, f part-payment

Teilzeitarbeit, tile-tsite-ahr-bite, f part-time work

Teint, teng, m complexion

Telefax, tay-le-fahcks, nt fax

Telefon, tay-le-fohn, nt telephone; **–anruf,** m telephone call; **–nummer,** f telephone number; **–zelle,** f telephone box; **–zentrale,** f switchboard

Teller, tel-er, m plate

Tempel, temp-el, m temple

Temperament, temp-er-ah-ment, nt temperament, liveliness

Tempo, temp-oh, nt time, measure; rhythm; **–limit,** nt speed limit

Tennis, ten-is, nt tennis; **–platz,** m tennis court; **–schläger,** m tennis racket

Teppich, tep-ik, m carpet; **–boden,** m carpeting

Termin, tairm-een, m appointment; (due-)date; hearing (court); term

Terpentin, tairp-en-teen, nt turpentine

Terrain, tair-reng, nt country; ground, plot

Terrasse, tair-ahss-e, f terrace, patio

Terrine, tair-reen-e, f tureen

Terrorist, tair-ohr-ist, m terrorist

Terzett, tairt-set, nt trio

Tesafilm®, tay-sah-film, m Sellotape®

teuer, toy-er, adj dear; expensive

Teu(e)rung, toy(-e)-roong, f rise in prices, inflation

Teufel, toyf-el, m devil

Teufelei, toyf-e-ly, f devilry

teuflisch, toyf-lish, adj devilish

Text, text, m text; words; libretto; wording; **–verarbeitung,** f word processing

Theater, tay-aht-er, nt theatre; stage; **–kasse,** f box-office; **–stück,** nt play

Thema, taym-ah, nt theme, subject; topic

Themse, tem-ze, f Thames

Therapie, tay-rah-pee, f therapy

Thermalbad, tair-mahl-baht, nt (thermal) spa; thermal bath

Thron, trohn, m throne; **–besteigung,** f accession to the throne; **–folger,** m successor to the throne

Thymian, tEEm-ee-ahn, m thyme

tief, teef, adj deep; profound; low

Tiefe, teef-e, f depth; profundity

Tiefebene, teef-ay-be-ne, f plain

Tiefgarage, teef-gah-rah-zhe, f underground car park

Tiefkühlkost, teef-kEEl-kost, f frozen food

Tiefsinn, teef-zin, m thoughtfulness; melancholy

Tiegel, teeg-el, m crucible

Tier, teer, nt animal, beast; **–arzt,** m vet; **–bändiger,** m animal trainer; **–garten,** m zoo

tierisch, teer-ish, adj bestial; of animals

Tierklinik, teer-kleen-ick, f veterinary clinic

Tierkunde, teer-koonn-de, f zoology

Tierpark, teer-park, m zoo

Tierquälerei, teer-kvayl-e-ry, f cruelty to animals

Tierreich, teer-ry'k, nt animal kingdom

Tierwelt, teer-velt, f wildlife

Tiger, teeg-er, m tiger

tilgen, tilg-en, v to destroy; to wipe out; to pay off

Tilgung, tilg-oong, f destruction; discharge (of debts)

Tinte, tin-te, f ink; **–nfaß,** nt inkstand; **–nfisch,** m cuttlefish, octopus; **–nklecks,** m ink-stain

tippen, tip-en, *v* to touch lightly; to type; to bet

Tisch, tish, *m* table; **–decke,** *f* table-cloth; **–gebet,** *nt* grace before/after meal; **–ler,** *m* joiner; **–tennis,** *nt* table tennis; **–tuch,** *nt* table-cloth; **–zeit,** *f* dinner-time

Titel, teet-el, *m* title; **–bild,** *nt* frontispiece

titulieren, tit-oo-**leer**-en, *v* to title, to style

toben, toh-ben, *v* to rage, to rave

Tobsucht, tohp-zookt, *f* frenzy

Tochter, tohk-ter, *f* daughter

töchterlich, terk-ter-lik, *adj* like a daughter

Tod, toht, *m* death

Todesstrafe, tohd-es-shtrahf-e, *f* capital punishment

Todfeind, toht-fine't, *m* mortal enemy

tödlich, tert-lik, *adj* mortal, fatal, deadly

todschick, toht-shick, *adj* flash, classy

Toilette, toy-**let**-e, *f* toilet; **–npapier,** *nt* toilet paper; **–ntisch,** *m* dressing table

toll, tol, *adj* foolish, mad; terrific

Tolle, tol-e, *f* head-dress; crest, tuft

tollen, tol-en, *v* to frolic

Tollheit, tol-hite, *f* madness; folly

tollkühn, tol-kEEn, *adj*

rash, foolhardy

Tollwut, tol-vooht, *f* hydrophobia, rabies

Tolpatsch, tol-pahtsh, *m* clumsy person

Tölpel, terl-pel, *m* fool

tölpelhaft, terl-pel-hahft, *adj* clumsy, awkward

Ton, tohn, *m* clay; tone, sound, note

tonangebend, tohn-ahnn-gayb-ent, *adj* leading

Tonart, tohn-art, *f* pitch; *mus* key

Tonband, tohn-bahnt, *nt* (magnetic) tape; **–gerät,** *nt* tape recorder

tönen, tern-en, *v* to sound, to ring

tönern, tern-ern, *adj* made of clay; clayey

Tonfall, tohn-fahll, *m* modulation

Tonkunst, tohn-koonst, *f* music

Tonleiter, tohn-ly-ter, *f mus* scale

Tonne, ton-e, *f* ton; tun, butt, barrel

Topf, top'f, *m* pot; vessel; saucepan; jug, jar

Töpfer, terpp-fer, *m* potter

Töpferei, terpp-fer-**i,** *f* pottery

töpfern, terpp-fern, *v* to make pottery

Tor, tohr, *nt* gate(way); *m* fool, simpleton

Torf, torf, *m* peat, turf

Torheit, tohr-hite, *f* folly, foolishness

Torhüter, tohr-hEEt-er, *m* gate-keeper; goalkeeper

töricht, terr-ikt, *adj* foolish; silly

torkeln, tork-eln, *v* to reel

Tornister, tor-**nist**-er, *m* satchel, knapsack, pack

Torte, tort-e, *f* tart, cake

Torwart, tohr-vart, *m* goalkeeper

Torweg, tohr-vayk, *m* gateway, archway

tosen, tohz-en, *v* to roar, to howl; to crash

tot, toht, *adj* dead, deceased

Tote(r), toht-e(r), *m & f,* dead person, corpse

töten, tert-en, *v* to kill

totenähnlich, toht-en-ayn-lik, *adj* deathlike

totenblaß, toht-en-blahss, *adj* deathly pale

Totenfeier, toht-en-fy-er, *f* funeral (ceremony)

Totengräber, toht-en-grayb-er, *m* grave-digger, sexton

Totengruft, toht-en-grooft, *f* tomb

Totenhemd, toht-en-hemt, *nt* shroud

Totenkopf, toht-en-kop'f, *m* skull

totenstill, toht-en-shtil, *adj* deathly still/quiet

totfahren, toht-fahr-en, *v* to run over

totlachen (sich), toht-lahk-en (zik), *v* to die laughing

totschießen, toht-shees-en, *v* to shoot dead

Totschlag, toht-shlahk, *m*

manslaughter

totschlagen, toht-shlahg-en, *v* to kill (also *fig*)

totschweigen, toht-shvy-gen, *v* to suppress (news, facts etc.)

Tötung, tert-oong, *f* manslaughter, killing

Trab, trahp, *m* trot

traben, trahb-en, *v* to trot

Tracht, trahkt, *f* dress, fashion; load

trachten, trahkt-en, *v* to strive (for)

Tragbahre, trahk-bahr-e, *f* litter, stretcher

tragbar, trahk-bar, *adj* portable; acceptable

träge, trayg-e, *adj* indolent, lazy; sleepy

tragen, trahg-en, *v* to carry, to bear, to support; to wear

Träger, trayg-er, *m* carrier; porter; girder; bearer

Tragetasche, trahg-e-tahsh-e, *f* carrier bag

Trägheit, trayk-hite, *f* laziness, indolence

Tragödie, trah-**gerd**-ye, *f* tragedy

traktieren, trahck-**teer**-en, *v* to maltreat

Traktor, trahck-tohr, *m* tractor

trällern, trel-ern, *v* to hum, to sing

trampeln, trahmm-peln, *v* to trample, to stamp

Trampeltier, trahmm-pel-teer, *nt* camel; *fam* clumsy

person

trampen, tramp-en, *v* to hitch-hike

Tran, trahn, *m* blubber, fish-oil

tranchieren, trahng-**sheer**-en, *v* to carve (meat)

Träne, train-e, *f* tear

tränen, train-en, *v* to run (with tears)

tranig, trahn-ik, *adj* like oil; sluggish

Trank, trahnk, *m* drink, beverage

tränken, treng-ken, *v* to give to drink; to soak, to drench

Transpiration, trahnn-spee-rahts-**yohn,** *f* perspiration

transpirieren, trahnn-spee-**reer**-en, *v* to perspire

Traube, trowb-e, *f* bunch of grapes

trauen, trow-en, *v* to trust; to rely; to marry

Trauer, trow-er, *f* mourning, sorrow, grief

trauern, trow-ern, *v* to mourn, to grieve

Trauerspiel, trow-er-shpeel, *nt* tragedy

Trauerweide, trow-er-vy-de, *f* weeping-willow

Traufe, trowf-e, *f* gutter

träufeln, troyf-eln, *v* to drip, to drop, to trickle

Traum, trowm, *m* dream

Trauma, trowm-ah, *nt* trauma

träumen, troym-en, *v* to dream

traurig, trow-rik, *adj* sad

Trauring, trow-ring, *m* wedding-ring

Trauschein, trow-shine, *m* marriage certificate

traut, trowt, *adj* beloved; intimate

Trauung, trow-oong, *f* wedding(-ceremony)

Treff, tref, *m* meeting-point

treffen, tref-en, *v* to hit (the mark), to strike; to meet

Treffer, tref-er, *m* good hit; goal

trefflich, tref-lik, *adj* excellent

Treffpunkt, tref-poonkt, *m* meeting place

treiben, try-ben, *v* to drive, to set in motion

Treibhaus, tripe-hows, *nt* conservatory, hot-house

Treibholz, tripe-holts, *nt* drift-wood

Treibstoff, tripe-shtof, *m* fuel

trennbar, tren-bar, *adj* separable

trennen, tren-en, *v* to separate, to detach

treppab, trep-**ahpp,** *adv* downstairs

treppauf, trep-**owf,** *adv* upstairs

Treppe, trep-e, *f* stairs, staircase; **–ngeländer,** *nt* banister(-rail)

treten, trayt-en, *v* to tread, to step; to kick

treu, troy, *adj* faithful, true; sincere

Treue, troy-e, f faithfulness; loyalty

treuherzig, troy-hairt-sik, adj frank; true-hearted

Tribüne, tree-bEEn-e, f platform; grandstand

Trichter, trik-ter, m funnel

Trieb, treep, m driving; momentum; force; impulse; shoot

Triebfeder, treep-fayd-er, f main spring; fig main motive

triefen, treef-en, v to drip; to be dripping

triftig, trift-ik, adj well-founded, cogent

Trikot, trick-oh, nt (cotton) jersey; (sports) shirt

trillern, tril-ern, v to trill, to warble

Trimester, tree-mest-er, nt (three month) term

trinken, trink-en, v to drink

Trinkgeld, trink-gelt, nt gratuity, tip

Trinkhalle, trink-hahll-e, f refreshment kiosk

Trinkwasser, trink-vahss-er, nt drinking water

trippeln, trip-eln, v to trip along

Tritt, trit, m tread; step; pace; kick; **–brett**, nt running-board; **–leiter**, f step-ladder

trocken, trock-en, adj dry; parched, arid

trocknen, trock-nen, v to dry

Trödel, trerd-el, m

lumber, rubbish

trödeln, trerd-eln, v to dawdle, to loiter

Trog, trohk, m trough

Trommel, trom-el, f drum; **–fell**, nt ear-drum; drum skin

trommeln, trom-eln, v to drum

Trompete, trom-payt-e, f trumpet

trompeten, trom-payt-en, v to (sound the) trumpet

Tropf, trop'f, m simpleton; wretch

tröpfeln, trerp-feln, v to fall in drops, to trickle

Tropfen, trop-fen, m drop

tropfen, trop-fen, v to drip, to trickle

Trost, trohst, m consolation, solace

trösten, trerst-en, v to console, to comfort

trostlos, trohst-lohs, adj bleak

Trottel, trot-el, m fam fool

Trottoir, trohtt-wahr, nt pavement

Trotz, trots, m stubbornness; defiance

trotz, trots, prep in spite of; **–dem**, adv nevertheless

trotzen, trots-en, v to defy; to sulk

trotzig, trots-ik, adj defiant, obstinate; haughty

trüb(e), trEEp (trEEb-e), adj gloomy, muddy, murky; sad

trüben, trEEb-en, v to dim;

to trouble; to make muddy

Trübsal, trEEp-zahl, f misery; affliction

trübselig, trEEp-zayl-ik, adj melancholy, sad

Trübsinn, trEEp-zin, m melancholy, sadness

Trug, troohk, m delusion; deception

trügen, trEEg-en, v to deceive, to delude

trügerisch, trEEg-er-ish, adj deceptive, deceitful

Trugschluß, troohk-shlooss, m false conclusion

Truhe, troo-e, f chest, trunk

Trümmer, trEEmm-er, pl debris, rubbish

Trumpf, troomp'f, m trump(s)

Trunk, troonk, m drink; draught; drunkenness

trunken, troonk-en, adj drunk, intoxicated

Trunkenbold, troonk-en-bolt, m drunkard

Trunkenheit, troonk-en-hite, f drunkenness

Trunksucht, troonk-zookt, f dipsomania, alcoholism

Truthahn, trooht-hahn, m turkey-cock

Tschechien, tshek-ee-en, nt Czech Republic

T-Shirt, tee-shirt, nt T-shirt

tschüs, tshEES, interj bye

Tuch, took, nt cloth, stuff, material; scarf; towel

tüchtig, tEEk-tik, adj (cap)able, efficient; thorough

Tücke, tEEck-e, *f* spite, malice; cunning

tückisch, tEEck-ish, *adj* spiteful; crafty

Tugend, toog-ent, *f* virtue

tugendhaft, toog-ent-hahft, *adj* virtuous

Tulpe, toolp-e, *f* tulip

tummeln (sich), toomm-eln (*zik*), *v* to stir, to exercise; to wheel

Tümpel, tEEmp-el, *m* pool, puddle

tun, toon, *v* to do, to make, to perform, to act

tünchen, tEEn-ken, *v* to whitewash

Tunke, toong-ke, *f* gravy

tunken, toong-ken, *v* to dip, to soak

tunlich, toon-lik, *adj* feasible; expedient; practical

tunlichst, toon-likst, *adv* if possible

Tüpfelchen, tEEpp-fel-ken, *nt* dot, point

Tupfen, toopp-fen, *m* dot, spot

tupfen, toopp-fen, *v* to touch lightly; to dab; to spot

Türkei, tEEr-ky, *f* Turkey

Tür(e), tEEr(-e), *f* door

Türkis, tEEr-kees, *m* turquoise

türkisch, tEErk-ish, *adj* Turkish

Türklinke, tEEr-kling-ke, *f* door-handle

Turm, toorm, *m* tower; castle

türmen, tEErm-en, *v* to tower; to pile up; to run away

turnen, toorn-en, *v* to do gymnastics

Turner, toorn-er, *m* gymnast

Turnhalle, toorn-hahll-e, *f* gym

Turnier, toorn-eer, *nt* tournament

Turnschuhe, toorn-shoo-e, *pl* trainers

Turnverein, toorn-fair-ine, *m* gymnastic club

Türschwelle, tEEr-shvel-e, *f* threshold

Tusch, toosh, *m* flourish (of trumpets)

Tusche, toosh-e, *f* Indian ink

tuschen, toosh-en, *v* to draw with Indian ink

tuscheln, toosh-eln, *v* to whisper

Tuschkasten, toosh-kahst-en, *m* paintbox

Tüte, tEEt-e, *f* paper-bag

TÜV, tEEf, *m abbr* Technischer Überwachungsverein, MOT

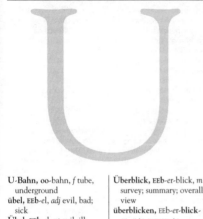

U-Bahn, oo-bahn, *f* tube, underground

übel, EEb-el, *adj* evil, bad; sick

Übel, EEb-el, *nt* evil, ill; malady; **–keit,** *f* nausea, (feeling of) sickness

übelnehmen, EEb-el-naym-en, *v* to take amiss

üben, EEb-en, *v* to practise; to exercise

über, EEb-er, *prep* over, above; about; via

überall, EEb-er-ahll, *adv* everywhere

überarbeiten, EEb-er-arb-ite-en, *v* to overwork; to revise

überaus, EEb-er-ows, *adv* extremely

überbieten, EEb-er-beet-en, *v* to outbid; to surpass

Überbleibsel, EEb-er-blipe-sel, *nt* remnant, remains

Überblick, EEb-er-blick, *m* survey; summary; overall view

überblicken, EEb-er-blick-en, *v* to survey; to overlook

überbringen, EEb-er-bring-en, *v* to convey, to deliver

überdies, EEb-er-dees, *adv* moreover

Überdruß, EEb-er-drooss, *m* weariness; surfeit

überdrüssig, EEb-er-drEEss-ik, *adj* weary of

überdurchschnittlich, EEb-er-doork-shnit-lik, *adj* above average; *adv* exceptionally

übereilen, EEb-er-ile-en, *v* to precipitate; to hurry too much

übereinander, EEb-er-ine-ahnn-der, *adv* one above the other

Übereinkommen, Übereinkunft, EEb-er-ine-kom-en, *nt* –koonft, *f* agreement, understanding

übereinstimmen, EEb-er-ine-shtim-en, *v* to agree

überfahren, EEb-er-fahr-en, *v* to run over; to pass over

Überfahrt, EEb-er-fahrt, *f* crossing

Überfall, EEb-er-fahll, *m* (sudden) attack, raid

überfallen, EEb-er-fahll-en, *v* to attack suddenly

überfällig, EEb-er-fel-ik, *adj* overdue

Überfluß, EEb-er-flooss, *m* abundance, plenty

überflüssig, EEb-er-flEEss-ik, *adj* superfluous, unnecessary; redundant

überfordern, EEb-er-ford-ern, *v* to ask too much; to overstrain

überführen, EEb-er-fEEr-en, *v* to transfer; to convict

überfüllen, EEb-er-fEEll-en, *v* to overcrowd

Übergabe, EEb-er-gahb-e, *f* handing over; surrender

Übergang, EEb-er-gahng, *m* crossing; transition

übergeben, EEb-er-gayb-en, *v* to hand over; to surrender; **sich –,** *v* to vomit

übergehen, EEb-er-gay-en, *v* to pass over; to omit

übergreifen, EEb-er-gry-fen, *v* to overlap; to encroach on

überhandnehmen, EEb-er-hahnnt-naym-en, v to gain ground

überhängen, EEb-er-heng-en, v to overhang

überhäufen, EEb-er-hoyf-en, v to overburden; to overwhelm

überhaupt, EEb-er-howpt, adv generally; actually; – **nicht,** not at all

überheblich, EEb-er-heb-lik, adj arrogant

überholen, EEb-er-hohl-en, v to overtake; to overhaul

überhören, EEb-er-her-en, v not to hear; to ignore

überkochen, EEb-er-kohk-en, v to boil over

überlassen, EEb-er-lahss-en, v to leave over; to relinquish

überlaufen, EEb-er-lowf-en, v to run over; to desert

überleben, EEb-er-layb-en, v to survive; to outlive

überlegen, EEb-er-layg-en, v to think over; adj superior

Überlegenheit, EEb-er-layg-en-hite, f superiority

Überlegung, EEb-er-layg-oong, f consideration; deliberation

überliefern, EEb-er-leef-ern, v to deliver; to hand down

Überlieferung, EEb-er-leef-er-oong, f tradition

überlisten, EEb-er-list-en, v to outwit; to dupe

überm, EEb-erm, = **über dem,** over the

Übermacht, EEb-er-mahkt, f superior strength

übermannen, EEb-er-mahnn-en, v to overpower

übermäßig, EEb-er-mace-ik, adj immoderate; profuse

Übermensch, EEb-er-mensh, m superman

übermitteln, EEb-er-mit-eln, v to transmit

übermorgen, EEb-er-morg-en, adv the day after tomorrow

Übermut, EEb-er-moot, m high spirits; impertinence

übermütig, EEb-er-mEEt-ik, adj high spirited; impertinent

übernachten, EEb-er-nahk-ten, v to pass the night

Übernachtung, EEb-er-nahkt-oong, f overnight stay

Übernahme, EEb-er-nahm-e, f taking over

übernehmen, EEb-er-naym-en, v to take over; to take on; **sich –,** v to take on too much, to overdo it

überqueren, EEb-er-kvayr-en, v to cross

überragen, EEb-er-rahg-en, v to tower above; to project, to protrude

überraschen, EEb-er-rahsh-en, v to surprise

überreden, EEb-er-rayd-en, v to persuade

überreichen, EEb-er-ry-ken, v to hand over

Überrest, EEb-er-rest, m remnant, remains; ruin

überrumpeln, EEb-er-roomp-eln, v to take by surprise

übers, EEb-ers, = **über das,** over the

überschätzen, EEb-er-shet-sen, v to over-estimate

überschreiten, EEb-er-shry-ten, v to overstep; to step over

Überschrift, EEb-er-shrift, f heading, title

Überschuß, EEb-er-shooss, m surplus; balance

überschüssig, EEb-er-shEEss-ik, adj surplus; left over

überschwemmen, EEb-er-shvem-en, v to flood; to overflow

Überschwemmung, EEb-er-shvem-oong, f flood

überschwenglich, EEb-er-shveng-lik, adj gushing; excessive

übersehen, EEb-er-say-en, v to overlook; to look over

übersenden, EEb-er-send-en, v to send; to transmit

übersetzen, EEb-er-set-sen, v to translate; EEb-er-sets-en, v to cross over

Übersicht, EEb-er-zikt, f survey; summary, sketch

übersichtlich, EEb-er-zikt-lik, adj clear

übersiedeln, EEb-er-zeed-eln, v to emigrate

überspringen, EEb-er-shpring-en, v to jump over; fig to skip

überstehen, EEb-er-shtay-en,

v to overcome; to endure

Überstunden, EEb-er-shtoond-en, *pl* overtime

überstürzen, EEb-er-**shtEErt**-sen, *v* to precipitate

übertragen, EEb-er-**trahg**-en, *v* to carry forward; to transfer; to broadcast

übertreffen, EEb-er-**tref**-en, *v* to excel, to eclipse

übertreiben, EEb-er-**try**-ben, *v* to exaggerate

übertreten, EEb-er-**trayt**-en, *v* to transgress; EEb-er-**trayt**-en, *v* to overstep; to convert

übertrieben, EEb-er-**treeb**-en, *adj* exaggerated

übervorteilen, EEb-er-**fohr**-tile-en, *v* to take advantage

überwachen, EEb-er-**vahk**-en, *v* to watch over; to superintend

überwältigen, EEb-er-**velt**-ig-en, *v* to overwhelm

überweisen, EEb-er-**vy**-zen, *v* to transfer; to refer (a patient)

überwiegen, EEb-er-**veeg**-en, *v* to outweigh; to prevail

überwinden, EEb-er-**vin**-den, *v* to overcome; to conquer

überwintern, EEb-er-**vint**-ern, *v* to hibernate

überwuchern, EEb-er-**voohk**-ern, *v* to overgrow

überzeugen, EEb-er-**tsoyg**-en, *v* to convince

Überzeugung, EEb-er-**tsoyg**-oong, *f* conviction

persuasion

überziehen, EEb-er-tsee-en, *v* to cover; to pull over; EEb-er-**tsee**-en, *v* to overdraw (account)

Überziehungskredit, EEb-er-**tsee**-oongs-kray-dit, *m* overdraft provision

Überzug, EEb-er-**tsook**, *m* cover, case, pillow-case; coating

üblich, EEb-lik, *adj* usual, customary

U-Boot, oo-boht, *nt abbr* **Unterseeboot,** U-boat

übrig, EEb-rik, *adj* over, left over, remaining

übrigens, EEb-rig-ens, *adv* by the way; moreover

Übung, EEb-oong, *f* exercise, practice

Ufer, oof-er, *nt* bank, beach, shore

Uhr, oor, *f* clock; watch; o'clock; **–macher,** *m* watchmaker; **im –zeigersinn,** *adv* clockwise; **gegen den –zeigersinn,** *adv* anti-clockwise; **–zeit,** *f* time of day

Ulk, oolk, *m* lark, practical joke

ulkig, oolk-ik, *adj* funny

Ulme, oolm-e, *f* elm(-tree)

Ultraschall, ool-trah-shahll, *m* ultrasound

um, oomm, *prep* (a)round; about; at; for; by; *conj* in order to

umändern, oomm-end-ern,

v to alter; to change

umarmen, oomm-**arm**-en, *v* to embrace

Umbau, oomm-bow, *m* reconstruction; rebuilding; conversion

umbauen, oomm-bow-en, *v* to rebuild

umbinden, oomm-bin-den, *v* to tie round; to put on

umblicken (sich), oomm-blick-en (zik), *v* to look round

umbringen, oomm-bring-en, *v* to kill

umbuchen, oomm-book-en, *v* to change one's booking

umdrehen, oomm-dray-en, *v* to turn round/over

umfallen, oomm-fahll-en, *v* to fall over

Umfang, oomm-fahng, *m* size, circumference; extent

umfangreich, oomm-fahng-rike, *adj* voluminous; extensive

umfassen, oomm-**fahss**-en, *v* to embrace, to clasp

Umfrage, oomm-frahg-e, *f* survey, poll

Umgang, oomm-gahng, *m* contact, dealings, relations, company

umgänglich, oomm-geng-lik, *adj* easy to get on with

Umgangssprache, oomm-gahngs-shprahk-e, *f* colloquial language

umgeben, oomm-gayb-en, *v* to surround

Umgebung, oomm-gayboong, f neighbourhood, surroundings

Umgegend, oomm-gayg-ent, f environs, vicinity

umgehen, oomm-**gay**-en, v to evade; to circumvent; **oomm**-gay-en, v to haunt; to have dealings (with)

Umgehungsstraße, oomm-**gay**-oongs-shtrahs-e, f bypass

umgekehrt, oomm-ge-kairt, adj contrary, reverse; adv vice versa

umgraben, oomm-grahb-en, v to dig (up)

umher, oomm-**hair**, adv around; on every side

umhüllen, oomm-**hEEll**-en, v to wrap; to veil

umkehren, oomm-kair-en, v to turn back/round

umkippen, oomm-kip-en, v to tip over, to upset

umklammern, oomm-**klahmm**-ern, v to clasp

Umkleide(raum), oomm-**kly**-de(-rowm), m & f, changing room

umkleiden (sich), oomm-**kly**-den (zik), v to change (clothes)

umkommen, oomm-**komm**-en, v to perish; to die

Umkreis, oomm-krice, m circumference; vicinity

Umlauf, oomm-lowf, m circulation; rotation; **–bahn**, f orbit

Umlaut, oomm-lowt, m umlaut (¨)

Umleitung, oomm-lite-oong, f (traffic) diversion

umrahmen, oomm-**rahm**-en, v to frame

Umrechnungskurs, oomm-rek-noongs-koors, m exchange rate

umringen, oomm-**ring**-en, v to surround

Umriß, oomm-riss, m outline; sketch

umrühren, oomm-**rEEr**-en, v to stir

ums, oomms, = um das, round the; for the

Umsatz, oomm-zahts, m turnover

Umschau, oomm-show, f look(ing) out

umschauen (sich), oomm-**show**-en (zik), v to look round

Umschlag, oomm-shlahk, m envelope, wrapper; poultice; change; comm turnover

umschließen, oomm-**shlees**-en, v to enclose

umschnallen, oomm-**shnahll**-en, v to buckle on

umschulen, oomm-**shool**-en, v to re-train

umschütten, oomm-**shEEtt**-en, v to spill, to overturn; to pour out

Umschwung, oomm-**shvoong**, m about-turn, sudden change

umsehen (sich), oomm-**zay**-en (zik), v to look round/about

umsetzen, oomm-zet-sen, v to transplant; to transpose; to convert; **sich –,** v to change places

umsichtig, oomm-zik-tik, adj circumspect, prudent

umsomehr, oomm-zoh-**mair**, adv all the more

umsonst, oomm-zonst, adv in vain; free, gratis

Umstand, oomm-shtahnt, m circumstance

umständlich, oomm-shtent-lik, adj fussy; complicated; troublesome

umsteigen, oomm-shty-gen, v to change (trains etc.)

umstoßen, oomm-shtohs-en, v to knock over; to overthrow; to cancel

Umsturz, oomm-shtoorts, m overthrow, crash

umtauschen, oomm-towsh-en, v to (ex)change

umwälzen, oomm-velt-sen, v to roll over; to overthrow; to revolutionize

umwechseln, oomm-veck-seln, v to (ex)change

Umweg, oomm-vayk, m roundabout way

Umwelt, oomm-velt, f environment

umweltbewußt, oomm-velt-be-voost, adj with concern for the environment

umweltfreundlich, oomm-velt-froynt-lik, adj environmentally friendly

umweltschädlich, oomm-

velt-shait-lik, *adj* harmful to the environment

Umweltschutz, oomm-velt-shoots, *m* environmental protection

Umweltschützer, oomm-velt-shEEts-er, *m* environmentalist

Umweltverschmutzung, oomm-velt-fair-shmoots-oong, *f* (environmental) pollution

umwenden, oomm-vend-en, *v* to turn over/round

umwerfen, oomm-vairf-en, *v* to knock over, to overturn, to upset

umzäunen, oomm-tsoyn-en, *v* to fence round/in

umziehen, oomm-tsee-en, *v* to move (house); **sich –,** *v* to change (clothes)

umzingeln, oomm-tsing-eln, *v* to surround

Umzug, oomm-tsook, *m* removal; procession

unabhängig, oonn-ahp-heng-ik, *adj* independent

unangenehm, oonn-ahnn-ge-naym, *adj* unpleasant

Unannehmlichkeit, oonn-ahnn-naym-lik-kite, *f* unpleasantness, inconvenience

unanständig, oonn-ahnn-shtend-ik, *adj* indecent

unartig, oonn-art-ik, *adj* naughty

unausstehlich, oonn-owss-shtay-lik, *adj* intolerable

unbedingt, oonn-be-dingt, *adj* unconditional; absolute; *adv* absolutely

unbeholfen, oonn-be-hol-fen, *adj* awkward, clumsy

unbeliebt, oonn-be-leept, *adj* unpopular

unberufen, oonn-be-roof-en, *adj* unauthorized; *interj* touch wood

unbesonnen, oonn-be-zon-en, *adj* careless; indiscreet

unbeweglich, oonn-be-vayk-lik, *adj* immobile; fixed

unbewußt, oonn-be-voost, *adj* unaware; unconscious

unbrauchbar, oonn-browk-bar, *adj* unusable

und, oont, *conj* and

Undank, oonn-dahnk, *m* ingratitude

undankbar, oonn-dahnk-bar, *adj* ungrateful

undenkbar, oonn-**denk**-bar, *adj* unthinkable; inconceivable

undeutlich, oonn-doyt-lik, *adj* indistinct

Unding, oonn-ding, *nt* absurdity

unduldsam, oonn-doolt-zahm, *adj* intolerant

undurchdringlich, oonn-doork-**dring**-lik, *adj* impenetrable

uneben, oonn-ayb-en, *adj* uneven, rough (ground)

unecht, oonn-ekt, *adj* spurious, counterfeit, sham

unehelich, oonn-ay-e-lik,

adj illegitimate

unehrlich, oonn-ayr-lik, *adj* dishonest

unendlich, oonn-ent-lik, *adj* infinite, endless

unentbehrlich, oonn-ent-bair-lik, *adj* indispensable

unentgeltlich, oonn-ent-gelt-lik, *adj* free (of charge)

unerfahren, oonn-air-fahr-en, *adj* inexperienced

unerhört, oonn-air-hert, *adj* unheard of

unermeßlich, oonn-air-mess-lik, *adj* immeasurable

unermüdlich, oonn-air-mEEt-lik, *adj* untiring

unerreicht, oonn-air-ry'kt, *adj* unequalled, unrivalled

unerschrocken, oonn-air-shrock-en, *adj* dauntless

unerwünscht, oonn-air-vEEnsht, *adj* undesired, unwelcome

Unfall, oonn-fahll, *m* accident, mishap

unfaßbar, oonn-**fahss**-bar, *adj* inconceivable

unfehlbar, oonn-**fayl**-bar, *adj* infallible

unförmig, oonn-ferm-ik, *adj* shapeless; monstrous

unfrankiert, oonn-frahng-keert, *adj* unstamped, not prepaid

unfreundlich, oonn-froynt-lik, *adj* unfriendly, unkind

Unfrieden, oonn-freed-en, *m* discord, strife

Unfug, oonn-fook, *m*

offence; mischief; wrong

Ungar, oonn-gar, *m* Hungarian (person)

Ungarn, oong-garn, *nt* Hungary

ungeachtet, oonn-ge-ahk-tet, *prep* irrespective of

ungebildet, oonn-ge-bild-et, *adj* uneducated

ungebührlich, oonn-ge-bEEr-lik, *adj* improper; undue

ungebunden, oonn-ge-boond-en, *adj* unattached

Ungeduld, oonn-ge-doolt, *f* impatience

ungeduldig, oonn-ge-dool-dik, *adj* impatient

ungeeignet, oonn-ge-ike-net, *adj* unsuitable

ungefähr, oonn-ge-fair, *adj* approximate; *adv* about, approximately

Ungeheuer, oonn-ge-hoy-er, *nt* monster

ungeheuer(lich), oonn-ge-hoy-er(-lik), *adj* huge, immense; monstrous

ungelegen, oonn-ge-layg-en, *adj* inopportune, inconvenient

ungemein, oonn-ge-mine, *adj* uncommon; extraordinary

ungemütlich, oonn-ge-mEEt-lik, *adj* uncomfortable; unsociable

ungeniert, oonn-zhay-neert, *adj* unceremonious, unrestrained

ungenießbar, oonn-ge-nees-bar, *adj* uneatable; undrinkable

ungerade, oonn-ge-rahd-e, *adj* uneven; odd (numbers); not straight

ungeraten, oonn-ge-raht-en, *adj* spoilt

ungerecht, oonn-ge-rekt, *adj* unjust, unfair

ungern, oonn-gairn, *adv* unwillingly, reluctantly

ungeschickt, oonn-ge-shickt, *adj* clumsy, awkward

ungeschliffen, oonn-ge-shlif-en, *adj* uncut; uncouth

ungestüm, oonn-ge-shtEEm, *adj* impetuous; hot-headed

Ungetüm, oonn-ge-tEEm, *nt* monster

ungewohnt, oonn-ge-vohnt, *adj* unaccustomed

Ungeziefer, oonn-ge-tseef-er, *nt* vermin

ungezogen, oonn-ge-tsohg-en, *adj* naughty; ill-mannered

ungezwungen, oonn-ge-tsvoong-en, *adj* unconstrained

Unglaube, oonn-glowb-e, *m* incredulity; lack of faith

ungläubig, oonn-gloyb-ik, *adj* disbelieving

unglaublich, oonn-glowp-lik, *adj* incredible, beyond belief

ungleich, oonn-gly'k, *adj* uneven, odd; varying, changeable; unequal

Unglück, oonn-glEEck, *nt* misfortune; bad luck; accident, disaster

unglücklich, oonn-glEEck-lik, *adj* unhappy; unfortunate; **–erweise,** *adv* unfortunately

unglückselig, oonn-glEEck-zayl-ik, *adj* disastrous

Unglücksfall, oonn-glEEcks-fahll, *m* misfortune, disaster, accident

Ungnade, oonn-g'nahd-e, *f* disfavour; disgrace

ungnädig, oonn-g'nayd-ik, *adj* ungracious; ill-humoured

ungünstig, oonn-gEEnst-ik, *adj* unfavourable

Unheil, oonn-hile, *nt* evil, trouble

unheimlich, oonn-hime-lik, *adj* uncanny, weird; sinister

Universität, oon-ee-vair-zee-tayt, *f* university

unkenntlich, oonn-kent-lik, *adj* unrecognizable

Unkenntnis, oonn-kent-niss, *f* ignorance

unklug, oonn-klook, *adj* unwise, imprudent

Unkosten, oonn-kost-en, *pl* expense(s)

Unkraut, oonn-krowt, *nt* weed(s)

unlängst, oonn-lengst, *adv* recently, not long since

unlauter, oonn-lowt-er, *adj* impure, unfair

unleserlich, oonn-lay-zer-

lik, *adj* illegible

Unmasse, oonn-mahss-*e*, *f* immense number/quantity

unmäßig, oonn-mace-ik, *adj* excessive; immoderate

Unmenge, oonn-meng-*e*, *f* huge number

Unmensch, oonn-mensh, *m* inhuman creature

unmenschlich, oonn-mensh-lik, *adj* inhuman, barbarous

unmittelbar, oonn-mit-el-bar, *adj & adv* immediate(ly); direct(ly)

unnötig, oonn-nert-ik, *adj* unnecessary

unnütz, oonn-nEEts, *adj* useless; idle; pointless

unordentlich, oonn-ord-ent-lik, *adj* messy, untidy

Unordnung, oonn-ort-noong, *f* disorder

unparteiisch, oonn-part-i-ish, *adj* impartial, unbiassed

unpassend, oonn-pahss-ent, *adj* unsuitable; improper

unpäßlich, oonn-pess-lik, *adj* indisposed, unwell

Unrat, oonn-raht, *m* rubbish; refuse

Unrecht, oonn-rekt, *nt* wrong; injury

unrecht, oonn-rekt, *adj* wrong; incorrect; unfair; **–mäßig**, *adj* illegal; illegitimate

unregelmäßig, oonn-rayg-el-mace-ik, *adj* irregular

unrein, oonn-rine, *adj* impure; unclean

unrichtig, oonn-rik-tik, *adj* wrong, incorrect

Unruhe, oonn-roo-*e*, *f* unrest, anxiety; commotion

unruhig, oonn-roo-ik, *adj* uneasy; alarmed; restless

uns, oons, *pron (accusative & dative)* us, to us

unsagbar, oonn-zahk-bar, *adj* unspeakable; unutterable

unsauber, oonn-zowb-er, *adj* unclean, impure

unschädlich, oonn-shayt-lik, *adj* harmless

unscheinbar, oonn-shine-bar, *adj* insignificant; plain

Unschuld, oonn-shoolt, *f* innocence; purity (of heart)

unschuldig, oonn-shoold-ik, *adj* innocent, not guilty

unser, unsere(r/s), oonn-zer, oonn-ze-re(r/s), *adj* our; *pron* ours

unsereiner, oonn-zer-ine-er, *pron* one of our kind

unsichtbar, oonn-zikt-bar, *adj* invisible

Unsinn, oonn-zin, *m* nonsense

unsinnig, oonn-zin-ik, *adj* nonsensical, absurd

unsozial, oonn-zo-tsee-ahl, *adj* anti-social

unsterblich, oonn-shtairp-lik, *adj* immortal

Unsterblichkeit, oonn-stairp-lik-kite, *f* immortality

unstet, oonn-shtayt, *adj* unstable, inconstant

Unsumme, oonn-zoomm-*e*, *f* immense sum

untauglich, oonn-towk-lik, *adj* unfit; unsuitable

unten, oonn-ten, *adv* below; underneath; down(stairs)

unter, oonn-ter, *prep* under(neath), beneath, below; among

Unterarm, oonn-ter-arm, *m* forearm

unterbleiben, oonn-ter-bly-ben, *v* not to happen; to cease

unterbrechen, oonn-ter-brek-en, *v* to interrupt

unterbringen, oonn-ter-bring-en, *v* to give/find shelter for; to lodge

unterdessen, oonn-ter-dess-en, *adv* meanwhile

unterdrücken, oonn-ter-drEEck-en, *v* to suppress, to oppress; to repress

untereinander, oonn-ter-ine-ahnn-der, *adv* together; one underneath the other

Unterernährung, oonn-ter-er-nair-oong, *f* malnutrition

unterfassen, oonn-ter-fahss-en, *v jdn –*, *v* to take sb's arm

Unterführung, oonn-ter-fEEr-oong, *f* underpass, subway

Untergang, oonn-ter-gahng,

m sinking; going down, setting; decline

Untergebene(r), oonn-ter-**gayb**-en-e(r), *m & f*, subordinate

untergehen, oonn-ter-**gay**-en, *v* to sink; to go down

untergeordnet, oonn-ter-ge-ord-net, *adj* inferior, subordinate

untergraben, oonn-ter-**grahb**-en, *v* to undermine

Untergrundbahn, oonn-ter-**groont**-bahn, *f* underground railway

unterhalb, oonn-ter-**hahlp**, *adv* below

Unterhalt, oonn-ter-**hahlt**, *m* maintenance; sustenance

unterhalten, oonn-ter-**hahlt**-en, *v* to maintain; to entertain; to keep; **sich –**, *v* to converse, to enjoy o.s.

Unterhaltung, oonn-ter-**hahlt**-oong, *f* conversation; entertainment

Unterhändler, oonn-ter-**hend**-ler, *m* negotiator

Unterhemd, oonn-ter-**hemt**, *nt* vest, undershirt

Unterhose(n), oonn-ter-**hoh**-ze(n), *f (pl)* (under)pants, briefs

unterirdisch, oonn-ter-**eerd**-ish, *adj* underground, subterranean

unterkommen, oonn-ter-**kom**-en, *v* to find shelter

Unterkühlung, oonn-ter-

kEEl-oong, *f* hypothermia

Unterkunft, oonn-ter-**koonft**, *f* accommodation

Unterlage, oonn-ter-**lahg**-e, *f* pad; layer; document

unterlassen, oonn-ter-**lahss**-en, *v* to refrain from

unterlegen, oonn-ter-**layg**-en, *v* to lay a thing under; oonn-ter-**layg**-en, *adj* inferior; defeated

Unterleib, oonn-ter-**lipe**, *m* abdomen

unterliegen, oonn-ter-**leeg**-en, *v* to succumb; to be subject to

Unterlippe, oonn-ter-**lip**-e, *f* lower lip

unterm, oonn-ter-m, = **unter dem**, under the

Unternehmen, oonn-ter-**naym**-en, *nt* enterprise, undertaking

unternehmen, oonn-ter-**naym**-en, *v* to undertake

Unternehmer, oonn-ter-**naym**-er, *m* contractor, entrepreneur

Unterredung, oonn-ter-**rayd**-oong, *f* conversation, conference

Unterricht, oonn-ter-**rikt**, *m* teaching, lesson

unterrichten, oonn-ter-**rikt**-en, *v* to instruct; to inform

Unterrock, oonn-ter-**rock**, *m* petticoat

unters, oonn-ters, = **unter das**, under the

untersagen, oonn-ter-**zahg**-en, *v* to prohibit; to forbid

Untersatz, oonn-ter-zahts, *m* base, stand, pedestal

unterscheiden, oonn-ter-**shy**-den, *v* to discern, to distinguish; to differ

Unterschied, oonn-ter-**sheet**, *m* difference

unterschlagen, oonn-ter-**shlahg**-en, *v* to embezzle; oonn-ter-shlahg-en, *v* to cross (legs)

Unterschlupf, oonn-ter-**shloop**'f, *m* refuge, hiding place

unterschreiben, oonn-ter-**shry**-ben, *v* to sign

Unterschrift, oonn-ter-**shrift**, *f* signature

Unterseeboot, oonn-ter-**zay**-boht, *nt* submarine

Untersetzer, oonn-ter-**zets**-er, *m* tablemat, coaster

untersetzt, oonn-ter-**zetst**, *adj* thick-set, squat

unterst(e/r), oonn-terst (-e/er), *adj* lowest

Unterstand, oonn-ter-**shtahnt**, *m* shelter; dug-out

unterstehen, oonn-ter-**shtay**-en, *v* to be subordinate to; **sich –**, *v* to dare (to)

unterstreichen, oonn-ter-**shtry**-ken, *v* to underline (also *fig*)

unterstützen, oonn-ter-**shtEtt**-sen, *v* to support

Unterstützung, oonn-ter-**shtEEtt**-soong, *f* support; relief

untersuchen, oonn-ter-**zook**-en, *v* to examine; to investigate

Untersuchung, oonn-ter-**zook**-oong, *f* inquiry; investigation; examination

Untertan, oonn-ter-tahn, *m* subject (of state)

untertänig, oonn-ter-tayn-ik, *adj* humble; submissive

Untertasse, oonn-ter-tahss-e, *f* saucer

untertauchen, oonn-ter-towk-en, *v* to submerge, to dip; *fig* to disappear

Untertitel, oonn-ter-tee-tel, *m* subtitle

Unterwäsche, oonn-ter-vaish-e, *f* underwear

unterwegs, oonn-ter-**vayks**, *adv* on the road/way

unterweisen, oonn-ter-vy-zen, *v* to instruct

unterwerfen, oonn-ter-**vairf**-en, *v* to subject

unterwürfig, oonn-ter-vEErf-ik, *adj* obsequious, humble

unterzeichnen, oonn-ter-tsy'k-nen, *v* to sign; to ratify

unterziehen, oonn-ter-**tsee**-en, *v* to subject to

Untier, oonn-teer, *nt* monster

untreu, oonn-troy, *adj* unfaithful; disloyal

untröstlich, oonn-trerst-lik, *adj* inconsolable

Untugend, oonn-toog-ent, *f* vice, bad habit

ununterbrochen, oonn-oonn-ter-brok-en, *adj* continuous

unverbesserlich, oonn-fair-bess-er-lik, *adj* incorrigible

unverbindlich, oonn-fair-bint-lik, *adj* not binding

unverblümt, oonn-fair-blEEmt, *adj* blunt, direct

unverdient, oonn-fair-deent, *adj* unmerited, undeserved

unverdorben, oonn-fair-dorb-en, *adj* unspoilt

unverdrossen, oonn-fair-dross-en, *adj* indefatigable

unvereinbar, oonn-fair-ine-bar, *adj* incompatible

unvergeßlich, oonn-fair-gess-lik, *adj* unforgettable

unvergleichlich, oonn-fair-gly'k-lik, *adj* incomparable

unverhofft, oonn-fair-hohft, *adj* unexpected, unforeseen

unverletzt, oonn-fair-letst, *adj* unharmed, uninjured

unvermeidlich, oonn-fair-mite-lik, *adj* inevitable

unvermutet, oonn-fair-moot-et, *adj* unsuspected, unlooked for

unvernünftig, oonn-fair-nEEnft-ik, *adj* unreasonable, absurd

unverschämt, oonn-fair-shaymt, *adj* impudent, brazen

Unverschämtheit, oonn-fair-shaymt-hite, *f* impertinence, impudence

unverschuldet, oonn-fair-shoold-et, *adj* through no fault of one's own; not in debt

unversehens, oonn-fair-zay-ens, *adv* unexpectedly

unversehrt, oonn-fair-zairt, *adj* unhurt, undamaged

Unverstand, oonn-fair-shtahnt, *m* lack of judgement; folly, foolishness

unverständlich, oonn-fair-shtent-lik, *adj* incomprehensible

unverträglich, oonn-fair-trayk-lik, *adj* incompatible

unverwundbar, oonn-fair-voont-bar, *adj* invulnerable

unverzagt, oonn-fair-tsahkt, *adj* intrepid, fearless

unverzeihlich, oonn-fair-tsy-lik, *adj* unpardonable

unverzüglich, oonn-fair-tsEEk-lik, *adj* without delay

Unwahrheit, oonn-vahr-hite, *f* untruth, lie

unwahrscheinlich, oonn-vahr-shine-lik, *adj* improbable, unlikely

unweit, oonn-vite, *prep* not far from, close to

Unwetter, oonn-vet-er, *nt* stormy/foul weather

unwiderruflich, oonn-veed-er-roof-lik, *adj* irrevocable

unwiderstehlich, oonn-veed-er-shtay-lik, *adj* irresistible

unwillig, oonn-vil-ik, *adj*
reluctant, unwilling

unwillkürlich, oonn-vil-
kEEr-lik, *adj* involuntary

unwirsch, oonn-veersh, *adj*,
surly, gruff; uncouth

unwissend, oonn-viss-ent,
adj ignorant;
unsuspecting;
inexperienced

Unwissenheit, oonn-viss-
en-hite, *f* ignorance

unwissentlich, oonn-viss-
ent-lik, *adj* unwitting

unwürdig, oonn-vEErd-ik,
adj unworthy

Unzahl, oonn-tsahl, *f*
immense number

unzählbar, oonn-tsayl-bar,
adj innumerable, countless

unzählig, oonn-tsayl-ik, *adj*
innumerable, countless

Unze, oont-se, *f* ounce

unzeitgemäß, oon-tsite-ge-
mace, *adj* ill-timed;
premature

unzertrennlich, oonn-tser-
trenn-lik, *adj* inseparable

Unzucht, oonn-tsookt, *f*
sexual offence;
prostitution

unzufrieden, oonn-tsoo-
free-den, *adj* dissatisfied

unzugänglich, oonn-tsoo-
geng-lik, *adj* inaccessible

unzulänglich, oonn-tsoo-
leng-lik, *adj* inadequate,
insufficient

Unzulänglichkeit, oonn-
tsoo-leng-lik-kite, *f*
inadequacy

unzurechnungsfähig, oonn-
tsoo-rek-noongs-fay-ik, *adj*
not responsible for one's
actions

unzureichend, oonn-tsoo-
ry-kent, *adj* insufficient

unzuverlassig, oonn-tsoo-
fair-less-ik, *adj* unreliable;
uncertain

unzweckmäßig, oon-tsveck-
mace-ik, *adj* inappropriate

unzweideutig, oonn-tsvy-
doyt-ik, *adj* simple;
unambiguous

unzweifelhaft, oonn-tsvy-
fel-hahft, *adj* undoubted

üppig, EEpp-ik, *adj*
luxuriant; rich; sensual,
voluptuous

Üppigkeit, EEpp-ik-kite, *f*
luxury; plenty;
voluptuousness

Urahn, oor-ahn, *m*
ancestor, great-
grandfather

uralt, oor-ahlt, *adj* ancient,
very old

Uranfang, oor-ahnn-fahng,
m very beginning

urbar, oor-bar, *adj* tilled;
arable

Urbedeutung, oor-be-doyt-
oong, *f* original meaning

Urbestandteil, oor-be-
shtahnt-tile, *m* original
component

Urbewohner, oor-be-vohn-
er, *m* native, original
inhabitant; Aborigine

Urbild, oor-bilt, *nt* original

ureigen, oor-eye-gen, *adj*

original, innate

Ureltern, oor-elt-ern, *pl*
ancestors

Urenkel, oor-eng-kel, *m*
great-grandchild

Urform, oor-form, *f* original
form

urgemütlich, oor-ge-mEEt-
lik, *adj* extremely
comfortable

Urgeschichte, oor-ge-shik-
te, *f* dawn of history

Urgroß–, oor-grohs, *pref*,
–eltern, *pl* great-
grandparents; **–mutter,** *f*
great-grandmother;
–vater, *m* great-
grandfather

Urheber, oor-hayb-er, *m*
originator, author; **–recht,**
nt copyright

urinieren, oor-ee-neer-en, *v*
to urinate

urkomisch, oor-kohm-ish,
adj very comical

Urkunde, oor-koonn-de, *f*
document, deed

urkundlich, oor-koont-lik,
adj documentary

Urlaub, oor-lowp, *m* leave
(of absence), holiday(s);
im –, on holiday

Urne, oorn-e, *f* urn

urnenförmig, oorn-en-ferm-
ik, *adj* urn-shaped

urplötzlich, oor-plerts-lik,
adj & adv very sudden(ly)

Urquell, oor-kvel, *m*
origin(al source)

Ursache, oor-zahk-e, *f*
cause, motive

ursächlich, oor-zek-lik, *adj* causative

Ursprung, oor-shproong, *m* origin; source

ursprünglich, oor-shprEEng-lik, *adj* original, primal

Ursprungsland, oor-shproongs-lahnt, *nt* country of origin

Urstoff, oor-shtof, *m* raw material

Urteil, oor-tile, *nt* judgement; verdict; opinion

urteilen, oor-tile-en, *v* to pass judgement; to judge

Urteilskraft, oor-tiles-krahft, *f* judgement; discernment

Urteilsspruch, oor-tiles-shprook, *m* sentence, judgement

Urtext, oor-text, *m* original text

urtümlich, oor-tEEm-lik, *adj* original

Urvater, oor-faht-er, *m* forefather

urväterlich, oor-fayt-er-lik, *adj* ancestral

Urvolk, oor-fohlk, *nt* primitive people

Urwald, oor-vahlt, *m* primeval forest; jungle

urwüchsig, oor-vEEks-ik, *adj* natural; original

Urzeit, oor-tsite, *f* primeval period; antiquity

Urzustand, oor-tsoo-shtahnt, *m* primitive condition

Urzweck, oor-tsveck, *m* original/chief purpose

Usus, ooz-ooss, *m* custom

usw., *abbr* und so weiter, etc.

V

Valentinstag, vah-len-teens-tahk, *m* Valentine's Day

Valuta, vah-loot-ah, *f* foreign currency; monetary standard

Vanille, vahn-ill-(y)e, *f* vanilla

Vater, faht-er, *m* father; **–land,** *nt* fatherland, motherland

väterlich, fayt-er-lik, *adj* fatherly

Vaterstadt, faht-er-shtaht, *f* native town

Vaterunser, faht-er-oonn-zer, *nt* Lord's Prayer

v. Chr., *abbr* **vor Christo/Christus,** B.C.

Vegetarier, vay-ge-**tar**-ee-er, *m* vegetarian

vegetarisch, vay-ge-**tar**-ish, *adj* vegetarian

vegetieren, vay-ge-**teer**-en, *v* to vegetate; to exist

Veilchen, file-*ke*n, *nt* violet

Vene, vayn-*e*, *f* vein

Venedig, ven-**ay**-dik, *nt* Venice

Ventil, ven-**teel**, *nt* valve; stop; piston

Ventilator, ven-tee-**laht**-ohr, *m* (electric) fan

verabreden, fair-**ahpp**-rayd-en, *v* to agree; to appoint (a time)

Verabredung, fair-**ahpp**-rayd-oong, *f* appointment; arrangement

verabreichen, fair-**ahpp**-ry-*ke*n, *v* to tender; to dispense

verabscheuen, fair-**ahpp**-shoy-en, *v* to loathe, to detest

verabschieden, fair-**ahpp**-sheed-en, *v* to dismiss; **sich –,** *v* to take leave

verachten, fair-**ahkt**-en, *v* to

despise; to disdain

verächtlich, fair-**ekt**-lik, *adj* contemptuous; contemptible

Verachtung, fair-**ahkt**-oong, *f* contempt; scorn

verallgemeinern, fair-ahll-ge-**mine**-ern, *v* to generalize

veralten, fair-**ahlt**-en, *v* to grow obsolete

veränderlich, fair-**end**-er-lik, *adj* changeable

verändern, fair-**end**-ern, *v* to change; to vary

Veränderung, fair-**end**-er-oong, *f* change; alteration

veranlagt, fair-**ahnn**-lahkt, *adj* suited to, gifted for; disposed to

Veranlagung, fair-**ahnn**-lahg-oong, *f* talent; disposition

veranlassen, fair-**ahnn**-lahss-en, *v* to cause

Veranlassung, fair-**ahnn**-lahss-oong, *f* cause, occasion, impulse

veranschaulichen, fair-**ahnn**-show-lik-en, *v* to make clear; to demonstrate

Veranschaulichung, fair-**ahnn**-show-lik-oong, *f* demonstration; illustration

veranstalten, fair-**ahnn**-shtahl-ten, *v* to organize; to arrange

verantworten, fair-**ahnt**-vort-en, *v* to be

responsible; **sich –**, v to justify oneself

Verantwortlichkeit, fair-**ahnt**-vort-lik-kite, f responsibility

Verantwortung, fair-**ahnt**-vort-oong, f responsibility, risk

verarbeiten, fair-**ahr**-by-ten, v to consume; to manufacture; to process

verärgert, fair-**airg**-ert, adj vexed, annoyed

verarmen, fair-**arm**-en, v to (be) impoverish(ed)

verausgaben, fair-**ows**-gahb-en, v to spend; **sich –**, v to exhaust oneself

veräußern, fair-**oys**-ern, v to dispose of

Verband, fair-**bahnt**, m bandage, dressing; union, association

verbannen, fair-**bahnn**-en, v to banish, to exile

Verbannung, fair-**bahnn**-oong, f exile; expulsion

verbergen, fair-**bairg**-en, v to hide, to conceal

verbessern, fair-**bess**-ern, v to improve, to (a)mend

verbeugen (sich), fair-**boyg**-en (zik), v to bow

Verbeugung, fair-**boyg**-oong, f bow

verbiegen, fair-**beeg**-en, v to bend out of shape

verbieten, fair-**beet**-en, v to forbid, to prohibit

verbilligen, fair-**bil**-ig-en, v to cheapen

verbilligt, fair-**bil**-ikt, adj reduced

verbinden, fair-**bin**-den, v to unite, to connect; to bandage

verbindlich, fair-**bint**-lik, adj binding; courteous

Verbindlichkeit, fair-**bint**-lik-kite, f courtesy; liability

Verbindung, fair-**bin**-doong, f communication, connection; compound

verbitten (sich), fair-**bit**-en (zik), v to refuse to tolerate

verbittern, fair-**bit**-ern, v to embitter

verblassen, fair-**blahss**-en, v to fade

Verbleib, fair-**blipe**, m whereabouts

verbleiben, fair-**bly**-ben, v to remain; to continue

verbleit, fair-**blite**, adj leaded (petrol)

verblenden, fair-**blend**-en, v to dazzle; to blind

Verblendung, fair-**blend**-oong, f delusion

verblüffen, fair-**blEEff**-en, v to dumbfound

verblühen, fair-**blEE**-en, v to fade, to wither

verbluten, fair-**bloot**-en, v to bleed to death

verbohrt, fair-**bohrt**, adj stubborn, cranky

verborgen, fair-**borg**-en, adj hidden

Verborgenheit, fair-**borg**-en-hite, f obscurity

Verbot, fair-**boht**, nt prohibition

verboten, fair-**boht**-en, adj prohibited, forbidden

Verbrauch, fair-**browk**, m consumption (of goods)

verbrauchen, fair-**browk**-en, v to use up, to consume

Verbraucher, fair-**browk**-er, m consumer

verbrechen, fair-**brek**-en, v to commit (a crime)

Verbrechen, fair-**brek**-en, nt crime

Verbrecher, fair-**brek**-er, m criminal

verbrecherisch, fair-**brek**-er-ish, adj criminal

verbreiten, fair-**bry**-ten, v to spread, to circulate, distribute

Verbreitung, fair-**bry**-toong, f spreading, circulation, distribution; radiation

verbrennen, fair-**bren**-en, v to burn up; to be consumed by fire

Verbrennung, fair-**bren**-oong, f burning (up); cremation

verbringen, fair-**bring**-en, v to spend time

verbrüdern (sich), fair-**brEEd**-ern (zik), v to fraternize

verbrühen, fair-**brEE**-en, v to scald

verbummeln, fair-**boomm**-eln, v to waste (time); to get lazy

verbunden, fair-**boonn**-den,
adj obliged; bandaged

verbünden (sich), fair-
bEEnn-den (zik), *v* to form
an alliance

Verbündete(r), fair-**bEEnn**-
de-te(r), *m & f,* ally

verbürgen, fair-**bEErg**-en, *v*
to warrant, to guarantee

Verdacht, fair-**dakt,** *m*
suspicion; distrust

verdächtig, fair-**dekt**-ik, *adj*
suspected, suspicious

verdächtigen, fair-**dek**-tig-
en, *v* to suspect

verdammen, fair-**dahmm**-en,
v to condemn

verdammt, fair-**dahmmt,** *adj
& interj* damned

Verdammung, fair-**dahmm**-
oong, *f* damnation,
condemnation

verdampfen, fair-**dahmp**-fen,
v to evaporate, to vaporise

verdanken, fair-**dahng**-ken,
v to be indebted to

verdauen, fair-**dow**-en, *v* to
digest

verdaulich, fair-**dow**-lik, *adj*
digestible

Verdauung, fair-**dow**-oong, *f*
digestion

Verdeck, fair-**deck,** *nt* deck;
roof, hood

verdecken, fair-**deck**-en, *v*
to cover up; to veil

Verderb(en), fair-**dairp**
(fair-**dairb**-en), *m* (*nt*),
ruin; decay

verderben, fair-**dairb**-en, *v*
to spoil; to ruin; to rot

verderblich, fair-**dairp**-lik,
adj fatal, pernicious;
corruptible

Verderbnis, fair-**dairp**-niss, *f*
depravity

verderbt, fair-**dairp't,** *adj*
demoralized; corrupt

verdeutlichen, fair-**doyt**-lik-
en, *v* to make clear

verdienen, fair-**deen**-en, *v* to
earn; to merit; to deserve

Verdienst, fair-**deenst,** *m*
earnings; merit

verdoppeln, fair-**dop**-eln, *v*
to double

verdorben, fair-**dorb**-en, *adj*
spoilt, bad, polluted;
corrupt

verdorren, fair-**dorr**-en, *v* to
wither, to dry up

verdrängen, fair-**dreng**-en, *v*
to displace; to push aside;
to repress

verdrehen, fair-**dray**-en, *v* to
distort

verdreht, fair-**drayt,** *adj*
crazy, cranky

verdrießen, fair-**drees**-en, *v*
to vex; to grieve

verdrießlich, fair-**drees**-lik,
adj vexed, annoyed;
grieved

Verdrießlichkeit, fair-**drees**-
lik-kite, *f* moroseness

verdrossen, fair-**dross**-en,
adj morose; unwilling;
reluctant

verdrucken, fair-**droock**-en, *v*
to misprint

Verdruß, fair-**drooss,** *m*
annoyance; indignation

verdunkeln, fair-**doong**-
keln, *v* to darken; to grow
dim; *fig* to obscure

verdünnen, fair-**dEEnn**-en, *v*
to dilute

verdursten, fair-**doorst**-en, *v*
to die of thirst

verdüstern, fair-**dEEst**-ern, *v*
to darken; to grow dim; *fig*
to obscure

verdutzt, fair-**dootst,** *adj*
taken aback

veredeln, fair-**ayd**-eln, *v* to
ennoble; to graft

verehelichen, fair-**ay**-e-lik-
en, *v* to marry

verehren, fair-**ayr**-en, *v* to
venerate; to admire

Verehrer, fair-**ayr**-er, *m*
admirer

Verehrung, fair-**ayr**-oong, *f*
veneration; admiration

vereidigen, fair-**ide**-ig-en, *v*
to swear in

Verein, fair-**ine,** *m* society,
association, club, union

vereinbaren, fair-**ine**-bar-en,
v to agree to

vereinen, fair-**ine**-en, *v* to
unite, to combine

vereinfachen, fair-**ine**-fahk-
en, *v* to simplify

vereinigen, fair-**ine**-ig-en, *v*
to unite, to combine

Vereinigte Staaten, fair-**ine**-
ick-te **shtaht**-en, *pl* United
States

Vereinte Nationen, fair-**ine**-
te nahts-**yohn**-en, *pl*
United Nations

vereiteln, fair-**ite**-eln,

v to frustrate

verenden, fair-**end**-en, *v* to perish, to die (animals)

verengen, fair-**eng**-en, *v* to (become/make) narrow

vererben, fair-**airb**-en, *v* to bequeath

verewigen, fair-**ay**-vig-en, *v* to immortalize

verfahren, fair-**fahr**-en, *v* to proceed; **sich –**, *v* to get lost

Verfahren, fair-**fahr**-en, *nt* process, proceeding, procedure

Verfall, fair-**fahll**, *m* decay, ruin; lapse; expiry (of card etc.)

verfallen, fair-**fahll**-en, *v* to decay; to expire (card etc.)

Verfallsdatum, fair-**fahls**-dah-toom, *nt* expiry date, sell-by date

verfälschen, fair-**felsh**-en, *v* to adulterate

verfärben, fair-**fairb**-en, *v* to discolour

verfassen, fair-**fahss**-en, *v* to compose, to draw up

Verfasser, fair-**fahss**-er, *m* author

Verfassung, fair-**fahss**-oong, *f* constitution; disposition

verfaulen, fair-**fowl**-en, *v* to rot, to decay

verfechten, fair-**fek**-ten, *v* to defend, to advocate, to champion

verfehlen, fair-**fayl**-en, *v* to miss; to fall

verfeinden, fair-**fine**-den, *v* to make enemies

verfeinern, fair-**fine**-ern, *v* to refine; to improve

verfertigen, fair-**fairt**-ig-en, *v* to manufacture, to prepare

verfinstern, fair-**finst**-ern, *v* to darken

verfliegen, fair-**fleeg**-en, *v* to fly off; to evaporate

verfließen, fair-**flees**-en, *v* to elapse

verfluchen, fair-**flook**-en, *v* to curse, to damn

verfolgen, fair-**foll**-gen, *v* to pursue; to follow

Verfolgung, fair-**folg**-oong, *f* persecution; pursuit

verfügbar, fair-**fEEg**-bar, *adj* available

verfügen, fair-**fEEg**-en, *v* to dispose; to decree

Verfügung, fair-**fEEg**-oong, *f* decree; disposition

verführen, fair-**fEEr**-en, *v* to tempt; to seduce

verführerisch, fair-**fEEr**-er-ish, *adj* tempting; seductive

Verführung, fair-**fEEr**-oong, *f* seduction

vergällen, fair-**gel**-en, *v* to spoil (enjoyment etc.); to embitter

vergangen, fair-**gahng**-en, *adj* past; bygone

Vergangenheit, fair-**gahng**-en-hite, *f* past; history

vergänglich, fair-**geng**-lik, *adj* transient, fleeting; perishable

vergeben, fair-**gayb**-en, *v* to forgive; to give away

vergebens, fair-**gayb**-ens, *adv* in vain; to no avail

vergeblich, fair-**gayp**-lik, *adj* futile, vain, fruitless

Vergebung, fair-**gayb**-oong, *f* forgiveness

vergehen, fair-**gay**-en, *v* to pass (of time), to elapse; **sich –**, *v* to commit an offence

Vergehen, fair-**gay**-en, *nt* trespass

vergelten, fair-**gelt**-en, *v* to repay, to requite

vergessen, fair-**gess**-en, *v* to forget

Vergessenheit, fair-**gess**-en-hite, *f* oblivion

vergeßlich, fair-**gess**-lik, *adj* forgetful

vergeuden, fair-**goyd**-en, *v* to squander; to lavish

vergewaltigen, fair-ge-**vahlt**-ig-en, *v* to assault; to rape

vergewissern, fair-ge-**viss**-ern, *v* to make sure

vergießen, fair-**gees**-en, *v* to shed (tears); to spill

vergiften, fair-**gift**-en, *v* to poison; to taint

Vergiftung, fair-**gift**-oong, *f* poisoning

Vergißmeinnicht, fair-**giss**-mine-nikt, *nt* forget-me-not

vergittern, fair-**git**-ern, *v* to fence in

Vergleich, fair-**gly'k**, *m*

comparison; agreement

vergleichen, fair-**gly**-ken, *v* to compare

verglühen, fair-**glEE**-en, *v* to fade/die away, to burn out

Vergnügen, fair-g'**nEEg**-en, *nt* amusement, pleasure

vergnügen, fair-gn**EEg**-en, *v* to amuse; **sich –,** *v* to enjoy o.s.

vergnüglich, fair-g'**nEEg**-lik, *adj* delightful; pleased

vergnügt, fair-g'**nEEgt,** *adj* delighted; cheerful

Vergnügung, fair-g'**nEEg**-oong, *f* amusement

vergolden, fair-**goll**-den, *v* to gild

vergönnen, fair-**gernn**-en, *v* to permit, to grant

vergöttern, fair-**gertt**-ern, *v* to idolize

vergraben, fair-**grahb**-en, *v* to bury; to burrow

vergreifen, fair-**gry**-fen, *v* to make a mistake; **sich an etw –,** to misappropriate; to lay hands on

vergriffen, fair-**grif**-en, *adj* out of print; out of stock

vergrößern, fair-**grers**-ern, *v* to enlarge; to increase

Vergrößerung, fair-**grers**-er-oong, *f* enlargement; **–sglas,** *nt* magnifying glass

vergünstigen, fair-g**EEnst**-ig-en, *v* to grant (privileges)

Vergünstigung, fair-g**EEnst**-ig-oong, *f* privilege; benefit

vergüten, fair-g**EEt**-en, *v* to

make good; to refund; to compensate

verhaften, fair-**hahft**-en, *v* to arrest

Verhaftung, fair-**hahft**-oong, *f* arrest

verhallen, fair-**hahll**-en, *v* to die away (sounds)

verhalten, fair-**hahlt**-en, *v* to suppress; **sich –,** *v* to behave; to be (in a position); *adj* restrained

Verhalten, fair-**hahlt**-en, *nt* conduct, behaviour

Verhältnis, fair-**helt**-niss, *nt* relation; proportion; (love) affair; **–se,** *pl* conditions, state of affairs

verhältnismäßig, fair-**helt**-niss-mace-ik, *adj* proportionate, relative; *adv* comparatively

verhandeln, fair-**hahnn**-deln, *v* to negotiate

Verhandlung, fair-**hahnd**-loong, *f* negotiation; trial

verhängen, fair-**heng**-en, *v* to cover; to decree; to impose

Verhängnis, fair-**heng**-niss, *nt* fate; doom

verhängnisvoll, fair-**heng**-niss-fol, *adj* fateful

verharmlosen, fair-**harm**-loh-zen, *v* to play down

verhaßt, fair-**hahsst,** *adj* hated, odious

verhätscheln, fair-**hayt**-sheln, *v* to pamper

verhauen, fair-**how**-en, *v* to thrash; to fail (exams)

verheben (sich), fair-**hayb**-en (zik), *v* to injure oneself by lifting

verheerend, fair-**hayr**-ent, *adj* disastrous

verhehlen, fair-**hayl**-en, *v* to dissemble, to conceal

verheimlichen, fair-**hime**-lik-en, *v* to conceal

verheiraten, fair-**hy**-raht-en, *v* to marry

Verheiratung, fair-**hy**-raht-oong, *f* marriage

verheißen, fair-**hy**-sen, *v* to hold out promise

Verheißung, fair-**hy**-soong, *f* promise

verhelfen, fair-**helf**-en, *v* to assist in obtaining

verherrlichen, fair-**hairr**-lik-en, *v* to glorify

verhexen, fair-**hecks**-en, *v* to bewitch

verhindern, fair-**hin**-dern, *v* to prevent

verhöhnen, fair-**hern**-en, *v* to mock; to jeer

Verhöhnung, fair-**hern**-oong, *f* derision; mockery

Verhör, fair-**her,** *nt* evidence, interrogation

verhören, fair-**her**-en, *v* to interrogate; to mishear

verhüllen, fair-**hEEll**-en, *v* to wrap up, to muffle

verhungern, fair-**hoong**-ern, *v* to starve (to death)

verhüten, fair-**hEEt**-en, *v* to prevent, to avert; to use contraceptives

Verhütung, fair-**hEEt**-oong, *f*

prevention; contraception; **–smittel,** *nt* contraceptive

verirren (sich), fair-**eerr**-en (zik), *v* to get lost

verjubeln, fair-**yoob**-eln, *v* to lavish

verjüngen, fair-**yEEng**-en, *v* to rejuvenate; to taper, to narrow

verkalken, fair-**kahlk**-en, *v* to calcify; *fam* to become senile

Verkauf, fair-**kowf**, *m* selling, sale

verkaufen, fair-**kowf**-en, *v* to sell; **sich –,** *v* to market o.s.; to present o.s.

Verkäufer, fair-**koyf**-er, *m* salesman; seller; shop assistant

verkäuflich, fair-**koyf**-lik, *adj* saleable

Verkehr, fair-**kair**, *m* traffic; contact, communication; business

verkehren, fair-**kair**-en, *v* to do business; to frequent; to associate (with)

Verkehrsamt, fair-**kairs**-ahmt, *nt* tourist office

Verkehrsberuhigung, fair-**kairs**-be-roo-ee-goong, *f* traffic calming

verkehrsgünstig, fair-**kairs**-gEEnst-ik, *adj* convenient, easy to reach (by car etc.)

Verkehrsmittel, fair-**kairs**-mit-el, *nt* means of transport

Verkehrsunfall, fair-**kairs**-oonn-fahll, *m* road accident

Verkehrsverein, fair-**kairs**-fair-ine, *m* tourist office

verkehrt, fair-**kairt**, *adj* wrong; inverted

verkennen, fair-**kenn**-en, *v* to mistake; to misjudge

verklagen, fair-**klahg**-en, *v* to sue

Verklärung, fair-**klair**-oong, *f* transfiguration; ecstasy

verkleiden (sich), fair-**kly**-den (zik), *v* to disguise o.s.

Verkleidung, fair-**kly**-doong, *f* disguise

verkleinern, fair-**kly**-nern, *v* to make small(er), to reduce

Verkleinerung, fair-**kly**-ner-oong, *f* reduction

verklingen, fair-**kling**-en, *v* to die away (sounds)

verknüpfen, fair-**k'nEEpp**-fen, *v* to connect

verkohlen, fair-**kohl**-en, *v* to char; to pull someone's leg

verkommen, fair-**kom**-en, *v* to decay; to go downhill

verkorken, fair-**kork**-en, *v* to cork up

verkörpern, fair-**kerp**-ern, *v* to embody

verkraften, fair-**krahft**-en, *v* to bear; to cope

verkriechen (sich), fair-**kreek**-en (zik), *v* to creep into hiding

verkrüppeln, fair-**krEEpp**-eln, *v* to cripple

verkümmern, fair-**kEEmm**-ern, *v* to pine, to atrophy (also *fig*)

verkünd(ig)en, fair-**kEENd**(-ig)-en, *v* to make known, to proclaim

Verkünd(ig)ung, fair-**kEENd**(-ig)-oong, *f* publication, announcement

verkupfern, fair-**koopp**-fern, *v* to copper(-plate)

verkuppeln, fair-**koopp**-eln, *v* to couple together

verkürzen, fair-**kEErt**-sen, *v* to shorten

Verkürzung, fair-**kEErt**-soong, *f* shortening

verladen, fair-**lahd**-en, *v* to load; to ship

Verlag, fair-**lahk**, *m* publishing house

verlangen, fair-**lahng**-en, *v* to demand; to long for

Verlangen, fair-**lahng**-en, *nt* desire; longing

verlängern, fair-**leng**-ern, *v* to lengthen; to extend

Verlängerung, fair-**leng**-er-oong, *f* prolongation; lengthening; extra time *sport*

verlangsamen, fair-**lahng**-zahm-en, *v* to retard; to slow down

Verlaß, fair-**lahss**, *m* reliance

verlassen, fair-**lahss**-en, *v* to leave, to quit; **sich –,** *v* to rely, to trust

verläßlich, fair-**less**-lik, *adj* reliable

Verlauf, fair-lowf, *m* passage of time; progress; course

verlaufen, fair-lowf-en, *v* to pass (time); **sich –**, *v* to get lost

verlegen, fair-layg-en, *v* to publish; to transfer; to mislay; **sich – auf**, to specialize in; *adj* embarrassed

Verlegenheit, fair-layg-en-hite, *f* embarrassment

Verleger, fair-layg-er, *m* publisher

verleiden, fair-ly-den, *v* to disgust; to spoil

Verleih, fair-ly, *m* hire service

verleihen, fair-ly-en, *v* to loan, to lend

verleiten, fair-ly-ten, *v* to lead astray

verlernen, fair-lairn-en, *v* to forget (something learned)

verlesen, fair-layz-en, *v* to read out; to misread; to sort out

verletzen, fair-lets-en, *v* to injure, to hurt; to damage

verletzlich, fair-lets-lik, *adj* vulnerable, sensitive

Verletzung, fair-lets-oong, *f* injury; damage; infringement

verleugnen, fair-loyg-nen, *v* to deny

Verleugnung, fair-loyg-noong, *f* denial

verleumden, fair-loym-den, *v* to defame, to slander

Verleumdung, fair-loym-doong, *f* defamation, slander, libel

verlieben (sich), fair-leeb-en (zik), *v* to fall in love

verliebt, fair-leept, *adj* in love, enamoured

verlieren, fair-leer-en, *v* to lose

Verließ, fair-leess, *nt* dungeon, keep

verloben (sich), fair-lohb-en (zik), *v* to become engaged

verlobt, fair-lohpt, *adj* betrothed, engaged

Verlobte(r), fair-lohpt-e(r), *m & f*, fiancé(e)

Verlobung, fair-lohb-oong, *f* betrothal, engagement

verlocken, fair-lock-en, *v* to allure, to entice

verlogen, fair-lohg-en, *adj* habitually untruthful

verlöschen, fair-lersh-en, *v* to extinguish

verlosen, fair-lohz-en, *v* to raffle

verlöten, fair-lert-en, *v* to solder

verlottern, fair-lott-ern, *v* to go to ruin

Verlust, fair-loost, *m* loss; bereavement

vermachen, fair-mahk-en, *v* to bequeath

Vermächtnis, fair-mekt-nis, *nt* legacy

vermählen, fair-mayl-en, *v* to marry; **sich –**, to get married

Vermählung, fair-mayl-oong, *f* marriage; wedding

vermarkten, fair-markt-en, *v* to market

vermehren, fair-mayr-en, *v* to increase

vermeiden, fair-my-den, *v* to avoid; to evade

vermengen, fair-meng-en, *v* to confuse; to mix up

Vermerk, fair-mairk, *m* remark, note; entry

vermerken, fair-mairk-en, *v* to note; to (re)mark

vermessen, fair-mess-en, *v* to survey; *adj* presumptuous

Vermessung, fair-mess-oong, *f* survey(ing)

vermieten, fair-meet-en, *v* to let

vermindern, fair-min-dern, *v* to lessen; to impair

vermischen, fair-mish-en, *v* to mix

vermissen, fair-miss-en, *v* to miss

vermitteln, fair-mit-eln, *v* to mediate; to intervene

vermittels(t), fair-mit-els(t), *prep* by means of

Vermittlung, fair-mit-loong, *f* mediation; intercession; agency; **–sgebühr**, *f* commission

Vermittler, fair-mit-ler, *m* intermediary; agent

vermodern, fair-mohd-ern, *v* to fall to dust

vermögen, fair-merg-en, *v* to be able (to)

Vermögen, fair-merg-en, *nt*

capability; fortune

vermögend, fair-**merg**-ent, *adj* well-to-do

vermuten, fair-**moot**-en, *v* to conjecture; to presume; to suppose

vermutlich, fair-**moot**-lik, *adj* probable; supposed

Vermutung, fair-**moot**-oong, *f* conjecture; supposition

vernachlässigen, fair-nahk-less-ig-en, *v* to neglect

vernageln, fair-**nahg**-eln, *v* to nail up

vernarben, fair-**nahrb**-en, *v* to (leave a) scar

vernarrt, fair-**nahrt,** *adj* infatuated

vernehmen, fair-**naym**-en, *v* to perceive, to understand, to learn; *law* to examine (in court)

Vernehmung, fair-**naym**-oong, *f law* examination

verneigen (sich), fair-**ny**-gen (zik), *v* to bow

verneinen, fair-**nine**-en, *v* to deny

Verneinung, fair-**nine**-oong, *f* denial; negation

vernichten, fair-**nik**-ten, *v* to destroy

Vernichtung, fair-**nik**-toong, *f* destruction

vernieten, fair-**neet**-en, *v* to rivet

Vernunft, fair-**noonft,** *f* reason, intellect; (common) sense

vernünftig, fair-**nEEnft**-ik, *adj* sensible; reasonable

veröden, fair-**erd**-en, *v* to lay waste; to become deserted

veröffentlichen, fair-**erff**-ent-lik-en, *v* to publish; to make known

verordnen, fair-**ord**-nen, *v* to prescribe; to order

Verordnung, fair-**ord**-noong, *f* order; edict

verpachten, fair-**pahk**-ten, *v* to lease

verpacken, fair-**pahck**-en, *v* to pack; to wrap

Verpackung, fair-**pahck**-oong, *f* packing

verpassen, fair-**pahss**-en, *v* to let slip; to miss up

verpfänden, fair-p'**fend**-en, *v* to pledge; to pawn

verpflanzen, fair-p'**flahnt**-sen, *v* to transplant

verpflegen, fair-p'**flayg**-en, *v* to look after; to nurse; to board

Verpflegung, fair-p'**flayg**-oong, *f* provisioning; board(ing); tending

verpflichten, fair-p'**flik**-ten, *v* to bind, to oblige

verpfuschen, fair-p'**foosh**-en, *v* to spoil; to botch

verpönt, fair-**pernt,** *adj* frowned (up)on

verprügeln, fair-**prEEg**-eln, *v* to thrash

Verrat, fair-**raht,** *m* treason; treachery

verraten, fair-**raht**-en, *v* to betray; to divulge

Verräter, fair-**rayt**-er, *m* traitor

verräterisch, fair-**rayt**-er-ish, *adj* treacherous; treasonable

verrauchen, fair-**rowk**-en, *v* to go up in smoke; to cool down

verrechnen, fair-**rek**-nen, *v* to adjust accounts; **sich –,** *v* to miscalculate

Verrechnung, fair-**rek**-noong, *f* miscalculation; adjustment; **–sscheck,** *m* crossed cheque

verrecken, fair-**reck**-en, *v* *fam* to perish, to die (like an animal)

verregnen, fair-**rayg**-nen, *v* to spoil by rain

verreisen, fair-**ry**-zen, *v* to go out of town, to travel

verrenken, fair-**reng**-ken, *v* to dislocate, to sprain

verrichten, fair-**rik**-ten, *v* to perform; to carry out

verriegeln, fair-**reeg**-eln, *v* to bolt (door)

verringern, fair-**ring**-ern, *v* to reduce, to diminish

verrinnen, fair-**rin**-en, *v* to elapse; to run off

verrosten, fair-**rost**-en, *v* to get rusty

verrucht, fair-**rookt,** *adj* villainous, infamous

verrücken, fair-**rEEck**-en, *v* to shift, to displace

verrückt, fair-**rEEckt,** *adj* mad, insane

Verrücktheit, fair-**rEEckt**-hite, *f* madness, insanity, lunacy

Verruf, fair-**roof**, m ill repute

verrufen, fair-**roof**-en, adj ill-reputed, notorious

Vers, fairs, m verse; poetry; stanza

versagen, fair-**zahg**-en, v to fail, to break down; to refuse

versalzen, fair-**zahlt**-sen, v to oversalt; fig to spoil

versammeln, fair-**zahmm**-eln, v to assemble

Versammlung, fair-**zahmm**-loong, f assembly, meeting

Versand, fair-**zahnt**, m export(ation), dispatch; –**haus**, nt mail-order business

versaufen, fair-**zowf**-en, v fam to spend on drink

versäumen, fair-**zoym**-en, v to neglect; to miss

verschachern, fair-**shahk**-ern, v to sell off

verschaffen, fair-**shahff**-en, v to provide, to supply; **sich –**, v to obtain, to acquire

verschämt, fair-**shaymt**, adj bashful; ashamed

verschärfen, fair-**shairf**-en, v to make more severe, to intensify

verscheiden, fair-**shy**-den, v to pass away

verschenken, fair-**sheng**-ken, v to give away

verscherzen, fair-**shairts**-en, v to forfeit

verscheuchen, fair-**shoyk**-en, v to scare away

verschicken, fair-**shick**-en, v to forward

verschieben, fair-**sheeb**-en, v to shift; to postpone

verschieden, fair-**sheed**-en, adj different; diverse; –**artig**, adj varied

Verschiedenheit, fair-**sheed**-en-hite, f difference; variety

verschiedentlich, fair-**sheed**-ent-lik, adj on several occasions

verschiffen, fair-**shif**-en v to ship, to dispatch

verschimmeln, fair-**shim**-eln, v to go mouldy

verschlafen, fair-**shlahf**-en, v to oversleep; fig to miss; adj drowsy, sleepy

Verschlag, fair-**shlahk**, m locker, shed; partition

verschlagen, fair-**shlahg**-en, v to board up; adj cunning, devious

verschlechtern, fair-**shlek**-tern, v to make worse; to worsen

verschleiern, fair-**shly**-ern, v to veil

Verschleiß, fair-**shlys**, m wear and tear

verschleißen, fair-**shly**-sen, v to wear out

verschleudern, fair-**shloy**-dern, v to squander; to sell off

verschließen, fair-**shlees**-en, v to lock; to shut

verschlimmern, fair-**shlim**-ern, v to aggravate; to demoralize

verschlingen, fair-**shling**-en, v to gulp; to gobble; to entangle

verschlucken, fair-**shloock**-en, v to swallow; **sich –**, v to swallow the wrong way

Verschluß, fair-**shlooss**, m lock; shutter; fastener

verschmähen, fair-**shmay**-en, v to scorn

verschmerzen, fair-**shmairt**-sen, v to forget/get over a loss

verschmitzt, fair-**shmitst**, adj mischievous

verschmutzen, fair-**shmoots**-en, v to soil; to pollute

verschnupft, fair-**shnoop**'ft, adj having a cold; fam to be miffed

verschollen, fair-**shol**-en, adj lost, forgotten

verschonen, fair-**shohn**-en, v to spare

verschöne(r)n, fair-**shern**-e(r)n, v to beautify, to improve

verschreiben, fair-**shry**-ben, v to prescribe; **sich –**, v to make a mistake in writing; to devote o.s. to

verschrotten, fair-**shrott**-en, v to scrap

verschüchtern, fair-**shEEk**-tern, v to intimidate

verschulden, fair-**shooll**-den, v to be guilty of

verschuldet, fair-**shooll**-det,

adj in debt

verschwägert, fair-shvay-gert, *adj* related by marriage

verschwenden, fair-shvend-en, *v* to waste, to squander

Verschwender, fair-shvend-er, *m* spendthrift

verschwenderisch, fair-shvend-er-ish, *adj* wasteful

verschwiegen, fair-shveeg-en, *adj* reserved, discreet

Verschwiegenheit, fair-shveeg-en-hite, *f* reticence; discretion

verschwimmen, fair-shvim-en, *v* to dissolve; to grow hazy

verschwinden, fair-shvin-den, *v* to disappear

verschwommen, fair-shvom-en, *adj* indistinct

verschwören, fair-shverr-en, *v* to conspire; to curse

Verschwörer, fair-shverr-er, *m* plotter

Verschwörung, fair-shverr-oong, *f* conspiracy

versehen, fair-zay-en, *v* to provide; to carry out; **sich –**, *v* to make a mistake

Versehen, fair-zay-en, *nt* oversight; mistake

versenden, fair-zend-en, *v* to send off; to export

versengen, fair-zeng-en, *v* to singe

versenken, fair-zeng-ken, *v* to sink; to lower

versessen, fair-zess-en, *adj*

keen (on), crazy (about)

versetzen, fair-zet-sen, *v* to misplace; to displace; to transfer; to pawn; to reply; to put

Versetzung, fair-zet-soong, *f* displacement; transfer

verseuchen, fair-zoyk-en, *v* to contaminate

versichern, fair-zik-ern, *v* to insure; to assure; to ensure; to ascertain

Versicherung, fair-zik-er-oong, *f* insurance; assurance

versiegeln, fair-zeeg-eln, *v* to seal up

versilbern, fair-zil-bern, *v* to silver

versinken, fair-zing-ken, *v* to sink

versoffen, fair-zof-en, *adj fam* drunk

versöhnen, fair-zern-en, *v* to reconcile

Versöhnung, fair-zern-oong, *f* reconciliation

versorgen, fair-zorg-en, *v* to provide (with)

Versorgung, fair-zorg-oong, *f* provision

verspäten (sich), fair-shpayt-en (zik), *v* to be late

Verspätung, fair-shpayt-oong, *f* delay; lateness

verspeisen, fair-shpy-zen, *v* to eat

versperren, fair-shpairr-en, *v* to obstruct

verspielen, fair-shpeel-en, *v*

to gamble away

verspotten, fair-shpot-en, *v* to mock; to tease

versprechen, fair-shprek-en, *v* to promise; **sich –**, *v* to make a slip of the tongue

Versprechen, fair-shprek-en, *nt* promise

verspüren, fair-shpEEr-en, *v* to feel; to perceive

Verstand, fair-shtahnt, *m* reason; understanding; mind; wit; intellect

verständig, fair-shten-dik, *adj* sensible, reasonable; prudent

verständigen, fair-shten-dig-en, *v* to advise; to inform; **sich –**, *v* to communicate; to agree on (sth)

verständlich, fair-shtent-lik, *adj* intelligible; understandable

Verständnis, fair-shtent-nis, *nt* comprehension; understanding

verstärken, fair-shtaik-en, *v* to strengthen

Verstärker, fair-shtaik-er, *m* amplifier

Verstärkung, fair-shtaik-oong, *f* strengthening; reinforcement; amplification

verstauben, fair-shtowb-en, *v* to get dusty

verstauchen, fair-shtowk-en, *v* to sprain

Versteck, fair-shteck, *nt* hiding-place; concealment

verstecken, fair-**shteck**-en, v
to hide

verstehen, fair-**shtay**-en, v
to understand

versteigern, fair-**shty**-gern, v
to auction

Versteigerung, fair-**shty**-ger-oong, f auction

verstellbar, fair-**shtel**-bar,
adj adjustable

verstellen, fair-**shtel**-en, v to
shift; to block (way); **sich
–,** v to dissemble, to
disguise

versteuern, fair-**shtoy**-ern, v
to tax

verstimmen, fair-**shtim**-en, v
to put out of tune; fam to
annoy

verstohlen, fair-**shtohl**-en,
adj stealthy, furtive

verstopfen, fair-**shtop**-fen, v
to stop up; to block

Verstopfung, fair-**shtop**-foong, f constipation;
obstruction

verstorben, fair-**shtorb**-en,
adj deceased; late

Verstörtheit, fair-**shtert**-hite, f bewilderment

Verstoß, fair-**shtohs**, m
offence, breach

verstoßen, fair-**shtohs**-en, v
to offend, to violate

verstreichen, fair-**shtry**-ken,
v to elapse

verstümmeln, fair-**shtEEmm**-eln, v to
mutilate

verstummen, fair-**shtoomm**-en, v to become

silent/dumb

Versuch, fair-**zook**, m
attempt; try, trial;
experiment

versuchen, fair-**zook**-en, v to
try; to attempt; to tempt

Versuchskaninchen, fair-**zooks**-kahn-een-ken, nt fig
guinea-pig

Versuchung, fair-**zook**-oong, f temptation

versumpfen, fair-**zoomp**-fen,
v to become boggy; to go
to pot

versündigen (sich), fair-**zEEnn**-dig-en (zik), v to
sin; to trespass

versüßen, fair-**zEEs**-en, v to
sweeten

vertagen, fair-**tahg**-en, v to
postpone; to adjourn

vertauschen, fair-**towsh**-en,
v to exchange; to mix up

verteidigen, fair-ty-dig-en, v
to defend

Verteidiger, fair-ty-dig-er, m
defender

Verteidigung, fair-ty-dig-oong, f defence

verteilen, fair-ty-len, v to
distribute; to apportion

verteuern, fair-toy-ern, v to
make dearer

verteufelt, fair-**toyf**-elt, adj
devilish; damned,
confounded

vertiefen, fair-teef-en, v to
deepen; **sich –,** v to
become engrossed

vertilgen, fair-tilg-en, v to
eradicate; to destroy; to

eat up

Vertilgung, fair-tilg-oong, f
extermination

Vertrag, fair-trahk, m
agreement, contract;
treaty

vertragen, fair-trahg-en, v to
bear, to endure; **sich –,** v
to get on (with sb); to go
well together

vertraglich, fair-trahk-lik,
adj & adv contractual(ly)

verträglich, fair-traik-lik, adj
sociable; compatible;
easily digestible

vertrauen, fair-trow-en, v to
trust

Vertrauen, fair-trow-en, nt
trust; confidence

vertraulich, fair-trow-lik,
adj in confidence

vertraut, fair-trowt, adj
familiar

vertreiben, fair-try-ben, v to
dispel; to sell; to pass
(time)

Vertreibung, fair-try-boong,
f exile, expulsion

vertreten, fair-trayt-en, v to
represent; to bar (way)

Vertreter, fair-trayt-er, m
representative; salesman

Vertretung, fair-trayt-oong,
f agency

Vertrieb, fair-treep, m sale;
distribution department

vertrocknen, fair-trock-nen,
v to dry up; to wither

vertrösten, fair-trerst-en, v
to put off with promises

vertun, fair-toon, v to waste;

sich –, v to make a mistake

vertuschen, fair-**toosh**-en, v to hush up; to gloss over

Vertuschung, fair-**toosh**-oong, f cover-up

verübeln, fair-**EEb**-eln, v to take amiss; to blame for

verüben, fair-**EEb**-en, v to commit (crime)

verunglücken, fair-oonn-**glEEck**-en, v to come to grief; to have an accident

verunreinigen, fair-oonn-**rine**-ig-en, v to pollute; to soil

verunstalten, fair-oonn-**shtahlt**-en, v to deface

verursachen, fair-oor-**zahk**-en, v to cause

verurteilen, fair-oor-**tile**-en, v to condemn; to sentence

Verurteilung, fair-oor-**tile**-oong, f (passing of) sentence, verdict; condemnation

vervielfachen, fair-**feel**-fak-en, v to multiply

vervielfältigen, fair-**feel**-felt-ig-en, v to copy, to duplicate

vervollkommnen, fair-**fol**-kom-nen, v to perfect

vervollständigen, fair-**fol**-shten-dig-en, v to complete

verwachsen, fair-**vahcks**-en, v to heal up; to outgrow; to interlace; adj deformed

verwahren, fair-**vahr**-en, v to guard; to keep (safe)

verwahrlosen, fair-**vahr**-lohz-en, v to be uncared for

Verwahrung, fair-**vahr**-oong, f safe keeping

verwaisen, fair-**vy**-zen, v to become orphaned

verwaist, fer-**vy'st**, adj orphaned; abandoned, deserted

verwalten, fair-**vahlt**-en, v to administer, to manage; to govern

Verwalter, fair-**vahlt**-er, m administrator; trustee

Verwaltung, fair-**vahlt**-oong, f management; administration

verwandeln, fair-**vahnn**-deln, v to transform

Verwandlung, fair-**vahnd**-loong, f transformation

verwandt, fair-**vahnt**, adj related

Verwandte(r), fair-**vahnt**-e(r), m & f, relative, relation

Verwandtschaft, fair-**vahnt**-shahft, f relationship; relatives, relations

verwarnen, fair-**vahrn**-en, v to caution

verwechseln, fair-**vecks**-eln, v to mistake for

Verwechslung, fair-**vecks**-loong, f mistake; confusion

verwegen, fair-**vayg**-en, adj bold, rash; daring

Verwegenheit, fair-**vayg**-en-hite, f audacity

verweigern, fair-**vy**-gern, v to refuse

Verweigerung, fair-**vy**-ger-oong, f refusal, denial

verweilen, fair-**vy**-len, v to stay, to remain

Verweis, fair-**vice**, m reproof, reprimand; reference

verweisen, fair-**vy**-zen, v to reprimand; to refer

verwelken, fair-**velk**-en, v to wither, to fade

verwenden, fair-**vend**-en, v to use; to utilize

Verwendung, fair-**vend**-oong, f use

verwerflich, fair-**vairf**-lik, adj reprehensible

verwerten, fair-**vairt**-en, v to utilize

verwesen, fair-**vayz**-en, v to decay, to rot

Verwesung, fair-**vayz**-oong, f putrefaction

verwickeln, fair-**vick**-eln, v to entangle, to involve

verwickelt, fair-**vick**-elt, adj complicated, complex

verwildern, fair-**vil**-dern, v to grow wild; to run to seed

verwirken, fair-**veerk**-en, v to forfeit

verwirklichen, fair-**veerk**-lik-en, v to realize

verwirren, fair-**veerr**-en, v to confuse; to (en)tangle

Verwirrung, fair-**veerr**-oong, f confusion

verwischen, fair-**vish**-en, v

to become blurred, to obscure

verwittern, fair-vit-ern, v to weather

verwöhnen, fair-vern-en, v to pamper; to spoil

verworren, fair-vorr-en, adj confused

verwundbar, fair-voont-bar, adj vulnerable

verwunden, fair-voonn-den, v to wound, to injure

verwundern, fair-voonn-dern, v to surprise

Verwunderung, fair-voonn-der-oong, f amazement, surprise, astonishment

Verwundung, fair-voond-oong, f wound, injury

verwünschen, fair-vEEnn-shen, v to curse; to enchant

verwüsten, fair-vEEst-en, v to devastate

Verwüstung, fair-vEEst-oong, f devastation

verzagen, fair-tsahg-en, v to despair; to lose courage

verzaubern, fair-tsowb-ern, v to bewitch

verzehren, fair-tsayr-en, v to devour; to absorb, to consume

verzeichnen, fair-tsy'k-nen, v to record

Verzeichnis, fair-tsy'k-nis, nt schedule, list, record, index

verzeihen, fair-tsy-en, v to pardon

verzeihlich, fair-tsy-lik, adj

pardonable

Verzeihung, fair-tsy-oong, f pardon, forgiveness; interj I'm sorry

verzerrt, fair-tsairt, adj distorted

Verzicht, fair-tsikt, m resignation; renunciation

verzichten, fair-tsikt-en, v to renounce

verziehen, fair-tsee-en, v to distort; to spoil (children)

verzieren, fair-tseer-en, v to decorate

Verzierung, fair-tseer-oong, f decoration, embellishment

verzinken, fair-tsing-ken, v to galvanize

verzinsen, fair-tsin-zen, v to pay interest on

verzögern, fair-tserg-ern, v to retard; to delay

verzollen, fair-tsol-en, v to pay duty on

verzuckern, fair-tsoock-ern, v to coat with sugar; to sweeten (also fig)

Verzug, fair-tsook, m delay

verzweifeln, fair-tsvy-feln, v to despair

Verzweiflung, fair-tsvy-floong, f despair

Vetter, fet-er, m (male) cousin

vgl., abbr vergleiche, cf.

Video, vee-day-oh, nt video; **–gerät**, nt video recorder

Vieh, fee, nt cattle; live stock; **–zucht**, f cattle-breeding

viel, feel, adj much; **–e**, feel-e, adj many

vielerlei, feel-er-ly, adj many kinds of

vielfach, feel-fahk, adj multiple; adv often

Vielfalt, feel-fahlt, f variety

Vielfraß, feel-frahs, m glutton

vielleicht, feel-ly'kt, adv perhaps, maybe

vielmals, feel-mahls, adv often, frequently

vielmehr, feel-mair, adv rather; on the contrary

vielseitig, feel-zy-tik, adj many-sided; versatile

vier, feer, num four

Viereck, feer-eck, nt square, quadrangle

viereckig, feer-eck-ik, adj square, four-cornered

Vierfüßler, feer-fEEs-ler, m quadruped

viermal, feer-mahl, adv four times

vierte(r), feert-e(r), adj fourth

Viertel, feert-el, nt quarter; fourth

Vierteljahr, feert-el-yahr, nt quarter (of a year)

vierteljährlich, feert-el-yair-lik, adj quarterly

Viertelstunde, feert-el-shtoonn-de, f quarter of an hour

vierzehn, feer-tsain, num fourteen

vierzig, feer-tsik, num forty

Villa, vil-ah, f villa

Violine, vee-oh-**leen**-*e*, *f* violin

Virus, vee-rooss, *nt* virus

Visitenkarte, vee-**zeet**-en-kart-*e*, *f* visiting-card

Visum, vee-zoomm, *nt* visa

Vitamin, vee-tah-**meen**, *nt* vitamin

Vogel, fohg-*el*, *m* bird; fowl; **–käfig,** *m* bird-cage; **–scheuche,** *f* scarecrow

Vokabel, voh-**kahb**-*el*, *f* word (usually in a foreign language); **–n,** *pl* vocabulary

Vokal, voh-**kahl**, *m* vowel

Volk, folk, *nt* people; nation; race; **–sabstimmung,** *f* referendum; **–sfest,** *nt* fair; **–slied,** *nt* folk-song

volkstümlich, folks-tEEm-lik, *adj* popular

Volksvertreter, folks-fair-trayt-*er*, *m* member of parliament

Volkswirtschaft, folks-veert-shahft, *f* political economy, economics

voll, fol, *adj* full; filled; complete; **–auf,** *adv* abundantly, in plenty

Vollbart, foll-bart, *m* (full) beard, whiskers

Vollblut, foll-bloot, *nt* thoroughbred

vollbringen, foll-bring-*en*, *v* to achieve; to carry out

vollenden, foll-end-*en*, *v* to complete; to finish

vollendet, foll-**end**-*et*, *adj* complete; perfect

vollends, foll-ends, *adv* entirely, wholly

Vollendung, foll-**end**-oong, *f* completion; perfection

Völlerei, ferll-*e*-**ry**, *f* gluttony

Vollgas, foll-gahs, *nt* full throttle; **mit –,** at full tilt

völlig, ferll-ik, *adj* complete; *adv* wholly, entirely

volljährig, foll-yayr-ik, *adj* of age

vollkommen, foll-kom-*en*, *adj* perfect; thorough; absolute

Vollkommenheit, foll-kom-en-hite, *f* perfection

Vollkorn, foll-korn, *nt* wholemeal; **–brot,** *nt* wholemeal bread

vollmachen, foll-mahk-*en*, *v* to fill

Vollmacht, foll-mahkt, *f* power of attorney

Vollmilch, foll-milk, *f* full-cream milk

Vollmond, foll-mohnt, *m* full moon

Vollpension, foll-pengs-yohn, *f* full-board

vollständig, foll-shten-dik, *adj* complete; *adv* altogether

vollstrecken, foll-shtreck-*en*, *v* to execute

Vollwertkost, foll-vairt-kost, *f* wholefood

vollzählig, foll-tsayl-ik, *adj* complete (numerically)

vollziehen, foll-tsee-*en*, *v* to

complete; to execute

Volontär, voll-on-**tair**, *m* volunteer; trainee

vom, fom, **= von dem,** of the, from the

von, fon, *prep* of; from; by

vor, for, *prep* before, in front of; previous; ago; because of

Vorabend, for-ahb-ent, *m* evening before

vorahnen, for-ahn-*en*, *v* to have a premonition

voran, for-**ahnn**, *adv* at the/in front; **–kommen,** *v* to make progress

voraus, for-**ows**, *adv* before, in advance

vorausahnen, for-ows-ahn-*en*, *v* to have a premonition

vorausgehen, for-ows-gay-*en*, *v* to lead the way; to precede

voraussagen, for-ows-zahg-*en*, *v* to predict

voraussetzen, for-ows-zet-sen, *v* to presume

Voraussetzung, for-ows-zet-soong, *f* assumption; prerequisite

voraussichtlich, for-ows-zikt-lik, *adj* prospective; *adv* probably

Vorbedacht, for-be-dahkt, *m* forethought

Vorbedingung, for-be-ding-oong, *f* precondition

Vorbehalt, for-be-hahlt, *m* reservation

vorbei, for-by, *adv* by, past;

over

vorbereiten, for-be-ry-ten, *v*
to prepare

vorbestellen, for-be-shtel-
en, *v* to book (in advance)

vorbeugen, for-boyg-en, *v*
to bend forward; to take
precaution

Vorbild, for-bilt, *nt* model,
pattern; prototype

vorbildlich, for-bilt-lik, *adj*
pattern, model;
representative

vordem, for-daym, *adv*
formerly

vordere(r), for-der-e(r), *adj*
(in) front

Vorderfuß, ford-er-foos, *m*
forefoot

Vordergrund, ford-er-
groont, *m* foreground

Vorderrad, ford-er-raht, *nt*
front wheel

vordrängen, for-dreng-en, *v*
to press forward

vordringen, for-dring-en, *v*
to push forward, to
advance

voreilig, for-ile-ik, *adj* rash,
overhasty

voreingenommen, for-ine-
ge-nomm-en, *adj*
prepossessed

vorenthalten, for-ent-hahlt-
en, *v* to withhold

vorerst, for-airst, *adv* for the
present; first of all

Vorfahr(e), for-fahr-(-e), *m*
ancestor

Vorfahrt, for-airst, *f* right of
way

Vorfall, for-fahll, *m*
incident, occurrence

vorfallen, for-fahll-en, *v* to
happen, to occur

vorfinden, for-fin-den, *v* to
find; to discover

Vorfreude, for-froy-de, *f*
anticipation

vorführen, for-fEEr-en, *v* to
demonstrate, to show

Vorgang, for-gahng, *m*
process; proceedings; file

Vorgänger, for-geng-er, *m*
predecessor

vorgehen, for-gay-en, *v* to
be fast (clock); to
proceed; to advance

vorgestern, for-gest-ern, *adv*
the day before yesterday

vorhaben, for-hahb-en, *v* to
intend; to have on

vorhanden, for-hahnn-den,
adj at hand; present;
existing

Vorhang, for-hahng, *m*
curtain

vorher, for-hair, *adv*
previously

vorhersagen, for-hair-zahg-
en, *v* to predict

vorhersehen, for-hair-zay-
en, *v* to foresee

vorhin, for-hin, *adv* just
now; recently

vorig(e/r), for-ik (**for**-ig-
e/er), *adj* last, previous;
past

Vorkehrung, for-kair-oong,
f provision; precautionary
measure

Vorkenntnis, for-kent-niss,

f previous knowledge

vorkommen, for-kom-en, *v*
to occur, to happen

vorläufig, for-loyf-ik, *adj*
provisional; preliminary

vorlaut, for-lowt, *adj*
cheeky, impertinent

vorlegen, for-layg-en, *v* to
lay before; to submit

vorlesen, for-layz-en, *v* to
read aloud

Vorlesung, for-layz-oong, *f*
lecture, reading

vorletzt(e/r), for-letst(-
e/er), *adj* last but one

Vorliebe, for-leeb-e, *f*
preference

vormals, for-mahls, *adv*
formerly

vormerken, for-mairk-en, *v*
to make a note; to mark

Vormittag, for-mit-ahg, *m*
morning

vormittags, for-mit-ahgs,
adv in the morning; a.m.

Vormund, for-moont, *m*
guardian

vorn(e), forn(-e), *adv* in
front

Vorname, for-nahm-e, *m*
first/Christian name

vornehm, for-naym, *adj*
elegant; aristocratic;
distinguished

vornehmen, for-naym-en, *v*
to do, to carry out; **sich –**,
v to resolve/intend (to do
sth)

Vorort, for-ort, *m* suburb(s)

Vorposten, for-post-en, *m*
outpost

Vorrat, for-raht, *m* stock; store; **–skammer**, *f* larder, store cupboard

Vorrichtung, for-rik-toong, *f* device, arrangement

vorrücken, for-rEEck-en, *v* to advance

Vorsaison, for-zay-zong, *f* early season

Vorsatz, for-zahts, *m* resolution; design; purpose

Vorschau, for-show, *f* preview; trailer

Vorschein, for-shine, *m* appearance

Vorschlag, for-shlahk, *m* proposal

vorschlagen, for-shlahg-en, *v* to propose; to suggest

vorschreiben, for-shry-ben, *v* to prescribe; to stipulate

Vorschrift, for-shrift, *f* order; prescription

Vorschule, for-school-e, *f* preparatory school

Vorschuß, for-shoos, *m* advance (of money)

vorschützen, for-shEEtt-sen, *v* to pretend

vorsehen, for-zay-en, *v* to provide for; **sich –**, *v* to be careful

Vorsehung, for-zay-oong, *f* (divine) providence

vorsetzen, for-zet-sen, *v* to place before; to move forward

Vorsicht, for-zikt, *f* foresight; care; caution

vorsichtig, for-zik-tik, *adj* careful, cautious

Vorsichtsmaßregel, for-zikts-mahs-rayg-el, *f* measure of precaution

Vorsitzende(r), for-zits-end-e(r), *m & f*, president, chair(person)

Vorsorge, for-zorg-e, *f* provision

vorsorgen, for-zorg-en, *v* to provide, to make provisions

Vorspeise, for-shpy-ze, *f* hors d'oeuvre, starter

vorspiegeln, for-shpeeg-eln, *v* to delude, to deceive

Vorspiel, for-shpeel, *nt* prelude; overture

vorsprechen, for-shprek-en, *v* to call on someone; to recite

Vorsprung, for-shproong, *m* projection; start, lead; advantage

Vorstadt, for-shtahtt, *f* suburb

Vorstand, for-shtahnt, *m* committee, board; director

vorstehen, for-shtay-en, *v* to superintend; to project

Vorsteher, for-shtay-er, *m* superintendent, chief

vorstellen, for-shtel-en, *v* to introduce; to represent; to personify; **sich –**, *v* to imagine, to visualize; to go for a (job) interview

Vorstellung, for-shtel-oong, *f* introduction; imagination; performance; show; **–sgespräch**, *nt* (job) interview

Vorstoß, for-shtohs, *m* push forward; advance, attack

vorstoßen, for-shtohs-en, *v* to project; to push forward

Vorstrafe, for-shtrah-fe, *f* previous conviction

vorstrecken, for-shtreck-en, *v* to stretch forward; to advance (money)

Vorteil, for-tile, *m* advantage, gain

vorteilhaft, for-tile-hahft, *adj* advantageous

Vortrag, for-trahk, *m* lecture; performance; recital

vortragen, for-trahg-en, *v* to carry forward; to recite; to express

vortrefflich, for-tref-lik, *adj* excellent; superior

vortreten, for-trayt-en, *v* to step forward

vorüber, for-EEb-er, *adv* past, over, gone; **–gehen**, *v* to go past; to pass

Vorurteil, for-oohr-tile, *nt* prejudice

Vorverkauf, for-fair-kowf, *m* advance sale

Vorwahl, for-vahl, *f* area code

Vorwand, for-vahnt, *m* pretext, subterfuge

vorwärts, for-vairts, *adv* forward(s); onward(s)

vorwerfen, for-vairf-en, *v* to throw in front of; to reproach

vorwiegend, for-veeg-ent,

adj predominant

Vorwort, for-vort, *nt*
preface

Vorwurf, for-voorf, *m*
reproach

vorzeigen, for-tsy-gen, *v* to
produce, to show; to
present

vorzeitig, for-tsy-tik, *adj*
premature

vorziehen, for-tsee-en, *v* to
draw forth; to prefer

Vorzimmer, for-tsim-*er, nt*
anteroom; reception
(area)

Vorzug, for-tsook, *m*
preference; privilege;
precedence

vorzüglich, for-tsEEk-lik, *adj*
excellent; choice

Waage, vahg-*e,* f scales

waagrecht, vahk-rekt, *adj* horizontal

Waagschale, vahk-shahl-*e,* f scale (of balance)

Wabe, vahb-*e,* f honeycomb

wach, vahk, *adj* awake; alive; brisk

Wache, vahk-*e,* f guard (-house); watch; police-station

wachen, vahk-*en,* v to watch; to be awake

Wachs, vahcks, *nt* wax

wachsam, vahk-zahm, *adj* watchful, vigilant

wachsen, vahcks-*en,* v to grow; to wax

Wachstuch, vahcks-took, *nt* American (wax) cloth

Wachstum, vahcks-toom, *nt* growth

Wachtel, vahk-tel, f quail (bird)

Wächter, vek-ter, m watchman; guard(ian)

Wachtmeister, vahkt-my-ster, m sergeant-major; police sergeant

wack(e)lig, vahck(-*e*)-lik, *adj* rickety; shaky

wackeln, vahck-*eln,* v to shake; to rock; to stagger

wacker, vahck-er, *adj* good, decent, honest

Wade, vahd-*e,* f calf (of leg)

Waffe, vahff-*e,* f weapon, arm

Waffel, vahff-*el,* f wafer; waffle

Waffenstillstand, vahff-en-shtil-shtahnt, m armistice; cease-fire

wagen, vahg-*en,* v to dare, to venture; to stake

Wagen, vahg-*en,* m carriage; car; vehicle

wägen, vayg-*en,* v to weigh (up)

Waggon, vahgg-ong, m railway-truck; carriage

Wagnis, vahg-nis, *nt* risk, hazard; venture

Wahl, vahl, f choice, selection; election

wählen, vayl-*en,* v to choose, to select; to elect

Wähler, vayl-er, m elector

wählerisch, vayl-er-ish, *adj* fastidious

Wahlkampf, vahl-kahmp'f, m election campaign

Wahlkreis, vahl-krise, m constituency

Wahlrecht, vahl-rekt, *nt* franchise; suffrage

Wahlstimme, vahl-shtim-*e,* f vote

Wahn, vahn, m delusion, illusion; mania

wähnen, vayn-*en,* v to fancy; to think wrongly

Wahnsinn, vahn-zin, m madness; insanity; far out!

wahnsinnig, vahn-zin-ik, *adj* mad, insane; *adj fam* incredibly

wahr, vahr, *adj* true; genuine; proper

wahren, vahr-*en,* v to preserve (from)

währen, vayr-*en,* v to last; to hold out

während, vayr-ent, *prep* during; *conj* while

wahrhaftig, vahr-hahft-ik,

223

adj true; *interj* really, actually

Wahrheit, vahr-hite, *f* truth; reality

wahrlich, vahr-lik, *adv* really; indeed

wahrnehmen, vahr-naym-en, *v* to perceive

wahrsagen, vahr-zahg-en, *v* to predict; to tell fortunes

Wahrsager, vahr-zahg-er, *m* fortune-teller

wahrscheinlich, vahr-shine-lik, *adj* probable; *adv* probably

Währung, vayr-oong, *f* currency; sterling

Waise, vy-ze, *f* orphan

Wal, vahll, *m* whale

Wald, vahlt, *m* wood, forest; **–brand**, *m* forest fire

Walfisch, vahll-fish, *m* whale

Waliser, vah-lee-zer, *m* Welshman; **–in**, *f* Welshwoman

walisisch, vah-lee-zish, *adj* Welsh

Wall, vahll, *m* rampart(s); dam

Wallach, vahll-ahk, *m* gelding

wallen, vahll-en, *v* to flow; to bubble up

Wallfahrt, vahll-fahrt, *f* pilgrimage

Walnuß, vahll-nooss, *f* walnut

Walroß, vahll-ross, *nt* walrus

walten, vahlt-en, *v* to rule;

to act

Walze, vahlt-se, *f* roller; cylinder; barrel

walzen, vahlt-sen, *v* to roll (flat)

wälzen, velt-sen, *v* to turn about; to roll over

Walzer, vahlt-ser, *m* waltz

Wand, vahnt, *f* wall; partition; side; panel

Wandel, vahnn-del, *m* change

wandeln, vahnn-deln, *v* to wander, to walk; to change

Wanderer, vahnn-de-rer, *m* traveller (on foot)

Wanderlust, vahnn-der-loost, *f* desire to travel

wandern, vahnn-dern, *v* to wander; to go walking

Wanderschaft, vahnn-der-shahft, *f* journey, travelling

Wandervogel, vahnn-der-fohg-el, *m* bird of passage; *fig* hiker

Wanderweg, vahnn-der-vayg, *m* footpath, trail

Wanduhr, vahnt-oor, *f* wall clock

Wange, vahng-e, *f* cheek

wanken, vahng-ken, *v* to flinch; to budge

wann, vahnn, *adv* when

Wanne, vahnn-e, *f* bath (-tub)

Wanze, vahnt-se, *f* bug

Wappen, vahpp-en, *nt* coat-of-arms; crest

Ware, vahr-e, *f* good(s),

ware, commodity; **–nhaus**, *nt* warehouse, department-store; **–nzeichen**, *nt* trademark

warm, varm, *adj* warm

Wärme, vairm-e, *f* warmth; heat

wärmen, vairm-en, *v* to warm; to heat

Wärmflasche, vairm-flahsh-e, *f* hot water bottle

warnen, varn-en, *v* to warn; to caution

Warnung, varn-oong, *f* warning; caution

Warschau, var-show, *nt* Warsaw

warten, vart-en, *v* to wait; to stay

Wärter, vairt-er, *m* attendant

Wartesaal, vart-e-zahl, *m* waiting-room

warum, vah-roomm, *adv* why

Warze, vart-se, *f* wart; nipple

was, vahss, *pron* what; (that) which, that

Waschbecken, vahsh-beck-en, *nt* wash-basin

Wäsche, vesh-e, *f* wash(ing); linen, clothes

waschecht, vahsh-ekt, *adj* (colour-)fast; *fig* genuine

waschen, vahsh-en, *v* to wash

Wäscherei, vesh-e-ry, *f* laundry

Waschküche, vahsh-KEEk-e, *f* laundry room

Waschlappen, vahsh-lahpp-en, m (face-) flannel

Waschmaschine, vahsh-mah-shee-ne, f washing machine

Waschmittel, vahsh-mit-el, nt detergent

Waschpulver, vahsh-pooll-fer, nt washing powder

Waschsalon, vahsh-sah-long, m launderette

Wasser, vahss-er, nt water

wasserdicht, vahss-er-dikt, adj water-tight, water-proof

Wasserfall, vahss-er-fahll, m waterfall

Wasserhahn, vahss-er-hahn, m water-tap

wässerig, vess-er-ik, adj watery

Wasserkessel, vahss-er-kess-el, m kettle; boiler

Wasserleitung, vahss-er-ly-toong, f water-supply

wässern, vess-ern, v to water

wasserscheu, vahss-er-shoy, adj afraid of water

Wassersport, vahss-er-shport, m watersports

Wasserstoff, vahss-er-shtof, m hydrogen

Wassersucht, vahss-er-zookt, f dropsy

wäßrig, vess-rik, adj watery

waten, vaht-en, v to wade

watscheln, vaht-sheln, v to waddle

Watt, vahtt, nt mud flats; watt

Watte, vahtt-e, f cotton-wool

weben, vayb-en, v to weave

Weber, vayb-er, m weaver

Weberei, vay-be-ry, f weaving (mill); woven article

Webstuhl, vayp-shtool, m loom

Wechsel, vecks-el, m change; fluctuation; fin bill of exchange; **–geld**, nt (small) change; **–jahre**, pl menopause; **–kurs**, m exchange rate

wechseln, vecks-eln, v to change; to interchange

wecken, veck-en, v to awaken, to rouse

Wecker, veck-er, m alarm-clock

wedeln, vayd-eln, v to wag (tail); to fan

weder, vayd-er, conj neither; **– ... noch**, neither ... nor

Weg, vayk, m way, path, track, road, street

weg, veck, adv away; gone; (far) off

wegbegeben (sich), veck-be-gayb-en (zik), v to go away, to drift away

wegbleiben, veck-bly-ben, v to remain/stay away

wegblicken, veck-blick-en, v to look away

wegbringen, veck-bring-en, v to take away

wegen, vayg-en, prep on account of, because of

wegfahren, veck-fahr-en, v to drive away; to depart

weggehen, veck-gay-en, v to go away, to leave

wegjagen, veck-yahg-en, v to chase/drive away

weglassen, veck-lahss-en, v to leave out; to allow someone to go

weglaufen, veck-lowf-en, v to run away

wegmüssen, veck-mEEss-en, v to be obliged to leave

wegnehmen, veck-naym-en, v to take away

wegräumen, veck-roym-en, v to clear away

wegreißen, veck-ry-sen, v to tear away/off

wegrennen, veck-ren-en, v to run away

wegschicken, veck-shick-en, v to send away

wegschleppen, veck-shlep-en, v to drag away

wegschließen, veck-shlees-en, v to lock away

wegsehen, veck-zay-en, v to look away

wegsenden, veck-zend-en, v to send off/away

wegsetzen, veck-zet-sen, v to move/put aside/away

wegstecken, veck-shteck-en, v to hide away; fig to cope

wegstellen, veck-shtel-en, v to put away

wegstürzen, veck-shtEErt-sen, v to dash/rush away

wegtragen, veck-trahg-en, v

to carry off/away

wegtreten, veck-trayt-*en*, *v* to step aside; to break ranks

wegtun, veck-toon, *v* to put away; to hide

Wegweiser, vayg-vy-*zer*, *m* sign-post

wegwerfen, veck-vairf-*en*, *v* to throw away

Wegwerfwindel, veck-vairf-vin-del, *f* disposable nappy

wegwollen, veck-vol-*en*, *v* to want to get away

wegziehen, veck-tsee-*en*, *v* to drag away; to move away

weh, vay, *adj* painful, sore; –**tun**, *v* to hurt

Weh, vay, *nt* pain, woe, pang; –**en**, *pl* labour pains

weh(e), vay(-*e*), *interj* alas! don't you dare!

wehen, vay-*en*, *v* to waft; to blow; to flutter

Wehgeschrei, vay-ge-shry, *nt* lamentation

wehklagen, vay-klahg-*en*, *v* to wail, to lament

Wehmut, vay-moot, *f* melancholy; sadness

wehmütig, vay-mEEt-ik, *adj* doleful

Wehr, vayr, *f* resistance, defence; guard, troop(s); *nt* weir; –**dienst**, *m* military service

wehren (sich), vay-ren, (zik), *v* to resist, to defend o.s.

wehrlos, vayr-lohs, *adj*

defenceless

Wehrpflicht, vayr-p'flikt, *f* compulsory military service

Weib, vipe, *nt* woman, female; wife; –**chen**, *nt* female animal

weiblich, vipe-lik, *adj* feminine

weich, vy'k, *adj* soft; mild, delicate

Weiche, vy-ke, *f* shunt(ing); switch

weichen, vy-ken, *v* to soften; to yield; to withdraw

weichherzig, vy'k-hairt-sik, *adj* soft-hearted

weichlich, vy'k-lik, *adj* flabby; effeminate

Weide, vy-de, *f* pasture (-land); willow(-tree)

weiden, vy-den, *v* to pasture, to graze

weigern(sich), vy-gern (zik), *v* to refuse, to decline

Weigerung, vy-ge-roong, *f* refusal

Weihe, vy-*e*, *f* dedication, ordination; inauguration

weihen, vy-en, *v* to consecrate, to ordain

Weiher, vy-er, *m* fish-pond

Weihnacht(en), vy-nahkt (-en), *f* (*nt*) Christmas; –**sabend**, *m* Christmas Eve; –**sbaum**, *m* Christmas-tree; **sfest**, *nt* Christmas celebration(s); –**skind**, *nt* child Jesus;

–**lied**, *nt* Christmas carol; –**smann**, *m* Santa Claus

Weihrauch, vy-rowk, *m* incense

weil, vile, *conj* because; since, as

Weile, vile-*e*, *f* while; short time

weilen, vile-*en*, *v* to abide; to stay; to linger

Wein, vine, *m* wine; vine; creeper; –**bau**, *m* cultivation of grapes; –**berg**, *m* vineyard

weinen, vine-*en*, *v* to weep, to cry

weinerlich, vine-er-lik, *adj* whining, whimpering

Weinfaß, vine-fahss, *nt* wine-cask

Weinkarte, vine-kart-*e*, *f* wine-list

Weinkelter, vine-kelt-*er*, *f* wine-press

Weinkrampf, vine-krahmpf, *m* fit of hysterical weeping

Weinlese, vine-lay-ze, *f* vintage

Weinrebe, vine-rayb-*e*, *f* (grape)vine

Weintraube, vine-trow-be, *f* (bunch of) grape(s)

weise, vy-ze, *adj* wise, prudent; shrewd

Weise, vy-ze, *f* manner, way; *mus* tune; *m* wise man, sage

weisen, vy-zen, *v* to point, to show

Weisheit, vice-hite, *f* wisdom, prudence

weismachen, vice-mahk-en, *v* jdm etw –, to make sb believe sth

weiß, vice, *adj* white

weissagen, vice-zahg-en, *v* to prophesy, to predict

Weißbier, vice-beer, *nt* pale ale

Weißbrot, vice-broht, *nt* white bread

Weiße(r), vice-e(r), *m & f,* white (wo)man

Weißkohl, vice-kohl, *m* (white) cabbage

Weisung, vy-zoong, *f* instruction(s); direction

weit, vite, *adj* distant; wide; extensive; broad

Weite, vite-e, *f* width, breadth; spaciousness; distance

weiten, vite-en, *v* to widen; to stretch

weiter, vite-er, *adj* wider; more distant; *adv* farther, further; **–gehen,** *v* to walk/go on; **–hin,** *adv* further/farther on

weitgreifend, vite-gry-fent, *adj* far-reaching

weither, vite-hair, *adv* from afar

weitläufig, vite-loyf-ik, *adj* extensive; spacious, rambling; long drawn-out; *adv* at great length

weitsichtig, vite-zik-tik, *adj* far-sighted; far-seeing

Weizen, vite-sen, *m* wheat; **–mehl,** *nt* wheat flour

welche(r/s), velk-e(r/s), *pron* who, which, what; some, any

welk, velk, *adj* faded, withered; wrinkled

Wellblech, vell-blek, *nt* corrugated iron

Welle, vell-e, *f* wave; billow; shaft; **–nlänge,** *f* wave-length

wellig, vell-ik, *adj* wavy

Welt, velt, *f* world; **–all,** *nt* universe

weltberühmt, velt-be-rEEmt, *adj* world-famous

welterfahren, velt-air-fahr-en, *adj* worldly wise

Weltgeschichte, velt-ge-shik-te, *f* world history

weltlich, velt-lik, *adj* worldly; temporal

Weltmacht, velt-mahkt, *f* world-power

Weltstadt, velt-shtahtt, *f* metropolis

weltweit, velt-vite, *adj* worldwide

wem, vaim, *pron (dative m & nt)* to whom, whom

wen, vain, *pron (accusative m)* whom

Wendeltreppe, ven-del-trep-e, *f* winding staircase

wenden, vend-en , *v* to turn; **sich – an,** to apply to, to turn to

Wendepunkt, vend-e-poonkt, *m* turning point

Wendung, vend-oong, *f* turn(ing); crisis; phrasing

wenig, vayn-ik, *adj* little; **–e,** few; **–er,** less; fewer

wenigstens, vayn-ig-stens, *adv* at least

wenn, ven, *conj* if, when

wer, vair, *pron* who

Werbegeschenk, vairb-e-ge-shenk, *nt* freebee

werben, vairb-en, *v* to woo; to recruit; to advertise

Werbung, vairb-oong, *f* advertising; promotion; publicity

werden, vaird-en, *v* to become; shall, will (future)

werfen, vairf-en, *v* to throw, to fling, to hurl

Werft, vairft, *f* shipyard; hangar

Werk, vairk, *nt* work; labour; enterprise; **–statt,** *f* workshop; **–tag,** *m* week-day; **–zeug,** *nt* tool, instrument

wert, vairt, *adj* worth

Wert, vairt, *m* value, worth; **–sachen,** *pl* valuables

wertvoll, vairt-fol, *adj* valuable; precious

Wesen, vayz-en, *nt* being; existence; condition; essence

wesentlich, vayz-ent-lik, *adj* essential

weshalb, ves-halp, *adv* why

Wespe, vesp-e, *f* wasp

wessen, ves-en, *pron* whose

West-, vest, *pref* West, western

Weste, vest-e, *f* waistcoat

Westen, vest-en, *m* West

westlich, vest-lik, *adj*

west(ern), westerly

weswegen, ves-vayg-en, *adv*
why

Wettbewerb, vet-be-vairp,
m competition

Wette, vet-e, *f* wager, bet

Wetteifer, vet-ife-er, *m*
emulation

wetten, vet-en, *v* to bet, to
wager

Wetter, vet-er, *nt* weather;
–bericht, *m* weather
report; **–karte,** *f* weather
chart; **–leuchten,** *nt* sheet-
lightning; **–vorhersage,** *f*
weather forecast

Wettfahrt, vet-fahrt, *f* race
(boat, cycle etc.)

Wettkampf, vet-kahmp'f, *m*
contest

Wettlauf, vet-lowf, *m*
(running) race

Wettrennen, vet-ren-en, *nt*
(horse)race

Wettstreit, vet-shtrite, *m*
competition; emulation;
match

wetzen, vet-sen, *v* to whet,
to sharpen

Wicht, vikt, *m* goblin; *fam*
titch, little devil

wichtig, vik-tik, *adj*
important, weighty

Wichtigkeit, vik-tik-kite, *f*
importance

wickeln, vick-eln, *v* to
wind; to coil; to reel

Wickelraum, vick-el-rowm,
m (nappy) changing room

wider, veed-er, *prep* against,
contrary to

widerfahren veed-er-**fahr**-
en, *v* to occur, to happen

Widerhall, veed-er-hahll, *m*
echo, reverberation

widerlegen, veed-er-**layg**-en,
v to refute, to disprove

widerlich, veed-er-lich, *adj*
repulsive; sickly

Widerrede, veed-er-rayd-e, *f*
contradiction, objection

widerrufen, veed-er-**roof**-en,
v to contradict; to retract

Widerschein, veed-er-shine,
m reflexion

widersetzen (sich), veed-er-
zets-en (zik), *v* to resist

widersinnig, veed-er-zin-ik,
adj contradictory;
paradoxical

widerspenstig, veed-er-
shpenst-ik, *adj* obstinate

widerspiegeln, veed-er-
shpeeg-eln, *v* to reflect

widersprechen, veed-er-
shprek-en, *v* to contradict

Widerspruch, veed-er-
shprook, *m* contradiction;
opposition

Widerstand, veed-er-
shtahnt, *m* resistance

widerstehen, veed-er-**shtay**-
en, *v* to resist

widerwärtig, veed-er-vairt-
ik, *adj* disgusting; adverse

Widerwille(n), veed-er-vil-
e(n), *m* repugnance;
aversion

widmen, vit-men, *v* to
dedicate

widrig, veed-rik, *adj*
contrary, adverse;

obnoxious

wie, vee, *adv* how; *conj*
(such) as; like

wieder, veed-er, *adv* again,
once more, afresh

wiederaufbereiten, veed-er-
owf-be-rite-en, *v* to
recycle

wiederbekommen, veed-er-
be-kom-en, *v* to get back

wiederbringen, veed-er-
bring-en, *v* to bring back

wiedererkennen, veed-er-
air-ken-en, *v* to recognize

wiederfinden, veed-er-fin-
den, *v* to find again; to
recover

wiedergeben, veed-er-gayb-
en, *v* to give back; to
repeat

wiederherstellen, veed-er-
hair-shtel-en, *v* to restore

wiederholen, veed-er-hohl-
en, *v* to repeat

Wiederkäuer, veed-er-koy-
er, *m* ruminant

wiederkehren, veed-er-kayr-
en, *v* to return

wiederkommen veed-er-
kom-en, *v* to come
back/again

wiedersehen, veed-er-zay-
en, *v* to see again

wiederum, veed-er-oomm,
adv again; on the other
hand

Wiedervereinigung, veed-
er-fair-ine-ee-goong, *f*
reunification

wiederverwerten, veed-er-
fair-vairt-en, *v* to recycle

Wiege, veeg-e, f cradle

wiegen, veeg-en, v to weigh; to have a weight; to rock

Wiegenlied, veeg-en-leet, nt cradle song; lullaby

wiehern, vee-ern, v to neigh

Wien, veen, nt Vienna

Wiese, veez-e, f meadow

Wiesel, veez-el, nt weasel

wieso, vee-zoh, adv why, how

wieviel, vee-feel, adv how much

wild, vilt, adj wild; savage

Wild, vilt, nt game, venison; **–bret,** nt game; venison; **–erer,** m poacher

wildern, vild-ern, v to poach

Wildleder, vilt-layd-er, nt suede

Wildnis, vilt-niss, f wilderness

Wildschwein, vilt-shvine, nt (wild) boar

Wille, vil-e, m will, desire, willingness

willig, vil-ik, adj willing; ready; docile

willkommen, vil-kom-en, adj welcome

Willkür, vil-kEEr, f free will; arbitrary power

willkürlich, vil-kEEr-lik, adj despotic, arbitrary

wimmeln, vim-eln, v to swarm, to abound in

wimmern, vim-ern, v to whine, to whimper

Wimper, vimp-er, f eyelash

Wind, vint, m wind, breeze; **–beutel,** m cream bun

Winde, vin-de, f winch, windlass

Windel, vin-del, f nappy

winden, vin-den, v to twist, to wind

Windenergie, vint-en-air-gee, f wind power

Windhund, vint-hoont, m greyhound

windig, vin-dik, adj windy, breezy

Windmühle, vint-mEEl-e, f windmill

Windschutzscheibe, vint-shoots-shy-be, f windscreen

windstill, vint-shtil, adj calm, without breeze

Windzug, vint-tsook, m draught, current of air

Wink, vink, m hint, beckoning; suggestion

Winkel, ving-kel, m angle; nook, quiet corner

winken, ving-ken, v to beckon, to wave (hand)

winseln, vin-zeln, v to whimper, to wail

Winter, vin-ter, m winter; **–garten,** m conservatory; **–schlaf,** m hibernation; **–sport,** m winter sports

Winzer, vint-ser, m wine-grower

winzig, vint-sik, adj minute, diminutive; petty

Wipfel, vip-fel, m tree-top

wippen, vip-en, v to rock, to balance; to tip

wir, veer, pron we

Wirbel, veerb-el, m whirl;

vertebra; top of head; fuss

wirbeln, veerb-eln, v to whirl; to warble

Wirbelsäule, veerb-el-zoyl-e, f spine

wirken, veerk-en, v to work; to be effective

wirklich, veerk-lik, adj real, actual, substantial

Wirklichkeit, veerk-lik-kite, f reality

wirksam, veerk-zahm, adj efficacious, effective; powerful

Wirksamkeit, veerk-zahm-kite, f efficacy

Wirkung, veerk-oong, f effect; result

wirr, veerr, adj confused, tangled

Wirre, veerr-e, f disorder, chaos; muddle

Wirrwarr, veerr-vahrr, m confusion, chaos

Wirsing(kohl), veer-zing (-kohl), m savoy cabbage

Wirt, veert, m landlord; host; master of house; **–schaft,** f inn; economy

wirtschaften, veert-shahft-en, v to manage

wirtschaftlich, veert-shahft-lik, adj economical; economic

Wirtshaus, veerts-hows, nt inn, pub(lic-house)

wischen, vish-en, v to wipe

wißbegierig, vis-be-geer-ik, adj thirsting for knowledge, inquisitive

wissen, vis-en, v to know, to

be aware

Wissenschaft, vis-en-shahft, f science

wissenschaftlich, vis-en-shahft-lik, adj scientific

wissenswert, vis-ens-vairt, adj worth knowing

wissentlich, vis-ent-lik, adj conscious; wilful

wittern, vit-ern, v to scent, to smell; to suspect

Witterung, vit-er-oong, f weather(-conditions); scent

Witwe, vit-ve, f widow; **–r,** m widower

Witz, vits, m joke, jest; wit; **–bold,** m joker, comedian

witzig, vits-ik, adj witty, funny

wo, voh, adv where

woanders, voh-ahn-ders, adv elsewhere

Woche, vok-e, f week; **–nende,** nt weekend

wochenlang, vok-en-lahng, adj for weeks (on end)

Wochentag, vok-en-tahg, m week-day

wöchentlich, verk-ent-lik, adj weekly

Wodka, vot-kah, m vodka

wodurch, voh-doohrk, adv through what; whereby, through which

Woge, vohg-e, f wave

wogen, vohg-en, v to surge, to swell

woher, voh-hair, adv where from; whence, from where

wohin, voh-hin, adv where

to; to where

wohingegen, voh-hin-**gayg-**en, conj whereas

wohl, vohl, adv well, in good health; indeed

Wohlbefinden, vohl-be-fin-den, nt well-being

Wohlbehagen, vohl-be-hahg-en, nt comfort

wohlbehalten, vohl-be-hahlt-en, adv safely

Wohlfahrt, vohl-fahrt, f welfare

Wohlgefallen, vohl-ge-fahll-en, nt liking; pleasure

Wohlgeruch, vohl-ge-rook, m scent, perfume

wohlhabend, vohl-hahb-ent, adj well-to-do

Wohlklang, vohl-klahng, m harmony, melody

Wohlstand, vohl-shtahnt, m wealth

Wohltäter, vohl-tayt-er, m benefactor

wohltätig, vohl-tayt-ik, adj charitable

Wohltätigkeit, vohl-tayt-ik-kite, f charity

wohlweislich, vohl-vice-lik, adv prudently

Wohlwollen, vohl-vol-en, nt goodwill

wohnen, voh-nen, v to live, to dwell, to reside

Wohngemeinschaft, vohn-ge-mine-shahft, f people sharing a flat/house

Wohnmobil, vohn-moh-beel, nt campervan

Wohnort, vohn-nort, m

dwelling-place

Wohnsitz, vohn-zits, m (place of) residence

Wohnstube, vohn-shtoob-e, f living-room

Wohnung, voh-noong, f dwelling; home; flat

Wohnwagen, vohn-vahg-en, m caravan

Wohnzimmer, vohn-tsim-er, nt living-room

wölben, verlb-en, v to vault, to arch

Wolf, volf, m wolf

Wolke, volk-e, f cloud; **–nbruch,** m cloud-burst, heavy shower; **–nkratzer,** m skyscraper

wolkig, volk-ik, adj cloudy, clouded

Wolle, vol-e, f wool

wollen, vol-en, v to want to; adj woollen

wollig, vol-ik, adj woolly

Wollust, vol-loost, f lust; sensuality

womit, voh-mit, adv what with; with/by which

Wonne, von-e, f bliss, joy, ecstasy

woran, voh-rahnn, adv at/by what; at/by which

worauf, voh-rowf, adv on what; on which

woraus, voh-rows, adv out of what; whence, out of which

worin, voh-rin, adv in what; wherein, in which

Wort, vort, nt word

Wörterbuch, vert-er-book,

nt dictionary

wörtlich, vert-lik, *adj* literal; verbal; verbatim

Wortschatz, vort-shahts, *m* vocabulary

worüber, voh-rEEb-er, *adv* about what; over/about which

worunter, voh-roont-er, *adv* under what; under/among which

wovon, voh-fon, *adv* what from; from which, whereof

wovor, voh-for, *adv* before what; before which

wozu, voh-tsoo, *adv* what for, why; for which

Wrack, vrahck, *nt* wreck(age); debris

wringen, vring-en, *v* to wring (out)

Wucherer, vook-e-rer, *m* usurer, profiteer

wuchern, vook-ern, *v* to grow rampant, to proliferate; to practise usury

Wuchs, voocks, *m* growth

Wucht, vookt, *f* impetus, force; weight

wuchtig, vook-tik, *adj* weighty, heavy

wühlen, vEEl-en, *v* to delve; to burrow; to agitate

wund, voont, *adj* sore, chafed

Wunde, voonn-de, *f* wound; hurt; injury

Wunder, voonn-der, *nt* miracle; marvel; wonder

wunderbar, voonn-der-bar,

adj wonderful

wunderhübsch, voonn-der-hEEpsh, *adj* very pretty

wunderlich, voonn-der-lik, *adj* strange, curious, odd

wundern, voonn-dern, *v* to astonish; **sich –,** *v* to marvel, to be astonished

wunderschön, voonn-der-shern, *adj* very beautiful, exquisite

wundervoll, voonn-der-fol, *adj* wonderful

Wunsch, voonsh, *m* wish, desire; request

wünschen, vEEnn-shen, *v* to wish; to request; **–swert,** *adj* desirable

Würde, vEErd-e, *f* dignity; honour; office; virtue

würdig, vEErd-ik, *adj* worthy; estimable; **–en,** *v* to deem worthy; to deign; to value

Wurf, voorf, *m* throw; cast; litter

Würfel, vEErf-el, *m* dice; cube

würfeln, vEErf-eln, *v* to throw dice; to jumble together

würgen, vEErg-en, *v* to choke; to swallow with difficulty

Wurm, voorm, *m* worm; serpent

wurmig, voorm-ik, *adj* wormy, worm-eaten

Wurst, voorst, *f* sausage

Würstchen, vEErst-ken, *nt* saveloy; small sausage

Würze, vEErt-se, *f* seasoning, flavouring

Wurzel, voort-sel, *f* root

wurzeln, voort-seln, *v* to take root

würzen, vEErt-sen, *v* to season, to spice

würzig, vEErt-sik, *adj* aromatic; piquant, spicy

Wust, voost, *m* confused heap; chaos

wüst, vEEst, *adj* desolate, deserted; waste; repulsive

Wüste, vEEst-e, *f* desert; wilderness

Wut, voot, *f* rage, anger, wrath; mania

wüten, vEEt-en, *v* to rage

wütend, vEEt-ent, *adj* raging, wrathful; furious

Wüterich, vEEt-er-ik, *m* tyrant; frantic person

X

Xanthippe, xahnn-**tip**-*e, f*
shrew

X-Beine, **icks**-by-ne, *pl*
knock-knees

x-beliebig, **icks**-*be*-lee-bik,
adj any old

x-mal, **icks**-mahl, *adv*
umpteen times

Y

Yacht, yah*k*t, *f* yacht
Yoghurt, yoh-goort, *m*
  yoghurt
Yucca, yook-ah, *f* yucca

Zacke(n), tsahck-*e*(n), *m & f,* tooth of comb; prong; peak

zackig, tsahck-ik, *adj* jagged; toothed

zaghaft, tsahk-hahft, *adj* timid; nervous

zäh, tsay, *adj* tough; gluey, glutinous; leathery

Zahl, tsahl, *f* number, figure

zahlen, tsahl-en, *v* to pay

zählen, tsayl-en, *v* to count; to reckon; to amount to

Zähler, tsayl-er, *m* meter (gas/electricity meter)

zahlreich, tsahl-ryk, *adj* numerous

Zahlung, tsahl-oong, *f* payment

Zählung, tsayl-oong, *f* counting; (e)numeration

zahm, tsahm, *adj* tame(d); domesticated

zähmen, tsaym-en, *v* to tame; to break in; to domesticate

Zähmung, tsaym-oong, *f* taming

Zahn, tsahn, *m* tooth; tusk; *mech* cog; **–arzt,** *m* dentist; **–bürste,** *f* tooth-brush; **–fleisch,** *nt* gums; **–pasta,** *f* tooth-paste; **–rad,** *nt* cogwheel; **–schmerz,** *m* toothache; **–stocher,** *m* toothpick; **–weh,** *nt* toothache

Zange, tsahng-e, *f* tongs; pliers; tweezers

Zank, tsahnk, *m* quarrel, altercation, dispute

zanken, tsahng-ken, *v* to quarrel; to scold

zänkisch, tseng-kish, *adj* quarrelsome; nagging

Zapfen, tsahpp-fen, *m* tap; bung, spigot; plug

zapfen, tsahpp-fen, *v* to tap (barrel)

Zapfenstreich, tsahpp-fen-stry'k, *m* lights-out; tattoo

Zapfsäule, tsahp'f-zoy-le, *f* petrol pump

zappelig, tsahpp-el-ik, *adj* fidgety

zappeln, tsahpp-eln, *v* to fidget; to jerk; to kick about

Zar, tsar, *m* Tsar

zart, tsart, *adj* tender; delicate; frail, weak

zartfühlend, tsart-fEEl-ent, *adj* tender-hearted

zärtlich, tsairt-lik, *adj* affectionate; tender

Zärtlichkeit, tsairt-lik-kite, *f* affection, tenderness; **–en,** *pl* affectionate words, sweet nothings

Zauber, tsowb-er, *m* magic, charm, enchantment

Zauberei, tsowb-e-ry, *f* magic; witchcraft

Zauberer, tsowb-e-rer, *m* magician; sorcerer

zauberhaft, tsowb-er-hahft, *adj* magical, enchanting

Zauberkünstler, tsowb-er-kEEnst-ler, *m* conjurer

zaubern, tsowb-ern, *v* to practise magic

zaudern, tsowd-ern, *v* to hesitate; to waver; to hang back

Zaum, tsowm, *m* bridle, rein

zäumen, tsoym-en, *v* to bridle

Zaumzeug, tsowm-tsoyk, *nt* bridle

Zaun, tsown, *m* fence; rail(ing); **–könig,** *m* wren

z.B., *abbr* **zum Beispiel,** e.g.

Zeche, tsek-*e,* *f* bill, reckoning; score; mine

zechen, tsek-en, *v* to carouse, to booze

Zechprellerei, tsek-prel-*e-ry,* *f* not paying one's bill

Zeder, tsay-der, *f* cedar

Zeh(e), tsay(-*e*), *m* (*f*), toe; **–enspitze,** *f* tip of toe

zehn, tsain, *num* ten; **–fach,** *adj* tenfold, ten times; **–te(r),** *adj* tenth

Zehntel, tsain-tel, *nt* tenth

zehren, tsayr-en, *v* to live off, to feed on; to weaken, to sap, to wear (sb) out

Zeichen, tsy-ken, *nt* sign, mark, brand; indication

zeichnen, tsy'k-nen, *v* to draw, to design; to sign

Zeichner, tsy'k-ner, *m* draughtsman

Zeichnung, tsy'k-noong, *f* drawing, sketch(ing)

Zeigefinger, tsy-*ge*-fing-er, *m* index finger, forefinger

zeigen, tsy-gen, *v* to show; to point; to manifest

Zeiger, tsy-ger, *m* hand (of clock/instrument); indicator

Zeile, tsy-le, *f* line (of print); row (of houses)

Zeit, tsite, *f* time; era, epoch; period; **–alter,** *nt* age; **–arbeit,** *f* temporary job; **–geist,** *m* spirit of the age; **–genosse,** *m* contemporary

zeitig, tsite-ik, *adj* timely; opportune; in good time

zeitigen, tsite-ig-en, *v* to mature; to come to a head

Zeitlang, tsite-lahng, *f* (for) some time

zeitlebens, tsite-layb-ens, *adv* for life

zeitlich, tsite-lik, *adj* temporal; earthly

Zeitlupe, tsite-loop-*e,* *f* slow motion

Zeitpunkt, tsite-poonkt, *m* moment; epoch

Zeitraum, tsite-rowm, *m* period (of time)

Zeitschrift, tsite-shrift, *f* periodical, journal

Zeitung, tsy-toong, *f* newspaper

Zeitverschwendung, tsite-fair-shvend-oong, *f* waste of time

Zeitvertreib, tsite-fair-tripe, *m* pastime

zeitweilig, tsite-vile-ik, *adj* temporary

zeitweise, tsite-vy-ze, *adv* for a time

Zeitwort, tsite-vort, *nt* verb

Zelle, tsel-*e,* *f* cell

Zelt, tselt, *nt* tent; awning; **–platz,** *m* campsite

zensieren, tsen-zee-ren, *v* to censure; to give marks (school)

Zensur, tsen-zoor, *f* censorship; (school) mark

Zentimeter, tsen-tee-mayt-er, *m* centimetre

Zentrale, tsent-**rahl**-*e,* *f* central office; (telephone) exchange

Zepter, tsep-ter, *nt* sceptre; mace

zerbrechen, tsair-brek-en, *v* to break to pieces

zerbrechlich, tsair-brek-lik, *adj* brittle; breakable; fragile

zerdrücken, tsair-drEEck-en, *v* to crush

Zerfall, tsair-fahll, *m* decay, ruin

zerfallen, tsair-fahll-en, *v* to fall to pieces

zerfetzen, tsair-fets-en, *v* to tear to shreds; to slit

zerfleischen, tsair-fly-shen, *v* to tear to pieces

zergehen, tsair-gay-en, *v* to dissolve

zergliedern, tsair-gleed-ern, *v* to dismember

zerhacken, tsair-hahck-en, *v* to hack to pieces

zerhauen, tsair-how-en, *v* to smash

zerkauen, tsair-kow-en, *v* to chew well

zerkleinern, tsair-klyn-ern, *v* to reduce to small pieces; to grind; to chop

zerknirscht, tsair-k'neersht, *adj* contrite, penitent

zerknittern, tsair-k'nitt-ern, *v* to crush

zerkratzen, tsair-krahtt-sen, *v* to spoil by scratching

zerlegen, tsair-layg-en, *v* to dissect

zerlumpt, tsair-**loompt,** adj
in rags, ragged

zermahlen, tsair-**mahl**-en, v
to grind up

zermalmen, tsair-**mahlm**-en,
v to grind to powder; to
smash up

zerplatzen, tsair-**plahtt**-sen,
v to explode; to burst

zerquetschen, tsair-**kvet**-
shen, v to crush, to squash

zerreiben, tsair-**ry**-ben, v to
rub to powder

zerreißen, tsair-**ry**-sen, v to
tear (to pieces)

zerren, tsairr-en, v to tug, to
drag

zerrinnen, tsair-**rin**-en, v to
dissolve; to melt (away)

Zerrung, tsair-oong, f
pulled muscle

zerrütten, tsair-**rEEt**-en, v to
ruin, to wreck

zerschellen, tsair-**shel**-en, v
to dash to pieces

zerschlagen, tsair-**shlahg**-en,
v to smash up; fig to
shatter

zerschmettern, tsair-**shmet**-
ern, v to shatter

zerschneiden, tsair-**shny**-
den, v to cut up

zersetzen, tsair-**zet**-sen, v to
disintegrate

zersplittern, tsair-**shplit**-ern,
v to splinter

zerspringen, tsair-**shpring**-
en, v to burst; to split

zerstampfen, tsair-**shtahmp**-
fen, v to pound

Zerstäuber, tsair-**shtoyb**-er,
m atomizer

zerstören, tsair-**shter**-en, v
to destroy

Zerstörung, tsair-**shter**-
oong, f destruction

zerstreuen, tsair-**shtroy**-en,
v to scatter; to divert

zerstreut, tsair-**shtroyt,** adj
scattered; absent-minded

Zerstreuung, tsair-**shtroy**-
oong, f diversion;
distraction

zerstückeln, tsair-**shtEEck**-
eln, v dismember; to chop
up

zerteilen, tsair-**ty**-len, v to
split up; to divide

zertreten, tsair-**trayt**-en, v to
tread under foot

zertrümmern, tsair-**trEEmm**-
ern, v to wreck; to
demolish

zerzausen, tsair-**tsowz**-en, v
to crumple; to crease; to
tousle

zetern, tsayt-ern, v to cry
out in protest; to nag

Zettel, tset-el, m label, slip
of paper; note; form

Zeug, tsoyk, nt stuff,
material; thing(s); utensils

Zeuge, tsoyg-e, m witness

zeugen, tsoyg-en, v to give
evidence; to witness; to
beget

Zeugnis, tsoyk-nis, nt
testimony; certificate

Zichorie, tseek-**ohr**-ye, f
chicory

Zicke, tsick-e, f goat; fam
silly cow

zickzack, tsick-tsahck, adv
(in) zigzag

Ziege, tseeg-e, f nanny-goat;
–nbock, m billy-goat

Ziegel, tseeg-el, m tile;
brick; –stein, m brick

ziehen, tsee-en, v to draw;
to pull; to be draughty; to
move; to rear; to train

Ziehharmonika, tsee-har-
mohn-ick-ah, f accordion

Ziel, tseel, nt goal; aim;
destination; target

zielen, tseel-en, v to (take)
aim

Zielscheibe, tseel-shy-be, f
target, butt

zielstrebig, tseel-shtraib-ik,
adj purposeful, determined

ziemen (sich), tseem-en
(zik), v to be seemly

ziemlich, tseem-lik, adj fair;
moderate; passable; adv
fairly, rather

Zierat, tseer-aht, m
decoration; ornament

Zier(de), tseer(-de), f
ornament

zieren, tseer-en, v to grace;
to decorate

zierlich, tseer-lik, adj dainty;
graceful; neat

Ziffer, tsif-er, f figure,
number; cypher; –blatt, nt
dial

Zigarette, tsee-gah-**ret**-e, f
cigarette

Zigarre, tsee-**gahrr**-e, f cigar

Zigeuner, tsee-**goyn**-er, m
gipsy

Zimmer, tsim-er, nt room,

chamber; **–mädchen**, *nt* chambermaid; **–mann**, *m* carpenter; **–service**, *m* room-service

zimmern, tsim-ern, *v* to do carpentry; to chop with an axe

zimperlich, tsimp-er-lik, *adj* squeamish; prudish

Zimt, tsimt, *m* cinnamon

Zink, tsink, *nt* zinc

Zinke, tsing-ke, *f* prong; (comb) tooth

Zinn, tsin, *nt* tin

Zinne, tsin-e, *f* battlement; pinnacle

Zins(en), tsins(-en), *m (pl)* interest; **–satz**, *m* rate of interest

Zipfel, tsip-fel, *m* tip, point; corner

zirka, tseer-kah, (*abbr* ca.) *adv* about, approximately

Zirkel, tseer-kel, *m* compasses; circle; society

zirkulieren, tseer-koo-leer-en, *v* to circulate

zirpen, tseer-pen, *v* to chirp; to squeak

zischeln, tsish-eln, *v* to whisper

zischen, tsish-en, *v* to hiss; to sizzle; to fizzle

Zitat, tsee-taht, *nt* quotation, quoted passage

Zither, tsit-er, *f* zither; lute

zitieren, tsee-teer-en, *v* to quote; to cite

Zitrone, tsee-trohn-e, *f* lemon

zittern, tsit-ern, *v* to

tremble; to shiver; to quake

Zitze, tsit-se, *f* nipple, teat

Zivil, tsee-veel, *nt* plain clothes; **–courage**, *f* courage of one's convictions; **–dienst**, *m* community service (as alternative to military service)

Zivilisation, tsee-vee-lee-zahts-yohn, *f* civilisation; **–skrankheit**, *f* stress caused by modern-living

zögern, tserg-ern, *v* to hesitate; to linger; to draw back

Zögling, tserk-ling, *m* pupil; charge

Zoll, tsol, *m* toll; (import) duty; customs; inch; **–amt**, *nt* customs house; **–beamte(r)**, *m & f* customs officer

zollen, tsol-en, *v* to acknowledge, to respect, to admire

zollfrei, tsol-fry, *adj* duty-free

Zoo, tsoh, *m* zoo

Zoom(objektiv), zoom(-op-yeck-teef), *nt* zoom lens

Zopf, tsop'f, *m* plait, pigtail

Zorn, tsorn, *m* wrath, anger, indignation

zornig, tsorn-ik, *adj* angry, indignant

Zote, tsoht-e, *f* obscenity, dirty joke

zotig, tsoht-ik, *adj* obscene, smutty

zottig, tsot-ik, *adj* shaggy; tousled

z.T., **abbr zum Teil**, *adv* partly

zu, tsoo, *prep* to, at, by, for, in; *adv* too

Zubehör, tsoo-be-her, *nt* equipment, accessories

zubereiten, tsoo-be-ry-ten, *v* to prepare

zubinden, tsoo-bin-den, *v* to tie/bind up

zubleiben, tsoo-bly-ben, *v* to remain shut

zubringen, tsoo-bring-en, *v* to spend (time)

Zubringer, tsoo-bring-er, *m* approach road

Zucchini, tsook-ee-nee, *pl* courgettes

Zucht, tsookt, *f* breeding; training; cultivation; discipline; decency

züchten, tsEEk-ten, *v* to breed; to grow

Züchter, tsEEk-ter, *m* breeder; keeper; cultivator

Zuchthaus, tsookt-hows, *nt* prison

züchtig, tsEEk-tik, *adj* chaste; demure, modest

züchtigen, tsEEk-tig-en, *v* to chastise; to punish

Züchtigung, tsEEk-tig-oong, *f* chastisement

Züchtung, tsEEk-toong, *f* breeding; cultivation; variety

zucken, tsoock-en, *v* to twitch; to quiver; to jerk

zücken, tsEEck-en, *v* to

draw (sword, dagger)

Zucker, tsoock-er, *m* sugar;
–guß, *m* icing

zuckerig, tsoock-er-ik, *adj*
sugary

Zuckerkrankheit, tsoock-
er-krahnk-hite, *f* diabetes

zuckern, tsoock-ern, *v* to
(sweeten with) sugar

Zuckerrohr, tsoock-er-rohr,
nt sugar-cane

Zuckerrübe, tsoock-er-rEEb-
e, *f* sugar-beet

zudecken, tsoo-deck-en, *v*
to cover (up)

zudem, tsoo-daym, *adv*
moreover, besides

zudrehen, tsoo-dray-en, *v* to
turn off (tap)

zudringlich, tsoo-dring-lik,
adj obtrusive; forward

Zudringlichkeit, tsoo-dring-
lik-kite, *f* forwardness

zudrücken, tsoo-drEEck-en,
v to press shut

zueinander, tsoo-ine-ahnn-
der, *adv* to one another

zuerst, tsoo-airst, *adv* (in
the) first (place)

Zufahrt, tsoo-fahrt, *f*
approach; drive(way)

Zufall, tsoo-fahll, *m* chance,
accident

zufallen, tsoo-fahll-en, *v* to
fall shut, to swing to; to
accrue to

zufällig, tsoo-fel-ik, *adj* by
chance, casual

zufassen, tsoo-fahss-en, *v* to
grasp hold of; to help

zufliegen, tsoo-fleeg-en, *v* to
fly towards; *fig* to come
easily

Zufluß, tsoo-flooss, *m*
influx; tributary

Zuflucht, tsoo-flookt, *f*
shelter, refuge

zufolge, tsoo-folg-e, *prep*
owing to, according to

zufrieden, tsoo-freed-en, *adj*
satisfied, content(ed)

Zufriedenheit, tsoo-freed-
en-hite, *f* contentment

zufriedenstellen, tsoo-freed-
en-shtel-en, *v* to satisfy

zufrieren, tsoo-freer-en, *v* to
freeze up

zufügen, tsoo-fEEg-en, *v* to
add (to); to inflict

Zug, tsook, *m* train;
drawing; draught (air);
march, procession; trait;
move

Zugabe, tsoo-gahb-e, *f*
supplement, make-weight;
encore

Zugang, tsoo-gahng, *m*
access, admittance

zugänglich, tsoo-geng-lik,
adj accessible;
approachable

zugeben, tsoo-gayb-en, *v* to
add; to admit; to grant

zugegen, tsoo-gayg-en, *adj* in
attendance

zugehen, tsoo-gay-en, *v* to
close (up); to reach; to
happen

zugehörig, tsoo-ge-her-ik,
adj proper; requisite;
belonging to

Zügel, tsEEg-el, *m* bridle

zügellos, tsEEg-el-lohs, *adj*
unbridled; unrestrained

zügeln, tsEEg-eln, *v* to bridle

Zugeständnis, tsoo-ge-
shtent-nis, *nt* concession

zugetan, tsoo-ge-tahn, *adj*
devoted, fond of

Zugführer, tsook-fEEr-er, *m*
guard (train)

zugig, tsoog-ik, *adj* draughty

zügig, tsEEg-ik, *adj* quick,
swift

zugleich, tsoo-gly'k, *adv* at
the same time

Zugluft, tsook-looft, *f*
draught (air)

zugraben, tsoo-grahb-en, *v*
to cover with earth

zugreifen, tsoo-gry-fen, *v* to
seize; to help oneself; **greif
zu!**, *fam* dig in!

zugrunde, tsoo-groonn-de,
adv to destruction; to the
bottom

Zugtier, tsook-teer, *nt*
draught animal

zugunsten, tsoo-goonn-sten,
prep in favour of

zugute, tsoo-goot-e, *adv* to
the benefit of

Zugvogel, tsook-fohg-el, *m*
bird of passage

zuhaken, tsoo-hahk-en, *v* to
fasten with a hook

zuhalten, tsoo-hahlt-en, *v*
to keep closed

Zuhälter, tsoo-helt-er, *m*
pimp

Zuhause, tsoo-how-se, *nt*
home

zuheilen, tsoo-hile-en, *v* to

heal up

zuhorchen, tsoo-hork-en, *v* to listen attentively

zuhören, tsoo-her-en, *v* to listen

zukehren (sich), tsoo-kayr-en (zik), *v* to turn to

zuklappen, tsoo-klahpp-en, *v* to close with a bang

zuknöpfen, tsoo-k'nerpp-fen, *v* to button up

zukommen, tsoo-kom-en, *v* to come up to; to be due to

Zukunft, tsoo-koonft, *f* future

zukünftig, tsoo-kEEnft-ik, *adj* future

zulächeln, tsoo-lek-eln, *v* to smile at

Zulage, tsoo-lahg-e, *f* bonus, raise

zulangen, tsoo-lahng-en, *v* to help o.s.

zulänglich, tsoo-leng-lik, *adj* adequate, sufficient

zulassen, tsoo-lahss-en, *v* to admit; to leave shut; to permit

zulässig, tsoo-less-ik, *adj* admissible

Zulauf, tsoo-lowf, *m* concourse, rush of people

zulaufen, tsoo-lowf-en, *v* to rush towards; to flock to

zulegen, tsoo-layg-en, *v* to add; **sich –,** *v* to provide o.s. with; to buy

zuleiten, tsoo-ly-ten, *v* to lead towards; to pass on

zuletzt, tsoo-letst, *adv* at

last; ultimately

zuliebe, tsoo-leeb-e, *adv* for love of; as a favour

zum, tsoomm, = zu dem, for/to the

zumachen, tsoo-mahk-en, *v* to shut, to close; to fasten

zumal, tsoo-mahl, *adv* especially; chiefly

zumauern, tsoo-mow-ern, *v* to brick up

zumeist, tsoo-my'st, *adv* for the most part

zumute, tsoo-moot-e, *adv* in a mood

zumuten, tsoo-moot-en, *v* **jdm etw –,** to ask/expect sb to do sth; **sich zu viel –,** to take on too much

Zumutung, tsoo-moot-oong, *f* unreasonable demand/expectation

zunächst, tsoo-naykst, *adv* first (of all)

zunageln, tsoo-nahg-eln, *v* to nail up

Zunahme, tsoo-nahm-e, *f* increase; growth

Zuname, tsoo-nahm-e, *m* family name, surname

zünden, tsEEnn-den, *v* to light, to ignite; to set fire to

Zündholz, tsEEnt-holts, *nt* match

Zündkerze, tsEEnt-kairt-se, *f* spark-plug

zunehmen, tsoo-naym-en, *v* to increase; to grow; to gain weight

Zuneigung, tsoo-ny-goong, *f*

inclination; sympathy

**Zunft, tsoonft, *f* guild, corporation

**Zunge, tsoong-e, *f* tongue

**züngeln, tsEEng-eln, *v* to leap up (fire)

**zungenfertig, tsoong-en-fairt-ik, *adj* fluent

zunichte, tsoo-nikt-e, *adv*; **–machen** *v* to ruin, to destroy

zunicken, tsoo-nick-en, *v* to nod towards someone

zuoberst, tsoo-oh-berst, *adv* right on top

zupfen, tsoopp-fen, *v* to pluck, to unravel; to pull

zuraten, tsoo-raht-en, *v* to advise to

zurechnen, tsoo-rek-nen, *v* to number among; to attribute to

zurechnungsfähig, tsoo-rek-noongs-fay-ik, *adj* accountable for one's actions; sane

zurecht, tsoo-rekt, *adv* in (good) order; right; **–kommen,** *v* to cope; **–legen, –machen,** *v* to prepare, to lay out; **–setzen,** *v* to set right; **–weisen,** *v* to reprimand

zureden, tsoo-rayd-en, *v* to advise; to urge; to comfort

zureiten, tsoo-ry-ten, *v* to break in (horses)

zurichten, tsoo-rik-ten, *v* to make ready; to dress; to injure badly

zuriegeln, tsoo-reeg-eln, *v*

to bolt (shut)

zürnen, tsEErn-en, *v* to be angry (with)

zurück, tsoo-rEEck, *adv* back, backward(s)

zurückbekommen, tsoo-rEEck-be-kom-en, *v* to get back; to recover

zurückbleiben, tsoo-rEEck-bly-ben, *v* to remain/lag behind

zurückdrängen, tsoo-rEEck-dreng-en, *v* to push back

zurückeilen, tsoo-rEEck-ile-en, *v* to hurry back

zurückerhalten, tsoo-rEEck-air-hahlt-en, *v* to receive back

zurückerstatten, tsoo-rEEck-air-shtahtt-en, *v* to return; to refund

zurückfahren, tsoo-rEEck-fahr-en, *v* to drive back; to recoil

zurückfinden, tsoo-rEEck-fin-den, *v* to find one's way back

zurückführen, tsoo-rEEck-fEEr-en, *v* to lead/trace back; to attribute to

zurückgezogen, tsoo-rEEck-ge-tsohg-en, *adj* secluded

zurückhalten, tsoo-rEEck-hahlt-en, *v* to keep/hold back

Zurückhaltung, tsoo-rEEck-hahlt-oong, *f* reserve, retention

zurückkehren, tsoo-rEEck-kair-en, *v* to return

zurückkommen, tsoo-

rEEck-kom-en, *v* to come back

zurücklassen, tsoo-rEEck-lahss-en, *v* to leave behind

zurücklegen, tsoo-rEEck-layg-en, *v* to cover (distance); to put back/by

zurücknehmen, tsoo-rEEck-naym-en, *v* to take back; to retract

zurückrufen, tsoo-rEEck-roof-en, *v* to call back; to recall

zurückschicken, tsoo-rEEck-shick-en, *v* to send back

zurückschlagen, tsoo-rEEck-shlahg-en, *v* to hit/throw back

zurückschrecken, tsoo-rEEck-shreck-en, *v* to shrink back; to frighten off

zurücksetzen, tsoo-rEEck-set-sen, *v* to set back; to slight; to reduce

zurückstehen, tsoo-rEEck-shtay-en, *v* to stand back; to be inferior

zurückstellen, tsoo-rEEck-shtel-en, *v* to put back

zurücktreten, tsoo-rEEck-trayt-en, *v* to step back; to retire

zurückweichen, tsoo-rEEck-vy-ken, *v* to recede, to yield

zurückweisen, tsoo-rEEck-vy-zen, *v* to reject

zurückzahlen, tsoo-rEEck-tsahl-en, *v* to repay

zurückziehen, tsoo-rEEck-tsee-en, *v* to withdraw

zurufen, tsoo-roof-en, *v* to call to, to call after

Zusage, tsoo-zahg-e, *f* promise; assent

zusagen, tsoo-zahg-en, *v* to promise; to assent

zusammen, tsoo-zahmm-en, *adv* together

zusammenarbeiten, tsoo-zahmm-en-ahr-by-ten, *v* to work together/in a team; to liaise

zusammenbrechen, tsoo-zahmm-en-brek-en, *v* to collapse

zusammenbringen, tsoo-zahmm-en-bring-en, *v* to bring together; to amass

zusammenfahren, tsoo-zahmm-en-fahr-en, *v* to be startled

zusammenfallen, tsoo-zahmm-en-fahll-en, *v* to collapse; to wither (away)

zusammenfassen, tsoo-zahmm-en-fahss-en, *v* to summarize

zusammenfinden (sich), tsoo-zahmm-en-fin-den (zik), *v* to meet

zusammenfügen, tsoo-zahmm-en-fEEg-en, *v* to join, to unite

zusammengesetzt, tsoo-zahmm-en-ge-zetzt, *adj* composed (of); compound, composite

Zusammenhalt, tsoo-zahmm-en-hahlt, *m*

holding together; coherence; solidarity; unity

zusammenhalten, tsoo-**zahmm**-en-hahlt-en, *v* to cling/hold together

Zusammenhang, tsoo-**zahmm**-en-hahng, *m* context, cohesion, connection

zusammenklappen, tsoo-**zahmm**-en-klahpp-en, *v* to fold up/together

Zusammenkunft, tsoo-**zahmm**-en-koonft, *f* meeting; conference

zusammenlegen, tsoo-**zahmm**-en-layg-en, *v* to place together; to fold; to combine; to club together

zusammennehmen, tsoo-**zahmm**-en-naym-en, *v* to take together; **sich –,** *v* to pull oneself together

zusammenschließen, tsoo-**zahmm**-en-shlees-en, *v* to combine; to chain together; **sich –,** *v* to join up

zusammenschrecken, tsoo-**zahmm**-en-shreck-en, *v* to startle

zusammenschrumpfen, tsoo-**zahmm**-en-shroompfen, *v* to shrink

zusammensetzen, tsoo-**zahmm**-en-zet-sen, *v* to put together; to combine; to compose: **sich –,** *v* to come together

zusammenstellen, tsoo-**zahmm**-en-shtel-en, *v* to assemble, to put together; to compile

Zusammenstoß, tsoo-**zahmm**-en-shtohs, *m* collision

Zusammensturz, tsoo-**zahmm**-en-shtoorts, *m* collapse, crash

zusammentreffen, tsoo-**zahmm**-en-tref-en, *v* to coincide; to meet (up)

zusammentun, tsoo-**zahmm**-en-toon, *v* to put together; **sich –,** *v* to unite

zusammenziehen, tsoo-**zahmm**-en-tsee-en, *v* to contract; to draw together; to move together

Zusatz, tsoo-**zahts,** *m* addition; additive; postscript

zuschauen, tsoo-**show**-en, *v* to watch; to look on

Zuschauer, tsoo-**show**-er, *m* spectator; **–raum,** *m* auditorium

zuschicken, tsoo-**shick**-en, *v* to send (to)

zuschieben, tsoo-**sheeb**-en, *v* to push to; to push shut

zuschießen, tsoo-**shees**-en, *v* to contribute

Zuschlag, tsoo-**shlahk,** *m* addition; surcharge

zuschlagen, tsoo-**shlahg**-en, *v* to slam; to close; to knock down; to add

zuschließen, tsoo-**shlees**-en, *v* to lock up

zuschneiden, tsoo-**shny**-den, *v* to cut (out)

zuschreiben, tsoo-**shry**-ben, *v* to attribute; to ascribe

Zuschrift, tsoo-**shrift,** *f* letter

Zuschuß, tsoo-**shooss,** *m* bonus; allowance; subsidy

zusehen, tsoo-**zay**-en, *v* to look on; to see to

zusehends, tsoo-**zay**-ents, *adv* visibly; more and more

zusetzen, tsoo-**zet**-sen, *v* to add to; to alloy with; to pester

zusichern, tsoo-**zik**-ern, *v* to assure of; to promise

zuspitzen, tsoo-**shpits**-en, *v* to point; to taper; to become critical

zusprechen, tsoo-**shprek**-en, *v* to cheer up, to comfort; to award

Zustand, tsoo-**shtahnt,** *m* condition, state, lot

zustandekommen, tsoo-**shtahnn**-de-kom-en, *v* to come about

zuständig, tsoo-**shten**-dik, *adj* competent; responsible

zustehen, tsoo-**shtay**-en, *v* to be proper/right

zustellen, tsoo-**shtel**-en, *v* to deliver

zustimmen, tsoo-**shtim**-en, *v* to agree; to assent

zustoßen, tsoo-**shtohs**-en, *v* to slam shut; to befall

zutage, tsoo-**tahg**-e, *adv* to the light of day

Zutat, tsoo-taht, *f*
ingredient; trimming

zuteilen, tsoo-tile-en, *v* to
apportion; to allot, to
allocate

zuträglich, tsoo-trayk-lik,
adj wholesome; useful,
beneficial

zutrauen, tsoo-trow-en, *v* to
think capable of

Zutrauen, tsoo-trow-en, *nt*
confidence

zutraulich, tsoo-trow-lik, *adj*
trusting; friendly

zutreffend, tsoo-tref-ent, *adj*
correct; apt

Zutritt, tsoo-trit, *m*
admittance; admission

Zutun, tsoo-toon, *nt*
assistance; action

zuverlässig, tsoo-fair-les-ik,
adj reliable

Zuversicht, tsoo-fair-zikt, *f*
confidence; faith, trust

zuvorkommen, tsoo-fohr-
kom-en, *v* to forestall

zuvorkommend, tsoo-fohr-
kom-ent, *adj* obliging,
courteous

Zuwachs, tsoo-vahcks, *m*
increase; growth

zuwege, tsoo-vayg-e, *adv*;
etw –bringen to achieve
sth

zuweisen, tsoo-vy-zen, *v* to
allot; to assign

zuwenden, tsoo-vend-en, *v*
to turn to; to bestow

zuwerfen, tsoo-vairf-en, *v* to
throw to; to slam

zuwider, tsoo-**veed**-er, *adj*

contrary; distasteful

zuziehen, tsoo-tsee-en, *v* to
draw together; to incur; to
consult; **sich –**, *v* to
tighten; to cloud over

zuzüglich, tsoo-tsEEk-lik,
prep plus

Zwang, tsvahng, *m*
compulsion; coercion

zwängen, tsveng-en, *v* to
force; to constrain; to
squeeze

zwanghaft, tsvang-hahft, *adj*
compulsive

zwanglos, tsvang-lohs, *adj*
informal, unceremonious

zwanzig, tsvahnt-sik, *num*
twenty

zwar, tsvahr, *adv* indeed, it's
true; **und –**, in fact,
actually

Zweck, tsveck, *m* purpose;
object, aim

zweckmäßig, tsveck-mace-
ik, *adj* suitable

zwecks, tsvecks, *prep* for the
purpose of

zwei, tsvy, *num* two;
–deutig, *adj* ambiguous;
–erlei, *adj* of two kinds

Zweifel, tsvy-fel, *m* doubt,
uncertainty

zweifelhaft, tsvy-fel-hahft,
adj doubtful

zweifeln, tsvy-feln, *v* to
doubt

Zweig, tsvike, *m* branch,
twig, bough; **–stelle**, *f*
branch (bank, shop)

Zweikampf, tsvy-kahmp'f,
m one-to-one combat

zweimal, tsvy-mahl, *adv*
twice

Zweirad, tsvy-raht, *nt*
bicycle

zweisprachig, tsvy-shprahk-
ik, *adj* bilingual

zweispurig, tsvy-shpoor-ik,
adj two-lane

zweite(r), tsvy-te(r), *adj*
second

zweitrangig, tsvite-rahng-ik,
adj of secondary
importance

Zwerg, tsvairk, *m* dwarf

Zwetsch(g)e, tsvetsh-(g)e, *f*
plum

zwicken, tsvick-en, *v* to
pinch, to nip

Zwieback, tsvee-bahck, *m*
rusk, biscuit

Zwiebel, tsveeb-el, *f* onion;
(plant) bulb

Zwiegespräch, tsvee-ge-
shprayk, *nt* dialogue

Zwiespalt, tsvee-shpahlt, *m*
disagreement; inner
conflict

Zwietracht, tsvee-trahkt, *f*
discord

Zwilling, tsvil-ing, *m* twin

Zwinge, tsving-e, *f* ferrule;
tip; clamp

zwingen, tsving-en, *v* to
compel, to force

Zwinger, tsving-er, *m*
kennel; cage (usually wild
animals)

zwinkern, tsving-kern, *v* to
wink; to twinkle

Zwirn, tsveern, *m* thread;
twine, yarn

zwischen, tsvish-en, *prep*
between; among(st)

Zwischenbericht, tsvish-en-be-rikt, *m* interim report

Zwischendeck, tsvish-en-deck, *nt* between decks

Zwischending, tsvish-en-ding, *nt* cross (between)

zwischendurch, tsvish-en-**doohrk**, *adv* in between times, in the meantime

Zwischenfall, tsvish-en-fahll, *m* incident

Zwischenglied, tsvish-en-gleet, *nt* connecting link

Zwischenhändler, tsvish-en-hend-ler, *m* middleman

zwischenher, tsvish-en-**hair**, *adv* in the meantime

zwischenmenschlich, tsvish-en-mensh-lik, *adj* interpersonal

Zwischenraum, tsvish-en-rowm, *m* gap, space

Zwischenwand, tsvish-en-vahnt, *f* partition

Zwist(igkeit), tsvist(-ik-kite), *m* (*f*), discord; quarrel

zwitschern, tsvit-shern, *v* to chirp, to twitter

zwo, tsvoh, = zwei, *num* two (used on telephone)

zwölf, tsverlf, *num* twelve; **–te(r),** *adj* twelfth

Zylinder, tsee-lin-der, *m* cylinder; top hat

Zypern, tsEEp-ern, *nt* Cyprus

ENGLISH · GERMAN
ENGLISCH · DEUTSCH

A

a, eh/e, *indefinite art* ein(e)
abandon, e-**bänn**-d'n, *v*
verlassen; (give up)
aufgeben; **–ed,** *adj*
verlassen; (morally)
verworfen
abate, e-**beht,** *v* nachlassen
abattoir, äbb-be-tu'ahr, *n*
Schlachthof *m*
abbey, äbb-i, *n* Abtei *f*
abbreviate, e-**brie-**wi-eht, *v*
abkürzen
abbreviation, e-brie-wi-eh-
sch'n, *n* Abkürzung *f*
abdicate, äbb-di-keht, *v*
abdanken; entsagen
abdomen, äbb-de-men, *n*
Bauch *m*, Unterleib *m*
abduction, äbb-**dack-**sch'n,
n Entführung *f*
abet, e-**bett,** *v* mithelfen
abhorrent, eb-ho-rent, *adj*
zuwider, verhaßt
abide, e-**beid,** *v* verweilen,
bleiben; **– by,** gehorchen,
sich halten an
ability, e-**bill**-i-ti, *n*
Fähigkeit *f*, Tüchtigkeit *f*
abject, äbb-dschekt, *adj*
erbärmlich, elend;
(poverty) bitter; (apology)
demütig
ablaze, e-**blehs,** *adj & adv*
brennend, lodernd
able, eh-b'l, *adj* fähig,
tüchtig; **to be – to,** *v*
können
ably, eh-bli, *adv* fähig,
geschickt
abnormal, äbb-**nor-**mel, *adj*
abnorm, regelwidrig;
(misshapen) mißgestaltet
aboard, e-bord, *adv* an Bord
abode, e-bohd, *n*
Wohnsitz *m*
abolish, e-**boll-**isch, *v*
abschaffen
abominable, e-bomm-in-e-

b'l, *adj* abscheulich
aborigine, äbb-e-**ridsch**-i-ni,
n Ureinwohner *m*
abortion, e-**bor-**sch'n, *n*
Abtreibung *f*;
(miscarriage) Fehlgeburt *f*
abound, e-**baund,** *v*
reichlich vorhanden sein
about, e-baut, *adv*
(approximately) etwa,
ungefähr; (around) (rings)
herum; *prep* (place) um;
(subject) über; **to be – to,**
v im Begriff sein
above, e-baw, *adv* oben;
prep über
abrasion, e-breh-sch'n, *n*
Hautabschürfung *f*
abreast, e-brest, *adv*
nebeneinander
abridge, e-**bridsch,** *v*
abkürzen, verkürzen
abroad, e-bro'ad, *adv* im
Ausland, ins Ausland
abrupt, e-**brapt,** *adj*
(manner) schroff; (step)
jäh
abscess, äbb-ssess, *n* Abszeß
m, Geschwür *nt*
abscond, eb-skond, *v*
durchgehen, flüchten
absence, äbb-ssenss, *n*
Abwesenheit *f*
absent, äbb-ssent, *adj*
abwesend; **–ee,** *n*
Abwesende(r) *m & f*;
– minded, *adj* zerstreut
absent, äbb-ssent, *v* –
oneself, fernbleiben
absolute, äbb-sse-luht, *adj*
absolut; unbedingt

absolve, eb-solw, v
lossprechen; – **from,**
freisprechen, entheben

absorb, eb-sorb, v
aufsaugen; *fig* ganz in
Anspruch nehmen

abstain, eb-stehn, v (parl
etc.) sich der Stimme
enthalten; – **from,** sich
enthalten

abstemious, eb-stie-mi-ess,
adj enthaltsam

abstention, eb-stenn-sch'n,
n (parl etc.)
Stimmenthaltung f

abstinence, äbb-sti-nenss, n
Enthaltsamkeit f

abstract, äbb-sträckt, *adj*
abstrakt; n
Zusammenfassung f

abstract, äbb-**sträckt,** v
wegnehmen;
zusammenfassen

absurd, eb-ssörd, *adj* albern;
unvernünftig

abundance, e-**bann**-denss, n
Überfluß m

abundant, e-**bann**-d'nt, *adj*
reichlich, im Überfluß

abuse, e-bjuhss, n
Mißbrauch m; (affront)
Beschimpfung f

abuse, e-bjuhs, v
mißbrauchen;
beschimpfen

abusive, e-bjuhss-iw, *adj*
beleidigend, Schimpf-

abyss, e-biss, n Abgrund m

academy, e-**kädd**-e-mi, n
Akademie f; Hochschule f

accede, eck-**ssied,** v
einwilligen; – **to,** (throne)
besteigen

accelerate, eck-ssell-e-reht,
v beschleunigen

accelerator, eck-ssell-e-reh-
ter, n Gaspedal nt

accent, äck-ssent, n Akzent
m; Betonung f

accept, eck-ssept, v
annehmen; akzeptieren;
–able, *adj* akzeptabel,
annehmbar; **–ance,** n
Annahme f;
Zustimmung, f

access, äck-ssess, n Zutritt
m, Zugang m

accessible, eck-ssess-i-b'l,
adj zugänglich

accessory, eck-ssess-e-ri, n
Accessoire nt, Zubehör nt

accident, äck-ssi-dent, n
Unfall m; Zufall m

accidental, äck-ssi-**denn**-t'l,
adj versehentlich, zufällig

acclaim, e-klehm, n Beifall
m; v Beifall zurufen

acclimatize, e-klei-me-tais, v
akklimatisieren; – **to,** sich
gewöhnen an

accommodate, e-komm-e-
deht, v (lodge)
unterbringen; – **(oneself)**
to, sich anpassen

accommodation, e-komm-e-
deh-sch'n, n (lodging)
Unterkunft f; (agreement)
Übereinkommen nt

accompany, e-**kamm**-pe-ni,
v begleiten

accomplice, e-**kamm**-pliss, n
Komplize m,

Mitschuldige(r) m & f

accomplish, e-**kamm**-plisch,
v vollführen; (purpose)
erreichen; **–ed,** *adj*
erreicht; kompetent;
–ment, n Vollendung f;
(performance) Leistung f

accord, e-kord, n
Übereinstimmung f; **of**
one's own –, freiwillig

accord, e-kord, v
übereinstimmen; – **with,**
entsprechen; **–ing to,** *prep*
gemäß; nach; **–ingly,** *adv*
demgemäß

accordance, e-kor-denss, n
in –ance with, *prep*
gemäß, entsprechend

accost, e-kosst, v
ansprechen; belästigen

account, e-kaunt, n (bill)
Rechnung f; (bank)
Konto nt; – **for,** v
Rechenschaft ablegen für,
verantwortlich sein für;
on –, auf Rechnung; **on**
no –, auf keinen Fall;
–able, *adj* verantwortlich

accountant, e-kaun-tent, n
Wirtschaftsprüfer m

accrue, e-kruh, v
erwachsen; **– from,**
entstehen aus

accumulate, e-kjuh-mju-
leht, v (gather)
ansammeln, anhäufen;
(collect) sich ansammeln,
sich anhäufen

accuracy, äck-ju-re-ssi, n
Genauigkeit f

accurate, äck-ju-ret, *adj*

genau; richtig

accuse, *e*-**kjuhs**, *v* anklagen, beschuldigen

accustom, *e*-**kass**-tem, *v* gewöhnen

ace, ehss, *n* As *nt*; *adj* Star-

ache, ehk, *n* Schmerz *m*; *v* schmerzen

achieve, *e*-**tschiew**, *v* vollbringen; erringen; **–ment**, *n* (attainment) Errungenschaft *f*; (performance) Leistung *f*

acid, äss-idd, *adj* sauer; *n* Säure *f*; **– rain**, *n* saurer Regen *m*

acidity, *e*-**ssidd**-i-ti, *n* Säure *f*

acknowledge, ek-**noll**-idsch, *v* anerkennen; (receipt) bestätigen

acknowledg(e)ment, ek-**noll**-idsch-ment, *n* Anerkennung *f*; (receipt) Bestätigung *f*

acne, **äck**-ni, *n* Akne *f*

acorn, eh-korn, *n* Eichel *f*

acoustics, *e*-**kuh**-sticks, *n* Akustik *f*

acquaint, *e*-**ku'ehnt**, *v* bekannt machen; (familiarize) vertraut machen

acquaintance, *e*-**ku'ehn**-tenss, *n* Bekanntschaft *f*; (person) Bekannte(r) *m & f*

acquiesce, äck-ku'i-**ess**, *v* einwilligen

acquire, *e*-**ku'eir**, *v* erwerben; erlangen

acquisition, äck-ku'i-**sisch**-'n, *n* Erwerb *m*; Akquisition *f*

acquit, *e*-**ku'itt**, *v* freisprechen, entlasten

acquittal, *e*-**ku'itt**-'l, *n* Freispruch *m*

acre, eh-ker, *n* (measurement) Morgen *m*

acrid, äck-ridd, *adj* beißend, scharf

acrobat, äck-re-bätt, *n* Akrobat *m*

across, *e*-kross, *adv* hinüber; *prep* durch; (quer) über

acrylic, *e*-**krill**-ick, *adj* Acryl *nt*

act, äckt, *n* Tat *f*; (of a play) Akt *m*; *law* Gesetz *nt*; *v* handeln; (in theatre) spielen

action, **äck**-sch'n, *n* Handlung *f*; *law* Prozeß *m*; *mil* Gefecht *nt*

activate, **äck**-ti-weht, *v* aktivieren

active, **äck**-tiw, *adj* wirksam; belebt; tätig

activity, äck-**tiw**-i-ti, *n* Betätigung *f*, Tätigkeit *f*

actor, **äck**-ter, *n* Schauspieler *m*

actress, **äck**-triss, *n* Schauspielerin *f*

actual, **äck**-tschu-el, *adj* tatsächlich; wirklich; **–ly**, *adv* tatsächlich

acute, *e*-**kjuht**, *adj* spitz; (pain) scharf; (senses) scharfsinnig; *med* akut

adamant, **ädd**-*e*-ment, *adj* beharrlich

adapt, *e*-**däpt**, *v* anpassen, umarbeiten, umbauen; (plays etc.) bearbeiten; **–er**, *n* (*elec* etc.) Adapter *m*, Zwischenstecker *m*

adaptation, ädd-**äpp-teh**-sch'n, *n* Anpassung *f*; (plays etc.) Bearbeitung *f*

add, ädd, *v* addieren; hinzufügen; beitragen

addict, **ädd**-ikt, *n* Süchtige(r) *m & f*

addicted, *e*-**dick**-tidd, *adj* süchtig

addiction, *e*-**dick**-sch'n, *n* Sucht *f*

addition, *e*-**disch**-'n, *n* Addition *f*; Zusatz *m*; **–al**, *adj* zusätzlich

additive, **ädd**-i-tiw, *n* Zusatz *m*

address, *e*-**dress**, *n* Anschrift *f*, Adresse *f*; (talk) Anrede *f*, Ansprache *f*; *v* adressieren; (orally) ansprechen

adept, **ädd**-ept, *adj* geschickt

adequate, **ädd**-i-ku'et, *adj* genügend; hinreichend

adhere, ed-**hier**, *v* anhaften; kleben; **– to**, festhalten an

adherent, ed-**hier**-ent, *n* Anhänger *m*

adhesive, ed-**hie**-ssiw, *adj* klebend; *n* Klebstoff *m*

adjacent, ed-**dscheh**-ss'nt, *adj* angrenzend

adjective, **ädd**-dscheck-tiw, *n* Adjektiv *nt*

adjoin, ed-**dscheun**, *v* angrenzen; **–ing**, *adj*

angrenzend

adjourn, ed-**dschörn**, *v*
vertagen, aufschieben;
–ment, *n* Vertagung *f*

adjust, ed-**dschast**, *v mech*
einstellen; **–** (**oneself**) **to**,
(sich) anpassen; **–able**, *adj*
verstellbar; **–ment**, *n*
Anpassung *f*; *mech*
Einstellung *f*

administer, ed-**minn**-iss-ter,
v verwalten; (medicine)
verabreichen

administration, ed-minn-iss-
treh-sch'n, *n* Verwaltung
f; Regierung *f*

admirable, **ädd**-mi-re-b'l, *adj*
bewundernswert

admiration, ädd-mi-**reh**-
sch'n, *n* Bewunderung *f*

admire, ed-**meir**, *v*
bewundern

admission, ed-**misch**-'n, *n*
(entry) Zutritt *m*, Einlaß
m; (confession)
Geständnis *nt*; **– fee**,
n Eintritt *m*,
Eintrittsgebühr *f*

admit, ed-**mitt**, *v* einlassen;
(concede) zugeben;
–tance, *n* Zulassung *f*;
(fee) Eintritt *m*,
Eintrittsgebühr *f*

admonish, ed-**monn**-isch, *v*
ermahnen; verweisen

ado, *e*-**duh**, *n* Tun *nt*;
Treiben *nt*

adolescence, ädd-*e*-less-'nss,
n Jugend *f*, Pubertät *f*

adolescent, ädd-*e*-less-'nt,
adj jugendlich; *n*

Jugendliche(r) *m & f*

adopt, *e*-**dopt**, *v* adoptieren,
annehmen; **–ion**, *n*
Adoption *f*, Annahme *f*

adore, *e*-**dor**, *v* schwärmen
(für), sehr lieben; (God)
anbeten

adorn, *e*-**dorn**, *v* schmücken,
verzieren

adrift, *e*-**drift**, *adv* (floating)
treibend; (lost) verloren

adroit, *e*-**dreut**, *adj* gewandt,
behende

adult, *e*-**dalt**/**ädd**-alt, *adj*
erwachsen; *n*
Erwachsene(r) *m & f*

adulterate, *e*-**dall**-te-reht, *v*
verfälschen, verpanschen

adultery, *e*-**dal**-te-ri, *n*
Ehebruch *m*

advance, ed-**wahnss**, *n*
(progress) Fortschritt *m*;
(money) Vorschuß *m*; *v*
(progress) vorrücken;
(lend) vorschießen; **in –**,
adv im voraus

advantage, ed-**wahn**-tidsch,
n Vorteil *m*

advantageous, ädd-wahn-
teh-**dschess**, *adj* vorteilhaft

advent, **ädd**-went, *n*
Ankunft *f*; Advent *m*

adventure, ed-**wenn**-tscher,
n Abenteuer *nt*

adventurous, ed-**wenn**-
tsche-ress, *adj*
abenteuerlich; (bold)
kühn

adverb, **ädd**-wörb, *n*
Adverb *nt*

adversary, **ädd**-wer-se-ri, *n*

Gegner *m*

adverse, **ädd**-wörss, *adj*
nachteilig; widrig

advert, **ädd**-wört, *n*
Annonce *f*, Anzeige *f*

advertise, **ädd**-wer-teis, *v*
werben, Reklame machen;
–ising, *n* Werbung *f*

advertisement, ed-**wör**-tiss-
ment, *n* Anzeige *f*

advice, ed-**weiss**, *n* Rat *m*;
(information)
Benachrichtigung *f*

advisable, ed-**weis**-*e*-b'l, *adj*
ratsam

advise, ed-**weis**, *v* raten;
(inform) benachrichtigen;
ill –d, *adj* unklug,
unüberlegt; **well –d**, *adj*
wohlüberlegt

adviser, ed-**wei**-ser, *n*
Ratgeber *m*

advocate, **ädd**-ve-ket, *n*
Befürworter *m*

advocate, **ädd**-ve-keht, *v*
befürworten

aerial, **ähr**-ri-el, *adj* Luft-; *n*
Antenne *f*

aerobics, ähr-**roh**-bicks, *n*
Aerobic *nt*

aerodynamic, ähr-roh-dei-
nämm-ick, *adj*
aerodynamisch

aeroplane, **ähr**-roh-plehn, *n*
Flugzeug *nt*

aerosol, **ähr**-roh-ssol, *n*
Aerosol *nt*, Sprühflasche *f*

afar, *e*-**fahr**, *adv* [von]
weither

affable, **äff**-*e*-b'l, *adj*
freundlich, umgänglich

affair, e-**fähr,** n (love)
Affäre f; (matter)
Angelegenheit f, Sache f

affect, e-**fekt,** v angehen,
betreffen; (move) rühren;
–ed, adj affektiert;
(moved) gerührt

affection, e-**feck**-sch'n, n
Zuneigung f, Liebe f; **–ate,**
adj liebevoll, zärtlich

affidavit, äff-i-**deh**-witt, n
eidliche Erklärung f

affiliate, e-**fill**-i-eht, v –
to/with, sich anschließen,
sich angliedern

affinity, e-**finn**-i-ti, n
(liking) Anziehung f;
(relationship)
Verwandtschaft f; chem
Affinität f

affirm, e-**förm,** v
bekräftigen, bestätigen

affirmation, äff-er-meh-
sch'n, n Bekräftigung f,
Bestätigung f

affirmative, e-**förm**-e-tiw,
adj bejahend, zustimmend;
n Bejahung f

affix, e-**ficks,** v anheften,
anbringen

afflict, e-**flikt,** v
heimsuchen; betrüben;
–ion, n Gebrechen nt,
Leiden nt

affluence, äff-luh-enss, n
(wealth) Reichtum m

affluent, äff-luh-ent, adj
(rich) wohlhabend

afford, e-**ford,** v
(time/money) sich leisten;
(opportunity) gewähren;

(pleasure) bereiten

Africa, äff-rick-e, n Afrika
nt; **–n,** adj afrikanisch; n
Afrikaner m

affront, e-**frant,** n
Beleidigung f; v beleidigen

afloat, e-**floht,** adj & adv
flott, schwimmend

afraid, e-**frehd,** adj
ängstlich, bange; **to be –
(of),** v sich fürchten,
Angst haben (vor); **I'm –
(that),** leider, ich fürchte
(daß)

afresh, e-**fresch,** adv von
neuem

after, ahf-ter, prep nach; adv
nachher, danach; conj
nachdem; **– sales service,**
n Kundendienst m

aftermath, ahf-ter-mahth, n
Auswirkungen pl Folgen pl

afternoon, ahf-ter-**nuhn,** n
Nachmittag m

aftershave, ahf-ter-schehw,
n Aftershave nt,
Rasierwasser nt

afterthought, ahf-ter-thort,
n nachträgliche Idee f

afterwards, ahf-ter-werds,
adv nachher, später,
danach

again, e-**gehn,** adv wieder,
nochmals; außerdem; **–
and –,** immer wieder

against, e-**genst,** prep gegen

age, ehdsch, n Alter nt;
(period) Zeitalter nt; **–
group,** n Altersgruppe f; **–
limit,** n Altersgrenze f; **to
be of –,** volljährig sein

aged, eh-dschidd, adj alt,
bejahrt

agency, eh-dschen-ssi, n
Agentur f, Vertretung f; fig
Vermittlung f

agenda, e-**dschenn**-de, n
Tagesordnung f

agent, eh-dschent, n
Vertreter m, Agent m

aggravate, ägg-re-weht, v
(person) ärgern;
(situation) verschlimmern

aggregate, ägg-ri-get, adj
gesamt; n Anhäufung f,
Summe f

aggregate, ägg-ri-geht, v
anhäufen, ansammeln

aggression, e-**gresch**-'n, n
Aggression f; (attack)
Angriff m, Überfall m

aggressive, e-**gress**-iw, adj
streitlustig; aggressiv

aghast, e-**gahst,** adj bestürzt,
entsetzt

agile, ädd-dscheil, adj
behende, flink

agitate, ädd-dschi-teht, v
(shake) schütteln; (upset)
erregen; (cause trouble)
agitieren

agitation, ädd-dschi-**teh**-
sch'n, n (mental)
Erregung f, Aufregung f;
(trouble) Agitation f

ago, e-**goh,** adv vor, her;
long –, adv lange her

agonize, ägg-e-neis, v sich
quälen, unentschlossen
sein

agony, ägg-e-ni, n Qual f,
Pein f

agree, *e-*grie, *v* einig sein, übereinstimmen; **– to**, einwilligen in; **–able**, *adj* angenehm; **–ment**, *n* Übereinstimmung *f*; (contract) Vertrag *m*

agricultural, ägg-ri-**kall**-tsche-rel, *adj* landwirtschaftlich

agriculture, ägg-ri-**kall**-tscher, *n* Landwirtschaft *f*

aground, *e-*graund, *adv* gestrandet

ahead, *e-*hedd, *adv* voran, voraus

aid, ehd, *n* Hilfe *f*; (money) Unterstützung *f*; *v* helfen

AIDS, ehds, *n* AIDS *nt*

ailing, eh-ling, *adj* kränklich

ailment, ehl-ment, *n* Leiden *nt*, Krankheit *f*

aim, ehm, *n* Ziel *nt*, Zweck *m*; *v* zielen; **–less**, *adj* ziellos

air, ähr, *n* Luft *f*; (manner) Miene *f*; *mus* Melodie *f*; *v* (clothes etc.) lüften; **– conditioning**, *n* Klimaanlage *f*; **– gun**, *n* Luftgewehr *nt*; **– mail**, *n* Luftpost *f*

aircraft, ähr-krahft, *n* Flugzeug *nt*

airline, ähr-lein, *n* Fluggesellschaft *f*

airplane, ähr-plehn, *n* Flugzeug *nt*

airport, ähr-port, *n* Flughafen *m*

airtight, ähr-teit, *adj* luftdicht

aisle, eil, *n* Gang *m*

ajar, *e-*dschahr, *adj* angelehnt, halboffen

akin, *e-*kinn, *adj* verwandt; gleicher Art

alabaster, **all**-*e-*bahss-ter, *n* Alabaster *m*

alarm, *e-*lahrm, *n* Alarm *m*; *v* beunruhigen; **– call**, *n* Weckruf *m*; **– clock**, *n* Wecker *m*

alarming, *e-*lahr-ming, *adj* beunruhigend

album, **äll**-bem, *n* Album *nt*; (record) Langspielplatte *f*

alcohol, **äll**-ke-holl, *n* Alkohol *m*; **– free**, *adj* alkoholfrei

alcoholic, äll-ke-**holl**-ick, *adj* alkoholisch; *n* Alkoholiker *m*

alcoholism, **äll**-ke-holl-ism, *n* Alkoholismus *m*

alert, *e-*lört, *adj* wachsam; **on the – (for)**, auf der Hut (vor); **–ness**, *n* Wachsamkeit *f*; (nimbleness) Flinkheit *f*

alias, eh-li-ess, *adv* alias; *n* Deckname *m*

alien, eh-li-en, *adj* fremd, ausländisch; (sci-fi) außerirdisch; *n* Fremde(r) *m & f*, Ausländer *m*; (sci-fi) Außerirdische(r) *m & f*

alienate, eh-li-en-eht, *v* entfremden

alight, *e-*leit, *adj* brennend; erleuchtet; *v* absteigen, aussteigen

align, *e-*lein, *v* ausrichten;

anpassen

alike, *e-*leik, *adj* gleich, ähnlich

alimony, **äll**-i-me-ni, *n* Unterhalt *m*

alive, *e-*leiw, *adj* (living) lebendig; (lively) lebendig, rege, munter

all, o'al, *adj* alle, alles; ganz; *adv* gänzlich; **– along**, die ganze Zeit; **– right**, in Ordnung, schon gut; **– the more**, um so mehr; **above –**, vor allem; **not at –**, gar nicht; gern geschehen

allay, *e-*leh, *v* beruhigen; beschwichtigen

allegation, äll-i-**geh**-sch'n, *n* Behauptung *f*

allege, *e-*ledsch, *v* aussagen; behaupten; **–d**, *adj* angeblich; **–dly**, *adv* angeblich

allegiance, *e-*lie-dschenss, *n* Treue *f*

allergy, **äll**-er-dschi, *n* Allergie *f*

allergic, *e-*lör-dschick, *adj* allergisch

alleviate, *e-*lie-wi-eht, *v* lindern

alley, **äll**-i, *n* Gasse *f*; **blind –**, Sackgasse *f*

alliance, *e-*lei-enss, *n* Bündnis *nt*, Allianz *f*

allied, **äll**-eid, *adj* verbündet, alliiert; **– to**, verwandt (mit)

allocate, **äll**-*e-*keht, *v* zuteilen

allot, *e-*lott, *v* zuteilen,

zuerkennen

allotment, e-lott-ment, n
Zuteilung f; (ground)
Schrebergarten m

allow, e-lau, v (permit)
erlauben; (concede)
zugeben; **– for,**
berücksichtigen

allowance, e-lau-enss, n
Unterstützung f,
Unterhaltsgeld nt; (pocket
money) Taschengeld nt;
(rebate) Nachlaß m; **to
make –ances,**
berücksichtigen,
Zugeständnisse machen

alloy, äll-eu, n Legierung f

all-round, o'al-raund, adj
Allround-

all-time, o'al-teim, adj aller
Zeiten

allude (to), e-luhd (tu), v
anspielen (auf)

alluring, e-luhr-ring, adj
verlockend; verführerisch

allusion, e-luh-sch'n, n
Anspielung f

ally, äll-ei, n Verbündete(r)
m & f, Alliierte(r) m

ally, e-lei, v – o.s. with, sich
vereinigen mit

almighty, o'al-**mei**-ti, adj
allmächtig; **the Almighty,**
n der Allmächtige m

almond, ah-mend, n
Mandel f

almost, o'al-mohst, adv fast,
beinahe

alms, ahms, npl Almosen pl;
–house, n Armenhaus nt

aloft, e-loft, adv in

der/die Luft

alone, e-lohn, adv allein,
nur

along, e-long, adv vorwärts;
prep längs, entlang; **–
with,** prep zusammen mit

alongside, e-long-sseid, adv
nebenher, daneben; prep
neben

aloof, e-luhf, adj unnahbar;
adv fern; **stay –,** sich
abseits halten

aloud, e-laud, adv laut;
hörbar

alphabet, äll-fe-bett, n
Alphabet nt

alphabetical(ly), äll-fe-bett-
i-k'l(-i), adj & adv
alphabetisch

alpine, äll-pein, adj Alpen-

Alps, älpss, npl Alpen pl

already, o'al-redd-i, adv
schon, bereits

also, o'al-ssoh, conj auch,
ebenfalls; außerdem

altar, o'al-ter, n Altar m

alter, o'al-ter, v ändern

alteration, o'al-te-reh-sch'n,
n Änderung f

alternate, o'al-tör-net, adj
abwechselnd; **on – days,**
jeden zweiten Tag

alternate, o'al-ter-neht, v
abwechseln

alternative, o'al-tör-ne-tiw,
adj Alternativ-, andere(r);
n Wahl f; Alternative f;
–ly, adv als Alternative,
oder

although, o'al-dhoh, conj
obwohl

altitude, äll-ti-tjuhd, n
Höhe, f

altogether, o'al-tu-gedh-er,
adv im ganzen;
vollkommen

aluminium, äll-juh-**minn**-
jem, n Aluminium nt

always, o'al-u'ehs, adv
immer, jederzeit

a.m. eh emm, adv (abbr ante
meridiem), vormittags

amass, e-mäss, v anhäufen,
ansammeln

amateur, ämm-e-tör, adj
Amateur-, Hobby-; n
Amateur m; pej Dilettant
m; **–ish,** adj dilettantisch

amaze, e-mehs, v in Staunen
(ver)setzen; **–d,** adj
erstaunt

amazement, e-mehs-ment, n
Erstaunen nt

amazing, e-meh-sing, adj
erstaunlich

ambassador, ämm-bäss-e-
der, n Botschafter m; fig
Vertreter m

amber, ämm-ber, n
Bernstein m; (traffic light)
Gelb nt

ambiguity, ämm-bi-gjuh-i-
ti, n Zweideutigkeit f

ambiguous, ämm-bigg-ju-
ess, adj zweideutig

ambition, ämm-bisch-'n, n
Ehrgeiz m

ambitious, ämm-bisch-ess,
adj ehrgeizig

ambulance, ämm-bju-lenss,
n Krankenwagen m

ambush, ämm-busch, n

Hinterhalt *m*, Überfall (aus dem Hinterhalt); *v* (aus dem Hinterhalt) überfallen

amenable, *e*-mie-ne-b'l, *adj* zugänglich; empfänglich

amend, *e*-mend, *v* (ab)ändern; **–ment**, *n* Änderung *f*

amends, *e*-mends, *npl* **make – (for)**, *v* wiedergutmachen

America, *e*-me-ri-ke, *n* Amerika; **–n**, *adj* amerikanisch; *n* Amerikaner *m*

amethyst, *ämm*-i-thist, *n* Amethyst *m*

amiable, *eh*-mi-e-b'l, *adj* liebenswürdig; freundlich

amicable, *ämm*-i-ke-b'l, *adj* freundschaftlich; (settlement) gütlich

amid(st), *e*-mid(st), *prep* inmitten, mitten in

amiss, *adj*-miss, *adj & adv* **there's something –**, da stimmt irgend etwas nicht; **to take sth –**, etw übelnehmen

ammonia, *e*-moh-ni-e, *n* Ammoniak *nt*

ammunition, *ämm*-ju-*nisch*-'n, *n* Munition *f*

amnesia, *ämm*-*nie*-si-e, *n* Gedächtnisschwund *m*

amnesty, *ämm*-niss-ti, *n* Amnestie *f*

amok, *e*-*mack*, *adv* **run –**, *v* Amok laufen

among(st), *e*-*mang*(st), *prep* unter, zwischen

amoral, *eh*-mo-rel, *adj* amoralisch

amorous, *ämm*-e-ress, *adj* verliebt

amount, *e*-maunt, *n* Menge *f*; (money) Betrag *m*; **– to**, *v* betragen, sich belaufen auf; *fig* hinauslaufen auf

amp(ere), *ämp*-(ähr), *n* Ampere *nt*

ample, *ämp*-'l, *adj* reichlich; (roomy) geräumig

amplifier, *ämp*-li-fei-er, *n* Verstärker *m*

amplify, *ämp*-li-fei, *v* verstärken

amputate, *ämp*-ju-teht, *v* amputieren

amuse, *e*-*mjuhs*, *v* amüsieren; (entertain) unterhalten

amusement, *e*-*mjuhs*-ment, *n* Belustigung *f*; (entertainment) Unterhaltung *f*; **–s**, *pl* Freizeitangebot *nt*; (slot machines) Spielhalle *f*

an, *an/en*, *art* ein, eine, ein

anaemia, *e*-*nie*-mi-e, *n* Anämie *f*, Blutarmut *f*

anaemic, *e*-*nie*-mick, *adj* blutarm

anaesthetic, *änn*-ess-*thett*-ick, *n* Betäubungsmittel *nt*; **general –**, Vollnarkose *f*

analogue, *änn*-e-logg, *adj* Analog-

analogy, *e*-*näll*-e-dschi, *n* Analogie *f*

analysis, *e*-*näll*-i-ssiss, *n* Analyse *f*

analyse, *änn*-e-leis, *v* analysieren

anarchy, *änn*-er-ki, *n* Anarchie *f*

ancestor, *änn*-ssess-ter, *n* Vorfahr *m*

ancestry, *änn*-ssess-tri, *n* Abstammung *f*, Herkunft *f*

anchor, *äng*-ker, *n* Anker *m*; *v* ankern; verankern

anchovy, *änn*-tsche-wi, *n* Sardelle *f*

ancient, *ehn*-sch'nt, *adj* alt; (clothes etc.) uralt; (monument) historisch

and, *ännd*, *conj* und; **– so on**, und so weiter; **bigger – bigger**, immer größer

Andes, *änn*-dies, *npl* Anden *pl*

anew, *e*-*njuh*, *adv* aufs neue, von neuem

angel, *ehn*-dsch'l, *n* Engel *m*

anger, *äng*-ger, *n* Zorn *m*, Ärger *m*; *v* ärgern

angle, *äng*-g'l, *n* Winkel *m*; *fig* Standpunkt *m*

angler, *äng*-gler, *n* Angler *m*, Fischer *m*

Anglican, *äng*-gli-k'n, *adj* anglikanisch; *n* Anglikaner *m*

angling, *äng*-gling, *n* Angeln *nt*, Fischen *nt*

angry, *äng*-gri, *adj* ärgerlich, böse; (enraged) zornig

anguish, *äng*-gu'isch, *n* Qual *f*

animal, *änn*-i-mel, *n* Tier *nt*;

adj tierisch

animate, änn-i-met, *adj*
lebendig

animate, änn-i-meht, *v*
beleben; animieren; **–d**,
adj lebhaft, belebt; **–d
film**, n Zeichentrickfilm *m*

animosity, änn-i-**moss**-i-ti, *n*
Feindseligkeit *f*

aniseed, änn-i-ssied, *n*
Anis *m*

ankle, äng-k'l, *n*
(Fuß)knöchel *m*

annex, änn-eks, *n* (to
document) Anhang *m*; (to
building) Anbau *m*

annex, e-neks, *v*
annektieren

annihilate, e-nei-i-leht, *v*
vernichten, zerstören

anniversary, änn-i-wör-se-
ri, n Jahrestag *m*;
(wedding) Hochzeitstag *m*

annotate, änn-e-teht, *v*
kommentieren

announce, e-naunss, *v*
ankündigen; **–ment**, *n*
Ankündigung *f*; (official)
Bekanntmachung *f*

announcer, e-naun-sser, *n*
Ansager *m*

annoy, e-neu, *v* ärgern;
be/get –ed, *v* sich ärgern;
–ance, *n* Verärgerung *f*;
–ing, *adj* ärgerlich

annual, änn-ju-el, *adj*
jährlich, Jahres-; n (plant)
einjährige Pflanze; (book)
Jahresalbum *nt*

annul, e-nall, *v* für ungültig
erklären, aufheben

anomalous, e-**nomm**-e-less,
adj anormal, abweichend

anomaly, e-**nomm**-e-li, *n*
Abweichung *f*

anonymous, e-**nonn**-i-mess,
adj anonym

anonymity, änn-e-ni-mi-ti,
n Anonymität *f*

anorak, änn-e-rack, *n*
Anorak *m*

anorexia, änn-e-reck-ssi-e, *n*
Magersucht *m*, Anorexie *f*

another, e-nadh-er, *adj &
pron* ein(e) andere(r/s),
noch ein(e); **one –**,
einander

answer, ahn-sser, *n* Antwort
f; *v* antworten; **– the door**,
aufmachen; **– the phone**,
das Telefon abnehmen

answerable, ahn-sse-re-b'l,
adj verantwortlich

answering machine, ahn-
sse-ring me-schien, *n*
Anrufbeantworter *m*

ant, ännt, *n* Ameise *f*

antagonism, än-tägg-e-
nism, n Antagonismus *m*

antagonize, än-tägg-e-neis,
v gegen sich aufbringen

Antarctic, änn-tark-tick,
adj antarktisch; **the –,
Antarctica**, *n* die
Antarktis *f*

antelope, änn-ti-lohp, *n*
Antilope *f*

antenatal, änn-ti-neh-t'l, *adj*
vor der Geburt,
Schwangerschafts-

anthem, änn-them, *n*
Hymne *f*

anti-, änn-ti, *pref* Anti-,
Gegen-

anti-aircraft, änn-ti-ähr-
krahft, *adj* Flugabwehr-

antibiotic, änn-ti-bei-ott-
ick, *adj* antibiotisch; n
Antibiotikum *nt*

anticipate, änn-tiss-i-peht, *v*
(expect) vorhersehen,
erwarten; (precede)
zuvorkommen

anticipation, änn-tiss-i-peh-
sch'n, *n* Erwartung *f*; **in –**,
im voraus

anticlimax, änn-ti-klei-
macks, *n* Enttäuschung *f*

anticlockwise, änn-ti-
klock-u'eis, *adj & adv*
gegen den Uhrzeigersinn

antidote, änn-ti-doht, *n*
Gegenmittel *nt*

antifreeze, änn-ti-fries, *n*
Frostschutzmittel *nt*

antihistamine, änn-ti-
hiss-te-mien, *n*
Antihistamin *nt*

antiquated, änn-ti-kueh-
tidd, *adj* antiquiert,
veraltet

antique, änn-tiek, *adj* antik;
n Antiquität *f*

antiseptic, änn-ti-ssepp-
tick, *adj* antiseptisch; n
Antiseptikum *nt*

antisocial, änn-ti-ssoh-sch'l,
adj unsozial

antlers, änt-lers, *npl*
Geweih *nt*

anvil, änn-will, *n* Amboß *m*

anxiety, äng-sei-i-ti, *n*
Besorgnis *f*, Sorge *f*; *med*

Angstneurose f

anxious, äng-schess, *adj*
besorgt, ängstlich; **be –
(about),** *v* sich Sorgen
machen (um)

any, enn-i, *adj & adv* (in
questions) etwas; welche
pl; (whichever) jede(r/s);
(any one) irgend eine(r/s);
not –, kein(e); (not) –
more, (nicht) mehr; **in –
case,** auf jeden Fall;
überhaupt

anybody, enn-i-bodd-i, *pron*
(irgend) jemand; **not –,**
niemand

anyhow, enn-i-hau, *conj* auf
jeden Fall, immerhin

anyone, enn-i-u'an, *pron*
(irgend) jemand; **not –,**
niemand

anything, enn-i-thing, *pron*
(irgend) etwas; alles; **not
–,** nichts

anyway, enn-i-u'eh, *adv* auf
jeden Fall, immerhin;
überhaupt

anywhere, enn-i-u'ähr, *adv*
irgendwo(hin); **not –,**
nirgendwo(hin)

apart, e-part, *adv* (aside)
abseits, beiseite;
(separated) auseinander; –
from, *prep* außer

apartheid, e-part-eit, *n*
Apartheid f

apartment, e-part-ment, *n*
Wohnung f

apathetic, äpp-e-thett-ick,
adj apathisch,
teilnahmslos

apathy, äpp-e-thi, *n* Apathie
f; Teilnahmslosigkeit f

ape, ehp, *n* Affe m; *v*
nachäffen

aperitif, e-pe-ri-tief, *n*
Aperitif m

aperture, äpp-er-tscher, *n*
Öffnung f; *photog*
Blende f

apex, eh-pecks, *n* Gipfel m;
Spitze f

apiece, e-piess, *adv* pro
Stück; pro Person

apologetic, e-poll-e-dsche-
tick, *adj* entschuldigend

apologize, e-poll-e-dscheis, *v*
sich entschuldigen

apology, e-poll-e-dschi, *n*
Entschuldigung f

apostle, e-poss-'l, *n* Apostel
m

apostrophe, e-poss-tre-fi, *n*
Apostroph m

appal, e-po'al, *v* entsetzen;
–ling, *adj* entsetzlich

apparatus, äpp-e-reh-tess, *n*
Apparat m, Geräte *pl*

apparent, e-pä-rent, *adj*
(obvious) offenbar, klar;
(seeming) scheinbar; **–ly,**
adv anscheinend

apparition, äpp-e-risch-'n, *n*
Erscheinung f

appeal, e-piel, *n* Aufruf m;
law Berufung f; *v*
(dringend) bitten; *law*
Berufung einlegen; **– to,**
(turn to) appellieren an;
(be attractive to) zusagen,
gefallen

appear, e-pier, *v* erscheinen;

(seem) scheinen; *theatre*
auftreten; **–ance,** *n*
Erscheinen nt; *theatre*
Auftritt m; (looks)
Aussehen nt

appease, e-pies, *v*
besänftigen,
beschwichtigen

appendage, e-pend-idsch, *n*
Anhang m, Zubehör m;
(limb) Gliedmaße f

appendicitis, e-pend-i-ssai-
tiss, *n*
Blinddarmentzündung f

appendix, e-pend-icks, *n* (to
book) Anhang m; *med*
Blinddarm m

appetite, äpp-i-teit, *n*
Appetit m; *fig* Lust f

appetizer, äpp-i-tei-ser, *n*
Appetitanreger m; (food)
Vorspeise f

appetizing, äpp-i-tei-sing,
adj appetitlich

applaud, e-plo'ad, *v*
applaudieren, Beifall
klatschen

applause, e-plo'as, *n*
Applaus m, Beifall m

apple, äpp-'l, *n* Apfel m; **–
tree,** Apfelbaum m

applicable, e-plick-e-b'l, *adj*
zutreffend

appliance, e-plei-enss, *n*
Gerät nt

applicant, äpp-li-kent, *n*
Bewerber m

application, äpp-li-keh-
sch'n, *n* (use) Anwendung
f, Gebrauch m;
(candidacy) Bewerbung f;

(effort) Fleiß m; – **form**, n Bewerbungsformular nt

apply, e-**plei**, v (be appropriate) zutreffen; (use) anwenden; (lay on) auflegen, auftragen; – **for**, sich bewerben um; – **to**, sich wenden an

appoint, e-**peunt**, v (to post) ernennen; (agree) festsetzen

appointment, e-**peunt**-ment, n (to post) Ernennung f; (meeting) Verabredung f; (post) Stelle f

appraisal, e-**preh**-s'l, n Abschätzung f, Beurteilung f

appreciable, e-**prie**-schi-e-b'l, adj merklich

appreciate, e-**prie**-schi-eht, v (recognize) anerkennen, einsehen; (value) schätzen, zu schätzen wissen; (be grateful) dankbar sein; (in value) im Wert steigen

appreciation, e-prie-schi-eh-sch'n, n Anerkennung f; Schätzung f; Steigerung f

apprehend, äpp-ri-**hend**, v (arrest) festnehmen; (understand) verstehen; (perceive) wahrnehmen

apprehension, äpp-ri-henn-sch'n, n (fear) Angst f; (arrest) Verhaftung f

apprehensive, äpp-ri-henn-ssiw, adj besorgt, ängstlich

apprentice, e-**prenn**-tiss, n Lehrling m; –**ship**, Lehre

f, Lehrzeit f

approach, e-**prohtsch**, n Annäherung f; (access) Zugang m, Zufahrt f; (to problem) Ansatz m; v sich nähern; (person) herantreten an; (problem) angehen

appropriate(ly), e-proh-**pri**-et(-li), adj & adv angemessen, passend

appropriate, e-**proh**-pri-eht, v sich aneignen

approval, e-**pruh**-wel, n Billigung f, Beifall m

approve, e-**pruhw**, v billigen

approximate(ly), e-prock-ssi-met(-li), adj & adv ungefähr, annähernd

approximate (to), e-prock-ssi-meht (tu), v nahekommen

apricot, eh-pri-kott, n Aprikose f

April, eh-prill, n April m

apron, eh-pren, n Schürze f

apse, äpps, n Apsis f

apt, äppt, adj (fit) passend; (inclined) geneigt; (capable) fähig

aptitude, äpp-ti-tjuhd, n Begabung f, Talent nt

aquarium, e-**kwähr**-ri-em, n Aquarium nt

Aquarius, e-**kwähr**-ri-ess, n Wassermann m

aquatic, e-**kwätt**-ick, adj Wasser-

Arab, ä-reb, adj arabisch; n Araber m

Arabic, ä-reb-bick, adj

(language) arabisch; n Arabisch nt

aqueduct, äck-u'i-dackt, n Aquädukt m/nt

arable, ä-re-b'l, adj bebaubar, nutzbar

arbitrary, ahr-bi-tre-ri, adj willkürlich

arbitrate, ahr-bi-treht, v schlichten, vermitteln

arbitration, ar-bi-treh-sch'n, n Schlichtung f

arbitrator, ahr-bi-treh-ter, n Schlichter m, Vermittler m

arc, ark, n Bogen m; – **lamp**, Bogenlampe f

arcade, ark-**ehd**, n Arkade f; (shopping) Passage f

arch, artsch, n Bogen m; v sich wölben

archaeologist, ar-ki-**oll**-e-dschist, n Archäologe m

archaeology, ar-ki-**oll**-e-dschi, n Archäologie f

archaic, ar-**keh**-ick, adj veraltet

archbishop, artsch-**bisch**-ep, n Erzbischof m

archer, artsch-er, n Bogenschütze m; –**y**, n Bogenschießen nt

archetype, ahr-ki-teip, n Urbild nt

archipelago, ar-ki-**pell**-e-goh, n Archipel m

architect, ahr-ki-tekt, n Architekt m, Baumeister m

architecture, ahr-ki-teck-tscher, n Architektur f

archive(s), ahr-keiw(s), n(pl) Archiv nt

archway, artsch-u'eh, n (Tor)bogen m

Arctic, ark-tick, adj arktisch, Polar-; **the –,** n die Arktis f

ardent, ahr-d'nt, adj feurig, glühend

ardour, ahr-der, n (passion) Leidenschaft f; (zest) Eifer m

arduous, ahr-djuh-ess, adj mühsam, schwierig

area, ähr-ri-e, n (expanse) Fläche f; (district) Gebiet nt, Gegend f

arena, e-rie-ne, n Arena f

Argentina, ar-djschen-tie-ne, n Argentinien nt

Argentinian, ar-djschen-tinn-jen, adj argentinisch; n Argentinier m

argue, ahr-gjuh, v (debate) diskutieren; (dispute) (sich) streiten

argument, ahr-gju-ment, n Diskussion f; Auseinandersetzung f; (reason) Begründung f

arise, e-reis, v (occur) entstehen, vorkommen; (of protest) sich erheben; (of question) sich stellen; **– from,** sich ergeben aus

aristocracy, ä-ri-stock-re-ssi, n Aristokratie f, Adel m

aristocratic, ä-ri-ste-krätt-ick, adj aristokratisch

arithmetic, e-rith-me-tick, n Rechnen nt

Ark, ark, n **– of the Covenant,** Bundeslade f; **Noah's –,** die Arche Noah f

arm, arm, n Arm m; (branch) Zweig m; v (sich) bewaffnen; (equip) ausrüsten; **–s,** npl (weapons) Waffen pl; **coat of –s,** Wappen nt

armament, ahr-me-m'nt, n Aufrüstung f; **–s,** npl Ausrüstung f

armchair, arm-tschähr, n Sessel m

armistice, ahr-miss-tiss, n Waffenstillstand m

armour, ahr-mer, n Rüstung f

armoured, ahr-merd, adj Panzer-

armoury, ahr-me-ri, n Waffenlager nt

armpit, arm-pitt, n Achselhöhle f

army, ahr-mi, n Heer nt Armee f

aromatic, ä-re-mätt-ick, adj würzig, aromatisch

aroma, e-roh-me, n Duft m, Aroma nt

around, e-raund, adv (rings) herum; prep um… herum

arouse, e-raus, v (auf)wecken; (excite) erregen

arrange, e-rehndsch, v (objects) (an)ordnen; (meeting) ansetzen; (obtain) besorgen; (agree) vereinbaren

array, e-reh, n (line-up) Aufstellung f; (collection) Ansammlung f

arrears, e-riers, n Rückstand m; **fall into –,** in Rückstand geraten

arrest, e-rest, n Verhaftung f, Festnahme f; v verhaften, festnehmen; (stop) anhalten

arrival, e-raiw-'l, n Ankunft f; (person) Ankömmling m; (goods) Lieferung f

arrive, e-raiw, v ankommen; **– at a decision,** zu einer Entscheidung kommen

arrogance, ä-re-genss, n Arroganz f

arrogant, ä-re-gent, adj arrogant

arrow, ä-roh, n Pfeil m

arse, arss, n vulg Arsch m

arsenal, ahr-ss'n-'l, n Arsenal nt, Waffenlager nt

arsenic, ahr-ss'n-ick, n Arsen nt

arson, ahr-ss'n, n Brandstiftung f

art, art, n Kunst f; (skill) Geschick nt; **–s,** Geisteswissenschaften pl

arterial road, ar-tier-ri-el rohd, n Verkehrsader f

artery, ahr-te-ri, n Schlagader f, Arterie f

artful, art-full, adj (sly) schlau

artichoke, ahr-ti-tschohk, n Artischocke f; **Jerusalem –,** Topinambur m

article, ahr-ti-k'l, n Artikel

m; – **of clothing**, Kleidungsstück nt

articulate, ar-**tick**-ju-let, *adj* (speech) deutlich; (speaker) gewandt; **to be** –, *v* sich gut ausdrücken

articulate, ar-**tick**-ju-leht, *v* artikulieren; (state) darlegen; **–d lorry**, Sattelschlepper m

artificial, ahr-ti-**fisch**-'l, *adj* künstlich

artillery, ar-**till**-e-ri, *n* Artillerie f

artisan, **ahr**-ti-sänn, *n* (Kunst)handwerker m

artist, **ahr**-tist, *n* Künstler m; **-ic**, *adj* künstlerisch

as, äs, *conj* (time) als; (manner) wie, so wie; (reason) da; *prep* als; **– for**, was… betrifft; – **if/though**, als ob; – **from/of**, ab; – **good** –, so gut wie; – **to**, in Bezug auf; – **well**, auch; – **well** –, sowohl… als auch; – **yet**, bis jetzt

asbestos, äs-**bess**-tess, *n* Asbest m

ascend, e-**ssend**, *v* besteigen; hinaufgehen

ascent, e-**ssent**, *n* Aufstieg m; Besteigung f

ascertain, äss-er-**tehn**, *v* feststellen

ascribe to, e-**skreib** tu, *v* zuschreiben

ash, äsch, *n* Asche f; (tree) Esche f; **–tray**, Aschenbecher m; **Ash**

Wednesday, Aschermittwoch m

ashamed, e-**schehmd**, *adj* beschämt; **be – (of)**, sich schämen (für)

ashore, e-**schohr**, *adv* an(s) Land

Asia, **eh**-sche, *n* Asien nt; **–n**, *adj* asiatisch; *n* Asiat m

aside, e-**sseid**, *adv* beiseite, abseits; *n* beiläufige Bemerkung f

ask, ahsk, *v* (enquire) fragen, (Frage) stellen; (permission, request) bitten; (invite) einladen; **– after**, fragen nach; – **for**, bitten um

askew, e-**skjuh**, *adv* schief

asleep, e-**sliep**, *adj* schlafend; **be –**, *v* schlafen; **fall –**, *v* einschlafen

asparagus, e-**spä**-re-gess, *n* Spargel m

aspect, **äss**-peckt, *n* Aspekt m, Seite f

aspen, **äss**-p'n, *n* Espe f

aspersion, äss-**pör**-sch'n, *n* **cast –s (on)**, *v* abfällige Bemerkungen machen (über)

asphyxiation, äss-fick-ssi-**eh**-sch'n, *n* Erstickung f

asphyxiate, äss-**fick**-ssi-eht, *v* ersticken; **be –d**, ersticken

aspiration, äss-pi-**reh**-sch'n, *n* Ziel nt; **have –s (towards)**, *v* streben (nach)

aspire to, e-**speir** tu, *v* streben nach

aspirin, **äss**-pi-rinn, *n* Aspirin nt

ass, äss, *n* Esel m

assail, e-**ssehl**, *v* angreifen; (of doubts) plagen

assailant, e-**sseh**-lent, *n* Angreifer m

assassin, e-**ssäss**-in, *n* Attentäter m

assassinate, e-**ssäss**-i-neht, *v* ermorden

assassination, e-ssäss-i-**neh**-sch'n, *n* (geglücktes) Attentat nt; **– attempt**, *n* Attentat nt

assault, e-**ssolt**, *n* Angriff m; *v* angreifen; (sexually) herfallen über

assemble, e-**ssemm**-b'l, *v* (people) versammeln; (parts) zusammensetzen; (of group) sich versammeln

assembly, e-**ssemm**-bli, *n* (meeting) Versammlung f; (construction) Zusammensetzen nt, Montage f

assent, e-**ssent**, *n* Zustimmung f; **– (to)**, *v* zustimmen

assert, e-**ssört**, *v* behaupten; **–ion**, *n* Behauptung f

assess, e-**ssess**, *v* (ein)schätzen; (tax) festsetzen; **–ment**, *n* Einschätzung f; (of tax) Festsetzung f; **–or**, *n* Schätzer m; Prüfer m

asset, äss-itt, n Vorteil m; fin Vermögenswert m; **–s,** pl fin Aktiva pl Vermögen nt

assiduous, e-**ssidd**-juh-ess, adj (hard-working) fleißig; (attentive) aufmerksam

assign, e-**ssein,** v zuteilen; übertragen; **–ment,** Übertragung f; (task) Aufgabe f

assist, e-**ssist,** v helfen; **–ance,** n Hilfe f; (money) Unterstützung f; **–ant,** Mitarbeiter m; (shop) –, Verkäufer m

associate, e-**ssoh**-ssi-et, n Kollege m; (partner) Teilhaber m; – **(member),** n außerordentliches Mitglied nt

associate (with), e-**ssoh**-ssi-siht (u'idh), v (ideas etc.) assoziieren (mit); (of people) verkehren (mit)

association, e-**ssoh**-ssi-eh-sch'n, n (link) Assoziation f, Zusammenhang m; (group) Verein m

assorted, e-**ssor**-tidd, adj gemischt

assortment (of), e-**ssort**-ment (ew), n Auswahl f (an), Sortiment nt (von)

assume, e-**ssjuhm,** v (presume, take on) annehmen; (responsibility) übernehmen; **–ing that,** angenommen/ vorausgesetzt, daß

assumption, e-**ssamp**-sch'n, n Annahme f

assurance, e-**schor**-renss, n (insurance) Versicherung f; (promise) Zusicherung f

assure, e-**schor,** v (promise, insure) versichern; (make certain) sichern

asterisk, äss-te-risk, n Sternchen nt

astern, e-**störn,** adv (nach) achtern, achteraus

astonish, e-**stonn**-isch, v erstaunen, in Erstaunen setzen; **–ment,** n Erstaunen nt

astound, e-**staund,** v verblüffen

astray, e-**streh,** adj verloren; **go –,** v fehlgehen; **lead –,** v irreführen

astride, e-**streid,** prep rittlings auf

astrologer, e-**stroll**-e-dscher, n Astrologe m

astrology, e-**stroll**-e-dschi, n Astrologie f

astronaut, äss-tre-no'at, n Astronaut m

astronomer, e-**stronn**-e-mer, n Astronom m

astronomy, e-**stronn**-e-mi, n Astronomie f

astute, e-**stjuht,** adj schlau

asylum, e-**ssei**-lem, n Asyl nt; (mental) Anstalt f

at, ätt/ett, prep an, zu, bei, in; (hour) um; (price) zu; (speed) mit; – **home,** zu Hause; – **once,** sofort; – **times,** manchmal

atheist, eh-thie-ist, n Atheist m

Athens, äth-ens, n Athen nt

athlete, äth-liet, n Athlet m, Sportler m

athletic, äth-lett-ick, adj athletisch; (person) sportlich; **–s,** pl Leichtathletik f

Atlantic, ätt-länn-tick, adj atlantisch; **the – (Ocean),** n der Atlantik

atlas, ätt-less, n Atlas m

atmosphere, ätt-mess-fier, n Atmosphäre f

atom, ätt-em, n Atom nt; **–ic,** adj atomar, Atom-; **–(ic) bomb,** n Atombombe f; **–ic energy,** n Atomenergie f

atone (for), e-**tohn** (for), v sühnen; **–ment,** n Sühne f

atrocious, e-**troh**-schess, adj scheußlich, gräßlich

atrocity, e-**tross**-i-ti, n (act) Greueltat f

attach (to), e-**tätsch,** v befestigen (an); (to a letter etc.) anheften; (value etc.) legen (auf), zuschreiben; **be –ed to,** (fond of) hängen an; **–ment,** n (accessory) Zusatzteil m; (fondness) Zuneigung f

attack, e-**täck,** n Angriff m; (illness) Anfall m; v angreifen; **–er,** n Angreifer m

attain, e-**tehn,** v erreichen, erlangen; **–ment,** n (act)

Erreichen nt, Erlangen nt; –ments, pl (talents) Kenntnisse pl

attempt, e-tempt, n Versuch m; (attack) Attentat nt; v versuchen

attend, e-tend, v (be at) anwesend sein; (regularly) besuchen; – to, (person) sich kümmern um; (task) erledigen; –ance, n (presence) Anwesenheit f; (number present) Teilnehmerzahl f

attendant, e-tenn-dent, adj damit verbunden; n (keeper) Wärter m, Wächter m; (companion) Begleiter m

attention, e-tenn-sch'n, n Aufmerksamkeit f; mil –!, Achtung!; for the – of, zu Händen von; pay – (to), v beachten

attentive, e-tenn-tiw, adj aufmerksam

attest (to), e-test (tu), v (testify) bescheinigen; (prove) bezeugen

attic, ätt-ick, n Dachboden m; – (room), Dachzimmer nt

attitude, ätt-i-tjuhd, n (mental) Einstellung f; (manner) Haltung f

attorney, e-tör-ni, n Rechtsanwalt m; power of –, Vollmacht f

attract, e-träkt, v anziehen; (attention) erregen, auf sich ziehen; –ion, n (power) Anziehungskraft f; (personal) Reiz m; (thing) Attraktion f; –ive, adj attraktiv, anziehend

attribute, ätt-ribb-juht, n Attribut nt

attribute (to), e-tribb-juht (tu), v zuschreiben, beimessen

aubergine, oh-ber-dschien, n Aubergine f

auburn, o'a-börn, adj rotbraun

auction, o'ak-sch'n, n Versteigerung f, Auktion f; v versteigern; –eer, n Auktionator m

audacious, o'a-deh-schess, adj (bold) verwegen; (impudent) dreist

audacity, o'a-däss-i-ti, n Kühnheit f; Dreistigkeit f

audible, o'a-di-b'l, adj hörbar

audience, o'a-di-enss, n (public) Publikum nt; (interview) Audienz f

audio, o'a-di-oh, adj Audio-; –visual, audiovisuell

audit, o'a-ditt, n Buchprüfung f; v prüfen; –or, n Buchprüfer m

audition, o'a-disch-'n, n theatre Vorsprechprobe f; mus Probespiel nt, Vorsingen nt

auditor, o'a-di-ter, n Buchprüfer m

augment, o'ag-ment, v vermehren, vergrössern

augur, o'a-ger, o'a – well (ill)

Gutes (nichts Gutes) verheißen

August, o'a-gest, n August m

aunt, ahnt, n Tante f

au pair, oh-pähr, n Au-pair-(Mädchen) nt

auspicious, o'ass-pisch-ess, adj günstig, glücklich

austere, oss-tier, adj (person) streng; (room etc.) karg, schmucklos

austerity, oss-te-ri-ti, n (severity) Strenge f; (simplicity) Schmucklosigkeit f; (hardship) Entbehrung f

Australia, oss-treh-li-e, n Australien nt; –n, adj australisch; n Australier m

Austria, oss-tri-e, n Österreich nt; –n, adj österreichisch; n Österreicher m

authentic, o'a-thenn-tick, adj authentisch; echt

author, o'a-ther, n Verfasser m, Schriftsteller m

authoritarian, o'a-tho-ri-tähr-ri-en, adj autoritär

authoritative, o'a-tho-ri-te-tiw, adj (definitive) maßgebend; (commanding) bestimmt

authority, o'a-tho-ri-ti, n Autorität f; the –s, pl die Verwaltung f

authorize, o'a-the-reis, v (empower) ermächtigen; (permit) genehmigen

autobiography, o'a-te-bei-

ogg-*re*-fi, n
Autobiographie f

autograph, o'a-*te*-grahf, n
Autogramm nt

automatic, o'a-*te*-mätt-ick,
adj automatisch; n
(engine) Automatik f;
(weapon)
Schnellfeuerwaffe f

automatically, o'a-*te*-mätt-ick-*e*-li, adv automatisch

automobile, o'a-*te*-me-biel,
n Auto(mobil) nt

autumn, o'a-tem, n
Herbst m

auxiliary, o'ag-*sill*-i-*e*-ri, adj
helfend, Hilfs-

avail, e-*wehl*, n to no –,
vergebens

available, e-*weh*-le-b'l, adj
(thing) verfügbar,
erhältlich; (person) frei,
erreichbar

availability, e-weh-le-*bill*-i-
ti, n (of thing)
Erhältlichkeit f

avalanche, äw-e-lahntsch, n
Lawine f

avarice, äw-e-riss, adj
Habsucht f, Geiz m

avenge, e-*wendsch*, v
rächen

avenue, äw-e-njuh, n Allee f

average, äw-e-ridsch, adj
durchschnittlich; n
Durchschnitt m; on –, adv
durchschnittlich

averse (to), e-*wörss* (tu),
adj abgeneigt

aversion (to), e-*wör*-sch'n
(tu), n (dislike)

Abneigung f (gegen);
(horror) Abscheu f (vor)

avert, e-*wört*, v (turn away)
abwehren, abwenden;
(prevent) abwenden,
verhüten

aviary, eh-wi-*e*-ri, n
Vogelhaus nt

aviation, eh-wi-*eh*-sch'n, n
Luftfahrt f

avid (for), äw-idd (for), adj
gierig (nach), süchtig
(nach)

avocado, äw-e-*kah*-doh, n
Avocado f

avoid, e-*weud*, v vermeiden;
(obstacle) ausweichen

avoidance, e-*weud*-'nss, n
Vermeidung f

await, e-*u'eht*, v erwarten

awake, e-*u'ehk*, adj wach; v
(wake up) aufwachen;
(arouse) aufwecken;
–ning, n Erwachen nt

award, e-*uord*, n Preis m;
(mil etc.) Auszeichnung f;
v (prize) zuerkennen;
(damages) zusprechen

aware (of), e-*u'ähr* (ew), adj
bewußt; be – (of), sich
bewußt sein

away, e-*u'eh*, adv weg, fort;
1 km –, 1 km entfernt

awe, o'ah, n Ehrfurcht f

awesome, o'a-s'm, adj
ehrfurchtgebietend

awful, o'a-full, adj furchtbar,
entsetzlich; –ly, adv
furchtbar; fam sehr

awhile, e-*u'eil*, adv eine
Weile, eine Zeitlang

awkward, o'ak-u'ed, adj
(inconvenient) ungünstig;
(embarrassing) peinlich;
(clumsy) ungeschickt;
–ness, n (embarrassment)
Verlegenheit f

awning, o'a-ning, n (of
shop) Markise f; (of
caravan) Vordach nt

awry, e-*rei*, adj & adv schief,
krumm; go –, v
schiefgehen

axe, äcks, n Axt f

axis, äck-ssiss, n (pl axes)
Achse f

axle, äck-ss'l, n mech
Achse f

azure, äs-juhr, adj
himmelblau

B & B, bie end bie (*abbr* **bed and breakfast**), Übernachtung *f* mit Frühstück, Gästezimmer *pl*

babble, bäbb-'l, *v* plappern; (stream) plätschern

baby, beh-bi, *n* Baby *nt*

baby-sit, beh-bi-ssitt, *n* babysitten; **-er,** *n* Babysitter *m*

bachelor, batsch-*e*-ler, *n* Junggeselle *m*; **Bachelor of Arts/Science,** *n* Bakkalaureus der philosophischen Fakultät/der Naturwissenschaften *m*

back, bäck, *adv* (nach) hinten; zurück; *n* (of person/animal) Rücken *m*; (of cheque etc.) Rückseite *f*; *v* (support) unterstützen; (bet) wetten auf; (go backwards) rückwärts

gehen/fahren; **– down,** nachgeben; **– out,** sich zurückziehen

backbone, bäck-bohn, *n* Rückgrat *nt*

background, bäck-graund, *n* Hintergrund *m*; (social) Verhältnisse *pl*

backing, bäck-ing, *n* (support) Unterstützung *f*

backlash, bäck-läsch, *n* Gegenreaktion *f*

backpack, bäck-päck, *n* Rucksack *m*

back seat, bäck ssieht, *n* Rücksitz *m*; **take a –,** *v fig* sich zurückhalten

backside, bäck-sseid, *n fam* Hinterteil *nt*

backstage, bäck-stehdsch, *adj & adv* hinter den Kulissen

back-up, bäck-app, *n* (support) Unterstützung *f*;

comp Sicherungskopie *f*

backward, bäck-u'ed, *adj* rückständig

backwards, bäck-u'eds, *adv* rückwärts

backwater, bäck-u'o'a-ter, *n* totes Wasser *nt*; *fig* hinterste Provinz *f*

backyard, bäck jahrd, *n* Hinterhof *m*

bacon, beh-k'n, *n* Speck *m*

bacteria, bäck-tier-ri-e, *npl* Bakterien *pl*

bad, bäd, *adj* schlecht; (grave) schlimm; (wicked) böse; (smell etc.) schlecht

badge, bädsch, *n* Abzeichen *nt*, Plakette *f*

badger, bädsch-er, *n* Dachs *m*; *v* (pester) belästigen

badly, bäd-li, *adv* schlecht, schlimm; **– injured,** schwerverletzt; **need –,** dringend brauchen

badminton, bädd-minn-t'n, *n* Badminton *nt*, Federball *nt*

baffle, bäff-'l, *v* verwirren, verblüffen

bag, bäg, *n* (sack) Beutel *m*; (handbag) Tasche *f*; (paper/plastic) Tüte *f*; **–s of,** *fam* eine Menge

baggage, bägg-idsch, *n* Gepäck *nt*

baggy, bägg-i, *adj* (zu) weit

bagpipes, bägg-peips, *npl* Dudelsack *m*

Bahamas, be-hah-mes, *npl* **the –,** die Bahamas *pl*

bail, behl, *n* Kaution *f*; *v*

gegen Kaution freilassen;
– **out,** die Kaution stellen
für; *fig* aus der Klemme
helfen

bailiff, beh-liff, *n*
Gerichtsvollzieher *m*

bait, beht, *n* Köder *m*; *v*
(hook) ködern; (animal)
hetzen

bake, behk, *v* backen; **–r,**
n Bäcker *m*; **–ry,** *n*
Bäckerei *f*

balance, báll-'nss, *n*
Gleichgewicht *nt*; (scales)
Waage *f*; *fin* Kontostand
m; **– of payments,**
Zahlungsbilanz *f*; *v*
balancieren; *m comm*
ausgleichen; **– the books,**
die Bilanz ziehen; **– sheet,**
n Bilanz *f*

balcony, báll-ke-ni, *n*
Balkon *m*

bald, bo'ald, *adj* kahl; *fig*
knapp; **be –,** *v* eine Glatze
haben

bale, behl, *n* (of hay) Ballen
m; **– out,** *v* (boat)
ausschöpfen; (from plane)
abspringen

ball, bo'al, *n* Ball *m*;
(billiards, bullet) Kugel *f*;
(wool) Knäuel *nt*

ballet, báll-eh, *n* Ballett *nt*;
– dancer, Ballettänzer *m*

balloon, be-**luhn,** *n*
Ballon *m*

ballot, báll-et, *n*
Abstimmung *f*, Wahl *f*; *v*
abstimmen

ballpoint (pen), bo'al-peunt

(penn), *n*
Kugelschreiber *m*

balm, bahm, *n* Balsam *m*

Baltic, bo'al-tick, *adj*
Ostsee-; **the – (Sea),** die
Ostsee *f*

bamboo, bämm-**buh,** *n*
Bambus *m*

ban, bänn, *n* Verbot *nt*; *v*
verbieten

banana, be-**nah**-ne, *n*
Banane *f*

band, bänd, *n* (strip) Band
nt; (group) Gruppe *f*;
(gang) Bande *f*; *mus* Band
f, Kapelle *f*; **– together,** *v*
sich zusammenschließen

bandage, bänn-didsch, *n*
Verband *m*; *v* verbinden;
(limb) bandagieren

bandy, bänn-di, *adj* **–
legged,** o-beinig; *v* **–
about,** herumerzählen

bang, bäng, *n* Knall *m*; *v*
knallen

Bangladesh, bäng-gle-**desch,**
n Bangladesch *nt*

bangle, bäng-g'l, *n*
Armreif(en) *m*

banish, bänn-isch, *v*
verbannen, ausweisen

banister(s), bänn-iss-ter(s),
n(pl) Treppengeländer *nt*

bank, bänk, *n* (fin etc.)
Bank *f*; (of river) Ufer *nt*;
(of earth) Damm *m*; *v*
(money) einzahlen; (of
plane) in die Querlage
gehen; **– on,** rechnen mit,
sich verlassen auf; **–
account,** *n* Bankkonto *nt*;

–(er's) card, *n*
Scheckkarte *f*; **– holiday,**
n öffentlicher Feiertag *m*;
–note, *n* Banknote *f*,
Geldschein *m*; **–
statement,** *n*
Kontoauszug *m*

banker, bäng-ker, *n*
Bankier *m*

bankrupt, bänk-rapt, *n*
adj bankrott; **go –,** *v*
Bankrott machen;
–cy, *n* Bankrott *m*

banner, bänn-er, *n*
Banner *nt*

banquet, bäng-ku'itt, *n*
Bankett *nt*, Festessen *nt*

baptism, bäpp-tism, *n*
Taufe *f*

baptize, bäpp-teis, *v* taufen

bar, bar, *n* (for drinks) Bar *f*;
(rod) Stange *f*; *mus* Takt
m; (of chocolate) Tafel *f*;
(fig obstacle) Hindernis
nt; *law* **the Bar,** die
Anwaltschaft *f*; *v* (route)
versperren; (person)
ausschließen; **– none,**
ohne Ausnahme; **behind
–s,** hinter Gittern

barbaric, bar-**bä**-rick, *adj*
barbarisch; (cruel)
grausam

barbarity, bar-**bä**-ri-ti, *n*
Barbarei *f*; (cruelty)
Grausamkeit *f*

barbecue, bar-bi-kjuh, *n*
Grillparty *f*, Barbecue *nt*; *v*
grillen

barbed wire, barbd u'eir, *n*
Stacheldraht *m*

barber, bar-ber, n
Herrenfriseur m
barcode, bar-kohd, n
Strichcode m
bare, bähr, adj nackt, bloss;
(country) kahl; v
entblößen; **–faced,**
schamlos; **–foot,** barfuß;
–headed, ohne Hut
barely, bähr-li, adv kaum
bargain, bar-ginn, n
(agreeement) Handel m;
(cheap item)
Schnäppchen nt; **– (for),**
v handeln (um); **get more
than one –ed for,** fig sein
blaues Wunder erleben
barge, bardsch, n (freight)
Lastkahn m; (houseboat)
Hausboot nt; **– in,** v
hereinplatzen; fig sich
einmischen; **– into,** v
(person) anrempeln
bark, bark, n (of dog) Bellen
nt; (of tree) Rinde f; v (of
dog) bellen
barley, bar-li, n Gerste f
barmaid, bar-mehd, n
Bardame f
barman, bar-männ, n
Barmann m, Barkellner m
barn, barn, n Scheune f
barometer, be-romm-i-ter, n
Barometer nt
barracks, bä-reks, npl
Kaserne f
barrage, bä-rahdsch, n (of
stones/words) Hagel m;
(dam) Talsperre f
barrel, bä-rel, n Faß nt,
Tonne f; (of gun) Lauf m

barren, bä-ren, adj
unfruchtbar; (land) öde
barricade, bä-ri-kehd, n
Barrikade f; v
verbarrikadieren
barrier, bä-ri-er, n Schranke
f; fig Hindernis nt
barrister, bä-riss-ter, n
Rechtsanwalt m
barrow, bä-roh, n
Schubkarren m
bartender, bar-tenn-der, n
Barkeeper m, Barkellner m
barter, bar-ter, v (exchange)
Tauschhandel treiben;
(bargain) handeln
base, behss, n Basis f;
(pedestal) Sockel m;
(centre) Stützpunkt m; **–
on,** v gründen/basieren
auf; **be –d on,** v
ruhen/basieren auf
baseball, behss-bo'al, n
Baseball m
basement, behss-ment, n
Untergeschoß nt,
Kellergeschoß nt
bash, bätt-er, v (fam)
(person) schlagen; (car
etc.) eindellen; **– down,**
einschlagen
bashful, bäsch-full, adj
schüchtern
basic, beh-ssick, adj
(fundamental)
grundsätzlich, Grund-;
(minimal) elementar; **the
–s,** npl das Wesentliche nt;
–ally, adv im Grunde
basil, bä-sill, n Basilikum nt
basin, beh-ss'n, n (dish)

Schüssel f; **(wash)–,**
Waschbecken nt
basis, beh-ssiss, n Basis f,
Grundlage f
bask, bahsk, v sich sonnen,
sich wärmen
basket, bahs-kitt, n Korb m
basketball, bahs-kitt-bo'al,
n Basketball m
bass, behss, n mus Baß m
bassoon, be-ssuhn, n
Fagott nt
bastard, bahss-ted, n
Bastard m; (fig, fam)
Scheißkerl m
bat, bätt, n (animal)
Fledermaus f; sport
Schläger m; v sport
schlagen; **not – an eyelid,**
nicht (mal) mit der
Wimper zucken
batch, bätsch, n (of work,
letters) Stoß m; (of goods)
Sendung f
bath, bahth, n Bad nt;
–(tub), n Badewanne f;
have a –, v baden;
(swimming) –s, npl
Schwimmbad nt
bathroom, bahth-rum, n
Bad nt, Badezimmer nt
bathe, behdh, v baden; **–r,** n
Badende(r) m, & f
batter, bätt-er, n Teig m; v
(strike) verprügeln;
(damage) verbeulen; **–
down,** v einschlagen; **–ed,**
adj (object) verbeult;
(wife) mißhandelt
battery, bätt-e-ri, n
Batterie f

battle, bätt-'l, n Schlacht f;
v kämpfen; **–field,** n
Schlachtfeld nt; **–ship,** n
Schlachtschiff nt

Bavaria, be-**vähr**-ri-e, n
Bayern nt; **–n,** adj
bay(e)risch; n Bayer m

bawl, bo'al, v laut schreien

bay, beh, n (of sea) Bucht f;
(horse) braunes Pferd nt; v
bellen; **–(leaf/tree),** n
Lorbeer(blatt/baum) nt/m

be, bie, v sein; (in passives)
werden, sein; (imperative)
sei!, seid!, seien Sie!; **how
are you?,** wie geht es
Ihnen?; **I'm hot/cold,** mir
ist heiß/kalt; **isn't
it?/aren't they?,** nicht
wahr?; **there is/are,** es gibt

beach, bietsch, n Strand m;
v auf Strand setzen

beacon, bie-k'n, n
Leuchtfeuer nt

bead, bied, n (of glass) Perle
f; (drop) Tropfen m

beak, biek, n Schnabel m

beaker, bie-ker, n Becher m

beam, biem, n (of wood)
Balken m; (of light) Strahl
m; v strahlen; **–ing,** adj
strahlend

bean, bien, n Bohne f

bear, bähr, n Bär m; v (carry,
produce) tragen; (endure)
aushalten, leiden;
(offspring) gebären; **–
left/right,** sich links/rechts
halten; **– out,** bestätigen

bearable, adj erträglich

beard, bierd, n Bart m; **–ed,**

adj bärtig

bearing, hähr-ring, n
(behaviour) Verhalten nt;
mech (Kugel)lager nt;
(relevance) **– on,** Bezug m
auf; **–s,** npl Orientierung f;
mech (Kugel)lager nt

beast, biest, n Tier nt;
(cattle) Vieh nt; fig Bestie
f; **–ly,** adv & adj fig roh,
gemein

beat, biet, n (stroke) Schlag
m; mus Takt m; v (strike,
defeat) schlagen; (thrash)
(ver)prügeln; **– it,** fam
abhauen; **– up,**
zusammenschlagen

beautiful, bjuh-ti-full, adj
schön; **–ly,** adv schön;
(well) hervorragend

beautify, bjuh-ti-fei, v
verschönern, schmücken

beauty, bjuh-ti, n Schönheit
f; **– spot,** (mole)
Schönheitsfleck m;
(place) schöne Gegend f

beaver, bie-wer, n Biber m

because, be-**kos,** conj weil; **–
of,** prep wegen

beckon (to), beck-en (tu), v
winken

become, bi-**kamm,** v
werden; **becoming,** adj
(conduct) schicklich;
(dress) kleidsam

bed, bedd, n Bett nt; (in
garden) Beet nt; **– clothes,**
npl Bettwäsche f; **–ding,** n
Bettzeug nt; **–ridden,** adj
bettlägerig; **–room,** n
Schlafzimmer nt; **–sit(ter),**

–sitting room, n
möbliertes Zimmer nt,
Wohnschlafzimmer nt

bee, bie, n Biene f

beech, bietsch, n Buche f

beef, bief, n Rindfleisch nt;
–burger, Hamburger m

beehive, bie-heiw, n
Bienenstock m

beer, bier, n Bier nt

beet, biet, n Rübe f

beetle, bie-t'l, n Käfer m

beetroot, biet-ruht, n rote
Beete/Rübe f

before, bi-**for,** adv vorher,
früher; (already) schon;
conj bevor; prep vor

beforehand, bi-**for**-händ,
adv im voraus

beg (for), beg (for), v
(request) dringend bitten
(um); (for alms) betteln;
–gar, n Bettler m

begin, bi-**ginn,** v beginnen,
anfangen; **–ner,** n
Anfänger m; **–ning,** n
Anfang m

begrudge, bi-**gradsch,** v
mißgönnen, beneiden

behalf, bi-**hahf,** n on **– of,**
im Namen von, für

behave, bi-**hehw,** v sich
benehmen, sich betragen

behaviour, bi-**hehw**-jer,
n Benehmen nt,
Verhalten nt

behead, bi-**hedd,** v
enthaupten, köpfen

behind, bi-**heind,** adv
hinten; n (inf) Hinterteil
nt; prep hinter; **–(hand),**

adv im Rückstand

behold, bi-**hohld**, *v*
erblicken; –!, siehe da!

being, bie-ing, *n* (existence)
Dasein *nt*; (creature)
Wesen *nt*

belated, bi-**leh**-tidd, *adj*
verspätet

belch, beltsch, *v* rülpsen,
aufstoßen; (smoke etc.)
ausspeien

belfry, bell-fri, *n*
Glockenturm *m*

Belgian, bell-dschen, *adj*
belgisch; *n* Belgier *m*

Belgium, bell-dschem, *n*
Belgien *nt*

belie, bi-**lei**, *v* Lügen strafen

belief, bi-**lief**, *n* (faith)
Glaube *m*; (opinion)
Meinung *f*

believable, bi-**liew**-e-b'l, *adj*
glaubhaft, glaubwürdig

believe (in), bi-**liew** (inn), *v*
glauben (an); –r, *n*
Gläubige(r) *m & f*

belittle, bi-**litt**-'l, *v*
schlechtmachen

bell, bell, *n* (church etc.)
Glocke *f*; (door etc.)
Klingel *f*

belligerent, bi-**lidsch**-e-rent,
adj (nation) kriegslustig;
(person) streitlustig

bellow, bell-oh, *v* brüllen

bellows, bell-ohs, *npl*
Blasebalg *m*

belly, bell-i, *n* Bauch *m*

belong (to), bi-**long** (tu), *v*
gehören; (club etc.)
angehören, Mitglied sein

belongings, bi-**long**-ings, *npl*
Sachen *pl* Besitz *m*

beloved, bi-**law**-idd, *adj*
geliebt, lieb; *n* Geliebte(r)
m & f

below, bi-**loh**, *adv* unten;
prep unter, unterhalb

belt, belt, *n* (clothing)
Gürtel *m*; *mech*
(Treib)riemen *m*; *v* den
Gürtel zumachen; (*fam*
hit) knallen; (*fam* run)
rasen; – up, *fam* die
Klappe halten

bench, bentsch, *n* Bank *f*;
law the –, (judges)
Richter *pl*; (in court)
Richterbank *f*

bend, bend, *n* Biegung *f*; (in
road) Kurve *f*; *v* biegen;
(back, knee, rules) beugen

beneath, bi-**nieth**, *adv*
unten; *prep* unter,
unterhalb

benefactor, benn-i-**fäck**-ter,
n Wohltäter *m*

beneficial, benn-i-**fisch**-'l,
adj vorteilhaft; (healing)
heilsam

beneficiary, be-ni-**fisch**-e-ri,
n Nutznießer *m*

benefit, benn-i-**fitt**, *n*
(advantage) Vorteil *m*,
Nutzen; (allowance)
Beihilfe *f*; (social security)
Sozialhilfe *f*; *v* nützen; –
(from), Nutzen ziehen
(aus)

benevolence, bi-**new**-e-
lenss, *n* Wohlwollen *nt*

benevolent, bi-**new**-e-lent,

adj wohlwollend

benign, bi-**nein**, *adj* (person)
gütig; (influence) günstig;
(tumour) gutartig

bent, bent, *adj* gebogen;
(*fam* dishonest) korrupt;
(*fam* homosexual) schwul;
n (inclination) Neigung *f*;
be – on (doing), *v*
entschlossen sein (zu tun)

bequeath (to), bi-**ku'iedh**
(tu), *v* vermachen,
hinterlassen

bequest, bi-**ku'est**, *n*
Vermächtnis *nt*

bereaved, bi-**riewd**, *adj* vom
Verlust betroffen; **the –,**
npl die Hinterbliebenen

bereavement, bi-**riew**-ment,
n Trauerfall *m*

Bermuda, ber-**mjuh**-de,
n; **the –s,** *npl* die
Bermudas *pl*

berry, be-ri, *n* Beere *f*

berth, börth, *n* (cabin) Koje
f; (on train) Bett *nt*;
(anchorage) Ankerplatz
m; *v* anlegen

beseech, bi-**ssietsch**, *v*
anflehen

beset, bi-**ssett**, *v* bedrängen;
– **with,** *adj* geplagt von

beside, bi-**sseid**, *prep* neben,
dicht bei; **be – o.s. (with),**
v außer sich sein (vor); **be
– the point,** *v* nicht zur
Sache gehören

besides, bi-**sseids**, *adv*
außerdem; *prep* außer

besiege, bi-**ssiedsch**, *v*
bedrängen; *mil* belagern

best, best, *adj* beste(r/s); *adv*
am besten; **all the –!**, alles
Gute!; **at –**, bestenfalls; **do
one's –**, *v* sein Bestes tun;
– man, *n* Trauzeuge *m*

bet, bett, *n* Wette *f*; *v*
wetten

betray, bi-treh, *v* verraten

better, bett-er, *adj & adv*
besser; (like, enjoy) mehr;
(healthy) gesund; *v*
verbessern; **get the – of**, *v*
unterkriegen; **you had –
(do)**, *v* Sie (tun)
lieber/besser

betting, bett-ing, *n*
Wetten *nt*

between, bi-tu'ien, *adv*
dazwischen; *prep*
zwischen; **– ourselves**,
unter uns gesagt

beverage, bew-e-ridsch, *n*
Getränk *nt*

bevy, bew-i, *n* Schwarm *m*,
Schar *f*

bewail, bi-u'ehl, *v* beklagen,
beweinen

beware (of), bi-u'ähr (ew),
v sich hüten (vor); **–!**,
Vorsicht!

bewildered, bi-u'ill-derd, *adj*
verwirrt

bewitched, bi-u'itscht, *v*
bezaubert

beyond, bi-jond, *adv*
jenseits, über… hinaus; **–
belief**, nicht zu glauben

bias, bei-ess, *n* (prejudice)
Vorurteil *nt*; (viewpoint)
Ausrichtung *f*; **–(s)ed**, *adj*
voreingenommen

Bible, bei-b'l, *n* Bibel *f*

bicker, bick-er, *v* zanken

bicycle, bei-ssick-'l, *n*
Fahrrad *nt*

bid, bidd, *n* (at sale, cards)
Gebot *nt*; (attempt)
Versuch *m*; *v* (at sale,
cards) bieten; **– farewell
to**, *v* Abschied nehmen
von

bidder, bidd-er, *n*
Bietende(r) *m & f*; **the
highest –**, *n* der/die
Meistbietende *m & f*

bide, beid, *v* abwarten

bifocal, bei-foh-k'l, *adj*
Bifokal-; **–s**, *npl*
Bifokalbrille *f*

big, bigg, *adj* groß;
(important) wichtig

bigot, bigg-et, *n* Frömmler
m; **–ed**, *adj* bigott,
borniert; **–ry**, *n* Bigotterie
f, Borniertheit *f*

bike, beik, *n* (Fahr)rad *nt*

bikini, bi-kie-ni, *n* Bikini *m*

bilberry, bill-be-ri, *n*
Heidelbeere *f*, Blaubeere *f*

bile, beil, *n* Galle *f*

bilingual, bei-ling-gu'el, *adj*
zweisprachig

bill, bill, *n* (account)
Rechnung *f*; *law*
Gesetzentwurf *m*; (of bird)
Schnabel *m*; *v* (charge)
berechnen; **– of fare**, *n*
Speisekarte *f*; **fill/fit the –**,
der/die/das richtige sein

billet, bill-itt, *n* Quartier *nt*

billiards, bill-jerds, *npl*
Billard *nt*

billion, bill-jen, *n* (in
Britain: 10^{12}) Billion *f*; (in
USA: 10^9) Milliarde *f*

bin, bin, *n* Kasten *m*;
(refuse) Mülleimer *m*

bind, beind, *v* binden;
(commit) verpflichten;
(person) fesseln; **–ing**, *adj*
verbindlich; *n* (of book)
Einband *m*

binge, bindsch, *n fam*
(drinking) Sauferei *f*;
(eating) Fresserei *f*

binoculars, bi-nock-ju-lers,
npl Fernglas *nt*

biography, bei-ogg-re-fi, *n*
Biographie *f*

biological, bei-e-lodsch-i-
k'l, *adj* biologisch

biology, bei-oll-e-dschi, *n*
Biologie *f*

birch, börtsch, *n* Birke *f*

bird, börd, *n* Vogel *m*; **–'s
eye view**, *n* (Blick aus der)
Vogelschau *f*; **– watcher**, *n*
Vogelbeobachter *m*

birth, börth, *n* Geburt *f*; **–
control**, *n*
Geburtenkontrolle *f*;
–day, *n* Geburtstag *m*;
–place, *n* Geburtsort *m*;
–rate, *n* Geburtsziffer *f*

biscuit, biss-kitt, *n* Keks *m*

bisect, bei-ssekt, *v*
halbieren

bishop, bisch-ep, *n* Bischof
m; (chess) Läufer *m*

bit, bitt, *n* (part) Stück *nt*;
(horse) Gebiß *nt*; *comp* Bit
nt; **a –**, etwas, ein bißchen

bitch, bitsch, *n* Hündin *f*;

(*pej woman*) Schlampe *f*; *v fam* meckern

bite, beit, *n* Biß *m*; (mouthful) Bissen *m*; *v* beißen

biting, beit-ing, *adj* beißend; (wind) schneidend

bitter, bitt-er, *adj* bitter; (struggle) erbittert; (person) verbittert; *n* (halb)dunkles Bier *nt*; **–ness,** *n* Bitterkeit *f*

black, bläck, *adj* schwarz; (dark, gloomy) finster, *v* schwärzen; (shoes) wichsen; (boycott) boykottieren; **– eye,** *n* blaues Auge *nt*; **– and blue,** grün und blau; **– and white,** (*photog* etc.) Schwarzweiß-; **B– Forest,** *n* Schwarzwald *f*; **– market,** *n* Schwarzmarkt *m*; **B– Sea,** *n* Schwarzes Meer *nt*

blackberry, bläck-be-ri, *n* Brombeere *f*

blackbird, bläck-börd, *n* Amsel *f*

blackcurrant, bläck-ka-rent, *n* schwarze Johannisbeere *f*

blacken, bläck-'n, *v* schwärzen; *fig* verleumden

blackleg, bläck-legg, *n* Streikbrecher *m*

blackmail, bläck-mehl, *n* Erpressung *f*; *v* erpressen; **–er,** *n* Erpresser *m*

blackout, bläck-aut, *n med* Ohnmachtsanfall *m*;

(wartime) Verdunkelung *f*

blacksmith, bläck-smith, *n* Schmied *m*

bladder, blädd-er, *n* Blase *f*

blade, blehd, *n* (of weapon) Klinge *f*; (of grass) Halm *m*; (of oar) Blatt *nt*

blame, blehm, *n* (censure) Tadel *m*; (fault) Schuld *f*, Verantwortung *f*; *v* **– (for),** die Schuld geben (an); **to be to – (for),** schuld sein (an)

blameless, blehm-liss, *adj* schuldlos, tadellos

bland, bländ, *adj* freundlich, mild; *pej* fade

blank, blänk, *n adj* (vacant) leer; (page) unbeschrieben; (look) ausdruckslos; *n* (space) Lücke *f*; (cartridge) Platzpatrone *f*; ; **– cheque,** *n* Blankoscheck *m*; *fig* Freibrief *m*; **– verse,** *n* Blankvers *m*; **go –,** *v fam* Mattscheibe haben

blanket, bläng-kitt, *n* Decke *f*; *v* bedecken

blare, blähr, *v* schmettern

blaspheme, bläss-fiem, *v* Gott lästern

blasphemy, bläss-fi-mi, *n* Gotteslästerung *f*

blast, blahst, *n* (of wind) Windstoß *m*; (explosion) Explosion *f*; *v* (explode) sprengen; **–!,** *fam* verdammt!; **–ed,** *adj fam* verdammt

blatant, bleh-t'nt, *adj*

offensichtlich, unverhohlen

blaze, blehs, *n* Feuer *nt*, Brand *m*; *v* lodern; **– a trail,** *v fig* den Weg bahnen; **– of light,** *n* Lichtstrahl *m*

bleach, blietsch, *v* bleichen; *n* Bleichmittel *nt*

bleak, bliek, *adj* (wind) rauh; (country) kahl, öde

bleary, blier-ri, *adj* (sleepy) verschlafen

bleat, bliet, *v* blöken; *fig* meckern

bleed, blied, *v* bluten; (draw blood) zur Ader lassen

blemish, blemm-isch, *n* Makel *m*; *v* beschädigen; *fig* beflecken

blend, blend, *v* (sich) vermischen; *n* Mischung *f*

bless, bless, *v* segnen; **– you!,** Gesundheit!; **–ed,** *adj* gesegnet; **–ing,** *n* Segen *m*; (good fortune) Glück *nt*

blight, bleit, *n* (on plant) Braunfäule *f*; (eyesore) Schandfleck *m*; *v* verderben

blind, bleind, *adj* blind; (corner) unübersichtlich; *n* (for window) Rouleau *nt*; (venetian) Jalousie *f*; *v* blenden; **– spot,** *n* toter Winkel *m*; *fig* schwacher Punkt *m*; **the –** *npl* die Blinden *pl*

blindfold, bleind-fohld, *n* Augenbinde *f*; *v* die

Augen verbinden

blindly, bleind-li, *adv*
blindlings

blindness, bleind-niss, *n*
Blindheit *f*

blink, blink, *v* (of eyes)
blinzeln; (of light)
blinken

blinkers, blink-ers, *npl* (for
horse) Scheuklappen *pl*

bliss, bliss, *n* Seligkeit *f*;
-ful, *adj* (person) selig;
(experience) herrlich

blister, bliss-ter, *n* Blase *f*; *v*
(paint) Blasen werfen;
(skin) Blasen bekommen

blitz, blitz, *n* Luftkrieg *m*

blizzard, bliz-erd, *n*
Schneesturm *m*

bloated, bloht-idd, *adj*
aufgedunsen; (*fig* full)
vollgestopft

blob, blob, *n fam* Klacks *m*,
Fleck *m*

block, block, *n* Block *m*; **–
of flats,** Wohnblock *m*;
mental –, geistige Sperre *f*

blockade, block-**ehd**, *n*
Blockade *f*

blockage, block-idsch, *n*
Verstopfung *f*

blockbuster, block-bass-ter,
n Knüller *m*

bloke, blohk, *n fam* Typ *m*

blond(e), blond, *adj* blond;
blonde, *n* Blondine *f*

blood, bladd, *n* Blut *nt*; **–
donor,** *n* Blutspender *m*; **–
group,** *n* Blutgruppe *f*; **–
pressure,** *n* Blutdruck *m*;
–shed, *n* Blutvergießen *nt*;

–shot, *adj* blutunterlaufen;
–thirsty, *adj* blutdürstig;
–y, *adj* blutig; *fam*
verdammt; **––minded,** *adj*
fam stur

bloom, bluhm, *n* Blüte *f*; *v*
blühen; **–ing,** *adj* blühend

blossom, bloss-em, *n* Blüte
f; *v* blühen

blot, blott, *n* Klecks *m*; *fig*
Fleck *m*; *v* beklecksen;
(dry) löschen; *fig*
verderben; **–ting paper,**
Löschpapier *nt*

blotchy, blotsch-i, *adj*
fleckig

blouse, blaus, *n* Bluse *f*

blow, bloh, *n* Schlag *m*; *v*
blasen; (of wind) wehen;
(nose) putzen; **– over,**
(storm, dispute) sich
legen; **– up,** (tyres etc.)
aufblasen; (explode)
sprengen

blow-dry, bloh-drei, *v*
fönen; **have a –,** *v* sich
föhnen lassen

blue, bluh, *adj* blau;
(obscene) Porno-; (*fam*
sad) melancholisch; **out
of the –,** aus heiterem
Himmel

bluebell, bluh-bell, *n*
Sternhyazinthe *f*;
(in Scotland)
Glockenblume *f*

blueprint, bluh-print, *n*
Blaupause *f*; *fig* Entwurf *m*

blues, bluhs, *npl* the **–,** *mus*
der Blues *m*; **have the –,** *fam*
melancholisch sein

bluff, blaff, *n* Bluff *m*; *v*
bluffen; **call sb's –,** *v* es
darauf ankommen lassen

blunder, blan-der, *n* grober
Fehler *m*; *v* einen Bock
schießen

blunt, blant, *adj* (blade)
stumpf; (words)
unverblümt; *v* (blade)
stumpf machen; (senses)
abstumpfen; **–ness,** *n*
Stumpfheit *f*;
Unverblümtheit *f*

blurred, blörd, *adj* (image)
verschwommen; (writing)
verschmiert

blurt out, blört aut, *v*
herausplatzen mit

blush, blasch, *n* Erröten *nt*;
v erröten

boar, bor, *n* Eber *m*; **wild –,**
Wildschwein *nt*

board, bord, *n* (of wood)
Brett *nt*; (black-) Tafel *f*;
(of company) Aufsichtsrat
m; (of officials) Behörde *f*;
v (lodge) (in Pension)
wohnen; (floor) mit
Brettern auslegen; (train,
bus) einsteigen in; (plane,
ship) besteigen; **– and
lodging,** *n* Unterkunft *f*
und Verpflegung *f*; **–er,** *n*
(guest) Pensionsgast *m*;
(pupil) Internatsschüler
m; **–ing house,** *n* Pension
f; **–ing-school,** *n* Internat
nt; **across the –,** *adv*
generell; **on –,** *adv* an
Bord

boast, bohst, *n* Prahlerei *f*; *v*

prahlen, sich rühmen; –er,
n Prahler m
boat, boht, n Boot nt;
(rowing) Kahn m; **--hook,**
n Bootshaken m; **–ing,**
n Boots-; n Bootfahren nt
boatswain, boh-ss'n, n
Bootsmann m
bob, bobb, v **– about,** bob
up and down, (auf dem
Wasser) schaukeln; **– up,**
auftauchen
bobbin, bobb-in, n Spule f
bobsleigh, bobb-slei, n
Bob m
bode, bohd, v **– well/ill,** ein
gutes/schlechtes Zeichen
sein
bodily, bodd-i-li, adj & adv
körperlich; (in one piece)
ganz
body, bodd-i, n Körper m;
(corpse) Leiche f; **–guard,**
Leibwächter m; (group)
Leibwache f; **–work,**
Karosserie f
bog, bogg, n Sumpf m; **get**
–ged down, v
steckenbleiben; **–gy,** adj
sumpfig
bogus, boh-gess, adj falsch
boil, beul, n med Geschwür
nt; v kochen; (of water)
sieden; **– down to,** fig
hinauslaufen auf
boiled, beuld, adj gekocht; **–**
potatoes, npl
Salzkartoffeln pl
boiler, beu-ler, n (domestic)
Boiler m; (in engine)
(Dampf)kessel m

boisterous, beuss-te-ress, adj
ausgelassen, wild
bold, bohld, adj (brave)
mutig; (impudent) dreist;
(pattern etc.) kräftig
bolster, bohl-ster, n
Nackenrolle f; **– up,** v
stützen; fig Mut machen
bolt, bohlt, n Riegel m;
(lightning) Blitzstrahl m;
v verriegeln; (of horse)
durchgehen; **– upright,**
adv kerzengerade
bomb, bomm, n Bombe f; v
bombardieren
bombard, bonm-**bahrd,** v
bombardieren
bond, bond, n (obligation)
Verpflichtung f; (fig link)
Band nt; (fin stock) Bond
m; **in –,** (customs) unter
Zollverschluß
bondage, bonn-didsch, n
Sklaverei f
bone, bohn, n Knochen m;
(of fish) Gräte f; v (meat)
die Knochen herauslösen,
entbeinen; (fish)
entgräten; **–d,** adj ohne
Knochen; ohne Gräten
bonfire, bonn-feir, n
(Freuden)feuer nt
bonnet, bonn-itt, n Haube f,
Häubchen nt; (of car)
Motorhaube f
bonus, bohn-ness, n (annual)
Prämie f; (supplement)
Zuschlag m; (special)
Bonus m
bony, boh-ni, adj knochig
book, buck, n Buch nt; v

(tickets) bestellen; **–case,**
n Bücherregal nt; **–ed**
(up), adj ausverkauft,
ausgebucht; **–ing office,** n
rail Fahrkartenschalter m;
theatre Vorverkaufsstelle f;
–keeper, n Buchhalter m;
–keeping, n Buchführung
f; **–mark,** n Lesezeichen
nt; **–seller,** n Buchhändler
m; **–shop,** n
Buchhandlung f; **–stall,** n
Bücherstand m; **–worm,** n
Bücherwurm m
boom, buhm, n comm
Hochkonjunktur f; naut
Baum m; (noise) Dröhnen
nt; v (of business) einen
Aufschwung nehmen; (of
noise) dröhnen
boon, buhn, n Segen m
boost, buhst, n (output etc.)
Auftrieb m; v (output etc.)
ankurbeln;
fig stärken; **give a – to,** v
Auftrieb geben; **–er,** n
(med injection)
Wiederholungsimpfung f
boot, buht, n Stiefel m; (of
car) Kofferraum m; v
(kick) einen Fußtritt
geben; comp laden; **– out,**
v fam rausschmeißen; **to –,**
adv noch dazu
booth, buhdh, n (voting
etc.) Kabine f; (fair) Bude
f; (telephone) Zelle f
booty, buh-ti, n Beute f
booze, buhs, fam n Alkohol
m; v saufen
border, bor-der, adj Grenz-;
n (frontier) Grenze f;

(edge) Rand m;
(flowerbed) Rabatte f; v
(country) grenzen an;
(surround) umschließen; –
on, v fig grenzen an; **–ing,**
adj angrenzend

borderline, bor-der-lein,
n Grenze f; **– case,**
Grenzfall m

bore, bor, v (drill) bohren;
(weary) langweilen; n (of
gun) Kaliber nt; (person)
Langweiler m; (thing)
Plage f

boring, bor-ring, adj
langweilig

born, born, adj geboren

borough, ba-re, adj Stadt-; n
(Stadt)bezirk m

borrow, bo-roh, v borgen

bosom, bus-em, n Busen m

boss, boss, n Boß m, Chef m;
– about/around, v
herumkommandieren; **–y,**
adj herrisch

botanist, bott-e-nist, n
Botaniker m

botany, bott-e-ni, n
Botanik f

botch (up), botsch (app), v
verpfuschen

both, bohth, adj beide,
beides; **– ... and ...,**
sowohl... als auch...

bother, bodh-er, n (trouble)
Mühe f; (nuisance) Plage
f; v (pester) belästigen;
(take trouble) sich Mühe
geben

bottle, bott-'l, n Flasche f; v
in Flaschen abfüllen; –

bank, n Altglascontainer
m; **– opener,** n
Flaschenöffner m

bottom, bott-em, adj
untere(r/s), unterste(r/s);
n Boden m, Grund m;
(fam of person) Hinterteil
m; **–less,** adj bodenlos

bough, bau, n Ast m,
Zweig m

bounce, baunss, n Aufprall
m; v (of ball)
(auf)springen; (fam of
cheque) platzen

bound, baund, adj (book,
hands) gebunden;
(obliged) verpflichtet; n
(jump) Sprung m; (limit)
Grenze f; v (jump)
springen; (border)
begrenzen; **be – for,** v auf
dem Weg sein nach; **out
of –s,** Betreten verboten

boundary, baun-de-ri, n
Grenze f

bounty, baun-ti, n (reward)
Kopfgeld nt

bouquet, bu-keh, n (of
flowers) Strauß m; (of
wine) Blume f

bout, baut, n (of illness)
Anfall m; (fight) Kampf m

bow, boh, n (archery, violin)
Bogen m; (tie, knot)
Schleife f

bow, bau, n (of body)
Verbeugung f, Verneigung
f; naut Bug m; v sich
verbeugen; **– to,** fig sich
beugen (vor)

bowel, bau-el, n Darm m;

–s, pl fig das Innere nt

bowl, bohl, n Schale f,
Schüssel f; (ball) Kugel f;
v die Kugel rollen;
(cricket) den Ball werfen

bowling, boh-ling, n
Bowling nt; Kegeln nt;
(cricket) Werfen nt; **–ing
alley,** n Kegelbahn f; **–ing
green,** n Rasenfläche f
zum Bowling

bowls, bohls, npl Bowling nt

bow tie, boh tei, n Fliege f

box, bocks, n Schachtel f;
(chest) Kiste f; theatre
Loge f; (fam TV) Glotze f;
v sport boxen; (pack)
verpacken; **– sb's ears,** v
jdm eine Ohrfeige geben

boxing, bock-ssing, n Boxen
nt; **Boxing Day,** n zweiter
Weihnachtstag m; **–
match,** Boxkampf m

box office, bocks-off-iss, n
(Theater/Kino)kasse f

boxroom, bocks-ruhm, n
Abstellraum m

boy, beu, n Junge m

boycott, beu-kott, n Boykott
m; v boykottieren

boyfriend, beu-frend, n
Freund m

bra, brah (abbr **brassière**),
n BH

brace, brehss, n mech Strebe
f; med Klammer f; (two)
Paar nt; v mech verstreben;
(invigorate) stärken; **–
oneself for,** v sich gefaßt
machen auf; **–s,** npl
Hosenträger pl

bracelet, brehss-let, n
Armband nt

bracing, breh-ssing, adj
stärkend, kräftigend

bracken, bräck-'n, n
Farnkraut nt

bracket, bräck-itt, n mech
(Regal)träger m;
(parenthesis) Klammer f;
(group) Gruppe f, Klasse f;
v einklammern; –
(together), v fig in
Verbindung bringen

brag, brägg, v prahlen;
–gart, n Prahler m

braid, brehd, n (of hair)
Flechte f; (trimming)
Borte f; v flechten

brain(s), brehn(s), n(pl)
(physical) Gehirn nt;
(mind) Verstand m;
–wave, n Geistesblitz m;
–y, adj gescheit; **have sth
on the –,** v etw im Kopf
haben

braise, brehs, v schmoren

brake, brehk, n Bremse f; v
bremsen

bramble, brämm-b'l, n
Brombeere f

bran, bränn, n Kleie f

branch, brahntsch, n Ast m,
Zweig, m; comm
Zweigstelle f; **– off,** v
abzweigen

brand, bränd, n comm
Marke f; (mark) Brandmal
m; v fig brandmarken

brandish, bränn-dish, v
schwingen

brand-new, bränd-njuh, adj
nagelneu

brandy, bränn-di, n Kognak
m, Branntwein m

brass, brahss, n Messing nt;
mus die Blechbläser pl; –
band, n Blaskapelle f

bravado, bre-vah-doh, n
Wagemut m

brave, brehw, adj tapfer,
mutig; v (weather) trotzen

bravery, breh-we-ri, n
Tapferkeit f

brawl, bro'al, n Schlägerei f;
v sich schlagen

brawn, bro'an, n (cooking)
Sülze f; (strength)
Muskelkraft m; **–y,** adj
muskulös, kräftig

bray, breh, v schreien

brazen, breh-s'n, adj
unverschämt

brazier, breh-si-er, n
Kohlenfeuer nt

Brazil, bre-sill, n Brasilien
nt; **–ian,** adj brasilianisch;
n Brasilianer m; **––nut,** n
Paranuß f

breach, brietsch, n (gap)
Lücke f; (of contract etc.)
Bruch m; (of law)
Übertretung f; (of
discipline) Verstoß m; v
durchbrechen

bread, bredd, n Brot nt; –
and butter, n Butterbrot
nt; fig tägliches Brot nt

breadth, bredth, n Breite f

break, brehk, n (fracture)
Bruch m; (gap) Lücke f;
(pause) Pause f; v
(zer)brechen,

kaputtmachen; (promise)
brechen; (habit) sich
abgewöhnen; (horse)
zureiten; (of glass etc.)
zerbrechen, kaputtgehen;
– down, v (of car) eine
Panne haben; (of
negotiatons) scheitern; –
even, v die Kosten
decken; **have a good/bad
–,** v Glück/Pech haben

breakage, brehk-kidsch, n
Bruch m

breakdown, brehk-daun, n
mech Panne f; (of person)
Zusammenbruch m

breakfast, breck-fest, n
Frühstück nt

breakthrough, brehk-thruh,
n Durchbruch m

breakwater, brehk-u'oa-ter,
n Wellenbrecher m

bream, briem, n Brassen m

breast, brest, n Brust f

breath, breth, n Atem(zug)
m; fig Hauch m; **under
one's –,** adv leise,
flüsternd

breathalyse, breth-e-leis, v
ins Röhrchen blasen
lassen; **Breathalyser ®** n
Alcotest ® m

breathe, briedh, v atmen

breathless, breth-less, adj
atemlos, außer Atem

breeches, brie-tschis, npl
Kniehosen f; (riding)
Reithosen f

breed, bried, n Rasse f; v
züchten; fig erzeugen; **–er,**
n Züchter m; **–ing,** n (of

stock) Zucht f;
(education) Bildung f

breeze, bries, n Brise f

breezy, brie-si, adj (weather)
windig; (manner) flott,
lustig

brevity, brew-i-ti, n Kürze f

brew, bruh, v brauen; **–er,**
n Brauer m; **–ery,** n
Brauerei f

bribe, breib, n Bestechung f,
Bestechungsgeld nt; v
bestechen; **–ry,** n
Bestechung f

brick, brick, n Backstein m,
Ziegelstein m; **–layer,** n
Maurer m

bridal, brei-d'l, adj Braut-

bride, breid, n Braut f;
–groom, Bräutigam m;
–smaid, Brautjungfer f

bridge, bridsch, n Brücke f;
(cards) Bridge nt; v
überbrücken

bridle, brei-d'l, n Zaum m; v
aufzäumen

brief, brief, adj kurz; n
Auftrag m; v informieren,
unterweisen; **–s,** npl
Slip m

briefcase, brief-keiss, n
Aktentasche f

brigadier, brigg-e-dier, n
Brigadegeneral m

bright, breit, adj (light) hell;
(clever) intelligent;
(lively) aufgeweckt;
(cheerful) heiter; **–en
(up),** v aufheitern; (of
weather) sich aufklären

brilliance, brill-jenss, n

Glanz m

brilliant, brill-jent, adj
glänzend; (achievement)
hervorragend

brim, brimm, n Rand m; (of
hat) Krempe f; **–full,** adj
randvoll; **– over,** v
überlaufen

brine, brein, n Salzwasser nt,
(Salz)lake f

bring, bring, v bringen;
– forward, comm
übertragen; **– in,**
hereinbringen; **– off,**
(succeed with) schaffen;
– up, (educate) erziehen;
(topic) erwähnen

brink, brink, n Rand m

brisk, brisk, adj (lively)
lebhaft; (agile) flink

brisket, briss-kitt, n
Bruststück nt

bristle, briss-'l, n Borste f; v
sich sträuben

British, britt-isch, adj
britisch; **the –,** npl die
Briten pl; **the – Isles,** npl
die Britischen Inseln pl

brittle, britt-'l, adj spröde,
zerbrechlich

broach, brohtsch, v
anschneiden

broad, bro'ad, adj (wide)
breit; (vague) grob, weit;
(accent) stark; **–cast,** n
(Rundfunk)sendung f; v
senden; **–en,** v (sich)
verbreitern; **–ly,** adv
allgemein gesagt;
–minded, adj tolerant

broccoli, brock-e-li, n

Brokkoli m

brochure, broh-scher, n
Broschüre f

broken, broh-k'n, adj
(object) kaputt; (bone,
heart, promise) gebrochen

broker, broh-ker, n
Makler m

bronchitis, brong-kei-tiss, n
Bronchitis f

bronze, brons, n Bronze f

brooch, brohtsch, n
Brosche f

brood, bruhd, n Brut f; v
brüten

brook, bruck, n Bach m; v
erdulden

broom, bruhm, n Besen m;
(plant) Ginster m

broth, broth, n Brühe f

brothel, broth-'l, n Bordell
nt

brother, bra-dher, n Bruder
m; **–hood,** Brüderschaft f;
– -in-law, Schwager m

brow, brau, n (eyebrow)
(Augen)braue f;
(forehead) Stirn f; (of
hill) (Berg)kuppe f

brown, braun, adj braun; v
bräunen; **– bread,** n
Mischbrot nt,
Vollkornbrot nt; **– paper,**
n Packpapier nt

browse, braus, v **– (around),**
sich umsehen; **– through,**
(book) schmökern in

bruise, bruhs, n blauer Fleck
m; v (body) einen blauen
Fleck verpassen; (feelings)
verletzen; (of body) einen

blauen Fleck bekommen

brunette, bru-**nett,** n
Brünette f

brunt, brant, n volle
Wucht f

brush, brasch, n Bürste f;
(paint) Pinsel m;
(skirmish) Zusammenstoß
m; v bürsten; (sweep)
fegen; **– up,** v auffrischen;
–wood, n Reisig nt

brusque, bruhsk, adj brüsk,
schroff

Brussels, brass-'ls, n Brüssel
nt; **– sprouts,** npl
Rosenkohl m

brutal, bruh-t'l, adj brutal,
roh

brutality, bru-**täll**-i-ti, n
Brutalität f, Roheit f

brute, bruht, n Bestie f; fig
Unmensch m

bubble, babb-'l, n Blase f; v
perlen, sprudeln; **– bath,** n
Schaumbad nt

buck, back, n Bock m; **–
up!,** (hurry up) halt dich
ran!; (cheer up) Kopf
hoch!; **pass the – (to),** v
die Verantwortung
abschieben (auf)

bucket, back-itt, n Eimer m

buckle, back-'l, n Schnalle
f; v zuschnallen; (bend)
verbiegen

bud, bad, n Knospe f; v
knospen, ausschlagen

budge, badsch, v sich
rühren; fig weichen

budget, badsch-itt, n Budget
nt; parl Haushaltsplan m; **–**

for, v einplanen

buff, baff, adj braungelb; n
(enthusiast) Fan m

buffalo, baff-e-loh, n Büffel
m

buffer, baff-er, n (railway)
Puffer m; comp
Pufferspeicher m

buffet, bu-feh, n (food)
Büfett nt; (bar)
Imbißstube f; **– car,**
Speisewagen m

buffet, baff-itt, v hin und
her stoßen

buffoon, be-fuhn, n
Hanswurst m

bug, bagg, n (also fig)
Wanze f

buggy, bagg-i, n
Kinderwagen m

bugle, bjuh-g'l, n Bügelhorn
nt

build, bild, n (Körper)bau
m; v bauen; **–er,**
Bauunternehmer m; **–ing,**
Gebäude nt, Bau m

built-in, bilt-inn, adj
eingebaut

built-up, bilt-app, adj
bebaut

bulb, balb, n (of plant)
Blumenzwiebel f; (lamp)
(Glüh)birne f

bulge, baldsch, n Wölbung f;
fig Anschwellen nt; v
anschwellen

bulk, balk, n (size) Größe f;
(major part) Großteil m;
in –, comm en gros; **–y,** adj
umfangreich

bull, bull, n Bulle m, Stier

m; **–dog,** Bulldogge f;
–dozer, Planierraupe f

bullet, bull-itt, n Kugel f

bulletin, bull-e-tinn, n
Bulletin nt, Bericht m

bulletproof, bull-itt-pruhf,
adj kugelsicher

bullion, bull-jen, n Gold-
/Silberbarren pl

bull's eye, buls-ei, n (target)
das Schwarze nt; (shot)
Volltreffer m

bully, bull-i, n Tyrann m; v
tyrannisieren

bum, bamm, n fam
(backside) Hinterteil m;
(good-for-nothing)
Rumtreiber m; **– (off),** v
(fam scrounge) schnorren
(bei)

bumble-bee, bamm-b'l-bie,
n Hummel f

bump, bamp, n (blow) Stoß
m; (swelling) Beule f; v
stoßen; **– into,** stoßen
gegen; fig treffen; **–y,** adj
holprig

bumper, bamm-per, adj
Rekord-, Sonder-; n (of
car) Stoßstange f

bunch, bantsch, n (of
flowers) Strauß m; (of
keys) Bund m; **– of
grapes,** Weintrauben pl

bundle, banm-d'l, n Bündel
nt; v (zusammen)bündeln

bung, bang, n Zapfen m; v
(fam throw) schmeißen; **–
(up),** verstopfen

bungalow, bang-ge-loh, n
Bungalow m

bungle, bang-g'l, n
Stümperei f; v
verpfuschen; **–r,** n
Stümper m

bunion, banm-jen, n
Entzündung f am
Fußballen

bunker, bang-ker, n
Bunker m

bunting, banm-ting, n
Wimpel pl

buoy, beu, n Boje f; **–ant,** adj
(floatable) schwimmfähig;
(cheerful) heiter

burden, bör-d'n, n Last f; fig
Bürde f; v belasten,
beladen; **–some,** adj
beschwerlich

bureau, bjue-roh, n (desk)
Sekretär m; (chest)
Kommode f; (office) Büro
nt; (official body) Amt nt

bureaucracy, bjue-rock-re-
ssi, n Bürokratie f

bureaucrat, bjue-re-krätt, n
Bürokrat m

burglar, bör-gler, n
Einbrecher m; **–y,** n
Einbruch m

burial, be-ri-el, n
Beerdigung f

burly, bör-li, adj stämmig,
stark

burn, börn, n Brandwunde f;
(stream) Bach m; v (of fire
etc.) brennen; (oneself,
food etc.) verbrennen; **–
down,** abbrennen,
niederbrennen; **–er,** n
Brenner m

burrow, ba-roh, n Bau m; v
graben

bursar, bör-sser, n
Schatzmeister m

burst, börst, n (in pipe)
Bruch m; (of anger etc.)
Ausbruch m; v platzen;
(pipe etc.) sprengen; **–
into,** (room) platzen in;
(tears) ausbrechen in;
(flames) aufgehen in; **–
out laughing,** in
Gelächter ausbrechen

bury, be-ri, v begraben;
(conceal) vergraben

bus, bass, n (Omni)bus m

bush, busch, n Busch m,
Strauch m; **–y,** adj buschig,
dicht

business, bis-niss, n comm
Geschäft nt; (concern)
Sache f; Angelegenheit f;
–-like, adj geschäftsmäßig;
–man, n Geschäftsmann
m; **–woman,** n
Geschäftsfrau f; **on –,** adv
geschäftlich; **that's none
of your –,** das geht dich
nichts an

busker, bass-ker, n
Straßenmusikant m

bus stop, bass stopp, n
Bushaltestelle f

bust, bast, adj (fam broken)
kaputt; (bankrupt) pleite;
n Büste f; **go –,** v pleite
machen

bustle, bass-'l, n Getriebe
nt; v geschäftig sein, hin
und her rennen

bustling, bass-ling, adj
(person) geschäftig;

(place) belebt

busy, bi-si, adj (person)
beschäftigt; (place)
belebt; (phone) besetzt; **–
oneself (with),** v sich
beschäftigen (mit)

busybody, bi-si-bodd-i, n
Wichtigtuer m

but, batt, conj aber; (on the
contrary) sondern; prep
außer; **all –,** so gut wie;
nothing –, nichts als, nur;
the last – one, der/die/das
vorletzte

butcher, butsch-er, n
Metzger m; v schlachten;
–'s (shop), n Metzgerei f

butler, batt-ler, n Butler m

butt, batt, n (for water)
Tonne f; (of gun) Kolben
m; (of cigarette) Stummel
m; v (mit dem Kopf
stoßen; **– in (on),** sich
einmischen (in)

butter, batt-er, n Butter f; v
mit Butter bestreichen,
buttern; **–cup,** n
Butterblume f; **–dish,** n
Butterdose f; **–fingers,** n
Schussel m; **–fly,** n
Schmetterling m

buttocks, batt-ecks, npl
Gesäß nt

button, batt-'n, n Knopf m;
v zuknöpfen; **–-hole,** n
Knopfloch nt

buttress, batt-riss, n
Strebepfeiler m; v stützen

buxom, back-ss'm, adj drall

buy, bei, v kaufen; **–er,** n
Käufer m

buzz, b*as,* n Summen *nt;*
v summen; **–er,** n
Summer m

buzzard, bas-*ed,* n Bussard m

by, bei, *prep* (agent) durch;
(means) mit, per; (via)
über, durch; (during) bei;
(near) neben, an; (before)
bis; **– oneself,** allein; **–
the way,** übrigens; **one –
one,** einer nach dem
anderen; *adv* **go/pass –,**
vorbeigehen

by(e)-law, bei-lo'a, n
Verordnung f

by(e)-election, bei-i-leck-
sch'n, n Nachwahl f

bypass, bei-pahss, n
Umgehungsstraße f; v
umgehen

bystander, bei-stänn-der, n
Umstehende(r) m & f,
Zuschauer m

byte, beit, n *comp* Byte *nt*

C

cab, käbb, n Taxi nt

cabaret, käbb-*e*-reh, n
Kabarett nt

cabbage, käbb-idsch, n Kohl
m; (head of cabbage)
Kohlkopf m

cabin, käbb-in, n (on ship)
Kabine f; (hut) Hütte f

cabinet, käbb-i-nitt, n
Schränkchen nt;
(display) Vitrine f; *parl*
Kabinett nt; **—maker**, n
Kunsttischler m

cable, keh-b'l, n Tau nt;
elec Kabel nt; (telegram)
Telegramm nt; v kabeln,
telegraphieren; **–
television**, n
Kabelfernsehen nt

cackle, käck-'l, n
Gackern nt; (chatter)
Geschwätz nt; (laughter)
Lachen nt; v gackern;
(chatter) schwatzen;

(laugh) lachen

cactus, käck-*t*ess, n
Kaktus m

caddie, kädd-i, n
Golfjunge m

caddy, kädd-i, n
(Tee)büchse f

cadet, ke-dett, n Kadett m

cadge, kädsch, v schnorren;
–r, n Schnorrer m

café, käff-eh, n Café nt

cafeteria, käff-i-tier-ri-*e*, n
Cafeteria f, Selbst-
bedienungsrestaurant nt

cage, kehdsch, n Käfig m;
–y, adj geheimnistuerisch,
ausweichend

cajole, ke-dschohl, **– sb
into sth**, v jdn zu etw
überreden

cake, kehk, n Kuchen m;
(of soap) Stück nt; v
verkrusten

calamity, ka-lämm-i-ti, n

Kalastrophe f; Unglück nt

calcium, käll-ssi-em, n
Kalzium nt

calculate, käll-kju-leht, v
berechnen, kalkulieren

calculation, käll-kju-leh-
sch'n, n Berechnung f

calculator, käll-kju-leh-ter,
n Rechner m

calendar, käll-in-der, n
Kalender m

calf, kahf, n (animal) Kalb
nt; (leg) Wade f

calibre, käll-i-ber, n
Kaliber nt

call, ko'al, n (shout) Ruf m;
(phone) Anruf m; v rufen;
(name) nennen; **– for**,
(collect) abholen;
(demand) erfordern; **– off**,
(cancel) absagen; **– on**,
(visit) besuchen; **be –ed**,
heißen

caller, ko'a-ler, n (visitor)
Besucher m; (phone)
Anrufer m

callous, käll-ess, adj
gefühllos, herzlos

calm, kahm, n Ruhe f, Stille
f; *naut* Flaute f; adj ruhig; v
beruhigen; **– down**, sich
beruhigen

calorie, käll-e-ri, n Kalorie f

camber, kämm-ber, n
Wölbung f

camcorder, kämm-kor-der, n
Camcorder m

camel, kämm-'l, n Kamel nt

cameo, kämm-i-oh, n
Kamee f

camera, kämm-e-re, n

(stills) Fotoapparat m;
(cine, TV) Kamera f; **in –**,
unter Ausschluß der
Öffentlichkeit
camouflage, kämm-e-
flahsch, n Tarnung f; v
tarnen
camp, kämp, adj fam
tuntenhaft; n Lager nt; v
zelten, campen
campaign, kämm-pehn, n
mil Feldzug m; fig
Kampagne f; v (in
election) den Wahlkampf
führen; – **(for/against)**,
sich einsetzen (für/gegen)
camper, kämm-per, n
(person) Camper m;
(vehicle) Wohnmobil nt
campsite, kämp-sseit, n
Campingplatz m
campus, kämm-pess, n
Campus m,
Universitätsgelände nt
can, känn, n Kanne f; (tin)
Dose f; v (preserve)
einmachen
can, känn, v (be able)
können; (be permitted)
können, dürfen
Canada, känn-e-de, n
Kanada nt
Canadian, ke-neh-di-en, adj
kanadisch; n Kanadier m
canal, ke-näll, n Kanal m
canary, ke-nähr-ri, n
Kanarienvogel m
cancel, känn-ss'l, v
(appointment) absagen;
(train) streichen; (ticket)
entwerten

cancellation, känn-sse-leh-
sch'n, n (of appointment)
Absage f; (of train)
Streichung f; (of ticket)
Entwertung f
cancer, känn-sser, n (med,
star sign) Krebs m
candid, känn-didd, adj
offen, ehrlich
candidate, känn-di-det, n
Kandidat m, Bewerber m
candle, känn-d'l, n Kerze f;
–stick, Kerzenhalter m
candour, känn-der, n
Offenheit f
candy, känn-di, n
Kandis(zucker) m;
(sweets) Bonbons pl; v
kandieren; **–floss,** n
Zuckerwatte f
cane, kehn, n Rohr nt;
(plant/walking stick)
Stock m; v prügeln
canine, keh-nein, adj
Hunde-; n (tooth)
Eckzahn m
canister, känn-iss-ter, n
Blechdose f
cannabis, kän-e-bis, n
Cannabis m
cannibal, kän-i-b'l, n
Kannibale m
cannon, känn-en, n
Kanone f
canny, känn-i, adj schlau
canoe, ke-nuh, n Kanu nt; v
Kanu fahren
can-opener, känn-oh-p'n-er,
n Dosenöffner m
canopy, känn-e-pi, n
Baldachin m

cantankerous, känn-täng-
ke-ress, adj zänkerisch
canteen, känn-tien, n
(restaurant) Kantine f;
(cutlery) Besteckkasten m
canter, känn-ter, n Kanter
m; v langsam galoppieren
canvas, känn-wess, n
Segeltuch nt; (painting)
Leinwand f; **under –**, im
Zelt
canvass, känn-wess, v comm
werben; (in election) um
Stimmen werben
canyon, kän-jen, n
Felsschlucht f
cap, käpp, n (hat) Mütze f;
(of bottle) Deckel m; (of
pen) Kappe f; (of
radiator/tank) Verschluß
m; v (close) verschließen;
(exceed) übertreffen;
(limit) einschränken
capable, keh-pe-b'l, adj
fähig; **– of,** imstande zu
capacity, ke-päss-i-ti, n
(size) Inhalt m; (ability)
Fähigkeit f; (position)
Eigenschaft f
cape, kehp, n geog Kap nt;
(cloak) Umhang m
caper, käh-per, n (pickle)
Kaper f; (prank)
Eskapade f
capital, käpp-i-t'l, n fin
Kapital nt; (city)
Hauptstadt f; (letter)
Großbuchstabe m; **–ism,**
Kapitalismus m; **–ist,** adj
kapitalistisch; n Kapitalist
m; **– punishment,**

Todesstrafe f

capitulate, ka-**pitt**-juh-leht, v kapitulieren

capricious, ke-**prisch**-ess, adj launisch, eigensinnig

capsize, käpp-**sseis**, v kentern

capsule, käpp-sjuhl, n Kapsel f

captain, käpp-tinn, n naut Kapitän m; mil Hauptmann m; v anführen; naut befehligen

captive, käpp-tiw, n Gefangene(r) m & f; adj gefangen

captivity, käpp-**tiw**-i-ti, n Gefangenschaft f

capture, käpp-tscher, n Eroberung f, Gefangennahme f; data –, Datenfassung f; v (person) gefangennehmen; (town) einnehmen; (interest) erregen

car, kahr, n Wagen m, Auto nt; rail Wagen m

carafe, ke-**räff,** n Karaffe f

caramel, kä-re-mel, n Karamel m; (toffee) Karamelle f

carat, kä-ret, n Karat nt

caravan, kä-re-wän, n Wohnwagen m; – site, n Campingplatz m für Wohnwagen

carbon, kahr-ben, n Kohlenstoff m; – copy, Durchschlag m; – paper, Kohlepapier nt

carburettor, kahr-be-**rett**-er, n Vergaser m

carcass, kahr-kess, n Kadaver m

card, kahrd, n Karte f; –board, Pappe f; –board box, Karton m

cardiac, kahr-di-ack, adj Herz-; – arrest, n Herzstillstand m

cardigan, kahr-di-gen, n Strickjacke f

cardinal, kahr-di-n'l, adj Haupt-; (number) Kardinal-; n Kardinal m

care, kehr, n (attention) Sorgfalt f; (caution) Vorsicht f; (anxiety) Sorge f; (tending) Pflege f; – (about), v sich kümmern (um); (like) mögen; **I don't –** das ist mir egal; **take –,** aufpassen; **take –!** Vorsicht!; **take – of,** sorgen für

career, ke-**rier,** n Karriere f, Laufbahn f

carefree, kehr-frie, adj sorglos

careful, kehr-full, adj vorsichtig, sorgfältig

careless, kehr-liss, adj nachlässig; **–ness,** n Nachlässigkeit f

caress, ke-ress, n Liebkosung f; v liebkosen

caretaker, kehr-teh-ker, n Hausmeister m

car ferry, kahr fe-ri, n Autofähre f

cargo, kahr-goh, n Ladung f

car hire, kahr heir, n Autovermietung f

Caribbean, kä-ri-**bie**-en, adj karibisch; n (Sea) Karibik f

caricature, kä-ri-ke-tjuhr, n Karikatur f

caring, kehr-ring, adj (person) warmherzig, liebevoll; (society) sozial

carnage, kahr-nidsch, n Blutbad nt

carnal, kahr-n'l, adj sinnlich, fleischlich

carnation, kar-**neh**-sch'n, n Nelke f

carnival, kahr-ni-w'l, n Karneval m, Fasching m

carnivorous, kar-**ni**-ve-ress, adj fleischfressend

carol, kä-rel, n (Weihnachts)lied nt

carp, kahrp, n (fish) Karpfen m; v nörgeln

car park, kahr pahrk, n Parkplatz m; (multi-storey) Parkhaus nt

carpenter, kahr-p'n-ter, n Zimmermann m

carpet, kahr-pitt, n Teppich m; (fitted) Teppichboden m; v (mit Teppichboden) auslegen

car phone, kahr fohn, n Autotelefon nt

carriage, kä-ridsch, n rail Wagen m; comm Beförderung(skosten) f(pl); (deportment) Haltung f

carrier, kä-ri-er, n comm

Spediteur m; (luggage rack) Gepäckhalter m; -- **bag,** Tragetasche f; -- **pigeon,** Brieftaube f

carrot, kä-ret, n Karotte f, Möhre f

carry, kä-ri, v tragen; **- on,** (continue) weitermachen; (fuss) Theater machen; (conduct) führen; **- out,** (order) ausführen; (plan) durchführen

cart, kahrt, n Wagen m; v schleppen

carton, kahr-ten, n Karton m; (of milk) Tüte f

cartoon, kahr-tuhn, n Karikatur f; (film) Zeichentrickfilm m; (strip) Comic m

cartridge, kahr-tridsch, n Patrone f

carve, kahrw, v (wood) schnitzen; (meat) tranchieren

carving, kahr-wing, n Schnitzerei f

car wash, kahr u'osch, n Autowäsche f

cascade, käss-kehd, n Wasserfall m, Kaskade f

case, kehss, n (matter) Fall m; (suitcase) Koffer m; (box) Kiste f; (spectacle etc.) Etui nt; **in any -,** auf jeden Fall; **in -,** im Falle, falls

cash, käsch, n Bargeld nt; v einlösen; **- book,** n Kassenbuch m; **- card,** n Geldautomatenkarte f; -

dispenser, n Geldautomat nt; **in -,** bar

cashier, käsch-ier, n Kassierer m

cashmere, käsch-mier, n Kaschmir m

casino, ke-**ssie-**noh, n Kasino nt

cask, kahsk, n Faß nt

casket, kahss-kitt, n Kästchen nt

casserole, käss-e-rohl, n Kasserolle f; (stew) Eintopf m

cassette, ke-**ssett,** n Kassette f; **- player,** n Kassettenspieler m; **- recorder,** n Kassettenrekorder m

cast, kahst, n (throw) Wurf m; *theatre* Besetzung f; (metal) Guß m; v (throw) werfen; (metal etc.) gießen; *theatre* besetzen

castanet, käss-te-nett, n Kastagnette f

caste, kahst, n Kaste f

cast iron, kahst **ei-**en, n Gußeisen nt

castle, kah-ss'l, n Schloß nt, Burg f; (chess) Turm m; v (chess) rochieren

castor, kahss-ter, n (wheel) Laufrolle

castor oil, kahss-ter eul, n Rizinusöl nt

casual, käsch-ju-el, adj (clothes) leger, Freizeit-; (attitude) ungezwungen; (meeting) zufällig; (work) Gelegenheits-

casualty, käsch-ju-el-ti, n Opfer nt; **- (department),** Unfallstation f

cat, kät, n Katze f; **tom-,** Kater m

catalogue, kätt-e-log, n Katalog m; v katalogisieren

catalytic converter, kätt-e-litt-ick ken-**wör-**ter, n Katalysator m

cataract, kätt-e-räkt, n (med) grauer Star; (rapids) Katarakt m

catarrh, ke-**tahr,** n Katarrh m

catastrophe, ke-**täss-**tre-fi, n Katastrophe f

catch, kätsch, n (of fish) Fang m; (snag) Haken m; (on door) Schnapper m; v fangen; (seize) fassen; (an illness) sich holen; **- fire,** Feuer fangen; **- up,** einholen

catching, kätt-sching, adj ansteckend

catch phrase, kätsch frehs, n Schlagwort nt

catchy, kätt-schi, adj eingängig

category, kätt-i-ge-ri, n Kategorie f, Klasse f

cater, keh-ter, v mit Speisen und Getränken versorgen; **- for,** (function) ausrichten; (needs) eingestellt sein auf; **-ing,** n Bewirtung f; (trade) Gastronomie f

caterer, keh-ter-er, n

Speiselieferant *m*

caterpillar, kätt-er-pill-er, *n* Raupe *f*

cathedral, ke-thie-drel, *n* Kathedrale *f*, Dom *m*

catholic, käth-*e*-lick, *adj* *relig* katholisch; (broad) vielseitig; *n* Katholik *m*

cattle, kätt-'l, *n* Vieh *nt*

cauliflower, koll-i-flau-er, *n* Blumenkohl *m*

cause, ko'as, *n* Grund *m*, Ursache *f*; (ideal) Sache *f*; *v* verursachen

causeway, ko'as-u'eh, *n* Damm *m*

caustic, ko'ass-tick, *adj* ätzend, kaustisch; *fig* bissig

caution, ko'a-sch'n, *n* (care) Vorsicht *f*; (warning) Verwarnung *f*; *v* verwarnen

cautious, ko'a-schess, *adj* vorsichtig

cavalier, käw-e-**lier,** *adj* unbekümmert; *n* Kavalier *m*

cavalry, käw-el-ri, *n* Kavallerie *f*

cave, kehw, *n* Höhle *f*; – **in,** *v* einstürzen; (give in) nachgeben

cavern, käw-ern, *n* Höhle *f*; –**ous,** *adj* (hollow) hohl; (gaping) gähnend

caviar(e), käw-i-**ahr,** *n* Kaviar *m*

cavity, käw-i-ti, *n* Höhlung *f*; (in tooth) Loch *nt*

CD, ssie-die (*abbr* compact disc), CD *f*; – **player,** *n*

CD-Spieler *m*; --**ROM,** *n* CD-ROM *f*

cease, ssiess, *v* aufhören; --**fire,** *n* Waffenruhe *f*; --**less,** *adj* unaufhörlich

cedar, ssie-der, *n* Zeder *f*

cede, ssied, *v* abtreten, überlassen

ceiling, ssie-ling, *n* Decke *f*; *fig* Höchstgrenze *f*

celebrate, ssell-i-breht, *v* feiern; –**d,** *adj* berühmt

celebration, ssell-i-**breh**-sch'n, *n* Feier *f*

celebrity, ssi-lebb-ri-ti, *n* (person) berühmte Persönlichkeit *f*; (fame) Berühmtheit *f*

celery, ssell-*e*-ri, *n* Sellerie *m & f*

celestial, ssi-less-ti-el, *adj* himmlisch

celibacy, ssell-i-be-ssi, *n* Zölibat *m/nt*

cell, ssell, *n* Zelle *f*

cellar, ssell-er, *n* Keller *m*

cello, tschell-oh, *n* (Violon)cello *nt*

cellphone, ssell-fohn, *n* Funktelefon *nt*

cellular, ssell-ju-ler, *adj* zellular, Zell-

celluloid, ssell-ju-leud, *n* Zelluloid *nt*

Celt, kelt/sselt, *n* Kelte *m*, Keltin *f*; –**ic,** *adj* keltisch

cement, ssi-ment, *n* Zement *m*; (glue) Klebstoff *m*; *v* zementieren; leimen; – **mixer,** *n* Betonmischmaschine *f*

cemetery, ssemm-i-tri, *n* Friedhof *m*

censor, ssenn-sser, *n* Zensor *m*; *v* zensieren; –**ship,** *n* Zensur *f*

census, ssenn-ssess, *n* Volkszählung *f*

centenary, ssenn-tie-ne-ri, *n* Jahrhundertfeier *f*

centigrade, ssenn-ti-grehd, *adj* Celsius-

centimetre, ssenn-ti-**mie**-ter, *n* Zentimeter *m*

central, ssenn-trel, *adj* zentral; (main) Haupt-; – **heating,** *n* Zentralheizung *f*

centralize, ssenn-tre-leis, *v* zentralisieren

centre, ssenn-ter, *n* Mittelpunkt *m*, Zentrum *nt*; *v* zentrieren

century, ssenn-tsche-ri, *n* Jahrhundert *nt*

ceramic, ssi-rämm-ick, *adj* keramisch; –**s,** *npl* Keramik *f*; Keramikwaren *pl*

cereal, ssier-ri-el, *n* (crop) Getreide *nt*; (food) Getreideflocken *pl*

ceremony, sse-ri-me-ni, *n* Zeremonie *f*; (formality) Förmlichkeit *f*

certain(ly), ssör-t'n(-li), *adj* *& adv* gewiß, sicher, bestimmt

certainty, ssör-t'n-ti, *n* Gewißheit *f*

certificate, sser-tidd-i-ket, *n* Bescheinigung *f*; (of

health, qualifications)
Zeugnis nt
certify, ssör-ti-fei, v
bescheinigen
cervical, ssör-wi-k'l, adj
Gebärmutterhals-
cervix, ssör-wicks, n
Gebärmutterhals m
cessation, sse-sseh-sch'n, n
Aufhören nt; (of
hostilities) Einstellung f
cf. (abbr = compare), vgl.
CFC ssie eff ssie (abbr
chlorofluorocarbon), n
FCKW
chafe, tschef, v (rub)
scheuern; (fret) aufgeregt
werden
chaffinch, tschäff-intsch, n
Buchfink m
chain, tschehn, n Kette f; –
up, v anketten
chair, tschehr, n Stuhl m;
(armchair) Sessel m; (of
committee) Vorsitz m; v
den Vorsitz führen
chairman, tschehr-men, n
Vorsitzende(r) m & f
chalet, schall-eh, n
Chalet nt
chalice, tschäll-iss, n
Kelch m
chalk, tscho'ak, n Kreide f
challenge, tschäll-indsch, n
Herausforderung f; (to
authority) Infragestellung
f; v herausfordern;
(authority) in Frage
stellen; fig fordern;
challenging, adj
(provocative)

herausfordernd;
(demanding)
anspruchsvoll
chamber, tschehm-ber, n
Kammer f; –maid, n
Zimmermädchen nt; –
music, n Kammermusik f;
–s, npl (of barrister)
Kanzlei f
chamois, schämm-u'a, adj, n
Gemse f, Waschleder nt
champagne, schämm-pehn,
n Champagner m;
(sparkling wine) Sekt m
champion, tschämm-pi-en,
n sport Meister m; (of
cause) Verfechter m;
–ship, n Meisterschaft f
chance, tschahnss, n (luck)
Zufall m; (opportunity)
Gelegenheit f;
(possibility) Möglichkeit
f; adj zufällig; v riskieren;
by –, adv zufällig
chancel, tschahn-ss'l, n
Chor m
chancellor, tschahn-ss'l-er,
n Kanzler m; – of the
Exchequer, n
Finanzminister m
chandelier, schänn-di-lier,
n Kronleuchter m
change, tschehndsch, n
(alteration) Veränderung
f; (small money)
Kleingeld nt; (money
returned) Wechselgeld nt;
v (alter) ändern;
(transform) verwandeln;
(money, gear, etc.)
wechseln; (swap)

tauschen; (trains etc.)
umsteigen; (clothes) sich
umziehen; – one's mind,
es sich anders überlegen;
–able, adj wechselhaft
changing room, tschehn-
dsching ruhm, n
Umkleideraum m
channel, tschänn-'l, n Kanal
m; v (water) leiten; fig
lenken; (English)
Channel, n Ärmelkanal,
m; Channel Islands, npl
Kanalinseln pl; Channel
Tunnel, n Kanaltunnel m
chant, tschahnt, n Gesang
m; v singen
chaos, keh-oss, n Chaos nt
chaotic, keh-ott-ick, adj
chaotisch
chap, tschäpp, n Kerl m
chapel, tschäpp-'l, n Kapelle
f
chaperon(e), schäpp-e-
rohn, n Anstandsdame f; v
begleiten
chaplain, tschäpp-linn, n
Kaplan m
chapped, tschäpt, adj
aufgesprungen, rauh
chapter, tschäpp-ter, n
Kapitel nt
char, tschar, n (charlady)
Putzfrau f; v (scorch)
verkohlen; (clean) putzen
character, kä-rick-ter, n
(nature) Charakter m;
(figure) Gestalt f; (letter)
Buchstabe m; –istic, adj
charakteristisch, typisch;
n Merkmal nt

charade, sche-**rahd,** n
Scharade f

charcoal, tschar-**kohl,** n
Holzkohle f

charge, tschardsch, n (price)
Preis m; (fee) Gebühr f;
(explosive) Ladung f; law
Anklage f; (bill)
berechnen; law anklagen;
mil angreifen; – **card,** n
Kundenkarte f; **free of –,**
kostenlos; **in – (of),**
verantwortlich (für)

charitable, tschä-ri-te-b'l,
adj wohltätig

charity, tschä-ri-ti, n (good
causes) Wohlfahrt f;
(organization)
Wohltätigkeitsverein nt;
(virtue) Nächstenliebe f

charlady, tschar-**leh-di,** n
Putzfrau f

charm, tscharm, n Charme
m, Reiz m; (spell) Bann m;
(amulet) Talisman m; v
bezaubern; **–ing,** adj
reizend, bezaubernd

chart, tschart, n (naut,
weather) Karte f;
(diagram) Schaubild nt; v
erfassen

charter, tschar-ter, n
Freibrief m; v chartern;
–ed accountant, n
Wirtschaftsprüfer m

charwoman, tschar-u'umm-
en, n Putzfrau f

chase, tschehss, n Jagd f; v
jagen; (pursue) verfolgen

chasm, käs-'m, n Abgrund m

chassis, schä-ssi, n

Fahrgestell nt

chaste, tschehst, adj keusch

chastity, tschäss-ti-ti, n
Keuschheit f

chat, tschätt, n Plauderei f; v
plaudern; **– show,** n
Talkshow f; **–ter,** n
Geschwätz nt; v
schwatzen; (of teeth)
klappern; **–terbox,** n
Quasselstrippe f; **–ty,** adj
geschwätzig

chauffeur, schoh-fer, n
Chauffeur m

chauvinist, schoh-wi-nist,
n Chauvinist m; fam
Chauvi m

cheap(ly), tschiep(-li), adj
& adv billig

cheat, tschiht, n Betrüger m;
v betrügen; **–ing,**
n Betrügen nt;
Falschspielen nt

check, tscheck, n (restraint)
Hemmung f; (chess)
Schach nt; (verification)
Kontrolle f; (pattern)
Karo nt; v hemmen; (stop)
einhalten; (verify)
kontrollieren; (examine)
prüfen; **– in,** v
einchecken, sich
anmelden; (luggage)
abfertigen lassen; **––in,** n
Abfertigung f; **–mate,** n
Schachmatt nt; v matt
setzen; **– out,** v sich
abmelden, abreisen; **––
out,** n Kasse f; **– up,** v
überprüfen; **–up,** n (med)
Untersuchung f

cheek, tschiek, n Backe f;
(impudence)
Unverschämtheit f; **–y,**
adj frech

cheer, tschier, n
Fröhlichkeit f; (applause)
Beifallsruf m; v (applaud)
zujubeln; (comfort)
aufmuntern; **–ful,** adj
fröhlich; **–less,** freudlos,
traurig; **–s!,** Prost!; **– up!**
Kopf hoch!

cheerio, tschier-i-**oh,** interj
tschüs

cheese, tschies, n Käse m;
–board, n Käseplatte f

chef, scheff, n
Küchenchef m

chemical, kemm-i-k'l, adj
chemisch; n Chemikalie f

chemist, kemm-ist, n
(expert) Chemiker m; (in
shop) Apotheker m,
Drogist m; **–ry,** n Chemie
f; **–'s,** n Apotheke f,
Drogerie f

cheque, tscheck, n Scheck
m; **–book,** n Scheckbuch nt;
– card, n Scheckkarte f

chequered, tscheck-erd, adj
(pattern) kariert; (career,
history) bewegt

cherish, tsche-risch, v
(person) lieben; (illusion)
sich hingeben

cherry, tsche-ri, n Kirsche f

chess, tschess, n
Schach(spiel) nt

chest, tschest, n Brust f;
(trunk) Truhe f; (box)
Kiste f; **– of drawers,**

Kommode f

chestnut, tschess-natt, n Kastanie f

chew, tschuh, v kauen; **–ing gum,** n Kaugummi m

chic, schiek, adj schick, elegant

chick, tschick, n Küken nt

chicken, tschick-inn, n (bird) Huhn nt; (food) Hähnchen nt; **– out,** v fam kneifen; **–pox,** n Windpocken pl

chief, tschief, n adj Haupt-; (boss) Chef m; (of tribe) Häuptling m; **– executive,** n Geschäftsführer m; **–ly,** adv hauptsächlich

chilblain, tschill-blehn, n Frostbeule f

child, tscheild, n (pl **children**) Kind nt; **–birth,** n Geburt f; **–ish,** adj kindisch; **–like,** adj kindlich; **–minder,** n Tagesmutter f

Chile, tschill-i, n Chile nt; **–an,** adj chilenisch; n Chilene m, Chilenin f

chill, tschill, n Frische f; (med) Erkältung f; fig Abkühlung f; v kühlen

chilli, tschill-i, adj Chili m

chilly, tschill-i, adj kühl; fig frostig

chime, tscheim, n Glockenspiel nt; v läuten; **– in,** sich einmischen

chimney, tschimm-ni, n Schornstein m; **– sweep,** Schornsteinfeger m

chimpanzee, tschimm-pänn-sie, n Schimpanse m

chin, tschinn, n Kinn nt

china, tschei-ne, n Porzellan nt

China, tschei-ne, n China nt

Chinese, tschei-**nies,** adj chinesisch; n Chinese m, Chinesin f; (language) Chinesisch nt

chink, tschink, n (gap) Spalt m, Ritze f; (clink) Klimpern nt; v klimpern

chip, tschipp, n (of wood etc.) Splitter m; v (cup etc.) anschlagen; (wood etc.) abstoßen; **– in,** v sich einmischen; **–s,** npl Pommes frites pl

chiropodist, ki-**ropp-**e-dist, n Fußpfleger m

chirp, tschörp, n Zwitschern nt; v zwitschern

chisel, tschis-'l, n Meißel m; v meißeln

chit, tschitt, n Zettel m

chitchat, tschitt-tschätt, n Geschwätz nt

chivalrous, schi-wel-ress, adj ritterlich

chives, tscheiws, npl Schnittlauch m

chlorine, klor-rien, n Chlor nt

chock, tschock, n Bremsklotz m; **– full,** adj knüppelvoll

chocolate, tschock-e-let, n Schokolade f

choice, tscheuss, n

(decision) Wahl f; (variety) Auswahl f; adj Qualitäts-, auserlesen

choir, ku'eir, n Chor m

choke, tschohk, v (suffocate) ersticken; (strangle) erwürgen

cholera, koll-e-re, n Cholera f

cholesterol, ko-**less-**te-rel, n Cholesterin f

choose, tschuhs, v wählen, auswählen

chop, tschopp, n Kotelett nt; v (wood) spalten; (food) (zer)hacken; **get the –,** fam rausgeschmissen werden

chopper, tschopp-er, n (axe) Hackbeil nt; (fam helicopter) Hubschrauber m

choppy, tschopp-i, adj bewegt

chopstick, tschopp-stick, n Stäbchen nt

choral, kor-rel, adj Chor-

chord, kord, n (string) Saite f; mus Akkord m

chore, tschor, n Pflicht f; **(domestic) –s,** npl Hausarbeit f

chorister, ko-**riss-**ter, n Chorsänger m

chorus, kor-ress, n (singers) Chor m; (in song) Refrain m

Christ, kreist, n Christus m

christen, kriss-'n, v taufen; **–ing,** n Taufe f

Christian, kriss-ti-en, adj

christlich; n Christ m; –
name, n Vorname m
Christianity, kriss-ti-**änn**-i-
ti, n Christentum nt
Christmas, kriss-mess, n
Weihnachten pl; – **card,** n
Weihnachtskarte f; – **Day,**
n erster Weihnachtstag m;
– **Eve,** n Heiligabend m;
Merry –! Frohe
Weihnachten!
chrome, krohm, n Chrom nt
chronic, kronn-ick, adj
chronisch
chronicle, kronn-i-k'l, n
Chronik f
chronological, kronn-e-
lodsch-ick-'l, adj
chronologisch
chubby, tschabb-i, adj
rundlich; (cheeks)
pausbäckig
chuck, tschakk, v fam
schmeißen; – **out,**
(person) rausschmeißen;
(object) wegschmeißen
chuckle, tschakk-'l, n
Kichern nt; v vor sich hin
lachen
chug, tschagg, v tuckern
chum, tschamm, n fam
Kumpel m
chunk, tschank, n (großes)
Stück nt
church, tschörtsch, n Kirche
f; –**yard,** Kirchhof m
churlish, tschör-lisch, adj
mürrisch, grob
churn, tschörn, n (butter)
Butterfaß nt; (milk)
Milchkanne f; v buttern; –

out, v massenweise
produzieren
chute, schuht, n Rutsche
f; (rubbish)
Müllschlucker m
cider, ssei-der, n
Apfelwein m
cigar, ssi-**gahr,** n Zigarre f
cigarette, ssi-ge-**rett,** n
Zigarette f
cinders, ssinn-ders, npl
Asche f
cine-camera, ssinn-i-kämm-
e-re, n (Schmal)
filmkamera f
cine-film, ssinn-i-film, n
Schmalfilm m
cinema, ssinn-i-me, n
Kino nt
cinnamon, ssinn-e-men, n
Zimt m
cipher, ssei-fer, n Chiffre f,
Code m
circle, ssör-k'l, n Kreis m;
theatre Rang m; v kreisen
(um); (surround)
umgeben
circuit, ssör-kitt, n (course)
Rennbahn f; (lap) Runde
f; elec Stromkreis m
circuitous, ssör-kjuh-itt-ess,
adj umständlich
circular, ssör-kju-ler, n
(letter) Rundschreiben nt;
(leaflet) Wurfsendung f;
adj kreisförmig; rund
circulate, ssör-kju-leht, v
(of blood, traffic) fließen;
(of news, rumour) sich
verbreiten; (memo)
zirkulieren lassen;

(rumour) in Umlauf
bringen
circulation, ssör-kju-leh-
sch'n, n Umlauf m; (of
blood) Kreislauf m; (of
newspaper) Auflage f
circumcise, ssör-kem-sseis,
v beschneiden
circumference, sser-kamm-
fe-renss, n Umfang m
circumspect, ssör-kem-
speckt, adj umsichtig
circumstances, ssör-kem-
sten-ssis, npl Umstände pl
Verhältnisse pl
circumstantial, ssör-kem-
stänn-sch'l, adj
umständlich; – **evidence,**
n Indizienbeweis m
circumvent, ssör-kem-went,
v umgehen
circus, ssör-kess, n Zirkus m
cistern, ssiss-tern, n (tank)
Zisterne f; (of WC)
Spülkasten m
cite, sseit, v zitieren
citizen, ssitt-i-s'n, n Bürger
m; –**ship,** n
Staatsbürgerschaft f
citrus, ssitt-ress, adj Zitrus-
city, ssitt-i, n Stadt f,
Großstadt f; – **centre,** n
Stadtmitte f; **City (of
London),** n das Londoner
Bankenviertel nt
civic, ssiw-ick, adj Stadt-,
Bürger-
civil, ssiw-il, adj (of society)
bürgerlich; (polite)
höflich; – **servant,** n
Staatsbeamte(r) m & f; –

war, n Bürgerkrieg m

civilian, ssi-**will**-jen, adj zivil; n Zivilist m

civilization, ssi-wi-lei-**seh**-sch'n, n Kultur f, Zivilisation f

civilized, ssiw-i-leisd, adj zivilisiert, zivil

claim, klehm, n (demand) Anspruch m; comm Forderung f; (assertion) Behauptung f; v (apply for) beantragen; (assert) behaupten; **–ant,** n Antragsteller m

clairvoyant, klähr-**weu**-ent, n adj hellseherisch; n Hellseher m

clamber, klämm-ber, v klettern

clammy, klämm-i, adj klamm, feucht

clamour, klämm-er, n Geschrei nt, Lärm m; **– for,** v schreien nach, fordern

clamp, klämp, n Schraubzwinge f; v einspannen; **– down (on),** v durchgreifen (gegen)

clan, klänn, n Clan m

clandestine, klänn-**dess**-tinn, adj geheim

clang, kläng, n Klappern nt; v klappern

clank, klänk, n Klirren nt; v klirren

clap, kläpp, n (of hands) Klatschen nt; (of thunder) Schlag m; v (Beifall) klatschen; **–ping,**

(Beifall)klatschen nt; **–– trap,** n Blödsinn m

claret, klä-ritt, n Bordeauxwein m

clarify, klä-ri-fei, v klären

clarinet, klä-ri-nett, n Klarinette f

clash, kläsch, n Zusammenstoß m; fig Konflikt m; v zusammenstoßen; (of colours) sich beißen; fig in Konflikt kommen

clasp, klahsp, n (catch) Spange f; (grasp) Griff m; v (grasp) ergreifen; (embrace) umarmen

class, klahss, n Klasse f; v klassifizieren

classic, kläss-ick, adj klassisch; n Klassiker m; **–al,** adj klassisch; (ancient) antik

classified, kläss-i-feid, adj klassifiziert; (secret) Geheim-; **ad(vertisement),** n Kleinanzeige f

classify, kläss-i-fei, v klassifizieren

classroom, klahss-ruhm, n Klassenzimmer nt

clatter, klätt-er, n Geklapper nt; v klappern

clause, klo'as, n law Klausel f; gram Satz m

claustrophobia, kloss-tre-**foh**-bi-e, n Klaustrophobie f

claw, klo'a, n Klaue f; (sharp) Kralle f; (of crab

etc.) Schere f; v kratzen; **– at,** sich krallen an

clay, kleh, n Lehm m; (potter's) Ton m; **–ey,** adj lehmig

clean, klien, adj sauber; v putzen; (clothes etc.) reinigen; **–er,** n (domestic) Putzfrau f; (office) Reiniger m; **–ing,** n Putzen nt; (clothes etc.) Reinigung f; **– out,** v (gründlich) saubermachen; **– up,** v saubermachen; (tidy) aufräumen

cleanliness, klenn-li-niss, n Reinlichkeit f

cleanse, klenns, v reinigen

clean-shaven, klien-**scheh**-wen, adj glattrasiert

clear, klier, adj klar; (unobstructed) frei; v (of weather) aufklaren; (of fog etc.) sich auflösen; (remove) beseitigen; (jump over) überspringen; (approve) abfertigen; (road) freimachen; (table) abräumen; (suspect) freisprechen; **–ance,** n Beseitigung f; (space) Spielraum m; (customs) Abfertigung f; (sale) Räumungsverkauf m; **–cut,** adj eindeutig; **–ing,** n Lichtung f; **–ly,** adv klar; fig selbstverständlich; **– off,** v fam abhauen; **– out,** v ausräumen; **– up,** v (tidy) aufräumen;

(mystery) aufklären
cleaver, klie-wer, n
Hackbeil nt
clef, kleff, n mus
(Noten)schlüssel m
cleft, kleft, n Spalte f
clematis, klemm-e-tiss, n
Klematis f
clemency, klemm-en-ssi, n
Milde f
clench, klentsch, v (teeth)
zusammenbeißen; (fist)
ballen
clergy, klör-dschi, n die
Geistlichen pl; **-man,** n
Geistlicher m
clerical, kle-ri-k'l, adj
(office) Schreib-, Büro-;
relig geistlich; **- error,** n
Schreibfehler m
clerk, klark, n
(Büro)angestellte(r) m & f
clever, klew-er, adj klug,
schlau; (dextrous)
geschickt; **-ness,** n
Klugheit f, Geschicktheit f
cliché, klie-scheh, n
Klischee nt
click, klick, n (of switch,
fingers) Knipsen nt; (of
joint) Knacken nt; v
knipsen; knacken; (of
heels) klappern; (fam
become clear) funken
client, klei-ent, n Kunde m,
Kundin f; Klient m; **-ele,**
n Kundschaft f
cliff, kliff, n Klippe f,
Felsen m
climate, klei-mitt, n
Klima nt

climax, klei-mäcks, n
Höhepunkt m
climb, kleim, n Aufstieg m;
v klettern; (mountain)
besteigen; **- down,** v
absteigen; (give in)
nachgeben; **-er,** n (rock)
Kletterer m; (mountain)
Bergsteiger m
clinch, klintsch, n Clinch
m; v (settle) abmachen
cling (to), kling (tu), v sich
festklammern (an); fig
sich festhalten (an)
clinic, klinn-ick, n Klinik f
clink, klink, n Klirren nt; v
klirren
clip, klipp, n Klammer f;
(clasp) Spange f; v
scheren; **-ping,** n (article)
Ausschnitt m
cloak, klohk, n Umhang m;
v bedecken, hüllen;
-room, n Garderobe f;
(WC) Toilette f
clock, klock, n Uhr f; **alarm
-,** Wecker m; **- in/on,** v
(den Arbeitsbeginn)
stempeln; **- off/out,** v (das
Arbeitsende) stempeln
clockwise, klock-u'eis, adv
im Uhrzeigersinn
clockwork, klock-u'örk, adj
(toy) zum Aufziehen; n
Uhrwerk m;
Aufziehmechanismus m;
like -, adv wie am
Schnürchen
clog, klogg, n Holzschuh m;
v - (up), verstopfen
cloister, kleuss-ter, n

Kreuzgang m
clone, klohn, n Klon m; v
klonen
close, klohss, adj nahe, in
der Nähe; (relative) nahe;
(friend, connection) eng;
(weather) schwül; (result)
knapp; (study) genau; adv
nahe; **- behind,** prep dicht
hinter; **- by,** adv in der
Nähe; **- to,** prep nahe bei,
dicht an, in der Nähe von
close, klohs, n Schluß m; v
schließen; **-d,** adj
geschlossen, zu; **- down,** v
schließen, stillegen
closet, klos-itt, n (cupboard)
Wandschrank m; (room)
Kabinett nt
closure, kloh-scher, n
Schließung f; (of road)
Sperrung f
clot, klott, n Klumpen nt;
(of blood) Blutgerinnsel
nt; (fool) Trottel m; v (of
blood) gerinnen
cloth, kloth, n Tuch nt, Stoff
m; (cleaning) Lappen m;
(table) Tischdecke f
clothe, klohdh, v kleiden
clothes, klohdhs, npl Kleider
pl; **bed-,** n Bettwäsche f;
-brush, n Kleiderbürste f;
-line, n Wäscheleine f
clothing, kloh-dhing, n
Kleidung f
cloud, klaud, n Wolke f; v fig
trüben; **-burst,** n
Wolkenbruch m; **-less,** adj
wolkenlos; **-y,** adj (sky)
bewölkt; (liquid) trüb

clout, klaut, n (*fam* blow) Schlag m; (strength) Schlagkraft f; v schlagen; *fam* hauen

clove, klohw, n Gewürznelke f; (of garlic) (Knoblauch)zehe f

clover, **kloh**-wer, n Klee m; v **to be in –**, üppig leben

clown, klaun, n Clown m; (fool) Hanswurst m; v – **(about/around)**, herumkaspern

club, klabb, n Klub m, Club m; (weapon) Keule f; (golf) Schläger m; **–house**, n Klubhaus nt; **–s**, npl (cards) Kreuz nt

cluck, klack, n Glucken nt; v glucken

clue, kluh, n Anhaltspunkt m; (crossword) Frage f; **I haven't (got) a –**, ich habe keine Ahnung

clump, klamp, n (of trees etc.) Gruppe f

clumsy, **klamm**-si, adj (person) ungeschickt; (unwieldy) plump

cluster, **klass**-ter, n (of trees, islands) Gruppe f; (of fruit) Büschel nt; v – **(round)**, sich drängen (um)

clutch, klatsch, n Griff m; (motor) Kupplung f; v (grasp) umklammern; (grab) packen

clutter, **klatt**-er, n Durcheinander nt; v (mind, room) vollstopfen;

(desk) übersäen

c/o (*abbr* care of), c/o, z. Hd.

coach, kohtsch, n (bus) (Reise)bus m; (horse-drawn) Kutsche f; sport Trainer m; (school) Nachhilfelehrer m; v sport trainieren; (school) Nachhilfeunterricht geben

coagulate, koh-**ägg**-ju-leht, v gerinnen

coal, kohl, n Kohle f; **– cellar**, n Kohlenkeller m

coalition, koh-e-**lisch**-'n, n Koalition f

coalmine, **kohl**-mein, n Kohlenbergwerk nt

coarse, korss, a, grob; (joke, laugh) derb

coast, kohst, n Küste f; v im Leerlauf fahren; **–guard**, n Küstenwache f; **–line**, n Küste(nlinie) f

coat, koht, n Mantel m; (of animal) Fell nt; (of paint) Schicht f; v (paint) überstreichen; **– hanger**, n Kleiderbügel m; **–ing**, n Überzug m; (of paint) Schicht f; **– of arms**, n Wappen nt

coax, kohkss, v überreden

cob, kobb, n (horse) kleines Pferd nt; (corn) (Mais)kolben m

cobble, **kobb**-'l, n Kopfstein m; **–s**, npl Kopfsteinpflaster nt

cobbler, **kobb**-ler, n (Flick)schuster m

cobblestone, **kobb**-'l-stohn, n Kopfstein m

cobweb, **kobb**-u'ebb, n (threads) Spinnenweben pl; (net) Spinnennetz nt

cocaine, koh-**kehn**, n Kokain nt

cock, kock, n (bird, tap, valve) Hahn m; (*vulg* penis) Schwanz m; v (gun) spannen; (ears) spitzen; **–erel**, junger Hahn m; **–eyed**, adj (crooked) schief; (absurd) widersinnig

cockle, **kock**-'l, n Herzmuschel f

Cockney, **kock**-ni, n eingeborener Londoner m

cockpit, **kock**-pitt, n Cockpit nt

cockroach, **kock**-rohtsch, n Küchenschabe f

cocktail, **kock**-tehl, n Cocktail m

cocoa, koh-koh, n Kakao m

coconut, koh-**ke**-natt, n Kokosnuß f

cocoon, ke-**kuhn**, n Kokon m; v einhüllen

cod, kodd, n Kabeljau m

coddle, kodd-'l, v verhätscheln

code, kohd, n law Gesetzbuch nt; (cipher) Kode m; comp Code m; v verschlüsseln; comp kodieren

cod-liver oil, kodd-li-wer eul, n Lebertran m

coerce, koh-**örss**, v zwingen

coffee, **koff**-i, n Kaffee m; **–**

pot, n Kaffeekanne f; – **table,** n Couchtisch m

coffin, koff-in, n Sarg m

cog, kogg, n Zahn m; – **wheel,** Zahnrad nt

cogent, koh-dschent, adj zwingend

cogitate, kodsch-i-teht, v nachdenken

cognac, konn-jäk, n Kognak m

coherent, koh-hier-rent, adj zusammenhängend

cohesion, koh-hie-sch'n, n Kohäsion f

coil, keul, n Rolle f; (contraceptive) Spirale f; elec Spule f; v aufrollen

coin, keun, n Münze f; v prägen; **–box,** n (phone) Münzfernsprecher m; **– operated,** adj Münz-

coincide, koh-inn-sseid, v zusammenfallen, übereinstimmen

coke, kohk, n Koks m; (carbonated drink) Cola f; (drug) Kokain nt; **– (up),** v verkoken

colander, koll-en-der, n Sieb nt

cold, kohld, n Kälte f; (med) Erkältung f; adj kalt; **catch –,** v sich erkälten; **I'm –,** mir ist kalt

coleslaw, kohl-slo'a, n Krautsalat m

collaborate, ke-**läbb**-e-reht, v zusammenarbeiten

collaboration, ke-läbb-e-**reh-sch'n,** n

Zusammenarbeit f; (with enemy) Kollaboration f

collapse, ke-**läps,** n (of person) Zusammenbruch m; (of building) Einsturz m; v (of person) zusammenbrechen; (of building) einstürzen

collar, koll-er, n Kragen m; (for dog) Halsband nt; **–bone,** n Schlüsselbein nt

collate, ke-**leht,** v kollationieren

collateral, ke-**lätt-**e-rel, adj nebensächlich; fin zusätzlich; n fin (zusätzliche) Sicherheit f

colleague, koll-ieg, n Kollege m

collect, ke-**lekt,** v sammeln; (fetch) abholen;**–ion,** n Sammlung f; (money) Kollekte f; (post) Leerung f; **–ive,** adj gemeinsam; **–or,** n Sammler m; (tax) (Steuer)einnehmer m

college, koll-idsch, n Hochschule f, Berufsschule f; (university) College nt

collide, ke-**leid,** v zusammenstoßen

colliery, kol-je-ri, n Zeche f

collision, ke-**lisch-'n,** n Zusammenstoß m

colloquial, ke-**loh-**ku'i-el, adj umgangssprachlich

collusion, ke-**luh-**sch'n, n (geheime) Absprache f

colon, koh-lonn, n (writing) Doppelpunkt m; (med)

Dickdarm m

colonel, köh-n'l, n Oberst m

colonial, ke-**loh**-ni-el, adj Kolonial-; n Bewohner m der Kolonien

colonnade, koll-e-nehd, n Säulengang m

colonize, koll-e-neis, v kolonisieren

colony, koll-e-ni, n Kolonie f

colossal, ke-**loss-**'l, adj kolossal, riesig

colour, kull-er, n Farbe f; v färben; **– bar,** n Rassenschranke f; **–-blind,** adj farbenblind; **–fast,** adj farbecht; **–ful,** adj bunt; **–ing,** n (complexion) Gesichtsfarbe f

colt, kohlt, n Fohlen nt

column, koll-em, n Säule f; (print) Spalte f; mil Kolonne f

coma, koh-me, n (med) Koma nt

comb, kohm, n Kamm m; (honey) (Honig)wabe f; v kämmen; fig durchkämmen

combat, komm-bätt, n Kampf m; v bekämpfen

combination, komm-bi-**neh-**sch'n, n Kombination f; **in –,** adv gemeinsam

combine, komm-bein, v comm Konzern m; **– (harvester),** n Mähdrescher m

combine, kem-**bein,** v verbinden

combustion, kem-**bass**-tsch'n, n Verbrennung f

come, kamm, v kommen; – **across,** (find) stoßen auf; – **down,** (of price) fallen; – **from,** herkommen, kommen aus; – **in,** hereinkommen; – **off,** (detach) abgehen; (succeed) gelingen; – **out,** herauskommen; – **round/to,** (med) wieder zu sich kommen; – **to,** (sum) sich belaufen auf; – **up,** hochkommen; (of sun) aufgehen; (of problem) auftauchen; – **up against,** stoßen auf

comedian, ke-**mie**-di-en, n Komiker m

comedy, komm-e-di, n Komödie f

comet, komm-itt, n Komet m

comfort, kamm-fet, n Komfort m; (consolation) Trost m; v trösten; **–able,** adj bequem; (income) ausreichend; (life) angenehm

comic, komm-ick, adj komisch; n (book) Comic m, Comic-Heft nt; (comedian) Komiker m

coming, kamm-ing, adj künftig; n Kommen nt

comma, komm-e, n Komma nt

command, ke-**mahnd,** n Befehl m; mil Kommando nt; (mastery)

Beherrschung f; v befehlen; beherrschen; mil kommandieren

commandeer, kamm-en-**dier,** v requirieren

commander, ke-**mahn**-der, n Kommandant m

commanding, ke-**mahn**-ding, adj mil befehlshabend; (tone) gebieterisch; (location) beherrschend

commandment(s), ke-**mahnd**-ment(s), n(pl) Gebot(e) nt(pl)

commemorate, ke-**memm**-e-reht, v gedenken

commence, ke-**menss,** v beginnen

commencement, ke-**menss**-ment, n Anfang m

commend, ke-**mend,** v (recommend) empfehlen; (praise) loben

commensurate (with), ke-**menn**-sju-ret (u'idh), adj entsprechend

comment, komm-ent, n Bemerkung f; v bemerken; **–ary,** n Kommentar m; **–ator,** n Kommentator m; (sports etc.) Reporter m; – **on,** v sich äußern über/zu

commerce, komm-örss, n Handel m

commercial, ke-**mör**-sch'l, adj kommerziell, Geschäfts-, Handels-; n (TV) Werbespot m; – **break,** (TV) Werbung f

commiserate (with), ke-mis-e-reht u'idh, v mitfühlen (mit)

commission, ke-**misch**-'n, n (fee) Provision f; (order) Auftrag m; mil Patent nt; (committee) Kommission f; v (person) beauftragen; (work) in Auftrag geben; (officer) ernennen; **–aire,** Portier m

commit, ke-**mitt,** v (resources) einsetzen; (crime) begehen; (to prison etc.) einweisen; **–ment,** n Verpflichtung f; – **oneself (to),** v sich festlegen (auf), sich verpflichten (zu)

committee, ke-**mitt**-i, n Ausschuß m

commodity, ke-**modd**-i-ti, n Ware f

common, komm-en, adj (usual; vulgar) gewöhnlich; (universal) allgemein; (communal) gemeinsam; n (public ground) Gemeindeland nt; **–er,** Bürgerliche(r) m & f; **–place,** adj alltäglich; – **room,** n Aufenthaltsraum m; **Commons,** npl parl Unterhaus nt; – **sense,** n gesunder Menschenverstand m; **Commonwealth,** n Commonwealth nt

commotion, ke-**moh**-sch'n, n Aufsehen nt

commune, komm-juhn, n Kommune f

communicate, ke-**mjuh**-ni-keht, v in Verbindung stehen; (be understood) sich verständigen; (news) mitteilen

communication, ke-mjuh-ni-**keh**-sch'n, n (act) Kommunikation f; (message) Mitteilung f

Communion, ke-**mjuh**-ni-en, n relig Abendmahl nt

communism, **komm**-ju-nism, n Kommunismus m

communist, **komm**-mju-nist, adj kommunistisch; n Kommunist m

community, ke-**mjuh**-ni-ti, n (group) Gemeinde f; (ideal) Gemeinschaft f; – **centre,** n Gemeindezentrum nt

commute, ke-**mjuht,** v * pendeln; –**r,** n Pendler m

compact, kem-**päckt,** adj kompakt; (soil) fest; – **disc,** n Compact Disc f, CD f

compact, **komm**-päckt, n (agreement) Vereinbarung f; (for powder) Puderdose f

companion, kem-**pänn**-jen, n Begleiter m; (spouse) Gefährte m; –**ship,** Gesellschaft f

company, **kamm**-pe-ni, n (people) Gesellschaft f; (firm) Firma f, Gesellschaft f, Unternehmen nt; mil Kompanie f; **keep sb –,** v jdm Gesellschaft leisten

comparative, kem-**pä**-re-tiw, adj relativ; n gram Komparativ m; –**ly,** adv verhältnismäßig

compare, kem-**pähr,** v vergleichen

comparison, kem-**pä**-ri-ss'n, n Vergleich m; **in – (with),** im Vergleich (zu)

compartment, kem-**pahrt**-ment, n rail Abteil nt; (in fridge etc.) Fach nt

compass, **kamm**-pess, n (magnetic) Kompaß m; (range) Umkreis m; (a pair of) –**es,** npl Zirkel m

compassion, kem-**päsch**-'n, n Mitleid nt; –**ate,** adj mitfühlend

compatible, kem-**pätt**-i-b'l, adj passend, entsprechend; comp kompatibel

compel, kem-**pell,** v zwingen

compensate, **komm**-pen-sseht, v entschädigen; – **for,** ausgleichen

compensation, komm-penn-**sseh**-sch'n, n Entschädigung f

compete, kem-**piet,** v (take part) teilnehmen; (vie) konkurrieren; – **for,** kämpfen um

competent, **komm**-pi-tent, adj fähig, kompetent

competition, komm-pe-**tisch**-'n, n (comm etc.) Konkurrenz f; sport Wettbewerb m

competitive, kem-**pett**-i-tiw, adj Konkurrenz-; (price

etc.) konkurrenzfähig

competitor, kem-**pett**-i-ter, n (participant) Teilnehmer m; comm Konkurrent m

compile, kem-**peil,** v zusammenstellen; (publication) verfassen

complacent, kem-**pleh**-ss'nt, adj selbstgefällig

complain, kem-**plehn,** v sich beklagen, sich beschweren

complaint, kem-**plehnt,** n Klage f; (formal) Beschwerde f; (med) Krankheit f

complement, **komm**-pli-ment, n Ergänzung f; v ergänzen

complete, kem-**pliet,** adj ganz, vollständig; (finished) fertig; v vervollständigen; (finish) abschließen; –**ly,** adv ganz

completion, kem-**plie**-sch'n, n Beendigung f; Abschluß m

complex, **komm**-plecks, adj verwickelt, kompliziert; n Komplex m

complexion, kem-**pleck**-sch'n, n Gesichtsfarbe f; fig **put a new – on,** v in einem neuen Licht erscheinen lassen

compliance, kem-**plei**-enss, n Einwilligung f; (with rules) Einhalten nt; – **with,** gemäß

complicate, **komm**-pli-keht, v komplizieren

compliment, **komm**-pli-

ment, *n* Kompliment *nt*;
–s, *npl* Grüße *pl*; –s slip, *n*
Empfehlungszettel *m*

compliment, komm-pli-
ment, *v* Komplimente
machen

comply (with), kem-plei
(u'idh), *v* entsprechen,
erfüllen

component, kem-poh-nent,
n Bestandteil *m*

compose, kem-pohs, *v*
(constitute) bilden;
(music) komponieren;
(poetry) verfassen; –d, *adj*
gefaßt; –r, *n* Komponist *m*

composite, komm-pe-sitt,
adj zusammengesetzt

composition, komm-pe-
sisch-'n, *n* (make-up)
Zusammensetzung *nt*;
(essay) Aufsatz *m*; (*mus,
art*) Komposition *f*

compost, komm-post, *n*
Kompost *m*

composure, kem-poh-scher,
n Fassung *f*

compound, komm-paund, *n*
chem Verbindung *f*;
(enclosure) Lager *nt*; *adj*
zusammengesetzt; –
fracture, *n* komplizierter
Bruch *m*; – interest, *n*
Zinseszins *m*

compound, kem-paund, *v*
chem mischen; (worsen)
verschlimmern

comprehend, komm-pri-
hend, *v* begreifen

comprehension, komm-
pri-henn-sch'n, *n*

Verständnis *nt*

comprehensive, komm-pri-
henn-siw, *adj* umfassend; –
(school), *n* Gesamtschule
f

compress, komm-press, *n*
Kompresse *f*

compress, kem-press, *v*
komprimieren

comprise, kem-preis, *v*
umfassen

compromise, komp-re-meis,
n Kompromiß *m*; *v*
kompromittieren; einen
Kompromiß schließen

compulsion, kem-pall-sch'n,
n Zwang *m*

compulsive, kem-pall-ssiw,
adj zwanghaft

compulsory, kem-pall-sse-ri,
adj obligatorisch

compute, kem-pjuht, *v*
berechnen

computer, kem-pjuh-ter, *n*
Computer *m*; – game, *n*
Computerspiel *nt*; –ize, *v*
(data) computerisieren;
(method, system) auf
Computer umstellen; –
programmer, *n*
Programmierer *m*

comrade, komm-ridd, *n*
Kamerad *m*; Genosse *m*

con, konn, *n* Schwindel;
v hereinlegen *m*

concave, konn-kehw/konn-
kehw, *adj* konkav

conceal, ken-ssiel, *v* (object,
feelings) verbergen; (fact)
verheimlichen

concede, ken-ssied, *v*

(admit) zugeben; (give
up) gewähren

conceit, ken-ssiet, *n*
Einbildung *f*; –ed, *adj*
eingebildet

conceive, ken-ssiew, *v*
(comprehend) sich
vorstellen; (med)
empfangen

concentrate, konn-ssen-
treht, *v* konzentrieren; –
(on), sich konzentrieren
(auf)

concentration, konn-ssen-
treh-sch'n, *n*
Konzentration *f*; – camp,
n Konzentrationslager *nt*,
KZ *nt*

concept, konn-ssept, *n*
Begriff *m*

conception, ken-ssepp-
sch'n, *n* Vorstellung *f*;
(med) Empfängnis *f*

concern, ken-ssörn, *n*
(affair) Sache *f*; (firm)
Unternehmen *nt*;
(disquiet) Sorge *f*; *v*
betreffen; be –ed (about),
sich Sorgen machen (um);
–ing, *prep* bezüglich

concert, konn-ssert, *n*
Konzert *nt*

concerted, ken-ssör-tidd, *adj*
gemeinsam

concerto, ken-tschähr-toh,
n Konzert *nt*, Concerto *nt*

concession, ken-ssesch-'n, *n*
Konzession *f*

conciliation, ken-ssill-i-eh-
sch'n, *n* Versöhnung *f*;
(procedure) Schlichtung *f*

conciliatory, ken-**ssill**-i-e-tri, *adj* besänftigend

concise, ken-**sseiss**, *adj* kurz, bündig

conclude, ken-**kluhd**, *v* (finish) beenden; (agree) abschließen; – **(from),** (infer, decide) schließen (aus)

conclusion, ken-**kluh**-sch'n, *n* Abschluß m; (inference, decision) Schluß m

conclusive, ken-**kluh**-ssiw, *adj* entscheidend

concoct, ken-**kokt,** *v* (cooking etc.) zusammenstellen; (scheme) aushecken; **–ion,** *n* (food) Kreation f; (drink) Gebräu nt

concourse, kong-**korss**, *n* Vorplatz m; **(station)** –, Bahnhofshalle f

concrete, kong-**kriet**, *adj* konkret; *n* Beton m

concur, ken-**kör,** *v* übereinstimmen

concurrent(ly), ken-**ka**-rent(-li), *adj & adv* gleichzeitig

concussion, ken-**kasch**-'n, *n* (med) Gehirnerschütterung f

condemn, ken-**demm**, *v* verurteilen; (building/food) abbruchreif/für den Verzehr ungeeignet erklären

condensation, konn-**denn**-sseh-sch'n, *n* (vaporization) Kondensation f

condense, ken-**denss,** *v chem* kondensieren; (book) abkürzen; **–d milk,** *n* Kondensmilch f

condescend, konn-di-**ssend**, *v* sich herablassen; **–ing,** *adj* herablassend

condition, ken-**disch**-'n, *n* Bedingung f; (state) Zustand m; **–al,** *adj* bedingt; **–er,** *n* (for hair) Spülung f; **–s,** *npl* Verhältnisse *pl*

condolences, ken-**doh**-len-ssis, *npl* Beileid nt

condom, konn-**domm**, *n* Kondom m/nt

condone, ken-**dohn**, *v* dulden

conducive (to), ken-**djuh**-ssiw (tu), *adj* förderlich, dienlich

conduct, konn-**dackt**, *n* Benehmen nt; (management) Führung f

conduct, ken-**dackt,** *v* (manage) leiten, führen; *mus* dirigieren; **–ed tour,** *n* Führung f; **–or,** *n elec* Leiter m; (bus) Schaffner m; *mus* Dirigent m

cone, kohn, *n* Kegel m; (for ice-cream) Tüte f; (fir-cone) Zapfen m

confectioner, ken-**feck**-sch'n-er, *n* Konditor m; **–'s,** *n* Konditorei f; **–y,** *n* Süßigkeiten *pl*

confederate, ken-**fedd**-e-ret,

n Verbündete(r) m

confederation, ken-**fedd**-erreh-sch'n, *n* Bund m

confer, ken-**för,** *v* konferieren; – **(on),** (bestow) verleihen

conference, konn-**fe**-renss, *n* Konferenz f

confess, ken-**fess,** *v* gestehen; *relig* beichten

confession, ken-**fesch**-'n, *n* Geständnis nt; *relig* Beichte f

confide, ken-**feid,** *v* anvertrauen; – **in sb,** sich jdm anvertrauen

confidence, konn-fi-denss, *n* (faith) Vertrauen nt; (self-) Selbstvertrauen nt; – **trick,** *n* Schwindel m

confident, konn-fi-dent, *adj* überzeugt; (self-) selbstsicher

confidential, konn-fi-**denn**-sch'l, *adj* vertraulich

confine (to), ken-**fein** (tu), *v* (limit) beschränken (auf); (lock up) einsperren (in); **–d,** *adj* beschränkt; **–ment,** *n* (childbirth) Wochenbett nt; (prison) Haft f

confines, konn-feins, *npl* Grenzen *pl*

confirm, ken-**förm**, *v* bestätigen; *relig* konfirmieren

confirmation, konn-fer-**meh**-sch'n, *n* Bestätigung f; *relig* Konfirmation f

confiscate, konn-fiss-keht, *v*

beschlagnahmen

conflagration, konn-fle-greh-sch'n, n Brand m

conflict, konn-flikt, n Konflikt m; (combat) Kampf m

conflict, ken-flikt, v im Widerspruch stehen; –ing, adj widersprechend

conform, ken-form, v sich anpassen; – to, sich richten nach, entsprechen

confound, ken-faund, v verwirren

confront, ken-frant, v (face) entgegentreten; – with, gegenüberstellen, konfrontieren mit

confrontation, konn-fren-teh-sch'n, n Konfrontation f

confuse, ken-fjuhs, v (bewilder) verwirren; (mix up) verwechseln

confusing, ken-fjuh-sing, adj verwirrend

confusion, ken-fjuh-sch'n, n (bewilderment) Verwirrung f; (disorder) Durcheinander nt

congeal, ken-dschiel, v (of blood) gerinnen; (of fat) fest werden

congenial, ken-dschie-ni-el, adj angenehm

congenital, ken-dschenn-i-tel, adj angeboren

congested, ken-dschess-tidd, adj überfüllt

congestion, ken-dschess-tsch'n, n Stau m,

Verstopfung f

conglomerate, ken-glomm-e-ret, n Konglomerat nt

congratulate, ken-grätt-ju-leht, v gratulieren; (on birthday etc.) beglückwünschen

congratulations, ken-grätt-ju-leh-sch'ns, npl Glückwünsche pl

congregate, kong-gri-geht, v sich versammeln

congregation, kong-gri-geh-sch'n, n Gemeinde f

congress, kong-gress, n Kongreß m

conical, konn-i-k'l, adj kegelförmig

conifer, konn-i-fer, n Nadelbaum m

conjecture, ken-dscheck-tscher, n Vermutung f; v vermuten

conjugal, konn-dschu-gel, adj ehelich

conjunction, ken-dschank-sch'n, n Verbindung f; gram Bindewort nt

conjunctivitis, ken-dschank-ti-wei-tiss, n Bindehautentzündung f

conjure, kann-dscher, v zaubern; – up, beschwören; fig heraufbeschwören; –r, n Zauberkünstler m

con man, konn männ, n Schwindler m

connect, ke-neckt, v verbinden; elec anschließen; –ion, n

Verbindung f; elec, rail Anschluß m

connive, ke-neiw, v (conspire) gemeinsame Sache machen; – at, (overlook) stillschweigend dulden

connoisseur, konn-e-ssör, n Kenner m

conquer, kong-ker, v (territory) erobern; (enemy, feelings) besiegen; –or, n Eroberer m

conquest, kong-ku'est, n Eroberung f; Sieg m

conscience, konn-sch'nss, n Gewissen nt

conscientious, konn-schi-enn-schess, adj gewissenhaft

conscious, konn-schess, adj bewußt; (med) bei Bewußtsein; –ness, n Bewußtsein nt

conscript, konn-skript, n Wehrpflichtige(r) m

consecrate, konn-ssi-kreht, v weihen

consecutive, ken-sseck-juh-tiw, adj aufeinanderfolgend

consensus, ken-ssen-ssess, n allgemeine Meinung f; (agreement) Übereinstimmung f

consent, ken-ssent, n Einwilligung f; v – (to), einwilligen (in)

consequence, konn-ssi-ku'enss, n (result) Folge f;

(importance)
Wichtigkeit f
consequently, konn-ssi-ku'ent-li, *adv* folglich
conservation, konn-sser-**weh**-sch'n, n Schutz m
conservative, ken-**ssör**-we-tiw, *adj* konservativ
conservatory, ken-**ssör**-we-tri, n Wintergarten m; *mus* Konservatorium nt
conserve, ken-**ssörw**, n Eingemachtes nt; v (maintain) erhalten; (fruit etc.) einmachen
consider, ken-**ssidd**-er, v (reflect) überlegen; (view) betrachten als; (take account of) berücksichtigen; **–able,** *adj* beträchtlich; **–ate,** rücksichtsvoll; **–ation,** n (reflection) Überlegung f; (thoughtfulness) Rücksicht f; **–ing,** *conj* eigentlich; *prep* in Anbetracht
consign, ken-**ssein**, v anvertrauen; **–ment,** n Sendung f
consist (of), ken-ssist (ew), v bestehen (aus)
consistency, ken-**ssiss**-ten-ssi, n (of substance) Konsistenz f; (logic) Konsequenz f
consistent, ken-ssiss-tent, *adj* konsequent
consolation, konn-sse-**leh**-sch'n, n Trost m
console, konn-ssohl, n

comp, mech Kontrollpult nt
console, ken-**ssohl**, v trösten
consolidate, ken-**ssoll**-i-deht, v konsolidieren
consonant, konn-sse-nent, n Konsonant m
consortium, ken-**ssor**-ti-em, n Konsortium nt
conspicuous, ken-**spick**-ju-ess, *adj* (striking) auffallend; (distinguished) hervorragend
conspiracy, ken-**spi**-re-ssi, n Verschwörung f
conspire, ken-**speir**, v sich verschwören
constable, ken-**ste**-b'l, n Polizist m
constabulary, ken-**stäbb**-ju-ler-ri, n Polizei f
constant, konn-stent, *adj* (continuous) ständig; (unchanging) konstant; (faithful) treu
constellation, konn-ste-**leh**-sch'n, n Sternbild nt
consternation, konn-ster-**neh**-sch'n, n Bestürzung f
constipation, konn-sti-**peh**-sch'n, n Verstopfung f
constituency, ken-**stitt**-ju-en-ssi, n Wahlkreis m
constituent, ken-**stitt**-ju-ent, n (part) Bestandteil m; (voter) Wähler m
constitute, konn-sti-tjuht, v ausmachen, bilden; (equate to) darstellen
constitution, konn-sti-**tjuh**-sch'n, n (administration)

Verfassung f; (health) Konstitution f; **–al,** *adj* Verfassungs-
constraint, ken-**strehnt,** n (force) Zwang m; (limit) Einschränkung f
constrict, ken-**strikt,** v einschränken
construct, ken-**strakt,** v bauen; (sentence) bilden; **–ion,** n Bau m; (interpretation) Auslegung f; **–ive,** *adj* konstruktiv
consul, konn-ss'l, n Konsul m; **–ate,** n Konsulat nt
consult, ken-**ssalt,** v konsultieren; **–ant,** n Berater m; (med) Facharzt m; **–ation,** n Beratung f
consume, ken-**ssjuhm,** v (food etc.) konsumieren; (fuel, money) verbrauchen; **–r,** n Verbraucher m; **–r goods,** npl Verbrauchsgüter pl; **–r society,** n Konsumgesellschaft f
consummate, konn-sse-met, *adj* vollkommen
consummate, konn-sse-meht, v vollziehen
consumption, ken-**ssamp**-sch'n, n Verbrauch m; (of food etc.) Konsum m; (med) Schwindsucht f
contact, konn-täckt, n Kontakt m, Verbindung; (physical) Berührung f; v sich in Verbindung setzen mit; **– lenses,** npl

Kontaktlinsen *pl*

contagious, ken-**teh**-dschess, *adj* ansteckend

contain, ken-**tehn,** *v* enthalten; **–er,** *n* Behälter; *comm* Container *m*

contaminate, ken-**tämm**-i-neht, *v* verunreinigen

contemplate, konn-**tem**-pleht, *v* nachdenken über

contemporary, ken-**temm**-pe-re-ri, *adj* zeitgenössisch; *n* Zeitgenosse *m*

contempt, ken-**tempt,** *n* Verachtung *f*; **–ible,** *adj* verachtenswert, verächtlich; **–uous,** *adj* verächtlich

contend, ken-**tend,** *v* (maintain) behaupten; – **(with sb for),** kämpfen/konkurrieren (mit jdn um); **–er,** *n* Kandidat *m*; *sport* Wettkämpfer *m*

content(ed), ken-**tent**(-idd), *adj* zufrieden; *v* befriedigen

content(s), konn-**tent**(s), *n*(pl) Inhalt *m*, Gehalt *m*

contention, ken-**tenn**-sch'n, *n* Behauptung *f*

contentious, ken-**tenn**-schess, *adj* (person) streitsüchtig; (issue) umstritten

contentment, ken-**tent**-ment, *n* Zufriedenheit *f*

contest, konn-**test,** *n* Kampf *m*; *sport* Wettkampf *m*

contest, ken-**test,** *v* bestreiten; *law* anfechten

contestant, ken-**test**-'nt, *n* (quiz, *parl*) Kandidat *m*; (sport, quiz) Teilnehmer *m*

context, konn-**tekst,** *n* Zusammenhang *m*

continent, konn-ti-nent, *n* Festland *nt*, Kontinent *m*

continental, konn-ti-**nenn**-t'l, *adj* kontinental; (European) europäisch

contingency, ken-**tinn**-dschen-ssi, *n* Eventualität *f*

contingent, ken-**tinn**-dschent, *adj* abhängig; *n* Kontingent *nt*

continual, ken-**tinn**-ju-el, *adj* fortwährend; **–ly,** *adv* immer wieder

continuation, ken-tinn-ju-**eh**-sch'n, *n* Fortsetzung *f*

continue, ken-**tinn**-juh, *v* (of person) weitermachen; (of event) weitergehen; (activity) fortsetzen

continuity, konn-tinn-**juh**-i-ti, *n* Kontinuität *f*

continuous, ken-**tinn**-ju-ess, *adj* ununterbrochen; – **stationery,** *n* Endlospapier *nt*

contortion, ken-**tor**-sch'n, *n* Verrenkung *f*

contraband, konn-tre-**bänd,** *n* Schmuggelware *f*

contraception, konn-tre-**ssepp**-sch'n, *n* Empfängnisverhütung *f*

contraceptive, konn-tre-**ssepp**-tiw, *adj*

empfängnisverhütend; *n* empfängnisverhütendes Mittel *nt*

contract, konn-**träckt,** *n* Vertrag *m*

contract, ken-**träckt,** *v* (shrink) (sich) zusammenziehen; (illness) erkranken an; **–ion,** *n* Zusammenziehung *f*; (med) Wehe *f*; **–or,** *n* Auftragnehmer *m*; (builder) Unternehmer *m*; **–ual,** *adj* vertraglich

contradict, konn-tre-**dikt,** *v* widersprechen; **–ion,** *n* Widerspruch *m*; **–ory,** *adj* widersprüchlich

contraption, ken-**träpp**-sch'n, *n* Apparat *m*

contrary, ken-**trähr**-ri, *adj* widerspenstig

contrary, konn-tre-ri, *adj* entgegengesetzt; *n* Gegenteil *nt*; **on the –,** im Gegenteil

contrast, konn-**trahst,** *n* Gegensatz *m*; (visual, TV) Kontrast *m*

contrast, ken-**trahst,** *v* gegenüberstellen; **– with,** in Kontrast stehen zu

contravene, konn-tre-**wien,** *v* verstoßen gegen

contribute (to), ken-**tribb**-juht (tu), *v* beitragen

contribution, kon-tri-**bjuh**-sch'n, *n* Beitrag *m*

contrivance, ken-**treiw**-'nss, *n* Vorrichtung *f*

contrive, ken-**treiw,** *v*

(scheme) ersinnen;
(arrange) arrangieren

control, ken-**trohl,** v
(manage) kontrollieren,
leiten; (master)
beherrschen; n Kontrolle
f; (of feelings etc.)
Beherrschung f; **–s,** npl
Kontrollpult nt; (of car)
Steuerung f; **out of –,**
außer Kontrolle; **under –,**
unter Kontrolle

controversial, kon-tre-**wör**-sch'l, adj umstritten

controversy, **konn**-tre-wör-ssi, n Kontroverse f

conurbation, konn-ör-**beh**-sch'n, n Ballungsgebiet nt

convalescence, konn-we-**less**-enss, n Genesung f

convalescent, konn-we-**less**-n't, adj genesend; n
Genesende(r) m & f

convector (heater), ken-**weck**-ter (**hie**-ter), n
Heizlüfter m

convene, ken-**wien,** v
(meeting)
zusammenrufen; (gather)
sich versammeln

convenience, ken-**wie**-ni-enss, n Annehmlichkeit f;
(WC) Toilette f; **with all
modern –s,** mit allem
Konfort

convenient, ken-**wie**-ni-ent,
adj praktisch, günstig

convent, **konn**-went, n
(Frauen)kloster nt

convention, ken-**wenn**-sch'n, n (gathering)

Versammlung f; (custom)
Konvention f, Brauch m;
–al, adj konventionell

converge, ken-**wördsch,** v
zusammenlaufen

conversant (with), ken-**wör**-ss'nt (u'idh), adj
vertraut (mit)

conversation, konn-wer-**sseh**-sch'n, n Gespräch nt,
Unterhaltung f

converse, ken-**wörss,** v sich
unterhalten

conversion, ken-**wör**-sch'n,
n Umwandlung f; (of
building etc.) Umbau m;
relig Bekehrung f

convert, konn-**wört,** n
Bekehrte(r) m & f

convert, ken-**wört,** v
umwandeln; umbauen;
bekehren; **–ible,** adj
umwandelbar; fin
konvertierbar; n
Kabriolett nt

convex, **konn**-weks, adj
konvex

convey, ken-**weh,** v (goods)
befördern; (message)
vermitteln; **–or (belt),** n
Fließband nt

convict, **konn**-wikt, n
Sträfling m

convict, ken-**wikt,** v
verurteilen; **–ion,** n
Verurteilung f; (belief)
Überzeugung f

convince, ken-**winss,** v
überzeugen

convoluted, **konn**-we-luh-tidd, adj verwickelt

convoy, **konn**-weu, n
Konvoi m

convulse, ken-**walss,** v
(muscles)
zusammenziehen; fig
erschüttern; **–d with
laughter,** gekrümmt vor
Lachen

convulsion, ken-**wall**-sch'n,
n Krampf m; fig
Erschütterung f

coo, kuh, v gurren; **–ing,** n
Gurren nt

cook, kuck, n Koch m,
Köchin f; v (do cooking)
kochen; (prepare)
zubereiten; **– book,**
Kochbuch n

cooker, kuck-er, n Herd m;
–y, n Kochen nt

cool, kuhl, adj kühl; v
abkühlen; **– down,** (sich)
abkühlen; **–ness,** n Kühle
f; (nerve) Kaltblütigkeit f

coop, kuhp, n Hühnerkorb
m; **– up,** v einsperren

co-operate, koh-**opp**-e-reht,
v zusammenarbeiten

co-operation, koh-opp-e-re-**reh**-sch'n, n
Zusammenarbeit f

co-operative, koh-opp-e-re-tiw, adj hilfsbereit; comm
Genossenschafts-; n
Kooperative f,
Genossenschaft f

co-ordinate, koh-**or**-di-neht, v koordinieren

co-ordination, koh-or-di-**neh**-sch'n, n
Koordination f

cop, kopp, n (fam policeman) Bulle m

cope, kohp, v; es schaffen; – with, fertig werden mit

copious, koh-pi-ess, adj reichlich; zahlreich

copper, kopp-er, n Kupfer nt; (fam policeman) Bulle m; –s, npl Kleingeld nt

coppice, kopp-iss, n Wäldchen nt

copse, kopps, n Wäldchen nt

copy, kopp-i, n Kopie f; (of book) Exemplar nt; v kopieren; (write out) abschreiben; –right, Copyright nt, Urheberrecht nt

coral, ko-rel, n Koralle f; – reef, n Korallenriff nt

cord, kord, n Schnur f; (belt) Kordel f

cordial, kor-di-el, adj herzlich; n (alcoholic) Likör m; (fruit) Fruchtsaft m

cordon, kor-den, n Kordon m; – off, v absperren

corduroy, kor-dju-reu, n Kord(samt) m

core, kor, n Kern m; v entkernen

cork, kork, n (material) Kork m; (stopper) Korken m; v zukorken; –screw, n Korkenzieher m

cormorant, kor-me-rent, n Kormoran m

corn, korn, n (wheat) Korn nt; (on foot) Hühnerauge

nt; –d beef, n Corned beef nt; – on the cob, n Maiskolben m; (sweet)–, n (maize) Mais m

corner, kor-ner, n Ecke f; (bend) Kurve f; v comm monopolisieren; (trap) in die Enge treiben

cornet, kor-nitt, n mus Kornett nt; (for ice-cream) Tüte f

cornflour, korn-flau-er, n Stärkemehl nt

corny, kor-ni, adj (joke) blöd; (sentimental) kitschig

coronary, ko-re-ne-ri, n Herzinfarkt m

coronation, ko-re-neh-sch'n, n Krönung f

coroner, ko-re-ner, n amtlicher Leichenschauer m

corporal, kor-pe-rel, n Obergefreite(r) m; adj körperlich; – punishment, n Prügelstrafe f

corporate, kor-pe-ret, adj gemeinsam; comm Firmen-

corporation, kor-pe-reh-sch'n, n comm Aktiengesellschaft f, Körperschaft f; (town) Gemeinde f

corps, kor, n Korps nt

corpse, korps, n Leiche f

corpuscle, kor-pass-'l, n Blutkörperchen nt

correct, ke-rekt, adj (right) richtig; (proper) korrekt; v berichtigen, korrigieren;

–ion, n Verbesserung f

correspond, ko-riss-pond, v – (to), (equate) entsprechen; – (with), (write) korrespondieren (mit); –ence, n Korrespondenz f; –ence course, n Fernkurs m; –ent, n Korrespondent m

corridor, ko-ri-dor, n Korridor m, Gang m

corroborate, ke-robb-e-reht, v bestätigen

corroboration, ke-robb-e-reh-sch'n, n Bestätigung f

corrode, ke-rohd, v korrodieren, zerfressen

corrosion, ke-roh-sch'n, n Korrosion f

corrugated, ko-re-geh-tidd, adj gewellt; – iron, n Wellblech nt; – paper, Wellpappe f

corrupt, ke-rapt, adj (bribable) korrupt, bestechlich; (text) verdorben; v korrumpieren; (bribe) bestechen; –ion, n (moral) Verdorbenheit f; (bribery) Bestechung f

corset, kor-ssitt, n Korsett nt

Corsica, kor-ssi-ke, n Korsika f

cortege, kor-tesch, n (funeral) Leichenzug m

cosh, kosch, n Totschläger m

cosmetic, kos-mett-ick, adj kosmetisch; –s, npl

Kosmetika pl

cosmic, kos-mick, adj kosmisch

cosmopolitan, kos-me-poll-i-t'n, adj kosmopolitisch, international

cosmos, kos-moss, n Kosmos m

cost, kost, n Preis m; (expense) Kosten pl; v kosten; —effective, adj rentabel; —ly, adj teuer; —of living, n Lebensunter-haltungskosten pl; —s, npl law Kosten pl; at all —s, um jeden Preis

costume, koss-tjuhm, n Kostüm nt

cosy, koh-si, adj gemütlich

cot, kott, n (child's) Kinderbett nt

cottage, kott-idsch, n kleines Haus nt, Häuschen nt; — cheese, n Hüttenkäse m; — industry, n Heimindustrie f

cotton, kott-'n, n Baumwolle f; (thread) Garn nt; — wool, Watte f

couch, kautsch, n Sofa nt, Couch f

couchette, ku-schett, n Liegewagen m

cough, koff, n Husten m; v husten; —drop/pastille, n Hustenbonbon nt

could, kudd, v (past & conditional of can)

council, kaun-ssil, n Rat m; — housing, n Sozialwohnung f; —lor, n

Stadtrat m, Stadträtin f

counsel, kaun-ss'l, v beraten; n law Anwalt; —lor, n Berater m

count, kaunt, v zählen; n (numbering) Zählung f; (aristocrat) Graf m; — on, v (rely on) zählen auf

countdown, kaunt-daun, n Countdown m

countenance, kaun-te-nenss, n face; v gutheißen

counter, kaun-ter, n (shop) Ladentisch m; (café) Theke f; (post office) Schalter m; (games) Spielmarke f; v kontern; —act, v entgegenwirken; —feit, adj gefälscht; n Fälschung f; v fälschen; —foil, n (Kontroll) abschnitt m; —mand, v widerrufen; —part, (person) Gegenüber nt; (object) Gegenstück nt; —sign, v gegenzeichnen; —to, prep gegen

countess, kaun-tiss, n Gräfin f

countless, kaunt-liss, adj zahllos

country, kant-ri, n Land nt; — dancing, n Volkstanz m; —man, Landmann m; (compatriot) Landsmann m; —side, n Landschaft f

county, kaun-ti, n Grafschaft f

coup, kuh, n Coup m; —

(d'état), n Putsch m

coupé, kuh-peh, n Coupé nt

couple, kapp-'l, n Paar nt; v (mate) (sich) paaren; (link) koppeln

coupon, kuh-ponn, n Gutschein m

courage, ka-ridsch, n Mut m

courageous, ke-reh-dschess, adj mutig

courgette, kur-schett, n Zucchini f

courier, ku-ri-er, n (messenger) Kurier m; (delivery) Zusteller m; (guide) Reiseleiter m

course, korss, n (river, direction) Lauf m; (tuition, naut) Kurs m; (of race) Bahn f; (golf) Platz m; (of meal) Gang m; of —, adv natürlich

court, kort, n (royal) Hof m; law Gericht nt; v (danger) herausfordern; (woman) den Hof machen

courteous, kör-ti-ess, adj höflich

courtesy, kör-ti-si, n Höflichkeit f

courtier, kort-i-er, n Höfling m

court-martial, kort-mahr-sch'l, n Kriegsgericht nt; v vor ein Kriegsgericht stellen

courtroom, kort-ruhm, n Gerichtssaal m

courtship, kort-schip, n (wooing) Werben nt

courtyard, kort-jahrd, n
Hof m

cousin, kas-inn, n Cousin
m, Kusine f

cove, kohw, n geog Bucht f

covenant, ka-we-nent, n
Abkommen nt; relig
Bund m

cover, ka-wer, n (cloth)
Decke f; (lid) Deckel m;
(of book, magazine)
Umschlag m; (insurance)
Versicherung f; mil
Deckung f; v bedecken;
(insure) versichern; (fin,
mi) decken; (distance)
zurücklegen; (report on)
berichten über; **–age,** n
Berichterstattung f; **–
charge,** n Bedienungsgeld
nt; **–ing,** n Decke f; **–
note,** n vorläufiger
Versicherungsschein m

covert, koh-wört, adj
geheim

cover up, ka-wer app, v
zudecken; (conceal)
verschleiern; **cover-up,** n
Verschleierung f

covet, ka-witt, v begehren

cow, kau, n Kuh f; v
einschüchtern

coward, kau-ed, n Feigling
m; **–ice,** Feigheit f; **–ly,** adj
feige

cowboy, kau-beu, n Cowboy
m

cower, kau-er, v kauern

coxswain, kock-ss'n, n
Steuermann m

coy, keu, adj (shy)

schüchtern; (coquettish)
neckisch

crab, kräb, n (food, large)
Krabbe f; (small) Krebs m;
–apple, n Holzapfel m

crack, kräck, n Riß m,
Sprung m; (noise) Knall
m; (drug) Crack nt; v (of
whip) knallen; (of china
etc.) springen; (nut, safe)
knacken; **–er,** n (firework)
Kracher m; (Christmas)
Knallbonbon nt; (biscuit)
Keks m; **–le,** v knistern; **–
up,** v fig
zusammenbrechen

cradle, kreh-d'l, n Wiege f; v
wiegen

craft, krahft, n (trade)
Gewerbe nt, Handwerk nt;
naut Schiff nt; (skill)
Handfertigkeit f; **–sman,**
Handwerker m

crafty, krahf-ti, adj schlau

crag, krägg, n Felsspitze f

cram, krämm, v vollstopfen;
(coach) einpauken; **–
into,** hineinstopfen in

cramp, krämp, n Krampf m;
v einengen; **–ed,** adj eng

cranberry, känn-be-ri, n
Preiselbeere f

crane, krehn, n (hoist)
Krahn m; (bird) Kranich

crank, känk, n mech Kurbel
f; (eccentric) Spinner m; v
kurbeln

crash, kräsch, n (collision)
Zusammenstoß m; (plane)
Absturz m; (noise) Krach
m; fin Zusammenbruch m;

v (collide)
zusammenstoßen;
(of plane) abstürzen;
(of stock market)
zusammenbrechen; **–
course,** n Intensivkurs m;
– helmet, n Sturzhelm m;
– landing, n
Bruchlandung f

crate, kreht, n Kiste f

crater, kreh-ter, n Krater m

crave, krehw, v sich sehnen
nach

craving, kreh-wing, n
Begierde f

crawl, kro'al, n Kriechen nt;
(swimming) Kraul nt; v
kriechen

crayfish, kreh-fisch, n
(freshwater) Krebs m;
(saltwater) Languste f

crayon, kreh-onn, n
Buntstift m

craze, krehs, n Fimmel m,
große Mode f

crazy, kreh-si, adj verrückt;
– paving, n Mosaikpflaster
nt

creak, kriek, v knarren

cream, kriem, n (dairy)
Rahm m, Sahne f;
(artificial, lotion) Creme
f; **– cheese,** n Frischkäse
m; **–y,** adj sahnig, cremig

crease, kriess, v zerknittern;
(deliberately) eine Falte
machen in; n Falte f

create, kri-eht, v erschaffen;
(cause) verursachen

creation, kri-eh-sch'n, n
Schöpfung f

creative, kri-**eh**-tiw, *adj*
(power) schöpferisch;
(attitude) kreativ

creator, kri-**eh**-ter, *n*
Schöpfer *m*

creature, **krie**-tscher, *n*
Geschöpf *nt*, Wesen *nt*

crèche, kresch, *n*
Kinderkrippe *f*

credentials, kri-
denn-sch'ls, *npl*
Beglaubigungsschreiben
nt, Zeugnis *nt*

credible, **kredd**-i-b'l, *adj*
glaubwürdig, glaubhaft

credit, **kredd**-itt, *n* Kredit
m; *v* glauben; *fin*
gutschreiben; **–able,** *adj*
lobenswert; **– card,** *n*
Kreditkarte *f*; **–or,** *n*
Gläubiger *m*

creed, kried, *n*
Glaubensbekenntnis *nt*

creek, kriek, *n* kleine
Bucht *f*

creep, kriep, *v* kriechen;
(glide) schleichen; **–er,** *n*
(plant) Kletterpflanze *f*;
–y, *adj* unheimlich

cremate, kri-**meht**, *v*
einäschern

cremation, kri-**meh**-sch'n, *n*
Einäscherung *f*

crematorium, kremm-*e*-**tor**-
ri-em, *n* Krematorium *nt*

crescent, **kres**-'nt, *n*
Halbmond *m*

cress, kress, *n* Kresse *f*

crest, krest, *n* (of hill, bird)
Kamm *m*; (heraldry)
Wappen *nt*; **–fallen,** *adj*

niedergeschlagen

Crete, kriet, *n* Kreta *nt*

crevice, **krew**-iss, *n* Spalte *f*

crew, kruh, *n* Besatzung *f*

crib, kribb, *n* Krippe *f*; *v* (
fam copy) abschreiben

crick, krick, *n* **– in one's
neck,** steifes Genick *nt*

cricket, **krick**-itt, *n* (insect)
Grille *f*; *sport* Kricket *nt*

crime, kreim, *n*
Verbrechen *nt*

criminal, **krimm**-i-n'l, *n*
Verbrecher *m*; *adj*
verbrecherisch, strafbar,
Straf-

crimson, **krimm**-s'n, *adj*
blutrot; (blushing)
knallrot

cringe, krindsch, *v*
schaudern; **– before sb,**
kriechen vor, kuschen

crinkle, **kring**-k'l, *n* Falte *f*;
v knittern

cripple, **kripp**-'l, *n* Krüppel
m; *v* verkrüppeln; *fig*
lahmlegen

crisis, **krei**-ssiss, *n* (*pl*
crises), Krise *f*

crisp, krisp, *adj* knusprig; *n*
Chip *m*

criterion, krei-**tier**-ri-en, *n*
(*pl* **criteria**), Kriterium *nt*

critic, **kritt**-ick, *n* Kritiker
m; **–al,** *adj* kritisch

criticism, **kritt**-i-ssism, *n*
Kritik *f*

criticize, **kritt**-i-sseis, *v*
kritisieren

croak, krohk, *v* (frog)
quaken; (crow, person)

krächzen

crochet, **kroh**-scheh, *v*
häkeln; *n* Häkelei *f*

crockery, **krock**-*e*-ri, *n*
Geschirr *nt*

crocodile, **krock**-*e*-deil, *n*
Krokodil *nt*

crocus, **kroh**-kes, *n*
Krokus *m*

crook, kruck, *n* (staff) Stab
m; (criminal) Gauner *m*

crooked, **kruck**-idd, *adj*
krumm; *fig* unehrlich

crop, kropp, *n* Ernte *f*; *v*
stutzen; **– up,** *v*
aufkommen

croquet, **kroh**-keh, *n*
Krocket *nt*

croquette, kre-**kett**, *n*
Krokette *f*

cross, kross, *adj* böse; *n*
Kreuz *nt*; *v* (road etc.)
überqueren; (legs)
übereinanderschlagen;
(arms) verschränken; **––
examine,** *v* ins
Kreuzverhör nehmen;
–ing, *n* (junction)
Kreuzung *f*; (sea)
Überfahrt *f*; **– out,** *v*
ausstreichen; **be at –
purposes,** aneinander
vorbeireden; **–road(s),** *n*
Kreuzung *f*; **–word
(puzzle),** *n*
Kreuzworträtsel *nt*

crotch, krotsch, *n* (body,
trousers) Schritt *m*

crotchet, **krott**-schitt, *n* *mus*
Viertelnote *f*; **–y,** *adj*
nörgelig

crouch, krautsch, *v* kauern

crow, kroh, *n* Krähe *f*; *v* krähen; (*fam* boast) sich brüsten

crowbar, kroh-bahr, *n* Brecheisen *nt*

crowd, kraud, *n* Menge *f*; *v* drängen; (room etc.) überfüllen

crown, kraun, *n* Krone *f*; (of head) Scheitel *m*; *v* krönen

crucial, kruh-sch'l, *adj* entscheidend

crucifix, kruh-ssi-ficks, *n* Kruzifix *nt*; **–ion,** *n* Kreuzigung *f*

crucify, kruh-ssi-fei, *v* kreuzigen; *fig* verreißen

crude, kruhd, *adj* (oil etc.) roh; (manners) grob; (implement etc.) primitiv

cruel, kru-el, *adj* grausam; **–ty,** *n* Grausamkeit *f*

cruet, kru-itt, *n* Gewürzständer *m*

cruise, kruhs, *n* Kreuzfahrt *f*; *v* eine Kreuzfahrt machen; **–r,** *n* *mil* Kreuzer *m*; (pleasure boat) Vergnügungsjacht *f*

crumb, kramm, *n* Krümel *nt*, Krume *f*

crumble, kramm-b'l, *v* zerbröckeln; (of resistance) sich auflösen

crumple, kramm-p'l, *v* zusammenknüllen, zerknittern

crunch, krantsch, *n* Knirschen *nt*; (*fig* crisis point) Knackpunkt *m*; *v* knirschen; **–y,** *adj* (apple) knackig; (biscuit) knusprig

crush, krasch, *n* Gedränge *nt*; *v* zerdrücken; (spices) zerstoßen; (opposition) unterdrücken

crust, krast, *n* Kruste *f*; **–y,** *adj* knusprig; *fig* barsch

crutch, kratsch, *n* Krücke *f*

cry, krei, *n* Schrei *m*; (call) Ruf *m*; *v* schreien; (call) rufen; (weep) weinen; **– off,** *v* absagen

crypt, kript, *n* Krypta *f*; **–ic,** *adj* rätselhaft; (clue) verschlüsselt

crystal, kriss-t'l, *n* Kristall *m*; (glass) Kristall *nt*; **–lize,** *v* *chem* kristallisieren; (fruit) kandieren; *fig* sich herauskristallisieren

cub, kab, *n* Junges *nt*

Cuba, kjuh-be, *n* Kuba *nt*

cube, kjuhb, *n* Würfel *m*; (maths) dritte Potenz *f*; *v* (maths) hoch drei nehmen

cubic capacity, kjuh-bick ke-**päss**-i-ti, *n* Fassungsvermögen *nt*

cubicle, kjuh-bi-k'l, *n* Kabine *f*

cuckoo, kuck-uh, *n* Kuckuck *m*; **– clock,** *n* Kuckucksuhr *f*

cucumber, kjuh-kamm-ber, *n* Gurke *f*

cuddle, kadd-'l, *v* liebkosen, schmusen

cue, kjuh, *n* *theatre* Stichwort *nt*; (billiards) Queue *m/nt*

cuff, kaff, *n* (of sleeve) Manschette *f*; (blow) Klaps *m*; *v* einen Klaps geben; **–link,** *n* Manschettenknopf *m*

culinary, kall-i-ne-ri, *adj* Koch-

cull, kall, *v* (flowers) pflücken; (seals, deer, etc.) abtöten

culminate, kall-mi-neht, *v* gipfeln

culpable, kall-pe-b'l, *adj* schuldig

culprit, kalp-ritt, *n* Schuldige(r) *m & f*, Täter *m*

cult, kalt, *n* Kult *m*

cultivate, kall-ti-weht, *v* kultivieren

cultural, kall-tsche-r'l, *adj* kulturell, Kultur-

culture, kall-tscher, *n* Kultur *f*

cumbersome, kamm-ber-ssem, *adj* (clothing) behinderlich; (parcel etc.) unhandlich; (procedure) beschwerlich

cumulative, kjuh-mju-le-tiw, *adj* kumulativ

cunning, kann-ing, *adj* listig, schlau; *n* Gerissenheit *f*, Schläue *f*

cup, kapp, *n* Tasse *f*; (mug) Becher *m*; (trophy) Pokal *m*

cupboard, kabb-erd, *n*

Schrank *m*

curate, kjuhr-ritt, *n* Vikar *m*

curator, kjuhr-reh-ter, *n*
Kustos *m*

curb, körb, *n* Beschränkung
f; *v* einschränken

curdle, kör-d'l, *v* gerinnen

cure, kjuhr, *n* (remedy)
Heilmittel *nt*; (treatment)
Heilverfahren *nt*; *v* (med)
heilen; (smoke) räuchern;
(salt) pökeln; (dry)
trocknen

curfew, kör-fjuh, *n*
Ausgangssperre *f*

curiosity, kjuhr-ri-oss-i-ti, *n*
(inquisitiveness) Neugier
f; (object) Kuriosität *f*

curious, kjuhr-ri-ess, *adj*
(inquisitive) neugierig;
(peculiar) seltsam

curl, körl, *n* Locke *f*; *v* (sich)
locken; **–er**, *n*
Lockenwickler *m*; **–y**,
adj lockig

currant, ka-rent, *n* (dried)
Korinthe *f*

currency, ka-ren-ssi, *n*
Währung *f*

current, ka-rent, *adj*
(present) aktuell;
(widespread)
gebräuchlich; *n* Strom *m*;
– account, *n* Girokonto *nt*

curriculum, ke-rick-ju-lem,
n Lehrplan *m*; **– vitae**, *n*
Lebenslauf *m*

curry, ka-ri, *n* Curry *m/nt*; *v*
mit Currygewürzen
zubereiten; **– favour
(with)**, sich

einschmeicheln (bei)

curse, körss, *n* Fluch *m*; *v*
fluchen, verwünschen

cursor, kör-sser, *n comp*
Cursor *m*

cursory, kör-sser-ri, *adj*
flüchtig

curt, kört, *adj* kurz, knapp,
barsch

curtail, ker-tehl, *v*
(ab)kürzen

curtain, kör-ten, *n* Vorhang
m, Gardine *f*

curts(e)y, kört-ssi, *n* Knicks
m; *v* knicksen

curve, körw, *n* Kurve *f*; *v*
sich biegen; (of road etc.)
einen Bogen machen

cushion, kusch-'n, *n* Kissen
nt; *v* dämpfen

custard, kass-terd, *n*
(runny) Vanillesoße *f*;
(set) Pudding *m*

custody, kass-te-di, *n*
(detention) Haft *f*; (care)
Aufsicht *f*

custom, kass-tem, *n* Brauch
m; (trade) Kundschaft *f*;
–ary, *adj* gebräuchlich,
üblich; **–er**, *n* Kunde *m*,
Kundin *f*; **–ize**, *v* speziell
ausrüsten; **–made**, *adj*
(clothes etc.) nach Maß;
(car) speziell angefertigt

customs, kass-tems, *n* Zoll
m; **–s duty**, Zoll *m*,
Zollabgabe *f*

cut, katt, *n* Schnitt *m*;
(share) Anteil *m*; (in
price) Herabsetzung *f*; (in
salary, hours, text)

Kürzung; *v* schneiden;
(grass) mähen; (price)
herabsetzen; (expenses,
wages, text) kürzen;
(production)
einschränken; (cards)
abheben; **– back (on)**,
einschränken; **– down**,
(tree) fällen; (expenses)
einschränken; **– off**,
abschneiden

cute, kjuht, *adj* niedlich

cuticle, kjuh-ti-k'l, *n*
Nagelhaut *f*

cutlery, katt-le-ri, *n*
Besteck *nt*

cutlet, katt-litt, *n*
Kotelett *nt*

cut-price, katt preiss, *adj*
herabgesetzt, ermäßigt

cut-throat, katt-throht, *adj*
mörderisch, gnadenlos

cutting, katt-ing, *adj*
schneidend; *n* (article)
Ausschnitt *m*; (plant)
Ableger *m*

CV, ssie wie (*abbr*
curriculum vitae),
Lebenslauf *m*

cycle, sei-k'l, *n* (bicycle)
Fahrrad *nt*; (sequence)
Zyklus *m*; *elec* Periode *f*

cycling, sei-kling, *n*
Radfahren *nt*

cyclist, sei-klist, *n*
Radfahrer *m*

cylinder, si-linn-der, *n*
Zylinder *m*

cymbals, simm-b'ls, *npl*
Becken *nt*

cynic, sinn-ick, *n* Zyniker *m*

m; **–al,** *adj* zynisch
cypress, sei-press, *n*
  Zypresse *f*
Cyprus, sei-press, Zypern *nt*
cyst, ssisst, *n* Zyste *f*; **–itis,** *n*
  Blasenentzündung *f*
czar, zahr, *n* Zar *m*
Czech, tscheck, *adj*
  tschechisch; *n* Tscheche
  m, Tschechin *f*; **–**
  Republic, *n* Tschechische
  Republik *f,* Tschechien *nt*

dab, däbb, n Tupfer m; v (be)tupfen

dabble, däbb-'l, v – **in,** sich in etw versuchen; –**r,** n Amateur m

dad(dy), dädd(-i), n Vati m

daffodil, däff-e-dill, n Osterglocke f, Narzisse f

daft, däft, adj doof

dagger, dägg-er, n Dolch m

dahlia, deh-li-e, n Dahlie f

daily, deh-li, adj & adv täglich, Tages-

dainty, dehn-ti, adj zierlich

dairy, dähr-ri, adj Milch-; n (works) Molkerei f; (shop) Milchgeschäft nt; – **produce,** n Molkereiprodukte pl

dais, deh-iss, n Podium nt

daisy, deh-si, n Gänseblümchen nt

dale, dehl, n Tal nt

dam, dämm, n Damm m; v stauen

damage, dämm-idsch, n Schaden m; v beschädigen; –**s,** npl Schadenersatz m

damn, dämm, fam n **I don't give a –,** das ist mir piepegal; v verdammen; – **(it)!** verdammt!

damning, dämm-ing, adj vernichtend

damp, dämp, adj feucht; n Feuchtigkeit f; v anfeuchten

dance, dahnss, n Tanz m; v tanzen; –**r,** n Tänzer m

dandelion, dänn-di-lei-en, n Löwenzahn m

dandruff, dänn-dreff, n Schuppen pl

Dane, dehn, n Däne m, Dänin f

danger, dehn-dscher, n Gefahr f; –**ous,** adj gefährlich

dangle, däng-g'l, v baumeln (lassen)

Danish, deh-nish, adj dänisch; n (language) Dänisch nt

Danube, dänn-juhb, n Donau f

dapper, däpp-er, adj fein, elegant

dare, dähr, v (have courage) es wagen; (challenge) herausfordern; **I – say,** es kann gut sein

daring, dähr-ring, adj (brave) waghalsig; (audacious) verwegen

dark, dahrk, adj dunkel; fig düster, –**ness,** n Dunkelheit f; –**room,** n Dunkelkammer f; **be in the – (about),** im Dunkeln sein (über)

darling, dahr-ling, adj sehr lieb; n Liebling m

darn, dahrn, v stopfen

dart, dahrt, n (weapon) Pfeil m; (in clothes) Abnäher m; v – (about), (herum)sausen; –**s,** n Darts nt

dash, däsch, n (punctuation) Gedankenstrich m; (small amount) bißchen; v (rush) stürzen; (destroy) zunichte machen; **make a – for,** stürzen auf

dashboard, däsch-bord, n Armaturenbrett nt

dashing, däsch-ing, adj

schneidig
data, deh-*te,* n*(pl)* Angaben
pl; *(comp* etc.) Daten pl; *-*
base, n Datenbank f; –
processing, n
Datenverarbeitung f
date, deht, n Datum nt;
(appointment)
Verabredung f; (fruit)
Dattel f; v (letter)
datieren; (go out with)
gehen mit; **–d,** adj
altmodisch; **– of birth,** n
Geburtsdatum nt; **out of**
–, überholt; **up to date,**
(clothes etc.) modisch;
(news etc.) aktuell
daughter, do'a-*ter,* n
Tochter f; **––in-law,** n
Schwiegertochter f
daunting, do'an-ting, adj
entmutigend
dawdle, do'a-d'l, v
bummeln, trödeln
dawn, do'an, n
(Morgen)dämmerung f; v
dämmern
day, deh, n Tag m; **the –**
after tomorrow,
übermorgen; **the – before**
yesterday, vorgestern; *–*
break, n Tagesanbruch
m; **–dream,** n Tagtraum m;
–light, n Tageslicht nt;
–time, n **in/during the –**
tagsüber; **––to-day,** adj
alltäglich
daze, deis, n **in a –,**
benommen; **–d,** adj
benommen
dazzle, däs-'l, v blenden

D-day, die-deh, n der
Tag X m
deacon, die-k'n, n Diakon m
dead, dedd, adj tot; (limb,
finger) abgestorben; adv
(exactly) genau; (*fam*
very) total; npl die Toten
pl; **–en,** v (pain) abtöten;
(sound) dämpfen; (blow)
auffangen; **––end,** n
Sackgasse f; **– heat,** n totes
Rennen nt; **–line,** n
Termin m; **–lock,** n
Stillstand m; **–ly,** adj
tödlich
deaf, deff, adj taub; **–en,** v
taub machen; **–ness,** n
Taubheit f
deal, diel, n comm Geschäft
nt; v (cards) geben,
austeilen; **–er,** n Händler
m; (cards) Geber m; **– in,**
v handeln mit; **– with,** v
comm verhandeln mit;
(attend to) sich befassen
mit; (sort out) fertig
werden mit; (of book etc.)
handeln von; **a great –**
(of), eine Menge f
dean, dien, n Dekan m
dear, dier, adj lieb; (costly)
teuer; n Liebling m; **Dear**
Mr X/Sir, Sehr geehrter
Herr X/Herr; **Dear James,**
Lieber James
death, deth, n Tod m;
(fatality) Todesfall m; **–**
penalty, n Todesstrafe f
debar (from), di-bahr
(frem), v ausschließen
(von)

debase, di-behss, v (person)
entwürdigen; (currency)
entwerten
debate, di-beht, n Debatte f;
v debattieren
debauchery, di-bo'a-tsche-
ri, n Ausschweifung f
debilitating, di-bill-i-teh-
ting, adj schwächend
debit, debb-itt, n fin Soll nt;
v (account) belasten
debris, debb-rie, n
Trümmer pl
debt, dett, n Schuld f; **–or,** n
Schuldner m; **in –,**
verschuldet
début, deh-bjuh, n Debüt nt
decade, deck-ehd, n
Jahrzehnt nt
decadence, deck-*e*-denss, n
Dekadenz f
decaffeinated, die-käff-ie-
neh-tidd, adj koffeinfrei
decanter, di-känn-ter, n
Karaffe f
decapitate, di-käpp-i-teht, v
köpfen, enthaupten
decay, di-keh, n (decline)
Verfall m; (rot) Fäule f; v
verfallen; (of food)
verderben
deceased, di-ssiesst, adj
verstorben
deceit, di-ssiet, n Betrug m,
Täuschung f; **–ful,** adj
falsch, hinterlistig
deceive, di-ssiew, v
täuschen
December, di-ssemm-ber, n
Dezember m
decency, die-ssen-ssi, n

Anstand m

decent, die-ssent, *adj*
anständig

deception, di-**ssepp-sch'n,** n
Betrug m, Täuschung f

deceptive, di-**ssepp-tiw,** *adj*
trügerisch

decide, di-**sseid,** v (sich)
entscheiden; **–d(ly),** *adj &*
adv (without question)
entschieden; (very)
ausgesprochen

deciduous, di-**ssidd-**ju-ess,
adj Laub-

decimal, dess-i-m'l, *adj*
Dezimal-; **– point,** n
Komma nt

decipher, di-**ssei-fer,** v
entziffern

decision, di-**ssisch-'n,** n
Entscheidung f,
Beschluß m

decisive, di-**ssei-**ssiw, *adj*
entscheidend

deck, deck, n Deck nt; **–
chair,** n Liegestuhl m; **–
out,** v schmücken

declaration, deck-le-**reh-**
sch'n, n Erklärung f

declare, di-**klähr,** v erklären;
(at customs) verzollen

declension, di-**klen-**sch'n, n
gram Deklination f

decline, di-**klein,** n
(reduction) Rückgang m;
(deterioration) Verfall m;
v (deteriorate) verfallen;
(reject) ablehnen; (be
reduced) zurückgehen;
gram deklinieren

declutch, die-**klatsch,** v

auskuppeln

decode, die-**kohd,** v
entschlüsseln; **–r,** n (TV
etc.) Decoder m

decompose, die-kom-**pohs,** v
(sich) zersetzen

décor, deh-**kor,** n (room)
Dekor m/nt; *theatre*
Dekor m/nt

decorate, deck-e-reht, v
(make festive)
schmücken; (paint)
(an)streichen; (paper)
tapezieren; (cake)
verzieren; (honour)
auszeichnen

decoration, deck-e-**reh-**
sch'n, n *mil* Auszeichnung
f; (ornament) Verzierung
f; **–s,** npl Schmuck m

decoy, die-keu, n
Lockvogel m

decrease, die-kriess, n
Abnahme f,
Verminderung f

decrease, di-**kriess,** v
abnehmen

decree, di-**krie,** n Erlaß m; v
verordnen

decrepit, di-**krepp-**itt, *adj*
altersschwach,
heruntergekommen

dedicate, dedd-i-keht, v
widmen; *relig* weihen; **–d,**
adj ergeben

deduce (from), di-**djuhss**
(frem), v ableiten (aus)

deduct, di-**dakt,** v
abziehen; **–ion,** n (of
money) Abzug m;
(conclusion) Folgerung f

deed, died, n (action) Tat f;
(document) Urkunde f

deem, diem, v halten für

deep, diep, *adj* tief; **–en,** v
vertiefen; **––frozen,** *adj*
tiefgefroren; (food)
Tiefkühl-; **––sea,** *adj*
(diving) Tiefsee-; (fishing)
Hochsee-; **––seated,** *adj*
tiefsitzend

deer, dier, n Hirsch m; (roe)
Reh nt

deface, di-**fehss,** v
verunstalten, entstellen

defamation, deff-e-**meh-**
sch'n, n Verleumdung f

default, di-**fo'alt,** n (non-
payment) Nichtzahlung f;
(non-performance)
Versäumnis f; v säumig
sein; *law* nicht erscheinen;
–er, n Säumige(r) m & f

defeat, di-**fiet,** n Niederlage
f; v schlagen, **–ist,** *adj*
defätistisch; n Defätist m

defect, die-fekt, n Fehler m;
mech Defekt m

defective, di-**feck-tiw,** *adj*
mangelhaft; *mech* defekt

defence, di-**fenss,** n
Verteidigung f; **–less,** *adj*
schutzlos, wehrlos

defend, di-**fend,** v
verteidigen; **–ant,** di-**fen-**
dent, n Angeklagte(r) m
& f; **–er,** n Verteidiger m

defensive, di-**fen-**ssiw, *adj*
defensiv

defer, di-**för,** v (delay)
verschieben; **– (to),**
(submit) sich fügen

deference, deff-e-renss, n
Achtung f; **in – to,** aus
Achtung vor

defiance, di-**fei**-enss, n Trotz
m; **in – of sb/sth,** jdm/etw
zum Trotz

defiant, di-**fei**-ent, adj
trotzig

deficiency, di-**fisch**-en-ssi,
(shortage) Mangel m;
(defect) Schwäche f

deficient, di-**fisch**-ent, adj
mangelhaft, unzulänglich

deficit, deff-i-ssitt, n
Defizit nt

defile, di-**feil,** v
verschmutzen

define, di-**fein,** v (word etc.)
definieren; (powers etc.)
bestimmen

definite, deff-i-nitt, adj
(agreed) fest; (positive)
bestimmt; (distinct)
eindeutig; **–ly,** adv fest,
eindeutig

definition, deff-i-**ni**-sch'n, n
(of word etc.) Definition
f; (of powers etc.)
Bestimmung f

deflect, di-**fleckt,** v
ablenken

deform, di-**form,** v
verunstalten, deformieren

defraud, di-**fro'ad,** v
betrügen

defray, di-**freh,** v
übernehmen

defrost, die-**frost,** v (fridge,
windscreen) abtauen;
(food) auftauen

deft, deft, adj flink

defunct, di-**fankt,** adj
(person) verstorben;
(machine etc.) überholt,
stillgelegt

defuse, die-**fjuhs,** v
entschärfen

defy, di-**fei,** v trotzen;
(challenge) herausfordern

degenerate, di-**dschenn**-e-
ret, adj entartet,
degeneriert

degenerate, di-**dschenn**-e-
reht, v entarten,
degenerieren

degradation, degg-re-**deh**-
sch'n, n Erniedrigung f

degrade, di-**grehd,** v
erniedrigen

degree, di-**grie,** n Grad m; **–
course,** n Universitätskurs
m

dehydrated, die-hei-**dreh**-
tidd, adj ausgetrocknet;
(food) Trocken-

de-ice, die-**eiss,** v enteisen;
–r, n Enteiser m

deity, die-i-ti, n Gottheit f

deject, di-**dscheckt,** v
niederschlagen; **–ion,** n
Niedergeschlagenheit f

delay, di-**leh,** n
(postponement) Aufschub
m; (lateness) Verspätung f;
v (postpone) verschieben;
(detain –) aufhalten;
without –, unverzüglich

delectable, di-**leck**-te-b'l, adj
(delicious) köstlich;
(delightful) reizend

delegate, dell-i-get, n
Delegierte(r) m & f

delegate, dell-i-geht, v
delegieren

delete, di-**liet,** v streichen

deliberate(ly), di-**libb**-e-
ret(-li), adj & adv
(intentional) absichtlich;
(slow) bedächtig

deliberate, di-**libb**-e-reht, v
nachdenken

delicacy, dell-i-ke-ssi, n
(food) Delikatesse f;
(sensitivity) Feingefühl nt;
(daintiness) Zartheit f

delicate, dell-i-ket, adj
(sensitive) feinfühlig;
(dainty, weak) zart

delicatessen, dell-i-ke-**tess**-
'n, n (food) Feinkost f;
(shop) Feinkostgeschäft nt

delicious, di-**lisch**-ess, adj
lecker

delight, di-**leit,** n Wonne f; v
entzücken; **–ed,** adj
entzückt; **–ful,** adj
entzückend, reizend

delinquency, di-**ling**-ku'en-
ssi, n Kriminalität f

delinquent, di-**ling**-ku'ent, n
Straffällige(r) m & f

delirious, di-**li**-ri-ess, adj
(med) im Delirium; fig im
Freudentaumel

deliver, di-**liw**-er, v (goods)
liefern; (letter) zustellen;
(speech) halten; (baby)
zur Welt bringen; **–y,** n (of
goods) Lieferung f; (of
letters) Zustellung f; (of
baby) Entbindung f

delude, di-**luhd,** v täuschen

deluge, dell-juhdsch, n

Überschwemmung f; fig
Flut f

delusion, di-**luh**-sch'n, n
Täuschung f

delve into, delw inn-tu, v
tief greifen in; fig sich
vertiefen in

demand, di-**mahnd,** n
Forderung f; comm
Nachfrage f; v verlangen,
fordern; **–ing,** adj
anspruchsvoll

demean (oneself), di-**mien**
(u'ann-sself), v (sich)
erniedrigen

demeanour, di-**mie**-ner, n
Benehmen nt

demented, di-**menn**-tidd, adj
verrückt

demise, di-**meis,** n Ableben
nt

demo, demm-oh, n (abbr
demonstration), Demo f

democracy, di-**mock**-re-ssi,
n Demokratie f

democrat, demn-e-krätt, n
Demokrat m

democratic, demn-e-**krätt**-
ick, adj demokratisch

demolish, di-**moll**-isch, v
(building) abreißen;
(theory) vernichten

demon, die-men, n
Dämon m

demonstrate, demm-en-
streht, v demonstrieren

demonstration, demm-en-
streh-sch'n, n
Demonstration f

demonstrator, demm-
en-streh-ter, n

Demonstrant m

demoralize, die-**mo**-re-leis, v
demoralisieren

demote, di-**moht,** v
degradieren

demure, di-**mjuhr,** adj
spröde, sittsam

den, den, denn, n (of animal)
Höhle f; (private room)
Bude f

denial, di-**nei**-el, n
Leugnung f; (official)
Dementi nt; (refusal)
Ablehnung f

denim, denn-imm, n
Denim-, Jeans-; **–s,** npl
(Blue) Jeans pl

Denmark, denn-mark, n
Dänemark nt

denomination, di-nomm-i-
neh-sch'n, n relig
Bekenntnis nt; fin Wert m

denominator, di-**nomm**-i-
neh-ter, n Nenner m

denote, di-**noht,** v
bezeichnen

denounce, de-**naunss,** v
(accuse) brandmarken;
(inform against)
denunzieren

dense, denss, adj dicht; (fam
stupid) dumm

density, denn-ssi-ti, n
Dichte f

dent, dent, n Delle f; v
(metal) einbeulen;
(wood) eine Delle
machen in

dental, dent-'l, adj Zahn-

dentist, denn-tist, n
Zahnarzt m; **–ry,** n

Zahnheilkunde f

dentures, denn-tschers, npl
Gebiß nt

denude, di-**njuhd,** v
entblößen

deny, di-**nei,** v (accusation)
ableugnen; (officially)
dementieren; (request)
abschlagen

deodorant, die-oh-de-rent, n
Deodorant nt

depart, di-**pahrt,** v abfahren;
fig abweichen

department, di-**pahrt**-ment,
n Abteilung f; **– store,**
Warenhaus nt

departure, di-**pahr**-tscher, n
(of train, bus) Abfahrt f;
(of plane) Abflug m; (of
person) Abreise f; fig neue
Richtung f; **– lounge,** n
Abflughalle f

depend (on), di-pend (onn),
v (be conditional on)
abhängen von; (rely on)
sich verlassen auf; **–ant,** n
Angehörige(r) m & f;
–ent, adj abhängig; **that
–s,** es kommt darauf an

depict, di-**pikt,** v darstellen

depleted, di-**plie**-tidd, adj
erschöpft

deplorable, di-**plor**-re-b'l, adj
bedauerlich

deplore, di-**plor,** v bedauern,
mißbilligen

deploy, di-**pleu,** v einsetzen

deport, di-**port,** v
abschieben

deportation, die-port-**eh**-
sch'n, n Abschiebung f

depose, di-**pohs,** *v* absetzen

deposit, di-**pos**-itt, *n*
(payment) Anzahlung *f*;
(security) Kaution *f*; (in
bank) Guthaben *nt*;
(sediment) Ablagerung *f*;
v (money) einzahlen;
(load) ablegen; **– account,**
n Sparkonto *nt*

depot, depp-oh, *n* Depot *nt*,
Lagerhaus *nt*

depraved, di-**prehwd,** *adj*
verdorben

depreciate, di-**prie**-schi-eht,
v an Wert verlieren

depreciation, di-prie-schi-
eh-sch'n, *n*
Wertminderung *f*

depress, di-**press,** *v* (press
down) niederdrücken; *fig*
deprimieren

depression, di-**presch**-'n, *n*
(low mood) Depression *f*;
(economic)
Wirtschaftskrise *f*; (in
ground) Vertiefung *f*;
(atmospheric) Tief *nt*

deprivation, depp-ri-**weh**-
sch'n, *n* (taking)
Beraubung *f*; (lack)
Entbehrung *f*

deprive (of), di-**preiw** (ew),
v berauben; **–d,** *adj*
benachteiligt

depth, depth, *n* Tiefe *f*

deputize (for), depp-ju-teis
(vor), *v* vertreten

deputy, depp-ju-ti, *n*
Stellvertreter *m*

derailed, di-**rehld, be –,** *v*
entgleisen

derailment, di-**rehl**-ment, *n*
Entgleisung *f*

deranged, di-**rehndschd,** *v*
geistesgestört

derelict, de-ri-lickt, *adj*
verlassen

deride, di-**reid,** *v* auslachen

derisory, di-**rei**-sse-ri, *adj*
(sum) lächerlich;
(laughter) spöttisch

derive (from), di-**reiw**
(frem), *v* (deduce)
ableiten (von); (obtain)
gewinnen (aus)

derogatory, di-**rogg**-e-tri, *adj*
abfällig

descend, di-**ssend,** *v*
(person) hinuntergehen;
(vehicle) hinunterfahren;
(lower o.s.) sich
erniedrigen; **–ant,** *n*
Nachkomme *m*; **be –ed
from,** *v* abstammen von

descent, di-**ssent,** *n* Abstieg
m; (ancestry)
Abstammung *f*

describe, di-**skreib,** *v*
beschreiben

description, di-**skripp**-sch'n,
n Beschreibung *f*

descriptive, di-**skripp**-tiw,
adj anschaulich

desecrate, dess-i-kreht, *v*
entweihen

desert, des-ert, *n* Wüste *f*

desert, di-**sört,** *v* verlassen;
mil desertieren; **–er,** *n mil*
Deserteur *m*; **–ion,** *n*
Verlassen *nt*; *mil*
Desertion *f*

deserve, di-**sörw,** *v*

verdienen

deserving, di-**sör**-wing, *adj*
verdienstvoll

design, di-**sein,** *n*
(intention) Absicht *f*;
(sketch) Entwurf *m*; (of
machine) Konstruktion *f*;
(pattern) Muster *nt*; *v*
(sketch) entwerfen;
(machine) konstruieren

designate, des-igg-net, *adj*
designiert

designate, des-igg-neht, *v*
ernennen

designer, di-**sei**-ner, *n*
Designer *m*

desirable, di-**seir**-re-b'l, *adj*
wünschenswert

desire, di-**seir,** *n* (wish)
Wunsch *m*; (craving)
Verlangen *nt*; *v* (sich)
wünschen; (sexually)
begehren

desist (from), di-**sist** (frem),
v absehen von

desk, desk, *n* Schreibtisch
m; (school) Pult *nt*;
(reception) Empfang *m*

desolate, dess-e-let, *adj*
trostlos

despair, diss-**pähr,** *n*
Verzweiflung *f*; **– (of),** *v*
verzweifeln (an)

despatch, diss-**pätsch,** *n*
(sending) Absendung *f*;
(message) Meldung *f*; *v*
abschicken

desperate, dess-pe-ret, *adj*
verzweifelt; (urgent)
dringend

desperation, dess-pe-**reh**-

sch'n, n Verzweiflung f

despicable, diss-**pick**-e-b'l, adj verächtlich

despise, diss-**peis,** v verachten

despite, diss-**peit,** prep trotz

despondent, diss-**ponn**-dent, adj niedergeschlagen

despot, dess-pet, n Despot m

dessert, di-**sört,** n Nachtisch m, Dessert nt

destination, dess-ti-**neh**-sch'n, n (of goods) Bestimmungsort m; (of person) Reiseziel nt

destiny, dess-ti-ni, n Schicksal nt

destitute, dess-ti-tjuht, adj mittellos

destroy, diss-**treu,** v zerstören, vernichten

destruction, diss-**track**-sch'n, n Zerstörung f

destructive, diss-**track**-tiw, adj zerstörend

detach, di-**tätsch,** v (loosen) loslösen; (take off) abnehmen; –ed, (house) Einzel-; (attitude) distanziert; –ment, n mil Sonderkommando nt; (attitude) Abstand m

detail, die-tehl, n Einzelheit f; v (relate) erzählen; (list) aufführen; –ed, adj detailliert

detain, di-tehn, v (delay) aufhalten; (imprison) in Haft halten

detect, di-**tekt,** v entdecken; –ion, n Entdeckung f;

–ive, n Detektiv m; –ive story, n Kriminalgeschichte f, Krimi m

détente, deh-**tahnt,** n Entspannung f

detention, di-**tenn**-sch'n, n (captivity) Haft f; (school) Nachsitzen nt

deter, di-**tör,** v abschrecken

detergent, di-**tör**-dschent, n Waschmittel nt

deteriorate, di-**tier**-ri-e-reht, v sich verschlechtern

determination, di-tör-mi-**neh**-sch'n, n Entschlossenheit f

determine, di-**tör**-minn, v bestimmen; –d, adj entschlossen

deterrent, di-**te**-rent, n Abschreckungsmittel nt

detest, di-**test,** v verabscheuen

detonate, dett-e-neht, v explodieren lassen

detour, die-tuhr, n Umweg m

detract (from), di-**träckt** (frem), v beeinträchtigen, schmälern

detrimental, dett-ri-menn-t'l, adj schädlich

devaluation, di-wäll-juh-**eh**-sch'n, n Abwertung f

devalue, di-**wäll**-juh, v abwerten

devastate, dew-ass-teht, v verwüsten; fig umhauen

develop, di-**well**-ep, v entwickeln; –ing country,

n Entwicklungsland nt; –ment, n Entwicklung f

deviate (from), die-wi-eht (frem), v abweichen (von)

device, di-weiss, n Gerät nt

devil, dew-'l, n Teufel m; –ish, adj teuflisch

devious, die-wi-ess, adj (method, act) fragwürdig; (person, mind) verschlagen

devise, di-weis, v sich ausdenken

devoid of, di-weud ew, prep ohne, frei von

devote (to), di-woht (tu), v (self, time) widmen; (resources) bestimmen (für); –d, adj ergeben

devotion, di-woh-sch'n, n (loyalty) Ergebenheit f; (duty) Hingabe f; –s, npl relig Andacht f

devour, di-wau-er, v verschlingen

devout, di-waut, adj fromm

dew, djuh, n Tau m

dexterity, decks-te-ri-ti, n Geschicklichkeit f

diabetes, dei-e-bie-ties, n Zuckerkrankheit f

diabetic, dei-e-bett-ick, adj (person) zuckerkrank; (food) Diabetiker-; n Diabetiker m

diabolical, di-e-boll-i-k'l, adj teuflisch

diagnose, dei-e-gnohs, v diagnostizieren

diagnosis, dei-e-gnoh-ssiss, n Diagnose f

diagonal, dei-**ägg**-e-n'l, *adj*
diagonal; *n* Diagonale *f*

diagram, **dei**-e-grämm, *n*
Diagramm *nt*

dial, **dei**-el, *n* (clock)
Zifferblatt *nt*; (telephone)
Wählscheibe *f*; *v* wählen

dialect, **dei**-e-lekt, *n*
Mundart *f*, Dialekt *m*

dialogue, **dei**-e-logg, *n*
Dialog *m*

diameter, dei-**ämm**-i-ter, *n*
Durchmesser *m*

diamond, **dei**-e-mend, *n*
Diamant *m*; **–s**, *npl* (cards)
Karo *nt*

diaphragm, **dei**-e-främm, *n*
(anatomy) Zwerchfell *nt*;
(contraceptive) Pessar *nt*

diarrhoea, dei-e-**rie**-e, *n*
Durchfall *m*

diary, **dei**-e-ri, *n* (for
appointments)
Terminkalender *m*;
(journal) Tagebuch *nt*

dice, deiss, *npl* Würfel *pl*

dictate, dick-**teht**, *v*
diktieren

dictation, dick-**teh**-sch'n, *n*
Diktat *nt*

dictator, dick-**teh**-ter, *n*
Diktator *m*; **–ship**, *n*
Diktatur *f*

dictionary, **dick**-schen-e-ri,
n Wörterbuch *nt*

die, dei, *n* Würfel *m*; *v*
sterben; **– away,** (of
sound) leiser werden; (of
wind, anger) sich legen; **–
out,** aussterben

diesel, **die**-s'l, *n* Diesel *m*

diet, **dei**-et, *n* (food)
Nahrung *f*; (slimming)
Abmagerungskur *f*;
(special) Diät *f*; *v* eine
Abmagerungskur machen

differ, **diff**-er, *v* (be
dissimilar) sich
unterscheiden; (disagree)
nicht übereinstimmen;
–ence, *n* Unterschied *m*;
(between amounts)
Differenz *f*; **–ent**, *adj*
verschieden

difficult, **diff**-i-k'lt, *adj*
schwer, schwierig; **–y**, *n*
Schwierigkeit *f*

diffident, **diff**-i-dent, *adj*
zaghaft, schüchtern

diffuse, diff-**juhss**, *adj*
weitschweifig

diffuse, diff-**juhs**, *v*
verbreiten

dig, dig, *v* graben; **– in**, *mil*
sich eingraben; (*fam* eat)
reinhauen; **– up,**
ausgraben

digest, di-**dschest**, *v*
verdauen; **–ion**, *n*
Verdauung *f*

digit, **didsch**-itt, *n* Ziffer *f*;
–al, *adj* Digital-

dignified, **digg**-ni-feid, *adj*
würdevoll

dignitary, **digg**-ni-te-ri, *n*
Würdenträger *m*

dignity, **digg**-ni-ti, *n*
Würde *f*

digress, dei-**gress**, *v*
abschweifen

dilapidated, di-**läpp**-i-deh-
tidd, *adj* verfallen

dilate, dei-**leht**, *v* (sich)
weiten

dilemma, dei-**lemm**-e, *n*
Dilemma *nt*

diligent, **dill**-i-dschent, *adj*
fleißig

dilute, dei-**luht**, *v*
verdünnen

dim, dimm, *adj* trüb,
schwach; (*fam* stupid)
dumm; *v* verdunkeln

dimension, dei-**menn**-sch'n,
n Dimension *f*

diminish, di-**minn**-isch, *v*
(sich) verringern

diminutive, di-**minn**-ju-tiw,
adj winzig

dimple, **dimm**-p'l, *n*
Grübchen *nt*

din, dinn, *n* Getöse *nt*

dine, dein, *v* speisen

dingy, **dinn**-dschi, *adj* düster

dinghy, **ding**-gi, *n* (sailing)
Dinghy *nt*; (inflatable)
Schlauchboot *nt*

dining car, **dei**-ning kahr, *n*
Speisewagen *m*

dining room, **dei**-ning
ruhm, *n* Eßzimmer *nt*,
Speisezimmer *nt*

dinner, **dinn**-er, *n* (evening)
Abendessen *nt*; (midday)
Mittagessen *nt*; (formal)
Essen *nt*; **– jacket,** *n*
Smoking *m*

dip, dipp, *n* (slope) Abfall
m; (swim) kurzes Bad *nt*; *v*
(of ground) sich senken;
(into liquid) eintauchen;
(headlights) abblenden

diploma, di-**ploh**-me, *n*

Diplom nt

diplomacy, di-**ploh**-me-ssi, n
Diplomatie f

diplomat, dipp-le-mätt, n
Diplomat m; **–ic,** adj
diplomatisch

dire, deir, adj entsetzlich

direct, dei-**reckt,** adj direkt;
v (manage) leiten; (order)
anweisen; (film) Regie
führen; **– sb (to),** jdm den
Weg sagen (zu); **–ion,** n
(way) Richtung f;
(management) Leitung f;
(of film) Regie f;
–ions, npl (to place)
Wegbeschreibung f;
(for use)
Bedienungsanleitung f

directly, di-**rekt**-li, adv
direkt; (immediately)
sofort

director, di-**reck**-ter, n
(manager) Direktor m,
Leiter m; (of film)
Regisseur m; **–y,** n
(telephone) Telefonbuch
nt; (trade) Verzeichnis nt

dirt, dört, n Schmutz m; **–
cheap,** adj spottbillig; **–y,**
adj schmutzig

disability, diss-e-**bill**-i-ti, n
Behinderung f

disabled, diss-**eh**-b'ld, adj
behindert

disadvantage, diss-ed-**wahn**-
tidsch, n Nachteil m

disagree, diss-e-**grie,** v nicht
übereinstimmen; **–able,**
adj unangenehm; **–ment,**
n (between opinions)

Uneinigkeit f; (between
figures etc.) Diskrepanz f

disallow, diss-e-**lau,** v nicht
zulassen

disappear, diss-e-**pier,** v
verschwinden; **–ance,** n
Verschwinden nt

disappoint, diss-e-**peunt,** v
enttäuschen; **–ment,** n
Enttäuschung f

disapproval, diss-e-**pruh**-w'l,
n Mißbilligung f

disapprove (of), diss-e-
pruhw (ew), v mißbilligen

disarm, diss-**ahrm,** v
(person) entwaffnen; mil
abrüsten; **–ament,** n
Abrüstung f

disaster, di-**sahss**-ter, n
Katastrophe f

disastrous, di-**sahss**-tress adj
verheerend

disc, disk, n Scheibe f;
(record) Platte f; (CD)
Compact Disc f

discard, diss-**kahrd,** v
(throw away)
ausrangieren; (reject)
verwerfen; (cards)
abwerfen

discern, di-**ssörn,** v
(distinguish)
unterscheiden; (perceive)
wahrnehmen; **–ing,** adj
kritisch

discharge, diss-tschardsch, n
(dismissal) Entlassung f;
(of gun) Abfeuern nt; med
Ausfluß m; elec Entladung
f; v (fulfil) nachkommen;
(release) freisprechen;

(dismiss) entlassen;
(cargo) ausladen; (gun)
abfeuern

disciple, di-**ssei**-p'l, n
Jünger m

discipline, di-ssi-plinn, n
Disziplin f

disc jockey, disk dscho-ki, n
Diskjockey m

disclaim, diss-**klehm,** v
abstreiten

disclose, diss-**klohs,** v
bekanntmachen,
enthüllen

disclosure, diss-**kloh**-scher,
n Enthüllung f

disco, diss-koh, n (abbr
discotheque), Disko f

discolour, diss-**kall**-er, v
verfärben

discomfort, diss-**kamm**-fert,
n Unbehagen nt

disconcerted, diss-ken-**ssör**-
tidd, adj beunruhigt

disconnect, diss-ke-**nekt,** v
(objects) trennen; (power
etc.) abstellen

discontent, diss-ken-**tent,** n
Unzufriedenheit f; **–ed,** adj
unzufrieden

discontinue, diss-ken-**tinn**-
juh, v (production)
einstellen; (conversation,
project) abbrechen

discord, diss-kord, n
Zwietracht f; mus
Dissonanz f

discordant, diss-**kor**-d'nt,
adj unharmonisch; mus
dissonant

discount, diss-kaunt, n

Skonto m/nt; (trade) Rabatt m; **at a –**, mit Rabatt

discount, diss-kaunt, v (reduce) diskontieren; (ignore) nicht berücksichtigen

discotheque, diss-ke-teck, n Diskothek f

discourage, diss-ka-ridsch, v (dishearten) entmutigen; (dissuade) abraten

discourteous, diss-kör-ti-ess, adj unhöflich

discover, diss-ka-wer, v entdecken; **–y,** n Entdeckung f

discredit, diss-kredd-itt, v unglaubwürdig machen

discreet, diss-kriet, adj diskret

discrepancy, diss-krepp-en-ssi, n Diskrepanz f

discriminate, diss-krimm-i-neht, v **– (between),** unterscheiden (zwischen); **– (against),** diskriminieren

discriminating, diss-krimm-i-neh-ting, adj kritisch

discrimination, diss-krimm-i-neh-sch'n, n (judgement) Urteilsvermögen nt; (unfair) Diskriminierung f

discuss, diss-kass, v diskutieren, besprechen; **–ion,** n Diskussion f, Besprechung f

disdain, diss-dehn, n Verachtung f; v verachten;

–ful, adj verächtlich

disease, di-sies, n Krankheit f; **–d,** adj krank

disembark, diss-imm-bark, v von Bord gehen

disenchanted, diss-inn-tschahn-tidd, adj desillusioniert

disengage, diss-inn-gehdsch, v (detach) losmachen; (clutch) auskuppeln

disentangle, diss-inn-täng-g'l, v entwirren

disfigure, diss-figg-er, v entstellen

disgrace, diss-grehss, n Schande f; v Schande bringen über; **–ful,** adj skandalös

disgruntled, diss-grann-t'ld, adj verstimmt

disguise, diss-geis, n Verkleidung f; v verkleiden; fig verschleiern

disgust, diss-gast, n Ekel m; v anekeln

dish, disch, n (bowl) Schüssel f; (food) Gericht nt; **–cloth,** Spüllappen m; **– up,** v auftischen

dishearten, diss-hahr-t'n, v entmutigen

dishevelled, di-schew-'ld, adj (hair) zerzaust; (clothes) unordentlich

dishonest, diss-onn-ist, adj unehrlich

dishonour, diss-onn-er, n Unehre f; v entehren

dishwasher, disch-u'osch-er,

n Geschirrspülmaschine f

disillusion, di-ssi-luh-sch'n, v ernüchtern, desillusionieren

disincentive, diss-inn-senn-tiw, n Entmutigung f

disinfect, diss-inn-fekt, v desinfizieren

disintegrate, diss-inn-ti-greht, v zerfallen

disjointed, diss-dscheun-tidd, adj zusammenhanglos

disk, disk, n comp (hard) Festplatte f; (floppy) Diskette f; **– drive,** n Diskettenlaufwerk nt

dislike, diss-leik, n Abneigung f; v nicht mögen

dislocate, diss-le-keht, v med verrenken; fig in Verwirrung bringen

dislodge, diss-lodsch, v entfernen, lösen

disloyal, diss-leu-el, adj treulos

dismal, dis-mel, adj (place) düster; (failure) kläglich

dismantle, diss-männ-t'l, v demontieren

dismay, diss-meh, n Bestürzung f; v bestürzen

dismiss, diss-miss, v (person) entlassen; (idea) abtun

dismount, diss-maunt, v absteigen

disobedient, diss-e-bie-di-ent, adj ungehorsam

disobey, diss-e-beh, v nicht gehorchen

disorder, di-ssor-der, n
(untidiness) Unordnung f;
(disturbance) Unruhen pl;
med Beschwerden pl; **–ly,**
adj (untidy) unordentlich;
(unruly) undiszipliniert

disorganized, di-ssor-ge-
neisd, adj chaotisch

disorientated, di-ssor-ri-en-
teh-tidd, adj verwirrt

disown, di-ssohn, v nicht
anerkennen; (person)
verstoßen

disparaging, diss-pä-ri-
dsching, adj geringschätzig

disparity, diss-pä-ri-ti, n
Ungleichheit f

dispatch, see **despatch**

dispel, diss-pell, v vertreiben

dispensary, diss-penn-se-ri,
n Apotheke f

dispense, diss-penss, v
verteilen; med abgeben; –
with, verzichten auf

dispensing chemist, diss-
penn-ssing kemm-ist, n
Apotheker m

disperse, diss-pörss, v (sich)
zerstreuen

displaced person, diss-
plehst pör-ss'n, adj
Verschleppte(r) m & f

display, diss-pleh, n (of
goods) Auslage f; (show)
Schau f; v (goods)
ausstellen; (interest etc.)
zeigen; (show off)
vorführen

displease, diss-plies, v
mißfallen; **–d,** adj
verstimmt

displeasure, diss-plesch-er, n
Mißfallen nt

disposable, diss-poh-se-b'l,
adj Wegwerf-; **– nappy,** n
Wegwerfwindel f

disposal, diss-poh-sel, n
(throwing away)
Beseitigung f, Entsorgung
f; **be at sb's –,** v (be
available) jdm zur
Verfügung stehen

dispose of, diss-pohs ew, v
(throw away) beseitigen,
entsorgen; (have
available) verfügen über

disposed, diss-pohsd, adj
geneigt

disposition, diss-pe-sisch-'n,
n Natur f

disproportionate, diss-pre-
por-sche-net, adj
unverhältnismäßig

disprove, diss-pruhw, v
widerlegen

dispute, diss-pjuht, n Streit
m; v bestreiten

disqualify, diss-ku'o-li-fai, v
disqualifizieren

disquiet, diss-ku'ai-et, n
Unruhe f; v beunruhigen

disregard, diss-ri-gahrd, n
Nichtbeachtung f; v nicht
beachten

disreputable, diss-repp-ju-
te-b'l, adj verrufen;
(appearance)
unansehnlich

disrepute, diss-ri-pjuht, n
Verruf m

disrespect, diss-ri-spekt, n

Respeklosigkeit f; **–ful,** adj
respektlos

disrupt, diss-rapt, v stören;
–ion, n Störung f

dissatisfied, diss-ssätt-iss-
feid, adj unzufrieden

dissect, di-ssekt, v sezieren

disseminate, di-ssemm-in-
eht, v verbreiten

dissent, di-ssent, n
Meinungsverschiedenheit
f; v anderer Meinung sein

dissident, diss-i-dent, adj
dissident; n Dissident m

dissimilar, diss-ssimm-i-ler,
adj unähnlich

dissipate, diss-i-peht, v (use
up) verschwenden;
(disappear) (sich)
auflösen

dissociate, di-ssoh-ssi-eht, v
trennen; **– o.s. from,** sich
distanzieren von

dissolute, diss-e-luht, adj
zügellos

dissolve, di-solw, v (sich)
auflösen

dissuade (from), di-ssu'ehd
(frem), v ausreden

distance, diss-tenss, n
Entfernung f; (gap)
Abstand m; v **– o.s. from,**
sich distanzieren von; **in
the –,** in der Ferne

distant, diss-tent, adj (in
space) entfernt, fern; (in
time) fern; (in attitude)
distanziert

distaste, diss-tehst, n
Widerwille m; **–ful,** adj
zuwider

distended, diss-**tenn**-didd, *adj* aufgebläht

distil, diss-**till**, *v* destillieren; **-lery,** n Brennerei *f*

distinct, diss-**tinkt**, *adj* (clear) deutlich; (different) verschieden; **-ion,** n (difference) Unterschied *m*; (eminence) Auszeichnung *f*; **-ive,** *adj* unverwechselbar

distinguish, diss-**ting**-gu'ish, *v* unterscheiden; **-ed,** *adj* berühmt; **-ing,** *adj* kennzeichnend; **– o.s.,** *v* sich auszeichnen

distort, diss-**tort**, *v* verdrehen, verrenken

distract, diss-**träckt**, *v* ablenken; **-ion,** n (interruption) Ablenkung *f*; (distress) Verstörung *f*

distress, diss-**tress**, n (danger) Not *f*; (worry) Sorge *f*; (pain) Leiden *nt*; *v* **– sb/o.s.,** jdm/sich Sorgen machen; **-ing,** *adj* bedrückend, bestürzend

distribute, diss-**tribb**-juht, *v* verteilen

distribution, diss-**tribb-juh**-sch'n, n Verteilung *f*

distributor, diss-**tribb**-juh-ter, n (car) Verteiler *m*; (wholesaler) Großhändler *m*

district, diss-**trikt**, n Bezirk *m*

distrust, diss-**trast**, n Mißtrauen *nt*; *v* mißtrauen

disturb, diss-**törb**, *v* (disrupt) stören; (worry) beunruhigen; **-ance,** n Störung *f*; (trouble) Unruhe *f*; **-ing,** *adj* störend; beunruhigend

disuse, diss-**juhss**, n **fall into –,** *v* außer Gebrauch kommen

disused, diss-**juhsd**, *v* außer Gebrauch; (building) leerstehend; (factory etc.) stillgelegt

ditch, ditsch, n Graben *m*; *v fam* fallenlassen

dither, didh-er, *v fam* zaudern

ditto, ditt-oh, *adv* gleichfalls, dito

dive, deiw, n (by swimmer) Kopfsprung *m*; (by plane) Sturzflug *m*; *v* (jump) springen; (under water) tauchen; **-r,** n (under water) Taucher *m*

diverge, dei-**wördsch**, *v* (voneinander) abweichen

diverse, dei-**wörss**, *adj* verschieden

diversion, dei-**wör**-sch'n, n (distraction) Ablenkung *f*; (from route) Umleitung *f*; (amusement) Zerstreuung *f*

diversity, dei-**wör**-ssi-ti, n Vielfalt *f*

divert, dei-**wört**, *v* (distract) ablenken; (re-route) umleiten; (amuse) zerstreuen

divide, di-**weid**, *v* (separate) trennen; (split up) (sich) teilen

diving, dei-wing, n (into water) Springen *nt*; (under water) Tauchen *nt*; **– board,** n Sprungbrett *nt*

divine, di-**wein**, *adj* göttlich

division, di-**wisch**-'n, n (separation) Teilung *f*; (part) Teil *m*; (maths, mil) Division *f*; (disagreement) Uneinigkeit *f*

divorce, di-**worss**, n Scheidung *f*; *v* sich scheiden lassen (von); **-d,** *adj* geschieden

divulge, dei-**waldsch**, *v* preisgeben

DIY, die ei u'ei, *abbr* do-it-yourself

dizzy, dis-i, *adj* schwindlig

DJ, die dschei, *abbr* disc jockey

do, duh, *v* tun, machen; (clean) putzen; (be suitable) passen; (be adequate) reichen; **– up,** (fasten) zumachen; (renovate) renovieren; **– without,** ohne auskommen; **can/could – with,** brauchen können; **he's -ing well/badly;** es geht ihm gut/schlecht; **how do you –?** Guten Tag; **make – (with),** auskommen (mit)

docile, doh-sseil, *adj* lenksam

dock, dock, n Dock *nt*; *law* Anklagebank *f*; *v* (of ship) anlegen; (of spaceship) docken; **–er,** n Hafenarbeiter m; **–s,** npl Hafen m; **–yard,** n Werft f

doctor, dock-ter, n (medical) Arzt m, Ärztin f; (title) Doktor m; v (evidence) verfälschen; (food, drink) etw beimischen

document, dock-ju-ment, n Urkunde f, Dokument nt; **–ary,** n (film) Dokumentarfilm m; adj urkundlich

dodge, dodsch, n Kniff m; v ausweichen

dog, dogg, n Hund m; **– collar,** n Hundehalsband nt; (vicar's) Kragen m

dogged, dogg-idd, adj hartnäckig

dogmatic, dogg-mätt-ick, adj dogmatisch

do-it-yourself, duh itt yor-**sself,** n Do-it-yourself nt

dole, dohl, n fam Stempelgeld nt; **be on the –,** v fam stempeln gehen; **– out,** v austeilen

doleful, dohl-full, adj traurig

doll, doll, n Puppe f

dollar, doll-er, n Dollar m

dolphin, doll-finn, n Delphin m

dome, dohm, n Kuppel f

domestic, de-**mess**-tick, n Hausangestellte(r) m & f; adj Haus-; (not international) Innen-, Binnen-; **–ated,** adj

häuslich

dominant, domm-i-nent, adj dominierend

dominate, domm-i-neht, v beherrschen

domineering, domm-i-nier-ring, adj tyrannisch

dominion, de-**minn**-jen, n (territory) Staatsgebiet nt

donate, doh-**neht,** v spenden

donation, doh-**neh**-sch'n, n Spende f

donkey, dong-ki, n Esel m

donor, doh-ner, n Spender m

doodle, duh-**d'l,** v kritzeln

doom, duhm, n Verhängnis nt; **be –ed,** v verdammt sein; **Doomsday,** n jüngster Tag m

door, dor, n Tür f; **–bell,** n Türklingel f; **on the –step,** fig direkt vor der Tür; **–way,** n Eingang m

dope, dohp, n fam Rauschgift nt; sport Aufputschmittel nt; v dopen; **–y,** adj (stupid) bekloppt; (sleepy) benebelt

dormant, dor-ment, adj ruhend

dormitory, dor-mi-tri, n Schlafsaal m; **– town,** n Schlafstadt f

dosage, doh-ssidsch, n Dosierung f

dose, dohss, n Dosis f

dot, dott, n Punkt m; **–ted,** adj (line) punktiert;

(scattered) verstreut; (patterned) übersät; **on the –,** pünktlich

double, dabb-'l, adj & adv doppelt; n Doppelte nt; (likeness) Doppelgänger m; v (sich) verdoppeln; **–bass,** n Kontrabaß m; **–bed,** n Doppelbett nt; **–cross,** v hintergehen; **–room,** n Doppelzimmer nt; **–s,** npl (tennis) Doppel nt

doubt, daut, n Zweifel m; v bezweifeln; **–ful,** adj zweifelhaft; **–less,** adv ohne Zweifel

dough, doh, n Teig m; **–nut,** n Berliner m

dove, daw, n Taube f; **–cot,** n Taubenschlag m

dowdy, dau-di, adj altmodisch

down, daun, adv & prep herunter, hinunter; n (feathers) Flaum m; **–and-out,** n Tramp m; **–cast,** adj niedergeschlagen; **–fall,** n Sturz m; **–hill,** adv bergab; **–pour,** n Platzregen m; **Downs,** npl (hills) Hügelland m; **–stairs,** adv (nach) unten; **–to-earth,** adj praktisch; **–wards,** adv abwärts, nach unten

doze, dohs, n Nickerchen nt; v dösen; **– off,** einnicken

dozen, das-en, n Dutzend nt

drab, dräbb, adj langweilig

draft, drahft, n (rough) Entwurf m; fin Wechsel m;

v entwerfen

drag, drägg, *v* (object)
schleppen; (behind)
hinterherhinken; *n fam*
Plage *f*; **in –,** in
Frauenkleidung

dragon, drägg-en, *n* Drache
m; **–fly,** Libelle *f*

drain, drehn, *n* Abfluß *m*; *fig*
Belastung *f*; *v* (land)
entwässern; (vegetables)
abtropfen lassen;
(resources) auslaugen;
–age, *n* Kanalisation *f*; **–
away,** *v* (of liquid)
ablaufen

drama, drah-me, *n* Drama *nt*

dramatic, dre-mätt-ick, *adj*
dramatisch

drastic, dräss-tick, *adj*
drastisch

draught, drahft, *adj* (beer)
vom Faß; *n* (air) Zug *m*;
(drink) Schluck *m*;
(sketch) Entwurf *m*; *naut*
Tiefgang *m*; **–board,**
Damebrett *nt*; **–s,** *pl*
Damespiel *nt*

draughtsman, drahfts-men,
n Zeichner *m*

draw, dro'a, *n* (lottery)
Ziehung *f*; (tie)
unentschiedenes Spiel *nt*;
v (pull) ziehen; (sketch)
zeichnen; (crowd)
anlocken; (money)
abheben; (cheque)
ausstellen; **–back,** *n*
Nachteil *m*

drawer, dro'a, *n* (furniture)
Schublade *f*; (bill)

Aussteller *m*; **–s,** *npl*
Unterhosen *pl*

drawing, dro'a-ing, *n*
(picture) Zeichnung *f*;
(act) Zeichnen *nt*; **–
room,** Salon *m*

drawl, dro'al, *v* schleppend
sprechen

dread, dredd, *n* Furcht *f*; *v*
fürchten; **–ful,** *adj*
furchtbar

dream, driem, *n* Traum *m*; *v*
träumen; **–y,** *adj* verträumt

dreary, drier-ri, *adj* (dull)
trüb; (boring) langweilig

dredge, dredsch, *v*
ausbaggern; **–r,** *n* Bagger *m*

dregs, dreggs, *npl*
(Boden)satz *m*; *fig*
Abschaum *m*

drench, drentsch, *v*
durchnässen

dress, dress, *n* (garment)
Kleid *nt*; (clothing)
Kleidung *f*; *v* (sich)
anziehen; (wound)
verbinden; **get –ed,** *v* sich
anziehen; **–ing,** *n med*
Verband *m*; (cooking)
(Salat)soße *f*, Dressing *nt*;
–ing gown, *n* Bademantel
m; **–ing room,** *n* (in
house) Ankleidezimmer
nt; *sport* Umkleideraum *m*;
theatre Garderobe *f*; **–
table,** *n* Toilettentisch *m*;
–maker, *n*
(Damen)schneider *m*; **–
up,** *v* (smart) sich
feinmachen; (disguise)
sich verkleiden

dribble, dribb-'l, *v* (saliva)
sabbern; *sport* dribbeln
(mit)

drift, drift, *n* (current)
Strömung *f*; (snow etc.)
Wehe *f*; (tendency)
Richtung *f*; *v* treiben; *fig*
sich treiben lassen

drill, drill, *n mil* Drill *m*;
(tool) Bohrer *m*; *v mil*
exerzieren; (bore) bohren

drink, drink, *n* Getränk, *nt*;
v trinken; **–ing water,** *n*
Trinkwasser *nt*

drip, dripp, *n* Tropfen *nt*; *v*
tropfen; **–ping,** *n*
Bratenfett *nt*

drive, dreiw, *n* (journey)
Fahrt *f*; (approach)
Einfahrt *f*; (energy)
Schwung *m*; *v* (set in
motion) treiben; (vehicle)
fahren; (machine)
antreiben; **–r,** *n* Fahrer *m*;
disk/CD-ROM –, *n*
Disketten-/CD-ROM-
Laufwerk *nt*

drivel, driw-'l, *n fam*
Blödsinn *m*

driving licence, drei-
wing lei-ssenss, *n*
Führerschein *m*

drizzle, dris-'l, *n*
Nieselregen *m*; *v* nieseln

droll, drohl, *adj* drollig

drone, drohn, *n* (of bee)
Summen *nt*; (of engine)
Brummen *nt*; *v* summen;
brummen

droop, druhp, *v* (of eyelids)
herunterhängen; (of head)

hängen lassen; (of plant)
verwelken

drop, dropp, n (fall) Fall m;
(of liquid) Tropfen m; v
(fall) fallen; (let fall)
fallen lassen; – **off,** v
einschlafen; **–out,** n
Aussteiger m

drought, draut, n Dürre f

drown, draun, v (be
drowned) ertrinken;
(cause to drown)
ertränken

drowsy, drau-si, adj schläfrig

drudgery, dradsch-e-ri, n
Schufterei f

drug, dragg, n med
Medikament nt;
(addictive) Droge f; v
betäuben; – **addict,** n
Rauschgiftsüchtige(r) m
& f

drum, dramm, n Trommel f;
v trommeln; **–s,** npl
Schlagzeug nt; **–mer,** n
Trommler m; – **up,** v
auftreiben

drunk, drank, adj
betrunken; n Säufer m;
–ard, n Trinker m;
–enness, Betrunkenheit f

dry, drei, adj trocken; v
trocknen; – **cleaning,** n
chemische Reinigung f; –
up, v (of well etc.)
austrocknen; (dishes)
abtrocknen

dual, djuh-el, adj doppelt; –
carriageway, n zweispurige
Fahrbahn f

dubious, djuh-bi-ess, adj
zweifelhaft

duchess, datsch-ess, n
Herzogin f

duck, dack, n Ente f; v sich
ducken

dud, dadd, adj fam (cheque)
ungedeckt; (bad) mies; n
(blank, person) Niete f

due, djuh, n (share) Anteil
m; (rights) Recht nt; adj
(owing) fällig; (fitting)
gebührend; – **east,** adv
nach Osten, östlich; – **to,**
prep wegen

duel, djuh-el, n Duell nt; v
sich duellieren

dues, djuhs, npl Gebühren
fpl

duet, dju-ett, n Duett nt

duke, djuhk, n Herzog m

dull, dall, adj (weather,
colour) trüb; (boring)
langweilig; (metal) matt;
(sound, pain) dumpf

duly, djuh-li, adv (properly)
gebührend; (officially)
ordnungsgemäß

dumb, damm, adj stumm;
(fam stupid) doof;
–founded, adj verblüfft

dummy, damm-i, n
(mannequin)
Schaufensterpuppe f;
(fake) Attrappe f; (cards)
Strohmann m; (baby's)
Schnuller m; – **run,** n
Probe f

dump, damp, n Müllplatz m;
(pej place) Kaff nt; **–ing,**
n Schuttabladen nt; (comm
of exports) Dumping nt

dumpling, damp-ling, n
Kloß m, Knödel m

dune, djuhn, n Düne f

dung, dang, n Dung m,
Dünger m

dungarees, dang-ge-**ries,** npl
Latzhose f

dungeon, dann-dschen, n
Verließ nt

dupe, djuhp, n
Angeführte(r) m & f; v
anführen

duplicate, djuh-pli-ket, adj
doppelt; n Duplikat nt

duplicate, djuh-pli-keht, v
(repeat) wiederholen;
(make copies) kopieren,
vervielfältigen

durable, djur-re-b'l, adj
(lasting) dauerhaft; (hard-
wearing) strapazierfähig

duration, djur-reh-sch'n, n
Dauer f

duress, djur-ress, n under –,
unter Zwang

during, djur-ring, prep
während

dusk, dask, n Dämmerung f

dust, dast, n Staub m; v
abstauben; (cooking)
bestäuben; **–bin,** n
Mülleimer m; **–er,** n
Staubtuch nt; **–man,** n
Müllmann m; **–y,** adj
staubig

Dutch, datsch, adj
holländisch;
niederländisch; n
(language) Niederländisch
nt; npl (people) Holländer
pl, Niederländer pl; **–man,**

n Holländer m,
Niederländer m

dutiful, djuh-ti-full, *adj*
pflichtbewußt

duty, djuh-ti, n Pflicht *f*;
(tax) Zoll *m*; **on –**, im
Dienst

duvet, duh-weh/**djuh**-weh,
n Federbett *nt*

dwarf, du'orf, n Zwerg *m*; *v*
überragen

dwell, duell, *v* wohnen; **–er**,
n Bewohner *m*; **–ing**,
Wohnung *f*; **– on**, grübeln
über

dwindle, du'inn-d'l, *v*
schwinden, abnehmen

dye, dei, n Farbstoff *m*; *v*
färben

dying, dei-ing, *adj* (person)
sterbend; (species)
aussterbend

dynamic, dei-**nämm**-ick, *adj*
dynamisch

dynamite, dei-*ne*-meit, n
Dynamit *nt*

dynamo, dei-*ne*-moh, n
Dynamo *m*

dyslexia, diss-**leck**-ssi-*e*, n
Legasthenie *f*

dyslexic, diss-**leck**-ssick, *adj*
legasthenisch; n
Legastheniker *m*

each, ietsch, *adj & pron*
jede(r/s); **– other,** uns/sich
(gegenseitig), einander;
two –, je zwei

eager(ly), ie-ger, *adj & adv*
eifrig; **–ness,** n Eifer *m*

eagle, ie-g'l, *n* Adler *m*

ear, ier, *n* Ohr *nt;* (of wheat)
Ähre *f*

earl, örl, *n* Graf *m*

early, ör-li, *adj & adv* früh

earmark, ier-mark, *v*
bestimmen

earn, örn, *v* verdienen

earnest, ör-nist, *adj*
ernsthaft; *n* Ernst *m;* **in –,**
im Ernst

earnings, ör-nings, *npl*
Verdienst *m*

earphones, ier-fohns, *npl*
Kopfhörer *m*

earring, ier-ring, *n*
Ohrring *m*

earshot, ier-schott, *n*

(with)in – in Hörweite *f*

earth, örth, *n* Erde *f; v*
(electricity) erden;
–enware, n Steingut *nt;*
–ly, *adj* irdisch; **no –
reason,** *fam* nicht der
geringste Grund

earthquake, örth-ku'ehk, *n*
Erdbeben *nt*

earwig, ier-u'igg, *n*
Ohrwurm *m*

ease, ies, *n* (comfort)
Behagen *nt;* (simplicity)
Leichtigkeit *f; v* (pain)
lindern; (mind, task)
erleichtern; **at (one's) –,**
ungezwungen

easel, ie-s'l, *n* Staffelei *f*

easily, ie-si-li, *adv* leicht

east, iest, *adj* östlich, Ost-;
adv östlich, nach Osten; *n*
Osten *m*

Easter, iess-ter, *adj* Oster-; *n*
Ostern *nt*

easterly, iess-ter-li, *adj*
östlich

eastern, iess-tern, *adj*
östlich, Ost-; orientalisch

easy, ie-si, *adj & adv*
(simple) leicht; (relaxed)
ungezwungen; **– chair,** n
Sessel *m;* **––going,** *adj*
gelassen

eat, iet, *v* essen; (of animals)
fressen; **– away,** (corrode)
zerfressen; **– into,**
(corrode) zerfressen; (use
up) angreifen

eavesdrop, iews-dropp, *v*
lauschen; **–er,** n Horcher
m; **– on,** *v* belauschen

ebb, ebb, *n* Ebbe *f; –
(away),** *v* abebben

ebony, ebb-*e*-ni, *n*
Ebenholz *nt*

ebullient, i-**ball**-jent, *adj*
übersprudelnd

eccentric, ek-**ssent**-rick,
adj exzentrisch; *n*
Exzentriker *m*

ecclesiastical, eck-lie-si-**äss**-
tick-'l, *adj* kirchlich

echo, eck-oh, *n* Echo *nt; v*
widerhallen

eclipse, i-**klipss,** *n* Finsternis
f; v verfinstern

ecology, i-**koll**-*e*-dschi, *n*
Ökologie *f*

economic, ie-ke-**nomm**-ick,
adj wirtschaftlich,
Wirtschafts-; **–al,** *adj*
wirtschaftlich; (thrifty)
sparsam; **–s,** *n*
Volkswirtschaft *f*

economize, i-**konn**-*e*-meis, *v*

sparen

economy, i-**konn**-*e*-mi, *n*
Wirtschaft *f*; (saving)
Sparmaßnahme *f*; (thrift)
Sparsamkeit *f*

ecstasy, **eck**-ste-ssi, *n*
Ekstase *f*, Verzückung *f*;
(drug) Ecstasy *f*

eczema, **eck**-si-me, *n*
Ekzem *nt*

eddy, edd-i, *n* Wirbel *m*; *v*
wirbeln

edge, edsch, *n* (of knife)
Schneide *f*; (brink) Rand
m; *v* (border) einfassen;
(move carefully) sich
vorsichtig bewegen; –
away, sich davonstehlen

edgy, edsch-i, *adj* nervös

edible, edd-i-b'l, *adj* eßbar,
genießbar

edifice, edd-i-fiss, *n*
Gebäude *nt*

edit, edd-itt, *v* (text)
redigieren; (film, tape)
schneiden; (publish)
herausgeben; –**ion**, *n*
Ausgabe *f*; (of book)
Auflage *f*; –**or**, *n*
Redakteur *m*; –**orial**,
adj Redaktions-; *n*
Leitartikel *m*

educate, edd-ju-keht, *v*
(aus)bilden; (child)
erziehen

education, ed-ju-**keh**-sch'n,
n Erziehung *f*;
(Aus)bildung *f*; –**al**, *adj*
pädagogisch, Erziehungs-

eel, iel, *n* Aal *m*

eerie, **ier**-ri, *adj* unheimlich

efface, eff-**ehss**, *v*
auswischen; *fig* tilgen

effect, eff-**ekt**, *n* Wirkung *f*;
v bewirken; –**ive**, *adj*
wirksam; **in –**, eigentlich;
take –, *v* in Kraft treten

effeminate, eff-**emm**-i-net,
adj unmännlich

effervescent, eff-er-**wess**-'nt,
adj sprudelnd

efficacious, eff-i-**keh**-schess,
adj wirksam

efficiency, eff-**isch**-en-ssi, *n*
Leistungsfähigkeit *f*

efficient, eff-**isch**-n't, *adj*
(person) tüchtig;
(machine) leistungsfähig

effort, eff-ert, *n*
Anstrengung *f*; –**less(ly)**,
adj & adv mühelos; **make
an –**, *v* sich anstrengen

effrontery, eff-**rann**-te-ri, *n*
Unverschämtheit *f*

effusive, eff-**juh**-ssiw, *adj*
überschwenglich

e.g., ie dschie, *abbr*, z.B.

egalitarian, egg-äll-i-**tähr**-ri-
en, *adj* egalitär,
Gleichheits-

egg, egg, *n* Ei *nt*; –**cup**,
Eierbecher *m*; – **on**, *v fam*
anstacheln

ego, ie-goh, *n* Ich *nt*; (self-
confidence)
Selbstbewußtsein *nt*

egotism, egg-*e*-tism, *n*
Ichbezogenheit *f*

egotist, egg-*e*-tist, *n*
Egozentriker *m*

Egypt, ie-dschipt, *n*
Ägypten *nt*

eiderdown, ei-der-daun, *n*
Federbett *nt*

eight, eht, *num* acht; –**een**,
num achtzehn; –**h**, *adj*
achte(r/s); *n* Achtel *nt*; –**y**,
num achtzig

Eire, ähr-re, *n* Irland *nt*

either, ei-dher, *adj & pron*
eine(r/s) von beiden; *adv*
(in negatives) auch nicht;
conj – **... or ...**, entweder
... oder ...

eject, i-**dscheckt**, *v*
ausstoßen, hinauswerfen

elaborate, i-**läbb**-*e*-ret, *adj*
kompliziert; (detailed)
sorgfältig ausgearbeitet

elaborate, i-**läbb**-*e*-reht, *v*
(work out) ausarbeiten;
(describe) ausführen

elapse, i-**läpps**, *v* vergehen

elastic, i-**läss**-tick, *n*
Gummiband *nt*; *adj*
elastisch; – **band**, *n*
Gummiband *nt*

elated, i-**leh**-tidd, *adj* freudig
erregt

elbow, **ell**-boh, *n* Ellbogen
m; – **one's way through**, *v*
sich durchdrängen

elder, **ell**-der, *adj* ältere(r/s);
n Ältere(r) *m & f*; (tree)
Holunder *m*; –**ly**, *adj*
ältlich, ältere(r/s); *npl*
Älteren *pl*

eldest, **ell**-dist, *adj*
älteste(r/s); *n* Älteste(r)
m & f

elect, i-**lekt**, *adj* designiert; *v*
wählen; –**ion**, *n* Wahl *f*;
–**or**, *n* Wähler *m*; –**orate**,

n Wählerschaft f

electric(al), i-leck-trick(-'l), *adj* elektrisch, Elektro-; – **blanket**, n Heizdecke f

electrician, i-leck-trisch-'n, n Elektriker m

electricity, i-leck-**triss**-i-ti, n Elektrizität f

electrify, i-leck-tri-fei, *v* elektrifizieren; *fig* elektrisieren

electrocute, i-leck-tre-kjuht, *v* durch Stromschlag töten

electronic, i-leck-**tronn**-ick, *adj* elektronisch; – **mail**, n E-Mail f; **–s**, n Elektronik f

elegance, ell-i-genss, n Eleganz f

elegant, ell-i-gent, *adj* elegant

element, ell-i-ment, n Element nt; **–ary**, *adj* elementar; (simple) einfach; (basic) Grund-

elephant, ell-i-fent, n Elefant m

elevate, ell-i-weht, *v* erhöhen; *fig* erheben

eleven, i-lew-en, *num* elf; **–th**, *adj* elfte(r/s)

elf, elf, n (*pl* **elves**), Elfe f, Kobold m

elicit, i-liss-itt, *v* entlocken

eligible, ell-i-dschi-b'l, *adj* (electable) wählbar; (entitled) berechtigt

eliminate, i-limm-i-neht, *v* ausscheiden

elite, i-liet, n Elite f

elm, elm, n Ulme f

elongated, ie-long-geh-tidd, *adj* langgestreckt

elope, i-lohp, *v* durchbrennen; **–ment**, n Durchbrennen nt

eloquence, ell-*e*-ku'enss, n Beredtheit f

eloquent, ell-*e*-ku'ent, *adj* beredt

else, elss, *adv* andere(r/s); sonst; **or –**, *conj* sonst, oder

elsewhere, elss-u'ähr, *adv* woanders(hin), sonstwo(hin)

elucidate, i-luh-ssi-deht, *v* erläutern; (mystery) aufklären

elude, i-luhd, *v* entkommen

elusive, i-luhss-iw, *adj* schwer faßbar; (vague) ausweichend

emaciated, i-meh-ssi-eh-tidd, *adj* abgezehrt

e-mail, ie-mehl, n (*abbr* **electronic mail**), E-Mail f

emanate (from), emm-*e*-neht (frem), *v* (flow out) ausströmen (von); (originate) stammen aus

emancipate, i-männ-ssi-peht, *v* emanzipieren; (slave) freilassen

embalm, im-bahm, *v* einbalsamieren

embankment, im-bänk-ment, n (river) Uferböschung f; (road) Straßendamm m; (railway) Bahndamm m

embargo, im-bar-goh, n Embargo nt

embark, im-bark, *v* (sich) einschiffen; **– on**, *fig* anfangen

embarrass, im-bä-ress, *v* in Verlegenheit bringen; **–ed**, *adj* verlegen; **–ing**, *adj* peinlich; **–ment**, n Verlegenheit f

embassy, emm-be-ssi, n Botschaft f

embedded, imm-bedd-idd, *adj* verankert

embellish, emm-bell-isch, *v* verschönern

embers, emm-bers, *npl* Glut f

embezzle, imm-bes-'l, *v* unterschlagen, veruntreuen; **–ment**, n Unterschlagung f

embitter, imm-bitt-er, *v* verbittern

embody, imm-bodd-i, *v* (personify) verkörpern; (include) aufnehmen

embrace, imm-brehss, *v* (hug) umarmen; (contain) umfassen

embroider, imm-breu-der, *v* (be)sticken; *fig* ausschmücken; **–y**, n Stickerei f

embroiled (in), imm-breuld (inn), *adj* verwickelt (in)

emerald, emm-*e*-reld, n Smaragd m

emerge, i-mördsch, *v* auftauchen; (truth) sich herausstellen

emergency, i-**mör**-dschen-ssi, n Notfall m; **– exit,** n Notausgang m; **– landing,** n Notlandung f

emetic, i-**mett**-ick, n Brechmittel nt

emigrant, emm-i-grent, n Auswanderer m

emigrate, emm-i-greht, v auswandern

eminence, emm-i-nenss, n (distinction) hoher Rang m; (title) Eminenz f

eminent, emm-i-nent, adj (hoch)angesehen

emission, i-**misch**-'n, n (of rays) Ausstrahlung f; (of heat, smoke) Abgabe f; (of gas) Ausströmen nt; **–s,** npl Emissionen pl

emit, i-**mitt,** v ausstrahlen; abgeben; ausströmen

emotion, i-**moh**-sch'n, n Gefühl nt; **–al,** adj emotional; (moving) gefühlsgeladen; (person) leicht erregbar

emperor, emm-pe-rer, n Kaiser m

emphasis, emm-fe-ssiss, n Betonung f, Nachdruck m

emphasize, emm-fe-sseis, v betonen

emphatic(ally), emm-**fätt**-ick-(e-li), adj & adv nachdrücklich

empire, emm-peir, n Reich nt

employ, imm-**pleu,** v (person) beschäftigen; (use) anwenden; **–ee,** n

Angestellte(r) m & f; **–er,** n Arbeitgeber m; **–ment,** n Beschäftigung f; (post) Arbeitsstelle f

empower, imm-**pau**-er, v ermächtigen

empress, emm-priss, n Kaiserin f

emptiness, emp-ti-niss, n Leere f

empty, emp-ti, adj leer; v leeren; (drain away) abfließen; (become empty) sich leeren

emulate, emm-ju-leht, v nachstreben

emulation, emm-ju-**leh**-sch'n, n Nacheiferung f

enable, i-**neh**-b'l, v – sb to do sth, es jdm ermöglichen, etw zu tun

enact, i-**näckt,** v (play) aufführen; (role) spielen; law erlassen

enamel, i-**nämm-**'l, n Email nt; (tooth) Zahnschmelz m; v emaillieren

encased (in), inn-**kehst** (inn), adj eingeschlossen (in)

enchant, inn-**tschahnt,** v bezaubern, entzücken; **–ing,** adj bezaubernd, entzückend

enchantment, inn-**tschahnt-**ment, n Entzücken nt

encircle, inn-**ssör-**k'l, v umgeben, umfassen

enclose, inn-**klohs,** v einschließen; (with letter)

beilegen; **–d,** adj & adv (with letter) beiliegend

enclosure, inn-**kloh-**scher, n (with letter) Anlage f; (fence) Umzäunung f; (for animals) Gehege nt

encompass, inn-**kamm-**pess, v umfassen

encore, ong-kohr, n Zugabe f

encounter, inn-**kaun**-ter, n Begegnung f; mil Zusammenstoß m; v treffen; (enemy, difficulties) stoßen auf

encourage, inn-**ka**-ridsch, v ermutigen; **–ment,** n Ermutigung f

encouraging, inn-**ka**-ridsch-ing, adj ermutigend

encroach, inn-**krohtsch** on, v (rights) eingreifen in; (time) in Anspruch nehmen

encrusted (with), inn-**krass**-tidd (u'idh), adj besetzt (mit)

encumbered, inn-**kamm**-berd, adj – by, (clothes etc.) behindert durch; – **with,** (load) beladen mit; (debts etc.) belastet mit

encumbrance, inn-**kamm**-brenss, n (load) Last f; (responsibility) Belastung f

encyclop(a)edia, inn-sseik-le-**pie**-di-e, n (Konversations)lexikon nt

end, endd, n Ende nt; (conclusion) Schluß m; v

(be)enden; **–less,** *adj*
endlos; **– up,** *v* landen,
enden; **in the –,** zum
Schluß; **on –,** (upright)
hochkant; **for days on –,**
tagelang

endanger, inn-**dehn**-dscher,
v gefährden

endear, inn-**dier, – o.s. to
sb,** *v* sich bei jdm beliebt
machen; **–ing,** *adj* reizend

endeavour, inn-**dew**-er, *n*
Bemühung *f; v* sich
bemühen

ending, enn-**ding,** *n* Ende *nt;*
(of story) Ausgang *m*

endive, enn-**diw,** *n*
Endiviensalat *m*

endorse, inn-**dorss,** *v* (sign)
unterzeichnen; (approve)
billigen; **–ment,** *n*
(approval) Billigung *f;* (on
driving licence)
Strafvermerk *m*

endow, inn-**dau,** *v* (pay for)
stiften; **– sb with,**
(money) jdm etw stiften;
(gift) jdm etw schenken

endurance, inn-**djuhr**-renss,
n Ausdauer *f*

endure, inn-**djuhr,** *v*
aushalten, ertragen

enema, enn-i-me, *n*
Einlauf *m*

enemy, enn-i-mi, *adj*
feindlich; *n* Feind *m*

energetic, enn-er-**dschett**-
ick, *adj* aktiv, tatkräftig

energy, enn-er-**dschi,** *n*
Energie *f*

enforce, inn-**forss,** *v*

(obedience) erzwingen;
(the law) durchsetzen

engage, inn-**gehdsch,** *v*
(employ) anstellen; *mil*
angreifen; *mech*
einschalten; **– sb in
conversation,** jdn in ein
Gespräch verwickeln; **– in,**
(take part) sich beteiligen
an

engaged, inn-**gehdschd,** *adj*
(to marry) verlobt; (busy)
beschäftigt; (toilet,
telephone) besetzt; ; **get –,**
v sich verloben

engagement, inn-**gehdsch**-
ment, *n* (appointment)
Verabredung *f;* (to
marry) Verlobung *f; mil*
Gefecht *nt*

engaging, inn-**geh**-dsching,
adj gewinnend

engender, inn-**dschen**-der, *v*
erzeugen

engine, enn-**dschinn,** *n*
Maschine *f;* (car) Motor
m; rail Lokomotive *f*

engineer, enn-dschi-**nier,** *n*
Ingenieur *m; v* (contrive)
arrangieren; **–ing,** *n*
Technik *f;* (trade)
Ingenieurswesen *nt*

England, ing-glend, *n*
England *nt*

English, ing-glisch, *adj*
englisch; *n* (language)
Englisch *nt;* **the –,** *npl* die
Engländer *pl;* **the –
Channel,** *n* der
Ärmelkanal *m;* **–man,** *n*
Engländer *m;* **–woman,** *n*

Engländerin *f*

engraving, inn-**greh**-wing, *n*
Stich *m*

engrossed, inn-**grohst,** *adj*
vertieft

engulf, inn-**galf,** *v*
verschlingen

enhance, inn-**hahnss,** *v*
steigern

enigma, i-**nigg**-me, *n* Rätsel
nt

enjoy, inn-**dscheu,** *v*
genießen; **– o.s.,** sich
amüsieren; **–ment,** *n*
Vergnügen *nt;* (of rights
etc.) Genuß *m*

enlarge, inn-**lahrdsch,** *v*
vergrößern, **–ment,** *n*
Vergrößerung *f*

enlighten, inn-**lei**-t'n, *v*
aufklären; **–ment,** *n*
Aufklärung *f*

enlist, inn-**list,** *v mil* sich
melden; (support,
sympathy) gewinnen

enliven, inn-**lei**-wen, *v*
beleben

enmity, enn-mi-ti, *n*
Feindschaft *f*

enormity, i-**nor**-mi-ti, *n*
Ungeheuerlichkeit *f*

enormous(ly), i-**nor**-mess(-
li), *adj & adv* enorm,
ungeheuer

enough, i-**naff,** *adj*
genügend, genug; *adv*
genug; **be –,** *v* reichen

enquire, inn-**ku'eir,** see
inquire

enrage, inn-**rehdsch,** *v*
wütend machen

enrol, inn-**rohl,** v (sich) einschreiben; (for course) sich anmelden **–ment,** n Einschreibung f; Anmeldung f

ensign, enn-**ssein,** n (naval flag) Flagge f; (rank) Fähnrich m

enslave, inn-**sslehw,** v zum Sklaven machen

ensue, inn-**sjuh,** v (darauf) folgen

entail, inn-**tehl,** v mit sich bringen

entangle, inn-**täng-g'l,** v verfangen; fig verstricken; **become –d (in),** sich verwickeln; sich verfangen in; fig sich verstricken in

enter, enn-**ter,** v (walk into, join) eintreten (in); (competition) sich melden (zu); (in book) eintragen; **– into,** (discussions) eingehen; (calculations) eine Rolle spielen bei

enterprise, enn-**ter-preis,** n (firm, project) Unternehmen nt; (initiative) Initiative f

enterprising, enn-**ter-prei-sing,** adj (person) unternehmungslustig; (idea) kühn

entertain, enn-ter-**tehn,** v (amuse) unterhalten; (guest) bewirten; (consider) erwägen; **–er,** n Entertainer m; **–ing,** adj

unterhaltsam; **–ment,** n Unterhaltung f

enthrall, inn-**thro'al,** v fesseln

enthusiasm, inn-**thjuh-si-äs-em,** n Begeisterung f

enthusiast, inn-**thjuh-si-äst,** n Enthusiast m; **–ic,** adj begeistert

entice, inn-**teiss,** v verführen

entire, inn-**teir,** adj ganz; **–ly,** adv völlig; **–ty,** n Gesamtheit f

entitled, inn-**tei-t'ld,** adj (book) mit dem Titel; (person) berechtigt; **be – (to),** v das Recht haben (auf); (have a claim) Anspruch haben auf

entitlement (to), inn-**tei-t'l-ment** (tu), n Berechtigung f (zu); Anspruch m (auf)

entrance, enn-**trenss,** n Eingang m; (for vehicles) Einfahrt f; (action) Eintritt m; **– fee,** n Eintrittsgeld nt

entrance, inn-**trahnss,** v entzücken

entrant, enn-**trent,** n sport Teilnehmer m; (for exam) Kandidat m

entreat, inn-**triet,** v anflehen

entrenched, inn-**trentscht,** adj verwurzelt

entrepreneur, onn-tre-pre-**nör,** n Unternehmer m

entrust, inn-**trast,** v **– to sb,** jdm anvertrauen; **– sb**

with, jdn betrauen mit

entry, enn-**tri,** n (way in) Eingang m, Einfahrt f; (entering) Eintritt m, Einfahrt f; (in book) Eintrag m; (in account) Eintragung f; **– form,** n Anmeldeformular nt; **– visa,** n Einreisevisum nt; **no –,** Eintritt/Einfahrt verboten

enumerate, i-**njuh-**me-reht, v aufzählen

envelop, inn-**well-**ep, v einhüllen

envelope, enn-we-**lohp,** n Umschlag m

enviable, inn-**wi-e-b'l,** adj beneidenswert

envious, enn-**wi-ess,** adj neidisch

environment, inn-**weir-**ren-ment, n (general) Umwelt f; (local) Umgebung f; **–al,** adj Umwelt-; **–ally friendly,** adj umweltfreundlich

environs, inn-**weir-**rens, npl Umgebung f

envisage, inn-**wi-**sidsch, v sich vorstellen

envoy, enn-**weu,** n Gesandte(r) m & f

envy, enn-**wi,** n Neid m; v beneiden

ephemeral, i-**femm-**e-rel, adj flüchtig

epic, epp-**ick,** adj episch; (achievement) gewaltig; n Epos nt

epidemic, epp-i-**demm-**ick,

n adj epidemisch;
Epidemie *f*

epilepsy, epp-i-lepp-ssi, *n*
Epilepsie *f*

epileptic, epp-i-**lepp**-tick,
adj epileptisch; *n*
Epileptiker *m*

episode, epp-i-ssohd, *n* (of
story) Episode *f*;
(incident) Begebenheit *f*

epoch, ie-pock, *n* Zeitalter
nt

equal, ie-ku'el, *n adj* gleich;
Gleichgestellte(r) *m & f*; *v*
gleichkommen; (maths)
gleichen

equality, i-**ku'oll**-i-ti,
n Gleichheit *f*;
(equal rights)
Gleichberechtigung *f*

equalize, ie-ku'e-leis, *v*
gleich machen; *sport*
ausgleichen

equally, ie-ku'e-li, *adv* gleich

equate (with), i-**ku'eht**
(u'idh), *v* gleichsetzen

equation, i-**ku'eh**-sch'n, *n*
Gleichung *f*

equator, i-**kueh**-ter, *n*
Äquator *m*

equilibrium, ie-ku'i-**libb**-ri-
em, *n* Gleichgewicht *nt*

equinox, ie-ku'i-nocks, *n*
Tagundnachtgleiche *f*

equip, i-**ku'ipp**, *v* ausrüsten;
–ment, *n* Ausrüstung *f*,
Ausstattung *f*;
(implements) Geräte *pl*

equitable, eck-u'i-te-b'l, *adj*
(just) gerecht; (fair) billig

equity, eck-u'i-ti, *n*

Gerechtigkeit *f*;
Billigkeit *f*

equivalent, i-**ku'iw**-*e*-lent,
adj (equal) gleichwertig;
(similar) entsprechend;
n (counterpart)
Gegenstück *nt*; (in
value) Gegenwert *m*

equivocal, i-**ku'iw**-*e*-k'l, *adj*
zweideutig

era, ier-re, *n* Epoche *f*

eradicate, i-**rädd**-i-keht, *v*
ausrotten

erase, i-rehs, *v* ausradieren;
(from tape, *comp*) löschen;
–r, *n* Radiergummi *m/nt*

erect, i-rekt, *adj* aufrecht; *v*
(building) errichten;
(sign, furniture, system)
aufstellen

erection, i-**reck**-sch'n, *n*
Errichten *nt*; Aufstellen
nt; (of penis) Erektion *f*

ergonomics, ör-ge-**nomm**-
icks, *n* Ergonomie *f*

erode, i-rohd, *v* (land)
auswaschen; (rock)
verwittern; (confidence)
untergraben

erotic, i-**rott**-ick, *adj*
erotisch

err, örr, *v* sich irren

errand, e-rend, *n*
Besorgung *f*

erratic, i-**rätt**-ick, *adj*
(unreliable)
unberechenbar; (irregular)
unregelmäßig

erroneous, i-**roh**-ni-ess, *adj*
irrig

error, e-rer, *n* Fehler *m*

erupt, i-**rapt**, *v* ausbrechen;
–ion, *n* Ausbruch *m*

escalate, ess-ke-leht, *v mil*
(sich) ausweiten; (costs)
(sich) schnell erhöhen

escalator, ess-ke-leh-ter, *n*
Rolltreppe *f*

escape, iss-**kehp**, *n* Flucht *f*;
(of gas) Ausströmen *nt*; *v*
entkommen, fliehen

escort, ess-kort, *n* (guard)
Eskorte *f*; (companion)
Begleiter *m*

escort, ess-**kort**, *v* begleiten;
mil eskortieren

especially, iss-**pesch**-*e*-li, *adv*
besonders

espionage, ess-pi-*e*-nahsch,
n Spionage *f*

essay, ess-eh, *n* Aufsatz *m*

essence, ess-enss, *n* (nature)
Wesen *nt*; (core)
Wesentliche(s) *nt*;
(extract) Essenz *f*

essential, i-**ssenn**-sch'l, *adj*
(fundamental) wesentlich;
(necessary) unbedingt
nötig; **–ly,** *adv* im
wesentlichen

establish, iss-**täbb**-lisch, *v*
(set up) gründen;
(determine) feststellen;
–ed, *adj* (belief,
government) herrschend;
(truth, method)
anerkannt; **–ment,** *n*
(institution) Anstalt *f*;
(setting up) Einrichtung *f*;
the Establishment,
Establishment *nt*

estate, iss-**teht**, *n* (land) Gut

nt; (of deceased) Nachlaß m; (housing) Siedlung f; **– agent,** n Grundstücksmakler m; **– car,** n Kombiwagen m

esteem, iss-**tiem,** n (opinion) Achtung f; (good opinion) Wertschätzung f; v schätzen

estimate, ess-ti-met, n Schätzung f; comm (of costs) (Kosten)- voranschlag m

estimate, ess-ti-meht, v schätzen

estranged, iss-**trehndschd**, adj entfremdet

estuary, ess-tju-e-ri, n Mündung f

etc., abbr et cetera, usw.

etching, ett-tsching, n Kupferstich m

eternal, i-tör-n'l, adj ewig

eternity, i-tör-ni-ti, n Ewigkeit f

ether, ie-ther, n Äther m

ethical, eth-ick-'l, adj ethisch

ethics, eth-icks, n (study) Ethik f; npl (morality) Moral f

ethnic, eth-nick, adj ethnisch, Volks-; – **minority,** n ethnische Minderheit f

etiquette, ett-i-kett, n Etikette f

EU, ie juh, n (abbr **European Union**), EU f

euphemism, juh-fe-mism, n

Euphemismus m

Euro, juhr-ro, n Euro m

Europe, juhr-rep, n Europa nt; **–an,** adj europäisch; n Europäer m

evacuate, i-wäck-ju-eht, v (people) evakuieren; (place) räumen

evade, i-wehd, v (blow, question) ausweichen; (pursuer, justice) sich entziehen

evaluate, i-wäll-ju-eht, v bewerten

evaporate, i-wäpp-e-reht, v verdunsten; fig schwinden; **–d milk,** Kondensmilch f

evasive, i-weh-ssiw, adj ausweichend

eve, iew, n Vorabend m; **Christmas Eve,** n Heiligabend m

even, ie-wen, adj (surface) eben; (layer) gleichmäßig; (score) unentschieden; (number) gerade; adv sogar; **– if,** selbst wenn; **get – (with),** heimzahlen; **– though,** obwohl; **– out,** v (sich) ausgleichen

evening, iew-ning, n Abend m; **– class(es),** n(pl), Abendkurs m; **– dress,** n (man's) Gesellschaftsanzug m; (woman's) Abendkleid nt

event, i-went, n (incident) Ereignis nt; (function) Veranstaltung f; **–ful,** adj ereignisreich; **in the –,** im Endeffekt; **in the – of,** im

Falle

eventual(ly), i-went-ju-el(-i), adj & adv schließlich; zum Schluß

ever, ew-er, adv (always) immer; (at any time) je(mals); **–green,** adj immergrün; **–lasting,** adj ewig; **– since,** adv & conj seitdem; prep seit; **for – (and ever),** für immer; **not –,** nie(mals)

every, ew-ri, adj & pron jede(r/s), alle; **–body/one,** adj jeder(mann); **–day,** adj alltäglich, Alltags-; **– other,** jeder(r/s) zweite; **–thing,** alles; **–where,** adv überall

evict, i-wikt, v ausweisen

eviction, i-wick-sch'n, n Räumung f

evidence, ew-i-denss, n (proof) Beweis(e) m(pl.); (testimony) Aussage f

evident, ew-i-dent, adj offensichtlich

evil, ie-wil, n Böse nt; adj schlecht

evoke, i-wohk, v hervorrufen

evolution, ie-we-luh-sch'n, n (of life) Evolution f; (development) Entwicklung f

evolve, i-wolw, v (sich) entwickeln

ewe, juh, n Mutterschaf nt

exacerbate, ick-säss-er-beht, v verschlimmern

exact, igg-säckt, adj genau; v

fordern; –**ing**, *adj*;
anspruchsvoll; –**ly**, *adv*
genau
exaggerate, igg-**sädd**-dsche-reht, *v* übertreiben
exaggeration, igg-sädd-dsche-**reh**-sch'n, *n*
Übertreibung *f*
exalted, igg-**soll**-tidd, *adj*
(rank) hoch; (mood)
exaltiert
exam, igg-**sämm**, *n* (*abbr*
examination), (test)
Prüfung *f*
examination, igg-sämm-i-**neh**-sch'n, *n* (test)
Prüfung *f*; (study, *med*)
Untersuchung *f*;
(inspection) Kontrolle *f*;
law Verhör *nt*
examine, igg-**sämm**-in, *v*
(test) prüfen; (study, *med*)
untersuchen; (inspect)
kontrollieren; *law*
verhören
example, igg-**sahm**-p'l, *n*
Beispiel, *nt*; **for –**, zum
Beispiel
exasperate, igg-**sahss**-pe-reht, *v* zur Verzweiflung
bringen
excavate, eks-ke-veht, *v*
ausgraben
exceed, ick-**ssied**, *v*
überschreiten
exceedingly, ick-**ssie**-ding-li, *adv* äußerst
excel, ick-**ssell**, *v* sich
auszeichnen
excellence, eck-**sse**-lenss, *n*
(quality/achievement)

hervorragende
Qualität/Leistung *f*;
Vortrefflichkeit *f*
excellent, eck-**sse**-lent, *adj*
ausgezeichnet, vortrefflich
except, ick-**ssept**, *prep*
außer; *v* ausnehmen; –**ion**,
n Ausnahme *f*; **take –ion
to**, *v* Anstoß nehmen an;
–**ional**, *adj*
außergewöhnlich
excerpt, eck-ssörpt, *n*
Auszug *m*
excess, eck-**ssess**, *n*
Übermaß *nt*; (charge)
Zuschlag *m*; **– baggage**,
Mehrgepäck *nt*; –**ive**, *adj*
übermäßig, übertrieben
exchange, iks-**tschehndsch**,
n (of objects) Tausch *m*;
(of views, prisoners)
Austausch *m*; (telephone)
Zentrale *f*; *v* tauschen;
(money, letters) wechseln;
(views) austauschen; **–
rate**, Wechselkurs *m*
Exchequer, iks-**tscheck**-er, *n*
Schatzamt *nt*
excise, eck-sseis, *n*
Verbrauchssteuer *f*
excise, ick-**sseis**, *v*
herausschneiden
excitable, ick-**sseit**-e-b'l, *adj*
leicht erregbar
excite, ick-**sseit**, *v* erregen;
–**d**, aufgeregt; –**ment**, *n*
Aufregung *f*; **get –d
(about)**, *v* (annoyed) sich
aufregen (über);
(enthusiastic) sich (für
etw) begeistern

exciting, ick-**ssei**-ting, *adj*
aufregend; (story)
spannend
exclaim, iks-**klehm**, *v*
ausrufen
exclamation, eks-kle-**meh**-sch'n, *n* Ausruf *m*; –
mark, *n* Ausrufezeichen *nt*
exclude, iks-**kluhd**, *v*
ausschließen
exclusion, iks-**kluh**-sch'n, *n*
Ausschluß *m*
exclusive, iks-**kluh**-ssiw, *adj*
(sole) ausschließlich;
(select) exklusiv; –**ly**, *adv*
ausschließlich
excrement, eks-kri-ment, *n*
Kot *m*
excruciating, iks-**kruh**-schi-eh-ting, *adj* fürchterlich
excursion, iks-**kör**-sch'n, *n*
Ausflug *m*
excuse, iks-**kjuhss**,
n Ausrede *f*,
Entschuldigung *f*
excuse, iks-**kjuhs**, *v*
entschuldigen; **– me!**
Entschuldigung!
execute, eck-ssi-**kjuht**, *v*
(carry out) ausführen;
(put to death) hinrichten
execution, eck-ssi-**kjuh**-sch'n, *n* Ausführung *f*;
Hinrichtung *f*; –**er**, *n*
Scharfrichter *m*
executive, igg-**seck**-ju-tiw,
adj Exekutiv-; *comm*
geschäftsführend; *n*
(government) Exekutive *f*;
comm Manager *m*
executor, igg-**seck**-ju-ter, *n*

Testamentsvollstrecker m

exemplary, igg-**semm**-ple-ri, *adj* musterhaft

exemplify, igg-**semm**-pli-fei, *v* erläutern

exempt, igg-**semmt**, *v* befreien; **–ion**, *n* Befreiung *f*

exercise, eck-**sser**-sseis, *n* Übung *f*; (physical) Bewegung *f*; *v* üben; *mil* exerzieren; (power) ausüben; (take exercise) sich Bewegung verschaffen; **– book**, *n* Heft *nt*

exert, igg-**sört**, *v* ausüben; **– o.s.**, sich anstrengen; **–ion**, *n* Anstrengung *f*

exhale, eks-**hehl**, *v* ausatmen

exhaust, igg-**so'ast**, *v* erschöpfen; **–ed**, *adj* erschöpft; *n mech* Auspuff *m*; (gases) Abgase *pl*; **–ion**, *n* Erschöpfung *f*; **–ive**, *adj* umfassend

exhibit, igg-**sibb**-itt, *n* Ausstellungsstück *nt*; *v* ausstellen

exhibition, eck-ssi-**bisch**-'n, *n* Ausstellung *f*; (shop) Auslage *f*; **–ist**, *n* Exhibitionist *m*

exhilarating, igg-**sil**-*e*-reh-ting, *adj* belebend, fröhlich stimmend

exhort, igg-**sort**, *v* ermahnen

exile, eck-**sseil**, *n* Exil *nt*, Verbannung *f*; (person)

Verbannte(r) *m & f*; *v* verbannen

exist, igg-**sist**, *v* existieren; **–ence**, *n* Existenz *f*; **–ing**, *adj* gegenwärtig

exit, eck-**ssitt**, *n* (way out) Ausgang *m*, Ausfahrt *f*; (departure) Abgang *m*; *v* hinausgehen

exodus, eck-**sse**-dess, *n* Auszug *m*

exonerate, igg-**sonn**-*e*-reht, *v* entlasten

exorbitant, igg-**sor**-bi-tent, *adj* übermäßig

exotic, igg-**sott**-ick, *adj* exotisch

expand, iks-**pänd**, *v* (sich) ausdehnen

expanse, iks-**pänss**, *n* Fläche *f*

expansion, iks-**pänn**-sch'n, *n* (physics) Ausdehnung *f*; (comm etc.) Erweiterung *f*

expect, iks-**pekt**, *v* (suppose) annehmen; (await, demand) erwarten; **–ant**, *adj* erwartungsvoll; **– mother**, *n* werdende Mutter *f*

expectation, eks-peck-**teh**-sch'n, *n* Erwartung *f*

expedience, expediency, iks-**pie**-di-enss, iks-**pie**-di-en-ssi, *n* Zweckdienlichkeit *f*

expedient, iks-**pie**-di-ent, *n* Hilfsmittel *nt*; *adj* zweckdienlich

expedition, eks-pi-**disch**-'n, *n* Expedition *f*

expel, iks-**pell**, *v* ausstoßen,

ausweisen

expend, iks-**pend**, *v* verwenden; **–iture**, *n* (spending) Ausgabe *f*; (money spent) Ausgaben *pl*

expense, iks-**penss**, *n* Kosten *pl*; **–s**, *npl* Unkosten *pl*; (account) Spesen *pl*

expensive, iks-**penn**-ssiw, *adj* teuer, kostspielig

experience, iks-**pier**-ri-enss, *n* (knowledge) Erfahrung *f*; (event) Erlebnis *nt*; *v* erleben; **–d**, *adj* erfahren

experiment, iks-pe-ri-ment, *n* Versuch *m*; *v* experimentieren

expert, eks-**pört**, *n* Fachmann *m*, Experte *m*, Expertin *f*; *adj* erfahren

expertise, eks-per-**ties**, *n* Sachverstand *m*

expire, iks-**peir**, *v* (run out) ablaufen; (die) versterben

expiry, iks-**peir**-ri, *n* Ablauf *m*

explain, iks-**plehn**, *v* erklären

explanation, eks-ple-**neh**-sch'n, *n* Erklärung *f*

explanatory, iks-**plänn**-*e*-te-ri, *n* erklärend

explicit, iks-**pli**-ssitt, *adj* deutlich

explode, iks-**plohd**, *v* explodieren; (cause to explode) sprengen

exploit, eks-**pleut**, *n* Heldentat *f*

exploit, iks-**pleut**, *v* (use)
ausnutzen; (treat unfairly)
ausbeuten

exploratory, iks-**plo**-*re*-te-ri,
adj Probe-

explore, iks-**plor**, *v*
erforschen

explosion, iks-**ploh**-sch'n, *n*
Explosion *f*

explosive, iks-**ploh**-ssiw, *adj*
explosiv; *n* Sprengstoff *m*

export, eks-port, *adj* Export-
; *n* Export *m*

export, eks-**port**, *v*
ausführen, exportieren;
-er, *n* Exporteur *m*

expose, iks-**pohs**, *v* (to
danger) aussetzen; (fraud
etc.) aufdecken; (person)
entlarven; *photog*
belichten

exposure, iks-**poh**-scher, *n*
(unmasking) Bloßstellung
f, Entlarvung *f*; *photog*
Belichtung *f*; *med*
Unterkühlung *f*

expound, iks-**paund**, *v*
auslegen, erläutern

express, iks-**press**, *adj* (fast)
Eil-; (explicit)
ausdrücklich; *n rail*
Schnellzug *m*; *v*
ausdrücken; **-ion**, *n*
Ausdruck *m*; **-ive**, *adj*
ausdrucksvoll; **-ly**, *adv*
ausdrücklich; **(by)** –, per
Expreß

expulsion, iks-**pall**-sch'n, *n*
Ausweisung *f*

exquisite, iks-**ku'is**-itt, *adj*
erlesen, köstlich

extend, iks-**tend**, *v* (enlarge)
erweitern; (house)
anbauen, ausbauen;
(hand, arm) ausstrecken;
(prolong) verlängern;
(cover) sich ausdehnen

extension, iks-**tenn**-sch'n, *n*
(enlargement)
Erweiterung *f*; (building)
Anbau *m*; (in time)
Verlängerung; (telephone)
Apparat *m*

extensive, iks-**tenn**-ssiw, *adj*
(area) weit; (research etc.)
umfangreich; (use)
weitgehend

extent, iks-**tent**, *n* (scope)
Umfang *m*; (degree) Maß
m; (area) Ausdehnung *f*

extenuating, eks-**tenn**-ju-
eh-ting, *adj* mildernd

exterior, iks-**tier**-ri-er, *adj*
äußere(r/s), Außen-; *n*
Äußere *nt*

exterminate, eks-**tör**-mi-
neht, *v* ausrotten

external, eks-**tör**-n'l, *adj*
äußere(r/s), Außen-

extinct, iks-**tinkt**, *adj*
(volcano) erloschen;
(species) ausgestorben

extinguish, iks-**ting**-gu'isch,
v auslöschen

extort, iks-**tort**, *v* erpressen;
-ion, *n* Erpressung *f*

extra, eks-tre, *adj* zusätzlich,
Zusatz-; *adv* besonders;
n (for car) Extra *nt*; **-s**,
npl comm zusätzliche
Kosten *pl*

extract, eks-**träckt**, *n*

(cooking) Extrakt *m*;
(from text) Auszug *m*

extract, iks-**träckt**, *v*
(her)ausziehen

extradite, eks-tre-deit, *v*
ausliefern

extramarital, eks-tre-mä-ri-
t'l, *adj* außerehelich

extraordinary, iks-**tror**-di-
ne-ri, *adj* (unusual)
außerordentlich; (special)
Sonder-; (strange) seltsam

extravagance, iks-**träw**-*e*-
genss, *n* Verschwendung *f*

extravagant, iks-**träw**-*e*-
gent, *adj* verschwenderisch;
(exaggerated) extravagant

extreme, iks-**triem**, *adj*
äußerste(r/s); (politics)
extrem; **-ly**, *adv* äußerst

extremity, iks-**tremm**-i-ti, *n*
(end) äußerstes Ende *nt*;
(need) Not *f*; (action)
äußerstes Mittel *nt*

extricate, eks-tri-keht, *v*
befreien

extrovert, eks-tre-vört, *n*
extravertierter Mensch *m*

exuberant, igg-**sjuh**-be-rent,
adj überschwenglich

eye, ei, *n* Auge *nt*; **-ball**, *n*
Augapfel *m*; **-brow**, *n*
Augenbraue *f*; **-drops**, *npl*
Augentropfen *pl*;
-lash, *n* Augenwimper *f*;
-let, *n* Schnürloch *nt*;
-lid, *n* Augenlid *nt*;
-shadow, *n* Lidschatten
m; **-sight**, *n* Sehkraft *f*; **-
witness**, *n* Augenzeuge *m*

F

fable, feh-b'l, n Fabel f,
Märchen nt; **-d,** adj
(famous) berühmt

fabric, fább-rick, n Gewebe
nt; (building) Struktur f

fabrication, fább-ri-keh-
sch'n, n Herstellung f;
(lie) Lüge f

fabulous, fább-ju-less, adj (
fam marvellous) fabelhaft

façade, fe-**ssahd,** n Fassade f

face, fehss, n Gesicht nt;
(clock) Zifferblatt nt; v
(opposite) gegenüber sein;
(deal with)
gegenübertreten; **-cream,**
n Gesichtscreme f; **-lift,** n
Facelifting nt; fig
Verschönerung f

facetious, fe-**ssie**-schess, adj
witzig, frech

facial, feh-schel, adj
Gesichts-

facile, fáss-eil, adj leicht;

(superficial) oberflächlich

facilitate, fe-**ssill**-i-teht, v
erleichtern

facilities, fe-**ssill**-i-tis, npl
(equipment)
Einrichtungen pl;
(opportunities)
Möglichkeiten pl

facsimile, fäck-**ssimm**-i-li, n
Faksimile nt; (message)
Telefax nt

fact, fäckt, n Tatsache f;
Wirklichkeit f

faction, fäck-sch'n, n
Splittergruppe f

factor, fäck-ter, n Faktor m

factory, fäck-te-ri, n Fabrik
f, Werk nt

faculty, fäck-'l-ti, n
Fähigkeit f; (university)
Fakultät f

fad, fäd, n fam Masche f

fade, fehd, v verwelken,
verblassen; (colour)

verschießen

fag, fägg, n fam Kippe f

fail, fehl, v fehlschlagen;
(voice, light etc.)
versagen; (neglect)
unterlassen; (go/get
wrong) mißlingen; (exam)
durchfallen; (bankrupt)
Konkurs machen; **– to do
sth,** v etw nicht tun, etw
unterlassen; **–ing,** n
Schwäche f; **-ure,** n
Mißerfolg m; (insolvency)
Konkurs m; **without –,** auf
jeden Fall

faint, fehnt, adj schwach; n
Ohnmacht f; v
ohnmächtig werden

fair, fähr, adj (just) fair;
(hair) blond; (weather)
heiter; n (trade) Messe f;
(funfair) Jahrmarkt m;
-ness, n Gerechtigkeit f

fairy, fähr-ri, n Fee f; **– tale,**
n Märchen nt

faith, fehth, n Glaube m;
(confidence) Vertrauen
nt; **-ful,** adj treu; **-less,**
treulos; **Yours –fully,** Mit
freundlichen Grüßen

fake, fehk, n Fälschung f; v
fälschen

falcon, foll-k'n, n Falke m

fall, fo'al, n Fall m, Sturz m;
v fallen, stürzen; **– for,**
(love) sich in jdn
verlieben; (be taken in)
auf etw hereinfallen; **–
through,** ins Wasser fallen

fallacy, fäll-e-ssi, n Irrtum m;
(false conclusion)

Trugschluß m

fallible, fäll-i-b'l, *adj* fehlbar

fallout, fo'al-aut, *n* radioaktiver Niederschlag m; (consequences) Konsequenzen *pl*

false, folss, *adj* falsch; – **teeth,** *npl* Gebiß *nt*

falsify, foll-ssi-fei, *v* (ver)fälschen

falter, foll-ter, *v* stocken; (speech) stammeln

fame, fehm, *n* Ruhm m; **–d,** *adj* berühmt

familiar, fe-**mill**-yer, *adj* vertraut; (intimate) intim

family, fämm-i-li, *n* Familie f; **– doctor,** *n* Hausarzt m, Hausärztin f

famine, fämm-inn, *n* Hungersnot f

famished, fämm-ischt, *adj* ausgehungert

famous, feh-mess, *adj* berühmt

fan, fänn, *n* Fächer m; Ventilator m; (admirer) Fan m; *v* fächeln

fanatic, fe-**nätt**-ick, *adj* fanatisch; *n* Fanatiker m

fancy, fänn-ssi, *adj* ausgefallen; *n* Idee f; (desire) Neigung f, Lust f; *v* (imagine) sich einbilden; (like) Lust haben zu/auf; **– dress,** *n* Maskenkostüm *nt*

fang, fäng, *n* Fang m; (snake) Giftzahn m

fantastic, fänn-**täss**-tick, *adj* phantastisch

fantasy, fänn-te-si, *n* Phantasie f

far, fahr, *adj & adv* weit; – **away,** weit entfernt

farce, fahrss, *n* Farce f

farcical, fahr-ssi-k'l, *adj* lächerlich

fare, fähr, *n* Fahrpreis m; (food) Kost f

farewell, fähr-**u'ell,** *n* Abschied m; *interj* lebe wohl!

Far East, fahr iest, *n* Ferner Osten m

farm, fahrm, *n* Bauernhof m; *v* bewirtschaften; **–er,** *n* Landwirt m; **–house,** *n* Bauernhaus *nt*; **–ing,** *n* Landwirtschaft f; **–yard,** *n* Bauernhof m

far-reaching, fahr-**riet**-tsching, *adj* weitreichend

fascinate, fäss-i-neht, *v* faszinieren, bezaubern

fascism, fäsch-ism, *n* Faschismus m

fashion, fäsch-'n, *n* Mode f; *v* bilden; **–able,** *adj* modisch; **in –,** modern

fast, fahst, *adj* schnell; (firm, fixed, tight) fest; (colour) farbecht; *n* Fasten *nt*; *v* fasten; **be –,** *v* (of clock) vorgehen; **– food,** *n* Fast food *nt*

fasten, fah-ss'n, *v* befestigen; fest zumachen; **–er,** *n* Verschluß m

fastidious, fäss-**tidd**-i-ess, *adj* pingelig

fat, fätt, *adj* fett, dick;

n Fett *nt*

fatal, feh-t'l, *adj* tödlich

fatality, fe-**täll**-i-ti, *n* tödliches Unglück *nt*

fate, feht, *n* Schicksal *nt*; **–d,** *adj* vorbestimmt; **–ful,** *adj* verhängnisvoll

father, fah-dher, *n* Vater m; **–in-law,** Schwiegervater m; **–ly,** *adj* väterlich

fathom, fädh-em, *n* Klafter f; *naut* Faden m; *v* ergründen; (to sound) sondieren

fatigue, fe-**tieg,** *n* Ermüdung f; *mil* Arbeitsdienst m; *v* ermüden

fatten (up), fätt-'n (app), *v* mästen

fault, fo'alt, *n* (blame, cause) Schuld f; (defect, mistake) Fehler m; **–less,** *adj* fehlerlos, tadellos; **–y,** *adj* fehlerhaft, mangelhaft

favour, feh-wer, *n* Gunst f; (kindness) Gefallen m; *v* begünstigen; **–able,** *adj* günstig

favourite, feh-we-ritt, *adj* Lieblings…; *n* Liebling m; *sport* Favorit m

fawn, fo'an, *adj* rehbraun; *n* Rehkalb *nt*; *v* kriechen

fax, fäcks, *n* (*abbr* **facsimile**), Fax *nt*; *v* faxen

fear, fier, *n* Furcht f; *v* fürchten; befürchten; **–ful,** *adj* schrecklich; (timid) furchtsam; **–less,** furchtlos

feasible, fie-si-b'l, *adj*

möglich, ausführbar

feast, fiest, n Fest nt; v
schmausen

feat, fiet, n Tat f;
(achievement) Leistung f

feather, fe-dher, n Feder f;
–s, pl Gefieder nt

feature, fiet-tscher, n
Merkmal nt; (face)
Gesichtszug m

February, febb-ru-e-ri, n
Februar m

federal, fedd-e-rel, adj
Bundes-

federation, fedd-e-reh-sch'n,
n Bund m, Verband m

fed up, fedd **app,** adj be –, v
die Nase voll haben

fee, fie, n Gebühr f; (for
person) Honorar nt

feeble, fie-b'l, adj schwach

feed, fied, v füttern, nähren.
n Futter nt; **–back,** n
Feedback nt

feel, fiel, v (sich) fühlen;
(touch) befühlen; n
Fühlen nt, Gefühl nt;
–er, n Fühler m; **–ing,** n
Gefühl nt

feet, fiet, pl of foot

feign, fehn, v heucheln, sich
verstellen

feline, fie-lein, adj
katzenartig

fell, fell, v fällen; (person)
niederschlagen

fellow, fell-oh, adj Mit-; n
Kerl m; (member)
Mitglied nt; **–ship,** n
Verbundenheit f

felony, fell-e-ni, n schweres

Verbrechen nt

felt, felt, n Filz m; **--tip pen,**
n Filzstift m

female, fie-mehl, adj
weiblich; n Weibchen nt

feminine, femm-i-ninn, adj
weiblich

feminist, femm-i-nist, adj
feministisch, Feministen-;
n Feministin f, Feminist m

fen, fenn, n Marschland nt

fence, fenss, n Zaun m; v
einzäunen; (combat)
fechten

fencing, fenn-ssing, n sport
Fechten nt; (fence) Zaun
m

fender, fenn-der, n (hearth)
Kaminschutz m; (ship)
Fender m

ferment, fer-ment, v gären,
gären lassen

fern, förn, n Farn m

ferocious, fe-roh-schess, adj
wild; (strong) heftig

ferret, fe-ritt, n Frettchen
nt; **– about,** v
herumstöbern

ferry, fe-ri, n Fähre f; v
übersetzen

fertile, för-teil, adj fruchtbar

fertilize, för-ti-leis, v
befruchten; (feed)
düngen; **–r,** n Dünger m

fervent, för-went, adj
leidenschaftlich

fester, fess-ter, v eitern

festival, fess-ti-w'l, n Fest
nt, Festtag m

festive, fess-tiw, adj festlich

festoon, fess-tuhn, n

Girlande f; v bekränzen

fetch, fetsch, v holen; (call
for) abholen

fête, feht, n Fest nt

feud, fjuhd, n Fehde f; **–al,**
adj feudal

fever, fie-wer, n Fieber nt;
–ish, adj fiebrig; (excited)
erregt

few, fjuh, adj wenige; **a –,**
einige, ein paar

fiancé, fi-onn-sseh, n
Verlobter m; **–e,** n
Verlobte f

fib, fibb, fam n Flunkerei f; v
flunkern, schwindeln

fibre, fei-ber, n Faser f

fickle, fick-'l, adj
unbeständig

fiction, fick-sch'n, n
erzählende Literatur f;
(book) Roman m; **–al,** adj
erdichtet

fictitious, fick-ti-schess, adj
erfunden; (false) unecht

fiddle, fidd-'l, n mus Geige f;
fam Gaunerei f; v mus
geigen; fig krumme Dinger
drehen; **– with,** v
herumspielen mit

fidelity, fi-dell-i-ti, n Treue f

fidget, fid-dschitt, n
Zappelphilipp m; v
zappelig sein

field, field, n Feld nt; v
aufstellen; (deal with)
fertig werden mit

fiend, fiend, n Teufel m;
–ish, adj teuflisch

fierce, fierss, adj wild;
(strong) heftig

fiery, feir-ri, *adj* feurig;
(temper) hitzig

fifteen, fiff-**tien,** *num*
fünfzehn; **–th,** *adj*
fünfzehnte(r/s)

fifth, fifth, *adj* fünfte(r/s); *n*
Fünftel *nt*

fifty, fiff-ti, *num* fünfzig

fig, figg, *n* Feige *f;* – -**tree,**
Feigenbaum *m*

fight, feit, *n* Kampf *m;*
Schlägerei *f; v* kämpfen;
–er, *n* Kämpfer *m;* (plane)
Kampfflugzeug *nt*

figment, figg-ment, *n* a – **of
the imagination,**
Hirngespinst *nt*

figure, figg-er, *n* Figur *f,*
Gestalt *f;* (number) Ziffer
f; v (sich) vorstellen;
–head, *n* Galionsfigur *f;* –
out, *v* verstehen,
herausfinden

filch, filtsch, *v* mausen,
stibitzen

file, feil, *n* (tool) Feile *f; mil*
Reihe *f;* (office) Ordner
m; v feilen; (letters etc.)
ablegen

filing, fei-ling, *n* Ablage
f; – **cabinet,** *n*
Aktenschrank *m*

fill, fill, *v* füllen; (teeth)
plombieren; – **in,** *v* (form)
ausfüllen; (details)
erläutern

filling, fill-ing, *n* Füllung *f;*
(teeth) Plombe *f;* –
station, *n* Tankstelle *f*

film, film, *n photog* Film *m;*
(cinema) Film *m;* (layer)

Belag *m; v* filmen,
verfilmen

filter, fill-ter, *n* Filter *m; v*
filtern

filth, filth, *n* Dreck *m;* **–y,**
adj schmutzig

fin, finn, *n* Flosse *f*

final, fei-nel, *adj* definitiv;
(last) letzte(r/s); **–ist,** *n*
Finalist *m;* **–ize,** *v*
abschließen(d
besprechen); **–ly,** *adv*
(lastly) schließlich; (in
the end) endlich

finance, fei-**nänss,** *n*
Finanzierung *f;*
(department)
Rechnungsabteilung *f; v*
finanzieren; **–s,** *npl*
Finanzlage *f*

financial, fei-**nän-**schel, *adj*
finanziell *m*

finch, fintsch, *n* Fink *m*

find, feind, *n* Fund *m; v* finden;
law erklären; – **out,** *v*
herausfinden; (person)
erwischen

fine, fein, *adj* fein; (weather)
schön; *n* Geldstrafe *f; v* zu
einer Geldstrafe
verurteilen; – **art(s),**
n(pl.), schöne Künste *pl*

finery, fei-ne-ri, *n* Glanz *m,*
Pracht *f*

finger, fing-ger, *n* Finger *m;*
v befühlen, betasten;
–nail, *n* Fingernagel *m;*
–print, *n* Fingerabdruck *m*

finish, finn-isch, *v* beenden;
(cease) aufhören; *n* Ende
nt, Schluß *m;* (goods)

Ausführung *f; sport* Finish
nt; **–ing line,** *n* Ziellinie *f*

finite, fei-neit, *adj* begrenzt

Finland, finn-lend, *n*
Finnland *nt*

Finn, finn, *n* Finne *m,*
Finnin *f;* **–ish,** *adj*
finnisch; *n* Finnisch *nt*

fir, för, *n* Tanne *f;* – **cone,**
Tannenzapfen *m*

fire, feir, *n* Feuer *nt;*
(conflagration) Brand *m;*
v anzünden; (inspire)
begeistern; (*fam* sack)
feuern; – **alarm,** *n*
Feuermelder *nt;* **–arm,** *n*
Schußwaffe *f* – **brigade,** *n*
Feuerwehr *f;* – **engine,** *n*
Feuerwehrauto *nt;* –
escape, *n* Feuertreppe *f;* –
exit, *n* Notausgang *m;* –
extinguisher, *n*
Feuerlöscher *m;* **–man,** *n*
Feuerwehrmann *m;*
(stoker) Heizer *m;* **–place,**
n offener Kamin *m;*
–proof, *adj* feuerfest;
–works, *npl* Feuerwerk *nt*

firing squad, feir-ring
sku'odd, *n*
Exekutionskommando *nt*

firm, förm, *adj* fest;
(resolute) standhaft; *n*
Firma *f*

first, först, *adj & n* erste(r/s);
adv zuerst; – **aid,** *n* Erste
Hilfe *f;* **–aid kit,** *n* Erste-
Hilfe-Kasten *m;* – **class,**
adj (travel) erster Klasse;
(excellent) erstklassig; –
name, *n* Vorname *m*

fish, fisch, n Fisch m; v fischen, angeln; **–bone,** n Gräte f; **–erman,** Fischer m; **– hook,** Angelhaken m; **–ing,** n Angeln nt; **–rod,** Angelrute f; **–monger,** Fischhändler m

fissure, fisch-er, n Spalte f

fist, fist, n Faust f

fit, fitt, adj passend, geeignet; n (paroxysm) Anfall m; v passen; (erect, set up, mount etc.) montieren; **–ness,** n Eignung f; sport Fitneß f; **–ted carpet,** n Teppichboden m; **–ting,** adj angemessen, geeignet; **–ting room,** n Anproberaum f; **–tings,** npl Ausstattung f

five, feiw, num fünf

fix, ficks, n fig Klemme f; v befestigen; **–ture,** n sport Spieldatum nt; **–tures,** npl, unbewegliches Inventar nt;

fizzle out, fis-'l aut, v im Sand verlaufen

fizzy, fis-i, adj sprudelnd, Sprudel-

flabby, flább-i, adj schlaff, schwammig

flag, flägg, n Fahne f, Flagge f; v (languish) erschlaffen; **– down,** v anhalten; **– up,** v hervorheben

flagrant, fleh-grent, adj flagrant, schamlos

flair, flähr, n Gespür nt, Talent nt

flake, flehk, n (of snow etc.) Flocke f; (of rust, paint) Schuppe f; **– (off),** v abbröckeln, abblättern

flamboyant, flämm-beu-ent, adj extravagant

flame, flehm, n Flamme f; v lodern

flammable, flämm-e-b'l, adj brennbar

flan, flänn, n Torte f

flank, flänk, n Flanke f; v flankieren

flannel, flänn-'l, n Flanell m; (facecloth) Waschlappen m

flap, fläpp, n (table etc.) Klappe f; v (wings) flattern

flare, flähr, n flackerndes Licht nt; (signal) Leuchtsignal nt; **– up,** v aufflackern; (break out) (wieder) ausbrechen

flash, fläsch, n Aufleuchten nt; photog Blitz m; v blitzen; **–back,** n Rückblende f; **–y,** adj auffallend

flask, flahsk, n Flachmann m; (Thermos ®) Thermosflasche f

flat, flätt, adj flach, platt; (business) flau; n; (dwelling) Wohnung f; mus b nt; **–ly,** adv rundweg, glatt; **–ten,** v flach machen, eben machen

flatter, flätt-er, v schmeicheln; **–ing,** adj

schmeichelhaft; **–y,** n Schmeichelei f

flavour, fleh-wer, n Geschmack m; (wine) Blume f; v würzen; **–ing,** Würze f

flaw, flo'a, n Fehler m; (crack) Riß m; **–less,** makellos

flax, fläcks, n Flachs m

flea, flie, n Floh m

fleck, fleck, n Tupfen m

flee, flie, v fliehen

fleece, fliess, n Flies nt; v fam ausnehmen

fleet, fliet, n Flotte f; **–ing,** adj flüchtig

flesh, flesch, n Fleisch nt

Flemish, flemm-isch, adj flämisch

flex, flecks, n Kabel nt; v beugen; **–ible,** adj biegsam, flexibel

flicker, flick-er, n Flackern nt; v flackern

flight, fleit, n Flug m

flimsy, flimm-si, adj (material, paper) dünn; (structure) schwach

flinch, flintsch, v (zusammen)zucken

fling, fling, v werfen, schleudern

flint, flint, n Feuerstein m

flip, flipp, v drehen; (go crazy) durchdrehen

flippant, flipp-'nt, adj leichtfertig

flipper, flipp-er, n Flosse f

flirt, flört, n Flirt m; v flirten

float, floht, n (raft) Floß nt;

(angler's) Schwimmer m;
v treiben; (ship) flott
machen; (stock exchange)
an die Börse gehen

flock, flock, n (cattle)
Herde f; (birds) Schwarm
m; v zusammenströmen

flog, flogg, v (whip)
peitschen; (fam sell)
verhökern, verscheuern

flood, fladd, n Flut f;
(inundation)
Überschwemmung f; v
überschwemmen; **–light**, n
Flutlicht nt

floor, flohr, n Boden m,
Fußboden m; (storey)
Stock m; v überfordern

flop, flopp, n (failure)
Reinfall m; v (fail)
durchfallen; (fall)
plumpsen; **–py**, adj schlaff;
– disk, n comp Diskette f

floral, flor-rel, adj Blumen-
florid, flo-ridd, adj blühend

florist, flo-rist, n
Blumenhändler m

flounder, flaun-der, n
Flunder f; v (stumble)
stolpern; (struggle) sich
quälen

flour, flau-er, n Mehl nt

flourish, fla-risch, n mus
Fanfare f; (writing)
Schnörkel m; v (brandish)
schwenken; (go well)
gutgehen, florieren

flout, flaut, v mißachten

flow, floh, n Strom m; v
fließen, strömen

flower, flau-er, n Blume f; v

blühen; **–bed**, n
Blumenbeet nt; **–pot**, n
Blumentopf m

flu, fluh, n (abbr **influenza**),
Grippe f

fluctuate, flack-tju-eht, v
schwanken

flue, fluh, n Rauchfang m

fluency, fluh-en-ssi, n
(Rede)gewandtheit f

fluent, fluh-ent, adj
gewandt; (language)
fließend

fluff, flaff, n Fussel f; **–y**, adj
flockig, flaumig

fluid, fluh-idd, adj flüssig; n
Flüssigkeit f

fluke, fluhk, n Glücksfall m

flurry, fla-ri, n Aufregung f;
v durcheinander bringen

flush, flasch, adj (level)
bündig; n Erröten nt; v
(redden) erröten; (rinse)
ausspülen; **–ed**, adj rot

flustered, flass-terd, adj
nervös

flute, fluht, n mus Flöte f;
–d, adj (grooved) gerillt

flutter, flatt-er, n Geflatter
nt; v flattern

fly, flei, n Fliege f; v fliegen;
(flag) wehen; **–ing**, n
Fliegen nt; **– saucer**, n
fliegende Untertasse f

foal, fohl, n Fohlen nt

foam, fohm, n Schaum m; v
schäumen

fob off, fobb off, v jdn mit
etw abspeisen

focal, foh-k'l, adj Brenn-; **–
point**, n Brennpunkt m

focus, foh-kess, n
Brennpunkt m; **– (on)**, v
(camera etc.) einstellen
(auf); (efforts etc.)
konzentrieren (auf); **in –**,
scharf; **out of –**, unscharf

fodder, fodd-er, n Futter nt

foe, foh, n Feind m

fog, fogg, n Nebel m;
–gy, adj neb(e)lig;
–lamp, n (car)
Nebelscheinwerfer m

foil, feul, n (metal) Folie f;
(fencing) Florett nt; v
vereiteln

foist on, feust on, v
aufhalsen

fold, fohld, n (clothes etc.)
Falte f; v falten; (arms)
kreuzen; **–er**, Mappe f;
–ing, adj Klapp-

foliage, foh-li-idsch, n
Laub nt

folk, fohk, adj Volks-;
Folklore-; n Leute pl
Volk nt

follow, foll-oh, v folgen; fig
befolgen; **–er**, n Anhänger
m; (disciple) Jünger m;
–ing, adj folgend; n
Anhängerschaft f

folly, foll-i, n Torheit f

fond, fond, adj **be – of**, v
gern haben

fondle, fonn-d'l, v
liebkosen, hätscheln

font, font, n Taufbecken nt

food, fuhd, n Speise f;
Nahrung f (for animals)
Futter nt; **– poisoning**, n
Lebensmittelvergiftung f;

– **processor,** n
Küchenmaschine f

fool, fuhl, n Narr m; v
täuschen, hereinlegen;
–hardy, adj tollkühn; **–ish,**
adj töricht, närrisch;
–proof, adj narrensicher

foot, futt, n Fuß m; **– the
bill,** v die Rechnung
bezahlen; **–ball,** n
Fußball m; **–baller,** n
Fußballspieler m; **–bridge,**
n Fußgängerbrücke f;
–hill, n (Gebirgs)ausläufer
m; **–hold,** n Halt m,
Stützpunkt m; **–man,** n
Diener m; **–path,** n
Fußweg m; **–print,** n
Fußabdruck m; **–step,** n
Schritt m

for, for, prep (purpose, future
time) für; (distance) auf,
weit; (purpose) zu;
(reason) aus; (past time)
seit; conj denn

forage, fo-ridsch, n
(Vieh)Futter nt; v nach
Nahrung suchen;
(rummage) stöbern

forbear, for-behr, v
unterlassen; (be patient)
sich gedulden; **–ance,** n
Nachsicht f

forbid, fe-bidd, v verbieten;
–den, adj verboten; **–ding,**
adj furchteinflößend;
(grim) unwirtlich

force, forss, n Gewalt f;
(power) Kraft f; v
(compel) zwingen; (break
open) aufbrechen; **–ful,**

adj stark; (person)
energisch; **–s,** npl
Streitkräfte pl

forceps, for-sseps, npl
(Geburts)zange f

forcibly, for-ssi-bli, adj
gewaltsam

ford, ford, n Furt f; v
durchwaten

fore, for, n Vordergrund m;
to the –, im/in den
Vordergrund

forearm, for-ahrm, n
Unterarm m

foreboding, for-boh-ding, n
Vorahnung f

forecast, for-kahst, n
Prognose f, Voraussage f;
(weather etc.)
Wetterbericht m; v
vorhersagen

forecourt, for-kort, n
Vorplatz m

forefathers, for-fah-dhers,
npl Vorfahren pl

forefinger, for-fing-ger, n
Zeigefinger m

forefront, for-frant, n **to be
in the –,** in vorderster
Linie stehen

forego, for-goh, v verzichten
auf

foregone, for-gonn, **it is a –
conclusion,** n es steht von
vornherein fest

foreground, for-graund, n
Vordergrund m

forehead, for-hedd, n Stirn f

foreign, fo-rinn, adj
ausländisch, fremd; **–er,** n
Ausländer m

foreman, for-men, n
Vorarbeiter m;
Werkmeister m; (law of
jury) Sprecher m

foremost, for-mohst, adj
vorderste(r/s); erste(r/s)

forensic, fe-renn-sick, s.,
gerichtsmedizinisch

forerunner, for-rann-er, n
Vorläufer m

foresee, for-ssie, v
vorhersehen; **–able,** adj
vorhersehbar

foreshadow, for-schädd-oh,
v vorausdeuten auf

foresight, for-sseit, n
Weitblick m, Voraussicht f

forest, fo-rist, n Wald m

forestall, for-sto'al, v
zuvorkommen

forestry, fo-riss-tri, n
Forstwirtschaft f

foretaste, for-tehst, n
Vorgeschmack m

foretell, for-tell, v
vorhersagen, prophezeien

forever, for-ew-er, adv
immer

foreword, for-u'örd, n
Vorwort nt

forfeit, for-fitt, v (life, goods
etc.) verlieren, verwirken;
n (games) Pfand nt; (fine)
Strafe f

forge, fohrdsch, n Schmiede
f; v schmieden; (falsify)
fälschen; **– ahead,** v
vorankommen

forger, for-dscher, n
Fälscher m; Falschmünzer
m; **–y,** n Fälschung f

forget, fe-gett, v vergessen;
  –ful, adj vergeßlich;
  –fulness, n Vergeßlichkeit
  f; **–me-not,**
  Vergißmeinnicht nt

forgive, fe-giw, v vergeben;
  –ness, n Verzeihung f,
  Vergebung f

fork, fork, n Gabel f; (road)
  Gabelung f; **– out,** v fam
  blechen

forlorn, fe-lorn, adj
  verlassen, einsam

form, form, n (shape) Form
  f; (class) Klasse f;
  Bank f; (to fill in)
  Formular nt; v bilden; (a
  plan) entwerfen; mil sich
  formieren

formal, for-mel, adj
  förmlich, formell; (stiff)
  steif

formality, fe-mäll-i-ti,
  n Förmlichkeit f,
  Formalität f

format, for-mätt, n Format
  nt; v comp formatieren

formation, for-meh-sch'n, n
  Gestaltung f; (mil &
  geological) Bildung f

former, for-mer, adj früher;
  –ly, adv vormals

formidable, for-mi-deb-'l,
  adj gewaltig,
  beeindruckend

formula, for-mju-le, n
  Formel f

formulate, for-muj-leht, v
  formulieren

forsake, fe-ssehk, v
  verzichten auf; (desert)

verlassen

fort, fort, n Fort nt

forth, forth, adv fort, weiter;
  (out) hervor; (ahead)
  vorwärts; **and so –,** und so
  weiter; **–coming,** adj
  bevorstehend; **–right,** adj
  direkt; **–with,** adv
  unverzüglich

fortification, for-ti-fi-keh-
  sch'n, n Befestigung f

fortify, for-ti-fei, v
  (military) befestigen;
  (strengthen) stärken

fortitude, for-ti-tjuhd, n
  innere Stärke f

fortnight, fort-neit, n
  vierzehn Tage mpl.

fortress, fort-riss, n
  Festung f

fortuitous, for-tjuh-i-tess,
  adj zufällig

fortunate, for-tju-net, adj
  glücklich

fortune, for-tjuhn, n
  Vermögen nt; (luck)
  Glück nt; **– teller,** n
  Wahrsager m

forty, for-ti, num vierzig

forward, for-u'erd, adj
  (advance) Voraus-;
  (advanced) frühreif;
  (cheeky) direkt; adv
  vorwärts; v (send)
  nachschicken; (further)
  vorantreiben

fossil, foss-'l, n Fossil nt

foster, foss-ter, v pflegen,
  fördern; **– parents,** npl
  Pflegeeltern pl

foul, faul, adj widerlich,

schmutzig; n sport Foul nt;
  v beschmutzen

found, faund, v gründen;
  –ation, n Gründung f;
  –ations, npl Fundament
  nt; **–er,** n Gründer m; **–ry,**
  n Gießerei f

fountain, faun-tin, n
  Springbrunnen m; **– pen,**
  Füller m

four, for, num vier; **–teen,**
  num vierzehn; **–th,** adj
  vierte(r/s); n Viertel nt

fowl, faul, n Huhn nt;
  (poultry) Geflügel nt

fox, focks, n Fuchs m; v
  täuschen; **–glove,** n
  Fingerhut m; **–terrier,** n
  Foxterrier m

foyer, feu-ei, n Foyer nt

fraction, fräck-sch'n, n
  Bruchstück nt;
  (mathematical) Bruch m

fracture, fräck-tscher, n
  Bruch m; v brechen

fragile, frädd-dscheil, adj
  zerbrechlich

fragment, frägg-ment, n
  Bruchstück nt

fragrance, freh-grenss, n
  Duft m

fragrant, freh-grent, adj
  duftend

frail, frehl, adj zart; (health)
  gebrechlich

frame, frehm, n Rahmen m;
  v einrahmen; **–work,** n
  Gerüst nt; (panelling)
  Fachwerk nt

France, frahnss, n
  Frankreich nt

franchise, fränn-tscheis, *n*
Wahlrecht *nt*; *comm*
Lizenz *f*

frank, fränk, *adj* aufrichtig;
–ly, *adv* offen gesagt;
–ness, *n* Offenheit *f*

frantic, fränn-tick, *adj*
hektisch, stürmisch; **be –,**
v außer sich sein

fraternal, fre-tör-n'l, *adj*
brüderlich

fraternity, fre-tör-ni-ti, *n*
Brüderlichkeit *f*; (club)
Vereinigung *f*

fraught (with), fro'at
(u'idh), *adj* -geladen

fraud, fro'ad, *n* Betrug *m*,
Schwindel *m*; **–ulent,** *adj*
betrügerisch

fray, freh, *n* (scuffle) Tumult
m; *v* abnützen; **–ed,** *adj*
(cuff etc.) abgescheuert;
fig angespannt

freak, friek, *n* Freak *m*;
(abnormal) Mißgeburt *f*;
–ish, *adj* launisch,
verrückt

freckle, freck-'l, *n*
Sommersprosse *f*

free, frie, *adj* frei; *v* befreien;
–dom, *n* Freiheit *f*; **–lance,**
adj freischaffend; **–mason,**
Freimaurer *m*; **––range,** *adj*
(egg) Land-; **– trade,**
Freihandel *m*; **of one's
own – will,** aus freien
Stücken

freeze, fries, *v* frieren,
gefrieren; **–r,** *n*
Tiefkühltruhe *f*

freezing, frie-sing, *adj* eisig;

– point, *n* Gefrierpunkt *m*

freight, freht, *n* Ladung *f*;
(cost) Fracht *f*; *v*
befrachten

French, frentsch, *adj*
französisch; *n*; (language)
Französisch *nt*; *npl*
(people) Franzosen *pl*; **–
bean,** *n* grüne Bohne *f*; **–
fries,** *npl* Pommes frites *pl*;
–man, *n* Franzose *m*;
–woman, *n* Französin *f*; **–
window,** Verandatür *f*

frenzied, frenn-sidd, *adj*
rasend

frenzy, frenn-si, *n* Raserei *f*,
Wahnsinn *m*

frequency, frie-ku'en-ssi, *n*
Häufigkeit *f*; (physics)
Frequenz *f*

frequent, frie-ku'ent, *adj*
häufig

frequent, fri-**ku'ent,** *v*
besuchen

fresh, fresch, *adj* frisch;
(cheeky) frech, keck; **–en
up,** *v* (sich) frischmachen;
–ness, *n* Frische *f*; **–water,**
adj Süßwasser-

fret, frett, *v* beunruhigt sein;
–ful, *adj* unruhig; (child)
quengelig; **–saw,** *n*
Laubsäge *f*

friar, frei-er, *n* Mönch *m*,
Frater *m*

friction, frick-sch'n, *n*
Reibung *f*, Friktion *f*

Friday, frei-deh, *n* Freitag *m*

fridge, fridsch, *n*
Kühlschrank *m*

friend, frend, *n* Freund *m*,

Freundin *f*; **–ly,** *adj*
freundschaftlich;
befreundet; **–ship,** *n*
Freundschaft *f*

frieze, fries, *n* Fries *m*

fright, freit, *n* Schreck *m*,
Furcht *f*; **–en,** *v* (people)
erschrecken; (animals)
verscheuchen; **–ening,** *adj*
schrecklich; **–ful,** *adj*
schrecklich, furchtbar; **be
–ened,** *v* Angst haben

frigid, fridd-dschidd, *adj*
eisig; *fig* frostig

frill, frill, *n* Krause *f*; *v*
kräuseln

fringe, frindsch, *n* Franse *f*;
(edge) Rand *m*; *v* säumen

frisk, frisk, *v* durchsuchen

frisky, friss-ki, *adj*
ausgelassen; (horse)
tänzeln

fritter, fritt-er, *n* (sweet)
Ausgebackenes *nt*; **–
away,** *v* vergeuden

frivolous, friw-e-less, *adj*
frivol, leichtfertig

frizzy, fris-i, *adj* kraus

fro, froh, *adv* **to and –,** hin
und her, auf und ab

frock, frock, *n* Kleid *nt*

frog, frogg, *n* Frosch *m*

frolic, froll-ick, *n* Spaß *m*; *v*
(herum)springen

from, fromm, *prep*
(distance) von; (origin)
aus; (cause) vor; (past
time) seit; **– ... to ...,** von
... bis ...; **where –?**
woher?

front, frant, *adj* Vorder-; *n*

Vorderteil nt, Vorderseite f; mil Front f; – door, Haustür f; in –, adv vorne; in – of, prep vor; front page, n Titelseite f

frontier, frann-tier, n Grenze f

frost, frost, n Frost m; v mit Reif überziehen –bitten, adj erfroren; –ed glass, n Milchglas nt; –y, adj frostig, eisig

froth, froth, n Schaum m; v schäumen

frown, fraun, n Stirnrunzeln nt; v die Stirne runzeln

frugal, fruh-g'l, adj (meal) spärlich; (person) sparsam

fruit, fruht, n (singly) Frucht f; (collectively) Obst nt; –erer, n Obsthändler m; –ful, adj fruchtbar

fruition, fru-isch-'n, n Reife f; fig Genuß m

fruitless, fruht-liss, adj unfruchtbar, fruchtlos

fruit machine, fruht me-schien, n Spielautomat m

frustrate, frass-treht, v vereiteln; –d, adj frustriert

fry, frei, v braten; –ing pan, n Bratpfanne f

fudge, fudsch, n Fondant m; v ausweichen

fuel, fju-el, n Brennstoff m; v treiben

fugitive, fjuh-dschi-tiw, n Flüchtling m

fulfil, full-fill, v erfüllen; –ment, n Erfüllung f

full, full, adj voll; – moon, n Vollmond m; –scale, adj (drawing) in Originalgröße; (complete) total; – stop, n Punkt m; –time, adj Ganztags-; –y, adv völlig, gänzlich; in –, vollständig

fulsome, full-sem, adj übertrieben

fume, fjuhm, v dampfen; (be angry) wütend sein; –s, npl Abgase pl

fun, fann, n Scherz m, Spaß m; make – of, v sich lustig machen über

function, fank-sch'n, n Veranstaltung f; Funktion f; v funktionieren; –al, adj zweckmäßig

fund, fand, n Fonds m; v finanzieren; –s, npl Mittel pl

fundamental, fan-de-menn-t'l, adj grundlegend, wesentlich

funeral, fjuh-ne-rel, n Beerdigung f; – service, n Trauergottesdienst m

funfair, fann-fähr, n Jahrmarkt m

fungus, fang-gess, n Pilz m

funnel, fann-'l, n Trichter m; (of engine, steamer) Schlot m; v schleusen

funny, fann-i, adj komisch, witzig

fur, för, n Pelz m, Fell nt

furbish, för-bisch, v ausstatten

furious, fjuhr-ri-ess, adj wütend, rasend

furlong, för-long, n Achtelmeile f

furlough, för-loh, n Urlaub m

furnace, för-niss, n Ofen m

furnish, för-nisch, v möblieren

furniture, för-nit-tscher, n Möbel npl

furrow, fa-roh, n Furche f

further, för-dher, adj weiter; adv überdies, ferner; v fördern; – education, n Weiterbildung f; (for adults) Erwachsenenbildung f; –more, adv ferner

furtive, för-tiw, adj verstohlen

fury, fjuhr-ri, n Wut f

fuse, fjuhs, n Zünder m; (electric) Sicherung f; v verschmelzen; durchbrennen; – box, n Sicherungskasten m

fuselage, fjuh-se-lahsch, n (Flugzeug) Rumpf m

fusion, fjuh-sch'n, n Verschmelzung f

fuss, fass, n Theater nt, Rummel m; v viel Aufhebens machen; –y, adj wählerisch

futile, fjuh-teil, adj vergeblich, nutzlos

futility, fju-till-i-ti, n Sinnlosigkeit f

future, fjuh-tscher, adj zukünftig; n Zukunft f

G

gabble, gäbb-'l, *v* brabbeln

gable, geh-b'l, *n* Giebel *m*

gadget, gädd-dschitt, *n* Gerät *nt*

Gaelic, geh-lick, *adj* gälisch; *n* (language) Gälisch *nt*

gaffe, gäff, *n* Fauxpas *m*, Fehler *m*

gag, gägg, *n* Knebel *m*; (joke) Gag *m*; *v* knebeln; (silence) zum Schweigen bringen; (choke) würgen

gaiety, geh-i-ti, *n* Fröhlichkeit *f*

gaily, geh-li, *adv* lustig

gain, gehn, *n* Gewinn *m*; *v* (win) gewinnen; (obtain) erhalten; (watch) vorgehen

gait, geht, *n* Gang *m*

gala, gah-le, *adj* Gala-; *n* Gala *f*, Fest *nt*

galaxy, gäll-äck-si, *n* Milchstraße *f*, Galaxis *f*

gale, gehl, *n* Sturm *m*

gall, go'al, *n* (cheek) Frechheit *f*

gallant, gäll-ant, *adj* tapfer; ritterlich; **-ry,** *n* (courage) Tapferkeit *f*; (manners) Aufmerksamkeit *f*

gallery, gäll-e-ri, *n* Galerie *f*

galling, go'a-ling, *adj* ärgerlich

gallon, gäll-en, *n* Gallone *f*

gallop, gäll-epp, *n* Galopp *m*; *v* galoppieren

gallows, gäll-ohs, *npl* Galgen *m*

galore, ga-lor, *adv* in Menge, in Fülle

galvanize, gäll-ve-neis, *v* (*fig* rouse) wachrütteln, galvanisieren

gamble, gämm-b'l, *n* Glücksspiel *nt*; (risk) Wagnis *v* spielen; (risk) riskieren, aufs Spiel

setzen; **-r,** *n* Spieler *m*

gambol, gämm-b'l, *n* Luftsprung *m*; *v* hüpfen

game, gehm, *n* Spiel *nt*; Partie *f*; (animals) Wild *nt*; (*fam* prostitution) Prostitution *f*; **-keeper,** Wildhüter *m*

gammon, gämm-en, *n* geräucherter Schinken *m*

gamut, gämm-et, *n* Tonleiter *f*; Umfang *m*

gang, gäng, *n* Trupp *m*; (of robbers etc.) Bande *f*

gangster, gäng-ster, *n* Gangster *m*

gangway, gäng-u'eh, *n* (passage) Gang *m*; (ship's) Gangway *f*

gaol, dschehl, *n* Gefängnis *nt*

gap, gäpp, *n* Lücke *f*

gape, gehp, *v* gaffen, glotzen

gaping, geh-ping, *adj* gähnend

garage, gä-rahsh, *n* Garage *f*

garb, gahrb, *n* Tracht *f*

garbage, gahr-bidsch, *n* Abfall *m*

garble, gahr-b'l, *v* durcheinanderbringen

garden, gahr-d'n, *n* Garten *m*; *v* im Garten arbeiten; **-er,** *n* Gärtner *m*; **-ing,** *n* Gartenarbeit *f*

gargle, gahr-g'l, *n* Gurgelwasser *nt*; *v* gurgeln

garish, gähr-risch, *adj* auffallend, grell

garlic, gahr-lick, *n* Knoblauch *m*

garment, gahr-ment, *n*
Kleidungsstück *nt*

garnish, gahr-nisch, *n*
Garnierung *f*; *v* garnieren

garret, gä-ritt, *n* Dachstube *f*

garrison, gä-ri-ss'n, *n*
Garnison *f*

garrulous, gä-rju-less, *adj*
schwatzhaft

garter, gahr-ter, *n*
Strumpfband *nt*

gas, gäss, *n* Gas *nt*; (petrol)
Benzin *nt*

gaseous, geh-ssi-ess, *adj*
gasig, gasartig

gash, gäsch, *n* klaffende
Wunde *f*; *v* tief ins Fleisch
schneiden

gasket, gäss-kitt, *n*
Dichtung *f*

gasp, gahsp, *n* Keuchen *nt*; *v*
nach Luft schnappen

gastric, gäss-trick, *adj*
gastrisch, Magen-

gate, geht, *n* (small) Pforte *f*;
(large) Tor *nt*; (airport)
Flugsteig *m*

gather, gädh-er, *v*
(ver)sammeln; (infer)
schließen, erfahren; **–ing,**
n Versammlung *f*

gauche, gohsch, *adj* linkisch;
(tactless) plump

gaudy, go'a-di, *adj* (colour)
grell; (appearance)
prunkhaft

gauge, gehdsch, *n* (size)
Normalmaß *nt*; (tool)
Maßstab *m*; (rails)
Spurweite *f*; (petrol)
Benzinuhr *f*; *v* ausmessen;

fig abschätzen

gaunt, go'ant, *adj* hager, dürr

gauntlet, go'ant-litt, *n*
Fehdehandschuh *m*

gauze, go'as, *n* Gaze *f*; (wire)
Drahtgeflecht *nt*

gawky, go'a-ki, *adj* linkisch;
(tall and thin) schlaksig

gay, geh, *adj* (happy)
fröhlich; (colour) lebhaft;
(homosexual) schwul

gaze, gehs, *n* Blick *m*; *v*
starren; **– at,** anstarren

GB, *abbr* **Great Britain**

gear, gier, *n mech* Getriebe
nt; (fam equipment)
Ausrüstung *f*; **–box,** *n*
Getriebekasten *m*; **be –ed
to,** *v* ausgerichtet sein auf;
bottom –, niedrigster
Gang *m*; **reverse –,**
Rückwärtsgang *m*; **top –,**
höchster Gang *m*

gelatine, dschell-e-tien, *n*
Gelatine *f*

gem, dschemm, *n*
Edelstein *m*

Gemini, dschemm-i-ni, *n*
Zwillinge *pl*

gender, dschenn-der, *n*
Geschlecht *nt*

general, dschenn-e-rel, *adj*
allgemein; *n* General *m*;
–ize, *v* verallgemeinern;
–ly, *adv* im allgemeinen; **–
practitioner,** *n* praktischer
Arzt *m*

generate, dschenn-e-reht, *v*
erzeugen

generation, dschenn-e-reh-
sch'n, *n* Generation *f*;

(production) Erzeugung *f*

generator, dschenn-e-reh-
ter, *n* Stromerzeuger *m*;
Generator *m*

generosity, dschenn-e-ross-
i-ti, *n* Großzügigkeit *f*;
(magnanimity) Großmut *f*

generous, dschenn-e-ress,
adj großzügig

genetic, dschi-nett-ick, *adj*
genetisch; **–s,** *n* Genetik *f*

Geneva, dschi-nie-we, *n*
Genf *nt*

genial, dschie-ni-el, *adj*
angenehm; (person)
liebenswürdig

genitals, dschenn-i-t'ls, *npl*
Genitalien *pl*

genius, dschie-ni-ess, *n*
Genie *nt*

genocide, dschenn-e-sseid, *n*
Völkermord *m*

genteel, dschenn-tiel, *adj*
fein, vornehm

gentle, dschenn-t'l, *adj*
sanft, mild; **–man,** *n*
Gentleman *m*, Herr *m*;
–ness, *n* Sanftheit *f*;
Milde *f*

gently, dschent-li, *adv* sanft

gents, dschents, *n* (toilet)
Herren *pl*

genuine, dschenn-ju-inn,
adj echt; **–ness,** *n*
Echtheit *f*

geographic(al), dschi-e-
gräff-ick(-'l), *adj*
geographisch

geography, dschi-ogg-re-fi, *n*
Geographie *f*

geological, dschi-e-lodsch-ik'l, *adj* geologisch

geology, dschi-**oll**-e-dschi, *n* Geologie *f*

geometric(al), dschi-e-**mett**-rick(-'l), *adj* geometrisch

geometry, dschi-**omm**-i-tri, *n* Geometrie *f*

geranium, dschi-**reh**-ni-em, *n* Geranie *f*

geriatric, dsche-ri-**ätt**-rick, *adj* Alten-; *n* alter Mensch *m*

germ, dschörm, *n* Keim *m*; *med* Bazillus *m*

German, dschör-men, *adj* deutsch; *n* (language) Deutsch *nt*; (person) Deutsche(r) *m & f*

Germany, dschör-me-ni, *n* Deutschland *nt*

germinate, dschör-mi-neht, *v* keimen, sprossen

gesticulate, dschess-**tick**-ju-leht, *v* gestikulieren

gesture, dschess-tscher, *n* Geste *f*

get, gett, *v* (obtain, catch) bekommen; (earn) verdienen; (fetch) bringen, holen; (become) werden; – **back,** (return) zurückkommen; – **by,** (manage) durchkommen; – **down,** (descend) ; (dismount) absteigen; – **down to,** in Angriff nehmen; – **in(to),** einsteigen (in); – **off,** (alight) aussteigen; (escape) loskommen; – **on,** (progress)

weiterkommen; – **out,** herauskommen; – **over,** (illness, shock) sich erholen von; – **round,** (circumvent) herumkommen um; – **round to** (it), dazu kommen; –**get sth done,** etw machen lassen; – **(to),** (arrive) ankommen (in); – **through** (to), durchkommen (zu); – **up,** aufstehen

ghastly, gahst-li, *adj* gräßlich

gherkin, gör-kinn, *n* Gewürzgurke *f*

ghetto, gett-oh, *n* G(h)etto *nt*; – **blaster,** *n fam* (lauter) Radiorekorder

ghost, gohst, *n* Gespenst *nt*; –ly, *adj* geisterhaft

giant, dschei-ent, *adj* riesig; *n* Riese *m*

gibberish, dschibb-e-risch, *n* Kauderwelsch *nt*

gibe, dscheib, *n* Spott *m*; *v* verspotten

giblets, dschibb-lits, *npl* (Geflügel)innereien *pl*

giddiness, gidd-i-niss, *n* Schwindelanfall *m*

giddy, gidd-i, *adj* schwindlig

gift, gift, *n* (present) Gabe *f*, Geschenk *nt*; (talent) Begabung *f*; –**ted,** *adj* begabt

gigantic, dschai-**gänn**-tick, *adj* riesenhaft; riesig

giggle, gigg-'l, *n* Gekicher *nt*; *v* kichern

gild, gild, *v* vergolden; –ing,

n Vergoldung *f*

gills, gills, *npl* Kiemen *pl*

gilt, gilt, *adj* vergoldet; *n* Vergoldung *f*

gimmick, gimm-ick, *n* Gag *m*

gin, dschinn, *n* (drink) Gin *m*, (Wacholder)schnaps *m*; (trap) Schlinge *f*

ginger, dschinn-dscher, *n* Ingwer *m*; – **beer,** *n* Ingwerbier *nt*; –**bread,** *n* Pfefferkuchen *m*; – **haired,** rothaarig; –ly, *adv* behutsam

gipsy, dschipp-ssi, *n* Zigeuner *m*

giraffe, dschi-rahf, *n* Giraffe *f*

girder, gör-der, *n* Träger *m*

girdle, gör-d'l, *n* Hüftgürtel *m*

girl, görl, *n* Mädchen *nt*; –**friend,** *n* Freundin *f*

giro, dschai-roh, *n* (bank) Giro *nt*; (post office) Postscheck *m*

girth, görth, *n* (strap) Sattelgurt *m*; (circumference) Umfang *m*

gist, dschist, *n* Wesentliches *nt*, Kern *m*

give, giw, *v* geben; (present) schenken; (confer) erteilen; – **away,** verschenken; – **in,** nachgeben; – **up,** aufgeben; – **way,** (to traffic) Vorfahrt gewähren; (collapse,

yield) nachgeben,
einstürzen

glacier, gläss-i-er, n
Gletscher m

glad, glädd, adj froh; (news)
erfreulich; **–ly**, adv gern(e)

glamorous, glämm-e-ress, adj
glamourös

glamour, glämm-er, n
Glanz m

glance, glahnss, n Blick m; v
blicken;**– off**, v abprallen
(von)

gland, gländ, n Drüse f

glare, glähr, n (brightness)
grelles Licht nt; (stare)
wilder Blick m; v blenden;
(stare) anstarren

glaring, glähr-ring, adj
blendend; (striking)
auffallend; (obvious) kraß

glass, glahss, adj Glas-; n
Glas nt, **–es**, npl
(spectacles) Brille f; **–
house**, n Gewächshaus nt;
– ware, n Glas nt; **–works**,
n Glashütte f; **–y**, adj
(stare) glasig; (smooth)
spiegelglatt

glaze, glehs, n Glasur f; v
(door etc.) verglasen;
(pottery etc.) glasieren; **–
over**, glasig werden

glazier, glehs-jer, n Glaser m

gleam, gliem, n Schimmer
m; (ray) Strahl m; v
schimmern, strahlen

glean, glien, v herausfinden

glee, glie, n Freude f

glib, glibb, adj pej aalglatt

glide, gleid, v gleiten; **–r**, n

(aircraft) Segelflugzeug nt

glimmer, glimm-er, n
Schimmer m; v
schimmern

glimpse, glimps, n flüchtiger
Blick m; v flüchtig sehen

glint, glint, n Lichtschein m;
v scheinen

glisten, gliss-'n, v glitzern,
glänzen

glitter, glitt-er, n Glitzern nt;
v glitzern

gloat (over), gloht (oh-
wer), v sich an etw
weiden; (sadistic pleasure)
schadenfroh sein

global, gloh-b'l, adj global,
Welt-; **– warming**, n
globale Erwärmung f

globe, glohb, n (sphere)
Kugel f; (earth) Erdball m;
(map) Globus m

globular, globb-ju-ler, adj
kugelförmig

gloom, gluhm, n
Düsterheit f

gloomy, gluh-mi, adj düster;
(person) schwermütig

glorify, glo'a-ri-fei, v
verherrlichen

glorious, glo'a-ri-ess, adj
glorreich; (excellent)
herrlich

glory, glo'a-ri, n Ruhm m;
(honour) Ehre f; **– in**, v
sich an etw rühmen; (take
pleasure) sich an etw
erfreuen

gloss, gloss, n Glanz m;
(paint) Lackfarbe f; **–
over**, v beschönigen; **–y**,

adj glänzend

glove, glaw, n Handschuh m

glow, gloh, n Glut f, Glühen
nt; (of sky) Röte f; v
glühen

glue, gluh, n Klebstoff m; v
kleben

glum, glamm, adj
mißgelaunt

glut, glatt, n Überfülle f; v
überschwemmen

glutton, glatt-'n, n Vielfraß
m; **–y**, n Völlerei f

gnarled, nahrld, adj knorrig

gnash, näsch, v knirschen

gnat, nätt, n Mücke f

gnaw, no'a, v nagen (an),
zernagen

go, goh, n Schwung m; v
gehen; (drive) fahren;
(travel) reisen; (depart)
abfahren; (function)
funktionieren; (become)
werden; **– away**,
weggehen; (on journey)
verreisen; **– back**,
zurückgehen; **– down**,
hinuntergehen; (sink)
untergehen; **– for**, holen;
(attack) angreifen; (like)
mögen; **– off**, (depart)
abgehen; (of light)
ausgehen; (explode)
losgehen; (go bad)
schlecht werden; (cease to
like) nicht mehr mögen; **–
on**, (continue)
weitergehen; pej reden
und reden; (of light)
angehen; (happen)
passieren; **– out**,

ausgehen; **– up,**
hinaufsteigen; **– with,**
passen zu; **– without,**
verzichten auf; **be –ing to,**
werden; **have a – (at),**
versuchen

goad, gohd, n v anstacheln

go-ahead, goh-*e*-hedd, adj
unternehmungslustig; n
(*fig* permission) grünes
Licht nt

goal, gohl, n (aim) Ziel nt;
sport Tor nt; **–keeper,** n
Torwart m

goat, goht, n Ziege f

gobble, gobb-'l, v
hinunterschlingen

goblet, gobb-litt, n Pokal m

goblin, gobb-linn, n
Kobold m

god, godd, n Gott m; **–child,**
n Patenkind nt; **–dess,** n
Göttin f; **–father,** n Pate
m; **– fearing,** adj
gottesfürchtig; **–forsaken,**
adj gottverlassen; **–liness,**
n Frömmigkeit f; **–ly,** adj
fromm; **–mother,** n Patin
f; **–send,** n Gottesgabe f

goggle-eyed, gogg-'l-eid, adj
glotzäugig

goggles, gogg-'ls, npl
Schutzbrille f

going, goh-ing, adj (current)
gängig; (viable)
gutgehend; in (progress)
Vorankommen nt

gold, gohld, adj golden,
Gold-; n Gold nt; **–en,** adj
golden; **–finch,** n Stieglitz
m; **–fish,** Goldfisch m;

–mine, Goldgrube f;
–smith, Goldschmied m

golf, golf, n Golf nt; **– club,**
n (organization) Golfklub
m; (stick) Golfschläger m;
– course, n Golfplatz m;
–er, n Golfspieler m

gondola, gonn-de-le, n
Gondel f

gong, gong, n Gong m

good, gudd, adj gut; n
(goodness) Güte nt; (use)
Nutzen m; (benefit) Wohl
nt; **– afternoon!** guten
Tag!; **–bye!** auf
Wiedersehen!; (on
telephone) auf
Wiederhören!; **– morning!**
guten Morgen!; **– night!**
gute Nacht!; **G– Friday,** n
Karfreitag m; **–looking,**
adj gutaussehend; **–
natured,** adj gutmütig

goodness, gudd-niss, n Güte
f; (virtue) Tugend f

goods, gudds, npl Waren pl
Güter pl; **– train,** n
Güterzug m

goodwill, gudd-u'ill, n
Wohlwollen nt; comm
Goodwill m

goose, guhss, n Gans f

gooseberry, gus-be-ri, n
Stachelbeere f

gooseflesh, guhss-flesch, n
Gänsehaut f

goose pimples, guhss pimm-
p'ls, npl Gänsehaut f

gore, gohr, n Blut nt; v
durchbohren

gorge, gordsch, n

Bergschlucht f; v **– (o.s.),**
sich vollstopfen

gorgeous, gor-dschess, adj
prächtig; (person)
hinreißend

gorilla, ge-rill-*e*, n Gorilla m

gorse, gorss, n Stechginster
m

gory, go'a-ri, adj blutig

gosling, gos-ling, n junge
Gans f, Gänschen nt

gospel, goss-p'l, n
Evangelium nt

gossip, goss-ipp, n (talk)
Klatsch m; (person)
Klatschbase f; v klatschen

gouge (out), gaudsch (aut),
v (aus)bohren

gout, gaut, n Gicht f; **–y,** adj
gichtkrank

govern, gaw-ern, v regieren;
–ess, n Gouvernante f;
–ment, Regierung f; **–or,**
Prinzipal m; (of province)
Statthalter m; mech
Regulator m

gown, gaun, n Kleid nt;
(official) Talar m;
(academic) Robe f

GP, dschie pie, abbr general
practitioner

grab, gräbb, v packen

grace, grehss, n (blessing)
Gnade f; (prayer)
Tischgebet nt; (charm)
Anmut f; v zieren; **–ful,**
adj graziös, anmutig;
–fulness, n Grazie f;
Anmut f; **–less,** adj
taktlos, schroff

gracious, greh-schess, adj

liebenswürdig; (merciful) gnädig

gradation, gre-**deh**-sch'n, *n* Abstufung *f*

grade, grehd, *n* Grad *m*, Rang *m*; (class) Klasse *f*; *v* einstufen

gradient, greh-di-ent, *n* Neigung *f*

gradual(ly), grädd-ju-el(-li), *adj & adv* allmählich

graduate, grädd-ju-et, *n* Akademiker *m*

graduate, grädd-ju-eht, *v* (from university) absolvieren

graft, grahft, *n* (botany) Edelreis *nt*; *med* Transplantat *nt*; (*fam* corruption) Schiebung *f*; (*fam* hard work) Schufterei *f*; *v* (tree) pfropfen; *med* transplantieren; (*fam* work hard) schuften

grain, grehn, *n* (of corn, salt, *photog* etc.) Korn *nt*; (cereal) Getreide *nt*; (of wood) Maserung *f*

gram, grämm, *n* Gramm *nt*

grammar, grämm-er, *n* Grammatik *f*; – **school,** *n* Gymnasium *nt*

gramme, grämm, *n* Gramm *nt*

granary, gränn-*e*-ri, *n* Kornspeicher *m*; – **bread,** *n* Vollkornbrot *nt*

grand, grähnd, *adj* grandios, großartig; –**child,** *n* Enkelkind *nt*; –**daughter,**

Enkelin *f*; –**father,** Großvater *m*; –**iose,** *adj* grandios; –**mother,** Großmutter *f*; –**parents,** *npl* Großeltern *pl*; – **piano,** *n* Flügel *m*; –**son,** Enkel *m*

grant, grahnt, *n* Zuschuß *m*; (scholarship) Stipendium *nt*; *v* bewilligen, gewähren; zugeben

granted, grahn-tidd, **take for –,** *v* als selbstverständlich hinnehmen

grape, grehp, *n* Traube *f*

grapefruit, grehp-fruht, *n* Pampelmuse *f*, Grapefruit *f*

graph, grahf, *n* Schaubild *nt*

graphic, gräff-ick, *adj* (vivid) anschaulich; (drawn) graphisch; –**s,** *n* Grafik *f*

grapple with, gräpp-'l u'idh, *fig.* ernstlich anpacken

grasp, grahsp, *n* Griff *m*; *v* greifen; (mentally) begreifen; –**ing,** *adj* habgierig

grass, grahss, *n* Gras *nt*; (lawn) Rasen *m*; –**hopper,** *n* Heuschrecke *f*; –**roots,** *adj* Basis-, von der Basis ausgehend; –**y,** *adj* grasig; *v* (*fam* tell) singen

grate, greht, *n* Kamin *m*; *v* (cheese etc.) reiben; (scrape) knirschen; (annoy) auf die Nerven gehen

grateful, greht-full, *adj*

dankbar

gratification, grätt-i-fi-keh-sch'n, *n* Genugtuung *f*; (satisfaction) Befriedigung *f*

gratify, grätt-i-fei, *v* freuen; (satisfy) befriedigen; –**ing,** *adj* erfreulich

grating, greh-ting, *adj* (rasping) knirschend; (shrill) schrill; *n* Gitter *nt*

gratis, greh-tiss, *adv* gratis, umsonst

gratitude, grätt-i-tjuhd, *n* Dankbarkeit *f*

gratuitous, gre-tjuh-i-tess, *adj* grundlos

gratuity, gre-tjuh-i-ti, *n* Geschenk *nt*; (tip) Trinkgeld *nt*

grave, grehw, *adj* ernst; *n* Grab *nt*

gravel, gräw-'l, *n* Kies *m*

gravestone, grehw-stohn, *n* Grabstein *m*

graveyard, grehw-jahrd, *n* Friedhof *m*

gravitate (towards), gräw-i-teht (tu-**u'ords**), *v* angezogen werden (von)

gravity, gräw-i-ti, *n* (physics) Schwere *f*; (seriousness) Ernsthaftigkeit *f*

gravy, greh-wi, *n* Soße *f*

graze, grehs, *n* Abschürfung *f*; *v* (touch) streifen; (scrape skin) aufschürfen; (feed) grasen

grease, griess, *n* Fett *nt*; (lubricant) Schmierfett *nt*;

v einfetten; (lubricate)
schmieren

greasy, grie-ssi, *adj* (oily)
fettig; (road) schlüpfrig

great, greht, *adj* groß;
(renowned) berühmt;
(*fam* good) toll

Great Britain, greht britt-
'n, *n* Großbritannien *nt*

great-grandfather, greht
gränd-fah-dher,
Urgroßvater *m*

great-grandmother, greht
gränd-madh-er,
Urgroßmutter *f*

greatly, greht-li, *adv* sehr

greatness, greht-niss, *n*
Größe *f*

Greece, griess, *n*
Griechenland *nt*

greed, gried, *n* Gier *f*;
(gluttony) Gefräßigkeit *f*;
–ily, *adv* gierig, gefräßig;
–iness, *n* Gier *f*; **–y,** *adj*
gierig, gefräßig

Greek, griek, *adj* griechisch;
n (language) Griechisch
nt; (person) Grieche *m*,
Griechin *f*

green, grien, *adj* grün;
(environmentally
friendly)
umweltfreundlich; *n* Grün
nt; (open ground) Wiese *f*;
v grünen; **–gage,** *n*
Reineclaude *f*; **–grocer,**
Gemüsehändler *m*;
–house, Gewächshaus *nt*;
–house gas, Treibhausgas
nt; **–ish,** *adj* grünlich; **–s,**
npl Grüngemüse *nt*

greet, griet, *v* begrüßen;
–ing, *n* Gruß *m*

gregarious, gri-gähr-ri-ess,
adj gesellig

grenade, gre-nehd, *n*
Granate *f*

grey, greh, *adj* grau; **–hound,**
n Windhund *m*

grief, grief, *n* Kummer *m*,
Trauer *f*

grievance, grie-wenss, *n*
Beschwerde *f*

grieve, griew, *v* trauern;
(vex) betrüben

grievous, griew-ess, *adj*
(serious) schwer;
(distressing) schmerzlich

grill, grill, *n* Rost *m*, Grill *m*;
v auf dem Rost braten,
grillen

grim, grimm, *adj* (dismal)
finster; (fierce) grimmig

grimace, gri-mehss, *n*
Grimasse *f*; *v* das Gesicht
verziehen

grime, greim, *n* Schmutz *m*

grin, grinn, *n* Grinsen *nt*; *v*
grinsen

grind, greind, *v* (coffee etc.)
mahlen; (knife) schleifen;
(teeth) knirschen mit;
–er, *n* Mühle *f*

grip, gripp, *n* Griff *m*; *v*
greifen, packen; **–ping,** *adj*
spannend

grisly, gris-li, *adj* gräßlich,
grausig

gristle, griss-'l, *n* Knorpel *m*

grit, gritt, *n* (gravel) Splitt
m; (*fam* courage) Schneid
m; *v* (teeth)

zusammenbeißen; (road)
streuen; **–ty,** *adj* sandig

groan, grohn, *n* Stöhnen *nt*,
Ächzen *nt*; *v* stöhnen

grocer, grohss-er, *n*
Lebensmittelhändler *m*;
–ies, *npl* Lebensmittel *pl*;
–'s, –y, *n*
Lebensmittelgeschäft *nt*

groin, greun, *n* Leisten *fpl.*

groom, gruhm, *n*
Pferdeknecht *m*;
(bridegroom) Bräutigam
m; *v* sich zurechtmachen;
(horse) striegeln; **well-
–ed,** *adj* gepflegt

groove, gruhw, *n* Rinne *f*,
Furche *f*

grope, grohp, *v* tasten,
tappen

gross, grohss, *adj* (thick)
dick; (coarse) grob; *comm*
brutto; *n* (12 dozen) Gros
nt; **– weight,**
Bruttogewicht *nt*; **–ly,** *adv*
ungeheuer

ground, graund, *v*
gründenen auf; *naut*
stranden; *n* Grund *m*,
Boden *m*; *sport* Platz *m*; **–
floor,** *n* Erdgeschoß *nt*;
–ing, *n* Grundlagen *pl*;
–less, *adj* grundlos; **–s,** *npl*
(park) Anlagen *fpl.*;
(coffee etc.) Satz *m*;
–sheet, *n* Zeltboden *m*;
–work, *n* Grundlage *f*;
(preparation) Vorarbeit *f*

group, gruhp, *n* Gruppe *f*; *v*
gruppieren

grouse, grauss, *n* Waldhuhn

nt; v fam murren

grove, grohw, n Hain m

grovel, grow-'l, v kriechen

grow, groh, v wachsen; (become) werden; (cultivate) anbauen; –er, n Produzent m; –n up, adj erwachsen; –th, n Wachstum nt; med Geschwür nt; (increase) Zunahme f; (of beard) Wuchs m

growl, graul, n Brummen nt; v brummen

grub, grabb, n Larve f; (fam food) Futter nt; –by, adj schmutzig

grudge, gradsch, n Groll m; v mißgönnen; bear a –, v einen Groll hegen

gruelling, gruh-e-ling, adj zermürbend

gruesome, gruh-sem, adj grausig, grauenhaft

gruff, graff, adj mürrisch; (voice) rauh

grumble, gramm-b'l, v murren

grumpy, gramm-pi, adj schlechtgelaunt

grunt, grant, n Grunzen nt; v grunzen

guarantee, gä-ren-tie, n Garantie f; v garantieren

guard, gahrd, n Wache f; (railway) Schaffner m; (machine) Schutzvorrichtung f; (corps) Garde f; v bewachen; –ed, adj zurückhaltend; (cautious)

vorsichtig; –ian, n Hüter m; (trustee) Vormund m

guerrilla, ge-rill-e, n Guerilla m; – war(fare), n Guerillakrieg m

guess, gess, n Vermutung f; v raten; –work, n Raten nt

guest, gest, n Gast m; –house, Pension f; –room, n Gästezimmer nt

guidance, gei-denss, n Leitung f, Führung f; (advice) Rat m

guide, geid, n Führer m; (book) Reiseführer m; v führen; –book, n Reiseführer m; – dog, n Blindenhund m; –lines, npl Richtlinien pl

guild, gild, n Gilde f

guile, geil, n Arglist f; –less, adj arglos

guilt, gilt, n Schuld f; –y, adj schuldig

guinea, ginn-i, n Guinee f; – pig, n Meerschweinchen nt; fig Versuchskaninchen nt

guise, geis, n in the – of sth, in Gestalt eines/des

guitar, gi-tahr, n Gitarre f

gulf, galf, n (sea) Golf m; (abyss) Abgrund m

gull, gall, n Möwe f

gullet, gall-itt, n Kehle f

gullible, gall-i-b'l, adj leichtgläubig

gulp, galp, n Schluck m; v schlucken

gum, gamm, n (glue) Klebstoff m; (in mouth) Zahnfleisch nt; v

gummieren

gun, gann, n Gewehr nt; (cannon) Geschütz nt; –down, v erschießen; –fire, n Geschützfeuer nt; –man, n mit einer Schutzwaffe bewaffneter Mann m; –powder, n Schießpulver nt

gurgle, gör-gl, v glucksen

gush, gasch, n Erguß m; v hervorströmen; (fig enthuse) schwärmen

gust, gast, n Windstoß m; –y, adj böig, stürmisch

gut, gatt, n Darm m; –s, npl (fam courage) Schneid m

gutter, gatt-er, n (in street) Gosse f; (on roof) Dachrinne f

guy, gei, n (fam man) Typ m; (effigy) Strohpuppe f; –rope, n Zeltschnur f

gym, dschimm, n (abbr gymnasium/gymnastics)

gymnasium, dschimm-neh-si-em, n Turnhalle f, Fitneßstudio nt

gymnast, dschimm-näst, n Turner m

gymnastics, dschimm-näss-tiks, n Turnen nt, Gymnastik f

gym shoes, dschimm schuhs, npl Turnschuhe pl

gynaecologist, gai-ni-koll-e-dschist, n Gynäkologe m, Frauenarzt m

gynaecology, gai-ni-koll-e-dschi, n Gynäkologie f, Frauenheilkunde f

haberdashery, häbb-er-däsch-e-ri, n Kurzwaren pl

habit, häbb-itt, n Gewohnheit f; (addiction) Sucht f

habitable, häbb-i-te-b'l, adj (be)wohnbar

habitat, häbb-i-tätt, n Lebensraum m

habitual, he-bitt-ju-el, adj gewohnt, gewohnheitsmäßig; **–ly,** adv gewöhnlich

hack, häck, n (pej writer) Schreiberling m; (pej horse) Gaul m; v comp hacken

hacker, häck-er, n comp Hacker m

hackneyed, häck-nidd, adj abgedroschen

haddock, hädd-ek, n Schellfisch m

haemorrhage, hemm-e-ridsch, n Blutung f

hag, hägg, n Hexe f; **–gard,** adj (worn) ausgezehrt; (worry) abgehärmt

haggle, hägg-'l, v handeln, feilschen

Hague, hehg, n The **–,** Den Haag nt

hail, hehl, n Hagel m; v hageln; (call) rufen; (welcome) zujubeln

hair, hähr, n Haar nt; **–brush,** n Haarbürste f; **–cut,** n Haarschnitt m; **–do,** n Frisur f; **–dresser,** n Friseur m; **–drier,** n Fön m; **–pin,** n Haarnadel f; **–pin bend,** n Haarnadelkurve f; **–-raising,** adj haarsträubend; **–style,** n Frisur f; **–y,** adj haarig;

hake, hehk, n Seehecht m

hale, hehl, adj gesund; (robust) kräftig

half, hahf, adj & adv halb; n Hälfte f; (beer) kleines Bier nt; (child's ticket) halbe Fahrkarte f; **– an hour,** eine halbe Stunde f; **– board,** n Halbpension f; **–-hearted,** adj halbherzig; **–-price,** adj zum halben Preis; **– term,** n Ferien pl in der Mitte des Trimesters; **– time,** n sport Halbzeit f; (work) Kurzarbeit f; **–way,** adj halb; adv zur Hälfte; **one and a –,** anderthalb; **two and a –,** zweieinhalb

halibut, häll-i-bet, n Heilbutt m

hall, ho'al, n (building) Halle f; (room) Saal m; (hallway) Flur m; **–mark,** n (Feingehalts)stempel m

hallo = hello

hallowed, häll-ohd, adj geheiligt, heilig

Hallowe'en, häll-oh-ien, n Halloween nt

hallucinate, he-lu-ssi-neht, v halluzinieren

hallucination, he-lu-ssi-neh-sch'n, n Halluzination f

hallway, ho'al-u'eh, n Flur m

halo, heh-loh, n Heiligenschein m; (moon's) Hof m

halt, hollt, n Halt m; v anhalten; (stop) stoppen

halve, hahw, v halbieren

ham, hämm, n Schinken m

hamburger, hämm-bör-ger,

n Hamburger m

hamlet, hämm-litt, n
Dörfchen nt

hammer, hämm-er, n
Hammer m; v hämmern

hammock, hämm-ek, n
Hängematte f

hamper, hämm-per, n
Picknickkorb m; v
hindern

hand, händ, n Hand f; (of
clock) Zeiger m; (worker)
Arbeiter m; v reichen; –
in, v abgeben; **–bag,** n
Handtasche f; **–bill,** n
Flugblatt nt; **–book,** n
Handbuch nt; **–cuffs,** npl
Handschellen pl; **–ful,** n
Handvoll f; (fam
nuisance) Plage f; **–icap,** n
(sport etc.) Handikap;
(physical/mental)
Behinderung; v
benachteiligen; **–icapped,**
adj behindert; **–icraft,** n
(Kunst)handwerk nt;
–kerchief, n Taschentuch
nt; **–le,** n Griff m; (knob)
Türknopf m; v
handhaben, anfassen; –
luggage, n Handgepäck nt;
––made, adj handgemacht;
–out, n (charity) Gabe f;
(leaflet) Flugblatt nt;
–rail, n Geländer nt; **at –,**
nahe, **in –,** (cash) auf die
Hand; (underway) in
Arbeit; **give/lend a –,**
helfen; **on (the) one –/on
the other hand,**
einerseits/andererseits; **out**

of –, außer Kontrolle

handsome, hänn-ss'm, adj
gutaussehend; ansehnlich

handy, hänn-di, adj
(convenient) praktisch;
(skilled) geschickt; **–man,**
n Bastler m

hang, häng, v aufhängen;
hängen; – **about/around,**
herumhängen, lungern; –
on, fam warten; – **up,**
(phone) auflegen; **get the
– of,** etw in Griff
bekommen, mit etw
klarkommen

hangar, häng-er, n Hangar m

hanger, häng-er, n
Kleiderbügel m

**hang-gliding, häng-glei-
ding,** n Drachenfliegen nt

hangover, häng-oh-wer, n
Kater m

**hanker (after), häng-ker
(ahf-ter),** v sich sehnen
(nach)

hanky, abbr **handkerchief**

haphazard, häpp-häs-erd,
adj willkürlich

happen, häpp-en, v
geschehen, passieren

happily, häpp-i-li, adv
(joyfully) glücklich;
(fortunately)
glücklicherweise

happiness, häpp-i-niss, n
Glück nt

happy, häpp-i, adj glücklich;
– **birthday!** Herzlichen
Glückwunsch zum
Geburtstag!; – **New Year!**
Frohes Neues Jahr!

harangue, he-räng, n Tirade
f; v fam predigen

harass, hä-ress, v plagen;
–ment, n Belästigung f

harbour, hahr-ber, n Hafen
m; v (criminal etc.)
beherbergen; (suspicion
etc.) hegen

hard, hahrd, adj hart;
(difficult) schwer;
(character) unbeugsam;
adv (work) hart; (push)
fest; **–back,** n gebundene
Ausgabe f, Hard-cover-
Ausgabe f; – **disk,** n comp
Festplatte f; **–en,** v härten;
hart werden; **–en o.s.,** sich
hartmachen; **–ly,** adv
kaum; **–ness,** n Härte f;
–ship, n Not f; – **shoulder,**
n Seitenstreifen m; – **up,**
adj knapp bei Kasse;
–ware, n Eisenwaren pl;
comp Hardware f; **––
working,** adj fleißig; **–y,**
adj (person) abgehärtet;
(plant) winterhart

hare, hähr, n Hase m; **––lip,**
n Hasenscharte f

harm, hahrm, n Schaden m;
v schädigen; **–ful,** adj
schädlich; **–less,** adj harmlos

**harmonious, har-moh-ni-
ess,** adj harmonisch

harmonize, hahr-me-neis, v
harmonieren; mus
harmonisieren; – **(with),**
harmonieren (mit)

harness, hahr-niss, n
Geschirr nt; v anschirren;
(forces) ausnützen

harp, hahrp, n Harfe f; – **on (about),** fam (immer wieder) über etw reden

harpoon, har-**puhn,** n Harpune f; v harpunieren

harrowing, hä-roh-ing, adj entsetzlich

harsh, hahrsch, adj (sound) barsch; (severe) streng; (colour) grell

harvest, hahr-wist, n Ernte f; v ernten

hash, häsch, n (meat) Haschee nt; (chaos) Wirrwarr m

hashish, häsch-isch, n Haschisch nt

hassle, häss-'l, n Ärger m

haste, hehst, n Eile f

hasten, heh-ss'n, v beschleunigen; eilen, sich beeilen

hastily, hehss-ti-li, adv rasch

hasty, hehss-ti, adj rasch; pej voreilig

hat, hätt, n Hut m

hatch, hätsch, n (in wall) Durchreiche f; n (naut) Luke f; v ausbrüten; (plot) aushecken; –**back,** n Schräghecklimousine f

hatchet, hätt-schitt, n Beil nt

hate, heht, n Haß m; v hassen; –**ful,** adj verhaßt; gehässig

hatred, heht-ridd, n Haß m

haughty, ho'a-ti, adj stolz, hochmütig

haul, ho'al, v ziehen; (tow) schleppen; n (catch) Fang m; –**age,** n Spedition f; **a long –,** ein weiter Weg m

haunch, ho'antsch, n Schenkel m; (meat) Keule f

haunt, ho'ant, n Treffpunkt m; v (of ghost) spuken in; (of memory etc.) plagen; (frequent) verkehren in

have, häw, v (possess) haben; (baby) bekommen; – **breakfast,** frühstücken; – **lunch/dinner,** zu Mittag/Abend essen; – **sth done,** etw machen lassen

haven, heh-wen, n Zufluchtsort m

havoc, häw-ek, n Verheerung f

hawk, ho'ak, n Habicht m; v hausieren; –**er,** n Hausierer m

hawthorn, ho'a-thorn, n Hagedorn m

hay, heh, n Heu nt; – **fever,** n Heuschnupfen m; –**stack,** n Heuschober m

hazard, häs-erd, n (danger) Gefahr f; (chance) Schicksal nt; (risk) Risiko nt; v riskieren; –**ous,** adj gefährlich

haze, hehs, n Dunst m

hazel, heh-s'l, adj (colour) hellbraun; n Haselnußstrauch m; –**nut,** n Hazelnuß f

hazy, heh-si, adj dunstig; (unclear) verschwommen

he, hie, pron er

head, hedd, adj Ober-; n Kopf m; (boss) Chef m; (forefront) Spitze f; v (lead) leiten; (ball) köpfen; –**ache,** n Kopfschmerzen pl; – **first,** adv mit dem Kopf zuerst/voran; kopfüber; –**(for),** v fahren in Richtung; –**ing,** n Überschrift f; –**lamp,** n Scheinwerfer m; –**land,** n Vorgebirge nt; –**light,** n Scheinwerfer m; –**line,** n Schlagzeile f; –**long,** adj ungestüm; kopfüber; –**master,** n Schuldirektor m; –**mistress,** n Schuldirektorin f; – **office,** n Zentrale f; –**phones,** npl Kopfhörer pl; –**quarters,** npl Zentrale f; mil Hauptquartier nt; –**s or tails,** Kopf oder Zahl; –**strong,** adj eigensinnig; – **waiter,** n Oberkellner m; –**way,** n Fortschritte pl; –**y,** adj berauschend

heal, hiel, v heilen; verheilen; –**ing,** adj heilsam

health, helth, n Gesundheit f; – **food,** n Reformkost f; –**y,** adj gesund

heap, hiep, n Haufen m; v häufen

hear, hier, v hören; –**ing,** n Gehör nt; law Verhandlung f; –**ing aid,** n Hörgerät nt; –**say,** n Hörensagen nt

hearse, hörss, n
Leichenwagen m

heart, hahrt, n Herz nt;
(core) Kern m; (cards)
Herz nt; **– attack,** n
Herzanfall m; **–breaking,**
adj herzzerreißend;
–broken, adj untröstlich;
–burn, n Sodbrennen nt;
–felt, adj aufrichtig

hearth, hahrth, n Herd m

heartily, hahr-ti-li, adv
herzlich

heartless, hahrt-liss, adj
herzlos

hearty, hahr-ti, adj (meal,
appetite) herzhaft;
(cheerful) herzlich

heat, hiet, n Hitze f; sport
Ausscheidungsrunde f; v
heizen, erhitzen; **–er,** n
(Heiz)ofen m

heath, hieth, n Heide f

heathen, hie-dhen, adj
heidnisch; n Heide m,
Heidin f

heather, hedh-er, n
Heidekraut nt

heating, hie-ting, n Heizung
f

heatstroke, hiet-strohk, n
Hitzschlag m

heatwave, hiet-u'eiw, n
Hitzewelle f

heave, hiew, n (throw)
Schwung m; (effort)
Anstrengung f; v (throw)
werfen; (lift) heben;
(drag) schleppen; (sigh)
ausstoßen

heaven, hew-en, n Himmel

m; **–ly,** adj himmlisch

heavy, hew-i, adj schwer

Hebrew, hie-bruh, adj
hebräisch; n (language)
Hebräisch nt

Hebrides, hebb-ri-dies, npl
Hebriden pl

heckle, heck-'l, v
dazwischenrufen

hectic, heck-tick, adj
hektisch

hedge, hedsch, n Hecke f; v
(be evasive) ausweichen;
– one's bets, sich
absichern

hedgehog, hedsch-hogg, Igel
m

heed, hied, v beachten; n
Acht f; **–ful,** adj achtsam;
–less, achtlos

heel, hiel, n (of foot) Ferse f;
(of shoe) Absatz m

hefty, heff-ti, adj kräftig,
groß

heifer, heff-er, n Färse f

height, heit, n (of object)
Höhe f; (of person) Größe
f; **–en,** v erhöhen;
(intensify) verstärken

heinous, heh-ness, adj
abscheulich

heir, ähr, n Erbe m; **–ess,** n
Erbin f; **–loom,** n Erbstück
nt

helicopter, hell-i-kop-ter, n
Hubschrauber m

hell, hell, n Hölle f; **–!**
verdammt!; **–ish,** adj
höllisch

hello, he-loh, interj hallo,
guten Tag

helm, helm, n Steuer nt;
–sman, n Steuermann m

helmet, hell-mitt, n Helm m

help, help, n Hilfe f; v
helfen; **–er,** n Helfer m
–ful, adj hilfreich; **–ing,** n
Portion f; **–less,** adj hilflos;
– oneself, v sich
bedienen; **I can't – it,** ich
kann nichts dafür

hem, hemm, n Saum m; v
säumen; **– in,**
einschließen

hemisphere, hemm-iss-fier,
n Halbkugel f

hemp, hemp, n Hanf m

hen, henn, n (chicken)
Henne f; (female bird)
Weibchen nt

hence, henss, adv (thus)
daher; **five years –,** in
fünf Jahren

henceforth, henss-forth, adv
von nun an

her, hör, adj ihr; pron
(accusative) sie; (dative)
ihr

herald, he-reld, n Vorbote
m; v ankündigen

heraldry, he-reld-ri, n
Wappenkunde f

herb, hörb, n Kraut nt;
(cookery) Gewürzkraut nt

herd, hörd, n Herde f; v
zusammenpferchen;
–sman, n Hirte m

here, hier, adv hier(her);
–abouts, adv ungefähr
hier; **–after,** adv künftig; n
Jenseits nt; **–by,** adv
hiermit

hereditary, hi-redd-i-te-ri, adj erblich; (property) ererbt

herewith, hier-u'idh, adv hiermit; (enclosed) anbei

heresy, he-ri-si, n Ketzerei f

heretic, he-ri-tick, n Ketzer m

heritage, he-ri-tidsch, n Erbschaft f, Erbe nt

hermetic(al), hörrmett-ick(-'l), adj hermetisch

hermit, hör-mitt, n Einsiedler m; **–age,** n Einsiedelei f

hernia, hör-ni-e, n Bruch m

hero, hier-roh, n Held m; **–ic,** adj heldenhaft

heroin, he-roh-in, n Heroin nt

heroine, he-roh-in, n Heldin f

heroism, he-roh-ism, n Heldentum nt

heron, he-ren, n Reiher m

herring, he-ring, n Hering m

hers, hörs, pron ihre(r/s)

herself, hör-sself, pron (refl) sich (selbst); (emphatic) selbst; **by –,** adv alleine

hesitant, he-si-tent, adj zögernd

hesitate, he-si-teht, v zögern

hesitation, he-si-teh-sch'n, n Zögern nt

heterosexual, he-te-roh-seck-ssju-el, adj heterosexuell; n Heterosexuelle(r) m & f

hew, hjuh, v hauen, hacken

hexagon, heck-sse-gen, n Sechseck nt

heyday, heh-deh, n Blüte f

hi, interj hallo

hiatus, hei-eh-tess, n Unterbrechung f

hibernate, hei-ber-neht, v Winterschlaf m halten

hiccough, hiccup, hick-app, n Schluckauf m

hidden, hidd-'n, adj verborgen

hide, heid, n Haut f, Fell nt; v (sich) verstecken, (sich) verbergen; (keep secret) verheimlichen

hideous, hidd-i-ess, adj scheußlich, gräßlich

hiding, hei-ding, n (beating) Tracht f Prügel.; **–place,** n Versteck nt; **in –,** versteckt

hi-fi, hei-fei, n Hi-Fi nt

high, hei, adj hoch; (wind) stark; **–brow,** adj intellektuell; **–er,** adj höher; **–er education,** n Hochschulbildung f; **–est,** adj höchste(r/s); **––heeled,** adj hochhackig; **H–lands,** npl schottisches Hochland nt; **–light,** n (in hair) Strähne f, fig Höhepunkt m; **–ness,** n Höhe f; **H–ness,** n (title) Hoheit f; **–rise building,** n Hochhaus nt; **– street,** n Hauptstraße f; **–way,** n öffentliche Straße f

hijack, hei-dschäck, v entführen; **–ing,** n Entführung f

hike, heik, n Wanderung f; v wandern; **–r,** n Wanderer m

hilarious, hi-lähr-ri-ess, n sehr lustig

hill, hill, n Berg m; (small) Hügel m; (incline) Steigung f; (slope) Berghang m; **–y,** adj hügelig

hilt, hilt, n Heft nt, Griff m; **up to the –,** voll und ganz

him, himm, pron (accusative) ihn; (dative) ihm; **–self,** pron (refl) sich (selbst); (emphatic) selbst; **by –,** adv alleine

hind, heind, adj hinter, Hinter-; n (deer) Hirschkuh f

hinder, hinn-der, v behindern

hindmost, heind-mohst, adj hinterste(r/s)

hindrance, hinn-drenss, n Hindernis nt

hindsight, heind-sseit, n **with (the benefit of) –,** im nachhinein

hinge, hindsch, n Scharnier nt; (on door) Angel f; **– on,** v abhängen von

hint, hint, n (indication) Hinweis m; (trace) Spur f; v andeuten

hip, hipp, adj fam in; n Hüfte f

hire, hei-er, n Miete f; (car) Verleih m; v (car etc.) mieten; (staff) anstellen; **– car,** n Leihwagen m; **–**

purchase, n Ratenkauf m

his, his, adj sein; pron
seine(r/s)

hiss, hiss, n Zischen nt; v
zischen

historian, hiss-tor-ri-en, n
Historiker m

historic, hiss-to-rick, adj
historisch

historical, hiss-to-rick-'l, adj
geschichtlich, historisch

history, hiss-te-ri, n
Geschichte f

hit, hitt, n (blow) Schlag m;
(score) Treffer m;
(success) Erfolg m; v
(strike) schlagen; (wound,
damage, score) treffen; **--
and-run accident,** n
Unfall m mit Fahrerflucht

hitch, hitsch, n Haken m; v
(pull up) hochziehen;
(hook on) anhängen;
(make fast) festmachen; **–
a lift,** v trampen

hitch-hike, hitsch-heik, v
trampen; **–r,** n Tramper m

hi-tech, hei-teck, adj Hi-
tech-

hitman, hitt-männ, n
Killer m

hither, hidh-er, adv hierher;
–to, adv bisher

hive, heiw, n Bienenstock
m; **– off,** v ausgliedern

hoard, hord, n Hort m; v
hamstern

hoarding, hor-ding, n
Bauzaun m

hoarse, horss, adj heiser

hoax, hohks, n Streich m; v

anführen

hob, hobb, n Kochplatte f,
Kochstelle f

hobble, hobb-'l, v humpeln

hobby, hobb-i, n Hobby nt;
--horse, n Steckenpferd nt

hock, hock, n (wine) weißer
Rheinwein m; (leg)
Hachse f

hoe, hoh, n Hacke f; v
hacken

hog, hogg, n Schwein nt; v
für sich beanspruchen; **go
the whole –,** v fam etw
konsequent durchziehen,
Nägel mit Köpfen machen

hoist, heust, n Winde f; v
hochheben; (flag) hissen

hold, hohld, n (grasp) Halt
m; (power) Macht f; naut
Laderaum m; (airplane)
Frachtraum m; v halten;
(contain) enthalten;
(possess) besitzen, haben;
(conversation) führen;
(on telephone) am
Apparat bleiben; **– back,**
zurückhalten; **– down,** v
festhalten; (job) behalten;
(prices) niedrig halten;
–er, n (receptacle)
Behälter m; (owner)
Inhaber m; **–ing,** n
Pachtgut nt; (share)
Anteil m; **– on,** v sich
festhalten; (wait) warten;
– one's own, v sich
behaupten; **– out,** v
(resist) aushalten; **– up,** v
(delay) aufhalten; (attack)
überfallen; **--up,** n (delay)

Verzögerung f; (attack)
Überfall m

hole, hohl, n Loch nt

holiday, holl-i-deh, n (day)
Feiertag m; (vacation)
Urlaub m; **– resort,** n
Ferienort m; **–s,** npl Ferien
pl

holiness, hoh-li-niss, n
Heiligkeit f

Holland, holl-end, n
Holland n

hollow, holl-oh, adj hohl;
(sound) dumpf; (fig
empty) leer; n Vertiefung
f; **– out,** v aushöhlen

holly, holl-i, n Stechpalme f

holocaust, holl-e-korst, n
Holocaust m

hologram, holl-e-grämm, n
Hologramm nt

holy, hoh-li, adj heilig; **H–
Week,** Karwoche f

homage, homm-idsch, n
Huldigung f; **pay – to,** v
huldigen

home, hohm, adv nach
Hause; (at home) zu
Hause; n Zuhause nt;
Heim nt; **at –,** adv zu
Hause; **–coming,** n
Heimkehr f; **–land,** n
Heimat f; **–less,** adj
obdachlos; **–ly,** adj
häuslich; **--made,** adj
selbstgemacht,
Hausmacher-; **–ward,** adj
Heim-, Rück-; adv nach
Hause, heimwärts; **be
–sick,** v Heimweh haben

homoeopathic, hoh-mi-o-

päth-ick, *adj*
homöopathisch

homosexual, hoh-moh-seck-ssju-el, *adj*
homosexuell; *n*
Homosexuelle(r) *m & f*

honest, onn-ist, *adj* ehrlich; **-y**, *n* Ehrlichkeit *f*

honey, hann-i, *n* Honig *m*; **-moon**, *n* Hochzeitsreise *f*, Flitterwochen *pl*; **-suckle**, *n* Geißblatt *nt*

honk, hongk, *v* hupen

honorary, onn-*e*-re-ri, *adj* Ehren-

honour, onn-er, *n* Ehre *f*; *v* ehren; **-able**, *adj* ehrenhaft

hood, hudd, *n* Kapuze *f*; (of car) Verdeck *nt*

hoodwink, hudd-u'ink, *v* täuschen

hoof, huhf, *n* Huf *m*

hook, huck, *n* Haken *m*; *v* festhaken; (catch) fangen; **– and eye**, *n* Haken und Öse *pl*

hooligan, huh-li-gen, *n* Rowdy *m*

hoop, huhp, *n* (toy) Reifen *m*; (band) Band *nt*

hooray, huh-rei, *interj* hurra; *n* Hurra *nt*

hoot, huht, *v* (of owl) heulen; (of horn) hupen; **-er**, *n* (car's) Hupe *f*; (fam nose) Zinken *m*

hoover ®, huh-wer, *n* Staubsauger *m*; *v* Staub saugen

hop, hopp, *n* Hüpfer *m*;

(plant) Hopfen *m*; *v* hüpfen

hope, hohp, *n* Hoffnung *f*; *v* hoffen; **-ful**, *adj* (person) hoffnungsvoll; (situation) vielversprechend; **-fully**, *adv* (with hope) hoffnungsvoll; (it is hoped) hoffentlich; **-less**, *adj* hoffnungslos

horizon, he-rei-sen, *n* Horizont *m*

horizontal, ho-ri-son-t'l, *adj* wagrecht, horizontal

hormone, hor-mohn, *n* Hormon *nt*

horn, horn, *n* Horn *nt*; (car's) Hupe *f*

hornet, hor-nitt, *n* Hornisse *f*

horny, hor-ni, *adj fam* geil

horrible, ho-ri-b'l, *adj* schrecklich

horrid, ho-ridd, *adj* entsetzlich; (person) gemein

horrify, ho-ri-fei, *v* entsetzen

horror, ho-rer, *n* Entsetzen *nt*; Greuel *m*; **– film**, *n* Horrorfilm *m*

hors d'oeuvre, or **dörw(r)**, *n* Vorspeise *f*

horse, horss, *n* Pferd *nt*; **– chestnut**, *n* Roßkastanie *f*; **-man**, *n* Reiter *m*; **-power**, *n* Pferdestärke *f*; **-racing**, *n* Pferderennen *nt*; **-radish**, *n* Meerrettich *m*; **-riding**, *n* Reiten *nt*; **-shoe**, *n* Hufeisen *nt*;

-woman, *n* Reiterin *f*; **on -back**, *adv* zu Pferde

horticulture, hor-ti-kall-tscher, *n* Gartenbau *m*

hose, hohs, *n* (rubber tube) Schlauch *m*; (stockings) Strümpfe *pl*

hosiery, hohs-je-ri, *n* Strumpfwaren *pl*

hospitable, hoss-pitt-*e*-b'l, *adj* gastfreundlich, gastlich

hospital, hoss-pit-'l, *n* Krankenhaus *nt*

hospitality, hoss-pi-täll-i-ti, *n* Gastfreundschaft *f*

host, hohst, *n* Gastgeber *m*; (innkeeper) Wirt *m*; (army) Heer *nt*; *relig* Hostie *f*

hostage, hoss-tidsch, *n* Geisel *f*

hostel, hoss-t'l, *n* Herberge *f*; (youth) Jugendherberge *f*; **-ry**, *n* Gasthof *m*

hostess, hohss-tess, *n* Gastgeberin *f*

hostile, hoss-teil, *adj* feindlich; (unfriendly) feindselig

hot, hott, *adj* heiß; (food, drink) warm; (spicy) scharf

hotel, hoh-tell, *n* Hotel *nt*

hothouse, hott-hauss, *n* Treibhaus *nt*

hotline, hott-lein, *n* heißer Draht *m*, Hotline *f*

hotly, hott-li, *adv* hitzig

hound, haund, *n* Jagdhund *m*; *v* hetzen

hour, au-er, *n* Stunde *f*; **-ly**,

adj stündlich

house, hauss, *n* Haus *nt*;
–boat, *n* Hausboot *nt*;
–hold, *n* Haushalt *m*;
–keeper, *n* Haushälterin *f*;
–keeping, *n*
Hauswirtschaft *f*; **H–** (of
Commons), *n* Unterhaus
nt; **––warming (party),** *n*
Einweihungsparty *f*;
–wife, *n* Hausfrau *f*;
–work, *n* Hausarbeit *f*

house, haus, *v* unterbringen

housing, hau-sing, *n*
Wohnungen *pl*; (cover)
Gehäuse *nt*; **– estate,** *n*
Wohnsiedlung *f*

hovel, how-'l, *n* elende
Hütte *f*

hover, how-er, *v* schweben;**–
about,** *v fig* herumhängen;
–craft, *n*
Luftkissenfahrzeug *nt*

how, hau, *adv* wie; **–ever,**
adv wie auch; *conj* jedoch;
– far? wie weit? **– much?**
wieviel? **– many?** wie
viele?

howl, haul, *n* Geheul *nt*; *v*
heulen

HQ, *abbr* **headquarters**

hub, habb, *n* Nabe *f*; *fig*
Mittelpunkt *m*

huddle (together), hadd-'l
(tu-gedh-er), *v* sich
(zusammen)drängen

hue, hjuh, *n* Farbton *m*; **–
and cry,** *n* Gezeter *nt*

hug, hagg, *n* Umarmung *f*; *v*
umarmen

huge, hjuhdsch, *adj* riesig

hulk, halk, *n naut* Hulk
m/nt; (*fam* person)
Klotz *m*

hull, hall, *n naut*
Schiffsrumpf *m*

hum, hamm, *n* (of insect)
Summen *nt*; (of engine)
Brummen *nt*; *v* summen;
brummen

human, hjuh-men, *adj*
menschlich; **– (being),** *n*
Mensch *m*

humane, hju-mehn, *adj*
human

humanitarian, hju-männ-i-
tähr-ri-en, *adj* humanitär

humanity, hju-**männ**-i-ti, *n*
Menschheit *f*; (kindness)
Humanität *f*

humble, hamm-b'l, *adj*
demütig; *v* demütigen

humbug, hamm-bagg, *n*
(nonsense) Humbug
m; (sweet)
Pfefferminzbonbon *nt*

humdrum, hamm-dramm,
adj Alltags-

humid, hjuh-midd, *adj*
feucht

humidity, hju-**midd**-i-ti, *n*
Feuchtigkeit *f*

humiliate, hju-**mill**-i-eht, *v*
erniedrigen

humiliation, hju-mill-i-**eh**-
sch'n, *n* Erniedrigung *f*

humorous, hjuh-me-ress, *adj*
lustig, komisch

humour, hjuh-mer, *n* (wit)
Humor *m*; (mood) Laune
f; **– sb** *v* jdm seinen
Willen lassen

hunch, hantsch, *n*
Buckel *m*; (suspicion)
Ahnung *f*; **–back,** *n*
Bucklige(r) *m & f*;
–ed, *adj* gekrümmt

hundred, **hann**-dred, *num*
hundert; **–th,** *adj*
hundertste(r/s), *n*
Hundertstel *nt*;
–weight, Zentner *m*

Hungarian, hang-**gähr**-ri-
en, *adj* ungarisch; *n*
(language) Ungarisch *nt*;
(person) Ungar *m*

Hungary, hang-ge-ri, *n*
Ungarn *nt*

hunger, hang-ger, *n* Hunger
m; **– after/for,** *v* hungern
nach

hungry, hang-gri, *adj*
hungrig; **be –,** *v* Hunger
haben

hunt, hant, *n* Jagd *f*; *v* jagen;
–er, *n* Jäger *m*; **– for,** *v*
suchen

hurdle, hör-d'l, *n* Hürde *f*

hurl, hörl, *v* schleudern

hurrah, he-**rah**, *interj* hurra

hurray = **hurrah**

hurricane, ha-ri-ken, *n*
Orkan *m*

hurried, ha-ridd, *adj* eilig;
–ly, *adv* hastig

hurry, ha-ri, *n* Eile *f*; *v*
eilen, sich beeilen; (rush)
übereilen; **be in a –,** *v* es
eilig haben

hurt, hört, *adj* verletzt; *v*
(pain) weh tun; (injure)
verletzen; **–ful,** *adj*
verletzend

hurtle, hör-t'l, *v* sausen

husband, has-bend, *n*
(Ehe)mann *m*

hush, hasch, *interj* Ruhe!; –
Stille *f*; **– up,** *v* (quieten)
zum Schweigen bringen;
(conceal) vertuschen

husk, hask, *n* Hülse *f*,
Schale *f*

husky, hass-ki, *adj* heiser; *n*
(dog) Husky *m*

hustle, hass-'l, *v* (jostle)
stoßen; (hurry) drängen

hut, hatt, *n* Hütte *f*

hutch, hatsch, *n* (rabbit)
Stall *m*; (hamster) Käfig *m*

hyacinth, hei-*e*-ssinth, *n*
Hyazinthe *f*

hybrid, hei-bridd, *adj*
Misch-; *n* Kreuzung *f*

hydrant, hei-drent, *n*
Hydrant *m*

hydraulic, hei-dro-lick, *adj*
hydraulisch

hydro-electric, hei-droh-i-
leck-trick, *adj* (power)
Wasserkraft-, durch
Wasserkraft erzeugt

hydrofoil, hei-dre-feul, *n*
Tragflügelboot *nt*

hydrogen, hei-dri-dschen, *n*
Wasserstoff *m*

hygiene, hei-dschien, *n*
Hygiene *f*

hygienic, hei-dschien-ick,
adj hygienisch

hymn, himm, *n* Hymne *f*

hype, heip, *n* Rummel *m*

hypermarket, heip-er-mahr-
kitt, *n* Hypermarket *m*

hyphen, hei-fen, *n*

Bindestrich *m*

hypnotic, hipp-nott-ick, *adj*
hypnotisch

hypnotize, hipp-ne-teis, *v*
hypnotisieren

hypocrisy, hi-pock-ri-ssi, *n*
Heuchelei *f*

hypocrite, hipp-e-kritt, *n*
Heuchler *m*

hypothermia, heip-oh-thör-
mje, *n* Unterkühlung *f*

hypothesis, hei-poth-i-ssiss,
n Hypothese *f*

hypothetic(al), heip-*e*-
thett-ick-'l, *adj*
hypothetisch

hysterical, hiss-te-rick-'l, *adj*
hysterisch

I

I, ei, *pers. pron* ich

ice, eiss, *n* Eis *nt;* **–berg,** *n* Eisberg *m;* **– cream,** *n* Eis *nt;* **– cube,** *n* Eiswürfel *m;* **– rink,** *n* Schlittschuhbahn *f;* **– skating,** *n* Schlittschuhlaufen *nt*

icicle, eiss-i-k'l, *n* Eiszapfen *m*

icing, eiss-ing, *n* Zuckerguß *m;* **– sugar,** *n* Puderzucker *m*

icon, ei-kon, *n* Ikone *f*

icy, eiss-i, *adj* eisig

idea, ei-di-e, *n* Idee *f,* Einfall *m*

ideal, ei-di-el, *adj* ideal; *n* Ideal *nt;* **–ist,** *n* Idealist *m*

identical, ei-denn-ti-k'l, *adj* gleichartig, identisch

identification, ei-denn-ti-fi-keh-sch'n, *n* Identifizierung *f;* **(means of) –,** Ausweispapiere *pl*

identify, ei-denn-ti-fai, *v* identifizieren

identity, ei-denn-ti-ti, *n* Identität *f;* **– card,** *n* Personalausweis *m*

idiom, idd-i-em, *n* (phrase) Redewendung *f;* (dialect) Idiom *nt*

idiomatic, idd-i-*e*-mätt-ick, *adj* idiomatisch

idiosyncratic, idd-i-oh-ssing-**krätt**-ick, *adj* eigenwillig

idiot, idd-i-et, *n* Idiot *m*

idiotic, idd-i-**ott**-ick, *adj* idiotisch

idle, ei-d'l, *adj* (lazy) faul; (inactive) tatenlos; (empty) leer; *v* faulenzen; **–ness,** *n* Untätigkeit *f;* **–r,** *n* Faulenzer *m*

idol, ei-d'l, *n* Idol *nt;* **–ize,** *v* vergöttern

idyllic, i-**dill**-ick, *adj* idyllisch

if, iff, *conj* wenn; (whether) ob; **– not,** wenn nicht; **– only,** wenn… nur; **– so,** wenn ja; **even –,** wenn

ignite, igg-**nait,** *v* (set fire to) anzünden; (catch fire) sich entzünden

ignition, igg-**ni**-sch'n, *n* Zündung *f;* **– key,** *n* Zündschlüssel *m*

ignorance, igg-ne-renss, *n* Unwissenheit *f*

ignorant, igg-ne-rent, *adj* unwissend

ignore, igg-**nor,** *v* ignorieren; unbeachtet lassen

ill, ill, *adj* (unwell) krank; (nauseous) übel; *n* Übel *nt*

illegal, i-**lie**-gel, *adj* illegal

illegible, i-**ledsch**-i-b'l, *adj* unleserlich

illegitimate, i-li-**dschitt**-i-met, *adj* (child) unehelich; (action, conclusion) unzulässig

ill feeling, ill **fie**-ling, *n* Verstimmung *f*

illiterate, i-**litt**-e-ret, *adj* analphabetisch; (uneducated) ungebildet

illness, ill-niss, *n* Krankheit *f*

illogical, i-**lodsch**-i-k'l, *adj* unlogisch

illuminate, i-**luh**-mi-neht, *v* beleuchten

illumination, i-lu-mi-**neh-**

sch'n, n Beleuchtung f

illusion, i-**luh**-sch'n, n
Täuschung f, Illusion f

illusory, i-**luh**-se-ri, adj
illusorisch

illustrate, ill-e-streht, v
(text) illustrieren;
(explain)
veranschaulichen

illustration, ill-e-**streh**-
sch'n, n (picture)
Illustration f; (example)
Beispiel nt

illustrious, i-**lass**-tri-ess, adj
berühmt

image, **imm**-idsch, n
(picture) Bild nt;
(reputation) Image nt

imaginary, i-**mädsch**-i-ne-ri,
adj Phantasie-; (not real)
eingebildet

imagination, i-mädsch-i-
neh-sch'n, n Phantasie f,
Einbildung(skraft) f

imagine, i-**mädsch**-inn, v
(picture to o.s.) sich
vorstellen; (delude o.s.)
sich einbilden

imbecile, **imm**-bi-ssiel, n
Schwachsinnige(r) m & f

imbibe, imm-**baibb**, v
trinken

imbue, imm-**bjuh**, v
durchdringen; fig erfüllen

imitate, **imm**-i-teht, v
nachahmen, imitieren

immaculate, i-**mäck**-ju-litt,
adj makellos; relig
unbefleckt

immaterial, i-me-**tier**-ri-el,
adj unwichtig

immature, i-me-**tjuhr**, adj
unreif

immediate, i-**mie**-di-et, adj
unmittelbar; sofortig; **–ly,**
adv (time) sofort; (place)
direkt

immense, i-**menss**, adj
ungeheuer

immensity, i-**menss**-i-ti, n
Ungeheuerlichkeit f

immerse (in), i-**mörss**
(inn), v (ein)tauchen (in)

immigrant, **imm**-i-grent, n
Einwanderer m,
Immigrant m

immigrate, **imm**-i-greht, v
einwandern, immigrieren

immigration, i-mi-**greh**-
sch'n, n Einwanderung f,
Immigration f

imminent, **imm**-i-nent, adj
unmittelbar bevorstehend

immobile, i-**moh**-beil, adj
unbeweglich

immobilize, i-**moh**-bi-lais, v
unbeweglich machen; fig
lähmen

immodest, i-**modd**-ist, adj
unbescheiden; (improper)
unanständig

immoral, i-**mo**-rel, adj
unmoralisch

immorality, i-me-**räll**-i-ti, n
Unsittlichkeit f

immortal, i-**mor**-t'l, adj
unsterblich; **–ize,** v
verewigen

immovable, i-**muh**-we-b'l,
adj unbeweglich, fest

immune, i-**mjuhn,** adj med
immun; (safe) geschützt

immunity, i-**mjuh**-ni-ti, n
(med, law) Immunität f

imp, imp, n Kobold m;
(rascal) Schelm m

impact, **imm**-päckt, n
(Zusammen)Stoß m; fig
Wirkung f

impair, imm-**pähr**, v
beeinträchtigen

impale, imm-**pehl**, v
aufspießen

impart, imm-**pahrt**, v
mitteilen

impartial, imm-**pahr**-schel,
adj unparteiisch

impassable, imm-**pah**-sse-b'l,
adj unpassierbar

impasse, **äm**-päss, n
Sackgasse f

impassive, imm-**päss**-iw, adj
ausdruckslos

impatience, imm-**peh**-
schenss, n Ungeduld f

impatient, imm-**peh**-schent,
adj ungeduldig

impeach, imm-**pietsch**, v
beschuldigen; **–ment,** n
Beschuldigung f

impeccable, imm-**peck**-e-b'l,
adj tadellos

impede, imm-**piedd**, v
behindern

impediment, imm-**pedd**-i-
ment, n Hindernis nt; (in
speech) Sprachfehler m

impending, imm-**penn**-ding,
adj bevorstehend;
(threatening) drohend

imperative, imm-pe-re-tiw,
adj gebieterisch;
(necessary) erforderlich; n

gram Imperativ *m*

imperfect, imm-**pör**-fikt, *adj* mangelhaft; *n gram* Imperfekt *nt*

imperfection, imm-per-**feck**-sch'n, *n* Unvollkommenheit *f*; Defekt *m*

imperial, imm-**pier**-ri-el, *adj* kaiserlich, Reichs-; **–ism**, *n* Imperialismus *m*

impersonal, imm-**pör**-sse-n'l, *adj* unpersönlich

impersonate, imm-**pör**-se-neht, *v* (pretend to be) sich ausgeben als; (mimic) imitieren

impertinence, imm-**pör**-ti-nenss, *n* Frechheit *f*

impertinent, imm-**pör**-ti-nent, *adj* unverschämt

impervious (to), imm-**pör**-vi-ess (to), *adj* unempfänglich (für)

impetuous, imm-**pett**-ju-ess, *adj* ungestüm, hitzig

impetus, imm-pi-tess, *adj* Antrieb *m*, Anstoß *m*

impinge (on), imm-**pindsch** (onn), *v* beeinträchtigen

implement, imm-pli-ment, *n* Gerät *nt*; *v* durchführen, umsetzen

implicate, imm-pli-keht, *v* belasten, verwickeln

implication, imm-pli-**keh**-sch'n, *n* (suggestion) Implikation *f*

implicit, imm-**pliss**-itt, *adj* (implied) implizit, unausgesprochen;

(unquestioning) unbedingt

implore, imm-**plor**, *v* anflehen

imply, imm-**plai**, *v* bedeuten; (suggest) andeuten

impolite, imm-pe-**lait**, *adj* unhöflich

import, **imm**-port, *n* (goods) Import *m*, Einfuhr *f*; (meaning) Bedeutung *f*; – **duty**, *n* Einfuhrzoll *m*

import, imm-**port**, *v* einführen

importance, imm-**port**-enss, *n* Wichtigkeit *f*

important, imm-**por**-tent, *adj* wichtig

importer, imm-**por**-ter, *n* Importeur *m*

impose (on), imm-**pohs** (onn), *v* auferlegen

imposing, imm-**poh**-sing, *adj* imposant

imposition, imm-pe-**si**-sch'n, *n* Auferlegung *f*, Erhebung *f*; (taking advantage) Ausnützung *f*

impossibility, imm-poss-i-**bill**-i-ti, *n* Unmöglichkeit *f*

impossible, imm-**poss**-i-b'l, *adj* unmöglich

impostor, imm-**poss**-ter, *n* Betrüger *m*

impotent, imm-pe-tent, *adj* (powerless) unfähig; (sexually) impotent

impound, imm-**paund**, *v* in Beschlag nehmen

impoverished, imm-**pow**-e-rischt, *adj* verarmt

impracticable, imm-**präck**-ti-ke-b'l, *adj* unpraktisch

imprecation, imm-pri-**keh**-sch'n, *n* Fluch *m*

impregnable, imm-**pregg**-ne-b'l, *adj* uneinnehmbar

impregnate, imm-**pregg**-neht, *v* imprägnieren

impress, imm-**press**, *v*(influence) Eindruck machen (auf); (mark) (ein)prägen; **–ion**, *n* Eindruck *m*; (mark) Abdruck *m*; **–ive**, *adj* eindrucksvoll

imprint, imm-**print**, *n* Abdruck *m*

imprison, imm-**pris**-'n, *v* einsperren; **–ment**, *n* Haft *f*

improbable, imm-**probb**-e-b'l, *adj* unwahrscheinlich

impromptu, imm-**promp**-tjuh, *adj & adv* improvisiert

improper, imm-**propp**-er, *adj* unschicklich

improve, imm-**pruhw**, *v* verbessern; **–ment**, *n* Verbesserung *f*

improvize, imm-**pre**-weis, *v* improvisieren

imprudent, imm-**pruh**-dent, *adj* unklug

impudence, imm-**pju**-denss, *n* Unverschämtheit *f*

impudent, imm-**pju**-dent, *adj* unverschämt, frech

impulse, imm-**palss**, *n*

Impuls *m*; (An)stoß *m*

impure, imm-**pjuhr**, *adj*
(dirty) unrein; (morally)
unkeusch

impurity, imm-**pjuhr**-ri-ti, *n*
Unreinheit *f*

in, inn, *adv* be –, (at
home/work) da sein; (in
fashion) in sein; **sb is –
for sth,** jdm steht etw
bevor; **be – on,** Bescheid
wissen über; **come –,**
(person) hereinkommen;
(train etc.) ankommen

in, inn, *prep* in; – 1960,
1960, im Jahre 1960; – **the
morning/afternoon,** am
Morgen/Nachmittag; –
German/English, auf
deutsch/englisch; 1 – 3,
jede(r/s) dritte

inability, inn-*e*-**bill**-i-ti, *n*
Unfähigkeit *f*

inaccessible, inn-äck-**ssess**-
i-b'l, *adj* unzugänglich

inaccuracy, i-**näck**-ju-re-ssi,
n Ungenauigkeit *f*

inaccurate, i-**näck**-ju-ret, *adj*
(wrong) unrichtig;
(imprecise) ungenau

inadequate, i-**nädd**-i-kuet,
adj unzulänglich

inadvertent(ly), inn-ed-**vört**-
ent(-li), *adj & adv*
versehentlich

inane, i-**nehn**, *adj* albern

inanimate, i-**nänn**-i-met, *adj*
leblos

inappropriate, inn-e-**prohp**-
pri-et, *adj* unpassend,
unangemessen

inasmuch as, inn-*es*-**matsch**
äs, *conj* insofern als

inaudible, i-**no'a**-di-b'l, *adj*
unhörbar

inaugurate, i-**no'a**-gju-reht,
v (building) einweihen;
(person, policy) einführen

inborn, inn-**born**, *adj*
angeboren

inbred, inn-**bred**, *adj*
angeboren

incalculable, inn-**käll**-kju-
le-b'l, *adj* unermeßlich;
(unpredictable)
unberechenbar

incapable, inn-**keh**-pe-b'l,
adj unfähig

incapacitate, inn-ke-**päss**-i-
teht, *v* unfähig machen

incapacity, inn-ke-**päss**-i-ti,
n Unfähigkeit *f*

incarnation, inn-kar-**neh**-
sch'n, *n* Verkörperung *f*;
relig Fleischwerdung *f*

incendiary, inn-**ssenn**-di-e-
ri, *adj* Brand-; *n*
Brandstifter *m*

incense, inn-**ssenss**, *n*
Weihrauch *m*

incense, inn-**ssenss**, *v*
erzürnen

incentive, inn-**ssenn**-tiw, *n*
Ansporn *m*;
(performance)
Leistungsanreiz *m*

incessant(ly), inn-**ssess**-
ent(-li), *adj & adv*
unaufhörlich

inch, intsch, *n* Zoll *m*; *v* sich
ganz langsam
voranbewegen

incident, inn-ssi-dent, *n*
Vorfall *m*

incidental, inn-ssi-**denn**-t'l,
adj beiläufig; (music)
Begleit-; **-ly,** *adv* übrigens

incinerator, inn-**ssinn**-*e*-
reh-ter, *n*
Verbrennungsofen *m*

incision, inn-**ssisch**-'n, *n*
Einschnitt *m*

incite, inn-**sseit**, *v*
aufstacheln

inclination, inn-kli-**neh**-
sch'n, *n* Neigung *f*

incline, inn-**klein**, *n*
Neigung *f*, Abhang *m*

incline, inn-**klein**, *v* sich
neigen; **be –ed (to),**
geneigt sein (zu)

include, inn-**kluhd**, *v*
einschließen

including, inn-**kluh**-ding,
prep einschließlich,
inbegriffen

inclusive (of), inn-**kluh**-
ssiw (ew), *adv*
einschließlich

incoherent, inn-ke-**hier**-
rent, *adj*
unzusammenhängend;
(rambling) unverständlich

income, inn-kamm, *n*
Einkommen *nt*; – **tax,** *n*
Einkommensteuer *f*

incoming, inn-kamm-ing,
adj (train etc.)
ankommend; (president
etc.) nachfolgend

incomparable, inn-**komm**-
pe-re-b'l, *adj*
unvergleichlich

incompatible, inn-kemm-**pätt**-i-b'l, *adj* unvereinbar

incompetence, inn-**komm**-pi-tenss, *n* Unfähigkeit *f*

incompetent, inn-**komm**-pi-tent, *adj* unfähig

incomplete, inn-kemm-**plieht**, *adj* unvollständig

incomprehensible, inn-komm-pri-**henn**-ssi-b'l, *adj* unbegreiflich, unverständlich

inconceivable, inn-kenn-**ssie**-we-b'l, *adj* unvorstellbar

inconclusive, inn-kenn-**kluh**-ssiw, *adj* ergebnislos, unschlüssig

incongruous, inn-**kong**-gru-ess, *adj* absurd; (inappropriate) unpassend

inconsiderate, inn-konn-**ssidd**-e-ret, *adj* rücksichtslos

inconsistent, inn-konn-**ssiss**-tent, *adj* (contradictory) widersprüchlich; (irregular) unbeständig; (self-contradictory) inkonsequent

inconsolable, inn-konn-**ssoh**-le-b'l, *adj* untröstlich

inconspicuous, inn-konn-**spick**-ju-ess, *adj* unauffällig

incontinent, inn-**konn**-ti-nent, *adj med* inkontinent

inconvenience, inn-konn-**wie**-ni-enss, *n* Unbequemlichkeit *f*; *v*

Unannehmlichkeiten bereiten

inconvenient, inn-konn-**wie**-ni-ent, *adj* unbequem, ungünstig

incorporate (into), inn-**kor**-pe-reht (**inn**-tu), *v* aufnehmen (in), einbringen (in)

incorrect, inn-ke-**rekt**, *adj* unrichtig

incorrigible, inn-ko-ri-dschi-b'l, *adj* unverbesserlich

increase, **inn**-kriess, *n* (in pay) Erhöhung *f*; (in size) Vergrößerung *f*; (in number) Zunahme *f*

increase, inn-**kriess**, *v* (raise) erhöhen; (in size) vergrößern; (in number) (sich) vermehren, zunehmen

incredible, inn-**kredd**-i-b'l, *adj* unglaublich

incredulous, inn-**kredd**-ju-less, *adj* skeptisch

incriminate, inn-**krimm**-i-neht, *v* beschuldigen

incubator, **inn**-kju-beh-ter, *n* Brutkasten *m*

incumbent, inn-**kamm**-bent, *adj* – **on**, obliegend; *n* Amtsinhaber *m*

incur, inn-**kör**, *v* sich zuziehen, erleiden

incurable, inn-**kjuhr**-re-b'l, *adj* unheilbar; *fig* unverbesserlich

indebted (to), inn-**dett**-id (tu), *adj* (owing money)

verschuldet; (obliged) verpflichtet

indecent, inn-**die**-ssent, *adj* unanständig

indecision, inn-di-**ssi**-sch'n, *n* Unentschlossenheit *f*

indecisive, inn-di-**ssei**-ssiw, *adj* ergebnislos, unschlüssig

indecorous, inn-di-**ko**-ress, *adj* unziemlich

indeed, inn-**died**, *adv* tatsächlich, in der Tat

indefensible, inn-di-**fenn**-ssi-b'l, *adj* unhaltbar; (inexcusable) nicht zu entschuldigen

indefinitely, inn-**deff**-i-nitt-li, *adv* auf unbestimmte Zeit

indelible, inn-**dell**-i-b'l, *adj* unauslöschlich; (stain) nicht zu entfernen

indemnify, inn-**demm**-ni-fai, *v* entschädigen

indemnity, inn-**demm**-ni-ti, *n* Entschädigung *f*

independence, inn-di-**penn**-dens, *n* Unabhängigkeit *f*

independent, inn-di-**penn**-dent, *adj* unabhängig

indescribable, inn-diss-**krei**-be-b'l, *adj* unbeschreiblich

indestructible, inn-diss-**track**-ti-b'l, *adj* unzerstörbar

indeterminate, inn-di-**tör**-mi-nitt, unbestimmt

index, **inn**-dex, *n* Index *m*; (in book) Register *nt*; **index finger**, *n*

Zeigefinger m

India, inn-di-*e*, n Indien nt;
–n, adj indisch; n
(language) Indisch nt;
Inder m; **(American) –,** n
Indianer m

indicate, inn-di-keht, v
andeuten

indication, inn-di-keh-
sch'n, n (An)zeichen nt

indicative, inn-**dick**-*e*-tiw,
adj be – **of,** v auf etw
schließen lassen; n gram
Indikativ m

indicator, inn-di-keh-ter, n
(sign) (An)zeichen nt;
(car's) Blinker m

indict, inn-**dait,** v anklagen;
–ment, n Anklage f

indifference, inn-**diff**-*e*-
renss, n Gleichgültigkeit f

indifferent, inn-**diff**-*e*-rent,
adj (uncaring)
gleichgültig; (mediocre)
mittelmäßig

indigestible, inn-di-**dschess**-
ti-b'l, adj unverdaulich

indigestion, inn-di-**dschess**-
tschen, n
Verdauungsstörung f

indignant, inn-**digg**-nent,
adj entrüstet

indignation, inn-digg-**neh**-
sch'n, n Entrüstung f

indignity, inn-**digg**-ni-ti, n
Demütigung f

indirect(ly), inn-di-**reckt**(-
li), adj & adv indirekt

indiscreet, inn-diss-**kriet,**
adj indiskret

indiscriminate, inn-diss-

krimm-i-net, adj
unkritisch; (random)
willkürlich

indispensable, inn-diss-
penn-sse-b'l, adj
unentbehrlich

indisposed, inn-diss-**pohsd,**
adj (disinclined)
abgeneigt; (unwell)
unwohl

indisputable, inn-diss-**pjuh**-
te-b'l, adj unbestreitbar

indistinct, inn-diss-**tinkt,**
adj undeutlich

indistinguishable, inn-diss-
ting-gu'isch-*e*-b'l, adj
ununterscheidbar

individual, inn-di-**widd**-
ju-el, adj individuell,
Einzel-; adv einzeln; n
Individuum nt

indolent, inn-de-lent, adj
träge

indoor, inn-dor, adj (plant,
game, etc.) Zimmer-;
(clothes) Haus-; sport
Hallen-

indoors, inn-**dors,** adv (in)
drinnen, im Hause; (into)
ins Haus

induce, inn-**djuhss,** v
(persuade) veranlassen;
(cause) herbeiführen;
–ment, n Anreiz m

induction, inn-**dack**-sch'n,
n Einführung f

indulge, inn-**daldsch,** v sich
hingeben; **– in,** sich etw
gönnen; **–nce,** n
(pleasure) Genuß m; **–nt,**
inn-**dall**-dschent, adj

genüßlich; (forgiving)
nachsichtig

industrial, inn-**dass**-tri-el,
adj industriell, Industrie-;
– estate, n Industriegebiet
nt

industrialization, inn-dass-
tri-*e*-lai-**seh**-sch'n, n
Industrialisierung f

industrious, inn-**dass**-tri-
ess, adj fleißig

industry, inn-dess-tri, n
Industrie f; (hard work)
Fleiß m

inebriated, i-**nie**-bri-eh-tidd,
adj betrunken

inedible, i-**nedd**-i-b'l, adj
ungenießbar

ineffective, i-ni-**feck**-tiw, adj
wirkungslos

ineffectual, i-ni-**feck**-tju-el,
adj untauglich

inefficiency, i-ni-**fisch**-en-
ssi, n Unfähigkeit f

inefficient, i-ni-**fisch**-ent,
adj unwirksam; unfähig

inept, i-**nept** adj
(inappropriate)
ungeeignet; (clumsy)
ungeschickt

inequality, i-ni-**ku'oll**-i-ti, n
Ungleichheit f

inert, i-**nört,** adj träge;
(chemical) inaktiv

inertia, i-**nör**-sche, n
Trägheit f

inescapable, i-niss-**keh**-pe-
b'l, adj unvermeidlich

inevitable, i-**new**-i-te-b'l, adj
unvermeidlich

inevitably, i-**new**-i-teb-li,

adv zwangsläufig

inexact, i-nigg-**säckt,** *adj*
(inaccurate) ungenau;
(incorrect) unrichtig

inexcusable, i-nicks-**kjuh**-se-b'l, *adj* unverzeihlich

inexhaustible, i-nigg-**so'ass**-ti-b'l, *adj* unerschöpflich

inexorable, i-**neckss**-*e*-re-b'l, *adj* unerbittlich

inexpensive, i-nickss-**penn**-ssiw, *adj* preiswert

inexperience, i-nickss-**pier**-ri-enss, *n* Unerfahrenheit *f*; **–d,** *adj* unerfahren

inexplicable, i-nickss-**plick**-e-b'l, *adj* unerklärlich

inextricable, i-nickss-**trick**-e-b'l, *adj* unentwirrbar

infallible, inn-**fäll**-i-b'l, *adj* unfehlbar

infamous, inn-**fe**-mess, *adj* berüchtigt

infamy, inn-**fe**-mi, *n* Unehre *f*; Schande *f*

infancy, inn-**fen**-ssi, *n* Kindheit *f*; **in its –,** *fig* noch in den Kinderschuhen

infant, inn-**fent,** *n* kleines Kind *nt*; *law* Unmündige(r) *m & f*; **–ile,** *adj* kindisch; **– school,** *n* Vorschule *f*

infantry, inn-**fen**-tri, *n* Infanterie *f*

infatuated (with), inn-**fätt**-ju-eh-tid (u'idh), *adj* vernarrt (in)

infect, inn-**feckt,** *v* anstecken; **–ed,** *adj*

(person) infiziert;
(wound) entzündet;
–ion, *n* Ansteckung *f*,
Infektion *f*; **–ious,** *adj* ansteckend

infer, inn-**för,** *v* ableiten, schließen (aus)

inference, inn-**fe**-renss, *n* Folgerung *f*, Schluß *m*

inferior, inn-**fier**-ri-er, *adj* minderwertig

inferiority, inn-**fier**-ri-o-ri-ti, *n* Minderwertigkeit *f*; **– complex,** *n* Minderwertigkeits-kom-plex *m*

infernal, inn-**för**-nel, *adj* teuflisch, höllisch

infertile, inn-**för**-teil, *adj* unfruchtbar

infertility, inn-fer-**till**-i-ti, *n* Unfruchtbarkeit *f*

infested, inn-**fess**-tidd, *adj* **be – with,** wimmeln von

infidelity, inn-fi-**dell**-i-ti, *n*, Untreue *f*

infinite(ly), inn-fi-nit(-li), *adj & adv* unendlich

infinity, inn-**finn**-i-ti, *n* Unendlichkeit *f*

infirm, inn-**förm,** *adj* gebrechlich; **–ary,** *n* Krankenhaus *nt*; (sick-quarters) Krankenstation *f*

inflame, inn-**flehm,** *v* (enrage) aufbringen; *med* entzünden

inflammable, inn-**flamm**-e-b'l, *adj* feuergefährlich, leicht entzündlich

inflammation, inn-fle-**meh**-sch'n, *n* Entzündung *f*

inflate, inn-**fleht,** *v* aufblasen; (tyre) aufpumpen; (price) steigern

inflation, inn-**fleh**-sch'n, *n* Inflation *f*

inflexible, inn-**fleck**-ssi-b'l, *adj* unbiegsam; *fig* unbeugsam

inflict (on), inn-**flickt** (onn), *v* zufügen; aufbürden

influence, inn-**fluh**-enss, *n* Einfluß *m*; *v* beeinflussen

influential, inn-fluh-**enn**-schel, *adj* einflußreich

influenza, inn-fluh-**enn**-se, *n* Grippe *f*

influx, inn-**flacks,** *n* Zufluß *m*

inform, inn-**form,** *v* benachrichtigen, informieren; **–al,** *adj* zwanglos; **–ant,** *n* Informant *m*

information, inn-fer-**meh**-sch'n, *n* Auskünfte *pl*, Information *f*; **a piece of –,** eine Auskunft *f*

informer, inn-**for**-mer, *n pej* Denunziant *m*

infrequent(ly), inn-**frie**-ku'ent(-li), *adj & adv* selten

infringe, inn-**frindsch,** *v* verstoßen gegen; *law* verletzen; **–ment,** *n* Verstoß *m*; Verletzung *f*

infuriate, inn-**fjuhr**-ri-eht, *v* wütend machen

infusion, inn-**fjuh**-sch'n, *n*

Aufguß m

ingenious, inn-**dschie**-ni-ess, adj geschickt; (cleverly designed) genial

ingenuity, inn-dschinn-**juh**-i-ti, n Einfallsreichtum m

ingenuous, inn-**dschenn**-juh-ess, adj naiv

ingot, ing-gett, n Barren m

ingrained, inn-**grehnd,** adj eingewurzelt; (person) eingefleischt

ingratiate oneself (with), inn-**greh**-schi-eht u'an**sself** (u'idh), v sich einschmeicheln (bei)

ingratitude, inn-**grätt**-i-tjuhd, n Undankbarkeit f

ingredient, inn-**grie**-di-ent, n Zutat f, Bestandteil m

ingrowing, inn-**groh**-ing, adj nach innen wachsend

inhabit, inn-**häbb**-itt, v bewohnen; **–able,** adj bewohnbar; **–ant,** n Einwohner m

inhale, inn-**hehl,** v einatmen, inhalieren

inherent (in), inn-**hier**-rent (inn), adj innewohnend; (natural) natürlich

inherit, inn-**he**-ritt, v erben; **–ance,** n Erbe nt

inhibited, inn-**hibb**-i-tidd, adj gehemmt

inhibition, inn-hi-**bi**-sch'n, n Hemmung f

inhospitable, inn-hoss-**pitt**-e-b'l, adj (climate etc.) unwirtlich; (person) ungastlich

inhuman, inn-**hju**-men, adj unmenschlich

inimitable, i-**nimm**-i-te-b'l, adj unnachahmlich

iniquitous, i-**nick**-u'i-tess, adj ungerecht

initial, i-**nisch**-el, adj Anfangs-, anfänglich; n Initiale f; **–ly,** adv anfangs, zu Anfang

initiate, i-**nisch**-i-eht, v (person) einweihen; (proceedings) einleiten

initiative, i-**nisch**-e-tiw, n Initiative f

inject, inn-**dscheckt,** v (ein)spritzen; **–ion,** n Spritze f

injunction, inn-**dschank**-sch'n, n law Verfügung f

injure, inn-**dscher,** v verletzen, schädigen

injury, inn-**dsche**-ri, n Verletzung f; fig Unrecht nt; **– time,** n sport Nachspielzeit f

injustice, inn-**dschass**-tiss, n Ungerechtigkeit f

ink, ink, n Tinte f

inkling, ink-ling, n Ahnung f

inlaid, inn-**lehd,** adj eingelegt

inland, inn-**länd,** adj inländisch, Binnen-; adv landeinwärts; **I– Revenue,** n Finanzamt nt

in-laws, inn-lo'as, npl (parents-in-law) Schwiegereltern pl; (family) angeheiratete

Verwandte pl

inlet, inn-lett, n mech Zuleitung f; geog Bucht f

inmate, inn-meht, n Insasse m

inn, inn, n Gasthaus m

innate, i-**neht,** adj angeboren

inner, inn-er, adj inner, Innen-; **– city,** n Innenstadt f

innkeeper, inn-**kie**-per, n Gastwirt m

innocent, inn-e-ssent, adj unschuldig

innocuous, i-**nock**-ju-ess, adj harmlos

innovation, i-ne-**weh**-sch'n, n Neuerung f

innuendo, inn-ju-**enn**-doh, n Anspielung f

innumerable, i-**njuh**-me-re-b'l, adj unzählig

inoculate, i-**nock**-ju-leht, v (ein)impfen

inoffensive, i-ne-**fenn**-ssiw, adj harmlos

inopportune, inn-**opp**-er-tjuhn, adj ungelegen

inordinately, i-**nor**-di-net-li, adj unmäßig

input, inn-putt, n (contribution) Beitrag m; comp Input m

inquest, inn-ku'est, n gerichtliche Untersuchung f; fig nachträgliche Analyse f

inquire (about), inn-**ku'air** (e-baut), v sich erkundigen (nach); –

into, untersuchen

inquiry, inn-**ku'air**-ri, n
Erkundigung f;
(investigation)
Untersuchung f; **– office,**
n Auskunftsbüro nt

inquisition, inn-ku'i-**sisch**-
'n, n Inquisition f

inquisitive, inn-**ku'i**-si-tiw,
adj neugierig

inroad, inn-rohd, n
Eingriff m

insane, inn-**ssehn,** adj
wahnsinnig; med
geisteskrank

insanity, inn-**ssänn**-i-ti, n
Wahnsinn m

insatiable, inn-**sseh**-schi-e-
b'l, adj unersättlich

inscribe, inn-**skraib,** v
einschreiben

inscription, inn-**skrip**-sch'n,
n Inschrift f

insect, inn-ssekt, n Insekt nt

insecure, inn-ssi-**kjuhr,** adj
unsicher

insemination, inn-semm-i-
neh-sch'n, n (artificial)
Befruchtung f

insensible, inn-**ssenn**-ssi-b'l,
adj unempfindlich;
(unconscious) bewußtlos

inseparable, inn-**ssepp**-e-re-
b'l, adj unzertrennlich;
gram untrennbar

insert, inn-**ssört,** v
einsetzen; (words)
einfügen; (advertisement)
setzen; **–ion,** n Einlegen
nt; (words) Einfügung f;
(advertisement) Anzeige

f, Inserat nt

inside, inn-**ssaid,** adj inner,
Innen-; adv drinnen; nach
innen; n Innenseite f,
Innere(s) nt; **inside out,**
adv (reversed) falsch
herum; (thoroughly) in-
und auswendig

insidious, inn-**ssidd**-i-ess,
adj hinterlistig

insight, inn-sseit, n Einsicht
f, Verständnis nt

insignificant, inn-ssigg-**niff**-
i-kent, adj unbedeutend

insincere, inn-ssinn-**ssier,**
adj unaufrichtig

insinuate, inn-**ssinn**-ju-eht,
v andeuten

insipid, inn-**ssipp**-idd, adj
fade, geschmacklos

insist (on), inn-**ssist** (onn),
v bestehen (auf); **–ent,** adj
beharrlich

insolence, inn-sse-lenss, n
Unverschämtheit f

insolent, inn-sse-lent, adj
unverschämt, frech

insolvent, inn-**ssoll**-went,
adj zahlungsunfähig

inspect, inn-**spekt,** v
inspizieren; **–ion,** n
Inspektion f; **–or,** n
Inspektor m; (bus, factory)
Kontrolleur m

inspiration, inn-spi-**reh**-
sch'n, n Inspiration f

inspire, inn-**speir,** v
einflößen; inspirieren

instal(l), inn-**sto'al,** v
einsetzen; installieren;
–ation, n Installation f;

mech Anlage f

instalment, inn-**sto'al**-ment,
n (payment) Rate f;
(episode) Fortsetzung f; **to
pay by –s,** v auf Rate
zahlen

instance, inn-stenss, n
Beispiel nt; Fall m; **for –,**
zum Beispiel

instant, inn-stent, adj
sofortig; n Augenblick m;
–aneous, adj
augenblicklich; **–ly,** adv
sofort

instead, inn-stedd, adv statt
dessen; **– of,** prep anstatt

instep, inn-stepp, n
Spann m

instigate, inn-sti-geht, v
anstiften

instil, inn-still, v einflößen

instinct, inn-stinkt, n
Instinkt m

institute, inn-sti-tjuht, n
Institut nt; v einleiten,
einführen

instruct, inn-**strakt,** v
(teach) unterrichten;
(direct) anweisen; **–ion,** n
(teaching) Unterricht m;
(direction) Anweisung;
–or, n Lehrer m

instrument, inn-stru-ment,
n Instrument nt

insubordination, inn-sse-
bor-di-**neh**-sch'n, n
Widersetzlichkeit f

insufferable, inn-**ssaff**-e-re-
b'l, adj unerträglich

insufficient, inn-sse-**fisch**-
ent, adj ungenügend

insular, inn-ssju-ler, *adj*
Insel-; *fig* engstirnig

insulation, inn-ssju-**leh**-sch'n, *n* Isolierung *f*

insulin, inn-ssju-linn, *n*
Insulin *nt*

insult, inn-ssalt, *n*
Beleidigung *f*

insult, inn-**ssalt**, *v*
beleidigen

insurance, inn-**schor**-renss, *n* Versicherung *f*

insure, inn-**schor**, *v*
versichern

insurrection, inn-sse-**reck**-sch'n, *n* Aufstand *m*

intact, inn-**takt**, *adj* intakt

intangible, inn-**tänn**-schib'l, nicht greifbar

integral, inn-**tegg**-rel, *adj*
wesentlich

integrate (into), inn-**tigg**-reht (**inn**-tu), *v*
eingliedern (in)

integrity, inn-**tegg**-ri-ti, *n*
Seriosität *f*

intellect, inn-ti-lekt, *n*
Verstand *m*

intelligence, inn-**tell**-i-dschenss, *n* Intelligenz *f*

intelligent, inn-**tell**-i-dschent, *adj* intelligent

intend, inn-**tend**, *v*
beabsichtigen

intense, inn-**tenss**, *adj* stark, intensiv; (person)
ernsthaft; **–ly**, *adv*
intensiv; (very) äußerst

intensify, inn-**tenn**-ssi-fei, *v*
verstärken

intensive, inn-**tenn**-ssiw, *adj*

intensiv; **– care (unit)**, *n*
Intensivstation *f*

intensity, inn-**tenn**-si-ti, *n*
Intensität *f*

intent (on), inn-**tent** (onn), *adj* (determined)
entschlossen;
(concentrating)
konzentriert (auf);**–ion**, *n*
Absicht *f*; **–ional**, *adj*
absichtlich; **–ly**, *adv*
konzentriert

interact, inn-te-**räkt**, *v*
gemeinsam handeln; *n*
Wechselwirkung *f*

intercept, inn-ter-**ssept**, *v*
auffangen

interchange, inn-ter-tschehndsch, *n*
(exchange) Austausch
m; (junction)
Verkehrskreuz *m*

interchange, inn-ter-**tschehndsch**, *v*
austauschen

intercom, inn-ter-komm, *n*
(Gegen)sprechanlage *f*

intercourse, inn-ter-korss, *n*
(sexual, social) Verkehr
m; *comm* Beziehungen *pl*

interest, inn-te-rest, *n*
Interesse *nt*; *fin* Zinsen *pl*;
comm Anteil *m*; *v*
interessieren; **–ed**,
interessiert; (involved)
beteiligt; **–ing**, *adj*
interessant; **be –ed in**, *v*
sich interessieren für

interface, inn-ter-feiss, *n*
Schnittstelle *f*; *comp*
Interface *nt*

interfere, inn-ter-**fier**, *v* –
(in), (meddle) sich
einmischen; **– with**,
(radio etc.) stören;
(property etc.) sich an etw
zu schaffen machen

interference, inn-ter-**fier**-renss, *n* (meddling)
Einmischung *f*; (radio
etc.) Störung *f*

interior, inn-**tier**-ri-er, *adj*
inner, Innen-; *n* Inneres
nt; **– designer**, *n*
Innenarchitekt *m*

intermediary, inn-ter-**mie**-di-e-ri, *n* Vermittler *m*

intermediate, inn-ter-**mie**-di-et, *adj* dazwischen
liegend; Mittel-,
Zwischen-

intermittent(ly), inn-ter-**mitt**-ent(-li), *adj & adv*
periodisch

intern, inn-**törn**, *v*
internieren

internal, inn-**tör**-nel, *adj*
inner, Innen-; (inland)
Inlands-; **–ly**, *adv*
innerlich, inner

international, *adj*
international; *n sport*
(player) Nationalspieler
m; (match) Länderspiel *nt*

interpret, inn-**tör**-pritt, *v*
(translate) dolmetschen;
(explain) deuten; *theatre*,
mus interpretieren;
–ation, *n* Interpretation *f*;
–er, *n* (translator)
Dolmetscher *m*; *theatre*,
mus Interpret *m*

interrogate, inn-**te**-re-geht, v verhören

interrogation, inn-te-re-**geh**-sch'n, n Verhör nt

interrupt, inn-te-**rapt,** v unterbrechen; **–ion,** n Unterbrechung f

intersect, inn-ter-**ssekt,** v (sich) schneiden; **–ion,** n (of roads) Kreuzung f

interspersed (with), inn-ter-**spörst** (u'idh), adj durchsetzt (mit)

interval, inn-ter-vel, n (distance) Abstand m; theatre etc. Pause f

intervene, inn-ter-**wien,** v (person) eingreifen; (space, time) dazwischenliegen

intervention, n Eingreifen nt

interview, Interview nt; **(job) –,** n Vorstellungsgespräch nt; v interviewen; **–er,** n Interviewer m

intestine, inn-**tess**-tin, n Darm m

intimacy, inn-ti-me-ssi, n Intimität f

intimate, inn-ti-met, adj (familiar, close) vertraut; (sexually) intim; (private) persönlich

intimate, inn-ti-meht, v andeuten

intimidate, inn-ti-mi-deht, v einschüchtern

intimidation, inn-ti-mi-**deh**-sch'n, n Einschüchterung f

into, inn-tu, prep in, in… hinein

intolerable, inn-**toll**-e-re-b'l, adj unerträglich

intolerance, inn-**toll**-e-renss, n Intoleranz f

intoxicate, inn-**tock**-ssi-keht, v berauschen; **–d,** adj betrunken

intractable, inn-**träck**-te-b'l, adj hartnäckig

intransigent, inn-**tränn**-si-dschent, adj unnachgiebig

in-tray, inn-treh, n Ablage f für Eingänge

intrepid, inn-**trepp**-idd, adj unerschrocken

intricate, inn-tri-ket, adj verwickelt

intrigue, inn-trieg, n Intrige f

intrigue, inn-trieg, v faszinieren

intriguing, inn-**trie**-ging, adj faszinierend

intrinsic, inn-**trinn**-sick, adj (inherent) innewohnend; (essential) wesentlich

introduce, inn-tre-**djuhss,** v (bring in) einführen; (person) vorstellen

introduction, inn-tre-**dak**-sch'n, n Einführung f; (to book etc.) Einleitung f; (to person) Vorstellung f

introductory, inn-tre-**dak**-te-ri, adj Einführungs-; einleitend

intrude (on), inn-**truhd** (onn), v stören; **–r,** n Eindringling m

intrusive, inn-**truh**-ssiw, adj aufdringlich, störend

intuition, inn-tju-**isch**-'n, n Intuition f

inundate, inn-an-deht, adj überschwemmen

invade, inn-**wehd,** v einfallen (in); **–r,** n Angreifer m

invalid, inn-**wäll**-idd, adj ungültig

invalid, inn-we-lidd, adj (disabled) invalide; (ill) krank; n (disabled) Invalide m; (ill) Kranke(r) m & f; **– chair,** n Rollstuhl m

invaluable, inn-**wäll**-ju-e-b'l, adj unschätzbar

invariable, inn-**wehr**-ri-e-b'l, adj unveränderlich

invariably, inn-**wehr**-ri-eb-li, adv ausnahmslos

invasion, inn-**weh**-sch'n, n Einfall m

invent, inn-**went,** v erfinden; **–ion,** n Erfindung f; **–ive,** adj erfinderisch; **–or,** n Erfinder m

inventory, inn-went-ri, n Inventar nt

invert, inn-**wört,** v umkehren, umdrehen; **–ed commas,** pl Anführungszeichen pl

invest, inn-**west,** v investieren

investigate, inn-**wess**-ti-geht, v untersuchen

investigation, inn-wess-ti-

geh-sch'n, *n* Untersuchung *f*

investment, inn-**west**-ment, *n* Investition *f*, Kapitalanlage *f*

investor, inn-**wess**-ter, *n* Investor *m*, Kapitalanleger *m*

inveterate, inn-**wett**-*e*-ret, *adj* eingefleischt

invigorating, inn-**wigg**-*e*-reh-ting, *adj* belebend

invincible, inn-**winn**-ssi-b'l, *adj* unüberwindlich

invisible, inn-**wis**-i-b'l, *adj* unsichtbar

invitation, inn-wi-**teh**-sch'n, *n* Einladung *f*

invite, inn-**weit**, *v* einladen

invoice, inn-**weuss**, *n* Rechnung *f*; *v* – **sb for sth,** jdm für etw eine Rechnung ausstellen

invoke, inn-**wohk**, *v* anrufen

involuntary, inn-**woll**-en-te-ri, *adj* unwillkürlich

involve, inn-**wolw**, *v* (entail) mit sich bringen; – **in,** verwickeln in; **–ed,** *adj* (complicated) verwickelt; **get –ed (in),** mitmachen (bei); sich verwickeln (in)

inward, inn-u'ed, *adj* inner, Innen-; *adv* nach innen; **–ly,** innerlich; **–s,** nach innen, einwärts

iodine, ei-o-dien, *n* Jod *nt*

IOU, ei oh juh, *n abbr* **I owe you**), Schuldschein *m*

IRA, ei ahr eh, *n* (*abbr* **Irish Republican Army**), IRA *f*

irate, ei-**reht**, *adj* wütend

Ireland, eir-lend, *n* Irland *nt*

iris, ei-riss, *n* (plant) Schwertlilie *f*; (eye) Regenbogenhaut *f*

Irish, ei-rish, *adj* irisch; **the –,** *npl* Iren *pl* Irländer *pl*; **–man,** Ire *m*, Irländer *m*; **–woman,** Irin *f*, Irländerin *f*

irksome, örk-sem, *adj* lästig

iron, ei-en, *adj* eisern, Eisen-; *n* (metal) Eisen *nt*; (appliance) Bügeleisen *nt*; *v* bügeln; **I– Curtain,** eiserner Vorhang *m*

ironic(al), ei-**ronn**-ick(-'l), *adj* ironisch

ironing, ei-*e*-ning, *n* (action) Bügeln *nt*; (clothes) Bügelwäsche *f*; – **board,** *n* Bügelbrett *nt*

ironmonger, ei-en-mang-ger, *n* Eisenwarenhandlung *f*

irony, ei-*ro*-ni, *n* Ironie *f*

irrational, i-**räsch**-*e*-nel, *adj* irrational

irreconcilable, i-reck-on-**sseil**-*e*-b'l, *adj* unvereinbar

irrefutable, i-ri-**fjuh**-te-b'l, *adj* unwiderlegbar

irregular, i-**regg**-ju-ler, *adj* (uneven, *gram*) unregelmäßig; (shape) ungleichmäßig; (extraordinary) unüblich

irrelevant, i-**rell**-*e*-went, *adj* nebensächlich

irreparable, i-**repp**-*e*-re-b'l,

adj nicht wiedergutzumachend

irreplaceable, i-ri-**pleh**-sse-b'l, *adj* unersetzlich

irreproachable, i-ri-**proh**-tsche-b'l, *adj* tadellos

irresistible, i-ri-**siss**-ti-b'l, *adj* unwiderstehlich

irrespective (of), i-riss-**peck**-tiw (ev), *adj* ungeachtet

irresponsible, i-riss-**ponn**-ssi-b'l, *adj* unverantwortlich; verantwortungslos

irretrievable, i-ri-**trie**-we-b'l, *adj* unwiederbringlich

irreverent, i-**rew**-*e*-rent, *adj* respektlos

irrigate, i-ri-geht, *v* bewässern

irritable, i-ri-te-b'l, *adj* reizbar

irritate, i-ri-teht, *v* irritieren; *med* reizen

Islam, is-lahm, *n* Islam *m*; **–ic,** *adj* islamisch

island, ei-lend, *n* Insel *f*; **–er,** *n* Inselbewohner *m*

isle, eil, *n* Eiland *nt*, Insel *f*

isolate, ei-sse-leht, *v* isolieren; **–d,** *adj* isoliert; (unique) einzeln, Einzel-

isolation, ei-sse-**leh**-sch'n, *n* Isolierung *f*

Israel, is-reh-el, *n* Israel *nt*; **–i,** *adj* israelisch; *n* Israeli *m & f*

issue, iss-juh, *n* (subject) Frage *f*, Thema *nt*; (of newspaper) Ausgabe *f*; (of

shares) Emission f; v
(publish) herausgeben;
(shares) emittieren;
(order) erteilen; (passport,
certificate) ausstellen

isthmus, iss-*mes, n*
Landenge f, Isthmus m

it, itt, *pron* er/sie/es;
ihn/sie/es; ihm/ihr/ihm

Italian, i-**täll**-jen, *adj*
italienisch; n (person)
Italiener m; (language)
Italienisch nt

italic, i-**täll**-ick, *adj* kursiv;
–s, *npl* Kursivschrift f

Italy, itt-*e*-li, n Italien nt

itch, itsch, n Krätze f; *fig*
Drang m; v jucken; –y, *adj*
juckend

item, ei-*tem, n* (thing)
Gegenstand m; (in list)
Posten m; (of news)
Artikel m; –ize, v einzeln
aufführen

itinerant, i-**tinn**-*e*-rent, *adj*
wandernd

itinerary, ei-**tinn**-*e*-re-ri, n
Reiseroute f

its, its, *adj* sein m/nt ihr f;
dessen

itself, itt-**sself,** *pron (refl)*
sich (selbst); *(emphatic)*
selbst

ivory, ei-*we*-ri, n
Elfenbein nt

ivy, ei-wi, n Efeu m

J

jab, dschäbb, n (blow)
Schlag m; (with needle)
Stich m; (fam injection)
Spritze f; v stechen

jabber, dschäbb-er, v
plappern

jack, dschäck, n mech
Wagenheber m; (cards)
Bube m; **– up,** v (car)
aufbocken

jackal, dschäck-'l, n
Schakal m

jacket, dschäck-itt, n Jacke
f; (of book)
Schutzumschlag m

jackknife, dschäck-neif, v
querstellen

jackpot, dschäck-pott, n
Hauptgewinn m

jade, dschehd, n Jade f

jaded, dscheh-didd, adj
(tired) abgespannt;
(worn) abgestumpft

jagged, dschägg-idd, adj
zackig

jail, dschehl, n Gefängnis nt;
–er, n Gefängniswärter m

jam, dschäm, n (conserve)
Marmelade f; (traffic)
Stau m; v (sich)
verklemmen; (broadcast)
stören; **– in(to),**
hineinzwängen (in)

jangle, dschäng-g'l, v klirren

January, dschänn-ju-e-ri, n
Januar m

Japan, dsche-pänn, n Japan
nt; **–ese,** adj japanisch; n
(person) Japaner m;
(language) Japanisch nt

jar, dschahr, n (container)
Glas nt; (jolt) Ruck m; v
(of sound) kreischen; (of
colours, opinions) nicht
harmonieren; (jolt)
erschüttern

jargon, dschahr-gen, n
Fachsprache f; pej Jargon
m

jaundice, dscho'an-diss, n
Gelbsucht f; **–d,** adj
zynisch

jaunt, dscho'ant, n Ausflug
m; **–y,** adj unbeschwert

javelin, dschäw-lin, n
Speer m

jaw, dscho'ah, n Kiefer m; v
fam schwatzen

jay, dscheh, n
Eichelhäher m

jazz, dschäs, n Jazz m; **–y,**
adj poppig

jealous, dschell-ess, adj
eifersüchtig; **–y,** n
Eifersucht f

jeans, dschiens, npl Jeans pl

jeer (at), dschier (et), v
höhnen, verhöhnen

jelly, dschell-i, n Gelee nt;
(sweet) Grütze f; **–fish,** n
Qualle f

jeopardize, dschepp-er-dais,
v gefährden

jeopardy, dschepp-er-di, n
Gefahr f

jerk, dschörk, n Ruck m; v
rucken; (fam idiot) Trottel
m

jersey, dschör-si, n Pullover
m; sport Trikot nt

jest, dschest, n Scherz m; v

scherzen

jet, dschett, n (of liquid) Strahl m; (nozzle) Mundstück nt; (plane) Düsenflugzeug nt; (mineral) Jett nt; **– engine,** n Düsentriebwerk nt; **–lag,** n Jet-lag m

jettison, dschett-i-ss'n, v über Bord werfen

jetty, dschett-i, n Mole f

jewel, dschuh-el, n Juwel nt; **–ler,** n Juwelier m; **–lery,** n Schmuck m

Jewish, dschuh-isch, adj jüdisch

jibe, dscheib, n Stichelei f

jig, dschigg, n Jig f; **– about,** v herumhüpfen

jigsaw, dschigg-so'a, n Puzzle nt

jingle, dsching-g'l, n (advertising) Werbespruch m; v klimpern

job, dschobb, n (position) Stellung f; (task) Arbeit f; **–less,** adj arbeitslos

jockey, dschock-i, n Jockei m

jocular, dschock-ju-ler, adj scherzhaft

jog, dschogg, v (run) joggen; (nudge) anstoßen; **–ging,** n Jogging m

join, dscheun, n Naht f; v verbinden; (club etc.) beitreten; **–er,** n Schreiner m; **– in,** v mitmachen (bei)

joint, dscheunt, adj

gemeinsam; n (of meat) Braten m; (carpentry) Verbindung nt; (anatomy) Gelenk nt; (fam bar etc.) Spelunke f; **–ly,** adv gemeinschaftlich

joke, dschohk, n Spaß m, Witz m; v scherzen; **–r,** n Witzbold m; (cards) Joker m

jolly, dscholl-i, adj lustig, munter; **– good!** fam prima!

jolt, dschohlt, n Stoß m; fig Schock m; v stoßen; fig aufrütteln

jostle, dschoss-'l, v anrempeln, anstoßen

journal, dschör-nel, n (periodical) Zeitschrift f; (diary) Tagebuch nt; **–ism,** n Journalismus m; **–ist,** n Journalist m

journey, dschör-ni, n Reise f, Fahrt f

jovial, dschoh-wi-el, adj heiter, jovial

joy, dscheu, n Freude f; **–ful,** adj freudig; **–ride,** n Spritztour f in einem gestohlenen Auto

jubilant, dschuh-bi-lent, adj jubelnd, freudestrahlend

jubilee, dschuh-bi-lie, n Jubiläum nt

judge, dschadsch, n law Richter m; (critic) Kenner m; v (assess) beurteilen; (law case) verhandeln; **–ment,** n law Urteil nt; relig Gericht nt; (opinion)

Meinung f

judicial, dschuh-disch-'l, adj gerichtlich

judicious, dschuh-disch-ess, adj verständig, weise

judo, dschuh-doh, n Judo nt

jug, dschagg, n Krug m

juggle, dschagg-'l, v jonglieren; **–r,** n Jongleur m

juice, dschuhss, n Saft m

juicy, dschuh-ssi, adj saftig

jukebox, dschuhk-bocks, n Jukebox f

July, dschu-lei, n Juli m

jumble, dschamm-b'l, n Wirrwarr m; v durcheinanderwerfen; **–d,** adj verwirrt; **– sale,** n Basar m

jumbo, dschamm-boh, n Jumbo m; **– (jet),** n Jumbo(-Jet) m

jump, dschamp, n Sprung m; v springen; (start) zusammenfahren; **–er,** n sport Springer m; (pullover) Pullover m

junction, dschank-sch'n, n (of roads) Kreuzung f; (of motorways) (Autobahn)kreuz nt; (railway) Knotenpunkt m

June, dschuhn, n Juni m

jungle, dschang-g'l, n Dschungel m

junior, dschuh-ni-er, adj (younger) jünger, Junioren-; (subordinate) untergeordnet; n Jüngere(r) m & f; **–**

school, n Grundschule f
junk, dsch*a*nk, n Trödel m;
 – food, n Junk-food nt; **–
 mail,** n Wurfsendung f
jurisdiction, dsch*u*hr-riss-
 dick-sch'n, n
 Gerichtsbarkeit f
juror, dsch*u*hr-rer, n *law*
 Geschworene(r) m & f
jury, dsch*u*hr-ri, n *law*
 Geschworene pl;
 (competition) Jury f
just, dsch*a*st, *adj* gerecht;
 adv (now) soeben, gerade;
 (only) nur; (exactly)
 genau; (simply) mal; **– as
 good,** genauso gut; **–ice,** n
 Gerechtigkeit f;
 –ification, Rechtfertigung
 f; **–ify,** v rechtfertigen; **–ly,**
 adv mit Recht
jut (out), dsch*o*tt (aut), v
 hervorragen
juvenile, dsch*u*h-we-neil,
 adj jugendlich, Jugend-;
 pej kindisch; n
 Jugendliche(r) m & f

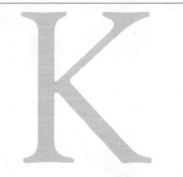

K

kangaroo, käng-ge-**ruh,** n
    Känguruh nt
karate, ke-**rah-**ti, n
    Karate nt
kebab, ki-**bäb,** n Kebab m
keel, kiel, n Kiel m
keen, kien, adj begeistert;
    (blade, intellect) scharf
keep, kiep, n Unterhalt f; v
    (retain) behalten;
    (preserve) erhalten;
    (animal, promise) halten;
    (remain) bleiben; (of
    food) sich halten; – **back,**
    zurückhalten; –**er,** n
    Wärter m; –**fit,** n
    Fitneßübungen pl; –
    left/right, v sich
    links/rechts halten; – **(on)**
    doing, v (continue)
    weitermachen; (repeat)
    immer wieder machen; –
    out! Eintritt verboten!;
    –**sake,** n Andenken nt; –

to, v daranhalten; – **up,** v
    (continue) fortsetzen; –
    up (with), v Schritt
    halten (mit)
keg, kegg, n Fäßchen nt
kennel, kenn-'l, n
    Hundehütte f
kerb, körb, n Bordstein m
kernel, körn-'l, n Kern m
kettle, kett-'l, n Kessel m;
    –**drum,** n Pauke f
key, kie, n Schlüssel m; (of
    typewriter etc.) Taste f;
    mus Tonart f; –**board,** n
    Tastatur f; –**hole,** n
    Schlüsselloch nt; –**ring,**
    n Schlüsselring m; v –
    (in), eingeben
khaki, kah-ki, adj k(h)aki;
    n K(h)aki nt
kick, kick, n Tritt m; (thrill)
    Kitzel m; v treten; (of
    horse) ausschlagen
kid, kidd, n (young goat)

Zicklein nt; (fam child)
    Kind nt; (leather)
    Glacéleder nt; v anführen,
    Spaß machen
kidnap, kidd-**näpp,** v
    entführen; –**er,** n
    Enführer m
kidney, kidd-ni, n Niere f
kill, kill, n (hunt) Erlegen
    nt; (prey) Beute f; v töten;
    (person) umbringen; –**er,**
    n Mörder m; –**ing,** n Mord
    m; (fam gain) Coup m
kiln, kiln, n Brennofen m
kilo, kie-loh, n (abbr
    kilogram(me)), Kilo nt
kilobyte, kill-e-beit, n comp
    Kilobyte nt
kilogram(me), kill-e-
    grämm, n Kilogramm nt
kilometre, ki-**lomm**-i-ter, n
    Kilometer m
kind, keind, adj
    liebenswürdig, freundlich;
    n Art f; **what – of,** was für
    (ein)
kindergarten, kinn-
    der-gahr-ten, n
    Kindergarten m
kindle, kinn-d'l, v
    anzünden; fig erwecken
kindly, keind-li, adj
    freundlich; adv
    freundlicherweise; **would**
    you –ly …? würden Sie
    bitte …?
kindness, keind-niss, n
    (goodness)
    Liebenswürdigkeit f;
    (favour) Gefallen m,
    Gefälligkeit f

king, king, n König m;
–dom, n Königreich nt

kinky, king-ki, adj (hair)
wellig; (bizarre) spleenig

kiosk, kie-osk, n Kiosk m;
(telephone) Telefonzelle f

kipper, kipp-er, n
Bückling m

kiss, kiss, n Kuß m; v (sich)
küssen

kit, kitt, n (equipment)
Ausrüstung f; (set) Satz m

kitchen, kitt-schinn, n
Küche f; **– sink,** n
Spülbecken nt

kite, keit, n (toy) Drachen
m; (bird) Milan m

kitten, kitt-'n, n
Kätzchen nt

kitty, kitt-i, n Kasse f; (fam
kitten) Mieze f

knack, näck, n Kniff m

knapsack, näpp-ssäck, n
Rucksack m; mil
Tornister m

knead, nied, v kneten

knee, nie, n Knie nt; **–cap,** n
Kniescheibe f

kneel, niel, v knien

knell, nell, n Grabgeläute nt

knickers, nick-ers, n
Schlüpfer m

knife, neif, n Messer nt; v
erstechen

knight, neit, n Ritter m;
(chess) Springer m;
–hood, n Ritterwürde f

knit, nitt, v stricken; **–ting,**
n Strickzeug nt; **–wear,** n
Strickwaren pl

knob, nobb, n Knopf m; (on

door) Griff m; **– of butter,**
n kleines Stück nt Butter

knock, nock, v (on door)
klopfen (an); (strike)
schlagen; (fam criticize)
kritisieren; **– against,** v
stoßen gegen; **– down,** v
niederschlagen; (with car)
anfahren; **–er,** n (door)
Türklopfer m; **– off,** v (do
quickly) schnell erledigen;
(fam steal) klauen; (stop
work) Feierabend
machen; **– out,** v k.o.-
schlagen

knock-out, nock-aut, adj
(fam great) toll; n (blow)
K.o.-Schlag m; fam
Wucht f

knot, nott, n Knoten m; v
(ver)knüpfen

knotty, nott-i, adj (problem)
verwickelt; (wood)
knorrig

know, noh, v (fact) wissen;
(be acquainted with)
kennen; (experience)
erleben; (language)
können; **– about,** v
Bescheid wissen über; **–
how to do sth,** etw tun
können

know-how, noh-hau, n
Know-how nt

knowledge, noll-idsch, n
Wissen nt; Kenntnis f

knuckle, nack-'l, n
Knöchel m

L

lab, läbb, n (*abbr* **laboratory**), Labor *nt*

label, leh-b'l, n Etikett *nt*; v etikettieren

laboratory, le-bo-re-te-ri, n Labor *nt*

laborious, le-bo-ri-ess, *adj* mühsam, anstrengend

labour, leh-ber, n Arbeit *f*; *med* Wehen *pl*; v (work hard) sich abmühen; (work with difficulty) sich quälen; **–ed**, *adj* schwer, mühsam; **–er**, n Arbeiter *m*; **go into –**, v *med* Wehen bekommen

laburnum, le-bör-nem, n Goldregen *m*

lace, lehss, n Spitze *f*; (shoe) Schnürsenkel *m*; v – (up), (zu)schnüren

lack, lack, n – **of**, Mangel *m* an; v – **sth**, kein(e, en)... haben; **be –ing**, fehlen

lacquer, läck-er, n Lack *m*; v lackieren

lad, lädd, n Junge *m*

ladder, lädd-er, n (steps) Leiter *f*; (in fabric) Laufmasche *f*

laden, leh-den, *adj* beladen

ladies, leh-dis, n (toilet) Damen *pl*

lady, leh-di, n Dame *f*; **–bird**, n Marienkäfer *m*; **–like**, *adj* damenhaft

lag, lägg, v isolieren; – **behind**, zurückbleiben

lair, lähr, n Unterschlupf *nt*

lake, lehk, n See *m*

lamb, lämm, n (animal) Lamm *nt*; (meat) Lamm(fleisch) *nt*; v lammen; – **chop**, n Lammkotelett *nt*

lame, lehmm, *adj* lahm; v lähmen; **–ness**, n Lahmheit *f*

lament, le-ment, n Klage *f*; v beklagen

lamp, lämp, n Lampe *f*; (in street) Laterne *f*; **–post**, n Laternenpfahl *m*; **–shade**, n Lampenschirm *m*

land, länd, n Land *nt*; (property) Grundstück *nt*; v landen; *naut* an Land gehen; (*fam* obtain) kriegen; **–fill**, n Müllgrube *f*; **–ing**, n Landung *f*; (on stairs) Treppenabsatz *m*; **–lady**, (lodgings) n Hauswirtin *f*; (pub) Wirtin *f*; **–lord**, (lodgings) n Hauswirt *m*; (pub) Wirt *m*; **–mark**, n Wahrzeichen *nt*; *fig* Markstein *m*; **–scape**, n Landschaft *f*; **–scape gardener**, n Gartengestalter *m*; **–slide**, n Erdrutsch *m*; (*fig* victory) Erdrutschsieg *m*

lane, lehn, n (narrow road) Weg *m*; (of carriageway) (Fahr)spur *f*; *sport* Bahn *f*

language, läng-gu'idsch, n Sprache *f*; **bad/strong –**, derbe Ausdrücke *pl*

languid, läng-gu'idd, *adj* schlaff

languish, läng-gu'isch, v schmachten

lank, länk, *adj* (tall) hager; (limp) glatt herabhängend; **–y**, lang und dünn

lantern, länn-tern, n Laterne *f*

lap, läpp, n Schoß *m*; *sport*

Runde f; v (of water) plätschern; sport überrunden; – **up,** (drink) auflecken

lapel, le-**pell,** n Revers nt

lapse, läpss, n (of time) Zeitraum m; (error) Fehler m; v verfallen

larceny, lahr-sse-ni, n Diebstahl m

lard, lahrd, n Schweineschmalz nt

large, lahrdsch, adj groß; **–ly,** adv größtenteils; **––scale,** adj (change, event) in großem Rahmen; (map) in großem Maßstab

lark, lahrk, n Lerche f; (fam fun) Scherz m; – **about,** v herumalbern

laryngitis, lä-rin-**dschei**-tiss, n Kehlkopfentzündung f

laser, leh-ser, n Laser m

lash, läsch, n (stroke) Hieb m; (eyelash) Augenwimper f; v (whip) peitschen; (tie) festbinden; – **out,** (fight) um sich schlagen; (spend heavily) sich etw leisten/gönnen

last, lahst, adj letzte(r/s); adv zuletzt; v (object) halten; (situation) dauern; (resources) ausreichen; **–ing,** adj dauerhaft; at **–,** adv endlich; – **but one,** adj vorletzte(r/s);

latch, lätsch, n Klinke f; **–key,** n Haussschlüssel m

late, leht, adj spät; (belated)

verspätet; (former) ehemalig; (deceased) verstorben; adv spät; (belatedly) zu spät

latecomer, leht-**kamm**-er, n Spätankömmling m

lately, leht-li, adv in letzter Zeit

lateral, lätt-e-rel, adj seitlich, Seiten-

latest, leh-tist, adj neueste(r/s)

lathe, lehdh, n Drehbank f

lather, lah-dher, n Seifenschaum m; v (ein)schäumen

Latin, lätt-in, adj lateinisch; n Latein nt; – **America,** n Lateinamerika nt

latitude, lätt-i-tjuhd, n geog Breite f; fig Spielraum m

latter, lätt-er, adj letztere(r/s)

lattice, lätt-iss, n Gitterwerk nt

laugh, lahf, n Lachen nt; – **(at),** v lachen (über); **–able,** adj lächerlich; **–ing stock,** n Gespött nt; **–ter,** n Gelächter nt

launch, lo'antsch, n (of ship) Stapellauf m; (of rocket) Start m; (of product, venture) Vorstellung f, Einführung f; v (ship) vom Stapel lassen; (product, venture) einführen

launderette, lo'an-de-rett, n Waschsalon m

laundry, lo'an-dri, n

Wäsche f; **do the –,** v (Wäsche) waschen

lavatory, läw-e-te-ri, n Toilette f

lavender, läw-in-der, n Lavendel m

lavish, läw-isch, adj freigebig; v – **(money) on sth,** (Geld) auf etw verschwenden; – **(gifts) on sb,** jdn mit (Geschenken) überhäufen

law, lo'ah, n (act) Gesetz nt; (study) Jura; **–abiding,** adj gesetzestreu; – **court,** n Gerichtshof m; **–ful,** adj rechtmäßig; **–less,** adj gesetzlos; (person) zügellos

lawn, lo'ahn, n Rasen m; **–mower,** n Rasenmäher m

lawsuit, lo'a-suht, n Prozeß m

lawyer, lo'a-jer, n Rechtsanwalt m, Rechtsanwältin f

lax, läcks, adj lose, locker

laxative, läx-e-tiw, n Abführmittel nt

lay, leh, adj Laien-; v (egg) legen; (table) decken; – **down,** v (arms) niederlegen; (rule, condition) festlegen; – **on,** (food etc.) bieten; (power, water) anschließen

layabout, leh-e-baut, n Faulenzer m

layby, leh-bei, n Haltebucht f

layer, leh-er, n Schicht f

layman, leh-men, n Laie m

layout, leh-aut, n
  (arrangement) Anlage f;
  (design) Layout nt

laze (about), lehs (e-baut),
  v faulenzen

laziness, leh-si-niss, n
  Faulheit f

lazy, leh-si, adj faul, träge

lb., abbr **pound** (weight)

lead, ledd, adj Blei-; n Blei
  nt; (for pencil) Mine f

lead, lied, n (distance
  ahead) Vorsprung m; (first
  position) Führung f;
  (example) Beispiel nt;
  (clue) Spur f; (theatre, mus
  role) Hauptrolle f; (dog's)
  Leine f; v führen, leiten;
  –er, n Leiter m, Führer m;
  (of party) Vorsitzende(r)
  m & f; (article) Leitartikel
  m; **–ership,** n Leitung f,
  Führung f

lead-free, ledd-frie, adj
  bleifrei

leading, adj führend;
  (principal) Haupt-; **–
  article,** n Leitartikel m

leaf, lief, n Blatt nt; **–
  through,** v durchblättern;
  turn over a new –, v
  einen neuen Anfang
  machen

leaflet, lief-litt, n (handout)
  Flugblatt nt; (instructions)
  Merkblatt nt

leafy, lief-i, adj belaubt

league, lieg, n Bund m; sport
  Liga f; naut Seemeile f

leak, liek, n Leck nt;
  (information) undichte

Stelle f; v (liquid) lecken;
  – out, (of liquid)
  auslaufen; (of
  information) durchsickern

lean, lien, adj mager; v **–
  against,** sich lehnen
  gegen; **– forward,** sich
  vorbeugen; **– on,** sich
  lehnen an; **– out,**
  hinauslehnen; **– towards,**
  fig tendieren zu

leaning, lie-ning, adj schräg;
  n Neigung f

leap, liep, n Sprung m; v
  springen; **– year,** n
  Schaltjahr nt

learn, lörnn, v lernen;
  (news, experience)
  erfahren; **–ed,** adj gelehrt;
  –er, n Lernende(r) m & f;
  (pupil) Schüler m;
  (beginner) Anfänger m;
  –ing, n Lernen nt;
  (knowledge) Wissen nt

lease, liess, n
  (accommodation)
  Mietvertrag m; (land etc)
  Pachtvertrag m; v mieten,
  pachten; **– (out),**
  vermieten, verpachten

leash, liesch, n Leine f

least, liest, adj geringste(r/s);
  adv am wenigsten; **at –,**
  mindestens, wenigstens;
  not in the –, gar nicht

leather, ledh-er, n Leder nt

leave, liew, n (permission)
  Erlaubnis f; (of absence)
  Urlaub m; v lassen;
  (depart) abreisen; (desert)
  verlassen; (bequeath)

hinterlassen; – behind,
  zurücklassen; (forget)
  liegenlassen; **– off,**
  aufhören; **– out,** auslassen;
  – to, (hand over)
  überlassen

lecherous, letsch-e-ress, adj
  lüstern

lecture, lek-tscher, n
  Vortrag m; (at university)
  Vorlesung f; (telling-off)
  Strafpredigt f; v einen
  Vortrag halten; (tell off)
  jdm eine Strafpredigt
  halten; **–r,** n (at
  university) Dozent m

ledge, ledsch, n (of window)
  Sims m; (of rock)
  Vorsprung m

ledger, ledsch-er, n
  Hauptbuch nt

leech, lietsch, n Blutegel m

leek, liek, n Lauch m

leer, lier, v fam angaffen

left, left, adj (side)
  linke(r/s); (remaining)
  übrig; adv links; n linke
  Seite; (politics) Linke f;
  – handed, adj linkshändig;
  –hand side, n linke Seite
  f; **– luggage (office),** n
  Gepäckaufbewahrung f;
  –overs, npl Reste pl; **be –
  (over),** v übrigbleiben; **on
  the –,** links; **to the –,**
  nach links

leg, legg, n Bein nt; (of
  meat) Keule f; (stage)
  Etappe f

legacy, legg-e-ssi, n
  Vermächtnis nt

legal, lie-g'l, *adj* (lawful)
legal; (imposed by law)
gesetzlich; (advice,
matter) juristisch; **–ize,** *v*
legalisieren; **– tender,** *n*
gesetzliches
Zahlungsmittel *nt*

legend, ledsch-end, *n* Sage *f*,
Legende *f*; **–ary,** *adj*
legendär; (famous)
berühmt

leggings, legg-ings, *npl*
Leggings *pl*

legible, ledsch-i-b'l, *adj*
leserlich

legion, lie-dschen, *n*
Legion *f*

legislate, ledsch-iss-leht, *v*
Gesetze erlassen

legislation, ledsch-iss-leh-
sch'n, *n* Gesetzgebung *f*

legitimate, le-**dschitt**-i-met,
adj legitim; (child)
ehelich

leisure, lesch-er, *n* Muße *f*,
Freizeit *f*; **– centre,** *n*
Freizeitzentrum *nt*; **–ly,**
adv gemächlich

lemon, lemm-en, *adj*
Zitronen-; *n* (fruit)
Zitrone *f*; (colour)
Zitronengelb *nt*; **–ade,**
Limonade *f*

lend, lend, *v* leihen

length, length, *n* Länge *f*;
(of time) Dauer *f*; (of
cloth etc.) Stück *nt*; **–en,**
v verlängern; **–ways,** *adj*
Längs-; *adv* der Länge
nach; **–y,** *adj* lang,
weitschweifig; **at –,** (fully)

ausführlich; (finally)
schließlich; **for the – of
...,** ... entlang

lenient, lie-ni-ent, *adj* mild,
gelind

lens, lens, *n* Linse *f*; *photog*
Objektiv *nt*

Lent, lent, *n* Fastenzeit *f*

lentil, lenn-till, *n* Linse *f*

Leo, lie-oh, *n* Löwe *m*

leopard, lepp-erd, *n* Leopard
m

leotard, lie-e-tahrd, *n*
Turnanzug *m*

leper, lepp-er, *n*
Leprakranke(r) *m & f*

leprosy, lepp-*re*-ssi, *n* Lepra *f*

lesbian, les-bi-en, *adj*
lesbisch; *n fam* Lesbe *f*;
Lesbierin *f*

less, less, *adj adv pron*
weniger; **– and less,**
immer weniger; **– than,**
weniger als

lessen, less-en, *v*
vermindern, abnehmen

lesser, less-er, *adj* geringer

lesson, less-en, *n* (school)
Stunde *f*; (in book etc.)
Lektion *f*; *fig* Lehre *f*

let, lett, *v* (allow) lassen;
(house etc.) vermieten;
(land) verpachten; **–
down,** (clothes) länger
machen; (disappoint)
enttäuschen; **– off,** (gun
etc.) abfeuern; (not
punish) laufenlassen; **–
out,** (clothes) weiter
machen; (prisoner)
entlassen; **– on,** (*fam* tell)

etw verraten; (*fam*
pretend) so tun, als ob; **–
up,** nachlassen

lethal, lie-thel, *adj* tödlich

lethargic, le-thahr-dschick,
adj träge

letter, lett-er, *n* (message)
Brief *m*; (of alphabet)
Buchstabe *m*; **–box,** *n*
Briefkasten *m*; **–ing,** *n*
Beschriftung *f*; **– of credit,**
n Kreditbrief *m*

lettuce, lett-iss, *n* Kopfsalat
m

leukaemia, lu-kie-mi-*e*,
Leukämie *f*

level, lew-el, *adj* (flat) eben;
(at same height) auf
gleicher Höhe; (head)
kühl; *adv* gleich, auf
gleicher Höhe; *n* (height)
Höhe *f*; (position) Niveau
nt; (instrument)
Wasserwaage *f*; *v* **–
(off/out),** (of ground)
eben werden; (of
inequalities) sich
ausgleichen; **– (out/up),**
(ground) einebnen;
(differences) ausgleichen;
– crossing, *n*
Bahnübergang *m*; **be –
with,** *v fam* ehrlich sein
mit; **on the –,** *adj fam*
ehrlich

lever, lie-wer, *n* Hebel *m*; *fig*
Druckmittel *nt*; **– open,** *v*
aufstemmen

levity, lew-i-ti, *n*
Leichtfertigkeit *f*

levy, lew-i, *n* (raising)

Erhebung f; (tax) Steuer f; v (tax) erheben; (fine) auferlegen

lewd, ljuhd, adj anzüglich; **–ness**, n Anzüglichkeit f

liability, lei-e-bill-i-ti, n (duty) Pflicht f; (responsibility) Haftung f; (burden) Belastung f; fin Verbindlichkeit f

liable, lei-e-b'l, adj – **for**, (responsible) haftbar; – **to**, (prone) anfällig; (subject) -pflichtig

liar, lei-er, n Lügner m

liaise (with), lie-**ehs** (u/idh), v zusammenarbeiten (mit), sich mit jdm absprechen

liaison, lie-**eh**-sonn, n Verbindung f; (sexual) Liaison f

libel, lei-b'l, n Verleumdung f; v verleumden; **–lous**, adj verleumderisch

liberal, libb-e-rel, adj (tolerant) liberal; (generous) freigebig; (tolerant person) liberal denkender Mensch m; (politics) Liberale(r) m & f

liberate, libb-e-reht, v befreien

liberty, libb-er-ti, n (freedom) Freiheit f; (cheek) Frechheit f; **take liberties (with)**, v sich etw herausnehmen

Libra, lie-bre, n Waage f

librarian, lei-**breht**-ri-en, n

Bibliothekar m

library, lei-bre-ri, n Bücherei f, Bibliothek f

licence, lei-ssenss, n Genehmigung f, Schein m; (driving) Führerschein m

license, lei-ssenss, v genehmigen; konzessionieren; **–d**, adj genehmigt; (to sell alcohol) mit Schankerlaubnis

licentious, lei-**ssenn**-shess, adj zügellos

lichen, lei-ken, n Flechte f

lick, lick, n Lecken nt; v lecken; **at a good –**, (fam fast) mit einem Affenzahn

lid, lidd, n Deckel m; (eye)–, (Augen)lid nt

lie, lei, n (untruth) Lüge f; v (rest) liegen; (tell lies) lügen; – **low**, untertauchen; – **down**, sich hinlegen

lieu, ljuh, n **in – of**, prep anstatt

lieutenant, lef-**tenn**-ent, n Leutnant m

life, leif, n Leben nt; **–belt**, n Rettungsring m; **–boat**, n Rettungsboot nt; – **cycle**, Lebenszyklus m; – **insurance**, n Lebensversicherung f; – **jacket**, n Schwimmweste f; **–less**, adj leblos; **–like**, adj lebensecht; – **long**, adj lebenslang; – **sentence**, n lebenslängliche

Freiheitsstrafe f; **–size(d)**, adj lebensgroß

lifetime, leif-teim, n Lebensdauer f; **in one's –**, während seines Lebens; **once in a –**, einmal im Leben, einmalig

lift, lift, n (elevator) Fahrstuhl m, Aufzug m, Lift m; v (object) hochheben; (restriction) aufheben; **give sb a –**, (in car) jdn mitnehmen; fig jdn aufmuntern; **–off**, n Abheben nt

light, leit, n Licht nt; (for cigarette) Feuer nt; adj (bright, pale) hell; (in weight) leicht; v (fire) anzünden; (illuminate) beleuchten; – **bulb**, n Glühbirne f; **–en**, (brighten) erhellen; (in weight) erleichtern; **–er**, n Feuerzeug nt; **–headed**, adj schwindlig; **–hearted**, adj leichtherzig; **–house**, n Leuchtturm m; **–ing**, n Beleuchtung f; **–ly**, adv (gently) leicht; (casually) leichthin; (unpunished) glimpflich; **–ness**, n (in colour) Helligkeit f; (in weight) Leichtheit f

lightning, leit-ning, n Blitz m; – **conductor**, n Blitzableiter m

lights, leits, npl (traffic lights) (Verkehrs)ampel f; (on car) Scheinwerfer pl

like, leik, adj (the same)

gleich; (similar) ähnlich;
prep (in comparisons) wie;
(similar to) ähnlich; *v*
gern haben, mögen;
–lihood, *n*
Wahrscheinlichkeit *f*; **–ly,**
adj wahrscheinlich; **–ness,**
n Ähnlichkeit *f*; (portrait)
Porträt *nt*; **– this,** *adv* so;
–wise, *adv* gleichfalls;
what (is it) like? wie (ist
es)?; **would –: I would –
...,** ich möchte ..., ich
hätte gern ...; **would you
– ...?** möchten Sie ...?,
hätten Sie gern ...?

liking, lei-king, *n* Vorliebe *f*

lilac, lei-lek, *n* (colour)
lila; *n* Flieder *m*

lilt, lilt, *n* singender
Tonfall *m*

lily, lill-i, *n* Lilie *f*; **– of the
valley,** Maiglöckchen *nt*

limb, limm, *n* Glied *nt*

limber up, limm-ber app, *v*
warm machen; (prepare)
sich vorbereiten

limbo, limm-bo, *n* **in –,** in
der Schwebe

lime, leim, *n* (substance)
Kalk *m*; (fruit) Limone *f*;
(tree) Linde *f*; **–light,** *n*
Rampenlicht *m*

limit, limm-itt, *n* Grenze *f*; *v*
begrenzen, beschränken;
–ation, *n* Einschränkung *f*;
–ed, *adj* beschränkt; **–ed
company,** *n* Gesellschaft *f*
mit beschränkter Haftung

limp, limp, schlaff; *n*
Hinken *nt*; *v* hinken

limpet, limm-pitt, *n*
Napfschnecke *f*; *fig*
Klette *f*

line, lein, *n* Linie *f*; (of
writing) Zeile *f*; (row)
Reihe *f*; (rope, fishing
etc.) Leine *f*; (railway)
Strecke *f*; Leitung *f*, Verbindung *f*;
(business) Branche *f*; *v*
(clothes) füttern; (street
etc.) säumen;

linear, linn-i-er, linear,
Längen-

lined, leind, *adj* (paper)
liniert; (face) faltig

line manager, lein männ-i-
dscher, *n* unmittelbarer
Vorgesetzter *m*

linen, linn-in, *n* (cloth)
Leinen *nt*; (laundry)
Wäsche *f*

liner, lei-ner, *n* Linienschiff
nt

line up, lein app, *v* (get in
line) sich aufstellen; (put
in line) aufstellen;
(prepare) planen,
arrangieren

linger, ling-ger, *v* (remain)
bleiben; (hesitate)
zaudern

lingerie, länn-dsche-rie, *n*
Damenunterwäsche *f*

lingering, *adj* (illness)
langwierig; (doubt)
anhaltend

linguist, ling-gu'ist, *n*
Sprachkundige(r) *m & f*;
–ic, *adj* sprachlich; **–s,** *n*
Sprachwissenschaft *f*

lining, lei-ning, *n* Futter *nt*

link, link, *n* (in chain)
Glied *nt*; (connection)
Verbindung *f*; *v*
verbinden; **–s,** *npl*
Golfplatz *m*; **– up,** *v* (bring
together) in Verbindung
bringen; (come together)
sich zusammenschließen

lino, lei-noh, *abbr* linoleum

linoleum, linn-oh-li-em, *n*
Linoleum *nt*

linseed oil, linn-ssied eul, *n*
Leinöl *n*

lint, lint, *n* (dressing) Mull
m; (fluff) Fussel *m*

lion, lei-en, *n* Löwe *m*; **–ess,**
n Löwin *f*

lip, lipp, *n* Lippe *f*; (of cup
etc.) Rand *m*; **–read,** *v*
von den Lippen ablesen;
give – service, ein
Lippenbekenntnis
ablegen; **–stick,** *n*
Lippenstift *m*

liqueur, li-kör, *n* Likör *m*

liquid, lick-u'idd, *adj* flüssig;
n Flüssigkeit *f*; **–ate,** *v*
liquidieren; (debts)
bezahlen; **–ation,** *n*
Liquidation *f*; **–ize,** *v*
pürieren; **–izer,** *n* Mixer *m*

liquor, lick-er, *n* Alkohol *m*;
–ice, *n* Lakritze *f*

lisp, lisp, *n* Lispeln *nt*; *v*
lispeln

list, list, *n* Liste *f*; *naut*
Schlagseite *f*; *v* (in
writing) aufschreiben;
(orally) aufzählen; *naut*
Schlagseite haben

listen, liss-'n, v horchen; –
to, zuhören; (radio)
hören; **–er,** n Zuhörer m;
(radio) Hörer m

literacy, litt-e-re-ssi, n Lese-
und Schreibfertigkeit f

**literal(ly), litt-e-rel(-i), adj
& adv** wörtlich

literary, litt-e-re-ri, adj
literarisch

literate, litt-e-ret, adj lese-
und schreibkundig;
(educated) gebildet

literature, lit-re-tscher, n
Literatur f

litigation, litt-i-geh-sch'n, n
Rechtsstreit m

litre, lie-ter, n Liter m

litter, litt-er, n (rubbish)
Abfall m; (stretcher)
Trage f; (animals) Wurf m;
v verstreuen; **– bin,** n
Abfalleimer m; **–ed with,**
übersät mit

little, litt-'l, adj (small)
klein; (not much) wenig;
adv & n wenig; **a –,** ein
wenig, ein bißchen

live, liw, v leben; (reside)
wohnen; **– down,** Gras
wachsen lassen über; **– up
to,** (expectation) gerecht
werden; (standard)
erreichen

live, leiw, adj (living)
lebend; (ammunition)
scharf; (electrically)
geladen; (broadcast) live;
adv live, direkt

livelihood, leiw-li-hud, n
Lebensunterhalt m

lively, leiw-li, adj lebhaft,
lebendig

liven up, leiw-en app, v
beleben

liver, liw-er, n Leber f

livid, liw-idd, adj (colour)
blau; (furious) wütend

living, liw-ing, adj
lebend(ig); n
Leben(sunterhalt m) nt; –
room, n Wohnzimmer nt;
– standards, npl
Lebensstandard m

lizard, lis-erd, n Eidechse f

load, lohd, n (cargo) Ladung
f; (burden) Last f; v
beladen; (comp, gun)
laden; **–s of, fam**
massenhaft; **–ed, adj**
beladen; (question)
suggestiv; (fam rich)
steinreich

loaf, lohf, n Laib m; v –
(about/around),
herumlungern

loam, lohm, n Lehm m; **–y,
adj** lehmig

loan, lohn, n Leihgabe f;
(public) Anleihe f; fin
Darlehen nt; v leihen; on
–, adj geliehen; adv
leihweise

loath (to), lohth (tu), **adj**
ungern

loathe, lohdh, v
verabscheuen

loathing, loh-dhing, n
Abscheu m, Ekel m

lobby, lobb-i, n (in house)
Vorhalle f; (in hotel,
theatre) Foyer nt;

(pressure group) Lobby f; v
– (for), sich für etw
einsetzen

lobe, lohb, n (of ear)
Ohrläppchen nt

lobster, lobb-ster, n
Hummer m

local, loh-k'l, adj Orts-,
hiesig; n (pub)
Stammkneipe f; (person)
Einheimische(r) m & f; **–
anaesthetic,** n örtliche
Betäubung f; **– call,** n
(telephone) Ortsgespräch
nt; **– government,** n
Kommunalverwaltung f;
–ly, loh-ke-li, adv am Ort

locality, loh-käll-i-ti, n Ort
m

locate, loh-keht, v auffinden

location, loh-keh-sch'n, n
Lage f; Stelle f; on –, vor
Ort

lock, lock, n Schloß nt; naut
Schleuse f; (of hair) Locke
f; v verschließen; **–er,** n
Schließfach nt; **–et,** n
Medaillon nt; **– out,** v
aussperren; **–smith,** n
Schlosser m; **– up,** v
einschließen

locomotive, loh-ke-moh-tiw,
n Lokomotive f

locust, loh-kest, n
Heuschrecke f

lodge, lodsch, n (gatehouse)
Pförtnerhaus nt;
(masonic) Loge f; v (stick)
stecken; **– (with),**
wohnen (bei); **–r,** n
Untermieter m

lodging, lodsch-ing, board and –, n Kost und Logis; **–s**, npl Unterkunft f; (flat) Wohnung f

loft, loft, n Dachboden m; **–y,** adj hoch m

log, logg, n (wood) Klotz m; **–(book)** Logbuch nt

logic, lodsch-ick, n Logik f; **–al,** adj logisch

loin, leun, n Lende f

loiter, leu-ter, v (go slowly) bummeln; (stand about) herumlungern; **–er,** n Herumlungerer m

London, lann-den, n London nt

lone, lohn, adj einzeln; **–liness,** n Einsamkeit f; **–ly,** adj einsam; **–r,** n Einzelgänger m

long, long, adj (time, size) lang; (journey) weit; adv lange; v **– (for),** sich sehnen (nach); **– distance,** adj Fern-; **–ing,** n Sehnsucht f, Sehnen nt; **–itude,** n Länge f; (degree of) Längengrad m; **– jump,** n Langsprung m; **– range,** adj (plane) Langstrecken-; (forecast) langfristig; **–suffering,** adj schwer geprüft; **–term,** adj langfristig; **–winded,** adj langatmig; **– a way (away),** weit (entfernt); **as – as,** solange; **before –,** bald; **no –er,** nicht mehr

loo, luh, n fam Klo nt

look, luck, n Blick m; v

schauen; (appear) aussehen; **– after,** v sorgen für; **– at,** v ansehen; **– down on,** v herabsehen auf; **– for,** v suchen; **– forward to,** v sich freuen auf; **–ing-glass,** n Spiegel m; **– into,** (investigate) untersuchen; **– out,** v hinaussehen; (take care) aufpassen; interj Achtung!; **–-out,** n (watch) Ausschau f; (person) Wachposten m; **– up,** aufblicken; (word) nachschlagen; **–s,** npl Aussehen nt

loom, luhm, n Webstuhl m; v bedrohlich werden

loony, luh-ni, adj verrückt

loop, luhp, n Schleife f; (rope) Schlaufe f; **–hole,** n fig Lücke f

loose, luhss, adj (fit, connection, conduct) lose; (knot, weave, morals) locker; (translation) frei; **– change,** n Kleingeld nt; **–n,** v lockern; **be at a – end,** nichts zu tun haben

loot, luht, n Beute f; v plündern

lop, lopp, v zustutzen; **– off,** v abhauen; **–sided,** adj schief

lord, lord, n Herr m; (title) Lord m; **the L–,** relig der Herr; **the L–s,** npl parl das Oberhaus f

lorry, lo-ri, n Lastwagen m

lose, luhs, v verlieren; (of watch) nachgehen; **–r,** n Verlierer m

loss, loss, n Verlust m; **be at a –,** v nicht weiter wissen

lost, lost, adj verloren; **– property,** n Fundsachen pl; **– property office,** n Fundbüro nt

lot, lott, n (item, fate) Los nt; (quantity) Menge f; **a –,** adv viel; **a – of, –s of,** eine Menge, viel(e); **the –,** alles; pl alle

lotion, loh-sch'n, n Lotion f

lottery, lott-e-ri, n Lotterie f; fig Glücksspiel m

loud, laud, adj (noise) laut; (colour, style) grell; **–speaker,** n Lautsprecher m

lounge, laundsch, n (in house) Wohnzimmer nt; (in hotel etc.) Gesellschaftszimmer nt; v **– (about),** herumsitzen; **– suit,** n Straßenanzug m

louse, lauss, n Laus f; pej Ratte f

lout, laut, n Lümmel m

love, law, adj Liebes-; n Liebe f; (person) Liebling m; (zero) null; v (person) lieben; (thing/activity) sehr gern haben/mögen; **– affair,** n Verhältnis nt; **–ly,** adj schön, reizend; **–r,** n Liebhaber m; (of animals etc.) Freund m; **in – (with),** adj verliebt (in); **make –,** v (sex) mit jdm schlafen

low, loh, *adj* niedrig; (note, level) tief; (voice) leise; (light) schwach; (morale) schlecht; (spirits) gedrückt; (density, quality) gering; *adv* (fly, sink, aim) tief; (quietly) leise; *n* (pressure) Tief *m*; (point) Tiefpunkt *m*; *v* (of cattle) muhen

lower, loh-er, *v* (price) herabsetzen; (load etc.) herunterlassen; (flag) einholen; (eyes, gun) senken; – **o.s.,** sich erniedrigen

low-cut, loh-**katt,** *adj* tiefausgeschnitten

low-fat, loh-**fatt,** *adj* fettarm

lowland(s), loh-lend(s), *n(pl.),* Tiefland *nt*

low tide, *n* Ebbe *f*

loyal, leu-*el,* *adj* treu; **–ty,** *n* Treue *f*

lozenge, los-indsch, *n* Pastille *f*

Ltd, limm-i-tidd, *n* (*abbr* **limited company**), GmbH

lubricant, luh-bri-kent, *n* Schmiermittel *nt*

lubricate, luh-bri-keht, *v* schmieren

lucid, luh-ssidd, *adj* klar

luck, lack, *n* Glück *nt*; **bad –,** Pech *nt*; **good –!** viel Glück!; **–ily,** *adv* glücklicherweise; **–y,** *adj* Glücks-; (chance) glücklich; **be –y,** Glück haben

lucrative, luh-kre-tiw, *adj* einträglich

ludicrous, luh-di-kress, *adj* lächerlich

lug, lagg, *v fam* schleppen

luggage, lagg-idsch, *n* Gepäck *nt*; **– office,** *n* Gepäckabgabe *f*; **– rack,** *n* Gepäckablage *f*

lukewarm, luhk-u'oarm, *adj* lau, lauwarm

lull, lall, *n* Pause *f*; *v* einlullen; beruhigen

lullaby, lall-e-bei, *n* Wiegenlied *nt*

lumbago, lamm-beh-goh, *n* Hexenschuß *m*

lumber, lamm-ber, *n* Gerümpel *nt*; (timber) Holz *nt*; **–jack,** *n* Holzfäller *m*; **– room,** *n* Abstellkammer *f*; *v* **– sb with sth,** jdm etw aufhalsen

luminous, luh-mi-ness, *adj* leuchtend

lump, lamp, *n* Klumpen *m*; (sugar) Stück *nt*; *med* Knoten *m*; **– it,** *v fam* sich mit etw abfinden; **– together,** *v* zusammenwerfen; **–y,** *adj* klumpig

lunacy, luh-ne-ssi, *n* Wahnsinn *m*

lunar, luh-ner, *adj* Mond-

lunatic, luh-ne-tick, *adj* wahnsinnig; *n* Wahnsinnige(r) *m & f*; **– asylum,** *n pej* Irrenanstalt *f*

lunch(eon), lantsch(-en), *n* Mittagessen *nt*

lunch hour, lantsch au-er, *n* Mittagspause *f*

lunchtime, lantsch-teim, *n* Mittag *m*; **at –,** mittags

lung, lang, *n* Lunge *f*

lurch, lörtsch, *n* Ruck *m*; *naut* Schlingern *nt*; *v* (of person) taumeln; (of vehicle) rucken; *naut* schlingern; **leave in the –,** *v* im Stich lassen

lure, ljuhr, *v* (an)locken

lurid, ljuhr-ridd, *adj* (colour) grell; (tale etc.) grausig

lurk, lörk, *v* lauern

luscious, lasch-ess, *adj* üppig; saftig

lust, last, *n* (desire) Wollust *f*; (greed) Gier *f*; **– (after/for),** *v* gelüsten (nach); **–ful,** *adj* lüstern

lusty, lass-ti, *adj* kräftig

lute, luht, *n* Laute *f*

luxuriant, lack-**schuhr**-ri-ent, *adj* üppig

luxurious, lack-**schuhr**-ri-ess, *adj* luxuriös

luxury, lack-sche-ri, *adj* Luxus-; *n* Luxus *m*

lying, lei-ing, *n* Lügen *nt*

lymph, limff, *n* Lymphe *f*

lynch, lintsch, *v* lynchen

lyric(al), li-rick(-'l), *adj* lyrisch

lyrics, li-ricks, *npl* Text *m*

mac, mäck, *abbr*
   mackintosh
macaroni, mäck-*e*-roh-ni, *n*
   Makkaroni *pl*
machine, me-**schien,** *n*
   Maschine *f*; **– gun,** *n*
   Maschinengewehr *nt*; **–ry,**
   n Maschinerie *f*
mackerel, mäck-*e*-rel, *n*
   Makrele *f*
mackintosh, mäck-inn-
   tosch, *n* Regenmantel *m*
mad, mädd, *adj* (crazy)
   verrückt; (angry) wütend;
   – about, vernarrt in
madam, mädd-em, *n* gnädige
   Frau *f*
madden, mädd-'n, *v* (make
   angry) wütend machen;
   (make crazy) verrückt
   machen
madly, mädd-li, *adv*
   wahnsinnig
madman, mädd-men, *n*

Verrückter *m*
madwoman, mädd-u'u-men,
   n Verrückte *f*
magazine, mäg-*e*-sien, *n*
   (periodical) Zeitschrift *f*;
   mil Magazin *nt*
madness, mädd-niss, *n*
   Wahnsinn *m*
maggot, mägg-et, *n* Made *f*
magic, mädsch-ick, *adj*
   magisch, Zauber-; *n*
   Zauberei *f*
magician, me-dschisch-'n, *n*
   Zauberer *m*
magistrate, mädsch-iss-
   treht, *n* Friedensrichter *m*
magnanimous, mägg-nänn-
   i-mess, *adj* großmütig
magnesium, mägg-nie-si-em,
   n Magnesium *nt*
magnet, mägg-nitt, *n*
   Magnet *m*; **–ic,** *adj*
   magnetisch; **–ism,** *n*
   Magnetismus *m*; *fig*

unwiderstehlich; **–ize,** *v*
   magnetisieren
magnificent, mägg-**ni**-fis-
   sent, *adj* prächtig
magnify, mägg-ni-fei, *v*
   vergrößern; **–ing glass,**
   n Lupe *f*,
   Vergrößerungsglas *nt*
magnitude, mägg-ni-**tjuhd,**
   n (size) Größe *f*;
   (importance) Bedeutung *f*
magpie, mägg-pei, *n* Elster *f*
mahogany, me-**hogg**-*e*-ni, *n*
   Mahagoni *nt*
maid, mehd, *n*
   Dienstmädchen *nt*; **old –,**
   n pej alte Jungfer *f*
maiden, meh-d'n, *adj*
   Jungfern-; *n* Maid *f*
mail, mehl, *n* Post *f*; *v*
   aufgeben; **– bag,** *n*
   Postsack *m*; **–box,** *n*
   Briefkasten *m*; **– order,** *adj*
   auf Bestellung, Katalog-,
   Versand-; *n*
   Versandhandel *m*
maim, mehm, *v*
   verstümmeln
main, mehn, *adj*
   hauptsächlich, Haupt-; *n*
   (water, gas) Hauptleitung
   f; **–land,** *n* Festland *nt*; **–ly,**
   adv hauptsächlich; **–s,** *npl*
   (water, gas)
   Versorgungsnetz *nt*;
   –stream, *n* (art, *mus*)
   Mainstream *m*; (trend)
   Trend *m*
maintain, mehn-**tehn,** *v*
   (claim) behaupten;
   (support) unterhalten;

(keep in repair) instand halten

maintenance, mehn-*te*-nenss, n (support) Unterhalt m; (repair) Instandhaltung f

maize, mehs, n Mais m

majestic, me-**dschess**-tick, adj majestätisch

majesty, mädsch-iss-ti, n Majestät f

major, meh-dscher, adj (important) Haupt-; (size) größer; (mus key) Dur nt; n mil Major m

Majorca, me-**jor**-ke, n Mallorca nt

majority, me-**dscho**-ri-ti, n Mehrheit f; (age) Volljährigkeit f

make, mehk, n Marke f; v machen; (manufacture) herstellen; (decision) treffen; (cause) dazu bringen; **--believe,** v Phantasie f; **- do (with),** v auskommen (mit); **- it,** v es schaffen; **-r,** n Fabrikant m; **--shift,** adj Behelfs-; **--up,** n Schminke f; v (face) schminken; (story) erfinden; (be reconciled) sich versöhnen

making, meh-king, n **in the -,** angehend

malaise, me-**lehs,** n Unbehagen nt

malaria, me-**lähr**-ri-e, n Malaria f

male, mehl, adj männlich; n

(animal) Männchen nt; (human) Mann m

malevolent, me-**lew**-e-lent, adj böswillig

malfunction, mäll-**fank**-sch'n, n Störung f; (machine) Funktionsstörung f; v nicht richtig funktionieren

malice, mäll-iss, n Groll m; Haß m

malicious, me-**lisch**-ess, adj boshaft; böswillig

malign, me-**lein,** adj böse; v verleumden

malignant, me-**ligg**-nent, adj bösartig

malinger, me-**ling**-ger, v sich krank stellen

mallet, mäll-itt, n Holzhammer m

malnutrition, mäll-njuh-**trisch**-'n, n Unterernährung f

malpractice, mäll-**präck**-tiss, n (law, med) Kunstfehler m

malt, mo'alt, n Malz nt

maltreat, mäll-triet, v mißhandeln

mammal, mämm-'l, n Säugetier nt

man, männ, n Mann m; (human race) Menschheit f; v bemannen

manage, männ-idsch, v (control) leiten, führen; (accomplish) fertigbringen; **-able,** adj machbar; **-ment,** n

Management nt, Leitung f, Führung f; (managers) Vorstand m; **-r,** n Manager m, Leiter m, Geschäftsführer m; **-ress,** n Managerin f, Leiterin f, Geschäftsführerin f

managerial, männ-idsch-**ier**-ri-el, adj leitend

mandate, männ-deht, n Verfügung f; law Mandat nt

mandatory, männ-de-te-ri, adj obligatorisch

mane, mehn, n Mähne f

manger, mehn-dscher, n Krippe f

mangle, mäng-g'l, n Rolle f; v mangeln

mango, mäng-goh, n Mango f

manhandle, männ-**hänn**-d'l, v (roughly) grob behandeln

manhole, männ-hohl, n Einstiegsluke f

manhood, n (quality) Männlichkeit f; (age) Mannesalter nt

mania, meh-ni-e, n Manie f, Sucht f; **-c,** n Verrückte(r) m & f

manic, männ-ick, adj manisch

manicure, männ-i-kjuhr, n Maniküre f

manifest, männ-i-fest, adj offenbar; v offenbaren; **-ation,** n Ausdruck m, Anzeichen nt

manifesto, männ-i-**fess**-toh,

n Manifest *nt*

manipulate, me-**nipp**-ju-leht, *v* handhaben

mankind, männ-**keind,** *n* Menschheit *f*

manly, **männ**-li, *adj* männlich

manner, **männ**-er, *n* Weise *f*; (kind) Art *f*; **–ism,** *n* Eigenart *f*; **–s,** *npl* Manieren *fpl*.

man-made, **männ**-mehd, *adj* künstlich, Kunst-

manoeuvre, me-**nuh**-wer, *n* Manöver *nt*; *mil* Feldzug *m*; *v* manövrieren

manor, **männ**-er, *n* Landgut *nt*; **– house,** *n* Herrenhaus *nt*

manpower, **männ**-pau-er, *n* Arbeitskräfte *pl*

mansion, **männ**-sch'n, *n* Herrensitz *m*

manslaughter, **männ**-slo'a-ter, *n* Totschlag *m*

mantelpiece, **männ**-t'l-piess, *n* Kaminsims *m*

manual, **männ**-ju-el, *adj* manuell, Hand-; *n* Handbuch *nt*; **– labour,** *n* manuelle Tätigkeit *f*

manufacture, männ-juh-**fäck**-tscher, *n* Herstellung *f*; *v* herstellen; **–r,** *n* Hersteller *m*

manure, me-**njuhr,** *n* Dung *m*; (fertilizer) Dünger *m*; *v* düngen

manuscript, **männ**-juh-skript, *n* Manuskript *nt*

many, **menn**-i, *adj & pron*

viele; **– a,** manch ein

map, mäpp, *n* Karte *f*; (of town) Plan *m*; *v* aufzeichnen; **– out,** planen

maple, **meh**-p'l, *n* Ahorn *m*

mar, mahr, *v* verderben; stören

marathon, **mä**-re-thonn, *n* *sport* Marathonlauf *m*; *fig* Marathon *m*

marble, mahr-**b'l,** *n* Marmor *m*; (toy) Murmel *f*

march, mahrtsch, *n* Marsch *m*; *v* marschieren

March, mahrtsch, *n* März *m*

mare, mähr, *n* Stute *f*

margarine, mahr-dsche-**rien,** *n* Margarine *f*

margin, **mahr**-dschin, *n* Rand *m*; **–al,** *adj* (in margin) Rand-; (slight) unbedeutend; **–al seat,** *n* mit knapper Mehrheit gewonnener Sitz *m*; **–alize,** *v* an den Rand drängen

marigold, **mä**-ri-gohld, *n* Ringelblume *f*

marijuana, mä-ri-u'ah-ne, *n* Marihuana *nt*

marina, me-**rie**-ne, *n* Yachthafen *m*

marinate, **mä**-ri-neht, *v* marinieren

marine, me-**rien,** *adj* See-; *n* Seesoldat *m*

marital, **mä**-ri-tel, *adj* Ehe-; **– status,** *n* Familienstand *m*

maritime, **mä**-ri-teim, *adj*

See-, Marine-

mark, mahrk, *n* (sign) Zeichen *nt*; (stain) Fleck *m*; (currency) Mark *f*; (in exam) Note *f*; *v* (identify) markieren; (characterize) kennzeichnen; (stain) Flecken machen; (exam) korrigieren; **–ed,** *adj* deutlich; **make one's –,** *v* sich einen Namen machen

market, **mahr**-kitt, *n* Markt *m*; *fin* Börse *f*; *v* vermarkten; **– gardening,** *n* Gemüseanbau *m*; **–ing,** *n* Marketing *nt*– **research,** *n* Marktforschung *f*

marksman, **mahrks**-men, *n* Scharfschütze *m*

marmalade, **mahr**-me-lehd, *n* Orangenmarmelade *f*

maroon, me-**ruhn,** *adj* kastanienbraun; *v* aussetzen

marriage, **mä**-ridsch, *adj* Heirats-; *n* (ceremony) Hochzeit *f*; (state) Ehe *f*

married, **mä**-ridd, *adj* verheiratet, **– couple,** *n* Ehepaar *nt*

marrow, **mä**-roh, *n* (bone) Mark *nt*; (vegetable) Kürbis *m*

marry, **mär**-i, *v* (get married to) heiraten; (perform ceremony) trauen

marsh, mahrsch, *n* Sumpf *m*

marshy, **mahr**-schi, *adj* sumpfig

martial, **mahr**-schel, *adj*

kriegerisch, Kriegs-; – **law**,
n Kriegsrecht nt

martyr, mahr-ter, n
Märtyrer m; v peinigen;
–dom, n Märtyrertum nt

marvel, mahr-wel, n
Wunder nt; v – **(at)**, sich
wundern (über); **–lous**, adj
wunderbar

Marxism, marck-ssism, n
Marxismus m

marzipan, mahr-si-pänn, n
Marzipan nt

mascara, mäss-kah-re, n
Wimperntusche f

masculine, mäss-kjuh-linn,
adj männlich

mash, mäsch, v zerdrücken;
–ed potato(es), n(pl.),
Kartoffelpüree nt

mask, mahsk, n Maske f; v
maskieren

mason, meh-ssen, n Maurer
m, Steinhauer m;
(freemason) Freimaurer m

masonic, me-ssonn-ick, adj
freimaurerisch

masonry, meh-ssen-ri, n
Mauerwerk nt

masquerade, mäss-ke-rehd,
n Maskerade f; v – **(as)**,
sich als etw/jd ausgeben

mass, mäss, adj Massen-;
Masse f, Menge f; relig
Messe f; v sich sammeln;
–es of, eine Menge; **the
–es**, npl die Massen pl

massacre, mäss-e-ker, n
Gemetzel nt; v
massakrieren

massage, mäss-ahsch, n

Massage f; v massieren

massive, mäss-iw, adj massiv

mast, mahst, n Mast m

master, mahss-ter, n Herr m;
(artist) Meister m;
(teacher) Lehrer m; **M–**,
(graduate) Magister m; v
beherrschen; **–ful**, adj
herrisch; **–ly**, adv
meisterhaft; **–mind**, n
(An)führer m; v
(an)führen; **–piece**, n
Meisterwerk nt; **–y**, n
Können nt

masticate, mäss-ti-keht, v
kauen, zerkauen

masturbate, mäss-ter-beht,
v masturbieren

mat, mätt, n Matte f

match, mätsch, n
Streichholz nt; sport
Spiel nt, Match nt;
(equal) Ebenbürtige(r)
m & f; v (go with)
passen zu; (go together)
zusammenpassen; (equal)
gleichkommen; **–ing**,
adj passend

mate, meht, n (friend)
Kumpel; (of animal)
Männchen nt, Weibchen
nt; naut Maat m; v (sich)
paaren

material, me-tier-ri-el, adj
(physical) materiell;
(significant) wesentlich; n
Material nt; (cloth) Stoff
m; **–istic**, adj
materialistisch; **–ize**, v
(plan etc.) sich
verwirklichen; (ghost

etc.) erscheinen; **–s**, npl
Materialien pl

maternal, me-tör-nel, adj
mütterlich, Mutter-

mathematics, mäth-i-mätt-
icks, n Mathematik f

maths, mäths, n (abbr
mathematics), Mathe f

matinée, mätt-i-neh, n
Frühvorstellung f

matrimonial, mätt-ri-moh-
ni-el, n ehelich, Ehe-

matrimony, mätt-ri-me-ni, n
Ehestand m

matrix, meh-tricks, n
Matrize f

matron, meh-tren, n
(hospital) Oberschwester
f; (school) Hausmutter f

matter, mätt-er, n
(substance) Materie f;
(substance) Stoff m;
(affair) Angelegenheit f; v
etwas ausmachen; **–of-
fact**, adj sachlich,
nüchtern; **it doesn't –**, es
macht nichts

matting, mätt-ing, n
Geflecht nt; (mats)
Matten pl

mattress, mätt-ress, n
Matratze f

mature, me-tjuhr, adj reif; v
reifen

maturity, me-tjuhr-ri-ti, n
Reife f

maul, mo'al, v verletzen

mauve, mohw, adj hell lila

maxim, mäck-ssimm, n
Grundsatz m

maximize, mäck-ssi-meis, v

maximieren

maximum, mäck-ssi-mem, *adj* maximal, Maximal-; *n* Maximum *nt*

may, meh, *v* (be permitted) dürfen; (be possible) können; (be probable) mögen

May, meh, *n* Mai *m*

maybe, meh-bie, *adj* vielleicht

May Day, meh deh, *n* der erste Mai *m*; (Labour Day) Tag *m* der Arbeit

mayhem, meh-hemm, *n* Chaos *nt*

mayonnaise, meh-*e*-nehs, *n* Mayonnaise *f*

mayor, meh-er, *n* Bürgermeister *m*

maze, mehs, *n* Irrgarten *m*

me, mie, *pron* (accusative) mich; (dative) mir; (emphatic) ich

meadow, medd-oh, *n* Wiese *f*

meagre, mie-ger, *adj* mager; (scanty) karg

meal, miel, *n* Essen *nt*, Mahlzeit *f*; (flour) Mehl *nt*; **–time,** *n* Essenszeit *f*

mean, mien, *adj* (miserly) geizig; (nasty) gemein; *n* Durchschnitt *m*; *v* (signify) bedeuten; (have in mind) meinen; (intend) wollen; **be –t to,** sollen

meander, mie-änn-der, *v* sich schlängeln; *fig* abschweifen

meaning, mie-ning, *n* Bedeutung *f*; (purpose) Sinn *m*; **–ful,** *adj* bedeutungsvoll, sinnvoll; **–less,** *adj* bedeutungslos, sinnlos

means, miens, *npl* Mittel *pl*; **by – of,** durch, mit Hilfe von; **by all –,** selbstverständlich; **by no –,** keineswegs

meantime, mien-teim, *adv* **(in the) –,** inzwischen

meanwhile, mien-u'eil, *adv* inzwischen

measles, mie-sels, *npl* Masern *pl*

measure, mesch-er, *n* (tool, unit) Maß *nt*; (step) Maßnahme *f*; *v* messen; **–d,** *adj* gemessen; **–ment,** Maß *nt*

meat, miet, *adj* Fleisch-; Fleisch *nt*; **–y,** *adj* fleischig; *fig* gehaltvoll

mechanic, mi-**känn**-ick, *n* Mechaniker *m*; **–al,** *adj* mechanisch; **–s,** *n* Mechanik *f*

mechanism, meck-*e*-nism, *n* Mechanismus *m*

mechanize, meck-*e*-neis, *v* mechanisieren

medal, medd-'l, *n* Medaille *f*

meddle (in), medd-'l (inn), *v* sich einmischen (in)

media, mie-di-*e*, *adj* Medien-; *npl* Medien *pl*

mediaeval = medieval

mediate, mie-di-eht, *v* vermitteln

mediator, mie-di-eh-ter, *n* Vermittler *m*

medical, medd-i-k'l, *adj* ärztlich, medizinisch; *n* (examination), (ärztliche) Untersuchung *f*

medication, medd-i-keh-sch'n, *n* Medikamente *pl*

medicinal, me-**diss**-i-n'l, *adj* medizinisch

medicine, medd-ssinn, *n* Medizin *f*, Arznei *f*

medieval, med-i-ie-vel, *adj* mittelalterlich

mediocre, mie-di-oh-ker, *adj* mittelmäßig

meditate, medd-i-teht, *v* meditieren; (think) nachdenken

Mediterranean, medd-i-te-reh-ni-en, *adj* Mittel-meer-; (person) südländisch; *n* (person) Südländer *m*; **the – (Sea),** das Mittelmeer *nt*

medium, mie-di-em, *adj* mittlere(r/s), Mittel-; **– (-sized),** mittelgroß; *n* (midpoint) Mittel *nt*; (person, channel) Medium *nt*

meek, miek, *adj* sanftmütig

meet, miet, *v* (by arrangement) sich treffen mit; (by chance) begegnen; (get to know) kennenlernen; (difficulty) begegnen; (obligation) nachkommen; **–ing,** *n* (chance) (Zusammen)treffen;

(formal) Besprechung f;
pleased to – you! es freut
mich!

mega-, megg-e, *pref*
Mega-; **–byte,** n *comp*
Megabyte nt; **–phone,** n
Megaphon nt

melancholy, mell-en-koll-i,
adj melancholisch; n
Melancholie f

mellow, mell-oh, adj mild;
(tone) weich; (mood)
heiter gestimmt; v reifen;
fig weicher werden

melodious, mi-**loh-**di-ess, adj
melodisch

melody, mell-e-di, n
Melodie f

melon, mell-en, n Melone f

melt, melt, v schmelzen; **–
away,** (person) sich
auflösen; (anger)
abklingen; **–down,** n
Kernschmelze f; **–ing
point,** n Schmelzpunkt m

member, memm-ber, n (of
club) Mitglied nt; **M– of
Parliament,**
Abgeordnete(r) m & f;
–ship, n Mitgliedschaft f;
–ship card, n
Mitgliedskarte f

membrane, memm-brehn, n
Membran f

memento, mi-**menn-**toh, n
Andenken f

memo, memm-oh, n (abbr
memorandum), Memo nt,
Mitteilung f; (on file)
Aktennotiz f

memoirs, memm-u'ahrs, npl

Memoiren pl

memorable, memm-e-re-b'l,
adj unvergeßlich

memorandum, memm-e-
ränn-dem, n
Memorandum nt,
Mitteilung f; (on file)
Aktennotiz f

memorial, mi-**mohr-**ri-el, adj
Gedenk-; n Denkmal nt

memorize, memm-e-reis, v
sich merken; (by heart)
auswendig lernen

memory, memm-e-ri, n
(faculty) Gedächtnis nt;
(thing recalled)
Erinnerung f; comp
Speicher m

menace, menn-iss, n
Drohung f; v bedrohen

menagerie, mi-**nädsch-**e-ri,
n Menagerie f

mend, mend, n reparierte
Stelle; v reparieren; (sew)
flicken; (of injury,
patient) kurieren

menial, mie-ni-el, adj
niedrig

meningitis, menn-in-
dschei-tiss, n
Hirnhautentzündung f

menopause, menn-e-po'as, n
Wechseljahre pl

menstruation, menn-stru-
eh-sch'n, n Menstruation f

mental, menn-t'l, adj geistig,
Geistes-; (fam mad)
verrückt; **– arithmetic,** n
Kopfrechnen nt; **–
breakdown,** n
Nervenzusammenbruch

m; **– cruelty,** n seelische
Grausamkeit; **– hospital,** n
Nervenklinik f

mentality, menn-**täll-**i-ti, n
Mentalität f

mention, menn-sch'n, n
Erwähnung f; v erwähnen;
don't – it! bitte (sehr)!

menu, menn-juh, n
Speisekarte f; comp Menü
nt

mercenary, mör-ssi-ne-ri,
adj geldgierig; n Söldner m

merchandise, mör-tschen-
deis, n Ware f

merchant, mör-tschent, n
Kaufmann m; **– navy,**
Handelsmarine f

merciful, mör-ssi-full, adj
gnädig; **–ly,** (kindly)
gnädig; (fortunately)
glücklicherweise

merciless, mör-ssi-liss, adj
erbarmungslos

mercury, mör-kju-ri, n
Quecksilber nt

mercy, mör-ssi, n (action)
Gnade f; (feeling)
Erbarmen nt

mere, mier, adj bloß; **–ly,** adv
bloß

merge, mördsch, v
verschmelzen; comm sich
zusammenschließen,
fusionieren; **–r,** n
Zusammenschluß m,
Fusion f

meridian, me-**ridd-**i-enn, n
Längengrad m

meringue, me-**räng,** n
Baiser nt

merit, me-ritt, n
(achievement) Verdienst
nt; (advantage) Vorzug m;
(distinction)
Auszeichnung f; v
verdienen

mermaid, mör-mehd, n
Meerjungfrau f

merry, me-ri, adj fröhlich,
heiter; – **Christmas!**
fröhliche Weihnachten!

mesh, mesch, n Masche f;
(netting) Geflecht nt

mesmerize, mes-me-reis, v
faszinieren

mess, mess, n (disorder)
Unordnung f; (dirt)
Schmutz m; (bungle)
Durcheinander f; mil
Kasino nt; –
about/around, v
herumalbern; –
about/around with, v an
etw herumbasteln;
(interfere) sich
einmischen; – **up,** v
(make untidy)
Unordnung machen;
(make dirty) schmutzig
machen; (bungle)
durcheinanderbringen

message, mess-idsch, n
Mitteilung f

messenger, mess-inn-
dscher, n Bote m

messy, adj (untidy)
unordentlich; (dirty)
schmutzig

metal, mett-'l, n Metall nt;
–**ic,** adj metallisch

metaphor, mett-e-for, n

Metapher f

meteor, mie-ti-er, n Meteor
m

meteorology, mie-ti-e-roll-e-
dschi, n Meteorologie f

meter, mie-ter, n (electricity
etc.) Zähler m

method, meth-edd, n
Methode f

methodical, mi-thodd-i-k'l,
adj methodisch

Methodist, meth-e-dist, n
Methodist m

meths, meths, abbr
methylated spirit(s)

methylated spirit(s), me-
thi-leh-tidd **spi**-ritt(s), n
Brennspiritus m

meticulous, mi-tick-ju-less,
n sorgfältig

metre, mie-ter, n Meter m/nt

metric, mett-rick, adj
metrisch

metropolis, mi-tro-pe-liss, n
Metropole f, Weltstadt f

metropolitan, mett-re-poll-
i-ten, adj Groß-;
großstädtisch

mew, mjuh, v miauen

mews, mjuhs, n Gasse f

Mexico, meck-ssi-koh, n
Mexiko m

micro-, mei-kroh, pref
Mikro-; –**chip,** n
Mikrochip m; –**computer,**
n Mikrocomputer m;
–**phone,** n Mikrophon nt;
–**scope,** n Mikroskop nt;
–**wave,** n Mikrowelle f; v
in der Mikrowelle
zubereiten; –**wave oven,** n

Mikrowellenherd nt

mid, midd, adj Mittel-; **in –
March,** Mitte März; **in –
air,** in der Luft

middle, midd-'l, adj
mittlere(r/s), Mittel-; n
Mitte f; –**aged,** adj
mittleren Alters; **M–
Ages,** npl Mittelalter nt;
M– East, n Naher Osten
m; –**class,** adj
Mittelstands-; pej spießig;
–**man,** Zwischenhändler
m; – **name,** n zweiter
Vorname m; **in the – of,**
prep mitten in, inmitten
von

middling, midd-ling, adj
mittelmäßig

midge, midsch, n Mücke f

midget, midsch-itt, n
Liliputaner m, Zwerg m

midnight, midd-neit, n
Mitternacht f

midst, midst, prep **in the –
of,** mitten in

midsummer, midd-samm-er,
n Hochsommer m

midweek, midd-wiek, adj &
adv in der Wochenmitte

midwife, midd-u'eif, n
Hebamme f

midwinter, midd-u'inn-ter,
n (Mitt)winter m

might, meit, n Macht f,
Gewalt f; v (past &
conditional of **may**) –**y,** adj
& adv mächtig

migraine, mie-grehn, n
Migräne f

migrate, mei-greht, v

(people) wandern; (birds) ziehen

migration, mei-**greh**-sch'n, n Wanderung f

Milan, mi-**länn,** n Mailand nt

mild, meild, adj (weather, flavour) mild; (medicine, beer) leicht; (person, criticism) sanft; (slight) leicht

mildew, mill-djuh, n Schimmel m

mile, meil, n Meile f; **–age,** (Anzahl f der) Meilen pl; **–stone,** n Meilenstein m

militant, mill-i-tent, adj militant; n Militante m

military, mill-i-te-ri, adj militärisch, Militär-; n Militär nt

militate (against), mill-i-teht (e-genst), v sich gegen etw aussprechen

militia, mi-**lisch-**e, n Miliz f

milk, milk, n Milch f; v melken; **– shake,** n Milkshake m; **–y,** adj milchig; **–y way,** n Milchstraße f

mill, mill, n Mühle f; (factory) Fabrik f; v mahlen; **– around/about,** durcheinanderlaufen

millennium, mi-**lenn-**i-em, n Jahrtausend nt

miller, mill-er, n Müller m

milli-, mill-i, pref Milli-; **–gram(e),** n Millgramm nt; **–metre,** n Millimeter m

million, mill-jen, n Million

f; **–aire,** n Millionär m

mime, meim, n (act) Pantomime f; (actor) Pantomime m; v pantomimisch darstellen

mimic, mimm-ick, v nachahmen; **–ry,** n Nachahmung f

mince, minss, n Hackfleisch nt; v zerhacken; **–meat,** n Hackfleisch nt; (sweet) süße Pastetenfüllung f; **– pie,** n Pastete f mit süßer Füllung

mind, meind, n Sinn m, Gemüt nt, Geist m; v aufpassen (auf); **–ful (of sth),** adj mit etw im Sinn; **–less,** adj sinnlos; **change one's –,** v es sich anders überlegen; **I don't mind,** es macht mir nichts aus; **make up one's –,** v sich entschließen; **never –!** macht nichts!, ist schlimm!

mine, mein, n (pit) Grube f; (explosive) Mine f; v Bergbau betreiben

mine, mein, pron meine(r/s)

miner, mei-ner, n Bergmann m

mineral, minn-e-rel, adj mineralisch, Mineral-; n Mineral nt; **– water,** n Mineralwasser nt

mingle (with), ming-g'l (u'idh), v sich mischen (unter)

miniature, minn-i-tscher, adj Miniatur-; n Miniatur f

minibus, minn-i-bass, n Kleinbus m

minim, minn-imm, n halbe Note f

minimal, minn-i-mel, adj minimal, Mindest-

minimize, minn-i-meis, v verringern

minimum, minn-i-mem, adj minimal, Mindest-; n Minimum nt; **– temperature,** n Tiefsttemperatur f

mini-skirt, minn-i-skört, n Minirock m

minister, minn-iss-ter, n (government) Minister m; relig Pfarrer m; **– to,** v sich kümmern um

ministry, minn-iss-tri, n (government) Ministerium nt; relig geistliches Amt nt

mink, mink, n Nerz m

minor, mei-ner, adj (unimportant) unbedeutend; (small) kleiner; (mus key) Moll nt; n Minderjährige(r) m & f

minority, mei-no-ri-ti, n Minderheit f

mint, mint, n (herb) Minze f; (sweet) Pfefferminzbonbon nt; (for coinage) Münze f; v (coins) prägen; **make a –,** v fam abstauben

minus, mei-ness, adv weniger, minus, Minus-

minute, mei-njuht, adj

(tiny) winzig; (precise) genau

minute, minn-itt, n (60 seconds) Minute f; (moment) Augenblick m; –s, pl Protokoll nt

miracle, mi-re-k'l, n Wunder nt

miraculous, mi-räck-ju-less, adj wunderbar

mirage, mi-rahsch, n Fata Morgana f

mire, meir, n Morast m

mirror, mi-rer, n Spiegel m; v widerspiegeln

mirth, mörth, n Frohsinn m; Heiterkeit f

misadventure, miss-ed-wenn-tscher, n Mißgeschick m

misanthropist, mi-sänn-thre-pist, n Menschenfeind m

misapprehension, miss-äpp-ri-henn-sch'n, n Mißverständnis nt

misappropriate, miss-e-proh-pri-eht, v unterschlagen

misbehave, miss-bi-hehw, v sich schlecht benehmen

miscalculate, miss-käll-klu-leht, v falsch berechnen; (misjudge) falsch einschätzen

miscarriage, miss-kä-ridsch, n med Fehlgeburt f; – of justice, n Justizirrtum m

miscellaneous, miss-e-leh-ni-ess, adj verschieden(erlei)

mischief, miss-tschiff, n (playfulness) Unfug m; (harm) Unheil nt

mischievous, miss-tschi-wess, adj (playful) spitzbübisch; (harmful) bösartig

misconduct, miss-konn-dakt, n schlechtes Betragen nt; (professional) unkorrektes Verhalten nt

misconstrue, miss-ken-struh, v mißdeuten; mißverstehen

miscount, miss-kaunt, v falsch rechnen

misdeed, miss-died, n Missetat f

misdemeanour, miss-di-mie-ner, n Vergehen nt

miser, mei-ser, n Geizhals m

miserable, mi-e-re-b'l, adj (poor) elend; (unhappy) unglücklich; (dreadful) elend

miserly, mei-ser-li, adj geizig

misery, mi-e-ri, n Elend nt

misfire, miss-feir, v (engine) fehlzünden; (gun) nicht losgehen; (plan) fehlschlagen

misfit, miss-fitt, n Außenseiter m

misfortune, miss-fohr-tjuhn, n Unglück nt

misgiving, miss-giw-ing, n Bedenken pl

misguided, miss-gei-didd, adj unangebracht

mishap, miss-häpp, n Mißgeschick nt

misinform, miss-in-form, v falsch informieren

misinterpret, miss-in-tör-pritt, v falsch auslegen

misjudge, miss-dschadsch, v falsch beurteilen

mislay, miss-leh, v verlegen

mislead, miss-lied, v irreleiten, irreführen

mismanage, miss-männ-idsch, v schlecht leiten

misnomer, miss-noh-mer, n falsche Bezeichnung f

misogynist, mi-ssodsch-i-nist, n Frauenfeind m

misplace, miss-plehss, v verlegen

misprint, miss-print, n Druckfehler m

misrepresent, miss-repp-ri-sent, v falsch darstellen

miss, miss, n Fehlschuß m; v (train, appointment etc.) versäumen; (person) vermissen; (not hit/catch) verfehlen; – out, auslassen

Miss, miss, n Fräulein nt

missile, miss-eil, n Geschoß nt

missing, adj (object) fehlend; (person) verloren; mil vermißt; be –, fehlen

mission, misch-en, n (delegation) Mission f; relig Mission f; (embassy) Gesandtschaft f; –ary, Missionar m

misspent, miss-spent, adj vergeudet

mist, mist, n Nebel m

mistake, miss-**tehk**, n Fehler m; – **for,** v verwechseln mit; **make a –,** v sich irren, einen Fehler machen

mistaken, miss-**teh**-k'n, adj (idea) falsch; – **identity,** n Verwechslung f; **be –,** v sich irren

mistletoe, miss-'l-toh, n Mistel f

mistress, miss-triss, n (house) Herrin f; (teacher) Lehrerin f; (lover) Geliebte f; (Mrs) Frau f

mistrust, miss-**trast**, n Mißtrauen nt; v mißtrauen

misty, miss-ti, adj neblig

misunderstand, miss-an-der-**ständ**, v mißverstehen; **–ing,** n Mißverständnis nt

misuse, miss-**juhs**, v mißbrauchen

mitigate, mitt-i-geht, v lindern, abschwächen

mitten, mitt-'n, n Fäustling m

mix, micks, v mischen, vermischen; **–ed,** adj gemischt; **–ed up,** adj (things) durcheinander; (person) verwirrt; **–er,** n Mixer m; **–ture,** n Mischung f; **– up,** v verwechseln; **– with,** v (associate with) mit jdm verkehren

moan, mohn, n (groan) Stöhnen nt; (complain) Beschwerde f; v (groan)

stöhnen; (complain) jammern, sich beschweren

moat, moht, n Burggraben m

mob, mobb, n Pöbel m; v belagern

mobile, moh-beil, adj beweglich, mobil; **– phone,** n Funktelefon nt

mobility, moh-**bill**-i-ti, n Beweglichkeit f

mobilize, moh-bi-leis, v mobilisieren

mock, mock, adj falsch, Schein-; v verspotten; **–ery,** n Spott m; **–ing(ly),** adj & adv spöttisch; **––up,** n (graphics) Layout nt; (three-dimensional) Modell nt

mode, mohd, n Weise f

model, modd-'l, adj (ideal) beispielhaft, Muster-; (toy etc.) Modell-; n (toy etc.) Modell nt; (ideal) Vorbild nt; (fashion) Model nt; v (make models) modellieren; (work as a model) als Model arbeiten; (clothes) vorführen, modeln

modem, moh-demm, n Modem nt

moderate, modd-e-ret, adj mäßig; n Gemäßigte(r) m & f

moderate, modd-e-reht, v (sich) mäßigen

moderation, modd-e-**reh**-sch'n, n Mäßigkeit f; **in –,** in/mit Maßen

modern, modd-ern, adj

modern, neu; **–ize,** v modernisieren

modest, modd-ist, adj bescheiden; **–y,** n Bescheidenheit f

modification, modd-i-fi-**keh**-sch'n, n Änderung f

modify, modd-i-fei, v ändern, modifizieren

moist, meust, adj feucht; **–en,** v anfeuchten; **–ure,** n Feuchtigkeit f

molar, moh-ler, n Backenzahn m

mole, mohl, n (animal) Maulwurf m; (mark) Muttermal nt; (jetty) Mole f

molecule, moll-i-kjuhl, n Molekül nt

molest, me-**lest**, v belästigen

molten, moh-'t'n, adj geschmolzen

moment, moh-ment, n Moment m, Augenblick m; **–ary,** adj kurz, vorübergehend

momentous, me-**menn**-tess, adj bedeutsam

momentum, me-**menn**-tem, n Schwung m

monarch, monn-erk, n Monarch m; **–y,** n Monarchie f

monastery, monn-ess-tri, n (Mönchs)kloster nt

Monday, mann-deh, n Montag m

monetary, mann-i-te-ri, adj Geld-

money, mann-i, n Geld nt;

–lender, n Geldverleiher m; **– order,** n Postanweisung f

mongrel, mang-grel, n (dog) Promenadenmischung f

monitor, monn-i-ter, n (observer) Beobachter m; (school) Aufsichtsschüler m; comp Monitor m; v überwachen

monk, mank, n Mönch m

monkey, mang-ki, n Affe m; **– nut,** n Erdnuß f

monochrome, monn-e-krohm, adj einfarbig

monopolize, me-**nopp-**e-leis, v monopolisieren

monopoly, mo-**nopp-**e-li, n Monopol nt

monotonous, me-**nott-**e-ness, adj eintönig

monster, monn-ster, n Ungeheuer nt

monstrosity, monn-**stross-**i-ti, n Monstrosität f

monstrous, monn-stress, adj (large) kolossal; (dreadful) schrecklich

month, manth, n Monat m; **–ly,** adj monatlich, Monats-; adv monatlich, einmal im Monat

monument, monn-ju-ment, n Denkmal nt

monumental, monn-ju-**menn-**t'l, adj gewaltig

mood, muhd, n Stimmung f; (temper) Laune f; gram Modus m; **–y,** adj launisch

moon, muhn, n Mond m; **–light,** n Mondlicht nt; v

schwarz arbeiten; **–lighting,** n Schwarzarbeit f

moor, mohr, n Heideland nt, Ödland nt; v (ship) festlegen; **–ing,** n Anlegeplatz m

mop, mopp, n Mop m; v wischen; **– up,** v aufwischen

mope, mohp, v fam Trübsal blasen

moral, mo-rel, adj moralisch; sittlich; n Moral f; **–s,** npl Moral f

morale, mo-**rahl,** n Moral f

morality, me-**räll-**i-ti, n Sittlichkeit f

morass, me-**räss,** n Morast m

morbid, mohr-bidd, adj krankhaft; (macabre) makaber

more, mohr, adj & pron (in number, size) mehr; (additional) noch (mehr); adv mehr; **– ... than,** ...er als; **– and –,** immer mehr, immer ...er; **no –,** adj kein... mehr; pron nichts mehr; **not any –,** (no longer) nicht mehr; **once –,** noch einmal

moreover, mohr-**roh-**wer, adv überdies, ferner

morning, mohr-ning n Morgen m; **in the –,** am Morgen, morgens

Morocco, me-**rock-**oh, n Marokko nt

moron, mohr-ronn, n pej Schwachkopf m

morose, me-**rohss,** adj vergrämt

morphine, mohr-fien, n Morphium nt

morsel, mohr-s'l, n Stückchen nt

mortal, mohr-t'l, adj sterblich; (fatal) tödlich; n Sterbliche(r) m & f

mortality, mohr-**täll-**i-ti, n Sterblichkeit f

mortar, mohr-ter, n (cement) Mörtel m; (gun) Mörser m

mortgage, mohr-gidsch, n Hypothek f; v, mit einer Hypothek belasten; **–e,** Hypothekar m

mortified, mohr-ti-feid, adj beschämt

mortuary, mohr-tju-e-ri, n Leichenhaus nt

mosaic, me-**seh-**ick, n Mosaik nt

Moscow, moss-koh, n Moskau nt

Moslem, mas-lem, adj moslemisch; n Moslem m

mosque, mosk, n Moschee f

mosquito, moss-**kie-**toh, n Mücke f

moss, moss, n Moos nt

most, mohst, adj meiste(r/s); (superlative) -ste(r/s); adv am meisten; (extremely) höchst, sehr; pron das meiste, die meisten; **–ly,** adv meistens, größtenteils

moth, moth, n Nachtfalter m; (in clothes) Motte f; **–ball,** n Mottenkugel f

mother, madh-er, n Mutter
f; v bemuttern; **–hood,** n
Mutterschaft f; **–in-law,** n
Schwiegermutter f; **–ly,** adj
mütterlich; **– of pearl,** n
Perlmutt nt; **– tongue,** n
Muttersprache f

motif, moh-tief, n Motiv nt

motion, moh-sch'n, n
Bewegung f; (proposal)
Antrag m; **–less,** adj
bewegungslos; **put/set in
–,** v in Gang bringen

motivation, moh-tiw-eh-
sch'n, n Motivierung f

motive, moh-tiw, n Motiv
nt, Beweggrund m

motor, moh-ter, adj Motor-;
n Motor m; (car) Auto nt;
–bike, n Motorrad nt;
–car, Auto nt; **–cycle,** n
Motorrad nt; **–ing,** n
Autofahren m; **–ist,** n
Autofahrer m; **–way,** n
Autobahn f

mottled, mott-l'd, adj
gesprenkelt

motto, mott-oh, n Motto nt,
Wahlspruch m

mould, mohld, n (pattern)
Form f; (mildew)
Schimmel m; v formen;
–er, v verschimmeln; **–y,**
adj schimmlig

moult, mohlt, v (sich)
mausern

mound, maund, n
Erdhügel m

mount, maunt, n (horse)
Pferd nt; (for picture)
Montierung f; (for jewel)

Fassung f; v (horse)
besteigen; (jewel) fassen;
(organize) organisieren; –
(up), (increase) sich
häufen

mountain, maun-tinn, n
Berg m; **– bike,** n
Mountainbike nt; **–eer,** n
Bergsteiger m; **–ous,** adj
bergig; **– range,** n
Bergkette f; **–side,** n
Berghang m

mourn, mohrn, v
(be)trauern; **–er,** n
Trauernde(r) m & f; **–ful,**
adj traurig; **–ing,** n Trauer
f; (clothes)
Trauerkleidung f

mouse, mauss, n (animal,
comp) Maus f; **–trap,** n
Mausefalle f

mousse, muhss, n (food)
Mousse f; (for hair)
Haarschaum m,
Schaumfestiger m

moustache, mess-tahsch, n
Schnurrbart m

mousy, mau-ssi, adj (colour)
mattbraun; (shy) scheu

mouth, mauth, n Mund m;
(of animal) Maul nt; (of
river) Mündung f; **–ful,** n
Mundvoll m; **–piece,** n
Mundstück nt; fig
Sprachrohr nt; **–
watering,** adj lecker

movable, muh-we-b'l, adj
beweglich

move, muhw, n (step)
Schritt m; (in game) Zug
m; (of house) Umzug m; v

(sich) bewegen; (house)
umziehen; (object)
bewegen, verstellen;
(affect) rühren; **– in,** v (to
house) einziehen; **–ment,**
n Bewegung f; (in clock)
Uhrwerk nt; **– on,** v
weitergehen; **– out,** v (of
house) ausziehen; **get a –
on,** v sich beeilen

movie, muh-wie, n fam Film
m; **go to the –s,** v ins Kino
gehen

moving, muh-wing, adj (in
motion) beweglich;
(affecting) rührend

mow, moh, v mähen; **–
down,** v niedermähen;
(lawn) –er, n Rasenmäher
m

Mr, miss-ter, n Herr m

Mrs, miss-is, n Frau f

Ms, mes, n Frau f

much, matsch, adj & pron
viel; adv viel, sehr; **as –
(as),** soviel; **how –?**
wieviel?; **too –,** zuviel

muck, mack, n Schmutz m;
– about, v fam
herumalbern; **–y,** adj
dreckig

mud, madd, n Schlamm m

muddle, madd-'l, n
Wirrwarr m; **– (up),** v
verwirren; **– through,** v
fam sich durchwursteln

muddy, madd-i, adj
schlammig, schmutzig

muffle, maff-'l, v (wrap)
einhüllen; (sound)
dämpfen

mug, magg, n (beaker)
Becher m; (fam face)
Fratze f; (fam idiot) Depp
m; v überfallen; **–ging**, n
Überfall m; **–gy**, adj
schwül

mule, mjuhl, n Maulesel m

mull over, mall oh-wer, v
nachdenken über

multi-, mall-ti, pref, Multi-;
–coloured, adj bunt,
mehrfarbig

multiple, mall-ti-p'l, adj
mehrfach; **– sclerosis**, n
multiple Sklerose f

multiplication, mall-ti-pli-
keh-sch'n, n
Multiplikation f

multiply, mall-ti-plei, v
(increase) sich
vermehren; **– (by)**,
(arithmetic)
multiplizieren (mit)

multi-purpose, mall-ti-pör-
pess, adj Mehrzweck-

multi-storey, mall-ti-stohr-
ri, adj mehrstöckig; **– car
park**, n Parkhaus nt

multitude, mall-ti-tjuhd, n
Menge f

mum, mamm, n Mutti f;
keep – (about), v den
Mund halten (über)

mumble, mamm-b'l, v
murmeln

mummy, mamm-i, n
(mother) Mutti f; (corpse)
Mumie f

mumps, mamps, n Mumps m

munch, mantsch, v kauen

mundane, mann-dehn, adj

banal

municipal, mju-niss-i-p'l,
adj städtisch, Gemeinde-

mural, muhr-rel, n
Wandgemälde nt

murder, mör-der, n Mord m;
v ermorden; **–er**, n Mörder
m; **–ess**, n Mörderin f;
–ous, adj mörderisch

murky, mör-ki, adj finster,
trüb

murmur, mör-mer, n
Gemurmel nt; v murmeln

muscle, mass-'l, n Muskel m

muscular, mass-kju-ler, adj
(of the muscle) Muskel-;
(strong) muskulös

muse, mjuhs, n Muse f; v
sinnen

museum, mjuh-sie-em, n
Museum nt

mushroom, mash-ruhm, n
Pilz m, Champignon m; v
wie Pilze aus dem Boden
schießen

music, mjuh-sick, n Musik f;
(score) Noten pl; **–al**, adj
musikalisch; **–al
instrument**, n
Musikinstrument nt

musician, mjuh-sisch-en, n
Musiker m

musk, mask, n Moschus m

Muslim, mas-limm, adj
moslemisch; n Moslem m

muslin, mas-linn, n
Musselin m

mussel, mass-'l, n Muschel f

must, mast, v müssen; **– not**,
nicht dürfen

mustard, mass-terd, n

Senf m

muster, mass-ter, v (sich)
zusammenrufen; fig
aufbringen

musty, mass-ti, adj muffig,
schimmelig

mute, mjuht, adj stumm; n
Stumme(r) m & f

mutilate, mjuh-ti-leht, v
verstümmeln

mutiny, mjuh-ti-ni, n
Meuterei f

mutter, matt-er, v murmeln,
murren

mutton, matt-'n, n
Hammelfleisch nt

mutual(ly), mjuh-tju-el(-i),
adj & adv gegenseitig

muzzle, mas-'l, n (for
animal) Maulkorb m;
(nose) Schnauze f; (of
gun) Mündung f; v
(animal) einen Maulkorb
anlegen; (silence) knebeln

my, mei, adj mein

myriad, mi-ri-ädd, n
Unzahl f

myself, mei-sself, pron (refl)
mich (selbst); mir (selbst);
(emphatic) selbst

mysterious, miss-tier-ri-ess,
adj geheimnisvoll

mystery, miss-te-ri, n
(secret) Geheimnis f;
(puzzle) Rätsel nt

mystify, miss-ti-fei, v
verwirren

myth, mith, n Mythos m; fig
Legende f; **–ical**, adj
mythisch; fig erfunden;
–ology, n Mythologie f

N

n/a, *abbr* not applicable, nicht zutreffend

nab, nӓbb, *v* (sich) schnappen

nag, nӓgg, *n* (horse) Gaul *m*; (person) Nörgler *m*; *v* nörgeln

nail, nehl, *n* Nagel *m*; *v* nageln; **–brush,** *n* Nagelbürste *f*; **– down,** *v* festnageln; **–file,** *n* Nagelfeile *f*; **– polish, – varnish,** *n* Nagellack *m*

naïve, nei-iew, *adj* naiv

naked, neh-kidd, *adj* nackt

name, nehm, *n* Name *nt*; (reputation) Ruf *m*; *v* nennen; (appoint) ernennen; **–less,** *adj* namenlos; **–ly,** *adv* nämlich; **–sake,** *n* Namensvetter *m*

nanny, nӓnn-i, *n* Kindermӓdchen *nt*;

(grandmother) Oma *f*

nap, nӓpp, *n* Schlӓfchen *nt*; (on cloth) Noppe *f*

nape, nehp, *n* Nacken *m*, Genick *nt*

napkin, nӓpp-kinn, *n* Serviette *f*

Naples, neh-p'ls, *n* Neapel *nt*

nappy, nӓpp-i, *n* Windel *f*; **– rash,** *n* Windelausschlag *m*

narcissus, nar-ssiss-ess, *n* Narzisse *f*

narcotic, nar-kott-ick, *n* Betӓubungsmittel *nt*

narrate, ne-reht, *v* erzӓhlen

narrative, nӓ-re-tiw, *n* Erzӓhlung *f*

narrator, ne-reh-ter, *n* Erzӓhler *m*

narrow, nӓ-roh, *adj* schmal, eng; *v* sich verengen; **– down (to),** *v* einengen

(auf); **–ly,** *adv* knapp; **– minded,** *adj* engstirnig; **have a – escape,** *v* mit knapper Not entkommen

nasal, neh-sel, *adj* nasal, Nasen-

nasty, nahss-ti, *adj* eklig

nation, neh-sch'n, *n* Nation *f*

national, nӓsch-en-el, *adj* national, National-; *n* Staatsangehörige(r) *m & f*; **–ism,** *n* Nationalismus *m*; **–ist(ic),** *adj* nationalistisch; **–ize,** *v* verstaatlichen

nationality, nӓsch-en-ӓll-i-ti, *n* Staatsangehörigkeit *f*

native, neh-tiw, *adj* (country etc.) Heimat-; (plant etc.) einheimisch; (person) gebürtig; (inborn) angeboren; *n* Einheimische(r) *m & f*; **– language, – tongue,** *n* Muttersprache *f*

natural, nӓtt-sche-rel, *adj* natürlich, Natur-; (inborn) angeboren; **–ist,** *n* Naturforscher *m*; **–ized,** *adj* eingebürgert; **–ly,** *adv* natürlich

nature, neh-tscher, *n* Natur *f*

naught, no'at, *n* Null *f*; **come to –,** *v* zunichte werden

naughty, no'a-ti, *adj* unartig, ungehörig

nausea, no'a-si-e, *n* (sickness) Übelkeit *f*;

(disgust) Ekel f; **–ting,** adj widerlich

nautical, no'a-ti-k'l, adj nautisch, See-

naval, neh-wel, Marine-; **– officer,** n Marineoffizier m

nave, nehw, n Kirchenschiff nt

navel, neh-wel, n Nabel m

navigate, näw-i-geht, v (in ship) befahren, navigieren; (in car) lotsen

navigation, näw-i-**geh-**sch'n, n Navigation f

navigator, näw-i-**geh-**ter, n (in ship) Seefahrer m; (in car) Lotse m

navvy, näw-i, n Bau-/Straßenarbeiter m

navy, neh-wi, n Marine f; **– (blue),** adj marineblau

Nazi, näh-zi, n Nazi m

near, nier, adj nahe; adv & prep in der Nähe; v sich nähern; **–by,** adj nahe; adv in der Nähe; **–ly,** adv beinahe, fast; **–side,** n Beifahrerseite f; **–sighted,** adj kurzsichtig

neat, niet, adj (tidy) ordentlich; (skilful) elegant; (undiluted) pur

necessarily, ness-e-sse-ri-li, adv notwendigerweise

necessary, ness-e-sse-ri, adj nötig, notwendig

necessitate, ni-**ssess-**i-teht, v erfordern

necessity, ni-**ssess-**i-ti, n Notwendigkeit f; (need) Not f

neck, neck, n Hals m; v fam knutschen; **– and –,** Kopf an Kopf; **–lace,** n Halskette f; **–tie,** Krawatte f

née, neh, adj geborene

need, nied, v brauchen; n (requirement) Bedürfnis nt; (necessity) Notwendigkeit f; (poverty) Not f; v brauchen; **– to,** müssen, brauchen zu; **be in – of,** v brauchen

needle, nie-d'l, n Nadel f; v fam ärgern

needless, nied-liss, adj unnötig; **– to say,** selbstverständlich

needy, nie-di, adj dürftig, arm

negation, ni-**geh-**sch'n, n Verneinung f

negative, negg-e-tiw, adj verneinend; n Negativ nt

neglect, ni-**gleckt,** n Vernachlässigung f; v vernachlässigen; **–ful,** adj nachlässig

negligence, negg-li-dschenss, n Nachlässigkeit f

negligible, negg-li-dschib-'l, adj unerheblich

negotiate, ni-**goh-**schi-eht, v (discuss) verhandeln; (get past) bewältigen; (corner) nehmen; comm einlösen

negotiation, ni-goh-schi-**eh-**sch'n, n (discussion) Verhandlung f; (getting

past) Bewältigung f

negotiator, n ni-goh-schi-eh-ter, n Unterhändler m

negro, nie-groh, n Neger m

neigh, neh, v wiehern

neighbour, neh-ber, n Nachbar m; **–hood,** n Nachbarschaft f; **–ing,** adj benachbart; **–ly,** adj nachbarlich

neither, nei-dher, adj & pron keine(r/s) (von beiden); adv & conj auch nicht; **– … nor,** weder… noch

neon, nie-onn, n Neon nt

nephew, neff-yuh, n Neffe m

nerve, nörw, n Nerv m; (courage) Mut m; (cheek) Frechheit f; **–racking,** adj nervenaufreibend

nervous, nör-wess, adj (of the nerves) Nerven-; (timid) nervös, befangen; **– breakdown,** n Nervenzusammenbruch m

nest, nest, n Nest n; v nisten

nestle (up to), ness-'l (app tu), v sich anschmiegen

net, nett, adj netto, Netto-; n Netz nt; v fangen; **–ball,** n Netzball m; **– curtain,** n Store m, Tüllgardine f

Netherlands, nedh-er-lends, npl Niederlande pl

nett, nett, adj netto, Netto-

nettle, nett-'l, n Nessel f

network, nett-u'erk, n Netz(werk) nt

neuralgia, njuhr-**räll-**dschi-e, n Nervenschmerz m

neurotic, njuhr-**rott**-ick, *adj* neurotisch; *n* Neurotiker *m*

neuter, njuh-ter, *adj gram* sächlich; *v* kastrieren

neutral, njuh-trel, *adj* neutral; *n* (person) Neutrale(r) *m & f*; (gear) Leerlauf *m*; **–ize,** *v* ausgleichen

never, new-er, *adv* nie(mals); **––ending,** *adj* endlos; **–theless,** *adv* trotzdem

new, njuh, *adj* neu; **––born,** *adj* neugeboren; **––fangled,** *adj pej* neumodisch; **–ly,** *adv* frisch; **–lyweds,** *npl* Frischvermählte *pl*

news, njuhs, *n* Nachrichten *pl*; (piece of) Neuigkeit *f*; **–agent,** *n* Zeitungshändler *m*; **– flash,** *n* Kurzmeldung *f*; **–letter,** *n* Rundschreiben *nt*; **–paper,** *n* Zeitung *f*; **–reader,** *n* Nachrichtensprecher *m*

new year, njuh jier, *n* neues Jahr *nt*; **N– Y–'s Day,** *n* Neujahr *nt*, Neujahrstag *m*; **N– Y–'s Eve,** *n* Silvester *m*

New Zealand, njuh sie-lend, *n* Neuseeland *nt*; **–er,** *n* Neuseeländer *m*

next, next, *adj* nächste(r/s); (following) folgend; *adv* dann; **–door,** *adj* von nebenan; *adv* nebenan; **– of kin,** *n* nächste(r) Verwandte(r) *m & f*; **–**

time, das nächste Mal; **– to,** *prep* neben

nib, nibb, *n* Feder *f*

nibble, nibb-'l, *v* nagen, annagen

nice, neiss, *adj* (pleasant) nett, sympathisch; (attractive) hübsch; (thing, idea) schön

nick, nick, *n* Kerbe *f*, Einschnitt *m*; *v fam* klauen; **in the – of time,** gerade rechtzeitig

nickel, nick-'l, *n* (metal) Nickel *m*; (5 cents) Nickel *m*

nickname, nick-nehm, *n* Spitzname *m*

nicotine, nick-*e*-tien, *n* Nikotin *nt*

niece, niess, *n* Nichte *f*

niggle, nigg-'l, *v* sich mit Einzelheiten aufhalten; (grumble about) herumnörgeln

night, neit, *n* Nacht *f*; **–cap,** *n* Schlummertrunk *m*; **–club,** *n* Nachtklub *m*; **–dress,** *n* Nachthemd *nt*; **–fall,** *n* Einbruch *m* der Nacht; **–ingale,** *n* Nachtigall *f*; **–life,** *n* Nachtleben *nt*; **–ly,** *adv* jede Nacht, jeden Abend; **–mare,** *n* Alptraum *m*; **–time,** *n* Nacht *f*; **at –,** *adv* nachts, abends

nil, nill, *n* Null *f*

Nile, neil, *n* Nil *m*

nimble, nimm-b'l, *adj* flink, gewandt

nine, nein, *num* neun; **–teen,** *num* neunzehn; **–ty,** *num* neunzig

ninth, neinth, *adj* neunte(r/s); *n* Neuntel *nt*

nip, nipp, *n* Biß *m*; *v* zwicken; **– out,** *v fam* kurz weggehen

nipple, nipp-'l, *n* Zitze *f*; Brustwarze *f*

nippy, nipp-i, *adj* (*fam* fast) flink; (cold) frisch

nitrogen, nei-tre-dschen, *n* Stickstoff *m*

no, noh, *adj* kein; *adv* nein; *n* Nein *nt*; **– parking,** Parken verboten

nobility, ne-bill-i-ti, *n* Adel *m*

noble, noh-b'l, *adj* (character etc.) edel; (rank) adlig

nobody, noh-be-di, *pron* niemand, keiner; *n* Null *f*

nocturnal, nock-tör-nel, *adj* Nacht-

nod, nodd, *n* Nicken *nt*; *v* nicken

noise, neus, *n* (loud) Lärm *m*; (sound) Geräusch *nt*; **–less(ly),** *adj & adv* geräuschlos

noisy, neu-si, *adj* laut

nominal, nomm-i-nel, *adj* nominell

nominate, nomm-i-neht, *v* (propose) nominieren; (appoint) ernennen

nominee, nomm-i-**nie,** *n* Kandidat *m*

none (of), nann (ev), *pron*

keine(r/s) (von)

nonentity, nonn-**enn**-ti-ti, n
Null f

non-fiction, nonn-**fick**-sch'n, n Sachbuch nt,
Sachbücher pl

nonetheless, nann-**dhe**-less,
adv trotzdem

nonplussed, nonn-**plasst**,
adj verwirrt

nonsense, nonn-**ssenss**, n
Unsinn m

non-smoker, nonn-**ssmoh**-ker, n Nichtraucher m

non-stop, nonn-**stopp**, adj
nonstop, Nonstop-;
(train) durchgehend

non-stick, nonn-**stick**, adj
mit Antihaftbeschichtung

noodles, nuh-**d'ls**, npl
Nudeln pl

nook, nuck, n Winkel m

noon, nuhn, n Mittag m

no one, noh u'an, pron
niemand, keiner

noose, nuhss, n Schlinge f

nor, nohr, adv & conj auch
nicht; **neither... –,**
weder... noch

norm, norm, n Norm f

normal, nohr-mel, adj
normal

north, north, adj nördlich,
Nord-; adv nördlich, nach
Norden; n Norden m; **–east,** n Nordosten m;
-erly, adj nördlich; **-ern,**
adj nördlich, Nord-;
N–ern Ireland, n
Nordirland nt; **N– Pole,** n
Nordpol m; **N– Sea,** n

Nordsee f; **–west,** n
Nordwesten m

Norway, nohr-u'ei, n
Norwegen nt

Norwegian, nor-**u'ie**-dschen, adj norwegisch; n
(person) Norweger m;
(language) Norwegisch nt

nose, nohs, n Nase f; **–
(about/around),** v
herumschnüffeln; **–bleed,**
n Nasenbluten nt

nostril, noss-trill, n
Nasenloch nt

nosy, noh-si, adj neugierig

not, nott, adv nicht; **– any,**
kein; **– only,** nicht nur; **–
yet,** noch nicht

notable, noh-te-b'l, adj
bemerkenswert

notch, notsch, n Kerbe f; v
kerben, einschneiden

note, noht, n mus Note f;
(letter) Briefchen nt;
(comment) Anmerkung f;
v (notice) bemerken; (in
writing) notieren; **–book,**
n Notizbuch nt; **–d,** adj
berühmt, bekannt; **–pad,** n
Notizblock m; **–paper,** n
Briefpapier nt; **take – of,** v
achten auf; **take –s,** v
Notizen machen

nothing, nath-ing, adv &
pron nichts; **for –,**
umsonst

notice, noh-tiss, n (to quit)
Kündigung f; (public)
Bekanntmachung; v
bemerken; **at short
notice,** adv kurzfristig; **be**

given **–,** gekündigt
werden; **give (one's) –,** v
kündigen; **take – of,** v
beachten; **–able, noh-tiss-**e-b'l, adj merklich;
–board, n Anschlagtafel f,
Schwarzes Brett nt

notify, noh-ti-fei, v
anzeigen, benachrichtigen

notion, noh-sch'n, n Idee f;
Begriff m

notorious, noh-**tohr**-ri-ess,
adj berüchtigt

notwithstanding, not-uidh-s'tänn-ding, adv trotzdem;
prep ungeachtet, trotz

nought, no'at, n Null f

noun, naun, n gram
Hauptwort nt

nourish, na-risch, v nähren,
ernähren; **–ing,** adj
nahrhaft; **–ment,** n
Nahrung f

novel, now-el, adj neuartig;
n Roman m; **–ist,** n
Romanautor m; **–ty,** n
Neuheit f

November, noh-**wemm**-ber,
n November m

novice, now-iss, n Neuling
m; relig Novize m & f

now, nau, adv nun, jetzt; **–
and again, – and then,** ab
und zu; **by –,** inzwischen;
just –, gerade; **right –,**
sofort, jetzt

nowadays, nau-e-dehs, adv
heutzutage

nowhere, noh-u'ähr, adv
nirgends, nirgendwo

noxious, nok-schess, adj

schädlich, giftig

nozzle, nos-'l, n
Mundstück nt

nuclear, njuh-klier, adj
Atom-, Kern-

nucleus, njuh-kli-ess, n
Kern m

nude, njuhd, adj nackt; **in
the –,** nackt

nudge, nadsch, n Stoß m; v
anstoßen

nudist, njuh-dist, n Nudist
m

nuisance, njuh-ssenss, n
Lästigkeit f; Unfug m

null, nall, adj null, nichtig; –
and void, null und
nichtig; **–ify,** v für null
und nichtig erklären;
(proof) entkräften

numb, namm, adj starr;
(sensation) gefühllos

number, namm-ber, n
Nummer f; (figure) Zahl f;
(quantity) Anzahl f; v
numerieren; (count)
zählen; **–less,** adj zahllos,
unzählig; **– plate,** n
Nummernschild nt; **a – of,**
mehrere

numerate, njuh-me-ret, adj
rechenkundig

numerical, njuh-me-ri-k'l,
adj numerisch

numerous, njuh-me-ress, adj
zahlreich

nun, nann, n Nonne f;
–nery, Nonnenkloster nt

nurse, nörss, n
Krankenpfleger m;
(children's)

Kindermädchen nt; v
pflegen; (suckle) säugen;
fig hegen

nursery, nör-sse-ri, n
(children's) Kinderstube f;
(for plants) Gärtnerei f; –
rhyme, Kinderlied nt; –
school, n Kindergarten m;
– slope, n fam
Idiotenhügel m

nursing, nör-ssing, n
Krankenpflege f; **– home,**
n Pflegeheim nt

nut, natt, n Nuß f; (for
screw) Mutter f; **–(case),** n
fam Verrückte(r) m & f

nutcrackers, natt-kräck-ers,
npl Nußknacker m

nutmeg, natt-megg, n
Muskatnuß f

nutrient, njuh-tri-ent, n
Nährstoff m

nutrition, njuh-trisch-en, n
Nahrung f

nutritious, njuh-trisch-ess,
adj nahrhaft

nutshell, natt-schell, n
Nußschale f; **in a –,** kurz
gesagt

nylon, nei-lonn, adj Nylon-;
n Nylon nt

oak, ohk, *a* Eichen-; *n*
Eiche *f*

oar, or, *n* Ruder *nt*; **–sman,** *n*
Ruderer *m*

oasis, oh-**eh**-ssiss, *n* Oase *f*

oath, ohth, *n* (declaration)
Eid *m*; (curse) Fluch *m*

oatmeal, oht-miel, *n*
Hafermehl *nt*

oats, ohts, *npl* Hafer *m*

obedience, e-**bie**-di-enss, *n*
Gehorsam *m*

obedient, e-**bie**-di-ent, *adj*
gehorsam

obese, oh-**biess,** *adj*
fett(leibig)

obesity, oh-**biess**-i-ti, *n*
Fettheit *f*, Fettleibigkeit *f*

obey, e-**beh,** *v* gehorchen,
folgen

obituary, e-**bitt**-ju-e-ri, *n*
Nachruf *m*; **– notice,** *n*
Todesanzeige *f*

object, obb-dschikt, *n*

(thing) Gegenstand *m*;
(purpose) Ziel *nt*; *gram*
Objekt *nt*; **money is no –,**
Geld spielt keine Rolle

object, eb-**dschekt,** *v* (be
opposed) dagegen sein; **–
(to),** (protest)
protestieren, Einspruch
erheben (gegen); **–ion,** *n*
Einwand *m*; **–ionable,** *adj*
unangenehm; (speech,
behaviour) anstößig; **–ive,**
adj objektiv; *n* Ziel *nt*

obligation, obb-li-**geh**-sch'n,
n Verpflichtung *f*; **without
–,** unverbindlich

obligatory, eb-**ligg**-e-te-ri,
adj verbindlich

oblige, eb-**leidsch,** *v* (please)
einen Gefallen tun;
(compel) zwingen; **–d,** *adj*
verbunden, dankbar

obliging, eb-**leidsch**-ing, *adj*
gefällig

oblique, eb-**liek,** *adj* (angle,
look) schief; (hint)
indirekt

obliterate, eb-**litt**-e-reht, *v*
auslöschen

oblivion, eb-**liw**-i-en, *n*
Vergessenheit *f*

oblivious (of/to), eb-**liw**-i-
ess (ew/tu), *adj* nicht
bewußt

oblong, obb-long, *adj*
länglich; *n* Rechteck *nt*

obnoxious, eb-**nock**-schess,
adj widerlich

obscene, eb-**ssien,** *adj*
obszön, widerlich

obscure, eb-**skjuhr,** *adj*
(unclear, indistinct)
unklar; (unknown)
unbekannt; *v* (hide)
verdecken; (confuse)
unverständlich machen

observance, eb-**sör**-wenss, *n*
Beachtung *f*; *relig*
Einhalten *nt*

observant, eb-**sör**-went, *adj*
aufmerksam

observation, obb-ser-**weh**-
sch'n, *n* Beobachtung *f*;
(remark) Bemerkung *f*

observatory, eb-**sör**-we-te-ri,
n Observatorium *f*,
Sternwarte *f*

observe, eb-**sörw,** *v* (watch)
beobachten; (notice,
remark) bemerken; (obey)
einhalten

obsess, eb-**ssess, –ed
(by/with),** *adj* besessen
(von); **be –ed (by/with),** *v*
besessen sein von; **–ion,** *n*

Besessenheit f; **–ive**, adj
zwanghaft

obsolete, obb-**sse**-liet, adj
veraltet

obstacle, obb-**ste**-k'l, n
Hindernis nt

obstinate, obb-**sti**-net, adj
stur

obstruct, eb-**strakt**, v
(hinder) hindern; (block)
sperren; (tube) verstopfen;
–ion, n Hindernis nt,
Sperre f; med Verstopfung
f, Obstruktion f

obtain, eb-**tehn**, v erhalten

obtrusive, eb-**truh**-ssiw, adj
aufdringlich

obtuse, eb-**tjuss**, adj stumpf,
dumm

obviate, obb-**wi**-eht, **– the
need of sth**, v etw unnötig
machen

obvious, obb-**wi**-ess, adj klar,
offenbar; **–ly**, adv
offensichtlich

occasion, e-**keh**-sch'n, n
Gelegenheit f; (event,
cause) Anlaß m; v
veranlassen; **–al(ly)**, adj &
adv gelegentlich

occult, e-**kalt**, adj
verborgen, geheim; n das
Okkulte nt

occupation, ock-ju-**peh**-
sch'n, n Beschäftigung f;
(job) Beruf m; mil
Besetzung f

occupied, ock-ju-peid, adj
(person) beschäftigt;
(seat, room) belegt

occupier, ock-ju-pei-er, n

(of post) Inhaber m; (of
property) Bewohner m

occupy, ock-ju-pei, v
(property) bewohnen;
(space, location)
einnehmen; (post)
innehaben; mil besetzen;
(use) gebrauchen; **–
oneself**, v sich
beschäftigen

occur, e-**kör**, v vorkommen;
– to sb, jdm einfallen

occurrence, e-**ka**-renss, n
Vorfall m

ocean, oh-sch'n, n Ozean m,
Meer nt, See f

o'clock, e-**klock**, adv it is
six **–**, es ist sechs Uhr

octagonal, ock-**tägg**-e-n'l, adj
achtseitig, achteckig

octave, ock-tiw, n Oktave f

October, ock-**toh**-ber, n
Oktober m

octopus, ock-te-puss, n
Tintenfisch m

odd, odd, adj (number)
ungerade; (single) einzeln;
(strange) seltsam; **–ity**, n
(object) Kuriosität f;
(person) Sonderling m; **–
job**, n Gelegenheitsarbeit
f; **–ly**, adv
seltsam(erweise); **be the –
one out**, (person)
überzählig sein; (thing)
nicht passen

odds, odds, npl (betting)
Odds pl; (chances)
Aussichten npl; **– and
ends**, pl allerlei Sachen

odious, oh-di-ess, adj

gehässig, abscheulich

odour, oh-der, n Geruch m;
(fragrant) Wohlgeruch m

of, ow, prep (belonging to)
von; (made of) aus; **a cup
– coffee**, eine Tasse
Kaffee; **a litre – milk**, ein
Liter Milch

off, off, adj (light etc.) aus;
(food) schlecht;
(cancelled) abgesagt; adv
(clothes) aus; (distant)
entfernt; prep ab, von; **–
and on**, ab und zu; **go –**,
(dislike) nicht mehr
mögen; (leave)
(weg)gehen; **day –**, freier
Tag m; **well –**, gut gestellt

offal, off-'l, n Innereien pl

offbeat, off-biet, adj
unkonventionell

offchance, off-tschahnss, n
on the –, in der vagen
Hoffnung

offence, e-**fenss**, n (insult)
Beleidigung f; (crime)
Verstoß m; **take –**, v
beleidigt sein

offend, e-**fend**, v (insult)
beleidigen; (commit
crime) ein Verbrechen
begehen; **–er**, n Täter m

offensive, e-**fenn**-ssiw, adj
(insulting) beleidigend;
(unpleasant) widerlich;
(weapon) Angriffs-; n
Angriff m

offer, off-er, v anbieten; n
Angebot nt; **–ing**, Gabe f;
(sacrifice) Opfer nt

offhand, off-händ, adj & adv

spontan

office, off-iss, n (place)
Büro nt; (post) Amt nt; **–
hours,** npl Dienstzeit f; **–r,**
n Beamte(r) m, Beamtin f;
mil Offizier m

official, e-fisch-'l, adj
amtlich, offiziell; n
Beamte(r) m, Beamtin f;

officious, e-fisch-ess, adj
übereifrig

off-licence, off-lei-ssenss, n
Wein- und
Spirituosenhandlung f

off-peak, off-piek, adj
außerhalb der Stoßzeiten

off-putting, off-putt-ing, adj
abstoßend

off-season, off-ssie-sen, adj
außerhalb der
Hauptsaison

offside, off-sseid, adj im
Abseits; adv abseits

offside, off-sseid, n (of car)
Fahrerseite f

offspring, off-spring, n
Nachwuchs m

off-stage, off-stehdsch, adv
hinter den Kulissen

off-the-cuff, off-dhe-kaff,
adj aus dem Stegreif

often, off-'n, adv oft, öfters

ogle, oh-g'l, v beäugeln

oh, oh, interj ach, oh

oil, eul, n Öl nt; v ölen, mech
schmieren; **–fired,** adj
Öl-; **–y,** adj ölig, ölhaltig

ointment, eunt-ment, n
Salbe f

OK, oh keh, adj in
Ordnung, OK; n

Zustimmung f; v
genehmigen

old, ohld, adj alt; **– age,** n
Alter nt; **–age pensioner,**
n Rentner m; **–fashioned,**
adj altmodisch

olive, oh-liw, adj Oliven-;
(colour) olivgrün; n
Olive f

Olympic, e-limm-pick,
adj olympisch; **the –
Games,** npl die
olympischen Spiele pl

omelet(te), omm-let, n
Omelett f

omen, oh-men, n Omen nt,
Vorbedeutung f

ominous, omm-i-ness, adj
unheilvoll

omission, e-misch-'n, n
(thing left out)
Auslassung f; (neglect)
Unterlassung f

omit, e-mitt, v (leave out)
auslassen; (neglect)
versäumen, unterlassen

omnibus, omm-ni-bess, n
(bus) Autobus m;
(compendium)
Sammelausgabe f

on, onn, adj (light etc.) an;
adv (clothes) an;
(onward) weiter; prep (on
top of) auf; (date, day,
TV) an; (foot, horseback)
zu; (train, bus) mit; **–
holiday,** im Urlaub; **–
Monday,** am Montag; **–
Mondays,** montags; **– the
left/right,** links/rechts; **–
to,** prep (movement) auf;

be –, v (of event)
stattfinden; (fam be
acceptable) in Ordnung
sein

once, u'anss, adv einmal; **all
at –,** plötzlich; **at –,** sofort,
sogleich; **– more,** noch
einmal; **– upon a time,** es
war einmal

oncoming, onn-kamm-ing,
adj entgegenkommend; **–
traffic,** n Gegenverkehr m

one, u'ann, num eins; (with
noun) ein(e); (only)
einzig; pron eine(r/s);
(impersonal) man; **– day,**
eines Tages; **– another,**
einander, sich; **a good –,**
ein(e) gute(r/s); **this –,**
diese(r/s); **that –,**
der/die/das

onerous, oh-ne-ress, adj
lästig, beschwerlich

oneself, u'ann-sself, pron
(refl) sich (selbst);
(emphatic) selbst; **by –,** adv
alleine

one-sided, u'ann-ssei-didd,
adj einseitig

one-way, u'ann-u'ei, adj
(street) Einbahn-; (ticket)
einfach

ongoing, onn-goh-ing, adj
andauernd; (current)
aktuell

onion, ann-jen, n Zwiebel f

online, onn-lein, adj comp
Online-

only, ohn-li, adj einzig;
(child) Einzel-; adv & conj
nur, bloß; **not – ... but**

also ..., nicht nur ..., sondern auch ...

onset, onn-ssett, n Beginn m; med Ausbruch m

onslaught, onn-slo'at, n (heftige) Attacke f

onto, onn-tu, (= **on to**) prep auf

onus, oh-ness, n Last f

onward(s), onn-u'erd(s), adv vorwärts, weiter; **from ... –,** von ... an

ooze, uhs, n Schlamm m; v (liquid) sickern; quellen

opaque, oh-**pehk,** adj undurchsichtig

open, oh-p'n, adj offen; auf; (to public) öffentlich; v öffnen, aufmachen; **–er,** n Öffner m; **–ing,** n Öffnung f; (hole) Loch nt; **– learning,** n Selbststudium nt mit Tutorenunterstützung; **––minded,** adj aufgeschlossen; ; **––plan,** adj offen ausgelegt; **––plan office,** n Großraumbüro nt

opera, oh-e-re, n Oper f; **– glass,** Opernglas nt; **– house,** Opernhaus nt

operate, opp-e-reht, v (of machine) funktionieren, laufen; ; (of business) aktiv sein; (activate) betätigen; **– (on),** (affect) hinwirken (auf); med operieren

operation, opp-e-**reh**-sch'n, n med Operation f; (business) Betrieb m; mil

Einsatz m

operator, opp-e-**reh**-ter, n (of machine) (Maschinen)bediener m; (telephone) Telefonist m, Operator m

opinion, **e-pinn**-jen, n Meinung f; **– poll,** n Meinungsumfrage f

opponent, **e-poh**-nent, n Gegner m, Opponent m

opportunity, opp-er-**tjuh**-ni-ti, n Gelegenheit f

oppose, **e-pohs,** v gegenüberstellen; (object) sich wenden gegen, sich aussprechen gegen; **as –d to,** im Gegensatz zu

opposing, **e-poh**-sing, adj entgegengesetzt; (team) gegnerisch

opposite, opp-e-sitt, adj entgegengesetzt; adv gegenüber; prep gegenüber; n Gegenteil nt

opposition, opp-e-**sisch**-'n, n (competition) Gegner m; (objection) Einrede f; (contrast) Gegensatz m; parl Opposition(spartei) f

oppress, **e-press,** v unterdrücken; **–ion,** n Unterdrückung f; **–ive,** adj (climate) drückend; (regime) repressiv

opt, opt, v **– for,** sich entscheiden für; **– out,** austreten aus

optical, opp-ti-k'l, adj optisch

optician, opp-**tisch**-'n, n

Optiker m

optimist, opp-ti-mist, n Optimist m; **–ic,** adj optimistisch

option, opp-sch'n, n Wahl f; (subject) Wahlfach nt; **–al,** adj (subject) wahlfrei; (feature) auf Wunsch

opulent, op-juh-lent, adj reich

or, or, conj oder; (in negative) noch; **– else,** sonst

oral, or-rel, adj mündlich

orange, o-rindsch, adj (colour) orange; n Apfelsine f, Orange f

orator, o-re-ter, n Redner m

orbit, or-bit, n Umlaufbahn f; v umkreisen

orchard, or-tscherd, n Obstgarten m

orchestra, or-kiss-tre, n Orchester nt

orchestral, or-kess-trel, adj orchestral, Orchester-

orchid, or-kidd, n Orchidee f

ordain, or-dehn, v bestimmen; relig ordinieren

ordeal, or-diel, n Qual f

order, or-der, n comm Bestellung f, Auftrag m; (command) Befehl m; (sequence) Reihenfolge f; (tidiness, civil) Ordnung f; (relig, decoration) Orden m; v (arrange) ordnen; comm bestellen; (command) befehlen; **–ly,**

adj ordentlich; *n med*
Krankenpfleger *m*; **in – to,**
um zu

ordinary, or-di-ne-ri, *adj*
gewöhnlich

ore, or, n Erz *nt*

organ, or-gen, *n mus* Orgel *f*;
(*med, fig*) Organ *nt*

organic, or-gänn-ick, *adj* aus
biologischem Anbau,
organisch

organization, or-ge-nei-seh-
sch'n, *n* Organisation *f*

organize, or-ge-neis, *v*
organisieren; **–r,** *n*
Organisator *m*,
Veranstalter *m*

orgasm, or-gäsm, *n*
Orgasmus *m*

orgy, or-dschi, *n* Orgie *f*

Orient, or-ri-ent, *n*
Orient *m*

oriental, or-ri-enn-t'l, *adj*
orientalisch

origin, o-ridsch-inn, *n*
Ursprung *m*

original, e-ri-dschinn-'l, *adj*
(earliest) ursprünglich;
(idea, person) originell; *n*
Original *nt*

originate, e-ridsch-i-neht, *v*
(arise) entstehen; (create)
schaffen; (invent)
erfinden

ornament, or-ne-ment, *n*
(decoration) Schmuck *m*;
(object) Ziergegenstand *m*

ornamental, or-ne-menn-t'l,
adj verzierend, Zier-

orphan, or-fen, *n* Waise *f*;
–age, Waisenhaus *nt*

orthodox, or-the-docks, *adj*
orthodox; **–y,** *n*
Orthodoxie *f*; *fig*
Konvention *f*

orthopaedic, or-the-pie-
dick, *adj* orthopädisch; **–s,**
n Orthopädie *f*

oscillate, oss-i-leht, *v*
schwanken

ostensible, oss-tenn-ssib-'l,
adj Schein-

ostentatious, oss-ten-teh-
schess, *adj* prahlerisch

ostrich, oss-tritsch, *n*
Strauß *m*

other, adh-er, *adj & pron*
andere(r/s); **–s,** *pl* andere;
– than, außer; **somehow
or –,** irgendwie

otherwise, adh-er-u'eis, *adv*
(or else) sonst;
(differently) anders

ought (to), o'at (tu), *v*
sollte(st, n); **– to have …,**
hätte … sollen

ounce, aunss, n Unze *f*

our, au-er, *adj* unser; **–s,**
pron unsere(r/s)

ourselves, aur-sselws, *pron*
(*refl*) uns (selbst);
(*emphatic*) selbst; **by –,** *adv*
alleine

out, aut, *adv* (absent) nicht
da, nicht zu Hause;
(outside) draußen;
(motion) hinaus, heraus;
(not lit) aus; **– of,** hinaus,
aus, außerhalb; **– of order,**
außer Betrieb; **be – of
(money),** *v* kein (Geld)
mehr haben

outback, aut-bäck, *n*
Hinterland *nt*

outboard, aut-bord, *adj*
Außenbord-

outbreak, aut-brehk, *n*
Ausbruch *m*

outburst, aut-börst, *n*
Ausbruch *m*

outcast, aut-kahst, *n*
Verstoßene(r) *m & f*

outcome, aut-kamm, *n*
Ergebnis *nt*

outcry, aut-krei, *n*
Aufschrei *m*

outdated, aut-deh-tidd, *adj*
überholt, altmodisch

outdo, aut-duh, *v*
übertreffen

outdoor, aut-dor, *adj*
Außen-; (pool) Frei-;
(sport, activity) im Freien;
–s, *adv* im Freien

outer, au-ter, *adj* äußere(r/s);
– space, n Weltraum *m*

outfit, aut-fitt, n (clothes)
Kleidung *f*; (*fam* business)
Laden *m*; **–ter,**
Herrenausstatter *m*

outgoing, aut-goh-ing, *adj*
(departing) (aus dem
Amt) scheidend;
(extrovert)
kontaktfreudig; **–s,** *npl*
Ausgaben *pl*

outgrow, aut-groh, *v*
entwachsen; (overcome)
überwinden

outing, au-ting, *n* Ausflug *m*

outlast, aut-lahst, *v*
überdauern

outlaw, aut-lor, *n*

Geächtete(r) m & f; v
ächten; (prohibit)
verbieten

outlay, aut-leh, n
Ausgaben npl

outlet, aut-lett, n Ablauf m;
(market) (Absatz)markt
m; fig Ventil nt

outline, aut-lein, n Umriß m

outlive, aut-liw, v überleben

outlook, aut-luck, n
Aussicht f

outlying, aut-lei-ing, adj
entfernt liegend

outnumber, aut-numm-ber,
v zahlenmäßig überlegen
sein

out-of-date, aut-ew-deht, adj
(outmoded) veraltet;
(expired) verfallen

outpatient, aut-peh-schent,
n ambulanter Patient m

outpost, aut-pohst, n
Vorposten m

output, aut-putt, n
Produktion f; comp
Ausgabe f

outrage, aut-rehdsch, n
(crime) Verbrechen);
(violation) Verstoß m

outrage, aut-rehdsch, v
empören; –ous, adj
(immoral) unverschämt;
(cruel) grausam

outright, aut-reit, adj
(complete) total;
(unashamed)
gereadeheraus; adv
(completely) ganz; (kill)
gleich; (deny) glatt

outset, aut-ssett, n

Anfang m

outside, aut-sseid, adj
Außen-; adv (nach)
draußen; prep außerhalb; n
Außenseite f; at the –,
höchstens

outsize, aut-sseis, adj
überdimensional;
(clothes) in Übergröße

outskirts, aut-skörts, npl
Randgebiete pl

outspoken, aut-spoh-k'n, adj
freimütig

outstanding, aut-stänn-
ding, adj (excellent)
hervorragend; (debts)
ausstehend; (work)
unerledigt

outstrip, aut-stripp, v
übertreffen

outward, aut-wed, adj
äußere(r/s); adv nach
außen; –bound, adj
(shipping) auslaufend;
(course) Abenteuer-; –ly,
adv äußerlich

outwit, aut-u'itt, v
überlisten

oval, oh-wel, adj oval; n
Oval nt

ovation, e-weh-sch'n, n
Ovation f, begeisterter
Beifall m

oven, aw-en, n (Back)ofen
m

over, oh-wer, adv (there)
drüben; (motion) hinüber,
herüber; (finished) vorbei;
(remainining) übrig; prep
über; (all) – again, wieder,
noch einmal; all –,

(everywhere) überall;
(finished) vorbei

overall, oh-we-ro'al, adj
(general) allgemein;
(total) gesamt, Gesamt-;
(majority) absolut

overall, oh-we-ro'al, adv
(generally) im großen und
ganzen; (in total)
insgesamt

overalls, oh-we-ro'als, npl
Overall m

overawed, oh-we-ro'ad, adj
eingeschüchtert

overbalance, oh-wer-bäll-
enss, v aus dem
Gleichgewicht kommen

overbearing, oh-wer-behr-
ring, adj arrogant

overboard, oh-wer-bord, adv
über Bord; go –, v es
übertreiben

overcast, oh-wer-kahst, adj
bewölkt

overcharge, oh-wer-
tschardsch, v zuviel
berechnen

overcoat, oh-wer-koht, n
Mantel m

overcome, oh-wer-kamm, v
überwinden

overcrowded, oh-wer-krau-
didd, adj überfüllt

overdo, oh-wer-duh, v
(exaggerate) übertreiben;
(overcook) verkochen

overdose, oh-wer-dohss, n
Überdosis f; v eine
Überdosis nehmen

overdraft, oh-wer-drahft, n
(Konto)überziehung f

overdrawn, oh-wer-**dro'an,** *adj* überzogen

overdue, oh-wer-**djuh,** *adj* (train) verspätet; (debt) überfällig

overflow, oh-wer-floh, *n* Überlaufrohr nt

overflow, oh-wer-**floh,** *v* überlaufen

overgrown, oh-wer-grohn, *adj* überwuchert

overhaul, oh-wer-**ho'al,** *v* überholen

overhear, oh-wer-**hier,** *v* (zufällig) hören

overjoyed, oh-wer-**dscheud,** *adj* überglücklich

overland, oh-wer-**länd,** *adj* Überland-

overlap, oh-wer-**läpp,** *v* (sich) überschneiden

overleaf, oh-wer-**lief,** *adv* umseitig

overload, oh-wer-**lohd,** *v* überladen

overlook, oh-wer-**luck,** *v* (miss) übersehen; (have view of) überblicken

overnight, oh-wer-neit, *adj* Nacht-; **– stay/stop,** *n* Übernachtung f

overnight, oh-wer-**neit,** *adv* über Nacht; **stay –,** *v* übernachten

overpower, oh-wer-**pau-er,** *v* überwältigen

overrated, oh-we-**reh-tidd,** *adj* überschätzt

overriding, oh-we-**rei-ding,** *adj* wichtigste(r/s)

overrule, oh-we-**ruhl,** *v* verwerfen

overrun, oh-we-**rann,** *v* länger dauern als vorgesehen; **– (with),** *adj* überlaufen von

overseas, oh-wer-**ssies,** *adj* Übersee-; *adv* nach/in Übersee

overshadow, oh-wer-**schädd-**oh, *v* überschatten

oversight, oh-wer-**sseit,** *n* Versehen nt

oversleep, oh-wer-**ssliep,** *v* verschlafen

overstatement, oh-wer-**steht-**ment, *n* Übertreibung f

overstep, oh-wer-**stepp,** *v* überschreiten

overt, oh-**wört,** *adj* unverhohlen

overtake, oh-wer-**tehk,** *n* (catch up) einholen; (pass) überholen

overthrow, oh-wer-**throh,** *v* stürzen; (defeat) besiegen

overtime, oh-wer-teim, *n* Überstunden pl

overture, oh-wer-**tjuhr,** *n* mus Ouvertüre f; (approach) Annäherungsversuch m

overturn, oh-wer-**törn,** *v* stürzen; (decision) aufheben

overweight, oh-wer-**u'eit,** *adj* übergewichtig

overwhelm, oh-wer-**u'elm,** *v* überwältigen

overwork, oh-wer-**u'örk,** *n* Überlastung f; *v* (somebody) mit Arbeit überlasten; (oneself) sich überarbeiten

overwrought, oh-we-**ro'at,** *adj* überreizt

owe, oh, *v* schulden

owing, oh-ing, *adj* schuldig; **– to,** *prep* wegen

owl, aul, *n* Eule f

own, ohn, *adj* eigen; *v* besitzen; (admit) gestehen; **–er,** *n* Besitzer m, Eigentümer m; **– up (to),** *v* zugeben; **get one's – back,** *v* sich revanchieren; **on one's –,** allein

ox, ocks, *n* Ochse m; **–tail soup,** *n* Ochsenschwanzsuppe f

oxygen, ock-ssi-dschen, *n* Sauerstoff m

oyster, euss-ter, *n* Auster f

ozone, oh-sohn, *n* Ozon nt; **––friendly,** *adj* ozonsicher; (without CFCs) FCKW-frei; **– layer,** *n* Ozonschicht f

pace, pehss, n (step) Schritt m; (speed) Tempo nt; v schreiten; (sport) Schritt machen; **–maker,** n Schrittmacher m

pacific, pe-ssi-fick, adj friedlich; **the P– (Ocean),** der Pazifik m

pacifist, päss-i-fist, n Pazifist m

pacify, päss-i-fei, v besänftigen

pack, päck, n (bundle) Pack m; (of cards) Spiel nt; (gang) Bande f; (of hounds) Meute f; v packen; **–age,** n Paket nt; **–age holiday,** n Pauschalreise f; **–ed lunch,** n Lunchpaket nt; **–et,** n Päckchen nt; **–ing,** n Verpackung f

pact, päkt, n Pakt m, Vertrag m

pad, pädd, n (wad) Polster nt; (of paper) Block m; v polstern; **–ding,** n Wattierung f

paddle, pädd-'l, n Paddel nt; v (boat) paddeln; (in water) planschen; **– steamer,** n Raddampfer m

paddock, pädd-eck, n (meadow) Wiese f; (at races) Sattelplatz m

padlock, pädd-lock, n Vorhängeschloß nt; v verschliessen

paediatrician, pie-di-e-trisch-'n, n Kinderarzt m

pagan, peh-gen, adj heidnisch; n Heide m, Heidin f

page, pehdsch, n Seite f; **–(boy),** n Page m; (haircut) Pagenkopf m; v ausrufen lassen

pageant, pädsch-ent, n Prunkaufzug m

pager, peh-dscher, n Pager m, Piepser m

pail, pehl, n Eimer m

pain, pehn, n Schmerz m; **–ful,** adj (physically) schmerzhaft; (distressing) schmerzlich; **–killer,** n Schmerzmittel nt; **–less,** adj schmerzlos; **take –s,** v sich Mühe geben

paint, pehnt, n Farbe f; v anstreichen; (art) malen; **–brush,** n Pinsel m; **–er,** n Maler m; **–ing,** n Gemälde nt

pair, pähr, n Paar nt; **– of glasses,** n Brille f; **– of trousers,** n Hose f

pal, päll, n fam Kumpel m

palace, päll-iss, n Palast m

palatable, päll-e-te-b'l, adj genießbar; (acceptable) akzeptabel

palate, päll-itt, n Gaumen m

pale, pehl, adj blaß; v erbleichen; **–ness,** n Blässe f

Palestine, päll-iss-tein, n Palästina nt

palette, päll-itt, n Palette f

pall, po'al, n Wolke f; v langweilig werden

pallid, päll-idd, adj bleich, blaß

palm, pahm, n (tree) Palme f; (of hand) Handfläche f; **– sth off on sb,** v etw auf jdn abschieben; **P– Sunday,** n Palmsonntag m

palpitation, päll-pi-teh-sch'n, n Herzklopfen nt

paltry, po'al-tri, adj
armselig, lumpig

pamper, pämm-per, v
verhätscheln

pamphlet, pämm-flitt, n
Broschüre f

pan, pänn, n Topf m; **frying
–**, n Bratpfanne f

panache, pe-näsch, n
Schwung m

pancake, pänn-kehk, n
Pfannkuchen m

panda, pänn-de, n Panda m

pandemonium, pänn-di-
moh-ni-em, n Chaos nt

pander (to), pänn-der (tu),
v allzu sehr
engegenkommen,
schmeicheln

pane, pehn, n Scheibe f

panel, pänn-'l, n (of wood
etc.) Tafel f; (of people)
Podium nt; **–ling**, n
Täfelung f

pang, päng, n (of hunger)
Stich; (of remorse) Reue

panic, pänn-ick, n Panik f; v
in Panik versetzen

pansy, pänn-si, n (flower)
Stiefmütterchen nt; (fam
homosexual man)
Schwuler m, (lesbian)
Lesbe f

pant, pänt, v keuchen; (of
dog) hecheln

panther, pänn-ther, n
Panther m

panties, pänn-tis, npl
(Damen)slip m

pantomime, pänn-te-meim,

n Pantomime f;
(entertainment)
Kinderstück nt; (fuss)
Aufhebens nt

pantry, pänn-tri, n
Speisekammer f

pants, pänts, npl
(underwear) Unterhose f;
(trousers) Hose f

papal, peh-pel, adj päpstlich

paper, peh-per, adj aus
Papier; n Papier nt;
(newspaper) Zeitung f; v
tapezieren; **–back**, n
Taschenbuch nt; **– bag**, n
Tüte f; **–clip**, n
Büroklammer f; **–
handkerchief**, n
Papiertaschentuch nt; **–s**,
npl Ausweis m, Papiere pl

par, pahr, n (golf) Par nt;
below –, nicht auf der
Höhe; **on a – with**,
gleichgestellt mit

parable, pä-re-b'l, n
Gleichnis nt

parachute, pä-re-schuht, n
Fallschirm m

parade, pe-rehd, n Parade f;
v paradieren; fig zur Schau
stellen

paradise, pä-re-deiss, n
Paradies nt

paradox, pä-re-docks, n
Paradox nt; **–ical**, adj
paradox

paraffin, pä-re-finn, n
Paraffin nt

paragraph, pä-re-grahf, n
Absatz m

parallel, pä-re-lell, adj

parallel

paralyse, pä-re-leis, v
lähmen

paralysis, pe-räll-i-ssiss, n
Lähmung f

parameter, pe-rämm-i-ter, n
Parameter m

paramount, pä-re-maunt, adj
höchter(r/s); von höchster
Bedeutung

paranoid, pä-re-neud, adj
paranoid

parapet, pä-re-pett, n
Brüstung f

paraphrase, pä-re-frehs, v
umschreiben

paraplegic, pä-re-plie-
dschick, n
Querschnittsgelähmte(r)
m & f

parasite, pä-re-sseit, n
Schmarotzer m, Parasit m

parasol, pä-re-ssoll, n
Sonnenschirm m

paratrooper, pä-re-truh-per,
n Fallschirmjäger m

parcel, pahr-s'l, n Paket nt

parched, pahrtscht, adj
ausgetrocknet; (person)
sehr durstig

parchment, pahrtsch-ment,
n Pergament nt

pardon, pahr-d'n, n
Verzeihung f; law
Begnadigung f; v
verzeihen; law
begnadigen; **(I beg your)
–?** wie bitte?; **I beg your
–!** Verzeihung!

parent, pähr-rent, n,
Elternteil m; **–s**, npl

Eltern *pl*

parental, pe-**renn**-t'l, *adj*
elterlich, Eltern-

parentheses, pe-**renn**-the-
ssies, *npl* Klammern *pl*

parish, pä-risch, *n*
Gemeinde *f*

park, pahrk, *n* Park *m*,
Anlagen *pl*; *v* parken;
–**ing,** *n* Parken *m*; –**ing**
meter, *n* Parkuhr *f*; –**ing**
place, *n* Parkplatz *m*; –
ticket, *n* Strafzettel *m*

parliament, pahr-le-ment, *n*
Parlament *nt*; –**ary,** *adj*
parlamentarisch,
Parlaments-

parlour, pahr-ler, *n* Salon *m*

parole, pe-rohl, *n*
Bewährung *f*

paroxysm, pä-reck-ssism, *n*
Anfall *m*

parrot, pä-ret, *n* Papagei *m*

parry, pä-ri, *v* parieren,
abwehren

parsimonious, pahr-ssi-
moh-ni-ess, *adj* geizig

parsley, pahrss-li, *n*
Petersilie *f*

parsnip, pahrss-nipp, *n*
Pastinake *f*

parson, pahr-ss'n, *n* Pfarrer
m; –**age,** *n* Pfarrhaus *nt*

part, pahrt, *n* (piece) Teil *m*;
mech Teil *nt*; *theatre* Rolle
f; *v* (divide) teilen;
(separate) sich trennen;
(the hair) scheiteln

partial, pahr-sch'l, *adj*
teilweise; **be – to,** *v* eine
Vorliebe haben für

participant, pahr-**tiss**-i-pent,
n Teilnehmer *m*

participate (in), pahr-**tiss**-i-
peht (inn), *v* teilnehmen
(an)

participle, pahr-tiss-i-p'l, *n*
Partizip *nt*

particle, pahr-tick-'l, *n*
Teilchen *nt*

particular, pe-tick-kju-ler,
adj besondere(r/s); (fussy)
wählerisch; (exact) genau;
–**s,** *npl* (details)
Einzelheiten *pl*; (personal)
Daten *pl*

parting, pahr-ting, *n*
(leaving) Abschied *m*; (of
hair) Scheitel *m*

partition, par-tisch-'n, *n*
(wall) Scheidewand *f*; (of
country) Teilung *f*

partly, pahrt-li, *adv*
teilweise, zum Teil

partner, pahrt-ner, *n*
Partner *m*; *comm*
Teilhaber *m*; –**ship,**
Partnerschaft *f*; *comm*
Teilhaberschaft *f*

partridge, pahrt-ridsch, *n*
Rebhuhn *nt*

part-time, pahrt-teim, *adj*
Teilzeit-; **work –,** *v*
Teilzeit arbeiten

party, pahr-ti, *n* (event)
Party *f*; (political) Partei *f*;
(person involved) Partei *f*

pass, pahss, *n* Paß *m*; *v*
vorbeigehen (an),
vorbeifahren (an); (not
speak) passen;
(examination) bestehen;

(time) verbringen; (hand
to) reichen; (of time)
verstreichen; – **away,** *v*
(die) versterben; – **up,** *v*
(renounce) ausschlagen

passage, päss-idsch, *n*
(corridor) Durchgang *m*;
(journey) Überfahrt *f*;
(text) Passage *f*

passbook, pahss-buck, *n*
Sparbuch *nt*

passenger, päss-in-dscher, *n*
Passagier *m*

passer-by, pahss-er-bei, *n*
Passant *m*

passing, pah-ssing,
adj (traffic) vorbei-
fahrend; (fleeting)
vorübergehend; – **place,** *n*
Ausweichstelle *f*

passion, päsch-'n, *n*
Leidenschaft *f*; (anger)
Zorn *m*; –**ate,** *adj*
leidenschaftlich

passive, päss-iw, *adj* passiv;
n gram Passiv *nt*

Passover, pahss-oh-wer, *n*
Passah *nt*

passport, pahss-port, *n*
(Reise)paß *m*

password, pahss-u'örd, *n*
Paßwort *nt*

past, pahst, *adj* vergangen;
adv vorbei, vorüber; *n*
Vergangenheit *f*; *prep* an
... vorbei; (telling time)
nach

pasta, päss-ter, *n* Pasta *f*,
Teigwaren *pl*

paste, pehst, *v* (glue)
Kleister *m*; Teig *m*; (gem)

Paste f; v kleben

pasteurized, pahss-tsche-reisd, adj pasteurisiert

pastime, pahss-teim, n Zeitvertreib m, Hobby nt

pastry, pehss-tri, n (dough) Teig m; (cakes) Gebäck nt

pasture, pahss-tscher, n Weide f

pat, pätt, n Klaps m; v streicheln

patch, pätsch, n (mend) Flicken m; (period) Phase f; v flicken; – **up,** v fig beilegen; –**y,** adj vereinzelt

pâté, pätt-eh, adj Pastete f

patent, peht-'nt, n Patent nt; v patentieren lassen; – **leather,** n Lackleder nt

paternal, pe-tör-n'l, adj väterlich

path, pahth, n Pfad m, Weg m; (course) Bahn f

pathetic, pe-thett-ick, adj herzergreifend; (contemptible) armselig

patience, peh-schenss, n Geduld f

patient, peh-schent, n Patient m; adj geduldig

patio, pätt-i-oh, n Terrasse f

patriot, peh-tri-et, n Patriot m

patriotic, peh-tri-ott-ick, adj patriotisch

patrol, pe-trohl, n Patrouille f; v die Runde machen; mil patrouillieren

patron, peh-tren, n (customer) Kunde m, Kundin f; (supporter)

Gönner m

patronize, pätt-re-neis, v (support) fördern; (condescend to) herablassend behandeln; (frequent) besuchen

patter, pätt-er, n (of feet) Trappeln nt; (talk) Gerede nt

pattern, pätt-ern, n Muster m

paunch, po'ansch, n Bauch m

pauper, po'a-per, n Arme(r) m & f

pause, po'as, n Pause f; v pausieren

pave, pehw, v pflastern; –**ment,** n Pflaster m; – **the way (for),** v den Weg bahnen (für)

paving, peh-wing, n Pflaster nt; – **stone,** n Pflasterstein m

paw, po'a, n Pfote f, Tatze f; v scharren; (fam touch) befummeln

pawn, po'an, n (pledge) Pfand nt; (chess) Bauer m; v versetzen; –**shop,** n Leihaus nt

pay, peh, n Lohn m; v (be)zahlen; (be profitable) sich lohnen; – **a visit to,** v besuchen; –**able,** adj zahlbar; – **attention (to),** v beachten, Aufmerksamkeit schenken; – **for,** v bezahlen; –**ment,** n Bezahlung f; –**phone,** n

(coins) Münzfernsprecher m; (public telephone) öffentliches Telefon nt

PC, pie ssie, abbr **personal computer**

pea, pie, n Erbse f

peace, piess, n Friede m; –**ful,** adj friedlich; – **keeping,** adj Friedens-

peach, pietsch, n Pfirsich m

peacock, pie-kock, n Pfau m

peak, piek, n Gipfel m

peal, piel, n (of bells) Geläute nt; (of thunder) Schlag m; – **of laughter,** n schallendes Gelächter nt

peanut, pie-natt, n Erdnuß f

pear, pähr, n Birne f

pearl, pörl, n Perle f

peasant, pes-'nt, n Bauer m; –**ry,** Landvolk nt

peat, piet, n Torf m

pebble, pebb-'l, n Kieselstein m

peck, peck, n (kiss) Küßchen nt; v picken; (kiss) flüchtig küssen; –**ish,** n hungrig

peculiar, pi-kjuh-li-er, adj sonderbar; –**ity,** n Eigenheit f

pedal, pedd-'l, n Pedal nt; v radfahren

pedantic, pi-dänn-tick, adj pedantisch, kleinlich

peddler, pedd-ler, n Hausierer m

pedestal, pedd-iss-t'l, n Sockel m

pedestrian, pi-dess-tri-en, adj Fußgänger-; fig

trocken, langweilig; *n*
Fußgänger *m*

pedigree, pedd-i-grie, *n*
Stammbaum *m*

pedlar, pedd-ler, *n*
Hausierer *m*

peel, piel, *n* Schale *f*, Rinde
f; *v* (fruit) schälen; (of
paint etc.) abblättern

peep, piep, *n* (look) Blick *m*;
(sound) Piepsen *nt*; *v*
(look) gucken; (make
sound) piepsen

peer, pier, *n* (noble) Peer *m*;
(equal) Gleichgestellte(r)
m & *f*; *v* gucken; **–age,** *n*
Adelsstand *m*; **–less,** *adj*
unvergleichlich

peeved, piewd, *adj* verärgert

peevish, pie-wisch, *adj*
verdrießlich

peg, pegg, *n* (for tent etc.)
Pflock *m*; (of violin)
Wirbel *m*; (for washing)
Klammer *f*; (for clothes)
Kleiderhaken *m*; *v* mit
Klammern aufhängen; *fig*
stabil halten

pellet, pell-itt, *n* Kügelchen
nt; (shot) Schrot *m*

pelt, pelt, *n* Fell *nt*; Pelz *m*; *v*
bewerfen; (of rain)
prasseln

pelvis, pell-wiss, *n* Becken
nt

pen, penn, *n* Feder *f*; (for
sheep) Pferch *m*

penal, pie-n'l, *adj* Straf-;
–ize, *v* bestrafen

penalty, penn-'l-ti, *n* Strafe
f; (football) Elfmeter *m*

penance, penn-enss, *n*
Buße *f*

pence, penss, *npl* Pence *pl*

pencil, penn-ssill, *n* Bleistift
m; **– sharpener,** *n*
Bleistiftspitzer *m*

pendant, penn-dent, *n*
Anhänger *m*

pending, penn-ding, *adj*
unerledigt; *prep* bis

pendulum, penn-dju-lem, *n*
Pendel *nt*

penetrate, penn-i-treht, *v*
durchdringen

penfriend, penn-frend, *n*
Brieffreund *m*

penguin, peng-gu'in, *n*
Pinguin *m*

penicillin, penn-i-ssill-in, *n*
Penizillin *nt*

peninsula, pi-ninn-ssju-le, *n*
Halbinsel *f*

penis, pie-niss, *n* Glied *nt*,
Penis *m*

penitent, penn-i-tent, *adj*
reuig

penknife, penn-neif, *n*
Taschenmesser *nt*

penniless, penn-i-liss, *adj*
mittellos

penny, penn-i, *n* Penny *m*

pension, penn-sch'n, *n*
Rente *f*; **–r,** *n* Rentner *m*

pensive, penn-ssiw, *adj*
nachdenklich

penthouse, pent-hauss, *n*
Penthouse *m*

penultimate, pi-nall-ti-met,
adj vorletzte(r/s)

people, pie-p'l, *n* (nation)
Volk *nt*; *npl* Leute *pl*; *v*

bevölkern

pepper, pepp-er, *n* (spice)
Pfeffer *m*; (vegetable)
Paprika *f*; **–mint,** *n*
(sweet) Pfefferminz *nt*;
(plant) Pfefferminze *f*

per, pör, *prep* pro, durch

perceive, per-ssiw, *v*
wahrnehmen

per cent, per ssent, *n*
Prozent *nt*

percentage, per-ssenn-
tidsch, *n* Prozentsatz *m*

perception, per-ssepp-sch'n,
n Wahrnehmung *f*

perceptive, per-ssepp-tiw,
adj aufmerksam

perch, pörtsch, *n* (of bird)
Stange *f*; (fish) Barsch *m*;
v hocken

percolate, pör-ke-leht, *v*
filtern

percussion, per-kasch-'n, *n*
Schlagzeug *nt*

peremptory, pe-remp-te-ri,
adj kategorisch

perennial, pe-renn-i-el, *adj*
(plant) mehrjährig;
(lasting) immerwährend;
n mehrjährige Pflanze *f*

perfect, pör-fikt, *adj*
vollkommen; *n gram*
Perfekt *nt*

perfect, per-fekt, *v*
vervollkommnen; **–ion,** *n*
Vollkommenheit *f*

perforate, pör-fe-reht, *v*
perforieren, durchlöchern

perform, per-form, *v* (task)
leisten; *theatre* etc.
aufführen; (operation)

ausführen; **–ance,** n *theatre* etc. Vorstellung f; (carrying out) Ausführung f; (productivity) Leistung f

perfume, pör-fjuhm, n Parfüm nt

perfunctory, per-fank-te-ri, adj oberflächlich

perhaps, per-häpss, adv vielleicht

peril, pe-rill, n Gefahr f; **–ous,** adj gefährlich

period, pier-ri-ed, n (time, menstruation) Periode f; **–ic(al),** adj periodisch; **–ical,** n Zeitschrift f

peripheral, pe-riff-e-rel, adj peripher

periscope, pe-ri-skohp, n Periskop nt

perish, pe-risch, v (spoil) verderben; (die) umkommen; **–able,** adj leicht verderblich

perjury, pör-dsche-ri, n Meineid m

perk, pörk, n Vergüngstigung f; **– up,** v (person) aufleben; fig in Gang kommen

perm, pörm, n Dauerwelle f

permanent, pör-me-nent, adj beständig, fest

permeate, pör-mi-eht, v durchdringen

permissible, per-miss-i-b'l, adj zulässig

permission, per-misch-'n, n Erlaubnis f

permissive, per-miss-iw, adj tolerant, großzügig

permit, pör-mitt, n Genehmigung f

permit, per-mitt, v erlauben

pernicious, pe-nisch-ess, adj übel

perpendicular, per-pen-dick-ju-ler, adj senkrecht

perpetrate, pör-pi-treht, v begehen

perpetual, per-pett-ju-el, adj immerwährend

perplex, per-plecks, v verwirren

persecute, pör-ssi-kjuht, v verfolgen

persecution, pör-ssi-**kjuh-**sch'n, n Verfolgung f

perseverance, pör-ssi-**wier-**renss, n Ausdauer f

persevere, pör-ssi-**wier,** v beharren

persist, per-ssist, v (insist) beharren; (remain) anhalten; **–ence,** n Beharrlichkeit f

person, pör-ss'n, n Person f; **–al(ly),** adj & adv persönlich; **–al computer,** n Computer m, Rechner m; **–ality,** n Persönlichkeit f; **–al stereo,** n Walkman ® m

personify, per-ssonn-i-fei, v verkörpern

personnel, per-se-nell, n Personal nt

perspective, per-speck-tiw, n Perspektive f

perspiration, per-spi-reh-sch'n, n Schweiß m

perspire, per-speir, v

schwitzen

persuade, per-ssu'ehd, v überreden

persuasion, per-ssu'eh-sch'n, n Überzeugung(skraft) f

pert, pört, adj frech; (pretty) hübsch

pertain (to), per-tehn (tu), v gehören (zu), betreffen

pertinent, pör-ti-nent, adj relevant

perturb, per-törb, v beunruhigen

pervade, per-wehd, v durchdringen

perverse, per-wörss, adj (perverted) pervers; (awkward) verstockt

pervert, pör-wört, n perverser Mensch m

pervert, per-wört, v verdrehen, entstellen

pessimist, pess-i-mist, n Pessimist m

pest, pest, n Pest f; **–er,** v plagen

pet, pett, n (animal) Haustier nt; (person) Liebling m; v liebkosen

petal, pett-'l, n Blumenblatt nt

petition, pi-tisch-'n, n Unterschriftensammlung f

petrify, pett-ri-fei, v versteinern; (terrify) erschrecken

petrol, pett-rel, n Benzin nt; Treibstoff m

petroleum, pi-troh-li-em, n Erdöl nt

petrol pump, pett-rel pamp, n Zapfsäule f

petrol station, pett-rel steh-sch'n, n Tankstelle f

petticoat, pett-i-koht, n Unterrock m

petty, pett-i, adj kleinlich; – cash, n Portokasse f

pew, pjuh, n Kirchenbank f; fam Platz m

pewter, pjuh-ter, n Zinn nt

pharmacy, fahr-me-ssi, n Apotheke f

phase, fehs, n Phase f; – in/out, v allmählich einführen/auslaufen lassen

pheasant, fes-'nt, n Fasan m

phenomenon, fi-nomm-i-nen, n Phänomen nt

philanthropist, fi-länn-thre-pist, n Menschenfreund m

philosopher, fi-loss-e-fer, n Philosoph m

philiosophy, fi-loss-e-fi, n Philosophie f

phlegm, flemm, n Phlegma nt; med Schleim m

phobia, foh-bi-e, n Phobie f

phone, fohn, n abbr telephone; —in, n Phone-in nt

photo, foh-toh, n Foto nt

photocopier, foh-te-kopp-i-er, n Kopiergerät nt

photocopy, foh-te-kopp-i, n Fotokopie f

photograph, foh-te-grahf, n Foto(grafie) f, Aufnahme f; v fotografieren

photographer, fe-togg-re-fer, n Fotograf m

phrase, frehs, n gram Phrase f; (expression) Ausdruck m; v formulieren; –book, n Sprachführer m

physical, fis-ick-'l, adj körperlich; – education, n Sportunterricht m

physician, fi-sisch-'n, n Arzt m, Ärztin f

physicist, fi-si-ssist, n Physiker m

physics, fi-sicks, n Physik f

physiotherapie, fi-si-oh-the-re-pi, n Physiotherapie f

pianist, pi-e-nist, n Pianist m

piano, pi-änn-oh, n Klavier nt; (grand) Flügel m

pick, pick, n (choice) Auswahl f; (tool) Pickel m; v (choose) wählen; (gather) pflücken; (teeth) stochern; – out, v aussuchen; – up, v aufheben; (collect) abholen; (fam learn) aufschnappen

pickle, pick-'l, v pökeln; –s, npl Pickles pl

pickpocket, pick-pock-itt, n Taschendieb m

picnic, pick-nick, n Picknick nt

picture, pick-tscher, n Bild nt; (painting) Gemälde nt; v sich vorstellen; –s, npl Kino nt; –sque, adj malerisch

pie, pei, n (savoury) Pastete f; (sweet) Torte f

piece, piess, n Stück nt;

–meal, adv stückweise; – together, v zusammenfügen; –work, n Akkordarbeit f

pier, pier, n Pier m

pierce, pierss, v durchstechen

piercing, pier-ssing, adj durchdringend

piety, pei-i-ti, n Frömmigkeit f

pig, pigg, n Schwein nt

pigeon, pidsch-inn, n Taube f; –hole, n Fach nt; v einordnen

pigheaded, pigg-hedd-idd, adj stur

piglet, pigg-litt, n Ferkel nt

pigsty, pigg-stei, n Schweinestall m

pike, peik, n (fish) Hecht m

pilchard, pill-tscherd, n Sardine f

pile, peil, n (heap) Haufen m, Stapel m; (stake) Pfahl m; (of carpet) Flor m; – (up), v (sich) anhäufen

piles, peils, n Hämorrhoiden pl

pile-up, peil-app, n Massenzusammenstoß m

pilfer, pill-fer, v stehlen

pilgrim, pill-grimm, n Pilger m; –age, n Wallfahrt f

pill, pill, n Pille f

pillage, pill-idsch, v plündern

pillar, pill-er, n Pfeiler m, Säule f

pillory, pill-e-ri, v an den Pranger stellen

pillow, pill-oh, n Kopfkissen nt; **–case,** n Kissenbezug m

pilot, pei-let, adj Versuchs-; n Pilot m; naut Lotse m; v führen; naut lotsen; **– light,** n Zündflamme f

pimp, pimp, n Zuhälter m

pimple, pimm-p'l, n Pickel m, Bläschen f

pin, pinn, n (sewing) Nadel f; (of brooch) Nadel f; (of bolt) Bolzen m; v stecken, heften; **–s and needles,** npl Kribbeln nt

pinafore, pinn-e-for, n Schürze f

pincers, pinn-ssers, npl Kneifzange f

pinch, pintsch, n Kniff m; (of salt etc.) Prise f; v kneifen; (of shoe) drücken; (fam steal) klauen

pine, pein, n Kiefer f; v sich grämen; **–apple,** n Ananas f; **– for,** v sich sehnen nach

ping, ping, n (bell) Klingeln nt; **–pong,** n Tischtennis nt

pink, pink, adj rosa; n (colour) Rosa nt; (flower) Nelke f

pinnacle, pinn-e-k'l, n Gipfel m

pinpoint, pinn-peunt, v genau bestimmen

pint, peint, n Schoppen m; (of beer) großes Bier nt

pioneer, pei-e-nier, n Pionier m; fig

Bahnbrecher m

pious, pei-ess, adj fromm

pip, pipp, n Kern m; **– sb at the post,** v jdn knapp schlagen

pipe, peip, n (tube) Rohr nt; (smoking) Pfeife f; v pfeifen, schrillen; **– down,** v fam ruhig sein; **–dream,** n Luftschloß nt; **–line,** n Pipeline f; **–r,** n mus Dudelsackbläser m

pirate, peir-ret, n Seeräuber m; **– radio,** n Piratensender m

Pisces, pei-ssies, n Fische pl

piss, piss, v fam pissen; **–ed,** adj fam besoffen

pistol, piss-t'l, n Pistole f

piston, piss-t'n, n Kolben m

pit, pitt, n Grube f; theatre Parkett nt; **– o.s. against,** v sich an etw messen

pitch, pitsch, n (tar) Pech nt; mus Tonhöhe f; (sport) Feld nt; v (throw) werfen; naut stampfen; (tent) aufschlagen; **–ed battle,** n offene Schlacht f

pitcher, pitsch-er, n Krug m

piteous, pitt-i-ess, adj kläglich

pitfall, pitt-fo'al, n Falle f

pith, pith, n Mark nt; **–y,** adj fig prägnant

pitiable, pitt-i-e-b'l, adj kläglich, elend

pitiful, pitt-i-full, adj elend

pitiless, pitt-i-liss, adj erbarmungslos

pittance, pitt-'nss, n

Hungerlohn m

pitted, pitt-idd, adj voller Vertiefungen

pity, pitt-i, n Mitleid nt; v bemitleiden; pej bedauern; **what a –!** wie schade!

pivot, piw-et, n Drehpunkt m; v sich drehen

pizza, pie-tse, n Pizza f

placard, plä-kahrd, n Plakat nt

placate, ple-keht, v besänftigen

place, plehss, n Platz m; (locality) Ort m; (home) Wohnung f; v (put) stellen; (lay) legen; **take –,** v stattfinden

placid, pläss-idd, adj gelassen, friedlich

plagiarism, pleh-dschje-rism, n Plagiat nt

plague, plehg, n Seuche f; fig Plage f; v plagen

plaice, plehss, n Scholle f

plain, plehn, adj (simple) einfach; (looks) unansehnlich; (clear) klar; n Ebene f; **–clothes,** adj in Zivil

plaintiff, plehn-tiff, n Kläger m

plaintive, plehn-tiw, adj klagend

plait, plätt, n Zopf m; v flechten

plan, plänn, n Plan m; (draft) Entwurf m; v planen; (intend) vorhaben

plane, plehn, n (aeroplane)

Flugzeug nt; (tool) Hobel
m; v hobeln; – **tree**, n
Platane f

planet, plänn-itt, n Planet m

plank, plänk, n Planke f,
Brett nt

plant, plahnt, n Pflanze f;
(factory) Fabrik f; mech
Anlage f; v pflanzen;
–ation, n Plantage f

plaque, plahk, n (board)
Gedenktafel f; (on teeth)
Belag m

plaster, plahss-ter, n Gips m;
(building) Verputz m; med
Gipsverband m; (sticking)
Pflaster nt; v (wall)
verputzen; (fig cover)
beschmieren

plastic, pläss-tick, adj (of
plastic) Plastik-; (arts)
plastisch; n Kunststoff m;
– **bag**, n Plastiktüte f; –
surgery, n plastische
Chirurgie f

plate, pleht, n (dish) Teller
m; (sheet) Platte f; (silver)
Silber nt; v (gold)
vergolden; (silver)
versilbern

plateau, plätt-oh, n
Hochebene f

plate glass, pleht glahss, n
Flachglas nt

platform, plätt-form, n (in
hall) Plattform f; Tribüne
f; (railway) Bahnsteig m

platinum, plätt-i-nem, n
Platin m

plausible, plo'a-si-b'l, adj
plausibel

play, pleh, n Spiel nt; theatre
Stück nt; v spielen; **–er**,
n Spieler m; **–ful**, adj
verspielt; (fun) scherzhaft;
–ground, n Spielplatz;
–group, n Krabbelgruppe
f; **–ing field**, n Spielfeld
nt; **–mate**, n Spiel-
kamerad m

plea, plie, n (request) Bitte
f; law Verteidigungsrede f

plead, plied, v (give as
excuse) sich
entschuldigen; law
plädieren; – **for sth**, v um
etw bitten; – **with sb**, v an
jdn appellieren

pleasant, ples-'nt, adj
angenehm

please, plies, v gefallen; **–!**
bitte!; **–d**, adj erfreut; **–d
to meet you**, angenehm; –
yourself! ganz wie du
willst!

pleasing, plie-sing, adj
angenehm

pleasure, plesch-er, n
Vergnügen nt; **with –**,
gern (geschehen)

pledge, pledsch, n (object)
Pfand nt; (oath) Gelübde
nt; v (pawn) verpfänden;
(promise) versprechen

plenty, plenn-ti, n Fülle f; –
of, viel, genügend

pleurisy, pluhr-ri-ssi, n
Rippenfellentzündung f

pliable, plei-e-b'l, adj
geschmeidig

pliers, plei-ers, npl
Drahtzange f

plight, pleit, n Notlage f

plimsoll, plimm-ss'l, n
Turnschuh m

plod, plodd, v (walk slowly)
trotten; (work) sich
abmühen; – **along**, v
dahintrotten; **–der**, n
Arbeitstier nt

plot, plott, n (conspiracy)
Komplott nt; (land)
Grundstück nt; (story)
Handlung f; v (heimlich)
planen

plotter, plott-er, n
(conspirator) Verschwörer
m; (machine) Plotter m

plough, plau, n Pflug m; v
pflügen; – **through**, v
(sich) durchkämpfen

ploy, pleu, n Trick m, Taktik
f

pluck, plack, n Mut m; v
(fruit) pflücken; (poultry)
rupfen; (string) zupfen; –
up the courage to do sth,
v den Mut zu etw finden

plug, plagg, n Pflock m;
elec Stecker m; (car)
Zündkerze f; v zustopfen;
(fam advertise) für etw
werben; – **in**, anschließen

plum, plamm, n Pflaume f

plumage, pluh-midsch, n
Gefieder nt

plumb, plamm, adj
senkrecht; n Senkblei nt; v
sondieren

plumber, plamm-er, n
Klempner m

plumbing, plamm-ing, n
(fittings) Rohre pl; (work)

Installationsarbeiten *pl*

plump, plamp, *adj* mollig; (animal) fett; **– for,** *v fam* sich entscheiden für

plunder, plann-der, *n* Beute *f*; *v* plündern

plunge, plandsch, *n* Sturz *m*; *v* tauchen; (dagger) stoßen

plural, pluhr-rel, *n* Mehrzahl *f*, Plural *m*

plus, plass, *prep* plus; **100 -,** mehr als hundert

plush(y), plasch(-i), *adj* feudal

ply, plei, *n* (wood) Sperrholz *nt*; *v* (travel) verkehren; (trade) betreiben; **–wood,** *n* Sperrholz *nt*; **3–,** *adj* (wool) dreifädig

PM, *abbr* **Prime Minister**

p.m., pie emm, *adv* (*abbr* **post meridiem**) nachmittags

pneumatic, nju-**mätt**-ick, *adj* pneumatisch, Luft-

pneumonia, nju-**moh**-ni-e, *n* Lungenentzündung *f*

poach, pohtsch, *v* (cook) pochieren; (for game) wildern; **–ed egg,** *n* verlorenes Ei *nt*; **–er,** *n* Wilddieb *m*

pocket, pock-itt, *n* Tasche *f*; *v* einstecken; **– money,** *n* Taschengeld *nt*

pod, podd, *n* Hülse *f*; (of peas) Schote *f*

poem, poh-imm, *n* Gedicht *nt*

poet, poh-itt, *n* Dichter *m*;

–ic, *adj* poetisch; **–ry,** *n* Lyrik *f*, Poesie *f*

poignant, peun-jent, *adj* ergreifend

point, peunt, *n* (tip) Spitze *f*; (score, position, *gram*) Punkt *m*; (purpose) Zweck *m*; (aspect) Seite *f*; *v* zeigen; **–ed,** *adj* spitz; **–er,** *n* Zeiger *m*; **–less,** *adj* zwecklos; **– out,** *v* hinweisen auf; **– to,** zeigen auf; **– of view,** *n* Standpunkt *m*; (opinion) Meinung *f*; **be on the – of,** *v* drauf und dran sein, etw zu tun; **come/get to the –,** *v* zur Sache kommen

poise, peus, *n* Haltung *f*

poison, peu-s'n, *n* Gift *nt*; *v* vergiften; **–ous,** *adj* giftig

poke, pohk, *n* Stoß *m*; *v* stoßen; (fire) schüren; **–r,** *n* Schüreisen *nt*; (cards) Poker *m*

poky, poh-ki, *adj* winzig, eng

Poland, poh-lend, *n* Polen *nt*

polar, poh-ler, *adj* polar, Polar-; **– bear,** *n* Eisbär *m*; **–ize,** *v* polarisieren

pole, pohl, *n* Stange *f*; (*geog, elec*) Pol *m*; **– vault,** *n* Stabhochsprung *m*

police, pe-**liess,** *n* Polizei *f*; **–man,** *n* Polizist *m*; **– station,** *n* Polizeiwache *f*; **–woman,** *n* Polizistin *f*

policy, poll-i-ssi, *n* Politik *f*; (insurance) Police *f*

polish, poll-isch, *n* (for

furniture) Politur *f*; (for floor) Wachs *nt*; (for shoes) Schuhcreme *f*; *fig* Glanz *m*; *v* polieren; wichsen; *fig* ausfeilen; **– off,** *v fam* verdrücken

polite, pe-**leit,** *adj* höflich; **–ness,** *n* Höflichkeit *f*

political, pe-**litt**-i-k'l, *adj* politisch

politician, poll-i-**tisch**-en, *n* Politiker *m*

politics, poll-i-ticks, *n* Politik *f*

poll, pohl, *n* (election) Wahl *f*; (of opinion) Umfrage *f*; *v* (votes) erhalten; **go to the –s,** *v* zur Wahl gehen

pollen, poll-en, *n* Pollen *m*

polling, poh-ling, *adj* Wahl-

pollute, pe-**luht,** *v* verunreinigen, verschmutzen

pollution, pe-**luh**-sch'n, *n* Verschmutzung *f*

polo, poh-loh, *n* Polo *nt*; **– neck,** *n* Rollkragenpullover *m*; **– shirt,** *n* Polohemd *nt*

polyester, poll-i-ess-ter, *n* Polyester *nt*

polystyrene, poll-i-**stei**-rien, *n* Styropor ® *nt*

polythene, poll-i-thien, *n* Plastik *nt*; **– bag,** *n* Plastiktüte *f*

pomegranate, pomm-i-gränn-itt, *n* Granatapfel *m*

pomp, pomp, *n* Prunk *m*; **–ous,** *adj* großspurig

pond, pond, n Teich m
ponder, ponn-der, v
nachdenken (über); **–ous,**
adj schwerfällig
pony, poh-ni, n Pony nt;
–tail, n Pferdeschwanz m
poodle, puh-d'l, n Pudel m
pool, puhl, n (swimming)
Bad nt; (of blood etc.)
Lache f; (kitty)
(gemeinsame) Kasse f;
(billiards) Poolspiel nt; v
zusammenlegen;
(**football**) **–s,** npl Toto nt
poor, por, adj (not rich,
unfortunate) arm; (not
good) schlecht, schwach;
–ly, adj & adv schlecht;
the –, npl die Armen pl
pop, popp, n (sound) Knall
m; mus Popmusik f;
(drink) Sprudel m, Brause
f; v (sound) knallen;
(burst) platzen; (fam put)
stecken; **–corn,** n Popcorn
nt; **– in/out,** v kurz
vorbeikommen/weggehen
Pope, pohp, n Papst m
poplar, popp-ler, n Pappel f
popper, popp-er, n
Druckknopf
poppy, popp-i, n Mohn m
populace, popp-ju-liss, n
Volk nt
popular, popp-ju-ler, adj
(liked) beliebt; (of the
people) Volks-, verbreitet
popularity, popp-ju-lä-ri-ti,
n Beliebtheit f,
Popularität f
populate, popp-ju-leht, v

bevölkern
population, popp-juh-leh-
sch'n, n Bevölkerung f
populous, popp-ju-less, adj
stark bevölkert
porcelain, por-ssi-linn, n
Porzellan nt
porch, portsch, n Vorhalle f;
Portal nt
porcupine, por-kju-pein, n
Stachelschwein nt
pore, por, n Pore f; **– over,** v
über etw (gründlich)
nachdenken
pork, pork, n
Schweinefleisch nt
pornography, por-nogg-re-fi,
n Pornographie f
porous, por-ress, adj porös
porpoise, por-pess, n
Schweinswal m
porridge, po-ridsch, n
Haferbrei m
port, port, n (wine)
Portwein m; (harbour)
Hafen m; (naut left)
Backbord nt; **–hole,** n
Bullauge nt
portable, port-e-b'l, adj
tragbar
portent, por-tent, n
Vorzeichen nt
porter, por-ter, n (doorman)
Portier m; (of luggage)
Träger m; **–age,** n
Trägerlohn m
portfolio, port-foh-li-oh, n
(case) Mappe f;
(ministerial, artist's)
Portefeuille nt
portion, por-sch'n, n (of

food) Portion f; (share)
(An)teil m
portly, port-li, adj beleibt,
korpulent
portrait, port-reht, n
Porträt nt
portray, por-treh, v
darstellen
Portugal, port-ju-gel, n
Portugal nt
Portuguese, port-ju-gies, adj
portugiesisch; n (person)
Portugiese m, Portugiesin
f; (language) Portugiesisch
nt
pose, pohs, n Stellung f; v
posieren; **– as,** v sich
ausgeben für
position, pe-sisch-'n, n Lage
f; (job) Stellung f;
(opinion) Standpunkt m;
v plazieren
positive, pos-i-tiw, adj
positiv; (certain) sicher
possess, pe-sess, v besitzen;
–ion, n Besitz m; **–ive,** adj
besitzergreifend
possibility, poss-i-bill-i-ti,
n Möglichkeit f
possible, poss-i-b'l, adj
möglich
possibly, poss-i-bli, adv
möglicherweise,
vielleicht; **not –,**
unmöglich
post, pohst, n (mail) Post f;
(pole) Pfosten m, Stange
f; (job) Stelle f; (place)
Posten m; v (letter)
aufgeben; (notice)
aushängen; **–age,** n Porto

nt; **–al order,** n
Postanweisung f; **–box,** n
Briefkasten m; **–card,** n
Postkarte f; **–code,** n
Postleitzahl f; **–date,** v
nachdatieren;
poster, poh-ster, n Plakat nt,
Poster nt
posterior, poss-**tier**-ri-er, n
Hinterteil nt
posterity, poss-**te**-ri-ti, n
Nachwelt f
postgraduate, pohst-
grädd-ju-et, n
Graduierte(r) m & f
posthumous, post-ju-mess,
adj postum
postman, pohst-men, n
Briefträger m
post-mortem, pohst-**mor**-
tem, n Obduktion f
post office, pohst off-iss, n
(organization) Post f;
(office) Postamt nt
postpone, pohss-**pohn,** v
aufschieben
postscript, pohst-skript, n
Nachschrift f
posture, poss-tscher, n
Stellung f, Positur f
pot, pott, n (plant, cooking)
Topf m; (coffee, tee)
Kanne f; (fam cannabis)
Hasch m; v (plant)
eintopfen
potato, pe-**teh**-toh, n
Kartoffel f
potent, poh-tent, adj kräftig,
stark
potential, pe-**tenn**-sch'l, adj
potentiell; n Potential nt

pothole, pott-hohl, n (cave)
Höhle f; (in road)
Schlagloch nt
potion, poh-sch'n, n
Trank m
potted, pott-idd, adj (plant)
Topf-; (food) eingemacht;
(condensed)
zusammengefaßt
potter, pott-er, n Töpfer m; **–y,**
n Steingut nt
potty, pott-i, adj verrückt; n
fam Töpfchen nt
pouch, pautsch, n Beutel m
poultry, pohl-tri, n
Geflügel nt
pounce (on), paunss (onn),
v sich stürzen (auf)
pound, paund, n (weight,
currency) Pfund nt;
(enclosure) Abstellplatz
m; (for dogs) Zwinger; v
zerstampfen
pour, por, v (rain, liquid)
gießen; (crowd) strömen;
–ing, adj strömend; **– out,**
(drink) einschenken
pout, paut, n Schmollmund
m; v schmollen
poverty, pow-er-ti, n Armut
f; **–stricken,** adj
notleidend
powder, pau-der, n Pulver
nt; (face) Puder m; v
pudern; **– room,** n
Damentoilette f
power, pau-er, n Macht f,
Gewalt f; (faculty)
Fähigkeit f; mech Kraft f;
elec Strom m; v betreiben;
– cut, n Stromausfall m;

–driven, adj Motor-,
Elektro-; **–ed,** adj
betrieben; **–ful,** adj
mächtig, stark; **–less,** adj
machtlos; **– point,** n
(elektrischer) Anschluß
m; **– station,** n
Kraftwerk nt
practicable, präck-ti-ke-b'l,
adj praktikabel
practical, präck-ti-k'l, adj
praktisch
practice, präck-tiss, n Praxis
f; (custom) Gebrauch m;
(exercise) Übung f;
(doctor's) Praxis f; **in –,** in
der Praxis; **out of –,** außer
Übung
practise, präck-tiss, v
(exercise) üben; med
praktizieren; (profession)
ausüben
practitioner, präck-**tisch**-e-
ner, n med praktischer
Arzt m, praktische
Ärztin f
pragmatic, prägg-**mätt**-ick,
adj pragmatisch
prairie, prehr-ri, n Prärie f
praise, prehs, n Lob nt; v
loben; **–worthy,** adj
lobenswert
pram, präm, n
Kinderwagen m
prance, prahnss, v
stolzieren; **– about,** v
herumhüpfen
prank, pränk, n Streich m
prattle, prätt-'l, n
Geschwätz nt; v schwatzen
prawn, pro'an, n Garnele f

pray, preh, *v* beten; *fig* bitten

prayer, prähr, *n* Gebet nt; **–book,** *n* Gebetbuch nt; **the Lord's P–,** Vaterunser nt

pre-, prie, *pref* Vor-, Voraus-

preach, prietsch, *v* predigen; **–er,** *n* Prediger m

precarious, pri-kehr-ri-ess, *adj* prekär, riskant

precaution, pri-ko'a-sch'n, *n* Vorsichtsmaßnahme f

precede, pri-ssied, *v* vorangehen

precedence, press-i-denss, *n* Priorität f, Vortritt m

precedent, press-i-dent, *n* Präzedenzfall m

precept, prie-ssept, *n* Lehre f, Regel f; *law* Befehl m

precinct, prie-ssinkt, *n* (district) Bezirk m; (surroundings) Gelände nt; **pedestrian –,** *n* Fußgängerzone f; **shopping –,** *n* Einkaufsviertel nt

precious, presch-ess, *adj* kostbar; Edel-

precipice, press-i-piss, *n* Abgrund m

precipitate, pri-ssipp-i-tet, *adj* übereilt

precipitate, pri-ssipp-i-teht, *v* schleudern; *fig* stürzen

precise, pri-sseiss, *adj* genau

precision, pri-ssisch-'n, *n* Präzision f

preclude, pri-kluhd, *v* ausschließen

precocious, pri-koh-schess, *adj* altklug, frühreif

preconceived, prie-ken-ssiewd, *adj* vorgefaßt

precursor, pri-kör-sser, *n* Vorgänger m

predator, predd-e-ter, *n* Raubtier nt

predecessor, prie-di-ssess-er, *n* Vorgänger m

predicament, pri-dick-e-ment, *n* Zwangslage f

predict, pri-dikt, *v* prophezeien, vorhersagen **–able,** *adj* vorhersagbar; **–ion,** *n* Vorhersage f

predominant, pri-domm-i-nent, *adj* vorherrschend; **–ly,** *adv* überwiegend

pre-eminent, prie-emm-i-nent, *adj* hervorragend

pre-empt, prie-empt, *v* vorwegnehmen

preface, preff-iss, *n* Vorwort m

prefect, prie-fekt, *n* Präfekt m; (in school) Aufseher m

prefer, pri-för, *v* vorziehen; bevorzugen; lieber tun/haben

preferably, preff-e-reb-li, *adv* lieber

preference, pref-e-renss, *n* Vorzug m

prefix, prie-ficks, *n* Vorsilbe f; *v* voransetzen

pregnancy, pregg-nen-ssi, *n* Schwangerschaft f

pregnant, pregg-nent, *adj* schwanger; (animal) trächtig

prejudice, predsch-ju-diss, *n* Vorurteil nt; *v* beeinträchtigen; **–d,** *adj* voreingenommen; **without –,** *comm* unter Vorbehalt

prejudicial, predsch-ju-disch-'l, *adj* nachteilig

preliminary, pri-limm-i-ne-ri, *adj* einleitend; *n* Vorbereitung f

prelude, prell-juhd, *n* Vorspiel nt; *fig* Auftakt m

premature, premm-e-tschuhr, *adj* vorzeitig

premeditated, prie-medd-i-teh-tidd, *adj* vorbedacht

premier, premm-i-er, *adj* erste(r/s); *n* Premierminister m

premise, premm-iss, *n* Voraussetzung f; **–s,** *npl* (building) Gebäude nt; (buildings and land) Gelände nt

premium, prie-mi-em, *adj* erstklassig; *n* Prämie f; **be at a –,** hoch im Kurs stehen

preparation, prepp-e-reh-sch'n, *n* Vorbereitung f

prepare, pri-pähr, *v* (sich) vorbereiten; **– for,** sich vorbereiten auf

preponderance, pri-ponn-de-renss, *n* Übergewicht nt

preposition, pre-pe-sisch-'n, *n* Präposition f

preposterous, pri-poss-te-ress, *adj* absurd

prerogative, pri-rogg-e-tiv, *n*

Vorrecht *nt*

prescribe, pri-**skreib,** *v*
vorschreiben; *med*
verschreiben

prescription, priss-**kripp**-
sch'n, *n med* Rezept *nt*

presence, pres-**enss,** *n*
Gegenwart *f*,
Geistesgegenwart *f*

present, pres-**ent,** *adj*
gegenwärtig; anwesend; *n*
Gegenwart *f*; (gift)
Geschenk *nt*; **–ation,** *n*
Vorstellung *f*; (of gift)
Überreichung *f*; **–ly,** *adv*
sofort

present, pri-**sent,** *v*
präsentieren, vorstellen; **–
sb with sth,** jdm etw
schenken

preservation, pres-er-**weh**-
sch'n, *n* Erhaltung *f*

preservative, pri-**sör**-we-tiw,
n Konservierungsmittel *nt*

preserve, pri-**sörw,** *n*
Eingemachtes *nt*; *v*
(maintain) erhalten; (fruit
etc.) einmachen

preside (over), pri-**seid** (oh-
wer), *v* vorsitzen

president, pres-**i**-dent, *n*
Präsident *m*; (chairman)
Vorsitzende(r) *m* & *f*

press, press, *n* Presse *f*; *v*
drücken; (clothes) bügeln;
(encourage) drängen; **–
conference,** *n*
Pressekonferenz *f*; **–ing,**
adj dringend

pressure, presh-**er,** *n* Druck
m; **– group,** *n* Pressure-

group *f*, Interessenverband
m

prestige, press-**tiesch,** *n*
Prestige *nt*

prestigious, press-**tidsch**-ess,
adj renommiert

presumably, pri-**sjuh**-meb-li,
adv vermutlich

presume, pri-**sjuhm,** *v*
vermuten

presumption, pri-**samp**-
sch'n, *n* (assumption)
Annahme *f*; (arrogance)
Anmaßung *f*

pretence, pri-**tenss,** *n*
Vorwand *m*

pretend, pri-**tend,** *v*
vorgeben

pretentious, pri-**tenn**-schess,
adj großspurig

pretext, prie-**tekst,** *n*
Vorwand *m*

pretty, pritt-**i,** *adj* hübsch;
adv fam ziemlich

prevail, pri-**wehl,** *v*
vorherrschen; **– upon sb,**
auf jdn einwirken

prevalent, prew-**e**-lent, *adj*
vorherrschend

prevent, pri-**went,** *v*
verhindern; **–ion,** *n*
Verhinderung *f*; **–ive,** *adj*
vorbeugend

preview, prie-**wjuh,** *n*
Vorschau *f*

previous(ly), prie-**wi**-ess(-
li), *adj & adv* früher

prey, preh, *n* Beute *f*, Raub
m; **– on,** *v* rauben; *fig* sehr
zusetzen

price, preiss, *n* Preis *m*;

–less, *adj* unschätzbar

prick, prick, *n* Stich *m*; *v*
stechen

prickle, prick-**'l,** *n*
Stachel *m*

prickly, prick-**li,** *adj*
stachelig

pride, preid, *n* Stolz *m*; **–
o.s. (on),** *v* sich brüsten
(mit)

priest, priest, *n* Priester *m*

prig, prigg, *n* Besserwisser *m*

prim, primm, *adj* steif

primary, prei-**me**-ri, *adj*
(original) ursprünglich;
(main) Haupt-; **– school,**
n Grundschule *f*

primate, prei-**mitt,** *n* (ape)
Primat *m*

prime, preim, *adj* (main)
Haupt-; (quality)
erstklassig; (number)
Prim-; *n* Blüte *f*; *v*
(prepare) vorbereiten;
(gun) laden; **P– Minister,**
n Premierminister *m*

primitive, primm-**i**-tiw, *adj*
primitiv

primrose, primm-**rohs,** *n*
Primel *f*

prince, prinss, *n* Prinz *m*,
Fürst *m*

princely, prinss-**li,** *adj*
fürstlich

princess, prinn-**ssess,** *n*
Prinzessin *f*, Fürstin *f*

principal, prinn-**ssi**-p'l, *adj*
hauptsächlich, Haupt-; *n*
(school) Direktor *m*;
(chief) Chef *m*

principle, prinn-**ssi**-p'l, *n*

Prinzip nt, Grundsatz m;
in –, im Prinzip; on –, aus
Prinzip

print, print, n Druck m;
photog Abzug m; v
drucken; (in capitals) in
Druckbuchstaben
schreiben; **–er**, n Drucker
m; **–ing**, n Druck m; photog
Abziehen nt; **–ing works**,
n Druckerei f; **out of –**, adj
vergriffen

prior, **prei**-er, adj früher; n
Prior m; **– to**, conj bevor;
prep vor

priority, prei-o-ri-ti, n
(precedence) Vorrang m;
(urgent thing) Priorität f

prise open, preis oh-pen, v
aufstemmen

prison, **pris**-'n, n Gefängnis
nt; **–er**, Gefangene(r)
m & f

pristine, **priss**-tien, adj
unberührt

privacy, **priw**-e-ssi, n
Zurückgezogenheit f,
Privatsphäre f

private, **prei**-witt, adj privat,
Privat-; n einfacher Soldat
m; **– eye**, n Privatdetektiv
m; **in –**, privat

privatize, **prei**-we-teis, v
privatisieren

privilege, **priw**-i-lidsch, n
Vorrecht nt, Privileg nt;
–d, adj privilegiert

prize, preis, n Preis m; v
schätzen; **– idiot**, n fam
Vollidiot m; **–winner**, n
Preisträger m

pro, proh, n Profi m; prep
für; **the –s and cons**, das
Für und Wider

probability, probb-e-**bill**-i-ti,
n Wahrscheinlichkeit f

probable, probb-e-b'l, adj
wahrscheinlich

probably, probb-e-bli, adv
wahrscheinlich

probation, pre-beh-sch'n, n
Probezeit f; law
Bewährung f

probe, prohb, v sondieren,
prüfen

problem, **probb**-lem, n
Problem nt, Aufgabe f

procedure, pre-**ssie**-dscher,
n Verfahren nt

proceed, pre-**ssied**, v (act)
vorgehen; (continue)
fortfahren; (go forward)
weiterfahren,
weitergehen; **–ings**, npl
(events) Vorgänge pl; law
Verfahren nt

proceeds, proh-ssieds, npl
Ertrag m

process, **proh**-ssess, n
Verfahren nt; chem
Prozeß m

procession, pre-**ssesch**-'n, n
Prozession f

proclaim, pre-klehm, v
bekanntmachen

proclamation, prock-le-
meh-sch'n, n
Proklamation f

procrastination, pre-krääss-
ti-neh-sch'n, n Aufschub
m, Verzögerung f

procure, pre-**kjuhr**, v

verschaffen; (sex) kuppeln

prod, prodd, n Stich m; v
stoßen, stechen

prodigal, prodd-i-g'l, adj
verschwenderisch; n
Verschwender m

prodigious, pre-**didsch**-ess,
adj ungeheuer

prodigy, prodd-i-dschi, n
Wunder nt; **child –**, n
Wunderkind nt

produce, prodd-juss, n
Erzeugnis nt

produce, pre-**djuss**, v (crop)
erzeugen; (goods)
herstellen; (effect)
hervorrufen; (play)
produzieren, inszenieren

producer, pre-**djuh**-sser, n
Produzent m; (theatre,
film) Produzent m

product, prodd-akt, n
Produkt nt, Erzeugnis nt

production, pre-**duck**-sch'n,
n Produktion f,
Herstellung f; theatre
Inszenierung f; **– line**, n
Fließband nt

profane, pre-fehn, adj
(secular) profan;
(language) profan

profess, pre-fess, v vorgeben

profession, pre-fesch-'n, n
Beruf m; **–al**, adj Berufs-; n
Profi m

professor, pre-fess-er, n
Professor m

proficiency, pre-fisch-en-ssi,
n Tüchtigkeit f

proficient, pre-fisch-ent, adj
bewandt

profile, proh-feil, n Profil nt;
fig Umriß m

profit, proff-itt, n Gewinn
m; v gewinnen; **–able,** adj
einträglich; **–eer,** n
Schieber m

profound, pre-**faund,** adj
tief; (thorough) gründlich

profuse, pre-**fjuss,** adj
reichlich; **–ly,** adv
(thanks)
überschwenglich; (sweat)
stark

profusion (of), pre-**fjuh**-
sch'n (ew), n Überfluß m
(an)

program, proh-grämm, n
comp Programm nt; v
programmieren

programme, proh-grämm, n
Programm nt; (broadcast)
Sendung f

programmer, proh-
grämm-er, n comp
Programmierer m

progress, proh-gress, n
Fortschritt m; **in –,** im
Gang

progress, pre-**gress,** v
vorwärts kommen

progression, pre-**gresch**-'n,
n (succession) Folge
f; (development)
Fortschritt m

prohibit, pre-**hibb**-itt, v
verbieten; **–ed,** adj
verboten

prohibition, proh-i-**bisch**-'n,
n Verbot nt

prohibitive, pro-**hibb**-i-tiw,
adj untragbar

project, prodsch-ekt, n
Projekt nt

project, pre-**dschekt,** v
(predict) prognostizieren;
(stick out) herausragen;
–ile, n Geschoß nt; **–ion,** n
(prediction) Prognose f;
(protrusion) Vorsprung m

proletariat, proh-li-**tähr**-ri-
et, n Proletariat nt

prolific, pre-**liff**-ick, adj
fruchtbar; fig produktiv

prologue, proh-logg, n
' Prolog m

prolong, pre-**long,** v
verlängern

prom, promm, abbr
promenade concert

promenade, prom-i-**nahd,** n
(walk) Spaziergang m;
(avenue) Promenade f; **–
concert,** n
Promenadenkonzert nt

prominent, promm-i-nent,
adj (important)
hervorragend; (striking)
auffallend

promiscuous, pre-**miss**-kju-
ess, adj häufig den Partner
wechselnd

promise, promm-iss, n
Versprechen nt; v
versprechen

promising, promm-iss-ing,
adj vielversprechend

promote, pre-**moht,** v
fördern

promoter, pre-**moh**-ter, n
Förderer m; (organiser)
Veranstalter m

promotion, pre-**moh**-sch'n,

n (of person) Beförderung
f; (of product) Werbung f

prompt, prompt, adj prompt;
v theatre souflieren;
(induce) anregen; **–er,** n
Souffleur m; **–ly,** adv
schnell; sofort

prone, prohn, adj
langgestreckt, liegend; **–
to,** geneigt zu

prong, prong, n Zinke f

pronoun, proh-naun, n
Pronomen nt, Fürwort nt

pronounce, pre-**naunss,** v
aussprechen; (judgement)
verkünden; **–d,** adj
ausgesprochen; **–ment,** n
Erklärung f

pronunciation, pre-nann-
ssi-**eh**-sch'n, n Aussprache
f

proof, pruhf, adj standhaft;
n Beweis m; (printer's)
Abzug m; (alcoholic
strength) Alkoholgehalt
m

prop, propp, n Stütze f;
theatre Requisite f; **– up,** v
stützen

propaganda, propp-e-**gänn**-
de, n Propaganda f

propagate, propp-e-geht, v
fortpflanzen; fig verbreiten

propel, pre-**pell,** v treiben;
–lant, n Treibmittel nt;
–ler, n Propeller m

proper, propp-er, adj
passend; (decent)
anständig; **–ly,** adv richtig

property, propp-er-ti, n
(possession) Eigentum nt;

(land) Immobilien pl;
(quality) Eigenschaft f

prophecy, proff-i-ssi, n
Prophezeiung f

prophesy, proff-i-ssei, v
prophezeien

prophet, proff-itt, n
Prophet m

proportion, pre-por-sch'n, n
Verhältnis nt; (share)
Anteil m; **–al,** adj
proportional; **–s,** npl
Proportionen pl

proposal, pre-poh-s'l, n
Vorschlag m; (of marriage)
Heiratsantrag m

propose, pre-pohs, v
vorschlagen; (marriage)
einen Heiratsantrag
machen

proprietor, pre-prei-e-ter, n
Besitzer m, Eigentümer m

proprietress, pro-prei-e-triss,
n Besitzerin f

propriety, pre-prei-e-ti, n
Schicklichkeit f

pro rata, proh rah-te, adv
anteilmäßig

prose, prohs, n Prosa f

prosecute, pross-i-kjuht, v
law anklagen

**prosecution, pross-i-kjuh-
sch'n,** n Anklage f

prospect, pross-pekt, n
Aussicht f

prospective, pre-speck-tiw,
adj zukünftig

prospectus, pre-speck-tess, n
Prospekt m; (university)
Studienführer m

prosper, pross-per, v

gedeihen

prosperity, pross-pe-ri-ti, n
Wohlstand m

prosperous, pross-pe-ress,
adj wohlhabend

prostitute, pross-ti-tjuht, n
Prostituierte f; v
prostituieren

prostrate, pross-treht, adj
(lying) ausgestreckt; fig
niedergeschlagen

protect, pre-tekt, v
beschützen; **–ion,** n
Schutz m; **–ive,** adj
schützend, Schutz-

protein, proh-tien, n
Protein nt

protest, proh-test, n
Einspruch m, Protest m

protest, pre-test, v (declare)
beteuern; **– (against),**
protestieren (gegen); **–er,**
n Demonstrant m

protracted, pre-träck-tidd,
adj langwierig

protrude, pre-truhd, v
herausragen

proud (of), praud (ew), adj
stolz (auf)

prove, pruhw, v
(demonstrate) beweisen;
(turn out) sich erweisen

proverb, prow-örb, n
Sprichwort nt; **–ial,** adj
stichwörtlich

provide, pre-weid, v
versorgen; **– for,**
vorsorgen für

**provided (that), pre-wei-
didd (dhet),** conj
vorausgesetzt (, daß)

providence, prow-i-denss, n
Vorsehung f

**providing (that), pre-wei-
ding (dhet),** conj
vorausgesetzt (, daß)

province, prow-inss, n
Provinz f; fig Bereich m

provincial, pre-winn-sch'l,
adj Provinz-; pej
provinzlerisch

provision, pre-wisch-'n, n
Vorkehrung f; **–al,** adj
provisorisch; **–s,** npl
Lebensmittel pl

proviso, pre-wei-soh, n
Bedingung f

**provocation, prow-e-keh-
sch'n,** n Provokation f,
Herausforderung f

**provocative, pre-wock-e-
tiw,** adj provozierend; –
(sexually) aufreizend

provoke, pre-wohk, v
(irritate) herausfordern,
reizen; (cause)
hervorrufen

prow, prau, n Bug m

prowess, prau-ess, n
(valour) Tapferkeit f;
(skill) Können nt

prowl, praul, v
herumstreifen; **–er,** n
jemand, der herumstreift

proximity, prock-ssi-mi-ti, n
Nähe f

proxy, prock-ssi, n
Stellvertreter m; **by –,** in
Vertretung; durch einen
Bevollmächtigten

prudence, pruh-denss, n
Überlegtheit f

prudent, pruh-dent, *adj*
vorsichtig, überlegt
prudish, pruh-disch, *adj*
prüde
prune, pruhn, *n*
Backpflaume *f*; *v*
(be)schneiden
pry (into), prei (**inn**-tu), *v*
herumschnüffeln
PS, pie ess, *abbr* **postscript**
psalm, ssahm, *n* Psalm *m*
pseudonym, sjuh-de-nimm,
n Pseudonym *nt*
psychiatric, sei-ki-**ätt**-rick,
adj psychiatrisch
psychiatrist, sei-**kei**-*e*-trist,
n Psychiater *m*
psychic, sei-kick, *adj*
(phenomenon, person)
übersinnlich; *n*
Hellseher *m*
psychoanalyst, sei-koh-
änn-*e*-list, *n*
Psychoanalytiker *m*
psychological, sei-ke-
lodsch-ick-'l, *adj*
psychologisch
psychology, sei-**koll**-*e*-dschi,
n Psychologie *f*
psychopath, sei-koh-päth, *n*
Psychopath *m*
PTO, pie tie oh, *abbr* **please
turn over,** bitte wenden
pub, pabb, *n* Kneipe *f*
public, pabb-lick, *adj*
öffentlich; *n*
Öffentlichkeit *f*
publican, pabb-li-ken, *n*
(Gast)wirt *m*
publication, pabb-li-**keh**-
sch'n, *n* Veröffentlichung *f*

public house, pabb-lick
hauss, *n* Wirtshaus *nt*
publicity, pabb-**liss**-i-ti, *n*
Werbung *f*
publish, pabb-lisch, *v*
veröffentlichen; **–er,** *n*
Verleger *m*; **–ing,** *n*
Verlagswesen *nt*
pucker, pack-er, *v* runzeln
pudding, pudd-ing, *n*
Pudding *m*; **black –,** *n*
Blutwurst *f*
puddle, padd-'l, *n* Pfütze *f*,
Lache *f*
puerile, pjuhr-reil, *adj*
kindisch
puff, paff, *n* (breath) Hauch
m; (of wind) Stoß *m*; (of
cigarette) Zug *m*; *v*
schnaufen; **–ed,** *adj fam*
außer Puste; **– pastry,** *n*
Blätterteig *m*; **– up,** sich
aufblasen; **–y,** *adj*
geschwollen; **powder–,** *n*
Puderquaste *f*
pull, pull, *n* Zug *m*;
(attraction)
Anziehungskraft *f*; *v*
ziehen; reißen; **– down,**
(demolish) abreißen; **–
one's weight,** sich voll
einsetzen; **– o.s. together,**
sich zusammenreißen; **–
sb's leg,** jdn anführen
pulley, pull-i, *n* Rolle *f*,
Flaschenzug *m*
pullover, pull-oh-wer, *n*
Pullover *m*
pulp, palp, *n* Brei *m*; (fruit)
Fruchtfleisch *nt*; *v* zu Brei
machen; **wood–,** *n*

Holzschliff *m*
pulpit, pull-pitt, *n* Kanzel *f*
pulse, palss, *n* Puls *m*
pulverize, pall-we-reis, *v*
pulverisieren
pumice-stone, pamm-iss-
stohn, *n* Bimsstein *m*
pump, pamp, *n* Pumpe *f*; *v*
pumpen; **– up,** aufpumpen
pun, pann, *n* Wortspiel *nt*
punch, pantsch, *n* (blow)
Schlag *m*; (tool)
Locheisen *nt*; (drink)
Punsch *m*; *v* schlagen,
boxen; **–line,** *n* Pointe *f*
punctual, pank-tju-el, *adj*
pünktlich
punctuate, pank-tju-eht, *v*
(text) mit Satzzeichen
versehen; (interrupt)
unterbrechen
punctuation, pank-tju-**eh**-
sch'n, *n* Zeichensetzung *f*
puncture, pank-tscher, *n*
Stich *m*; (in tyre)
Reifenpanne *f*; *v*
durchstechen; (tyre) platt
werden
pungent, pann-dschent, *adj*
scharf, beißend
punish, pann-isch, *v*
bestrafen, strafen; **–able,**
adj strafbar; **–ment,** *n*
Strafe *f*
punitive, pjuh-ni-tiw, *adj*
rigoros
punt, pant, *n* Stechkahn *m*;
v staken; **–er,** *n fam*
Zocker *m*
puny, pjuh-ni, *adj*
schwächlich

pupil, pjuh-pill, n (at school) Schüler m; (of eye) Pupille f

puppet, papp-itt, n Marionette f

puppy, papp-i, n Hündchen nt

purchase, pör-tschiss, n (buy) Einkauf m; (grasp) Halt m; v einkaufen; **-r**, n Käufer m

pure(ly), pjuhr(-li), adj & adv rein

puree, pjuhr-reh, n Püree nt; v pürieren

purgatory, pör-ge-te-ri, n Fegefeuer nt

purge, pördsch, v reinigen; med abführen

purify, pjuhr-ri-fei, v reinigen

purity, pjuhr-ri-ti, n Reinheit f

purple, pör-p'l, adj lila, violett; n Lila nt, Violett nt

purport, per-port, v besagen

purpose, pör-pess, n (intention) Absicht f; (goal) Zweck m; **-ful**, adj zielstrebig; **-ly**, adv absichtlich; **on -**, adv absichtlich

purr, pörr, v schnurren

purse, pörss, n Geldbeutel m; Portemonnaie nt; v kräuseln

purser, pör-sser, n Zahlmeister m

pursue, per-ssjuh, v (prey) verfolgen; (aim)

nachstreben

pursuit, per-ssjuht, n (chase) Verfolgung f; (occupation) Beschäftigung f

purveyor, per-weh-er, n Lieferant m

pus, pass, n Eiter m

push, pusch, n Stoß m, Schub m; v stoßen, schieben; (press) drücken; (put forward) fördern; **-y**, adj (allzu) ehrgeizig

puss(y), puss(-i), n Miezekatze f

put, putt, v (lay) legen; (stand) stellen; (set) setzen; **- across**, erklären; **- away**, wegräumen; **- down**, (animal) einschläfern; (rebellion) unterdrücken; **- off**, (delay) aufschieben; **- sb off sth**, (discourage) jdn von etw abbringen; **- on**, (clothes) anziehen; (event) veranstalten; (light etc.) anschalten; **- out**, (light etc.) ausschalten; (circulate) verbreiten; **- up**, (lodge) unterbringen; **- up with**, sich gefallen lassen

putrefy, pjuh-tri-fei, v verfaulen

putrid, pjuh-tridd, adj faul

putt, patt, n Putt m; v putten; **-ing**, n Putten nt

putty, patt-i, n Kitt m

puzzle, pas-'l, n Rätsel nt; Puzzle(spiel) nt; v

verwirren; **- over**, v herumrätseln an;

crossword -, n Kreuzworträtsel nt

pyjamas, pi-dschah-mes, npl Schlafanzug m, Pyjama m

pylon, pei-len, n Pylon m, Mast m

pyramid, pi-re-midd, n Pyramide f

Pyrenees, pi-re-nies, npl Pyrenäen pl

python, pei-then, n Python m, Riesenschlange f

quack, ku'äck, n (sound) Quaken nt; (pej doctor) Quacksalber m; v quaken

quadrangle, ku'odd-räng-g'l, n (courtyard) Hof m; (shape) Viereck nt

quadruple, ku'odd-ru-p'l, adj vierfach

quadruplets, ku'odd-ruh-plet, npl, Vierlinge pl

quagmire, ku'ägg-meir, n Sumpf m

quail, ku'ehl, n Wachtel f; v verzagen

quaint, ku'ehnt, adj drollig, kurios

quake, ku'ehk, v beben; (earth)–, n Erdbeben nt

qualification, ku'oll-i-fi-keh-sch'n, n

(achievement) Qualifikation f; (limitation) Einschränkung f

qualified, k'uoll-i-feid, adj qualifiziert; (limited) eingeschränkt

qualify, ku'oll-i-fei, v sich qualifizieren; (entitle) berechtigen; (limit) einschränken

quality, ku'oll-i-ti, n Qualität f; (characteristic) Eigenschaft f

qualms, ku'ahms, npl Bedenken pl

quandary, ku'onn-de-ri, n Dilemma nt

quantity, ku'onn-ti-ti, n Menge f

quarantine, ku'o-ren-tien, n Quarantäne f

quarrel, ku'o-rel, n Streit m; v sich streiten; **–some,** adj streitsüchtig

quarry, ku'o-ri, n (pit) Steinbruch m; (prey) Beute f

quart, ku'ort, n Quart nt

quarter, ku'or-ter, n Viertel nt; (period) Vierteljahr nt; v vierteln; (mil lodge) einquartieren; **–ly,** adj & adv vierteljährlich; **–final,** n Viertelfinale nt; **–master,** n Quartiermeister m; **–s,** npl Quartier nt

quartet, ku'or-tett, n Quartett nt

quartz, ku'orts, n Quarz m

quash, ku'osch, v law aufheben

quaver, ku'eh-wer, n mus Achtelnote f; v zittern

quay, kie, n Kai m, Ufermauer f

queasy, ku'ie-si, adj übel

queen, ku'ien, n Königin f

queer, ku'ier, adj sonderbar; (homosexual) schwul; n (homosexual man) Schwuler m; (lesbian) Lesbe f

quell, ku'ell, v (rebellion) unterdrücken; (fears) stillen

quench, ku'entsch, v löschen

querulous, ku'e-ru-less, adj gereizt

query, ku'ier-ri, n Frage f; v in Frage stellen

quest, ku'est, n Suche f

question, ku'ess-tschen, n Frage f; v (doubt) bezweifeln; (enquire) fragen; (interrogate) verhören; **–able,** adj fraglich; **– mark,** n Fragezeichen nt; **–naire,** n Fragebogen m; **out of the –,** ausgeschlossen

queue, kjuh, n Schlange f; v anstehen, Schlange stehen

quibble, ku'ibb-'l, v streiten

quick, ku'ick, adj schnell; (wit) lebhaft; **cut to the –,** v tief treffen; **–en,** v beschleunigen; **–ly,** adv schnell; **–sand,** n Treibsand m; **–silver,** n Quecksilber nt; **–-witted,** adj schlagfertig

quiet, ku'ei-et, adj (peaceful) ruhig, still; (not loud) leise; n Ruhe f, Stille f; **–en,** v beruhigen; **–ly,** adj leise, ruhig

quilt, ku'ilt, n Steppdecke f; **–ing,** n Steppen nt; (material) gesteppter Stoff m

quince, ku'inss, n Quitte f

quinine, ku'i-nien, n Chinin nt

quintuplets, ku'inn-tjuh-plet, npl Fünflinge pl

quit, ku'itt, v (leave) verlassen; (resign) kündigen; (give up)
aufgeben; (stop) aufhören

quite, ku'eit, adv (totally) ganz, völlig; (fairly) ziemlich; **–! **genau!

quits, ku'itts, adj quitt

quiver, ku'iw-er, n (sheath) Köcher m; v beben, zittern

quiz, ku'is, n Quiz nt; v befragen; **–zical,** adj fragend; (mocking) spöttisch

quota, ku'oh-te, n Quote f

quotation, ku'oh-teh-sch'n, n (text) Zitat nt; (price) Kostenvoranschlag m; **– marks,** npl Anführungszeichen pl

quote, ku'oht, n Kostenvoranschlag m; v (give price) (den Preis) angeben; (cite) zitieren

rabbi, räbb-ei, n Rabbiner m

rabbit, räbb-it, n Kaninchen nt

rabble, räbb-'l, n Gesindel nt, Pöbel m

rabid, reh-bidd, adj tollwütig; fig rasend, wütend

rabies, reh-bies, n Tollwut f

race, rehss, n (breed) Rasse f; (contest) Wettrennen nt; (motor) Rennen nt; v rennen; –course, n Rennstrecke f; –horse, n Rennpferd nt; –s, npl Pferderennen nt; –track, n Rennstrecke f

racial, reh-sch'l, adj rassisch

racism, reh-ssism, n Rassismus m

racist, reh-ssist, adj rassistisch; n Rassist m

rack, räck, n Gestell nt; (for luggage) Ablage f; (on vehicle) Gepäckträger m; v – one's brains, sich den Kopf zerbrechen

racket, räck-itt, n (noise) Lärm m; (swindle) Schwindel m; (tennis) (Tennis)schläger m

racquet, räck-itt, n (Tennis)schläger m

radar, reh-dar, n Radar m/nt

radial, reh-di-el, adj radial

radiant, reh-di-ent, adj strahlend

radiate, reh-di-eht, v ausstrahlen; – from, (of roads) strahlenförmig ausgehen von

radiation, reh-di-eh-sch'n, n Strahlung f

radiator, reh-di-eh-ter, n Heizkörper m; (in car) Kühler m

radical, rädd-i-k'l, adj radikal; n Radikale(r)

m & f

radio, reh-di-oh, n Radio nt; –active, adj radioaktiv; – station, n Rundfunkstation f

radiotherapy, reh-di-oh-the-re-pi, n Strahlentherapie f

radish, rädd-isch, n Radieschen nt; (mooli) Rettich m

radius, reh-di-ess, n Radius m; (area around) Umkreis m

raffle, räff-'l, n Verlosung f; v verlosen

raft, rahft, n Floß nt

rafter, rahf-ter, n Sparren m

rag, rägg, n Lumpen m; (fam newspaper) Käseblatt nt

rage, rehdsch, n Wut f; v wüten, rasen; all the –, der letzte Schrei

ragged, rägg-idd, adj ausgefranst, kaputt

raid, rehd, n Überfall m; mil Angriff m; (police) Razzia f; v überfallen

rail, rehl, adj Eisenbahn-; n (railway) Schiene f; (stairs) Geländer nt; –way, n Eisenbahn f; –way station, n Bahnhof m; by –, mit dem Zug

rain, rehn, n Regen m; v regnen; –bow, n Regenbogen m; –coat, n Regenmantel m; –fall, n Niederschlag m; – forest, n Regenwald f; –y, adj regnerisch

raise, rehs, v (hoch)heben;

(increase) erhöhen;
(family) großziehen;
(money) aufbringen;
(voice) erheben

raisin, reh-sinn, n Rosine f

rake, rehk, n Rechen m;
(person) Draufgänger m; v
rechen; (fire) schüren;
(with gunfire) bestreichen

rally, räll-i, n (political)
Versammlung f; (car)
Rallye f; v (collect)
sammeln; **– round**, sich
zusammentun

ram, rämm, n (animal)
Widder m; (weapon)
Rammklotz m; v rammen

ramble, rämm-b'l, n
Wanderung f; v wandern;
(of mind) irre sein; (talk)
zusammenhanglos
quasseln

ramp, rämp, n Rampe f

rampage, rämm-pedsch, n
go on the –, v randalieren

rampant, rämm-pent, adj
zügellos

rampart, rämm-pahrt, n
(Festungs)wall m

rancid, ränn-ssidd, adj
ranzig

random, ränn-dem, adj
willkürlich; **at –**, adv
willkürlich, aufs
Geratewohl

randy, ränn-di, adj fam geil

range, rehndsch, n (choice)
Auswahl f, Sortiment nt;
(of mountains) Kette f;
(extent) Umfang m; (of
weapon) Schußweite f;

(cooker) Herd m; v
(roam) umherziehen;
(extend) reichen; (line
up) ordnen; **rifle –**, n
Schießplatz m

ranger, rehndsch-er, n
Aufseher m; (forest)
Förster m

rank, ränk, adj (offensive)
stark, stinkend; (utter)
total; n (grade) Rang m;
(row) Reihe f; v
klassifizieren; **– among**, v
gehören zu; **– and file**, n
Basis f; **taxi –**,
n Taxistand m

rankle, räng-k'l, v fam
wurmen

ransack, ränn-ssäck, v
durchstöbern,
durchwühlen

ransom, ränn-ssem, n
Lösegeld nt; v auslösen

rant, ränt, v wettern

rap, räpp, n (blow) Schlag
m; mus Rap m; v (hit)
schlagen; (knock) klopfen

rape, rehp, n
Vergewaltigung f; (plant)
Raps m; v vergewaltigen

rapid, räpp-idd, adj rasch,
schnell; **–ity**, n
Schnelligkeit f; **–s**, npl
Stromschnelle f

rapist, reh-pist, n
Vergewaltiger m

rapture, räpp-tscher, n
Entzücken nt

rare, rähr, adj rar, selten;
(lightly cooked) englisch
(gebraten); **–ly**, adv selten

rarity, rähr-ri-ti, n
Seltenheit f

rascal, rahss-k'l, n Schelm
m, Spitzbube m

rash, räsch, adj unbesonnen;
n Hautausschlag m

rasher, räsch-er, n
Speckscheibe f

rasp, rahsp, n Raspel f; v
raspeln; (voice) rasseln

raspberry, rahs-be-ri, n
Himbeere f

rat, rätt, n Ratte f; (pej
person) Ratte f

rate, reht, n (speed) Tempo
nt; fin Kurs m; (charge)
Preis m; (proportion)
Verhältnis nt; (tax)
Grundsteuer f; v schätzen

rather, rah-dher, adv (fairly)
ziemlich; (preferably)
lieber

ratify, rätt-i-fei, v
bestätigen, ratifizieren

ratio, reh-schi-oh, n
Verhältnis nt

ration, räsch-en, n Ration f;
v rationieren

rational, räsch-en-'l, adj
vernünftig, rational; **–ize**,
v rationalisieren

rattle, rätt-'l, n (noise)
Gerassel nt; (toy) Rassel f;
v rasseln, klappern;
–snake, n
Klapperschlange f

raucous, ro'a-kess, adj wild

ravage, räw-idsch, v
verwüsten

rave, rehw, v (rage) rasen; **–
about**, (enthuse)

schwärmen über

raven, reh-wen, n Rabe m

ravenous, räw-en-ess, adj
heißhungrig

ravine, re-wien, n
Schlucht f

raving, reh-wing, adj
(furious) rasend; (mad)
wahnsinnig

ravishing, räw-isch-ing, adj
entzückend, hinreißend

raw, ro'a, adj roh; (wound)
wund; **a – deal,** n (fam
unfair treatment)
ungerechte Behandlung f;
(bad luck) Pech nt

ray, reh, n Strahl m

raze, rehs, v vernichten

razor, reh-ser, n
Rasierapparat m; **– blade,**
n Rasierklinge f

reach, rietsch, n (stretch)
Reichweite f; (length)
Strecke f; v langen nach;
(arrive at) erreichen;
(pass) reichen; **(with)in –,**
erreichbar

react, ri-äkt, v reagieren;
–ion, n Reaktion f;
(nuclear) –or, n
(Kern)reaktor m

read, ried, v lesen; **–er,** n
(person) Leser m; (book)
Schmöker m

readily, redd-i-li, adv
(willingly) bereitwillig;
(easily) leicht

reading, rie-ding, n Lesen nt

read out, ried aut, v
vorlesen

ready, redd-i, adj bereit,

fertig; **–made,** adj Fertig-;
(clothes) Konfektions-; –
meal, n Fertigmahlzeit f

real, ri-el, adj (actual)
wirklich; (genuine) echt;
– estate, n Immobilien pl;
–istic, adj realistisch

reality, ri-äll-i-ti, n
Wirklichkeit f

realize, ri-e-leis, v
(understand) begreifen;
(plan) verwirklichen;
(income) (er)bringen

really, ri-e-li, adv wirklich,
tatsächlich

realm, relm, n Reich nt

reap, riep, v ernten; **the
grim –er,** n der Schnitter
(Tod) m

rear, rier, adj hintere(r & s),
Hinter-; n (back)
Rückseite f; mil Nachhut
f; v (child) großziehen;
(prance) sich bäumen;
bring up the –, v die
Nachhut bilden; **in the –,**
adv hinten

rearmament, rie-ahr-me-
ment, n Wiederaufrüstung
f

reason, rie-sen, n (cause,
motive) Grund m;
(intellect) Verstand m;
(sense) Vernunft f; v
diskutieren; **–able,** adj
vernünftig; (price) mäßig;
–ably, adj (sensibly)
vernünftig; (fairly)
ziemlich; **–ing,** n
Argumentation f

reassurance, rie-e-**schor-**

renss, n Beruhigung f

reassure, rie-e-**schor,** v
beruhigen

rebate, rie-beht, n Rabatt m,
Nachlaß m

rebel, rebb-'l, n Rebell m

rebel, ri-bell, v rebellieren,
sich auflehnen; **–lion,** n
Aufstand m; **–lious,** adj
rebellisch

rebirth, ri-börth, n
Wiedergeburt f

rebound, rie-baund, n
Rückprall m

rebound, ri-baund, v
zurückprallen

rebuff, ri-baff, n Abweisung
f; v abweisen

rebuke, ri-bjuhk, n Rüge f,
Tadel m; v rügen, tadeln

recalcitrant, ri-käll-ssi-
trent, adj aufsässig

recall, rie-ko'al, n
(summons) Rückruf m;
(memory)
Erinnerungsvermögen nt

recall, ri-ko'al, v (call back)
zurückrufen; (remember)
sich erinnern an

recap, rie-käpp, =
recapitulate

recapitulate, rie-ke-pitt-ju-
leht, v rekapitulieren,
(kurz) zusammenfassen

recede, ri-ssied, v
zurückweichen

receipt, ri-ssiet, n comm
Quittung f; (receiving)
Empfang m; **–s,** npl comm
Einnahmen pl

receive, ri-ssiew, v erhalten;

(visitor) empfangen; **–r,** n
(telephone) Hörer m;
(official)
Konkursverwalter m; (of
stolen goods) Hehler m
recent, rie-ssent, adj
(period) letzte(r/s);
(event) neueste(r/s);
(invention etc.) neu; adv
kürzlich, neulich
receptacle, ri-ssepp-te-k'l, n
Behälter m
reception, ri-ssepp-sch'n, n
Empfang m; (hotel)
Rezeption f; **–ist,** n
Empfangsschef m,
Empfangsdame f;
(doctor's)
Sprechstundenhilfe f
receptive, ri-ssepp-tiw, adj
empfänglich
recess, ri-ssess, n (niche)
Nische f; parl Ferien pl
recharge, rie-tschahrdsch, v
(wieder)aufladen
recipe, ress-i-pi, n Rezept nt
reciprocal, ri-ssipp-re-kel,
adj gegenseitig
recital, ri-ssei-t'l, n mus
Konzert nt
recite, ri-sseit, v rezitieren;
(list) aufzählen
reckless, reck-liss, adj
(careless) leichtsinnig;
(driving) fahrlässig
reckon, reck-'n, v
(calculate) rechnen;
(think) meinen
reclaim, ri-klehm, v
(expenses) zurückfordern;
(land) urbar machen

recline, ri-klein, v sich
lehnen, zurücklehnen
recluse, ri-kluhss, n
Einsiedler m
recognition, reck-eg-nisch-
'n, n Wiedererkennen nt;
(appreciation)
Anerkennung f
recognize, reck-eg-neis, v
erkennen; (appreciate)
anerkennen
recoil, ri-keul, v
zurückprallen; fig
zurückschrecken
recollect, reck-e-lekt, v sich
erinnern (an); **–ion,** n
Erinnerung f
recommend, reck-e-mend, v
empfehlen; **–ation,** n
Empfehlung f
recompense, reck-emm-
penss, n Entschädigung f;
(reward) Belohnung f; v
entschädigen; (reward)
belohnen
reconcile, reck-en-sseil, v
(people) versöhnen;
(facts) in Einklang
bringen; (dispute)
beilegen
reconditioned, rie-ken-
disch-'nd, adj überholt
reconnoitre, reck-e-neu-ter,
v auskundschaften
reconsider, rie-ken-ssidd-er,
v (noch einmal)
überdenken
reconstruct, rie-ken-strakt,
v wiederaufbauen; **–ion,** n
Wiederaufbau m
record, reck-ord, n (sport)

Rekord m; mus
Schallplatte f; (account)
Protokoll nt,
Aufzeichnung f;
(achievement) Leistung f
record, ri-kord, v mus
aufnehmen; (document)
festhalten
recording, ri-kor-ding, n
Aufnahme f
record player, reck-ord
pleh-er, n Plattenspieler m
recoup, ri-kuhp, v
zurückgewinnen
recourse, ri-korss, n
Zuflucht f
recover, ri-kaw-er, v
(retrieve)
zurückgewinnen; (health)
sich erholen
re-cover, rie-kaw-er, v neu
überziehen
recovery, ri-kaw-e-ri, n (of
health) Erholung f; (of
belongings) Wiederfinden
nt
recreate, rie-krie-eht, v neu
bilden
recreation, reck-ri-eh-sch'n,
n Erholung f; **–al,** adj
Erholungs-; **– ground,** n
Freizeitgelände nt;
(playground) Spielplatz m
recrimination, ri-krimm-i-
neh-sch'n, n
Beschuldigung f
recruit, ri-kruht, n Rekrut
m; v werben
rectangle, reck-täng-g'l, n
Rechteck nt
rectangular, reck-täng-gju-

ler, *adj* rechteckig

rectify, reck-ti-fei, *v* berichtigen

rector, reck-ter, *n* Pfarrer *m*; **-y**, Pfarrhaus *nt*

recuperate, ri-kuh-pe-reht, *v* sich erholen

recur, ri-kör, *v* wiedervorkommen; **-rence**, *n* Wiederholung *f*; **-rent**, *adj* wiederkehrend

recycle, rie-ssei-k'l, *v* recyceln, wiederverwerten; **-d**, *adj* recycelt; (paper) Alt-

recycling, rie-sseik-ling, *n* Recycling *nt*, Wiederverwertung *f*

red, redd, *adj* rot; *n* Rot *nt*; (communist) Rote(r) *m* & *f*; **R– Cross**, *n* Rotes Kreuz *nt*; **-den**, *v* rot werden; (blush) erröten; **-dish**, *adj* rötlich

redeem, ri-diem, *v* (pledge) einlösen; (soul) erlösen; **-ing**, *adj* ausgleichend

red-handed, redd **hänn**-didd, *adv* auf frischer Tat

red herring, redd **he**-ring, *n* falsche Spur *f*

red-hot, redd hott, *adj* rotglühend

red-light district, *n* Amüsierviertel *nt*

redo, rie-duh, *v* neu machen

redouble, rie-dabb-'l, *v* verdoppeln

redress, ri-dress, *n* Abhilfe *f*; *v* abhelfen

red tape, red tehp, *n*

(unnötige) Bürokratie *f*

reduce, ri-djuhss, *v* vermindern; (price) herabsetzen; (size) verkleinern

reduction, ri-dack-sch'n, *n* Verminderung *f*; (of price) Ermäßigung *f*

redundant, ri-dann-dent, *adj* überflüssig; (worker) arbeitslos

reed, ried, *n* (Schilf)rohr *nt*

reef, rief, *n* Riff *nt*; *naut* Reff *nt*; *v* reffen

reek, riek, *n* Gestank *m*; (of), *v* stinken (nach)

reel, riel, *n* Rolle *f*, Haspel *m*; *v* (wind) aufspulen; (stagger) taumeln

refer to, ri-för tu, *v* (mention) sich beziehen auf; (send to) verweisen an; (consult) nachschlagen in

referee, reff-e-rie, *n* (sport) Schiedsrichter *m*; (guarantor) Referenz *f*; *v* (sport) schiedsrichtern; (mediate) schlichten

reference, reff-e-renss, *n* (mention) Erwähnung *f*; (allusion) Anspielung *f*; (testimonial) Zeugnis *nt*, Referenz *f*; (identification) Zeichen *nt*; **– book**, *n* Nachschlagewerk *nt*; **terms of –**, Aufgabenbereich *m*; **with – to**, mit Bezug auf

referendum, reff-e-renn-

dem, *n* Volksabstimmung *f*

refill, rie-fill, *n* Nachfüll-; (for pencil, ballpoint) Ersatzmine *f*

refill, rie-fill, *v* nachfüllen

refine, ri-fein, *v* raffinieren; *fig* verfeinern; **-d**, *adj* fein, gebildet; **-ment**, *n* (person) Kultiviertheit *f*; (improvement) Verbesserung *f*

refit, ri-fitt, *v* überholen

reflect, ri-flekt, *v* (light) zurückstrahlen; *fig* widerspiegeln; **- (on)**, nachdenken (über); **-ion**, *n* (image) Spiegelbild *nt*; (thought) Überlegung *f*; (criticism) Kritik *f*; **-ive**, *adj* reflektierend; (thoughtful) nachdenklich

reflex, rie-flecks, *adj* Reflex-; *n* Reflex *m*; **-ive**, *adj* *gram* reflexiv

reform, ri-form, *n* Reform *f*; *v* (system etc.) reformieren; (person) (sich) bessern; **R–ation**, *relig* Reformation *f*

refrain, ri-frehn, *n* Refrain *m*; **– (from)**, *v* unterlassen

refresh, ri-fresch, *v* erfrischen; **-er course**, *n* Auffrischungskurs *m*; **-ing**, *adj* erfrischend; **-ment**, *n* Erfrischung *f*

refrigerator, ri-fridsch-e-reh-ter, *n* Kühlschrank *m*

refuel, rie-fju-el, *v* tanken

refuge, reff-juhdsch, *n*

Zufluchtsort m; **take –
(in),** v sich flüchten (in)
refugee, reff-juh-dschie, n
Flüchtling m
refund, rie-fand, n
Rückzahlung f
refund, ri-fandd, v
zurückzahlen
refusal, ri-fjuh-sel, n
Verweigerung f
refuse, ri-fjuhs, v
verweigern
refuse, reff-juhss, n Abfall
m, Müll m; **– disposal,** n
Müllbeseitigung f; **–
dump,** n Mülldeponie f
regain, ri-gehn, v
zurückgewinnen;
zurückbekommen; **–
consciousness,** v wieder
zu sich kommen
regal, rie-gel, adj königlich
regale, ri-gehl, v festlich
bewirten; (entertain)
unterhalten
regard, ri-gahrd, n (esteem)
Achtung f; (look) Blick
m; v betrachten; **–ing,** prep
in bezug auf; **–less,** adv
trotzdem; **–less of,** prep
ungeachtet, ohne
Rücksicht auf; **kind –s,**
herzliche Grüße
regenerate, ri-dschen-e-
reht, v neu beleben
regent, rie-dschent, n
Regent m
régime, reh-dschiem, n
Regime nt
regiment, redsch-i-ment, n
Regiment nt

regiment, redsch-i-ment, v
reglementieren
region, rie-dschen, n
Gegend f, Region f; **–al,**
adj regional; **in the – of,**
(so) ungefähr
register, redsch-iss-ter, n
Verzeichnis nt; Register nt;
v (course) einschreiben;
(record) eintragen; (sign
up) sich melden; (show)
zeigen; **–ed,** adj (letter)
eingeschrieben;
(trademark) eingetragen
registrar, redsch-iss-trar, n
Standesbeamter m;
Standesbeamtin f
registration, redsch-iss-treh-
sch'n, n Eintragung f;
Anmeldung f; **– number,**
n (on car)
amtliches/polizeiliches
Kennzeichen nt
registry office, redsch-iss-tri
off-iss, n Standesamt m
regret, ri-grett, n Bedauern
nt; v bedauern; **–table,** adj
bedauerlich
regular, regg-ju-ler, adj
regelmäßig; n
Stammkunde m
regulate, regg-ju-leht, v
regulieren
regulation, regg-ju-leh-
sch'n, n (rule) Vorschrift f;
(control) Regelung f
rehabilitation, rie-he-bill-i-
teh-sch'n, n
Rehabilitierung f
rehearsal, ri-hör-ss'l, n
Probe f

rehearse, ri-hörss, v proben
reign, rehn, n Herrschaft f; v
regieren
reimburse, rie-im-börss, v
(money) zurückzahlen;
(person) entschädigen
rein, rehn, n Zügel m; v
zügeln
reincarnation, rie-inn-kahr-
neh-sch'n, n Wiedergeburt
f
reindeer, rehn-dier, n
Ren(tier) nt
reinforce, rie-inn-forss, v
verstärken; **–ment,** n
Verstärkung f; **–ments,** npl
(mil etc.) Verstärkung f
reinstate, rie-inn-steht, v
wieder einsetzen
reiterate, rie-itt-e-reht, v
betonen
reject, rie-dschekt, n
Ausschuß m
reject, ri-dschekt, v
verwerfen; **–ion,** n
Ablehnung f
rejoice, ri-dscheuss, v sich
freuen
rejuvenate, ri-dschu-wen-
eht, v verjüngen
relapse, ri-läpss, n Rückfall
m; v (illness) einen
Rückfall bekommen;
(crime) rückfällig werden
relate, ri-leht, v (tell)
erzählen; (make
connection) einen
Zusammenhang
herstellen; **–d,** adj
verwandt
relation, ri-leh-sch'n, n

(connection) Beziehung f;
(relative) Verwandte(r) m
& f; –ship, n (connection)
Zusammenhang f; (family)
Verwandtschaft f;
(couple) Beziehung f

relative, rell-e-tiw, adj
relativ; n Verwandte(r) m
& f; –ly, adv
verhältnismäßig

relax, ri-**läcks,** v (sich)
entspannen; –ation, n
Erholung f; –ing, adj
erholsam

relay, rie-leh, n (sport)
Staffel f; v (signal)
übertragen; (message)
ausrichten

release, ri-**liess,** n
Entlassung f; v (prisoner)
entlassen; (news)
bekanntgeben

relent, ri-**lent,** v nachgeben;
–less(ly), adj & adv
unbarmherzig

relevant, rel-i-went, adj
relevant

reliable, ri-**lei-**e-b'l, adj
zuverlässig

reliance, ri-**lei-**enss, n Verlaß
m, Vertrauen nt

relic, rell-ick, n
Überbleibsel nt; relig
Reliquie f

relief, ri-**lief,** n
Erleichterung f; (of
pain) Linderung f; mil
Ablösung f

relieve, ri-**liew,** v
erleichtern; (pain)
lindern; mil ablösen; – sb

of sth, jdm etw
abnehmen

religion, ri-**lidsch-**en, n
Religion f

religious, ri-**lidsch-**ess, adj
fromm, religiös

relinquish, ri-**link-**u'isch, v
aufgeben

relish, rell-isch, n (spice)
Relish nt; (enjoyment)
Geschmack; v genießen

relocate, rie-**loh-keht,** v
umziehen; (business)
verlegen

reluctance, ri-**lack-**tenss, n
Widerwillen m

reluctant, ri-**lack-**tent, adj
unwillig, widerwillig

rely on, ri-**lei** on, v sich
verlassen auf

remain, ri-**mehn,** v (stay)
bleiben; (be left over)
übrigbleiben; –der, n Rest
m; –s, npl (human)
Überreste pl

remand, ri-**mahnd,** n
Untersuchungshaft; v – in
custody, in
Untersuchungshaft
behalten

remark, ri-**mahrk,** n
Bemerkung f; v bemerken;
–able, adj bemerkenswert

remedial, ri-**mie-**di-el, adj
med Heil-; (measure)
Hilfs-; (teaching)
Nachhilfe-

remedy, rem-i-di, n Mittel
nt; v (ver)bessern,
abhelfen

remember, ri-**memm-**ber, v

sich erinnern (an)

remembrance, ri-**memm-**
brenss, n Erinnerung f

remind (of), ri-**meind,** v
erinnern (an)

reminiscence, remm-i-**niss-**
enss, n Erinnerung f

reminiscent, remm-i-**niss-**
ent, adj be – of, v erinnern
an

remiss, ri-**miss,** adj
nachlässig; –ion, n med
Remission f

remit, ri-**mitt,** v (money)
überweisen; (fine, etc.)
erlassen; –tance, n (of
money) Überweisung f

remnant, remm-nent, n
Rest m

remorse, ri-**morss,** n Reue f;
–less(ly), adj & adv
unerbittlich

remote, ri-**moht,** adj
(distant) entfernt;
(isolated) abgelegen; –
control, n Fernsteuerung;
–-**controlled,** adj
ferngesteuert

removal, ri-**muh-**wel, n
(taking away) Beseitigung
f; (house move) Umzug m;
– **van,** n Möbelwagen m

remove, ri-**muhw,** v (take
away) beseitigen;
(dismiss) entlassen

remuneration, ri-mjuh-ne-
reh-sch'n, n Entlohung f

rend, rend, v (zer)reißen

render, renn-der, v (make)
machen; (assistance)
leisten; (interpret)

wiedergeben; **–ing**, n (*mus* etc.) Wiedergabe f, Interpretation f

rendezvous, ronn-deh-vuh, n Rendezvous nt; v sich treffen

renew, ri-njuh, v erneuern; **–al**, n Erneuerung f

renounce, ri-naunss, v (abandon) verzichten auf; (give up) aufgeben

renovate, renn-*e*-veht, v renovieren, restaurieren

renown, ri-naun, n Ruhm m; **–ed,** adj berühmt

rent, rent, n Miete f; v mieten; (let out) vermieten; **–al,** n Miete f

renunciation, ri-nun-ssi-eh-sch'n, n Verzicht m

reorganize, rie-or-g*e*-neis, v umorganisieren

rep, repp, n abbr comm **representative**

repair, ri-pähr, n (mend) Reparatur f; (state) Zustand m; v reparieren

repartee, repp-ahr-tie, n (witty remark) schlagfertige Antwort; (quality) Schlagfertigkeit f

repay, ri-pei, v zurückzahlen; **–ment,** n Zurückzahlung f

repeal, ri-piel, n Aufhebung f; v aufheben

repeat, ri-piet, n Wiederholung f; v wiederholen

repel, ri-pell, v zurückschlagen; fig abstoßen; **–lent,** adj

abstoßend; **insect –ent,** n Insektenschutzmittel nt

repent (of), ri-pent (ew), v bereuen

repercussions, rie-per-kasch-'ns, npl Nachwirkungen pl, Konsequenzen pl

repetition, repp-i-tisch-'n, n Wiederholung f

repetitive, ri-pett-i-tiw, adj eintönig

replace, ri-plehss, v ersetzen; **–ment,** n Ersatz m

replenish, ri-plenn-isch, v (wieder) auffüllen

replica, repp-lick-*e*, n Nachbildung f

reply, ri-plei, n Antwort f; v antworten

report, ri-port, n (account) Bericht m; (school) Zeugnis nt; v (give account) berichten; (notify police) anzeigen; (present o.s.) sich melden; **–er,** n Reporter m

repose, ri-pohs, n Ruhe f

represent, repp-ri-sent, v darstellen; (act for) vertreten; (quality) Darstellung f; (agency) Vertretung f; **–ative,** adj repräsentativ; n Vertreter m

repress, ri-press, n unterdrücken; **–ion,** n Unterdrückung f

reprieve, ri-priew, n Begnadigung f; v

begnadigen

reprimand, repp-ri-mahnd, n Verweis m; v tadeln

reprint, rie-print, n Nachdruck m

reprint, rie-print, v nachdrucken

reprisal, ri-prei-s'l, n Vergeltungsakt m, Repressalie f

reproach, ri-prohtsch, n Vorwurf m; v – sb with sth, jdm etw vorwerfen

reproduce, rie-pre-djuhss, v reproduzieren

reproduction, rie-pre-dack-sch'n, n Reproduktion f

reptile, repp-teil, n Reptil nt

republic, ri-pabb-lick, n Republik f

repudiate, ri-pjuh-di-eht, v zurückweisen

repugnant, ri-pagg-nent, adj widerlich

repulse, ri-palss, v (enemy) zurückschlagen; (approach) abweisen

repulsive, ri-pall-ssiw, adj widerwärtig

reputable, repp-juh-te-b'l, adj angesehen

reputation, repp-juh-teh-sch'n, n Ruf m

repute, ri-pjuht, n Ansehen nt; **–ed(ly),** adj & adv angeblich

request, ri-ku'est, n Bitte f; v bitten um

require, ri-ku'eir, v (need) benötigen; (demand) verlangen; **–ment,** n

(need) Bedarf m;
(demand) Anforderung f
requisite, reck-u'i-sitt,
adj erforderlich; n
Erfordernis nt
requisition, reck-u'i-sisch-
'n, v beschlagnahmen
rescue, ress-kjuh, n Rettung
f; v retten; **–r,** n Retter m
research, ri-ssörtsch, n
Forschung f; v forschen,
erforschen; **–er,** n
Forscher m
resemblance, ri-semm-
blenss, n Ähnlichkeit f
resemble, ri-semm-b'l, v
gleichen, ähnlich sein
resent, ri-sent, v
übelnehmen; **–ful,** adj
nachtragend; **–ment,** n
Groll m
reservation, res-e-weh-
sch'n, n (booking)
Reservierung f;
(qualification)
Vorbehalt m
reserve, ri-sörw, n (stock)
Reserve f; (reticence)
Zurückhaltung f;
(nature/game) Reservat
nt; v (book) reservieren;
(right) sich vorbehalten;
–d, adj reserviert
reservoir, res-er-wu'ahr, n
Reservoir m
reside, ri-seid, v wohnen
residence, res-i-denss, n
(home) Wohnung f; (stay)
Aufenthalt m
resident, res-i-dent, adj
wohnhaft; n (of house)

Bewohner m; (in area)
Einwohner m
residential, res-i-denn-sch'l,
adj Wohn-
resign, ri-sein, v
zurücktreten, kündigen;
–o.s. (to), sich mit etw
abfinden
resignation, res-igg-neh-
sch'n, n Rücktritt m,
Kündigung f
resilient, ri-sill-jent, adj
unverwüstlich
resin, res-inn, n Harz nt
resist, ri-sist, v sich wehren
gegen; **–ance,** n
Widerstand m
resolute, res-e-luht, adj
entschlossen
resolution, res-e-luh-sch'n,
n (decision) Beschluß m;
(intention) Vorsatz m;
(determination)
Entschlossenheit f
resolve, ri-solw, v (decide)
beschließen; (solve) lösen
resort, ri-sort, n (place)
Urlaubsort m; **– to,** v
Zuflucht nehmen zu; **last
–,** n letzter Ausweg m
resounding, ri-saun-ding,
adj überwältigend
resource, ri-sorss, n
Hilfsmittel nt; **–s,** npl
(natural) Ressourcen pl;
(money) Geldmittel pl;
–ful, adj findig
respect, ri-spekt, n (aspect)
Hinsicht f; (esteem)
Respekt m; v achten;
–able, adj angesehen; **–ful,**

adj respektvoll; **–ing,** prep
bezüglich; **–ive,** adj
jeweils; **–ively,** adv
beziehungsweise; **with –
to,** hinsichtlich
respite, ress-peit, n
Aufschub m; (break)
(Ruhe)pause f
respond (to), ri-spond (tu),
v (answer) antworten
(auf); (react) reagieren
response, riss-ponss, n
(answer) Antwort f;
(reaction) Reaktion f
responsibility, riss-ponn-ssi-
bill-i-ti, n
Verantwortlichkeit f,
Verantwortung f
responsible, riss-ponn-ssib-
'l, adj (answerable)
verantwortlich; (reliable)
verantwortungsvoll
rest, rest, n (repose) Ruhe f;
(remainder) Rest m;
(break) Pause f; (sleep)
Schlaf m; v (repose) sich
ausruhen; (take break)
Pause machen; **– on,** v
beruhen auf
restaurant, ress-te-rong, n
Restaurant nt; **– car,** n
Speisewagen m
restful, rest-full, adj ruhig
restive, ress-tiw, adj unruhig
restless, rest-liss, adj ruhelos
restore, riss-tor, v (give
back) zurückgeben;
(renovate) restaurieren;
(health, order)
wiederherstellen
restrain, riss-trehn, v

441

zurückhalten; **–ed**, *adj*
zurückhaltend; **–t**, *n*
(control) Zurückhaltung *f*;
(arrest) Haft *f*
restrict, riss-**trikt**, *v*
einschränken; **–ion**, *n*
Einschränkung *f*
result, ri-**salt**, *n* Resultat *nt*;
Folge *f*; *v* – **from sth**, aus
etw folgern; – **in**, zur Folge
haben
resume, ri-**sjuhm**, *v*
wiederaufnehmen
resumption, ri-**samp**-sch'n,
n Wiederaufnahme *f*
resurgence, ri-**ssör**-
dschenss, *n*
Wiederaufleben *nt*
resurrection, res-*e*-**reck**-
sch'n, *n* Auferstehung *f*
retail, **rie**-tehl, *adj*
Einzelhandels-; *n*
Einzelhandel *m*; *v* im
Einzelhandel verkaufen;
–er, *n* Einzelhändler *m*
retain, ri-**tehn**, *v* behalten;
–er, *n* (fee) Kaution *f*
retaliate, ri-**täll**-i-eht, *v*
vergelten
retarded, ri-**tahr**-didd, *adj*
zurückgeblieben
retch, retsch, *v* würgen
reticent, **rett**-i-ssent, *adj*
zurückhaltend
retinue, **rett**-i-njuh, *n*
Gefolge *nt*
retire, ri-**teir**, *v* (from work)
in Rente/Pension gehen;
(withdraw) sich
zurückziehen; **–d**, *adj* in
Rente/Pension; **–ment**, *n*

(from work) Ruhestand *m*;
(from world)
Zurückgezogenheit *f*
retort, ri-**tort**, *n* Erwiderung
f; *v* erwidern
retract, ri-**träkt**, *v* (take
back) zurücknehmen;
(pull back) zurückziehen
retreat, ri-**triet**, *v*
(withdrawal) Rückzug *m*;
(place) Zufluchtsort *m*; *v*
sich zurückziehen
retribution, rett-ribb-**juh**-
sch'n, *n* Vergeltung *f*
retrieve, ri-**triew**, *v* (get
back) zurückgewinnen;
(rescue) retten; (of dog)
zurückholen
return, ri-**törn**, *adj* Rück-;
(of person) Rückkehr *f*;
(of object) Rückgabe *f*;
(profit) Ertrag *m*; *v* (come
back) zurückkommen; (go
back) zurückgehen; (give
back) zurückgeben; **–s**, *npl*
comm Umsatz *m*; –
(ticket), *n* Rückfahrkarte
f; (plane) Rückflugkarte *f*
reunion, rie-**juh**-ni-*e*n, *n*
(school) Treffen *nt*;
(politics)
Wiedervereinigung *f*
reunite, rie-ju-**neit**, *v*
wiedervereinigen
rev, rew, *n* Umdrehungen *pl*;
v (den Motor) auf Touren
bringen
reveal, ri-**wiel**, *v* offenbaren,
enthüllen; **–ing**, *adj*
aufschlußreich
revel (in), rew-'l (inn), *v*

schwelgen in
revelation, rew-*e*-**leh**-sch'n,
n Offenbarung *f*
revenge, ri-**wendsch**, *n*
Rache *f*; *v* – **o.s. (on)**,
sich rächen (an)
revenue, **rew**-*e*-njuh, *n*
Einkünfte *pl*; Umsatz *m*
reverence, **rew**-*e*-renss, *n*
Ehrfurcht *f*
Reverend, **rew**-*e*-rend, *adj*
ehrwürdig; *n* Pfarrer *m*
reverse, ri-**wörss**, *adj*
umgekehrt; *n* (back)
Rückseite *f*; (contrary)
Gegenteil *nt*; (gear)
Rückwärtsgang *m*; *v* (turn
over) umdrehen; (go
backwards) rückwärts
fahren
revert to, ri-**wört** (tu), *v*
zurückkommen auf
review, ri-**wjuh**, *n*
(checking) Überprüfung *f*;
(events) Rückschau *f*;
(critique) Rezension *f*;
theatre Revue *f*; *v* (check)
überprüfen; (critique)
rezensieren; *mil* mustern;
(reconsider) revidieren;
–er, *n* Rezensent *m*
revile, ri-**weil**, *v* schmähen,
lästern
revise, ri-**weis**, *v* revidieren
revision, ri-**wisch**-'n, *n*
(reconsideration)
Revision *f*; (for exam)
Wiederholung *f*, Lernen *nt*
revitalize, rie-**wei**-te-leis, *v*
neu beleben
revival, ri-**wei**-wel, *n*

Wiederbelebung f

revive, ri-weiw, v (play, custom) wiederaufnehmen; (recover) wieder aufleben

revoke, ri-wohk, v widerrufen

revolt, ri-wohlt, n Aufstand m; v (rebel) rebellieren; (disgust) anekeln; –ing, adj ekelhaft

revolution, rew-e-luh-sch'n, n (uprising) Revolution f; (turn) Umdrehung f

revolve, ri-wolw, v sich drehen; –r, n Revolver m

reward, ri-u'ord, n Belohnung f; v belohnen; –ing, adj lohnend

rheumatism, ruh-me-tism, n Rheuma nt

Rhine, rein, n Rhein m

rhinoceros, rei-noss-e-ress, n Nashorn nt

rhubarb, ruh-barb, n Rhabarber m

rhyme, reim, n Reim m; v reimen

rhythm, ridh-'m, n Rhythmus m

rib, ribb, n Rippe f

ribbon, ribb-en, n Band nt

rice, reiss, n Reis m

rich, ritsch, adj reich; (food) schwer; –es, npl Reichtum m

rickety, rick-itt-i, adj wackelig

rid, ridd, v befreien; to get – of, loswerden

riddle, ridd-'l, n Rätsel nt;

–d with, durchlöchert von

ride, reid, n (in vehicle) Fahrt f; (on horse) Ritt m; v (horse) reiten; (bicycle) radfahren; (in vehicle) fahren; –r, n (on horse) Reiter m; (vehicle) Fahrer m

ridge, ridsch, n (mountain) Kamm m; (roof) First m

ridicule, ridd-i-kjuhl, n Spott m; v lächerlich machen

ridiculous, ri-dick-juh-less, adj lächerlich

riding, n Reiten nt; – school, n Reitschule f

rife, adj weit verbreitet

rifle, reif-'l, n Gewehr nt; – through, v durchstöbern

rift, rift, n Spalte f; fig Unstimmigkeit f

rig, rigg n naut Takelung f; v naut auftakeln; (election) manipulieren; oil –, n Ölbohrinsel f

right, reit, adj (correct) recht, richtig; (side) rechte(r/s); adv (to the right) rechts; (correctly) richtig; (directly) genau; n rechte Seite; (justice) Recht nt; (politics) Rechte f; (put) –, v wiedergutmachen; – away, adv sofort; –-handed, adj rechtshändig; –-hand side, n rechte Seite f; – now, adv sofort; – of way, n Vorfahrt f; (all) –, gut; be –, (of person) recht

haben; (of fact) stimmen; on/to the –, nach rechts

rigid, ridsch-idd, adj starr, steif, fest

rigorous, rigg-e-ress, adj streng

rigour, rigg-er, n Strenge f

rile, reil, v reizen

rim, rimm, n Rand m; (of hat) Krempe f; (of wheel) (Rad)felge f

rind, reindd, n Rinde f

ring, ring, n (object) Ring m; (of bell, telephone) Klingeln nt; (circle) Kreis m; v (bell) klingeln; (up), (on telephone) anrufen; –leader, n Rädelsführer m; – road, n Ringstraße f

rink, rink, n (ice) Eisbahn f; (roller-skating) Rollschuhbahn f

rinse, rinss, v spülen, ausspülen

riot, rei-ett, n Aufruhr m; fig Explosion f; v randalieren; –er, n Aufrührer m

rip, ripp, n Riß m; v reißen

ripe, reip, adj reif; –n, v reifen

rip-off, ripp-off, n fam Nepp m

ripple, ripp-'l, n kleine Welle f; v (sich) kräuseln

rise, reis, n (slope) Steigung f; (in salary) Erhöhung f; (in price) Steigerung f; v (in price) steigen; (stand up) aufstehen; (revolt) sich erheben; (of sun)

aufgehen; **give – to,** v
führen zu

risk, risk, n Risiko nt,
Gefahr f; v riskieren; **take
a –,** v ein Risiko eingehen;
–y, adj riskant; **at –,**
gefährdet, in Gefahr

rite, reit, n Ritus m

rival, rei-w'l, adj
rivalisierend; n Rivale m;
(competitor) Konkurrent
m; v rivalisieren mit; **–ry,**
n Rivalität f;
(competition) Konkurrenz
f

river, riw-er, adj Fluß-; n
Fluß m; (large) Strom m

rivet, riw-itt, n Niete f; v
nieten

road, rohd, adj Straßen-; n
Straße f; **– map,** n
Straßenkarte f; **– sign,** n
Straßenschild m; **–works,**
npl Straßenbauarbeiten pl,
Baustelle f

roam, rohm, v
umherwandern

roar, ror, n Gebrüll nt; v
brüllen; (of storm)
brausen; **do a –ing trade,** v
ein Bombengeschäft
machen

roast, rohst, n Braten m; v
braten

rob, robb, v berauben; **–ber,**
n Räuber m; **–bery,** n
Raubüberfall m

robe, rohb, n (dress) Kleid
nt; (of office) Talar m;
(dressing gown)
Bademantel m

robin, robb-in, n
Rotkehlchen nt

robot, roh-bott, n Roboter
m

robust, re-bast, adj (health,
appetite) robust; (build)
kräftig; (flavour, manner)
ausgeprägt

rock, rock, n Felsen m; mus
Rock m; (sweet)
Zuckerstange f; v
schaukeln; (cradle)
wiegen; **– and roll,** n Rock
and Roll m; **–ery,**
Steingarten m; **on the –s,**
(marriage, business)
wackelig; (drink) mit Eis

rocket, rock-it, n Rakete f; v
(of prices) in die Höhe
schießen

rocking, rock-ing, adj
Schaukel-

rocky, rock-i, adj (stony)
felsig; (wobbly) wackelig

rod, rodd, n Stange m;
(cane) Rute f

roe, roh, n (deer) Reh nt; (of
fish) Rogen m

rogue, rohg, n Gauner m;
(in fun) Schelm m; **–ry,** n
Gaunerei f

roll, rohl, n Rolle f; (bread)
Brötchen f; v rollen; **–
call,** n Aufrufen nt; **–er,** n
Walze f; **–er skate,** n
Rollschuh m; **–ing,** adj
wellig; **–ing pin,** n
Wellholz nt; **– over,** v
(sich) umdrehen; **– up,** v
aufrollen; (fam arrive)
kommen

Roman, roh-men, adj
römisch; n Römer m; **–
Catholic,** adj (römisch-)
katholisch; n Katholik m

romance, roh-mänss, n
(affair) Romanze f; (story)
Liebesroman m

romantic, roh-männ-tick,
adj romantisch

romanticism, roh-männ-ti-
ssism, n Romantik f

Rome, rohm, n Rom nt

romp, romp, v
(herum)tollen

roof, ruhf, n Dach nt; (of
mouth) Gaumen m; **–
rack,** n Dachständer m

rook, ruk, n Saatkrähe f;
(chess) Turm m

room, ruhm, n Zimmer nt;
(space) Platz m; **– service,**
n Zimmerservice m; **–y,** adj
geräumig

roost, ruhst, n
Hühnerstange f; v
schlafen; **–er,** n Hahn m

root, ruht, n Wurzel f; v **–
(about),** (herum)wühlen

rope, rohp, n Seil nt; **– in,** v
einspannen; **get –ed in,** v
eingespannt werden

rosary, roh-se-ri, n
Rosenkranz m

rose, rohs, adj rosa; n Rose f

rosé, roh-seh, adj rosé

rosemary, rohs-me-ri, n
Rosmarin m

rostrum, rost-rem, n
Tribüne f; mus
Dirigentenpult nt

rosy, rohs-i, adj rosig

rot, rott, n Fäulnis f; v
verfaulen

rota, roh-te, n
Arbeitsplan m

rotate, roh-teht, v (sich)
drehen; (take turns) sich
abwechseln

rotten, rott-'n, adj verfault,
faul; (person, act) gemein

rough, raff, adj (not smooth)
rauh; (treatment, finish)
grob; (approximate)
ungefähr; (sea) stürmisch;
(bumpy) holperig; **–age,** n
Ballaststoffe pl; **– copy,** n
Entwurf m; **–ly,** adj
(treatment) grob;
(approximately) ungefähr;
–ness, n Rauheit f,
Grobheit f

round, raund, adj rund; adv
ringsherum; prep (corner)
um; (area) um … herum;
n Runde f; (shot) Schuß
m; v abrunden; **– about,**
adv ringsherum; **–about,**
adj umständlich; n
(traffic) Kreisverkehr m;
(child's) Karussell nt; **–ly,**
adv entschieden; **–ness,** n
Rundheit f; (figure)
Rundlichkeit f; **– up,** v
(criminals) hochnehmen;
(figure, price) aufrunden;
go –, v herumgehen um;
(visit sb) besuchen; (be
enough) ausreichen

rouse, raus, v aufwecken

route, ruht, n Route f, Weg
m; (bus) Linie f

routine, ruh-tien, adj

Routine-, routinemäßig; n
Routine f

rove, rohw, v herumstreifen

row, roh, n Reihe f; v rudern

row, rau, n (dispute) Streit
m; (noise) Lärm m; v sich
streiten

rowdy, rau-di, adj rowdyhaft

royal, reu-el, adj königlich;
Königs-; **–ty,** n Königshaus
nt; (fee) Tantieme f

rub, rabb, v reiben; **– off,** v
abreiben; fig abfärben; **–
out,** n ausradieren; **– sb
(up) the wrong way,** v
jdn reizen

rubber, rabb-er, n Gummi
m/nt; (eraser)
Radiergummi m; **– band,** n
Gummiband nt

rubbish, rabb-isch, n
(refuse) Abfall m;
(nonsense) Quatsch m; **–
bin,** n Mülleimer m; **–
dump/tip,** n Mülldeponie f

rubble, rabb-'l, n Schutt m

ruby, ruh-bi, adj rubinfarbig;
n Rubin m; **– wedding,** n
vierzigster Hochzeitstag m

rucksack, rack-ssäck, n
Rucksack m

rudder, radd-er, n
(Steuer)ruder nt

ruddy, radd-i, adj rötlich;
fam verdammt

rude, ruhd, adj (impolite)
unhöflich; (rough) grob;
(awakening, reminder)
unsanft

rudimentary, ruh-di-menn-
te-ri, adj (knowledge)

elementar; (tool etc.)
primitiv

rue, ruh, v bereuen; **–ful,** adj
(person) reuevoll;
(situation) kläglich

ruffian, raff-jen, n
Rohling m

ruffle, raff-'l, n Kräuseln f; v
kräuseln; (upset) aus der
Fassung bringen

rug, ragg, n (blanket) Decke
f; (carpet) Teppich m,
Läufer m

rugby, ragg-bi, n Rugby nt

rugged, ragg-idd, adj
(landscape) zerklüftet;
(features) zerfurcht

ruin, ruh-in, n (building)
Ruine f; (downfall) Ruin
m; v ruinieren; **in –s,**
zerstört

rule, ruhl, n (regulation)
Regel nt; (reign)
Herrschaft f;
(government) Amtszeit f;
(ruler) Lineal nt; v (king)
herrschen (über);
(government) amtieren;
(decide) enscheiden;
(draw lines on) linieren;
–r, n Lineal nt; (royal)
Herrscher m

rumble, ramm-b'l, n
(thunder etc.) Rollen nt;
(stomach) Knurren nt; v
rollen; knurren

rummage, ramm-idsch, v
herumstöbern

rumour, ruh-mer, n
Gerücht nt

rump, ramp, n fam

Hinterteil nt; – **steak,** n Rumpsteak nt

run, rann, n Lauf m; (race) Rennen nt; v rennen, laufen; (flow) fließen; (of train etc.) fahren; – **away,** v weglaufen; **–away,** n (person, horse) Ausreißer m; – **down,** v (of battery) leer werden; (with car) überfahren; (reduce) abbauen; – **into,** v (meet) begegnen; (trouble, debt) geraten in; (collide with) fahren gegen; **–ning,** adj fließend; n (management) Leitung f; (sport) Rennen nt, Jogging nt; **–ny,** adj (liquid) flüssig; (nose) laufend; – **out,** v (expire) ablaufen; (be exhausted) ausgehen; – **out of sth,** v kein … mehr haben; – **over,** v überfahren; – **through,** v (read/explain quickly) durchgehen; **–way,** n (take-off) Startbahn f; (landing) Landebahn f

rupture, rap-tscher, n Bruch m

rural, ruhr-rel, adj ländlich

rush, rasch, n (panic) Gedränge nt; (surge) Andrang m; (reed) Binse f; v (hurry) stürzen; (move quickly) schnell transportieren; – **hour,** n Stoßzeit f; (traffic) Hauptverkehrszeit f

Russia, rasch-e, n Rußland

nt; **–n,** adj russisch; n (person) Russe m, Russin f; (language) Russisch nt

rust, rast, n Rost m; v (ver)rosten

rustic, rass-tick, adj ländlich

rustle, rass-'l, v rauschen, rascheln; (steal cattle) stehlen

rusty, rass-ti, adj rostig; fig eingerostet

rut, rat, n Furche f, Spur f; fig Trott m

ruthless, ruhth-less, adj rücksichtslos

rye, rei, n Roggen m

sabbath, ssä́bb-eth, n
Sabbat m

sabotage, ssä́bb-e-tahdsch, n
Sabotage f; v sabotieren

sachet, ssä́sch-eh, n
Beutel m

sack, ssäck, n Sack m; v
(dismiss) entlassen; mil
plündern; **–ing**, n
(dismissal) Entlassung f;
(cloth) Sackleinen nt; **get
the –**, v entlassen werden

sacrament, ssack-re-ment, n
Sakrament nt

sacred, sseh-kridd, adj heilig

sacrifice, ssä́ck-ri-feiss, n
Opfer nt; v opfern

sacrilege, ssä́ck-ri-lidsch, n
Sakrileg nt

sad, ssäd, adj traurig; **–den**,
traurig machen

saddle, ssä́dd-'l, n Sattel m;
v (horse) satteln; **– sb
with sth**, v jdm etw

aufbürden; **–bag**, n
Satteltasche f

sadistic, sse-diss-tick, adj
sadistisch

sadly, ssä́dd-li, adv
(unfortunately) leider;
(with sadness) traurig

sadness, ssä́dd-niss, n
Traurigkeit f

safe, ssehf, adj sicher; n
Geldschrank m; **–-deposit
box**, n Banksafe m;
–guard, n Schutz m; v
beschützen; **–-keeping**, n
sichere Verwahrung f; **–
sex**, n Safer Sex m

safety, ssehf-ti, n Sicherheit
f; **– belt**, n Sicherheitsgurt
m; **– pin**, n
Sicherheitsnadel f

sag, ssägg, v durchhängen

sage, ssehdsch, n (herb)
Salbei m; (wise person)
Weise(r) m & f

Saggitarius, ssädsch-i-tä́hr-
ri-ess, n Schütze m

sail, ssehl, n Segel nt; v
segeln; (leave) abfahren;
– through, v fam etw
spielend schaffen; **–ing**, n
Segeln nt; **–or**, n Matrose
m, Seemann m

saint, ssehnt, n Heilige(r) m
& f; **–ly**, adj heilig

sake, ssehk, **for … sake**, um
… willen

salad, ssä́ll-ed, n Salat m;
– dressing, n Salatsoße f

salami, sse-lah-mi, n
Salami f

salary, ssä́ll-e-ri, n Gehalt nt

sale, ssehl, n Verkauf m;
(bargain) Ausverkauf m;
–able, adj verkäuflich; **–s
assistant**, n Verkäufer m;
–sman, n Verkäufer m;
–woman, n Verkäuferin f;
for –, zu verkaufen

salient, sseh-li-ent, adj
auffallend

saliva, sse-lei-we, n
Speichel m

sallow, ssä́ll-oh, adj bleich

salmon, ssä́mm-en, n
Lachs m

saloon, sse-luhn, n (car)
Limousine f; (lounge)
Salon m

salt, ssolt, adj salzig, Salz-; n
Salz nt; v salzen; (cure)
pökeln; **– away**, v auf die
hohe Kante legen; **–
cellar**, n Salzstreuer m; **–
water**, n Salzwasser nt; **–y**,
adj salzig

salute, sse-**luht,** n mil Salut m; v – **sb,** mil jdn salutieren; (admire) sich vor jdm verneigen

salvage, ssäll-widsch, n Bergung f; v bergen

salvation, ssäll-**weh**-sch'n, n Rettung f; relig Seligkeit f; **S– Army,** n Heilsarmee f

same, ssehm, adj (identical) (der/die/das)selbe; (equivalent) (der/die/das) gleiche; **all the –,** trotzdem; **at the – time,** (simultaneously) gleichzeitig; (however) andererseits

sample, ssahm-p'l, n Muster nt; v probieren

sanctify, ssänk-ti-fei, v heiligen, weihen

sanction, ssänk-sch'n, n Genehmigung f; law Sanktion f; v sanktionieren

sanctity, ssänk-ti-ti, n Heiligkeit f

sanctuary, ssänk-tju-e-ri, n (refuge) Zufluchtsort m; (in church) Altarraum m

sand, ssänd, n Sand m

sandal, ssänn-d'l, n Sandale f

sandcastle, ssänd-kah-ss'l, n Sandburg f

sand dune, ssänd djuhn, n Sanddüne f

sandpaper, ssänd-peh-per, n Sandpapier nt

sandwich, ssänd-u'itsch, n Sandwich m/nt, belegtes Brot nt; v – **(between),** einklemmen (zwischen); – **course,** n Ausbildung f mit theoretischen und praktischen Bestandteilen

sandy, ssänn-di, adj sandig; (hair) rötlich

sane, ssehn, adj geistig gesund; vernünftig

sanitary, ssänn-i-te-ri, adj Gesundheits-; – **towel,** n Damenbinde f

sanity, ssänn-i-ti, n geistige Gesundheit f

sap, ssäpp, n Saft m; v unterhöhlen

sapphire, ssäff-eir, n Saphir m

sarcasm, ssahr-käsm, n Sarkasmus m

sarcastic, ssar-käss-tick, adj sarkastisch

sardine, ssar-dien, n Sardine f

sash, ssäsch, n Schärpe f

satchel, ssätsch-'l, n Schultasche f

satellite, ssätt-i-leit, n Satellit m; – **dish,** n Satellitenschüssel f; – **television,** n Satellitenfernsehen nt

satin, ssätt-inn, n Satin m

satire, ssätt-eir, n Satire f

satisfaction, ssätt-iss-**fäck**-sch'n, n Befriedigung f

satisfactory, ssätt-iss-**fäck**-te-ri, adj befriedigend

satisfy, ssätt-iss-fei, v (content) befriedigen; (fulfil) erfüllen

satsuma, ssätt-**suh**-me, n Mandarine f

saturate, ssätsch-e-reht, v durchtränken

Saturday, ssätt-er-deh, n Samstag m, Sonnabend m

sauce, sso'ass, n Soße f, Sauce f; **–pan,** n (Koch)topf m

saucer, sso'a-sser, n Untertasse f

saucy, sso'a-ssi, adj frech

sauna, sso'a-ne, n Sauna f

saunter, sso'an-ter, v schlendern

sausage, ssoss-idsch, n Wurst f

sauté, ssoh-teh, adj anbraten

savage, ssäw-idsch, adj wild; n Barbar m

savagery, ssäw-idsch-e-ri, n Grausamkeit f

save, ssehw, n sport Abwehr f; v (rescue) retten; (economize) sparen; (keep) aufbewahren; comp speichern; – **up,** sparen

saving, sseh-wing, n Ersparnis f; **–s,** npl Ersparnisse pl; **–s account,** n Sparkonto nt

Saviour, ssehw-jer, n relig Erlöser m

savour, sseh-wer, v genießen; **–y,** adj pikant; n Pikantes nt

saw, sso'a, n Säge f; v sägen

say, sseh, v sagen; **–ing,** n Spruch m; **have a – in,** v Mitspracherecht haben bei; **that is to –**, das heißt

scab, skäbb, n Schorf m

scaffold, skäff-ohld, n Schaffot nt; **–ing**, n Baugerüst nt

scald, sko'ald, n Verbrühung f; v verbrühen

scale, skehl, adj (drawing, model) maßstabgetreu; n(pl), (of fish) Schuppe f; (measure) Skala f; (ratio) Maßstab m; mus Tonleiter f; v (fish) abschuppen; (mountain) besteigen; **–s**, npl Waage f

scallop, skäll-ep, n Jakobsmuschel f

scalp, skälp, n Kopfhaut f

scamp, skämp, n Schlingel m

scamper, skämm-per, v **– away/off**, davoneilen, ausreißen

scampi, skämm-pi, npl Scampi pl

scan, skänn, n med Scan m; v (examine, med) untersuchen; (skim) überfliegen; (of verse) skandieren; comp scannen

scandal, skänn-d'l, n Skandal m; **–ous**, adj skandalös

Scandinavia, skänn-di-neh-wi-e, n Skandinavien nt; **–n**, adj skandinavisch; n Skandinavier m

scanty, skänn-ti, adj knapp, dürftig

scapegoat, skehp-goht, n Sündenbock m

scar, skahr, n Narbe f; v vernarben

scarce, skährss, adj rar, selten; **–ly**, adv kaum

scarcity, skähr-ssi-ti, n Knappheit f

scare, skähr, n Schreck m; v erschrecken; **– away**, v verscheuchen; **–crow**, n Vogelscheuche f; **bomb –**, n Bombendrohung f

scarf, skarf, n Schal m; (headscarf) Kopftuch nt

scarlet, skahr-let, adj scharlachrot; n Scharlachrot nt; **– fever**, n Scharlach m

scary, skähr-ri, adj fam furchterregend

scathing, skeh-dhing, adj scharf, verletzend

scatter, skätt-er, v (sich) zerstreuen, ausstreuen; **–brain**, n Schussel m

scavenger, skäw-in-dscher, n fam Aasgeier m

scene, ssien, n (place, theatre) Szene f; (view) Anblick m; **–ry**, n theatre Bühnenbild nt; (view) Landschaft f

scent, ssent, n Parfüm nt; (of flowers) Duft m; (trail) Spur f; v parfümieren

sceptical, skepp-ti-k'l, adj skeptisch

schedule, schedd-juhl, n (list) Liste f, Verzeichnis nt; (timetable) Zeitplan m; v ansetzen; **on –**, adv planmäßig; **–ed flight**, n

Linienflug m

scheme, skiem, n Plan m; pej Intrige f; v planen; pej aushecken

scholar, skoll-er, n Gelehrte(r) m & f; (pupil) Schüler m; **–ship**, n (prize) Stipendium nt; (learning) Gelehrsamkeit f

school, skuhl, n Schule f; **–child**, n Schulkind nt; **– days**, npl Schulzeit f; **–master**, n Lehrer m; **–mistress**, n Lehrerin f; **– teacher**, n Lehrer(in f) m

sciatica, ssei-ätt-i-ke, n Ischias m/nt

science, ssei-enss, n Wissenschaft f

scientific, ssei-en-tiff-ick, adj wissenschaftlich

scientist, ssei-en-tist, n Wissenschaftler m

scissors, ssis-ers, npl Schere f

scoff, skoff, v spotten; (fam eat) fressen; **– at**, verspotten

scold, skohld, v (aus)schimpfen

scoop, skuhp, n Schippe f, Schaufel f; v **– out**, (hollow) aushöhlen; (liquid) ausschöpfen

scooter, skuh-ter, n (motor) Motorroller m

scope, skohp, n (opportunity) Spielraum m; (extent) Rahmen m

scorch, skortsch, v sengen, anbrennen

score, skor, n (result)
Ergebnis nt; (points)
Punktzahl f; mus Partitur
f; (twenty) zwanzig; v
(goal) (ein Tor) schießen;
(points) bekommen;
(scratch) kerben; (keep
count) zählen

scorn, skorn, n Verachtung
f; v verachten; **–ful,** adj
verächtlich

Scorpio, skor-pi-oh, n
Skorpion m

Scot, skott, n Schotte m,
Schottin f

scotch, skotsch, n (whisky)
Scotch m

Scotland, skott-lend, n
Schottland nt

Scots, skots, adj schottisch;
–man, n Schotte m;
–woman, n Schottin f

Scottish, skott-isch, adj
schottisch

scoundrel, skaun-drel, n
Schurke m

scour, skau-er, v (scrub)
scheuern; (search)
durchkämmen

scourge, skördsch, n (whip)
Geißel f; fig Plage f

scout, skaut, n mil Späher m;
v – **(for),** Ausschau
halten nach; **boy –,** n
Pfadfinder m

scowl, skaul, n finsterer
Blick m; v finster blicken

scrabble, skräbb-'l, v
kratzen; **– around,** wühlen
nach

scraggy, skrägg-i, adj dürr,

hager

scramble, skrämm-b'l, n
(struggle) Getümmel nt;
(climb) klettern; v **– up,**
hochklettern; **– for,** sich
reißen um

scrap, skräpp, n (food)
Bissen m; (paper etc)
Fetzen m; (metal) Schrott
m; (fam fight) Rauferei f; v
(throw out) aufgeben;
(fam fight) raufen

scrape, skrehp, n (scratch)
Kratzen nt; (fam trouble)
Klemme f; v kratzen;
(vegetables) schaben; **–r,**
n (boots) Abstreifer m;
(ice) Schaber m; **–
through,** v gerade noch
durchkommen

scrap heap, skräpp hiep, n
Schutthaufen m; fig altes
Eisen nt

scrap merchant, skräpp
mör-tschent, n
Schrotthändler m

scraps, skräps, npl Reste pl

scratch, skrätsch, adj (team)
zusammengeworfen;
(without handicap) ohne
Vorgabe f; n Schramme f;
v kratzen; sport streichen;
start from –, v von vorne
anfangen; **up to –,** adj auf
Vordermann

scrawl, skro'al, n Gekritzel
nt; v kritzeln

scream, skriem, n Schrei m;
v schreien

screen, skrien, n Schirm m;
(TV) Bildschirm m; comp

Monitor m; (cinema)
Leinwand f; v
(be)schirmen; (film etc.)
zeigen; (check)
überprüfen; **–ing,** n
(check) Überprüfung f;
(of film etc.) Vorführung
f; **– off,** v abtrennen

screw, skruh, n Schraube f; v
schrauben; vulg bumsen;
–driver, n
Schraubenzieher m; **– up,**
v (crumple) zerknüllen;
(fam ruin) vermasseln

scribble, skribb-'l, n
Gekritzel nt; v kritzeln

script, skript, n (writing)
Handschrift f; theatre
Regiebuch nt; (film)
Drehbuch nt

Scripture, skripp-tscher, n
Heilige Schrift f

scroll, skrohl, n Rolle f;
(sculptural) Schnörkel m

scrounge, skraundcsh, v
schnorren; **–r,** n Schnorrer
m

scrub, skrabb, n Gestrüpp
nt; v scheuern

scruff, skraff, n **– of the
neck,** Genick nt; **–y,** adj
schäbig

scrum, skramm, n Gedränge
nt

scruple, skruh-p'l, n
Skrupel m

scrupulous, skruh-pju-less,
adj peinlich, gewissenhaft

scrutinize, skruh-ti-neis, v
prüfen, untersuchen

scrutiny, skruh-ti-ni, n

Prüfung f

scuff, skaff, v abstoßen

scuffle, skaff-'l, n
Handgemenge nt

scullery, skall-e-ri, n
Spülküche f

sculptor, skalp-ter, n
Bildhauer m

sculpture, skalp-tscher, n
(art) Bildhauerei f;
(statue) Skulptur f

scum, skammm, n
Abschaum m

scupper, skapp-er, v naut
versenken; fig zunichte
machen

scurry, ska-ri, v hasten

scuttle, skatt-'l, n
(Kohlen)eimer m; v naut
versenken; (scamper)
trippeln

scythe, sseidh, n Sense f

sea, ssie, n See f, Meer nt;
–food, n Meeresfrüchte pl;
–gull, n Möwe f

seal, ssiel, n (stamp) Siegel
nt; (animal) Seehund m; v
versiegeln

sea level, ssie lew-'l,
Meeresspiegel m

sea lion, ssie lei-en, n
Seelöwe m

seam, ssiem, n (sewing)
Naht f; (in mine) Lager nt

seamy, ssie-mi, adj
zwielichtig

search, ssörtsch, n Suche f;
(examination)
Durchsuchung f; v suchen;
durchsuchen; – for, v
suchen nach; –ing, adj

forschend; –light, n
Scheinwerfer m; – party, n
Suchtrupp m

seasick, ssie-ssick, adj
seekrank; –ness, n
Seekrankheit f

seaside, ssie-sseid, n Küste f;
at the –, am Meer

season, ssie-s'n, n Jahreszeit
f; (fashionable) Saison f; v
(food) würzen; (timber)
austrocknen; –al, adj
Saison-; –ed, adj erfahren;
–ing, n Würze f; – ticket,
n theatre Abonnement nt;
(public transport)
Dauerkarte f

seat, ssiet, n Sitz m,
(Sitz)platz m; (bench)
Bank f; (of trousers)
Hosenboden m; (estate)
Landsitz m; v (guests,
public) Sitzplätze bieten
für; – belt, n
Sicherheitsgurt m

seaweed, ssie-u'ied, n
Seetang m

seaworthy, ssie-u'ör-dhi, adj
seefest

secluded, ssi-kluh-didd, adj
einsam, abgeschlossen

seclusion, ssi-kluh-sch'n, n
Abgeschiedenheit f

second, sseck-end, adj
zweite(r/s); n (time, mus)
Sekunde f; comm zweite
Wahl f; (supporter)
Sekundant m; v
unterstützen; –ary, adj
untergeordnet; –hand, adj
aus zweiter Hand,

gebraucht; – hand, n
Sekundenzeiger m; –ly,
adv zweitens; —rate, adj
zweitklassig; have –
thoughts, v es sich anders
überlegen

secrecy, ssie-kriss-i, n
Heimlichkeit f

secret, ssie-kritt, adj
geheim, Geheim-; n
Geheimnis nt

secretarial, sseck-re-tähr-ri-
el, adj Sekretariats-

secretary, sseck-re-te-ri, n
Sekretär m

secretion, ssi-krie-sch'n, n
Ausscheidung f

secretive, ssie-kritt-iw, adj
geheimnisvoll

sect, ssekt, n Sekte f; –arian,
adj Konfessions-

section, sseck-sch'n, n
Abschnitt m; v
unterteilen

sector, sseck-ter, n Sektor m

secular, sseck-ju-ler, adj
Säkular-; weltlich

secure, ssi-kjuhr, adj (safe)
sicher; (fixed) fest; v
(make safe, obtain)
sichern; (fix) befestigen

security, ssi-kjuhr-ri-ti, n
(safety) Sicherheit f;
(pledge) Pfand nt

sedate, ssi-deht, adj gesetzt,
ruhig; v med ruhigstellen,
sedieren

sedative, ssedd-e-tiw, n
Beruhigungsmittel nt

sedentary, ssedd-'n-te-ri, adj
sitzend

sediment, ssedd-i-ment, *n*
Ablagerung *f*; (in liquid)
Satz *m*

sedition, ssi-disch-'n, *n*
Aufruhr *m*

seduce, ssi-djuhss, *v*
verführen

seduction, ssi-dack-sch'n, *n*
Verführung *f*

see, ssie, *v* sehen;
(understand) verstehen;
(visit) besuchen; **– that,**
dafür sorgen, daß; **–
through,** durchschauen; **–
to,** erledigen

seed, ssied, *n* Samen *m*; *sport*
gesetzter Spieler *m*; **–y,** *adj*
zwielichtig; **go/run to –,** *v*
fig herunterkommen

seek, ssiek, *v* suchen; (strive
for) streben nach

seem, ssiem, *v* scheinen;
–ingly, *adv* anscheinend;
–ly, *adj* anständig

seep, ssiep, *v* sickern

seethe, ssiedh, *v* (crowds)
wimmeln; (with anger)
kochen

seize, ssies, *v* ergreifen,
packen; (power) ergreifen;
(confiscate)
beschlagnahmen

seizure, ssie-scher, *n*
(confiscation)
Beschlagnahme *f*; *med*
Anfall *m*

seldom, ssell-dem, *adv*
selten

select, ssi-lekt, *adj* exklusiv;
v auswählen; **–ion,** *n*
Auswahl *f*

self, sself, *adj* Selbst-; **(one**
etc.)**–,** *pron* (*refl*) sich;
(*emphatic*) selber, selbst; **—
catering,** *adj* für
Selbstversorger; **—
centred,** *adj* egozentrisch;
—confidence, *n*
Selbstvertrauen *nt*; **—
conscious,** *adj* unsicher; **—
contained,** *adj*
abgeschlossen; **– defence,**
n Selbstverteidigung *f*; **—
employed,** *adj* selbständig;
–ish, *adj* selbstsüchtig;
–ishness, *n* Selbstsucht *f*;
–less, *adj* selbstlos; **—pity,**
n Selbstmitleid *nt*; **—
portrait,** *n* Selbstbildnis
nt; **—righteous,** *adj*
selbstgerecht; **—sacrifice,**
n Selbstaufopferung *f*; **—
service,** *n*
Selbstbedienung *f*; **—
sufficient,** *adj* unabhängig

sell, ssell, *v* verkaufen; **—by
date,** *n* Verfallsdatum; **—
out (of),** *v* ausverkaufen

Sellotape ®, sell-oh-tehp, *n*
Tesafilm ® *m*

semblance, ssemm-blenss, *n*
Anschein *m*

semi, ssemm-i, *pref* Halb-;
–circle, *n* Halbkreis *m*;
—colon, *n* Semikolon *nt*; **—
-detached house,** *n*
Doppelhaushälfte *f*;
–final, *n* Halbfinale *nt*

semolina, ssemm-e-lie-ne, *n*
Grieß *m*

senate, ssenn-itt, *n* Senat *m*

send, ssend, *v* senden;

schicken; **–er,** *n* Absender
m; **– for,** *v* holen lassen; **–
off,** *v* abschicken; *sport*
vom Platz stellen; **– up,** *v*
(satirize) parodieren

senile, ssie-neil, *adj*
altersschwach

senior, ssie-ni-er, *adj* (older)
älter; (higher)
höhergestellt; *n* (in age)
Ältere(r) *m* & *f*; (in rank)
Höhergestellte(r) *m* & *f*; **–
citizen,** *n* Rentner *m*

seniority, ssie-ni-o-ri-ti, *n*
(in age) höheres Alter *nt*;
(in rank) höherer Rang *m*

sensation, ssenn-sseh-sch'n,
n Gefühl *f*; (stir)
Aufsehen *nt*, Sensation *f*

sense, ssenss, *n* (faculty,
meaning) Sinn *m*;
(reason) Verstand *m*;
(feeling) Gefühl *nt*; *v*
spüren; **–less,** *adj* sinnlos;
(unconscious) bewußtlos;
make –, *v* Sinn ergeben

sensible, ssenn-ssi-b'l, *adj*
vernünftig

sensitive, ssenn-ssi-tiw, *adj*
empfindlich

sensual, ssenn-ssju-el, *adj*
sinnlich

sentence, ssenn-tenss, *n*
gram Satz *m*; *law* Urteil *nt*;
v verurteilen

sentiment, ssenn-ti-ment, *n*
Gefühl *nt*, Empfindung *f*;
(conviction) Gesinnung *f*;
–al, *adj* sentimental

sentry, ssenn-tri, *n* Posten
m; **– box,** Wachhaus *nt*

separate, ssepp-e-ret, *adj*
einzeln

separate, ssepp-e-reht, *v*
(sich) trennen; **–ly,** *adv*
getrennt

separation, ssepp-e-reh-
sch'n, *n* Trennung *f*

September, ssepp-**temm**-ber,
n September *m*

septic, ssepp-tick, *adj*
septisch

sequel, ssie-ku'el, *n* Folge *f*

sequence, ssie-ku'enss, *n*
Reihenfolge *f*

serenade, sse-re-nehd, *n*
Ständchen *nt*

serene, ssi-**rien,** *adj* heiter;
(still) ungetrübt

sergeant, ssahr-dschent, *n*
mil Feldwebel *m*; (police)
Wachtmeister *m*

serial, ssier-ri-el, *adj* Serien-
; *n* (TV, radio) Serie *f*;
–ize, *v* in Fortsetzungen
bringen

series, ssier-ris, *n* Serie *f*,
Reihe *f*

serious(ly), ssier-ri-ess(-li),
adj & adv ernst(haft);
(injury) schwer

sermon, ssör-men, *n*
Predigt *f*

serpent, ssör-pent, *n*
Schlange *f*

servant, ssör-went, *n*
Diener *m*

serve, ssörw, *v* (be)dienen;
(food) servieren; (tennis)
aufschlagen; (sentence)
verbüßen; **it –s you right!**
das geschieht dir recht!

service, ssör-wiss, *n* Service
m, Dienst *m*; (hotel etc.)
Bedienung *f*; (trains etc.)
Verbindung *f*; *relig*
Gottesdienst *m*; *mech*
Wartung *f*; *v mech* warten;
– area, *n* Raststätte *f*; **–
charge,** *n* Bedienung *f*;
S–s, *npl mil* Streitkräfte *pl*;
– station, *n* Tankstelle *f*

serviette, ssör-wi-ett, *n*
Serviette *f*

servile, ssör-weil, *adj*
unterwürfig

session, sse-sch'n, *n* Sitzung
f; **be in –,** *v* tagen

set, ssett, *adj* (fixed)
festgesetzt; (ready) bereit;
n (collection, tennis) Satz
m; (radio, TV) Apparat *m*;
(of china) Service *nt*;
theatre Bühnenbild *nt*; *v*
setzen; (trap, clock, task)
stellen; (example) geben;
(table) decken; (hair)
legen; (bone) einrenken;
(solidify) fest werden;
(jewel) fassen; (of sun)
untergehen; **–back,** *n*
Rückschlag *m*; **–
meal/menu,** *n* Tagesmenü
nt; **– off,** *v* (depart)
losfahren; (alarm, bomb)
losgehen lassen; **– on fire,**
v anzünden; **– out,** *v*
(arrange) arrangieren;
(explain) erklären;
(depart) losfahren; **– up,** *v*
(organization) einrichten;
(statue) aufstellen

settee, ssett-**ie,** *n* Sofa *nt*

setting, ssett-ing, *n*
Umgebung *f*; (of jewel)
Fassung *f*

settle, ssett-'l, *v* (calm)
beruhigen; (pay)
bezahlen; (decide)
entscheiden; (make one's
home) sich niederlassen;
(of dust, sediment) sich
setzen; **– down,** *v* (calm
down) sich beruhigen;
(get used to) sich
eingewöhnen; **– for,** *v* sich
zufriedengeben mit;
–ment, *n* (payment)
Begleichung *f*; (colony)
Siedlung *f*; (of
foundations) Senken *nt*;
(agreement) Vereinbarung
f; (bequest) Vermächtnis
nt; **– on,** *v* sich
entscheiden für; **–r,** *n*
Siedler *m*

seven, ssew-en, *num* sieben;
–teen, *num* siebzehn; **–th,**
adj siebte; *n* Siebtel *nt*;
–ty, *num* siebzig

sever, ssew-er, *v* trennen;
(break off) abbrechen

several, ssew-'rel, *adj & pron*
mehrere

severe, ssi-**wier,** *adj* (person)
streng; (injury) schwer;
(weather) rauh

severity, ssi-we-ri-ti, *n*
Strenge *f*; Schwere *f*

sew, ssoh, *v* nähen

sewage, ssjuh-idsch, *n*
Abwasser *nt*

sewer, ssjuh-er, *n*

Abwasserkanal m

sex, sseks, n Sex m;
Geschlecht nt; **–ist,** adj
sexistisch; n Sexist m,
Sexistin f; **–ual,** adj
geschlechtlich,
Geschlechts-; **–y,** adj sexy;
have – (with), v
Geschlechtsverkehr
haben (mit)

shabby, schäbb-i, adj
schäbig; (action) gemein

shack, schäck, n Hütte f

shackle, schäck-'l, n Fessel
f; v fesseln

shade, schehd, n Schatten
m; (colour) Farbton m;
(for lamp, eyes etc.)
Schirm m; v beschatten

shadow, schädd-oh, n
Schatten m; v nachspüren;
–y, adj schattenhaft

shady, scheh-di, adj
schattig; fig verdächtig

shaft, schahft, n (of spear)
Schaft m; mech Welle f;
(in mine) Schacht m; (of
light) Strahl m

shaggy, schägg-i, adj zottig

shake, schehk, v schütteln;
(tremble) zittern; (shock)
erschüttern; **–n,** adj
erschüttert

shaky, scheh-ki, adj
wackelig; (unreliable)
unzuverlässig

shall, schäll, v (future)
werden; (obligation)
sollen

shallow, schäll-oh, adj
seicht; fig oberflächlich

sham, schämm, adj falsch; n
Heuchelei f

shame, schehm, n (disgrace)
Schande f; (sense of)
Scham f; v beschämen;
–ful, adj schändlich; **–less,**
adj schamlos; **it's a –,** es ist
schade; **what a –!** schade!

shampoo, schämm-puh, n
Shampoo nt; v Haare
waschen

shamrock, schämm-rock, n
Klee m; (leaf) Kleeblatt nt

shandy, schänn-di, n
Radlermaß f

shape, schehp, n Form f; v
formen, bilden; **–ed,**
suffix -förmig; **–less,** adj
formlos; **–ly,** adj
wohlgeformt; **take –,** v
Form annehmen

share, schähr, n Teil m,
Anteil m; fin Aktie f; v
teilen; **–holder,** n
Aktionär m

shark, schark, n Haifisch m;
fig Geschäftemacher m

sharp, scharp, adj scharf;
spitz; (mind) scharfsinnig;
mus erhöht; n mus Kreuz
nt; **–en,** v schärfen;
(point) spitzen; **–ener,** n
Schleifgerät nt; (pencil)
Anspitzer m; **–ly,** adj
(clearly) deutlich;
(suddenly) plötzlich;
(harshly) scharf; **–ness,** n
Schärfe f

shatter, schätt-er, v
zerschmettern; (nerves)
erschüttern; **–ed,** adj

(exhausted) erledigt

shave, schehw, n Rasur f; v
(sich) rasieren; **–r,** n
Rasierapparat m

shaving, scheh-wing, n
Rasieren nt; **– brush,** n
Rasierpinsel m; **– cream,** n
Rasiercreme f; **– foam,** n
Rasierschaum m

shavings, scheh-wings, npl
Hobelspäne mpl

shawl, scho'al, n Stola f

she, schie, adj weiblich, -
weibchen; pron sie

sheaf, schief, n (of corn)
Garbe f; (of papers)
Bündel nt

shear, schier, v scheren; **–s,**
npl (große) Schere f;
(garden) Gartenschere f

sheath, schieth, n
(scabbard) Scheide f;
(condom) Kondom m/nt

shed, schedd, n Schuppen
m; v (tears, blood)
vergießen; (hair, leaves
etc.) verlieren

sheen, schien, n Glanz m

sheep, schiep, n Schaf nt

sheer, schier, adj (pure)
lauter, rein; (steep) steil;
(fine) fein; adv steil

sheet, schiet, n (for bed)
Bettuch nt, Laken nt; (of
paper) Bogen m; (of metal
etc.) Platte f; (of water,
ice) Fläche f; **– lightning,**
Wetterleuchten nt

shelf, schelf, n Brett nt; (set
of shelves) Regal nt

shell, schell, n (of nut)

Schale f; (of pea) Hülse f;
(seashell) Muschel f; mil
Geschoß nt, Granate f; v
schälen; pulen; mil
bombardieren; **–fish**, n
Schalentier nt; pl
Meeresfrüchte pl

shelter, schell-ter, n Schutz
m; (mountain) Hütte f;
(air raid etc.) Bunker m; v
(take shelter) sich
unterstellen; (give shelter)
schützen; **night –**, n
Obdachlosenheim nt

shelve, schelw, v
aufschieben; **–s**, npl see
shelf

shepherd, schepp-erd, n
Schäfer m

sherry, sche-ri, n Sherry m

Shetland, schett-lend, n **the
Shetlands**, npl die
Shetlandinseln pl

shield, schield, n Schild nt;
fig Schirm m; v schützen

shift, schift, n (work)
Schicht f; (change)
Wandel m; v (move)
(sich) bewegen; (change)
wechseln; **– work**, n
Schichtarbeit f; **–y**, adj
(untrustworthy)
verschlagen; (evasive)
ausweichend

shin, schinn, n
Schienbein nt

shine, schein, n Schein m;
Glanz m; v scheinen,
leuchten, glänzen

shingle, sching-g'l, n
(pebbles) Kiesel m; (on

roof) Schindel f; **–s**, n med
Gürtelrose f

shiny, schei-ni, adj glänzend

ship, schipp, n Schiff nt; v
versenden; **–ment**, n
Sendung f; **–per**, n
Spediteur m; **–ping**, n
(traffic) Schiffahrt f;
(sending) Versand m;
–wreck, n Schiffbruch m;
–yard, n Werft f

shire, scheir, n Grafschaft f

shirk, schörk, v ausweichen;
–er, n Drückeberger m

shirt, schört, n Hemd nt; **–y**,
adj sauer

shit, schitt, vulg n Scheiße f;
v scheißen

shiver, schiw-er, n Schauer
m; v zittern

shoal, scho'al, n (of fish)
Schwarm m; (shallows)
Sandbank f

shock, schock, n Stoß m;
(fright) Schreck m; elec
Schlag m; v (frighten)
erschüttern; (offend)
schockieren; **– absorber**, n
Stoßdämpfer m; **–ing**, adj
schrecklich, schockierend

shoddy, schodd-i, adj (work)
schludrig; (goods)
minderwertig

shoe, schuh, n Schuh m;
(horse's) Hufeisen nt; v
(horse) beschlagen;
–horn, n Schuhanzieher
m; **–lace**, n Schnürsenkel
m; **– polish**, n
Schuhcreme f

shoot, schuht, n (growth)

Sprößling m; (hunt) Jagd
f; v schießen; (kill)
erschießen; (film) drehen;
– up, v aufschießen; **–ing**,
n Schießen nt; **–ing star**, n
Sternschnuppe f

shop, schopp, n Laden m,
Geschäft nt; v einkaufen
gehen; **–assistant**, n
Verkäufer m; **–keeper**, n
Ladeninhaber m; **–lifting**,
n Ladendiebstahl m; **–per**,
n Käufer m; **–ping**, n (act)
Einkaufen nt; (goods)
Einkäufe pl; **– ping centre**,
n Einkaufszentrum nt

shore, schor, n Ufer nt,
Strand m; v **– up**, v
abstützen

shorn, schorn, adj geschoren

short, schort, adj kurz;
(person) klein; (supply)
knapp; n (film) Kurzfilm
m; elec Kurzschluß m;
–age, n Mangel m; **–
circuit**, n Kurzschluß m;
–coming n Fehler m; **–
cut**, n Abkürzung f; **–en**, v
(ab)kürzen; **–fall**, n Defizit
nt; **–hand**, n Kurzschrift f;
–list, n engere Wahl f; **–ly**,
adv bald; **–sighted**, adj
kurzsichtig; **–tempered**,
adj aufbrausend; **–term**,
adj kurzfristig; **be – for
sth**, v die Kurzform von
etw sein; **be – of ...**, v
nicht genug ... haben

shot, schott, n Schuß m;
(person) Schütze m;
(pellet) Schrot m; photog

Aufnahme f; (fam attempt) Versuch m; like a –, wie der Blitz; **–gun,** n Schrotflinte f

should, schudd, v (past & conditional of **shall**)

shoulder, schohl-der, n Schulter f, v schultern; fig auf sich nehmen; **– blade,** n Schulterblatt nt; **hard –,** n Seitenstreifen m

shout, schaut, n Schrei m; Ruf m; v schreien; rufen

shove, schaw, n Schub m; v schieben

shovel, scha-w'l, n Schaufel f; v schaufeln

show, schoh, n (display) Schau f; theatre Vorstellung f; (exhibition) Ausstellung f; v zeigen; ausstellen; (pity etc.) erweisen; (be visible) sichtbar sein; **– off,** v angeben; **––off,** n Angeber m; **– up,** v (be visible) zu sehen sein; (arrive) erscheinen; (expose) bloßstellen

shower, schau-er, n (of rain) Schauer m; (wash) Dusche f; v duschen; **– with,** schadd-en mit; **–proof,** adj regendicht; **–y,** adj regnerisch

show jumping, schoh dschamm-ping, n Turnierreiten nt

showroom, schoh-ruhm, n Ausstellungsraum m

showy, schoh-i, adj

auffallend; (ostentatious) protzig

shred, schredd, n Fetzen m; v zerfetzen; (cooking) raspeln

shrewd, schruhd, adj scharfsinnig

shriek, schriek, n Kreischen nt; v kreischen

shrill, schrill, adj schrill, gellend

shrimp, schrimp, n Garnele f

shrine, schrein, n Schrein m

shrink, schrink, v schrumpfen; **– from,** zurückschrecken vor

shrivel, schri-w'l, v **– (up),** (zusammen)schrumpfen

shroud, schraud, n Leichentuch nt; v einhüllen

Shrove Tuesday, schrohw tjuhs-deh, n Faschingsdienstag m

shrub, schrabb, n Strauch m; **–bery,** n Gebüsch nt

shrug, schragg, n Achselzucken nt; v die Achseln zucken; **– off,** v fig als unwichtig abtun

shudder, schadd-er, n Schauder m; v schaudern

shuffle, schaff-'l, v (feet) schlurfen; (cards) mischen

shun, schann, v meiden

shunt, schant, v rangieren

shut, schatt, v zumachen, schließen; **– up,** v fam den Mund halten; **–ter,** n Fensterladen m; photog

Verschluß m

shuttle, schatt-'l, n (train) Pendelzug m; (bus) Pendelbus m; (spaceship) Shuttle f; **–cock,** n Federball m; **– service,** n Pendelverkehr m

shy, schei, adj schüchtern; v (of horse) scheuen; **– away from,** fig zurückweichen vor; **–ness,** n Schüchternheit f

sick, ssick, adj (unwell) krank; (nauseous) übel; (in bad taste) makaber; **be –,** v (unwell) krank sein; (vomit) brechen, sich übergeben; **be – of sth,** v fam etw satt haben; **feel –,** v sich übel fühlen; **–en,** v (fall ill) krank werden; (disgust) anekeln; **–ening,** adj ekelhaft

sickle, ssick-'l, n Sichel f

sickly, ssick-li, adj (unwell) kränklich; (too sweet) zu süß

sickness, n Krankheit f

sick pay, ssick peh, n Krankengeld nt

side, sseid, adj Seiten-; n Seite f; (team) Mannschaft f; v **– with sb,** jds Partei ergreifen; **–board,** n Anrichte nt; **–boards,** npl Koteletten pl; **– by –,** nebeneinander; **–car,** n Beiwagen m; **– effect,** n Nebenwirkung f; **–light,** adj Standlicht nt;

–step, v ausweichen; **–street,** n Nebenstraße f; **get –tracked,** v abgelenkt werden; **–ways,** adv seitwärts

siding, sseid-ing, n Nebengleis nt

siege, ssiedsch, n Belagerung f

sieve, ssiw, n Sieb nt; v sieben; fig durchsieben

sift, ssift, v sieben; fig prüfen

sigh, ssei, n Seufzer m; v seufzen

sight, sseit, n (faculty) Sehkraft f; (view, spectacle) Anblick m; (of gun) Visier nt; v erblicken; **at –,** vom Blatt; **by –,** vom Sehen; **in/out of –,** in/außer Sicht

sights, sseitss, npl Sehenswürdigkeiten pl

sightseeing, sseit-ssie-ing, n Sightseeing nt

sign, ssein, n (symbol) Zeichen nt; (notice) Schild nt; v unterschreiben

signal, ssigg-nel, n Signal nt; v signalisieren

signature, ssigg-ne-tscher, n Unterschrift f

significance, ssigg-niff-i-kenss, n Bedeutung f

significant, ssigg-niff-i-kent, adj bedeutend

signify, ssigg-ni-fei, v bedeuten

sign language, ssein läng-gu'idsch, n

Zeichensprache f

signpost, ssein-pohst, n Wegweiser m

silence, ssei-lenss, n (quiet) Stille f; (not speaking) Schweigen nt; v zum Schweigen bringen; **–!** Ruhe!; **–r,** ssei-len-sser, n Schalldämpfer m

silent, ssei-lent, adj (quiet) still; (not speaking) schweigsam; **be/keep –,** v schweigen

silhouette, sill-uh-ett, n Schattenbild nt

silicon, ssill-i-ken, n Silicium nt; **– chip,** n Siliciumchip m

silk, ssilk, adj seiden, Seiden-; n Seide f; **–y,** adj seidig

silly, ssill-i, adj albern

silver, ssill-wer, adj silbern, Silber-, aus Silber; n Silber nt; v versilbern; **–plated,** adj versilbert; **–smith,** n Silberschmied m; **–y,** adj silbern

similar, ssimm-i-ler, adj ähnlich

similarity, ssimm-i-lä-ri-ti, n Ähnlichkeit f

similarly, ssimm-i-ler-li, adv ebensogut

simile, ssimm-i-li, n Gleichnis nt

simmer, ssimm-er, v sieden (lassen)

simper, ssimm-per, v gekünstelt lächeln

simple, ssimm-p'l, adj

einfach; **–minded,** adj einfältig

simplicity, ssimm-pliss-i-ti, n Einfachheit f

simplify, ssimm-pli-fei, v vereinfachen

simply, ssimp-li, adv einfach

simultaneous(ly), ssimm-el-teh-ni-ess(-li), adj & adv gleichzeitig

sin, ssinn, n Sünde f; v sündigen

since, ssinss, adv seitdem; conj (time) seit(dem); (because) da, weil; prep seit

sincere, ssinn-ssier, adj aufrichtig; **Yours –ly,** Mit freundlichen Grüßen

sincerity, ssinn-sse-ri-ti, n Aufrichtigkeit f

sinew, ssinn-juh, n Sehne f

sinful, ssinn-full, adj sündhaft

sing, ssing, v singen

singe, ssindsch, v versengen

singer, ssing-er, n Sänger m

single, ssing-g'l, adj (only) einzig; (unmarried) ledig; (ticket) einfach; n (ticket) einfache Fahrkarte f; (unmarried person) Single m; **– bed,** n Einzelbett nt; **– file,** n Gänsemarsch m; **–handed,** adj & adv allein; **–minded,** adj zielstrebig; **– out,** v aussondern; **– room,** n Einzelzimmer nt; **–s,** n (tennis) Einzel nt

singly, ssing-gli, adv einzeln;

(piece by piece)
stückweise

singular, ssing-gju-ler, *adj*
einmalig; *n* Einzahl *f*,
Singular *m*

sinister, ssinn-iss-ter, *adj*
unheilvoll

sink, ssink, *n* Waschbecken
nt; *v* sinken; (ship)
versenken; (shaft) senken;
– **in**, einsinken;
(comprehend) verstehen

sinner, ssinn-er, *n* Sünder *m*

sinus, ssei-ness, *n* Sinus *m*

sip, ssipp, *n* Schlückchen *nt*;
v schlückchenweise
trinken

siphon, ssei-fen, *n* Siphon
m; *v* – **off**, ablassen; *fig*
abzweigen

sir, ssör, *n* (address) mein
Herr *m*; (title) Sir *m*

siren, sseir-ren, *n* Sirene *f*

sirloin, ssör-leun, *n*
Lendenstück *nt*

sister, ssiss-ter, *n* Schwester
f; –**in-law**, *n* Schwägerin *f*

sit, ssitt, *v* sitzen; (of
committee etc.) tagen; –
down, *v* sich (hin)setzen;
– **up**, *v* (straight) sich
gerade setzen

sitcom, ssitt-komm, *n* (*abbr*
situation comedy),
Situationskomödie *f*

site, sseit, *n* (land)
Grundstück *nt*; (location)
Lage *f*, Standort *m*; *v*
legen; **building** –, *n*
Baustelle *f*

sitting, ssitt-ing, *n* Sitzung *f*;

– **room**, *n* Wohnzimmer *nt*

situated, ssitt-juh-eh-
tidd, *adj* gelegen; **be** –, *v*
liegen

situation, ssitt-juh-**eh**-sch'n,
n Lage *f*; (post) Stelle *f*

six, ssiks, *num* sechs; –**teen**,
num sechzehn; –**th**, *adj*
sechste(r/s); *n* Sechstel *nt*;
–**ty**, *num* sechzig

size, sseis, *n* Größe *f*;
(measure) Maß *nt*; –**able**,
adj beträchtlich; – **up**, *v*
einschätzen

skate, skeht, *n* Schlittschuh
m; (fish) Rochen *m*; *v*
Schlittschuh laufen;
–**board**, *n* Skateboard *nt*;
–**r**, *n* Schlittschuhläufer *m*

skating, skeh-ting, *n* (ice)
Schlittschuhlaufen *nt*;
(roller skates)
Rollschuhlaufen *nt*; –
rink, *n* (ice) Eisbahn *f*;
(roller skates)
Rollschuhbahn *f*

skeleton, skell-i-ten, *n*
Skelett *nt*; *fig* Gerippe *nt*

sketch, sketsch, *n* Skizze *f*;
theatre Sketch *m*; *v*
skizzieren

skewer, skjuh-er, *n* Spieß *m*;
v (auf)spießen

ski, skie, *n* Ski *m*; *v* Ski
laufen; – **boot**, *n* Skistiefel
m

skid, skidd, *v* ausrutschen;
(of car) schleudern

skier, skie-er, *n* Skiläufer *m*

skilful, skill-full, *adj*
geschickt, gewandt

skiing, skie-ing, *n*
Skilaufen *nt*

ski lift, skie lift, *n* Skilift *m*

skill, skill, *n*
Geschicklichkeit *f*; –**ed**, *n*
(worker) gelernt; (expert)
geschickt

skim, skimm, *v*
abschäumen; –**med milk**,
n Magermilch *f*

skimp, skimp, *v* knausern,
sparen; –**py**, *adj* knapp

skin, skinn, *n* Haut *f*; (peel)
Schale *f*; *v* abhäuten;
(peel) schälen; –**ny**, *adj*
dünn

skip, skipp, *n* (jump) Sprung
m; (container) Container
m; *v* (jump) hüpfen; (with
rope) seilspringen; (omit)
auslassen; –**per**, *n* Kapitän
m

skirmish, skör-misch, *n*
Rangelei *f*; (fight)
Gefecht *nt*; *v* streiten;
(fight) sich Gefechte
liefern

skirt, skört, *n* Rock *m*; *v*
umgehen

ski slope, skie slohp, *n*
Skipiste *f*

skittle, skitt-'l, *n* Kegel *m*;
–**s**, *n* Kegeln *pl*

skive, skeiw, *v* *fam*
schwänzen

skull, skall, *n* Schädel *m*

skunk, skank, *n* Skunk *m*,
Stinktier *nt*

sky, skei, *n* Himmel *m*;
–**light**, *n* Oberlicht *nt*;
–**scraper**, *n*

Wolkenkratzer m

slab, släbb, n Platte f

slack, släck, adj (loose) lose, schlaff; (careless) nachlässig; (business) flau; v (not work) bummeln; **–en**, v (work loose) locker werden; (loosen) lockern; (slow down) verlangsamen; **–er**, n Faulenzer m

slam, slamm, n (cards) Schlemm m; v zuschlagen

slander, slahn-der, n Verleumdung f; v verleumden; **–er**, n Verleumder m

slang, släng, n Slang m

slant, slahnt, n Schräge f; fig Neigung f; v schräg laufen; **–ing**, adj schief, schräg

slap, släpp, n Klaps m; v schlagen, klopfen

slash, släsch, n (cut) Schnitt m; (wound) Schnittwunde f; v aufschlitzen; (fig price) drastisch reduzieren; (spending) drastisch kürzen

slate, sleht, n (material) Schiefer m; (on roof) Dachziegel m; (list of candidates) Kandidatenliste f; v in der Luft zerreißen

slaughter, slo'a-ter, n (of animals) Schlachten nt; (massacre) Metzelei f; v schlachten; (massacre) niedermetzeln; **–house**, n Schlachthof m

slave, slehw, n Sklave m, Sklavin f; v sich schinden; **–ry**, n Sklaverei f; (hard work) Schinderei f

slay, sleh, v erschlagen, umbringen

sledge, sledsch, n Schlitten m; **–hammer**, n Schmiedehammer m

sleek, sliek, adj (smooth) glatt; (well fed) wohlgenährt

sleep, sliep, n Schlaf m; v schlafen; **–ing bag**, n Schlafsack m; **–ing car**, n Schlafwagen m; **–ing pill**, n Schlaftablette f; **–less**, adj schlaflos; **–lessness**, n Schlaflosigkeit f; **–walker**, n Schlafwandler m; **–y**, adj schläfrig

sleet, sliet, n Schneeregen m

sleeve, sliew, n Ärmel m; **–less**, adj ärmellos

sleigh, sleh, n Schlitten m

sleight, sleit, n **– of hand**, Taschenspielerei f

slender, slenn-der, adj schlank; fig karg

slice, sleiss, n Schnitte f, Scheibe f; v in Scheiben schneiden

slick, slick, adj glatt; (polished) professionell; n (oil) **–**, Ölteppich m

slide, sleid, n (children's) Rutschbahn f; photog Dia nt; v rutschen, gleiten; **hair –**, n Haarspange f

slight, sleit, adj (small) gering; (figure) zierlich; n

Beleidigung f; v beleidigen

slim, slimm, adj (thin) schlank; (small) gering; v (diet) eine Schlankheitskur machen; (reduce) reduzieren

slime, sleim, n Schlamm m

slimming, slimm-ing, adj Schlankheits-; n (diet) Abnehmen nt; (reduction) Kürzen nt

slimy, slei-mi, adj schlammig, fig schmierig

sling, sling, n Schlinge f; v schleudern

slink, slink, v schleichen

slip, slipp, n (error) Fehler m; (petticoat) Unterrock m; v (glide) gleiten; (fall) ausrutschen; **– away**, v sich davonstehlen; **– off**, v sich davonstehlen; (clothes) abstreifen; **– on**, v (clothes) überstreifen; **– one's mind**, v vergessen; **give sb the –**, v jdm entkommen

slipped disc, slipt disk, n Bandscheibenvorfall m

slipper, slipp-er, n Pantoffel m, Hausschuh m

slippery, slipp-e-ri, adj schlüpfrig

slip-road, slipp-rohd, n (on) Auffahrt f; (off) Ausfahrt f

slit, slitt, n Schlitz m; v aufschlitzen

sliver, sliw-er, n Streifen m; (food) dünne Scheibe f

slob, slobb, n (fam lazy) fauler Sack m; (fam fat)

Fettsack m

slog, slogg, v *fam* schuften

slogan, sloh-gen, n Slogan m, Schlagwort nt

slope, slohp, n Abhang m; v schräg laufen

slot, slott, n Schlitz m; (for coins) Einwurf m; **– in,** v (insert) einfügen; (fit in) passen; **– machine,** n Automat m

sloth, slohth, n Faulheit f; (animal) Faultier nt

slouch, slautsch, v lümmeln

slovenly, slaw-en-li, adj schlampig

slow, sloh, adj langsam; (stupid) dicht; (business) flau; **– down,** v nachlassen, (sich) verlangsamen; **–ly,** adv langsam; **be –,** v (of watch) nachgehen

slug, slagg, n Nacktschnecke f; (fam sip) Schlückchen nt; (fam bullet) Kugel f; **–ish,** adj träge

sluice, sluhss, n Schleuse f; **–gate,** n Schleusentor nt

slum, slamm, n Armenviertel nt

slumber, slamm-ber, n Schlummer m; v schlummern

slump, slamp, n Rückgang m, Sturz m; comm stark zurückgehen

slur, slör, n Verleumdung f; **–red,** adj undeutlich; v undeutlich sprechen

slush, slasch, n

Schneematsch m; **–y,** adj matschig; (sentimental) sentimental

slut, slatt, n Schlampe f

sly, slei, adj schlau, listig

smack, smäck, n Schlag m; v schlagen; **– one's lips,** schmatzen

small, smo'al, adj klein; **– ad,** n Kleinanzeige f; **– change,** n Kleingeld nt; **– hours,** npl früher Morgen m; **–pox,** n Pocken pl; **–print,** n das Kleingedruckte nt

smart, smart, adj (clever) clever; (elegant) schick; (quick) flink; v schmerzen; **– card,** n Chipkarte f; **–en up,** v (make elegant) sich herrichten; (fam get clever) sich am Riemen reißen; **–ly,** adv (quickly) schnell; (elegantly) schick

smash, smäsch, n (collision) Zusammenstoß m; fin Einbruch m; v zerschlagen, zerschmettern; **–ing,** adj fam toll

smattering, smätt-e-ring, n oberflächliche Kenntnis f

smear, smier, n Fleck m; (defame) Beschmutzung f; v (be)schmieren; (defamation) in den Schmutz ziehen

smell, smell, n Geruch m; v riechen; (good) duften

smile, smeil, n Lächeln nt; v lächeln

smirk, smörk, n Grinsen nt; v grinsen

smith, smith, n Schmied m

smithy, ssmidh-i, n Schmiede f

smog, smogg, n Smog m

smoke, smohk, n Rauch m; v rauchen; (cure) räuchern; **–d glass,** n Rauchglas nt; **–less,** adj rauchlos; **–r,** n Raucher m; **–screen,** n fig Vernebelung f

smoking, smoh-king, n Rauchen nt

smoky, smoh-ki, adj (flavour) rauchig; (room) verraucht

smooth, smuhdh, adj glatt; v glätten

smother, smadh-er, n ersticken

smoulder, smohl-der, v glimmen; **–ing,** adj glühend

smudge, smadsch, n (Schmutz)fleck m; v beschmutzen, beschmieren

smug, smagg, adj selbstzufrieden

smuggle, smagg-'l, v schmuggeln; **–r,** n Schmuggler m

smuggling, smagg-ling, n Schmuggeln nt

smut, smatt, n Rußfleck m; (lewd) Schund m; **–ty,** adj schmutzig

snack, snäck, n Snack m, Imbiß m

snail, snehl, n Schnecke f

snake, snehk, n Schlange f

snap, snapp, n (sound) Schnappen nt; (breaking) Knack m; *photog* Schnappschuß m; v (break) brechen; (of person, animal) schnappen; *photog* knipsen; **–shot,** n Schnappschuß m

snare, snähr, n Schlinge f; v fangen; (ensnare) in eine Falle locken

snarl, snarl, v knurren; **– up,** durcheinanderbringen; (traffic) stocken

snatch, snätsch, n (grab) Griff m; (snippet) Stückchen nt; v (grab) wegnehmen; (steal) klauen; (sleep, meal) sich (schnell) genehmigen

sneak, sniek, n (*fam* telltale) Petze f; v schleichen; **–er,** n Turnschuh m

sneer, snier, v spöttisch lächeln

sneeze, snies, n Niesen nt; v niesen

sniff, sniff, n Schnüffeln nt; v schnüffeln; (smell) schnuppern

snip, snipp, n Schnitt m; (*fam* bargain) Schnäppchen nt; v schnippeln; **– off,** v abschnippeln

sniper, snei-per, n Heckenschütze m

snippet, snipp-itt, n

Schnipsel m

snivel, sniw-'l, v schnüffeln

snob, snobb, n Snob m; **–bish,** adj snobistisch

snooker, snuh-ker, n Snooker nt

snooze, snuhs, n Nickerchen nt; v dösen

snore, snor, v schnarchen

snorkel, snor-k'l, n Schnorchel m; v schnorcheln

snort, snort, n Schnauben nt; v schnauben

snout, snaut, n Schnauze f

snow, snoh, n Schnee m; v schneien; **–ball,** n Schneeball m; v *fig* schnell zunehmen; **–bound,** adj eingeschneit; **–drop,** n Schneeglöckchen nt; **–flake,** n Schneeflocke f; **–plough,** n Schneepflug m; **–storm,** n Schneesturm m

snub, snabb, n Abfuhr f; v vor den Kopf stoßen; **– nosed,** adj stupsnasig

snuff, snaff, n Schnupftabak m

snug, snagg, adj mollig, behaglich

so, ssoh, adv so; conj (therefore) also; (so that) so daß; **– as to ...,** conj damit; (in order to) um ... zu; **– do I** (etc.), ich auch; **– far,** adv bis jetzt; **– that,** conj (purpose) damit; (result) so daß; **– what?** na und; **... or –,** etwa ...

soak, ssohk, v einweichen; (drench) durchnässen

soap, ssohp, n Seife f; **– opera,** n (TV) Seifenoper f; **– powder,** n Waschpulver nt; **–y,** adj seifig

soar, ssor, v auffliegen; (of prices) steil ansteigen

sob, ssobb, n Schluchzen nt; v schluchzen

sober, ssoh-ber, adj nüchtern; v **– up,** nüchtern werden

so-called, ssoh-ko'ald, adj sogenannte(r/s)

sociable, ssoh-sche-b'l, adj gesellig

social, ssoh-schel, adj sozial; **– club,** n Klub m für geselliges Zusammensein; **– evening,** n gesellige Abendveranstaltung f; **–ism,** n Sozialismus m; **–ize with sb,** v mit jdm Umgang pflegen/verkehren; **– security,** n Sozialversicherung f; **– worker,** n Sozialarbeiter m

society, sse-ssei-i-ti, n Gesellschaft f; (club) Verein m

sock, ssock, n Socke f; (*fam* blow) Schlag m

socket, ssock-itt, n elec Steckdose f; (for eye, tooth) Höhle f

sod, ssodd, n (grass) Rasensode f; *vulg* Sau f

soda, ssoh-de, n Soda nt; **–**

water, n Sodawasser nt

sofa, ssoh-fe, n Sofa nt

soft, ssoft, adj weich; (quiet) leise; (lenient) nachsichtig; **– drink,** n alkoholfreies Getränk nt; **–en,** v (make soft) aufweichen; (get soft) weich werden; (blow) lindern; **–ness,** n Weichheit f; **–ware,** n comp Software f

soil, sseul, n Erde f, Boden m; v beschmutzen

solace, ssol-iss, n Trost m; v trösten

solar, ssoh-ler, adj Sonnen-; **– panel,** n Sonnenkollektor m; **– power,** n Sonnenenergie f

solder, ssohl-der, n Lötmetall nt; v löten

soldier, ssohl-dscher, n Soldat m; v **– on,** sich durchkämpfen

sole, ssohl, adj einzig; n (of foot etc.) Sohle f; (fish) Seezunge f; **–ly,** adv allein

solemn, ssoll-em, adj (occasion) feierlich; (person) ernst

solicit, sse-liss-itt, v bitten um; (of prostitute) sich anbieten; **–or,** n Rechtsanwalt m, Rechtsanwältin f

solid, ssoll-idd, adj (hard) fest; (not hollow) massiv

solidarity, ssoll-i-dä-ri-ti, n Solidarität f

solidify, sse-lidd-i-fei, v fest werden

solitary, ssoll-i-te-ri, adj einsam; (single) einzeln; **– confinement,** n Einzelhaft f

solitude, ssoll-i-tjuhd, n Einsamkeit f

solo, ssoh-loh, adj Solo-; n Solo nt; **–ist,** n Solist m

soluble, ssoll-ju-b'l, adj löslich; (problem) lösbar

solution, sse-luh-sch'n, n Lösung f

solve, ssolw, v lösen; (puzzle) erraten

solvency, ssoll-wen-ssi, n Zahlungsfähigkeit f

solvent, ssoll-went, adj fin zahlungsfähig; n chem Lösungsmittel nt

sombre, ssomm-ber, adj düster

some, ssamm, adj & pron etwas, pl einige, manche, ein paar; (a little) ein wenig; (some or other) (irgend)ein; adv etwa

somebody, ssamm-be-di, pron jemand

somehow, ssamm-hau, adv irgendwie

someone, ssamm-u'ann, pron jemand

somersault, ssamm-er-ssolt, n Purzelbaum m

something, ssamm-thing, pron etwas

sometime, ssamm-teim, adj (former) ehemalig(e, r); adv irgendwann

sometimes, ssamm-teims, adv manchmal

somewhat, ssamm-u'ott, adv etwas

somewhere, ssamm-u'ähr, adv irgendwo

son, ssann, n Sohn m

sonar, ssoh-nahr, n Sonar nt

sonata, sse-nah-te, n Sonate f

song, ssong, n Lied nt

son-in-law, sann-inn-lor, n Schwiegersohn m

soon, ssuhn, adv bald; **– after(wards),** kurz danach; **as – as,** sobald; **–er,** adv (earlier) früher; (rather) lieber

soot, ssutt, n Ruß m

soothe, ssuhdh, v (person) beruhigen; (pain) lindern

sophisticated, sse-fiss-ti-keh-tidd, adj (person) kultiviert; (elaborate) ausgeklügelt

sopping wet, ssopp-ing u'ett, adj patschnaß

soppy, ssopp-i, adj schmalzig

sorcerer, ssor-sse-rer, n Zauberer m

sorcery, ssor-sse-ri, n Zauberei f, Hexerei f

sordid, ssor-didd, adj (squalid) schmutzig; (base) dreckig

sore, ssor, adj schmerzhaft; n wunde Stelle f

sorrow, sso-roh, n Kummer m; **–ful,** adj kummervoll

sorry, sso-ri, adj elend; **–?** wie bitte?; **(I am) –,** es tut mir leid; **I am/I feel – for**

sb, v jd tut mir leid
sort, ssort, n Sorte f; v –
  (out), (arrange) sortieren;
  (solve) lösen; **a – of ...**,
  eine Art ..., so ein(e) ...
soul, ssohl, n Seele f; mus
  Soul m; **--destroying**, adj
  nervtötend
sound, ssaund, adj (healthy)
  gesund; (thorough)
  gründlich; (sensible)
  vernünftig; (sleep) fest; n
  Laut m; (musical) Klang
  m; (of voice) Ton m; v
  ertönen; (seem) klingen; –
  barrier, n Schallmauer f;
  –bite, n
  (Nachrichten)happen m;
  – effects, npl Toneffekte
  pl**–ing**, n naut Lotung f;
  (investigation)
  Sondierung f; **–track**, n
  Soundtrack m; **– like**, v
  sich anhören wie
soup, ssuhp, n Suppe f;
  –spoon, n Suppenlöffel m
sour, ssau-er, adj sauer
source, ssorss, n Quelle f;
  (origin) Ursprung m
south, ssauth, adj südlich,
  Süd-; adv südlich, nach
  Süden; n Süden m; **S–
  Africa**, n Südafrika nt; **S–
  America**, n Südamerika
  nt; **--east**, n Südosten m;
  --erly, adj südlich; **--ern**,
  adj südlich, Süd-; **S– Pole**,
  n Südpol m; **--west**, n
  Südwesten m
souvenir, ssuh-we-**nier**, n
  Andenken nt, Souvenir n

sovereign, ssow-rin, adj
  souverän; n Herrscher m;
  –ty, n Souveränität f
soviet, ssoh-wi-et, adj
  sowjetisch; **the – Union**,
  Sowjetunion f
sow, ssau, n Sau f
sow, ssoh, v (be)säen; **–er**, n
  Sämann m
soya, **sseu-e**, **– bean**, n
  Sojabohne f
space, spehss, n Raum m;
  (universe) All nt,
  Weltraum m; (time
  interval) Zeitraum m;
  (gap) Zwischenraum m;
  (distance) Abstand m;
  –craft, **–ship**, n
  Raumschiff nt
spacious, speh-schess, adj
  geräumig, umfangreich
spade, spehd, n Spaten m;
  (cards) Pik nt
Spain, spehn, n Spanien nt
span, spänn, n Spanne f; (of
  arch) Spannweite f; v
  überspannen
Spaniard, spänn-jerd, n
  Spanier m
spaniel, spänn-jel, n Spaniel
  m
Spanish, spänn-isch, adj
  spanisch; n (language)
  Spanisch nt; npl (people)
  Spanier pl
spank, spänk, v hauen
spanner, spänn-er, n
  Schraubenschlüssel m
spar, spahr, n naut Spiere f; v
  boxen; (fight) kämpfen
spare, spähr, adj

(replacement) Ersatz-;
  (thin) dürr; (left over)
  übrig; n Ersatzteil nt; v
  (time, money) übrig
  haben; (person, feelings)
  (ver)schonen; **– part**, n
  Ersatzteil nt; **– time**, n
  Freizeit f
sparing(ly), spähr-ring(-li),
  adj & adv sparsam
spark, spark, n Funken m; v
  Funken sprühen; **–(ing)
  plug**, n Zündkerze f
sparkle, spark-'l, v funkeln,
  glänzen
sparkling, spark-ling, adj
  funkelnd, glänzend;
  (wine) Schaum-; (water)
  mit Kohlensäure
sparrow, spä-roh, n Spatz m,
  Sperling m
sparse, sparss, adj spärlich
spasm, späsm, n Krampf m
spasmodic, späs-modd-ick,
  adj sporadisch
spate, speht, n (fig series)
  Serie f
spatter, spätt-er, v
  (be)spritzen
spawn, spo'an, n Laich m; v
  hervorbringen; (frog)
  laichen
speak, spiek, v sprechen;
  (talk) reden; **–er**, n
  (person) Redner m;
  (loudspeaker)
  Lautsprecher m; **– to**, v
  sprechen mit
spear, spier, n Speer m; v
  aufspießen
special, spesch-'l, adj

besondere(r/s); **–ist,** n
Experte m, Expertin f; med
Facharzt m, Fachärztin f;
–ity, n Spezialität f;
(subject) Fachgebiet nt; **–
ize (in),** v sich
spezialisieren (auf);
–ly, adv (particularly)
besonders; (purposely)
speziell; **–ty,** n
Fachgebiet nt

species, spie-schies, n Art f
specific(ally), spe-**ssi-**fick(-
e-li), adj & adv spezifisch
specification, spess-i-fi-**keh-**
sch'n, n Angabe f; comm
Spezifikation f
specify, spess-i-fei, v (list)
spezifizieren; (stipulate)
vorschreiben
specimen, spess-i-minn, adj
Probe-; n Exemplar nt;
med Probe f
speck, speck, n Fleck m;
–led, adj gesprenkelt
spectacle, speck-te-k'l, n
Anblick m; **(pair of) –s,**
npl Brille f
spectacular, speck-**täck-**ju-
ler, adj sensationell
spectator, speck-teh-ter, n
Zuschauer m
spectre, speck-ter, n
Gespenst nt
speculate, speck-juh-leht, v
spekulieren
speech, spietsch, n Sprache
f; (discourse) Rede f;
–less, adj sprachlos
speed, spied, n
Geschwindigkeit f; v

eilen; (in car) zu schnell
fahren; **–ing,** n
Geschwindigkeitsüber-
schreitung f; **– limit,** n
Geschwindigkeits-
beschränkung f; **–ometer,**
n Tacho m; **– up,** v (make
faster) beschleunigen; (get
faster) schneller werden;
–y, adj schnell

spell, spell, n (magic)
Zauber m; (period)
Zeitlang f; v
buchstabieren; **–ing,** n
Schreibweise f
spend, spend, v ausgeben;
–thrift, n Verschwender m
sphere, sfier, n (shape,
globe) Kugel f; (area)
Gebiet nt
spherical, sfe-rick-'l, adj
kugelförmig
spice, speiss, n Gewürz nt; v
würzen
spicy, speiss-i, adj pikant
spider, spei-der, n Spinne f
spike, speik, n Stachel m;
(shoe) Spike m; v (fam
add to drink) etw in den
Drink tun
spill, spill, n Auslaufen nt; v
verschütten; (run over)
überlaufen
spin, spinn, n (outing)
Spazierfahrt f; v (turn)
sich drehen; (thread)
spinnen; **– out,** v in die
Länge ziehen
spinach, spinn-itsch, n
Spinat m
spinal, spei-n'l, adj

Wirbelsäulen-
spindly, spind-li, adj
spindeldürr
spin doctor, spinn-dock-ter,
n Wortkünstler m (in der
Politik)
spin-drier, spinn-drei-er, n
Wäscheschleuder f
spine, speinn, n Wirbelsäule
f; fig Rückgrat nt
spinning, spinn-ing, adj
Spinn-; n Spinnen nt
spin-off, spinn-off, n
Konsequenz f
spinster, spinn-ster, n
unverheiratete Frau f; pej
alte Jungfer f
spiral, spei-rel, adj
spiralförmig; n Spirale
f; **– staircase,** n
Wendeltreppe f
spire, speir, n Turmspitze f
spirit, spi-ritt, n Geist m;
(alcohol) Spirituosen pl;
(vitality) Lebhaftigkeit f;
–ed, adj (lively) lebhaft;
(bold) mutig; **–s,** npl
Spirituosen pl; **–ual,** adj
geistig; **–ualist,** n Spiritist
m; **in good –s,** guten
Mutes
spit, spitt, n (saliva) Spucke
f; (cooking) Spieß m; v
spucken; (rain) sprühen
spite, speit, n Groll m; v
ärgern; **–ful,** adj boshaft;
in – of, conj trotz
spittle, spitt-'l, n Speichel m
splash, spläsch, n Spritzer m;
v (be)spritzen
splendid, splenn-didd, adj

prächtig, glänzend

splendour, splenn-der, n
Pracht f, Glanz m

splint, splint, n Schiene f

splinter, splinn-ter, n
Splitter m; v zersplittern

split, splitt, n Spalte f; fig
Trennung f; v spalten; fig
trennen; **– up,** sich
trennen

spoil, speul, v verderben;
(indulge) verwöhnen; **–s,**
npl Beute f

spoke, spohk, n Speiche f

spokesman, spohkss-men, n
Sprecher m

spokeswoman, spohkss-wu-
men, n Sprecherin f

sponge, spandsch, n
Schwamm m; v schnorren;
– bag, n Kulturbeutel m; **–
on sb,** v von jdm
schnorren

sponsor, sponn-ser, n
Sponsor m; v sponsern;
–ship, n Sponsoring nt,
Sponsorschaft f

**spontaneous(ly), sponn-
teh**-ni-ess(-li), adj & adv
spontan

spooky, spuh-ki, adj
gespenstisch

spool, spuhl, n Spule f; v
spulen

spoon, spuhn, n Löffel m;
–ful, n Löffel(voll) m

sport, sport, n Sport m;
–ing, adj fair; **–s car,** n
Sportwagen m; **–sman,** n
Sportler m; **–swoman,** n
Sportlerin f; **–y,** adj

sportlich

spot, spott, n (mark) Fleck
m; (dot) Punkt m; (place)
Ort m, Stelle f; v (mark)
beflecken; (notice)
bemerken; **– check,** n
Stichprobe f; **–less,** adj
fleckenlos; **–light,** n
Scheinwerfer(licht nt) m;
(limelight) Rampenlicht
nt; **–ted,** adj gefleckt;
getüpfelt; **–ty,** adj (skin)
pickelig

spout, spaut, n (of gutter)
Ausguß m; (of jug)
Schnabel m; (of water)
Ausfluß m; v spritzen

sprain, sprehn, n
Verrenkung f; v verrenken

sprawl, spro'al, v sich
spreizen, sich rekeln

spray, spreh, n (sea) Gischt
m; (on road) Spritzen nt;
(for hair etc.) Spray m/nt;
(of flowers) Strauß m; v
(be)sprühen; (hair)
sprayen

spread, spredd, n (for bread)
Aufstrich m; (expanse)
Verbreitung f; v (expand)
(sich) ausbreiten; (butter
etc.) (ver)streichen;
(news) verbreiten

spree, sprie, n (shopping)
Einkaufsorgie f

sprig, sprigg, n Reis nt,
Sproß m

sprightly, spreit-li, adj
munter, lebhaft

spring, spring, n (season)
Frühling m; (leap) Sprung

m; (source) Quelle f; mech
Feder f; v springen;
–cleaning, n Frühjahrsputz
m; **–y,** adj elastisch

sprinkle, spring-k'l, v
(water) sprengen; (sugar
etc.) streuen; **–r,** n
Sprinkler m; (garden)
Sprenger m; **– with,** v
(liquid) besprengen mit;
(sugar etc.) bestreuen mit

sprint, sprint, n Sprint m; v
sprinten, rennen

sprout, spraut, n Sprößling
m; (vegetable) Rosenkohl
m; v sprossen

spruce, spruhss, adj gepflegt;
n Fichte f

spur, spör, n Sporn m; fig
Ansporn m; v **– (on),**
anspornen

spurious, spjuhr-ri-ess, adj
unecht, falsch

spurn, spörn, v
verschmähen

spurt, spört, n (jet) Spurt m;
(speed) Endspurt m; v
spritzen

spy, spei, n Spion m; v
spionieren; **–ing,** n
Spionage f

squabble, sku'obb-'l, n Zank
m; v (sich) zanken

squad, sku'odd, n mil Trupp
m; sport Mannschaft f;
–ron, n (air) Staffel f;
(naval) Geschwader nt

squalid, sku'oll-idd, adj
schäbig; (dirty) schmutzig

squall, sku'o'al, n Bö f

squalor, sku'oll-er, n Elend

nt; (dirtiness) Schmutz m

squander, sku'onn-der, v
verschwenden

square, sku'ähr, adj
viereckig; (meal)
anständig; (fam old-
fashioned) spießig;
(maths) Quadrat-; n
Quadrat nt; (open space)
Platz m; v (maths)
quadrieren; **–ed,** adj
(paper) kariert; (maths)
(im) Quadrat; **– metre,** n
Quadratmeter m; **– with,**
v (agree) übereinstimmen
mit; (make agree)
abstimmen; **all –,** quitt

squash, sku'osch, n sport
Squash nt; (drink)
Fruchtsaftgetränk nt; v
(zer)quetschen; fig
erdrücken

squat, sku'ott, adj untersetzt;
v hocken; **–ter,** n
Hausbesetzer m

squeak, sku'iek, v (of
animal) quieken; (of
door) quietschen

squeeze, sku'ies, n Druck m;
v drücken; (fruit)
auspressen

squiggle, sku'igg-'l, n
Schnörkel m

squint, sku'int, n Schielen
nt; v schielen

squirrel, sku'i-rel, n
Eichhörnchen nt

squirt, sku'ört, n Spritze f; v
spritzen

St, abbr Street or Saint

stab, stäbb, n Stich m; (fam

attempt) Versuch m; v
stechen; (fatally)
erstechen

stability, ste-bill-i-ti, n
Stabilität f

stabilize, steh-bill-eis, v
(sich) stabilisieren

stable, steh-b'l, adj fest,
stabil; n Stall m

stack, stäck, n (of paper)
Stapel m; (of hay)
Schober m; (chimney)
Schornstein m; v
aufstapeln

stadium, steh-di-em, n
Stadion nt

staff, stahf, n (employees)
Personal nt; (teachers)
Lehrerschaft f; (stick, mil)
Stab m; v besetzen

stag, stägg, n Hirsch m

stage, stehdsch, n theatre
Bühne f; (point)
(Zeit)punkt m; (of
journey) Etappe f; v
veranstalten; theatre
aufführen; **– manager,** n
Inspizient m

stagger, stägg-er, v taumeln;
(astonish) verblüffen;
(offset) staffeln

stagnate, stägg-neht, v
stocken, stillstehen

stag party, stägg pahr-ti, n
Männerabend m (vor der
Hochzeit)

staid, stehd, adj gesetzt

stain, stehn, n (colour)
Beize f; (mark) Fleck m; v
(colour) beizen; (mark)
beflecken; **–ed glass,** n

Farbglas nt; **–ed glass
window,** n Fenster nt mit
Glasmalereien; **–less,** adj
(steel) rostfrei; **– remover,**
n Fleckentferner m

stair, stähr, n (Treppen)stufe
f; **–s,** npl Treppe f; **–case,** n
Treppenhaus nt

stake, stehk, n (post) Pfahl
m; (wager) Einsatz m;
(interest) Anteil m; v
(wager) setzen; **at –,** auf
dem Spiel

stale, stehl, adj alt; (bread)
altbacken; (beer) schal;
–mate, n Patt nt

stalk, sto'ak, n Stengel m; v
(game) pirschen; (person)
jdm hinterherschleichen;
–er, n jd, der einer Person
hinterherschleicht

stall, sto'al, n Stand m; v (of
car) abwürgen; (stop)
stehenbleiben; (be
evasive) ausweichen; **–s,**
npl theatre Parkett nt

stalwart, sto'al-u'ert, adj
wacker, standhaft; n treuer
Anhänger m

stamina, stämm-i-ne, n
Ausdauer f

stammer, stämm-er, n
Stottern nt; v stottern;
–er, n Stotterer m

stamp, stämp, n (rubber
etc.) Stempel m; (postage)
Briefmarke f; v stempeln;
(post) frankieren; (foot)
stampfen; (memory)
einprägen; **– collecting,** n
Briefmarkensammeln nt

stampede, stämm-**pied,** n
wilde Flucht f

stance, stänss, n Haltung f

stand, ständ, n (platform)
Tribüne f; (support)
Ständer m; (resistance)
Widerstand m; v stehen;
(put) stellen; (endure)
aushalten; (for election)
kandidieren; – **down,** v
(resign) zurücktreten; –
for, v (mean) bedeuten;
(tolerate) dulden; – **up,** v
aufstehen

standard, stann-derd, adj
Normal-; n (norm) Norm
f; (level) Niveau nt; (flag)
Fahne f; –**ize,** v normen; –
of living, n
Lebensstandard m; –**s,** npl
(moral) Maßstäbe pl; (of
achievement) Maß nt

standing, adj (permanent)
ständig; (upright)
stehend; n Ansehen nt; –
order, n fin Dauerauftrag
m; – **room,** n Stehplatz m

standpoint, ständ-peunt, n
Standpunkt m

standstill, ständ-still, n
Stillstand m

staple, steh-p'l, adj Haupt-;
n (clip) Heftklammer f;
(food)
Hauptnahrungsmittel nt; v
(clip) klammern; –**r,** n
Hefter m

star, stahr, n Stern m;
(person) Star m; v
auftreten

starboard, stahr-berd, n

Steuerbord nt

starch, startsch, n Stärke f; v
stärken

stare, stähr, n Starren nt; v –
(at), (an)starren

stark, stark, adj (reality etc.)
kraß; (landscape) kahl; –
naked, adj splitternackt

starling, stahr-ling, n Star m

starry, adj sternenübersät

start, start, n (beginning)
Anfang m; sport Start m;
(shock) Schreck m; v
(begin) anfangen; sport
starten; (car) anspringen;
(journey) antreten;
(jump) sich erschrecken;
–**er,** n (dish) Vorspeise f;
mech Anlasser m

startle, start-'l, v
erschrecken

starvation, stahr-weh-sch'n,
n Verhungern nt

starve, stahrw, v
(ver)hungern

state, steht, n (country)
Staat m; (condition)
Zustand m; v angeben,
erklären; –**ly,** adj stattlich;
–**ment,** n Erklärung f;
(account) Aufstellung f;
–**sman,** n Staatsmann m

static, adj stillstehend; elec
statisch

station, steh-sch'n, n rail
Bahnhof m; (police)
Wache f; (position) Rang
m; v stationieren; (place)
stellen; –**ary,** adj
stillstehend

stationer, steh-sch'n-er, n

Schreibwarenhändler m;
–**y,** n Schreibwaren fpl

statistics, ste-tiss-ticks,
n Statistik f; npl
Statistiken pl

statue, stätt-juh, n
Standbild nt, Statue f

status, steh-tess, n Status m,
Ansehen nt

statute, stätt-juht, n Statut
nt, Gesetz nt

staunch, stoansch, adj treu,
fest; v stillen

stave, stehw, n (stick) Stab
m; mus Notenlinien pl; –
in, v einschlagen; – **off,** v
abwehren

stay, steh, n Aufenthalt m; v
(remain) bleiben; (lodge)
wohnen; – **the night,** v
übernachten

stead, stedd, n Stelle f; **in
good –,** zustatten

steadfast, stedd-fahst, adj
standhaft, fest

steadily, stedd-i-li, adv
(rain) ununterbrochen;
(balance, gaze) fest

steady, stedd-i, adj (stable)
stabil, fest; (reliable)
solide; (unshaking) ruhig;
(gradual) stetig; (rain)
ununterbrochen

steak, stehk, n Steak nt

steal, stiel, v stehlen;
(creep) sich stehlen

stealth, stelth, n
Heimlichkeit f; –**y,** adj
verstohlen

steam, stiem, n Dampf m; v
dampfen; (cooking)

dämpfen; **-er,** Dampfer m

steel, stiel, n Stahl m; v –
o.s., sich wappnen

steep, stiep, adj steil; v
einweichen

steeple, stie-p'l, n
Kirchturm m

steer, stier, v steuern; – **clear
of,** v fam aus dem Weg
gehen, vermeiden; **-ing
wheel,** n Steuerrad nt,
Lenkrad nt

stem, stemm, n Stiel m; v
(stop) stemmen; – **from,** v
stammen von

stench, stentsch, n Gestank
m

step, step, n (pace, measure)
Schritt m; (stair) Stufe f; v
schreiten; – **down,** v
(resign) abtreten; –
brother/daughter/father,
n Stiefbruder m/-tochter
f/-vater m; **-ladder,** n
Trittleiter f;
-mother/sister/son,
Stiefmutter f/-schwester
f/-sohn m

stereo, ste-ri-oh, adj Stereo-;
n Stereoanlage f

stereotype, ste-ri-oh-teip, n
Stereotyp nt; fig Klischee
nt; v fig in ein Klischee
zwängen

sterile, ste-reil, adj
unfruchtbar; med steril

sterilize, ste-ri-leis, v
sterilisieren

sterling, stör-ling, adj
(silver) Sterling-; (pound)
Sterling; fig gediegen; n

Pfund Sterling nt

stern, störn, adj ernst,
streng; n naut Heck nt

stew, stjuh, n Ragout nt,
Eintopf m; v schmoren

steward, stjuh-erd, n
Steward m; **-ess,** n
Stewardeß f

stick, stick, n Stock m; v
stecken; (paste) ankleben;
(fam bear) dabeibleiben; –
out, v hervorstehen; – **up
for sb/sth,** v sich für
jdn/etw einsetzen; **-er,** n
Ankleber m; **-ing plaster,**
n Heftpflaster nt; **-y,** adj
klebrig

stiff, stiff, adj steif; (thick)
dick; (strong) stark, **-en,** v
(sich) versteifen

stifle, steif-'l, v ersticken; fig
unterdrücken

stigma, stigg-me, n Stigma
nt

stigmatize, stigg-me-teis, v
brandmarken

stile, steil, n Zauntritt m

still, still, adj still; adv
(immer) noch; (anyway)
trotzdem; conj trotzdem; –
Destillierapparat m; v
beruhigen; **birth,** n
Totgeburt f; **-born,** adj
totgeboren

stilted, still-tidd, gestelzt

stilts, stilts, npl Stelzen pl

stimulate, stimm-juh-leht, v
anregen

stimulus, stimm-juh-less, n
Anreiz m

sting, sting, n Stich m;

(barb) Stachel m; v
stechen; (be sore)
brennen

stingy, stinn-dschi, adj
geizig, filzig

stink, stink, n Gestank m; v
stinken

stint, stint, n Pensum nt; v
sparen

stipulate, stipp-ju-leht, v
fordern

stir, stör, n (excitement)
Aufsehen nt; v (sich)
rühren; – **up,** v fig wecken

stirrup, sti-rep, n Steigbügel
m

stitch, stitsch, n Stich m;
(knitting) Masche f; med
Faden m; (pain)
Seitenstiche pl; v nähen

stock, stock, adj Standard-;
n (store) Vorrat m; comm
Warenbestand m; (of gun)
Kolben m; (broth) Brühe
f; (animals) Vieh nt;
(flower) Levkoje f; v
(goods) führen; **in –,**
vorrätig; **out of –,** nicht
vorrätig; **take –,** v
Inventur machen; fig
Bilanz ziehen

stockbroker, stock-broh-
ker, n Börsenmakler m

stock cube, stock kjuhb, n
Brühwürfel m

stock exchange, stock iks-
tschehndsch, n Börse f

stocking, stock-ing, n
Strumpf m

stock market, stock **mahr-**
kitt, n Börse f

stockpile, stock-peil, n
Vorrat m; v horten,
anhäufen

stocks, stocks, npl Aktien pl;
– and shares, Effekten pl

stocktaking, stock-teh-king,
n Inventur f

stoke, stohk, v heizen; **–r,** n
Heizer m

stolid, stoll-idd, adj stur

stomach, stamm-ek, n
Magen m; **– ache,** n
Magenschmerzen pl

stone, stohn, n Stein m;
(pebble) Kieselstein m; (of
fruit) Kern m; (weight)
6,35 kg; v (fruit)
entkernen; (throw stones
at) steinigen; **–deaf,** adj
stocktaub

stool, stuhl, n Hocker m;
med Stuhlgang m

stoop, stuhp, v sich bücken,
sich beugen

stop, stopp, n Halt m,
Haltestelle f;
(punctuation) Punkt m; v
anhalten; (payment)
einstellen; (hole)
verschließen; (cease)
aufhören; (doing sth)
aufhören mit; **–gap,** n
Notbehelf m; **–page,** n
Unterbrechung; (traffic,
blockage) Stau m; (strike)
Streik m; **–per,** n Stöpsel
m; **– press,** n letzte
Meldung f

storage, stor-ridsch, n
Lagerung f

store, stor, n (supply) Vorrat

m; (warehouse) Lager nt;
(shop) Kaufhaus nt, Laden
m; v lagern

storey, stor-ri, n Stock m,
Etage f

stork, stork, n Storch m

storm, storm, n Sturm m; v
stürmen; **–y,** adj stürmisch

story, stor-ri, n Geschichte
f; (untruth) Lüge f; **–book,**
n Kinderbuch nt; (fairy
tales) Märchenbuch nt

stout, staut, adj (fat)
dick; (brave) tapfer; n
Malzbier nt

stove, stohw, n Ofen m;
(cooker) Herd m

stow, stoh, v verstauen;
–away, n blinder Passagier
m

straddle, strädd-'l, v rittlings
sitzen; fig überspannen

straggle, strägg-'l, v
nachhinken; **–r,** n
Nachzügler m; **–y,** adj
zottig

straight, streht, adj gerade;
(honest) erhlich;
(undiluted) pur; adv
direkt; **– away,** adv sofort;
–en, v gerade machen;
–forward, adj einfach;
(honest) redlich; **– on,**
adv geradeaus

strain, strehn, n (tension)
Spannung f; (effort)
Anstrengung f; (type) Art
f; mus Klang m; v sich
anstrengen; (make tense)
spannen; (ankle)
verrenken; (liquid)

durchseihen; (water)
abgießen; **– ed,** adj (tense)
gespannt; (forced)
gezwungen; **–er,** n Sieb nt

strait, streht, n Meerenge f;
–jacket, n Zwangsjacke f

strand, stränd, n Faden m;
(of hair) Strähne f; **–ed,**
adj (naut, fig) gestrandet

strange, strehndsch, adj
fremd; (peculiar) seltsam;
–r, n Fremde(r) m & f

strangle, sträng-g'l, v
erwürgen

strap, sträpp, n Riemen m; v
festschnallen; **–ping,** adj
stramm

strategic, stre-**tie**-dschick, a,
strategisch

strategy, strätt-e-dschi, n
Strategie f

straw, stro'a, n Stroh nt;
(drinking) Strohhalm m;
–berry, n Erdbeere f; **be
the last –,** v das Faß zum
Überlaufen bringen

stray, streh, adj (animal)
verirrt; (rare) vereinzelt; v
vom Weg abgehen

streak, striek, n Streifen m;
(in hair) Strähne f;
(characteristic)
Eigenschaft f; v (go
quickly) flitzen; (run
naked) blitzen; **–er,** n
Blitzer m; **–y,** adj gestreift;
(bacon) durchwachsen

stream, striem, n (small
river) Bach m; (current,
fig) Strom m; v strömen;
–line, v rationalisieren;

–lined, *adj*
stromlinienförmig;
(simplified) rationalisiert

street, striet, *adj* Straßen-; *n*
Straße *f*; **– map,** *n*
Stadtplan *m*; **be –wise,** *v*
wissen, wo's langgeht

strength, strength, *n* Stärke
f, Kraft *f*; **–en,** *v*
verstärken

strenuous, strenn-juh-*ess,*
adj (task) anstrengend;
(denial, effort) heftig

stress, stress, *n med* Streß *m*;
mech Belastung *f*;
(emphasis) Gewicht *nt*; *v*
betonen; belasten

stretch, stretsch, *n* Strecke *f*;
v (sich) strecken; **–er,** *n*
Tragbahre *f*; **– out,** *v*
(sich) ausstrecken

strew, struh, *v* übersäen

strict(ly), strikt(-li), *adj &*
adv (severe) streng;
(precise) genau

stride, streid, *n* Schritt *m*; *v*
schreiten

strident, strei-dent, *adj*
schrill

strife, streif, *n* Streit *m*

strike, streik, *n* Streik *m*; *v*
(hit) schlagen; (stop
work) streiken; (occur to)
einfallen; (chime)
schlagen; (match)
anstreichen; **– out,**
(delete) ausstreichen; (set
off) aufbrechen; **–r,** *n*
Streiker *m*

string, string, *n* Schnur *f*;
mus Saite *f*; (series) Reihe

f; **– out,** *v* (delay) in die
Länge ziehen; **–s,** *npl*
Streichinstrumente *pl*; **–**
(together), *v*
aneinanderreihen

stringent, strinn-dschent,
adj streng

strip, stripp, *n* Streifen *m*; *v*
(undress) (sich)
ausziehen; **– cartoon,** *n*
Comic(strip) *m*

stripe, streip, *n* Streifen *m*;
–d, *adj* gestreift

strive (for), streiw (for), *v*
streben (nach)

stroke, strohk, *n* Schlag *m*;
sport Stoß *m*; (of pen) Zug
m; *mech* Hub *m*; *med*
Schlaganfall *m*; *v*
streicheln

stroll, strohl, *n* Spaziergang
m; *v* spazierengehen,
schlendern

strong, strong, *adj* stark;
(firm) fest; (bright) grell;
–hold, *n* Hochburg *f*;
–room, *n* Tresor *m*

stroppy, *adj fam* pampig

structure, strack-tscher, *n*
(construction) Struktur *f*;
(building) Bau *m*

struggle, stragg-'l, *n* Kampf
m; *v* **– (for),** kämpfen
(um)

strut, stratt, *n* Strebe *f*; *v*
stolzieren

stub, stabb, *n* (of pencil
etc.) Stummel *m*; (of
cigarette) Kippe *f*; (of
cheque, ticket) Abschnitt
m; *v* **– one's toe (on),** sich

den Zeh stoßen (an); **–**
out, ausdrücken

stubble, stabb-'l, *n*
Stoppeln *pl*

stubborn, stabb-ern, *adj*
hartnäckig

stud, stadd, *n* (earring)
Ohrstecker *m*; (on boot)
Stollen *m*; (stallion)
Deckhengst *m*; (for
horses) Gestüt *nt*; *v*
übersäen

student, stjuh-dent, *adj*
Studenten-; *n* (university)
Student *m*; (school)
Schüler *m*

studio, stjuh-di-oh, *n*
Studio *nt*; **– apartment,**
– flat, *n*
Einzimmerwohnung *f*

studious, stjuh-di-ess, *adj*
lernbegierig

study, stadd-i, *n* (work)
Studium *nt*; (room)
Arbeitszimmer *nt*;
(investigation)
Untersuchung *f*; *v*
studieren; (investigate)
untersuchen

stuff, staff, *n* Stoff *m*; *fam*
Zeug *nt*; *v* stopfen;
(animal) ausstopfen, **–ing,**
n Füllung *f*; **–y,** *adj* schwül

stumble, stamm-b'l, *v*
stolpern; **– across/on,**
stoßen auf

stump, stamp, *n* Stumpf *m*;
(cricket) Torstab *m*; *v fam*
verwirren; **– up,** *v fam*
blechen

stun, stann, *v* betäuben;

–ning, *adj* (looks) toll;
(shocking) bestürzend
stunt, stant, *n* Stunt *m*; **–ed,**
adj verkümmert
stupefied, stjuh-pi-feid, *adj*
verblüfft
stupendous, stjuh-**penn**-
dess, *adj* kolossal
stupid, stjuh-pidd, *adj*
dumm; **–ity,** *n* Dummheit
f
stupor, stjuh-per, *n*
Betäubung *f*
sturdy, stör-di, *adj* kräftig
stutter, statt-er, *n* Stottern
nt; *v* stottern
sty, stei, *n* Schweinestall *m*
style, steil, *n* Stil *m*, Art *f*;
(fashion) Mode *f*
stylish, stei-lisch, *adj*
modisch, elegant
subdue, sseb-**djuh**, *v* (quell)
unterwerfen; (soften)
dämpfen; **–d,** *adj* gedämpft
subject, ssabb-dschikt, *n*
(topic) Thema *nt*;
(school) Fach *nt*; *gram*
Subjekt *nt*; (person)
Untertan *m*; **– to,** *adj*
(exposed to) ausgesetzt;
(subordinate to)
unterwerfen; (depending
on) abhängig von
subject (to), ssabb-**dschekt**
(tu), *v* (rule) unterwerfen;
(suffering, criticism)
aussetzen
subjective, *adj* subjektiv
subjunctive, sseb-**dschank**-
tiw, *n* Konjunktiv *m*
sublime, sseb-**leim**, *adj*

erhaben
submarine, ssabb-me-rien,
adj unterseeisch; *n*
Unterseeboot *nt*
submerge, sseb-**mördsch**, *v*
untertauchen
submission, sseb-misch-'n, *n*
(proposal) Vorschlag *m*;
(yielding) Unterwerfung *f*
submit, sseb-mitt, *v* (yield)
nachgeben; (proposal)
vorlegen
subordinate, sse-bor-di-net,
adj untergeordnet; *n*
Untergebene(r) *m* & *f*
subscribe (to), sseb-skreib
(tu), *v* (support) sich etw
anschließen; (donate)
beitragen; (to journal)
abonnieren; **–r,** *n*
Abonnent *m*
subscription, sseb-skripp-
sch'n, *n* (donation)
Beitrag *m*; (to journal)
Abonnement *nt*
subsequent, ssabb-ssi-
ku'ent, *adj* folgend; **–ly,**
adv später
subside, sseb-sseid, *v* sich
senken; (abate)
abnehmen; **–nce,** *n*
Senkung *f*; (liquid)
Senken *nt*
subsidiarity, ssabb-ssidd-i-ä-
ri-ti, *n* Subsidiarität *f*
subsidiary, sseb-ssidd-i-e-ri,
adj Neben-; *n comm*
Tochtergesellschaft *f*
subsidize, ssabb-ssi-deis, *v*
subventionieren
subsidy, ssabb-ssi-di, *n*

Subvention *f*, Hilfsgeld *nt*
subsistence, sseb-ssiss-tenss,
n Unterhalt *m*
substance, ssabb-stenss, *n*
Substanz *f*
substantial, sseb-stänn-sch'l,
adj beträchtlich; (solid)
kräftig
substantiate, sseb-stänn-
schi-eht, *v* erhärten
substitute, ssabb-sti-tjuht, *n*
Ersatz *m*; *sport*
Ersatzspieler *m*; *v* **– for**
sb/sth, für jdn/etw
einspringen; **– X for Y,** Y
durch X ersetzen
subterfuge, ssabb-ter-
fjuhdsch, *n* List *f*
subterranean, ssabb-te-reh-
ni-en, *adj* unterirdisch
subtle, ssatt-'l, *adj* subtil,
fein
subtitle, ssabb-tei-t'l, *n*
Untertitel *m*
subtotal, ssabb-toh-t'l, *n*
Zwischensumme *f*
subtract (from), sseb-träkt
(frem), *v* abziehen (von)
suburb, ssabb-örb, *n* Vorort
m
suburban, sseb-ör-ben, *adj*
Vororts-; **–ia,** *n* Stadtrand
m
subway, ssabb-u'eh, *n*
Unterführung *f*;
(underground train) U-
Bahn *f*
succeed, ssek-ssied, *v*
(person) Erfolg haben;
(plan) gelingen; (heir)
nachfolgen; **–ing,** *adj*

nachfolgend

success, ssek-ssess, n Erfolg m; **–ful,** adj erfolgreich; **be – (in),** v Erfolg haben (bei)

succession, ssek-sesch-'n, n (sequence) Folge f; (inheritance) Nachfolge f; **–or,** n Nachfolger m

successive, ssek-ssess-iw, adj aufeinanderfolgende (r/s)

succinct, ssek-ssinkt, adj knapp; (clear) prägnant

succumb (to), sse-kamm (tu), v erliegen

such, ssatsch, adj solche(r/s); **– a,** solch ein(e), ein solche(r/s); (so great) so ein(e); adv so; **– a lot,** so viel(e); **– as,** wie (etwa)

suck, ssack, v saugen; **–le,** v säugen

suction, ssack-sch'n, n Saugkraft f

sudden(ly), ssadd-'n(-li), adj & adv plötzlich

sue, ssuh, v verklagen

suede, ssu'ehd, n Wildleder nt

suet, ssuh-itt, n Talg m

suffer, ssaff-er, v (er)leiden; **–er,** n Betroffene(r) m & f; (illness) Leidende(r) m & f; **–ing,** adj leidend; n Leiden nt

suffice, sse-feiss, v genügen

sufficient(ly), sse-fisch-ent(-li), adj & adv genügend, genug

suffocate, ssaff-e-keht, v

ersticken

suffrage, ssaff-ridsch, n Wahlrecht nt

sugar, schugg-er, n Zucker m; v zuckern; **–y,** adj süßlich

suggest, sse-dschest, v (imply) andeuten; (propose) vorschlagen; **–ion,** n (hint) Andeutung f; (proposal) Vorschlag m; **–ive,** adj andeutend; (indecent) zweideutig

suicide, ssuh-i-sseid, n (act) Selbstmord m; (person) Selbstmörder m; **commit –,** v Selbstmord begehen

suit, ssuht, n (man's) Anzug m; (woman's) Kostüm m; law Prozeß m; (cards) Farbe f; v passen; **–able,** adj passend; **–case,** n Koffer m

suite, ssu'iet, n (rooms) Suite f; (furniture) Garnitur f; (followers) Gefolge nt; mus Suite f

sulk, ssalk, v schmollen; **–y,** adj mürrisch

sullen, ssall-en, adj mürrisch

sulphur, ssall-fer, n Schwefel m

sultry, ssalt-ri, adj schwül; (sensual) sinnlich

sum, ssamm, n Summe f; (arithmetic) Ergebnis nt; **– up,** v (kurz) zusammenfassen

summarize, ssamm-e-reis, v zusammenfassen

summary, ssamm-e-ri, adj

summarisch; n Zusammenfassung f

summer, ssamm-er, adj Sommer-; n Sommer m

summit, ssamm-itt, n Gipfel m

summon, ssamm-en, v law vorladen; (people)einberufen; (strength etc.) aufbringen; **–s,** n law Vorladung f

sumptuous, ssamp-tju-ess, adj prächtig, kostbar

sun, ssann, n Sonne f; **–bathe,** v sich sonnen; **–beam,** n Sonnenstrahl m; **–burn,** n Sonnenbrand m; **– cream,** n Sonnencreme f

Sunday, ssann-deh, n Sonntag m

sundial, ssann-deil, n Sonnenuhr f

sundries, ssann-dris, npl Verschiedenes nt

sunglasses, ssann-glah-ssis, npl Sonnenbrille f

sunlight, ssann-leit, n Sonnenlicht nt

sunny, ssann-i, adj sonnig

sunrise, ssann-reis, n Sonnenaufgang m

sunroof, ssann-ruhf, n (elec elektrisches) Schiebedach nt, Sonnendach nt

sunscreen, ssann-skrien, n Sonnenschutz m

sunset, ssann-ssett, n Sonnenuntergang m

sunshine, ssann-schein, n Sonnenschein m

sunstroke, ssann-strohk, *n*
Sonnenstich *m*

suntan, ssann-tänn, *n*
(Sonnen)bräune *f*; –
lotion,) *n* Sonnenmilch *f*

super, ssuh-per, *adj fam*
prima

superb, ssuh-**pörb,** *adj*
herrlich, ausgezeichnet

supercilious, ssuh-per-**ssill**-
i-ess, *adj* hochnäsig

superficial, ssuh-per-**fisch**-'l,
oberflächlich

superfluous, ssuh-**pör**-flu-
ess, *adj* überflüssig

superintend, ssuh-pe-rinn-
tend, *v* überwachen; **–ent,**
n (police) Kommissar *m*;
(hostel etc.) Leiter *m*

superior, ssuh-**pier**-ri-er, *adj*
(tool, goods) besser; (skill,
intellect) überlegen;
(authority) höher; *n*
Vorgesetzte(r) *m* & *f*

supermarket, ssuh-
per-mahr-kitt, *n*
Supermarkt *m*

superlative, ssuh-**pör**-le-tiw,
adj überragend; *n gram*
Superlativ *m*

supernatural, ssuh-per-
nätsch-e-rel, *adj*
übernatürlich

superpower, ssuh-per-pau-
er, *n* Weltmacht *f*

supersede, ssuh-per-**ssied,** *v*
ersetzen

supersonic, ssuh-per-**ssonn**-
ick, *adj* Überschall

superstition, ssuh-per-
stisch-'n, *n* Aberglaube *f*

superstitious, ssuh-per-
stisch-ess, *adj*
abergläubisch

supervise, ssuh-per-weis, *v*
beaufsichtigen

supervision, ssuh-per-
wisch-'n, *n* Aufsicht *f*

supervisor, ssuh-per-weis-er,
n Aufseher *m*; (manual
work) Vorarbeiter *m*;
(clerical work) Büroleiter
m

supper, ssapp-er, *n*
Abendessen *nt*

supplant, sse-**plahnt,** *v*
verdrängen

supple, ssapp-'l, *adj*
geschmeidig, biegsam

supplement, ssapp-li-ment,
n (to book) Nachtrag *m*;
(to newspaper) Beilage *f*;
(food) Zusatz *m*

supplement, ssapp-li-ment,
v ergänzen

supplier, sse-**plei**-er, *n*
Lieferant *m*

supplies, sse-**pleis,** *npl*
Vorräte *pl*

supply, sse-**plei,** *n* Vorrat *m*;
(with), *v* versehen,
versorgen (mit); (deliver)
liefern

support, sse-**port,** *n* (prop)
Stütze *f*; (aid)
Unterstützung *f*; *v* stützen,
unterstützen; **–er,** *n*
Anhänger *m*

suppose, sse-**pohs,** *v*
vermuten, annehmen;
–edly, *adv* angeblich; **be
–d to,** *v* sollen

supposing, sse-**poh**-sing, *conj*
angenommen

supposition, ssapp-e-**sisch**-
'n, *n* Annahme *f*

suppress, sse-**press,** *v*
unterdrücken; **–ion,** *n*
Unterdrückung *f*

supremacy, ssuh-**premm**-e-
ssi, *n* Souveränität *f* (over
others) Vorherrschaft *f*

supreme, ssuh-**priem,** *adj*
höchste(r/s), oberste(r/s)

surcharge, ssör-tschardsch,
n Zuschlag *m*; (postage)
Strafporto *nt*

sure, schor, *adj* sicher,
gewiß; *adv fam* klar; **make
– (of),** *v* sich
vergewissern; (check)
nachprüfen

surf, ssörf, *n* Brandung *f*; *v*
surfen; **–en,** *n* Surfer *m*

surface, ssör-fiss, *adj*
Oberflächen-; (mail) auf
dem Landweg; *n*
Oberfläche *f*; *v* auftauchen

surfboard, ssörf-bord, *n*
Surfboard *nt*

surfing, ssör-fing, Surfen *nt*

surge, ssördsch, *n* Woge *f*; *v*
(auf)schwellen, wogen

surgeon, ssör-dschen, *n*
Chirurg *m*

surgery, ssör-dsche-ri, *n*
(specialty) Chirurgie *f*;
(operation) Operation *f*;
(place) Praxis *f*; –
hours/times, *npl*
Sprechstunden *pl*

surgical, ssör-dschick-'l, *adj*
chirurgisch; **– spirit,** *n*

Wundalkohol *nt*

surly, ssör-li, *adj* mürrisch, schroff, grob

surmount, sser-maunt, *v* überwinden

surname, ssör-nehm, *n* Familienname *m*

surpass, sser-pahss, *v* übertreffen

surplus, ssör-pless, *n* Überschuß *m*

surprise, sser-preis, *n* Überraschung *f*; *v* überraschen

surrender, sse-renn-der, *n* Kapitulation *f*; (of weapon) Übergabe *f*; *v* sich ergeben; (weapon) aufgeben

surround, sse-raund, *v* umgeben

surrounding, sse-raun-ding, *adj* umliegende(r/s); **–s,** *npl* Umgebung *f*

survey, ssör-weh, *n* (report) Bericht *m*; (opinion poll) (Meinungs)umfrage *f*; (measurement) Vermessung *f*

survey, sser-weh, *v* (measure) vermessen; (question) befragen; (look over) überblicken; **–or,** *n* Landvermesser *m*

survival, sser-wei-wel, *n* Überleben *nt*

survive, sser-weiw, *v* überleben

survivor, sser-wei-wer, *n* Überlebende(r) *m* & *f*

susceptible (to) , sse-ssepp-

ti-b'l (tu), *adj* (receptive) empfänglich (für); (sensitive) empfindlich (gegen)

suspect, ssass-pekt, *adj* verdächtig; *n* Verdächtige(r) *m* & *f*

suspect, ssass-pekt, *v* verdächtigen

suspend, ssess-pend, *v* (halt) einstellen; (defer) verschieben; (worker) suspendieren; (hang up) hängen; **–er belt,** *n* Strumpfhaltergürtel *m*; **–ers,** *npl* (Brit) Strumpfbänder *pl*; (US) Hosenträger *m*

suspense, ssess-penss, *n* Spannung *f*

suspension, ssess-penn-sch'n, *n* (of worker) Suspendierung *f*; (on car) Federung *f*; **– bridge,** Hängebrücke *f*

suspicion, ssess-pisch-'n, *n* Verdacht *m*

suspicious, ssess-pisch-ess, *adj* (person) mißtrauisch; (thing) verdächtig

sustain, ssess-tehn, *v* (suffer) erleiden; (nourish) ernähren; (maintain) (aufrecht)erhalten; **–able,** *adj* nachhaltig

sustenance, ssass-ti-nenss, *n* Nahrung *f*

swagger, ssu'agg-er, *n* Großtuerei *f*; *v* (walk) stolzieren; (boast) großtun

swallow, ssu'oll-oh, *n*

Schluck *m*; (bird) Schwalbe *f*; *v* (ver)schlucken

swamp, ssu'omp, *n* Sumpf *m*; *v* überschwemmen

swan, ssu'onn, *n* Schwan *m*

swap, ssu'opp, *n* Tausch *m*; *v* **– (for),** tauschen (gegen)

swarm, ssu'orm, *n* Schwarm *m*; *v* schwärmen; (with people) wimmeln

swastika, ssu'oss-tick-e, *n* Hakenkreuz *nt*

swat, ssu'ott, *v* schlagen

sway, ssu'eh, *n* (power) Herrschaft *f*; (influence) Einfluß *m*; *v* (swing) schaukeln; (influence) beeinflussen; (rock) schwanken

swear, ssu'ähr, *v* (affirm) schwören; (curse) fluchen; **–word,** *n* Schimpfwort *nt*, Fluch *m*

sweat, ssu'ett, *n* Schweiß *m*; *v* schwitzen; **–er,** *n* Pullover *m*; **–shirt,** *n* Sweatshirt *nt*; **–y,** *adj* verschwitzt

swede, su'ied, *n* Steckrübe *f*

Swede, su'ied, *n* Schwede *m*, Schwedin *f*

Sweden, ssu'ie-den, *n* Schweden *nt*

Swedish, ssu'ie-disch, *adj* schwedisch; *n* Schwedisch *nt*

sweep, ssu'iep, *n* Schornsteinfeger *m*; *v* (clean) kehren; (go fast) rauschen; **–ing,** *adj*

(statement) umfassend;
(movement) ausholend

sweet, ssu'iet, *adj* süß; *n*
(confectionery) Bonbon
nt; (dessert) Nachtisch *m*;
–corn, *n* Zuckermais *m*;
–en, *v* (ver)süßen; **–ener,**
n (artificial) Süßstoff *m*;
(bribe) (kleine)
Bestechung *f*; **–heart,** *n*
Geliebte(r) *m & f*; **–ness,**
n Süße *f*; **– pea,**
Gartenwicke *f*

swell, ssu'ell, *n* Dünung *f*; *v*
aufschwellen; **–ing,** *n*
Geschwulst *f*

swerve, ssu'örw, *v* ausbiegen,
abweichen

swift, ssu'ift, *adj* schnell,
geschwind, rasch; *n* (bird)
Mauersegler *m*

swim, ssu'imm, *v*
schwimmen; **–mer,** *n*
Schwimmer *m*; **–ming,** *n*
Schwimmen *nt*; **–ming
baths,** *npl* Schwimmbad
nt; **–ming costume,** *n*
Badeanzug *m*; **–ming pool,**
n Schwimmbad *nt*; **–ming
trunks,** *n* Badehose *f*;
–suit, *n* Badeanzug *m*

swindle, ssu'ind-'l, *n*
Schwindel *m*; *v*
beschwindeln; **–r,** *n*
Schwindler *m*

swine, ssu'ein, *n* Schwein *nt*

swing, ssu'ing, *n* Schwung
m; (child's) Schaukel *f*;
mus Swing *m*; *v*
schwingen, schaukeln

Swiss, ssu'iss, *adj*

schweizerisch; *n*
Schweizer *m*

switch, ssu'itsch, *n elec*
Schalter *m*; (change)
Wechsel *m*; *v* (change)
wechseln; (swap)
tauschen; **–board,** *n*
Zentrale *f*; **– off,** *v*
ausschalten; **– on,** *v*
einschalten

Switzerland, ssu'itt-zer-
lend, *n* Schweiz *f*

swivel, ssu'iw-'l, *n*
Drehgelenk *nt*; *v* (sich)
drehen

swoon, ssu'uhn, *v* in
Ohnmacht fallen

swoop, ssu'uhp, *n* Sturz *m*;
(raid) Razzia *f*; *v* **–
(down),** *v* (herab)stürzen

swot, ssu'ott, *fam n* Streber
m; *v* büffeln

sword, ssord, *n* Schwert *nt*

sworn, ssu'orn, *adj*
eingeschworen

syllable, ssill-e-b'l, *n* Silbe *f*

syllabus, ssill-e-bess, *n*
Lehrplan *m*

symbol, ssimm-b'l, *n*
Symbol *nt*

symbolic(ally), ssimm-**boll**-
ick(-e-li), *adj & adv*
symbolisch

symmetry, ssimm-itt-ri, *n*
Symmetrie *f*

sympathetic, ssimm-pe-
thett-ick, *adj* mitfühlend

sympathize (with), ssimm-
pe-**theis** (u'idh), *v*
mitfühlen mit, Mitleid
haben mit

sympathy, ssimm-pe-thi, *n*
Mitleid *nt*, Mitgefühl
nt; (on bereavement)
Beileid *nt*

symphony, ssimm-fe-ni, *n*
Symphonie *f*

symptom, ssimp-tem, *n*
Symptom *nt*

synagogue, ssinn-e-gogg, *n*
Synagoge *f*

synchronize, ssing-kre-neis,
v synchronisieren

syncopated, ssing-ke-peh-
tidd, *adj* synkopiert

syndicate, ssinn-di-ket, *n*
Konsortium *nt*

synonym, ssinn-e-nimm, *n*
Synonym *nt*

synonymous, ssi-nonn-i-
mess, *adj* gleichbedeutend,
synonym

synopsis, ssi-nopp-ssiss, *n*
Zusammenfassung *f*

synthetic, ssinn-thett-ick,
adj synthetisch; (fibre)
Kunst-

syphon, ssei-fen, *n* Siphon
m; *v* **– off,** ablassen; *fig*
abzweigen

syringe, ssi-rindsch, *n*
Spritze *f*; *v* (aus)spritzen

syrup, ssi-rep, *n* Sirup *m*; **–y,**
adj pej zuckersüß

system, ssiss-tem, *n* System
nt; **–atic(ally),** *adj & adv*
systematisch; **–s analyst,** *n*
comp Systemanalytiker *m*

T

ta, tah, *interj fam* danke

table, teh-b'l, *n* Tisch *m*; (list) Tabelle *f*; **–cloth**, *n* Tischtuch *nt*; **–spoon**, *n* Eßlöffel *m*

tablet, tább-let, *n* Tafel *f*; (pill) Tablette *f*

table tennis, teh-b'l tenn-iss, *n* Tischtennis *nt*

tabloid, tább-leud, *adj* – **(newspaper)**, *n* Boulevardzeitung *f*

tacit, täss-itt, *adj* stillschweigend

tack, täck, *n* (nail) Stift *m*; (stitch) Heftstich *m*; (direction) Kurs *m*; *v* (nail) anschlagen; (sew) anheften; *naut* lavieren

tackle, täck-'l, *n* Ausrüstung *f*; *sport* Angriff *m*; *v* (task) anpacken; (person) in Angriff nehmen; *sport* angreifen

tacky, täck-i, *adj* (sticky) klebrig; (*fam* shoddy) geschmacklos

tact, täkt, *n* Takt *m*; **–ful**, *adj* taktvoll

tactic, täck-tick, *n* Taktik *f*; **–al**, *adj* taktisch; **–s**, *n* Taktik *f*; *npl* Taktiken *pl*; **–less**, *adj* taktlos

tadpole, tädd-pohl, *n* Kaulquappe *f*

tag, tägg, *n* Aufhänger *m*; *v* (goods) anhängen; (criminal) überwachen

tail, tehl, *n* Schwanz *m*; *v* beschatten; **– off**, *v* abfallen; **–or**, *n* Schneider *m*; **–coat**, *n* Frack *m*; **–gate**, *n* Heckklappe *f*; **–s**, (of coin) Zahl(seite) *f*; (tailcoat) Frack *m*

taint, tehnt, *v* verderben; *fig* beschmutzen

take, tehk, *v* nehmen; (*med*, *comm*, fortress) einnehmen; (accept) annehmen; (along) mitnehmen; (accommodate) Platz haben für; *gram* dazugehören; **– away**, *v* wegnehmen; **–away**, *adj* zum Mitnehmen; *n* Imbißstube *f*; **-home pay**, *n* Nettolohn *m*; **– in**, *v* (understand) begreifen; (fool) einwickeln; (dress) enger machen; **– it (that)**, davon ausgehen (, daß); **– off**, *v* (of plane) starten; (of project) in Schwung kommen; (clothes) ausziehen; (mimic) parodieren; **– on**, *v* (worker) einstellen; (task) übernehmen; **– over**, *v* übernehmen; **–over**, *n* Übernahme *f*; **– up**, *v* (dress) kürzer machen; (hobby) anfangen

takings, teh-kings, *npl* Einnahmen *pl*

talc, tälk, *abbr* **talcum powder**

talcum powder, täll-kem pau-der, *n* Talkumpuder *m*

tale, tehl, *n* Erzählung *f*; (fairy) Märchen *nt*; **tell –s**, *v* (betray confidence) petzen; (lie) schwindeln

talent, täll-ent, *n* Talent *nt*, Begabung *f*; **–ed**, *adj* begabt

talk, to'ak, *n* Gespräch *nt*; (speech) Vortrag *m*; *v* –

476

(about), sprechen (über);
reden (über); **–ative,** adj
gesprächig

tall, to'al, adj (high) hoch;
(big) groß

tally, täll-i, v
übereinstimmen; **keep a
–,** v mitschreiben, Buch
führen

talon, täll-en, n Kralle f

tame, tehm, adj (animal)
zahm; (dull) lahm; v
zähmen

tamper (with), tämm-per
(u'idh), v herumpfuschen
(an)

tampon, tämm-ponn, n
Tampon m

tan, tänn, adj (hell)braun; n
Bräune f; v (hides) gerben;
(make brown) bräunen;
(go brown) braun werden

tangerine, tänn-dsche-rien,
n Mandarine f

tangible, tänn-dschi-b'l, adj
greifbar; (real) wirklich

tangle, täng-g'l, n
Verwicklung f

tank, tänk, n Tank m; mil
Panzer m

tankard, täng-kerd, n
Krug m

tanker, täng-ker, n (ship)
Tanker m; (lorry)
Tankwagen m

tantalize, tänn-te-leis, v
quälen

tantamount to, tänn-te-
maunt tu, adj
gleichbedeutend mit

tap, täpp, n (cock) Hahn m;

(knock) Klopfen nt; v
(knock) klopfen; (barrel,
tree) anzapfen; (wire)
abhören

tape, tehp, n Band nt;
(adhesive) Klebeband nt;
(recording) Tonband nt; v
(record) auf Band
aufnehmen; **– measure,** n
Bandmaß m; **red –,** n
(unnötige) Bürokratie f

taper, teh-per, n Wachsstock
m; v spitz zulaufen

tape recorder, tehp ri-**kor-**
der, n Tonbandgerät nt

tapestry, täpp-iss-tri, n
Wandteppich m,
Gobelin m

tar, tahr, n Teer m; v teeren

tardy, tahr-di, adj (slow)
langsam; (late) spät

target, tahr-gitt, n Scheibe
f; fig Ziel nt

tariff, tä-riff, n Tarif m; (tax)
Zolltarif m

tarnish, tahr-nisch, v matt
machen, matt werden; fig
beflecken

tarpaulin, tar-**po'a-**linn, n
Persenning f

tart, tart, adj herb; n Torte f;
(fam prostitute) Nutte f

tartan, tahr-ten, adj
Schotten-; n
Schottenstoff m

task, tahsk, n Aufgabe f;
–force, n Sondertruppe f;
take to –, v zur
Rechenschaft nehmen

tassel, täss-'l, n Quaste f,
Troddel f

taste, tehst, n Geschmack
m; v schmecken, kosten;
–ful, adj geschmackvoll;
–less, adj geschmacklos

tasty, tehss-ti, adj
schmackhaft

tattered, tätt-erd, adj zerfetzt

tatters, tätt-ers, n Fetzen pl

tattoo, te-**tuh,** n (on skin)
Tätowierung f; mil
Zapfenstreich m; v (skin)
tätowieren

tatty, tätt-i, adj schäbig

taunt, to'ant, n Hohn m; v
verhöhnen

Taurus, to'a-ress, n Stier m

taut, to'at, adj gespannt

tavern, täw-ern, n Schenke
f, Wirtshaus nt

tawdry, to'a-dri, adj
geschmacklos

tax, täcks, n Steuer f; v
besteuern; (strain)
belasten; **– with,** v
beschuldigen

taxation, täcks-eh-sch'n, n
Besteuerung f

tax-free, täcks-frie, adj
steuerfrei

taxi, täck-ssi, n Taxi nt; **–
rank, – stand,** n
Taxistand m

tea, tie, n (drink) Tee m;
(meal) Nachmittagstee m;
–bag, n Teebeutel m

teach, tietsch, v lehren;
(subject) unterrichten;
–er, n Lehrer m; **–ing,** n
Lehren nt, Unterricht m;
(relig etc.) Lehre f

team, tiem, n sport

Mannschaft *f*; (animals)
Gespann *nt*; (workers)
Team *nt*; **–work**, *n*
Teamarbeit *f*
teapot, *n* Teekanne *f*
tear, tähr, *n* Riß *m*; *v*
(zer)reißen; (muscle)
zerren; (go fast) rasen
tear, tier, *n* Träne *f*; **–ful**, *adj*
tränenüberströmt; **– gas**, *n*
Tränengas *nt*
tease, ties, *n* Quälgeist *m*; *v*
necken
teaspoon, tie-spuhn, *n*
Teelöffel *m*
teat, tiet, *n* Zitze *f*; (for
baby) Sauger *m*
tea towel, tie tau-el,
Geschirrtuch *nt*
technical, teck-nick-'l, *adj*
technisch
technician, teck-nisch-'n, *n*
Techniker *m*
technique, teck-niek, *n*
Technik *f*
technology, teck-noll-e-
dschi, *n* Technologie *f*
teddy (bear), tedd-i bähr, *n*
Teddy(bär) *m*
tedious, tie-di-ess, *adj*
langweilig; (tiring)
ermüdend
tedium, tie-di-em, *n*
Langeweile *f*
teem (with), tiem (u'idh), *v*
wimmeln (von); (rain)
gießen
teenage, tien-ehdsch, *adj*
jugendlich, Teenie-; **–r**, *n*
Teenie *m*, Teenager *m*,
Jugendliche(r) *m* & *f*

teens, tiens, *npl*
Teenageralter *nt*
teeter, tie-ter, *v* wanken
teeth, tieth, *pl of* **tooth**
teething, tie-dhing, *n*
Zahnen *nt*; **– troubles**, *npl*
fig Anlaufprobleme *pl*
teetotal, tie-toh-t'l, *adj*
abstinent; **–ler**, *n*
Abstinenzler *m*
telecommunications, tell-i-
ke-mjuh-ni-**keh**-sch'ns,
npl Fernmeldewesen *n*
telegram(me), tell-i-grämm,
n Telegramm *nt*
telegraph, tell-i-grahf, *n*
Telegraf *m*; *v* telegrafieren
telephone, tell-i-fohn, *n*
Telefon *nt*; *v* anrufen; **–
booth, – box**, *n*
Telefonzelle *f*; **– call**, *n*
Anruf *m*; **– conversation**,
n Telefongespräch *nt*; **–
directory**, *n* Telefonbuch
nt; **– number**, *n*
Telefonnummer *f*
telephonist, ti-**leff**-*e*-nist, *n*
Telefonist *m*
telephoto (lens), tell-i-
foh-toh (lens), *n*
Teleobjektiv *nt*
telescope, tell-i-skohp, *n*
Fernrohr *nt*
televise, tell-i-weis, *v* (im
Fernsehen) übertragen
television, tell-i-**wisch**-'n, *n*
Fernsehen *nt*; **– (set)**, *n*
Fernseher *m*;
Fernsehapparat *m*
telex, tell-ecks, *n* Telex *nt*
tell, tell, *v* (fact) sagen,

mitteilen; (story)
erzählen; (secret)
verraten; **– (by)**,
(recognize) erkennen
(an); **–ing**, *adj* (effective)
schlagend; (revealing)
vielsagend; **– off**, *v*
ausschimpfen; **–tale**, *n* Petzer *m*
vielsagend; *n* Petzer *m*
temper, temm-per, *n*
(character) Naturell *nt*;
(mood) Laune *f*; (angry
mood) Wutanfall *m*; *v*
(steel) härten; (reduce)
mäßigen; **be in a (bad) –**,
wütend sein; **lose one's –**,
die Geduld verlieren
temperament, temm-pe-re-
ment, *n* Temperament *nt*
temperamental, temm-pe-
re-**menn**-t'l, *adj* launisch
temperance, temm-pe-renss,
n Mäßigkeit *f*;
(abstinence) Abstinenz *f*
temperate, temm-pe-ret, *adj*
gemäßigt
temperature, temm-pritt-
tscher, *n* Temperatur *f*;
med Fieber *nt*
tempest, temm-pist, *n*
Sturm *m*, Ungewitter *nt*
template, temm-plet, *n*
Schablone *f*
temple, temp-p'l, *n* Tempel
m; (forehead) Schläfe *f*
temporarily, temm-pe-*re*-ri-
li, *adv* vorübergehend
temporary, temm-pe-*re*-ri,
adj vorübergehend
tempt, temmpt, *v* (attract)
verlocken; (urge)

verleiten; **–ation,** n
Versuchung f; **–ing,** adj
verlockend

ten, tenn, num zehn

tenable, tenn-e-b'l, adj
haltbar

tenacious, ti-**neh**-schess, adj
zäh, beharrlich

tenacity, ti-**näss**-i-ti, n
Zähigkeit f

tenancy, tenn-en-ssi, n
(rent) Mietverhältnis nt

tenant, tenn-ent, n Mieter
m; (of land) Pächter m

tend, tend, v (nurse)
pflegen; **– to do sth,** (be
inclined) dazu neigen,
etw zu tun; (have a habit)
etw gewöhnlich tun, etw
oft tun

tendency, tenn-den-ssi, n
(inclination) Neigung f;
(habit) Angewohnheit f

tender, tenn-der, adj zart;
(painful) empfindlich;
(loving) zärtlich; n comm
Angebot nt; (public)
Ausschreibung f; rail
Tender m; **––hearted,** adj
weichherzig; **–ness,** n
Zartheit f; (soreness)
Empfindlichkeit f;
(affection) Zärtlichkeit f

tenement, tenn-i-ment, n
Mietshaus nt

tennis, tenn-iss, n Tennis nt;
– court, n Tennisplatz m;
– racket/racquet, n
Tennisschläger m; **– shoe,**
n Tennisschuh m

tenor, tenn-er, n Tenor m

tense, tenss, adj (tight)
gespannt; fig angespannt;
n gram Zeitform f

tension, tenn-sch'n, n
Spannung f,
Anspannung f

tent, tent, n Zelt nt

tentative, tenn-te-tiw, adj
(hesitant) unsicher;
(provisional)
unverbindlich

tenth, tenth, adj zehnte(r/s);
n Zehntel nt

tenure, tenn-jer, n (of
property) Besitz m; (of
office) Amtszeit f

tepid, tepp-idd, adj lauwarm

term, törm, n (expression)
Ausdruck m; (period)
Zeitraum m; (school,
university) Trimester nt;
(expiry) Laufzeit f; **–s,** npl
comm Bedingungen f; **be
on good –s with,** v gut
auskommen mit; **come to
–s with,** v sich abfinden
mit; **in the long/short –,**
auf lange/kurze Sicht

terminal, tör-mi-n'l, adj
Schluß-, End-; med
unheilbar; n (bus station)
Endstation f; (airport)
Terminal m; comp
Terminal m/nt

terminate, tör-mi-neht, v
beenden

terminus, tör-mi-ness, n
Endstation f

terrace, te-ress, n Terrasse f;
(of houses) (Häuser)reihe
f; **–d,** adj terrassenförmig

angelegt; **–d house,** n
Reihenhaus nt

terrain, te-rehn, n
Gelände nt

terrible, te-ri-b'l, adj
schrecklich

terrific, te-**riff**-ick, adj
irrsinnig; fam toll

terrify, te-ri-fei, v
(er)schrecken

territory, te-ri-te-ri, n
Gebiet nt

terror, te-rer, n Schrecken
m; (terrorism) Terror m;
–ism, n Terrorismus m;
–ist, n Terrorist m; **–ize,** v
terrorisieren

terse, törss, adj kurz und
bündig

test, test, n Versuch m,
Probe f; (examination)
Prüfung f; v probieren,
prüfen

testicle, tess-ti-k'l, n
Hoden m

testify, tess-ti-fei, v
aussagen; **– that/to,**
bezeugen

testimonial, tess-ti-**moh**-ni-
el, n (recommendation)
Referenz f; (presentation)
Geschenk nt

testimony, tess-ti-me-ni, n
Zeugnis nt; law Aussage f

test tube, test tjuhb,
Reagenzglas nt; **test-tube
baby,** n Retortenbaby nt

text, tekst, n Text m; **–book,**
n Lehrbuch nt

textile, tecks-teil, adj
Textil-; n Stoff m; **–s,** npl

Textilien pl

texture, tecks-tscher, n Struktur f

Thames, tems, n Themse f

than, dhänn/dhen, conj als

thank, thänk, v danken; – **sb for sth,** jdm für etw danken; **–ful,** adj dankbar; **–less,** adj undankbar; **–s,** interj danke; npl Dank m; **–s to,** prep dank; **T–sgiving,** n (festival) Erntedankfest nt; – **you (very much)!** interj danke (schön)!

that, dhätt, adj der/die/das, jene(r/s); pron (demonstrative) das; (relative) der/die/das, welche(r/s), was; conj daß; – **good/much,** so gut/soviel; – **one,** jene(r/s); **after/before –,** danach/davor; **who is –?** wer ist da?

thatch, thätsch, n Strohdach nt; v mit Stroh decken

thaw, tho'a, n Tauwetter nt; v tauen; (frozen food) auftauen lassen

the, dhie/dhe, definite art der/die/das; – **more ...,** – **more ...,** je mehr ..., desto mehr ...; **so much –** ..., umso ...

theatre, thie-ter, n Theater nt; med Operationssaal m

theatrical, thie-ätt-rick-'l, adj Theater-; fig theatralisch

theft, theft, n Diebstahl m

their, dhähr, adj ihr; **–s,** pron ihre(r/s)

them, dhem, pron (accusative) sie; (dative) ihnen

theme, thiem, n Thema nt; mus Motiv nt; – **park,** n Themenpark m

themselves, dhem-sselws, pron (refl) sich (selbst); (emphatic) selbst

then, dhenn, adj damalig; adv (next) dann, darauf; (at that time) damals; conj also; **by –,** bis dahin

theology, thi-oll-e-dschi, n Theologie f

theoretical(ly), thi-e-rett-ick-'l(-i), adj & adv theoretisch

theory, thi-e-ri, n Theorie f; **in –,** adv theoretisch

therapist, the-re-pist, n Therapeut m

therapy, the-re-pi, n Therapie f

there, dhähr, adv da, dort; (movement) dahin, dorthin; – **is/are,** es ist/sind; (in existence) es gibt

thereabouts, dhähr-re-bauts, adv (place) dort irgendwo; **... or –,** (quantity) ungefähr ...

thereafter, dhähr-ahf-ter, adv danach

thereby, dhähr-bei, adv dadurch, damit

therefore, dhähr-for, adv

deshalb, daher

thermal, thör-m'l, adj thermal

thermometer, ther-**momm**-i-ter, n Thermometer nt

thermostat, thör-moh-stätt, n Thermostat nt

these, dhies, adj & pron, pl of **this**

thesis, thie-ssiss, n These f; (university) Doktorarbeit f

they, dheh, pron sie; (impersonal) man

thick, thick, adj dick; (liquid) dickflüssig; (hair, smoke, forest) dicht; (fam stupid) dumm; **–en,** v (of liquid) eindicken; (of smoke etc.) dichter werden; (of plot) kompliziert werden; **–et,** n Dickicht nt; **–ness,** n Dicke f; (density) Dichte f

thief, thief, n Dieb m

thieve, thiew, v stehlen

thieving, thie-wing, adj diebisch; n Stehlen nt

thigh, thei, n Schenkel m

thimble, thimm-b'l, n Fingerhut m

thin, thinn, adj dünn; (person) mager; (sparse) spärlich; v – **(down),** verdünnen

thing, thing, n (object) Ding nt; (matter) Sache f; **–s,** npl (belongings) Sachen pl; **first – (in the morning),** früh am Morgen; **the – is,** das

Problem ist
think, think, *v* denken;
(believe) glauben; –
about, (consider)
überlegen; (ponder)
nachdenken über; – **of,**
denken an; (opinion)
halten von; (intend)
vorhaben; – **over,**
überlegen; – **up,** sich
ausdenken
third, thörd, *adj* dritte(r/s); *n*
Drittel *nt*; –**ly,** *adv*
drittens; **the T– World,** *n*
die Dritte Welt *f*
thirst, thörrst, *n* Durst *m*; *v*
– **for,** dürsten nach; –**y,**
adj durstig
thirteen, thör-tien, *num*
dreizehn; –**th,** *adj*
dreizehnte(r/s)
thirty, thör-ti, *num* dreißig
this, dhiss, *adj* diese(r/s);
pron (demonstrative) dies,
das; – **big/high,** so
groß/hoch; –
morning/evening, heute
morgen/abend; – **one,**
diese(r/s)
thistle, thiss-'l, *n* Distel *f*
thorn, thorn, *n* Dorn *m*; –**y,**
adj dornig; (problem)
schwierig
thorough, tha-re, *adj*
gründlich; (real) wirklich;
–**bred,** *adj* reinrassig; *n*
Vollblut *nt*; –**fare,** *n*
Hauptstraße *f*; **no –fare,**
gesperrt
those, dhohs, *pl adj* die,
jene; *pl pron* die (da), jene

though, dhoh, *adv* aber,
doch; *conj* obwohl
thought, tho'at, *n* (idea)
Gedanke *m*; (thinking)
Denken *nt*; –**ful,** *adj*
nachdenklich;
(considerate)
rücksichtsvoll; (attentive)
aufmerksam; –**less,** *adj*
(inconsiderate)
rücksichtslos, achtlos
thousand, thau-send, *num*
tausend; –**s (of),** Tausende
(von); –**th,** *adj*
tausendste(r/s); *n*
Tausendstel *nt*
thrash, thräsch, *v*
verdreschen; (*fam* sport
etc.) vernichtend
schlagen; – **about,** sich
hin- und herwerfen; –**ing,**
n Tracht Prügel *f*
thread, thredd, *n* Faden *m*;
(of screw) Gewinde *nt*; *v*
einfädeln; –**bare,** *adj*
fadenscheinig
threat, thrett, *n* Drohung *f*;
(danger) Gefahr *f*; –**en,** *v*
(be)drohen
three, thrie, *num* drei
thresh, thresch, *v* dreschen
threshold, thresch-hohld, *n*
Schwelle *f*
thrift, thrift, *n* Sparsamkeit
f; –**less,** *adj*
verschwenderisch; –**y,** *adj*
sparsam
thrill, thrill, *n* Aufregung *f*;
v aufregen; –**ed,** *adj*
entzückt; –**ing,** *adj*
aufregend

thrive (on), threiw (onn), *v*
gedeihen; *comm*
erfolgreich sein
throat, throht, *n* Kehle *f*,
Hals *m*
throb, throbb, *v* pochen,
klopfen; –**bing,** *n* Pochen
nt, Klopfen *nt*
throes, throhs, *npl* **in the –
of,** mitten in etw
throne, throhn, *n* Thron *m*
throng, throng, *n* Gedränge
nt; *v* sich drängen (in)
throttle, thrott-'l, *n mech*
Gas(pedal) *nt*; *v*
erdrosseln
through, thruh, *adj* (train)
durchgehend; (finished)
fertig; *adv* durch; *prep*
(place, means) durch;
(time) während; – **and –,**
durch und durch; –**out,**
adv (place) überall; (time)
die ganze Zeit; *prep* (time)
überall in; (place)
der/die/das ganze …
hindurch; –**put,** *n*
Durchsatz *m*; **no – road,**
keine Durchfahrt
throw, throh, *n* Wurf *m*; *v*
werfen; – **a party,** eine
Party geben; – **up,** *v*
brechen
thrush, thrasch, *n* Drossel *f*
thrust, thrast, *n* Stoß *m*;
mech Schubkraft *f*; *v*
stoßen
thud, thadd, *n* dumpfer
Schlag *m*
thumb, thamm, *n* Daumen
m; *v* durchblättern; – **a**

lift, per Anhalter fahren

thump, thamp, n (noise) Pochen nt; (blow) Schlag m; v schlagen

thunder, thann-der, n Donner m; v donnern; –bolt, n Donnern nt; –storm, n Gewitter nt; –y, adj gewittrig

Thursday, thörs-dei, n Donnerstag m

thus, dhass, adv (in this way) so; (therefore) also, daher

thwart, thu'ort, v (plan) vereiteln; (person) jdm in die Quere kommen

thyme, teim, n Thymian m

tick, tick, n (sound) Ticken nt; (mark) Häkchen nt; v (of clock) ticken; (mark) anhaken; – off, v fam rüffeln; – over, v (of engine) im Leerlauf laufen; fig weiterlaufen

ticket, tick-itt, n (transport) Fahrkarte f; (admission) Eintrittskarte f; (price) Schild nt; (luggage) Schein m; (lottery) Schein m; – office, n (transport) Fahrkartenschalter m; theatre Kasse f; parking –, (for car park) Parkschein m; (fine) Strafzettel m; ´season –, n Dauerkarte f

tickle, tick-'l, n Kitzeln nt; v kitzeln

ticklish, tick-lisch, adj kitzlig

tidal, tei-d'l, adj Flut-

tide, teid, n fig Trend m; high –, Flut f; low–, Ebbe f

tidy, tei-di, adj ordentlich; v – (up), aufräumen

tie, tei, n (for neck) Krawatte f; (band) Band nt; sport Unentschieden nt; v (fasten) binden; (draw) unentschieden spielen; – a knot in, einen Knoten machen; – up, v (person) beschäftigen; (animal, boat) anbinden; –d up, adj beschäftigt

tier, tier, n Rang m

tiff, tiff, n Streit m

tiger, tei-ger, n Tiger m

tight, teit, adj (close) dicht, fest; (clothes) eng; (control) streng; (fam drunk) blau; –en, v anziehen; (controls) verschärfen; (rope), n Drahtseil m; fig Balanceakt m; –s, npl Strumpfhose f

tile, teil, n (on roof) Ziegel m; (glazed) Kachel f; (on floor) Fliese f; v mit Ziegeln decken; mit Fliesen belegen

till, till, conj = until; n Kasse f; v (earth) bestellen; prep = until

tiller, till-er, n naut Ruderpinne f

tilt, tilt, n Neigung f; v kippen

timber, timm-ber, n

Bauholz nt

time, teim, n Zeit f; (period) Zeitdauer f; (occasion) Mal nt; (hour) Uhr f; mus Takt m; v zeitlich abstimmen; sport stoppen; – bomb, n Zeitbombe f; –less, adj zeitlos; – limit, n Frist f; –ly, adj rechtzeitig; –r, n (device) Schaltuhr f; –scale, n Frist f; –table, n (transport) Fahrplan m; (school) Stundenplan m; – zone, n Zeitzone f; have a good –, sich amüsieren; in –, rechtzeitig; on –, pünktlich; what – is it?/what is the –? wieviel Uhr ist es?

timid, timm-idd, adj zaghaft, furchtsam

timing, tei-ming, n Timing nt

tin, tinn, n (metal) Zinn nt; (can) Dose f, Büchse f; v einmachen; –foil, n Alufolie f

tinge, tindsch, n Färbung f; fig Anflug m; v leicht färben; –d with, fig angehaucht mit

tingle, ting-g'l, n Prickeln nt; v prickeln

tinkle, tink-'l, n Geklingel nt; v klingeln

tinned, tind, adj Dosen-

tin opener, tinn-oh-p'n-er, n Dosenöffner m

tinsel, tinn-ss'l, n Lametta nt

tint, tint, n Farbton m; v

tönen; **–ed glass,** n getöntes Glas nt

tiny, tei-ni, adj winzig

tip, tipp, n Spitze f; (hint) Wink m; (money) Trinkgeld nt; v kippen; (give money) ein Trinkgeld geben; **––off,** n Tip m; **–** over, umkippen

tipsy, tipp-si, adj beschwipst

tiptoe, tipp-toh, n on **–,** auf Zehenspitzen

tire, teir, v ermüden; **–d,** adj müde; **be –d of,** v satt haben; **–less(ly),** adj & adv unermüdlich; **–some,** adj lästig

tiring, teir-ring, adj ermüdend

tissue, tisch-uh, n Gewebe nt; (handkerchief) Papiertaschentuch nt; **– paper,** n Seidenpapier nt

tit, titt, n (bird) Meise f; (vulg n breast) Titte f; **– for tat,** wie du mir, so ich dir

titillate, titt-i-leht, v erregen

title, tei-t'l, n Titel m; (right) Rechtstitel m; **– deed,** Eigentumsurkunde f; **– page,** Titelblatt nt

titter, titt-er, n Gekicher nt; v kichern

to, tuh, adv (shut) zu; prep (a place) zu; (town, country, direction) nach; (person) an; (per) pro; (as far as) bis; (attached) an; (before verb) zu; (purpose) um … zu; **– and fro,** hin und her;

try – do sth, versuchen, etw zu tun; **want –,** wollen

toad, tohd, n Kröte f; **–stool,** n (nicht eßbarer) Pilz m

toast, tohst, n Toast m; v (bread) toasten; (drink to) trinken auf; **–er,** n Toaster m

tobacco, te-bäck-oh, n Tabak m; **–nist,** n Tabakhändler m

toboggan, te-bogg-en, n Rodelschlitten m; v rodeln

today, tu-deh, adv heute; (nowadays) heutzutage; **–'s,** adj der/die/das heutige

toddler, todd-ler, n Kleinkind nt

toe, toh, n Zeh m, Zehe f; (of sock, shoe) Spitze f; **–nail,** n Zehennagel m

toffee, toff-ie, n Karamelbonbon nt

together, tu-gedh-er, adv zusammen

toil, teul, n Plackerei f; v schwer arbeiten

toilet, teu-litt, n Toilette f; **– bag,** n Kulturbeutel m; **– paper,** n Toilettenpaper nt; **–ries,** npl Toilettenartikel pl

token, toh-k'n, n Zeichen nt; (gift token) Gutschein m

tolerable, toll-e-re-b'l, adj (bearable) erträglich; (good enough) annehmbar

tolerance, toll-e-renns, n

Toleranz f, Duldsamkeit f

tolerant, toll-e-rent, adj duldsam

tolerate, toll-e-reht, v dulden

toll, tohl, n Gebühr f; (road) Maut f; v läuten

tomato, te-mah-toh, n Tomate f

tomb, tuhm, n Grab nt

tomboy, tomm-beu, n Wildfang m

tombstone, tuhm-stohn, n Grabstein m

tomcat, tomm-kätt, n Kater m

tomfoolery, tom-fuh-le-ri, n Blödsinn m

tomorrow, tu-mo-roh, adv morgen; **– morning,** morgen früh; **the day after –,** übermorgen

ton, tann, n Tonne f; **–s of,** fam eine Unmenge (von)

tone, tohn, n Ton m; v (muscles) Fitneß f; **– down,** mäßigen; **– up,** (ver)stärken; **– with,** in Einklang sein mit

tongs, tongs, npl Zange f

tongue, tang, n Zunge f; **–in-cheek,** scherzhaft; **– tied,** adj stumm; **–twister,** n Zungenbrecher m

tonic, tonn-ick, n Stärkungsmittel nt; **– (water),** Tonic nt

tonight, tu-neit, adv heute abend, heute nacht

tonsil, tonn-ssill, n Mandel f; **–litis,** n

483

Mandelentzündung f

too, tuh, *adv* (excessively) zu; (also) auch; **– much**, zuviel

tool, tuhl, *n* Werkzeug *nt*

toot, tuht, *n* Hupen *nt*; *v* hupen

tooth, tuhth, *n* Zahn *m*; **–ache**, *n* Zahnschmerzen *pl*; **–brush**, *n* Zahnbürste *f*; **–paste**, *n* Zahnpasta *nt*; **–pick**, *n* Zahnstocher *m*

top, topp, *adj* oberste(r/s); *n* Spitze *f*; (of mountain) Gipfel *m*; (of tree) Wipfel *m*; (toy) Kreisel *m*; *v* übertreffen; **– hat**, *n* Zylinderhut *m*; **––heavy**, *adj* kopflastig; **– up**, *v* auffüllen; **on top**, *adv* oben; **on – of**, *prep* darüber hinaus

topic, topp-ick, *n* Gesprächsstoff *m*, Thema *nt*; **–al**, *adj* aktuell

topless, topp-liss, *adj* oben ohne

topple, topp-'l, *v* stürzen; **– over**, umstürzen

topsy-turvy, topp-ssi-tör-wi, *adv* durcheinander

torch, tortsch, *n* (electric) Taschenlampe *f*; (burning) Fackel *f*

torment, tor-ment, *n* Qual *f*

torment, tor-ment, *v* quälen

tornado, tor-neh-doh, *n* Wirbelsturm *m*

torpedo, tor-pie-doh, *n* Torpedo *m*

torrent, to-rent, *n* reißender

Strom *m*

torrential, te-renn-tsch'l, *adj* strömend

torrid, to-ridd, *adj* heiß

tortoise, tor-tess, *n* Schildkröte *f*; **–shell**, *n* Schildpatt *nt*

tortuous, tort-ju-ess, *adj* gequält

torture, tor-tscher, *n* Folter *f*; *v* foltern

toss, toss, *n* Wurf *m*; *v* werfen; (coin) losen; **– and turn**, **– about**, sich wälzen; **– up**, eine Münze werfen

tot, tott, *n* (child) kleines Kind *nt*; (small drink) Gläschen *nt*

total, toh-t'l, *adj* Gesamt-, total; *n* Gesamtheit *f*; (sum) Endsumme *f*; *v* (add up) zusammenrechnen; (come to) auf … kommen

totalitarian, toh-tall-i-tähr-ri-en, *adj* totalitär

totally, toh-te-li, *adv* total

totter, tott-er, *v* wanken, wackeln

touch, tatsch, *n* (touching) Berührung *f*; (faculty) (Tast)gefühl *nt*; *v* berühren; (emotionally) rühren; **–ing**, *adj* (emotional) rührend; **– on**, *v* erwähnen; **–y**, *fig* empfindlich; **get in – with sb**, mit jdm Kontakt aufnehmen; **keep in – with sb**, mit jdm in Kontakt bleiben

tough, taff, *adj* zäh; (fam difficult) schwierig; (fam unfair) hart; **–!** Pech!

tour, tuhr, *n* Reise *f*, Tour *f*; *v* bereisen; **–ism**, *n* Tourismus *m*, Fremdenverkehr *m*; **–ist**, *n* Tourist *m*; **–ist office**, *n* Verkehrsamt *nt*, Verkehrsbüro *nt*

tournament, tor-ne-ment, *n* Turnier *nt*

tout, taut, *n* Anlocker *m*; *v* **– for**, Kunden schleppen

tow, toh, *v* schleppen; (car) abschleppen

toward(s), tu-u'ord(s), *prep* (time) gegen; (direction) nach; (a place) auf … zu

towel, tau-el, *n* Handtuch *nt*

tower, tau-er, *n* Turm *m*; **– block**, *n* Hochhaus *nt*; **–ing**, *adj* hoch aufragend

town, taun, *n* Stadt *f*; **– centre**, *n* Stadtzentrum *nt*, Stadtmitte *f*; **– hall**, *n* Rathaus *nt*

towrope, toh-rohp, *n* Abschleppseil *nt*

toy, teu, *n* Spielzeug *nt*; *v* **– with**, spielen mit; **–shop**, *n* Spielwarengeschäft *nt*

trace, trehss, *n* (track) Spur *f*; *v* (follow track of) nachspüren; (copy) durchpausen; (find) aufspüren

tracing paper, treh-ssing peh-per, *n* Pauspapier *nt*

track, träck, *n* (path) Weg *m*; (trace) Spur *f*; (for race) Bahn f; rail Gleis nt; v verfolgen; –suit, n Trainingsanzug m

tract, träkt, n (area) Gebiet nt; relig Traktat m

traction, träck-sch'n, n mech Zugkraft f; med Streckverband m; – engine, n Zugmaschine f

tractor, träck-ter, n Traktor m

trade, trehd, n (commerce) Handel m; (occupation) Gewerbe nt; (skilled work) Handwerk nt; v – (in), handeln (mit); – in, v in Zahlung geben; –mark, n Warenzeichen nt; –r, n Händler m; –sman, n (shopkeeper) Händler m; (worker) Handwerker m; – union, n Gewerkschaft f

tradition, tre-disch-'n, n Tradition f; –al, adj traditionell

traffic, träff-ick, n Verkehr m; – jam, n (Verkehrs)stau m; – light(s), n(pl), (Verkehrs)ampel f

tragedy, trädsch-i-di, n Tragödie f

tragic, trädsch-ick, adj tragisch

trail, trehl, n (path) Weg f; (trace) Spur f; (of smoke) Wolke f; v (follow) verfolgen; (drag) schleppen; (hang) hängenbleiben; (be left behind) zurückbleiben;

–er, n (vehicle) Anhänger m; (TV, film) Vorschau f

train, trehn, n rail Zug m; (of dress) Schleppe f; v (teach) ausbilden; sport trainieren; (animal) dressieren; (study) eine Ausbildung machen; mil einexerzieren; –ed, adj ausgebildet; –ee, n Lehrling m; –er, n (person) Trainer m; (shoe) Sportschuh m; –ing, n Ausbildung f; (further education) Weiterbildung f; sport Training nt

trait, treht, n Zug m

traitor, treh-ter n Verräter m

tram, trämm, n Straßenbahn f

tramp, trämp, n (beggar) Landstreicher m; v marschieren

trample, trämp-'l, v niedertreten

trance, trahnss, n Trance f

tranquil, träng-ku'ill, adj ruhig; (mind) gelassen; –lizer, n Beruhigunsmittel nt

transact, tränn-säkt, v verrichten, durchführen; –ion, n Verrichtung f; (business) Geschäft nt

transcend, trann-ssend, v übersteigen

transcribe, träns-kreib, v abschreiben

transcript, tränn-skript, v Abschrift f; law Protokoll nt

transfer, tränss-fer, n (drawing) Abziehbild nt; (of money) Überweisung f; (of premises) Verlegung f; (of person) Versetzung f

transfer, tränss-för, v (money) überweisen; (premises) verlegen; (person) versetzen

transform, tränss-form, v umgestalten

transfusion, tränss-fjuh-sch'n, n Blutübertragung f

transient, tränn-si-ent, adj vergänglich

transistor, tränn-siss-ter, n Transistor m; – (radio), n Transistorradio nt

transit, tränn-sitt, n Transit m; in –, unterwegs

transition, tränn-sisch-'n, n Übergang m

transitory, tränn-sitt-e-ri, adj flüchtig

translate, träns-leht, v übersetzen

translation, träns-leh-sch'n, n Übersetzung f

translator, träns-leh-ter, n Übersetzer m

transmission, träns-misch-'n, Übersendung f; (elec, TV) Übertragung f, Sendung f

transmit, träns-mitt, v übersenden; (elec, TV) übertragen, senden; –ter, n Sender m

transparent, tränss-pä-rent, adj durchsichtig; fig offenkundig

transpire, tränss-**peir**, v sich herausstellen

transplant, tränss-plahnt, n med Transplantation f

transplant, tränss-**plahnt**, v (plant) umpflanzen; (med, fig) verpflanzen

transport, tränss-port, n Transport m

transport, tränss-**port**, v transportieren

transportation, tränss-porteh-sch'n, n Transport m, Beförderung f

transverse, tränss-**wörss**, adj querlaufend

trap, träpp, n Falle f; (pej mouth) Klappe f; v (catch) fangen; (trick) überlisten; **–door**, n Falltür f

trappings, **träpp**-ings, npl äußere Zeichen pl

trash, träsch, n (rubbish) Plunder m; (nonsense) Unsinn m; **–y**, adj wertlos

trauma, tro'a-me, n Trauma nt

traumatic, tro'a-**mätt**-ick, adj traumatisch

travel, träw-el, v reisen; **– agent**, n (office) Reisebüro nt; (person) Reisebürokaufmann m/- kauffrau f; **–ler**, n Reisende(r) m & f; **–ler's cheque**, n Reisescheck m; **– sickness**, n Reisekrankheit f

trawler, tro'a-ler, n Trawler m

tray, treh, n Tablett nt; **ash–**, Aschenbecher m

treacherous, tretsch-e-ress, adj (untrustworthy) verräterisch; (dangerous) gefährlich

treachery, tretsch-e-ri, n Verrat m

treacle, trie-k'l, n Sirup m

tread, tredd, n (of feet) Tritt m; (on tyre) Profil nt; (of stair) Stufe f; v – (on), treten (auf)

treason, trie-sen, n Verrat m

treasure, tresch-er, n Schatz m; v schätzen; **–r**, n Schatzmeister m

treasury, tresch-e-ri, n Schatzamt nt

treat, triet, n (reward) Belohnung f; (enjoyment) Genuß m; v behandeln; **– sb to sth**, jdm etw gönnen

treatise, trie-tiss, n Abhandlung f

treatment, triet-ment, n Behandlung f

treaty, trie-ti, n Vertrag m

treble, trebb-'l, adj dreifach; (mus clef) Violin-; n mus Diskant m; v verdreifachen

tree, trie, n Baum m; **family –**, n Stammbaum m

trek, treck, n Treck m; v trecken

trellis, trell-iss, n Spalier nt

tremble, tremm-b'l, v zittern

tremendous, tri-menn-dess, adj ungeheuer; fam

großartig

tremor, tremm-er, n Zittern nt; (earthquake) Beben nt

trench, trentsch, n Graben m; mil Schützengraben m

trend, trend, n Tendenz f, Trend m; **–y**, adj modisch

trespass (on), tress-pess (onn), v unbefugt betreten; **–er**, n Unbefugte(r) m & f

trestle, tress-'l, n Gestell nt, Bock m

trial, trei-el, n (test) Probe f; (hardship) Kraftprobe f; law Prozeß m; **– and error**, Ausprobieren

triangle, trei-äng-g'l, n Dreieck nt; mus Triangel f

triangular, trei-äng-gju-ler, adj dreieckig

tribal, trei-b'l, adj Stammes-

tribe, treib, n Stamm m

tribunal, trei-bjuh-n'l, n Tribunal nt

tributary, tribb-ju-te-ri, n Nebenfluß m

tribute, tribb-juht, n (praise) Lob nt; (gift) Abgabe f

trick, trick, n (trap) Falle f; (joke) Streich m; (ruse) Trick m; (cards) Stich m; v überlisten; **–ery**, n Gaunerei f; **–ster**, Gauner m

trickle, trick-'l, n Tröpfeln nt; v tröpfeln

tricky, trick-i, adj (difficult) schwierig; (sensitive) delikat

trifle, trei-f'l, n Kleinigkeit
f; (dessert) Trifle nt

trifling, treif-ling, adj
geringfügig

trigger, trigg-er, n Drücker;
v – (off), auslösen

trill, trill, n Triller m; v
trillern

trim, trimm, adj proper; n
(on car) Verzierung f; v
(decorate) besetzen; (clip)
stutzen; –ming, n (for
clothes) Besatz m; –s, npl
(extras) Zubehör nt

Trinity, trinn-i-ti, n
Dreieinigkeit f

trinket, tring-kitt, n
Schmuckstück nt

trio, trie-oh, n Trio nt,
Terzett nt

trip, tripp, n (journey) Reise
f; (stumble) Stolpern nt; v
(stumble) stolpern

tripe, treip, n Kaldaunen pl;
Gedärme pl; (rubbish)
Quatsch m

triple, tripp-'l, adj dreifach;
v verdreifachen

triplets, tripp-litts, n
Drillinge pl

tripod, trei-podd, n photog
Stativ nt

trite, treit, adj banal

triumph, trei-emf, n
Triumph m; v – (over),
triumphieren (über)

trivial, tri-wi-el, adj
belanglos

trolley, troll-i, n Karren
m; (shopping)
Einkaufswagen m

trombone, tromm-bohn, n
Posaune f

troop, truhp, n mil Trupp m;
v sich scharen; –s, npl
Truppen pl

trophy, troh-fi, n Trophäe f

tropical, tropp-ick-'l, adj
tropisch

tropics, tropp-icks, npl
Tropen pl

trot, trott, n Trab m; v
traben

trouble, trabb-'l, n (worry)
Sorge f; (inconvenience)
Mühe f; (disturbance)
Unruhen pl; (difficulty)
Schwierigkeit f; med
Beschwerde f; v (bother)
sich bemühen; (disturb)
stören; –maker, n
Unruhestifter m; –some,
adj lästig; (difficult)
beschwerlich; be in –, v
Probleme haben; make –,
v Unruhe stiften

trough, troff, n Trog m; (low
pressure) Tief nt

trounce, traunss, v
verprügeln

trousers, trau-sers, npl Hose
f

trout, traut, n Forelle f

trowel, trau-el, n Kelle f

truant, truh-ent, n
(Schul)schwänzer m; play
–, v die Schule schwänzen

truce, truhss, n
Waffenstillstand m

truck, track, n (lorry)
Lastwagen m; rail
Güterwagen m

truculent, track-ju-lent, adj
aufsässig

trudge, tradsch, v sich
schleppen

true, truh, adj (correct)
wahr; (faithful) treu;
(genuine) echt

truffle, traff-'l, n Trüffel f

truly, truh-li, adj wirklich;
Yours –, Mit freundlichen
Grüßen

trump, tramp, n Trumpf m; v
trumpfen; –ed-up, adj
übertrieben

trumpet, tramm-pitt, n
Trompete f

truncheon, trann-tsch'n, n
Knüttel m

trunk, trank, n (of tree)
Stamm m; (elephant's)
Rüssel m; (of body)
Rumpf m; (box) Truhe f; –
call, n Fernruf m; –s, npl
Badehose f

truss, trass, n Bündel nt; med
Bruchband nt; v fesseln;
(poultry) dressieren

trust, trast, n Vertrauen nt;
(law, fin) Trust m; v
trauen; –ee, n (law, fin)
Treuhänder m; –ing, adj
vertrauensvoll; – to, v sich
verlassen auf; –worthy, adj
zuverlässig

truth, truhth, n Wahrheit f;
–ful, adj ehrlich

try, trei, v (attempt)
versuchen, probieren;
(taste) kosten; law (einen
Fall) verhandeln; –ing, adj
schwierig; – on, v

(clothes) anprobieren

tub, tabb, n Kübel m; (bath) Wanne f

tube, tjuhb, n (pipe) Rohr nt, Röhre f; (paint etc.) Tube f; (London underground) U-Bahn f; **inner –,** n Schlauch m

tuck, tack, n Falte f; v (gather) falten; (put) stecken; **– in,** (sheet etc.) einwickeln; (fam eat) es sich schmecken lassen

Tuesday, tjuhs-dei, n Dienstag m

tuft, taft, n Büschel nt

tug, tagg, n Ruck m; v (drag) schleppen; (pull) zerren; **–(boat),** n Schlepper m; **–of-war,** n Seilziehen nt

tuition, tjuh-**isch-**'n, n Unterricht m

tulip, tjuh-lipp, n Tulpe f

tumble, tamm-b'l, n Sturz m; v stürzen; **–down,** adj baufällig; **–drier,** n Trockner m; **–r,** n Wasserglas nt

tummy, tamm-i, n fam Bauch m, Magen m

tumour, tjuh-mer, n Tumor m

tumultuous, tjuh-**malt-**ju-ess, adj stürmisch

tuna, tjuh-ne, n Thunfisch m

tune, tjuhn, n Melodie f; v stimmen; **–ful,** adj melodisch; **– in (to),** v einschalten; **–r,** n (for radio) Tuner m; **be in**

tune/out of tune with, v fig in Einklang/nicht in Einklang stehen mit

tunic, tjuh-nick, n Kittel m; mil Waffenrock m

tuning fork, tjuh-ning fork, n Stimmgabel f

tunnel, tann-'l, n Tunnel m; v einen Tunnel graben

turbulent, tör-bju-lent, adj stürmisch

tureen, tu-**rien,** n Terrine f, (Suppen)schüssel f

turf, törf, n Rasen m; (piece of) Sode f; v mit Fertigrasen auslegen; **– out,** fam rausschmeißen

turkey, tör-ki, n Truthahn m, Puter m

Turkey, tör-ki, n Türkei f

turmoil, tör-meul, n Aufruhr f

turn, törn, n Drehung f; (of century, tide) Wende f; (shock) Schrecken m; v (rotate) (sich) drehen; (turn round) wenden; (become) werden; (page) umblättern; **– back,** v zurückkehren; (clock) zurückstellen; **– into,** v (sich) verwandeln in; **– off,** v (light) ausschalten; (tap) zudrehen; (in car) abbiegen; **– on,** (light) einschalten; (tap) aufdrehen; **– out,** v (develop) sich herausstellen als; (produce) produzieren; (expel) hinauswerfen; (light)

ausschalten; **– up,** v (appear) auftauchen; (volume) lauter stellen; **– to,** v sich wenden an; **do (sb) a good –,** (jdm) etw Gutes tun; **in –,** abwechselnd; **it's my –,** ich bin an der Reihe f; **take –s,** v abwechseln

turning, tör-ning, n Abzweigung f; **– point,** n Wendepunkt m

turnip, tör-nipp, n weiße Rübe f

turnout, tör-naut, n theatre etc. Publikum nt; (election) Wahlbeteiligung f

turnover, tör-noh-ver, n (income) Umsatz m; (of stock) Umschlag m; (of staff) Personalwechsel m

turnstile, törn-steil, n Drehkreuz nt

turntable, törn-teh-b'l, n Plattenteller m

turnup, tör-napp, n Aufschlag m

turpentine, tör-pen-tein, n Terpentin m

turquoise, tör-ku'eus, n adj türkisfarben; n (gem) Türkis m

turret, ta-ret, n Türmchen nt; mil Panzerturm m

turtle, tör-t'l, n Schildkröte f; **– dove,** n Turteltaube f; **– neck,** n Pullover m mit Stehbundkragen

tusk, task, n Stoßzahn m

tussle, tass-'l, n Kampf m,

Rauferei *f*; *v* kämpfen

tutor, tjuh-ter, *n* Lehrer *m*; (private) Hauslehrer *m*; *v* schulen

TV, tie wie, *n abbr* **television,** TV *nt*

twang, tu'äng, *n* (voice) näselnde Sprache *f*; (sound) heller Ton *m*

tweezers, tu'ie-sers, *npl* Pinzette *f*

twelfth, tu'elfth, *adj* zwölfte(r/s), *n* Zwölftel *nt*

twelve, tu'elw, *num* zwölf

twenty, tu'enn-ti, *num* zwanzig

twice, tu'eiss, *adv* zweimal; – **as much/good,** doppelt soviel/so gut

twig, tu'igg, *n* Zweig *m*; *v fam* kapieren

twilight, tu'ei-leit, *n* Zwielicht *nt*

twin, tu'inn, *adj* Zwillings-; *fig* Doppel-; *n* Zwilling *m*; *n* (towns) Partnerstadt *f*; – **beds,** *npl* zwei Einzelbetten *pl*

twine, tu'ein, *n* Bindfaden *m*; *v* sich winden

twinge, tu'indsch, *n* Stechen *nt*, Stich *m*; *v* stechen

twinkle, tu'ing-k'l, *n* Funkeln *nt*; *v* flimmern; (of eyes) funkeln

twin town, tu'inn taun, *n* Partnerstadt *f*

twirl, tu'örl, *v* (herum)wirbeln

twist, tu'ist, *n* Drehung *f*; (in road) Biegung *f*, Kurve *f*; *v* (sich) drehen; (contort) verdrehen; **–ing, –y,** *adj* kurvenreich

twit, tu'itt, *n fam* Idiot *m*

twitch, tu'itsch, *n* Zucken *nt*; *v* zucken

twitter, tu'it-ter, *n* Gezwitscher *nt*; *v* zwitschern

two, tuh, *num* zwei; **--faced,** *adj* falsch; **–fold,** *adj* zweifach; **--seater,** *n* Zweisitzer *m*; **–some,** *n* Paar *nt*; **--way,** *adj* (traffic) Gegen-; (communication) in beide Richtungen; **--wheeler,** *n* Zweirad *nt*

tycoon, tei-**kuhn**, *n* Magnat *m*

type, teip, *n* (sort) Art *f*; (printing) Schrift *f*; *v* mit der Maschine schreiben, tippen; **–writer,** *n* Schreibmaschine *f*; **–written,** *adj* maschinegeschrieben

typhoid, tei-feud, *n* Typhus *m*

typical (of), tipp-ick-'l (ew), *adj* typisch (für)

typing, tei-ping, *n* Tippen *nt*, Maschineschreiben *nt*

typist, tei-pist, *n* Schreibkraft *f*

tyrannical, ti-**ränn**-ick-'l, *adj* tyrannisch

tyrant, teir-rent, *n* Tyrann *m*

tyre, teir, *n* Reifen *m*; – **pressure,** *n* Reifendruck *m*

U

U-bend, juh-bend, n (pipe) U-Rohr nt

ubiquitous, ju-bick-u'i-tess, adj allgegenwärtig

udder, add-er, n Euter nt

UFO, juh-foh, n (abbr unidentified flying object), UFO nt

ugliness, agg-li-niss, n Häßlichkeit f

ugly, agg-li, adj häßlich; (situation) unangenehm

UK, juh kei, abbr United Kingdom

ulcer, all-sser, n Geschwür nt

ulterior, all-tier-ri-er, adj – motive, n Hintergedanke m

ultimate, all-ti-met, adj allerletzte(r/s); –ly, adv letztendlich

ultimatum, all-ti-meh-tem, n Ultimatum nt

ultrasound, all-tre-ssaund, n Ultraschall m

umbrella, amm-brell-e, n Regenschirm m

umpire, amm-peir, n Schiedsrichter m

umpteen, amp-tien, num x; –th, adj x-te(r/s)

UN, juh enn, abbr United Nations

unabashed, ann-e-bäscht, adj ungeniert

unable, ann-eh-b'l, adj unfähig, unvermögend; be – to, v nicht können

unacceptable, ann-ek-ssepp-te-b'l, adj unannehmbar, nicht akzeptabel

unaccountable, ann-ä-kaun-te-b'l, adj unerklärlich

unaided, ann-eh-didd, adj ohne fremde Hilfe

unanimity, juh-ne-nim-i-ti, n Einmütigkeit f

unanimous(ly), juh-nänn-i-mess(-li), adj & adv einstimmig

unanswerable, ann-ahn-sse-re-b'l, adj nicht beantwortbar; (argument) unwiderlegbar

unapproachable, ann-e-prohtsch-e-b'l, adj unnahbar

unarmed, ann-ahrmd, adj unbewaffnet

unashamed, ann-e-schehmd, adj schamlos

unassuming, ann-e-sjuh-ming, adj bescheiden

unattached, ann-e-tätscht, adj ungebunden

unattainable, ann-e-teh-ne-b'l, adj unerreichbar

unattended, ann-e-tenn-didd, adj unbewacht

unauthorized, ann-o'a-the-reisd, adj unbefugt

unavoidable, ann-e-weu-de-b'l, adj unvermeidlich

unaware, ann-e-u'ähr, adj nicht bewußt; –s, adv unerwartet

unbearable, ann-bähr-re-b'l, adj unerträglich

unbeatable, ann-bie-te-b'l, adj unschlagbar

unbeknown(st), ann-bi-nohn(st), adj – to sb, ohne jds Wissen

unbelievable, ann-bi-lie-we-b'l, adj unglaublich

unbend, ann-bend, v (make

straight) geradebiegen; (fig
open up) aus sich
herausgehen; –ing, adj
unnachgiebig, unbeugsam
unbiased, ann-**bai**-est, adj
unvoreingenommen
unbleached, ann-**blietscht**,
adj ungebleicht
unbreakable, ann-**brehk**-e-
b'l, adj unzerbrechlich
unbridled, ann-**brei**-d'ld, adj
zügellos
unburden, ann-**börr**-d'n, v –
o.s. (of), sich von etw
befreien
unbutton, ann-**batt**-'n, v
aufknöpfen
uncalled-for, ann-**ko'ald**-for,
adj unangebracht
uncanny, ann-**känn**-i, adj
unheimlich
uncared-for, ann-**kährd**-for,
adj (unloved) ungeliebt;
(unheeded) vernachlässigt
unceasing, ann-**ssie**-ssing,
adj unaufhörlich
unceremonious, ann-sse-ri-
moh-ni-ess, adj formlos;
(rude) brüsk
uncertain, ann-**ssörr**-t'n, adj
unsicher; –ty, n
Unsicherheit f
unchanging, ann-**tschehn**-
dsching, adj
unveränderlich
uncivilized, ann-**ssiw**-i-
leisd, adj unzivilisiert
uncle, ang-k'l, n Onkel m
uncomfortable, ann-**kammf**-
fer-te-b'l, adj unbequem
uncommon, ann-**komm**-en,

adj ungewöhnlich
uncompromising, ann-
komm-pre-mei-sing, adj
kompromißlos
unconcerned, ann-ken-
ssörnd, adj gleichgültig
unconditional, ann-ken-
disch-e-n'l, adj
bedingungslos
uncongenial, ann-ken-
dschie-ni-el, adj
unsympathisch
unconscious, ann-**konn**-
schess, adj med bewußtlos;
(unintended) unbewußt;
–ly, adv unbewußt
uncontrollable, ann-ken-
trohl-e-b'l, adj
unkontrollierbar
unconventional, ann-ken-
wenn-schen-'l, adj
zwanglos
uncork, ann-**kork**, v
entkorken
uncouth, ann-**kuhth**, adj
grob
uncover, ann-**kaw**-er, v
aufdecken; (reveal)
entblößen
uncultivated, ann-**kall**-ti-
weh-tidd, adj unkultiviert
undecided, ann-di-**ssai**-didd,
adj unentschieden
undeniable, ann-di-**nai**-e-
b'l, adj unleugbar
under, ann-der, adj unten,
darunter; (movement)
nach unten; prep unter; –
age, adj nicht volljährig
undercarriage, ann-der-kä-
ridsch, n Untergestell nt

underclothing, ann-der-
kloh-dhing, n
Unterwäsche f
undercover, ann-der-kaw-er,
adj Geheim-
undercurrent, ann-der-ka-
rent, n Unterströmung f;
fig Unterton m
undercut, ann-der-**katt**, v
unterbieten
underdeveloped, ann-der-
di-**well**-ept, adj
unterentwickelt; –
country, n
Entwicklungsland nt
underdog, ann-der-dogg, n
Benachteiligte(r) m & f
underdone, ann-der-**dann**,
adj halbgar, blutig
underestimate, ann-de-**ress**-
ti-met, n Unterschätzung f
underestimate, ann-de-**ress**-
ti-meit, v unterschätzen
underexposed, ann-de-rick-
spohsd, adj photog
unterbelichtet
underfed, ann-der-**fedd**, adj
unterernährt
undergo, ann-der-**goh**, v
durchmachen; med sich
unterziehen
undergraduate, ann-der-
grädd-ju-et, n Student m
underground, ann-der-
graund, adj unterirdisch; n
rail U-Bahn f
undergrowth, ann-der-
grohth, n Unterholz nt,
Gestrüpp nt
underhand, ann-der-händ,
adj hinterlistig

underline, ann-der-**lein,** v unterstreichen

underlying, ann-der-**lei**-ing, adj zugrundeliegend

undermine, ann-der-**mein,** v untergraben; (health) angreifen

underneath, ann-der-**nieth,** adv unten; (movement) nach unten; prep unter

underpaid, ann-der-**pehd,** adj unterbezahlt

underpants, **ann**-der-pänts, npl Unterhose f

underpass, ann-der-pahss, n Unterführung f

underprivileged, ann-der-**priw**-i-lidschd, adj benachteiligt

underrated, ann-de-**reh**-tidd, adj unterschätzt

underside, ann-der-sseid, n Unterseite f

understand, ann-der-**ständ,** v verstehen, begreifen; (believe) glauben; **–ing,** n Verständnis nt; (accord) Einverständnis nt; (supposition) Annahme f

understatement, **ann**-der-steht-ment, n Untertreibung f

understudy, ann-der-stadd-i, n theatre zweite Besetzung f; fig Stellvertreter m

undertake, ann-der-**tehk,** v unternehmen

undertaker, **ann**-der-teh-ker, n Leichenbestatter m

undertaking, **ann**-der-teh-

king, n Unternehmen nt; (task) Aufgabe f

undertone, **ann**-der-tohn, n Flüsterton m

underwater, ann-der-u'o'a-ter, adj Unterwasser-; adv unter Wasser

underwear, ann-der-u'ähr, n Unterwäsche f

underworld, **ann**-der-u'örld, n Unterwelt f

underwriter, ann-de-rei-ter, n Versicherer m

undeserved, ann-di-sörwd, adj unverdient

undesirable, ann-di-**sair**-re-b'l, adj unerwünscht

undies, **ann**-dis, npl fam Unterwäsche f

undignified, ann-**digg**-ni-feid, adj würdelos

undisclosed, ann-diss-**klohsd,** adj geheim(gehalten)

undisputed, ann-diss-**pjuh**-tidd, adj unbestritten

undisturbed, ann-diss-törbd, adj ungestört

undo, ann-**duh,** v (unfasten) aufmachen; (negate) zunichte machen; **–ing,** n Verderben nt

undoubted, ann-**dau**-tidd, adj unzweifelhaft; **–ly,** adv zweifellos

undress, ann-**dress,** v (sich) ausziehen

undue, **ann**-djuh, adj übermäßig

undulating, **ann**-dju-leh-ting, adj (countryside)

sanft hügelig

unduly, ann-**djuh**-li, adv übermäßig

unearned, ann-**örnd,** adj unverdient

unearth, ann-**örth,** v ausgraben; fig aufstöbern; **–ly,** adj unheimlich

uneasy, ann-**ie**-si, adj unruhig

uneconomic(al), ann-ie-ke-**nomm**-ick(-'l), adj unwirtschaftlich

uneducated, ann-**edd**-ju-keh-tidd, adj ungebildet

unemployed, ann-imm-**pleud,** adj arbeitslos

unemployment, ann-imm-**pleu**-ment, n Arbeitslosigkeit f

unending, ann-**enn**-ding, adj endlos

unequal, ann-**iek**-u'el, adj ungleich; **–led,** adj unvergleichlich

unerring, ann-**ör**-ring, adj unfehlbar

uneven, ann-**ie**-wen, adj (not level) uneben; (irregular) unregelmäßig

unexpected, ann-ick-**speck**-tidd, adj unerwartet

unfailing, ann-**feh**-ling, adj unerschöpflich; **–ly,** adv stets

unfair, ann-**fähr,** adj unfair

unfaithful, ann-**fehth**-full, adj untreu

unfamiliar, ann-fe-**mill**-je, adj (strange) ungewohnt; (unknown) unbekannt; **be**

– with, v nicht kennen

unfashionable, ann-**fäsch**-e-ne-b'l, *adj* unmodern

unfasten, ann-**fah**-ss'n, *v* aufmachen

unfavourable, ann-**feh**-we-re-b'l, *adj* ungünstig

unfeeling, ann-**fie**-ling, *adj* gefühllos

unfinished, ann-**finn**-ischt, *adj* unvollendet

unfit, ann-**fitt**, *adj* (unsuitable) ungeeignet; (not well) nicht fit

unfold, ann-**fohld**, *v* (sich) entfalten

unforeseen, ann-for-**ssien**, *adj* unvorhergesehen

unforgettable, ann-fer-**gett**-e-b'l, *adj* unvergeßlich

unforgivable, ann-fer-**giw**-e-b'l, *adj* unverzeihlich

unfortunate, ann-**for**-tju-net, *adj* unglücklich; –ly, *adv* unglücklicherweise, leider

unfounded, ann-**faun**-didd, *adj* unbegründet

unfriendly, ann-**frend**-li, *adj* unfreundlich

unfurnished, ann-**för**-nischt, *adj* unmöbliert

ungainly, ann-**gehn**-li, *adj* unbeholfen

ungrateful, ann-**greht**-full, *adj* undankbar

unguarded, ann-**gahr**-didd, *adj* unbewacht; *fig* unvorsichtig

unhappiness, ann-**häpp**-i-niss, *n* Bekümmertheit *f*

unhappy, ann-**häpp**-i, *adj* (sad) unglücklich; (dissatisfied) unzufrieden

unharmed, ann-**harmd**, *adj* unverletzt

unhealthy, ann-**hell**-thi, *adj* ungesund

unheard-of, ann-**hör**-dow, *adj* unbekannt; (outrageous) unerhört

unhurt, ann-**hört**, *adj* unverletzt

unidentified, ann-ei-**denn**-ti-feid, *adj* unbekannt; (body) nicht identifiziert

unification, juh-ni-fi-**keh**-sch'n, *n* Vereinigung *f*

uniform, juh-ni-**form**, *n* Uniform *f; adj* gleichförmig; –ity, *n* Gleichförmigkeit *f*

unify, juh-ni-**fei**, *v* vereinigen

unilateral, juh-ni-**lätt**-e-rel, *adj* einseitig

unimaginative, ann-i-**madsch**-i-ni-tiw, *adj* phantasielos

uninhabited, ann-inn-**habb**-i-tidd, *adj* unbewohnt

unintentional, ann-inn-**tenn**-sche-n'l, *adj* unabsichtlich

union, juh-ni-en, *n* (joining) Vereinigung *f;* (association) Union *f;* (trade) –, *n* Gewerkschaft *f*

unique, juh-**niek**, *adj* (only) einzig; (unequalled) einzigartig

unison, juh-ni-ss'n, *n* Einklang *m*; in –, einstimmig

unit, juh-nitt, *n* Einheit *f*

unite, juh-**nait**, *v* (sich) vereinigen; –d, *adj* geschlossen; U–d Kingdom, *n* Vereinigtes Königreich *nt*; U–d Nations (Organization), *n* Vereinte Nationen *pl*; U–d States (of America), *n* Vereinigte Staaten *pl*

unity, juh-ni-ti, *n* Einigkeit *f*

universal, juh-ni-**wör**-ss'l, *adj* universal, Universal-

universe, juh-ni-wörss, *n* (Welt)all *nt*

university, juh-ni-**wör**-ssi-ti, *n* Universität *f*

unjust, ann-**dschast**, *adj* ungerecht

unkind, ann-**kaind**, *adj* unfreundlich

unknown, ann-**nohn**, *adj* unbekannt

unlawful, ann-**lo'a**-full, *adj* gesetzwidrig

unleaded, ann-**ledd**-idd, *adj* bleifrei, unverbleit

unless, en-**less**, *conj* wenn nicht, es sei denn

unlike, ann-**laik**, *adj* unähnlich; *prep* im Gegensatz zu; –ly, *adv* unwahrscheinlich

unlimited, ann-**limm**-i-tidd, *adj* unbegrenzt

unload, ann-**lohd**, *v* abladen

unlock, ann-**lock**, *v*

aufschließen

unlucky, ann-**lack**-i, *adj*
unglücklich

unmarried, ann-**mä**-ridd, *adj*
ledig

unmistakable, ann-miss-
teh-ke-b'l, *adj*
unverkennbar

unmitigated, ann-**mitt**-i-
geh-tidd, *adj* (severity)
ungemildert; (disaster)
vollkommen

unnatural, ann-**nätt**-tsche-
rel, *adj* unnatürlich

unnecessary, ann-**ness**-e-
sse-ri, *adj* unnötig

unnoticed, ann-**noh**-tist, *adj*
unbemerkt

unobtainable, ann-eb-**teh**-
ne-b'l, *adj* nicht erhältlich

unobtrusive, ann-eb-**truh**-
ssiw, *adj* unauffällig

unofficial, ann-e-**fisch**-'l, *adj*
inoffiziell

unopposed, ann-e-**pohsd,**
adj (progress)
ungehindert; (proposal)
unbestritten

unorthodox, ann-or-**the**-
docks, *adj*
unkonventionell

unpack, ann-**päck,** *v*
auspacken

unpleasant, ann-**ples**-'nt, *adj*
unangenehm

unpopular, ann-**popp**-ju-ler,
adj unpopulär; (person)
unbeliebt

unprecedented, ann-**press**-i-
den-tidd, *adj* beispiellos

unpredictable, ann-pri-

dick-e-b'l, *adj*
unvorhersehbar;
(unreliable)
unberechenbar

unprofessional, ann-pre-
fesch-en-'l, *adj*
unprofessionell

unqualified, ann-**kwoll**-i-
feid, *adj* (person)
unqualifiziert; (complete)
uneingeschränkt

unquestionably, ann-
ku'ess-tsche-neb-li, *adv*
fraglos

unravel, ann-**räw**-'l, *v*
entwirren; *fig* lösen

unreal, ann-**riel,** *adj*
unwirklich; –**istic,** *adj*
unrealistisch

unreasonable, ann-**rie**-se-
ne-b'l, *adj* unvernünftig

unrelated, ann-ri-**leh**-tidd,
adj (people) nicht
verwandt; (events)
unzusammenhängend

unrelenting, ann-ri-**lenn**-
ting, *adj* unerbittlich

unreliable, ann-ri-**lei**-e-b'l,
adj unzuverlässig

unremitting, ann-ri-**mitt**-
ing, *adj* unablässig

unreserved, ann-ri-**sörwd,**
adj nicht reserviert; –**ly,**
adv uneinschränkt

unrest, ann-**rest,** *n*
Unruhen *pl*

unroll, ann-**rohl,** *v* (sich)
aufrollen

unruly, ann-**ruh**-li, *adj*
ungehorsam

unsafe, ann-**ssehf,** *adj* nicht

sicher; (dangerous)
gefährlich

unsatisfactory, ann-ssätt-iss-
fäck-te-ri, *adj*
unbefriedigend

unsavoury, ann-**sseh**-we-ri,
adj abstoßend

unscrew, ann-**skruh,** *v*
aufschrauben

unscrupulous, ann-**skruh**-
pju-less, *adj* skrupellos

unselfish, ann-**ssell**-fisch,
adj selbstlos

unsettled, ann-**ssett**-l'd, *adj*
wechselhaft, unsicher

unshaven, ann-**scheh**-ven,
adj unrasiert

unshrinking, ann-**schring**-
king, *adj* unverzagt

unsightly, ann-**ssait**-li, *adj*
hässlich

unskilled, ann-**skild,** *adj*
ungelernt

unsolved, ann-**ssolwd,** *adj*
ungelöst

unstable, ann-**steh**-b'l, *adj*
(structure, economy)
unsicher; (mentally) labil

unstuck, ann-**stack,** *adj*
come –, *v* sich lösen; *fig* in
die Binsen gehen

unsuccessful, ann-ssek-
ssess-full, *adj* erfolglos

unsuitable, ann-**ssuh**-te-b'l,
adj unpassend

unsuited (to), ann-**ssuh**-
tidd (tu), *adj* ungeeignet

unsuspecting, ann-ssess-
peck-ting, *adj*
nichtsahnend

unsympathetic, ann-simm-

pe-**thett**-ick, *adj* wenig
mitfühlend

unthinkable, ann-**think**-*e*-b'l, *adj* unvorstellbar

unthinking, ann-**thing**-king, *adj* gedankenlos

untidy, ann-**tai**-di, *adj* unordentlich

untie, ann-**tai**, *v* (knot) lösen; (lace etc.) aufbinden

until, en-**till**, *conj prep* bis

untimely, ann-**taim**-li, *adv* (inopportune) ungelegen; (death) vorzeitig

untold, ann-**tohld**, *adj* (wealth) unermeßlich; (countless) unzählig

untouched, ann-**tatscht**, *adj* unberührt

untoward, ann-te-u'ord, *adj* ungünstig

unusual, ann-**juh**-schu-el, *adj* ungewöhnlich

unveil, ann-**wehl**, *v* enthüllen

unwarranted, ann-u'o-ren-tidd, *adj* ungerechtfertigt

unwavering, ann-u'eh-we-ring, *adj* standhaft

unwelcome, ann-u'ell-kem, *adj* (visitor) unwillkommen; (news etc.) unangenehm

unwell, ann-u'ell, *adj* be –, *v* sich nicht wohl fühlen

unwieldy, ann-u'iel-di, *adj* unhandlich

unwilling, ann-u'ill-ing, *adj* widerwillig; **be – to do sth**, nicht bereit sein, etw

zu tun

unwind, ann-u'aind, *v* abwickeln, abwinden; *fig* sich entspannen

unwise, ann-u'ais, *adj* unklug

unwittingly, ann-u'itt-ing-li, *adv* unwissentlich

unworthy (of), ann-u'ör-dhi (ew), *adj* unwürdig

unwrap, ann-**räpp**, *v* auswickeln, auspacken

unwritten, ann-**ritt**-'n, *adj* ungeschrieben

unyielding, ann-**jiel**-ding, *adj* unbeugsam

up, app, *adv* (position) oben; (movement) nach oben; *prep* hinauf; **–coming**, *adj* aufstrebend; **– and down**, *adv* auf und nieder; **–s and downs**, *npl* Höhen und Tiefen *pl*; **– here**, *adv* (position) hier oben; (movement) herauf; **– there**, *adv* (position) dort oben; (movement) hinauf; **– to**, *prep* bis; **be – to**, *v* (capable of) zu etw in der Lage sein; **be – to sth**, *fam* etw aushecken; **it's – to you**, das ist deine/Ihre Sache

upbringing, **a**pp-bring-ing, *n* Erziehung *f*

update, app-**deht**, *v* auf den neuesten Stand bringen

upgrade, app-**grehd**, *v* (product) verbessern; (person) befördern

upheaval, app-**hie**-w'l, *n*

Aufruhr *m*

uphill, **a**pp-**hill**, *adj* (path) bergauf führend; (task) mühsam; *adv* bergauf

uphold, app-**hohld**, *v* aufrechterhalten; (support) stützen

upholster, app-**hohl**-ster, *v* polstern; **–y**, *n* Polsterung *f*

upkeep, **a**pp-kiep, *n* Instandhaltung *f*

uplifting, app-**liff**-ting, *adj* erhebend

upon, e-**ponn**, *prep* auf

upper, **a**pp-er, *adj* obere(r/s), höhere(r/s), Ober-; **– class**, *adj* Oberschicht-; **– hand**, *n* Oberhand *f*; **–most**, *adj* oberste(r/s), höchste(r/s)

upright, **a**pp-rait, *adj* aufrecht; (honest) rechtschaffen; *adv* aufrecht; *n* **– (piano)**, Klavier *nt*

uprising, **a**pp-rei-sing, *n* Aufstand *m*

uproar, **a**pp-ror, *n* Aufruhr *m*

uproot, app-**ruht**, *v* entwurzeln

upset, app-**ssett**, *adj* (person) bestürzt, aufgeregt; (stomach) verdorben; *v* (knock over) umwerfen; (worry) aufregen

upshot, **a**pp-shott, *n* Ergebnis *nt*

upside-down, app-sseid-

daun, *adv* verkehrt herum; (untidy) drunter und drüber

upstairs, app-**stährs,** *adj* obere(r/s); *adv* oben; *n* Obergeschoß *nt*; **go –,** *v* nach oben gehen, hinaufgehen

upstart, app-**start,** *n* Emporkömmling *m*

upstream, app-**striem,** *adv* stromaufwärts

uptake, app-**tehk,** *n* **be quick/low on the –,** *v* schnell verstehen/schwer von Begriff sein

uptight, app-**teit,** *adj* nervös

up-to-date, app-tu-**deht,** *adj & adv* auf dem neuesten Stand, aktuell

upward, app-**u'erd,** *adj* steigend; **–s,** *adv* aufwärts

uranium, juhr-**reh**-ni-em, *n* Uran *nt*

urban, ör-ben, *adj* städtisch, Stadt-

urchin, ör-tschinn, *n* Strolch *m*

urge, ördsch, *n* Drang *m*; *v* drängen

urgency, ör-dschen-ssi, *n* Dringlichkeit *f*

urgent, ör-dschent, *adj* dringend

urinate, juhr-ri-neht, *v* urinieren

urine, juhr-rinn, *n* Urin *m*, Harn *m*

urn, örn, *n* Urne *f*

us, ass, *pron* uns; (emphatic) wir

US, *abbr* United States

USA, *abbr* United States of America

usage, juhss-idsch, *n* Gebrauch *m*

use, juhss, *n* Gebrauch *m*; (utility) Nutzen *m*; **–ful,** *adj* nützlich; **–less,** *adj* nutzlos; **it's no –,** (pointless) es hat keinen Zweck; (useless) es ist nutzlos

use, juhs, *v* gebrauchen; (apply) anwenden; **–d,** *adj* gebraucht; **I –d to …,** früher habe ich …; **– up,** *v* verbrauchen; **be –d to sth,** *v* etw gewohnt sein

usher, asch-er, *n* (court) Gerichtsdiener *m*; (cinema etc.) Platzanweiser *m*; **– in,** *v* einführen

usual, juh-schu-el, *adj* gewöhnlich, gebräuchlich; **–ly,** *adv* gewöhnlich

usurp, juh-sörp, *v* sich widerrechtlich aneignen; **–er,** *n* Usurpator *m*

utensil, juh-tenn-ssill, *n* Gerät *nt*

utility, juh-till-i-ti, *n* (usefulness) Nützlichkeit *f*; (service provider) öffentlicher Versorgungsbetrieb *m*; **– room,** *n* Hausarbeitsraum *m*

utilize, juh-ti-lais, *v* benutzen, verwerten

utmost, att-mohst, *adj*

äußerste(r/s); **to the –,** (exertion) bis zum äußersten; (enjoy) völlig

utter, att-er, *adj* höchster(r/s), völlig; *v* äußern; ausstoßen; **–ance,** *n* Äußerung *f*; **–ly,** *adv* äußerst, völlig

U-turn, juh-törn, *n* (in car, fig) Wende *f* (um 180 Grad)

V

vacancy, weh-ken-ssi, n (job) freie Stelle; (room) (freies) Zimmer nt; (emptiness) Leere f

vacant, weh-kent, adj leer; (available) frei; (house) unbewohnt

vacate, we-keht, v räumen

vacation, we-keh-sch'n, n Ferien pl

vaccinate, wäck-ssi-neht, v impfen

vaccination, wäck-ssi-neh-sch'n, n Impfung f

vacuum, wäck-ju-em, n Vakuum nt; v Staub saugen; – **cleaner,** n Staubsauger m; – **flask,** n Thermosflasche ® f

vagina, we-dschei-ne, n Scheide f

vagrant, weh-grent, n (homeless person) Obdachlose(r) m & f

vague, wehg, adj (shape, question) vage; (person) zerstreut

vain, wehn, adj eitel; (attempt) vergeblich; **in –,** umsonst

valentine, wäll-en-tein, n – (**card**), n Valentinskarte f

valet, wäll-eh, n Diener m

valiant, wäll-jent, adj tapfer

valid, wäll-idd, adj (ticket etc.) gültig; (excuse) triftig; (argument) stichhaltig; (objection) berechtigt

valley, wäll-i, n Tal nt

valour, wäll-er, n Tapferkeit f

valuable, wäll-ju-e-b'l, adj wertvoll; **–s,** npl Wertsachen pl

valuation, wäll-ju-eh-sch'n, n Schätzung f

value, wäll-juh, n Wert m; v schätzen; – **added tax,** n Mehrwertsteuer f; **–d,** adj geschätzt; **–r,** n Schätzer m

valve, wälw, n Ventil m; (of heart) Klappe f; (radio) Röhre f

vampire, wämm-peir, n Vampir m

van, wänn, n Lieferwagen m; mil Vorhut f

vandal, wänn-d'l, n Vandale m; fig Rowdy m; **–ism,** n (mutwillige) Zerstörung f; **–ize,** n (mutwillig) beschädigen

vanguard, wänn-gard, n mil Vorhut f; fig Spitze f

vanilla, we-nill-e, n Vanille f

vanish, wänn-isch, v verschwinden

vanity, wänn-i-ti, n Eitelkeit f; **– bag,** n Kosmetiktäschchen nt

vantage point, wahn-tidsch peunt, n Aussichtspunkt m

vapour, weh-per, n Dunst m

variable, wehr-ri-e-b'l, adj veränderlich; (adjustable) regulierbar

variance, wehr-ri-ens, n Unterschied m; **be at –** (**with**), v uneinig sein (mit); (opinions) nicht übereinstimmen

variation, wehr-ri-eh-sch'n, n Veränderung f, Variation f; (fluctuation) Schwankung f

varicose veins, wä-ri-kohss wehns, npl Krampfadern pl

varied, wehr-ridd, *adj*
(mixed) gemischt;
(eventful) bewegt

variegated, wehr-ri-geh-
tidd, *adj* buntfarbig; (leaf)
geflammt

variety, we-rei-i-ti, *n*
(mixture) Vielfalt *f*;
(change) Abwechslung *f*;
(type) Art *f*; *theatre*
Variété *nt*

various, wehr-ri-ess, *adj*
(different) verschieden;
(several) mehrere

varnish, wahr-nisch, *n* Lack
m; *v* lackieren

vary, wehr-ri, *v* (make
different) ändern;
(become different) sich
verändern; (be different)
sich unterscheiden;
(fluctuate) schwanken

vase, wahs, *n* Vase *f*

vast, wahst, *adj*
unermeßlich, riesig

vat, watt, *n* großes Faß *nt*

vault, wo'alt, *n* Gewölbe *nt*;
(burial) Gruft *f*;
(strongroom) Tresorraum
m; (jump) Sprung *m*; *v* –
(over), überspringen

veal, wiel, *n* Kalbfleisch *nt*

veer, wier, *v* (of wind) sich
drehen; (of car)
ausscheren

vegetable, wedsch-i-te-b'l, *n*
Gemüse *nt*; **–s**, *npl*
Gemüse *nt*

vegetarian, wedsch-i-**tähr**-
ri-en, *n* Vegetarier *m*

vegetation, wedsch-i-**teh**-
sch'n, *n* Vegetation *f*

vehement, wie-i-ment, *adj*
heftig, gewaltig

vehicle, wie-i-k'l, *n*
Fahrzeug *nt*

veil, wehl, *n* Schleier *m*; *v*
verschleiern

vein, wehn, *n* Ader *f*;
(mood) Stimmung *f*

velocity, wi-loss-i-ti, *n*
Geschwindigkeit *f*

velvet, well-witt, *adj* Samt-;
n Samt *m*

vending machine, wenn-
ding me-schien, *n*
(Verkaufs)automat *m*

vendor, wenn-der, *n*
Verkäufer *m*

veneer, we-nier, *n* Furnier
nt; *fig* Fassade *f*; *v*
furnieren

venereal, wi-nier-ri-el,
–disease, *n*
Geschlechtskrankheit *f*

vengeance, wenn-dschenss,
n Rache *f*; **with a –**,
gewaltig

Venice, wenn-iss, *n*
Venedig *nt*

venison, wenn-i-s'n, *n*
Reh(fleisch) *nt*

venom, wenn-em, *n* Gift *nt*;
fig Groll *m*; **–ous**, *adj* giftig

vent, went, *n* Öffnung *f*; (in
cask) Spundloch *nt*; (in
coat) Schlitz *m*; *v*
abreagieren; **give – to**, *v*
etw freien Lauf lassen

ventilate, wenn-ti-leht, *v*
lüften; (discuss) erörtern

ventilator, wenn-ti-leh-ter,

n Ventilator *m*; *med*
Beatmungsgerät *nt*

ventriloquist, wenn-trill-e-
ku'ist, *n* Bauchredner *m*

venture, wenn-tscher, *n*
Unternehmung *f*; *v* (sich)
wagen

venue, wenn-juh, *n*
(Austragungs)ort *m*

verb, wörb, *n* Zeitwort *nt*,
Verb *nt*; **–al(ly)**, *adj & adv*
mündlich

verbatim, wer-beh-timm, *adj
& adv* wortwörtlich

verbose, wer-bohss, *adj*
wortreich, schwülstig

verdict, wör-dikt, *n* Urteil
nt

verge, wördsch, *n* Rand *m*; *v*
– on, grenzen an

verify, we-ri-fei, *v* (confirm)
bestätigen; (check)
überprüfen

veritable, we-ritt-e-b'l, *adj*
wahrhaftig

vermin, wör-minn, *n*
Ungeziefer *nt*; *fig*
Abschaum *m*

vernacular, wer-näck-ju-ler,
n Landessprache *f*

versatile, wör-sse-teil, *adj*
vielseitig

verse, wörss, *adj* Vers-; *n*
(stanza) Strophe *f*;
(poetry) Dichtung *f*,
Poesie *f*; *relig* Vers *m*

versed (in), wörst (inn), *adj*
bewandert in

version, wör-sch'n, *n*
Version *f*

versus, wör-ssess, *prep* gegen

vertebrate, wör-ti-bret, *adj*
Wirbel-; *n* Wirbeltier *nt*

vertical, wör-tick-'l, *adj*
senkrecht

vertigo, wör-ti-goh, *n*
Schwindel(anfall) *m*

very, we-ri, *adj* (exact)
genau; *adv* (extremely)
sehr; (absolutely) aller-; –
much, sehr; **thank you –
much,** vielen Dank

vessel, wess-'l, *n* Gefäß *nt*;
naut Schiff *nt*

vest, west, *n* Unterhemd *nt*

vested, wess-tidd, *adj* **have a
– interest in,** *v* (financial)
finanziell beteiligt sein an;
(personal) ein
persönliches Interesse
haben an

vestige, wess-tidsch, *n* Spur
f, Zeichen *nt*

vestry, wess-tri, *n* Sakristei *f*

vet, wett, *n* (*abbr* **veterinary
surgeon**) Tierarzt *m*,
Tierärztin *f*; *v* überprüfen

veteran, wett-e-ren, *n*
Veteran *m*

veterinary, wett-ri-ne-ri, *adj*
tierärztlich, Veterinär-; –
surgeon, *n* Tierarzt *m*,
Tierärztin *f*

veto, wie-toh, *n* Veto *nt*; *v*
sein Veto einlegen

vex, wecks, *v* ärgern; **–ation,**
n Ärger *m*; **–ed,** *adj*
(person) verärgert;
(question) umstritten

via, wei-e, *prep* über

viable, wei-e-b'l, *adj* (plan)
durchführbar; (business)

rentabel; (foetus,
economy) lebensfähig

viaduct, wei-e-dakt, *n*
Viadukt *m*

vibrate, wei-breht, *v*
vibrieren; (shake) beben

vibration, wei-breh-sch'n, *n*
Schwingung *f*, Vibrieren
nt

vicar, wick-er, *n* Pfarrer
m;**–age,** *n* Pfarrhaus *nt*

vice, weiss, *adj*
stellvertretend; *n* Laster
m; *mech* Schraubstock *m*;
–-president, *n*
Vizepräsident *m*

vice versa, wei-ssi wör-sse,
adv umgekehrt

vicinity, wi-ssinn-i-ti, *n*
Nähe *f*, Nachbarschaft *f*

vicious, wisch-ess, *adj*
(nasty) gemein; (wicked)
übel; (dog etc.) bösartig; –
circle, *n* Teufelskreis *m*

victim, wick-timm, *n* Opfer
nt; **–ize,** *v* schikanieren

victor, wick-ter, *n* Sieger *m*

victorious, wick-tor-ri-ess,
adj siegreich

victory, wick-te-ri, *n* Sieg *m*

video, widd-i-oh, *adj* Video-;
n (film) Video *nt*;
(recorder) Videorekorder
m; *v* (auf Video)
aufnehmen; **– cassette,** *n*
Videokassette *f*; **– tape,** *n*
Videoband *nt*

vie (for), wei (for), *v*
wetteifern (um)

Vienna, wi-enn-e, *n*
Wien *nt*

view, wjuh, *n* (sight)
Aussicht *f*; (opinion)
Ansicht *f*; (intention)
Absicht *f*; *v* betrachten;
–er, *n* (TV) Zuschauer *m*;
(for film) Filmbetrachter
m; (for slides)
Diabetrachter *m*; **–finder,**
n photog Sucher *m*; **–point,**
n Standpunkt *m*; **in – of,**
angesichts

vigil, widsch-ill, *n*
Nachtwache *f*; **–ance,** *n*
Wachsamkeit *f*; **–ant,** *adj*
wachsam

vigorous, wigg-e-ress, *adj*
energisch

vigour, wigg-er, *n* Kraft *f*,
Energie *f*

vile, weil, *adj* (thought,
remark) gemein; (food,
weather) scheußlich

vilify, will-i-fei, *v*
verunglimpfen

villa, will-e, *n* Villa *f*

village, will-idsch, *n* Dorf *nt*;
–r, *n* Dorfbewohner *m*

villain, will-en, *n* Schurke
m, Schuft *m*; **–ous,** *adj*
gemein, abscheulich

vindicate, winn-di-keht, *v*
rechtfertigen

vindictive, winn-dick-tiw,
adj rachsüchtig, rachgierig

vine, wein, *n* Rebstock *m*

vinegar, winn-i-ger, *n* Essig
m

vineyard, winn-jahrd, *n*
Weinberg *m*

vintage, winn-tidsch, *adj*
(car) Oldtimer-; (wine)

edel; n Jahrgang m

vinyl, wei-nill, n Vinyl nt

viola, wi-oh-le, n Bratsche f

violate, wei-e-leht, v
(disturb) schänden; (rape)
vergewaltigen; (law,
rights) verletzen; (treaty)
brechen

violence, wei-e-lenss, n
(brutality) Gewalt f;
(force) Heftigkeit f

violent, wei-e-lent, adj
(strong) heftig; (brutal)
gewaltsam

violet, wei-e-let, adj violett;
n Veilchen nt

violin, wei-e-linn, n Violine
f, Geige f; –ist, Geiger m

VIP, wie ei pie, n (abbr very
important person), VIP m

virgin, wör-dschinn, adj fig
unberührt; n Jungfrau f

Virgo, wör-goh, n Jungfrau f

virile, wi-reil, adj männlich,
maskulin

virtual, wör-tju-el, adj
(near) praktisch; (math,
comp) virtuell; –lly, adv
praktisch, so gut wie

virtue, wör-tjuh, n
(goodness) Tugend f;
(advantage) Vorteil m; by
– of, aufgrund

virtuous, wör-tju-ess, adj
tugendhaft

virulent, wi-rju-lent, adj
med bösartig; fig heftig

virus, wei-ress, n (med,
comp) Virus m

visa, wi-se, n Visum nt

visibility, wis-i-bill-i-ti, n

Sicht(weite) f

visible, wis-i-b'l, adj
sichtbar

visibly, wis-ibb-li, adv
sichtlich

vision, wisch-'n, n (faculty)
Sehvermögen nt; (image)
Vision f; (foresight)
Weitblick m

visit, wis-itt, n Besuch m;
v besuchen; –or, n
Besucher m

visor, wei-ser, n (on helmet)
Visier nt; (in car) Blende f

vista, wiss-te, n Ausblick m

visual, wisch-ju-el, adj Seh-,
visuell; –ize, v sich
vorstellen

vital, wei-t'l, adj (of life)
Lebens-; (essential)
unerläßlich, unbedingt
notwendig; (lively) vital;
–ity, n Vitalität f; –ly, adv
äußerst

vitamin, witt-e-minn, n
Vitamin nt

vivacious, wi-weh-schess,
adj lebhaft

vivacity, wi-wäss-i-ti, n
Lebhaftigkeit f

vivid, wi-widd, adj lebhaft;
(bright) leuchtend

V-neck, wie-neck, n V-
Ausschnitt m

vocabulary, we-käbb-ju-le-
ri, n Wortschatz f

vocal, woh-k'l, adj mus
Vokal-; (vociferous)
lautstark; – cords, npl
Stimmbänder pl

vocation, we-keh-sch'n, n

(profession) Beruf m;
(calling) Berufung f; –al,
adj Berufs-

vociferous, we-ssiff-e-ress,
adj lautstark

vodka, wodd-ke, n Wodka m

vogue, wohg, n Mode f; in
–, modisch

voice, weuss, n Stimme f; v
äußern

void, weud, adj (empty) leer;
(invalid) ungültig; n Leere
f

volatile, woll-e-teil, adj
(substance) flüchtig;
(person) impulsiv;
(situation) brisant

volcano, woll-keh-noh, n
Vulkan m

volley, woll-i, n mil Salve f;
(tennis) Volley m; (of
stones, insults) Hagel m; v
(tennis) einen Volley
schlagen; –ball, n
Volleyball m

volt, wohlt, n Volt nt; –age,
n Spannung f

voluble, woll-ju-b'l, adj
beredt; (chatty) redselig

volume, woll-juhm, n
(loudness) Lautstärke f;
(book) Band m; (bulk)
Volumen nt

voluminous, we-luh-mi-
ness, adj groß,
umfangreich

voluntary, woll-en-te-ri, adj
freiwillig

volunteer, woll-en-tier, n
Freiwillige(r) m & f; v sich
(freiwillig) melden

voluptuous, we-**lapp**-tju-ess,
  adj üppig
vomit, womm-itt, *n*
  Erbrochenes *nt*; *v* (sich)
  erbrechen
vote, woht, *n* (voice)
  Stimme *f*; (election) Wahl
  f; (franchise) Wahlrecht
  nt; *v* wählen; –
  for/against, stimmen
  für/gegen
voter, woh-ter, *n* Wähler *m*
voucher, wautsch-er, *n*
  Gutschein *m*
vouch for, wautsch for, *v*
  einstehen für
vow, wau, *n* Versprechen *nt*;
  relig Gelübde *nt*; *v* geloben
vowel, wau-el, *n* Vokal *m*
voyage, weu-idsch, *n* Reise
  f; *v* reisen
vulgar, wall-ger, *adj* vulgär
vulnerable, wall-ne-re-b'l,
  adj (helpless) wehrlos;
  (unprotected)
  ungeschützt; – **to,** anfällig
  für
vulture, wall-tscher, *n*
  Geier *m*

W

wacky, u'äck-i, *adj fam*
verrückt

wad, u'odd, *n* (paper)
Bündel *nt*; (cotton wool)
Bausch *m*; **–ding,** *n*
Füllmaterial *nt*

waddle, u'odd-'l, *v*
watscheln

wade, u'ehd, *v* waten

wafer, u'eh-fer, *n* Waffel *f*;
relig Hostie *f*

wag, u'ägg, *n* Spaßvogel *m*; *v*
wedeln (mit)

wage, u'ehdsch, *n* Lohn *m*; *v*
– war (on), Krieg führen
(gegen)

wager, u'eh-dscher, *n* Wette
f; *v* wetten

wages, u'ehdsch-is, *npl*
Lohn *m*, Gehalt *nt*

waggle, u'ägg-'l, *v* wackeln;
(tail) wedeln mit

wag(g)on, u'ägg-en, *n rail*
Wagen *m*; (horse-drawn)
Fuhrwerk *nt*

wail, u'ehl, *n* klagender
Schrei *m*; *v* jammern

waist, u'ehst, *n* Taille *f*;
–coat, *n* Weste *f*; **–line,** *n*
Taille *f*

wait, u'eht, *n* Wartezeit *f*; *v*
warten; **– at table,** *v*
servieren; **–er,** *n* Kellner
m, Bedienung *f*; **– for,** *v*
warten auf; **–ing,** *n*
Warten *nt*; (service) *n*
Bedienung *f*; **–ing room,** *n*
rail Wartesaal *m*;
(doctor's) Wartezimmer
nt; **–ress,** *n* Bedienung *f*; **–
on,** *v* bedienen; **lie in –
for,** *v* auflauern

waive, u'ehw, *v* verzichten
auf, aufgeben

wake, u'ehk, *n naut*
Kielwasser; *v* (self)
aufwachen; (sb else)
aufwecken; **– up to sth,**

fig sich etw bewußt
werden

Wales, u'ehls, *n* Wales *nt*

walk, u'o'ak, *n* Spaziergang
m; *v* gehen; (stroll)
spazierengehen; (hike)
wandern; **–er,** *n* Wanderer
m, Spaziergänger *m*; **–ing,**
adj Wander-; Gehen *nt*;
Wandern *nt*; **–ing stick,** *n*
Spazierstock *m*; **–over,** *n*
fam Spaziergang *m*

wall, u'o'al, *n* (exterior)
Mauer *f*; (interior) Wand
f; **–ed,** *adj* mit Mauern
umgeben

wallet, u'oll-itt, *n*
Brieftasche *f*

wallflower, u'o'al-flau-er, *n*
Goldlack *m*; *fig*
Mauerblümchen *nt*

wallop, u'oll-ep, *fam n*
Schlag *m*; *v* hauen

wallow, u'oll-oh, *v* sich
wälzen

wallpaper, u'o'al-peh-per, *n*
Tapete *f*

wally, u'oll-i, *n fam* Depp *m*

walnut, u'o'al-natt, *n*
Walnuß *f*

walrus, u'o'al-ress, *n* Walroß
nt

waltz, u'olts, *n* Walzer *m*; *v*
Walzer tanzen

wander, u'onn-der, *v*
wandern; (from subject)
abschweifen

wane, u'ehn, *v* abnehmen

want, u'ont, *n* (lack)
Mangel *m*; (distress) Not
f; *v* (need) brauchen; **–**

(to), wollen; **–ed,** *adj*
gesucht; **–ing,** *adj*
unzulänglich

wanton, u'onn-ten, *adj*
zügellos; (lustful)
liederlich

war, u'or, *n* Krieg *m*; **–like,**
adj kriegerisch; **make –,** *v*
Krieg führen

ward, u'ord, *n* (minor)
Mündel *nt*; (in hospital)
Krankensaal *m*; **–en,** *n*
(guard) Aufseher *m*; (of
college) Rektor *m*; **–er,** *n*
Wärter *m*; **– off,** *v*
abwehren; **–ress,** *n*
Wärterin *f*

wardrobe, u'ord-rohb, *n*
(cupboard)
Kleiderschrank *m*;
(clothes) Garderobe *f*

warehouse, u'ähr-hauss, *n*
Lagerhaus *nt*

wares, u'ährs, *npl* Waren *pl*

warhead, w'or-hedd, *n*
Sprengkopf *m*

warily, u'ähr-ri-li, *adv*
vorsichtig, behutsam

warm, u'orm, *adj* warm; *v*
wärmen; **– up,** *v* (get
warm) warm werden;
(make warm) aufwärmen
–th, *n* Wärme *f*

warn (against), u'orn (*e-*
genst), *v* warnen (vor);
–ing, *adj* Warn–; *n*
Warnung *f*

warp, u'orp, *v* sich werfen;
–ed, *adj* verzogen; *fig*
pervers

warrant, u'o-rent, *n* (for

search)
Durchsuchungsbefehl *m*;
(for arrest) Haftbefehl *m*;
comm Garantie *f*; **–y,** *n*
Garantie *f*

warren, u'o-ren, *n* (rabbit's)
Kaninchenbau *m*; *fig*
Labyrinth *nt*

warrior, u'o-ri-er, *n* Krieger
m

Warsaw, u'or-so'a, *n*
Warschau *nt*

warship, u'or-schipp, *n*
Kriegsschiff *nt*

wart, u'ort, *n* Warze *f*

wartime, u'or-teim, *adj*
Kriegs–; *n* Krieg *m*; **in –,** in
Kriegszeiten

wary, u'ähr-ri, *adj*
bedachtsam

wash, u'osch, *v* (sich)
waschen; (crockery)
abwaschen; **–able,** *adj*
waschbar; **– basin,** *n*
Waschbecken *nt*; **–er,** *n*
mech Dichtungsring *m*;
(machine)
Waschmaschine *f*; **–ing,** *n*
(laundry) Wäsche *f*; **–ing
machine,** *n*
Waschmaschine *f*; **–ing
powder,** *n* Waschpulver
nt; **–ing-up,** *n* Abwasch *m*;
–ing-up liquid, *n*
Spülmittel *nt*; **–out,** *n fam*
Reinfall *m*; **– up,** *v* spülen

wasp, u'osp, *n* Wespe *f*

waste, u'ehst, *adj* Abfall–; *n*
Verschwendung *f*;
(rubbish) Abfall *m*; *v*
verschwenden; (time)

vergeuden; **– away,** *v*
dahinschwinden; **–
disposal unit,** *n*
Müllschlucker *m*; **–ful,** *adj*
(person)
verschwenderisch;
(process)
unwirtschaftlich; **–land,** *n*
Einöde *f*; **—paper basket,**
n Papierkorb *m*

watch, u'otsch, *n*
(timekeeper) Uhr *f*,
Armbanduhr *f*; (lookout)
Wache *f*; *v* (TV)
fernsehen; (guard)
(be)wachen; (observe)
beobachten; (look)
zusehen; **–dog,** *n*
Wachthund *m*; *fig*
Aufsicht(sbehörde) *f*;
–ful, *adj* wachsam;
–maker, *n* Uhrmacher *m*;
–man, *n* Wächter *m*; **–
out,** *v* (be careful)
aufpassen; **– television,** *v*
fernsehen

water, u'o'a-ter, *n* Wasser *nt*;
v (plant) gießen; (animal)
tränken; (of eye) tränen;
(hot) – bottle, *n*
Wärmflasche *f*; **– closet,** *n*
Toilette *f*; **–colour,** *n*
Aquarell *nt*; **–cress,** *n*
Brunnenkresse *f*; **–fall,** *n*
Wasserfall *m*; **–ing can,** *n*
Gießkanne *f*; **– level,** *n*
Wasserstand *m*; **–lily,** *n*
Seerose *f*; **–line,** *n*
Wasserlinie *f*; **–logged,** *adj*
vollgesogen; **–mark,** *n* (in
paper) Wasserzeichen *nt*;

–proof, *adj* wasserdicht; *n* Regenhaut *f*; **–shed,** *n fig* Wendepunkt *m*; **––skiing,** *n* Wasserskilaufen *nt*; **– tank,** *n* Wasserbehälter *m*; **–tight,** *adj* wasserdicht; **–y,** *adj* wässerig

wave, u'ehw, *n* (sea, *elec*) Welle *f*; (hand) Winken *nt*; *v* (of flag) wehen; (with hand) winken; (hair) wellen; **–length,** *n* Wellenlänge *f*

waver, u'eh-wer, *v* zaudern; **–ing,** *adj* unschlüssig

wavy, u'eh-wi, *adj* wellig

wax, u'äks, *n* Wachs *nt*; *v* wachsen, wichsen; (of moon) zunehmen; (become) werden; **–works,** *npl* Wachsfigurenkabinett *nt*

way, u'eh, *adv fam* weit; *n* (route, path) Weg *m*; (direction) Richtung *f*; (manner) Weise *f*, ; **– in,** *n* Eingang *m*, Einfahrt *f*; **–lay,** *v* auflauern; **– out,** *n* Ausgang *m*, Ausfahrt *f*; **–ward,** *adj* ungezügelt; **a long –,** weit; **by the –,** übrigens; **on the –,** unterwegs, auf dem Weg; **lose one's –,** sich verirren

we, u'ie, *pron* wir

weak, u'iek, *adj* schwach; **–en,** *v* (make weak) schwächen; (grow weak) schwach werden; **–ling,** *n* Schwächling *m*; **–ness,** *n* Schwäche *f*

wealth, u'elth, *n* (richness) Reichtum *m*; (abundance) Fülle *f*; **–y,** *adj* reich

wean, u'ien, *v* entwöhnen; *fig* abgewöhnen

weapon, u'epp-'n, *n* Waffe *f*

wear, u'ähr, *n* (wear and tear) Abnützung *f*; (clothes) Kleidung *f*; *v* tragen; (last) sich tragen; **– off,** *v* (layer) abgehen; *fig* nachlassen; **– out,** *v* verbrauchen; (clothes) abnützen; (person) erschöpfen

weary, u'ier-ri, *adj* müde; *v* (tire) ermüden; (bore) langweilen

weasel, u'ie-s'l, *n* Wiesel *nt*

weather, u'edh-er, *n* Wetter *nt*; *v* (survive) überstehen; (become worn) verwittern; **––beaten,** *adj* wettergegärbt; **– forecast,** *n* Wettervorhersage *f*; **– report,** *n* Wetterbericht *m*; **under the –,** *fam* nicht ganz auf dem Posten

weave, u'iew, *v* (cloth) weben; (zigzag) sich schlängeln; **–r,** *n* Weber *m*

web, u'ebb, *n* Gewebe *nt*; **–bing,** *n* Gurtband *nt*; **–bed,** *adj* Schwimm-

wed, u'edd, *v* heiraten

wedding, u'edd-ing, *n* Hochzeit *f*; **– ring,** *n* Ehering *m*

wedge, u'edsch, *n* Keil *m*; *v* einkeilen; **– in,** einzwängen

wedlock, u'edd-lock, *n* Ehestand *m*

Wednesday, u'ens-dei, *n* Mittwoch *m*

weed, u'ied, *n* Unkraut *nt*; *v* jäten; **–killer,** *n* Unkrautvertilgungsmittel *nt*; **–s,** *npl* Unkraut *nt*; **–y,** *adj* (*fam* feeble) schmächtig

week, u'iek, *n* Woche *f*; **–day,** *n* Wochentag *m*; (on timetable) Werktag *m*; **–end,** *n* Wochenende *nt*; **–ly,** *adj* wöchentlich, Wochen-; *adv* wöchentlich; *n* (magazine) Wochenzeitschrift *f*

weep, u'iep, *v* weinen; **–ing willow,** *n* Trauerweide *f*

weigh, u'eh, *v* wiegen; **– down,** niederdrücken; **– up,** erwägen

weighing-machine, u'eh-ing me-schien, *n* Waage *f*

weight, u'eht, *n* Gewicht *nt*; **–y,** *adj* gewichtig; **lose –,** *v* abnehmen; **put on –,** *v* zunehmen

weir, u'ier, *n* Wehr *nt*

weird, u'ierd, *adj* unheimlich; (*fam* odd) sonderbar

welcome, u'ell-kem, *adj* willkommen; *n* Willkommen *nt*; *v* willkommen heißen; **you're –,** nichts zu danken

weld, u'eld, n Schweißnaht f; v schweißen; **–er,** n Schweißer m; **–ing,** n Schweißen nt

welfare, u'ell-fähr, n (wellbeing) Wohl nt; (support) Fürsorge f; **– state,** n Wohlfahrtsstaat m

well, u'ell, adj gesund; adv gut; n (water) Brunnen m; (oil) Quelle f; **–being,** n Wohl nt; **– -bred,** adj wohlerzogen; **–built,** adj kräftig gebaut; **– done,** adj (food) durchgebraten; **– known,** adj bekannt; **– meaning,** adj wohlmeinend; **–off,** adj wohlhabend; **–wisher,** n Gönner m; **as –,** auch; **... as – as ...,** sowohl ... als auch ...; **I'm well,** es geht mir gut

Welsh, u'elsch, adj walisisch; n (language) Walisisch nt; pl (people) Waliser pl; **–man,** n Waliser m; **–woman,** n Waliserin f

west, u'est, adj westlich, West-; adv westlich, nach Westen; n Westen m; **–erly,** adj westlich; **–ern,** adj westlich, West-; n Western m; **the W–Indies,** npl die Westindischen Inseln pl

wet, u'ett, adj naß; (fam weak) weichlich; n Nässe f; v naß machen; **–suit,** n Taucheranzug m

whack, u'äck, n Schlag m; v schlagen

whale, u'ehl, n Wal m; **–r,** n Walfänger m

wharf, u'orf, n Kai m

what, u'ott, adj (which) welche(r/s); (what sort) was für ein(e); pron was; **– a ...!** was für ein(e) ...!; **– is your name/are you called?** wie heißen Sie?; **–ever,** adj welche(r/s) auch immer; pron was auch (immer); **– kind/sort of,** was für ein(e)

wheat, u'iet, n Weizen m

wheedle, u'ie-d'l, v beschwatzen

wheel, u'iel, n Rad nt; v schieben; (wheelchair) fahren; **–barrow,** n Schubkarren m; **–chair,** n Rollstuhl m; **– clamp,** n Parkkralle f

wheeze, u'ies, v keuchen

when, u'enn, adv wann; conj (question) wann; (future, whenever) wenn; (past) als; **–ever,** adv (any time) wann auch immer; (every time) jedesmal; conj (any time) wenn (auch immer); (every time) jedesmal wenn

where, u'ähr, adv wo; (movement) wohin; **–about(s),** adv wo; n Verbleib m; **–as,** conj während, wo hingegen; **–by,** adv woran, wodurch, womit; **– from,** adv woher;

– to, adv wohin; **–upon,** conj worauf

wherever, u'ähr-ew-er, adv wo auch immer; (movement) wohin auch immer

wherewithal, u'ähr-u'idh-o'al, n (Geld)mittel pl

whet, u'ett, v (blade) wetzen; (appetite) anregen

whether, u'edh-er, conj ob

which, u'itsch, pron (interrogative) welche(r/s); (relative) der/die/das; was; **–ever,** pron welche(r/s) auch immer

while, u'eil, n Weile f, Zeitlang f; conj während; **– away,** v (sich) die Zeit vertreiben

whim, u'imm, n Grille f

whimper, u'imm-per, n Gewinsel nt; v winseln

whine, u'ein, n Heulen nt; v wimmern

whip, u'ipp, n Peitsche f; v peitschen; (cream, egg) schlagen; **–ped cream,** Schlagsahne f

whirl, u'örl, n Wirbel m; v wirbeln; **–pool,** n Strudel m; **–wind,** n Wirbelwind m

whirr, u'ör, v surren

whisk, u'isk, n Schneebesen m; v (cream, egg) schlagen; **– away,** schnell wegziehen

whiskers, u'iss-kers, npl (cat etc) Schnurrhaare pl;

(man's) Backenbart m

whisky, u'iss-ki, n Whisky m

whisper, u'iss-per, n Geflüster nt; v flüstern

whistle, u'iss-'l, n (instrument) Pfeife f; (sound) Pfiff m; v pfeifen

white, u'eit, adj weiß; (drink) mit Milch; n Weiß nt; (of egg) Eiweiß nt; – **elephant,** n nutzloser Besitz m; – **lie,** n Notlüge f; **–ness,** n Weiße f; **–wash,** n Tünche f; fig Schönfärberei f; v tünchen; fig übertünchen

whiting, u'ei-ting, n Weißfisch m

Whitsun, u'itt-ssen, n Pfingsten nt

whiz, u'is, v zischen, sausen

who, huh, pron (interrogative) wer, wen, wem; (relative) der/die/das; **–ever,** pron wer/wen/wem auch immer

whole, hohl, adj ganze(r/s); n Ganze(s) nt; **–heartedly,** adv mit ganzem Herzen; **–meal,** adj Vollkorn-; **–sale,** adj Großhandels-; fig Massen-; adv ohne weiteres; n Großhandel m; **–some,** adj gesund; **on the –,** im großen und ganzen; **the – of the ...,** der/die/das ganze ...

wholly, hoh-li, adv gänzlich, völlig

whom, huhm, pron (accusative, dative) (interrogative) wen, wem; (relative) den/die/das, dem/der/dem

whooping cough, huh-ping-koff, n Keuchhusten m

whore, hor, n Hure f

whose, huhs, adj wessen; pron (possessive) (interrogative) wessen; (relative) dessen/deren/dessen; – **is that?** wem gehört das?

why, u'ei, adv warum, weshalb; conj that is –, deshalb, deswegen

wick, u'ick, n Docht m

wicked, u'ick-idd, adj böse; **–ness,** n Bosheit f

wicker, u'ick-er, n Korbgeflecht nt; – **basket,** n Weidenkorb m

wicket, u'ick-itt, n Wicket nt

wide, u'eid, adj breit; (clothes, world) weit; (interests) vielfältig; adv (open, spread) weit; (throw) daneben; **–angle lens,** n Weitwinkelobjektiv nt; **–awake,** adj hellwach; **–ly,** adv weit; (known) überall; **–n,** v (sich) erweitern; **–spread,** adj weitverbreitet

widow, u'idd-oh, n Witwe f; **–ed,** adj verwitwet; **–er,** n Witwer m

width, u'idth, n Breite f, Weite f

wield, u'ield, v schwingen; (power) ausüben

wife, u'eif, n Frau f, (formal) Gattin f

wig, u'igg, n Perücke f

wild, u'eild, adj wild; (angry) wütend; (mad) verrückt

wilderness, u'ill-der-niss, n Wildnis f, Wüste f

wildlife, u'eild-leif, n Tierwelt f

wildly, u'eild-li, adv wild; **not –,** fam nicht so sehr

wilful, u'ill-full, adj (person) eigenwillig; (act) vorsätzlich

will, u'ill, n Wille m; law Testament nt v (in future) werden; (be willing) wollen

willing, u'ill-ing, adj bereit; **–ly,** adv bereitwillig; **–ness,** n Bereitwilligkeit f

willow, u'ill-oh, n Weide f

willpower, u'ill-pau-er, n Willenskraft f

wily, u'ei-li, adj schlau, listig

win, u'inn, n Sieg m; v gewinnen

wince, u'inss, v zucken, zusammenfahren

winch, u'intsch, n Winde f

wind, u'ind, adj mus Blas-; n Wind m; med Blähung f; mus Blasinstrumente pl

wind, u'eind, v winden; (meander) sich winden; (clock) aufziehen; – **up,** v (clock) aufziehen; (business) liquidieren

windfall, u'ind-fo'al, n

(luck) unverhoffte(r) Glücksfall m; (fruit) Fallobst nt

winding, u'ein-ding, adj gewunden

windmill, u'ind-mill, n Windmühle f

window, u'inn-doh, n Fenster nt – **box,** n Blumenkasten m; –**dressing,** n Schaufensterdekoration f; fig Schönfärberei f; – **ledge,** n Fensterbank f; – **pane,** n Fensterscheibe f; – **sill,** n Fensterbank f

windpipe, u'ind-peip, n Luftröhre f

wind power, u'ind pau-er, n Windenergie f

windscreen, u'ind-skrien, n Windschutzscheibe f; – **washer,** n Scheibenwaschanlage f; – **wiper,** n Scheibenwischer m

windswept, u'ind-ssu'ept, adj (person) zerzaust; (landscape) windgepeitscht

windy, u'inn-di, adj windig

wine, u'ein, n Wein m; –**glass,** n Weinglas nt – **list,** n Weinkarte f; – **merchant,** n Weinhändler m; – **tasting,** n Weinprobe f

wing, u'ing, n Flügel m; (of car) Kotflügel m; –**s,** npl Seitenkulisse f

wink, u'ink, n Zwinkern nt;

v zwinkern, blinzeln

winner, u'inn-er, n Gewinner m; sport Sieger m

winning, u'inn-ing, adj (team) siegreich; (shot) entscheidend; (smile) einnehmend; – **post,** n Ziel nt; –**s,** npl Gewinn m

winter, u'inn-ter, adj Winter-; n Winter m; v überwintern; – **sport(s),** n(pl), Wintersport m

wintry, u'int-ri, adj winterlich, rauh

wipe, u'eip, v (ab)wischen; – **out,** v (erase) löschen; (destroy) vernichten

wire, u'eir, n Draht m; (telegram) Telegramm nt; v telegrafieren

wireless, u'eir-liss, n Funk m; (set) Radio nt

wiring, u'eir-ring, n (elektrische) Leitungen pl

wisdom, u'is-dem, n Weisheit f, Verstand m; – **tooth,** n Weisheitszahn m

wise, u'eis, adj weise, klug

wish, u'isch, n Wunsch m; v wünschen; **best –es,** (in letter) herzliche Grüße; (on birthday etc.) herzliche Glückwünsche; –**ful thinking,** n Wunschdenken nt

wisp, u'isp, n Wölkchen nt; (of hair) Strähne f

wistful, u'ist-full, adj sehnsüchtig

wit, u'itt, n (intelligence)

Verstand; (humour) Witz m; (funny person) Spaßvogel m

witch, u'itsch, n Hexe f; –**craft,** n Hexerei f

with, u'idh, prep mit; (in the company of) bei; (as a result of) vor

withdraw, u'idh-dro'a, v zurückziehen; (money) abheben; –**n,** adj verschlossen

wither, u'idh-er, v verwelken; –**ing,** adj (look) vernichtend

withhold (from), u'idh-hohld (frem), v vorenthalten

within, u'idh-inn, adv innen; prep innerhalb

with it, u'idh itt, adj auf dem Laufenden

without, u'idh-aut, adv draußen; prep ohne; – …**ing,** ohne zu …en

withstand, u'idh-ständ, v widerstehen

witness, u'itt-niss, n Zeuge m, Zeugin f; v (see) sehen; (signature) bestätigen; – **to,** bezeugen

wits, u'itts, npl Verstand m

witticism, u'itt-i-ssism, n Witzelei f

witty, u'itt-i, adj witzig

wizard, u'is-erd, n Zauberer m

wobble, u'obb-'l, v wackeln

woe, u'oh, n Jammer m; –**ful,** adj jammervoll, elend

wolf, u'ulf, n Wolf m
woman, u'umm-en, n Frau f;
  -ly, adj weiblich, feminin
womb, u'uhm, n
  Gebärmutter f
women's lib, wimm-ins libb,
  n Frauenbewegung f
wonder, u'ann-der, n
  (astonishment)
  Verwunderung f; (marvel)
  Wunder nt; v (ask oneself)
  sich fragen; **– at**, sich
  wundern über; **–ful(ly)**,
  adj & adv wunderbar; **no
  –!** kein Wunder!
woo, u'uh, v umwerben
wood, u'udd, n Holz nt;
  (forest) Wald m; **-ed**, adj
  bewaldet; **–en**, adj hölzern,
  Holz-; **–pecker**, n Specht
  m; **–wind**, n adj Holzblas-;
  n Holzblasinstrumente pl;
  –work, n Arbeiten pl mit
  Holz
wool, u'ull, adj Woll-;
  Wolle f; **–len**, adj Woll-;
  –lens, npl Wollsachen pl;
  –ly, adj wollig; (vague)
  undeutlich
word, u'örd, n Wort nt;
  (news) Bescheid m; v
  verfassen; **–ing**, n
  Wortlaut m; **– processing**,
  n Textverarbeitung f; **–
  processor**, n Text-
  verarbeitungsprogramm
  nt; **give one's –**, v sein
  Wort geben; **in other –s**,
  anders gesagt
work, u'örk, n Arbeit f; (of
  art) Werk nt; v (labour)

arbeiten; (function)
  funktionieren; (succeed)
  klappen; **– loose**, v sich
  lockern; **– out**, v (solve)
  lösen; (devise)
  ausarbeiten; (succeed)
  klappen; sport sich fit
  halten; **get –ed up**, sich
  aufregen
workable, u'ör-ke-b'l, adj
  durchführbar, machbar
worker, u'ör-ker, n
  Arbeiter m
workforce, u'örk-forss, n
  Personal nt
working, u'ör-king, adj
  (functioning)
  betriebsfähig; (in work)
  berufstätig; n (effect)
  Wirken nt; **– class**, n
  Arbeiterklasse f
workman, u'örk-men, n
  Arbeiter m; **–ship**, n
  Ausführung f
workplace, u'örk-pleiss, n
  Arbeitsplatz m
works, u'örks, n Fabrik f; pl
  mech Werk nt
workshop, u'örk-schopp, n
  Werkstatt f
work station, u'örk-steh-
  sch'n, n Arbeitsplatz m
world, u'örld, adj Welt-; n
  Welt f; **–ly**, adj weltlich;
  –wide, adj & adv weltweit
worm, u'örm, n Wurm m;
  (screw) Gewinde nt
worry, u'a-ri, n Sorge f; v
  (be worried) sich sorgen;
  (make worried)
  beunruhigen

worse, u'örss, adj & adv
  schlechter, schlimmer; n
  Schlimmeres nt,
  Schlechteres nt; **–n**, v
  (sich) verschlimmern
worship, u'ör-schipp, n
  Verehrung f; v anbeten
worst, u'örst, adj
  schlechteste(r/s),
  schlimmste(r/s); adv am
  schlechtesten, am
  schlimmsten; n
  Schlimmste(s),
  Schlechteste(s) nt
worsted, u'uss-tidd, n
  Kammgarn nt
worth, u'örth, adj wert; n
  Wert m; **–less**, adj wertlos;
  (person) nichtswürdig;
  –while, adv der Mühe
  wert
worthy, u'ör-dhi, adj würdig
would, u'udd, v (past &
  conditional of **will**); **––be**,
  adj Möchtegern-
wound, u'uhnd, n Wunde f;
  v verletzen
wrangle, räng-g'l, n Streit
  m; v streiten
wrap, räpp, n (shawl)
  Umhang m; (cover)
  Verhüllung f; v
  einwickeln; **– up**, (sich)
  einwickeln
wrapper, räpp-er, n (of
  book) Umschlag m
wrapping paper, räpp-ing
  peh-per, Packpapier nt;
  (gifts) Geschenkpapier nt
wrath, roth, n Zorn m; **–ful**,
  adj zornig

wreak, riek, *v* (havoc)
anrichten; (vengeance)
üben

wreath, rieth, *n* Kranz *m*

wreck, reck, *n* Wrack *nt*; *v*
zerstören; **–age,** *n*
Trümmer *pl*

wren, renn, *n* Zaunkönig *m*

wrench, rentsch, *n* (jar)
Ruck *m*; (sprain)
Verrenkung *f*; (tool)
Schraubenschlüssel *m*; *v*
(sprain) verrenken; (pull)
reißen

wrestle, ress-'l, *v* ringen;
–r, *n* Ringer *m*,
Ringkämpfer *m*

wretch, retsch, *n* Elende(r)
m & f; **–ed,** *adj* elend; *fam*
elend

wriggle, rigg-'l, *n* Windung
f; *v* sich winden, sich
schlängeln

wring, ring, *v* (clothes)
(aus)wringen; (neck)
umdrehen; (hands) ringen

wrinkle, ring-k'l, *n* Falte *f*; *v*
(crumple) verknittern;
(get wrinkled) Falten
bekommen

wrist, rist, *n* Handgelenk *nt*;
–watch, *n* Armbanduhr *f*

writ, ritt, *n* Verfügung *f*

write, reit, *v* schreiben;
(cheque) ausstellen; **– off,**
(debt, car) abschreiben;
–r, *n* Schreiber *m*;
(author) Schriftsteller *m*

writhe, reidh, *v* sich
krümmen

writing, rei-ting, *n*

Schreiben *nt*; **(hand)–,**
(Hand)schrift *f*; **in –,** *adv*
schriftlich; **– paper,** *n*
Schreibpapier *nt*

written, ritt-en, *adj*
schriftlich

wrong, rong, *adj* falsch;
(morally) unrecht; *n*
Unrecht *nt*; *v* Unrecht
zufügen; **be –,** unrecht
haben, sich irren; **be in
the –,** im Unrecht sein;
what's – (with …)? was
ist (mit …) los?

wrought iron, ro'at **ei-**en, *n*
Schmiedeeisen *nt*

wry, rei, *adj* (joke, humour)
fein; (grin) ironisch

X

xenophobic, zenn-*e*-foh-
bick, *adj* fremdenfeindlich
Xmas, *abbr* **Christmas**
X-ray, ecks-reh, *adj*
Röntgen-; *n* (image)
Röntgenaufnahme *f*; *v*
röntgen; **–s,** *npl*
Röntgenstrahlen *pl*
xylophone, sai-*le*-fohn, *n*
Xylophon *nt*